THE PENGUIN
ATLAS
OF THE
WORLD

VIKING

In association with Rand McNally & Company Chicago/New York/San Francisco

VIKING

Published by the Penguin Group
27 Wrights Lane, London W8 5TZ, England
Viking Penguin Inc., 40 West 23rd Street, New York, New York 10010, USA
Penguin Books Australia Ltd, Ringwood, Victoria, Australia
Penguin Books Canada Ltd, 2801 John Street, Markham, Ontario, Canada L3R 1B4
Penguin Books (NZ) Ltd, 182–190 Wairau Road, Auckland 10, New Zealand

Penguin Books Ltd, Registered Offices: Harmondsworth, Middlesex, England

This edition first published by Viking 1987
Reprinted 1988

Copyright © Rand McNally & Company, 1987
Maps, tables and index copyright © Rand McNally & Company, Chicago, Illinois, U.S.A., 1986
Preface copyright © Penguin Books Ltd, 1987
The maps are from *The New International Atlas*, copyright © Rand McNally
& Company, 1986, 1980; and *The New International Atlas*, copyright ©
Rand McNally & Company, 1978, 1969

Printed in Italy by Olivotto

British Library Cataloguing in Publication Data available

ISBN 0-670-81715-5

Table of Contents

Preface

The history of maps is as old as travel, discovery and curiosity about the world. Since the earliest times cartographers have provided mariners with guidance for their explorations, monarchs with portraits of their territories and scholars with a record of the Earth's surface. Today maps play an even more important role by supplying us all with the evidence of the ties that link the world's countries and peoples with one another.

The prime function of a map is to portray the Earth's surface and the patterns of human occupancy that have developed upon it. If a map were no more than an objective record, it would not need revision; however, a map is more than just a simple picture. Greatly reduced in scale from the reality it represents, it must abstract and generalize from that reality, selecting and interpreting the facts deemed to be of greatest significance. The maps in this atlas not only depict the regions of the world, but they also reflect improvements in the techniques of portraying geographical information.

The present century has offered a great challenge to map-makers. It has witnessed an increasing demand for specialized map information from governments, teachers and scientists; it has also seen growing numbers of non-specialists eager to use maps for business, for travel or simply for enjoyment. This atlas has been developed to meet the needs of all those who are interested in a factual world volume of reference.

The metric system of measurement is used, and there is a strong emphasis on local forms of geographical names – English is used only for names of major features that extend across international borders. The names of countries appear on most of the maps both in English and in the locally official forms.

The world is covered by maps that fit into even-scale increments. The continents are portrayed at 1:24,000,000, in natural colours, as they might appear from about 4,000 miles in space. The major

world regions are uniformly portrayed at 1:12,000,000. These maps are political in style and content. The maps at the scales of 1:3,000,000 and 1:6,000,000 cover the more important areas in greater detail. The largest scale, that of 1:1,000,000, has been used to portray the British Isles.

The sequence of reference maps in the atlas begins with the series of world and continent maps. Next are maps arranged by geographical region, from smallest scale (1:12,000,000) to largest (1:1,000,000). The individual maps have been planned to portray geographical and economic regions rather than individual countries. Thus there are maps of the Iberian Peninsula and of Southeastern Europe but no separate maps of Portugal or Romania. In a few instances this has necessitated the omission of some small portion of the region or country described in the map title. Inset maps have generally been avoided, though exceptions have been made to portray certain isolated islands or island groups.

The map symbols used for given features (pages 16–17) are generally alike on all of the map scales, though reduced in size on smaller scales.

No aspect of map design has shown more dramatic advances in recent years than the cartographic rendering of relief. The Editors believe that the most effective method of depicting this is the bird's-eye-view or hill-shading technique, which uses variation from light through dark tones to indicate pictorially the slope and shape of relief features. There is shaded relief on all maps in this atlas.

In the concluding portion of the atlas are tables and summaries for general reference. The World Information Table lists area, population and political status for each major political unit. The world's largest metropolitan areas are also listed. And, finally, the Index provides location references – map page, latitude and longitude – for more than 40,000 names.

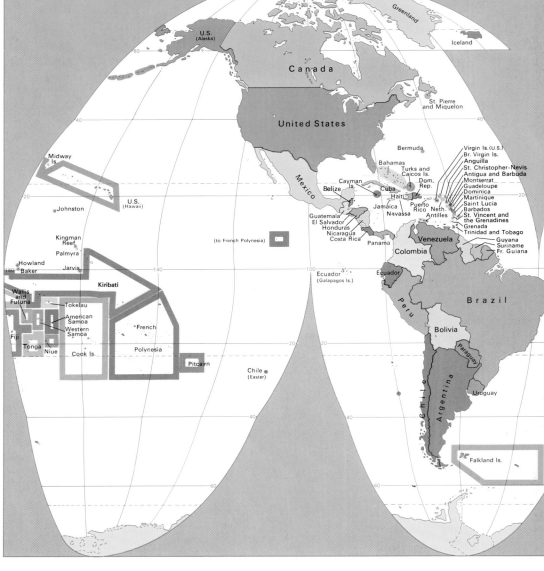

The World, January 1, 1987

Every political entity that has a separate administration, whether it is independent or dependent, is named here and is distinguished from adjacent units by color. In all, over 200 political units are named. A noncontiguous part of a country has the same color as the country. If it lies at any distance, it is identified (for example, Alaska, a state of the United States), but if it lies close by, it is not (for example, the island of Corsica, which comprises two departments of France).

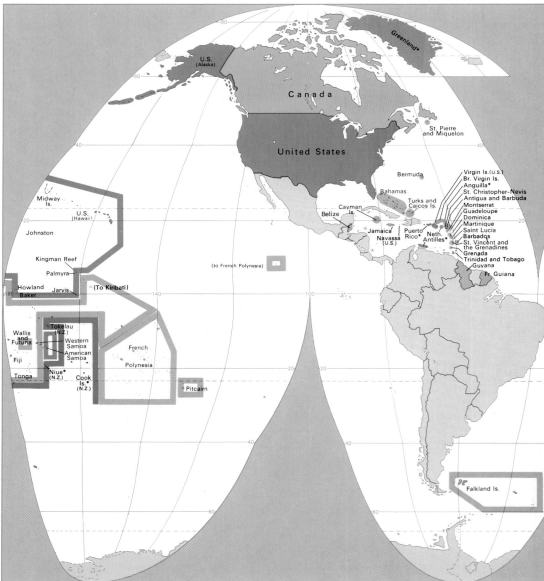

Politically Related Areas

United Kingdom and related areas

Member of the Commonwealth of Nations

Areas related to a Commonwealth Nation other than the United Kingdom

France and related areas

Part of Danish Realm

Part of Netherlands Realm

United States and related areas

*Virtually independent: major country primarily responsible for foreign relations and defense.

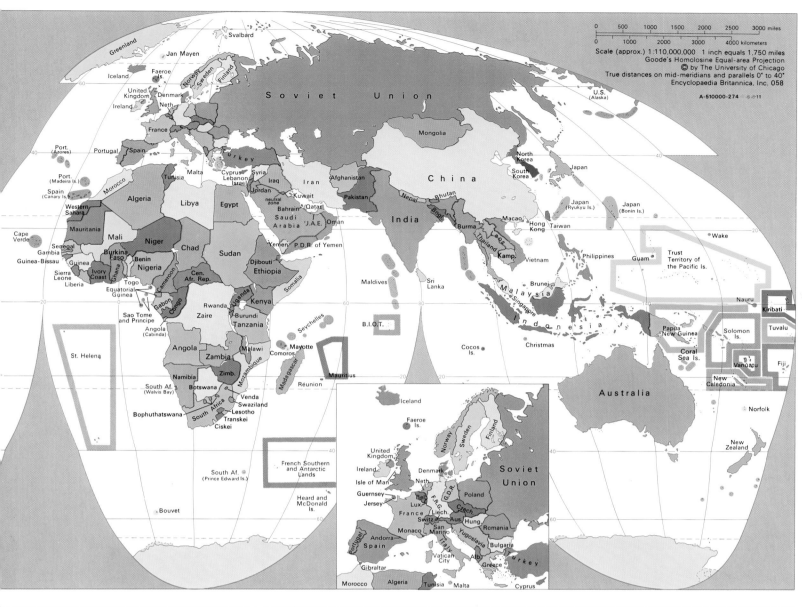

Scale (approx.) 1:110,000,000 1 inch equals 1,750 miles
Goode's Homolosine Equal-area Projection
© by The University of Chicago
True distances on mid-meridians and parallels 0° to 40°
Encyclopaedia Britannica, Inc. 058

A-510000-274 6-011

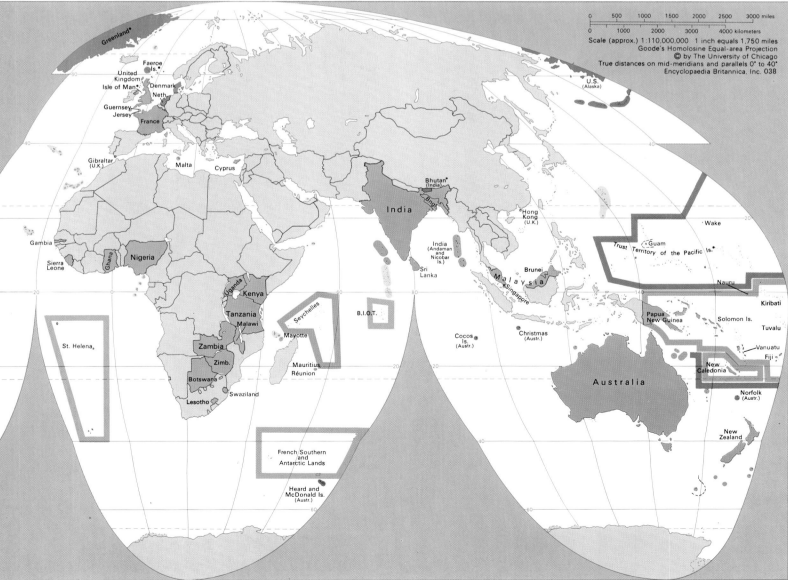

Scale (approx.) 1:110,000,000 1 inch equals 1,750 miles
Goode's Homolosine Equal-area Projection
© by The University of Chicago
True distances on mid-meridians and parallels 0° to 40°
Encyclopaedia Britannica, Inc. 038

Population

Extent of urbanization
Percent of total population urban

- 80% and more
- 60 to 79%
- 40 to 59%
- 20 to 39%
- Less than 20%

Major metropolitan areas

- ◯ 5,000,000 and more persons
- ◯ 3,000,000 to 4,999,999
- ◦ 2,000,000 to 2,999,999

The increase in the proportion of urban to total population reflects the change from a dispersed pattern of human settlement to a concentrated one. In industrialized countries the proportion of people living in cities increases mainly through movement from country to city, due to the attraction of higher wages and greater opportunities, a process which in most cases started about 100 years ago. In the underdeveloped countries, where in recent years the number of people living in cities has risen sharply, the proportion of urban population has not increased appreciably; here the urban growth is generally due not so much to rural-urban migration as it is to the natural population increase in both urban and rural areas, and to the decline in the urban mortality rate.

In population studies the definitions of "urban" differ from country to country, but generally take into account the total number of people in a settlement and the percent of the population engaged in nonagricultural activities. The map shows the degree of urbanization (the proportion of urban to total population), considering as urban those communities having no fewer than 2,000 inhabitants, more than half of them dependent on nonfarm occupations. Also indicated are selected metropolitan areas where cities have expanded beyond their boundaries into the surrounding regions in patterns of continuous settlement oriented toward the central cities.

Age and sex composition

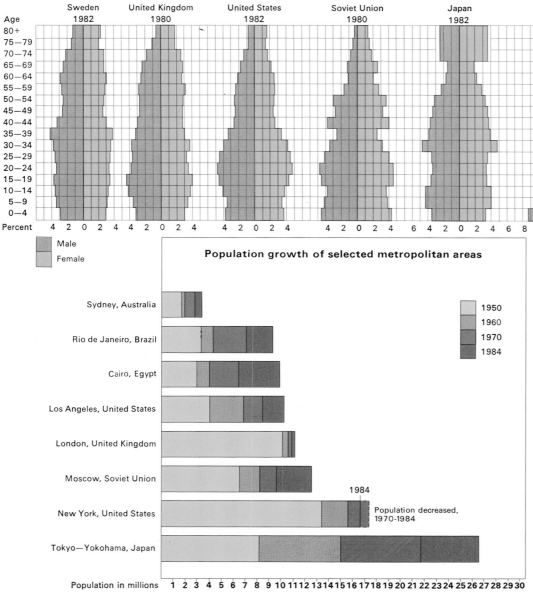

Age	Sweden 1982	United Kingdom 1980	United States 1982	Soviet Union 1980	Japan 1982	Brazil 1980	Egypt 1976	Philippines 1975

- Male
- Female

Population growth of selected metropolitan areas

1950
1960
1970
1984

Sydney, Australia
Rio de Janeiro, Brazil
Cairo, Egypt
Los Angeles, United States
London, United Kingdom
Moscow, Soviet Union
New York, United States — 1984 Population decreased, 1970-1984
Tokyo—Yokohama, Japan

Population in millions 1 2 3 4 5 6 7 8 9 10 11 12 13 14 15 16 17 18 19 20 21 22 23 24 25 26 27 28 29 30

World population

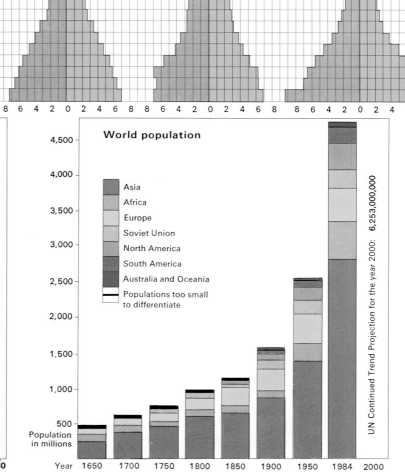

- Asia
- Africa
- Europe
- Soviet Union
- North America
- South America
- Australia and Oceania
- Populations too small to differentiate

UN Continued Trend Projection for the year 2000: 6,253,000,000

Population in millions

Year 1650 1700 1750 1800 1850 1900 1950 1984 2000

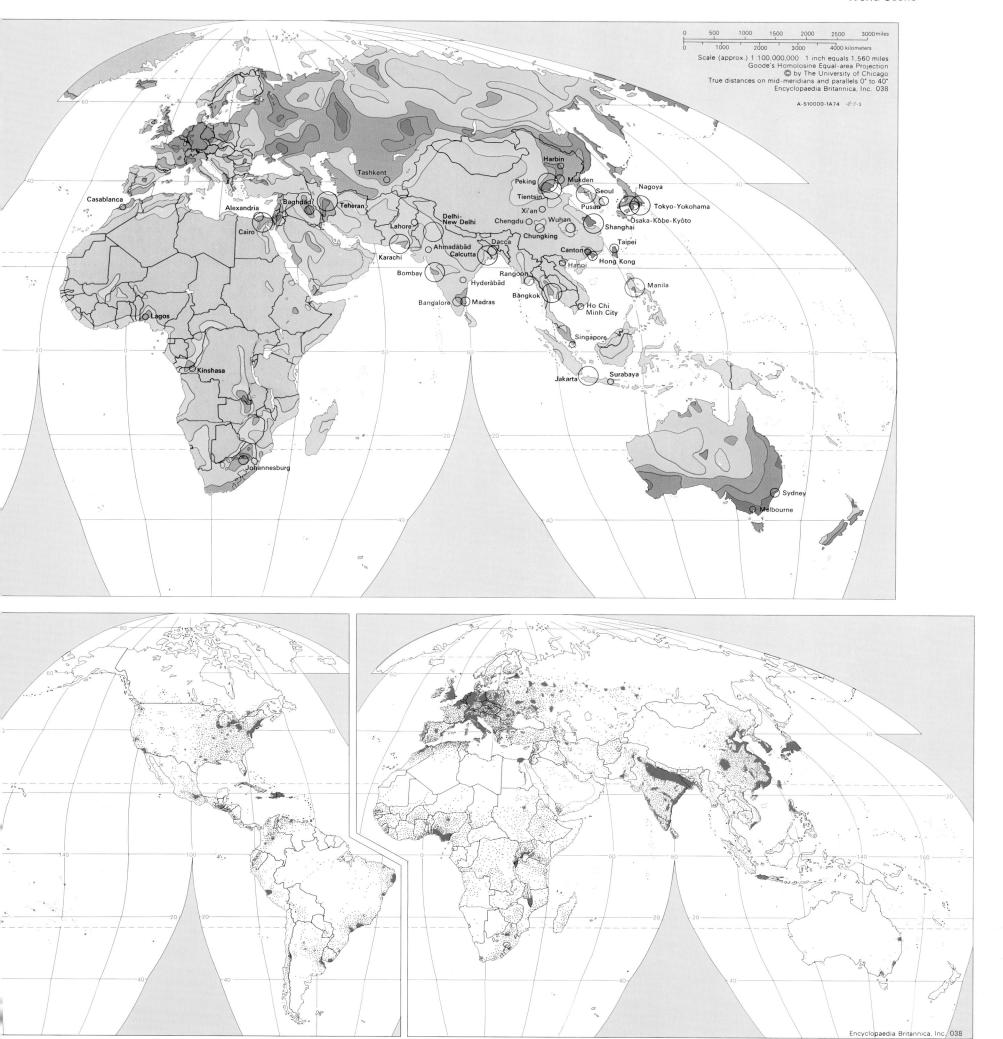

Scale (approx.) 1:100,000,000 1 inch equals 1,560 miles
Goode's Homolosine Equal-area Projection
© by The University of Chicago
True distances on mid-meridians and parallels 0° to 40°
Encyclopaedia Britannica, Inc. 038

A-510000-1A74

Casablanca
Alexandria
Baghdād
Teheran
Tashkent
Cairo
Lahore
Delhi-New Delhi
Chengdu
Xi'an
Wuhan
Chungking
Karachi
Ahmadābād
Calcutta
Dacca
Peking
Tientsin
Harbin
Mukden
Seoul
Pusan
Nagoya
Tokyo-Yokohama
Ōsaka-Kōbe-Kyōto
Shanghai
Taipei
Canton
Hong Kong
Hanoi
Bombay
Hyderābād
Rangoon
Bangalore
Madras
Bangkok
Ho Chi Minh City
Manila
Lagos
Singapore
Kinshasa
Jakarta
Surabaya
Johannesburg
Sydney
Melbourne

Encyclopaedia Britannica, Inc. 038

Distribution

Each dot represents 100,000 persons. The dots show the location of concentrated areas of population rather than the location of cities.

Religions

The majority of the inhabitants in each of the areas colored on the
map share the religious tradition indicated. Letter symbols show
religious traditions shared by at least 25% of the inhabitants
within areal units no smaller than one thousand square miles.
Therefore minority religions of city-dwellers have generally not been
represented.

	R	Roman Catholicism
	P	Protestantism
	E	Eastern Orthodox religions (including Armenian, Coptic, Ethiopian, Greek, and Russian Orthodox)
	M	Mormonism
	C	Christianity, undifferentiated by branch (chiefly mingled Protestantism and Roman Catholicism, neither predominant)
	I	Islam, predominantly Sunni
	Sh	Islam, predominantly Shia
		Theravada Buddhism
	L	Lamaism
	H	Hinduism
	J	Judaism
	Ch	Chinese religions*
	Ja	Japanese religions*
		Korean religions*
		Vietnamese religions*
	T	Simple ethnic (tribal) religions
	Sk	Sikhism
		Countries under Communist regimes; traditional religions often subject to restraint
		Uninhabited

*In certain Eastern Asian areas, most of the people have plural
religious affiliations. Chinese, Korean, and Vietnamese religions
include Mahayana Buddhism, Taoism, Confucianism, and folk cults.
The Japanese religions include Shinto and Mahayana Buddhism.

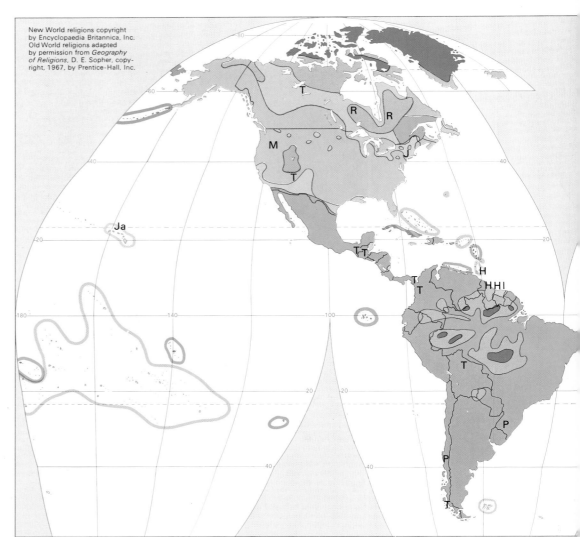

New World religions copyright
by Encyclopaedia Britannica, Inc.
Old World religions adapted
by permission from *Geography
of Religions*, D. E. Sopher, copyright, 1967, by Prentice-Hall, Inc.

Languages

Languages of Europe

The following languages are ranked in descending order by
number of speakers. Languages spoken by more than
4.5 million people are indicated by color. Others listed, spoken
by fewer than 4.5 million persons, are named on the map.

Russian	Norwegian	Basque	Karelian
German	Lithuanian	Irish-Gaelic	Icelandic
Italian	Chuvash	Mari	Adyge
English	Slovenian	Welsh	Scots-Gaelic
French	Macedonian	Friulian	Romansh
Ukrainian	Latvian	Komi	Lappish
Polish	Mordvinian	Frisian	Lusatian
Spanish	Estonian	Sardinian	Ladin
Romanian	Breton	Maltese	
Serbo-Croatian			
Dutch-Flemish			
Hungarian			
Portuguese			
Czech			
Belorussian			
Greek			
Bulgarian			
Swedish			
Catalan			
Danish			
Turkish			
Slovak			
Albanian			
Finnish			
All others			

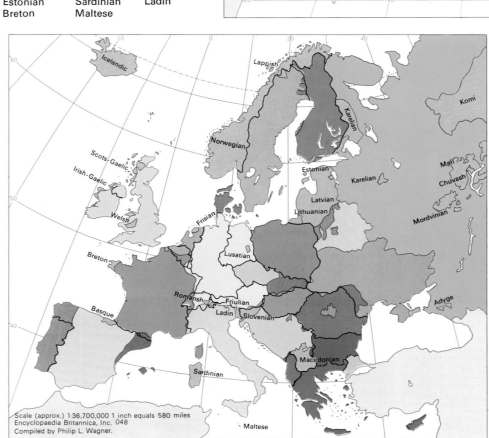

Scale (approx.) 136,700,000 1 inch equals 580 miles
Encyclopaedia Britannica, Inc. 048
Compiled by Philip L. Wagner.

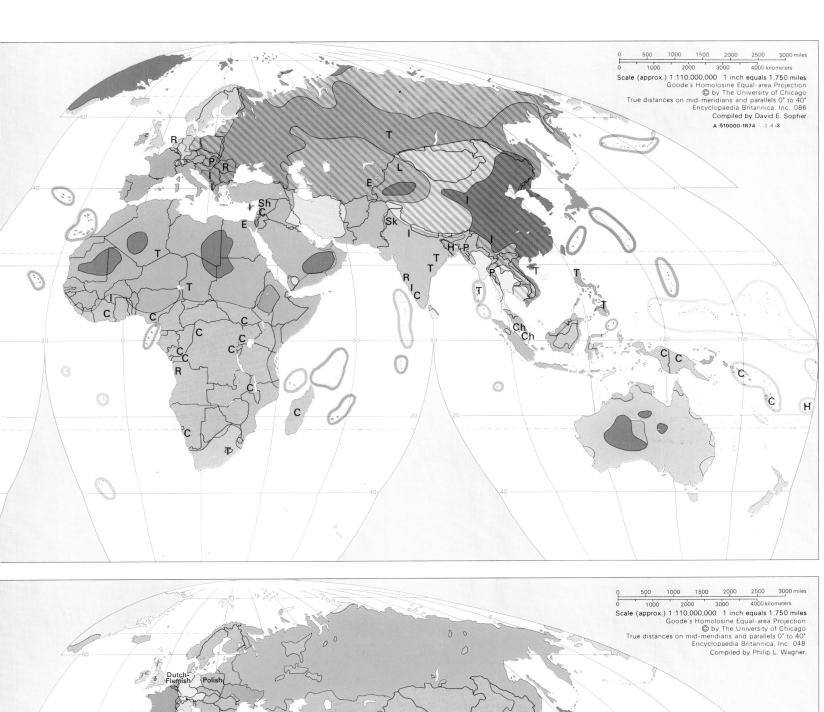

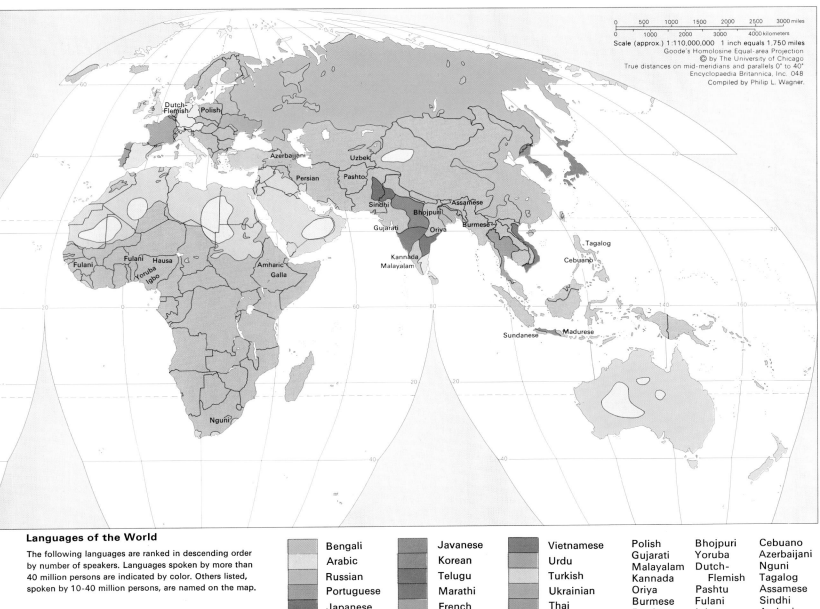

Languages of the World

The following languages are ranked in descending order
by number of speakers. Languages spoken by more than
40 million persons are indicated by color. Others listed,
spoken by 10-40 million persons, are named on the map.

Chinese	English	
Spanish	Hindi	

Bengali	Javanese	Vietnamese
Arabic	Korean	Urdu
Russian	Telugu	Turkish
Portuguese	Marathi	Ukrainian
Japanese	French	Thai
German	Italian	All others
Punjabi	Tamil	Uninhabited

Polish	Bhojpuri	Cebuano
Gujarati	Yoruba	Nguni
Malayalam	Dutch-	Azerbaijani
Kannada	Flemish	Tagalog
Oriya	Pashtu	Assamese
Burmese	Fulani	Sindhi
Persian	Igbo	Amharic
Hausa	Uzbek	Madurese
Sundanese	Galla	

11

Climate Graphs

Each graph below shows temperature and rainfall at a weather station that was selected to illustrate one of the climate regions described in the legend at the right. The weather stations are keyed by number to the maps. The elements of the graphs are identified in the sample graph at the top, with a temperature scale in degrees Fahrenheit and Celsius (Centigrade), and a precipitation scale in inches and millimeters.

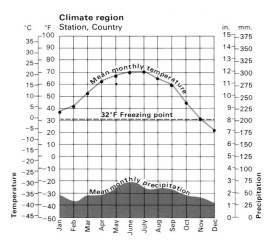

Climate Regions

Rainy tropical At most, one or two dry months; all months warm or hot

Wet and dry tropical A well-developed dry season with one or two rainy seasons; all months warm or hot

Semiarid tropical Light precipitation, rapid evaporation; all months warm or hot

Hot arid Negligible precipitation, rapid evaporation; all months warm or hot

Humid subtropical Precipitation in all seasons with maximum in summer; long warm summers, cool winters

Dry subtropical Hot dry summers; cool, moderately rainy winters

Humid mid-latitude Precipitation in all seasons with maximum in summer; warm or hot summers, cold winters

Temperate marine Numerous rainy days in all seasons with moderate total precipitation, higher precipitation in highland areas; warm summers, cool winters

Semiarid mid-latitude Light precipitation; warm or hot summers, cool or cold winters

Arid mid-latitude Extremely light precipitation; warm or hot summers, cool or cold winters

Subarctic Light precipitation; short cool summers, long very cold winters

Arctic margin Extremely light precipitation; very short cold summers, extremely long cold winters

High altitude Climate varies with elevation, latitude, and exposure

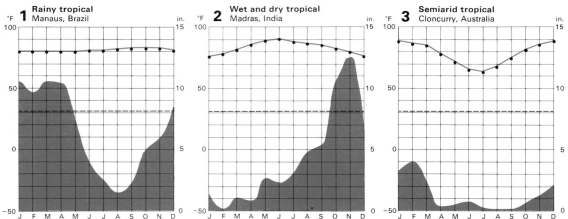

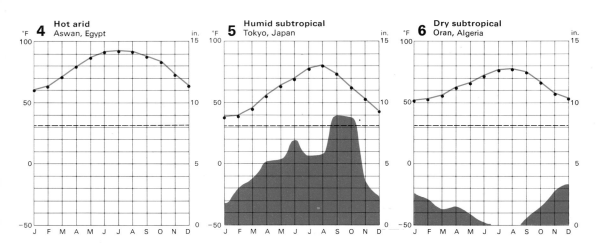

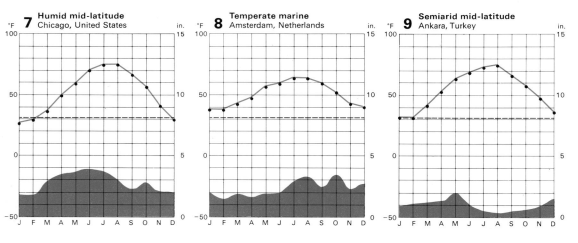

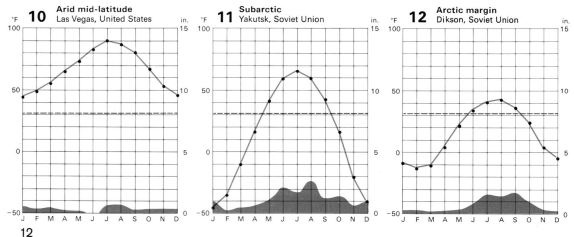

Mean Annual Temperature

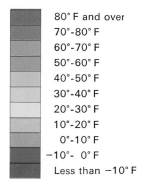

80° F and over
70°-80° F
60°-70° F
50°-60° F
40°-50° F
30°-40° F
20°-30° F
10°-20° F
0°-10° F
−10°- 0° F
Less than −10° F

Mean Annual Precipitation

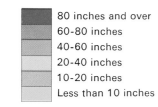

80 inches and over
60-80 inches
40-60 inches
20-40 inches
10-20 inches
Less than 10 inches

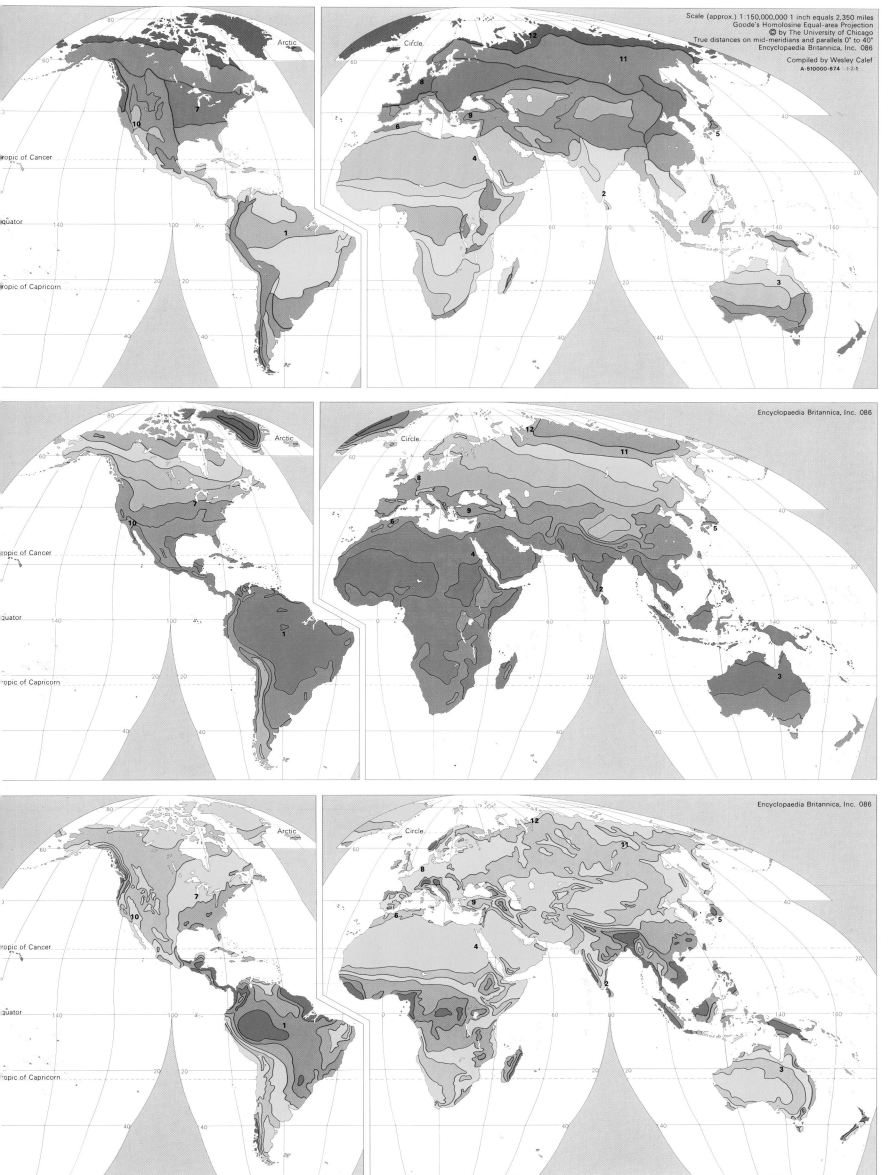

Scale (approx.) 1:150,000,000 1 inch equals 2,350 miles
Goode's Homolosine Equal-area Projection
© by The University of Chicago
True distances on mid-meridians and parallels 0° to 40°
Encyclopaedia Britannica, Inc. 086
Compiled by Wesley Calef
A-510000-674 -1-2-1

Encyclopaedia Britannica, Inc. 086

Encyclopaedia Britannica, Inc. 086

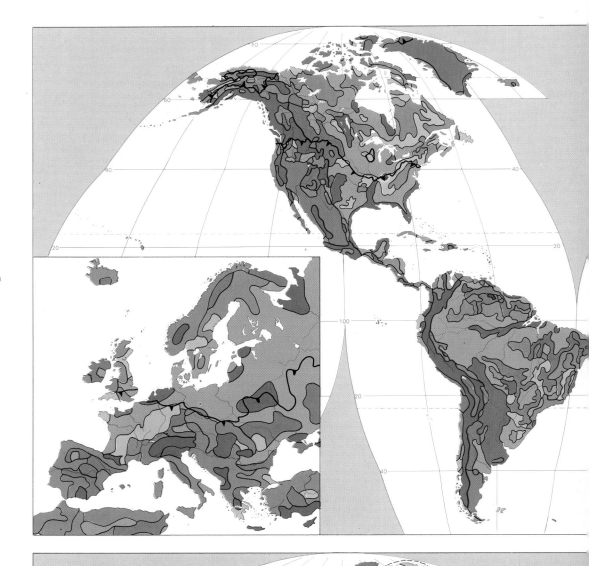

Surface Configuration

Smooth lands

Level plains: nearly all slopes gentle; local relief less than 100 ft. (30 m.)

Irregular plains: majority of slopes gentle; local relief 100-300 ft. (30-90 m.)

Broken lands

Tablelands and plateaus: majority of slopes gentle, with the gentler slopes on the uplands; local relief more than 300 ft. (90 m.)

Hill-studded plains: majority of slopes gentle, with the gentler slopes in the lowlands; local relief 300-1,000 ft. (90-300 m.)

Mountain-studded plains: majority of slopes gentle, with the gentler slopes in the lowlands; local relief more than 1,000 ft. (300 m.)

Rough lands

Hill lands: steeper slopes predominate; local relief less than 1,000 ft. (300 m.)

Mountains: steeper slopes predominate; local relief 1,000-5,000 ft. (300-1,500 m.)

Mountains of great relief: steeper slopes predominate; local relief more than 5,000 ft. (1,500 m.)

Other surfaces

Ice caps: permanent ice

Maximum extent of glaciation

Earth Structure and Tectonics

Precambrian stable shield areas

Exposed Precambrian rock

Paleozoic and Mesozoic flat-lying sedimentary rocks

Principal Paleozoic and Mesozoic folded areas

Cenozoic sedimentary rocks

Principal Cenozoic folded areas

Lava plateaus

Major trends of folding

Geologic time chart

Precambrian—from formation of the earth (at least 4 billion years ago) to 600 million years ago

Paleozoic—from 600 million to 200 million years ago

Mesozoic—from 200 million to 70 million years ago

Cenozoic—from 70 million years ago to present time

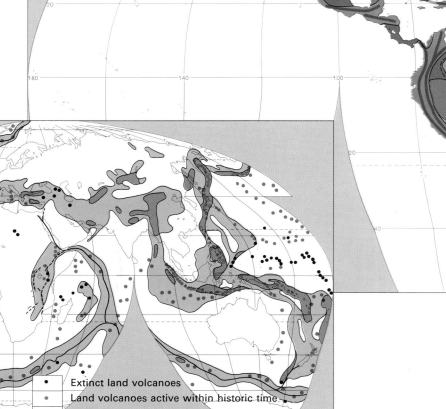

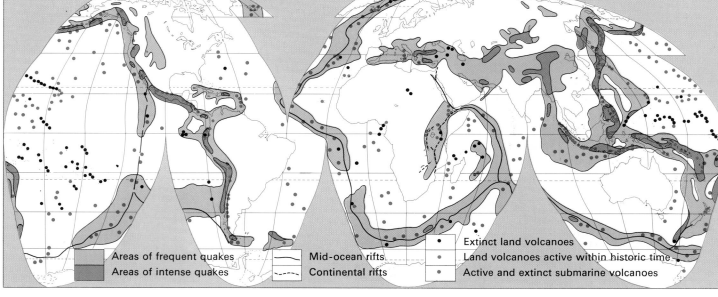

Areas of frequent quakes

Areas of intense quakes

Mid-ocean rifts

Continental rifts

Extinct land volcanoes

Land volcanoes active within historic time

Active and extinct submarine volcanoes

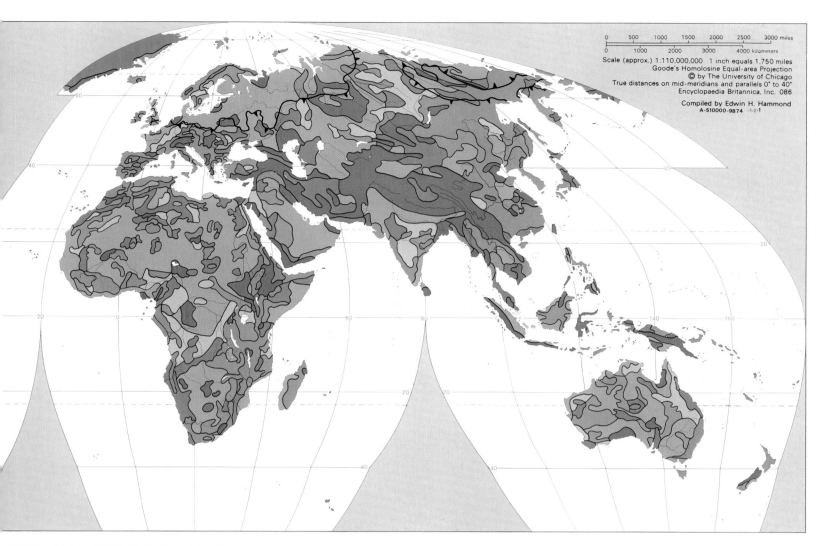

Scale (approx.) 1:110,000,000 1 inch equals 1,750 miles
Goode's Homolosine Equal-area Projection
© by The University of Chicago
True distances on mid-meridians and parallels 0° to 40°
Encyclopaedia Britannica, Inc. 086

Compiled by Edwin H. Hammond
A-510000-9874 -1-0-1

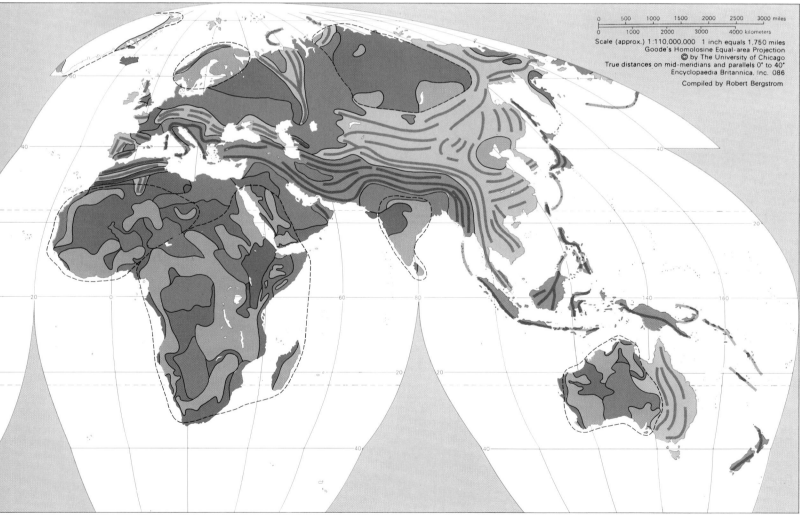

Scale (approx.) 1:110,000,000 1 inch equals 1,750 miles
Goode's Homolosine Equal-area Projection
© by The University of Chicago
True distances on mid-meridians and parallels 0° to 40°
Encyclopaedia Britannica, Inc. 086

Compiled by Robert Bergstrom

Development of the earth's structure

The earth is in process of constant transformation.
Movements in the hot, dense interior of the earth result
in folding and fracture of the crust and transfer of molten
material to the surface. As a result, large structures
such as mountain ranges, volcanoes, lava plateaus, and
rift valleys are created. The forces that bring about these
structural changes are called *tectonic forces*.

The present continents have developed from stable
nuclei, or *shields*, of ancient (Precambrian) rock.
Erosive forces such as water, wind, and ice have worn

away particles of the rock, depositing them at the edges
of the shields, where they have accumulated and
ultimately become sedimentary rock. Subsequently,
in places, these extensive areas of flat-lying rock have
been elevated, folded, or warped, by the action of tectonic
forces, to form mountains. The shape of these mountains
has been altered by later erosion. Where the forces of
erosion have been at work for a long time, the mountains
tend to have a low relief and rounded contours, like the
Appalachians. Mountains more recently formed are high

and rugged, like the Himalayas.

The map above depicts some of the major geologic
structures of the earth and identifies them according to the
period of their formation. A geologic time chart is included in
the legend. The inset map shows the most important areas
of earthquakes, rifts, and volcanic activity. Comparison of
all the maps will show the close correlation between
present-day mountain systems, recent (Cenozoic)
mountain-building, and the areas of frequent earthquakes
and active volcanoes.

Legend to Maps

Inhabited Localities

The symbol represents the number of inhabitants within the locality

1:300,000	•	0—10,000	1:12,000,000	•	0—50,000
1:1,000,000	○	10,000—25,000		⊚	50,000—100,000
1:3,000,000	⊙	25,000—100,000		⊡	100,000—250,000
1:6,000,000	⊡	100,000—250,000		▣	250,000—1,000,000
	▣	250,000—1,000,000		■	>1,000,000
	■	>1,000,000			

Urban Area (area of continuous industrial, commercial, and residential development)

Northland Center ■ **Major Shopping Center**

Major Industrial Area

Wooded Area

Local Park or Recreational Area

The size of type indicates the relative economic and political importance of the locality

Écommoy	Lisieux	**Rouen**
Trouville	**Orléans**	**PARIS**

Hollywood □   **Section of a City, Neighborhood**
Westminster

Bi'r Safājah ○   **Inhabited Oasis**   *Kumdah* ○   **Uninhabited Oasis**

Capitals of Political Units

BUDAPEST   Independent Nation

Cayenne   Dependency   (Colony, protectorate, etc.)

GALAPAGOS   **Administering Country**
(Ecuador)

Villarica   State, Province, etc.

White Plains   County, Oblast, etc.

Iserlohn   Okrug, Kreis, etc.

Alternate Names

Basel	**MOSKVA**	English or second official language names are shown
Bâle	MOSCOW	in reduced size lettering

Ventura	Volgograd	Historical or other alternates in the local language
(San Buenaventura)	(Stalingrad)	are shown in parentheses

Political Boundaries

International (First-order political unit)

	1:1,000,000
	1:3,000,000
1:300,000	1:6,000,000
	1:12,000,000

Demarcated, Undemarcated, and Administrative

Disputed de jure

Indefinite or Undefined

Demarcation Line

Internal

Okrug, Kreis, etc.
(Fourth-order political unit)

City or Municipality
(may appear in combination with another boundary symbol)

GUAIRA   State, Province, etc. (Second-order political unit)

WESTCHESTER   County, Oblast, etc. (Third-order political unit)

ANDALUCIA   Historical Region   (No boundaries indicated)

Miscellaneous Cultural Features

PARQUE NACIONAL CANAIMA	**National or State Park or Monument**	*STEINHAUSEN*	Church, Monastery
FORT CLATSOP NAT. MEM.	**National or State Historic(al) Site, Memorial**	*UXMAL*	Ruins
BLACKFOOT IND. RES.	**Indian Reservation**	*WINDSOR CASTLE*	Castle
FORT DIX	**Military Installation**	*AMISTAD DAM*	Dam
			Quarry or Surface Mine
TANGLEWOOD	**Point of Interest** (Battlefield, cave, historical site, etc.)		Subsurface Mine
		GREENWOOD CEMETERY	Cemetery
			Lighthouse
‹›	**Lock**	*Crib*	Water Intake Crib

Transportation

1:12,000,000	1:3,000,000 1:6,000,000	1:300,000 1:1,000,000	
		PENNSYLVANIA TURNPIKE	Primary Road
			Secondary Road
			Tertiary Road
			Minor Road, Trail
		CANADIAN NATIONAL	Primary Railway
			Secondary Railway
		DULLES INTERNATIONAL F: AIRPORT	Airport
		LONDON (HEATHROW) AIRPORT	Airport
		SÜD-BAHNHOF ◼	Rail or Air Terminal

MACKINAC BRIDGE — Bridge

TUNNEL DU GRAND-SAINT-BERNARD — Tunnel

TO CALAIS — Ferry

Shipping Channel

Canal du Midi — Navigable Canal

Intracoastal Waterway

Metric-English Equivalents

Areas represented by one square centimeter at various map scales

1:300,000
9 km²
3.48 square miles

1:6,000,000
3,600 km²
1,390 square miles

1:1,000,000
100 km²
39 square miles

1:12,000,000
14,400 km²
5,558 square miles

1:3,000,000
900 km²
348 square miles

Meter=3.28 feet
Kilometer=0.62 mile

Meter² (m²)=10.76 square feet
Kilometer² (km²)=0.39 square mile

Hydrographic Features

Shoreline

Undefined or Fluctuating Shoreline

Amur — River, Stream

Intermittent Stream

Rapids, Falls

Irrigation or Drainage Canal

Reef

764 ▽ Depth of Water

Los Angeles Aqueduct — Aqueduct

The Everglades — Swamp

SEWARD GLACIER — Glacier

L. Victoria — Lake, Reservoir

Tuz Gölü — Salt Lake

Intermittent Lake, Reservoir

Dry Lake Bed

(395) Lake Surface Elevation

Pier, Breakwater

Topographic Features

Mt. Rainier △ 4392 — Elevation Above Sea Level

76 ▽ — Elevation Below Sea Level

Mount Cook ▲ 3764 — Highest Elevation in Country

Khyber Pass ⚍ 1067 — Mountain Pass

133 ▼ — Lowest Elevation in Country

(106) — Elevation of City

⋆ Rock

Elevations and depths are given in meters

Highest Elevation and Lowest Elevation of a continent are underlined

Lava

Sand Area

Salt Flat

A N D E S
KUNLUNSHANMAI — Mountain Range, Plateau, Valley, etc.

BAFFIN ISLAND
NUNIVAK ISLAND — Island

POLUOSTROV
KAMČATKA — Peninsula, Cape, Point, etc.
CABO DE HORNOS

ARCTIC OCEAN

GREENLAND
(Den.)

Beaufort Sea

Thule

Baffin
Bay

ICELAND
FAEROE
ISLANDS
(Den.)

UNITED STATES
Arctic Circle

Inuvik

VICTORIA
ISLAND

BAFFIN ISLAND

Godhavn

Angmagssalik

Reykjavik

Nome

Fairbanks

Yellowknife

Davis Strait

Godthåb

Anchorage
Mount
McKinley

Gulf of
Alaska

Bering Sea

ALEUTIAN
ISLANDS

U.S.S.R.

Juneau

Hudson
Bay

Churchill

Goose Bay

Glasgow

Dublin

UNITED
KINGDOM
LONDON

ALEUTIAN
ISLANDS

CANADA

Edmonton

Calgary

Winnipeg

Lake
Superior

Ottawa

Québec

NEWFOUNDLAND

St. John's

IRELAND

PACIFIC

Vancouver

Seattle

Portland

NORTH AMERICA

UNITED STATES

Minneapolis

CHICAGO

Lake
Michigan

DETROIT

Toronto

Montréal

Lake
Huron

Boston

NEW YORK

PHILADELPHIA

Halifax

ATLANTIC OCEAN

PORTUGAL

Porto

SPAIN

Madr

OCEAN

San Francisco

LOS ANGELES

San Diego

Salt
Lake City

Denver

St.
Louis

Phoenix

El Paso

Dallas

Atlanta

Washington

AÇORES AZORES
(Port.)

BERMUDA
(U.K.)

Lisboa

GIBRALTAR
(U.K.)

Rabat

Wahre

MOROCCO

MIDWAY ISLANDS
(U.S.)

OCEAN

Tropic of Cancer

CABO SAN LUCAS

Houston

New
Orleans

Monterrey

Gulf of Mexico

Miami

BAHAMAS

ISLAS CANARIAS
CANARY ISLANDS
(Sp.)

WESTERN
SAHARA

AL

HAWAIIAN
ISLANDS
(U.S.)

Honolulu

MEXICO

Guadalajara

CIUDAD
DE MÉXICO

La Habana

CUBA

HAITI

DOMINICAN
REPUBLIC

PUERTO RICO (U.S.)

S

MAURI-
TANIA

JOHNSTON ATOLL
(U.S.)

P
O
L
Y
N
E
S
I
A

GUATEMALA

Guatemala

BELIZE

Port-au-Prince

JAMAICA

Kingston

Santo
Domingo

San Juan

GUADELOUPE (Fr.)

Nouakchott

Tómbouctou

CAPE VERDE

SENEGAL

Dakar

MA

CLIPPERTON
(Fr. Poly.)

HONDURAS

Tegucigalpa

EL SALVADOR

San Salvador

NICARAGUA

Managua

COSTA
RICA

San José

Caribbean
Sea

MARTINIQUE (Fr.)

BARBADOS

TRINIDAD AND
TOBAGO

Port of Spain

GUINEA-BISSAU

GAMBIA

Banjul

BURKIN

Bamako

Ouagadougo

FASO

LINE ISLANDS

Equator

ARCHIPIÉLAGO DE COLÓN
GALÁPAGOS ISLANDS
(Ec.)

Panamá

PANAMA

Medellín

Cali

Bogotá

Caracas

VENEZUELA

GUYANA

Georgetown

Paramaribo

SURI-
NAME

FRENCH
GUIANA

Conakry

GUINEA

SIERRA
LEONE

Freetown

Yamoussoukro

IVORY
COAST

Abidjan

Equator

PHOENIX
ISLANDS

COLOMBIA

ECUADOR

Quito

Guayaquil

Manaus

Amazon

Belém

Fortaleza

CABO DE SÃO ROQUE

Natal

LIBERIA

Monrovia

TOKELAU ISLANDS
(N.Z.)

ÎLES MARQUISES

Iquitos

P
E
R
U

Trujillo

A
N
D
E
S

B R A Z I L

Recife

ATLANTIC OCEAN

WALLIS
AND
FUTUNA
(Fr.)

W.
SAMOA

AM.
SAMOA

Apia

ÎLES
TUAMOTU

ÎLES

Lima

SOUTH AMERICA

Salvador

FIJI

NIUE
(N.Z.)

ÎLES DE LA SOCIÉTÉ
SOCIETY ISLANDS

FRENCH
POLYNESIA

Arequipa

La Paz

BOLIVIA

Sucre

Goiânia

Brasília

Belo Horizonte

TONGA

COOK
ISLANDS
(N.Z.)

Tropic of Capricorn

PARAGUAY

SÃO PAULO

RIO DE JANEIRO

PITCAIRN
(U.K.)

Antofagasta

ISLA
SAN AMBROSIO
(Chile)

Asunción

Santos

Curitiba

PACIFIC

ISLA DE PASCUA
EASTER ISLAND
(Chile)

CHILE

Co. Aconcagua
6959

A
N
D
E
S

Córdoba

Pôrto Alegre

ISLAS JUAN FERNÁNDEZ
(Chile)

Valparaiso

Santiago

Rosario

BUENOS AIRES

URUGUAY

Montevideo

CHATHAM ISLAND
(N.Z.)

OCEAN

Concepción

ARGENTINA

Mar del Plata

Bahía Blanca

International Date Line

FALKLAND ISLANDS
ISLAS MALVINAS
(U.K.)

Punta Arenas

CABO DE HORNOS
CAPE HORN

SOUTH GEORGIA
(Falk. Is.)

Antarctic Circle

SOUTH ORKNEY
ISLANDS
(B.A.T.)

Bellingshausen Sea

ANTARCTIC
PENINSULA

Weddell
Sea

Ross Sea

Vinson Massif
5140

A N T A R

One centimetre represents 750 kilometres.

Robinson Projection

Scale 1:75,000,000

19

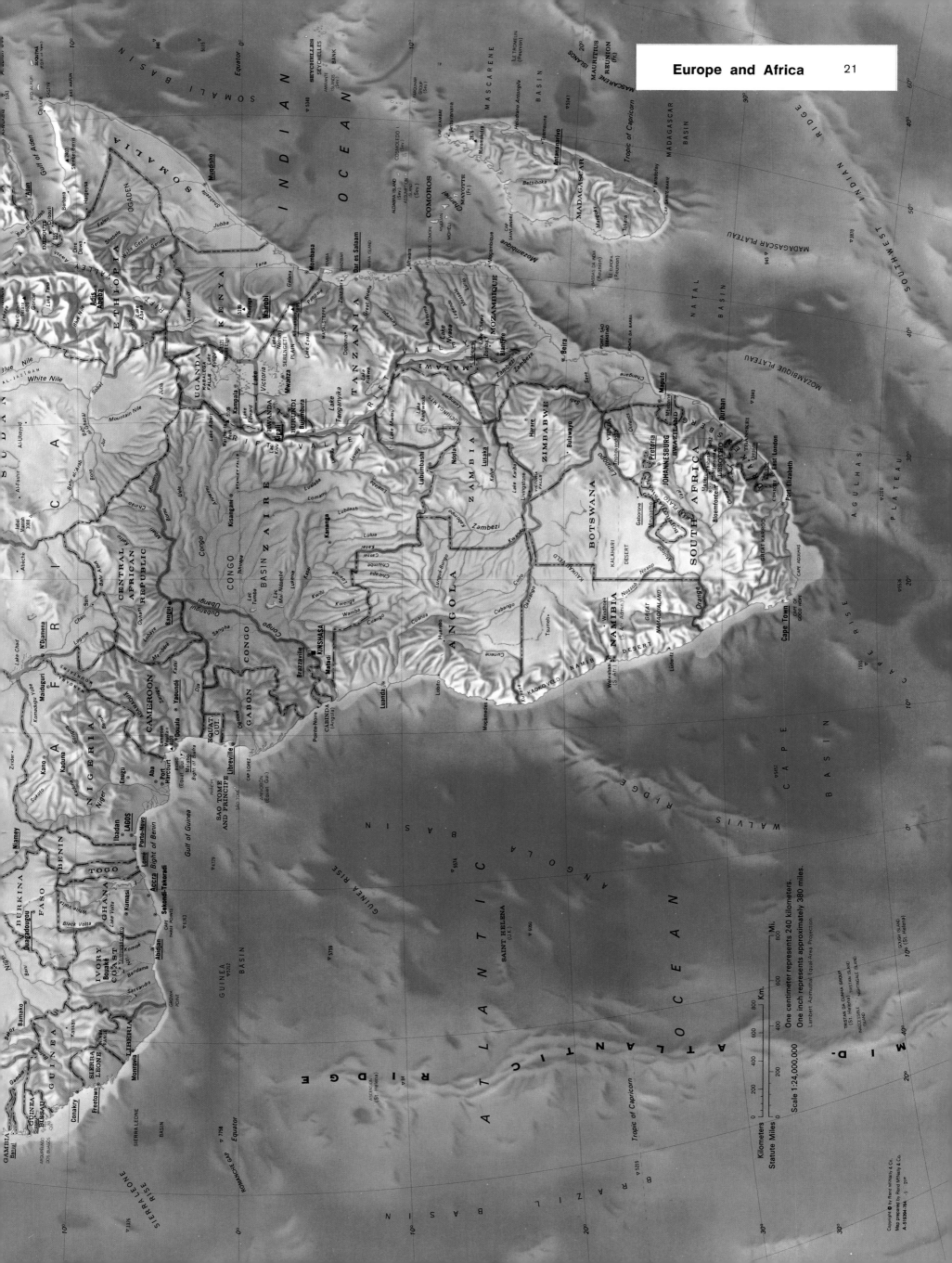

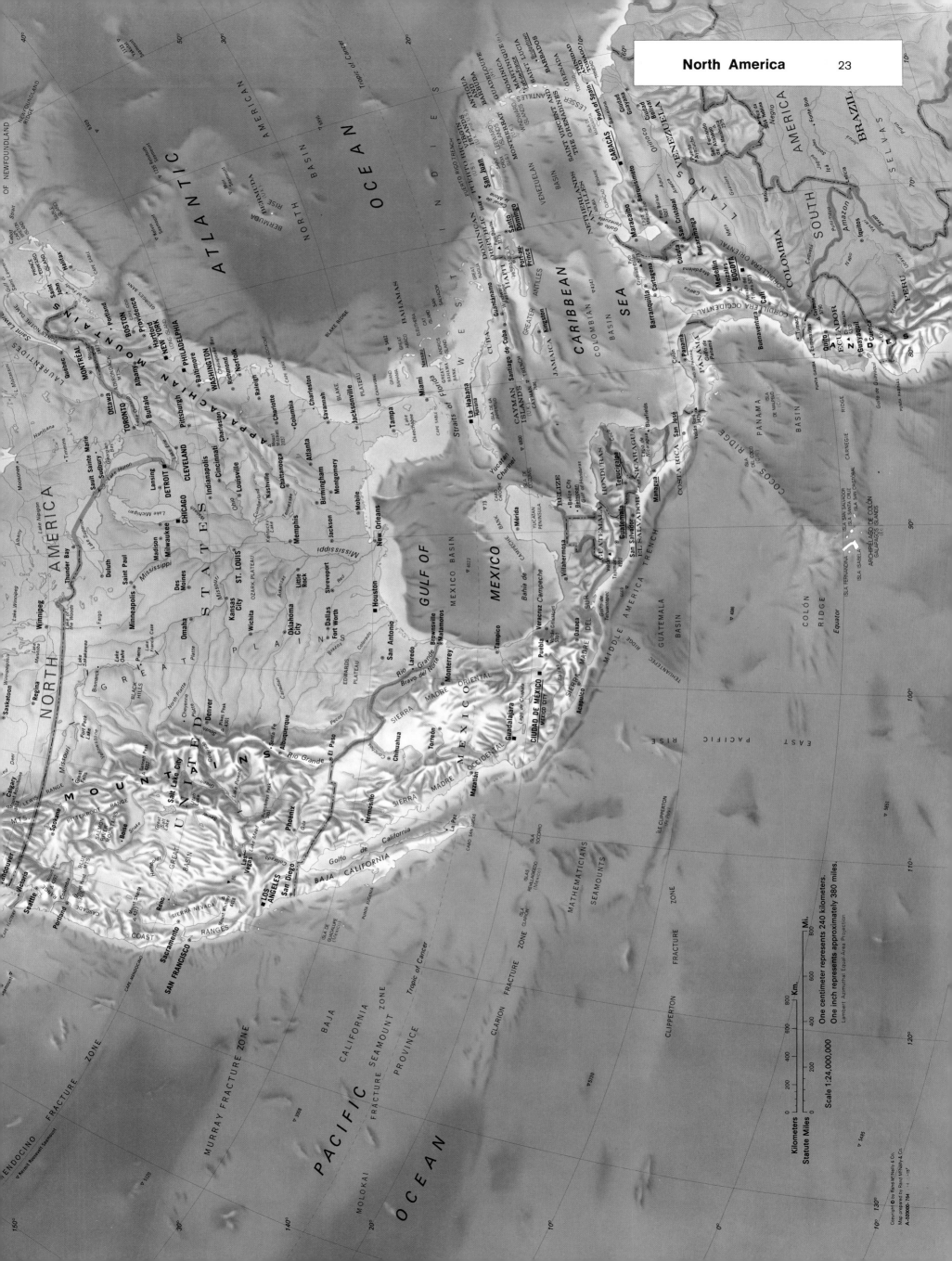

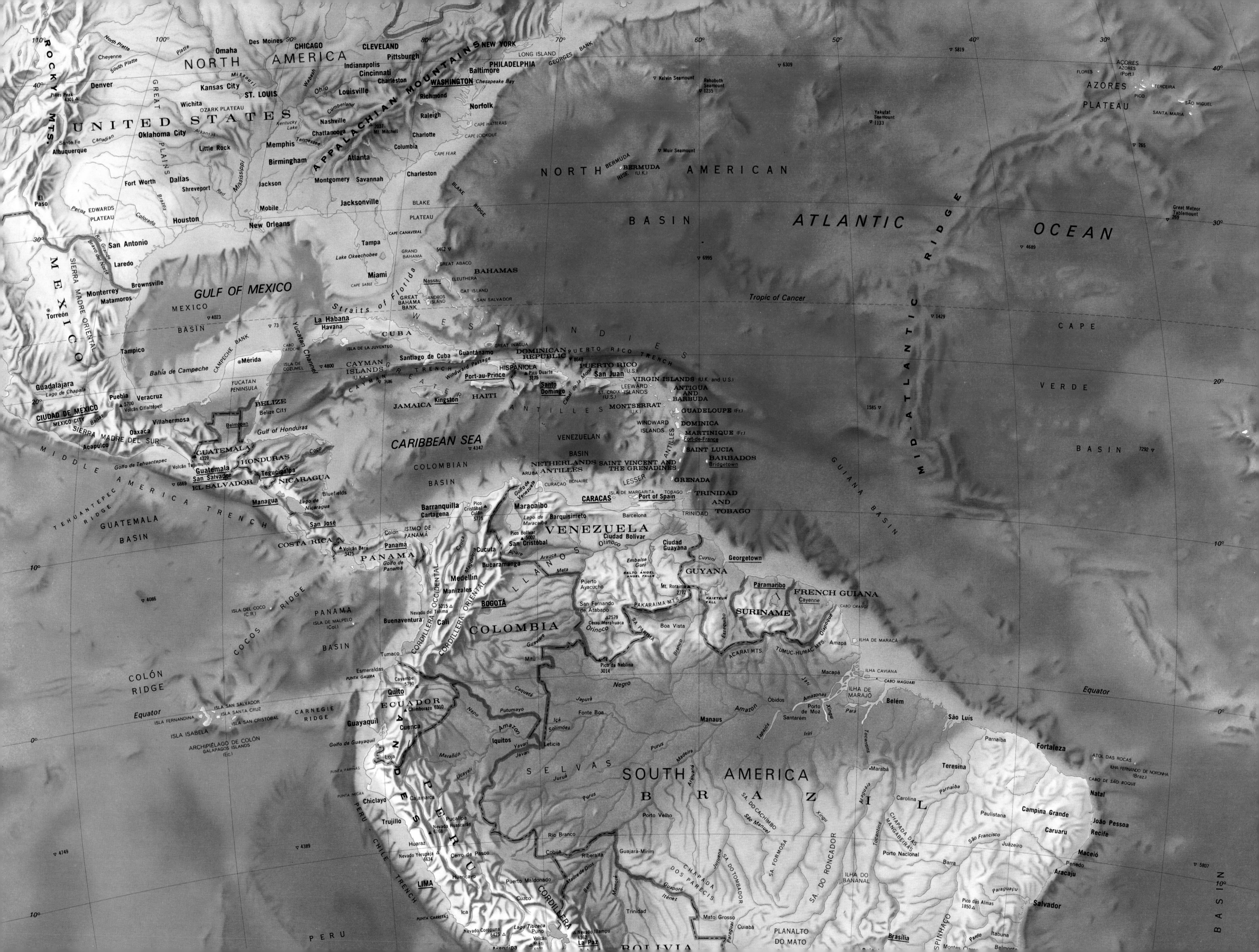

AZORES PLATEAU

FLORES AÇORES (Port.) TERCEIRA SANTA MARIA
PICO SÃO MIGUEL

ATLANTIC OCEAN

CAPE VERDE

MID-ATLANTIC RIDGE

NORTH AMERICAN BASIN

NORTH AMERICA

UNITED STATES

ROCKY MOUNTAINS   APPALACHIAN MOUNTAINS

Cheyenne North Platte Omaha Des Moines CHICAGO CLEVELAND Pittsburgh NEW YORK LONG ISLAND
Denver Kansas City Indianapolis Cincinnati PHILADELPHIA Baltimore
Colorado Springs Wichita St. Louis Louisville Charleston WASHINGTON Chesapeake Bay
Pueblo OZARK PLATEAU Nashville Chattanooga Richmond Norfolk
Santa Fe Oklahoma City Memphis Knoxville Charlotte Raleigh CAPE HATTERAS
Albuquerque Little Rock Birmingham Atlanta Columbia CAPE LOOKOUT
Fort Worth Dallas Shreveport Jackson Montgomery Savannah CAPE FEAR
El Paso Brazos Jacksonville CAPE CANAVERAL
Laredo Houston Mobile New Orleans Tampa Lake Okeechobee Miami CAPE SABLE
San Antonio Brownsville Mississippi

GREAT PLAINS EDWARDS PLATEAU

Rio Grande Bravo del Norte

MEXICO

Monterrey Matamoros Tampico
Guadalajara Torreón
CIUDAD DE MÉXICO MEXICO CITY Puebla Veracruz
Lago de Chapala Acapulco Oaxaca Villahermosa
SIERRA MADRE ORIENTAL SIERRA MADRE DEL SUR
Golfo de Tehuantepec

GULF OF MEXICO

MEXICO BASIN CAMPECHE BANK Bahía de Campeche YUCATAN PENINSULA Mérida

Straits of Florida
Florida
BAHAMAS GREAT BAHAMA GRAND BAHAMA ABACO GREAT ABACO
Nassau ELEUTHERA CAT ISLAND SAN SALVADOR
ANDROS ISLAND BLAKE PLATEAU BLAKE RIDGE

BERMUDA (U.K.)

NORTH AMERICAN BASIN

WEST INDIES

CUBA La Habana Havana ISLA DE LA JUVENTUD Santiago de Cuba Guantánamo
CAYMAN ISLANDS CAYMAN TRENCH
JAMAICA Kingston

HISPANIOLA HAITI Port-au-Prince DOMINICAN REPUBLIC Santo Domingo
PUERTO RICO (U.S.) San Juan PUERTO RICO TRENCH
VIRGIN ISLANDS (U.K. and U.S.)
LEEWARD ISLANDS
ANTIGUA AND BARBUDA
MONTSERRAT (U.K.)
GUADELOUPE (Fr.)
DOMINICA
MARTINIQUE (Fr.) Fort-de-France
SAINT LUCIA
BARBADOS Bridgetown
SAINT VINCENT AND THE GRENADINES
WINDWARD ISLANDS
GRENADA
NETHERLANDS ANTILLES
ARUBA CURAÇAO BONAIRE
LESSER ANTILLES

CARIBBEAN SEA

COLOMBIAN BASIN VENEZUELAN BASIN

BELIZE Belmopan Belize City
GUATEMALA Guatemala Villahermosa
HONDURAS Tegucigalpa San Pedro Sula
EL SALVADOR San Salvador
NICARAGUA Managua Lago de Nicaragua Lago de Managua Bluefields
COSTA RICA San José
PANAMA Panamá Colón Golfo de Panamá ISTMO DE PANAMÁ
Gulf of Honduras

MIDDLE AMERICA TRENCH
TEHUANTEPEC

COCOS RIDGE COLÓN RIDGE CARNEGIE RIDGE PANAMA BASIN
ISLA DEL COCO ISLA DE MALPELO
ARCHIPIÉLAGO DE COLÓN (GALÁPAGOS ISLANDS) ISLA ISABELA ISLA SANTA CRUZ ISLA SAN CRISTÓBAL

Equator

SOUTH AMERICA

VENEZUELA CARACAS Maracaibo Lago de Maracaibo Barquisimeto Barcelona Ciudad Bolívar Ciudad Guayana
San Cristóbal LLANOS ORINOCO San Fernando de Atabapo Puerto Ayacucho
MARGARITA TRINIDAD AND TOBAGO Port of Spain
PARIA TOBAGO

COLOMBIA BOGOTÁ Medellín Cali Barranquilla Cartagena Cúcuta Bucaramanga Manizales Buenaventura
CORDILLERA OCCIDENTAL CORDILLERA ORIENTAL
Mitú Leticia

GUYANA Georgetown
SURINAME Paramaribo
FRENCH GUIANA Cayenne
GUIANA BASIN
ACARAI MTS. PAKARAIMA MTS. Mt. Roraima KAIETEUR FALL
TUMUC-HUMAC MTS.

ECUADOR Quito Guayaquil Cuenca Esmeraldas Golfo de Guayaquil

PERU LIMA Iquitos Trujillo Chiclayo Nevado Huascarán
ANDES CORDILLERA

PERU - CHILE TRENCH

BRAZIL BRASIL
SELVAS Manaus Belém ILHA DE MARAJÓ ILHA CAVIANA
Boa Vista Macapá Santarém
Fortaleza Teresina São Luís Natal João Pessoa Recife Maceió Salvador Aracaju Campina Grande Caruaru
PLANALTO DO MATO GROSSO CHAPADA DOS PARECIS
SA. DO RONCADOR SA. DOS PARECIS SA. DO TOMBADOR SA. DO CACHIMBO SA. FORMOSA
CABO DE SÃO ROQUE
Amazonas Negro Branco Madeira Tapajós Xingu Tocantins Japurá Purus Juruá

BOLIVIA

Rio Grande

Tropic of Cancer

Equator

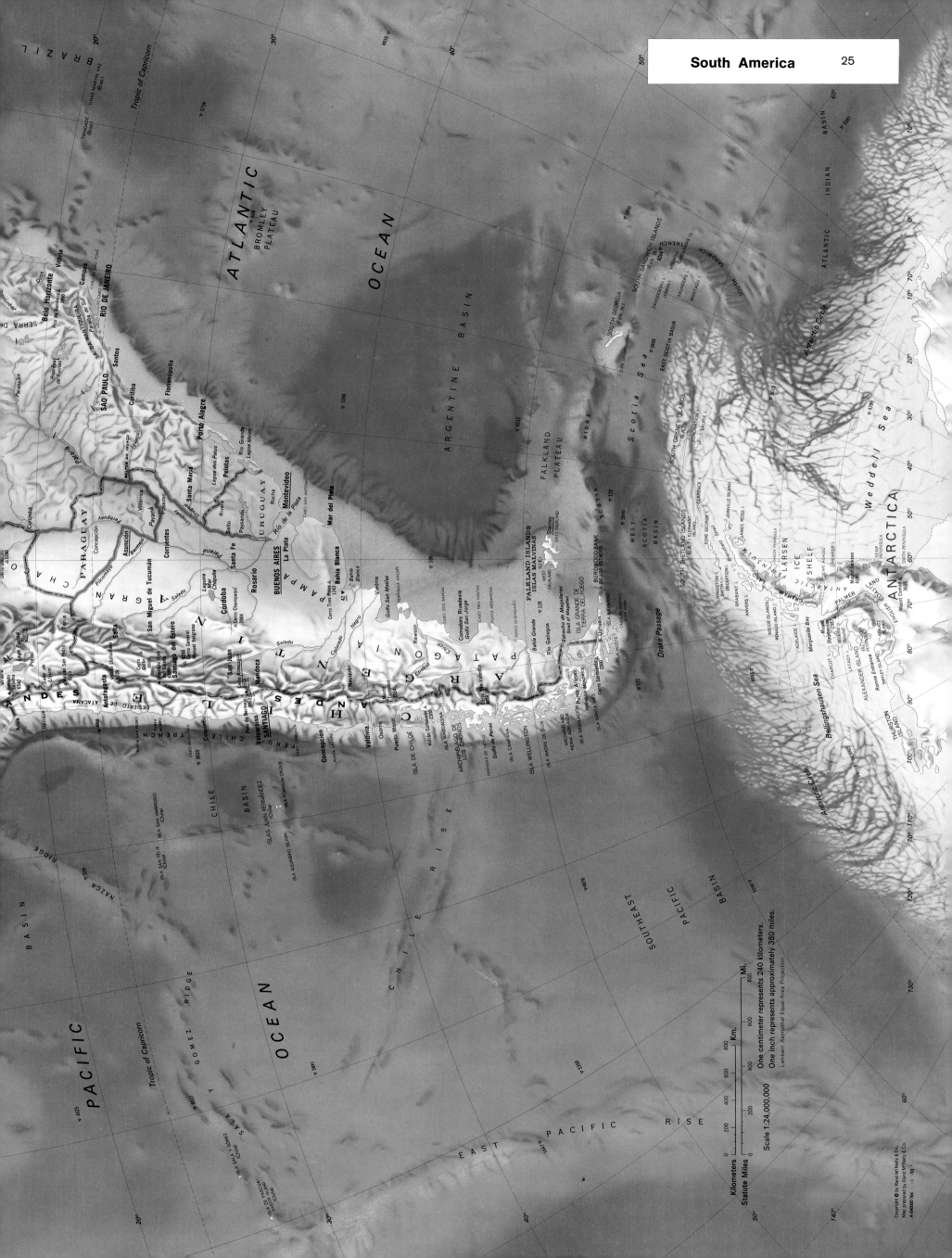

ATLANTIC

OCEAN

Tropic of Capricorn

BROMLEY PLATEAU

ARGENTINE BASIN

SCOTIA SEA

SOUTH SANDWICH ISLANDS

SOUTH GEORGIA

SOUTH ORKNEY ISLANDS

FALKLAND PLATEAU

WEST SCOTIA BASIN

EAST SCOTIA BASIN

WEDDELL Sea

ANTARCTICA

LARSEN ICE SHELF

GRAHAM LAND

PALMER LAND

ELLSWORTH LAND

SOUTH SHETLAND ISLANDS

Antarctic Circle

BRAZIL

SERRA DA MANTIQUEIRA

Belo Horizonte
Vitória
RIO DE JANEIRO
SÃO PAULO
Santos
Curitiba
Florianópolis
Porto Alegre
Rio Grande
Pelotas

PARAGUAY

URUGUAY

Asunción
Concepción
Corrientes
Santa Fe
Paraná
Rosario
Córdoba
Santa María
Rivera
Salto
Paysandú
Rocha
Montevideo
Mar del Plata
Bahía Blanca

BUENOS AIRES
La Plata

PAMPA

San Miguel de Tucumán
Santiago del Estero
San Juan
Mendoza
SANTIAGO
Valparaíso
Concepción
Valdivia
Puerto Montt
ISLA DE CHILOÉ

Antofagasta
ATACAMA
DESIERTO DE ATACAMA

CHILE

PERU - CHILE TRENCH

ANDES

PATAGONIA

ARGENTINA

Neuquén
Bahía Blanca
Viedma
Rawson
Comodoro Rivadavia
Gallo San Jorge
Río Gallegos
Bahía Grande
Estrecho de Magallanes
Strait of Magellan
Punta Arenas
Ushuaia
ISLA GRANDE DE TIERRA DEL FUEGO
Cabo de Hornos

FALKLAND ISLANDS
ISLAS MALVINAS
Stanley
BURDWOOD BANK

Drake Passage

PACIFIC

OCEAN

NAZCA BASIN

CHILE BASIN

ISLAS JUAN FERNÁNDEZ (Chile)

GOMEZ RIDGE

SALA Y GOMEZ RIDGE

CHILE RISE

SOUTHEAST PACIFIC BASIN

EAST PACIFIC RISE

Tropic of Capricorn

Scale 1:24,000,000

One centimeter represents 240 kilometers.
One inch represents approximately 380 miles.

Lambert Azimuthal Equal-Area Projection

Kilometers
Statute Miles
Km.
Mi.

Copyright © by Rand McNally & Co.
Map prepared by Rand McNally & Co.
A-640000-394

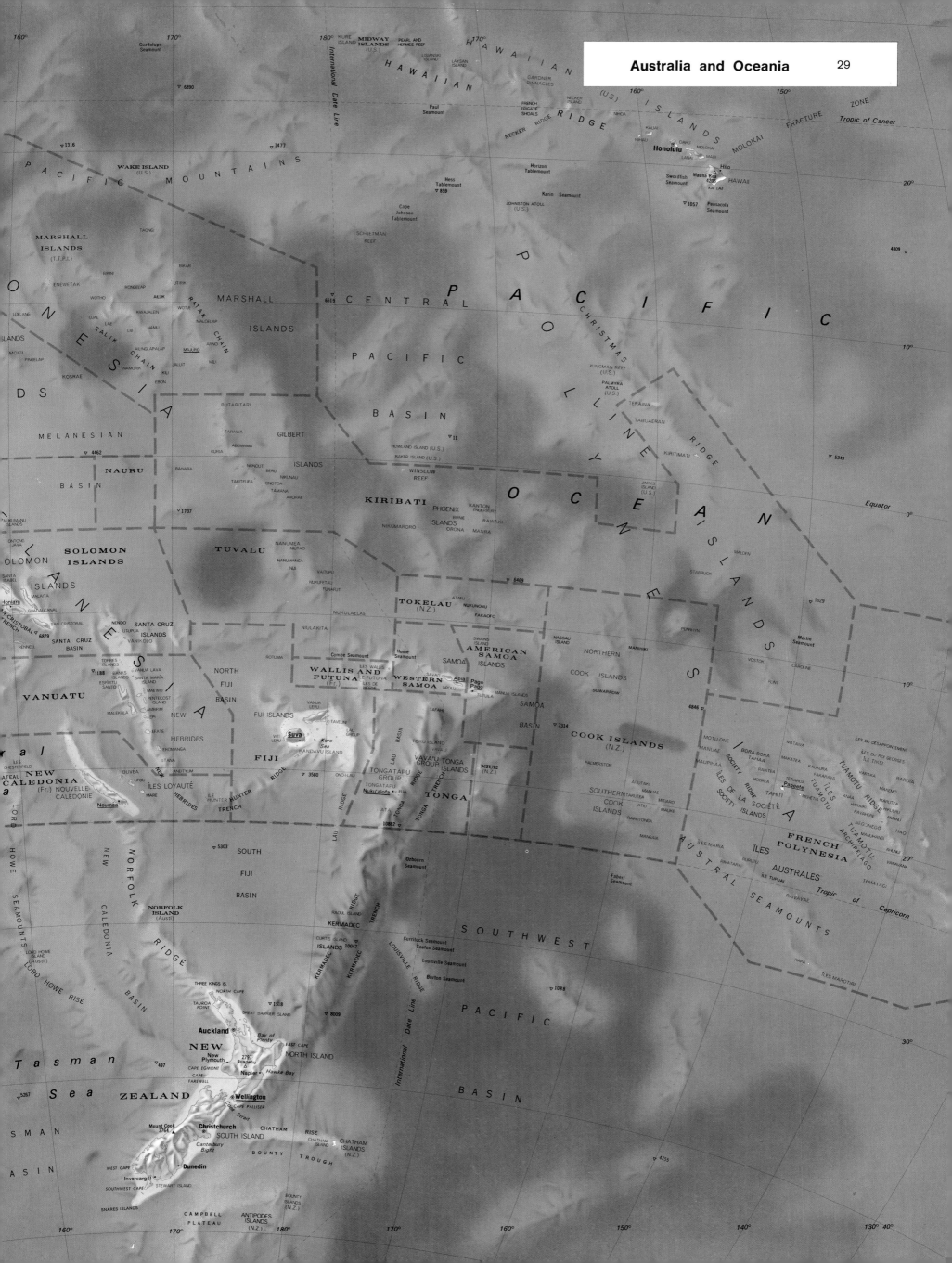

Kilometers

Statute Miles

Scale 1:12,000,000

0   200   400   600
Km.

0   200   400   600
Mi.

One centimeter represents 120 kilometers.
One inch represents approximately 190 miles.
Miller Oblated Stereographic Projection

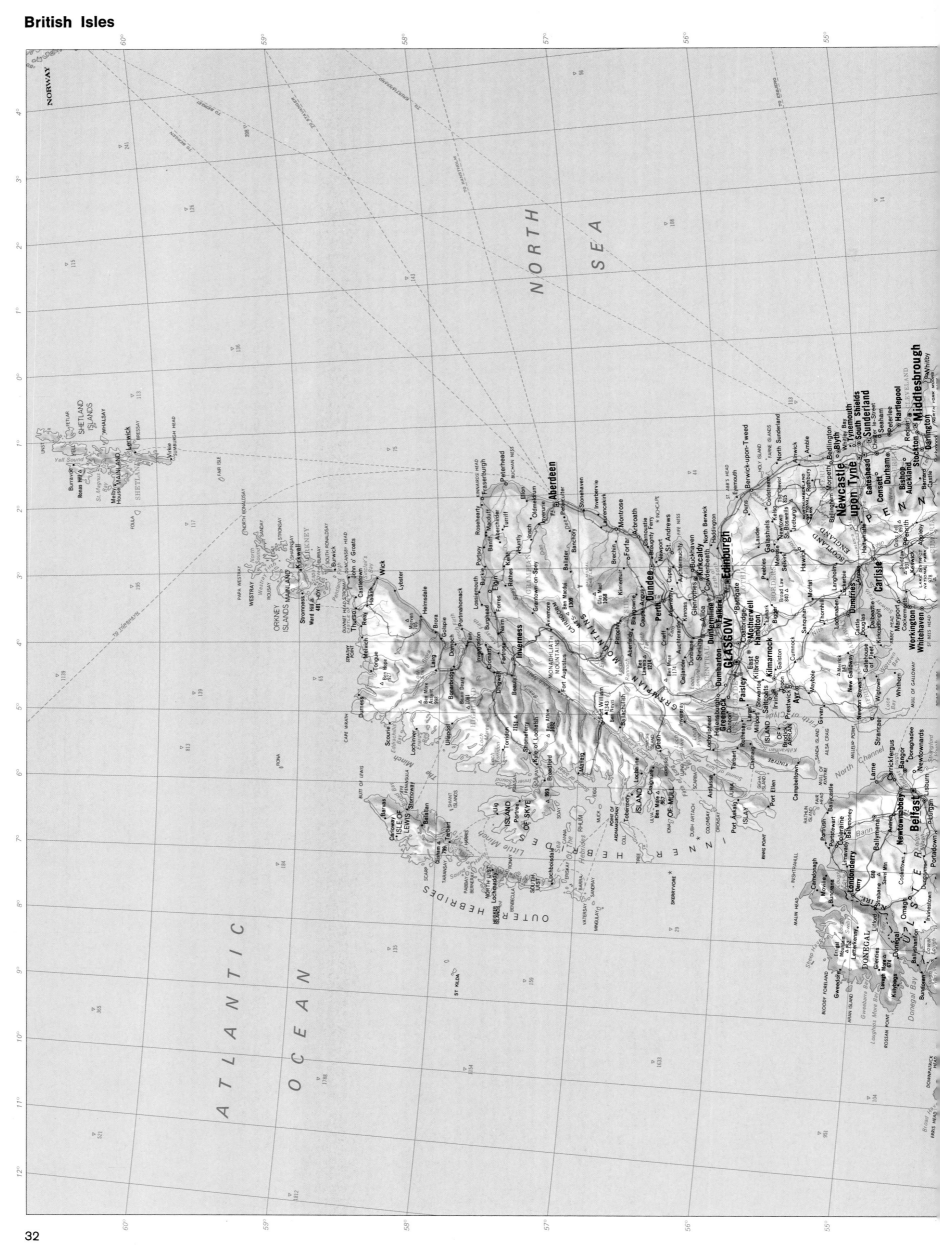

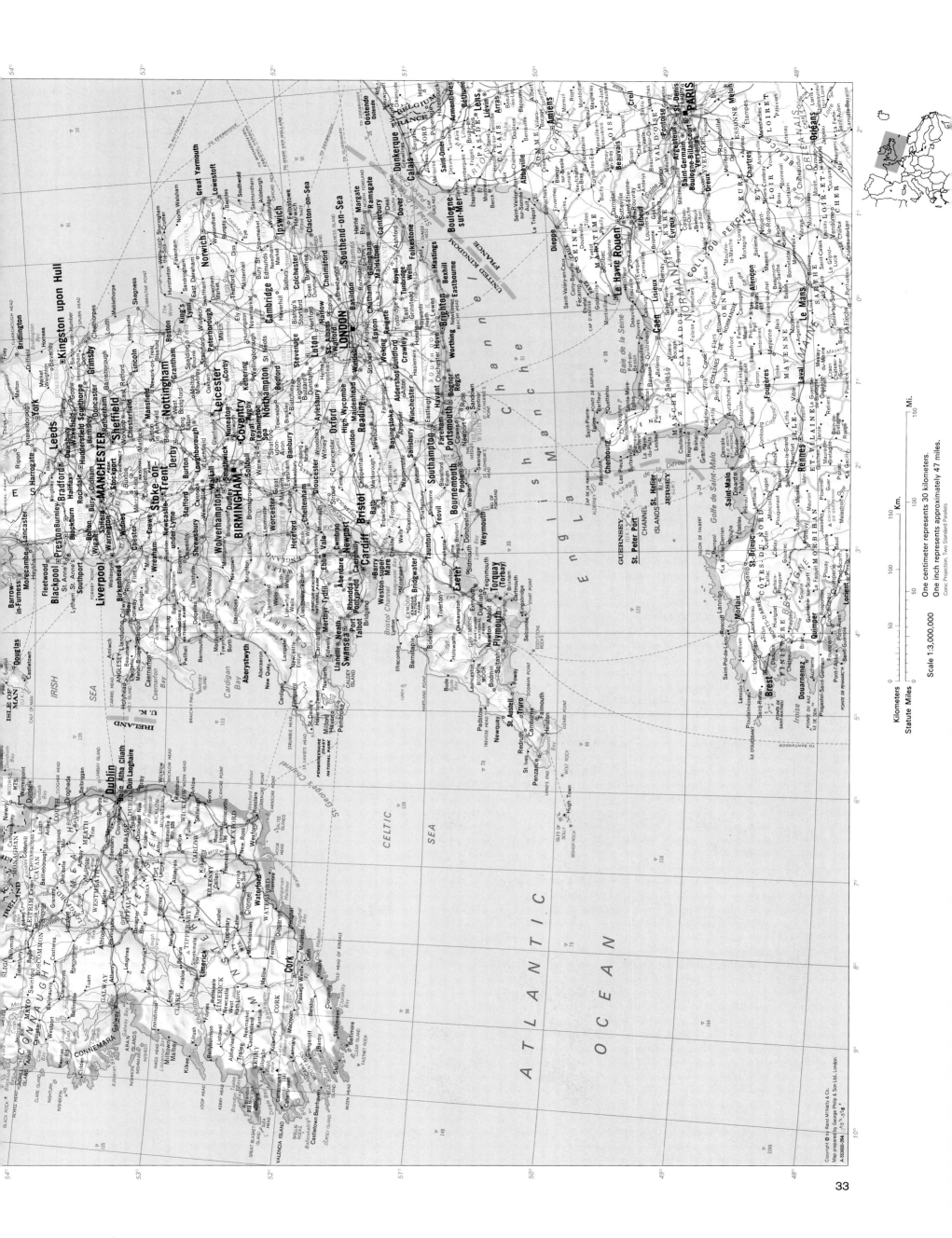

Kilometers

Statute Miles

Mi.

Km.

Scale 1:3,000,000

One centimeter represents 30 kilometers.
One inch represents approximately 47 miles.

Conic Projection. Two Standard Parallels.

England and Wales, South

Map prepared by Rand McNally & Co.

Copyright by Rand McNally & Co.
A-556900-264

ISLES OF SCILLY

North Channel

NORTH CHANNEL

North Channel

NORTHERN IRELAND

SCOTLAND

IRISH

SEA

DONEGAL

Lough Foyle

Londonderry Derry

NORTHERN IRELAND

Lough Neagh

Belfast

MONAGHAN

IRELAND ÉIRE N.K.

CAVAN

LOUTH

MEATH

An Uaimh (Navan)

Drogheda Droichead Átha

KILDARE

DUBLIN BAILE ÁTHA CLIATH

Dún Laoghaire

Bray

WICKLOW

WICKLOW MOUNTAINS

CARLOW

WEXFORD

ISLAND OF ARRAN

Campbeltown

Ayr

STRATHCLYDE

Kilmarnock

THE GLENKENS

GALLOWAY

THE MOORS

Stranraer

THE RHINS

THE MACHARS

Luce Bay

MULL OF GALLOWAY

Dumfries

Solway Firth

Maryport

Workington

Whitehaven

LAKE DISTRICT

Barrow-in-Furnes

CUMB

ISLE OF MAN (U.K.)

Douglas

Peel

Port Erin

IRELAND ÉIRE
UNITED KINGDOM

ANGLESEY

Holyhead

Bangor

Llandudno

Colwyn Bay

Rhyl

SNOWDONIA NATIONAL PARK

Caernarfon

Caernarfon Bay

LLEYN PENINSULA

Tremadog Bay

BERWYN

MYNYDD HIRETHOG

Copyright © by Rand McNally & Co.
Map prepared by Rand McNally & Co.
A-556800-264

36

Kilometers 0 10 20 30 40 50 Km.

Statute Miles 0 10 20 30 40 50 Mi.

Scale 1:1,000,000

One centimeter represents 10 kilometers.
One inch represents approximately 16 miles.

Lambert Conformal Conic Projection

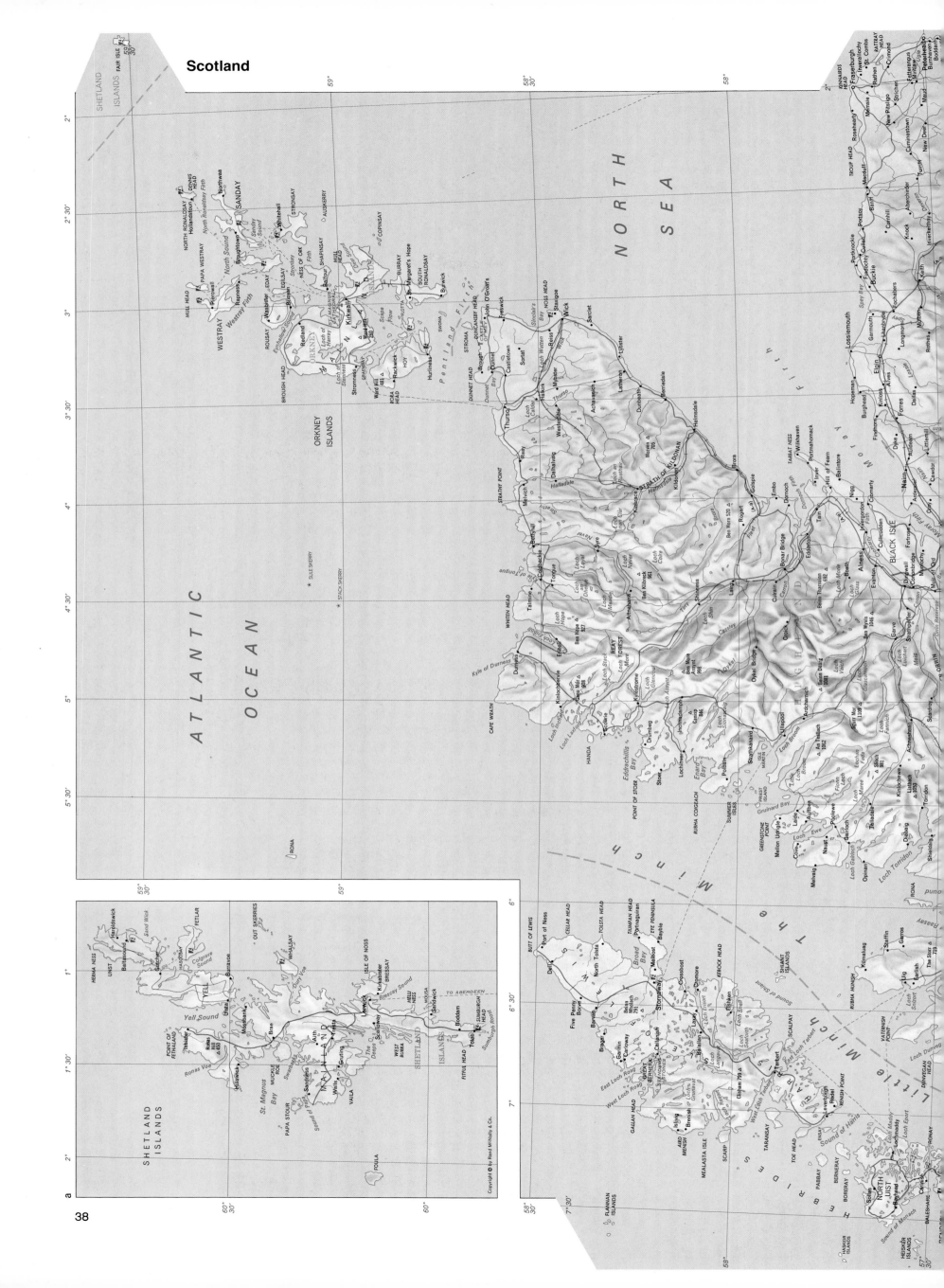

Scotland

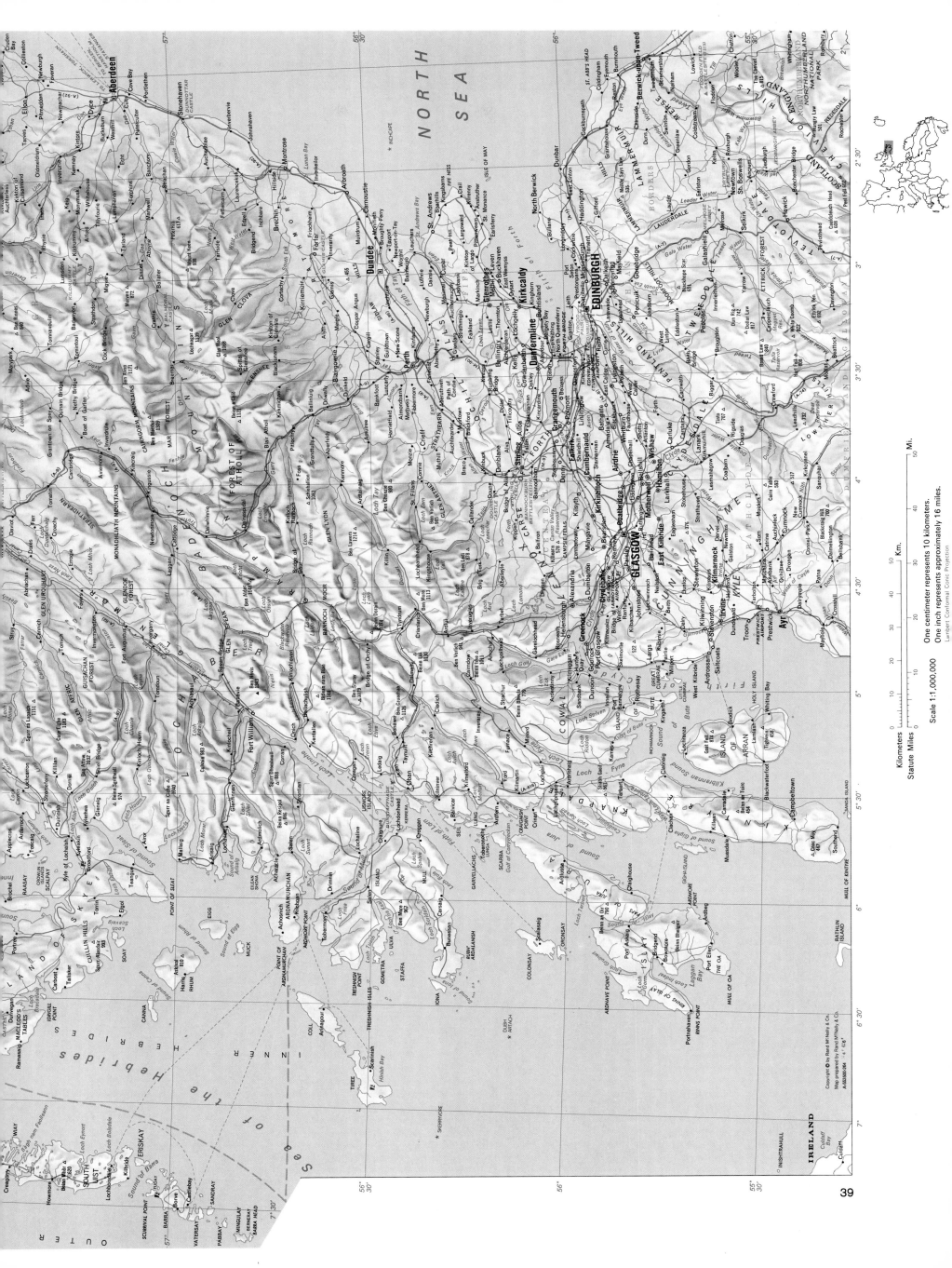

Scale 1:1,000,000

One centimeter represents 10 kilometers.
One inch represents approximately 16 miles.

Lambert Conformal Conic Projection

Copyright © by Rand McNally & Co.
Map prepared by Rand McNally & Co.
A-583500-864 — 4 - 416 *

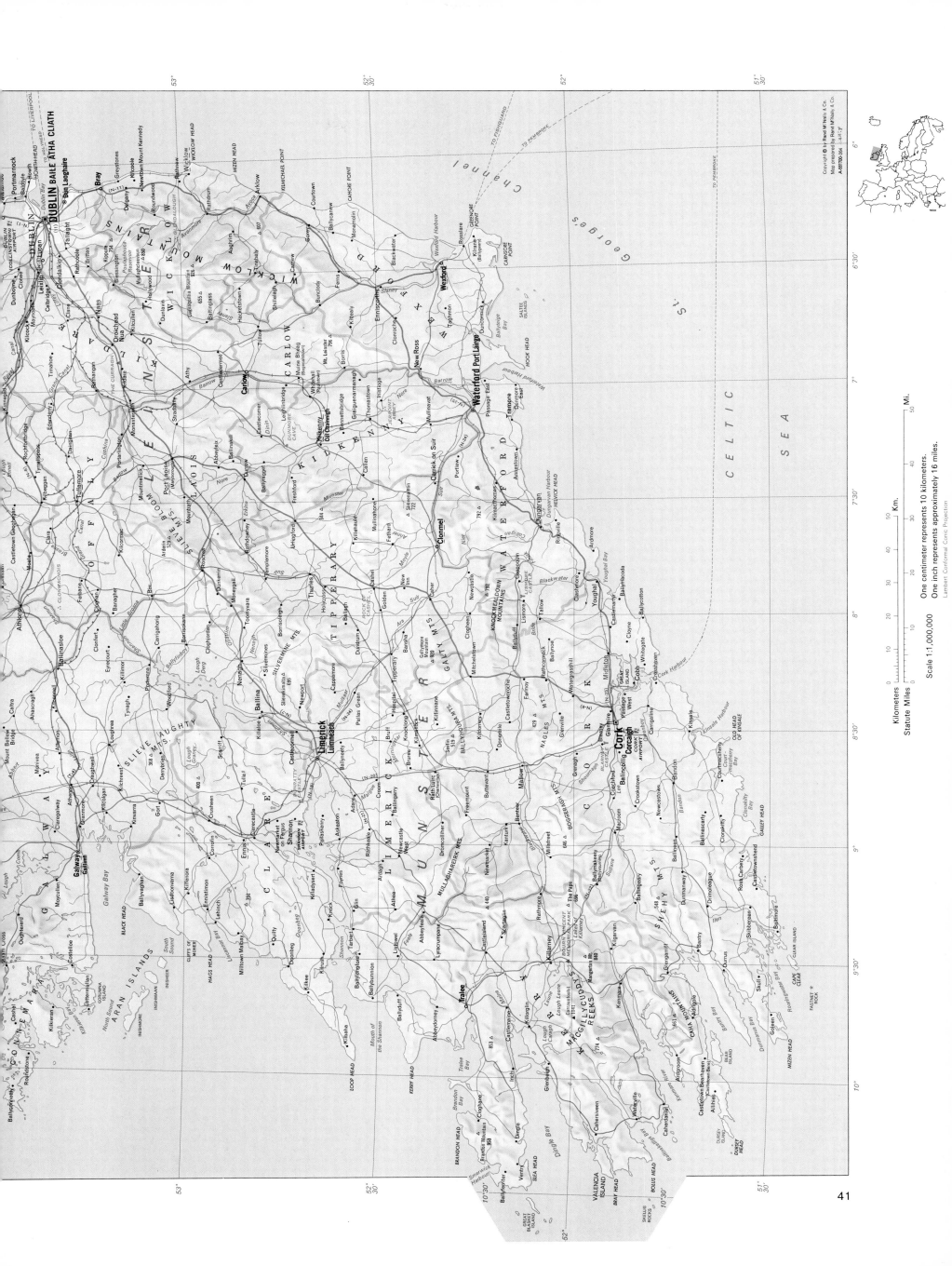

DUBLIN BAILE ÁTHA CLIATH

Dún Laoghaire

Bray

Wicklow
WICKLOW HEAD

MIZEN HEAD

CAHORE POINT

Arklow

KILMICHAEL POINT

Courtown

Blackwater

Rosslare
GREENORE
POINT

CARNSORE
POINT

Wexford

SALTEE
ISLANDS

Waterford Port Láirge

HOOK HEAD

Tramore

Dungarvan

HELVICK HEAD

Youghal

Cork
Corcaigh
Cobh

CELTIC   SEA

St. George's Channel

TO FISHGUARD

TO PEMBROKE

TO PEMBROKE

WICKLOW MOUNTAINS

LEINSTER

WICKLOW

KILDARE

CARLOW

KILKENNY
Cill Chainnigh

WEXFORD

New Ross

Carrick on Suir

Clonmel

WATERFORD

Tipperary

TIPPERARY

MUNSTER

Limerick
Luimneach

GALTY MTS.

COMERAGH MTS.

KNOCKMEALDOWN MOUNTAINS

CORK

Mallow

Tralee

Killarney

MACGILLYCUDDY'S REEKS

Cork Harbour

Kinsale

OLD HEAD
OF KINSALE

GALLEY HEAD

MIZEN HEAD

FASTNET
ROCK

VALENCIA
ISLAND

SKELLIG
ROCKS

GREAT BLASKET
ISLAND

SLEA HEAD

DINGLE BAY

Dingle

BRANDON HEAD

LOOP HEAD

KERRY HEAD

ARAN ISLANDS

GALWAY
Gaillimh

Galway Bay

CONNEMARA

CLARE

SLIEVE AUGHTY MTS.

Ennis

Shannon
AIRPORT

Ballinasloe

OFFALY

LAOIS

Athlone

Copyright © by Rand McNally & Co.
Map prepared by Rand McNally & Co.
A-661700-264   1-41-7

Kilometers

Statute Miles

Scale 1:11,000,000

One centimeter represents 10 kilometers.
One inch represents approximately 16 miles.

Lambert Conformal Conic Projection

Km.

Mi.

Kilometers
Statute Miles

| | 0 | 100 | 200 | 300 | Km. |

100 200 300 Mi.

Scale 1:6,000,000   One centimeter represents 60 kilometers.
One inch represents approximately 95 miles.
Lambert Conformal Conic Projection

Copyright © by Rand McNally & Co.
Map compiled by Esselte Map Service AB, Stockholm.
Map produced by Rand McNally & Co.
A-SS4400-264

Kilometers | 0 | 50 | 100 | 150 | Km.

Statute Miles | 0 | 50 | 100 | 150 | Mi.

Scale 1:3,000,000

One centimeter represents 30 kilometers.
One inch represents approximately 47 miles.
Conic Projection, Two Standard Parallels

45

Kilometers 0 50 100 150 Km.

Statute Miles 0 50 100 150 Mi.

Scale 1:3,000,000

One centimeter represents 30 kilometers.
One inch represents approximately 47 miles.

Conic Projection, Two Standard Parallels.

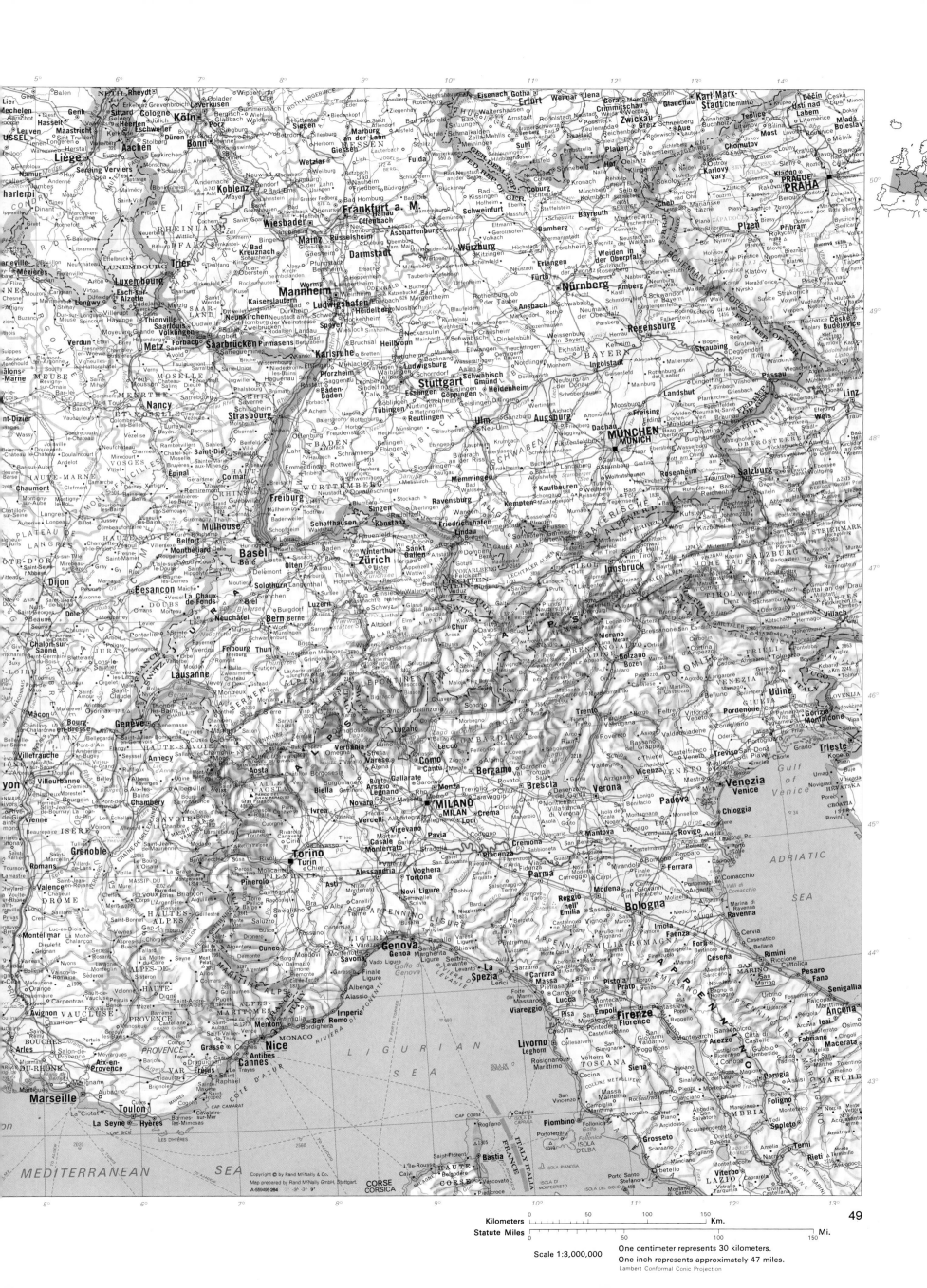

Kilometers | | | | | Km.
0   50   100   150

Statute Miles | | | Mi.
0   50   100   150

Scale 1:3,000,000

One centimeter represents 30 kilometers.
One inch represents approximately 47 miles.
Lambert Conformal Conic Projection

Copyright © by Rand McNally & Co.
Map prepared by Rand McNally GmbH, Stuttgart.
A-589496 264

Kilometers 0 50 100 150 Km.

Statute Miles 0 50 100 150 Mi.

Scale 1:3,000,000

One centimeter represents 30 kilometers.
One inch represents approximately 47 miles.

Conic Projection, Two Standard Parallels

51

Italy

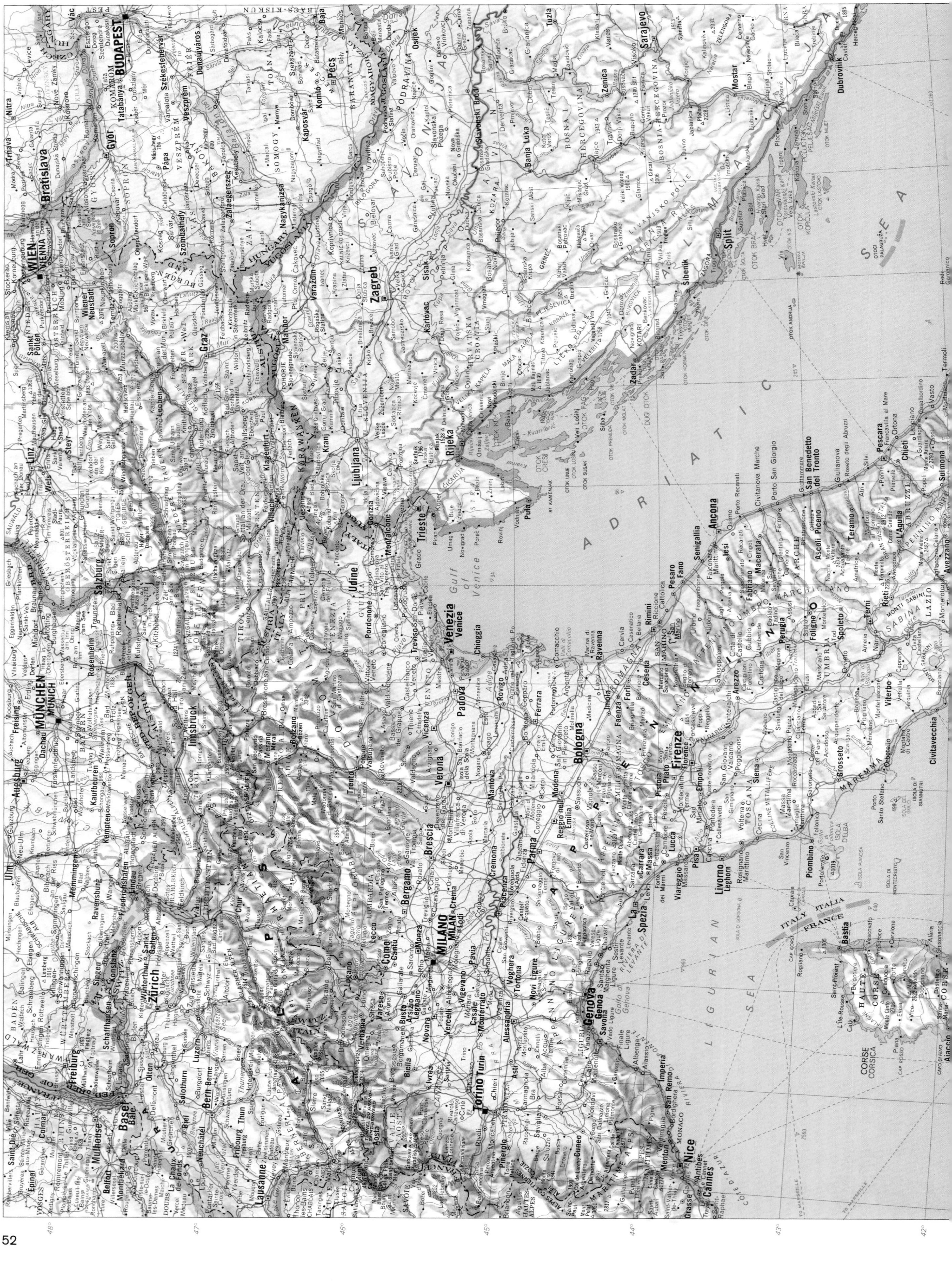

BUDAPEST
Bratislava
WIEN
VIENNA
Graz
Zagreb
Ljubljana
Rijeka
Split
Sarajevo
Mostar
Dubrovnik
Zadar
Klagenfurt
Salzburg
Linz
MÜNCHEN
MUNICH
Innsbruck
Augsburg
Ulm
Zürich
Basel
Bern
Luzern
Lausanne
Trieste
Udine
Venezia
Venice
Padova
Verona
Trento
Bolzano
Brescia
Bergamo
MILANO
MILAN
Torino
Turin
Genova
Parma
Bologna
Firenze
Pisa
Livorno
Ancona
Pescara
Nice
Cannes
Bastia
Ajaccio
A D R I A T I C
S E A
L I G U R I A N
Gulf of Venice
ITALY
FRANCE

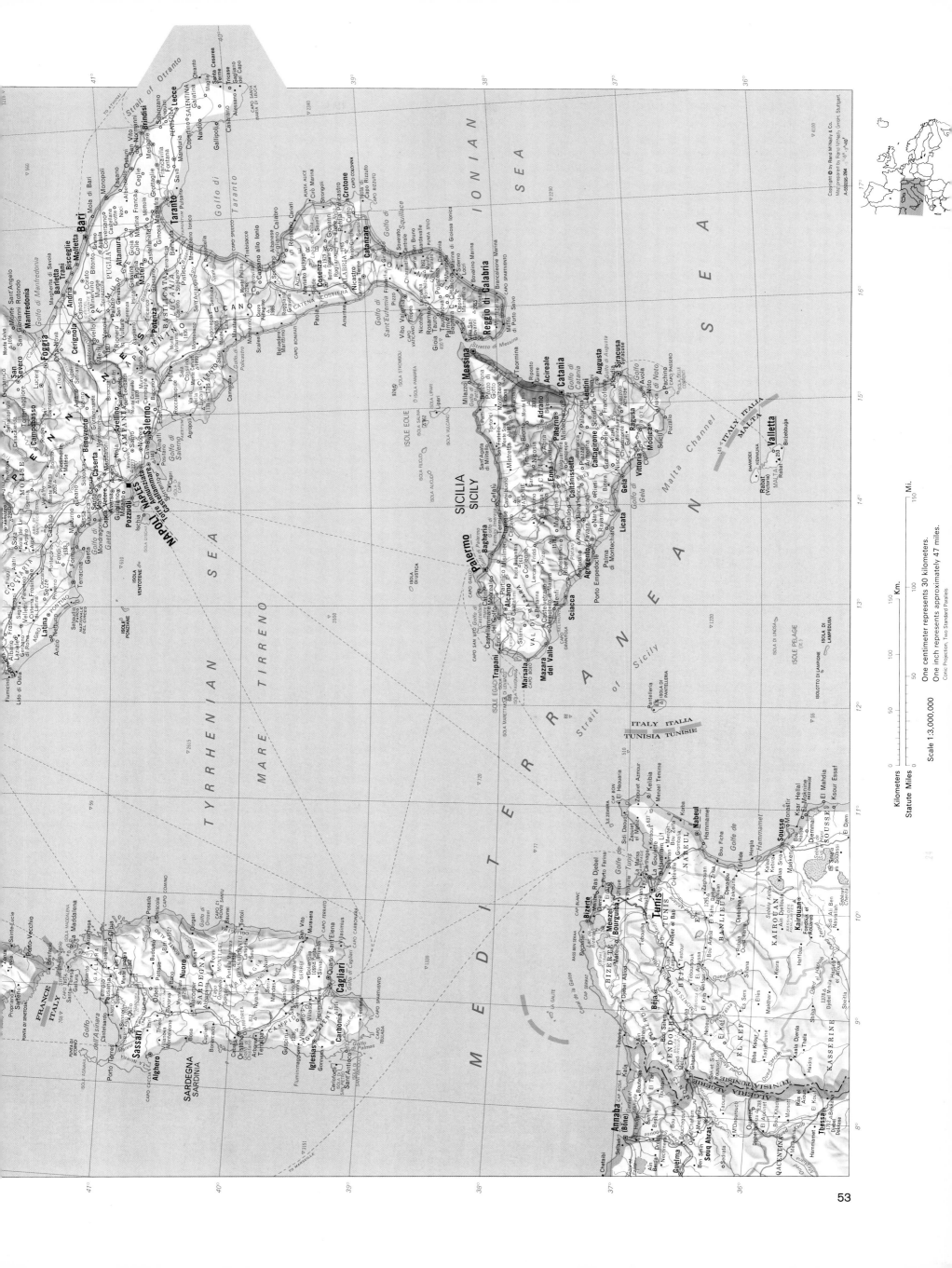

Kilometers
Statute Miles

Scale 1:3,000,000

One centimeter represents 30 kilometers.
One inch represents approximately 47 miles.

Conic Projection, Two Standard Parallels

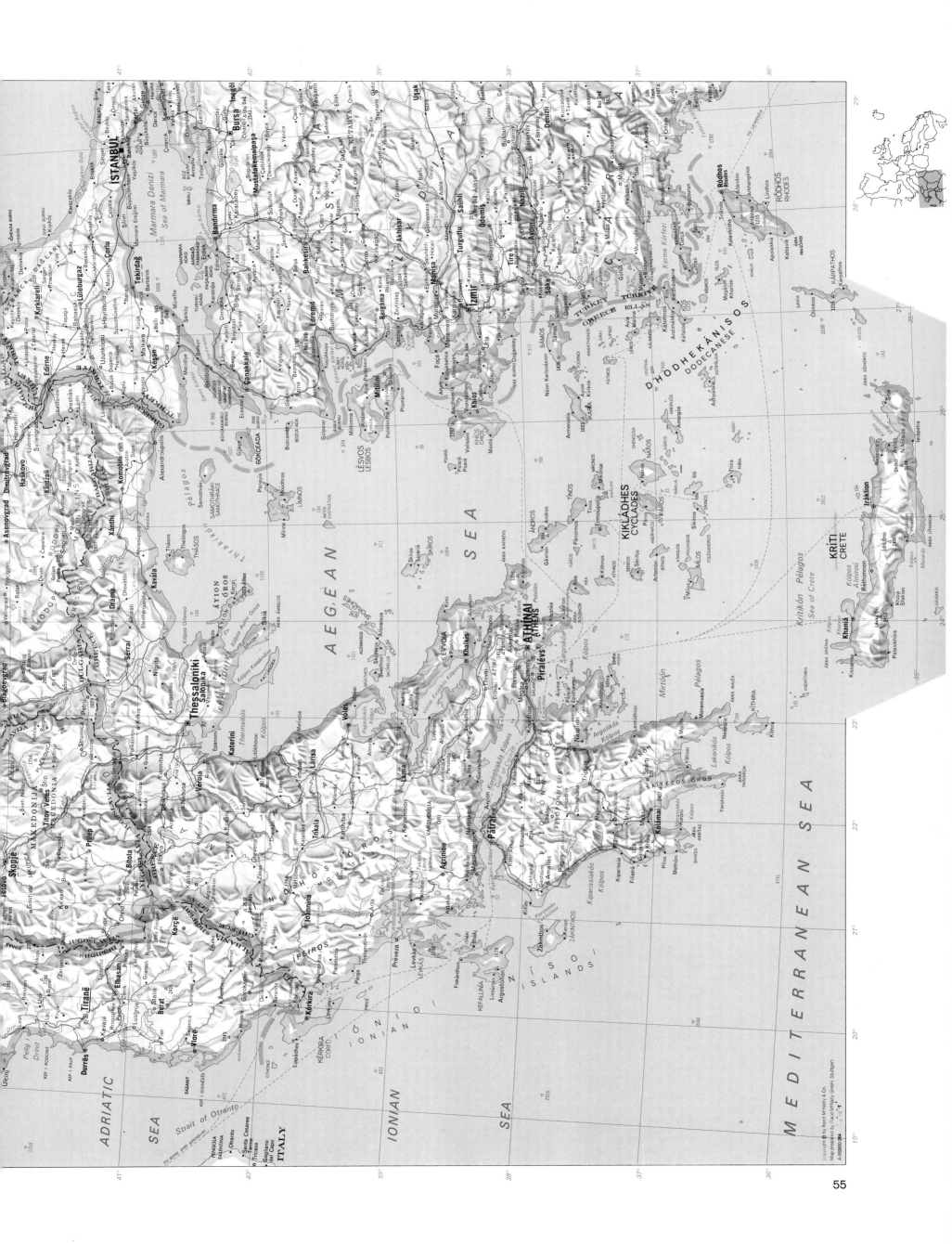

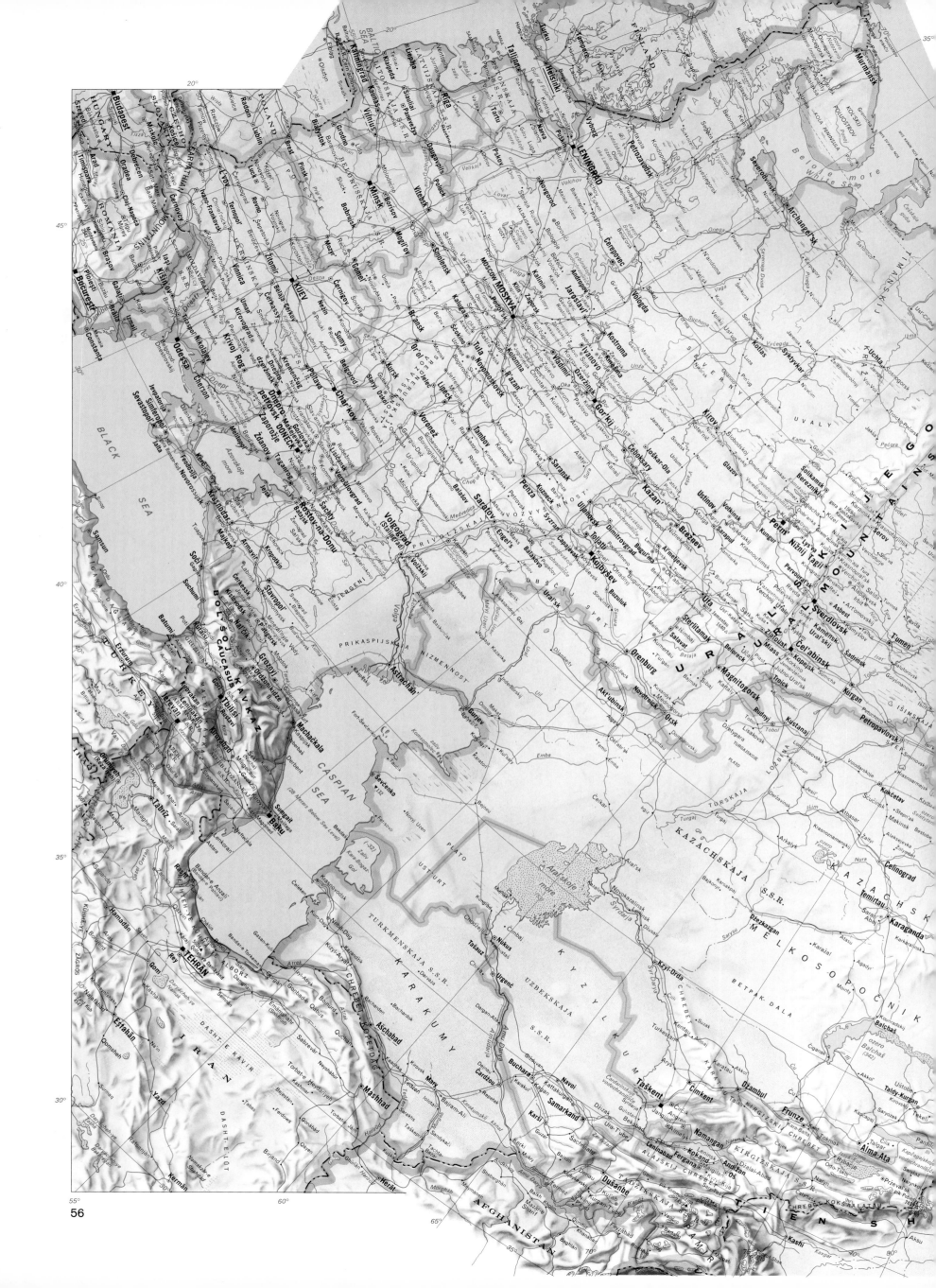

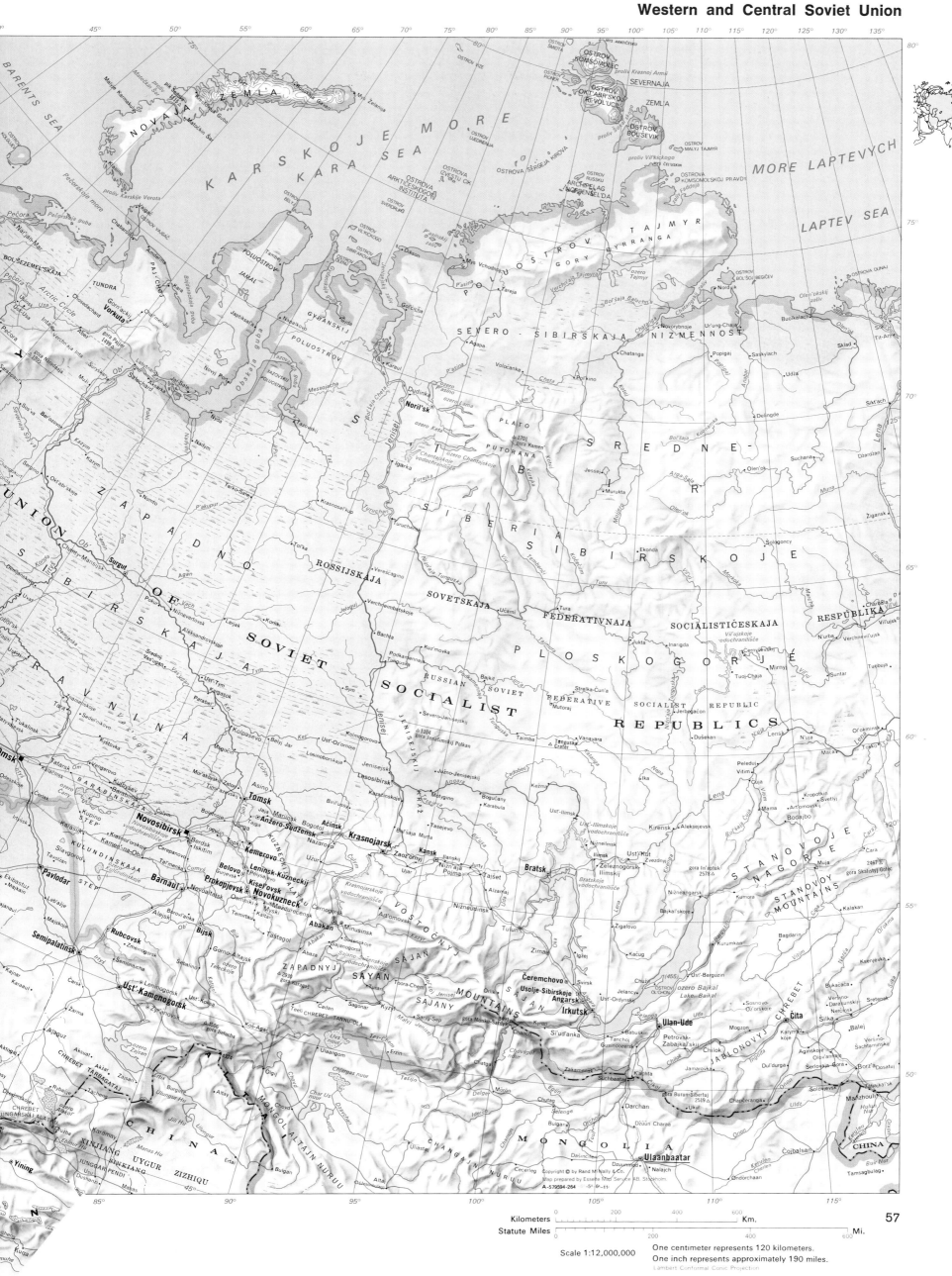

Scale 1:12,000,000

Kilometers
Statute Miles

One centimeter represents 120 kilometers.
One inch represents approximately 190 miles.

Lambert Conformal Conic Projection

Copyright © by Rand McNally & Co.
Map prepared by Esselte Map Service AB, Stockholm
A-579594-264

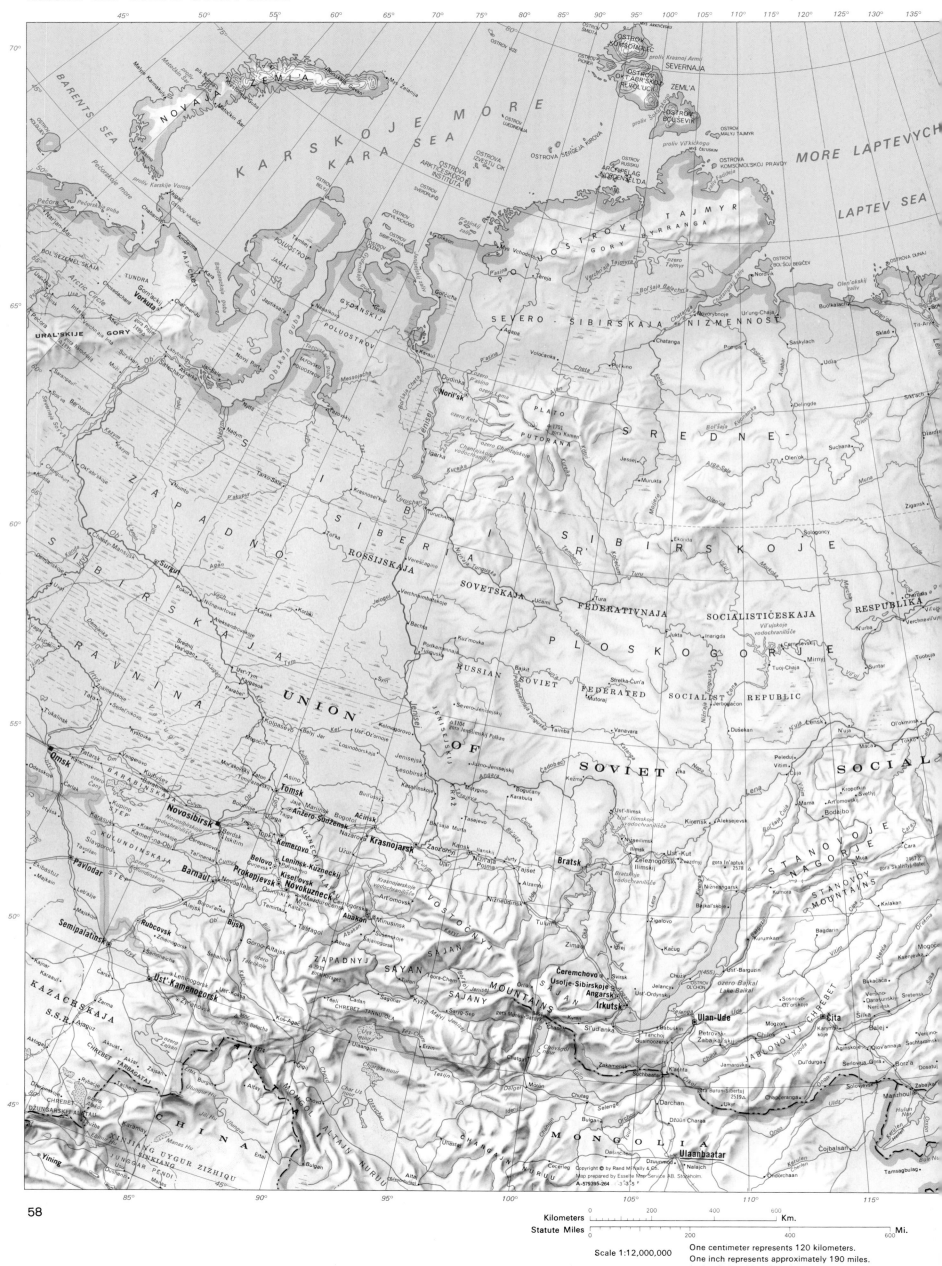

Kilometers
Statute Miles

Scale 1:12,000,000

One centimeter represents 120 kilometers.
One inch represents approximately 190 miles.
Lambert Conformal Conic Projection

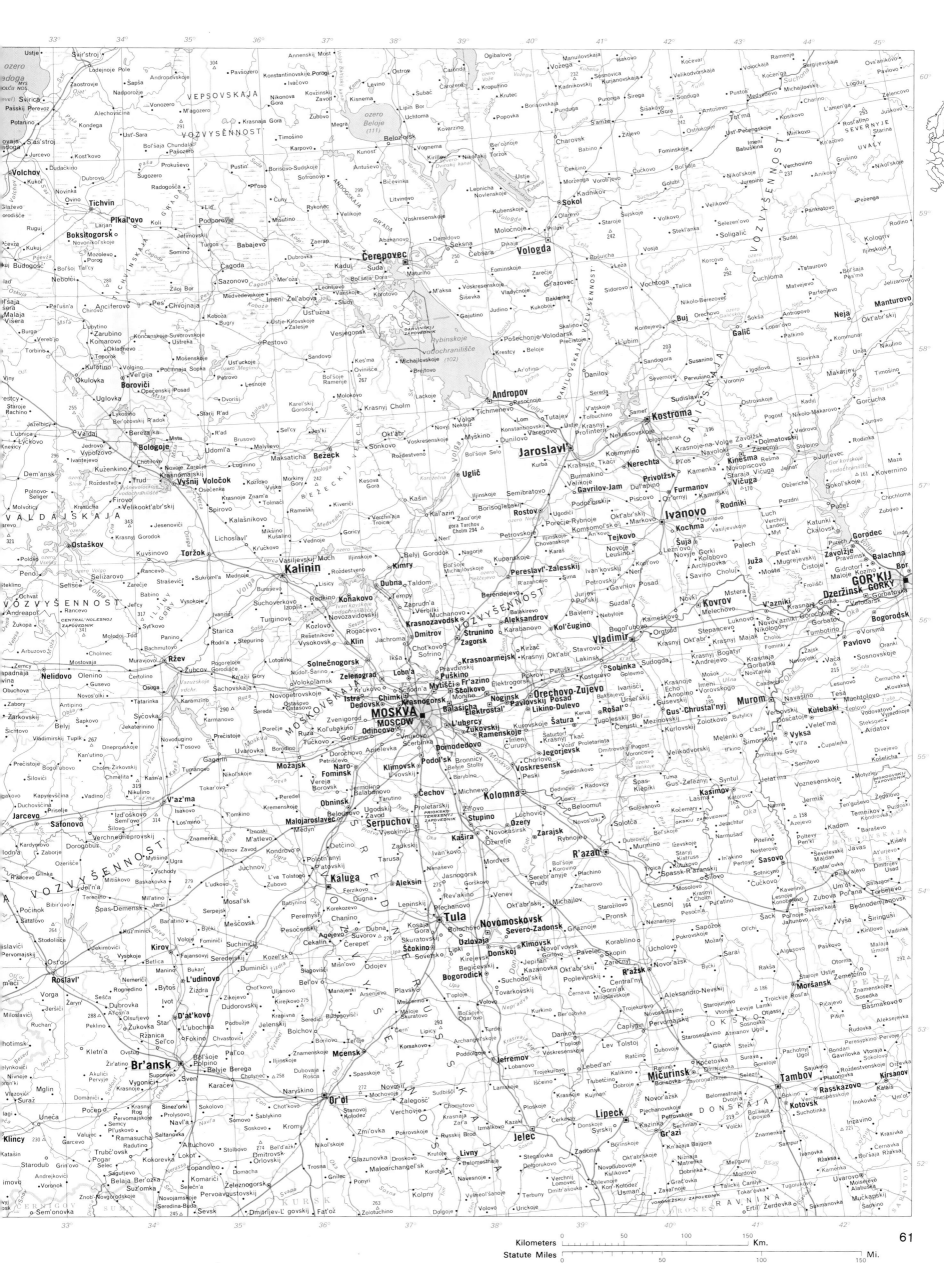

61

Kilometers 0 50 100 150 Km.

Statute Miles 0 50 100 150 Mi.

Scale 1:3,000,000

One centimeter represents 30 kilometers.
One inch represents approximately 47 miles.
Lambert Conformal Conic Projection

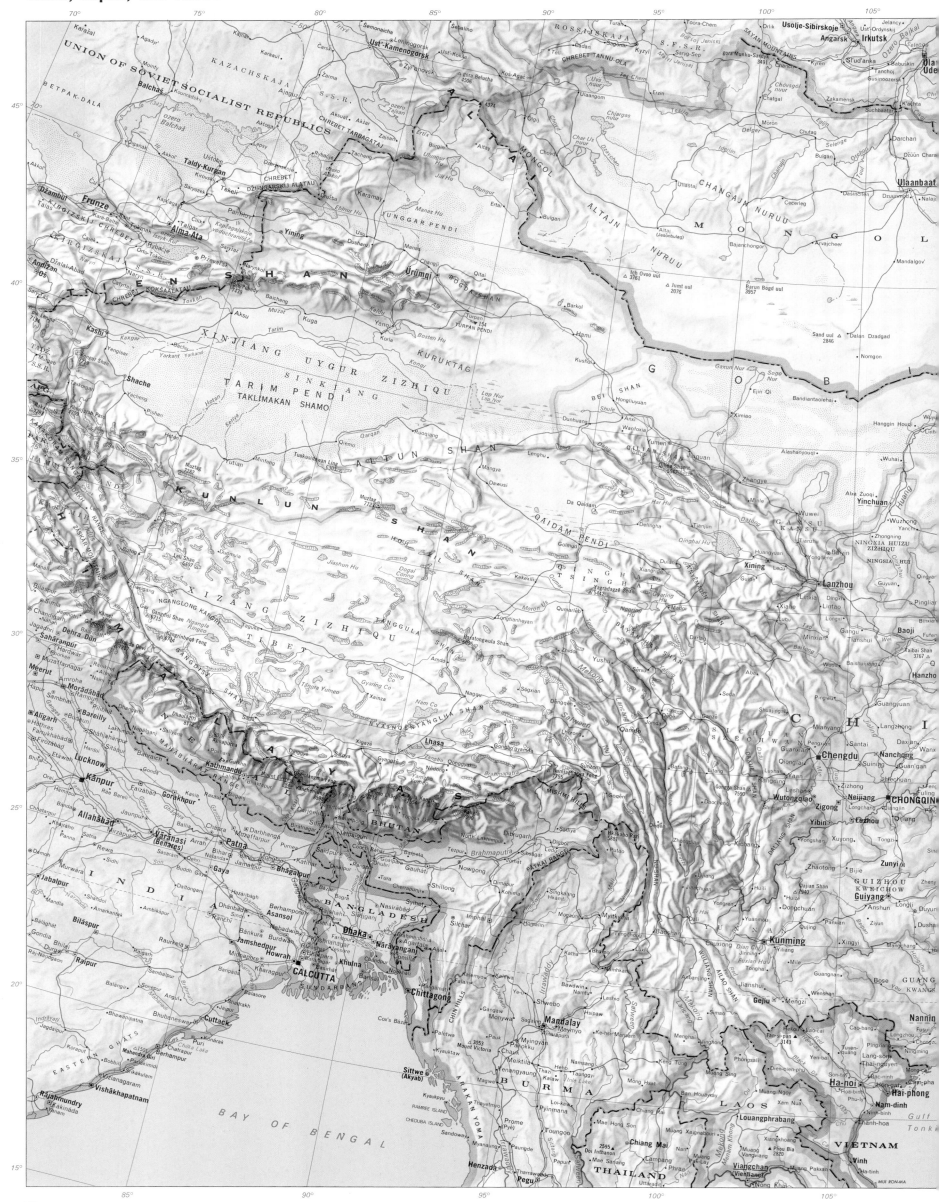

Kilometers 0   200   400   600   Km.

Statute Miles 0   200   400   600   Mi.

Scale 1:12,000,000

One centimeter represents 120 kilometers.
One inch represents approximately 190 miles.

Lambert Conformal Conic Projection

Copyright © by Rand McNally & Co.

Map prepared by Esselte Map Service AB, Stockholm.

A-569700-264

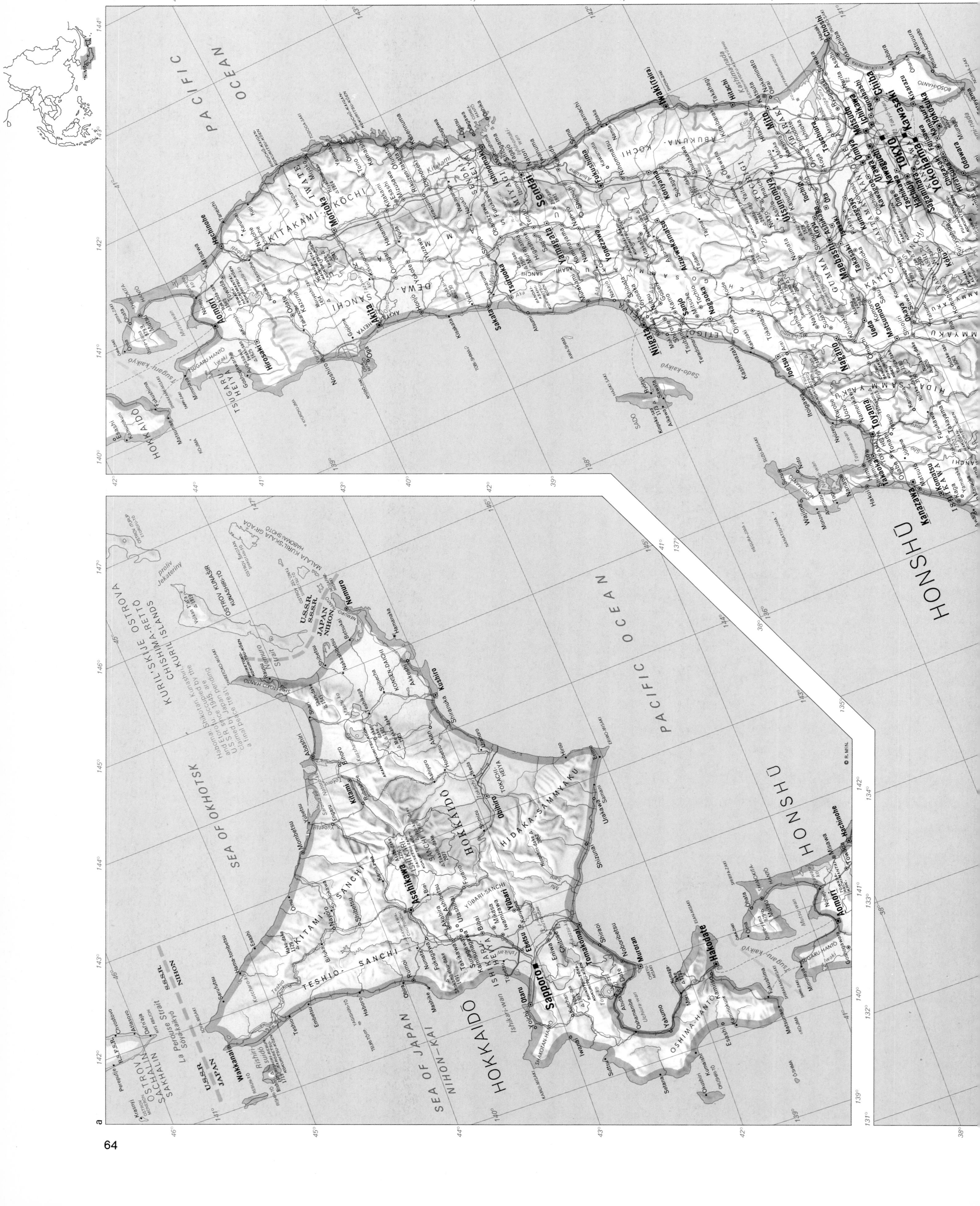

PACIFIC OCEAN

HOKKAIDO

HONSHŪ

TOKYO

Yokohama
Kawasaki
Chiba
Nagano
Niigata
Nagaoka
Toyama
Kanazawa
Sendai
Morioka
Hachinohe
Akita
Hirosaki
Aomori

KITAKAMI

KŌCHI

IWATE

DEWA SANCHI

MIYAGI

GUMMA

KANTŌ

ECHIGO

HIDA

SAMMYAKU

TSUGARU-HANTO
TSUGARU HEIYA

SADO

SEA OF JAPAN
NIHON-KAI

SEA OF OKHOTSK

KURILSKIJE OSTROVA
KURIL ISLANDS
CHISHIMA-RETTŌ

MALAJA KURIL'SKAJA GRJADA
HABOMAI-SHOTŌ

OSTROV KUNAŠIR
KUNASHIRI-TŌ

U.S.S.R.
S.S.S.R.
JAPAN
NIHON

Nemuro
Kushiro
Obihiro
Asahikawa
Kitami
Sapporo
Tomakomai
Muroran
Hakodate
Wakkanai

HOKKAIDO

HIDAKA SAMMYAKU

TESHIO SANCHI
KITAMI SANCHI
ISHIKARI HEIYA
KONSEN-DAICHI
TOKACHI HEIYA
YŪBARI-SANCHI

OSHIMA-HANTŌ

SHIRETOKO-HANTŌ

OSTROV SACHALIN
SAKHALIN
SSSR
U.S.S.R.

La Perouse Strait
Sōya-kaikyō

PACIFIC OCEAN

HONSHŪ

Hachinohe
Aomori

TSUGARU-HANTO

Tsugaru-kaikyō

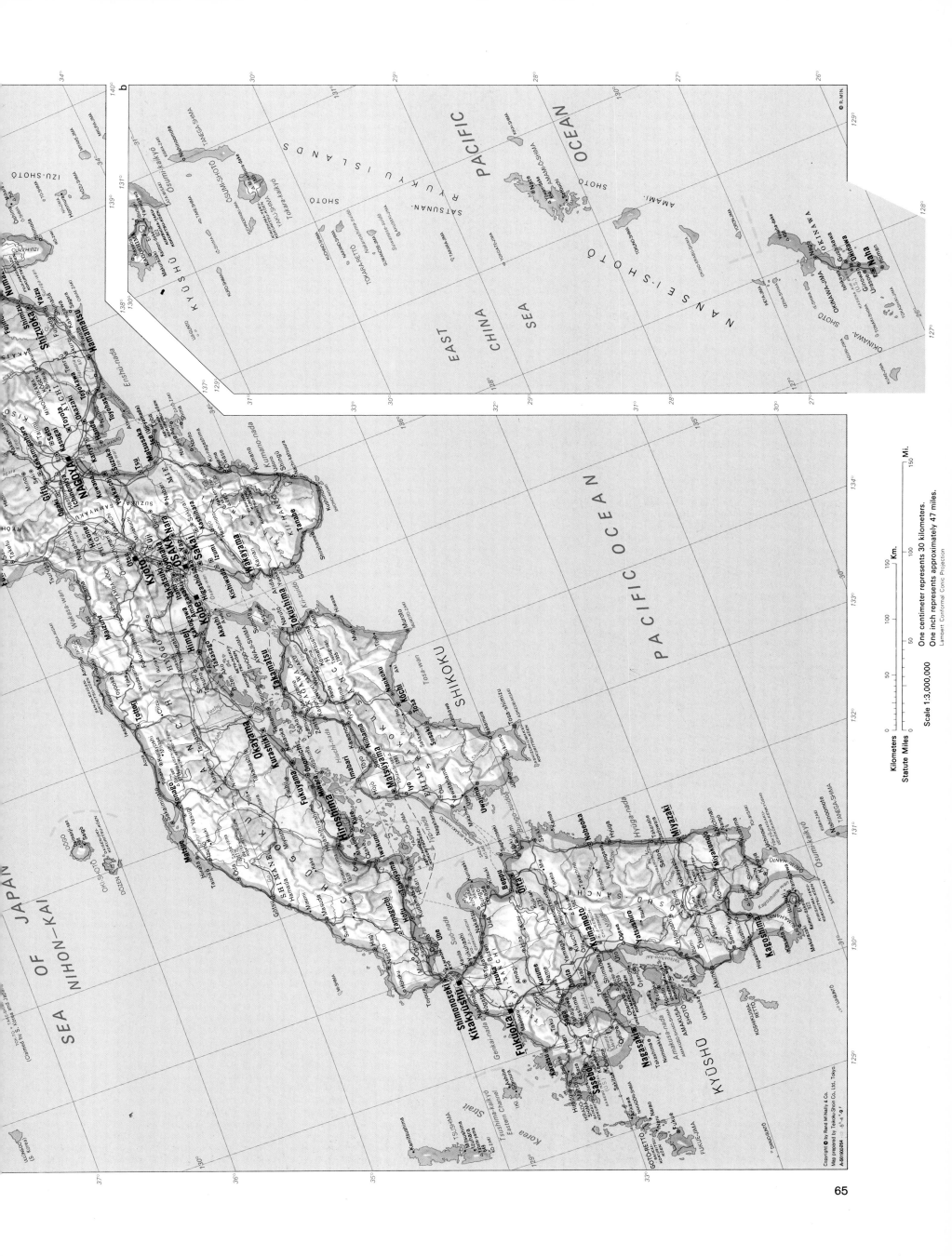

Scale 1:3,000,000

One centimeter represents 30 kilometers.
One inch represents approximately 47 miles.
Lambert Conformal Conic Projection

Copyright © by Rand McNally & Co.
Map prepared by Teikoku-Shoin Co., Ltd., Tokyo.
A-561002054

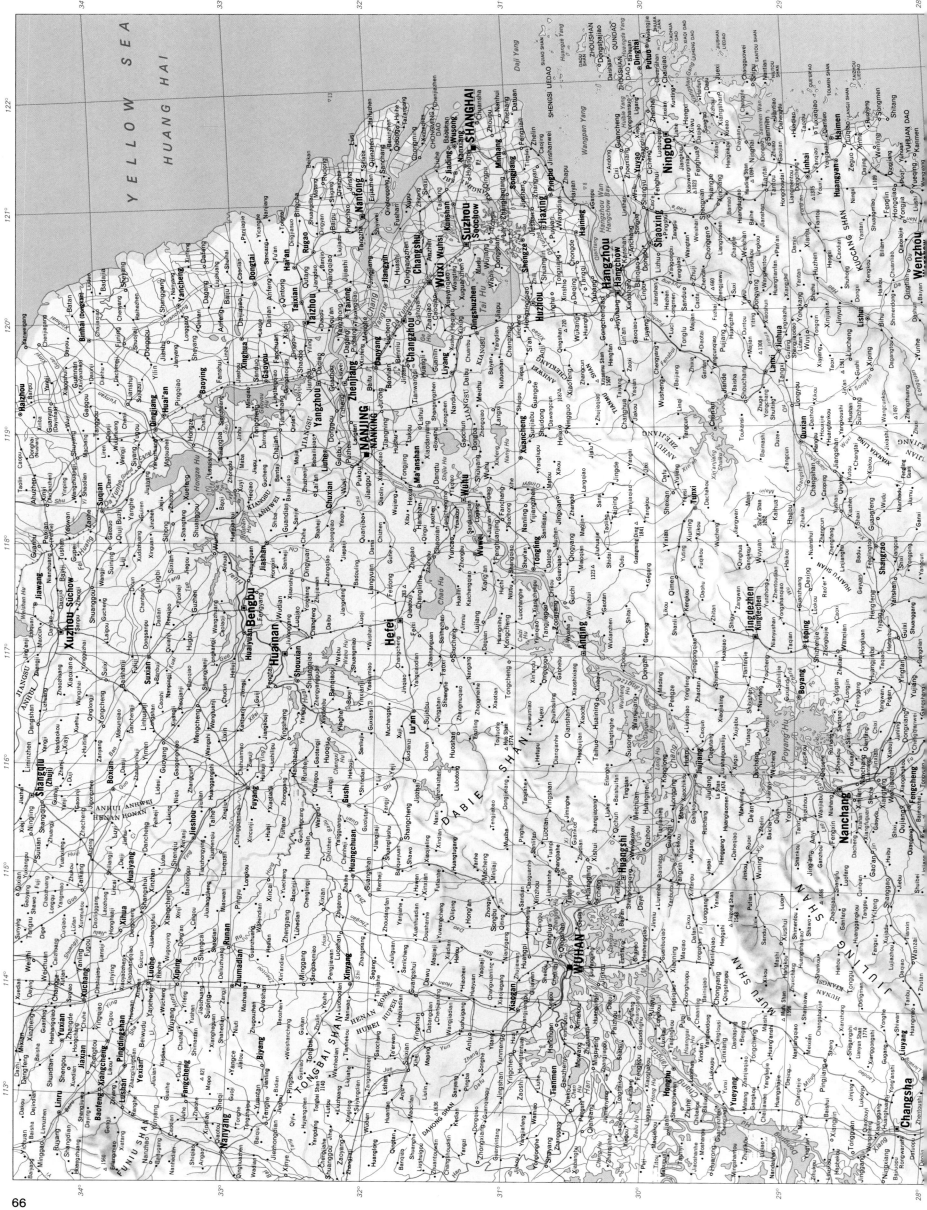

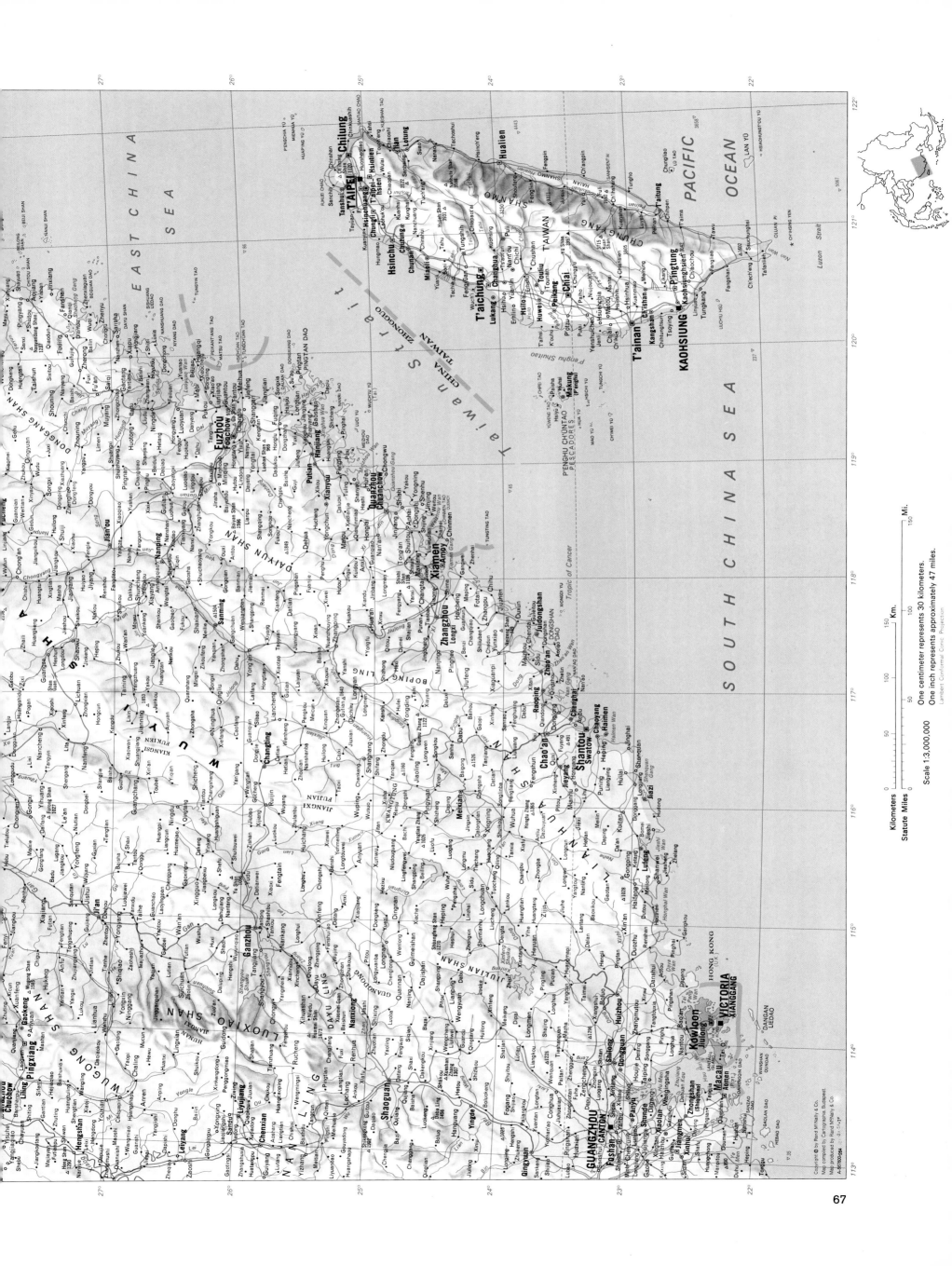

NCHU NANYING
kung
Chiai ▲3997 Hualien
Yü Shan TAIWAN
T'ainan P'ingtung
AOHSIUNG T'aitung T'AIWAN

OUAN PI
*Y'AMI ISLAND
Basco *ITBAYAT ISLAND
*BATAN ISLAND BATAN ISLANDS
*SABTANG ISLAND

CAPE BOJEADOR
DALUPIRI ISLAND *BABUYAN ISLAND
ISLAND *CALAYAN ISLAND BABUYAN ISLANDS
FUGA *CAMIGUIN ISLAND
ISLAND
ESCARPADA
POINT
Laoag Aparri
Tuguegarao
Vigan Ilagan
Bontoc Lagawe
San Fernando ▲2934
Mount Polos LUZON
Baguio
Dagupan
San Carlos
Tarlac Cabanatuan
Angeles San Fernando POLILLO ISLANDS
Olongapo PHILIPPINES
MANILA Quezon City
Cavite Laguna Lamon Bay
Matrola Bay Tagaytay San Pablo Lucena
Lipa Lucena
Batangas
Calapan Naga Virac CATANDUANES ISLAND
Mamburao Mayon Volcano
MINDORO BURIAS ▲2462
San Jose LEGARPI Sorsogon
MARINDUQUE ISLAND
TABLAS Bulan Laoang
San Agustin ISLAND Bernardino Strait
Sibuyan MASBATE Catarman
ROMBLON ISLAND Catbalogan SAMAR
Kalibo ISLAND Basey
Roxas Visayan Calbayog Tacloban
PANAY Sea Guiuan
Iloilo Bacolod LEYTE Leyte Gulf
GUIMARAS San Carlos
ISLAND CEBU Ormoc DINAGAT ISLAND
NEGROS Bais SIARGAO ISLAND
Santander BOHOL
Dumaguete Tagbilaran Surigao
Mindanao Sea Tandag
Dipolog Butuan
Liloy Cagayan
Ozamiz de Oro Bislig
Pagadian Iligan Malaybalay
MINDANAO
Zamboanga Cotabato ▲2954 Davao
Datu Mount Apo
BASILAN ISLAND Piang Davao
Lebak Kiamba Gulf
CAPE SAN AGUSTIN
Jolo TINACA POINT
JOLO ISLAND SARANGANI ISLANDS
SULU ARCHIPELAGO
TAWITAWI
ISLAND

PHILIPPINE

SEA

PACIFIC

OKINO-TORI-SHIMA
(Japan)

FARALLON DE PAJAROS
MAUG ISLANDS

NORTHERN
MARIANA
ISLANDS
(T.T.P.I.)
*AGRIHAN
*PAGAN
MARIANA ISLANDS *ALAMAGAN
*GUGUAN
TRUST TERRITORY OF *SARIGAN
THE PACIFIC ISLANDS *ANATAHAN
(U.S.)
FARALLON DE MEDINILLA *
SAIPAN
TINIAN
AGUIJAN
ROTA

Agana GUAM
(U.S.)

OCEAN

TRUST TERRITORY OF THE PACIFIC ISLANDS
(U.S.)
ULITHI
YAP *FAIS GAFERUT
FEDERATED STATES OF MICRONESIA
(T.T.P.I.) FARAULEP
NGULU SOROL
KAYANGEL ISLANDS OLIMARAO
PALAU ISLANDS BABELTHUAP WOLEAI FALIK
URUKTHAPEL Koror *EAURIPIK
PELELIU EIL MALK
ANGAUR

CAROLINE ISLANDS

PULO ANNA
MERIR
BELAU PALAU
(T.T.P.I.)
TOBI
HELEN ISLAND
SONSOROL ISLANDS

PULAU MIANGAS

PULAU-PULAU NANUSA
PULAU KARAKELONG KEPULAUAN TALAUD
PULAU
SALEBABU PULAU KABURUANG
Tahuna PULAU SANGHE

CELEBES

SEA

KEPULAUAN ASIA
KEPULAUAN
MAPIA

PULAU SIAU
SANGIHE
PULAU TAHULANDANG
PULAU BIARO
Wayabula MOROTAI
Galela
Manado Bitung Tobelo KEPULAUAN AYU
MINAHASA 2022 Gunung Klabat
Tondano Jailolo
Bukit Malino HALMAHERA
▲2440 Kotamobagu Ternate
Gorontalo Tidore Weda
Tomini Moutong PULAU GEBE
PULAU WAIGEO
PULAU Laut Selat Dampier
KEPULAUAN WAIGEO
TOGIAN Halmahera
Palu KEPULAUAN KASIRUTA PULAU Halmahera Manokwari
Poso BACAN Sea JAZIRAH DOBERAI
Teluk PULAU MANDIOLI PULAU BATANTA
Poso PULAU BISA SALAWATI Teminabuan
Luwuk PULAU OBI PULAU Sorong
Banggai MISOOL Ransiki
SULAWESI KEPULAUAN PULAU OBI Teluk
CELEBES BANGGAI Inanwatan Cenderawasih
PULAU PELENG Waren
Poso Danau Towuti KEPULAUAN PULAU Teluk Nabire
N D A SULA MANGOLE Berau
Kendari PULAU TALIABU Kaimana
Watampone PULAU SANANA Wahai
PULAU Namlea SERAM CERAM
Sinjai BUTUNG BURU Piru
Ujung Pandang PULAU Ambon
WOWONI SERAM CERAM SEA
PULAU PULAU AMBON
KABAENA Geser
Baubau PULAU ADI
Bantaeng KEPULAUAN
Bulukumba BANDA
PULAU KEPULAUAN
Tanahampea SELAYAR WATUBELA
PULAU SELAYAR
PULAU
WANGIWANGI
LUCIPARA PENYU
KEPULAUAN KAI
Flores Sea FUKANGBESI KAI KECIL Tual
PULAU KEPULAUAN KEPULAUAN
Tanahjampea LAUT BANDA LUCIPARA KAI BESAR
BANDA SEA DAYA Dobo PULAU WOKAM
PULAU BININGGOLO PULAU NILA PULAU SERUA KEPULAUAN
KEPULAUAN PULAU TEUN ARU
BARAT PULAU DAMAR PULAU TRANGAN
PULAU WETAR PULAU ROMANG PULAU WULIARU
PULAU PULAU SERMATA PULAU SELU PULAU
Larantuka KISAR PULAU MOA LARAT YAMDENA
Maumere PULAU LAKOR PULAU SELARU KEPULAUAN TANIMBAR
FLORES PULAU KAMBING KEPULAUAN
Reo Ende LOMBLEN PULAU SERMATA BABAR Saumlaki
Ruteng PULAU PANTAR KEPULAUAN
Dili LETI
ENGGARA Ocussi
INDA ISLANDS Soe TIMOR
SUMBA Kupang
Waingapu Baing PULAU SEMAU
Laut Sawu PULAU SAWU
Savu Sea PULAU ROTI
TIMOR SEA

Equator

BIAK
Bosnik
Ransiki PULAU YAPEN TANJUNG PERKAM NINIGO GROUP
Sarmi WUVULU ISLAND
Denta PEGUNUNGAN VAN REES Jayapura (Sukarnapura) PAPUA
Nabire Waren Babo Bomberai Tariku Taritatu Vanimo NEW GUINEA
Wasior Tariku Aitape
Steenkool Wasior JAZIRAH Dagua Wewak MANAM
Faktak BOMBERAI Kokonau ▲5030 Puncak Jaya ISLAND
JAZIRAH Karufa Puncak Trikora Angoram Sepik
Kaimana ▲4750 Ambunti
Idenburg ▲4760 Puncak Wabag Mendi Mount MAOKE Mandala Telefomin Hagen ▲4368 Wilhelm
Kepi PEGUNUNGAN Mount Giluwe Goroka ▲4509
PULAU Mapi NEW Mount Ialibu
YOS GUINEA Mount Bosavi
SUDARSA Ohabu ▲2397 Kikori
TANAH MERAH Lake Murray Daru
Merauke Baling
Gulf
of Papua
TANJUNG VALS

BOIGU ISLAND
SASAI ISLAND
MABUDUAN WARRIOR REEF
PRINCE OF WALES ISLAND CAPE YORK
CAPE CROKER Torres Strait Endeavour Strait
ARAFURA SEA CAPE WESSEL AUSTRALIA CAPE YORK PENINSULA
CAPE YORK GREAT BARRIER REEF

69

Kilometers 0 200 400 600
Km.
Statute Miles 0 200 400 600
Mi.

Scale 1:12,000,000
One centimeter represents 120 kilometers.
One inch represents approximately 190 miles.
Lambert Conformal Conic Projection

Burma, Thailand, and Indochina

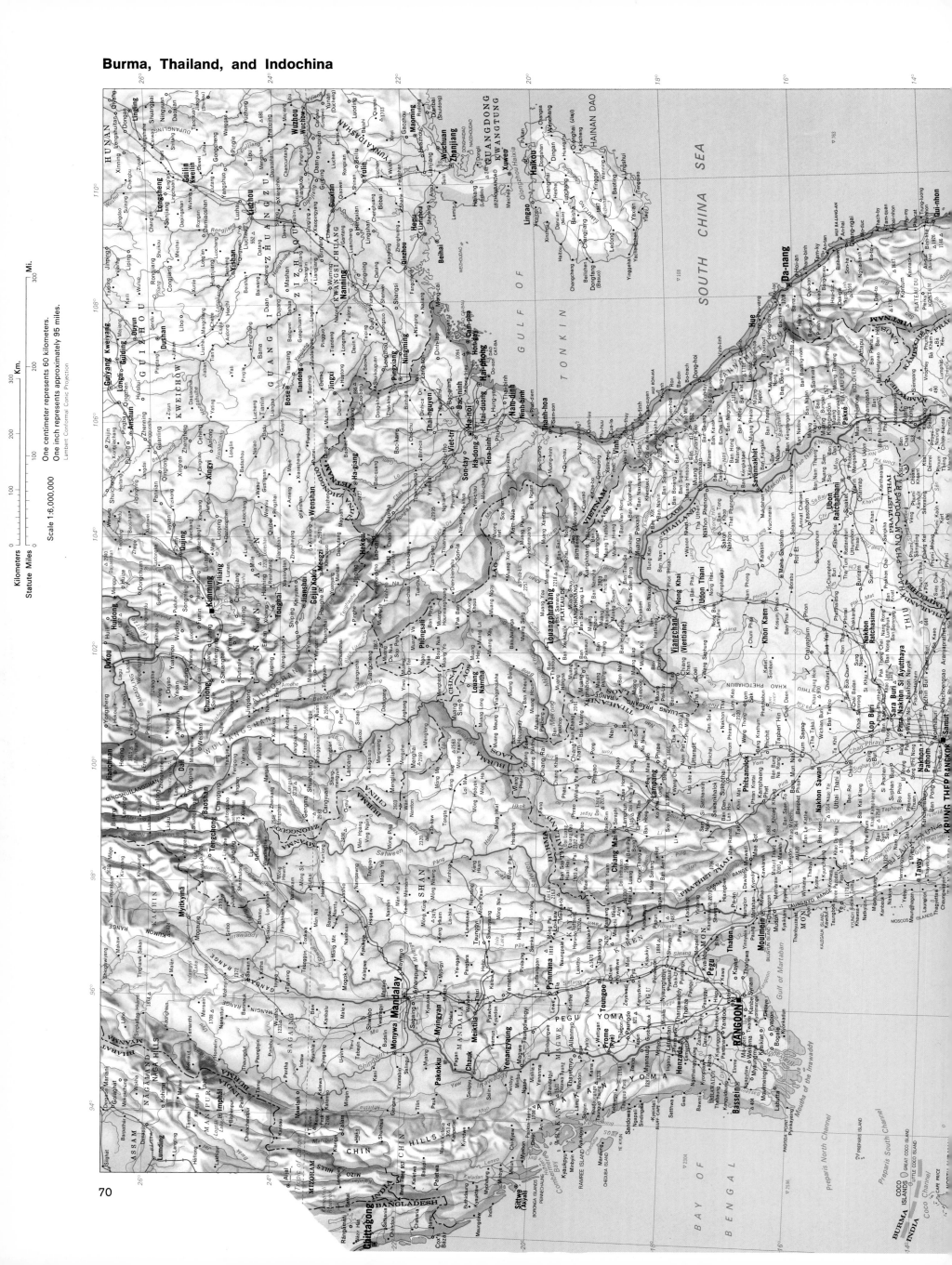

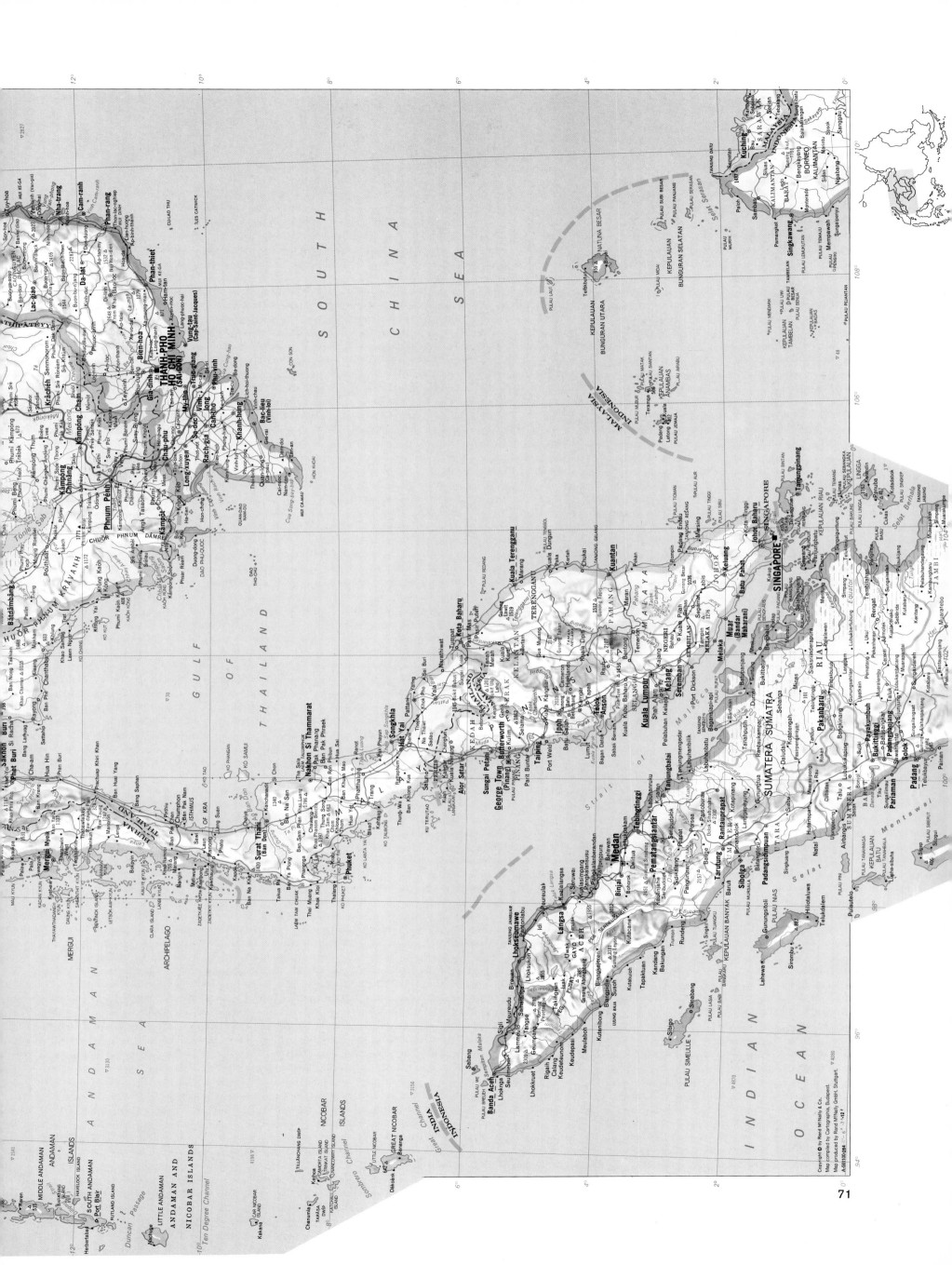

71

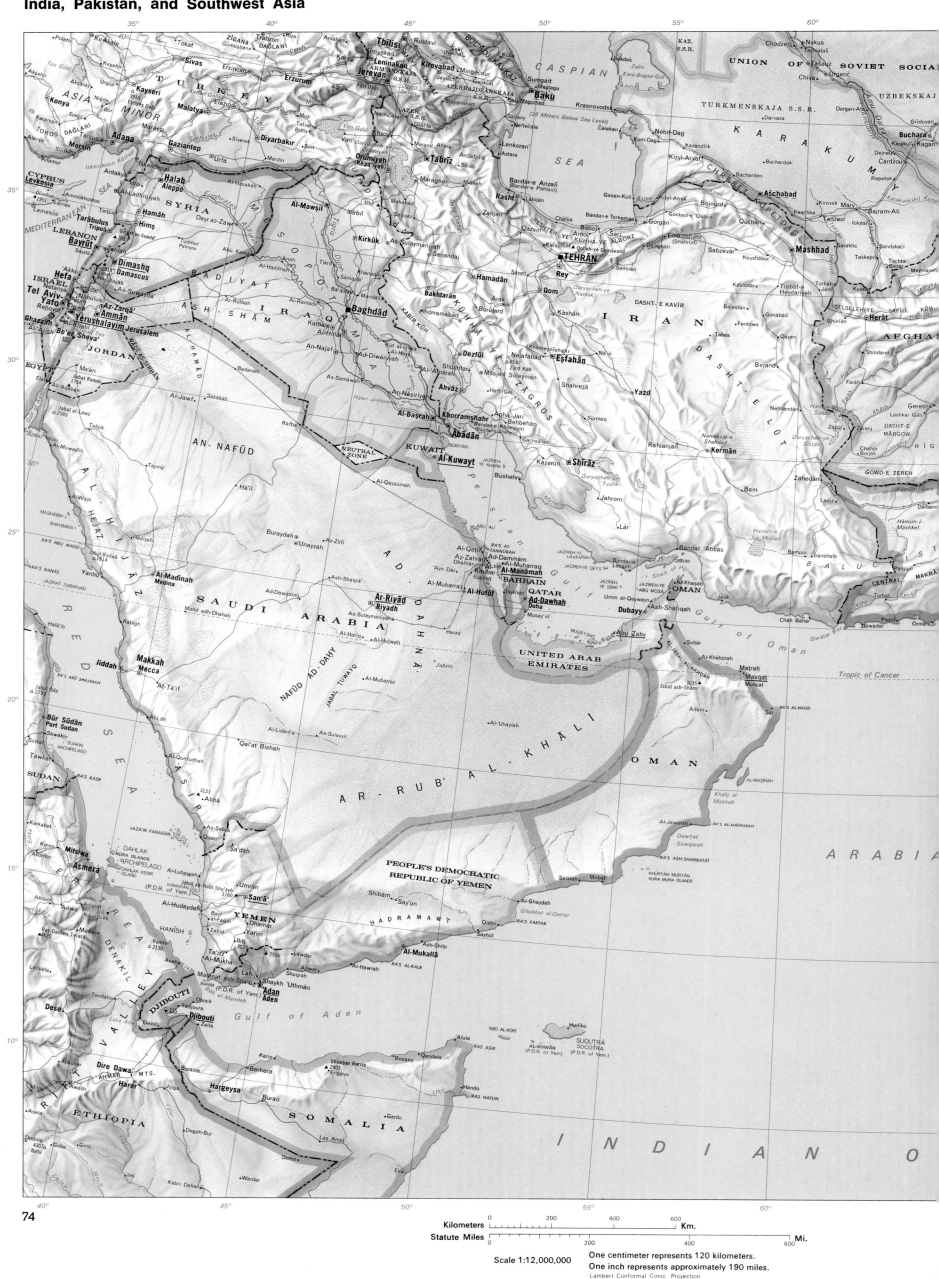

Kilometers 0 200 400 600 Km.

Statute Miles 0 200 400 600 Mi.

Scale 1:12,000,000
One centimeter represents 120 kilometers.
One inch represents approximately 190 miles.
Lambert Conformal Conic Projection

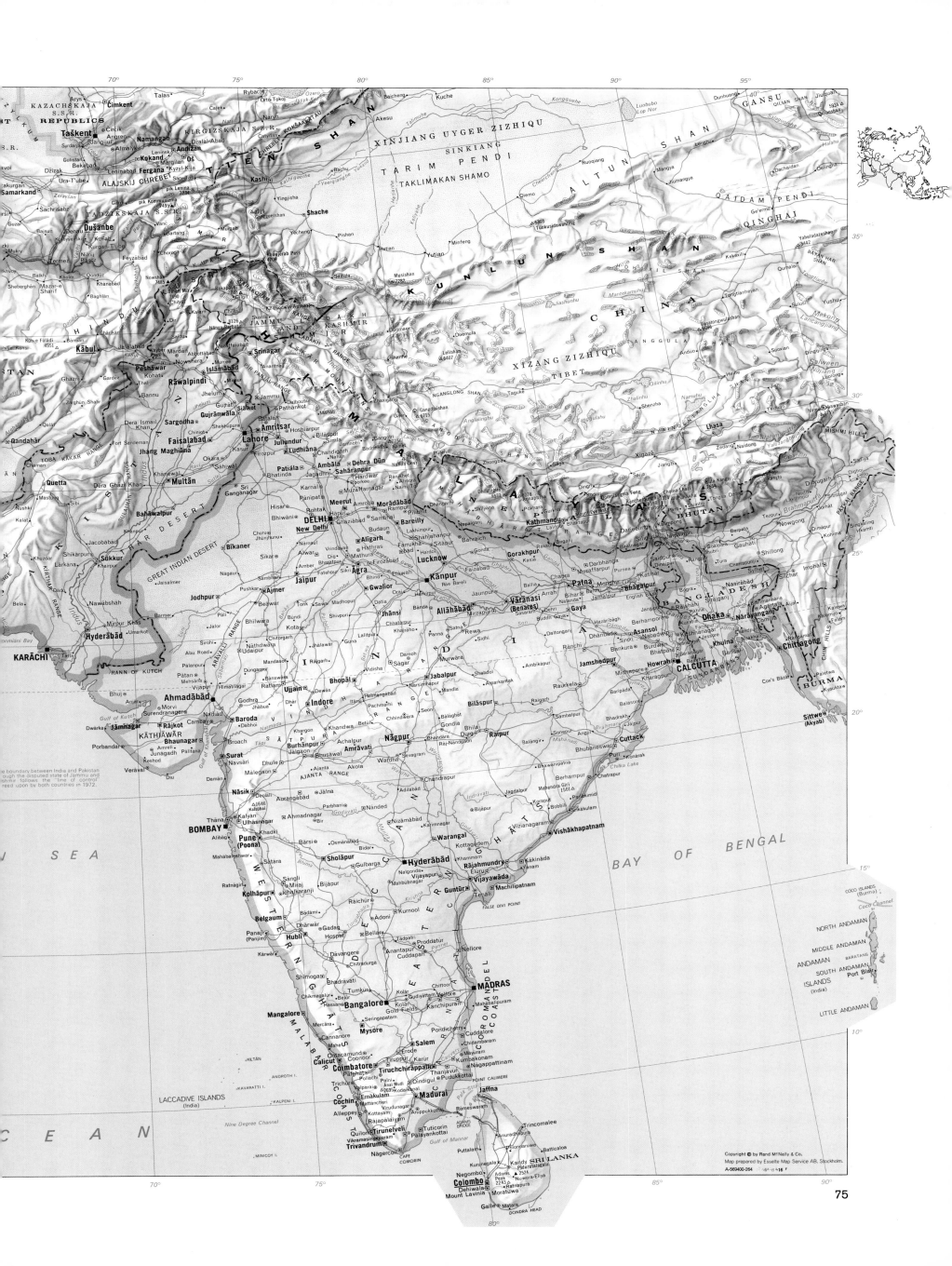

75

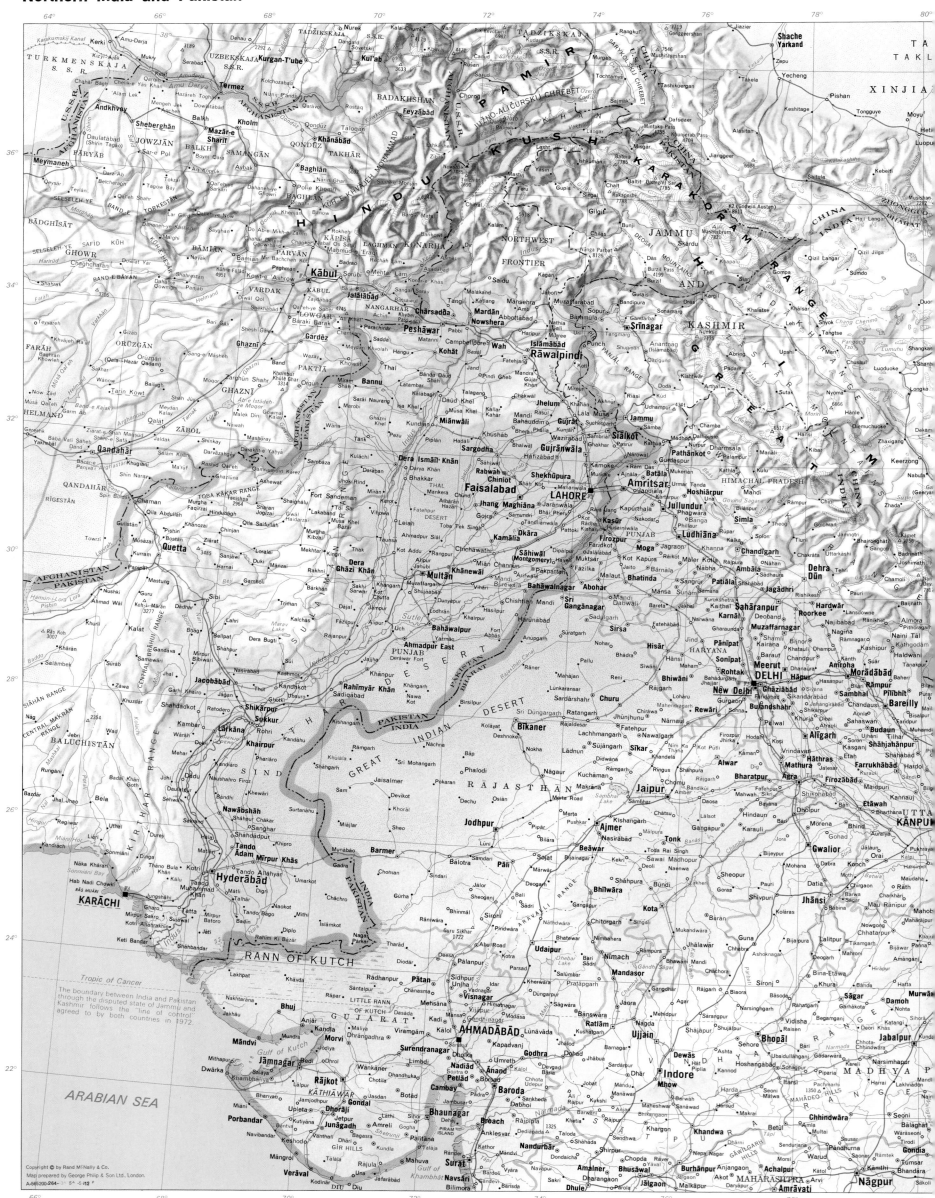

Kilometers 0 100 200 300 Km.
Statute Miles 0 100 200 300 Mi.

Scale 1:6,000,000   One centimeter represents 60 kilometers.
One inch represents approximately 95 miles.
Lambert Conformal Conic Projection

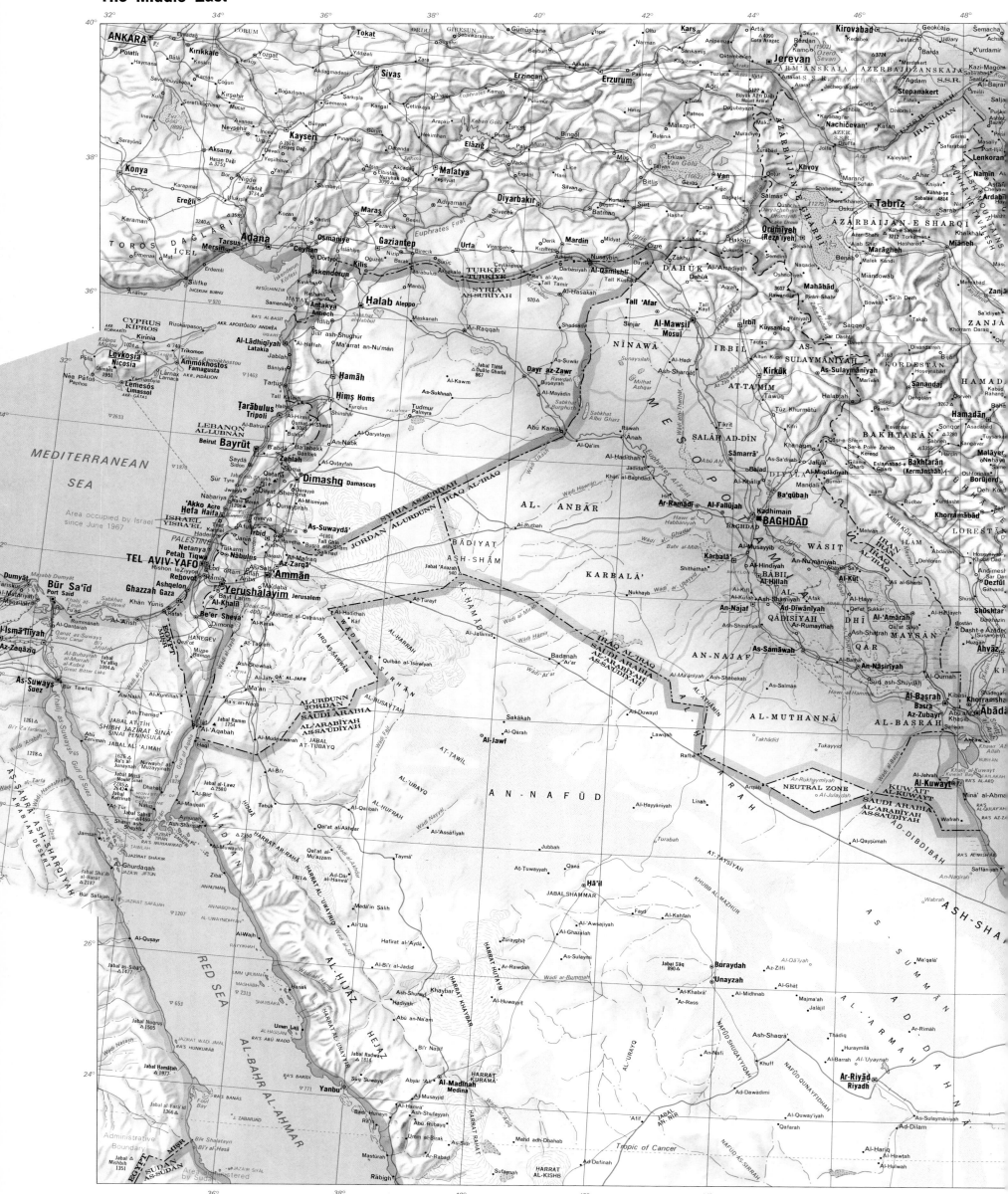

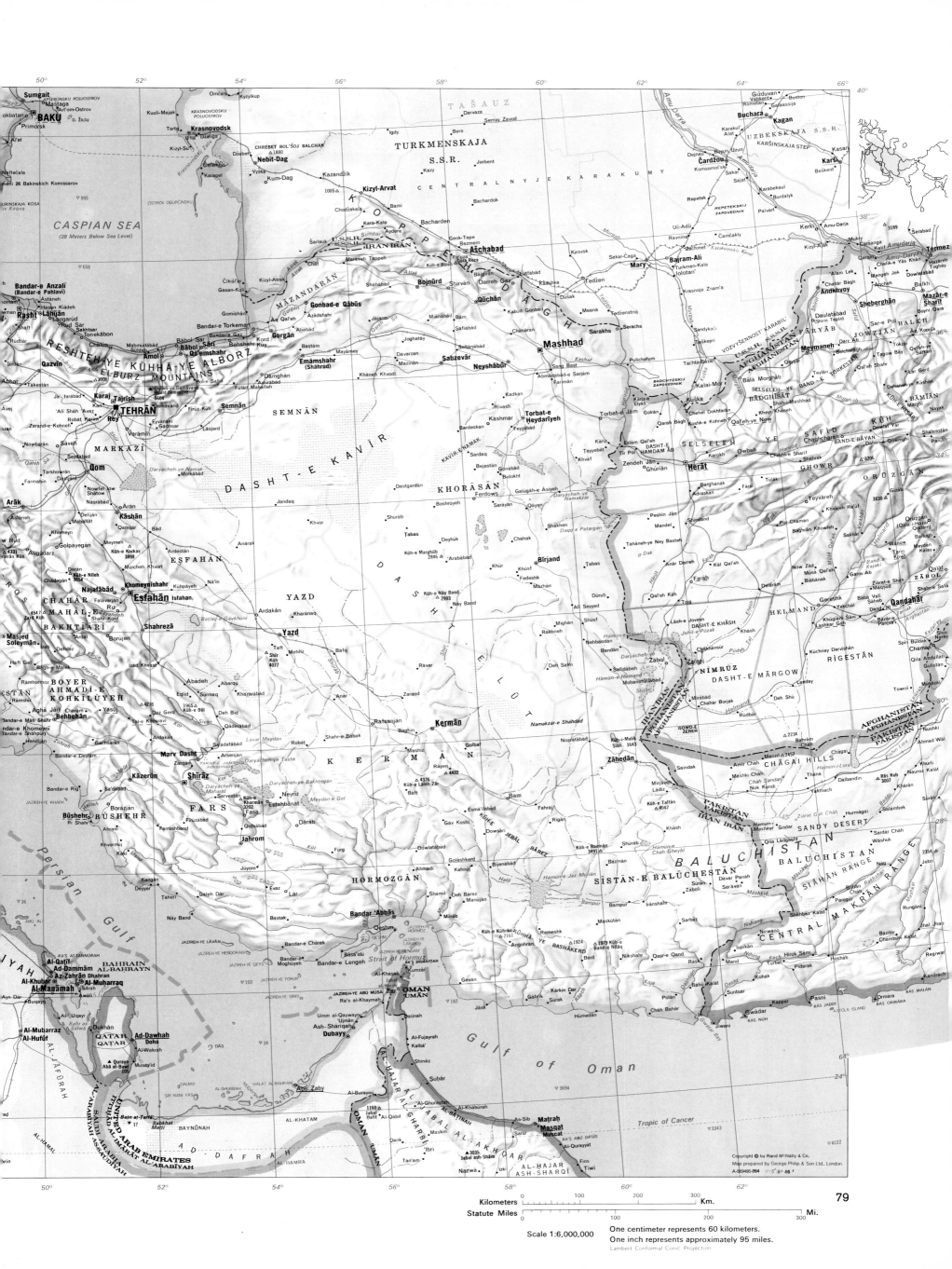

Western North Africa

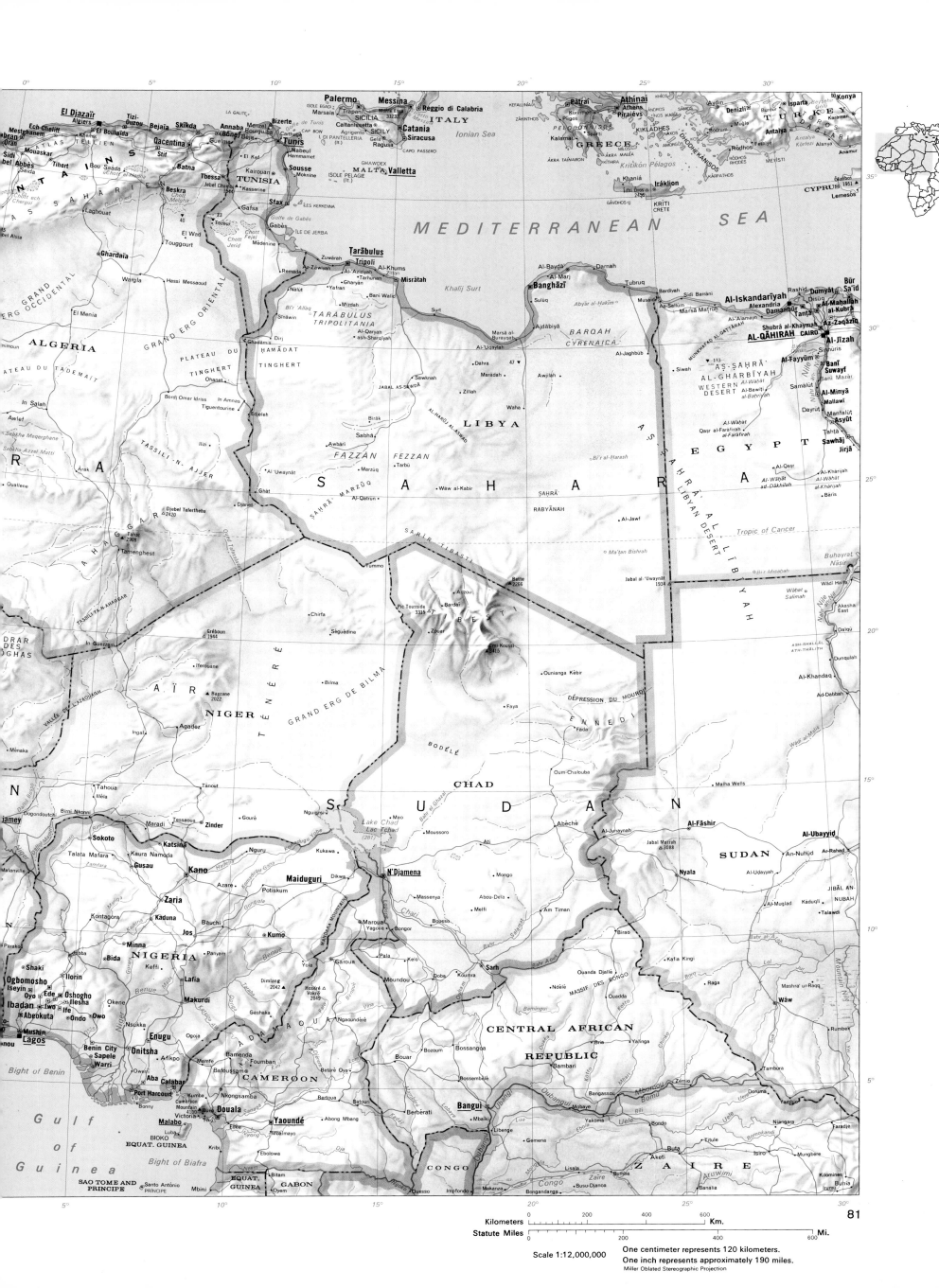

MEDITERRANEAN SEA

ALGERIA

LIBYA

TARĀBULUS
TRIPOLITANIA

FAZZAN   FEZZAN

SAHARA

EGYPT

NIGER

AÏR

TÉNÉRÉ

GRAND ERG DE BILMA

TIBESTI

ENNEDI

BODÉLÉ

CHAD

SUDAN

NIGERIA

CAMEROON

CENTRAL AFRICAN REPUBLIC

ZAIRE

Gulf of Guinea

Bight of Benin

Bight of Biafra

CONGO

GABON

EQUAT. GUINEA

SAO TOME AND PRINCIPE

Kilometers
Statute Miles

Scale 1:12,000,000
One centimeter represents 120 kilometers.
One inch represents approximately 190 miles.
Miller Oblated Stereographic Projection

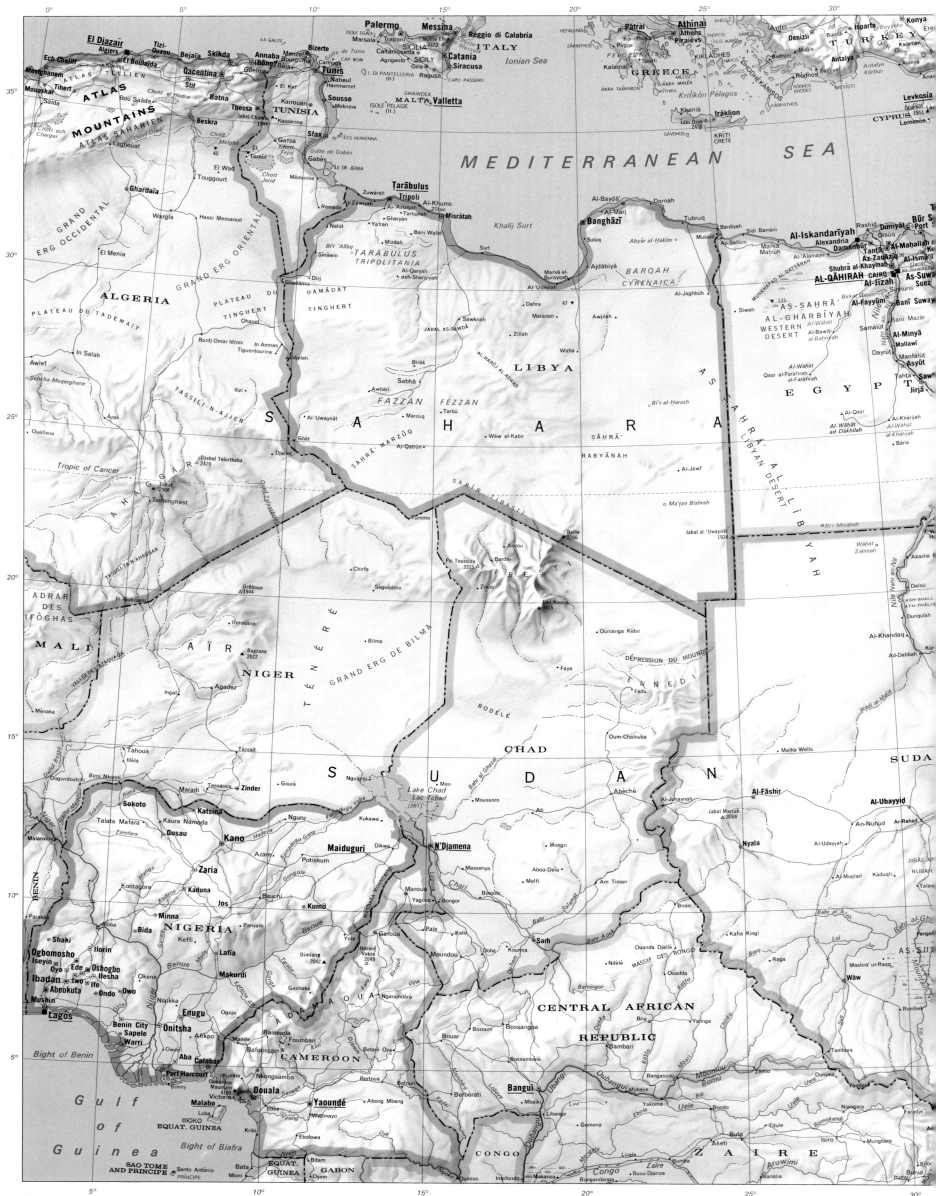

Kilometers 0   200   400   600
Km.
Statute Miles 0   200   400   600
Mi.

Scale 1:12,000,000
One centimeter represents 120 kilometers.
One inch represents approximately 190 miles.
Miller Oblated Stereographic Projection

Copyright © by Rand M&Nally & Co.
Map prepared by Esselte Map Service AB, Stockholm.
A-589391 -264 -4''16''

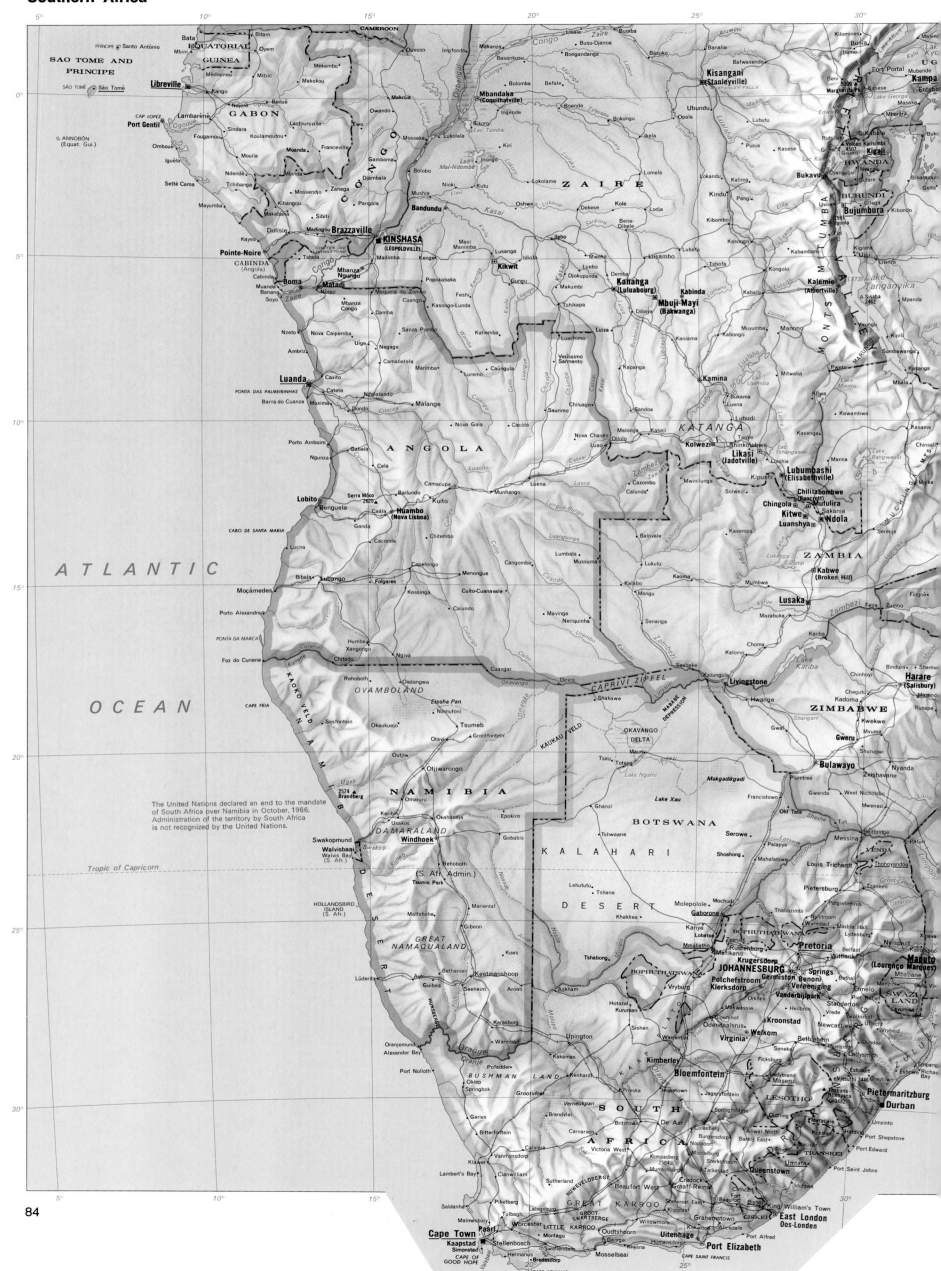

The United Nations declared an end to the mandate
of South Africa over Namibia in October, 1966.
Administration of the territory by South Africa
is not recognized by the United Nations.

INDIAN OCEAN

Equator 0°

SOMALIA
Baraawe

KENYA
Nairobi
Machakos
Mombasa

TANZANIA
Zanzibar
Dar es Salaam

5°

SEYCHELLES
PRASLIN ISLAND ◦ LA DIGUE
SILHOUETTE ◦ **Victoria**
MAHÉ ISLAND

AMIRANTE ISLANDS (Sey.) ◦ ÎLE DESROCHES (Sey.) ◦ PLATTE ISLAND (Sey.)

ALPHONSE ISLAND (Sey.) COETIVY ISLAND (Sey.)

10°

AGALEGA ISLANDS (Mauritius)

ALDABRA ISLAND (Sey.) COSMOLEDO I. (Sey.) SAINT PIERRE ISLAND (Sey.) ◦ PROVIDENCE ISLAND (Sey.)
CERF ISLAND (Sey.)
ASSUMPTION ISLAND (Sey.) ◦ ASTOVE ISLAND (Sey.) ◦ FARQUHAR GROUP (Sey.)

MALAWI
Blantyre

MOZAMBIQUE

ÎLES GLORIEUSES (Reunion)
GRANDE COMORE
Moroni **COMOROS**
Fomboni ARCHIPEL DES COMORES MOHÉLI
ANJOUAN Mutsamudu
Dzaoudzi MAYOTTE (Fr.)

CAP D'AMBRE
CAP SAINT-SÉBASTIEN **Antsiranana**
NOSY MITSIO
NOSY BE
Hell-Ville Ambilobe Vohimarina
Ambanja MASSIF DU Maromokotro 2876 TSARATANANA
NOSY LAVA Doany Sambava
Analalava Antsohihy Andapa
Baie de Narinda Befandriana Antalaha
CAP EST
Mahajanga Port-Bergé Maroantsetra PRESQU'ÎLE DE MASOALA
Marovoay Mampikony Mandritsara
Helodranon' i Mahajamba Tsaratanana
Maevatanana NOSY BORAHA
Ambodifototra
Soalala Andriamena Fenoarivo Atsinanana
MADAGASCAR Morafenobe Ambatondrazaka
Maintirano Ankazobe **Toamasina**
NOSY BARREN Tsiroanomandidy
Belo Ankavandra **Antananarivo**
Ambatolampy Vohibinany
Morondava Miandrivazo Vatomandry
Mahabo Malaimbandy **Antsirabe**
Manja Ambositra Mahanoro
Mandabe NOSY VARIKA
Morombe Ambalavao Mananjary
Beroroha **Fianarantsoa**
Ankazoabo Pic Boby 2658 Manakara
Ihosy
Farafangana
Toliara Betioky Vangaindrano
Bekily Midongy Sud
Ampanihy
Androka
Tsihombe Ambovombe Faradofay
CAP SAINTE-MARIE

15°

ÎLE TROMELIN (Reunion)

ÎLE CHESTERFIELD (Reunion)
ÎLE JUAN DE NOVA (Reunion)
Tambohorano

BASSAS DA INDIA (Reunion)

ÎLE EUROPA (Reunion)
CAP SAINT-VINCENT

Tropic of Capricorn

20°
Port Louis
Curepipe ® Mahébourg
MAURITIUS
Le Port Saint-Denis
Saint-Paul **REUNION**
Saint-Pierre (Fr.)

MASCARENE ISLANDS

25°

INDIAN OCEAN

30°

35° 40° 45° 50° 55° 60°

Kilometers |0 200 400 600| Km.
Statute Miles |0 200 400 600| Mi.

Scale 1:12,000,000

One centimeter represents 120 kilometers.
One inch represents approximately 190 miles.

Miller Oblated Stereographic Projection

85

Southern Africa and Madagascar

The United Nations declared
an end to the mandate of
South Africa over Namibia in
October, 1966. Administration
of the territory by South Africa
is not recognized by the United Nations.

Copyright © by Rand McNally & Co.
Map prepared by George Philip & Son Ltd. London.
A-589292-264

Kilometers   0   100   200   300   Km.
Statute Miles   0   100   200   300   Mi.

Scale 1:6,000,000

One centimeter represents 60 kilometers.
One inch represents approximately 95 miles.
Lambert Azimuthal Equal-Area Projection

Australia

Kilometers
Km.

Statute Miles
Mi.

0   200   400   600

0   200   400   600

Scale 1:12,000,000

One centimeter represents 120 kilometers.
One inch represents approximately 190 miles.
Lambert Conformal Conic Projection

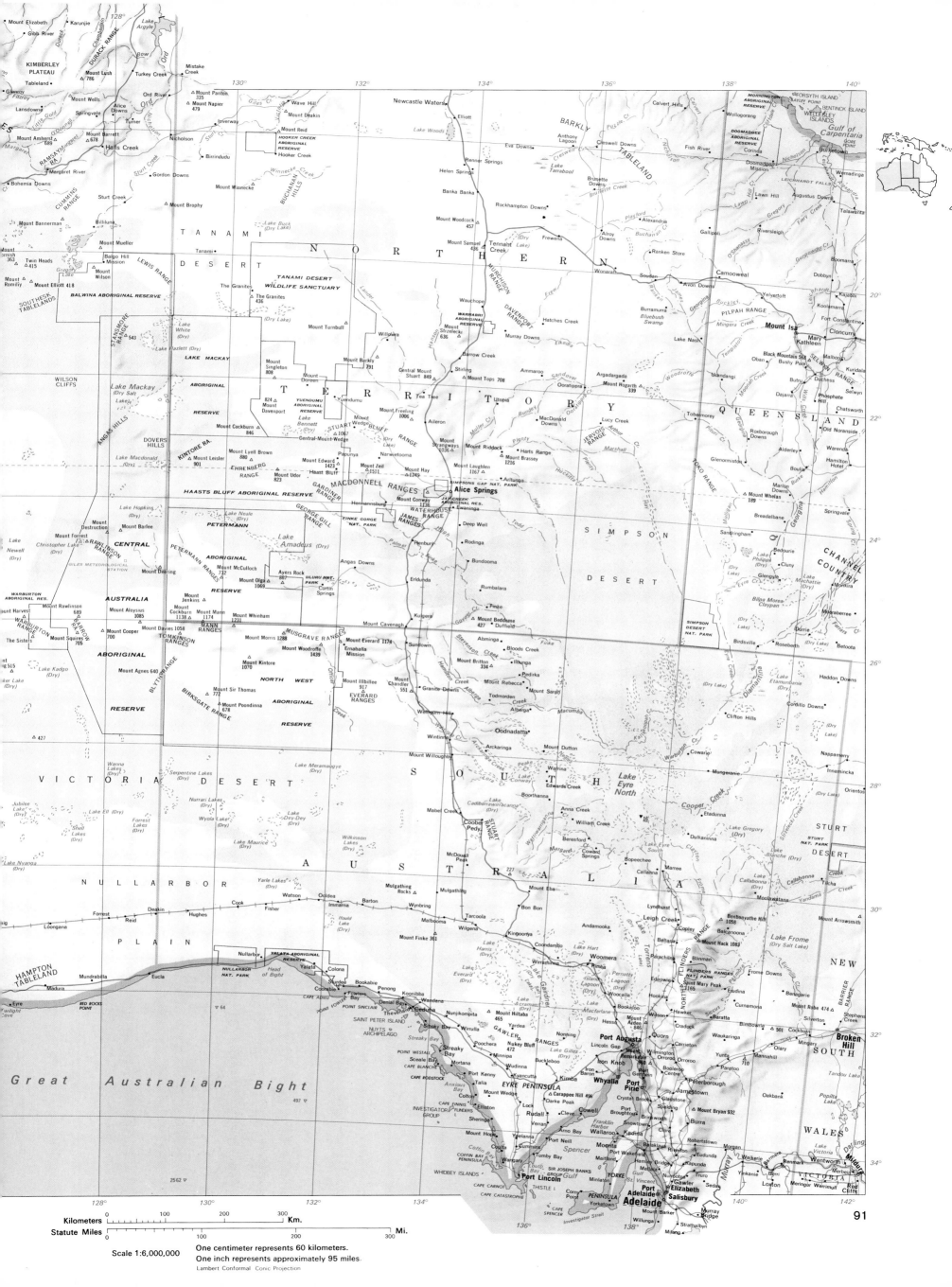

Kilometers 0 100 200 300 Km.

Statute Miles 0 100 200 300 Mi.

Scale 1:6,000,000   One centimeter represents 60 kilometers.
One inch represents approximately 95 miles.
Lambert Conformal Conic Projection

Kilometers

Statute Miles

Scale 1:6,000,000

One centimeter represents 60 kilometers.
One inch represents approximately 95 miles.
Lambert Conformal Conic Projection

0   100   200   300 Km.

0   100   200   300 Mi.

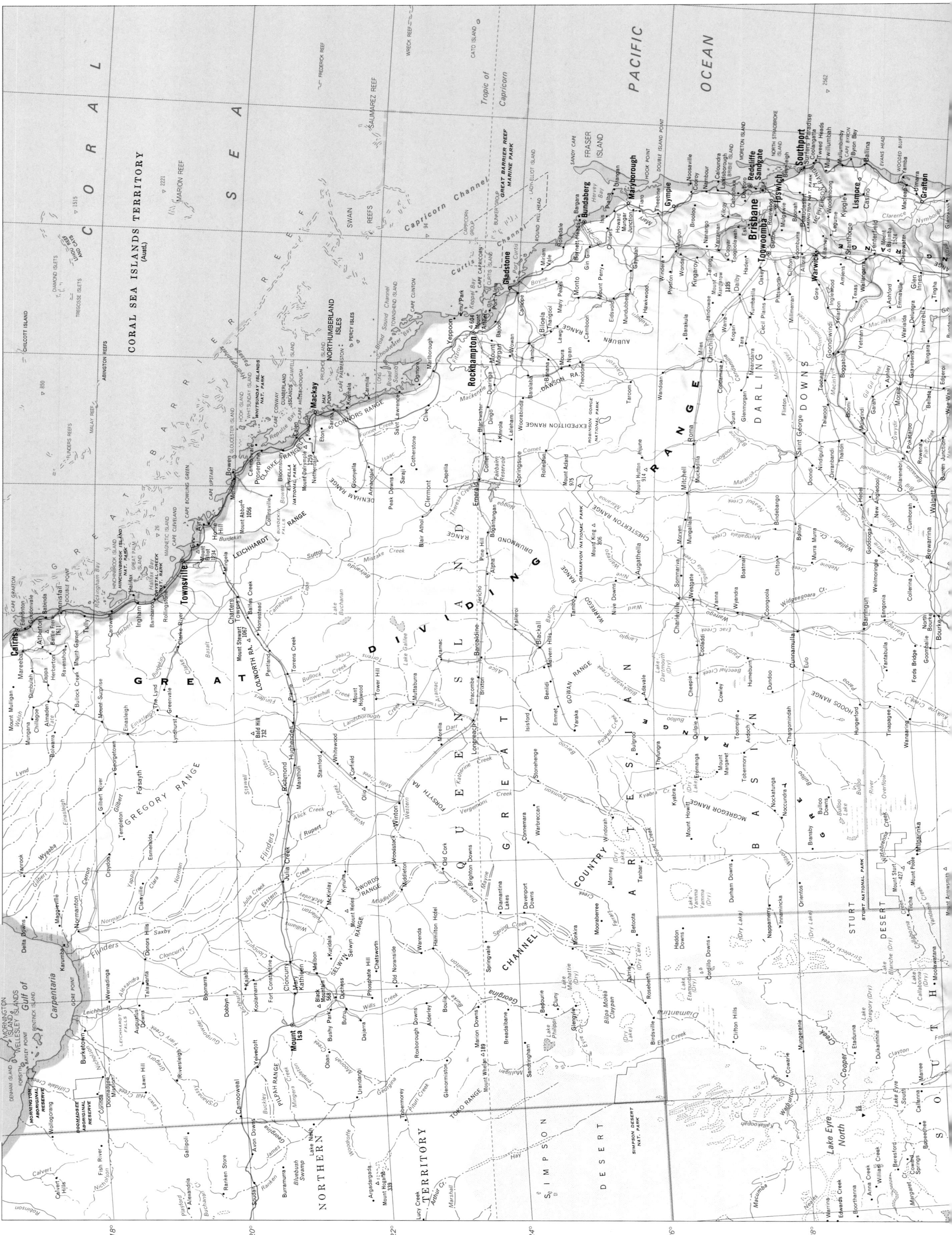

Eastern Australia

PACIFIC OCEAN

CORAL SEA

CORAL SEA ISLANDS TERRITORY (Aust.)

GREAT BARRIER REEF MARINE PARK

Tropic of Capricorn

GULF of Carpentaria

GREAT DIVIDING RANGE

GREAT ARTESIAN BASIN

QUEENSLAND

NORTHERN TERRITORY

SOUTH

SIMPSON DESERT

STURT DESERT

DARLING DOWNS

GREGORY RANGE

SELWYN RANGE

Brisbane
Southport
Ipswich
Warwick
Toowoomba
Gympie
Maryborough
Bundaberg
Gladstone
Rockhampton
Mackay
Bowen
Townsville
Cairns
Charters Towers
Mount Isa
Cloncurry
Longreach
Roma
Walgett
Lismore
Grafton
Redcliffe
Sandgate

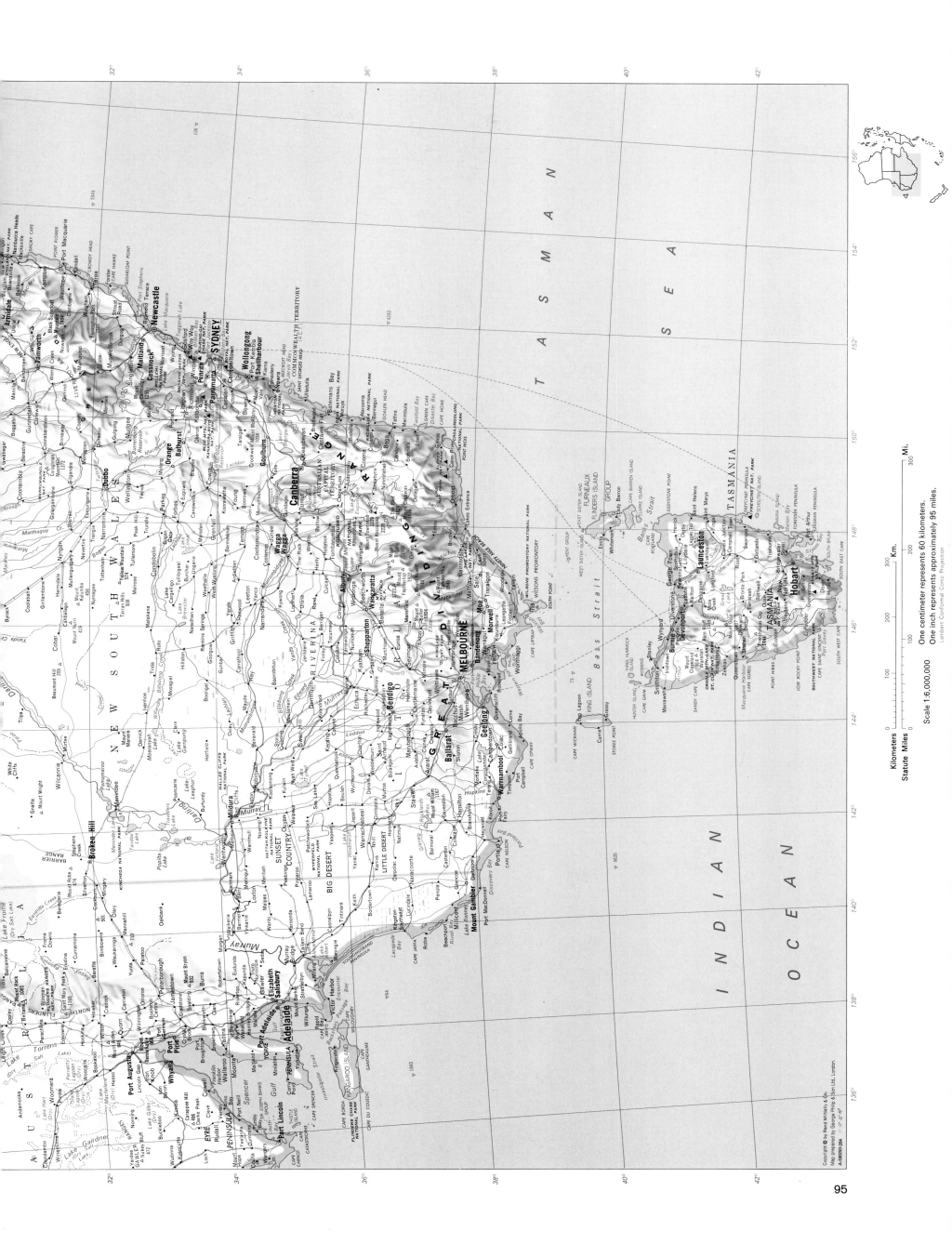

Scale 1:6,000,000

One centimeter represents 60 kilometers.
One inch represents approximately 95 miles.
Lambert Conformal Conic Projection

Kilometers

Statute Miles

Km.

Mi.

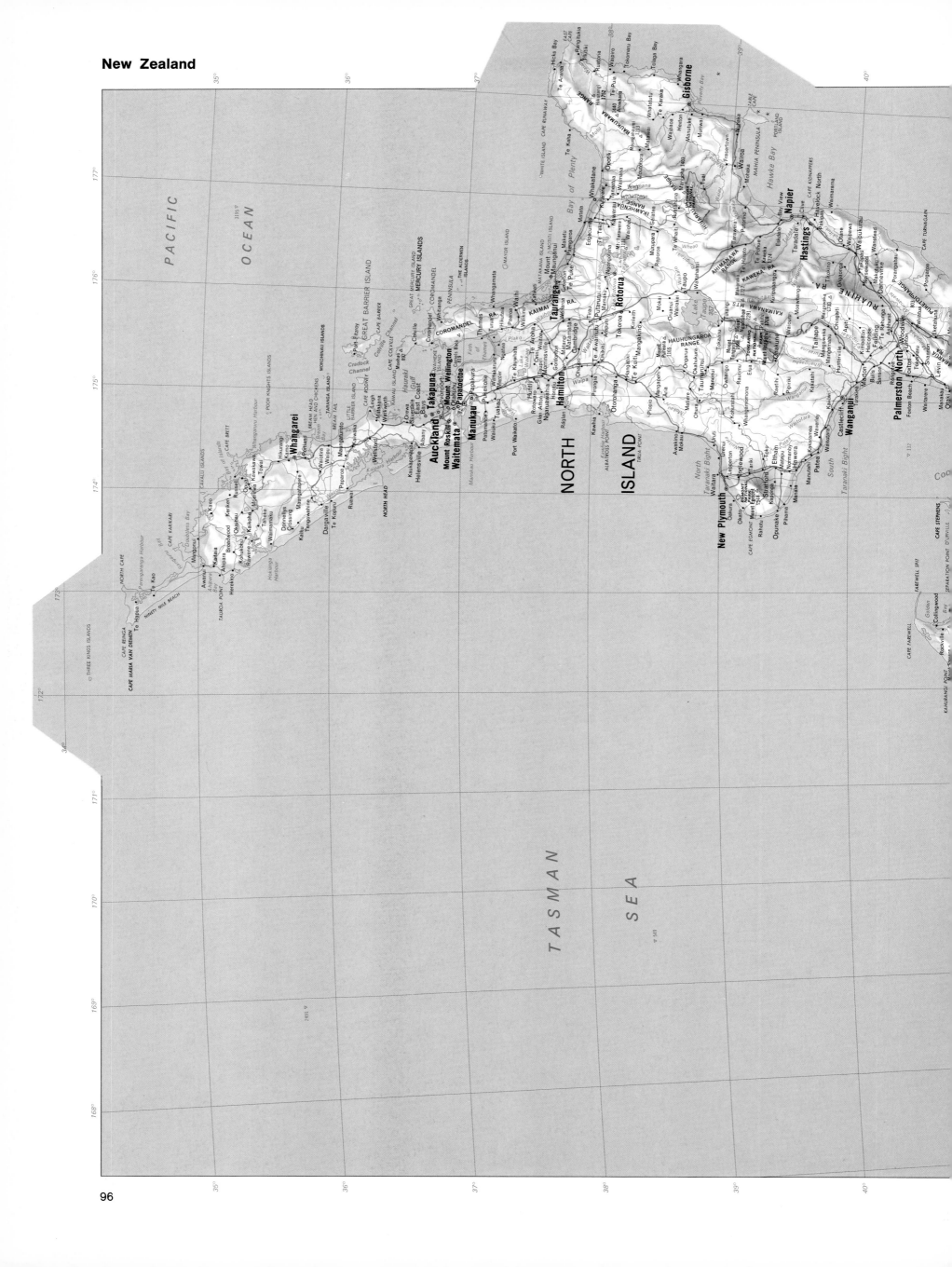

New Zealand

PACIFIC

OCEAN

TASMAN

SEA

NORTH

ISLAND

Auckland
Manukau
Hamilton
Rotorua
Gisborne
Napier
Hastings
Tauranga
New Plymouth
Wanganui
Palmerston North
Whangarei

Bay of Plenty

Hawke Bay

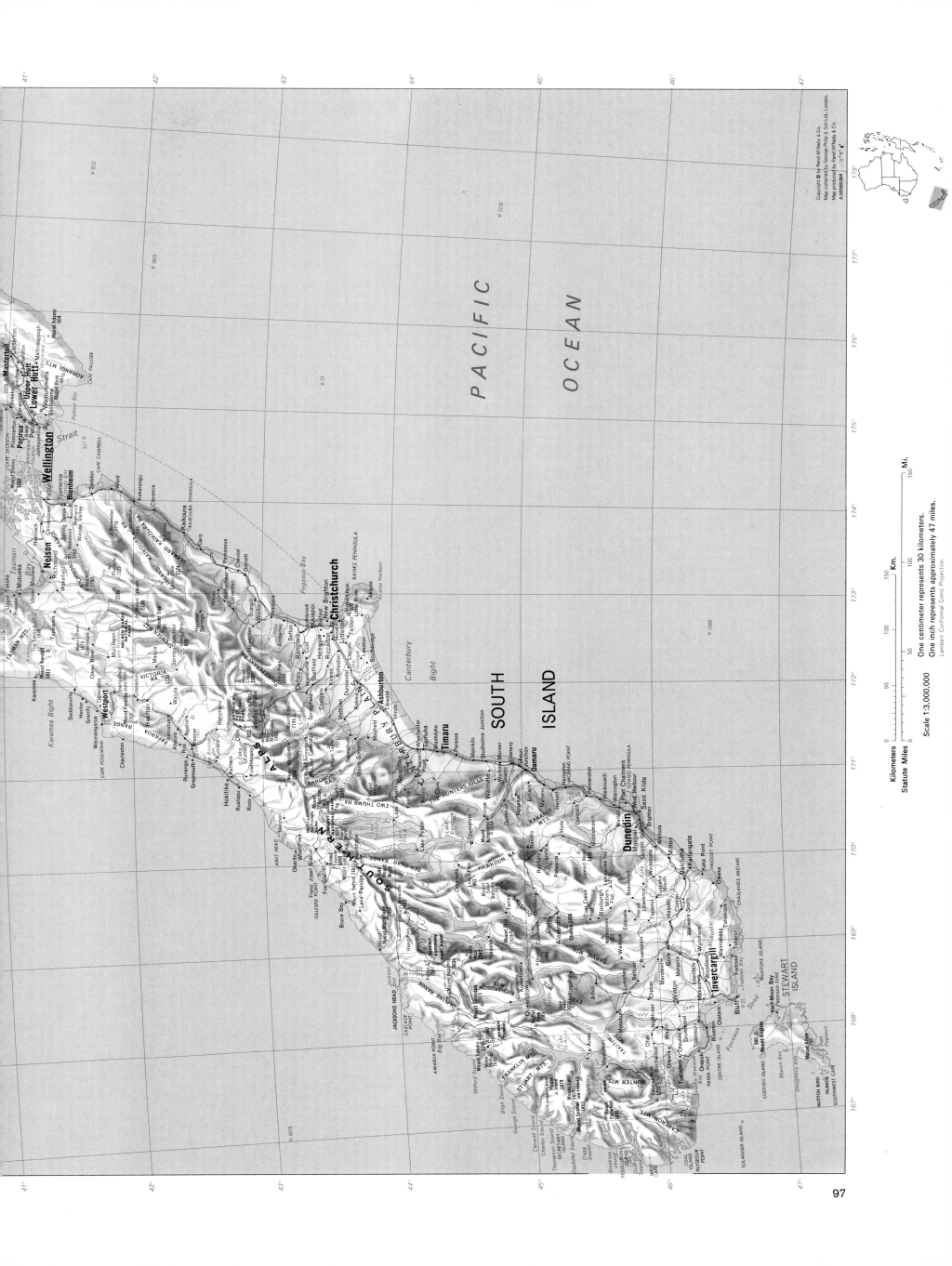

PACIFIC

OCEAN

SOUTH

ISLAND

STEWART
ISLAND

Wellington
Lower Hutt
Upper Hutt
Porirua
Masterton
Nelson
Blenheim
Picton
Westport
Kaikoura
Christchurch
Ashburton
Timaru
Oamaru
Dunedin
Invercargill

SOUTHERN ALPS

Tasman Bay

Tasman Mts.

Canterbury Bight

Foveaux Strait

Km.
Kilometers
0   50   100   150
Statute Miles
0   50   100   150
Mi.

Scale 1:3,000,000
One centimeter represents 30 kilometers.
One inch represents approximately 47 miles.
Lambert Conformal Conic Projection

Baffin Bay

GREENLAND (Denmark)

Davis Strait

Labrador Sea

ATLANTIC OCEAN

Hudson Bay

QUEBEC

LABRADOR

James Bay

ONTARIO

NEWFOUNDLAND

St. John's

ST. PIERRE AND MIQUELON

NEW BRUNSWICK

PRINCE EDWARD ISLAND

NOVA SCOTIA

Halifax

Saint John

MAINE

APPALACHIAN MTS

MONTREAL

Ottawa

Quebec

Thunder Bay

Sault Ste. Marie

Sudbury

TORONTO

BOSTON

NEW YORK

PHILADELPHIA

DETROIT

CHICAGO

Cleveland

MICHIGAN

WISCONSIN

ILLINOIS

Milwaukee

Madison

99

Kilometers 0 200 400 600 Km.

Statute Miles 0 200 400 600 Mi.

Scale 1:12,000,000   One centimeter represents 120 kilometers.
One inch represents approximately 190 miles.

Lambert Conformal Conic Projection

Kilometers

Statute Miles

Scale 1:12,000,000   One centimeter represents 120 kilometers.
One inch represents approximately 190 miles.
Albers Conical Equal-Area Projection

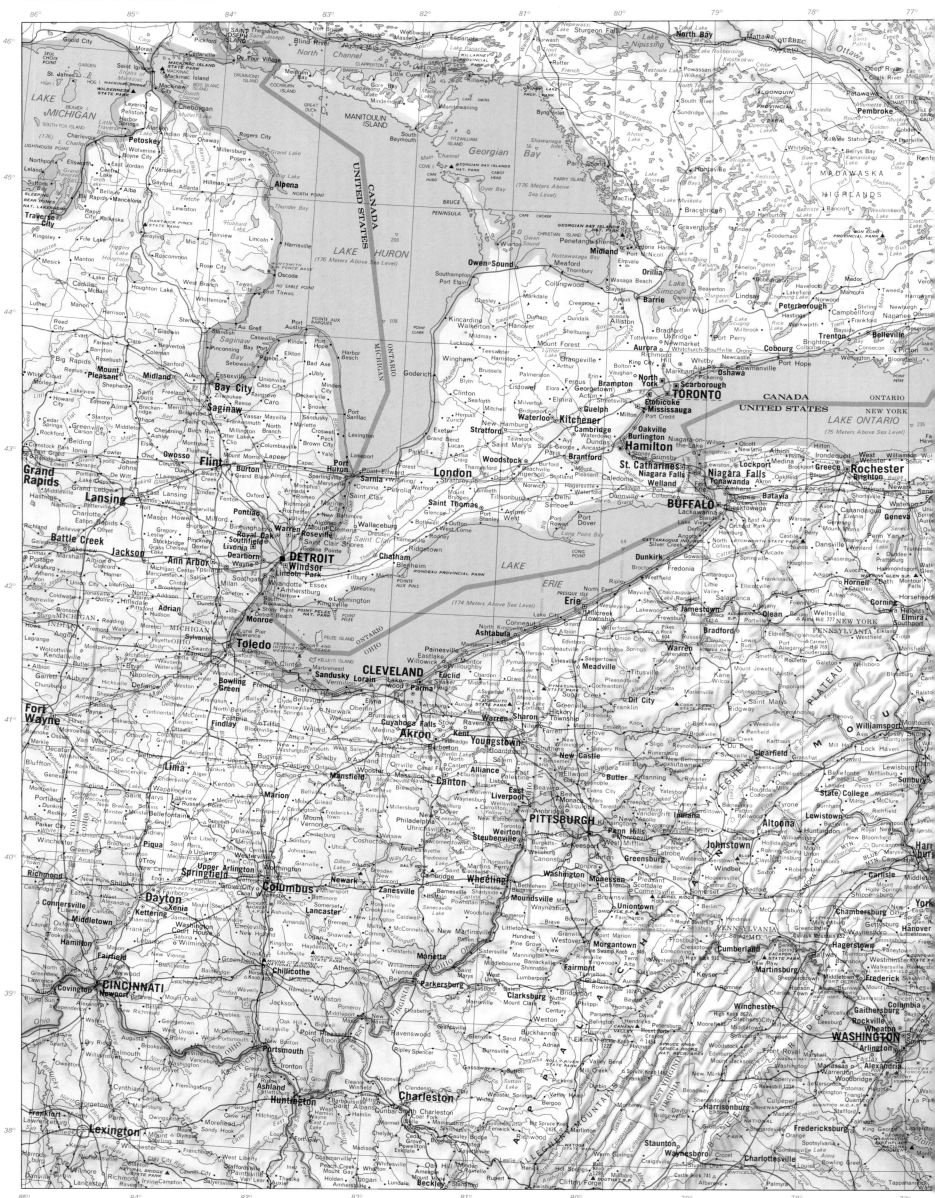

Kilometers
Statute Miles

Scale 1:3,000,000
One centimeter represents 30 kilometers.
One inch represents approximately 47 miles.
Albers Conical Equal-Area Projection

ATLANTIC

OCEAN

California and Nevada, Hawaii

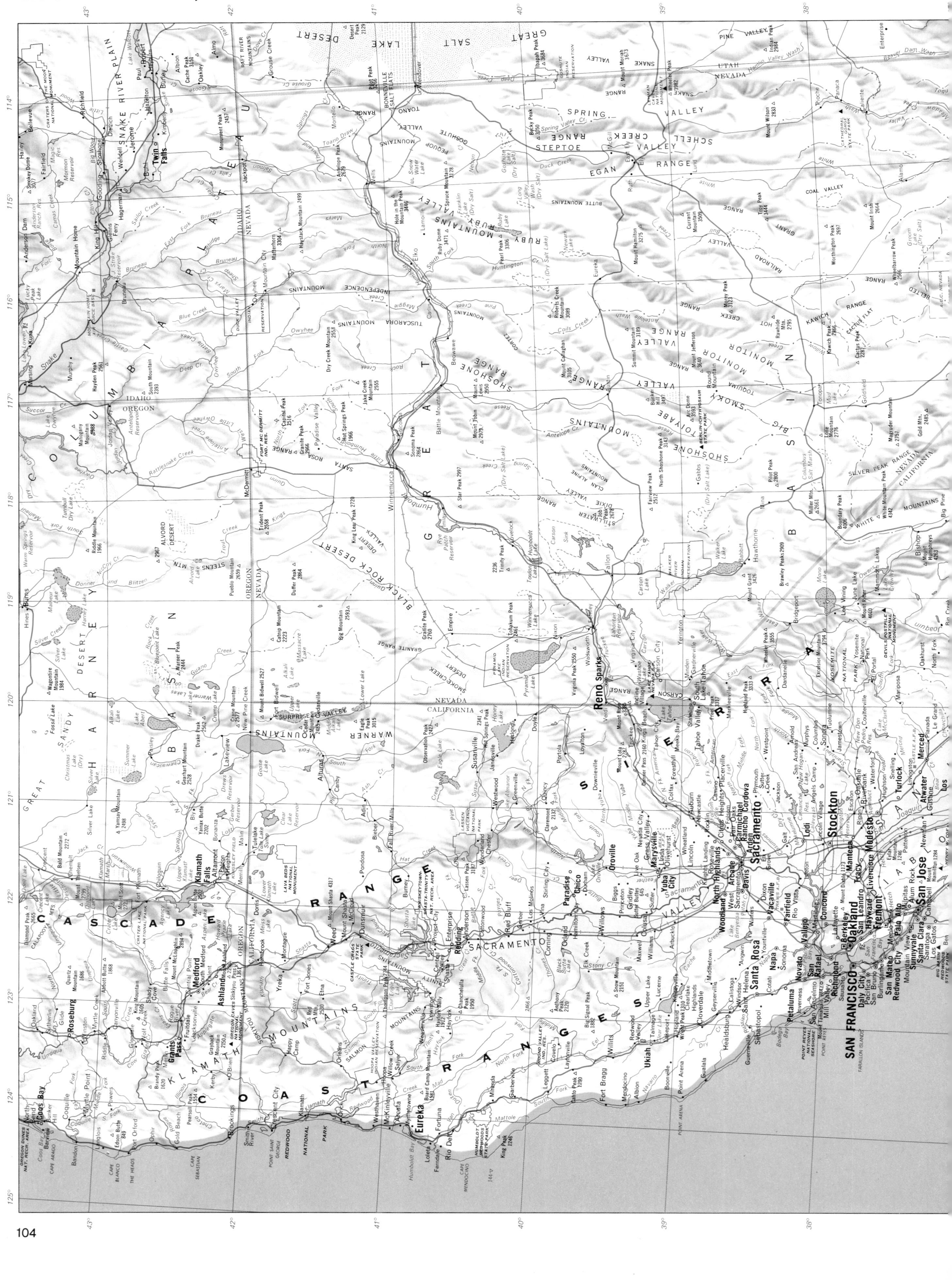

Kilometers $\overline{0\hspace{2cm}50\hspace{2cm}100\hspace{2cm}150}$ Km.

Statute Miles $\overline{0\hspace{2cm}50\hspace{2cm}100\hspace{2cm}150}$ Mi.

Scale 1:3,000,000

One centimeter represents 30 kilometers.
One inch represents approximately 47 miles.

Albers Conical Equal-Area Projection

Islands of the West Indies

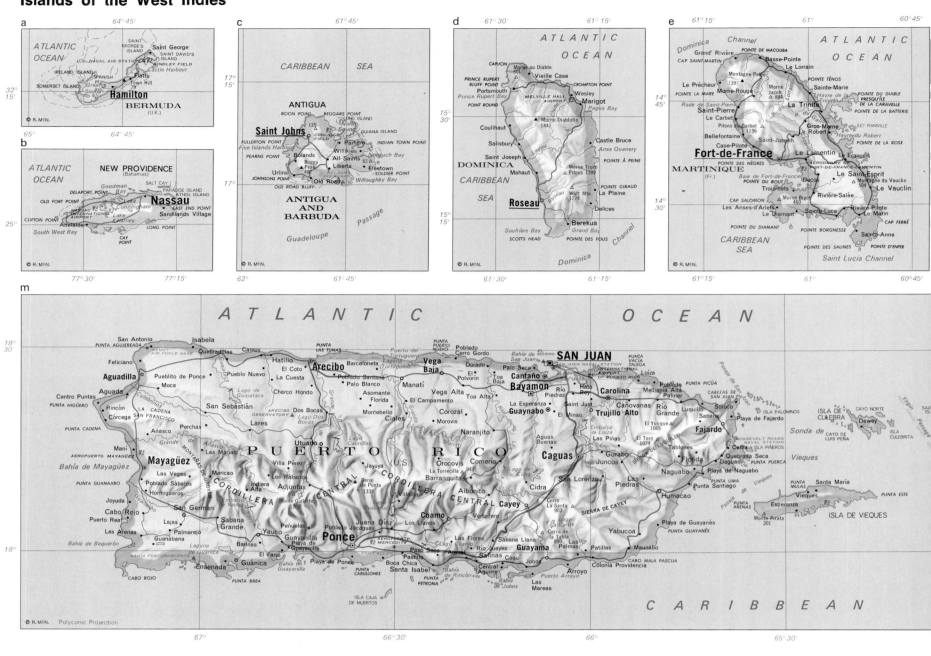

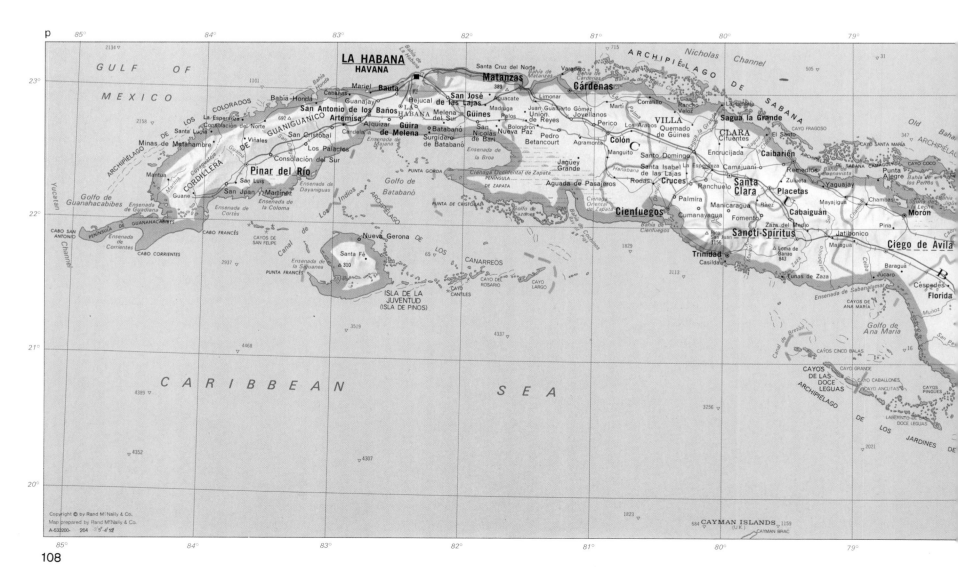

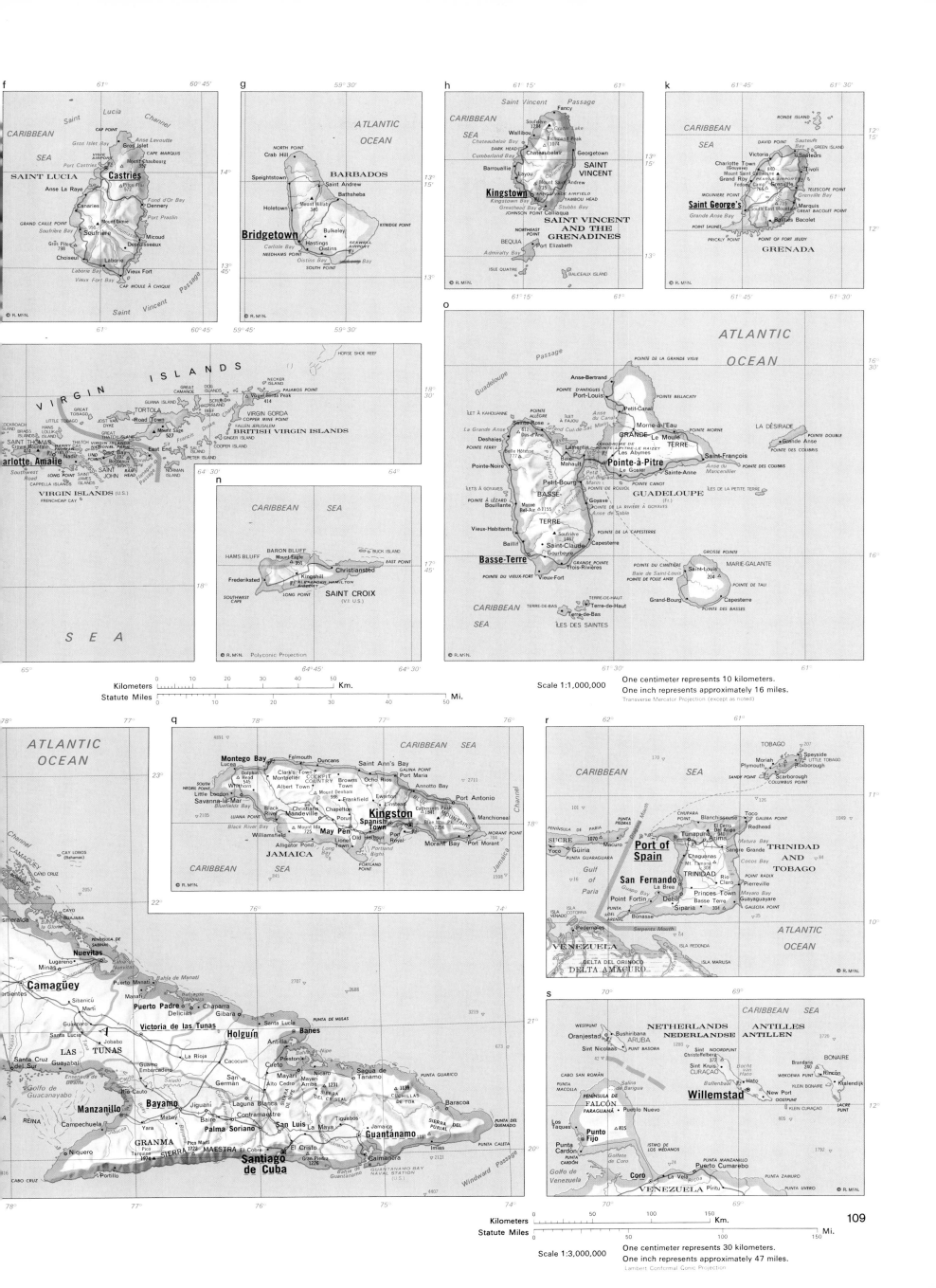

Northern South America

CARIBBEAN SEA

PACIFIC OCEAN

COLOMBIA

VENEZUELA

ECUADOR

PERU

BOLIVIA

NICARAGUA

COSTA RICA

CHILE

ARGENTINA

Kilometers

Statute Miles

Scale 1:12,000,000
One centimeter represents 120 kilometers.
One inch represents approximately 190 miles.
Oblique Conic Conformal Projection

Copyright © by Rand McNally & Co.
Map prepared by Esselte Map Service AB, Stockholm.
A-549100-264

ATLANTIC OCEAN

BARBADOS
Bridgetown

OBAGO

Morawhanna

Charity
Spring Garden
Parika
Hyde Park
Georgetown
Bartica
Rosignol
New Amsterdam
Totness
Rockstone
Mackenzie
Wismar
Nieuw Nickerie
Wismar

GUYANA

Paramaribo
Nieuw Amsterdam
Paranam
Onverwacht
Albina
Moengo
Kwakoegron
Brokopondo
Sinnamary
ÎLE DU DIABLE

W. J. van
Blommestein
Meer
Saint-Élie
Regina
Cayenne

SURINAME

FRENCH
GUIANA

Juliana Top
1230

Saint-Georges

Saül
830

TUMUC-HUMAC MTS.

ACARAI MTS.

Oiapoque

Cunani

Amapá

Calçoene

Serra do Navio

ILHA DE MARACÁ

Macapá

ILHA CAVIANA
ILHA MEXIANA
CABO MAGUARI

Mazagão

ILHA
GRANDE
DO GURUPÁ

ILHA DE MARAJÓ

Gurupá

Marapanim
Curuçá

Breves

Belém

Bragança

Abaetetuba

Portel

Cametá

Camiranga

Caturupu

Alenquer
Monte Alegre

Oriximiná
Óbidos
Porto de
Móz

Carrajinho

Pinheiro

Alcântara

São Luís

Tutóia

Santarém

São Bento

Viana

Rosário

Camocim

Acaraú

Tucuruí

Hapecuru-Mirim
Monção

Parnaíba

Brejo

Sobral

Maranguape

Baturité

Fortaleza

Parintins
Maués

Itaituba

Altamira

Imperatriz

Bacabal
Pedreiras
Codó

Barras

Ipu
Pedro II

Campo Maior

Quixadá

Aracati

Areia Branca

Borba

Tucuruí

São João
do Araguaia
Araguaína

Marabá

Barra
do Corda

Caxias

União

Teresina

Crateús

Senador
Pompeu

Mossoró

Russas

Macau

Itaituba

SERRA DOS CARAJÁS

Grajaú

Colinas

Amarante

Iguatu

Icó

Sousa

Currais Novos

Angicos

Lajes

Natal

CABO DE SÃO ROQUE

Tocantinópolis

Carolina

Loreto

Benedito Leite

Oeiras

Picos

Caicó

Cajazeiras

Patos

Campina Grande

Guarabira
Sapé
Goiana

João Pessoa

Gradaús

Conceição do Araguaia

Riachão

Balsas

Floriano

Crato
Juazeiro
do Norte

Serra
Talhada

Itabaiana

Cabedelo

Olinda

Recife

Araguacema

Pedro
Afonso

Alto Parnaíba
Santa Filomena

São Raimundo Nonato

Flores

Sertânia
Pesqueira

Nazaré da
Mata
Limoeiro

Caruaru

Jaboatão

Barreiros

Miracema do Norte
Tocantínia

Gilbués

Remanso

Petrolina

Juazeiro

Arcoverde

Palmares

Porto de Pedras

Pium
Cristalândia

Parnaguá

Paulistana

Cabrobó

União dos Palmares
Palmeira
dos Índios
Arapiraca

Rio Largo

Maceió

Porto Nacional

Natividade

Senhor
do Bonfim

Tucano

Propriá

Penedo

BRAZIL

ILHA
DO
BANANAL

Gurupiá

Dianópolis

Xique-Xique

Jacobina

Itabaianinha

Aracaju
São Cristóvão

Serra do Escurial
1229

Morro do Chapéu

Estância

Inhambupe

Paranã

Taguatinga

Barreiras

Serrinha

Feira de Santana

Alagoinhas

Arraias

São Domingos

Lençóis

Mucugê

Santo Amaro
Candeias

Maragogipe

Cachoeira

Porangatu

Cavalcante

Posse

Bom Jesus
da Lapa

Santo Antônio de Jesus

Aratuípe

Nazaré

Salvador

Pilar de Goiás

Aruanã

Carinhanha

Guanambi

Paramirim
Pico das
Almas
1850

Jequié

Valença

ILHA DE TINHARÉ

PLANALTO DO
MATO GROSSO

Rosário Oeste

Goiás

Formosa

Monte Azul

Januária

Vitória
da Conquista

Ibicaraí

Ilhéus

Itabuna

Cuiabá

Poxoréo

Aragarças

Brasília

São Francisco

Rio Pardo
de Minas

Pedra Azul

Itapetinga

Canavieiras

PLANALTO

Guiratinga

Anápolis

Luziânia

Pirenópolis

Silvânia

Grão Mogol

Belmonte

Rondonópolis

Alto Araguaia

Goiânia

CENTRAL

Araçuaí

Minas Novas

Porto Seguro

Mineiros

Montes
Claros

Pirapora

Diamantina

Prado
Alcobaça
Caravelas

Jataí
Rio Verde

Morrinhos
Campo Alegre de Goiás

Corinto

Pedra Azul

Nunque

ILHA CAÇUMBA

Humaitá
Caiapônia

Pires do Rio

Araçatuba

Catalão

Ipameri

Diamantina

Peçanha

Pôrto Seguro

Governador
Valadares

São Mateus

Tupaciguara
Araguari

Patrocínio

Aimorés

Campo Grande
Três Lagoas

Ituiutaba

Patos
de Minas

Dores
do Indaiá

Bom Despacho

Caratinga

Colatina

Vitória
Vila Velha

Aquidauana

Uberlândia

Araxá

SA. DA CANASTRA

Divinópolis

Belo
Horizonte

Ponte
Nova

Cachoeiro de
Itapemirim

Presidente Prudente

Uberaba

Sete
Lagoas

Ouro
Prêto

Itabira

Itapemirim

Andradina
Paulicéia

Fernandópolis

Franca

Passos

Formiga

São João
del Rei
Barbacena

Conselheiro
Lafaiete

Leopoldina

Campos

Voturoporanga

Barretos
Olímpia

Poços
de Caldas

Varginha

Juiz de Fora

Campos
dos Goytacazes

CABO FRIO

Lins
Tupã

Araraquara
Marília
São Carlos

Ribeirão
Prêto

Jaú

Limeira

Itajubá

MANTIQUEIRA

Nova
Friburgo

Niterói

Bauru

Piracicaba

Campinas

Jundiaí

São José
dos Campos

Nova
Iguaçu

Petrópolis

RIO DE JANEIRO

Sorocaba

Mogi das Cruzes

Botucatu

SÃO PAULO

Santo André

Santos

São Vicente

ILHA DE SÃO SEBASTIÃO

ILHA
GRANDE

Tropic of Capricorn

111

A T L A N T I C

O C E A N

Tropic of Capricorn

BRAZIL

SÃO PAULO
RIO DE JANEIRO

Ribeirão Prêto
Campinas
Curitiba
Joinvile
Blumenau
Florianópolis
Passo Fundo
Caxias do Sul
Pôrto Alegre
Pelotas
Rio Grande

URUGUAY
Montevideo

Presidente Prudente
Maringá
Londrina
Ponta Grossa

Santos

SHAG ROCKS
BLACK ROCK
BIRD ISLAND   SOUTH GEORGIA
ANNENKOV ISLAND   (Falkland Is.)
                  Mount Paget
CAPE DISAPPOINTMENT
                  CLERKE ROCKS

Kilometers 0   200   400   600 Km.
Statute Miles 0   200   400   600 Mi.

Scale 1:12,000,000

One centimeter represents 120 kilometers.
One inch represents approximately 190 miles.

Oblique Conic Conformal Projection

Kilometers
Statute Miles

Scale 1:6,000,000   One centimeter represents 60 kilometers.
One inch represents approximately 95 miles.
Oblique Conic Conformal Projection

WORLD INFORMATION TABLE

This table gives the area, population, population density, capital, and political status for every country in the world. The political units listed are categorized by political status in the last column of the table, as follows: A—independent countries; B—internally independent political entities which are under the protection of another country in matters of defence and foreign affairs; C—colonies and other dependent political units; and D—the major administrative subdivisions of Australia, Canada, China, the Soviet Union, the United Kingdom, and the United States. For comparison, the table also includes the continents and the world. For units categorized B, the protecting countries are identified in the political status column. For units categorized C, the names of administering countries are given in parentheses in the first column. A key to abbreviations of country names appears on page 121. All footnotes to this table appear on page 119.

The populations are estimates for January 1, 1987, made by Rand McNally & Company on the basis of official data, United Nations estimates, and other available information. Area figures include inland water.

English Name	Local Name	Area in sq. km.	Area in sq. mi.	Population	Pop. per sq. km.	Pop. per sq. mi.	Capital	Political Status
†Afghanistan	Afghānestān	636,266	245,664	18,950,000	30	77	Kābol	A
Africa	...	30,300,000	11,700,000	600,600,000	20	51		...
Alabama, U.S.	Alabama	133,913	51,704	4,065,000	30	79	Montgomery	D
Alaska, U.S.	Alaska	1,530,693	591,004	530,000	0.3	0.9	Juneau	D
†Albania	Shqipëri	28,748	11,100	3,045,000	106	274	Tiranë	A
Alberta, Can.	Alberta	661,190	255,287	2,395,000	3.6	9.4	Edmonton	D
†Algeria	Algérie (French) / Djazaïr (Arabic)	2,381,741	919,595	23,135,000	9.7	25	El Djazaïr (Algiers)	A
American Samoa (U.S.)	American Samoa (English) / Amerika Samoa (Samoan)	199	77	37,000	186	481	Pago Pago	C
Andorra	Andorra	453	175	50,000	110	286	Andorra	B(Sp., Fr.)
†Angola	Angola	1,246,700	481,354	9,150,000	7.3	19	Luanda	A
Anguilla	Anguilla	91	35	7,000	77	200	The Valley	B(U.K.)
Anhwei, China	Anhui	140,000	54,054	52,720,000	377	975	Hefei	D
Antarctica	...	14,000,000	5,400,000	(1)	0.0	0.0		...
†Antigua and Barbuda	Antigua and Barbuda	443	171	83,000	187	485	St. John's	A
†Argentina	Argentina	2,780,092	1,073,400	31,300,000	11	29	Buenos Aires	A
Arizona, U.S.	Arizona	295,264	114,002	3,220,000	11	28	Phoenix	D
Arkansas, U.S.	Arkansas	137,764	53,191	2,395,000	17	45	Little Rock	D
Armenian S.S.R., U.S.S.R.	Arm'anskaja S.S.R.	29,800	11,506	3,370,000	113	293	Jerevan	D
Aruba	Aruba	193	75	77,000	399	1,027	Oranjestad	B(Neth.)
Asia	...	44,900,000	17,300,000	2,985,000,000	66	173		...
†Australia	Australia	7,682,300	2,966,153	16,065,000	2.1	5.4	Canberra	A
Australian Capital Territory, Austl.	Australian Capital Territory	2,400	927	260,000	108	280	Canberra	D
†Austria	Österreich	83,855	32,377	7,550,000	90	233	Wien (Vienna)	A
Azerbaijan S.S.R., U.S.S.R.	Azerbajdžanskaja S.S.R.	86,600	33,436	6,710,000	77	201	Baku	D
†Bahamas	Bahamas	13,939	5,382	235,000	17	44	Nassau	A
†Bahrain	Al-Bahrayn	662	256	435,000	657	1,699	Al-Manāmah	A
†Bangladesh	Bangladesh	143,998	55,598	102,510,000	712	1,844	Dhaka (Dacca)	A
†Barbados	Barbados	430	166	255,000	593	1,536	Bridgetown	A
†Belgium	Belgique (French) / België (Flemish)	30,518	11,783	9,855,000	323	836	Bruxelles (Brussels)	A
†Belize	Belize	22,963	8,866	170,000	7.4	19	Belmopan	A
†Benin	Bénin	112,622	43,484	4,095,000	36	94	Porto-Novo and Cotonou	A
Bermuda (U.K.)	Bermuda	54	21	59,000	1,093	2,810	Hamilton	C
†Bhutan	Druk-Yul	47,000	18,147	1,445,000	31	80	Thimbu	B(India)
†Bolivia	Bolivia	1,098,581	424,165	6,700,000	6.1	16	Sucre and La Paz	A
Bophuthatswana(2)	Bophuthatswana	40,000	15,444	1,730,000	43	112	Mmabatho	B(S. Afr.)
†Botswana	Botswana	582,000	224,711	1,155,000	2.0	5.1	Gaborone	A
†Brazil	Brasil	8,511,965	3,286,488	140,440,000	16	43	Brasilia	A
British Columbia, Can.	British Columbia (English) / Colombie-Britannique (French)	947,800	365,948	2,925,000	3.1	8.0	Victoria	D
British Indian Ocean Territory (U.K.)	British Indian Ocean Territory	60	23	300	5.0	13	...	C
†Brunei	Brunei	5,765	2,226	235,000	41	106	Bandar Seri Begawan	A
†Bulgaria	Bâlgarija	110,912	42,823	8,985,000	81	210	Sofija (Sofia)	A
†Burkina Faso	Burkina Faso	274,000	105,792	7,195,000	26	68	Ouagadougou	A
†Burma	Myanmä	676,577	261,228	37,970,000	56	145	Rangoon	A
†Burundi	Burundi	27,830	10,745	5,000,000	180	465	Bujumbura	A
†Byelorussian S.S.R., U.S.S.R.	Belorusskaja S.S.R.	207,600	80,155	10,110,000	49	126	Minsk	D
California, U.S.	California	411,041	158,704	26,715,000	65	168	Sacramento	D
†Cameroon	Cameroun (French) / Cameroon (English)	475,442	183,569	10,145,000	21	55	Yaoundé	A
†Canada	Canada	9,970,610	3,849,674	25,740,000	2.6	6.7	Ottawa	A
†Cape Verde	Cabo Verde	4,033	1,557	320,000	79	206	Praia	A
Cayman Islands (U.K.)	Cayman Islands	259	100	22,000	85	220	Georgetown	C
†Central African Republic	République centrafricaine	622,984	240,535	2,785,000	4.5	12	Bangui	A
†Chad	Tchad	1,284,000	495,755	5,265,000	4.1	11	N'Djamena	A
Chekiang, China	Zhejiang	102,000	39,382	41,170,000	404	1,045	Hangzhou	D
†Chile	Chile	756,626	292,135	12,330,000	16	42	Santiago	A
†China (excl. Taiwan)	Zhongguo	9,631,600	3,718,783	1,069,410,000	111	288	Beijing (Peking)	A
Christmas Island (Austl.)	Christmas Island	135	52	3,900	29	75	...	C
Ciskei(2)	Ciskei	5,386	2,080	770,000	143	370	Bisho	B(S. Afr.)
Cocos (Keeling) Islands (Austl.)	Cocos (Keeling) Islands	14	5.4	700	50	130	...	C
†Colombia	Colombia	1,141,748	440,831	29,340,000	26	67	Bogotá	A
Colorado, U.S.	Colorado	269,602	104,094	3,265,000	12	31	Denver	D
†Comoros	Comores (French) / Al-Qumur (Arabic)	2,171	838	435,000	200	519	Moroni	A
†Congo	Congo	342,000	132,047	2,000,000	5.8	15	Brazzaville	A
Connecticut, U.S.	Connecticut	12,999	5,019	3,195,000	246	637	Hartford	D
Cook Islands	Cook Islands	236	91	18,000	76	198	Avarua	B(N.Z.)
†Costa Rica	Costa Rica	51,100	19,730	2,690,000	53	136	San José	A
†Cuba	Cuba	110,861	42,804	10,225,000	92	239	La Habana (Havana)	A
†Cyprus	Kípros (Greek) / Kıbrıs (Turkish)	9,251	3,572	675,000	73	189	Levkosia (Nicosia)	A
†Czechoslovakia	Československo	127,903	49,384	15,525,000	121	314	Praha (Prague)	A
Delaware, U.S.	Delaware	5,297	2,045	630,000	119	308	Dover	D
†Denmark	Danmark	43,080	16,633	5,120,000	119	308	København	A
District of Columbia, U.S.	District of Columbia	179	69	630,000	3,520	9,130	Washington	D
†Djibouti	Djibouti	23,000	8,880	310,000	13	35	Djibouti	A
†Dominica	Dominica	752	290	75,000	100	259	Roseau	A
†Dominican Republic	República Dominicana	48,442	18,704	6,460,000	133	345	Santo Domingo	A
†Ecuador	Ecuador	283,561	109,484	9,770,000	34	89	Quito	A
†Egypt	Misr	1,001,450	386,662	50,540,000	50	131	Al-Qāhirah (Cairo)	A
†El Salvador	El Salvador	21,041	8,124	5,000,000	238	615	San Salvador	A
England, U.K.	England	130,439	50,363	46,975,000	360	933	London	D
†Equatorial Guinea	Guinea Ecuatorial	28,051	10,831	325,000	12	30	Malabo	A
Estonian S.S.R., U.S.S.R.	Estonskaja S.S.R.	45,100	17,413	1,545,000	34	89	Tallinn	D
†Ethiopia	Ityopiya	1,223,600	472,435	45,110,000	37	96	Adis Abeba	A
Europe	...	9,900,000	3,800,000	680,100,000	69	179		...
Faeroe Islands	Føroyar	1,399	540	46,000	33	85	Tórshavn	B(Den.)
Falkland Islands (excl. Dependencies) (U.K.)(3)	Falkland Islands (English) / Islas Malvinas (Spanish)	12,173	4,700	2,000	0.2	0.4	Stanley	C
†Fiji	Fiji	18,333	7,078	720,000	39	102	Suva	A
†Finland	Suomi (Finnish) / Finland (Swedish)	338,145	130,559	4,950,000	15	38	Helsinki (Helsingfors)	A
Florida, U.S.	Florida	151,949	58,668	11,520,000	76	196	Tallahassee	D
†France (excl. Overseas Departments)	France	547,026	211,208	55,500,000	101	263	Paris	A
French Guiana, Fr.	Guyane française	91,000	35,135	85,000	0.9	2.4	Cayenne	D

English Name	Local Name	Area in sq. km.	Area in sq. mi.	Population	Pop. per sq. km.	Pop. per sq. mi.	Capital	Political Status
French Polynesia (Fr.)	Polynésie française	4,000	1,544	185,000	46	120	Papeete	C
Fukien, China	Fujian	123,000	47,491	27,700,000	225	583	Fuzhou	D
†Gabon	Gabon	267,667	103,347	1,030,000	3.8	10	Libreville	A
†Gambia	Gambia	11,295	4,361	780,000	69	179	Banjul	A
Georgia, U.S.	Georgia	152,587	58,914	6,050,000	40	103	Atlanta	D
Georgian S.S.R., U.S.S.R.	Gruzinskaja S.S.R.	69,700	26,911	5,280,000	76	196	Tbilisi	D
†German Democratic Republic	Deutsche Demokratische Republik	108,333	41,828	16,595,000	153	397	Berlin, Ost- (East Berlin)	A
†Germany, Federal Republic of	Bundesrepublik Deutschland	248,717	96,032	60,925,000	245	634	Bonn	A
†Ghana	Ghana	238,533	92,098	13,630,000	57	148	Accra	A
Gibraltar (U.K.)	Gibraltar	6.0	2.3	31,000	5,167	13,478	Gibraltar	C
†Greece	Ellás	131,944	50,944	9,995,000	76	196	Athínai (Athens)	A
Greenland	Kalaallit Nunaat (Eskimo) / Grønland (Danish)	2,175,600	840,004	54,000	0.0	0.1	Godthåb	B(Den.)
†Grenada	Grenada	344	133	86,000	250	647	St. George's	A
Guadeloupe (incl. Dependencies), Fr.	Guadeloupe	1,780	687	335,000	188	488	Basse-Terre	D
Guam (U.S.)	Guam	541	209	125,000	231	598	Agana	C
†Guatemala	Guatemala	108,889	42,042	8,310,000	76	198	Guatemala	A
Guernsey (incl. Dependencies) (U.K.)	Guernsey	77	30	79,000	1,026	2,633	St. Peter Port	C
†Guinea	Guinée	245,857	94,926	6,330,000	26	67	Conakry	A
†Guinea-Bissau	Guiné-Bissau	36,125	13,948	880,000	24	63	Bissau	A
†Guyana	Guyana	214,969	83,000	795,000	3.7	9.6	Georgetown	A
†Haiti	Haïti	27,750	10,714	5,925,000	214	553	Port-au-Prince	A
Hawaii, U.S.	Hawaii	16,765	6,473	1,065,000	64	165	Honolulu	D
Heilungkiang, China	Heilongjiang	460,000	177,607	33,795,000	73	190	Harbin	D
Honan, China	Henan	167,000	64,479	78,820,000	472	1,222	Zhengzhou	D
†Honduras	Honduras	112,088	43,277	4,710,000	42	109	Tegucigalpa	A
Hong Kong (U.K.)	Hong Kong	1,068	412	5,535,000	5,183	13,434	Hong Kong (Victoria)	C
Hopeh, China	Hebei	203,000	78,379	56,680,000	279	723	Shijiazhuang	D
Hunan, China	Hunan	211,000	81,468	57,430,000	272	705	Changsha	D
†Hungary	Magyarország	93,036	35,921	10,655,000	115	297	Budapest	A
Hupeh, China	Hubei	188,000	72,587	50,370,000	268	694	Wuhan	D
†Iceland	Ísland	103,000	39,769	245,000	2.4	6.2	Reykjavík	A
Idaho, U.S.	Idaho	216,435	83,566	1,015,000	4.7	12	Boise	D
Illinois, U.S.	Illinois	149,888	57,872	11,690,000	78	202	Springfield	D
†India (incl. part of Jammu and Kashmir)	India (English) / Bharat (Hindi)	3,203,975	1,237,062	773,430,000	241	625	New Delhi	A
Indiana, U.S.	Indiana	94,320	36,417	5,565,000	59	153	Indianapolis	D
†Indonesia	Indonesia	1,919,443	741,101	168,460,000	88	227	Jakarta	A
Inner Mongolia, China	Nei Monggol	1,200,000	463,323	20,535,000	17	44	Hohhot	D
Iowa, U.S.	Iowa	145,752	56,275	2,930,000	20	52	Des Moines	D
†Iran	Īrān	1,648,000	636,296	46,130,000	28	72	Tehrān	A
†Iraq	Al-'Irāq	438,317	169,235	16,250,000	37	96	Baghdād	A
†Ireland	Ireland (English) / Éire (Gaelic)	70,283	27,136	3,590,000	51	132	Dublin (Baile Átha Cliath)	A
Isle of Man	Isle of Man	588	227	65,000	111	286	Douglas	B(U.K.)
†Israel	Yisra'el (Hebrew) / Isrā'īl (Arabic)	20,235	7,848	4,220,000	196	508	Yerushalayim (Jerusalem)	A
Israeli Occupied Areas[4]	. . .	7,000	2,703	1,730,000	247	640	. . .	. . .
†Italy	Italia	301,266	116,319	57,300,000	190	493	Roma (Rome)	A
†Ivory Coast	Côte d'Ivoire	320,763	123,847	10,680,000	33	86	Abidjan and Yamoussoukro[5]	A
†Jamaica	Jamaica	10,991	4,244	2,305,000	210	543	Kingston	A
†Japan	Nihon	377,708	145,834	121,770,000	322	835	Tōkyō	A
Jersey (U.K.)	Jersey	117	45	55,000	470	1,222	St. Helier	C
†Jordan	Al-Urdunn	91,000	35,135	2,795,000	31	80	'Ammān	A
†Kampuchea (Cambodia)	Kâmpǔchéa Prâcheathipâtéyy	181,035	69,898	6,465,000	36	92	Phnum Pénh	A
Kansas, U.S.	Kansas	213,109	82,282	2,495,000	12	30	Topeka	D
Kansu, China	Gansu	390,000	150,580	20,855,000	53	138	Lanzhou	D
Kazakh S.S.R., U.S.S.R.	Kazachskaja S.S.R.	2,717,300	1,049,156	16,090,000	5.9	15	Alma-Ata	D
Kentucky, U.S.	Kentucky	104,672	40,414	3,775,000	36	93	Frankfort	D
†Kenya	Kenya	582,646	224,961	24,555,000	42	109	Nairobi	A
Kiangsi, China	Jiangxi	165,000	63,707	35,395,000	215	556	Nanchang	D
Kiangsu, China	Jiangsu	102,000	39,382	63,520,000	623	1,613	Nanjing (Nanking)	D
Kirghiz S.S.R., U.S.S.R.	Kirgizskaja S.S.R.	198,500	76,641	4,045,000	20	53	Frunze	D
Kiribati	Kiribati	712	275	65,000	91	236	Bairiki	A
Kirin, China	Jilin	187,000	72,201	23,525,000	126	326	Changchun	D
Korea, North	Chosŏn-minjujuǔi-inmīn-konghwaguk	120,538	46,540	20,745,000	172	446	P'yŏngyang	A
Korea, South	Taehan-min'guk	98,484	38,025	42,200,000	428	1,110	Sŏul (Seoul)	A
†Kuwait	Al-Kuwayt	17,818	6,880	1,800,000	101	262	Al-Kuwayt	A
Kwangsi Chuang, China	Guangxi Zhuangzu	237,000	91,506	39,570,000	167	432	Nanning	D
Kwangtung, China	Guangdong	231,000	89,190	63,950,000	277	717	Guangzhou (Canton)	D
Kweichow, China	Guizhou	174,000	67,182	30,370,000	175	452	Guiyang	D
†Laos	Lao	236,800	91,429	3,720,000	16	41	Viangchan (Vientiane)	A
Latvian S.S.R., U.S.S.R.	Latvijskaja S.S.R.	63,700	24,595	2,640,000	41	107	Rīga	D
†Lebanon	Al-Lubnān	10,400	4,015	2,700,000	260	672	Bayrūt (Beirut)	A
†Lesotho	Lesotho	30,355	11,720	1,575,000	52	134	Maseru	A
Liaoning, China	Liaoning	151,000	58,301	37,645,000	249	646	Shenyang (Mukden)	D
†Liberia	Liberia	111,369	43,000	2,290,000	21	53	Monrovia	A
†Libya	Lībiyā	1,759,540	679,362	3,930,000	2.2	5.8	Tarābulus (Tripoli)	A
Liechtenstein	Liechtenstein	160	62	28,000	175	452	Vaduz	A
Lithuanian S.S.R., U.S.S.R.	Litovskaja S.S.R.	65,200	25,174	3,625,000	56	144	Vilnius	D
Louisiana, U.S.	Louisiana	123,672	47,750	4,550,000	37	95	Baton Rouge	D
†Luxembourg	Luxembourg	2,586	998	365,000	141	366	Luxembourg	A
Macau (Port.)	Macau	16	6.2	405,000	25,313	65,323	Macau	C
†Madagascar	Madagasikara (Malagasy) / Madagascar (French)	587,041	226,658	10,375,000	18	46	Antananarivo	A
Maine, U.S.	Maine	86,156	33,265	1,185,000	14	36	Augusta	D
†Malawi	Malaŵi	118,484	45,747	7,405,000	62	162	Lilongwe	A
†Malaysia	Malaysia	330,228	127,502	15,975,000	48	125	Kuala Lumpur	A
†Maldives	Maldives	298	115	190,000	638	1,652	Male	A
†Mali	Mali	1,240,000	478,767	7,985,000	6.4	17	Bamako	A
†Malta	Malta	314	121	355,000	1,131	2,934	Valletta	A
Manitoba, Can.	Manitoba	649,950	250,947	1,085,000	1.7	4.3	Winnipeg	D
Marshall Islands (Trust Territory)	Marshall Islands	181	70	37,000	204	529	Majuro (island)	B(U.S.)
Martinique, Fr.	Martinique	1,100	425	330,000	300	776	Fort-de-France	D
Maryland, U.S.	Maryland	27,094	10,461	4,455,000	164	426	Annapolis	D
Massachusetts, U.S.	Massachusetts	21,461	8,286	5,905,000	275	713	Boston	D
†Mauritania	Mauritanie (French) / Mūrītāniyā (Arabic)	1,030,700	397,956	1,710,000	1.7	4.3	Nouakchott	A
†Mauritius (incl. Dependencies)	Mauritius	2,040	788	1,025,000	502	1,301	Port Louis	A
Mayotte, Fr.[6]	Mayotte	373	144	60,000	161	417	Dzaoudzi and Mamoudzou[5]	D
†Mexico	México	1,972,547	761,605	81,230,000	41	107	Ciudad de México (Mexico City)	A
Michigan, U.S.	Michigan	251,506	97,107	9,220,000	37	95	Lansing	D

WORLD INFORMATION TABLE

English Name	Local Name	Area in sq. km.	Area in sq. mi.	Population	Pop. per sq. km.	Pop. per sq. mi.	Capital	Political Status
Micronesia, Federated States of (Trust Territory)	Federated States of Micronesia	702	271	99,000	141	365	Kolonia	B(U.S.)
Midway Islands (U.S.)	Midway Islands	5.2	2.0	500	96	250	. . .	C
Minnesota, U.S.	Minnesota	224,329	86,614	4,260,000	19	49	St. Paul	D
Mississippi, U.S.	Mississippi	123,519	47,691	2,640,000	21	55	Jackson	D
Missouri, U.S.	Missouri	180,514	69,697	5,105,000	28	73	Jefferson City	D
Moldavian S.S.R., U.S.S.R.	Moldavskaja S.S.R.	33,700	13,012	4,185,000	124	322	Kišin'ov (Kishinev)	D
Monaco	Monaco	1.5	0.6	28,000	18,667	46,667	Monaco	A
†Mongolia	Mongol Ard Uls	1,565,000	604,250	1,965,000	1.3	3.3	Ulaanbaatar (Ulan Bator)	A
Montana, U.S.	Montana	380,845	147,045	845,000	2.2	5.7	Helena	D
Montserrat (U.K.)	Montserrat	103	40	12,000	117	300	Plymouth	C
†Morocco (excl. Western Sahara)	Al-Magrib	446,550	172,414	23,915,000	54	139	Rabat	A
†Mozambique	Moçambique	799,379	308,642	14,210,000	18	46	Maputo	A
Namibia (excl. Walvis Bay)(S. Afr.)[7]	Namibia	824,292	318,261	1,180,000	1.4	3.7	Windhoek	C
Nauru	Nauru (English) / Naoero (Nauruan)	21	8.1	9,000	429	1,111	Yaren District	A
Nebraska, U.S.	Nebraska	200,336	77,350	1,620,000	8.1	21	Lincoln	D
†Nepal	Nepāl	147,181	56,827	17,310,000	118	305	Kathmandu	A
†Netherlands	Nederland	41,548	16,042	14,570,000	351	908	Amsterdam and 's-Gravenhage (The Hague)	A
Netherlands Antilles	Nederlandse Antillen	800	309	235,000	294	761	Willemstad	B(Neth.)
Nevada, U.S.	Nevada	286,354	110,562	945,000	3.3	8.5	Carson City	D
New Brunswick, Can.	New Brunswick (English) / Nouveau-Brunswick (French)	73,440	28,355	725,000	9.9	26	Fredericton	D
New Caledonia, Fr.	Nouvelle-Calédonie	19,079	7,366	155,000	8.1	21	Nouméa	D
Newfoundland, Can.	Newfoundland (English) / Terre-Neuve (French)	405,720	156,649	585,000	1.4	3.7	St. John's	D
New Hampshire, U.S.	New Hampshire	24,030	9,278	1,015,000	42	109	Concord	D
New Jersey, U.S.	New Jersey	20,168	7,787	7,670,000	380	985	Trenton	D
New Mexico, U.S.	New Mexico	314,927	121,594	1,475,000	4.7	12	Santa Fe	D
New South Wales, Austl.	New South Wales	801,600	309,500	5,585,000	7.0	18	Sydney	D
New York, U.S.	New York	136,588	52,737	18,025,000	132	342	Albany	D
†New Zealand	New Zealand	268,103	103,515	3,315,000	12	32	Wellington	A
†Nicaragua	Nicaragua	130,000	50,193	3,390,000	26	68	Managua	A
†Niger	Niger	1,267,000	489,191	6,820,000	5.4	14	Niamey	A
†Nigeria	Nigeria	923,768	356,669	107,250,000	116	301	Lagos and Abuja[5]	A
Ningsia Hui, China	Ningxia Huizu	66,000	25,483	4,280,000	65	168	Yinchuan	D
Niue	Niue	263	102	3,000	11	29	Alofi	B(N.Z.)
Norfolk Island (Austl.)	Norfolk Island	36	14	2,000	56	143	Kingston	C
North America	. . .	24,400,000	9,400,000	407,200,000	17	43	. . .	. . .
North Carolina, U.S.	North Carolina	136,412	52,669	6,340,000	46	120	Raleigh	D
North Dakota, U.S.	North Dakota	183,117	70,702	700,000	3.8	9.9	Bismarck	D
Northern Ireland, U.K.	Northern Ireland	14,122	5,453	1,575,000	112	289	Belfast	D
Northern Mariana Islands (Trust Territory)	Northern Mariana Islands	477	184	21,000	44	114	Saipan (island)	B(U.S.)
Northern Territory, Austl.	Northern Territory	1,346,200	519,771	145,000	0.1	0.3	Darwin	D
Northwest Territories, Can.	Northwest Territories (English) / Territoires du Nord-Ouest (French)	3,426,320	1,322,910	52,000	0.0	0.0	Yellowknife	D
†Norway (incl. Svalbard and Jan Mayen)	Norge	386,317	149,158	4,170,000	11	28	Oslo	A
Nova Scotia, Can.	Nova Scotia (English) / Nouvelle-Écosse (French)	55,490	21,425	890,000	16	42	Halifax	D
Oceania (incl. Australia)	. . .	8,500,000	3,300,000	25,100,000	3.0	7.6	. . .	. . .
Ohio, U.S.	Ohio	115,995	44,786	10,890,000	94	243	Columbus	D
Oklahoma, U.S.	Oklahoma	181,188	69,957	3,340,000	18	48	Oklahoma City	D
†Oman	'Umān	212,457	82,030	1,285,000	6.0	16	Masqaṭ (Muscat)	A
Ontario, Can.	Ontario	1,068,580	412,581	9,225,000	8.6	22	Toronto	D
Oregon, U.S.	Oregon	251,426	97,076	2,735,000	11	28	Salem	D
Pacific Islands, Trust Territory of the	Trust Territory of the Pacific Islands	1,857	717	170,000	92	237	Saipan (island)	B(U.S.)
†Pakistan (incl. part of Jammu and Kashmir)	Pākistān	879,902	339,732	103,510,000	118	305	Islāmābād	A
Palau (Trust Territory)	Palau (English) / Belau (Palauan)	497	192	13,000	26	68	Koror	B(U.S.)
†Panama	Panamá	77,082	29,762	2,250,000	29	76	Panamá	A
†Papua New Guinea	Papua New Guinea	462,840	178,704	3,440,000	7.4	19	Port Moresby	A
†Paraguay	Paraguay	406,752	157,048	4,070,000	10	26	Asunción	A
Peking, China	Beijing	16,800	6,487	9,840,000	586	1,517	Beijing (Peking)	D
Pennsylvania, U.S.	Pennsylvania	119,261	46,047	12,000,000	101	261	Harrisburg	D
†Peru	Perú	1,285,216	496,225	20,435,000	16	41	Lima	A
†Philippines	Pilipinas	300,000	115,831	55,930,000	186	483	Manila	A
Pitcairn (incl. Dependencies) (U.K.)	Pitcairn	49	19	55	1.1	2.9	Adamstown	C
†Poland	Polska	312,683	120,728	37,635,000	120	312	Warszawa (Warsaw)	A
†Portugal	Portugal	91,985	35,516	10,320,000	112	291	Lisboa (Lisbon)	A
Prince Edward Island, Can.	Prince Edward Island (English) / Île-du Prince-Édouard (French)	5,660	2,185	130,000	23	59	Charlottetown	D
Puerto Rico	Puerto Rico	9,104	3,515	3,310,000	364	942	San Juan	B(U.S.)
†Qatar	Qatar	11,000	4,247	310,000	28	73	Ad-Dawḥah (Doha)	A
Quebec, Can.	Québec	1,540,680	594,860	6,675,000	4.3	11	Québec	D
Queensland, Austl.	Queensland	1,727,200	666,876	2,600,000	1.5	3.9	Brisbane	D
Reunion, Fr.	Réunion	2,504	967	540,000	216	558	Saint-Denis	D
Rhode Island, U.S.	Rhode Island	3,139	1,212	990,000	315	817	Providence	D
†Romania	România	237,500	91,699	22,905,000	96	250	Bucureşti (Bucharest)	A
Russian Soviet Federative Socialist Republic, U.S.S.R.	Rossijskaja S.F.S.R.	17,075,400	6,592,849	145,470,000	8.5	22	Moskva (Moscow)	D
†Rwanda	Rwanda	26,338	10,169	6,505,000	247	640	Kigali	A
†St. Christopher-Nevis	St. Christopher-Nevis	269	104	40,000	149	385	Basseterre	A
St. Helena (incl. Dependencies) (U.K.)	St. Helena	419	162	8,100	19	50	Jamestown	C
†St. Lucia	St. Lucia	616	238	139,000	226	584	Castries	A
St. Pierre and Miquelon, Fr.	Saint-Pierre-et-Miquelon	242	93	6,100	25	66	Saint-Pierre	D
†St. Vincent and the Grenadines	St. Vincent and the Grenadines	388	150	104,000	268	693	Kingstown	A
San Marino	San Marino	61	24	23,000	377	958	San Marino	A
†Sao Tome and Principe	São Tomé e Príncipe	964	372	110,000	114	296	São Tomé	A
Saskatchewan, Can.	Saskatchewan	652,330	251,866	1,030,000	1.6	4.1	Regina	D
†Saudi Arabia	Al-'Arabīyah as-Su'ūdīyah	2,149,690	830,000	11,685,000	5.4	14	Ar-Riyāḍ (Riyadh)	A
Scotland, U.K.	Scotland	77,167	29,794	5,150,000	67	173	Edinburgh	D
†Senegal	Sénégal	196,722	75,955	6,515,000	33	86	Dakar	A
†Seychelles	Seychelles	453	175	65,000	143	371	Victoria	A
Shanghai, China	Shanghai	5,800	2,239	12,405,000	2,139	5,540	Shanghai	D
Shansi, China	Shanxi	157,000	60,618	26,840,000	171	443	Taiyuan	D
Shantung, China	Shandong	153,000	59,074	78,600,000	514	1,331	Jinan	D
Shensi, China	Shaanxi	196,000	75,676	30,690,000	157	406	Xi'an (Sian)	D
†Sierra Leone	Sierra Leone	72,325	27,925	3,795,000	52	136	Freetown	A
†Singapore	Singapore	620	239	2,620,000	4,226	10,962	Singapore	A

English Name	Local Name	Area in sq. km.	Area in sq. mi.	Population	Pop. per sq. km.	Pop. per sq. mi.	Capital	Political Status
Sinkiang Uighur, China	Xinjiang Uygur	1,647,000	635,910	13,900,000	8.4	22	Ürümqi	D
†Solomon Islands	Solomon Islands	29,800	11,506	285,000	9.6	25	Honiara	A
†Somalia	Somaliya	637,657	246,201	7,935,000	12	32	Muqdisho (Mogadishu)	A
†South Africa (incl. Walvis Bay)	South Africa (English) / Suid-Afrika (Afrikaans)	1,123,226	433,680	33,585,000	30	77	Pretoria, Cape Town, and Bloemfontein	A
South America	. . .	17,800,000	6,900,000	276,700,000	16	40	. . .	. . .
South Australia, Austl.	South Australia	984,000	379,925	1,390,000	1.4	3.7	Adelaide	D
South Carolina, U.S.	South Carolina	80,590	31,116	3,390,000	42	109	Columbia	D
South Dakota, U.S.	South Dakota	199,740	77,120	725,000	3.6	9.4	Pierre	D
South Georgia (incl. Dependencies) (Falk. Is.)	. . .	3,755	1,450	20	0.0	0.0	. . .	C
†Spain	España	504,750	194,885	39,680,000	79	204	Madrid	A
Spanish North Africa (Sp.)[8]	Plazas de Soberanía en el Norte de África	32	12	150,000	4,688	12,500	. . .	C
†Sri Lanka	Sri Lanka	64,652	24,962	16,195,000	250	649	Colombo and Sri Jayawardenapura [5]	A
†Sudan	As-Sūdān	2,505,813	967,500	23,730,000	9.5	25	Al-Khartūm (Khartoum)	A
†Suriname	Suriname	163,265	63,037	405,000	2.5	6.4	Paramaribo	A
†Swaziland	Swaziland	17,364	6,704	700,000	40	104	Mbabane	A
†Sweden	Sverige	410,929	158,661	8,350,000	20	53	Stockholm	A
Switzerland	Schweiz (German) / Suisse (French) / Svizzera (Italian)	41,293	15,943	6,465,000	157	406	Bern (Berne)	A
†Syria	As-Sūrīyah	185,180	71,498	10,790,000	58	151	Dimashq (Damascus)	A
Szechwan, China	Sichuan	569,000	219,692	104,160,000	183	474	Chengdu	D
Taiwan	T'aiwan	36,002	13,900	19,685,000	547	1,416	T'aipei	A
Tajik S.S.R., U.S.S.R.	Tajikskaja S.S.R.	143,100	55,251	4,575,000	32	83	Dušanbe	D
†Tanzania	Tanzania	945,087	364,900	22,810,000	24	63	Dar es Salaam and Dodoma[5]	A
Tasmania, Austl.	Tasmania	67,800	26,178	450,000	6.6	17	Hobart	D
Tennessee, U.S.	Tennessee	109,150	42,143	4,815,000	44	114	Nashville	D
Texas, U.S.	Texas	691,022	266,805	16,600,000	24	62	Austin	D
†Thailand	Prathet Thai	513,115	198,115	52,690,000	103	266	Krung Thep (Bangkok)	A
Tibet, China	Xizang	1,222,000	471,817	2,030,000	1.7	4.3	Lhasa	D
Tientsin, China	Tianjin	11,000	4,247	8,235,000	749	1,939	Tianjin (Tientsin)	D
†Togo	Togo	56,785	21,925	3,165,000	56	144	Lomé	A
Tokelau (N.Z.)	Tokelau	12	4.6	1,500	125	326	. . .	C
Tonga	Tonga	699	270	99,000	142	367	Nuku'alofa	A
Transkei[2]	Transkei	43,553	16,816	2,765,000	63	164	Umtata	B(S. Afr.)
†Trinidad and Tobago	Trinidad and Tobago	5,128	1,980	1,215,000	237	614	Port of Spain	A
Tsinghai, China	Qinghai	721,000	278,380	4,170,000	5.8	15	Xining	D
†Tunisia	Tunisie (French) / Tunis (Arabic)	163,610	63,170	7,500,000	46	119	Tunis	A
†Turkey	Türkiye	779,452	300,948	53,450,000	69	178	Ankara	A
Turkmen S.S.R., U.S.S.R.	Turkmenskaja S.S.R.	488,100	188,456	3,230,000	6.6	17	Ašchabad	D
Turks and Caicos Islands (U.K.)	Turks and Caicos Islands	430	166	8,900	21	54	Grand Turk	C
Tuvalu	Tuvalu	26	10	8,400	323	840	Funafuti	A
†Uganda	Uganda	241,139	93,104	15,505,000	64	167	Kampala	A
†Ukrainian S.S.R., U.S.S.R.	Ukrainskaja S.S.R.	603,700	233,090	51,675,000	86	222	Kijev (Kiev)	D
†Union of Soviet Socialist Republics	Sojuz Sovetskich Socialističeskich Respublik	22,274,900	8,600,387	280,830,000	13	33	Moskva (Moscow)	A
†United Arab Emirates	Ittihād al-Imārāt al-'Arabīyah	83,600	32,278	1,345,000	16	42	Abū Zaby (Abu Dhabi)	A
†United Kingdom	United Kingdom	242,496	93,629	56,510,000	233	604	London	A
†United States	United States	9,529,202	3,679,245	241,960,000	25	66	Washington	A
†Uruguay	Uruguay	176,215	68,037	2,965,000	17	44	Montevideo	A
Utah, U.S.	Utah	219,895	84,902	1,670,000	7.6	20	Salt Lake City	D
Uzbek S.S.R., U.S.S.R.	Uzbekskaja S.S.R.	447,400	172,742	18,280,000	41	106	Taškent	D
†Vanuatu	Vanuatu	12,189	4,706	138,000	11	29	Port-Vila	A
Vatican City	Città del Vaticano	0.4	0.2	700	1,750	3,500	Città del Vaticano (Vatican City)	A
Venda[2]	Venda	6,198	2,393	410,000	66	171	Thohoyandou	B(S. Afr.)
†Venezuela	Venezuela	912,050	352,145	17,990,000	20	51	Caracas	A
Vermont, U.S.	Vermont	24,900	9,614	530,000	21	55	Montpelier	D
Victoria, Austl.	Victoria	227,600	87,877	4,200,000	18	48	Melbourne	D
†Vietnam	Viet Nam	329,556	127,242	62,670,000	190	493	Ha-noi	A
Virginia, U.S.	Virginia	105,576	40,763	5,785,000	55	142	Richmond	D
Virgin Islands (U.S.)	Virgin Islands (U.S.)	344	133	116,000	337	872	Charlotte Amalie	C
Virgin Islands, British (U.K.)	British Virgin Islands	153	59	12,000	78	203	Road Town	C
Wake Island (U.S.)	Wake Island	7.8	3.0	300	38	100	. . .	C
Wales, U.K.	Wales	20,768	8,019	2,810,000	135	350	Cardiff	D
Wallis and Futuna (Fr.)	Wallis et Futuna	255	98	14,000	55	143	Mata-Utu	C
Washington, U.S.	Washington	176,479	68,139	4,475,000	25	66	Olympia	D
Western Australia, Austl.	Western Australia	2,525,500	975,101	1,435,000	0.6	1.5	Perth	D
Western Sahara	. . .	266,000	102,703	95,000	0.4	0.9	El Aaiún	. . .
†Western Samoa	Western Samoa (English) / Samoa i Sisifo (Samoan)	2,842	1,097	165,000	58	150	Apia	A
West Virginia, U.S.	West Virginia	62,771	24,236	1,960,000	31	81	Charleston	D
Wisconsin, U.S.	Wisconsin	171,491	66,213	4,840,000	28	73	Madison	D
Wyoming, U.S.	Wyoming	253,322	97,808	510,000	2.0	5.2	Cheyenne	D
†Yemen	Al-Yaman	195,000	75,290	9,495,000	49	126	San'ā'	A
†Yemen, People's Democratic Republic of	Jumhūrīyat al-Yaman ad-Dīmuqrātīyah ash-Sha'bīyah	332,968	128,560	2,400,000	7.2	19	'Adan (Aden)	A
†Yugoslavia	Jugoslavija	255,804	98,766	23,365,000	91	237	Beograd (Belgrade)	A
Yukon Territory, Can.	Yukon Territory	483,450	186,661	23,000	0.0	0.1	Whitehorse	D
Yunnan, China	Yunnan	436,000	168,341	34,865,000	80	207	Kunming	D
†Zaire	Zaïre	2,345,409	905,568	31,740,000	14	35	Kinshasa	A
†Zambia	Zambia	752,614	290,586	6,965,000	9.3	24	Lusaka	A
†Zimbabwe	Zimbabwe	390,759	150,873	8,800,000	23	58	Harare (Salisbury)	A
WORLD	. . .	149,800,000	57,800,000	4,975,000,000	33	86	. . .	. . .

† Member of the United Nations (1986).
. . . None, or not applicable.
(1) No permanent population.
(2) Bophuthatswana, Ciskei, Transkei, and Venda are not recognized by the United Nations.
(3) Claimed by Argentina.
(4) Includes West Bank, Golan Heights, and Gaza Strip.
(5) Future capital.
(6) Claimed by Comoros.
(7) In October 1966 the United Nations terminated the South African mandate over Namibia, a decision which South Africa did not accept.
(8) Comprises Ceuta, Melilla, and several small islands.

METROPOLITAN AREAS TABLE

This table lists the major metropolitan areas of the world according to their estimated population on January 1, 1987. For convenience in reference, the areas are grouped by major region with the total for each region given. The number of areas by population classification is given in parentheses

with each size group.

For ease of comparison, each metropolitan area has been defined by Rand McNally & Company according to consistent rules. A metropolitan area includes a central city,

neighbouring communities linked to it by continuous built-up areas, and more distant communities if the bulk of their population is supported by commuters to the central city. Some metropolitan areas have more than one central city; in such cases each central city is listed.

CLASSIFICATION	ANGLO-AMERICA	LATIN AMERICA	EUROPE	U.S.S.R.	WEST ASIA	EAST ASIA	AFRICA-OCEANIA
OVER 15,000,000 (5)	New York	Ciudad de México (Mexico City) São Paulo				Ōsaka-Kōbe-Kyōto Tōkyō-Yokohama	
10,000,000-15,000,000 (8)	Los Angeles	Buenos Aires Rio de Janeiro	London	Moskva (Moscow)	Bombay Calcutta	Sŏul (Seoul)	
5,000,000-10,000,000 (19)	Chicago Philadelphia-Trenton- Wilmington San Francisco- Oakland-San Jose	Lima	Paris	Leningrad	Delhi-New Delhi Istanbul Karāchi Madras Tehrān	Beijing (Peking) Jakarta Krung Thep (Bangkok) Manila Shanghai Tianjin (Tientsin) T'aipei	Al-Qāhirah (Cairo)
3,000,000-5,000,000 (34)	Boston Dallas-Fort Worth Detroit-Windsor Houston Miami-Fort Lauderdale Toronto Washington	Belo Horizonte Bogotá Caracas Santiago	Athinai (Athens) Barcelona Berlin Essen-Dortmund- Duisburg (The Ruhr) Madrid Milano (Milan) Roma (Rome)		Baghdād Bangalore Dhaka (Dacca) Hyderābād, India Lahore	Nagoya Pusan Rangoon Shenyang (Mukden) Thanh-pho Ho Chi Minh (Sai-gon) Victoria (Hong Kong) Wuhan	Al-Iskandariyah (Alexandria) Johannesburg Lagos Sydney
2,000,000-3,000,000 (47)	Atlanta Cleveland Minneapolis-St. Paul Montréal Pittsburgh St. Louis San Diego-Tijuana Seattle-Tacoma	Guadalajara La Habana (Havana) Medellín Monterrey Porto Alegre Recife Salvador	Birmingham Bruxelles (Brussels) Bucuresti (Bucharest) Budapest Hamburg Katowice-Bytom- Gliwice Lisboa (Lisbon) Manchester Napoli (Naples) Warszawa (Warsaw)	Baku Doneck-Makejevka Kijev (Kiev) Taškent	Ahmadābād Ankara Colombo Kānpur Pune (Poona)	Bandung Chongqing (Chungking) Guangzhou (Canton) Harbin Nanjing (Nanking) Singapore Surabaya Taegu	Cape Town Casablanca El Djazair (Algiers) Kinshasa Melbourne
1,500,000-2,000,000 (49)	Baltimore Denver Phoenix	Brasília Curitiba Fortaleza San Juan Santo Domingo	Amsterdam Beograd (Belgrade) Frankfurt am Main Glasgow Köln (Cologne) Leeds-Bradford München (Munich) Stuttgart Torino (Turin) Wien (Vienna)	Char'kov (Kharkov) Dnepropetrovsk Gor'kij (Gorkiy) Kujbyšev (Kuybyshev) Minsk Novosibirsk Sverdlovsk	Bayrūt (Beirut) Chittagong Dimashq (Damascus) Izmir Nāgpur Tel Aviv-Yafo	Changchun (Hsinking) Chengdu (Chengtu) Fukuoka Ha-noi Hiroshima-Kure Kaohsiung Kitakyūshū-Shimonoseki Kuala Lumpur Lüda (Dairen) (Dalian) Medan P'yongyang Sapporo Taiyuan Xi'an (Sian)	Abidjan Al-Khartūm (Khartoum)- Umm Durmān (Omdurman) Dakar Durban
1,000,000-1,500,000 (107)	Buffalo-Niagara Falls- Saint Catharines Cincinnati El Paso-Ciudad Juárez Hartford-New Britain Indianapolis Kansas City Milwaukee New Orleans Portland San Antonio Vancouver	Barranquilla Belém Cali Campinas Córdoba Goiânia Guatemala Guayaquil La Paz Maracaibo Montevideo Puebla Quito Rosario Santos	Antwerpen (Anvers) Dublin (Baile Átha Cliath) Düsseldorf Hannover København (Copenhagen) Lille-Roubaix Liverpool Łódź Lyon Mannheim Marseille Newcastle- Sunderland Nürnberg Porto Praha (Prague) Rotterdam Sofija (Sofia) Stockholm Valencia	Alma-Ata Čel'abinsk (Chelyabinsk) Jerevan Kazan' Odessa Omsk Perm Rostov-na-Donu Saratov Tbilisi Ufa Volgograd	Al-Kuwayt 'Amman Ar-Riyad (Riyadh) Asansol Coimbatore Esfahān Faisalabad Halab (Aleppo) Indore Jaipur Jiddah Kābul Lucknow Madurai Mashhad Patna Rāwalpindi-Islāmābād Surat Vārānasi (Benares)	Anshan Changsha Fushun Guiyang (Kweiyang) Hangzhou (Hangchow) Jilin (Kirin) Jinan (Tsinan) Kunming Lanzhou (Lanchow) Nanchang Qingdao (Tsingtao) Qiqihar (Tsitsihar) Semarang Sendai Shijiazhuang Tangshan Ürümqui Zhengzhou (Chengchow)	Accra Adelaide Adis Abeba Brisbane Dar es Salaam Harare Ibadan Luanda Nairobi Perth Pretoria Tarābulus (Tripoli) Tunis
Total (269)	34	36	48	25	42	57	27

This universal index includes in a single alphabetical list more than 46,000 names of features that appear on the reference maps. Each name is followed by a page reference and approximate geographic coordinates.

Names Local official names are used on the maps and in the index. The names are shown in full, including diacritical marks. Features that extend beyond the boundaries of one country and have no single official name are usually named in English. Many conventional English names and former names are cross-referenced to the official names. Names that appear in shortened versions on the maps due to space limitations are spelled out in full in the index. The portions of these names omitted from the maps are enclosed in brackets — for example, Acapulco [de Juárez].

Transliteration For names in languages not written in the Roman alphabet, the locally official transliteration system has been used where one exists. Thus, names in the Soviet Union and Bulgaria have been transliterated according to the systems adopted by the academies of science of these countries. Similarly, the transliteration for mainland Chinese names follows the Pinyin system, which has been officially adopted in mainland China. For languages with no one locally accepted system, notably Arabic, transliteration closely follows a system adopted by the United States Board on Geographic Names.

Abbreviation and Capitalization Abbreviations of names on the maps have been standardized as much as possible. Names that are abbreviated on the maps are generally spelled out in full in the index. Periods are used after all abbreviations regardless of local practice. The abbreviation 'St.' is used only for 'Saint.' 'Sankt' and other forms of this term are spelled out.
Most initial letters of names are capitalized, except for generic terms in the Soviet Union and a few Dutch names, such as ''s-Gravenhage'. Capitalization of noninitial words in a name generally follows local practice.

Alphabetization Names are alphabetized in the order of the letters of the English alphabet. Spanish *ll* and *ch*, for example, are not treated as distinct letters. Furthermore, diacritical marks are disregarded in alphabetization — German or Scandinavian *ä* or *ö* are treated as *a* or *o*.
The names of physical features may appear inverted, since they are always alphabetized under the proper, not the generic, part of the name, thus: 'Gibraltar, Strait of u'. Otherwise every entry, whether consisting of one word or more, is alphabetized as a single continuous entity. 'Lakeland,' for example, appears after 'La Crosse' and before 'La Salle.' Names beginning with articles (Le Havre, Den Helder, Al-Qāhirah, As-Suways) are not inverted. Names beginning 'Mc' are alphabetized as though spelled 'Mac,' and names beginning 'St.', 'Ste.' and 'Sainte' as though spelled 'Saint.'
In the case of identical names, towns are listed first, then political divisions, then physical features. Entries that are completely identical (including symbols, discussed below) are distinguished by abbreviations of their official country names. The country abbreviations used for places in the United States, Canada and United Kingdom indicate the state, province or political division in which the feature is located. (See List of Abbreviations below).

Symbols City names are not followed by symbols. The names of all other features are followed by symbols that graphically represent broad categories of features, for example, ▲ for mountain (Everest, Mount ▲). Superior numbers indicate finer distinctions, for example, $▲^1$ for volcano (Fuji-san $▲^1$). A complete list of symbols, including those with superior numbers, follows the List of Abbreviations.
All cross-references are indicated by the symbol →.

Page References and Geographical Coordinates Each name is followed by a page reference and by the location of the feature on the map.
The page number generally refers to the map that shows the feature at the best scale. Countries, mountain ranges and other extensive features are usually indexed to maps that both show the features completely and also show them in their relationship to broad areas. Page references to two-page maps always refer to the left-hand page. If a page contains several maps or insets, a lowercase letter identifies the specific map or inset.
The map location is designated by latitude and longtitude coordinates. Coordinates for point features, such as cities and mountain peaks, indicate the locations of the symbols. For extensive areal features, such as countries or mountain ranges, locations are given for the approximate centre of the feature. Those for linear features, such as canals and rivers, are given for the location of the name.

LIST OF ABBREVIATIONS

	LOCAL NAME	ENGLISH
Ab., Can.	Alberta	Alberta
Afg.	Afghānestān	Afghanistan
Afr.	—	Africa
Ak., U.S.	Alaska	Alaska
Al., U.S.	Alabama	Alabama
Alg.	Algérie / Djazaïr	Algeria
Am. Sam.	American Samoa / Amerika Samoa	American Samoa
And.	Andorra	Andorra
Ang.	Angola	Angola
Anguilla	Anguilla	Anguilla
Ant.	—	Antarctica
Antig.	Antigua and Barbuda	Antigua and Barbuda
Ar., U.S.	Arkansas	Arkansas
Arc. O.	—	Arctic Ocean
Arg.	Argentina	Argentina
Ar. Su.	Al-'Arabīyah as-Su'ūdīyah	Saudi Arabia
Aruba	Aruba	Aruba
Asia	—	Asia
Atl. O.	—	Atlantic Ocean
Austl.	Australia	Australia
Az., U.S.	Arizona	Arizona
Ba.	Bahamas	Bahamas
Baḥr.	Al-Baḥrayn	Bahrain
Barb.	Barbados	Barbados
B.A.T.	British Antarctic Territory	British Antarctic Territory
B.C., Can.	British Columbia /Colombie-Britannique	British Columbia
Bdi.	Burundi	Burundi
Bel.	Belgique / België	Belgium
Belize	Belize	Belize
Bénin	Bénin	Benin
Ber.	Bermuda	Bermuda
Ber. S.	—	Bering Sea
B.I.O.T.	British Indian Ocean Territory	British Indian Ocean Territory
Blg.	Bâlgarija	Bulgaria
Bngl.	Bangladesh	Bangladesh
Bol.	Bolivia	Bolivia
Boph.	Bophuthatswana	Bophuthatswana
Bots.	Botswana	Botswana
Bra.	Brasil	Brazil
B.R.D.	Bundesrepublik Deutschland	Federal Republic of Germany
Bru.	Brunei	Brunei
Br. Vir. Is.	British Virgin Islands	British Virgin Islands
Burkina	Burkina Faso	Burkina Faso
Ca., U.S.	California	California
Cam.	Cameroun / Cameroon	Cameroon
Can.	Canada	Canada
Carib. S.	—	Caribbean Sea
Cay. Is.	Cayman Islands	Cayman Islands
Centraf.	République centrafricaine	Central African Republic
Česko.	Československo	Czechoslovakia
Chile	Chile	Chile
Christ. I.	Christmas Island	Christmas Island
Ciskei	Ciskei	Ciskei
C. Iv.	Côte d'Ivoire	Ivory Coast
C.M.I.K.	Chosŏn-minjujuŭi-inmīn-konghwaguk	North Korea
Co., U.S.	Colorado	Colorado
Cocos Is.	Cocos (Keeling) Islands	Cocos (Keeling) Islands
Col.	Colombia	Colombia
Comores	Comores / Al-Qumur	Comoros
Congo	Congo	Congo
Cook Is.	Cook Islands	Cook Islands
C.R.	Costa Rica	Costa Rica
Ct., U.S.	Connecticut	Connecticut
Cuba	Cuba	Cuba
C.V.	Cabo Verde	Cape Verde
Dan.	Danmark	Denmark
D.C., U.S.	District of Columbia	District of Columbia
D.D.R.	Deutsche Demokratische Republik	German Democratic Republic
De., U.S.	Delaware	Delaware
Dji.	Djibouti	Djibouti
Dom.	Dominica	Dominica
D.Y.	Druk-Yul	Bhutan
Ec.	Ecuador	Ecuador
Ellás	Ellás	Greece
El Sal.	El Salvador	El Salvador
Eng., U.K.	England	England
Esp.	España	Spain
Europe	—	Europe
Falk. Is.	Falkland Islands / Islas Malvinas	Falkland Islands
Fiji	Fiji	Fiji
Fl., U.S.	Florida	Florida
För.	Føroyar	Faeroe Islands
Fr.	France	France
Ga., U.S.	Georgia	Georgia
Gabon	Gabon	Gabon
Gam.	Gambia	Gambia
Ghana	Ghana	Ghana
Gib.	Gibraltar	Gibraltar
Gren.	Grenada	Grenada
Guad.	Guadeloupe	Guadeloupe
Guam	Guam	Guam
Guat.	Guatemala	Guatemala
Guernsey	Guernsey	Guernsey
Gui.-B.	Guiné-Bissau	Guinea-Bissau
Gui. Ecu.	Guinea Ecuatorial	Equatorial Guinea
Guinée	Guinée	Guinea
Guy.	Guyana	Guyana
Guy. fr.	Guyane française	French Guiana
Haï.	Haïti	Haiti
Hi., U.S.	Hawaii	Hawaii
H.K.	Hong Kong	Hong Kong
Hond.	Honduras	Honduras
Ia., U.S.	Iowa	Iowa
Id., U.S.	Idaho	Idaho
I.I.A.	Ittiḥād al-Imārāt al-'Arabīyah	United Arab Emirates
Il., U.S.	Illinois	Illinois
In., U.S.	Indiana	Indiana
India	India / Bharat	India
Ind. O.	—	Indian Ocean
Indon.	Indonesia	Indonesia
I. of Man	Isle of Man	Isle of Man
Īrān	Īrān	Iran
'Irāq	Al-'Īrāq	Iraq
Ire.	Ireland / Éire	Ireland
Ísland	Ísland	Iceland
Isr. Occ.	—	Israeli Occupied Areas
It.	Italia	Italy
Ityo.	Ityopiya	Ethiopia
Jam.	Jamaica	Jamaica
Jersey	Jersey	Jersey
Jugo.	Jugoslavija	Yugoslavia
J.Y.D.S.	Jumhūrīyat al-Yaman ad-Dīmuqrāṭīyah ash-Sha'bīyah	People's Democratic Republic of Yemen
Kal. Nun.	Kalaallit Nunaat / Grønland	Greenland
Kam.	Kâmpŭchéa Prâchéathĭpâtéyy	Kampuchea (Cambodia)
Kenya	Kenya	Kenya
Kípros	Kípros / Kıbrıs	Cyprus
Kiribati	Kiribati	Kiribati
Ks., U.S.	Kansas	Kansas
Kuwayt	Al-Kuwayt	Kuwait
Ky., U.S.	Kentucky	Kentucky
La., U.S.	Louisiana	Louisiana
Lao	Lao	Laos
Leso.	Lesotho	Lesotho
Liber.	Liberia	Liberia
Lībiyā	Lībiyā	Libya
Liech.	Liechtenstein	Liechtenstein
Lubnān	Al-Lubnān	Lebanon
Lux.	Luxembourg	Luxembourg
Ma., U.S.	Massachusetts	Massachusetts
Macau	Macau	Macau
Madag.	Madagasikara / Madagascar	Madagascar
Magreb	Al-Magreb	Morocco
Magy.	Magyarország	Hungary
Malaŵi	Malaŵi	Malawi
Malay.	Malaysia	Malaysia
Mald.	Maldives	Maldives
Mali	Mali	Mali
Malta	Malta	Malta
Mart.	Martinique	Martinique
Maur.	Mauritanie / Mūrītāniyā	Mauritania
Maus.	Mauritius	Mauritius
Mayotte	Mayotte	Mayotte
Mb., Can.	Manitoba	Manitoba
Md., U.S.	Maryland	Maryland
Me., U.S.	Maine	Maine
Medit. S.	—	Mediterranean Sea
Méx.	México	Mexico
Mi., U.S.	Michigan	Michigan
Mid. Is.	Midway Islands	Midway Islands
Miṣr	Miṣr	Egypt
Mn., U.S.	Minnesota	Minnesota
Mo., U.S.	Missouri	Missouri
Moç.	Moçambique	Mozambique
Monaco	Monaco	Monaco
Mong.	Mongol Ard Uls	Mongolia
Monts.	Montserrat	Montserrat
Ms., U.S.	Mississippi	Mississippi
Mt., U.S.	Montana	Montana
Mya.	Myanmā	Burma
N.A.	—	North America
Namibia	Namibia	Namibia
Nauru	Nauru / Naoero	Nauru
N.B., Can.	New Brunswick / Nouveau-Brunswick	New Brunswick
N.C., U.S.	North Carolina	North Carolina
N. Cal.	Nouvelle-Calédonie	New Caledonia
N.D., U.S.	North Dakota	North Dakota
Ne., U.S.	Nebraska	Nebraska
Ned.	Nederland	Netherlands
Ned. Ant.	Nederlandse Antillen	Netherlands Antilles
Nepāl	Nepāl	Nepal
Nf., Can.	Newfoundland / Terre-Neuve	Newfoundland
N.H., U.S.	New Hampshire	New Hampshire
Nic.	Nicaragua	Nicaragua
Nig.	Nigeria	Nigeria
Niger	Niger	Niger
Nihon	Nihon	Japan
N. Ire., U.K.	Northern Ireland	Northern Ireland
Niue	Niue	Niue
N.J., U.S.	New Jersey	New Jersey
N.M., U.S.	New Mexico	New Mexico
Nor.	Norge	Norway
Norf. I.	Norfolk Island	Norfolk Island
N.S., Can.	Nova Scotia / Nouvelle-Écosse	Nova Scotia
N.T., Can.	Northwest Territories / Territoires du Nord-Ouest	Northwest Territories
Nv., U.S.	Nevada	Nevada
N.Y., U.S.	New York	New York
N.Z.	New Zealand	New Zealand
Oc.	—	Oceania
Oh., U.S.	Ohio	Ohio
Ok., U.S.	Oklahoma	Oklahoma
On., Can.	Ontario	Ontario
Or., U.S.	Oregon	Oregon
Öst.	Österreich	Austria
Pa., U.S.	Pennsylvania	Pennsylvania
Pac. O.	—	Pacific Ocean
Pāk.	Pākistān	Pakistan
Pan.	Panamá	Panama
Pap. N. Gui.	Papua New Guinea	Papua New Guinea
Para.	Paraguay	Paraguay
P.E., Can.	Prince Edward Island / Île-du Prince-Édouard	Prince Edward Island
Perú	Perú	Peru
Pil.	Pilipinas	Philippines
Pit.	Pitcairn	Pitcairn
Pol.	Polska	Poland
Poly. fr.	Polynésie française	French Polynesia
Port.	Portugal	Portugal
P.Q., Can.	Québec	Quebec
P.R.	Puerto Rico	Puerto Rico
P.S.N.Á.	Plazas de Soberanía en el Norte de África	Spanish North Africa
Qaṭar	Qaṭar	Qatar
Rep. Dom.	República Dominicana	Dominican Republic
Réu.	Réunion	Reunion
R.I., U.S.	Rhode Island	Rhode Island
Rom.	România	Romania
Rw.	Rwanda	Rwanda
S.A.	—	South America
S. Afr.	South Africa / Suid-Afrika	South Africa
S.C., U.S.	South Carolina	South Carolina
S. Ch. S.	—	South China Sea
Schw.	Schweiz / Suisse / Svizzera	Switzerland
Scot., U.K.	Scotland	Scotland
S.D., U.S.	South Dakota	South Dakota
Sén.	Sénégal	Senegal
Sey.	Seychelles	Seychelles
Shq.	Shqīpëri	Albania
Sing.	Singapore	Singapore
Sk., Can.	Saskatchewan	Saskatchewan
S.L.	Sierra Leone	Sierra Leone
S. Lan.	Sri Lanka	Sri Lanka
S. Mar.	San Marino	San Marino
Sol. Is.	Solomon Islands	Solomon Islands
Som.	Somaliya	Somalia
S.S.S.R.	Sojuz Sovetskich Socialističeskich Respublik	Union of Soviet Socialist Republics
St. C.-N.	St. Christopher-Nevis	St. Christopher-Nevis
St. Hel.	St. Helena	St. Helena
St. Luc.	St. Lucia	St. Lucia
S. Tom./P.	São Tomé e Príncipe	Sao Tome and Principe

Introduction to the Index

KEY TO SYMBOLS

- ⋏ **Mountain**
- ⋏¹ **Volcano**
- ⋏² **Hill**
- ⋇ **Mountains**
- ⋇¹ **Plateau**
- ⋇² **Hills**
- ⋉ **Pass**
- ⋎ **Valley, Canyon**
- ≃ **Plain**
- ≃¹ **Basin**
- ≃² **Delta**

- ⋗ **Cape**
- ⋗¹ **Peninsula**
- ⋗² **Spit, Sand Bar**
- ı **Island**
- ı¹ **Atoll**
- ı² **Rock**
- ıı **Islands**
- ıı¹ **Rocks**
- ⊥ **Other Topographic Features**
- ⊥¹ **Continent**

- ±² **Coast, Beach**
- ±³ **Isthmus**
- ±⁴ **Cliff**
- ±⁵ **Cave, Caves**
- ±⁶ **Crater**
- ±⁷ **Depression**
- ±⁸ **Dunes**
- ±⁹ **Lava Flow**
- ≈ **River**
- ≈¹ **River Channel**
- ≊ **Canal**

- ⌶¹ **Aqueduct**
- ∟ **Waterfall, Rapids**
- ⋃ **Strait**
- ⊂ **Bay, Gulf**
- ⊂¹ **Estuary**
- ⊂² **Fjord**
- ⊂³ **Bight**
- ⊜ **Lake, Lakes**
- ⊜¹ **Reservoir**
- ∷ **Swamp**
- ⋈ **Ice Features, Glacier**

- ⊤ **Other Hydrographic Features**
- ⊤¹ **Ocean**
- ⊤² **Sea**
- ⊤³ **Anchorage**
- ⊤⁴ **Oasis, Well, Spring**
- ⊹ **Submarine Features**
- ⊹¹ **Depression**
- ⊹² **Reef, Shoal**
- ⊹³ **Mountain, Mountains**
- ⊹⁴ **Slope, Shelf**

- □ **Political Unit**
- □¹ **Independent Nation**
- □² **Dependency**
- □³ **State, Canton, Republic**
- □⁴ **Province, Region, Oblast**
- □⁵ **Department, District, Prefecture**
- □⁶ **County**
- □⁷ **City, Municipality**

- □⁸ **Miscellaneous**
- □⁹ **Historical**
- ⊍ **Cultural Institution**
- ⊍¹ **Religious Institution**
- ⊍² **Educational Institution**
- ⊍³ **Scientific, Industrial Facility**
- ⊥ **Historical Site**
- ♦ **Recreational Site**
- ⊗ **Airport**

- ▪ **Military Installation**
- ⋆ **Miscellaneous**
- ⋆¹ **Region**
- ⋆² **Desert**
- ⋆³ **Forest, Moor**
- ⋆⁴ **Reserve, Reservation**
- ⋆⁵ **Transportation**
- ⋆⁶ **Dam**
- ⋆⁷ **Mine, Quarry**
- ⋆⁸ **Neighbourhood**

INDEX

122

Name	Page	Lat.°′	Long.°′
Alajuela	108	10.01N	84.13W
Alajuela, Lago ⊜[1]	108	9.15N	79.35W
Alakol', ozero ⊜	58	46.10N	81.45 E
Alalakeiki Channel ⊔	105a	20.35N	156.30W
Al-'Alamayn	82	30.49N	28.57 E
Al-'Amādīyah	78	37.06N	43.29 E
Alamagan I	68	17.36N	145.50 E
Al-'Amārah	78	31.50N	47.09 E
Alameda, Esp.	50	37.12N	4.39W
Alameda, Ca., U.S.	104	37.45N	122.14W
Alamein →Al-'Alamayn	82	30.49N	28.57 E
Alamo	104	37.21N	115.09W
Alamo ≃	104	33.14N	115.39W
Alamogordo	100	32.53N	105.57W
Alamosa	100	37.28N	105.52W
Alanäs	44	64.10N	15.42 E
Al-Anbār □[4]	78	33.45N	41.45 E
Aland Sea ⊤[2]	44	60.00N	19.30 E
Alanson	102	45.26N	84.47W
Alanya	30	36.33N	32.01 E
Alaotra, Lac ⊜	87b	17.30S	48.30 E
Alapajevsk	56	57.52N	61.42 E
Al-'Aqabah	78	29.31N	35.00 E
Alarcón	50	39.33N	2.05W
Alarcón, Embalse de ⊜[1]	50	39.36N	2.10W
Al-'Arīsh	82	31.08N	33.48 E
Alasdair, Sgurr ∧	38	57.12N	6.14W
Alaşehir	54	38.21N	28.32 E
Alashanyouqi	62	40.02N	103.33 E
Alaska □[3]	98	64.00N	149.00W
Alaska, Gulf of C	98	58.00N	146.00W
Alaska Peninsula ≻[1]	22	57.00N	158.00W
Alaska Range ✱	98	62.30N	150.00W
Alassio	52	44.00N	8.10 E
Alastaro	44	60.56N	22.55 E
Al'at	78	39.57N	49.25 E
Alatri	52	41.43N	13.21 E
Alatyr'	42	54.51N	46.36 E
Alausí	110	2.12S	78.50W
Alava □[4]	50	42.50N	2.45W
Alavieska	44	64.10N	24.18 E
Alavus	44	62.35N	23.37 E
Alaw ≃	36	53.18N	4.32W
Alaw, Llyn ⊜[1]	36	53.20N	4.22W
Alayor	50	39.56N	4.08 E
Alazeja ≃	58	70.51N	153.34 E
Al-'Azīzīyah	82	32.32N	13.01 E
Alba, It.	52	44.42N	8.02 E
Alba, Mi., U.S.	102	44.58N	84.58W
Alba □[6]	54	46.15N	23.30 E
Albacete	50	38.59N	1.51W
Alba de Tormes	50	40.49N	5.31W
Ålbæk	44	57.36N	10.25 E
Albaida	50	38.51N	0.31W
Alba-Iulia	54	46.04N	23.35 E
Alban	48	43.54N	2.28 E
Albanel, Lac ⊜	98	50.55N	73.12W
Albania (Shqipëri) □[1]	30	41.00N	20.00 E
Albano Laziale	52	41.44N	12.39 E
Albany, Austl.	90	35.02S	117.53 E
Albany, N.Z.	96	36.43S	174.42 E
Albany, Ga., U.S.	100	31.34N	84.09W
Albany, In., U.S.	102	40.18N	85.14W
Albany, N.Y., U.S.	102	42.39N	73.45W
Albany, Oh., U.S.	102	39.13N	82.12W
Albany, Or., U.S.	100	44.38N	123.06W
Albany ≃	98	52.17N	81.31W
Albardón	114	31.26S	68.32W
Albarracín	50	40.25N	1.26W
Al-Baṣrah (Basra)	78	30.30N	47.47 E
Al-Baṣrah □[4]	78	30.20N	47.35 E
Albatross Bay C	92	12.45S	141.43 E
Albatross Point ≻	96	38.06S	174.41 E
Al-Batrūn	78	34.15N	35.39 E
Al-Bawīṭī	82	28.21N	28.52 E
Al-Bayḍā'	82	32.46N	21.43 E
Albegna ≃	52	42.30N	11.11 E
Albemarle Sound ⊔	100	36.03N	76.12W
Albenga	52	44.03N	8.13 E
Albens	48	45.47N	5.57 E
Alberche ≃	50	39.58N	4.46W
Alberdi	114	26.10S	58.09W
Alberene	102	37.53N	78.37W
Alberga	90	27.12S	135.28 E
Alberga Creek ≃	90	27.06S	135.33 E
Albergaria-a-Velha	50	40.42N	8.29W
Alberique	50	39.07N	0.31W
Alberobello	52	40.47N	17.15 E
Albert	48	50.00N	2.39 E
Albert, Lake ⊜, Afr.	84	1.40N	31.00 E
Albert, Lake ⊜, Austl.	94	35.38S	139.17 E
Alberta □[4]	98	54.00N	113.00W
Albert Edward, Mount ∧	92	8.23S	147.24 E
Albert Edward Bay C	98	69.32N	103.00W
Alberti	114	35.02S	60.16W
Al'bertin	60	53.05N	25.23 E
Albertinia	86	34.13S	21.36 E
Albertirsa	46	47.15N	19.38 E
Albert Lea	100	43.38N	93.22W
Albert Nile ≃	82	3.36N	32.02 E
Albertville, Fr.	48	45.41N	6.23 E
Albertville →Kalemie, Zaïre	84	5.56S	29.12 E
Albi	48	43.56N	2.09 E
Albina	110	5.30N	54.03W
Albino	52	45.46N	9.47 E
Albion, Ca., U.S.	104	39.13N	123.46W
Albion, Id., U.S.	104	42.24N	113.34W
Albion, In., U.S.	102	41.23N	85.25W
Albion, Mi., U.S.	102	42.14N	84.45W
Albion, N.Y., U.S.	102	43.14N	78.11W
Albion, Pa., U.S.	102	41.53N	80.22W
Albo, Monte ∧	52	40.32N	9.35 E
Albocácer	50	40.21N	0.02 E
Alborán, Isla de I	50	35.58N	3.02W
Ålborg	44	57.03N	9.56 E
Ålborg Bugt C	44	56.45N	10.30 E
Alborz, Reshteh-ye Kūhhā-ye ✱	78	36.00N	53.00 E
Albrighton	34	52.38N	2.16W
Albufeira	50	37.05N	8.15W
Ālbū Gharz, Sabkhat ⊜	78	34.45N	41.15 E
Albuñol	50	36.47N	3.12W
Albuquerque	100	35.05N	106.39W
Albuquerque, Cayos de II	108	12.10N	81.50W
Alburg	102	44.58N	73.18W
Alburquerque	50	39.13N	7.00W
Albury, Austl.	94	36.05S	146.55 E
Albury, N.Z.	96	44.14S	170.52 E
Alby	44	62.30N	15.28 E
Alcácer do Sal	50	38.22N	8.30W
Alcains	50	39.55N	7.27W
Alcalá de Guadaira	50	37.20N	5.50W
Alcalá de Henares	50	40.29N	3.22W
Alcalá la Real	50	37.28N	3.56W
Alcamo	52	37.59N	12.58 E
Alcanadre ≃	50	41.37N	0.12 E
Alcanar	50	40.33N	0.29 E
Alcañices	50	41.42N	6.21W
Alcañiz	50	41.03N	0.08W
Alcântara, Bra.	110	2.24S	44.24W
Alcántara, Esp.	50	39.43N	6.53W
Alcántara, Embalse de ⊜[1]	50	39.45N	6.25W
Alcantarilla	50	37.58N	1.13W
Alcaraz	50	38.40N	2.29W
Alcarrache ≃	50	38.16N	7.24W
Alcaudete	50	37.36N	4.05W
Alcázar de San Juan	50	39.24N	3.12W
Alcester	34	52.13N	1.52W
Alcira (Gigena), Arg.	114	32.45S	64.20W
Alcira, Esp.	50	39.09N	0.26W
Alcobaça, Bra.	110	17.30S	39.13W
Alcobaça, Port.	50	39.33N	8.59W
Alcobendas	50	40.32N	3.38W
Alcolea del Pinar	50	41.02N	2.28W
Alconbury Brook ≃	34	52.19N	0.12W
Alconchel	50	38.31N	7.04W
Alcorta	114	33.32S	61.07W
Alcoutim	50	37.28N	7.28W
Alcoy	50	38.42N	0.28W
Alcubierre	50	41.48N	0.27W
Alcudia	50	39.52N	3.07 E
Alcudia, Bahía de C	50	39.48N	3.13 E
Aldabra Island I	84	9.25S	46.22 E
Aldan	58	58.37N	125.24 E
Aldan ≃	58	63.28N	129.35 E
Aldanskoje nagorje ✱[1]	58	57.00N	127.00 E
Aldbourne	34	51.31N	1.37W
Aldbrough	36	53.50N	0.07W
Aldbury	34	51.48N	0.36W
Alde ≃	34	52.03N	1.28 E
Aldeburgh	34	52.09N	1.35 E
Aldeia Nova de Santo Bento	50	37.55N	7.25W
Alder, Ben ∧	38	56.48N	4.28W
Alderley	94	22.39S	139.44 E
Alderley Edge	36	53.18N	2.15W
Aldermaston	34	51.23N	1.09W
Alderney I	35b	49.43N	2.12W
Aldershot	34	51.15N	0.47W
Aldridge	34	52.36N	1.55W
Aled ≃	34	53.14N	3.34W
Aleg	80	17.03N	13.55W
Alegrete	114	29.46S	55.46W
Alejandro Roca	114	33.21S	63.43W
Alejandro Selkirk, Isla (Isla Más Afuera) I	112	33.45S	80.46W
Alejo Ledesma	114	33.37S	62.37W
Alejsk	56	52.58N	82.45 E
Aleksandro-Nevskij	60	53.28N	40.13 E
Aleksandrov	60	56.24N	38.43 E
Aleksandrov Gaj	56	50.09N	48.34 E
Aleksandrovskoje	56	60.26N	77.50 E
Aleksandrovsk-Sachalinskij	58	50.54N	142.10 E
Aleksandrów Kujawski	46	52.52N	18.42 E
Aleksandrów Łódzki	46	51.49N	19.19 E
Aleksejevka, S.S.S.R.	56	51.59N	70.59 E
Aleksejevka, S.S.S.R.	56	50.37N	38.42 E
Aleksejevsk	58	57.50N	108.23 E
Aleksin	60	54.31N	37.05 E
Aleksinac	54	43.32N	21.43 E
Alemania, Arg.	114	25.36S	65.38W
Alemania, Chile	114	25.10S	69.55W
Alençon	48	48.26N	0.05 E
Alenquer	110	1.56S	54.46W
Alentejo □[9]	50	38.00N	8.00W
Alenuihaha Channel ⊔	105a	20.26N	156.00W
Aleppo →Halab	78	36.12N	37.10 E
Alert Bay	98	50.35N	126.55W
Alès	48	44.08N	4.05 E
Aleşd	54	47.04N	22.24 E
Alessandria	52	44.54N	8.37 E
Alessano	52	39.53N	18.20 E
Ålestrup	44	56.42N	9.30 E
Ålesund	44	62.28N	6.09 E
Aleutian Basin ⊶[1]	22	57.00N	177.00 E
Aleutian Islands II	22	52.00N	176.00W
Aleutian Trench ⊶[1]	22	51.00N	170.00W
Aleutka	58	45.57N	150.10 E
Alevina, mys ≻	58	58.50N	151.20 E
Ale Water ≃	38	55.31N	2.35W
Alexander, Mount ∧	90	22.39S	115.32 E
Alexander Bay	86	28.40S	16.30 E
Alexander City	100	32.56N	85.57W
Alexander Island I	24	71.00S	70.00W
Alexandra	96	45.15S	169.24 E
Alexandra ≃	94	18.14S	139.54 E
Alexandra Falls ↳	98	60.29N	116.18W
Alexandretta →İskenderun	78	36.37N	36.07 E
Alexandretta, Gulf of →İskenderun Körfezi C	30	36.30N	35.40 E
Alexandria, Austl.	94	19.05S	136.40 E
Alexandria, On., Can.	102	45.19N	74.38W
Alexandria →Al-Iskandarīyah, Miṣr	82	31.12N	29.54 E
Alexandria, Rom.	54	43.58N	25.20 E
Alexandria, S. Afr.	86	33.40S	26.24 E
Alexandria, Scot., U.K.	38	55.59N	4.36W
Alexandria, Ky., U.S.	102	38.57N	84.23W
Alexandria, La., U.S.	100	31.18N	92.26W
Alexandria, Va., U.S.	102	38.48N	77.02W
Alexandria Bay	102	44.20N	75.55W
Alexandrina, Lake ⊜	94	35.26S	139.10 E
Alexandroúpolis	54	40.50N	25.52 E
Al-Fallūjah	78	33.20N	43.46 E
Alfambra	50	40.33N	1.02W
Alfambra ≃	50	40.21N	1.07W
Alfaro, Ec.	110	2.12S	79.50W
Alfaro, Esp.	50	42.11N	1.45W
Alfarrás	50	41.49N	0.35 E
Al-Fāshir	82	13.38N	25.21 E
Alfatar	54	43.57N	27.17 E
Al-Fayyūm	82	29.19N	30.50 E
Alfeld	46	51.59N	9.50 E
Alfenas	114	21.25S	45.57W
Alfiós ≃	54	37.40N	21.33 E
Alfonsine	52	44.30N	12.03 E
Alford, Eng., U.K.	36	53.16N	0.10 E
Alford, Scot., U.K.	38	57.13N	2.42W
Ålfotbreen ⊼	44	61.45N	5.40 E
Alfred, On., Can.	102	45.34N	74.53W
Alfred, Me., U.S.	102	43.28N	70.43W
Alfred, N.Y., U.S.	102	42.15N	77.47W
Alfreton	36	53.06N	1.23W
Alfriston	34	50.48N	0.10 E
Alfta	44	61.21N	16.05 E
Al-Fujayrah	78	25.06N	56.21 E
Alga	56	49.46N	57.20 E
Ålgård	44	58.46N	5.51 E
Algarrobal	114	28.08S	70.39W
Algarrobo, Arg.	114	38.53S	63.08W
Algarrobo, Chile	114	33.22S	71.40W
Algarrobo del Águila	114	36.26S	67.09W
Algarrobo Verde	114	31.44S	68.18W
Algarve □[9]	50	37.10N	8.15W
Algeciras	50	36.08N	5.30W
Algemesí	50	39.11N	0.26W
Alger	102	40.42N	83.50W
Algeria (Algérie) □[1]	80	28.00N	3.00 E
Al-Ghayḍah	74	16.12N	52.15 E
Alghero	52	40.34N	8.19 E
Al-Ghubbah I	78	24.18N	53.18 E
Al-Ghurdaqah	82	27.14N	33.50 E
Algiers →El Djazaïr	80	36.47N	3.03 E
Alginet	50	39.16N	0.28W
Algoabaai C	86	33.50S	25.50 E
Algodor ≃	50	39.55N	3.53W
Algoma Mills	102	46.10N	82.50W
Algonac	102	42.37N	82.31W
Algorta, Esp.	50	43.22N	3.01W
Algorta, Ur.	114	32.25S	57.23W
Al-Ḥadīthah	78	34.07N	42.23 E
Al-Ḥamād ≚	78	32.00N	39.30 E
Alhama de Granada	50	37.00N	3.59W
Alhama de Murcia	50	37.51N	1.25W
Al-Ḥamrā' ⊶[1]	78	22.40N	55.05 E
Al-Ḥarīq	78	23.37N	46.31 E
Al-Harūj al-Aswad ✱[2]	82	27.00N	17.10 E
Al-Ḥasakah	78	36.29N	40.45 E
Alhaurín el Grande	50	36.38N	4.41W
Al-Ḥawrah	74	13.49N	47.37 E
Al-Ḥayy	78	32.10N	46.03 E
Al-Ḥijāz ⊶[1]	78	24.30N	38.30 E
Al-Ḥillah	78	32.29N	44.25 E
Al-Hirmil	78	34.23N	36.23 E
Al-Hoceïma	80	35.15N	3.55W
Al-Ḥudaydah	74	14.48N	42.57 E
Al-Hufūf	78	25.22N	49.34 E
Al-Ḥulwah	78	23.27N	46.47 E
Alía	50	39.27N	5.13W
Aliaga	50	40.40N	0.42W
Aliákmon ≃	54	40.30N	22.36 E
Alībāg	74	18.39N	72.54 E
Ali-Bajramly	78	39.56N	48.56 E
Alibunar	54	45.05N	20.58 E
Alicante	50	38.21N	0.29W
Alice, Ciskei	86	32.47S	26.50 E
Alice, Tx., U.S.	100	27.45N	98.04W
Alice ≃	94	24.02S	144.50 E
Alicedale	86	33.19S	26.05 E
Alice Downs	90	17.45S	127.56 E
Alice Springs	90	23.42S	133.53 E
Alice Town	108	25.44N	79.17W
Alick Creek ≃	94	20.25S	142.00 E
Alicudi, Isola I	52	38.32N	14.21 E
Alīgarh	76	27.53N	78.05 E
Alīgūdarz	78	33.24N	49.41 E
Al-Ikhwān II	74	12.09N	53.12 E
Alima ≃	84	1.36S	16.36 E
Alingsås	44	57.56N	12.31 E
Alīpur Duār	76	26.29N	89.44 E
Aliquippa	102	40.38N	80.14W
Aliseda	50	39.26N	6.41W
Al-Iskandarīyah (Alexandria)	82	31.12N	29.54 E
Al-Ismā'īlīyah	82	30.35N	32.16 E
Alistráti	54	41.04N	23.57 E
Alivérion	54	38.24N	24.02 E
Aliwal North	86	30.45S	26.45 E
Al-Jafr	78	30.18N	36.13 E
Al-Jaghbūb	82	29.45N	24.31 E
Al-Jahrah	78	29.20N	47.40 E
Al-Jawārah	74	18.55N	57.17 E
Al-Jawf, Ar. Su.	78	29.50N	39.52 E
Al-Jawf, Lībiyā	82	24.11N	23.19 E
Al-Jazīrah ⊶[1]	82	14.25N	33.00 E
Aljezur	50	37.19N	8.48W
Al-Jīzah	82	30.01N	31.13 E
Aljucén ≃	50	38.56N	6.25W
Al-Julaydah ⊤[4]	78	29.03N	45.38 E
Al-Junaynah	82	13.27N	22.27 E
Aljustrel	50	37.52N	8.10W
Alkali Lake ⊜, Nv., U.S.	104	41.42N	119.50W
Alkali Lake ⊜, Or., U.S.	104	42.58N	120.02W
Al-Karak	78	31.11N	35.42 E
Al-Khābūrah	78	23.59N	57.08 E
Al-Khalīl	78	31.32N	35.06 E
Al-Khandaq	82	18.36N	30.34 E
Al-Khārijah	82	25.26N	30.33 E
Al-Kharṭūm (Khartoum)	82	15.36N	32.32 E
Al-Khaṣab	78	26.12N	56.15 E
Al-Khatam ⊶[1]	78	24.16N	55.10 E
Al-Khubar	78	26.17N	50.12 E
Al-Khums	82	32.39N	14.16 E
Alkmaar	46	52.37N	4.44 E
Al-Kūfah	78	32.02N	44.24 E
Al-Kūt	78	32.25N	45.49 E
Al-Kuwayt	78	29.20N	47.59 E
Allach-Jun'	58	61.08N	138.03 E
Al-Lādhiqīyah (Latakia)	78	35.31N	35.47 E
Allāhābād	76	25.27N	81.51 E
Allanche	48	45.14N	2.56 E
Allanmyo	70	19.22N	95.13 E
Allanridge	86	27.55S	26.44 E
Allanton	38	55.47N	3.51W
Allan Water ≃	38	56.08N	3.56W
'Allāq, Bi'r ⊤[4]	82	31.05N	11.42 E
Allariz	50	42.11N	7.48W
Alldays	86	22.44S	29.04 E
Allegany	102	42.05N	78.29W
Allegheny ≃	102	40.27N	80.00W
Allegheny Mountains ✱	102	38.30N	80.00W
Allegheny Plateau ✱[1]	102	41.30N	78.00W
Allegheny Reservoir ⊜[1]	102	42.00N	78.56W
Allen	114	38.58S	67.50W
Allen ≃	36	54.58N	2.19W
Allen, Lough ⊜	40	54.08N	8.08W
Allen, Mount ∧	96	47.05S	167.48 E
Allendale Town	36	54.54N	2.15W
Allende	106	28.20N	100.51W
Allenstein →Olsztyn	46	53.48N	20.29 E
Allentown	102	40.36N	75.28W
Allentsteig	46	48.42N	15.20 E
Alleppey	74	9.29N	76.19 E
Aller ≃	46	52.57N	9.11 E
Allestree	34	52.57N	1.29W
Allevard	48	45.24N	6.04 E
Allgäu ⊶[1]	46	47.35N	10.10 E
Allgäuer Alpen ✱	48	47.20N	10.25 E
Alliance, Ne., U.S.	100	42.12N	102.58W
Alliance, Oh., U.S.	102	40.54N	81.06W
Al-Lidām	74	20.29N	44.50 E
Allier □[5]	48	46.25N	3.00 E
Allier ≃	48	46.58N	3.04 E
Allihies	40	51.38N	10.03W
Allinge	44	55.16N	14.49 E
Alliston	102	44.09N	79.52W
Al-Līth	74	20.09N	40.16 E
Alloa	38	56.07N	3.49W
Allonby	36	54.46N	3.25W
Allora	94	28.02S	151.59 E
Allos	48	44.14N	6.38 E
Allott, Mount ∧[2]	90	26.06S	124.46 E
Al-Luḥayyah	74	15.42N	42.42 E
Allumette Lake ⊜	102	45.53N	77.13W
Allumettes, Île des I	102	45.50N	77.05W
Alma, P.Q., Can.	98	48.33N	71.39W
Alma, Mi., U.S.	102	43.22N	84.39W
Alma-Ata	56	43.15N	76.57 E
Almada	50	38.41N	9.09W
Almaden, Austl.	94	17.20S	144.41 E
Almadén, Esp.	50	38.46N	4.50W
Almadén de la Plata	50	37.52N	6.04W
Al-Madīnah (Medina)	78	24.28N	39.36 E
Al-Mafraq	78	32.21N	36.12 E
Almafuerte	114	32.12S	64.15W
Almagro	50	38.53N	3.43W
Al-Maḥallah al-Kubrā	82	30.58N	31.10 E
Alma Hill ∧[2]	102	42.03N	78.01W
Almăjului, Munţii ✱	54	44.43N	22.12 E
Almalyk	56	40.50N	69.35 E
Al-Manāmah	78	26.13N	50.35 E
Almanor, Lake ⊜	104	40.15N	121.08W
Almansa	50	38.52N	1.05W
Almansor ≃	50	38.56N	8.54W
Almanza	50	42.39N	5.02W
Al-Manzilah	78	31.09N	31.56 E
Almanzor, Pico de ∧	50	40.15N	5.18W
Almanzora ≃	50	37.14N	1.46W
Almar ≃	50	40.54N	5.29W
Al-Marj	82	32.30N	20.54 E
Almaş ≃	54	47.14N	23.19 E
Almas, Pico das ∧	110	13.33S	41.56W
Al-Maṣīrah I	74	20.25N	58.50 E
Al-Maṭarīyah	78	31.11N	32.02 E
Al-Mawṣil (Mosul)	78	36.20N	43.08 E
Almazán	50	41.29N	2.32W
Almazora	50	39.57N	0.03W
Almeida	50	40.43N	6.54W
Almeirim	50	39.12N	8.38W
Almelo	46	52.21N	6.39 E
Almenara	110	16.11S	40.42W
Almenar de Soria	50	41.41N	2.12W
Almendra, Embalse de ⊜[1]	50	41.15N	6.10W
Almendralejo	50	38.41N	6.24W
Almería	50	36.50N	2.27W
Almería, Golfo de C	50	36.46N	2.30W
Al'metjevsk	42	54.53N	52.20 E
Älmhult	44	56.33N	14.08 E
Al-Minyā	82	28.06N	30.45 E
Almirante	108	9.18N	82.24W
Almirante Latorre	114	29.38S	70.58W
Almirós	54	39.11N	22.46 E
Almiroú, Kólpos C	54	35.23N	24.20 E
Almo	104	42.06N	113.37W
Almodôvar	50	37.31N	8.04W
Almodóvar del Campo	50	38.43N	4.10W
Almond ≃, Scot., U.K.	38	55.58N	3.18W
Almond ≃, Scot., U.K.	38	56.25N	3.27W
Almondbank	38	56.24N	3.33W
Almondsbury	34	51.34N	2.34W
Almont	102	42.55N	83.02W
Almonte, On., Can.	102	45.14N	76.12W
Almonte, Esp.	50	37.15N	6.31W
Almonte ≃	50	39.42N	6.28W
Almora	76	29.37N	79.40 E
Al-Mubarraz	78	25.55N	49.36 E
Al-Mudawwarah	78	29.19N	35.59 E
Almudébar	50	42.03N	0.35W
Al-Muglad	82	11.02N	27.44 E
Al-Muḥarraq	78	26.16N	50.37 E
Al-Mukallā	74	14.32N	49.08 E
Al-Mukhā	74	13.19N	43.15 E
Almuñécar	50	36.43N	3.41W
Al-Muthannā □[4]	78	30.30N	45.15 E
Al-Muwayliḥ	78	27.41N	35.27 E
Aln ≃	36	55.23N	1.37W
Alne ≃	34	52.13N	1.52W
Alness	38	57.41N	4.15W
Alnmouth	36	55.23N	1.36W
Alnön I	44	62.25N	17.26 E
Alnwick	36	55.25N	1.42W
Alónnisos	54	39.08N	23.50 E
Alónnisos I	54	39.13N	23.55 E
Alor, Pulau I	72	8.15S	124.45 E
Álora	50	36.48N	4.42W
Alor Setar	72	6.07N	100.22 E
Alosno	50	37.33N	7.07W
Alost →Aalst	46	50.56N	4.02 E
Aloysius, Mount ∧	90	26.01S	128.34 E
Alpachiri	114	37.22S	63.46W
Alpaugh	104	35.53N	119.29W
Alpena	102	45.03N	83.25W
Alpes-de-Haute-Provence □[5]	48	44.10N	6.00 E
Alpes Maritimes □[5]	48	44.00N	7.10 E
Alpha	94	23.39S	146.38 E
Alphington	34	50.42N	3.31W
Alphonse Island I	84	7.00S	52.45 E
Alpiarça	50	39.15N	8.35W
Alpine, Ca., U.S.	104	32.50N	116.47W
Alpine, Tx., U.S.	100	30.21N	103.39W
Alps ✱	30	46.25N	10.00 E
Al-Qaḍārif	82	14.02N	35.24 E
Al-Qādisīyah □[4]	78	31.55N	45.00 E
Al-Qāhirah (Cairo)	82	30.03N	31.15 E
Al-Qāmishlī	78	37.02N	41.14 E
Al-Qanṭarah	78	30.52N	32.19 E
Al-Qaryah ash-Sharqīyah	82	30.24N	13.36 E
Al-Qaṣr	82	25.42N	28.53 E
Al-Qaṭīf	78	26.33N	50.00 E
Al-Qaṭrūn	82	24.56N	14.38 E
Al-Qayṣūmah	78	28.16N	46.03 E
Al-Quds →Yerushalayim	78	31.46N	35.14 E
Al-Qunayṭirah	78	33.07N	35.49 E
Al-Qunfudhah	74	19.08N	41.05 E
Al-Qurnah	78	31.00N	47.26 E
Al-Quṣayr	82	26.06N	34.17 E
Alroy Downs	90	19.18S	136.04 E
Als I	44	54.59N	9.55 E
Alsace □[9]	48	48.30N	7.30 E
Alsager	36	53.06N	2.17W
Alsasua	50	42.54N	2.10W
Alsfeld	46	50.45N	9.16 E
Alsh, Loch C	38	57.15N	5.39W
Alsina	114	33.54S	59.23W
Alsterbro	44	56.57N	15.55 E
Alston	36	54.49N	2.26W
Alt ≃	36	53.32N	3.03W
Alta	42	69.55N	23.12 E
Alta, Mount ∧	96	44.30S	168.58 E
Alta Gracia, Arg.	114	31.40S	64.26W
Altagracia, Ven.	110	10.43N	71.32W
Altagracia de Orituco	108	9.52N	66.23W
Altai ✱	62	48.00N	90.00 E
Altaj (Jesönbulag)	62	46.20N	96.18 E
Altamaha ≃	100	31.19N	81.17W
Altamira, Bra.	110	3.12S	52.12W
Altamira, Chile	114	25.47S	69.51W
Altamont	104	42.12N	121.44W
Altamura	52	40.50N	16.33 E
Altar, Desierto de ⊶[2]	104	32.00N	114.30W
Altarnun	34	50.37N	4.30W
Altata	106	24.38N	107.55W
Altay	62	47.52N	88.07 E
Altdorf	48	46.53N	8.39 E
Alteelva ≃	42	69.58N	23.23 E
Altenburg	46	50.59N	12.26 E
Altentreptow	46	53.42N	13.14 E
Alter do Chão	50	39.12N	7.40W
Altevatnet ⊜	42	68.32N	19.30 E
Althofen	46	46.54N	14.27 E
Altiplano ✱[1]	110	18.00S	68.00W
Altkirch	48	47.37N	7.15 E
Altmark □[9]	46	52.40N	11.20 E
Altmühl ≃	46	48.54N	11.54 E
Altnaharra	38	58.16N	4.27W
Alto Araguaia	110	17.19S	53.12W
Alto Cedro	108	20.31N	75.58W
Alto del Carmen	114	28.46S	70.30W
Altomünster	46	48.23N	11.15 E
Alton, Eng., U.K.	34	51.09N	0.59W
Alton, Il., U.S.	100	38.53N	90.11W
Alton, N.H., U.S.	102	43.27N	71.13W
Altona, Austl.	90	27.34S	120.00 E
Altona, Mb., Can.	98	49.06N	97.33W
Altoona	102	40.31N	78.23W
Alto Paraná □[5]	114	25.00S	54.50W
Alto Parnaíba	110	9.06S	45.57W
Alto Río Senguerr	112	45.02S	70.50W
Altötting	46	48.13N	12.40 E
Altrincham	36	53.24N	2.21W
Altstätten	48	47.23N	9.33 E
Altuchovo	60	52.40N	34.20 E
Altun Shan ✱	62	38.00N	88.00 E
Alturas	104	41.29N	120.32W
Altus	100	34.38N	99.20W
Al-'Ubaylah	74	21.59N	50.57 E
Al-Ubayyiḍ	82	13.11N	30.13 E
Al-Uḍayyah	82	12.03N	28.17 E
Alūksne	60	57.25N	27.03 E
Aluminé, Lago ⊜	114	38.55S	71.09W
Alum Rock	104	37.21N	121.49W
Alunda	44	60.04N	18.05 E
Al-'Uqaylah	82	30.16N	19.12 E
Al-Uqṣur (Luxor)	82	25.41N	32.39 E
Al-'Uwaynāt	82	25.46N	10.34 E
Alva, Scot., U.K.	38	56.09N	3.48W
Alva, Ok., U.S.	100	36.48N	98.39W
Alva ≃	50	40.18N	8.15W
Alvaiázere	50	39.49N	8.23W
Älvängen	44	57.58N	12.07 E
Alvarado	106	18.46N	95.46W
Alvdal	44	62.07N	10.39 E
Älvdalen	44	61.14N	14.02 E
Alvear	114	29.06S	56.33W
Alvechurch	34	52.21N	1.57W
Alverca	50	38.54N	9.02W
Alvernia, Mount ∧[2]	108	24.15N	75.24W
Alves	38	57.38N	3.27W
Alvesta	44	56.54N	14.33 E
Alveston	34	51.36N	2.32W
Ålvik, Nor.	44	60.26N	6.26 E
Alvik, Sve.	44	62.25N	17.24 E
Alvito	50	38.15N	7.59W
Älvkarleby	44	60.34N	17.27 E
Alvord Desert ⊶[2]	104	42.30N	118.25W
Alvord Lake ⊜	104	42.23N	118.36W
Älvros	44	62.03N	14.39 E
Älvsborgs Län □[6]	44	58.00N	12.30 E
Älvsbyn	42	65.39N	20.59 E
Al-Wajh	78	26.15N	36.26 E
Al-Wakrah	78	25.10N	51.36 E
Alwar	76	27.34N	76.36 E
Alwen ≃	34	52.58N	3.24W
Alxa Zuoqi	62	38.50N	105.32 E
Alyth	38	56.37N	3.13W
Alytus	60	54.24N	24.03 E
Alzamaj	56	55.33N	98.39 E
Alzey	46	49.45N	8.07 E
Amadeus, Lake ⊜	90	24.50S	130.45 E
Amadjuak Lake ⊜	98	65.00N	71.00W
Amagansett	102	40.58N	72.08W
Amagasaki	64	34.43N	135.25 E
Amager I	44	55.37N	12.37 E
Amagi	64	33.25N	130.39 E
Amahai	92	3.20S	128.55 E
Amaichá del Valle	114	26.36S	65.55W
Amakusa-nada ⊤[2]	64	32.35N	130.05 E
Amakusa-shotō II	64	32.20N	130.15 E
Amakuso-Shimo-shima I	64	32.20N	130.05 E
Åmål	44	59.03N	12.42 E
Amalfi, Col.	110	6.55N	75.04W
Amalfi, It.	52	40.38N	14.36 E
Amaliás	54	37.49N	21.23 E
Amalner	76	21.03N	75.04 E
Amambaí	114	23.05S	55.13W
Amambay □[5]	114	23.00S	56.00W
Amambay, Cordillera de ✱	114	23.10S	55.30W
Amami-Ō-shima I	65b	28.15N	129.20 E
Amami-shotō II	65b	28.16N	129.21 E
Amana ≃	108	9.45N	62.39W
Amanda	102	39.38N	82.44W
Amantea	52	39.08N	16.05 E
Amanu I[1]	28	17.48S	140.46W
Amapá	110	2.03N	50.48W
Amarante	110	6.14S	42.50W
Amarapura	70	21.54N	96.03 E
Amărăştii-de-Jos	54	43.59N	24.10 E
Amareleja	50	38.12N	7.14W
Amares	50	41.38N	8.21W
Amargosa ≃	104	36.13N	116.48W
Amargosa Range ✱	104	36.15N	116.45W
Amarillo	100	35.13N	101.49W
Amarkantak	74	22.40N	81.45 E
Amaro, Monte ∧	52	42.05N	14.05 E
Amarume	64	38.50N	139.55 E
Amasya	30	40.39N	35.51 E
Amatikulu	86	29.06S	31.27 E
Amatrice	52	42.38N	13.17 E
Amatsu-kominato	64	35.07N	140.10 E
Amazon (Solimões) (Amazonas) ≃	110	0.10S	49.00W
Amazonas →Amazon ≃	110	0.10S	49.00W
Ambāla	76	30.21N	76.50 E
Ambalavao	87b	21.50S	46.56 E
Ambanja	87b	13.41S	48.27 E
Ambarawa	72	7.15S	110.24 E
Ambarčik	58	69.39N	162.20 E
Ambargasta, Salinas de ≚	114	29.15S	64.30W
Ambato	110	1.15S	78.37W
Ambatolampy	87b	19.23S	47.25 E
Ambatondrazaka	87b	17.50S	48.25 E
Ambelau, Pulau I	92	3.51S	127.12 E
Ámbelos, Ákra ≻	54	39.56N	23.55 E
Amber	76	26.59N	75.52 E
Amber ≃	36	53.04N	1.29W
Amberg	46	49.27N	11.52 E
Ambérieu-en-Bugey	48	45.57N	5.21 E
Amberley	96	43.10S	172.44 E
Ambert	48	45.33N	3.45 E
Ambikāpur	76	23.07N	83.12 E
Ambilobe	87b	13.12S	49.04 E
Ambjörby	44	60.30N	13.10 E
Amble	36	55.20N	1.34W
Amblecote	34	52.28N	2.09W
Ambleside	36	54.26N	2.58W
Ambodifototra	87b	16.59S	49.52 E
Amboina →Ambon	92	3.43S	128.12 E
Amboise	48	47.25N	0.59 E
Ambon	92	3.43S	128.12 E
Ambon, Pulau I	92	3.40S	128.10 E
Ambositra	87b	20.31S	47.15 E
Ambovombe	87b	25.11S	46.05 E
Ambre, Cap d' ≻	87b	11.57S	49.17 E
Ambridge	102	40.35N	80.13W
Ambrières	48	48.24N	0.38W
Ambrim I	28	16.15S	168.10 E
Ambriz	84	7.50S	13.06 E
Ambuntentimur	72	6.54S	113.45 E
Ambunti	92	4.14S	142.50 E
Amderma	56	69.45N	61.39 E
Amdo	62	32.18N	91.04 E
Ameagle	102	37.56N	81.25W
Ameca	106	20.33N	104.02W
Amecameca	106	19.07N	98.46W
Ameghino	114	34.50S	62.27W
Ameland I	46	53.25N	5.45 E
Amelia	52	42.33N	12.25 E
American, North Fork ≃	104	38.43N	121.09W
American, South Fork ≃	104	38.43N	121.09W
Americana	114	22.45S	47.20W
American Falls Reservoir ⊜[1]	100	42.55N	112.45W
American Samoa □[2]	28	14.20S	170.00W
Americus	100	32.04N	84.13W
Amersfoort, Ned.	46	52.09N	5.24 E
Amersfoort, S. Afr.	86	27.01S	29.51 E
Amersham	34	51.40N	0.38W
Amery	90	31.09S	117.05 E
Ames	100	42.02N	93.37W
Amesbury, Eng., U.K.	34	51.10N	1.45W
Amesbury, Ma., U.S.	102	42.51N	70.55W
Amfiklia	54	38.38N	22.35 E
Amfilokhía	54	38.51N	21.10 E
Ámfissa	54	38.31N	22.24 E
Amga	58	60.53N	132.00 E
Amga ≃	58	62.38N	134.32 E
Amgun' ≃	58	52.56N	139.40 E
Amherst, N.S., Can.	98	45.49N	64.14W
Amherst, Ma., U.S.	102	42.22N	72.31W
Amherst, N.Y., U.S.	102	42.58N	78.48W
Amherst, Oh., U.S.	102	41.23N	82.13W
Amherst, Mount ∧	90	18.11S	126.59 E
Amherstburg	102	42.06N	83.06W
Amherstdale	102	37.47N	81.48W
Amherst Island I	102	44.08N	76.45W
Amiens, Austl.	94	28.35S	151.49 E
Amiens, Fr.	48	49.54N	2.18 E
Aminga	114	28.50S	66.54W
Amino	64	35.41N	135.02 E
Amirante Islands II	84	6.00S	53.10 E
Amistad Reservoir ⊜[1]	100	29.34N	101.15W
Åmli	44	58.47N	8.30 E
Amlwch	36	53.25N	4.20W
'Ammān	78	31.57N	35.56 E
Ammanford	34	51.48N	3.59W
Ämmänsaari	44	64.53N	28.55 E
Ammarnäs	42	65.56N	16.09 E
Ammaroo	90	21.45S	135.15 E
Åmmeberg	44	58.52N	15.00 E
Ammerån ≃	44	63.09N	16.13 E
Ammókhostos (Famagusta)	78	35.07N	33.57 E
Ammonoosuc ≃	102	44.10N	72.02W
Amne Machin Shan →A'nyêmaqên Shan ✱	62	34.30N	100.00 E
Amo ≃	76	26.16N	89.36 E
Āmol	78	36.23N	52.20 E
Amorgós	54	36.50N	25.54 E
Amorgós I	54	36.50N	25.59 E
Amos	98	48.35N	78.07W
Åmot, Nor.	44	59.35N	8.00 E
Åmot, Nor.	44	59.54N	9.54 E
Åmotfors	44	59.46N	12.22 E
Amoy →Xiamen	66	24.28N	118.07 E
Ampanihy	87b	24.42S	44.45 E
Amparo	114	22.42S	46.45W
Ampezzo	52	46.25N	12.48 E
Ampleforth	36	54.12N	1.06W
Amposta	50	40.43N	0.35 E
Ampthill	34	52.02N	0.30W
Amraoti →Amrāvati	76	20.56N	77.45 E
Amrāvati	76	20.56N	77.45 E
Amreli	76	21.37N	71.14 E
Amritsar	76	31.35N	74.53 E
Amroha	76	28.55N	78.28 E
Amrum I	46	54.39N	8.21 E
Åmsele	44	64.32N	19.20 E
Amsterdam, Ned.	46	52.22N	4.54 E
Amsterdam, S. Afr.	86	26.35S	30.45 E
Amsterdam, N.Y., U.S.	102	42.56N	74.11W
Amstetten	46	48.07N	14.53 E
Am Timan	82	11.02N	20.17 E
Amu Darya (Amudarja) ≃	56	43.40N	59.01 E
Amulree	38	56.30N	3.47W
Amundsen Gulf C	98	71.00N	124.00W
Amungen ⊜	44	61.09N	15.39 E
Amuntai	72	2.26S	115.15 E
Amur (Heilong) ≃	58	52.56N	141.10 E
Amurang	72	1.11N	124.35 E
Amurrio	50	43.04N	3.00W
Amvrakikós Kólpos C	54	39.00N	21.00 E
Anaa I[1]	28	17.25S	145.30W
Anabar ≃	58	73.08N	113.36 E
Anaco	108	9.27N	64.28W
Anaconda	100	46.07N	112.56W
Anadyr'	58	64.45N	177.29 E
Anadyr' ≃	58	64.55N	176.05 E
Anadyrskij zaliv C	58	64.00N	179.00W
Anadyrskoje ploskogorje ✱[1]	58	67.00N	172.00 E
Anáfi I	54	36.21N	25.50 E
Anagni	52	41.44N	13.09 E
'Ānah	78	34.28N	41.56 E
Anaheim	104	33.50N	117.54W
Ānai Mudi ∧	74	10.10N	77.04 E
Analalava	87b	14.38S	47.45 E
Ana María, Golfo de C	108	21.25N	78.40W
Anambas, Kepulauan II	72	3.00N	106.00 E
Anamizu	64	37.14N	136.54 E
Anamur	78	36.06N	32.50 E
Anamur Burnu ≻	78	36.03N	32.48 E
Anan	64	33.55N	134.39 E
Ānand	76	22.34N	72.56 E
Anantapur	74	14.41N	77.36 E
Anantnāg (Islāmābād)	76	33.44N	75.09 E
Anápolis	110	16.20S	48.58W
Ånäset	44	64.16N	21.03 E
Anatahan I	68	16.22N	145.40 E
Añatuya	114	28.28S	62.50W
Anauá ≃	110	0.58N	61.21W
Anaurilândia	114	22.03S	52.45W
Anbanjing	62	23.57N	100.55 E
Anbu	66	23.28N	116.44 E
Ancaster, On., Can.	102	43.12N	80.00W
Ancaster, Eng., U.K.	34	52.59N	0.32W
Ancasti	114	28.49S	65.30W
Ancasti, Sierra de ✱	114	28.50S	65.39W
Ancenis	48	47.22N	1.11W
Anchang	66	30.09N	120.30 E
Anch'ing →Anqing	66	30.31N	117.02 E
Ancholme ≃	36	53.41N	0.32W
Anchorage	98	61.13N	149.54W
Anchorena	114	35.41S	65.27W
Anchuras	50	39.29N	4.50W
Anciferovo	60	58.58N	34.01 E
Ancona	52	43.38N	13.30 E
Ancrum	38	55.31N	2.35W
Ancud	112	41.52S	73.50W
Ancud, Golfo de C	112	42.05S	73.00W
Ancy-le-Franc	48	47.46N	4.10 E
Anda	62	46.24N	125.19 E
Andacollo, Arg.	114	37.11S	70.41W
Andacollo, Chile	114	30.14S	71.06W
Andalgalá	114	27.36S	66.19W
Åndalsnes	44	62.34N	7.42 E
Andalusia	100	31.19N	86.29W
Andaman Basin ⊶[1]	26	10.00N	94.00 E
Andaman Islands II	70	12.00N	92.45 E
Andaman Sea ⊤[2]	70	10.00N	95.00 E
Andamooka	94	30.27S	137.12 E
Andapa	87b	14.39S	49.39 E
Andarax ≃	50	36.48N	2.26W
Andelot	48	48.15N	5.18 E
Andenes	42	69.16N	16.08 E
Andenne	46	50.29N	5.06 E
Andermatt	48	46.38N	8.36 E
Andernach	46	50.26N	7.24 E
Anderslöv	44	55.26N	13.22 E
Anderson, Ca., U.S.	104	40.26N	122.17W
Anderson, In., U.S.	100	40.06N	85.40W
Anderson, S.C., U.S.	100	34.30N	82.39W
Anderson ≃	98	69.43N	128.58W
Anderson Dam	104	43.30N	115.30W
Anderson Ranch Reservoir ⊜[1]	104	43.25N	115.20W
Anderstorp	44	57.17N	13.38 E
Andes ✱	24	20.00S	67.00W

Symbols in the Index entries are identified on page 122.

Name	Page	Lat.	Long.

Andfjorden ⋃ 42 69.10 N 16.20 E
Andikíthira I 54 35.52 N 23.18 E
Andímákhia 54 36.48 N 27.07 E
Andímeshk 78 32.27 N 48.21 E
Ándissa 54 39.14 N 25.59 E
Andižan 56 40.45 N 72.22 E
Andkhvoy 76 36.56 N 65.08 E
Andoam 92 12.40 S 141.55 E
Andong 62 36.35 N 128.44 E
Andorra 50 42.30 N 1.31 E
Andorra □¹ 50 42.30 N 1.30 E
Andover, Eng., U.K. 34 51.13 N 1.28 W
Andover, Me., U.S. 102 44.38 N 70.45 W
Andover, Ma., U.S. 102 42.39 N 71.08 W
Andover, N.Y., U.S. 102 42.09 N 74.47 W
Andover, Oh., U.S. 102 41.36 N 80.34 W
Andøya 42 69.08 N 15.54 E
Andradina 110 20.54 S 51.23 W
Andreapol' 60 56.39 N 32.15 E
Andreas 36 54.22 N 4.26 W
Andrejevo 60 55.56 N 41.08 E
Andrew, Mount ∧ 90 32.52 S 122.56 E
Andrews Air Force Base ✈ 102 38.48 N 76.52 W
Andria 52 41.13 N 16.18 E
Andriamena 87b 17.26 S 47.30 E
Andrija, Otok I 52 43.02 N 15.45 E
Andrijevica 54 42.44 N 19.46 E
Androka 87b 25.02 S 44.05 E
Andropov (Rybinsk) 60 58.03 N 38.52 E
Ándros 54 37.50 N 24.57 E
Ándros I 54 37.45 N 24.42 E
Androscoggin ≃ 102 43.55 N 69.55 W
Andros Island I 108 24.26 N 77.57 W
Andros Town 108 24.43 N 77.47 W
Androth Island I 74 10.49 N 73.41 E
Andrychów 46 49.52 N 19.21 E
Anduljar 50 38.03 N 4.04 W
Anduze 48 44.03 N 3.59 E
Aneby 44 57.50 N 14.48 E
Anécho 80 6.14 N 1.36 E
Anegada I 108 18.45 N 64.20 W
Anegada Passage ⋃ 108 18.30 N 63.40 W
Aneityum I 28 20.12 S 169.45 E
Añelo 114 38.21 S 68.47 W
Aneto, Pico de ∧ 50 42.38 N 0.40 E
Anfeng, Zhg. 66 33.06 N 120.24 E
Anfeng, Zhg. 66 32.44 N 120.21 E
Anfengying 70 24.59 N 102.18 E
Anfu 66 27.23 N 114.37 E
Angamos, Punta > 114 23.01 S 70.32 W
Angara ≃ 58 58.06 N 93.00 E
Angarsk 58 52.34 N 103.54 E
Angas Downs 90 24.49 S 132.14 E
Angas Hills ⋏² 90 22.55 S 128.00 E
Angastaco 114 25.38 S 66.11 W
Angathonisi I 54 37.28 N 27.00 E
Angatuba 114 23.29 S 48.25 W
Angaur I 28 6.54 N 134.09 E
Ånge 44 62.31 N 15.37 E
Ángel, Salto (Angel Falls) ∟ 110 5.57 N 62.30 W
Ángel de la Guarda, Isla I 106 29.20 N 113.25 W
Angeles 68 15.09 N 120.35 E
Angel Falls
→Ángel, Salto ∟ 110 5.57 N 62.30 W
Ängelholm 44 56.15 N 12.51 E
Angelo ≃ 90 23.43 S 117.45 E
Angels Camp 104 38.04 N 120.33 W
Ångermanälven ≃ 44 62.48 N 17.56 E
Ångermanland □⁹ 44 63.30 N 18.05 E
Angermünde 46 53.01 N 14.00 E
Angers 48 47.28 N 0.33 W
Angerville 48 48.19 N 2.00 E
Ångesön I 44 63.43 N 20.55 E
Angicos 110 5.40 S 36.36 W
Angijak Island I 98 65.40 N 62.15 W
Angikuni Lake 🝔 98 62.13 N 99.50 W
Angkor, Ruines d' ⊥ 70 13.26 N 103.52 E
Ångk Tasaôm 70 11.01 N 104.41 E
Anglainghu ≃ 70 31.40 N 83.00 E
Angle 34 51.41 N 5.06 W
Anglem, Mount ∧ 96 46.44 S 167.56 E
Anglesey I 36 53.17 N 4.22 W
Anglona ←¹ 52 40.50 N 8.45 E
Angmagssalik 98 65.36 N 37.41 W
Angmering 34 50.48 N 0.28 W
Angoche 84 16.15 S 39.54 E
Angoche, Ilha I 84 16.20 S 39.50 E
Angol 114 37.48 S 72.43 W
Angola, In., U.S. 102 41.38 N 84.59 W
Angola, N.Y., U.S. 102 42.38 N 79.01 W
Angola □¹ 84 12.30 S 18.30 E
Angola Basin ←¹ 20 15.00 S 3.00 E
Angora
→Ankara 78 39.56 N 32.52 E
Angoram 92 4.04 S 144.04 E
Angostura, Presa de la 🝔¹ 106 16.10 N 92.40 W
Angoulême 48 45.39 N 0.09 E
Angoumois □⁹ 48 45.30 N 0.05 E
Angren 56 41.01 N 70.12 E
Angualasto 114 30.03 S 69.09 W
Anguema ≃ 58 68.14 N 177.30 W
Anguilla □² 108 18.15 N 63.05 W
Anguilla Cays II 108 23.31 N 79.33 W
Angul 76 20.51 N 85.06 E
Angus 102 44.19 N 79.53 W
Angwin 104 38.34 N 122.26 W
Anhai 66 24.44 N 118.27 E
Anholt 44 56.42 N 11.34 E
Anhui □⁴ 66 32.00 N 117.00 E
Anhwei
→Anhui □⁴ 66 32.00 N 117.00 E
Anie, Pic d' ∧ 48 42.57 N 0.43 W
Ánimas, Cerro de las ∧ 114 34.46 S 55.19 W
Anina 54 45.05 N 21.51 E
Aniva, zaliv C 58 46.16 N 142.48 E
Anjan 58 63.41 N 12.49 E
Anjangaon 76 21.10 N 77.18 E
Anjār 76 23.08 N 70.01 E
Anji 66 30.43 N 119.41 E
Anjou □⁹ 48 47.20 N 0.30 W
Anjouan I 87a 12.15 S 44.25 E
Anju 62 39.36 N 125.40 E
Ankang 78 32.42 N 109.05 E
Ankara 78 39.56 N 32.52 E
Ankaratra ⋏ 87b 19.25 S 47.12 E
Ankarsrum 44 57.42 N 16.19 E
Ankavandra 87b 18.46 S 45.18 E
Ankazoabo 87b 22.18 S 44.31 E
Ankazobe 87b 18.21 S 47.07 E
Anking
→Anqing 66 30.31 N 117.02 E
Anklam 46 53.51 N 13.41 E
Anklesvar 76 21.36 N 73.00 E
Ankober 82 9.35 N 39.44 E
An-loc 70 11.39 N 106.36 E
Anlu 70 25.02 N 105.31 E
Anlu 66 31.17 N 113.40 E
Ann 🝔 44 63.16 N 12.34 E
Anna, Lake 🝔¹ 102 38.04 N 77.45 W
Annaba (Bône) 80 36.54 N 7.46 E
Annaberg-Buchholz 46 50.35 N 13.00 E
An-Nabk 78 34.01 N 36.44 E
Anna Creek 90 28.51 S 136.08 E
An-Nafūd ←² 78 28.30 N 41.00 E
Annagassan 40 53.53 N 6.20 W
An-Najaf 78 31.59 N 44.20 E
An-Najaf □⁴ 78 31.00 N 44.00 E
Annalee ≃ 40 54.03 N 7.24 W
Annalong 40 54.06 N 5.53 W

Annamitique, Chaîne ⋏ 70 17.00 N 106.00 E
Annan 36 54.59 N 3.16 W
Annan ≃ 36 54.59 N 3.16 W
Annandale 94 21.57 S 148.22 E
Annandale ∨ 36 55.10 N 3.25 W
Anna Plains 90 19.17 S 121.37 E
Annapolis 102 38.58 N 76.29 W
Annapurna ∧ 76 28.34 N 83.50 E
Ann Arbor 102 42.16 N 83.43 W
An-Nāsirīyah 78 31.02 N 46.16 E
Annbank 36 55.28 N 4.30 W
Annean, Lake 🝔 90 26.54 S 118.14 E
Annecy 48 45.54 N 6.07 E
Annecy, Lac d' 🝔 48 45.51 N 6.11 E
Annemasse 48 46.12 N 6.15 E
Annenkov Island I 112 54.29 S 37.05 W
Anner ≃ 40 52.22 N 7.39 W
Annet I 34a 49.54 N 6.21 W
Annfield Plain 36 54.51 N 1.45 W
An-nhon 70 13.53 N 109.06 E
Anniston 100 33.39 N 85.49 W
Annobón I 84 1.25 S 5.36 E
Annonay 48 45.14 N 4.40 E
Annopol 46 50.54 N 21.52 E
An-Nuhūd 82 12.42 N 28.26 E
Annville 102 40.19 N 76.30 W
Anopino 60 55.42 N 40.40 E
Anori 110 3.45 S 61.38 W
Anqing 66 30.31 N 117.02 E
Anren 66 26.42 N 113.16 E
Ansager 44 55.42 N 8.45 E
Ansbach 46 49.17 N 10.34 E
Anse-d'Hainault 108 18.30 N 74.27 W
Anshan 62 41.08 N 122.59 E
Anshun 70 26.15 N 105.56 E
Ansina 114 31.54 S 55.28 W
Anson Bay C 92 13.20 S 130.06 E
Ansongo 80 15.40 N 0.30 E
Ansted 102 38.08 N 81.05 W
Anstey 34 52.40 N 1.11 W
Anstruther 38 56.13 N 2.42 W
Antakya (Antioch) 78 36.14 N 36.07 E
Antalaha 87b 14.53 S 50.16 E
Antalya 30 36.53 N 30.42 E
Antalya, Gulf of
→Antalya Körfezi C 30 36.30 N 31.00 E
Antalya Körfezi C 30 36.30 N 31.00 E
Antananarivo 87b 18.55 S 47.31 E
Antarctica ±¹ 18 80.00 S 15.00 E
Antarctic Peninsula ⟩¹ 24 69.30 S 65.00 W
An Teallach ∧ 38 57.48 N 5.14 W
Antela, Laguna de 🝔 50 42.07 N 7.41 W
Antelope Creek ≃ 104 40.00 N 117.24 W
Antelope Peak ∧ 104 41.39 N 114.58 W
Antelope Reservoir 🝔¹ 104 42.54 N 117.13 W
Antelope Wash ∨ 104 39.33 N 116.17 W
Antequera, Esp. 50 37.01 N 4.33 W
Antequera, Para. 114 24.08 S 57.07 W
Anthony Creek ≃ 102 37.54 N 80.20 W
Anthony Lagoon 90 17.59 S 135.32 E
Anthony Peak ∧ 104 39.51 N 122.58 W
Anti-Atlas ⋏ 80 30.00 N 8.30 W
Antibes 48 43.35 N 7.07 E
Anticosti, Île d' I 98 49.30 N 63.00 W
Antifer, Cap d' > 48 49.41 N 0.10 E
Antigua 48 45.35 N 61.55 W
Antigua I 108 17.03 N 61.48 W
Antigua and Barbuda □¹ 106 17.03 N 61.48 W
Antilla, Arg. 114 26.07 S 64.36 W
Antilla, Cuba 108 20.50 N 75.45 W
Antioch
→Antakya 78 36.14 N 36.07 E
Antioquia 110 6.33 N 75.50 W
Antipodes Islands II 28 49.40 S 178.47 E
Antofagasta 114 23.39 S 70.24 W
Antofagasta □⁴ 114 23.39 S 70.24 W
Antofagasta de la Sierra 114 26.04 S 67.25 W
Antofalla, Salar de ⋍ 114 25.45 S 67.45 W
Antofalla, Volcán ⋏¹ 114 25.34 S 67.55 W
Antongila, Helodrano C 87b 15.45 S 49.50 E
Antonina 114 25.27 S 48.43 W
António João 114 23.15 S 55.31 W
Antônio Prado 114 28.51 S 51.17 W
Antopol' 60 52.12 N 24.47 E
Antrain 48 48.27 N 1.29 W
Antrim 40 54.43 N 6.13 W
Antrodoco 52 42.25 N 13.05 E
Antsirabe 87b 19.51 S 47.02 E
Antsiranana 87b 12.16 S 49.17 E
Antsiranana □⁴ 87b 13.30 N 49.10 E
Antsla 60 57.50 N 26.32 E
Antsohihy 87b 14.52 S 47.59 E
Anttis 42 67.16 N 22.52 E
Antwerp
→Antwerpen, Bel. 46 51.13 N 4.25 E
Antwerp, Oh., U.S. 102 41.10 N 84.44 W
Antwerpen (Anvers) 46 51.13 N 4.25 E
An Uaimh (Navan) 40 53.39 N 6.41 W
An'ujsk 58 68.18 N 161.38 E
An'ujskij chrebet ⋏ 58 67.30 N 166.00 E
Anūpgarh 76 29.11 N 73.13 E
Anuradhapura 74 8.21 N 80.23 E
Anvers
→Antwerpen 46 51.13 N 4.25 E
Anvers Island I 24 64.33 S 63.35 W
Anxi, Zhg. 66 30.42 N 95.51 E
Anxi, Zhg. 62 40.32 N 95.51 E
Anxi, Zhg. 66 25.06 N 118.12 E
Anxious Bay C 90 33.25 S 134.35 E
Anyang 62 36.06 N 114.21 E
A'nyêmaqên Shan ⋏ 62 34.30 N 100.00 E
Anyi 72 6.04 S 105.53 E
Anyi 66 28.50 N 115.31 E
Anykščiai 60 55.32 N 25.06 E
Anyuan, Zhg. 66 27.37 N 113.54 E
Anyuan, Zhg. 66 25.08 N 115.28 E
Anžero-Sudžensk 58 56.07 N 86.00 E
Anzhen 66 31.36 N 120.28 E
Anzio 52 50.22 N 3.30 E
Anzio 52 41.27 N 12.37 E
Anzoátegui □³ 108 9.00 N 64.30 W
Anžu, ostrova II 58 75.30 N 143.00 E
Aoga-shima I 62 32.28 N 139.46 E
Aoiz 50 42.47 N 1.22 W
Aojiang 66 27.37 N 120.33 E
Aonla 76 28.17 N 79.09 E
Aôral, Phnum ∧ 70 12.02 N 104.10 E
Aorangi Mountains ⋏ 96 41.25 S 175.20 E
Aorere ≃ 96 40.41 S 172.40 E
Aosta 52 45.44 N 7.20 E
Aouk, Bahr ≃ 82 8.51 N 18.53 E
Aoukâr ←¹ 80 18.00 N 9.30 W
Aozou 82 21.49 N 17.25 E
Apa ≃ 114 22.06 S 58.00 W
Apalachicola ≃ 100 29.44 N 84.59 W
Apaporis ≃ 110 1.23 S 69.25 W
Aparima ≃ 96 46.20 S 168.01 E
Aparri 68 18.22 N 121.39 E
Apatin 54 45.40 N 18.59 E
Apatity 42 67.34 N 33.18 E
Apatzingán 106 19.05 N 102.21 W
Ape 60 57.32 N 26.40 E
Ape Dale ∨ 34 52.30 N 2.45 W
Apeldoorn 46 52.13 N 5.58 E

Apennines
→Appennino ⋏ 52 43.00 N 13.00 E
Apia 28 13.50 S 171.44 W
Apiacás, Serra dos ⋏¹ 110 10.15 S 57.15 W
Apiaí 114 24.31 S 48.50 W
Apiti 96 39.58 S 175.53 E
Apo, Mount ∧ 68 6.59 N 125.16 E
Apolakkiá 54 36.06 N 27.50 E
Apolda 46 51.01 N 11.31 E
Apolinario Saravia 114 24.25 S 64.02 W
Apollo 102 40.34 N 79.34 W
Apollo Bay 94 38.45 S 143.40 E
Apolo 110 14.43 S 68.31 W
Apón ≃ 108 10.06 N 72.23 W
Aporé ≃ 110 19.27 S 50.57 W
Apostle Islands II 100 46.50 N 90.30 W
Apóstoles 114 27.55 S 55.46 W
Apostólou Andréa, Akrotírion > 78 35.42 N 34.35 E
Appalachian Mountains ⋏ 100 41.00 N 77.00 W
Äppelbo 44 60.30 N 14.00 E
Appennino (Apennines) ⋏ 52 43.00 N 13.00 E
Appennino Abruzzese ⋏ 52 42.00 N 14.00 E
Appennino Calabrese ⋏ 52 39.00 N 16.30 E
Appennino Ligure ⋏ 52 44.30 N 9.00 E
Appennino Lucano ⋏ 52 40.30 N 16.00 E
Appennino Tosco-Emiliano ⋏ 52 44.00 N 11.30 E
Appennino Umbro-Marchigiano ⋏ 52 43.00 N 13.00 E
Appenzell 48 47.20 N 9.25 E
Appiano 52 46.28 N 11.15 E
Appleby 36 54.36 N 2.29 W
Applecross 38 57.25 N 5.49 W
Appledore 34 51.03 N 4.10 W
Applegate ≃ 104 42.26 N 123.27 W
Appleton 100 44.15 N 88.24 W
Aprelevka 60 55.33 N 37.04 E
Apt 48 43.53 N 5.24 E
Apucarana 114 23.33 S 51.29 W
Apure ≃ 110 7.37 N 66.25 W
Apurímac ≃ 110 11.48 S 74.03 W
Aqaba, Gulf of C 78 29.00 N 34.40 E
Aquidabán ≃ 114 23.11 S 57.30 W
Aquidauana 110 20.28 S 55.48 W
Aquin 108 18.17 N 73.24 W
Ara ≃, Esp. 50 42.25 N 0.09 E
Ara ≃, Ire. 40 52.24 N 7.56 W
Ara ≃, Nihon 64 35.39 N 139.51 E
'Arab, Bahr al- ≃ 82 9.02 N 29.28 E
'Arab, Shatt al- ≃ 78 29.57 N 48.34 E
Arabian Basin ←¹ 26 11.30 N 65.00 E
Arabian Peninsula >¹ 26 25.00 N 45.00 E
Arabian Sea ⊤² 26 15.00 N 65.00 E
Aracá ≃ 110 0.25 S 62.55 W
Aracaju 110 10.55 S 37.04 W
Aracataca 108 10.36 N 74.12 W
Aracati 110 4.34 S 37.46 W
Aracena 50 37.53 N 6.33 W
Araçuaí 110 16.52 S 42.04 W
Arad 46.11 N 21.20 E
Arafura Sea ⊤² 92 9.00 S 133.00 E
Aragarças 110 15.55 S 52.15 W
Arago, Cape > 104 43.18 N 124.25 W
Aragón □⁹ 50 41.25 N 1.00 W
Aragón ≃ 50 42.13 N 1.44 W
Aragona 52 37.24 N 13.37 E
Aragua □³ 108 10.00 N 67.10 W
Araguacema 110 8.50 S 49.34 W
Aragua de Barcelona 108 9.28 N 64.49 W
Aragua de Maturín 108 9.58 N 63.29 W
Araguaia ≃ 110 5.21 S 48.41 W
Araguao, Caño ≃¹ 108 9.15 N 60.50 W
Araguari 110 18.38 S 48.11 W
Araguari ≃ 110 1.15 N 49.55 W
Araguatins 110 5.38 S 48.07 W
Arai 64 37.01 N 138.15 E
Ārak, Alg. 80 25.18 N 3.45 E
Arāk, Īrān 78 34.05 N 49.41 E
Arakan □⁸ 70 19.00 N 94.15 E
Arakan Yoma ⋏ 70 19.00 N 94.40 E
Arákhova 54 38.29 N 22.35 E
Araks (Aras) ≃ 56 40.01 N 48.28 E
Aral Sea
→Aral'skoje more ⊤² 56 45.00 N 60.00 E
Aral'sk 56 46.48 N 61.40 E
Aral'skoje more ⊤² 56 45.00 N 60.00 E
Aramac 94 22.59 S 145.14 E
Aramac ≃ 94 23.02 S 144.31 E
Arāmbāgh 76 22.53 N 87.47 E
Āran 78 34.04 N 51.29 E
Arana, Sierra ⋏ 50 37.20 N 3.30 W
Aranda de Duero 50 41.41 N 3.41 W
Arandelovac 54 44.18 N 20.35 E
Aran Fawddwy ∧ 34 52.47 N 3.41 W
Arang 76 21.12 N 81.58 E
Aran Island I 40 54.58 N 8.33 W
Aran Islands II 40 53.07 N 9.43 W
Aranjuez 50 40.02 N 3.36 W
Aranyaprathet 70 13.41 N 102.30 E
Arao 64 32.59 N 130.26 E
Arapawa Island I 96 41.11 S 174.19 E
Arapey 114 30.58 S 57.32 W
Arapey Chico ≃ 114 30.57 S 57.30 W
Arapey Grande ≃ 114 30.55 S 57.49 W
Arapiraca 110 9.45 S 36.39 W
Arapongas 114 23.23 S 51.27 W
Arapoti 114 24.08 S 49.50 W
Araquari 94 26.23 S 48.43 W
Araquil ≃ 50 42.54 N 1.45 W
Araraquara 114 21.47 S 48.10 W
Araraquará 114 21.47 S 48.10 W
Araras 114 22.22 S 47.23 W
Ararat 94 37.17 S 142.56 E
Ararat, Mount
→Ağrı Dağı ∧ 30 39.42 N 44.18 E
Araria 76 26.08 N 87.24 E
Aras (Araks) ≃ 56 40.01 N 48.28 E
Aratiba 114 27.24 S 52.19 W
Aratos 54 41.05 N 25.33 E
Arauca 110 7.05 N 70.45 W
Arauca ≃ 110 7.24 N 66.35 W
Araucania □⁴ 114 38.36 S 72.00 W
Araucária 114 25.35 S 49.25 W
Arauco, Golfo de C 114 37.15 S 73.19 W
Arauquita 110 7.02 N 71.25 W
Āravalli Range ⋏ 76 25.00 N 73.30 E
Araxá 110 19.35 S 46.55 W
Araya, Punta de > 108 10.34 N 64.18 W
Arba Minch 82 6.02 N 37.33 E
Arboga 44 59.24 N 15.50 E
Arbois 48 46.54 N 5.46 E
Arboledas 114 37.06 S 61.28 W
Arbon 48 47.31 N 9.26 E
Arborea ←¹ 52 39.50 N 8.35 E
Arbrá 44 61.29 N 16.23 E
Arbroath 38 56.34 N 2.35 W
Arbuckle 104 39.01 N 122.03 W

Arcachon 48 44.37 N 1.12 W
Arcachon, Bassin d' C 48 44.40 N 1.10 W
Arcade, Ca., U.S. 104 34.02 N 118.15 W
Arcade, N.Y., U.S. 102 42.32 N 78.25 W
Arcadia, Ca., U.S. 104 34.08 N 118.02 W
Arcadia, Pa., U.S. 102 40.47 N 78.51 W
Arcanum 102 39.59 N 84.33 W
Arcata 104 40.52 N 124.04 W
Arce 52 41.35 N 13.34 E
Arcevia 52 43.30 N 12.56 E
Archbold 102 41.31 N 84.18 W
Archer ≃ 92 13.28 S 141.41 E
Archer, Mount ∧ 94 23.20 S 150.34 E
Archer Bay C 92 13.25 S 141.43 E
Archiac 48 45.31 N 0.18 W
Archidona 50 37.05 N 4.23 W
Arcidosso 52 42.52 N 11.33 E
Arcis-sur-Aube 48 48.32 N 4.08 E
Arckaringa ≃ 90 28.10 S 135.22 E
Arckaringa Creek ≃ 90 28.10 S 135.22 E
Arco 52 45.55 N 10.53 E
Arco de Baúlhe 50 41.29 N 7.58 W
Arcos de la Frontera 50 36.45 N 5.48 W
Arcoverde 110 8.25 S 37.04 W
Arctic Ocean ⊤¹ 22 85.00 N 170.00 E
Arctic Red ≃ 98 67.27 N 133.46 W
Ard, Loch 🝔 38 56.11 N 4.28 W
Arda ≃ 54 41.39 N 26.29 E
Ardabīl 78 38.15 N 48.18 E
Ardagh 40 52.28 N 9.04 W
Ardahan 30 41.07 N 42.41 E
Ardakān 78 32.19 N 53.59 E
Ardalanish, Rubh' > 38 56.17 N 6.18 W
Ardalstangen 44 61.12 N 7.30 E
Ardara 40 54.46 N 8.25 W
Ardarroch 38 57.25 N 5.38 W
Ardatov 60 55.15 N 43.06 E
Ardbeg 38 55.39 N 6.05 W
Ardcharnich 38 57.51 N 5.05 W
Ardee 40 53.52 N 6.33 W
Ardèche □⁵ 48 44.40 N 4.20 E
Ardee 40 53.52 N 6.33 W
Arden, Forest of ←³ 34 52.23 N 1.42 W
Ardennes □⁵ 48 49.40 N 4.40 E
Ardennes ←¹ 46 50.10 N 5.45 E
Arderin ∧² 40 53.02 N 7.40 W
Ardersier 38 57.34 N 4.02 W
Ardfern 38 56.10 N 5.32 W
Ardglass 40 54.16 N 5.37 W
Ardgroom 40 51.42 N 9.52 W
Ardila ≃ 50 38.12 N 7.28 W
Ardino 54 41.35 N 25.08 E
Ardlethan 94 34.21 S 146.54 E
Ardlui 38 56.18 N 4.43 W
Ardlussa 38 56.02 N 5.47 W
Ardmolich 38 56.49 N 5.41 W
Ardmore, Ire. 40 51.57 N 7.43 W
Ardmore, Ok., U.S. 100 34.10 N 97.08 W
Ardmore, Pa., U.S. 102 40.01 N 75.18 W
Ardmore Point >, Scot., U.K. 38 56.39 N 6.07 W
Ardmore Point >, Scot., U.K. 38 55.42 N 6.01 W
Ardnamurchan >¹ 38 56.43 N 6.00 W
Ardnamurchan, Point of > 38 56.44 N 6.13 W
Ardoch ≃ 94 27.26 S 144.08 E
Ardrishaig 38 56.01 N 5.27 W
Ardrossan 38 55.39 N 4.49 W
Ardsley 38 53.32 N 1.29 W
Åre 44 63.24 N 13.04 E
Areado 114 21.21 S 46.09 W
Arecibo 108 18.28 N 66.43 W
Areguá 114 25.18 S 57.25 W
Areia Branca 110 4.56 S 37.07 W
Areial 110 7.07 S 35.57 W
Arena, Point > 104 38.57 N 123.44 W
Arena, Punta > 106 23.33 N 109.28 W
Arenas de San Pedro 50 40.12 N 5.05 W
Arenberg 44 58.27 N 8.48 E
Arendal 44 58.27 N 8.46 E
Arenenberg 44 51.29 N 9.01 E
Arenys de Mar 50 41.35 N 2.33 E
Arequipa 110 16.24 S 71.33 W
Arequito 114 33.09 S 61.28 W
Ares 44 44.46 N 1.08 W
Åreskutan ∧ 44 63.26 N 13.06 E
Arévalo 50 41.04 N 4.43 W
Arezzo 52 43.25 N 11.53 E
Arga ≃ 50 42.18 N 1.47 W
Argadargada 90 21.40 S 136.40 E
Argamasilla de Alba 50 39.07 N 3.06 W
Arganda 50 40.18 N 3.26 W
Arga-Sala ≃ 58 68.30 N 112.12 E
Argelès-Gazost 48 43.01 N 0.06 E
Argelès-sur-Mer 48 42.33 N 3.01 E
Argens ≃ 48 43.24 N 6.44 E
Argent, Côte d' ±² 48 44.30 N 1.30 W
Argenta 52 44.37 N 11.50 E
Argentan 48 48.45 N 0.01 W
Argentat 48 45.06 N 1.56 E
Argentera ∧ 52 44.10 N 7.18 E
Argenteuil 48 48.57 N 2.15 E
Argentina □¹ 112 34.00 S 64.00 W
Argentino, Lago 🝔 112 50.13 S 72.25 W
Argenton-Château 48 46.59 N 0.27 W
Argenton-sur-Creuse 48 46.35 N 1.31 E
Argentré 48 48.05 N 0.39 W
Arges □⁴ 54 45.00 N 24.45 E
Argeş ≃ 54 44.12 N 26.25 E
Arghandāb ≃ 76 31.27 N 64.23 E
Argolikós Kólpos C 54 37.33 N 22.45 E
Argonne ⊥ 48 49.30 N 5.00 E
Árgos 54 37.39 N 22.44 E
Árgos Orestikón 54 40.28 N 21.16 E
Argostólion 54 38.10 N 20.30 E
Arguello, Point > 104 34.35 N 120.39 W
Argun' (Ergun) ≃ 58 53.20 N 121.28 E
Argyle, Lake 🝔¹ 92 16.15 S 128.45 E
Århus 44 56.09 N 10.13 E
Ariake-kai C 64 33.05 N 130.20 E
Ariano Irpino 52 41.09 N 15.05 E
Ariano nel Polesine 52 44.56 N 12.07 E
Arias 114 33.38 S 62.25 W
Arica, Chile 110 18.29 S 70.20 W
Arica, Col. 110 2.08 S 71.47 W
Arid, Cape > 90 34.00 S 123.09 E
Aridaia 54 40.59 N 22.03 E
Ariège □⁵ 48 43.00 N 1.30 E
Ariège ≃ 48 43.31 N 1.25 E
Ariguaní ≃ 108 9.35 N 73.48 W
Arīhā (Jericho) 78 31.52 N 35.27 E
Arikawa 64 32.59 N 129.07 E
Arima 108 10.38 N 61.17 W
Arinos ≃ 110 10.25 S 58.20 W
Ariogala 60 55.16 N 23.30 E
Aripuanã 110 9.10 S 60.38 W
Aripuanã ≃ 110 5.07 S 60.25 W
Ariquemes 110 9.56 S 63.04 W
Arisaig 38 56.51 N 5.51 W

Arisaig, Sound of C 38 56.51 N 5.51 W
Arizaro, Salar de ⋍ 114 24.42 S 67.45 W
Arizgoiti 50 43.13 N 2.54 W
Arizona 114 35.43 S 65.18 W
Arizona □³ 100 34.00 N 112.00 W
Ärjäng 44 59.23 N 12.08 E
Arjeplog 42 66.00 N 17.58 E
Arjona, Col. 108 10.15 N 75.21 W
Arjona, Esp. 50 37.56 N 4.03 W
Arjuna ∧ 72 7.45 S 112.35 E
Arkadelphia 100 34.07 N 93.03 W
Arkaig, Loch 🝔 38 56.58 N 5.08 W
Arkalyk 56 50.13 N 66.50 E
Arkansas □³ 100 34.50 N 93.40 W
Arkansas ≃ 100 33.48 N 91.04 W
Arkansas City 100 37.03 N 97.02 W
Arkhángelos 54 36.12 N 28.08 E
Árki I 54 37.22 N 26.45 E
Arklow 40 52.48 N 6.09 W
Arkona, Kap > 46 54.41 N 13.26 E
Arkösund 44 58.30 N 16.56 E
Arl ≃ 48 43.22 N 77.41 W
Arlanc 48 45.25 N 3.44 E
Arlanza ≃ 50 42.06 N 4.09 W
Arlanzón ≃ 50 42.03 N 4.17 W
Arles 48 43.40 N 4.38 E
Arlesey 34 52.01 N 0.14 W
Arlington, S. Afr. 86 28.02 S 27.54 E
Arlington, Oh., U.S. 102 40.53 N 83.39 W
Arlington, Tx., U.S. 102 32.45 N 73.09 W
Arlington, Va., U.S. 102 38.52 N 77.06 W
Arlon 46 49.41 N 5.49 E
Arltunga 90 23.26 S 134.41 E
Armadá 102 42.50 N 82.53 W
Armadale, Austl. 90 32.09 S 116.00 E
Armadale, Scot., U.K. 38 55.54 N 3.42 W
Armagh 40 54.21 N 6.39 W
Armagnac □⁹ 48 43.45 N 0.10 E
Armançon ≃ 48 47.57 N 3.30 E
Armavir 56 45.00 N 41.08 E
Armenia 108 4.31 N 75.41 W
Armenia
→Arm'anskaja Sovetskaja Socialističeskaja Respublika □³ 56 40.00 N 45.00 E
Armenís 54 45.12 N 22.19 E
Armentières 48 50.41 N 2.53 E
Armidale 94 30.31 S 151.39 E
Armilla 50 37.09 N 3.37 W
Armit Lake 🝔 98 64.10 N 91.32 W
Armona 104 36.19 N 119.42 W
Armoy 40 55.08 N 6.20 W
Armstrong, Mount ∧ 98 63.12 N 133.16 W
Armstrong Station 98 50.18 N 89.02 W
Armthorpe 36 53.32 N 1.03 W
Arnaía 54 40.29 N 23.35 E
Arnarfjörður C² 42a 65.45 N 23.40 W
Arnay-le-Duc 48 47.08 N 4.29 E
Arnedo 50 42.13 N 2.06 W
Arnes 44 60.09 N 11.28 E
Arnesby 34 52.34 N 7.37 W
Arnett 98 51.59 N 5.55 E
Arnhem 46 51.59 N 5.55 E
Arnhem, Cape > 92 12.21 S 136.21 E
Arnhem Bay C 92 12.20 S 136.12 E
Arnhem Land ←¹ 92 13.10 S 134.30 E
Ärnissa 54 40.48 N 21.50 E
Arno ≃ 52 43.41 N 10.17 E
Arno Bay 94 33.54 S 136.34 E
Arnold, Eng., U.K. 34 53.00 N 1.08 W
Arnold, Ca., U.S. 104 38.15 N 120.21 W
Arnold ≃ 114 55.19 S 134.06 E
Arnoldstein 46 46.33 N 13.43 E
Arnoya ≃ 50 42.15 N 8.09 W
Arnprior 102 45.26 N 76.21 W
Arnsberg 46 51.24 N 8.03 E
Arnside 36 54.12 N 2.50 W
Arnstadt 46 50.50 N 10.57 E
Aroab 86 26.47 S 19.40 E
Arolsen 46 51.23 N 9.01 E
Aroostook ≃ 102 46.48 N 67.45 W
Arorae I 28 2.38 S 176.49 E
Aroroa ∧ 96 40.10 S 175.11 E
Arosa 48 46.47 N 9.41 E
Arosa, Ría de C¹ 50 42.28 N 8.57 W
Arpaçay 30 40.50 N 43.20 E
Arpajon 48 48.35 N 2.15 E
Arra ≃ 40 52.39 N 8.09 W
Arra-Sala 114 28.04 S 64.14 W
Arrah 76 25.34 N 84.40 E
Arraias 110 12.56 S 46.57 W
Ar-Rahad 82 12.43 N 30.39 E
Ar-Ramādī 78 33.25 N 43.17 E
Ar-Ramthā 78 32.34 N 36.00 E
Arran, Island of I 38 55.35 N 5.15 W
Ar-Rank 82 11.45 N 32.48 E
Arras 48 50.17 N 2.47 E
Arrats ≃ 48 44.06 N 0.52 E
Ar-Riyāḍ (Riyadh) 78 24.38 N 46.43 E
Arrochar 38 56.12 N 4.44 W
Arroio Grande 114 32.14 S 53.05 W
Aronches 50 39.07 N 7.17 W
Arroyo de la Luz 50 39.29 N 6.35 W
Arroyo Grande 104 35.07 N 120.35 W
Arroyos y Esteros 114 25.04 S 57.06 W
Ar-Rub' al-Khālī ←² 74 20.00 N 51.00 E
Ar-Rukhaymīyah ⊤⁴ 78 29.22 N 45.35 E
Ar-Rusayris 82 11.51 N 34.23 E
Ar-Rutbah 78 33.02 N 40.17 E
Arsenjev 58 44.10 N 133.15 E
Ārs 44 56.48 N 9.32 E
Ars-en-Ré 48 46.12 N 1.31 W
Arta, Ellás 54 39.09 N 20.59 E
Arta, Esp. 50 39.41 N 3.21 E
Artemisa 108 22.49 N 82.46 W
Artemovsk 56 48.36 N 38.00 E
Artenay 48 48.05 N 1.53 E
Artern 46 51.22 N 11.18 E
Artesia 100 32.50 N 104.24 W
Arthabaska 102 46.02 N 71.55 W
Arthur ≃ 94 41.02 S 144.40 E
Arthur, Lake 🝔 102 40.56 N 80.06 W
Arthur Creek ≃ 94 22.55 S 136.45 E
Arthur's Pass 96 42.54 S 171.34 E

Arthur's Pass)(96 42.54 S 171.34 E
Arthurs Town 108 24.38 N 75.42 W
Artibonite ≃ 108 19.15 N 72.47 W
Artigas 114 30.24 S 56.28 W
Artik 78 40.37 N 43.58 E
Artillery Lake 🝔 98 63.09 N 107.52 W
Artney, Glen ∨ 38 56.20 N 4.04 W
Artois □⁹ 48 50.30 N 2.30 E
Art'omovsk 56 43.22 N 132.13 E
Art'omovsk 58 54.21 N 93.26 E
Art'omovskij, S.S.S.R. 56 57.21 N 61.54 E
Art'omovskij, S.S.S.R. 58 58.12 N 114.45 E
Artvin 30 41.11 N 41.49 E
Artyk 58 64.12 N 145.06 E
Aru, Kepulauan II 92 6.00 S 134.30 E
Aru, Tanjung > 72 1.13 S 116.34 E
Arua 84 3.01 N 30.55 E
Aruanã 110 14.54 S 51.05 W
Aruba I 108 12.30 N 69.58 E
Aru Basin ←¹ 28 5.00 S 134.00 E
Arun ≃ 34 50.48 N 0.33 W
Arunachal Pradesh □⁸ 76 28.30 N 95.00 E
Arundel 34 50.51 N 0.34 W
Aruppukkottai 74 9.31 N 78.06 E
Arusha 84 3.22 S 36.41 E
Aruwimi ≃ 84 1.13 N 23.36 E
Arvagh 40 53.55 N 7.34 W
Arvajcheer 62 46.15 N 102.48 E
Arvi 76 20.59 N 78.14 E
Arvidsjaur 42 65.35 N 19.07 E
Arvika 44 59.39 N 12.36 E
Årväs 104 35.12 S 118.49 W
Ārvorezinha 114 28.53 S 52.10 W
Arxan 62 47.11 N 119.57 E
Arys' 56 42.26 N 68.48 E
Arzachena 52 41.05 N 9.23 E
Arzamas 60 55.23 N 43.50 E
Arzew 50 35.51 N 0.19 W
Arzignano 52 45.31 N 11.20 E
Arzúa 50 42.56 N 8.09 W
Aš, Česko. 46 50.13 N 12.10 E
Ås, Nor. 44 59.40 N 10.48 E
Aša 56 55.00 N 57.16 E
Asadābād 76 34.52 N 71.09 E
Asahi 64 35.43 N 140.29 E
Asahi ≃ 64 34.36 N 133.58 E
Asahi-dake ∧ 64a 43.40 N 142.51 E
Asahigawa
→Asahikawa 64a 43.46 N 142.22 E
Asahikawa 64a 43.46 N 142.22 E
Asahi-sanchi ⋏ 64 38.25 N 139.50 E
Asamankese 80 5.52 N 0.42 W
Asama-yama ∧ 64 36.24 N 138.31 E
Asansol 76 23.41 N 86.59 E
Asarna 44 62.39 N 14.21 E
Asarum 44 56.12 N 14.50 E
Asbesberg ⋏ 86 28.55 S 23.15 E
Asbest 56 57.00 N 61.30 E
Asbestos 102 45.46 N 71.57 W
Asbury Park 102 40.13 N 74.01 W
Ascensión 20 7.57 S 14.22 W
Ascensión, Bahía de la C 108 19.40 N 87.30 W
Aschabad 56 37.57 N 58.23 E
Aschaffenburg 46 49.59 N 9.09 E
Aschendorf 46 51.45 N 7.27 E
Aschersleben 46 51.45 N 11.27 E
Asciano 52 43.14 N 11.33 E
Áscoli Piceno 52 42.51 N 13.34 E
Ascoli Satriano 52 41.12 N 15.34 E
Ascona 48 46.09 N 8.46 E
Ascot 34 51.25 N 0.41 W
Ascotán 114 21.44 S 68.18 W
Aseb 82 13.00 N 42.45 E
Åseda 44 57.10 N 15.20 E
Asela 82 7.59 N 39.08 E
Åsele 42 64.10 N 17.20 E
Äsele 44 64.10 N 17.20 E
Asenovgrad 54 42.01 N 24.52 E
Åsensbruk 44 58.48 N 12.25 E
Asfordby 34 52.46 N 0.57 W
Åsgårdstrand 44 59.21 N 10.28 E
Ash, Eng., U.K. 34 51.17 N 1.16 E
Ash, Eng., U.K. 34 51.15 N 0.44 W
Ash ≃ 34 51.48 N 0.02 W
Ashbourne, Ire. 40 53.31 N 6.24 W
Ashbourne, Eng., U.K. 34 53.02 N 1.44 W
Ashburton, N.Z. 96 43.55 S 171.45 E
Ashburton ≃, N.Z. 90 21.40 S 114.56 E
Ashburton ≃, Austl. 90 21.40 S 114.56 E
Ashburton Downs 90 23.24 S 117.04 E
Ashby-de-la-Zouch 34 52.46 N 1.28 W
Ashchurch 34 52.00 N 2.07 W
Ash Creek ≃ 104 41.05 N 121.08 W
Ashdown Forest ←³ 34 51.04 N 0.03 E
Asheville 100 35.36 N 82.33 W
Asheweig ≃ 98 54.17 N 87.12 W
Ashford, Austl. 94 29.20 S 151.06 E
Ashford, Eng., U.K. 34 51.08 N 0.53 E
Ashford, Eng., U.K. 34 51.26 N 0.27 W
Ashhurst 96 40.18 S 175.45 E
Ashibe 64a 33.48 N 129.46 E
Ashibetsu 64a 43.31 N 142.11 E
Ashikaga 64 36.20 N 139.27 E
Ashington 36 55.11 N 1.34 W
Ashio 64 36.38 N 139.27 E
Ashiyoro 64a 43.15 N 143.30 E
Ashizuri-misaki > 64 32.44 N 133.01 E
Ashkhabad
→Aschabad 56 37.57 N 58.23 E
Ashland, Ky., U.S. 102 38.28 N 82.38 W
Ashland, N.H., U.S. 102 43.41 N 71.37 W
Ashland, Oh., U.S. 102 40.52 N 82.19 W
Ashland, Or., U.S. 104 42.12 N 122.42 W
Ashland, Wi., U.S. 100 46.35 N 90.53 W
Ashland, Mount ∧ 104 42.05 N 122.43 W
Ashley, Austl. 94 29.19 S 149.49 E
Ashley, Oh., U.S. 102 40.24 N 82.57 W
Ashley ≃ 96 43.17 S 172.43 E
Ashmore Islands II 88 12.14 S 123.05 E
Ashoknagar 76 24.34 N 77.43 E
Ashqelon 78 31.40 N 34.35 E
Ash-Shariqah 78 25.22 N 55.23 E
Ash-Sharqāt 78 35.27 N 43.16 E
Ash-Shaqrā' 82 13.50 N 45.11 E
Ash-Shatrah 78 31.25 N 46.10 E
Ash-Shihr 74 14.45 N 49.36 E
Asht 56 40.29 N 70.21 E
Ashta 76 23.01 N 76.43 E
Ashtabula 102 41.51 N 80.47 W
Ashtead 34 51.19 N 0.18 W
Ashton-in-Makerfield 36 53.29 N 2.39 W
Ashton-under-Lyne 36 53.29 N 2.06 W
Ashuanipi Lake 🝔 98 52.35 N 66.10 W
Asia ±¹ 30 50.00 N 100.00 E
Asia, Kepulauan II 68 1.03 N 131.18 E
Asia Minor □⁹ 30 39.00 N 32.00 E
Asinara, Golfo dell' C 52 41.00 N 8.32 E
Asinara, Isola I 52 41.04 N 8.16 E
Asino 56 57.00 N 86.09 E
Asíós 54 57.00 N 86.09 E
'Asīr ←¹ 74 19.00 N 42.00 E
Askam in Furness 36 54.11 N 3.13 W

Symbols in the Index entries are identified on page 122

Name	Page	Lat. °′	Long. °′
Ballybogy	40	55.07N	6.34W
Ballybunnion	40	52.31N	9.40W
Ballycanew	40	52.36N	6.19W
Ballycastle, Ire.	40	54.16N	9.23W
Ballycastle, N. Ire., U.K.	40	55.12N	6.15W
Ballyclare	40	54.45N	6.00W
Ballyconneely	40	53.26N	10.02W
Ballyconnell	40	54.07N	7.35W
Ballycotton	40	51.50N	8.01W
Ballycroy	40	54.01N	9.51W
Ballyduff, Ire.	40	52.27N	9.40W
Ballyduff, Ire.	40	52.09N	8.03W
Ballyferriter	40	52.09N	10.26W
Ballyfinboy ≃	40	53.02N	8.15W
Ballygar	40	53.32N	8.20W
Ballygawley	40	54.28N	7.02W
Ballygorman	40	55.22N	7.21W
Ballygowan	40	54.30N	5.48W
Ballyhaise	40	54.03N	7.19W
Ballyhalbert	40	54.30N	5.28W
Ballyhaunis	40	53.46N	8.46W
Ballyhoura Mountains ⋀	40	52.20N	8.35W
Ballyjamesduff	40	53.52N	7.12W
Ballylongford	40	52.33N	9.28W
Ballymacoda	40	51.57N	7.54W
Ballymahon	40	53.34N	7.45W
Ballymakeery (Ballyvourney)	40	51.55N	9.09W
Ballymena	40	54.52N	6.17W
Ballymoe	40	53.42N	8.29W
Ballymoney	40	55.04N	6.31W
Ballymote	40	54.06N	8.31W
Ballymurray	40	53.35N	8.08W
Ballynahinch	40	54.24N	5.54W
Ballyneety	40	52.35N	8.33W
Ballynoe	40	52.03N	8.05W
Ballyquintin Point ›	40	54.20N	5.30W
Ballyragget	40	52.47N	7.20W
Ballysadare	40	54.13N	8.31W
Ballyshannon	40	54.30N	8.11W
Ballyteige Bay c	40	53.23N	9.51W
Ballyvaghan	40	53.07N	9.07W
Ballyvoy	40	55.12N	6.12W
Ballywalter	40	54.33N	5.30W
Balmaceda	112	45.55S	71.41W
Balmerino	38	56.24N	3.02W
Balmoral	94	37.15S	141.51 E
Balnacra	38	57.28N	5.23W
Balnearia	114	31.00S	62.40W
Baloda Bāzār	76	21.40N	82.10 E
Balonne ≃	94	28.47S	147.56 E
Bālotra	76	25.50N	72.14 E
Balovale	84	13.33S	23.06 E
Balrāmpur	76	27.26N	82.11 E
Balranald	94	34.38S	143.33 E
Balş	54	44.21N	24.06 E
Balsam Lake ⊜	102	44.35N	78.50W
Balsas	110	7.31S	46.02W
Balsas ≃	106	17.55N	102.10W
Balsas, Rio das ≃	110	7.14S	44.33W
Balsham	34	52.08N	0.20 E
Bålsta	44	59.35N	17.30 E
Balta	56	47.55N	29.37 E
Baltanás	50	41.56N	4.15W
Baltasar Brum	114	30.44S	57.19W
Baltasound	38a	60.45N	0.52W
Baltic Sea ≂2	42	57.00N	19.00 E
Baltijsk	60	54.39N	19.55 E
Baltijskaja kosa ›2	46	54.25N	19.35 E
Baltimore, Ire.	40	51.29N	9.22W
Baltimore, S. Afr.	86	23.15S	28.20 E
Baltimore, Md., U.S.	102	39.17N	76.36W
Baltimore, Oh., U.S.	102	39.50N	82.36W
Baltinglass	40	52.55N	6.41W
Baluchistān □4	76	29.00N	67.00 E
Baluchistan □9	74	28.00N	63.00 E
Bālurghāt	76	25.13N	88.46 E
Balvicar	38	56.14N	5.38W
Balygyčan	58	63.56N	154.12 E
Balykši	56	47.05N	51.54 E
Bam	78	29.06N	58.21 E
Bama	70	24.21N	107.08 E
Bamaga	92	10.52S	142.24 E
Bamako	80	12.39N	8.00W
Bamba	80	17.02N	1.24W
Bambana ≃	108	13.27N	83.50W
Bambari	82	5.45N	20.40 E
Bambaroo	94	18.52S	146.12 E
Bamberg	46	49.53N	10.53 E
Bambezi	86	20.00S	28.56 E
Bamboo Creek	90	20.56S	120.13 E
Bamboo Springs	90	22.04S	119.38 E
Bamburgh	36	55.36N	1.42W
Bamenda	80	5.56N	10.10 E
Bāmīān	76	34.50N	67.50 E
Bāmīān □4	76	34.45N	67.15 E
Bamingui ≃	82	8.33N	19.05 E
Bampton, Eng., U.K.	34	51.00N	3.29W
Bampton, Eng., U.K.	34	51.44N	1.33W
Bampūr	78	27.12N	60.27 E
Baña, Punta de la ›	50	40.34N	0.38 E
Banaba I	28	0.52S	169.35 E
Banagher	40	53.11N	7.59W
Banalia	84	1.33N	25.20 E
Banana, Austl.	94	24.28S	150.07 E
Banana, Zaïre	84	6.01S	12.24 E
Bananal, Ilha do I	110	11.30S	50.15W
Banaras →Vārānasi	74	25.20N	83.00 E
Banās ≃	76	25.54N	76.45 E
Banās, Ra's ›	82	23.54N	35.48 E
Banat ◆1	54	45.20N	20.40 E
Banavie	38	56.47N	5.07W
Banbridge	40	54.21N	6.16W
Banbury	34	52.04N	1.20W
Banchory	38	57.30N	2.30W
Bancroft, On., Can.	102	45.03N	77.51W
Bancroft →Chililabombwe, Zam.	84	12.18S	27.43 E
Bānda	76	25.29N	80.20 E
Banda, Kepulauan II	92	4.35S	129.55 E
Banda, Laut (Banda Sea) ≂2	68	5.00S	128.00 E
Banda Aceh	70	5.34N	95.20 E
Banda del Río Salí	114	26.50S	65.10W
Bandai-san ∧	64	37.36N	140.04 E
Bandak ⊜	44	59.24N	8.15 E
Bandama ≃	80	5.10N	5.00W
Bandama Blanc ≃	80	6.54N	5.31W
Bandama Rouge ≃	80	6.54N	5.31W
Bandar →Machilīpatnam	74	16.10N	81.08 E
Bandar-e 'Abbās	78	27.11N	56.17 E
Bandar-e Anzalī (Bandar-e Pahlavī)	78	37.28N	49.27 E
Bandar-e Khomeynī (Bandar-e Shāhpūr)	78	30.25N	49.05 E
Bandar-e Lengeh	78	26.33N	54.53 E
Bandar-e Māh Shahr	78	30.33N	49.12 E
Bandar-e Torkeman	78	36.56N	54.06 E
Bandar Seri Begawan	72	4.56N	114.55 E
Bande	50	42.02N	7.58W
Bandeira, Pico da ∧	110	20.26S	41.47W
Bandeirantes	114	23.06S	50.21W
Bandera	114	28.54S	62.16W
Bandera, Alto ∧	108	18.49N	70.37W
Bandera Bajada	114	27.14S	63.31W
Bandiantaolehai	62	41.41N	104.06 E
Bāndikūi	76	27.03N	76.34 E
Bandipura	76	34.25N	74.39 E
Bandırma	30	40.20N	27.58 E
Bandon, Ire.	40	51.45N	8.45W
Bandon, Or., U.S.	104	43.07N	124.24W
Bandon ≃	40	51.42N	8.30W
Bandundu	84	3.18S	17.20 E
Bandung	72	6.54S	107.36 E
Băneasa	54	44.04N	27.42 E
Banes	108	20.58N	75.43W
Banff, Ab., Can.	98	51.10N	115.34W
Banff, Scot., U.K.	38	57.40N	2.33W
Banga	76	31.11N	75.59 E
Bangalore	74	12.58N	77.36 E
Bangaon	76	23.04N	88.49 E
Bangassou	82	4.50N	23.07 E
Bangeta, Mount ∧	92	6.15S	147.04 E
Banggai (Luwuk)	72	1.34S	123.30 E
Banggai, Kepulauan II	72	1.30S	123.15 E
Banggi, Pulau I	72	7.17N	117.12 E
Banghāzī	82	32.07N	20.04 E
Bangil	72	7.36S	112.47 E
Bangka I	72	2.15S	106.00 E
Bangka, Selat ʉ	72	2.20S	105.45 E
Bangkalan	72	7.02S	112.44 E
Bangkinang	72	0.21N	101.02 E
Bangko	72	2.05S	102.17 E
Bangkok →Krung Thep	70	13.45N	100.31 E
Bangladesh □1	74	24.00N	90.00 E
Bang Mun Nak	70	16.02N	100.23 E
Bangor, Ire.	40	54.09N	9.45W
Bangor, N. Ire., U.K.	40	54.40N	5.40W
Bangor, Wales, U.K.	36	53.13N	4.08W
Bangor, Me., U.S.	102	44.48N	68.46W
Bangor, Pa., U.S.	102	40.51N	75.12W
Bāngriposi	76	22.10N	86.32 E
Bangs, Mount ∧	104	36.48N	113.51W
Bangui	82	4.22N	18.35 E
Bangweulu, Lake ⊜	84	11.05S	29.45 E
Ban Houayxay	70	20.18N	100.26 E
Bani, Burkina	80	14.02N	0.02W
Baní, Rep. Dom.	108	18.17N	70.20W
Bani ≃	80	14.30N	4.12W
Baniara	92	9.46S	149.53 E
Banie	46	53.08N	14.38 E
Banī Mazār	82	28.30N	30.48 E
Banī Suwayf	82	29.05N	31.05 E
Banī Walīd	82	31.45N	14.01 E
Banja Luka	52	44.46N	17.11 E
Banjarmasin	72	3.20S	114.35 E
Banjul	80	13.28N	16.39W
Bānka	76	24.53N	86.55 E
Banka Banka	90	18.48S	134.01 E
Bankeryd	44	57.51N	14.07 E
Bankfoot	38	56.30N	3.30W
Banks	36	53.41N	2.55W
Banks Island I, B.C., Can.	98	53.25N	130.10W
Banks Island I, N.T., Can.	98	73.15N	121.30W
Banks Islands II	28	13.50S	167.30 E
Banks Peninsula ›1	96	43.45S	173.00 E
Banks Strait ʉ	94	40.40S	148.07 E
Bānkura	76	23.15N	87.04 E
Bann ≃	40	55.10N	6.46W
Ban Na San	70	8.48N	99.22 E
Bannerman, Mount ∧2	90	19.26S	127.10 E
Banning	104	33.55N	116.52W
Bannockburn	38	56.06N	3.55W
Bannu	76	32.59N	70.36 E
Bañolas	50	42.07N	2.46 E
Banon	48	44.02N	5.38 E
Baños	110	1.24S	78.25W
Baños de Cerrato	50	41.55N	4.28W
Bánovce nad Bebravou	46	48.43N	18.14 E
Ban Pak Phraek	70	8.13N	100.12 E
Ban Pong	70	13.49N	99.53 E
Banqiao	66	30.06N	120.27 E
Banqiaoji	66	32.19N	116.37 E
Bānsda	76	20.45N	73.22 E
Bansha	40	52.28N	8.04W
Banská Bystrica	46	48.44N	19.07 E
Banská Štiavnica	46	48.28N	18.56 E
Bansko	54	41.50N	23.29 E
Banstead	34	51.19N	0.12W
Bānswāra	76	23.33N	74.27 E
Banteer	40	52.07N	8.54W
Bantry	40	51.41N	9.27W
Bantry Bay c	40	51.38N	9.48W
Bāntva	76	21.29N	70.05 E
Banwell	34	51.20N	2.52W
Banwy ≃	34	52.42N	3.16W
Banyak, Kepulauan II	70	2.10N	97.15 E
Banyuwangi	72	8.12S	114.21 E
Bao'an	66	22.34N	114.07 E
Baode	62	39.06N	111.11 E
Baoding	62	38.52N	115.29 E
Baofeng	66	33.55N	113.02 E
Bao-ha	70	22.11N	104.21 E
Baoji	62	34.23N	107.09 E
Bao-loc	70	11.32N	107.48 E
Baoshan, Zhg.	66	31.25N	121.29 E
Baoshan, Zhg.	70	25.09N	99.09 E
Baoting	70	18.42N	109.45 E
Baotou	62	40.40N	109.59 E
Baoying	66	33.16N	119.20 E
Bāp	76	27.23N	72.21 E
Bapaume	48	50.06N	2.51 E
Baptiste Lake ⊜	102	45.07N	78.02W
Ba'qūbah	78	33.45N	44.38 E
Baquedano	114	23.20S	69.51W
Bar	54	42.05N	19.05 E
Baraawe	82	1.06N	44.03 E
Barabinsk	56	55.21N	78.21 E
Barabinskaja step' ≚	58	55.00N	79.00 E
Baracoa	108	20.21N	74.30W
Baradero	114	33.48S	59.30W
Baradine	94	30.56S	149.04 E
Baraka v	82	18.13N	37.35 E
Barakī Barak	76	33.56N	68.55 E
Bārākot	76	21.33N	85.01 E
Barakula	94	26.26S	150.31 E
Baralaba	94	24.11S	149.49 E
Baram ≃	72	4.36N	113.59 E
Bāramūla	76	34.12N	74.21 E
Bārān, India	76	25.06N	76.31 E
Baran', S.S.S.R.	60	54.29N	30.18 E
Baranagar	76	22.38N	88.22 E
Baranoa	108	10.48N	74.55W
Baranof Island I	98	56.45N	135.10W
Baranoviči	60	53.08N	26.02 E
Baranów Sandomierski	46	50.30N	21.33 E
Baranya □6	46	46.05N	18.15 E
Barão de Melgaço	110	16.13S	55.58W
Baraolt	54	46.05N	25.36 E
Baraoltului, Munţii ⋀	54	46.15N	25.45 E
Baratang Island I	70	12.13N	92.45 E
Barat Daya, Kepulauan II	92	7.25S	128.00 E
Baratta	94	31.59S	139.06 E
Baraut	76	29.06N	77.16 E
Barbacena	110	21.14S	43.46W
Barbacoas	110	1.41N	78.09W
Barbadillo del Mercado	50	42.02N	3.21W
Barbados □1	106	13.10N	59.32W
Barbagia ◆1	52	40.00N	9.10 E
Barbar	82	18.01N	33.59 E
Barbas, Cap ›	80	22.18N	16.41W
Barbastro	50	42.02N	0.08 E
Barbate ≃	50	36.11N	5.55W
Barbate de Franco	50	36.12N	5.55W
Barbeau Peak ∧	22	81.54N	75.01W
Barberton, S. Afr.	86	25.48S	31.03 E
Barberton, Oh., U.S.	102	41.00N	81.36W
Barbezieux	48	45.28N	0.09W
Barbil	76	22.06N	85.20 E
Barboursville	102	38.24N	82.17W
Barbuda I	108	17.38N	61.48W
Barby	46	51.58N	11.53 E
Barcaldine	94	23.33S	145.17 E
Barcarrota	50	38.31N	6.51W
Barcellona Pozzo di Gotto	52	38.09N	15.13 E
Barcelona, Esp.	50	41.23N	2.11 E
Barcelona, Ven.	110	10.08N	64.42W
Barcelos, Bra.	110	0.58S	62.57W
Barcelos, Port.	50	41.32N	8.37W
Barcin	46	52.52N	17.57 E
Barcoo ≃	94	25.30S	142.50 E
Barcs	46	45.58N	17.28 E
Barczewo	46	53.50N	20.42 E
Barda	78	40.23N	47.08 E
Barda del Medio	114	38.43S	68.10W
Bardaï	82	21.22N	16.59 E
Bardawīl, Sabkhat al- ∷	78	31.10N	33.10 E
Bardejov	46	49.18N	21.16 E
Bárdenas Reales ⋀1	50	42.10N	1.25W
Bardi	52	44.38N	9.44 E
Bardīyah	82	31.46N	25.06 E
Bardney	36	53.12N	0.21W
Bardoc	90	30.20S	121.17 E
Bardoli	76	21.07N	73.07 E
Bardonecchia	52	45.05N	6.42 E
Bardsey Island I	34	52.45N	4.45W
Bardsey Sound ʉ	34	52.47N	4.45W
Bardu	42	68.52N	18.21 E
Bardufoss	42	69.04N	18.30 E
Bareilly	76	28.21N	79.25 E
Barengapāra	76	25.14N	90.14 E
Barentin	48	49.33N	0.57 E
Barents Sea (Barencevo more) ≂2	42	69.00N	40.00 E
Barents Trough ✢1	20	75.00N	29.00 E
Bareo	72	3.45N	115.27 E
Bareta	76	29.52N	75.42 E
Barfleur	48	49.40N	1.15W
Barfleur, Pointe de ›	48	49.42N	1.16W
Bargara	94	24.49S	152.27 E
Bargarh	76	21.20N	83.37 E
Bargas	50	39.56N	4.03W
Barge	52	44.43N	7.20 E
Bargoed	34	51.43N	3.15W
Barguzin ≃	58	53.27N	109.00 E
Bārh	76	25.29N	85.43 E
Bar Harbor	102	44.23N	68.12W
Barharwa	76	24.52N	87.47 E
Barhi	76	24.18N	85.25 E
Bar Hill	34	52.15N	0.01 E
Bāri, India	76	23.03N	78.05 E
Bāri, India	76	26.39N	77.36 E
Bari, It.	52	41.07N	16.52 E
Bariloche →San Carlos de Bariloche	112	41.09S	71.18W
Barīm I	74	12.40N	43.25 E
Barinas	110	8.38N	70.12W
Baring, Cape ›	98	70.05N	117.20W
Baripāda	76	21.56N	86.43 E
Bariri	114	22.04S	48.44W
Bārīs	82	24.40N	30.36 E
Bari Sādri	76	24.25N	74.28 E
Barisāl	76	22.42N	90.22 E
Barisan, Pegunungan ⋀	72	3.00S	102.15 E
Barito ≃	72	3.32S	114.29 E
Barjac	48	44.18N	4.21 E
Barjols	48	43.33N	6.00 E
Barking ◆8	34	51.33N	0.06 E
Bark Lake ⊜	102	45.27N	77.51W
Barkley Sound ʉ	98	48.53N	125.20W
Barkly, Mount ∧2	90	21.34S	132.28 E
Barkly East	86	30.58S	27.33 E
Barkly Tableland ⋀1	90	18.00S	136.00 E
Barkly West	86	28.05S	24.31 E
Barkol	62	43.50N	93.30 E
Barlaston	34	52.57N	2.10W
Barlby	36	53.48N	1.03W
Bar-le-Duc	48	48.47N	5.10 E
Barlee, Lake ⊜	90	29.10S	119.30 E
Barlee, Mount ∧2	90	24.37S	128.06 E
Barlee Range ⋀	90	23.35S	116.00 E
Barletta	52	41.19N	16.17 E
Barlinek	46	53.00N	15.12 E
Barmedman	94	34.09S	147.23 E
Barmer	76	25.45N	71.23 E
Barmera	94	34.15S	140.28 E
Barmouth	34	52.43N	4.03W
Barmouth Bay c	34	52.42N	4.08W
Barnagar	76	23.03N	75.22 E
Barnard Castle	36	54.33N	1.55W
Barnaul	56	53.22N	83.45 E
Barn Bluff ∧	94	41.43S	145.56 E
Barnegat	102	39.45N	74.13W
Barnegat Bay c	102	39.52N	74.07W
Barnesboro	102	40.39N	78.46W
Barnesville	102	39.59N	81.10W
Barnet ◆8	34	51.40N	0.13W
Barnetby le Wold	36	53.35N	0.25W
Barneville-Carteret	48	49.23N	1.47W
Barnoldswick	36	53.55N	2.11W
Barnsley	36	53.34N	1.28W
Barnstable	102	41.42N	70.18W
Barnstaple	34	51.05N	4.04W
Barnstaple Bay c	34	51.05N	4.20W
Barnt Green	34	52.22N	1.59W
Baro ≃	82	8.26N	33.13 E
Baroda	76	22.18N	73.12 E
Baroe	86	33.13S	24.33 E
Barpathār	76	26.17N	93.53 E
Barpeta	76	26.19N	91.00 E
Barqah (Cyrenaica) □9	82	31.00N	22.30 E
Barque Canada Reef ✢2	68	8.12N	113.19 E
Barques, Pointe aux ›	102	44.04N	82.58W
Barquisimeto	110	10.04N	69.19W
Barra	110	11.05S	43.10W
Barra I	38	56.58N	7.29W
Barra, Ponta da ›	86	23.47S	35.32 E
Barra, Sound of ʉ	38	57.05N	7.25W
Barraba	94	30.22S	150.36 E
Barracão	114	26.15S	53.38W
Barrackville	102	39.30N	80.10W
Barra de Río Grande	108	12.54N	83.32W
Barra do Corda	110	5.30S	45.15W
Barra do Cuanza	84	9.09S	13.00 E
Barra do Ribeiro	114	30.18S	51.18W
Barra Falsa, Ponta da ›	86	22.55S	35.37 E
Barrafranca	52	37.22N	14.12 E
Barra Head ›	38	56.46N	7.38W
Barra Mansa	110	22.32S	44.11W
Barranca	110	10.45S	77.46W
Barrancabermeja	110	7.03N	73.52W
Barrancas, Chile	114	33.27S	70.46W
Barrancas, Col.	108	10.57N	72.50W
Barrancas, Ven.	110	8.42N	62.11W
Barrancas ≃	114	36.52S	69.45W
Barranco do Velho	50	37.14N	7.56W
Barrancos	50	38.08N	6.59W
Barranqueras	114	27.29S	58.56W
Barranquilla	110	10.59N	74.48W
Barra Punta Gorda	108	11.31N	83.47W
Barras	110	4.15S	42.18W
Barrax	50	39.03N	2.12W
Barre	102	44.11N	72.30W
Barreal	114	31.38S	69.28W
Barreiras	110	12.08S	45.00W
Barreiro	50	38.40N	9.05W
Barreiros	110	8.49S	35.12W
Barrême	48	43.57N	6.22 E
Barren, Nosy II	87b	18.25S	43.40 E
Barren Islands II	98	58.55N	152.15W
Barretos	110	20.33S	48.33W
Barrett, Mount ∧	90	18.10S	127.33 E
Barrhead	38	55.48N	4.24W
Barrhill	36	55.07N	4.46W
Barrie	102	44.24N	79.40W
Barrie Island I	102	45.55N	82.40W
Barrier, Cape ›	96	36.21S	175.31 E
Barrier Range ⋀	94	31.25S	141.25 E
Barrier Reef ✢2	92	11.36S	153.00 E
Barrington Tops ∧	94	32.00S	151.28 E
Barringun	94	29.01S	145.43 E
Barrow	114	38.18S	60.14W
Barrow ≃	40	52.15N	7.00W
Barrow, Point ›	22	71.23N	156.30W
Barrow Creek	90	21.33S	133.53 E
Barrowford	36	53.52N	2.13W
Barrow-in-Furness	36	54.07N	3.14W
Barrow Island I	90	20.48S	115.23 E
Barrow Range ⋀	90	26.04S	127.28 E
Barrow Strait ʉ	98	74.21N	94.10W
Barrow upon Humber	36	53.41N	0.23W
Barry	34	51.24N	3.18W
Barrys Bay	102	45.29N	77.41W
Barryton	102	43.45N	85.08W
Bārsi	74	18.14N	75.42 E
Barsinghausen	46	52.18N	9.27 E
Barstow	104	34.53N	117.01W
Bar-sur-Aube	48	48.14N	4.43 E
Bar-sur-Seine	48	48.07N	4.22 E
Bartang	56	38.05N	71.51 E
Barth	46	54.22N	12.43 E
Bartica	110	6.24N	58.37W
Bartle Frere ∧	94	17.23S	145.49 E
Bartlesville	100	36.44N	95.58W
Bartlett	102	44.04N	71.17W
Bartolomé de las Casas	114	25.24S	59.34W
Bartolomeu Dias	86	21.10S	35.09 E
Barton, Austl.	90	30.31S	132.39 E
Barton, Vt., U.S.	102	44.44N	72.10W
Barton-le-Clay	34	51.57N	0.25W
Barton Mills	34	52.20N	0.31 E
Barton-under-Needwood	34	52.45N	1.43W
Barton-upon-Humber	36	53.41N	0.27W
Bartoszyce	46	54.16N	20.49 E
Barú, Volcán ∧1	108	8.48N	82.33W
Barun Bogd uul ∧	62	44.57N	100.15 E
Bāruni	76	25.29N	85.59 E
Baruun-Urt	62	46.42N	113.15 E
Barvas	38	58.22N	6.32W
Barview	104	43.21N	124.18W
Barwāh	76	22.16N	76.03 E
Barwāni	76	22.02N	74.54 E
Barwell	34	52.32N	1.21W
Barwice	46	53.45N	16.22 E
Barwidgee	90	27.02S	120.54 E
Barwon ≃	94	30.00S	148.05 E
Barycz ≃	46	51.42N	16.15 E
Baryš	42	53.39N	47.08 E
Basail	114	27.52S	59.18W
Basalt ≃	94	19.38S	145.52 E
Basankusu	84	1.14N	19.48 E
Basarabi	54	44.10N	28.24 E
Basatongwula Shan ∧	62	33.05N	91.30 E
Basavilbaso	114	32.22S	58.53W
Basco	68	20.27N	121.58 E
Bascuñán, Cabo ›	114	28.51S	71.30W
Basel (Bâle)	48	47.33N	7.35 E
Basella	50	42.01N	1.18 E
Basento ≃	52	40.21N	16.50 E
Başeu ≃	54	47.44N	27.15 E
Basey	68	11.17N	125.04 E
Bashākerd, Kūhhā-ye ⋀	78	26.42N	59.00 E
Bashi Channel ʉ	68	22.00N	121.00 E
Basilan	68	6.42N	121.58 E
Basilan Island I	68	6.34N	122.03 E
Basilan Strait ʉ	72	6.49N	122.05 E
Basildon	34	51.35N	0.25 E
Basilicata □4	52	40.30N	16.10 E
Basílio	114	31.53S	53.01W
Basingstoke	34	51.15N	1.05W
Basīrhāt	76	22.40N	88.53 E
Baška	52	44.58N	14.46 E
Baskahegan Lake ⊜	102	45.30N	67.48W
Baskatong, Réservoir ⊜1	98	46.48N	75.50W
Baslow	36	53.15N	1.38W
Bašmakovo	60	53.12N	43.02 E
Bāsoda	76	23.51N	77.56 E
Basoko	84	1.14N	23.36 E
Basque Provinces →Vascongadas □9	50	43.00N	2.45W
Basra →Al-Baṣrah	78	30.30N	47.47 E
Bas-Rhin □5	48	48.35N	7.40 E
Bassano del Grappa	52	45.46N	11.44 E
Bassari	80	9.15N	0.47 E
Bassas da India ✢2	84	21.25S	39.42 E
Bassein	70	16.47N	94.44 E
Bassenthwaite	36	54.41N	3.12W
Bassenthwaite Lake ⊜	36	54.38N	3.13W
Basse-Terre, Guad.	108	16.00N	61.44W
Basseterre, St. C.-N.	108	17.18N	62.43W
Basse-Terre I	108	16.10N	61.40W
Bass Harbor	102	44.14N	68.20W
Bassingbourn	34	52.04N	0.03W
Bass Strait ʉ	94	39.20S	145.30 E
Basswood Lake ⊜	98	48.06N	91.40W
Båstad	44	56.26N	12.51 E
Basti	76	26.48N	82.43 E
Bastia	48	42.42N	9.27 E
Bastogne	46	50.00N	5.43 E
Bastrop	100	32.46N	91.54W
Bastuträsk	44	64.47N	20.02 E
Basutoland →Lesotho □1	84	29.30S	28.30 E
Bata	84	1.51N	9.45 E
Batabanó, Golfo de c	108	22.15N	82.30W
Batagaj	58	67.38N	134.38 E
Batagaj-Alyta	58	67.48N	130.25 E
Bataguaçu	114	21.42S	52.22W
Bataiporã	114	22.20S	53.17W
Batajsk	56	47.10N	39.44 E
Batak	54	41.57N	24.13 E
Batak, Jazovir ⊜1	54	41.59N	24.11 E
Batāla	76	31.48N	75.12 E
Batalha	50	39.39N	8.50W
Batamaj	58	63.31N	129.27 E
Batan	66	34.10N	120.04 E
Batang	62	30.02N	99.02 E
Batangas	68	13.45N	121.03 E
Batanghari ≃	72	1.16S	104.05 E
Batan Island I	68	20.26N	121.58 E
Batan Islands II	68	20.30N	121.50 E
Batanta, Pulau I	92	0.50S	130.40 E
Bátaszék	46	46.12N	18.44 E
Batavia, Arg.	114	34.47S	65.41W
Batavia, N.Y., U.S.	102	42.59N	78.11W
Batavia, Oh., U.S.	102	39.04N	84.10W
Batchelor	92	13.04S	131.01 E
Bătdâmbâng	70	13.06N	103.12 E
Batemans Bay	94	35.43S	150.11 E
Bates Range ⋀	90	27.25S	121.13 E
Bath, Eng., U.K.	34	51.23N	2.22W
Bath, Me., U.S.	102	43.54N	69.49W
Bath, N.Y., U.S.	102	42.20N	77.19W
Bathgate	38	55.55N	3.39W
Bathsheba	108	13.13N	59.31W
Bathurst, Austl.	94	33.25S	149.35 E
Bathurst, N.B., Can.	98	47.36N	65.39W
Bathurst →Banjul, Gam.	80	13.28N	16.39W
Bathurst, S. Afr.	86	33.30S	26.50 E
Bathurst, Cape ›	98	70.35N	128.00W
Bathurst Inlet	98	66.50N	108.01W
Bathurst Inlet c	98	68.10N	108.50W
Bathurst Island I, Austl.	92	11.37S	130.23 E
Bathurst Island I, N.T., Can.	22	76.00N	100.30W
Bathurst Island Mission	92	11.45S	130.38 E
Batina	54	45.51N	18.51 E
Batley	36	53.44N	1.37W
Batlow	94	35.31S	148.09 E
Batman	78	37.52N	41.07 E
Batna	80	35.34N	6.11 E
Baton Rouge	100	30.27N	91.09W
Batouri	80	4.26N	14.22 E
Battambang →Bătdâmbâng	70	13.06N	103.12 E
Batticaloa	74	7.43N	81.42 E
Battle	34	50.55N	0.29 E
Battle ≃	98	52.43N	108.15W
Battle Creek	102	42.19N	85.10W
Battle Creek ≃, Ca., U.S.	104	40.21N	122.11W
Battle Creek ≃, Id., U.S.	104	42.14N	116.32W
Battle Harbour	98	52.16N	55.35W
Battle Mountain	104	40.38N	116.56W
Battonya	46	46.17N	21.01 E
Batu ∧	82	6.55N	39.46 E
Batu, Bukit ∧	72	2.16N	113.43 E
Batu, Kepulauan II	70	0.18S	98.28 E
Batu Berinchang, Gunong ∧	72	4.30N	101.24 E
Batu Gajah	72	4.28N	101.03 E
Batumi	56	41.38N	41.38 E
Batu Pahat	72	1.51N	102.56 E
Baturaja	72	4.08S	104.10 E
Baturité	110	4.20S	38.53W
Batusangkar	72	0.27S	100.35 E
Bau	72	1.25N	110.08 E
Baubau	72	5.28S	122.38 E
Bauchi	80	10.19N	9.50 E
Baud	48	47.52N	3.01W
Baudh	76	20.50N	84.19 E
Bauld, Cape ›	98	51.38N	55.25W
Baume-les-Dames	48	47.21N	6.22 E
Baun	72	10.18S	123.43 E
Baunei	52	40.02N	9.40 E
Bauru	114	22.19S	49.04W
Bauska	60	56.24N	24.14 E
Bautzen	46	51.11N	14.26 E
Bavaria →Bayern □3	46	49.00N	11.30 E
Båven ⊜	44	59.01N	16.56 E
Bavleny	60	56.24N	39.34 E
Bawdeswell	34	52.45N	1.01 E
Bawdwin	70	23.06N	97.18 E
Bawean, Pulau I	72	5.46S	112.40 E
Bawtry	36	53.26N	1.01W
Bay, Laguna de ⊜	68	14.23N	121.15 E
Bayamo	108	20.23N	76.39W
Bayamón	108	18.24N	66.09W
Bayan	72	8.16S	116.26 E
Bayāna	76	26.54N	77.17 E
Bayan Har Shan ⋀	62	33.48N	98.10 E
Bayano, Lago ⊜1	108	9.10N	78.40W
Bayan Obo	62	41.58N	110.02 E
Bayard	102	39.16N	79.21W
Bayble	38	58.12N	6.13W
Bayburt	78	40.16N	40.15 E
Bay City, Mi., U.S.	102	43.35N	83.53W
Bay City, Tx., U.S.	100	28.58N	95.58W
Baydhabo	82	3.07N	43.39 E
Bayern □3	46	49.00N	11.30 E
Bayeux	48	49.16N	0.42W
Bayhead	38	57.33N	7.24W
Bayiji	66	34.18N	117.41 E
Bayındır	54	38.13N	27.40 E
Baykonur →Bajkonyr	56	47.50N	66.03 E
Bayley Point ›	92	16.56S	139.02 E
Baynūnah ◆1	78	23.50N	52.45 E
Bayo	50	43.09N	8.58W
Bayon	48	48.29N	6.19 E
Bayona	50	42.07N	8.51W
Bayonne	48	43.29N	1.29W
Bayóvar	110	5.50S	81.03W
Bay Port	102	43.50N	83.22W
Bayreuth	46	49.57N	11.35 E
Bayrischzell	46	47.40N	12.00 E
Bayrūt (Beirut)	78	33.53N	35.30 E
Bays, Lake of ⊜	102	45.15N	79.04W
Bay Shore	102	40.43N	73.14W
Bayside	102	44.07N	77.30W
Bayston Hill	34	52.40N	2.45W
Bayt al-Faqīh	74	14.32N	43.20 E
Bayt Laḥm	78	31.43N	35.12 E
Baytown	100	29.44N	94.58W
Bay View	96	39.25S	176.53 E
Baza	50	37.29N	2.46W
Baza, Sierra de ⋀	50	37.15N	2.45W
Bazargic →Tolbuhin	54	43.34N	27.50 E
Bazaruto, Ilha do I	86	21.40S	35.28 E
Bazas	48	44.26N	0.13W
Baziège	48	43.27N	1.37 E
Be, Nosy I	87b	13.20S	48.15 E
Beach Haven	102	39.33N	74.14W
Beachport	94	37.30S	140.01 E
Beachville	102	43.05N	80.49W
Beachy Head ›	34	50.44N	0.16 E
Beacon, Austl.	90	30.26S	117.51 E
Beacon, N.Y., U.S.	102	41.30N	73.58W
Beacon Hill ∧2	34	52.23N	3.12W
Beaconsfield, Austl.	94	41.12S	146.48 E
Beaconsfield, Eng., U.K.	34	51.37N	0.39W
Beagh, Slieve ∧2	40	54.21N	7.12W
Beagle Bay Mission	90	16.58S	122.40 E
Beagle Gulf c	92	12.00S	130.20 E
Beagle Reef ✢2	88	15.20S	123.29 E
Bealanana	87b	14.33S	48.44 E
Beaminster	34	50.49N	2.45W
Bear ≃	104	38.57N	121.35W
Bear Bay c	98	75.47N	87.00W
Bear Creek ≃	104	42.26N	122.58W
Beardmore	98	49.36N	87.57W
Bear Island I	40	51.40N	9.48W
Bear Island →Bjørnøya I	26	74.25N	19.00 E
Bear Lake ⊜	100	42.00N	111.20W
Béarn □9	48	43.20N	0.45W
Bearsden	38	55.56N	4.20W
Beasain	50	43.03N	2.11W
Beas de Segura	50	38.15N	2.53W
Beata, Cabo ›	108	17.36N	71.25W
Beata, Isla I	108	17.35N	71.31W
Beatrice	100	40.16N	96.44W
Beatrice, Cape ›	92	14.15S	136.59 E
Beattock	38	55.18N	3.28W
Beatton ≃	98	56.10N	120.25W
Beatty	104	36.54N	116.45W
Beaucaire	48	43.48N	4.38 E
Beauce ◆1	48	48.22N	1.50 E
Beaudesert	94	27.59S	153.00 E
Beaufort, Malay.	72	5.20N	115.45 E
Beaufort, S.C., U.S.	100	32.25N	80.40W
Beaufort, Cape ›	90	34.26S	115.32 E
Beaufort Sea ≂2	98	72.00N	130.00W
Beaufort West	86	32.18S	22.36 E
Beaugency	48	47.47N	1.38 E
Beauharnois	102	45.19N	73.52W
Beaujolais, Monts du ⋀	48	46.00N	4.30 E
Beaulieu	34	50.49N	1.27W
Beauly	38	57.29N	4.29W
Beauly ≃	38	57.28N	4.28W
Beauly Firth c1	38	57.30N	4.23W
Beaumaris	36	53.16N	4.05W
Beaumont, Fr.	48	49.40N	1.51W
Beaumont, N.Z.	96	45.49S	169.32 E
Beaumont, Ca., U.S.	104	33.55N	116.58W
Beaumont, Tx., U.S.	100	30.05N	94.06W
Beaumont Hill ∧2	94	31.33S	145.13 E
Beaumont-sur-Sarthe	48	48.13N	0.08 E
Beaune	48	47.02N	4.50 E
Beaune-la-Rolande	48	48.04N	2.26 E
Beaupré	98	47.03N	70.54W
Beaupréau	48	47.12N	1.00W
Beaurepaire	48	45.20N	5.03 E
Beausejour	98	50.04N	96.33W
Beauvais	48	49.26N	2.05 E
Beauville	48	44.17N	0.52 E
Beauvoir-sur-Mer	48	46.55N	2.02W
Beauvoir-sur-Niort	48	46.11N	0.28W
Beaver	102	40.41N	80.18W
Beaver ≃, Can.	98	59.43N	124.16W
Beaver ≃, Can.	98	55.25N	107.45W
Beaver ≃, N.Y., U.S.	102	43.54N	75.30W
Beaver ≃, Pa., U.S.	102	40.40N	80.18W
Beaver Falls	102	40.45N	80.19W
Beaver Island I	102	45.40N	85.31W
Beaverton, On., Can.	102	44.26N	79.09W
Beaverton, Mi., U.S.	102	43.52N	84.29W
Beāwar	76	26.06N	74.19 E
Beazley	114	33.45S	66.39W
Bebington	36	53.23N	3.01W
Bécancour ≃	102	46.22N	72.27W
Beccles	34	52.28N	1.34 E
Bečej	54	45.37N	20.03 E
Beceni	54	45.23N	26.46 E
Becerreá	50	42.51N	7.10W
Béchar	80	31.37N	2.13W
Bechet	54	43.46N	23.58 E
Bechuanaland →Botswana □1	84	22.00S	24.00 E
Bechuanaland ◆1	86	27.10S	22.10 E
Bechyně	46	49.18N	14.29 E
Beckington	34	51.16N	2.18W
Beckley	102	37.46N	81.11W
Beckum	46	51.45N	8.02 E
Becky Peak ∧	104	39.58N	114.36W
Beclean	54	47.11N	24.10 E
Bedale	36	54.17N	1.35W
Bédarieux	48	43.37N	3.09 E
Beddgelert	36	53.01N	4.06W
Beddome, Mount ∧	90	25.50S	134.22 E
Bedele	82	8.33N	36.23 E
Bedford, P.Q., Can.	102	45.07N	72.59W
Bedford, S. Afr.	86	32.41S	26.05 E
Bedford, Eng., U.K.	34	52.08N	0.29W
Bedford, Pa., U.S.	102	40.01N	78.30W
Bedford, Cape ›	92	15.14S	145.21 E
Bedford Harbour c	90	33.35S	120.35 E
Bedford Level ≚	34	52.27N	0.02W
Bedfordshire □6	34	52.05N	0.30W
Bedi	76	22.30N	70.02 E
Bedlington	32	55.08N	1.35W
Bedlington ≃	36	55.10N	1.34W
Bednodemjanovsk	60	53.56N	43.10 E
Bedourie	94	24.21S	139.28 E
Bedwas	34	51.35N	3.13W
Bedworth	34	52.28N	1.29W
Beechworth	94	36.22S	146.41 E
Beecroft Head ›	94	35.01S	150.51 E
Beela ≃	36	54.13N	2.47W
Beelitz	46	52.14N	12.58 E
Beenleigh	94	27.43S	153.12 E
Beeringgnurding ∧	90	29.53S	117.55 E
Beersheba →Be'er Sheva'	78	31.14N	34.47 E
Be'er Sheva'	78	31.14N	34.47 E
Beeskow	46	52.10N	14.14 E
Beestekraal	86	25.23S	27.38 E
Beeston	34	52.56N	1.12W
Beeville	100	28.24N	97.44W
Befale	84	0.28N	20.58 E
Befandriana	87b	15.16S	48.32 E
Beg, Lough ⊜	36	54.47N	6.28W
Bega	94	36.40S	149.50 E
Bega (Begej) ≃	54	45.13N	20.19 E
Begamganj	76	23.36N	78.20 E
Begej (Bega) ≃	54	45.13N	20.19 E
Begičevskij	60	53.47N	38.15 E
Beglés	48	44.47N	0.34W
Begoml'	60	54.44N	28.04 E
Begusarai	76	25.25N	86.08 E
Behbehān	78	30.35N	50.14 E
Behshahr	78	36.43N	53.34 E
Bei ≃	62	23.09N	112.48 E
Bei'an	62	48.16N	126.36 E
Beida →Al-Bayḍā'	82	32.46N	21.43 E
Beighton	36	53.20N	1.20W
Beigi	82	9.20N	34.29 E
Beihai	70	21.29N	109.05 E
Beijing (Peking)	62	39.55N	116.25 E
Beijing Shi (Peking Shih) □7	62	40.15N	116.30 E
Beiliu	70	22.42N	110.22 E
Beipiao	62	41.49N	120.46 E
Beira	86	19.49S	34.52 E
Beira Baixa □9	50	39.45N	7.30W
Beira Litoral □9	50	40.15N	8.25W
Beirut →Bayrūt	78	33.53N	35.30 E
Bei Shan ⋀	62	41.30N	96.00 E
Beitbridge	86	22.13S	30.00 E
Beith	38	55.45N	4.38W
Beitstadfjorden c2	44	63.53N	11.00 E
Beiuş	54	46.40N	22.21 E
Beiwudu	66	33.39N	113.39 E
Beja, Port.	50	38.01N	7.52W
Béja, Tun.	80	36.44N	9.11 E
Bejaïa	80	36.45N	5.05 E
Béjar	50	40.23N	5.46W
Bejestān	78	34.31N	58.10 E
Bejneu	56	45.15N	55.07 E
Bejuma	108	10.11N	68.16W
Bekabad	56	40.13N	69.14 E
Bekdaš	56	41.34N	52.32 E
Békés	46	46.46N	21.08 E
Békés □6	46	46.46N	21.08 E
Békéscsaba	46	46.41N	21.06 E
Bekily	87b	24.13S	45.19 E
Bela, India	76	25.56N	81.59 E
Bela, Pāk.	76	26.14N	66.19 E
Bélâbre	48	46.33N	1.09 E
Bela Crkva	54	44.54N	21.26 E
Belaga	72	2.42N	113.47 E
Bel Air	102	39.32N	76.20W
Belaja ≃	56	55.54N	53.33 E
Belaja Cerkov'	56	49.49N	30.07 E
Belaja Cholunica	42	58.50N	50.48 E
Bel'ajevka	54	46.29N	30.12 E
Belalcázar	50	38.34N	5.10W
Belambanganumpu	72	4.54S	105.03 E
Bela Palanka	54	43.13N	22.19 E
Belau (Palau) □2	28	5.00N	137.00 E

Symbols in the Index entries are identified on page 122.

Name	Page	Lat. °′	Long. °′
Bela Vista, Bra.	114	22.06 S	56.31 W
Bela Vista, Moç.	86	26.20 S	32.40 E
Bela Vista do Paraiso	114	23.00 S	51.12 W
Belawan	70	3.47 N	98.41 E
Belayan ≃	72	0.14 S	116.36 E
Bełchatów	46	51.22 N	19.21 E
Belcher Islands II	98	56.20 N	79.30 W
Belchite	50	41.18 N	0.45 W
Belcoo	40	54.17 N	7.52 W
Bel'cy	56	47.46 N	27.56 E
Belding	102	43.05 N	85.13 W
Belebej	56	54.07 N	54.07 E
Beled Weyne	82	4.45 N	45.12 E
Belém	110	1.27 S	48.29 W
Belén, Arg.	114	27.39 S	67.02 W
Belén, Nic.	108	11.30 N	85.53 W
Belén, Para.	114	23.30 S	57.06 W
Belen, N.M., U.S.	100	34.39 N	106.46 W
Belén, Ur.	114	30.47 S	57.47 W
Belén ≃	114	28.00 S	66.52 W
Belén de Escobar	114	34.21 S	58.47 W
Belene	54	43.39 N	25.07 E
Belesar, Embalse de ⊜1	50	42.45 N	7.40 W
Belfast, N.Z.	96	43.27 S	172.38 E
Belfast, S. Afr.	86	25.43 S	30.03 E
Belfast, N. Ire., U.K.	40	54.35 N	5.55 W
Belfast, Me., U.S.	102	44.25 N	69.00 W
Belfast Lough ⊂	40	54.40 N	5.50 W
Belford	36	55.36 N	1.49 W
Belfort	48	47.38 N	6.52 E
Belgaum	74	15.52 N	74.31 E
Belgium □1	30	50.50 N	4.00 E
Belgodère	52	42.35 N	9.01 E
Belgorod	56	50.36 N	36.35 E
Belgorod-Dnestrovskij	56	46.12 N	30.20 E
Belgrade →Beograd	54	44.50 N	20.30 E
Beli Drim ≃	54	42.06 N	20.25 E
Beli Manastir	54	45.46 N	18.36 E
Belin	48	44.30 N	0.47 W
Belington	102	39.01 N	79.56 W
Belitung I	72	2.50 S	107.55 E
Belize □1	106	17.15 N	88.45 W
Belize City	106	17.30 N	88.12 W
Bel'kovskij, Ostrov I	58	75.32 N	135.44 E
Bell ≃	98	49.48 N	77.38 W
Bella Bella	98	52.09 N	128.07 W
Bellac	48	46.07 N	1.02 E
Bella Coola	98	52.22 N	126.46 W
Bellagio	52	45.59 N	9.15 E
Bellahy	40	53.58 N	8.48 W
Bellaire, Mi., U.S.	102	44.58 N	85.12 W
Bellaire, Oh., U.S.	102	40.00 N	80.45 W
Bellaria	52	44.09 N	12.28 E
Bellary	74	15.09 N	76.56 E
Bellata	94	29.55 S	149.47 E
Bella Unión	114	30.15 S	57.35 W
Bella Vista, Arg.	114	27.02 S	65.18 W
Bella Vista, Arg.	114	28.30 S	59.03 W
Bella Vista, Para.	114	22.08 S	56.31 W
Bellavista, Perú	110	7.04 S	76.35 W
Bellavista, Perú	110	4.54 S	80.42 W
Bellbrook	94	30.49 S	152.31 E
Bell Crags ∧2	36	55.03 N	2.22 W
Belle	102	38.13 N	81.32 W
Belle ≃	102	42.43 N	82.30 W
Belledonne, Chaîne de ✶	48	45.18 N	6.08 E
Belleek	40	54.28 N	8.06 W
Bellefontaine	102	40.21 N	83.45 W
Bellefonte	102	40.54 N	77.46 W
Belle Fourche	100	44.40 N	103.51 W
Bellegarde	48	46.06 N	5.49 E
Belle Glade	100	26.41 N	80.40 W
Belle-Île I	48	47.20 N	3.10 W
Belle Isle I	98	51.55 N	55.20 W
Belle Isle, Strait of ⋓	98	51.35 N	56.30 W
Bellême	48	48.22 N	0.34 E
Belleville, On., Can.	102	44.10 N	77.23 W
Belleville, Il., U.S.	100	38.31 N	89.59 W
Belleville, Ks., U.S.	100	39.49 N	97.37 W
Belleville, Pa., U.S.	102	40.36 N	77.43 W
Belleville-sur-Saône	48	46.06 N	4.45 E
Bellevue, Id., U.S.	104	43.27 N	114.15 W
Bellevue, Mi., U.S.	102	42.26 N	85.01 W
Bellevue, Oh., U.S.	102	41.16 N	82.50 W
Belley	48	45.46 N	5.41 E
Bellingen	94	30.27 S	152.54 E
Bellingham, Eng., U.K.	36	55.09 N	2.16 W
Bellingham, Wa., U.S.	100	48.45 N	122.29 W
Bellingshausen Sea ∓2	24	71.00 S	85.00 W
Bellinzona	48	46.11 N	9.02 E
Bello	110	6.20 N	75.33 W
Bellona Plateau ✦3	28	20.30 S	158.30 E
Bellona Reefs ✦2	88	21.30 S	159.00 E
Bellot Strait ⋓	98	71.58 N	94.45 W
Bellows Falls	102	43.08 N	72.26 W
Bell Peninsula ›1	98	63.50 N	82.00 W
Bellsbank	36	55.18 N	4.23 W
Bells Corners	102	45.19 N	75.50 W
Bellshill	38	55.49 N	4.01 W
Belluno	52	46.09 N	12.13 E
Bell Ville, Arg.	114	32.37 S	62.42 W
Bellville, S. Afr.	86	33.53 S	18.36 E
Bellville, Oh., U.S.	102	40.37 N	82.30 W
Bellwood	102	40.36 N	78.19 W
Bélmez	50	38.16 N	5.12 W
Belmont, S. Afr.	86	29.28 S	24.22 E
Belmont, N.H., U.S.	102	43.26 N	71.28 W
Belmont, N.Y., U.S.	102	42.13 N	78.02 W
Belmonte, Bra.	110	15.51 S	38.54 W
Belmonte, Esp.	50	43.17 N	6.14 W
Belmonte, Esp.	50	39.34 N	2.42 W
Belmonte, Port.	50	40.21 N	7.21 W
Belmopan	106	17.15 N	88.46 W
Belmullet	40	54.14 N	10.00 W
Belo	87b	19.42 S	44.33 E
Belogorsk	58	50.57 N	128.25 E
Belogradčik	54	43.38 N	22.41 E
Belo Horizonte	110	19.55 S	43.56 W
Beloit	100	42.30 N	89.01 W
Beloje, ozero ⊜	60	60.11 N	37.37 E
Beloje more (White Sea) ∓2	42	65.30 N	38.00 E
Belomorsk	42	64.32 N	34.48 E
Beloomut	60	54.57 N	39.20 E
Beloozersk	60	52.28 N	25.11 E
Belorado	50	42.25 N	3.11 W
Belorečensk	56	44.46 N	39.52 E
Beloreck	56	53.58 N	58.24 E
Belorusskaja Sovetskaja Socialističeskaja Respublika □3	56	53.50 N	28.00 E
Belot, Lac ⊜	98	66.55 N	126.18 W
Bel'ov	60	53.48 N	36.08 E
Belovo	56	54.25 N	86.18 E
Beloz'orsk	60	60.02 N	37.48 E
Belpasso	52	37.50 N	14.58 E
Belper	34	53.01 N	1.29 W
Belpre	102	39.16 N	81.34 W
Beltana	94	30.48 S	138.25 E
Belted Range ✶	104	37.25 N	116.10 W
Belton, Eng., U.K.	34	52.34 N	1.41 E
Belton, Eng., U.K.	36	53.33 N	0.49 W
Beltra	40	54.13 N	8.37 W
Beltrán	114	27.50 S	64.04 W
Belturbet	40	54.06 N	7.28 W
Belucha, gora ∧	58	49.48 N	86.40 E
Belūr	74	13.10 N	75.52 E
Beluran	72	5.54 N	117.33 E
Belvedere Marittimo	52	39.37 N	15.52 E
Belvès	48	44.47 N	1.00 E
Belvidere	102	40.49 N	75.04 W
Belvis de la Jara	50	39.45 N	4.57 W
Belvoir, Vale of ∨	34	52.57 N	0.53 W
Belyando ≃	94	21.38 S	146.50 E
Belyj	60	55.50 N	32.56 E
Belyj, ostrov I	56	73.10 N	70.45 E
Belyje Berega	60	53.12 N	34.40 E
Belyj Gorodok	60	56.58 N	37.30 E
Belyj Jar	58	58.26 N	85.01 E
Belyniči	60	53.59 N	29.42 E
Belz	48	47.41 N	3.10 W
Bełżec	46	50.24 N	23.26 E
Belzig	46	52.08 N	12.35 E
Bełżyce	46	51.11 N	22.18 E
Bembézar ≃	50	37.45 N	5.13 W
Bembridge	34	50.41 N	1.05 W
Bemidji	100	47.28 N	94.52 W
Benāb	78	37.20 N	46.04 E
Benabarre	50	42.07 N	0.29 E
Bena-Dibele	84	4.07 S	22.50 E
Benagerie	94	31.25 S	140.24 E
Benalla	94	36.33 S	145.59 E
Benamejí	50	37.16 N	4.32 W
Benares →Vārānasi	74	25.20 N	83.00 E
Benavente, Esp.	50	42.00 N	5.41 W
Benavente, Port.	50	38.59 N	8.48 W
Benbane Head ›	40	55.15 N	6.28 W
Benbecula I	38	57.26 N	7.21 W
Benbonyathe Hill ∧	94	30.24 S	139.11 E
Bencubbin	90	30.48 S	117.52 E
Bend	100	44.03 N	121.18 W
Bendemeer	94	30.53 S	151.10 E
Bendery	56	46.48 N	29.29 E
Bendigo	94	36.46 S	144.17 E
Bendorf	46	50.25 N	7.34 E
Benedito Leite	110	7.13 S	44.34 W
Benemérita de San Cristóbal	108	18.25 N	70.06 W
Beneraird ∧2	36	55.04 N	4.57 W
Benešov	46	49.47 N	14.43 E
Bénestroff	48	48.55 N	6.45 E
Bénévent-l'Abbaye	48	46.07 N	1.38 E
Benevento	52	41.08 N	14.45 E
Benfeld	48	48.22 N	7.36 E
Bengal, Bay of ⊂	26	15.00 N	90.00 E
Bengbu	66	32.58 N	117.24 E
Benghazi →Banghāzī	82	32.07 N	20.04 E
Bengkalis	72	1.28 N	102.07 E
Bengkayang	72	0.50 N	109.29 E
Bengkulu	72	3.48 S	102.16 E
Bengkulu □4	72	4.00 S	102.30 E
Bengtsfors	44	59.02 N	12.13 E
Benguela	84	12.35 S	13.25 E
Beni	84	0.30 N	29.28 E
Beni ≃	110	10.23 S	65.24 W
Béni Abbas	80	30.08 N	2.10 W
Benicarló	50	40.25 N	0.26 E
Benidorm	50	38.32 N	0.08 W
Beni-Mellal	80	32.22 N	6.29 W
Benin (Bénin) □1	80	9.30 N	2.15 E
Benin, Bight of ⊂3	80	5.30 N	3.00 E
Benin City	80	6.19 N	5.41 E
Benisa	50	38.34 N	0.03 E
Benjamín Aceval	114	24.58 S	57.34 W
Benjamin Constant	110	4.22 S	70.02 W
Benjamín Zorrilla	114	39.06 S	65.29 W
Benkovac	52	44.02 N	15.37 E
Benlidi	94	24.34 S	144.52 E
Benllech	36	53.19 N	4.13 W
Ben Lomond	104	37.05 N	122.05 W
Benmore, Lake ⊜1	96	44.25 S	170.15 E
Bennett, Lake ⊜	90	22.55 S	130.57 E
Bennetta, ostrov I	58	76.21 N	148.56 E
Bennettsbridge	40	52.36 N	7.12 W
Bennington	102	42.52 N	73.11 W
Benniu	66	31.52 N	119.48 E
Ben Ohau Range ✶	96	44.00 S	170.00 E
Benom, Gunong ∧	72	3.49 N	102.04 E
Benoni	86	26.11 S	28.19 E
Bénoué (Benue) ≃	80	7.48 N	6.46 E
Bensheim	46	49.41 N	8.37 E
Benson	34	51.38 N	1.05 W
Benteng (Salayar)	72	6.08 S	120.27 E
Bentinck Island I	94	17.04 S	139.30 E
Bentley	36	53.33 N	1.09 W
Bento Gonçalves	114	29.10 S	51.31 W
Benton	102	41.11 N	76.23 W
Bentong	72	3.32 N	101.55 E
Benton Harbor	100	42.07 N	86.26 W
Benue (Bénoué) ≃	80	7.48 N	6.46 E
Benwee ∧	40	53.35 N	9.31 W
Benwee Head ›	40	54.20 N	9.50 W
Benxi	62	41.18 N	123.45 E
Beograd (Belgrade)	54	44.50 N	20.30 E
Beohāri	76	24.03 N	81.23 E
Beowawe	104	40.35 N	116.28 W
Beppu	64	33.17 N	131.30 E
Bequia I	108	13.01 N	61.13 W
Berat	54	40.42 N	19.57 E
Berau, Teluk ⊂	92	2.30 S	132.30 E
Berbera	82	10.25 N	45.02 E
Berbérati	82	4.16 N	15.47 E
Berbería, Cabo ›	50	38.38 N	1.23 E
Berbice ≃	110	6.17 N	57.32 W
Berceto	52	44.31 N	9.59 E
Berchtesgaden	46	47.38 N	13.01 E
Berck	48	50.24 N	1.34 E
Berd'ansk	56	46.45 N	36.49 E
Berdičev	56	49.54 N	28.36 E
Berdigest'ach	58	62.06 N	126.40 E
Berdsk	56	54.47 N	83.02 E
Berea	102	41.21 N	81.51 W
Bere Alston	34	50.29 N	4.11 W
Berekua	108	15.14 N	61.19 W
Berendejevo	60	56.36 N	39.01 E
Berens ≃	98	52.21 N	97.02 W
Berens River	98	52.22 N	97.02 W
Bere Regis	34	50.46 N	2.14 W
Beresford	94	29.14 S	136.40 E
Bereşti	54	46.06 N	27.53 E
Beretău (Berettyó) ≃	54	46.59 N	21.07 E
Berettyó (Beretău) ≃	54	46.59 N	21.07 E
Berettyóújfalu	46	47.14 N	21.32 E
Berezajka	60	57.59 N	33.54 E
Berezino	60	53.49 N	28.59 E
Berezniki	56	59.24 N	56.46 E
Berg	42	69.26 N	17.15 E
Berga	50	42.06 N	1.51 E
Bergama	30	39.07 N	27.11 E
Bergamo	52	45.41 N	9.43 E
Bergantín	108	10.01 N	64.22 W
Bergby	44	60.56 N	17.02 E
Bergen, B.R.D.	46	52.53 N	10.58 E
Bergen, Ned.	46	52.40 N	4.41 E
Bergen, Nor.	44	60.23 N	5.20 E
Bergen, N.Y., U.S.	102	43.05 N	77.56 W
Bergen [auf Rügen]	46	54.25 N	13.26 E
Bergen op Zoom	46	51.30 N	4.17 E
Bergerac	48	44.51 N	0.29 E
Bergisch	46	51.09 N	7.15 E
Bergisch Gladbach	46	50.59 N	7.07 E
Bergkvara	44	56.23 N	16.05 E
Bergö I	44	62.58 N	21.11 E
Bergoo	102	38.29 N	80.18 W
Bergsjö	44	61.59 N	17.04 E
Bergslagen ✦1	44	59.55 N	15.00 E
Berguent	80	34.03 N	2.02 W
Bergues	48	50.58 N	2.26 E
Bergville	86	28.52 S	29.18 E
Berhala, Selat ⋓	72	0.48 S	104.25 E
Berhampore	76	24.06 N	88.15 E
Berhampur	74	19.19 N	84.47 E
Beringa, ostrov I	58	55.00 N	165.15 E
Beringovskij	58	63.03 N	179.19 E
Bering Sea ∓2	22	60.00 N	175.00 W
Bering Strait ⋓	22	65.30 N	169.00 W
Berinsfield	34	51.40 N	1.11 W
Berja	50	36.51 N	2.57 W
Berkåk	44	62.50 N	10.00 E
Berkeley, Eng., U.K.	34	51.42 N	2.27 W
Berkeley, Ca., U.S.	104	37.52 N	122.16 W
Berkeley, Vale of ∨	34	51.43 N	2.25 W
Berkeley Springs	102	39.37 N	78.13 W
Berkhamsted	34	51.46 N	0.35 W
Berkshire □6	34	51.30 N	1.20 W
Berkshire Downs ✶1	34	51.33 N	1.24 W
Berkshire Hills ✶2	102	42.20 N	73.10 W
Berlaimont	48	50.12 N	3.49 E
Berlanga de Duero	50	41.28 N	2.51 W
Berlenga I	50	39.25 N	9.30 W
Berlevåg	42	70.51 N	29.06 E
Berlin (West), B.R.D.	46	52.31 N	13.24 E
Berlin (Ost), D.D.R.	46	52.30 N	13.25 E
Berlin, S. Afr.	86	32.54 S	27.35 E
Berlin, Md., U.S.	102	38.19 N	75.13 W
Berlin, N.H., U.S.	102	44.28 N	71.11 W
Berlin, N.J., U.S.	102	39.47 N	74.55 W
Berlin, Pa., U.S.	102	39.55 N	78.57 W
Berlin □5	46	52.33 N	13.30 E
Berlinguet Inlet ⊂	98	71.10 N	85.35 W
Berlin Lake ⊜1	102	41.00 N	81.00 W
Bermagui	94	36.25 S	150.04 E
Bermejo	114	31.37 S	67.39 W
Bermejo ≃, Arg.	114	31.52 S	67.22 W
Bermejo ≃, S.A.	114	26.51 S	58.23 W
Bermejo, Paso de)(	114	32.50 S	70.05 W
Bermen, Lac ⊜	98	53.35 N	68.55 W
Bermeo	50	43.26 N	2.43 W
Bermillo de Sayago	50	41.22 N	6.06 W
Bermo	76	23.47 N	85.57 E
Bermuda □2	100	32.20 N	64.45 W
Bermuda Rise ✦3	22	32.30 N	65.00 W
Bern (Berne)	48	46.57 N	7.26 E
Bernalda	52	40.24 N	16.41 E
Bernasconi	114	37.54 S	63.43 W
Bernau bei Berlin	46	52.40 N	13.35 E
Bernaville	32	50.08 N	2.10 E
Bernay	48	49.06 N	0.36 E
Bernburg	46	51.48 N	11.44 E
Berndorf	46	47.57 N	16.08 E
Berne →Bern, Schw.	48	46.57 N	7.26 E
Berne, In., U.S.	102	40.39 N	84.57 W
Berner Alpen ✶	48	46.30 N	7.30 E
Berneray I	38	57.43 N	7.12 W
Bernier Bay ⊂	98	71.00 N	87.30 W
Bernier Island I	90	24.52 S	113.08 E
Bernina, Piz ∧	48	46.21 N	9.51 E
Bernisdale	38	57.27 N	6.24 W
Bernkastel-Kues	46	49.55 N	7.04 E
Bernsdorf	46	51.22 N	14.04 E
Beromünster	48	47.12 N	8.11 E
Berón de Astrada	114	27.33 S	57.32 W
Beroroha	87b	21.41 S	45.10 E
Beroun	46	49.58 N	14.04 E
Berounka ≃	46	50.00 N	14.24 E
Berovo	54	41.42 N	22.51 E
Ber'oza	60	52.32 N	24.59 E
Ber'ozovka, S.S.S.R.	42	65.00 N	56.26 E
Ber'ozovka, S.S.S.R.	60	53.43 N	25.30 E
Ber'ozovo	56	63.56 N	65.02 E
Berre, Étang de ⊂	48	43.27 N	5.08 E
Berri	94	34.17 S	140.36 E
Berriedale	38	58.11 N	3.29 W
Berrigan	94	35.40 S	145.49 E
Berry □9	48	47.20 N	2.10 E
Berryessa, Lake ⊜1	104	38.35 N	122.14 W
Berry Head ›	34	50.24 N	3.29 W
Berry Islands II	108	25.34 N	77.45 W
Bersenbrück	46	52.33 N	7.56 E
Bertam	72	5.09 N	102.03 E
Bertinoro	52	44.09 N	12.08 E
Bertoua	80	4.35 N	13.41 E
Beru I	28	1.20 S	176.00 E
Berwick, Me., U.S.	102	43.15 N	70.51 W
Berwick, Pa., U.S.	102	41.03 N	76.14 W
Berwick-upon-Tweed	36	55.46 N	2.00 W
Berwyn ✶	34	52.53 N	3.24 W
Besalampy	87b	16.45 S	44.30 E
Besançon	48	47.15 N	6.02 E
Besar, Gunong ∧	72	2.30 N	103.10 E
Besaya ≃	50	43.21 N	4.04 W
Beskid Mountains ✶	46	49.40 N	20.00 E
Beskra	80	34.51 N	5.44 E
Beslan	56	43.12 N	44.33 E
Bessacarr	36	53.30 N	1.04 W
Bessarabia □9	54	47.00 N	28.30 E
Bessbrook	40	54.12 N	6.25 W
Bessemer, Al., U.S.	100	33.24 N	86.57 W
Bessemer, Pa., U.S.	102	40.58 N	80.29 W
Bessheim	44	61.31 N	8.51 E
Best	46	51.31 N	5.24 E
Best'ach	58	61.52 N	129.55 E
Bestobe	56	52.30 N	73.05 E
Betanzos	50	43.17 N	8.12 W
Betanzos, Ría de ⊂1	50	43.23 N	8.15 W
Betaré Oya	80	5.36 N	14.05 E
Betarsjön ⊜	44	63.44 N	16.52 E
Bétera	50	39.35 N	0.27 W
Bethal	86	26.27 S	29.28 E
Bethanien	86	26.32 S	17.11 E
Bethanien □5	86	26.30 S	17.00 E
Bethel, Ct., U.S.	102	41.22 N	73.24 W
Bethel, Me., U.S.	102	44.24 N	70.47 W
Bethel, Oh., U.S.	102	38.57 N	84.04 W
Bethelsdorp	86	33.52 S	25.34 E
Bethersden	34	51.08 N	0.48 E
Bethesda, Wales, U.K.	36	53.11 N	4.03 W
Bethesda, Oh., U.S.	102	40.00 N	81.04 W
Bethlehem, S. Afr.	86	28.15 S	28.15 E
Bethlehem, Pa., U.S.	102	40.37 N	75.22 W
Bethlehem, W.V., U.S.	102	40.02 N	80.41 W
Bethlehem →Bayt Laḥm, Urd.	78	31.43 N	35.12 E
Bethulie	86	30.32 S	25.59 E
Béthune	48	50.32 N	2.38 E
Beticos, Sistemas ✶	50	37.00 N	4.00 W
Betijoque	108	9.23 N	70.44 W
Betioky	87b	23.42 S	44.22 E
Betong, Malay.	72	1.24 N	111.31 E
Betong, Thai	70	5.45 N	101.05 E
Betoota	94	25.42 S	140.44 E
Betpak-Dala ✦2	56	46.00 N	70.00 E
Betroka	87b	23.16 S	46.06 E
Betsiamites ≃	98	48.56 N	68.38 W
Betsiboka ≃	87b	16.03 S	46.36 E
Betsukai	64a	43.23 N	145.17 E
Bette ∧	82	22.00 N	19.12 E
Bettiah	76	26.48 N	84.30 E
Bettyhill	38	58.32 N	4.14 W
Betūl	76	21.55 N	77.54 E
Betwa ≃	76	25.55 N	80.12 E
Betws-y-Coed	36	53.05 N	3.48 W
Betzdorf	46	50.47 N	7.53 E
Beulah	94	35.56 S	142.26 E
Beult ≃	34	51.14 N	0.25 E
Bevensen	46	53.05 N	10.34 E
Beverley, Austl.	90	32.06 S	116.56 E
Beverley, Eng., U.K.	36	53.52 N	0.26 W
Beverley Springs	92	16.43 S	125.28 E
Beverly	102	42.33 N	70.52 W
Beverly Hills	104	34.04 N	118.23 W
Beverly Lake ⊜	98	64.36 N	100.30 W
Beverungen	46	51.39 N	9.22 E
Beverwijk	46	52.28 N	4.40 E
Bewani Mountains ✶	92	3.10 S	141.25 E
Bewdley	34	52.22 N	2.19 W
Bewl Bridge Reservoir ⊜1	34	51.04 N	0.24 E
Bexhill	32	50.50 N	0.29 E
Bexhill on Sea	34	50.50 N	0.29 E
Bexley	102	39.58 N	82.56 W
Bexley ✦8	34	51.26 N	0.10 E
Beykoz	54	41.08 N	29.05 E
Beyşehir Gölü ⊜	30	37.40 N	31.30 E
Bežanicy	60	56.58 N	29.53 E
Bezau	46	47.23 N	9.54 E
Bežeck	60	57.47 N	36.39 E
Béziers	48	43.21 N	3.15 E
Bhadohi	76	25.25 N	82.34 E
Bhādra	76	29.07 N	75.10 E
Bhadrakh	76	21.03 N	86.30 E
Bhadrāvati	74	13.52 N	75.43 E
Bhāgalpur	76	25.15 N	87.00 E
Bhaironghāti	76	31.01 N	78.53 E
Bhakkar	76	31.38 N	71.04 E
Bhaktapur	76	27.42 N	85.27 E
Bhamo	70	24.16 N	97.14 E
Bhandāra	76	21.10 N	79.39 E
Bhānvad	76	21.56 N	69.47 E
Bharatpur	76	27.13 N	77.29 E
Bharthana	76	26.45 N	79.14 E
Bhātāpāra	76	21.44 N	81.56 E
Bhatewar	76	24.38 N	74.00 E
Bhatinda	76	30.12 N	74.57 E
Bhātpāra	76	22.52 N	88.24 E
Bhaunagar	76	21.46 N	72.09 E
Bhawāni Mandi	76	24.25 N	75.50 E
Bhawānipatna	74	19.54 N	83.10 E
Bheigeir, Beinn ∧2	38	55.44 N	6.05 W
Bheula, Beinn ∧	38	56.08 N	4.58 W
Bhikangaon	76	21.52 N	75.57 E
Bhilai	76	21.13 N	81.26 E
Bhilainagar →Bhilai	76	21.13 N	81.26 E
Bhīlwāra	76	25.21 N	74.38 E
Bhīma ≃	74	16.24 N	77.18 E
Bhind	76	26.34 N	78.48 E
Bhīnmāl	76	25.00 N	72.15 E
Bhiwāni	76	28.47 N	76.08 E
Bhopāl	76	23.16 N	77.24 E
Bhuban	76	20.53 N	85.50 E
Bhubaneswar	76	20.14 N	85.50 E
Bhuj	76	23.16 N	69.40 E
Bhusāwal	76	21.03 N	75.46 E
Bhutan (Druk-Yul) □1	74	27.30 N	90.30 E
Bia, Phou ∧	70	18.59 N	103.09 E
Biafra, Bight of ⊂3	80	4.00 N	8.00 E
Biak I	92	1.00 S	136.00 E
Biała	46	50.23 N	17.40 E
Biała ≃	46	50.03 N	20.55 E
Biała Piska	46	53.37 N	22.04 E
Biała Podlaska	46	52.02 N	23.06 E
Biała Rawska	46	51.49 N	20.29 E
Białobrzegi	46	51.40 N	20.57 E
Białogard	46	54.01 N	16.00 E
Biały Bór	46	53.54 N	16.51 E
Białystok	46	53.09 N	23.09 E
Bian, Bidean nam ∧	38	56.38 N	5.02 W
Bianco, Monte (Mont Blanc) ∧	48	45.50 N	6.52 E
Biaora	76	23.55 N	76.54 E
Biaro, Pulau I	72	2.05 N	125.20 E
Biarritz	48	43.29 N	1.34 W
Biasca	48	46.22 N	8.58 E
Bibai	64a	43.19 N	141.52 E
Bibala	84	14.46 S	13.21 E
Biberach an der Riss	46	48.06 N	9.47 E
Bibey ≃	50	42.24 N	7.13 W
Bicaz	54	46.54 N	26.05 E
Bicaz, Lacul ⊜1	54	47.00 N	26.00 E
Bicester	34	51.54 N	1.09 W
Bickerton Island I	92	13.45 S	136.12 E
Bickle Knob ∧	102	38.56 N	79.44 W
Bicknacre	34	51.41 N	0.35 E
Bicske	46	47.29 N	18.37 E
Bida	80	9.05 N	6.01 E
Bīdar	74	17.54 N	77.33 E
Biddeford	102	43.29 N	70.27 W
Biddenden	34	51.07 N	0.39 E
Biddulph	36	53.08 N	2.10 W
Bideford	34	51.01 N	4.13 W
Bidford-on-Avon	34	52.10 N	1.51 W
Bidwell	102	38.55 N	82.17 W
Bidwell, Mount ∧	104	41.58 N	120.10 W
Bieber	104	41.07 N	121.08 W
Biebrza ≃	46	53.13 N	22.25 E
Biecz	46	49.44 N	21.14 E
Biedenkopf	46	50.55 N	8.32 E
Biei	64a	43.35 N	142.28 E
Biel (Bienne)	48	47.10 N	7.12 E
Bielawa	46	50.41 N	16.38 E
Bielefeld	46	52.01 N	8.31 E
Bieler Lake ⊜	98	70.20 N	73.00 W
Bielersee ⊜	48	47.05 N	7.10 E
Biella	52	45.34 N	8.03 E
Bielsk	46	52.40 N	19.49 E
Bielsko-Biała	46	49.49 N	19.02 E
Bielsk Podlaski	46	52.47 N	23.12 E
Bien-hoa	70	10.57 N	106.49 E
Bienne →Biel	48	47.10 N	7.12 E
Bienville, Lac ⊜	98	55.05 N	72.40 W
Bierné	32	47.49 N	0.32 W
Bieruń Stary	46	50.06 N	19.06 E
Bierutów	46	51.08 N	17.32 E
Bietigheim	46	48.58 N	9.07 E
Biferno ≃	52	41.59 N	15.02 E
Bifuka	64a	44.29 N	142.21 E
Biga	54	40.13 N	27.14 E
Big Bay ⊂	96	44.18 S	168.05 E
Big Bear Lake	104	34.15 N	116.53 W
Big Bear Lake ⊜	104	34.15 N	116.55 W
Big Bell	90	27.21 S	117.40 E
Big Bend	86	26.50 S	31.57 E
Bigbury Bay ⊂	34	50.16 N	3.48 W
Big Creek	104	37.12 N	119.14 W
Big Creek ≃	102	42.36 N	80.27 W
Big Desert ✦2	94	35.40 S	141.00 E
Bigelow Bight ⊂3	102	43.15 N	70.30 W
Biggar, Sk., Can.	98	52.04 N	108.00 W
Biggar, Scot., U.K.	38	55.38 N	3.32 W
Bigge Island I	92	14.35 S	125.10 E
Biggin Hill ✦8	34	51.18 N	0.04 E
Biggleswade	34	52.05 N	0.17 W
Biggs	104	39.24 N	121.42 W
Big Gull Lake ⊜	102	44.50 N	76.58 W
Bighorn ≃	100	46.09 N	107.28 W
Bighorn Mountains ✶	100	44.00 N	107.30 W
Bight, Head of ›	90	31.30 S	131.10 E
Big Island I	98	62.43 N	70.43 W
Big Lake ⊜	102	45.10 N	67.40 W
Big Mountain ∧	104	41.17 N	119.04 W
Bignasco	48	46.20 N	8.36 E
Big Pine	104	37.09 N	118.17 W
Big Pine Mountain ∧	104	34.42 N	119.39 W
Big Quill Lake ⊜	98	51.55 N	104.22 W
Big Rapids	102	43.41 N	85.29 W
Big Rideau Lake ⊜	102	44.45 N	76.14 W
Big Sand Lake ⊜	98	57.45 N	99.42 W
Big Sandy ≃	102	38.25 N	82.36 W
Big Signal Peak ∧	104	39.31 N	123.06 W
Big Smoky Valley ∨	104	38.30 N	117.15 W
Big Spring	100	32.15 N	101.28 W
Big Spruce Knob ∧	102	38.16 N	80.12 W
Big Squaw Mountain ∧	102	45.30 N	69.45 W
Big Trout Lake ⊜	98	53.45 N	90.00 W
Biguaçu	114	27.30 S	48.40 W
Big Warrambool ≃	94	30.05 S	147.33 E
Big Wood ≃	104	42.52 N	114.54 W
Bihać	52	44.49 N	15.52 E
Bihār	76	25.11 N	85.31 E
Bihār □3	76	25.00 N	86.00 E
Biharamulo	84	2.38 S	31.20 E
Bihor □6	54	47.00 N	22.15 E
Bihoro	64a	43.49 N	144.07 E
Bihu	66	28.21 N	119.48 E
Bija ≃	58	52.25 N	85.05 E
Bijagós, Arquipélago dos II	80	11.25 N	16.20 W
Bijainagar	76	25.56 N	74.38 E
Bijaipura	76	24.46 N	77.48 E
Bijāpur, India	74	16.50 N	75.42 E
Bījāpur, India	74	18.48 N	80.49 E
Bījār	78	35.52 N	47.36 E
Bijeljina	54	44.45 N	19.13 E
Bijelo Polje	54	43.02 N	19.44 E
Bijeypur	76	26.03 N	77.22 E
Bijiang	70	26.30 N	98.55 E
Bijie	62	27.18 N	105.20 E
Bijsk	56	52.34 N	85.15 E
Bīkaner	76	28.01 N	73.18 E
Bikar I1	28	12.15 N	170.06 E
Bikeqi	62	40.45 N	111.17 E
Bikin	58	46.48 N	134.16 E
Bikin ≃	58	46.51 N	134.02 E
Bikini I1	28	11.35 N	165.23 E
Bikoro	84	0.45 S	18.07 E
Bilāra	76	26.10 N	73.42 E
Bilāri	76	28.38 N	78.48 E
Bilāsipāra	76	26.14 N	90.14 E
Bilāspur	76	22.05 N	82.09 E
Bilauktaung Range ✶	70	13.00 N	99.00 E
Bilauri	76	28.41 N	80.21 E
Bilbao	50	43.15 N	2.58 W
Bileća	54	42.53 N	18.26 E
Biłgoraj	46	50.34 N	22.43 E
Bilgrām	76	27.11 N	80.02 E
Bili ≃	82	4.09 N	22.29 E
Bilimora	76	20.45 N	72.57 E
Bílina	46	50.35 N	13.45 E
Biliran Island I	68	11.35 N	124.28 E
Billabong Creek ≃	94	35.06 S	144.02 E
Billericay	34	51.38 N	0.25 E
Billesdon	34	52.37 N	0.55 W
Billiluna	90	19.37 S	127.41 E
Billingham	36	54.36 N	1.17 W
Billings	100	45.46 N	108.30 W
Billingsfors	44	58.59 N	12.15 E
Billingshurst	34	51.01 N	0.28 W
Billom	48	45.44 N	3.21 E
Bilma	80	18.41 N	12.56 E
Biloela	94	24.24 S	150.30 E
Bilo Gora ✶	52	46.06 N	16.46 E
Biloxi	100	30.23 N	88.53 W
Bilpa Morea Claypan ≚	94	25.00 S	140.00 E
Bilston	34	52.34 N	2.04 W
Bilugyun Island I	70	16.24 N	97.32 E
Bilwaskarma	108	14.45 N	83.53 W
Bimbowrie	94	32.03 S	140.09 E
Bimini Islands II	108	25.42 N	79.15 W
Bīna-Etāwa	76	24.11 N	78.11 E
Binche	46	50.24 N	4.10 E
Bindal	42	65.06 N	12.30 E
Bindebango	94	27.45 S	147.24 E
Bindki	76	26.02 N	80.36 E
Bindura	84	17.19 S	31.20 E
Binéfar	50	41.51 N	0.18 E
Binga, Monte ∧	86	19.45 S	33.04 E
Bingara	94	29.52 S	150.34 E
Bingcha	66	32.30 N	120.52 E
Bingen	46	49.57 N	7.54 E
Bingham, Eng., U.K.	34	52.57 N	0.57 W
Bingham, Me., U.S.	102	45.03 N	69.52 W
Binghamton	102	42.05 N	75.55 W
Bingley	36	53.51 N	1.50 W
Bingöl	78	38.53 N	40.29 E
Binhai (Dongkan)	66	34.03 N	119.51 E
Binjai, Indon.	70	3.36 N	98.30 E
Binjai, Indon.	72	3.48 N	108.14 E
Binnaway	94	31.33 S	149.23 E
Binongko, Pulau I	72	5.57 S	124.02 E
Bintan, Pulau I	72	1.05 N	104.30 E
Bintimani ∧	80	9.13 N	11.07 W
Bintuhan	72	4.48 S	103.22 E
Bintulu	72	3.10 N	113.02 E
Binxian	62	35.00 N	108.08 E
Binyang	70	23.18 N	108.46 E
Biobío □4	114	37.00 S	72.30 W
Biobío ≃	114	36.49 S	73.10 W
Biograd	52	43.56 N	15.27 E
Bioko I	80	3.30 N	8.40 E
Bīr	74	18.59 N	75.46 E
Birāk	82	27.32 N	14.16 E
Birao	82	10.17 N	22.47 E
Birātnagar	76	26.29 N	87.17 E
Bîrca	54	43.58 N	23.37 E
Birch ≃, Ab., Can.	98	58.30 N	112.15 W
Birch ≃, W.V., U.S.	102	38.35 N	80.53 W
Birchington	34	51.23 N	1.19 E
Birch Mountains ✶2	98	57.30 N	112.30 W
Birch Run	102	43.15 N	83.47 W
Birchwood, N.Z.	96	45.56 S	167.52 E
Birchwood, Eng., U.K.	36	53.13 N	0.36 W
Bird Island I	112	54.00 S	38.05 W
Bird Islet I	88	22.10 S	155.28 E
Birdsville	94	25.54 S	139.22 E
Birdum	92	15.39 S	133.13 E
Bireuen	70	5.12 N	96.41 E
Bīrganj	76	27.00 N	84.52 E
Biril'ussy	58	57.07 N	90.32 E
Bīrjand	78	32.53 N	59.13 E
Birkeland	44	58.20 N	8.14 E
Birkenfeld	46	49.39 N	7.10 E
Birkenhead	36	53.24 N	3.02 W
Birkerød	44	55.50 N	12.26 E
Birkfeld	46	47.21 N	15.42 E
Birksgate Range ✶	90	27.10 S	129.45 E
Bîrlad	54	46.14 N	27.40 E
Bîrlad ≃	54	45.36 N	27.31 E
Birmingham, Eng., U.K.	34	52.30 N	1.50 W
Birmingham, Al., U.S.	100	33.31 N	86.48 W
Birmingham, Mi., U.S.	102	42.32 N	83.12 W
Birmitrapur	76	22.24 N	84.46 E
Bîr Mogreïn	80	25.14 N	11.35 W
Birnie I1	28	3.35 S	171.31 W
Birni Nkonni	80	13.48 N	5.15 E
Birobidžan	58	48.48 N	132.57 E
Birr	40	53.05 N	7.54 W
Birrie ≃	94	29.43 S	146.37 E
Birrindudu	90	18.22 S	129.27 E
Birsilpur	76	28.10 N	72.15 E
Birsk	56	55.25 N	55.32 E
Birstall	34	52.41 N	1.07 W
Birtley	36	54.54 N	1.34 W
Bir'usa ≃	58	57.43 N	95.24 E
Biržai	60	56.12 N	24.45 E
Bîrzava ≃	54	45.16 N	20.49 E
Birzebbuga	52	35.49 N	14.32 E
Bisa, Pulau I	92	1.15 S	127.28 E
Bisaccia	52	41.01 N	15.22 E
Bīsalpur	76	28.18 N	79.48 E
Biscarosse, Étang de ⊂	48	44.20 N	1.10 W
Biscarrosse	48	44.24 N	1.10 W
Biscay, Bay of ⊂	48	44.00 N	4.00 W
Bisceglie	52	41.14 N	16.31 E
Bischofshofen	46	47.25 N	13.13 E
Bischofswerda	46	51.07 N	14.10 E
Biscucuy	108	9.22 N	69.59 W
Bishenpur	76	24.38 N	93.46 E
Bisho	86	32.50 S	27.20 E
Bishop	104	37.21 N	118.23 W
Bishop Auckland	36	54.40 N	1.40 W
Bishop Rock I2	34a	49.52 N	6.27 W
Bishop's Castle	34	52.29 N	3.00 W
Bishop's Cleeve	34	51.57 N	2.04 W
Bishop's Falls	98	49.01 N	55.30 W
Bishops Frome	34	52.08 N	2.29 W
Bishops Lydeard	34	51.04 N	3.12 W
Bishop's Stortford	34	51.53 N	0.09 E
Bishopsteignton	34	50.34 N	3.31 W
Bishopstoke	34	50.59 N	1.19 W
Bishopston	34	51.35 N	4.03 W
Bishop's Waltham	34	50.58 N	1.12 W
Bishopthorpe	36	53.55 N	1.06 W
Bishrah, Ma'ṭan ∓4	82	22.58 N	22.39 E
Biskupiec	46	53.52 N	20.58 E
Bisley	34	51.45 N	2.08 W
Bislig	68	8.13 N	126.19 E
Bismarck	100	46.48 N	100.47 W
Bismarck Archipelago II	92	5.00 S	150.00 E
Bismarck Range ✶	92	5.30 S	144.45 E
Bismarck Sea ∓2	92	4.00 S	148.00 E
Bismo	44	61.53 N	8.16 E
Bispgården	44	63.02 N	16.37 E
Bissau	80	11.51 N	15.35 W
Bissett	98	51.02 N	95.40 W
Bistcho Lake ⊜	98	59.40 N	118.40 W
Bistra ≃	54	45.29 N	22.11 E
Bistreţ	54	43.54 N	23.30 E
Bistriţa	54	47.08 N	24.30 E
Bistriţa ≃	54	46.30 N	26.57 E
Bistriţa-Năsăud □6	54	47.15 N	24.30 E
Biswān	76	27.30 N	81.00 E
Bisztynek	46	54.06 N	20.55 E
Bitam	84	2.05 N	11.29 E
Bitburg	46	49.58 N	6.31 E
Bitche	48	49.03 N	7.26 E
Bitlis	78	38.22 N	42.06 E
Bitola	54	41.01 N	21.20 E
Bitolj →Bitola	54	41.01 N	21.20 E
Bitonto	52	41.06 N	16.42 E
Bitterfeld	46	51.37 N	12.20 E
Bitterfontein	86	31.00 S	18.32 E
Bitterness, Mount ∧	96	44.45 S	170.18 E
Bitterroot Range ✶	100	47.06 N	115.10 W
Bitti	52	40.29 N	9.23 E
Bitung	72	1.27 N	125.11 E
Bituruna	114	26.10 S	51.34 W
Biwa-ko ⊜	64	35.15 N	136.05 E
Biyang	66	32.44 N	113.20 E
Bizen	64	34.44 N	134.09 E
Bizerte	80	37.17 N	9.52 E
Bjala	54	43.27 N	25.44 E
Bjala Slatina	54	43.28 N	23.56 E
Bjargtangar ›	42a	65.31 N	24.32 W
Bjärnum	44	56.17 N	13.42 E
Bjästa	44	63.12 N	18.30 E
Bjelovar	52	45.54 N	16.51 E
Bjerringbro	44	56.23 N	9.40 E
Bjørkelangen	44	59.53 N	11.34 E
Björkö I	44	59.53 N	19.00 E
Björköby	44	63.21 N	21.19 E
Björna	44	63.34 N	18.33 E
Bjørnafjorden ⊂2	44	60.06 N	5.22 E
Bjornesfjorden ⊜	44	60.10 N	7.41 E
Bjørnøya (Bear Island) I	26	74.25 N	19.00 E
Bjurholm	44	63.56 N	19.13 E
Bjuv	44	56.05 N	12.54 E
Blaby	34	52.34 N	1.09 W
Blace	54	43.17 N	21.18 E
Black (Lixianjiang) (Da) ≃, Asia	70	21.15 N	105.20 E
Black ≃, On., Can.	102	44.42 N	79.19 W
Black ≃, On., Can.	102	44.32 N	77.22 W
Black ≃, Ak., U.S.	98	66.39 N	144.50 W
Black ≃, Mi., U.S.	102	45.39 N	84.29 W
Black ≃, Mi., U.S.	102	43.00 N	82.25 W
Black ≃, N.Y., U.S.	102	43.59 N	76.04 W
Black ≃, Vt., U.S.	102	43.16 N	72.27 W
Black ≃, Vt., U.S.	102	44.55 N	72.13 W
Blackadder Water ≃	38	55.46 N	2.15 W
Blackall	94	24.25 S	145.28 E
Blackburn, Eng., U.K.	36	53.45 N	2.29 W
Blackburn, Scot., U.K.	38	55.52 N	3.38 W
Black Butte Lake ⊜1	104	39.45 N	122.20 W
Blackcraig Hill ∧	36	55.20 N	4.08 W
Black Devon ≃	38	56.06 N	3.47 W
Black Down Hills ✶2	34	50.57 N	3.09 W
Black Duck ≃	98	56.51 N	89.02 W
Black Esk ≃	36	55.12 N	5.10 W
Blackford	38	56.15 N	3.46 W
Black Forest →Schwarzwald ✶	46	48.00 N	8.15 E
Blackhall Colliery	36	54.44 N	1.14 W
Black Head ›, Ire.	40	53.08 N	9.17 W
Black Head ›, Eng., U.K.	34	50.01 N	5.06 W
Black Hills ✶	100	44.00 N	104.00 W
Blackhope Scar ∧	38	55.44 N	3.05 W
Black Isle ›1	38	57.35 N	4.15 W
Black-Lake	102	46.03 N	71.21 W
Black Lake ⊜, Sk., Can.	98	59.10 N	105.20 W
Black Lake ⊜, Mi., U.S.	102	45.28 N	84.15 W
Black Lake ⊜, N.Y., U.S.	102	44.31 N	75.35 W
Blacklunans	38	56.44 N	3.22 W
Blackmoor ✶1	34	50.24 N	4.46 W
Blackmoor Vale ∨	34	50.56 N	2.25 W
Black Mountain ∧, Wales, U.K.	34	51.52 N	3.46 W
Black Mountain ∧, Ca., U.S.	104	35.24 N	120.21 W
Black Mountain ∧2	94	21.08 S	139.41 E
Black Mountains ✶	34	51.57 N	3.08 W
Black Peak ∧	104	34.08 N	114.13 W
Blackpool	36	53.50 N	3.03 W
Black River	102	44.00 N	75.47 W
Black Rock I2	40	54.05 N	10.22 W
Black Rock II1	112	53.39 S	41.48 W
Black Rock Desert ✦2	104	41.10 N	119.00 W
Black Sea ∓2	30	43.00 N	35.00 E
Blacks Harbour	102	45.03 N	66.47 W
Blacksod Bay ⊂	40	54.08 N	10.00 W
Blackstone ≃	98	65.51 N	137.12 W
Black Sugarloaf Mountain ∧	94	31.20 S	151.33 E
Black Volta (Volta Noire) ≃	80	8.41 N	1.33 W
Blackwater, Austl.	94	23.35 S	148.53 E
Blackwater, Ire.	40	52.26 N	6.21 W
Blackwater ≃, Europe	40	54.31 N	6.34 W
Blackwater ≃, Ire.	40	53.39 N	6.43 W
Blackwater ≃, Ire.	40	51.51 N	7.50 W
Blackwater ≃, Eng., U.K.	34	51.45 N	1.00 E
Blackwaterfoot	38	55.30 N	5.19 W
Blackwater Lake ⊜	98	64.00 N	123.05 W
Blackwater Reservoir ⊜1	38	56.41 N	4.46 W
Blackwood ≃	90	34.19 S	115.11 E
Bladgrond	86	28.52 S	19.57 E
Bladnoch ≃	36	54.51 N	4.25 W
Blaenau Ffestiniog	34	52.59 N	3.56 W
Blaenavon	34	51.48 N	3.05 W

Symbols in the Index entries are identified on page 122.

Name	Page	Lat. °′	Long. °′
Bláfell ∧	42a	64.32N	19.53W
Blagaj	52	43.15N	17.50 E
Blagdon	34	51.20N	2.43W
Blagodarnyj	56	45.06N	43.27 E
Blagoevgrad	54	42.01N	23.06 E
Blagoveščensk	58	50.17N	127.32 E
Blåhø ∧	44	62.45N	9.19 E
Blain	48	47.29N	1.46W
Blaina	34	51.46N	3.10W
Blaine Creek ≃	102	38.11N	82.37W
Blair Athol	94	22.42S	147.33 E
Blair Atholl	38	56.46N	3.51W
Blairgowrie	38	56.36N	3.21W
Blairsville	102	40.25N	79.15W
Blaj	54	46.11N	23.55 E
Blakeney, Eng., U.K.	34	52.58N	1.00 E
Blakeney, Eng., U.K.	34	51.46N	2.29W
Blake Plateau + [4]	22	31.00N	79.00W
Blake Ridge + [3]	22	29.00N	73.30W
Blanc, Mont (Monte Bianco) ∧	48	45.50N	6.52 E
Blanca, Bahía c	112	38.55S	62.10W
Blanca Grande, Laguna ⊜	114	38.26S	63.55W
Blanca Peak ∧	100	37.35N	105.29W
Blanchard ≃	102	41.02N	84.18W
Blanche, Cape ›	90	33.01S	134.09 E
Blanche, Lake ⊜	94	29.15S	139.39 E
Blanchester	102	39.17N	83.59W
Blanco	86	33.57S	22.24 E
Blanco ≃	114	30.12S	69.05W
Blanco, Cabo ›	108	9.34N	85.07W
Blanco, Cape ›	104	42.50N	124.34W
Blanda ≃	42a	65.39N	20.18W
Blandford Forum	34	50.52N	2.11W
Blanes	50	41.41N	2.48 E
Blangkejeren	70	3.59N	97.20 E
Blangy-sur-Bresle	48	49.56N	1.38 E
Blankenburg	46	51.48N	10.58 E
Blankenheim	46	50.26N	6.39 E
Blanquefort	48	44.53N	0.39W
Blanquilla, Isla I	110	11.51N	64.37W
Blansko	46	49.22N	16.39 E
Blantyre	84	15.47S	35.00 E
Blarney	40	51.56N	8.34W
Blasdell	102	42.47N	78.49W
Błaszki	46	51.39N	18.27 E
Blatná	46	49.26N	13.53 E
Blatnica	54	43.42N	28.31 E
Blaubeuren	46	48.24N	9.47 E
Blaufelden	46	49.18N	9.58 E
Blåvands Huk ›	44	55.33N	8.05 E
Blaydon	36	54.58N	1.42W
Blaye-et-Sainte-Luce	48	45.08N	0.39W
Blayney	94	33.32S	149.15 E
Blaze, Point ›	92	12.56S	130.12 E
Błażowa	46	49.54N	22.05 E
Blean	34	51.19N	1.02 E
Bled	52	46.22N	14.06 E
Blefjell ∧	44	59.48N	9.10 E
Blega	72	7.08S	113.03 E
Bleiburg	46	46.35N	14.48 E
Blekinge ☐ [9]	44	56.20N	15.05 E
Blekinge Län ☐ [6]	44	56.20N	15.20 E
Blenheim, On., Can.	102	42.20N	82.00W
Blenheim, N.Z.	96	41.31S	173.57 E
Bléré	48	47.20N	1.00 E
Blessington	40	53.10N	6.32W
Bletchley	34	52.00N	0.46W
Bletterans	48	46.45N	5.27 E
Bleus, Monts ⋀	82	1.30N	30.30 E
Blidö I	44	59.37N	18.54 E
Blidworth	36	53.06N	1.07W
Bligh Sound ʊ	96	44.50S	167.32 E
Blind River	102	46.10N	82.58W
Blinman	94	31.06S	138.41 E
Blissfield	102	41.49N	83.51W
Blitar	72	8.06S	112.09 E
Blithe ≃	34	52.45N	1.50W
Blithfield Reservoir ⊜ [1]	34	52.48N	1.53W
Block Island	102	41.10N	71.33W
Block Island I	102	41.11N	71.35W
Blockley	34	52.01N	1.45W
Bloemfontein	86	29.12S	26.07 E
Bloemhof	86	27.38S	25.32 E
Bloemhofdam ⊜ [1]	86	27.40S	25.40 E
Blois	48	47.35N	1.20 E
Blokhus	44	57.15N	9.35 E
Blomstermåla	44	56.59N	16.20 E
Blönduós	42a	65.39N	20.15W
Bloods Creek	90	26.28S	135.17 E
Bloodvein ≃	98	51.45N	96.44W
Bloody Foreland ›	40	55.09N	8.17W
Bloomfield	102	43.59N	77.14W
Bloomington, Il., U.S.	100	40.29N	88.59W
Bloomington, In., U.S.	100	39.09N	86.31W
Bloomsburg	102	41.00N	76.27W
Bloomsbury	94	20.43S	148.35 E
Bloomville	102	41.03N	83.00W
Blora	72	6.57S	111.25 E
Blossburg	102	41.40N	77.03W
Blouberg	86	23.08S	28.56 E
Blouberg ∧	86	23.01S	28.59 E
Blovice	46	49.35N	13.33 E
Blowering Reservoir ⊜ [1]	94	35.30S	148.15 E
Bloxham	34	52.02N	1.22W
Bludenz	46	47.09N	9.49 E
Bluebush Swamp ⩩	94	20.30S	137.25 E
Blue Creek ≃	104	42.02N	116.08W
Bluefield	100	37.16N	81.13W
Bluefields	108	12.00N	83.45W
Blue Hill	102	44.24N	68.35W
Blue Hill Bay c	102	44.15N	68.30W
Bluejoint Lake ⊜	104	42.35N	119.40W
Blue Mountain ∧, N.H., U.S.	102	44.47N	71.28W
Blue Mountain ∧, Pa., U.S.	102	40.15N	77.30W
Blue Mountain Peak ∧	108	18.03N	76.35W
Blue Mountains ⋀, U.S.	100	45.30N	118.15W
Blue Mountains ⋀, Me., U.S.	102	44.50N	70.35W
Blue Mountains National Park ♠	94	33.40S	150.25 E
Blue Mud Bay c	92	13.26S	135.56 E
Blue Nile (Al-Baḥr al-Azraq) (Abay) ≃	82	15.38N	32.31 E
Bluenose Lake ⊜	98	68.25N	119.45W
Blue Ridge ⋀	100	37.00N	82.00W
Blue Stack Mountains ⋀	40	54.45N	8.05W
Bluff	96	46.36S	168.20 E
Bluff Knoll ∧	90	34.23S	118.20 E
Bluff Point ›	90	27.50S	114.06 E
Bluffton, In., U.S.	102	40.44N	85.10W
Bluffton, Oh., U.S.	102	40.53N	83.53W
Blumberg	46	47.50N	8.31 E
Blumenau	114	26.56S	49.03W
Blupblup Island I	92	3.30S	144.37 E
Bly	104	42.23N	121.02W
Blyth, On., Can.	102	43.44N	81.26W
Blyth, Eng., U.K.	36	55.07N	1.30W
Blyth ≃, Austl.	92	12.04S	134.35 E
Blyth ≃, Eng., U.K.	34	52.18N	1.40 E
Blyth ≃, Eng., U.K.	36	55.08N	1.31W
Blyth Bridge	38	55.42N	3.24W
Blythe	104	33.36N	114.35W
Blythe ≃	34	52.31N	1.42W
Blytheville	100	35.55N	89.55W
Blyth Range ⋀	90	26.50S	129.00 E
Bø, Nor.	42	68.37N	14.33 E
Bø, Nor.	44	59.25N	9.04 E
Bo, S.L.	80	7.56N	11.21W
Boaco	108	12.28N	85.40W
Board Camp Mountain ∧	104	40.42N	123.43W
Boardman	102	41.01N	80.39W
Boardman ≃	102	44.46N	85.38W
Boarhills	38	56.19N	2.42W
Boath	38	57.44N	4.23W
Boatman	94	27.16S	146.55 E
Boat of Garten	38	57.20N	3.44W
Boa Vista, Bra.	110	2.49N	60.40W
Boa Vista, Bra.	114	26.17S	48.50W
Boa Vista I	80	16.05N	22.50W
Bobai	70	22.12N	109.52 E
Bobbili	74	18.34N	83.22 E
Bobbio	52	44.46N	9.23 E
Bobcaygeon	102	44.33N	78.33W
Böblingen	46	48.41N	9.01 E
Bobo Dioulasso	80	11.12N	4.18W
Bobolice	46	53.57N	16.36 E
Bóbr ≃	46	52.04N	15.04 E
Bobrujsk	60	53.09N	29.14 E
Bobs Lake ⊜	102	44.40N	76.35W
Bobtown	102	39.45N	79.58W
Bobures	108	9.15N	71.11W
Boby, Pic ∧	87b	22.12S	46.55 E
Boca del Pozo	108	11.00N	64.23W
Bôca do Acre	110	8.45S	67.23W
Boca Raton	108	26.21N	80.05W
Bocas del Toro	108	9.20N	82.15W
Bocay	108	14.19N	85.10W
Bochnia	46	49.58N	20.26 E
Bocholt	46	51.50N	6.36 E
Bochum, B.R.D.	46	51.28N	7.13 E
Bochum, S. Afr.	86	23.17S	29.07 E
Bocognano	52	42.05N	9.03 E
Boconó	108	9.15N	70.16W
Böda, Sve.	44	57.15N	17.03 E
Boda, Sve.	44	61.01N	15.13 E
Bodafors	44	57.30N	14.42 E
Boda Glasbruk	44	56.44N	15.40 E
Bodajbo	58	57.51N	114.10 E
Bodalla	94	36.05S	150.03 E
Bodallin	90	31.22S	118.52 E
Boddam, Scot., U.K.	38	57.28N	1.47W
Boddam, Scot., U.K.	38	59.55N	1.17W
Bodega Bay c	104	38.15N	123.00W
Bodélé + [1]	82	16.30N	16.30 E
Boden	44	65.50N	21.42 E
Bodensee ⊜	48	47.35N	9.25 E
Boderg, Lough ⊜	40	53.52N	7.58W
Bodiam	34	51.00N	0.33 E
Bodmin	34	50.29N	4.43W
Bodmin Moor + [3]	34	50.33N	4.33W
Bodø	42	67.17N	14.23 E
Bodrog ≃	54	48.07N	21.25 E
Bodrum	30	37.02N	27.26 E
Bodzentyn	46	50.56N	20.57 E
Boende	84	0.13S	20.52 E
Boën-sur-Lignon	48	45.44N	3.59 E
Boesmanland ☐ [5]	86	19.30S	20.00 E
Boesmans ≃	86	33.42S	26.39 E
Bofors	44	59.20N	14.32 E
Bogale	70	16.17N	95.24 E
Bogalusa	100	30.47N	89.50W
Bogan ≃	94	29.57S	146.21 E
Bogan Gate	94	33.07S	147.48 E
Bogantungan	94	23.39S	147.18 E
Bogda Shan ⋀	62	43.30N	89.45 E
Bogen	46	48.55N	12.43 E
Bogense	44	55.34N	10.06 E
Boggabilla	94	28.37S	150.21 E
Boggabri	94	30.42S	150.02 E
Boggeragh Mountains ⋀	40	52.03N	8.55W
Boggola, Mount ∧	90	23.48S	117.40 E
Bognes	42	68.10N	16.00 E
Bognor Regis	34	50.47N	0.41W
Bogo	68	11.03N	124.00 E
Bogol'ubovo	60	56.13N	40.31 E
Bogomila	54	41.36N	21.28 E
Bogong, Mount ∧	94	36.45S	147.18 E
Bogor	72	6.35S	106.47 E
Bogorodick	60	53.46N	38.08 E
Bogorodsk	60	56.06N	43.31 E
Bogotá	110	4.36N	74.05W
Bogotol	58	56.12N	89.33 E
Bogra	76	24.51N	89.22 E
Bogrie Hill ∧ [2]	36	55.08N	3.55W
Bogučany	58	58.23N	97.29 E
Bogué	80	16.35N	14.16W
Bo Hai c	62	38.30N	120.00 E
Bohai Haixia ʊ	62	38.15N	121.00 E
Bohain-en-Vermandois	48	49.59N	3.27 E
Bohemia →Čechy ☐ [9]	46	49.50N	14.00 E
Bohemia Downs	90	18.53S	126.14 E
Bohemian Forest ⋀	46	49.15N	12.45 E
Bohinjska Bistrica	52	46.17N	13.57 E
Bohol I	68	9.50N	124.10 E
Bohuslän ☐ [9]	44	58.15N	11.50 E
Boiano	52	41.29N	14.29 E
Boigu Island I	92	9.16S	142.12 E
Boiro	50	42.39N	8.54W
Bois, Lac des ⊜	98	66.40N	125.15W
Bois Blanc Island I	102	45.45N	84.28W
Boisdale, Loch c	38	57.08N	7.19W
Bois du Roi ∧	48	47.00N	4.02 E
Boise	100	43.36N	116.12W
Boise, South Fork ≃	104	43.36N	115.51W
Boissevain	98	49.14N	100.03W
Boizenburg	46	53.22N	10.43 E
Boja	72	7.06S	110.16 E
Bojadła	46	51.57N	15.50 E
Bojeador, Cape ›	68	18.30N	120.34 E
Bojnūrd	78	37.28N	57.19 E
Bojonegoro	72	7.09S	111.52 E
Bojuru	114	31.38S	51.26W
Boké	80	10.56N	14.18W
Bokes Creek ≃	102	40.19N	83.10W
Bokhara	86	27.57S	20.30 E
Bokhara ≃	94	29.55S	146.42 E
Boknafjorden c [2]	44	59.10N	5.35 E
Boksitogorsk	60	59.28N	33.51 E
Bokungu	84	0.41S	22.19 E
Bol	52	43.16N	16.40 E
Bolama	80	11.35N	15.28W
Bolangum	94	36.46S	142.53 E
Bolaños de Calatrava	50	38.54N	3.40W
Bolbec	48	49.34N	0.29 E
Bolchov	60	53.27N	36.01 E
Boldon	36	54.57N	1.27W
Bolesławiec	46	51.16N	15.34 E
Boleszkowice	46	52.44N	14.36 E
Bolgart	90	31.16S	116.30 E
Bolgatanga	80	10.46N	0.52W
Boli	62	45.46N	130.31 E
Boliden	44	64.52N	20.23 E
Bolívar, Arg.	112	36.15S	61.06W
Bolívar, Col.	110	4.21N	76.10W
Bolivar, N.Y., U.S.	102	42.04N	78.10W
Bolívar ☐ [5]	108	9.50N	75.15W
Bolívar, Cerro ∧	110	7.28N	63.25W
Bolívar, Pico ∧	110	8.30N	71.02W
Bolivia ☐ [1]	110	17.00S	65.00W
Boljarovo	54	42.09N	26.49 E
Bollène	48	44.17N	4.45 E
Bollin ≃	36	53.23N	2.28W
Bollington	36	53.18N	2.06W
Bollnäs	44	61.21N	16.25 E
Bollon	94	28.05S	147.15 E
Bollstabruk	44	63.00N	17.39 E
Bollullos par del Condado	50	37.20N	6.32W
Bolmen ⊜	44	56.55N	13.40 E
Bolobo	84	2.10S	16.14 E
Bolochovo	60	54.05N	37.50 E
Bologna	52	44.29N	11.20 E
Bologoje	60	57.54N	34.02 E
Bolomba	84	0.29N	19.12 E
Bolotnoje	56	55.41N	84.23 E
Bolovens, Plateau des ⋀ [1]	70	15.20N	106.20 E
Bol'šaja Balachn'a ≃	58	73.37N	107.05 E
Bol'šaja Cheta ≃	58	69.33N	84.15 E
Bol'šaja Čuja ≃	58	58.56N	112.13 E
Bol'šaja Ižora	60	59.56N	29.34 E
Bol'šaja Kuonamka ≃	58	70.45N	113.24 E
Bol'šaja Murta	58	56.55N	93.07 E
Bolsena	52	42.39N	11.59 E
Bolsena, Lago di ⊜	52	42.36N	11.56 E
Bol'šereck	58	52.25N	156.24 E
Bol'ševik, S.S.S.R.	58	62.44N	147.30 E
Bol'ševik, S.S.S.R.	60	52.34N	30.53 E
Bol'ševik, ostrov I	58	78.40N	102.30 E
Bol'šezemel'skaja Tundra + [1]	56	67.30N	56.00 E
Bol'šoj An'uj ≃	58	68.30N	160.49 E
Bol'šoj Begičev, ostrov I	58	74.20N	112.30 E
Bol'šoje Polpino	60	53.14N	34.30 E
Bol'šoj Jenisej ≃	58	51.43N	94.26 E
Bol'šoj Kavkaz (Caucasus) ⋀	56	42.30N	45.00 E
Bol'šoj L'achovskij, ostrov I	58	73.35N	142.00 E
Bol'šoj Uzen' ≃	56	48.50N	49.40 E
Bolsover	36	53.14N	1.18W
Bolsward	46	53.03N	5.31 E
Boltaña	50	42.27N	0.04 E
Bolton, On., Can.	102	43.53N	79.44W
Bolton, Eng., U.K.	36	53.35N	2.26W
Bolton Abbey	36	53.59N	1.53W
Bolton Bridge	36	53.58N	1.57W
Bolton-le-Sands	36	54.06N	2.47W
Bolton upon Dearne	36	53.31N	1.19W
Bolu	30	40.44N	31.37 E
Boluo	66	23.11N	114.17 E
Bolus Head ›	40	51.46N	10.21W
Bolwarra	94	17.24S	144.11 E
Bóly	46	45.58N	18.32 E
Bolzano (Bozen)	52	46.31N	11.22 E
Boma	84	5.51S	13.03 E
Bomaderry	94	34.51S	150.37 E
Bomarsund	44	60.13N	20.15 E
Bombala	94	36.54S	149.14 E
Bombarral	50	39.16N	9.09W
Bombay	74	18.58N	72.50 E
Bomberai, Jazirah › [1]	92	3.00S	133.00 E
Bom Despacho	110	19.43S	45.15W
Bom Jesus da Lapa	110	13.15S	43.25W
Bømlafjorden c [2]	44	59.39N	5.20 E
Bømlo I	44	59.46N	5.12 E
Bomnak	58	54.46N	128.51 E
Bom Retiro	114	27.48S	49.31W
Bom Retiro do Sul	114	29.37S	51.56W
Bom Sucesso	114	23.42S	51.45W
Bomu (Mbomou) ≃	82	4.08N	22.26 E
Bon, Cap ›	80	37.05N	11.03 E
Bonaigarh	76	21.50N	84.57 E
Bonaire I	108	12.10N	68.15W
Bonanza, Nic.	108	14.01N	84.35W
Bonanza, Or., U.S.	104	42.11N	121.24W
Bonao	108	18.56N	70.25W
Bonar Bridge	38	57.53N	4.21W
Bonarcado	52	40.04N	8.38 E
Bonavista	98	48.39N	53.07W
Bonavista Bay c	98	48.45N	53.20W
Bonawe	38	56.26N	5.13W
Bon Bon	90	30.26S	135.28 E
Bonchester Bridge	38	55.24N	2.40W
Bondeno	52	44.53N	11.25 E
Bondo	82	3.49N	23.40 E
Bondoukou	80	8.02N	2.48W
Bondowoso	72	7.55S	113.49 E
Bône →Annaba, Alg.	80	36.54N	7.46 E
Bone →Watampone, Indon.	72	4.32S	120.20 E
Bone, Teluk c	72	4.00S	120.40 E
Bo'ness	38	56.01N	3.37W
Bonete, Cerro ∧	114	27.51S	68.47W
Bonete Chico, Cerro ∧	114	28.01S	68.45W
Bongaigaon	76	26.28N	90.34 E
Bongandanga	84	1.30N	21.03 E
Bongo, Massif des ⋀	82	8.40N	22.25 E
Bongon	72	6.35N	116.52 E
Bongor	82	10.17N	15.22 E
Bonhomme, Morne ∧	108	19.05N	72.18W
Bonifacio	52	41.23N	9.10 E
Bonifacio, Strait of ʊ	52	41.20N	9.15 E
Bonifati, Capo ›	52	39.35N	15.52 E
Bonin Islands →Ogasawara-guntō II	28	27.00N	142.10 E
Bonito, Pico ∧	108	15.38N	86.55W
Bonn	46	50.44N	7.05 E
Bonnechere ≃	102	45.31N	76.33W
Bonnétable	48	48.11N	0.26 E
Bonnet Plume ≃	98	65.55N	134.58W
Bonneval	48	48.11N	1.24 E
Bonneville	48	46.05N	6.25 E
Bonneville Salt Flats ⊻	104	40.45N	113.52W
Bonney, Lake ⊜	94	37.48S	140.22 E
Bonnie Rock	90	30.32S	118.21 E
Bonny	80	4.27N	7.10 E
Bonnyrigg	38	55.52N	3.08W
Bono	52	40.25N	9.02 E
Bonorva	52	40.25N	8.46 E
Bonsecours	48	49.26N	1.08 E
Bonthain	72	5.32S	119.56 E
Bonthe	80	7.32N	12.30W
Bontoc	68	17.05N	120.58 E
Bonyhád	46	46.19N	18.32 E
Boogardie	90	28.02S	117.47 E
Bookabie	90	31.50S	132.41 E
Bookaloo	94	31.55S	137.22 E
Boolaloo	90	22.35S	115.51 E
Booleroo Centre	94	32.53S	138.21 E
Booligal	94	33.52S	144.53 E
Boologooro	90	24.21S	114.02 E
Boom	46	51.05N	4.22 E
Boomarra	94	19.33S	140.20 E
Boomer	102	38.09N	81.17W
Boomi	94	28.44S	149.35 E
Boonah	94	28.00S	152.41 E
Boone	100	42.03N	93.52W
Boonsboro	102	39.30N	77.39W
Boonville, Ca., U.S.	104	39.00N	123.21W
Boonville, N.Y., U.S.	102	43.29N	75.20W
Boorama	82	9.56N	43.11 E
Boorindal	94	30.21S	146.08 E
Booroorban	94	34.56S	144.46 E
Boorowa	94	34.26S	148.43 E
Boorthanna	94	28.38S	135.54 E
Boosaaso	82	11.17N	49.11 E
Boot	36	54.24N	3.17W
Boothbay Harbor	102	43.51N	69.37W
Boothia, Gulf of c	98	71.00N	91.00W
Boothia Peninsula › [1]	98	70.30N	95.00W
Bootle	36	53.28N	3.00W
Booué	84	0.06S	11.56 E
Bopeechee	94	29.36S	137.23 E
Bophuthatswana ☐ [1]	86	26.00S	25.35 E
Boquerón ☐ [5]	114	21.30S	60.00W
Bor, Česko.	46	49.43N	12.47 E
Bor, Jugo.	54	44.05N	22.07 E
Bor, S.S.S.R.	60	56.22N	44.05 E
Bor, Sūd.	82	6.12N	31.33 E
Bor, Tür.	78	37.54N	34.34 E
Bora-Bora I	28	16.30S	151.45W
Boraha, Nosy I	87b	16.50S	49.55 E
Borah Peak ∧	100	44.08N	113.48W
Borås	44	57.43N	12.55 E
Borāzjān	78	29.16N	51.12 E
Borba, Bra.	110	4.24S	59.35W
Borba, Port.	50	38.48N	7.27W
Borborema	114	21.37S	49.04W
Borcea ≃	54	44.40N	27.53 E
Borda, Cape ›	94	35.45S	136.34 E
Bordeaux	48	44.50N	0.34W
Borden	90	34.05S	118.16 E
Borden Peninsula › [1]	98	73.00N	83.00W
Border Mountains ⋀	92	3.40S	141.05 E
Borders ☐ [4]	38	55.37N	3.15W
Bordertown	94	36.19S	140.47 E
Bordesholm	46	54.11N	10.01 E
Borđeyri	42a	65.15N	21.10W
Bordighera	52	43.46N	7.39 E
Bordj Bou Arreridj	50	36.04N	4.46 E
Bordj Menaïel	50	36.44N	3.43 E
Bordj Omar Idriss	80	28.09N	6.43 E
Borehamwood	34	51.40N	0.16W
Borensberg	44	58.34N	15.17 E
Boreray I	38	57.42N	7.18W
Borgå (Porvoo)	44	60.24N	25.40 E
Borgarnes	42a	64.35N	21.53W
Borger	100	35.40N	101.23W
Borgholm	44	56.53N	16.39 E
Borghorst	46	52.07N	7.23 E
Borgo	52	46.03N	11.27 E
Borgomanero	52	45.42N	8.28 E
Borgo San Dalmazzo	52	44.20N	7.30 E
Borgo San Lorenzo	52	43.57N	11.23 E
Borgosesia	52	45.43N	8.16 E
Borgo Val di Taro	52	44.29N	9.46 E
Borisoglebsk	56	51.23N	42.06 E
Borisoglebskij	60	57.16N	39.09 E
Borisov	60	54.15N	28.30 E
Borja	50	41.50N	1.32W
Borjas Blancas	50	41.31N	0.52 E
Borken	46	51.51N	6.51 E
Borkum I	46	53.35N	6.41 E
Borlänge	44	60.29N	15.25 E
Bormes-les-Mimosas	48	43.09N	6.20 E
Bormio	52	46.28N	10.22 E
Borna	46	51.19N	13.11 E
Borne	46	52.18N	6.45 E
Borneo (Kalimantan) I	72	0.30N	114.00 E
Bornholm I	44	55.10N	15.00 E
Bornos, Embalse de ⊜ [1]	50	36.50N	5.30W
Bornova	54	38.27N	27.14 E
Boro ≃	82	8.52N	26.11 E
Borogoncy	58	62.42N	131.08 E
Boron	104	34.59N	117.38W
Boronga Islands II	70	19.58N	93.06 E
Boroughbridge	36	54.06N	1.23W
Borough Green	34	51.17N	0.19 E
Borovan	54	43.26N	23.45 E
Boroviči	60	58.24N	33.55 E
Borovl'anka	56	52.38N	84.29 E
Borovoj	42	59.55N	51.38 E
Borovsk	60	55.12N	36.30 E
Borrazópolis	114	23.56S	51.36W
Borrby	44	55.27N	14.10 E
Borris	40	52.35N	6.06W
Borrisokane	40	52.59N	8.07W
Borrisoleigh	40	52.45N	7.57W
Borroloola	92	16.04S	136.17 E
Borrowdale	36	54.31N	3.10W
Borş	54	47.07N	21.49 E
Borşa, Rom.	54	46.56N	23.40 E
Borşa, Rom.	54	47.39N	24.40 E
Borsad	76	22.25N	72.54 E
Borsod-Abaúj-Zemplén ☐ [6]	46	48.15N	21.00 E
Borth	34	52.29N	4.03W
Borthwick Water ≃	38	55.24N	2.50W
Bort-les-Orgues, Fr.	48	43.49N	2.53 E
Bort-les-Orgues, Fr.	48	45.24N	2.30 E
Borūjen	78	31.59N	51.18 E
Borūjerd	78	33.54N	48.46 E
Borve	38	56.58N	7.32W
Borz'a	58	50.24N	116.31 E
Borzyszkowy	46	54.03N	17.22 E
Bosa	52	40.18N	8.30 E
Bosanska Dubica	52	45.11N	16.49 E
Bosanska Gradiška	52	45.09N	17.15 E
Bosanska Krupa	52	44.53N	16.10 E
Bosanski Novi	52	45.03N	16.23 E
Bosanski Petrovac	52	44.33N	16.22 E
Bosanski Šamac	54	45.03N	18.28 E
Bosansko Grahovo	52	44.11N	16.22 E
Bosavi, Mount ∧	92	6.35S	142.50 E
Boscastle	34	50.41N	4.42W
Bose	62	23.54N	106.37 E
Bosham	34	50.49N	0.52W
Boshan	62	36.29N	117.50 E
Boshoek	86	25.30S	27.09 E
Boshof	86	28.34S	25.04 E
Bosilegrad	54	42.29N	22.28 E
Boskovice	46	49.29N	16.40 E
Bosna ≃	54	45.04N	18.29 E
Bosna i Hercegovina (Bosnia-Hercegovina) ☐ [3]	54	44.15N	17.50 E
Bosnik	92	1.10S	136.14 E
Bōsō-hantō › [1]	64	35.18N	140.10 E
Bosporus →İstanbul Boğazı ʊ	54	41.06N	29.04 E
Bossangoa	82	6.29N	17.27 E
Bossembélé	82	5.16N	17.39 E
Bossier City	100	32.30N	93.43W
Bosso, Dallol ∨	80	12.25N	2.50 E
Bossut, Cape ›	90	18.43S	121.38 E
Bosten Hu ⊜	62	42.00N	87.00 E
Boston, Eng., U.K.	34	52.59N	0.01W
Boston, Ma., U.S.	102	42.21N	71.03W
Boston Mountains ⋀	100	35.50N	93.20W
Boston Spa	36	53.54N	1.21W
Bosut ≃	54	44.57N	19.22 E
Boswell	102	40.09N	79.01W
Botād	76	22.10N	71.40 E
Botany Bay c	94	33.59S	151.12 E
Botesdale	34	52.20N	1.01 E
Boteti ≃	86	20.08S	23.23 E
Botev ∧	54	42.43N	24.55 E
Botevgrad	54	42.54N	23.47 E
Botha's Hill	86	29.45S	30.45 E
Bothaville	86	27.27S	26.36 E
Bothnia, Gulf of c	44	63.00N	20.00 E
Bothwell, Austl.	94	42.23S	147.00 E
Bothwell, On., Can.	102	42.38N	81.52W
Boticas	50	41.41N	7.40W
Botkins	102	40.28N	84.10W
Botoşani	54	47.45N	26.40 E
Botoşani ☐ [6]	54	48.00N	26.45 E
Botoşaniţa	54	47.53N	26.07 E
Botrange ∧	46	50.30N	6.08 E
Botswana ☐ [1]	84	22.00S	24.00 E
Botte Donato ∧	52	39.17N	16.26 E
Bottenhavet (Selkämeri) c	44	62.00N	20.00 E
Bottenviken (Perämeri) c	44	65.00N	23.00 E
Bottesford	34	52.56N	0.48W
Bottineau	100	48.49N	100.26W
Bottisham	34	52.13N	0.16 E
Bottrop	46	51.31N	6.55 E
Botucatu	114	22.52S	48.26W
Botwood	98	49.09N	55.21W
Bouaflé	80	6.59N	5.45W
Bouaké	80	7.41N	5.02W
Bouar	82	5.57N	15.36 E
Bouaye	48	47.09N	1.42W
Bouches-du-Rhône ☐ [5]	48	43.30N	5.00 E
Bougainville I	28	6.00S	155.00 E
Bougainville, Cape ›	92	13.54S	126.06 E
Bougainville Reef + [2]	92	15.30S	147.06 E
Boughton	36	53.12N	1.00W
Bougouni	80	11.25N	7.29W
Bouillon	46	49.48N	5.04 E
Boujdour, Cap ›	80	26.08N	14.30W
Boulay-Moselle	48	49.11N	6.30 E
Boulder, Austl.	90	30.47S	121.29 E
Boulder, Co., U.S.	100	40.00N	105.16W
Boulder City	104	35.58N	114.49W
Boulia	94	22.54S	139.54 E
Boulogne-Billancourt	48	48.50N	2.15 E
Boulogne-sur-Gesse	48	43.18N	0.39 E
Boulogne-sur-Mer	48	50.43N	1.37 E
Bouloire	32	47.58N	0.33 E
Boulsworth Hill ∧	36	53.48N	2.06W
Bouna	80	9.16N	3.00W
Boundary Peak ∧	104	37.51N	118.21W
Bounty Islands II	28	47.42S	179.04 E
Bounty Trough + [1]	28	46.00S	178.00 E
Bourbon-Lancy	48	46.38N	3.46 E
Bourbonnais ☐ [9]	48	46.20N	3.00 E
Bourbonne-les-Bains	48	47.57N	5.45 E
Bourem	80	16.57N	0.21W
Bourganeuf	48	45.57N	1.46 E
Bourg-en-Bresse	48	46.12N	5.13 E
Bourges	48	47.05N	2.24 E
Bourget	102	45.26N	75.09W
Bourget, Lac du ⊜	48	45.44N	5.52 E
Bourg-Lastic	48	45.39N	2.33 E
Bourgneuf-en-Retz	48	47.02N	1.57W
Bourgogne ☐ [9]	48	47.00N	4.30 E
Bourgogne, Canal de ⌅	48	47.58N	3.30 E
Bourgoin	48	45.35N	5.17 E
Bourg-Saint-Andéol	48	44.22N	4.39 E
Bourg-Saint-Maurice	48	45.37N	6.46 E
Bourgueil	48	47.17N	0.10 E
Bourke	94	30.05S	145.56 E
Bourne	34	52.46N	0.23W
Bourne ≃	34	51.02N	1.47W
Bournemouth	34	50.43N	1.54W
Bourton-on-the-Water	34	51.53N	1.45W
Bou Saâda	80	35.12N	4.11 E
Bouse	104	33.55N	114.00W
Boussac	48	46.21N	2.13 E
Bousso	82	10.29N	16.43 E
Boussu	48	50.26N	3.48 E
Boutilimit	80	17.33N	14.42W
Bouvard, Cape ›	90	32.41S	115.37 E
Bov	44	54.50N	9.23 E
Bøvågen	44	60.40N	4.58 E
Bovalino Marina	52	38.10N	16.11 E
Bovec	52	46.20N	13.33 E
Bøverdal	44	61.43N	8.21 E
Bovey ≃	34	50.34N	3.37W
Bovey Tracey	34	50.36N	3.40W
Bovingdon	34	51.44N	0.32W
Bovington Camp	34	50.42N	2.14W
Bovril	114	31.21S	59.26W
Bow ≃, Austl.	92	16.32S	128.39 E
Bow ≃, Ab., Can.	98	49.56N	111.42W
Bo-Wadrif	86	32.26S	20.07 E
Bow Brook ≃	34	52.04N	2.07W
Bowburn	36	54.43N	1.31W
Bowelling	90	33.25S	116.29 E
Bowen, Arg.	114	35.00S	67.31W
Bowen, Austl.	94	20.01S	148.15 E
Bowen ≃	94	20.24S	147.21 E
Bowers Ridge + [3]	26	54.00N	179.00 E
Bowgreave	36	53.52N	2.45W
Bowie	102	39.00N	76.46W
Bowland, Forest of + [3]	36	53.58N	2.32W
Bowling Green, Ky., U.S.	100	36.59N	86.26W
Bowling Green, Oh., U.S.	102	41.22N	83.39W
Bowling Green, Va., U.S.	102	38.02N	77.20W
Bowling Green, Cape ›	94	19.19S	145.25 E
Bowman	100	46.10N	103.23W
Bowmanville	102	43.55N	78.41W
Bowmont Water ≃	36	55.34N	2.09W
Bowmore	38	55.45N	6.17W
Bowness-on-Windermere	36	54.22N	2.55W
Bowral	94	34.28S	150.25 E
Bowraville	94	30.39S	152.51 E
Box	34	51.26N	2.15W
Boxholm	44	58.12N	15.03 E
Boxian	66	33.53N	115.45 E
Boxtel	46	51.35N	5.20 E
Boyalık	54	41.15N	28.37 E
Boyang	66	28.59N	116.40 E
Boyanup	90	33.29S	115.44 E
Boyd ≃	94	29.51S	152.35 E
Boyertown	102	40.20N	75.38W
Boyle	40	53.58N	8.18W
Boyne ≃, Austl.	94	23.56S	151.21 E
Boyne ≃, On., Can.	102	44.10N	79.49W
Boyne ≃, Ire.	40	53.43N	6.15W
Boyne City	102	45.12N	85.00W
Boyup Brook	90	33.50S	116.24 E
Bozel	48	45.27N	6.39 E
Bozeman	100	45.40N	111.02W
Bozhen	62	38.07N	116.32 E
Bozoum	82	6.19N	16.23 E
Bozovici	54	44.55N	21.59 E
Bra	52	44.42N	7.51 E
Braan ≃	38	56.33N	3.35W
Braås	44	57.04N	15.03 E
Brabant Island I	24	64.15S	62.20W
Brač, Otok I	52	43.20N	16.40 E
Bracadale, Loch c	38	57.19N	6.30W
Bracciano	52	42.06N	12.10 E
Bracciano, Lago di ⊜	52	42.07N	12.14 E
Bracebridge	102	45.02N	79.19W
Bracebridge Heath	36	53.13N	0.33W
Bracieux	48	47.33N	1.33 E
Bracigovo	54	42.01N	24.22 E
Bräcke	44	62.43N	15.27 E
Brački Kanal ʊ	52	43.24N	16.40 E
Brackley	34	52.02N	1.09W
Bracknell	34	51.26N	0.45W
Braco	38	56.15N	3.53W
Braço do Norte	114	28.17S	49.11W
Brad	54	46.08N	22.47 E
Bradano ≃	52	40.23N	16.51 E
Bradenton	100	27.29N	82.34W
Bradford, On., Can.	102	44.07N	79.34W
Bradford, Eng., U.K.	36	53.48N	1.45W
Bradford, Oh., U.S.	102	40.08N	84.26W
Bradford, Pa., U.S.	102	41.57N	78.38W
Bradford, Vt., U.S.	102	43.59N	72.09W
Bradford-on-Avon	34	51.20N	2.15W
Brading	34	50.41N	1.09W
Bradninch	34	50.50N	3.25W
Bradwell-on-Sea	34	51.44N	0.54 E
Bradworthy	34	50.54N	4.22W
Brae	38a	60.23N	1.21W
Brædstrup	44	55.58N	9.37 E
Braemar	38	57.01N	3.23W
Braeside	90	21.12S	121.01 E
Braga	50	41.33N	8.26W
Bragado	114	35.08S	60.30W
Bragança, Bra.	110	1.03S	46.46W
Bragança, Port.	50	41.49N	6.45W
Bragança Paulista	114	22.57S	46.34W
Bragar	38	58.24N	6.40W
Brāhmanbāria	76	23.59N	91.07 E
Brāhmani ≃	74	20.39N	86.46 E
Brahmaputra (Yaluzangbujiang) ≃	76	24.02N	90.59 E
Braich y Pwll ›	34	52.48N	4.36W
Braidwood	94	35.27S	149.48 E
Brăila	54	45.16N	27.58 E
Brăila ☐ [6]	54	45.00N	27.40 E
Brain ≃	34	51.48N	0.39 E
Braine-l'Alleud	46	50.41N	4.22 E
Braine-le-Comte	46	50.36N	4.08 E
Brainerd	100	46.21N	94.12W
Braint ≃	36	53.08N	4.19W
Braintree	34	51.53N	0.32 E
Brak ≃	86	29.35S	22.55 E
Brake	46	53.19N	8.28 E
Brålanda	44	58.34N	12.22 E
Bramford	34	52.04N	1.06 E
Bramhope	36	53.53N	1.37W
Bramming	44	55.28N	8.42 E
Brampton, On., Can.	102	43.41N	79.46W
Brampton, Eng., U.K.	34	52.19N	0.14W
Brampton, Eng., U.K.	36	54.57N	2.43W
Bramsche	46	52.24N	7.58 E
Bran, Pasul)(	54	45.26N	25.17 E
Brancaleone Marina	52	37.58N	16.06 E
Brancaster	34	52.58N	0.39 E
Brancaster Roads ∓ [3]	34	53.05N	0.45W
Branco ≃	110	1.24S	61.51W
Brandberg ∧	86	21.10S	14.33 E
Brandbu	44	60.28N	10.30 E
Brande	44	55.57N	9.07 E
Brandenburg	46	52.24N	12.32 E
Brandenburg ☐ [9]	46	52.00N	13.30 E
Brand-Erbisdorf	46	50.52N	13.19 E
Brandfort	86	28.47S	26.30 E
Brandon, Mb., Can.	98	49.50N	99.57W
Brandon, Eng., U.K.	34	52.27N	0.37 E
Brandon, Eng., U.K.	36	54.46N	1.39W
Brandon, Vt., U.S.	102	43.47N	73.05W
Brandon Bay c	40	52.15N	10.05W
Brandon Head ›	40	52.16N	10.14W
Brandon Mountain ∧	40	52.14N	10.15W
Brandsen	114	35.10S	58.14W
Brandvlei	86	30.25S	20.30 E
Brandy Peak ∧	104	42.36N	123.53W
Brandýs nad Labem	46	50.10N	14.41 E
Braniewo	46	54.24N	19.50 E
Bransby	94	28.14S	142.04 E
Bransgore	34	50.47N	1.44W
Brańsk, Pol.	46	52.45N	22.51 E
Br'ansk, S.S.S.R.	60	53.15N	34.22 E
Brant ≃	36	53.09N	0.35W
Brantford	102	43.08N	80.16W
Brant Lake	102	43.40N	73.45W
Brantôme	48	45.22N	0.39 E
Branxholme	94	37.51S	141.47 E
Bras d'Or Lake ⊜	98	45.52N	60.50W
Brasiléia	110	11.00S	68.44W
Brasília	110	15.47S	47.55W
Braslav	60	55.38N	27.02 E
Braşov	54	45.39N	25.37 E
Braşov ☐ [6]	54	45.45N	25.15 E
Brassey, Binjaran ⋀	72	4.54N	117.30 E
Brassey, Mount ∧	90	23.05S	134.38 E
Brastad	44	58.23N	11.29 E
Břasy	46	49.50N	13.35 E
Bratca	54	46.56N	22.37 E
Brateş, Lacul ⊜	54	45.30N	28.05 E
Bratislava	46	48.09N	17.07 E
Bratsk	58	56.05N	101.48 E
Bratskoje vodochranilišče ⊜ [1]	58	56.10N	102.10 E
Brattleboro	102	42.51N	72.33W
Brattvåg	44	62.36N	6.27 E
Braunau [am Inn]	46	48.15N	13.02 E
Braunlage	46	51.44N	10.37 E
Braunschweig	46	52.16N	10.31 E
Braunston	34	52.17N	1.12W
Braunton	34	51.07N	4.10W
Brava I	80	14.52N	24.43W
Brava, Costa ⊥ [2]	50	41.45N	3.04 E
Brava, Laguna ⊜	114	28.22S	68.50W
Brava, Punta ›	114	34.56S	56.10W
Brave	102	39.44N	80.16W
Bråviken c	44	58.38N	16.32 E
Bravo del Norte (Rio Grande) ≃	100	25.55N	97.09W
Brawley	104	32.58N	115.31W
Brawley Peaks ⋀	104	38.15N	118.55W
Bray, Bel.	48	50.26N	4.06 E
Bray, Ire.	40	53.12N	6.06W
Bray ≃	34	50.59N	3.53W
Bray Head ›	40	51.53N	10.26W
Bray Island I	98	69.20N	76.45W
Bray [-sur-Seine]	48	48.25N	3.14 E
Brayton	36	53.46N	1.05W
Brazeau ≃	98	52.55N	115.15W
Brazil (Brasil) ☐ [1]	110	10.00S	55.00W
Brazil Basin + [1]	24	15.00S	25.00W
Brazos ≃	100	28.53N	95.23W
Brazzaville	84	4.16S	15.17 E
Brčko	54	44.53N	18.48 E
Brda ≃	46	53.07N	18.08 E
Brea	104	33.55N	117.53W
Breadalbane	94	23.49S	139.35 E
Breaksea Sound ʊ	96	45.35S	166.40 E
Bream	34	51.45N	2.34W
Bream Bay c	96	35.55S	174.30 E
Breamish ≃	36	55.31N	1.56W
Bream Tail ›	96	36.03S	174.35 E
Brea Pozo	114	28.15S	63.57W
Breaston	36	52.54N	1.19W
Breaza	54	45.11N	25.40 E
Brebes	72	6.53S	109.03 E
Brécey	48	48.44N	1.10W
Brechfa	34	51.54N	4.36W
Brechin	38	56.44N	2.40W
Breckenridge	102	43.24N	84.28W
Breckland + [1]	34	52.28N	0.37 E
Břeclav	46	48.46N	16.53 E
Brecon	34	51.57N	3.24W
Brecon Beacons ∧	34	51.53N	3.31W
Brecon Beacons National Park ♠	34	51.52N	3.25W
Breda	46	51.35N	4.46 E
Bredaryd	44	57.10N	13.44 E
Bredasdorp	86	34.32S	20.02 E
Bredbyn	44	63.27N	18.06 E
Bredon Hill ∧ [2]	34	52.06N	2.03W
Bredstedt	46	54.37N	8.59 E
Breë ≃	86	34.24S	20.50 E
Breedoge ≃	40	53.55N	8.27W
Breeza Plains	92	14.50S	144.07 E
Bregalnica ≃	54	41.43N	22.09 E
Bregenz	46	47.30N	9.46 E
Bregovo	54	44.09N	22.39 E
Breguzzo	52	46.00N	10.42 E
Bréhal	48	48.54N	1.31W
Breiđafjörđur c	42a	65.15N	23.15W
Breil-sur-Roya	48	43.56N	7.30 E
Breisach	46	48.01N	7.40 E

Symbols in the Index entries are identified on page 122.

Symbols in the Index entries are identified on page 122.

Symbols in the Index entries are identified on page 122.

Name	Page	Lat.°′	Long.°′
Castell'Arquato	52	44.51 N	9.52 E
Castelli	114	36.06 S	57.47 W
Castellón □4	50	40.10 N	0.10 W
Castellón de la Plana	50	39.59 N	0.02 W
Castellote	50	40.48 N	0.19 W
Castelmassa	52	45.01 N	11.18 E
Castelmoron-sur-Lot	48	44.24 N	0.30 E
Castelnaudary	48	43.19 N	1.57 E
Castelnau-Montratier	48	44.16 N	1.21 E
Castelnovo ne'Monti	52	44.26 N	10.24 E
Castelnuovo di Garfagnana	52	44.06 N	10.24 E
Castelo Branco	50	39.49 N	7.30 W
Castel San Giovanni	52	45.04 N	9.26 E
Castelsardo	52	40.55 N	8.43 E
Castelsarrasin	48	44.02 N	1.06 E
Casteltermini	52	37.32 N	13.39 E
Castelvetrano	52	37.41 N	12.47 E
Casterton	94	37.35 S	141.24 E
Castets	48	43.53 N	1.09 W
Castiglione del Lago	52	43.07 N	12.03 E
Castiglione della Pescaia	52	42.46 N	10.53 E
Castiglion Fiorentino	52	43.20 N	11.55 E
Castile	102	42.37 N	78.03 W
Castilla	110	5.12 S	80.38 W
Castilla, Playa de ⊥2	50	37.00 N	6.33 W
Castilla la Nueva □9	50	40.00 N	3.45 W
Castilla la Vieja □9	50	41.30 N	4.00 W
Castillon-la-Bataille	48	44.51 N	0.03 W
Castillos	114	34.12 S	53.50 W
Castillos, Laguna de ⊜	114	34.20 S	53.54 W
Castine	102	44.23 N	68.48 W
Castle Acre	34	52.42 N	0.41 E
Castlebar	40	53.52 N	9.17 W
Castlebay	38	56.57 N	7.28 W
Castlebellingham	40	53.54 N	6.23 W
Castleblayney	40	54.07 N	6.44 W
Castle Cary	34	51.06 N	2.31 W
Castlecliff	96	39.57 S	174.59 E
Castlecomer	40	52.48 N	7.12 W
Castleconnell	40	52.43 N	8.30 W
Castle Creek ≃	104	43.06 N	116.16 W
Castlederg	40	54.42 N	7.36 W
Castledermot	40	52.55 N	6.50 W
Castle Dome Peak ∧	104	33.05 N	114.08 W
Castle Donington	34	52.51 N	1.19 W
Castle Douglas	36	54.57 N	3.56 W
Castlefinn	40	54.47 N	7.35 W
Castleford	36	53.44 N	1.21 W
Castlegar	98	49.19 N	117.40 W
Castleisland	40	52.14 N	9.27 W
Castlemaine, Austl.	94	37.04 S	144.13 E
Castlemaine, Ire.	40	52.09 N	9.43 W
Castlemartyr	40	51.55 N	8.03 W
Castle Mountain ∧	98	64.32 N	135.27 W
Castlepoint	96	40.54 S	176.13 E
Castlepollard	40	53.40 N	7.17 W
Castlerea	40	53.46 N	8.29 W
Castlereagh ≃	94	30.12 S	147.32 E
Castle Rock ∧	102	37.57 N	78.44 W
Castleside	36	54.50 N	1.52 W
Castleton, Eng., U.K.	36	53.21 N	1.46 W
Castleton, Eng., U.K.	36	54.28 N	0.56 W
Castleton, Vt., U.S.	102	43.36 N	73.10 W
Castletown, I. of Man	36	54.04 N	4.40 W
Castletown, Scot., U.K.	38	58.35 N	3.23 W
Castletown Bearhaven (Castletown Bere)	40	51.39 N	9.55 W
Castletown Geoghegan	40	53.26 N	7.38 W
Castletownroche	40	52.10 N	8.28 W
Castletownshend	40	51.32 N	9.11 W
Castlewellan	40	54.16 N	5.57 W
Castres	48	43.36 N	2.15 E
Castries	108	14.01 N	61.00 W
Castro, Bra.	114	24.47 S	50.00 W
Castro, Chile	114	42.29 S	73.46 W
Castro Barros	114	30.35 S	65.44 W
Castro Daire	50	40.54 N	7.56 W
Castro del Río	50	37.41 N	4.28 W
Castrojeriz	50	42.17 N	4.08 W
Castro Marim	50	37.13 N	7.26 W
Castronuño	50	41.23 N	5.16 W
Castropol	50	43.32 N	7.02 W
Castro-Urdiales	50	43.23 N	3.13 W
Castro Verde	50	37.42 N	8.05 W
Castrovillari	52	39.49 N	16.13 E
Castroville	104	36.45 N	121.45 W
Castuera	50	38.43 N	5.33 W
Casupá	114	34.07 S	55.39 W
Caswell Sound ᑌ	96	45.00 S	167.10 E
Catacamas	108	14.54 N	85.56 W
Catacaos	110	5.16 S	80.41 W
Catalão	110	18.10 S	47.57 W
Catalina	114	25.13 S	69.43 W
Catamarca	112	28.28 S	65.47 W
Catamarca □4	114	27.00 S	67.00 W
Catanduanes Island I	68	13.45 N	124.15 E
Catanduva	110	21.08 S	48.58 W
Catania	52	37.30 N	15.06 E
Catania, Golfo di c	52	37.24 N	15.09 E
Catanzaro	52	38.54 N	16.36 E
Catarman	68	12.30 N	124.38 E
Catarroja	50	39.24 N	0.24 W
Catastrophe, Cape ⟩	94	34.59 S	136.00 E
Catatumbo ≃	108	9.22 N	71.45 W
Catbalogan	68	11.46 N	124.53 E
Caterham	34	51.17 N	0.04 W
Catete	84	9.06 S	13.43 E
Cathcart	86	32.18 S	27.09 E
Cathedral City	104	33.46 N	116.27 W
Cat Island I	108	24.27 N	75.30 W
Catlettsburg	102	38.24 N	82.36 W
Catlins ≃	96	46.29 S	169.43 E
Catlodge	38	57.00 N	4.15 W
Catnip Mountain ∧	104	41.52 N	119.23 W
Catoche, Cabo ⟩	106	21.35 N	87.05 W
Cato Island I	94	23.15 S	155.32 E
Caton	36	54.04 N	2.43 W
Catonsville	102	39.16 N	76.43 W
Catriló	114	36.26 S	63.24 W
Catrimani ≃	110	0.28 N	61.44 W
Catrine	38	55.30 N	4.20 W
Catshill	34	52.22 N	2.03 W
Catskill	102	42.13 N	73.51 W
Catskill Creek ≃	102	42.12 N	73.51 W
Catskill Mountains ✱	102	42.10 N	74.30 W
Cattaraugus	102	42.19 N	78.52 W
Cattaraugus Creek ≃	102	42.35 N	79.10 W
Catterick	36	54.22 N	1.38 W
Catterick Garrison	36	54.22 N	1.43 W
Cattolica	52	43.58 N	12.44 E
Catton	36	54.55 N	2.15 W
Catus	48	44.34 N	1.20 E
Čatyrtaš	56	40.55 N	76.26 E
Cauca ≃	110	8.54 N	74.28 W
Caucasus →Bol'šoj Kavkaz ✱	56	42.30 N	45.00 E
Cauchari, Salar de ≚	114	23.50 S	66.50 W
Caudry	48	50.08 N	3.25 E
Cauldcleuch Head ∧	36	55.18 N	2.51 W
Caulkerbush	36	54.54 N	3.40 W
Caulonia	52	38.23 N	16.25 E
Caúngula	84	8.25 S	18.40 E
Čaunskaja guba c	58	69.20 N	170.00 E
Cauquenes	114	35.58 S	72.21 W
Caura ≃	110	7.38 N	64.53 W
Caussade	48	44.10 N	1.32 E
Cauto ≃	108	20.33 N	77.14 W
Cauvery ≃	74	11.09 N	79.52 E
Caux, Pays de ✦1	48	49.40 N	0.40 E
Cava [de'Tirreni]	52	40.42 N	14.42 E
Cavaillon	48	43.50 N	5.02 E
Cavalaire-sur-Mer	48	43.10 N	6.32 E
Cavalcante	110	13.48 S	47.30 W
Cavalese	52	46.17 N	11.27 E
Cavalla (Cavally) ≃	80	4.22 N	7.32 W
Cavalli Islands II	96	35.02 S	173.58 E
Cavan	40	54.00 N	7.21 W
Cavan □6	40	53.55 N	7.30 W
Cavarzere	52	45.08 N	12.05 E
Cave	96	44.19 S	170.57 E
Caveiras ≃	114	27.35 S	50.56 W
Cavendish	94	37.31 S	142.02 E
Caviana, Ilha I	110	0.10 N	50.10 W
Cavite	68	14.29 N	120.55 E
Cavtat	54	42.35 N	18.13 E
Cawdor	38	57.31 N	3.56 W
Cawood	36	53.50 N	1.07 W
Cawston	34	52.46 N	1.10 E
Caxias	110	4.50 S	43.21 W
Caxias do Sul	114	29.10 S	51.11 W
Caxito	84	8.33 S	13.36 E
Cayambe	110	0.03 N	78.08 W
Cayambe ∧1	110	0.02 N	77.59 W
Cayenne	110	4.56 N	52.20 W
Cayey	108	18.07 N	66.10 W
Caylus	48	44.14 N	1.46 E
Cayman Brac I	108	19.43 N	79.49 W
Cayman Islands □2	106	19.30 N	80.40 W
Cayman Trench ✦1	22	19.00 N	80.00 W
Cayucos	104	35.27 N	120.54 W
Cayuga	102	42.56 N	79.51 W
Cayuga Heights	102	42.27 N	76.29 W
Cayuga Lake ⊜	102	42.45 N	76.45 W
Cayuta Creek ≃	102	41.59 N	76.30 W
Cazalla de la Sierra	50	37.56 N	5.45 W
Căzăneşti	54	44.37 N	27.01 E
Cazaux, Étang de c	48	44.30 N	1.10 W
Cazenovia	102	42.55 N	75.51 W
Cazères	48	43.13 N	1.05 E
Cazin	52	44.58 N	15.57 E
Čazma	52	45.45 N	16.37 E
Cazombo	84	11.54 S	22.52 E
Cazorla	50	37.55 N	3.00 W
Cchinvali	56	42.13 N	43.56 E
Cea ≃	50	42.00 N	5.36 W
Ceanannus Mór	40	53.44 N	6.53 W
Ceará-Mirim	110	5.38 S	35.26 W
Čeboksary	42	56.09 N	47.15 E
Cebollar	114	29.06 S	66.33 W
Cebollati	114	33.16 S	53.47 W
Cebollati ≃	114	33.09 S	53.38 W
Cebreros	50	40.27 N	4.28 W
Cebu	68	10.18 N	123.54 E
Cebu I	68	10.20 N	123.45 E
Ceccano	52	41.34 N	13.20 E
Čecerleg	62	48.52 N	101.14 E
Čečersk	60	52.55 N	30.55 E
Čechov	60	55.09 N	37.27 E
Čechtice	46	49.37 N	15.03 E
Čechy □9	46	49.50 N	14.00 E
Cecil Plains	94	27.32 S	151.12 E
Cecil Rhodes, Mount ∧	90	25.26 S	121.26 E
Cecina	52	43.19 N	10.31 E
Cecita, Lago di ⊜	52	39.24 N	16.30 E
Cedar ≃, Mi., U.S.	102	43.53 N	84.29 W
Cedar ≃, N.Y., U.S.	102	43.51 N	74.11 W
Cedar Creek ≃	104	42.24 N	114.49 W
Cedar Falls	102	42.31 N	92.26 W
Cedar Grove	102	38.13 N	81.25 W
Cedar Lake ⊜	102	46.02 N	78.30 W
Cedar Lake ⊜1	98	53.20 N	100.10 W
Cedar Mountain ∧	104	41.36 N	120.16 W
Cedar Rapids	102	41.59 N	91.40 W
Cedar Springs	102	43.13 N	85.33 W
Cedarville, S. Afr.	86	30.23 S	29.03 E
Cedarville, Ca., U.S.	104	41.31 N	120.10 W
Cedarville, Mi., U.S.	102	46.00 N	84.22 W
Cedarville, N.J., U.S.	102	39.19 N	75.12 W
Cedeira	50	43.39 N	8.03 W
Cedillo, Embalse de ⊜1	50	39.40 N	7.25 W
Cedrino ≃	52	40.23 N	9.44 E
Cedrón ≃	50	39.48 N	3.33 W
Cedros, Isla I	106	28.12 N	115.15 W
Ceduna	90	32.07 S	133.40 E
Cedynia	46	52.50 N	14.14 E
Cefalù	52	38.02 N	14.01 E
Cefn-mawr	34	52.58 N	3.04 W
Cega ≃	50	41.33 N	4.46 W
Čegdomyn	58	51.07 N	133.05 E
Cegléd	46	47.10 N	19.48 E
Ceglie Messapico	52	40.39 N	17.31 E
Cehegín	50	38.06 N	1.48 W
Ceheng	70	25.10 N	105.48 E
Cehu-Silvaniei	54	47.25 N	23.11 E
Ceiriog ≃	34	52.57 N	3.02 W
Ceirw ≃	34	52.59 N	3.27 W
Čekalin	60	54.06 N	36.15 E
Čel'abinsk	56	55.10 N	61.24 E
Čeläkovice	46	50.10 N	14.46 E
Celano	52	42.05 N	13.33 E
Celanova	50	42.09 N	7.58 W
Celaya	106	20.31 N	100.49 W
Celbridge	40	53.20 N	6.33 W
Cele	76	37.00 N	80.47 E
Celebes →Sulawesi I	72	2.00 S	121.00 E
Celebes Basin ✦1	28	4.00 N	122.00 E
Celebes Sea ▼2	72	3.00 N	122.00 E
Čeleken	56	39.26 N	53.07 E
Celina	102	40.32 N	84.34 W
Celinograd	56	51.10 N	71.30 E
Celje	52	46.14 N	15.16 E
Čelkar	56	47.50 N	59.36 E
Cellar Head ⟩	38	58.26 N	6.10 W
Celldömölk	46	47.16 N	17.09 E
Celle	46	52.37 N	10.05 E
Celorico da Beira	50	40.38 N	7.23 W
Celtic Sea ▼2	32	51.00 N	6.30 W
Celtic Shelf ✦4	20	49.15 N	7.00 W
Čel'uskin, mys ⟩	58	77.45 N	104.20 E
Cemaes Head ⟩	34	52.07 N	4.44 W
Čemerno	52	43.11 N	18.37 E
Čemerno)(	54	43.14 N	18.37 E
Cemmaes	34	52.37 N	3.42 W
Cenderawasih, Teluk c	92	2.30 S	135.20 E
Ceno ≃	52	44.41 N	10.05 E
Cenovo	54	43.32 N	25.39 E
Centenario	114	38.48 S	68.08 W
Centenário do Sul	114	22.48 S	51.37 W
Centerburg	102	40.18 N	82.41 W
Center Moriches	102	40.48 N	72.47 W
Centerville, In., U.S.	102	39.49 N	84.59 W
Centerville, Pa., U.S.	102	40.02 N	79.58 W
Cento	52	44.43 N	11.17 E
Central □4	38	56.05 N	4.20 W
Central □5, Bots.	86	21.30 S	26.00 E
Central □5, Para.	114	25.30 S	57.30 W
Central, Cordillera ✱, Col.	110	5.00 N	75.00 W
Central, Cordillera ✱, Perú	110	8.00 S	77.00 W
Central, Cordillera ✱, P.R.	108	18.10 N	66.35 W
Central, Massif ✱	48	45.00 N	3.10 E
Central, Planalto ✱1	110	18.00 S	47.00 W
Central, Sistema ✱	50	40.30 N	5.00 W
Central African Republic □1	82	7.00 N	21.00 E
Central Brāhui Range ✱	76	29.20 N	66.55 E
Central City	102	40.06 N	78.48 W
Centralia	100	46.42 N	122.57 W
Central Lake	102	45.04 N	85.15 W
Central Makrān Range ✱	74	26.40 N	64.30 E
Central Mount Stuart ∧	90	21.54 S	133.27 E
Central Mount Wedge ∧	90	22.51 S	131.50 E
Central'nyj	60	53.41 N	39.38 E
Central Pacific Basin ✦1	28	5.00 N	175.00 W
Central Point	104	42.22 N	122.54 W
Central Range ✱, Leso.	86	29.35 S	28.35 E
Central Range ✱, Pap. N. Gui.	92	5.00 S	142.30 E
Central Square	102	43.17 N	76.08 W
Central Valley	104	40.40 N	122.22 W
Centre, Canal du ≍	48	46.27 N	4.07 E
Centre Island I	96	46.28 S	167.51 E
Centreville, Md., U.S.	102	39.02 N	76.04 W
Centreville, Mi., U.S.	102	41.55 N	85.31 W
Century	102	39.05 N	80.11 W
Čepelare	54	41.44 N	24.41 E
Cepu	72	7.09 S	111.35 E
Ceram →Seram I	92	3.00 S	129.00 E
Ceram Sea →Seram, Laut ▼2	68	2.30 S	128.00 E
Čerčany	46	49.51 N	14.43 E
Čerdyn'	42	60.23 N	56.24 E
Cère ≃	48	44.55 N	1.53 E
Cereales	114	36.49 S	63.51 W
Čeremchovo	58	53.09 N	103.05 E
Čerepanovo	58	54.13 N	83.22 E
Čerepovec	60	59.08 N	37.54 E
Ceres, Arg.	114	29.53 S	61.57 W
Ceres, S. Afr.	86	33.21 S	19.18 E
Ceresole Reale	52	45.26 N	7.15 E
Céret	48	42.29 N	2.45 E
Cerf Island I	84	9.32 S	50.59 E
Ceri ≃	34	52.03 N	4.29 W
Cerignola	52	41.16 N	15.54 E
Cérilly	48	46.37 N	2.49 E
Cerisiers	48	48.08 N	3.29 E
Čerkassy	56	49.26 N	32.04 E
Čerkessk	56	44.14 N	42.04 E
Cerknica	52	45.48 N	14.22 E
Čerlak	56	54.09 N	74.48 E
Cermei	54	46.33 N	21.51 E
Čermez	56	58.53 N	56.08 E
Cerna, Jugo.	54	45.11 N	18.42 E
Cerna, Rom.	54	45.04 N	28.18 E
Čern'achovsk (Insterburg)	60	54.38 N	21.49 E
Černá hora ∧	46	48.58 N	13.48 E
Cernavodă	54	44.21 N	28.01 E
Cernay	48	47.49 N	7.10 E
Cerne Abbas	34	50.49 N	2.29 W
Cernei, Munţii ✱	54	45.02 N	22.31 E
Černigov	56	51.30 N	31.18 E
Černi vrăh ∧	54	42.34 N	23.17 E
Černogorsk	58	53.49 N	91.18 E
Černovcy	56	48.18 N	25.56 E
Černyševskij	58	63.00 N	112.15 E
Cerralvo, Isla I	106	24.15 N	109.55 W
Cerrigydrudion	34	53.02 N	3.33 W
Cërrik	54	41.02 N	19.57 E
Cerrillos	114	24.54 S	65.29 W
Cerritos	106	22.26 N	100.17 W
Cêrro Azul, Arg.	114	27.38 S	55.29 W
Cêrro Azul, Bra.	114	24.50 S	49.15 W
Cerro Chato	114	33.06 S	55.08 W
Cerro Colorado	114	33.52 S	55.33 W
Cerro de Pasco	110	10.41 S	76.16 W
Cêrro Largo	114	28.09 S	54.45 W
Cerro Moreno	114	23.28 S	70.25 W
Cerron, Cerro ∧	108	10.19 N	70.39 W
Cerro Prieto	104	32.27 N	115.17 W
Cerros Colorados, Embalse ⊜1	114	38.35 S	68.40 W
Cerro Vera	114	33.11 S	57.28 W
Čerskij	58	68.45 N	161.45 E
Čerskogo, chrebet ✱	58	65.00 N	144.00 E
Cervaro ≃	52	41.30 N	15.52 E
Cervati, Monte ∧	52	40.17 N	15.29 E
Červen Brjag	54	43.16 N	24.06 E
Červený Kostelec	46	50.29 N	16.06 E
Cervera	50	41.40 N	1.17 E
Cervera del Río Alhama	50	42.01 N	1.57 W
Cervera de Pisuerga	50	42.52 N	4.30 W
Cerveteri	52	42.00 N	12.06 E
Cervia	52	44.15 N	12.22 E
Cervialto, Monte ∧	52	40.47 N	15.08 E
Cervignano del Friuli	52	45.49 N	13.20 E
Cervione	52	42.20 N	9.31 E
Cervo	50	43.40 N	7.25 W
Červonograd	56	50.24 N	24.14 E
César □5	108	10.00 N	73.40 W
César ≃	108	9.00 N	73.58 W
Cesena	52	44.08 N	12.15 E
Cesenatico	52	44.12 N	12.24 E
Cēsis	60	57.18 N	25.15 E
Česká Kamenice	46	50.47 N	14.26 E
Česká Lípa	46	50.42 N	14.32 E
Česká Socialistická Republika □3	46	49.40 N	15.10 E
Česká Třebová	46	49.54 N	16.27 E
České Budějovice	46	48.59 N	14.28 E
Českomoravská vrchovina ✱1	46	49.20 N	15.30 E
Český Brod	46	50.02 N	14.58 E
Český Krumlov	46	48.49 N	14.19 E
Český Těšín	46	49.45 N	18.37 E
Češskaja guba c	42	67.30 N	46.30 E
Cessnock	94	32.50 S	151.21 E
Cestos ≃	80	5.40 N	9.10 W
Cetate	54	44.06 N	23.03 E
Cetina ≃	52	43.26 N	16.42 E
Cetinje	54	42.23 N	18.55 E
Ceuta	80	35.53 N	5.19 W
Ceva	52	44.23 N	8.02 E
Cévennes ✦1	48	44.00 N	3.30 E
Ceyhan	78	37.04 N	35.47 E
Ceylon →Sri Lanka □1	74	7.00 N	81.00 E
Chabanais	48	45.52 N	0.43 E
Chabarovo	56	69.39 N	60.24 E
Chabarovsk	58	48.27 N	135.06 E
Chabás	114	33.15 S	61.22 W
Chabeuil	48	44.54 N	5.01 E
Chabjuwardoo Bay c	90	22.57 S	113.48 E
Chablais ✦1	48	46.18 N	6.39 E
Chablis	48	47.49 N	3.48 E
Chacabuco	114	34.38 S	60.29 W
Chachani, Nevado ∧	110	16.12 S	71.33 W
Chachapoyas	110	6.13 S	77.51 W
Chachoengsao	70	13.42 N	101.05 E
Chāchora	76	24.10 N	76.59 E
Chaco □4	114	26.25 S	60.30 W
Chaco Austral ✦1	114	26.30 S	61.30 W
Chaco Boreal ✦1	114	23.00 S	60.00 W
Chaco Central ✦1	114	25.00 S	59.45 W
Chad (Tchad) □1	82	15.00 N	19.00 E
Chad, Lake (Lac Tchad) ⊜	82	13.20 N	14.00 E
Chadderton	36	53.33 N	2.08 W
Chadron	100	42.49 N	103.00 W
Chāgai Hills ✱2	78	29.30 N	64.15 E
'Chaghcharān	76	34.32 N	65.15 E
Chagny	48	46.55 N	4.45 E
Chagos Archipelago II	26	6.00 S	72.00 E
Chagos-Laccadive Plateau ✦3	26	3.00 N	73.00 E
Chaguaramas	108	9.20 N	66.16 W
Chaguaya	114	21.49 S	64.50 W
Chahār Borjak	78	30.17 N	62.03 E
Chaibāsā	76	22.34 N	85.49 E
Chaillé-les-Marais	48	46.24 N	1.01 W
Chaiqiao	66	29.51 N	121.56 E
Chaiyaphum	70	15.48 N	102.02 E
Chajarí	114	30.46 S	57.59 W
Chajian	66	32.40 N	118.46 E
Chākdaha	76	23.05 N	88.31 E
Chākia	76	26.25 N	85.03 E
Chakradharpur	76	22.42 N	85.38 E
Chakrāta	76	30.42 N	77.51 E
Chalais	48	45.16 N	0.02 E
Chalbi Desert ✦2	82	3.00 N	37.20 E
Chalfont Saint Peter	34	51.37 N	0.33 W
Chalford	34	51.45 N	2.09 W
Chaling	66	26.47 N	113.33 E
Chalk River	102	46.01 N	77.27 W
Challans	48	46.51 N	1.53 W
Challenger Deep ✦1	28	11.21 N	142.12 E
Chal'mer-Ju	42	67.58 N	64.50 E
Chalonnes-sur-Loire	48	47.21 N	0.46 W
Châlons-sur-Marne	48	48.57 N	4.22 E
Chalon-sur-Saône	48	46.47 N	4.51 E
Chalosse ✦1	48	43.45 N	0.30 W
Chalturin	42	58.33 N	48.50 E
Châlus, Fr.	48	45.39 N	0.59 E
Chālūs, Īrān	78	36.38 N	51.26 E
Cham	46	49.13 N	12.41 E
Chamaicó	114	35.03 S	64.58 W
Chaman	76	30.55 N	66.27 E
Chamba	76	32.34 N	76.08 E
Chambal ≃	76	26.30 N	79.15 E
Chamberlain	100	43.48 N	99.19 W
Chamberlain ≃	90	15.08 S	128.06 E
Chambersburg	102	39.56 N	77.39 W
Chambéry	48	45.34 N	5.56 E
Chambi, Jebel ∧	80	35.11 N	8.42 E
Chambley-Bussières	48	49.03 N	5.54 E
Chambon-sur-Voueize	48	46.11 N	2.25 E
Chambri Lake ⊜	92	4.16 S	143.08 E
Chamdo →Qamdo	62	31.11 N	97.15 E
Chamical	114	30.21 S	66.19 W
Chamo, Lake ⊜	82	5.50 N	37.33 E
Chamoli	76	30.24 N	79.21 E
Chamonix-Mont-Blanc	48	45.55 N	6.52 E
Chāmpa	76	22.03 N	82.39 E
Champagne □9	48	49.00 N	4.30 E
Champagne Castle ∧	86	29.06 S	29.20 E
Champagnole	48	46.45 N	5.55 E
Champaign	100	40.06 N	88.14 W
Champaqui, Cerro ∧	114	31.59 S	64.56 W
Champasak	70	14.53 N	105.52 E
Champdeniers	48	46.29 N	0.24 W
Champdoré, Lac ⊜	98	55.55 N	65.49 W
Champeix	48	45.36 N	3.08 E
Champéry	48	46.10 N	6.52 E
Champion	102	41.17 N	80.51 W
Champlain	102	44.59 N	73.26 W
Champlain, Lake ⊜	102	44.45 N	73.15 W
Champlitte-et-le-Prélot	48	47.37 N	5.31 E
Champotón	106	19.21 N	90.43 W
Chamusca	50	39.21 N	8.29 W
Chañar	114	30.32 S	65.58 W
Chañaral	114	26.21 S	70.37 W
Chañaral, Isla I	114	29.02 S	71.35 W
Chānasma	76	23.43 N	72.07 E
Chanch	62	51.30 N	100.40 E
Chanchelulla Peak ∧	104	40.28 N	122.59 W
Chanco	114	35.44 S	72.32 W
Chandalar ≃	98	66.36 N	145.48 W
Chandan Chauki	76	28.33 N	80.47 E
Chandausi	76	28.27 N	78.46 E
Chāndbāli	76	20.47 N	86.45 E
Chandīgarh	76	30.44 N	76.55 E
Chāndil	76	22.58 N	86.03 E
Chandler's Ford	34	50.59 N	1.23 W
Chandos Lake ⊜	102	44.49 N	78.00 W
Chāndpur, Bngl.	76	23.13 N	90.39 E
Chāndpur, India	76	29.09 N	78.16 E
Chandrapur	74	19.57 N	79.18 E
Chandyga	58	62.40 N	135.36 E
Chang (Yangtze) ≃	62	31.48 N	121.10 E
Chang, Ko I	70	12.05 N	102.20 E
Changajn nuruu ✱	62	47.30 N	100.00 E
Changan →Xi'an	62	34.15 N	108.52 E
Changane ≃	86	24.43 S	33.32 E
Changchou →Zhangzhou	66	24.33 N	117.39 E
Changchow →Changzhou	66	31.47 N	119.57 E
Changchun	62	43.53 N	125.19 E
Changde	62	29.02 N	111.41 E
Changge	66	34.15 N	113.50 E
Changhua, T'aiwan	66	24.05 N	120.32 E
Changhua, Zhg.	66	30.11 N	119.13 E
Changji	62	44.01 N	87.19 E
Changjiang	70	19.17 N	109.02 E
Changle	66	26.00 N	119.31 E
Changli	62	39.43 N	119.11 E
Changlinhe	66	31.40 N	117.29 E
Changlun	72	6.26 N	100.26 E
Changning	70	24.55 N	99.35 E
Changokurt	56	61.58 N	64.18 E
Changsha	66	28.12 N	112.58 E
Changshan	66	28.55 N	118.30 E
Changshu	66	31.39 N	120.45 E
Changtai	66	24.40 N	117.46 E
Changting	66	25.52 N	116.20 E
Changxing	66	31.01 N	119.54 E
Changzhi	62	36.11 N	113.08 E
Changzhou (Changchow)	66	31.47 N	119.57 E
Chanino	60	54.13 N	36.37 E
Chanka, ozero (Xingkai Hu) ⊜	62	45.00 N	132.24 E
Channel Country ✦1	94	24.45 S	141.00 E
Channel Islands II, Europe	32	49.20 N	2.20 W
Channel Islands II, Ca., U.S.	104	33.30 N	119.15 W
Channel-Port-aux-Basques	98	47.34 N	59.09 W
Chantada	50	42.37 N	7.46 W
Chantajskoje, ozero ⊜	58	68.20 N	91.00 E
Chantajskoje vodochranilišče ⊜1	58	68.00 N	88.00 E
Chanthaburi	70	12.36 N	102.09 E
Chantilly	48	49.12 N	2.28 E
Chantonnay	48	46.41 N	1.03 W
Chantrey Inlet c	98	67.48 N	96.20 W
Chanty-Mansijsk	56	61.00 N	69.06 E
Chanujn ≃	62	49.22 N	102.22 E
Chanute	100	37.40 N	95.27 W
Chao'an	66	23.41 N	116.38 E
Ch'aochou	66	22.33 N	120.32 E
Chao Hu ⊜	66	31.31 N	117.33 E
Chao Phraya ≃	70	13.32 N	100.36 E
Chaoxian	66	31.36 N	117.52 E
Chaoyang, Zhg.	62	41.35 N	120.28 E
Chaoyang, Zhg.	66	23.17 N	116.37 E
Chapala, Lago de ⊜	106	20.15 N	103.00 W
Chāparmukh	76	26.12 N	92.32 E
Chaparra	108	21.10 N	76.29 W
Chaparral	110	3.43 N	75.28 W
Chapčeranga	58	49.42 N	112.24 E
Chapecó	114	27.06 S	52.36 W
Chapel-en-le-Frith	36	53.20 N	1.54 W
Chapelfell Top ∧	36	54.41 N	2.13 W
Chapelhall	38	55.50 N	3.56 W
Chapel Point ⟩	34	50.16 N	4.46 W
Chapel Saint Leonards	36	53.13 N	0.19 E
Chapeltown	36	53.28 N	1.28 W
Chapicuy	114	31.39 S	57.54 W
Chapleau	98	47.50 N	83.24 W
Chapman, Cape ⟩	98	69.12 N	88.59 W
Chapmanville	102	37.58 N	82.01 W
Chāpra	76	25.46 N	84.45 E
Chapultepec, Méx.	104	31.50 N	116.38 W
Chapultepec, Méx.	104	32.22 N	115.05 W
Chaquiago	114	27.32 S	66.21 W
Char ≃	34	50.44 N	2.53 W
Charadai	114	27.38 S	59.54 W
Charata	114	27.13 S	61.12 W
Charbala	58	64.07 N	120.19 E
Chard	34	50.53 N	2.58 W
Chardon	102	41.36 N	81.08 W
Charduār	76	26.52 N	92.46 E
Charente □5	48	45.40 N	0.10 E
Charente ≃	48	45.57 N	1.05 W
Charente-Maritime □5	48	45.30 N	0.45 W
Charenton-du-Cher	48	46.44 N	2.38 E
Chari ≃	82	12.58 N	14.31 E
Chārīkār	76	35.01 N	69.11 E
Charing	34	51.13 N	0.48 E
Charity	110	7.24 N	58.36 W
Charkhāri	76	25.24 N	79.45 E
Char'kov	56	50.00 N	36.15 E
Charlbury	34	51.53 N	1.29 W
Charleroi	46	50.25 N	4.26 E
Charles, Peak ∧	90	32.52 S	121.11 E
Charles City	100	43.03 N	92.40 W
Charles Island I	98	62.40 N	74.15 W
Charles Point ⟩	92	12.23 S	130.36 E
Charles Sound ᑌ	96	45.02 S	167.04 E
Charleston, N.Z.	96	41.54 S	171.26 E
Charleston, S.C., U.S.	100	32.46 N	79.55 W
Charleston, W.V., U.S.	102	38.20 N	81.37 W
Charleston Peak ∧	104	36.16 N	115.42 W
Charlestown, Ire.	40	53.57 N	8.49 W
Charlestown, St. C.-N.	108	17.08 N	62.37 W
Charlestown, S. Afr.	86	27.30 S	29.55 E
Charlestown, N.H., U.S.	102	43.14 N	72.25 W
Charles Town, W.V., U.S.	102	39.17 N	77.51 W
Charleville	94	26.24 S	146.15 E
Charleville →Ráth Luirc	40	52.21 N	8.41 W
Charleville-Mézières	48	49.46 N	4.43 E
Charlevoix	102	45.19 N	85.15 W
Charlevoix, Lake ⊜	102	45.15 N	85.08 W
Charlieu	48	46.10 N	4.10 E
Charlotte, Mi., U.S.	102	42.33 N	84.50 W
Charlotte, N.C., U.S.	100	35.13 N	80.50 W
Charlotte Amalie	108	18.21 N	64.56 W
Charlotte Harbor c	108	26.45 N	82.12 W
Charlottenberg	44	59.53 N	12.17 E
Charlottesville	102	38.01 N	78.28 W
Charlottetown	98	46.14 N	63.08 W
Charlton	94	36.16 S	143.21 E
Charlton Island I	98	52.00 N	79.30 W
Charlton Kings	34	51.53 N	2.03 W
Charly-sur-Marne	48	48.58 N	3.17 E
Charmes	48	48.22 N	6.17 E
Charminster	34	50.43 N	2.28 W
Charmouth	34	50.45 N	2.55 W
Charnley ≃	92	16.25 S	124.57 E
Charnwood Forest ✦3	34	52.43 N	1.15 W
Charolles	48	46.26 N	4.17 E
Charovsk	60	59.57 N	40.11 E
Charroux	48	46.09 N	0.24 E
Chārsadda	76	34.09 N	71.44 E
Charters Towers	94	20.05 S	146.16 E
Chartres	48	48.27 N	1.30 E
Char Us nuur ⊜	62	48.00 N	92.10 E
Chasav'urt	56	43.15 N	46.37 E
Chascomús	114	35.34 S	58.01 W
Chase, Mount ∧	102	46.07 N	68.29 W
Chaslands Mistake ⟩	96	46.38 S	169.22 E
Chatanbulag	62	43.09 N	109.08 E
Chatanga	58	71.58 N	102.30 E
Chatanga ≃	58	72.55 N	106.00 E
Chatangskij zaliv c	58	73.30 N	109.00 E
Châteaubriant	48	47.43 N	1.23 W
Château-Chinon	48	47.04 N	3.56 E
Château d'Oex	48	46.28 N	7.08 E
Château-du-Loir	48	47.42 N	0.25 E
Châteaudun	48	48.05 N	1.20 E
Chateaugay	102	44.55 N	74.04 W
Château-Gontier	48	47.50 N	0.42 W
Châteauguay ≃	102	45.24 N	73.45 W
Château-Landon	48	48.09 N	2.42 E
Château-la-Vallière	48	47.33 N	0.19 E
Châteaulin	48	48.12 N	4.05 W
Châteaumeillant	48	46.34 N	2.12 E
Châteauneuf-de-Randon	48	44.39 N	3.40 E
Châteauneuf-en-Thymerais	48	48.35 N	1.15 E
Châteauneuf-sur-Charente	48	45.36 N	0.03 W
Châteauneuf-sur-Loire	48	47.52 N	2.14 E
Châteauneuf-sur-Sarthe	48	47.41 N	0.30 W
Château-Renault	48	47.35 N	0.55 E
Châteauroux	48	46.49 N	1.42 E
Château-Salins	48	48.49 N	6.30 E
Château-Thierry	48	49.03 N	3.24 E
Châtellerault	48	46.49 N	0.33 E
Châtel-sur-Moselle	48	48.18 N	6.24 E
Châtelus-Malvaleix	48	46.18 N	2.01 E
Chatgal	62	50.26 N	100.09 E
Chatham, N.B., Can.	98	47.02 N	65.28 W
Chatham, On., Can.	102	42.24 N	82.11 W
Chatham, Eng., U.K.	34	51.23 N	0.32 E
Chatham, Ma., U.S.	102	41.40 N	69.57 W
Chatham, N.Y., U.S.	102	42.21 N	73.35 W
Chatham Islands II	28	43.55 S	176.30 W
Chatham Rise ✦3	28	43.30 S	178.00 W
Chatham Strait ᑌ	98	57.30 N	134.45 W
Châtillon	52	45.45 N	7.37 E
Châtillon-Coligny	48	47.50 N	2.51 E
Châtillon-en-Bazois	48	47.03 N	3.40 E
Châtillon-sur-Chalaronne	48	46.07 N	4.58 E
Châtillon-sur-Indre	48	46.59 N	1.11 E
Châtillon-sur-Seine	48	47.51 N	4.33 E
Chatra	76	24.13 N	84.52 E
Chatrapur	74	19.21 N	84.59 E
Chātsu	76	26.36 N	75.57 E
Chatsworth	94	21.58 S	140.19 E
Chattahoochee ≃	100	30.52 N	84.57 W
Chattanooga	100	35.02 N	85.18 W
Chatteris	34	52.27 N	0.03 E
Chatton	36	55.33 N	1.55 W
Chatyrka	58	62.03 N	175.15 E
Chaudes-Aigues	48	44.51 N	3.00 E
Chauk	70	20.54 N	94.50 E
Chaumont	48	48.07 N	5.08 E
Chaumont-en-Vexin	48	49.16 N	1.53 E
Chaumont-Porcien	48	49.39 N	4.15 E
Chauncey	102	39.23 N	82.07 W
Chauny	48	49.37 N	3.13 E
Chaupāran	76	24.23 N	85.15 E
Chau-phu	70	10.42 N	105.07 E
Chaussin	48	46.58 N	5.25 E
Chautauqua Lake ⊜	102	42.12 N	79.27 W
Chauvigny	48	46.34 N	0.39 E
Chavanges	48	48.31 N	4.34 E
Chavarría	114	28.57 S	58.35 W
Chaves	50	41.44 N	7.28 W
Chayuan	66	27.40 N	112.57 E
Chazy	102	44.53 N	73.26 W
Cheadle	34	52.59 N	1.59 W
Cheat ≃	102	39.45 N	79.54 W
Cheat, Shavers Fork ≃	102	39.06 N	79.33 W
Cheb	46	50.01 N	12.25 E
Cheboygan	102	45.38 N	84.28 W
Chech, Erg ✦2	80	25.00 N	2.15 W
Chęciny	46	50.48 N	20.28 E
Cheddar	34	51.17 N	2.46 W
Cheddleton	36	53.04 N	2.02 W
Cheduba Island I	70	18.48 N	93.38 E
Cheektowaga	102	42.55 N	78.46 W
Cheepie	94	26.39 S	145.01 E
Chef-Boutonne	48	46.07 N	0.04 W
Chegutu	86	18.10 S	30.14 E
Cheiron, Cime du ∧	48	43.49 N	6.58 E
Cheju	62	33.31 N	126.32 E
Cheju-do I	62	33.20 N	126.30 E
Chekiang →Zhejiang □4	62	29.00 N	120.00 E
Chelforó	114	39.04 S	66.32 W
Chelghoum el Aïd	50	36.10 N	6.10 E
Chellaston	34	52.53 N	1.27 W
Chełm	46	51.10 N	23.28 E
Chelmer ≃	34	51.48 N	0.40 E
Chełmno	46	53.22 N	18.26 E
Chelmsford	34	51.44 N	0.28 E
Chełmża	46	53.12 N	18.37 E
Chelsea, Mi., U.S.	102	42.19 N	84.01 W
Chelsea, Vt., U.S.	102	43.59 N	72.26 W
Cheltenham	34	51.54 N	2.04 W
Chelva	50	39.45 N	0.59 W
Chelyabinsk →Čel'abinsk	56	55.10 N	61.24 E
Chelyan	102	38.11 N	81.29 W
Chemax	108	20.39 N	87.56 W
Chemillé	48	47.13 N	0.44 W
Chemnitz →Karl-Marx-Stadt	46	50.50 N	12.55 E
Chemult	104	43.13 N	121.46 W
Chemung Lake ⊜	102	44.25 N	78.22 W
Chenāb ≃	76	29.23 N	71.02 E
Chenango ≃	102	42.05 N	75.55 W
Chenango Bridge	102	42.10 N	75.51 W
Chenchiang →Zhenjiang	62	32.13 N	119.26 E
Chencun	66	22.58 N	113.13 E
Chendai	66	23.48 N	117.24 E
Chenderoh, Tasek ⊜	72	4.58 N	100.57 E
Chénéville	102	45.53 N	75.03 W
Cheney	100	47.29 N	117.34 W
Chengde	62	40.58 N	117.53 E
Chengdu	62	30.39 N	104.04 E
Chengele	76	28.47 N	96.16 E
Chenghai	66	23.30 N	116.46 E
Chengjiang	70	24.45 N	102.54 E
Chengmai	70	19.48 N	110.02 E
Chengshan Jiao ⟩	62	37.24 N	122.42 E
Chengtu →Chengdu	62	30.39 N	104.04 E
Chenxian	66	25.48 N	112.59 E
Chepén	110	7.13 S	79.27 W
Chepes	114	31.21 S	66.36 W
Chepo	108	9.10 N	79.06 W
Chepstow	34	51.39 N	2.41 W
Cher □5	48	47.05 N	2.30 E
Cher ≃	48	47.21 N	0.29 E
Cherbourg	48	49.39 N	1.39 W
Cherchell	50	36.36 N	2.12 E
Cherepovets →Čerepovec	60	59.08 N	37.54 E
Chergui, Chott ech ⊜	80	34.21 N	0.30 E
Cheribon →Cirebon	72	6.44 S	108.34 E
Cherkassy →Čerkassy	56	49.26 N	32.04 E
Cherokee Sound	108	26.17 N	77.04 W
Cherquenco	114	38.41 S	72.00 W
Cherrabun	90	18.29 S	125.19 E
Cherrapunji	76	25.18 N	91.42 E
Cherry Hill	102	39.56 N	75.01 W
Cherson	56	46.38 N	32.35 E
Chertsey	34	51.24 N	0.30 W
Cherwell ≃	34	51.44 N	1.15 W
Chesaning	102	43.11 N	84.06 W
Chesapeake	100	36.49 N	76.16 W
Chesapeake Bay c	100	38.40 N	76.25 W
Chesapeake Beach	102	38.41 N	76.32 W
Chesapeake City	102	39.31 N	75.48 W
Chesham	34	51.43 N	0.38 W
Cheshire	102	42.33 N	73.09 W
Cheshire □6	36	53.23 N	2.30 W
Cheshire Plain ≚	36	53.17 N	2.40 W
Cheshunt	34	51.43 N	0.02 W
Chesil Beach ⊥2	34	50.38 N	2.33 W
Chesley	102	44.17 N	81.05 W
Chest Creek ≃	102	40.53 N	78.44 W
Chester, Eng., U.K.	36	53.12 N	2.54 W
Chester, Ca., U.S.	104	40.18 N	121.13 W
Chester, Pa., U.S.	102	39.50 N	75.21 W
Chester, Vt., U.S.	102	43.15 N	72.35 W
Chesterfield	36	53.15 N	1.25 W
Chesterfield, Île I	87b	16.20 S	43.58 E
Chesterfield, Îles II	88	19.30 S	158.00 E
Chesterfield Inlet	98	63.21 N	90.42 W
Chesterfield Inlet c	98	63.25 N	90.45 W
Chesterhill	102	39.29 N	81.51 W
Chester-le-Street	36	54.52 N	1.34 W
Chesterton Range ✱	94	25.30 S	147.27 E
Chestertown	102	39.12 N	76.04 W
Chesterville	102	45.06 N	75.14 W
Chest Peak ∧	96	43.06 S	172.01 E
Chesuncook Lake ⊜	102	46.00 N	69.20 W
Chet ≃	34	52.33 N	1.32 E
Cheta ≃	58	71.54 N	102.06 E
Chetco ≃	104	42.03 N	124.16 W
Cheval Blanc, Pointe du ⟩	108	19.41 N	73.27 W
Chevington Drift	36	55.17 N	1.36 W
Cheviot, N.Z.	96	42.49 S	173.16 E
Cheviot, Oh., U.S.	102	39.09 N	84.36 W
Cheviot Hills ✱2	38	55.22 N	2.22 W
Chew Bahir (Lake Stefanie) ⊜	82	4.40 N	36.50 E
Chew Magna	34	51.22 N	2.35 W
Cheyenne	100	41.08 N	104.49 W
Cheyenne ≃	100	44.40 N	101.15 W
Cheyne Bay c	90	34.35 S	118.50 E
Cheyne Point ⟩	90	33.58 S	122.34 E
Chhabra	76	24.40 N	76.50 E
Chhatarpur, India	76	24.55 N	79.36 E
Chhatarpur, India	76	24.23 N	84.11 E
Chhindwāra	76	22.04 N	78.56 E
Chhota-Chhindwāra	76	23.03 N	79.29 E
Chhota Udepur	76	22.19 N	74.01 E
Chi ≃	70	15.11 N	104.43 E
Chiai	66	23.29 N	120.27 E
Chiali	66	23.10 N	120.10 E
Chian →Ji'an	66	27.07 N	114.58 E

Name	Page	Lat. °′	Long. °′
Chianciano Terme	52	43.03N	11.50 E
Chiang Khan	70	17.52N	101.36 E
Chiang Mai	70	18.47N	98.59 E
Chiang Rai	70	19.54N	99.50 E
Chiaramonte Gulfi	52	37.02N	14.42 E
Chiaravalle Centrale	52	38.41N	16.25 E
Chiari	52	45.32N	9.56 E
Chiasso	48	45.50N	9.01 E
Chiavari	52	44.19N	9.19 E
Chiavenna	52	46.19N	9.24 E
Chiba	64	35.36N	140.07 E
Chibougamau	98	49.55N	74.22W
Chibuto	86	24.44S	33.33 E
Chibuzhangchuhu ⊜	76	33.25N	90.15 E
Chicago	100	41.51N	87.39W
Chicapa ≃	84	6.26S	20.47 E
Chichagof Island I	98	57.30N	135.30W
Chīchāwatni	76	30.32N	72.42 E
Chichester	34	50.50N	0.48W
Chichester Range ⋏	90	22.00S	118.50 E
Chichi	66	23.50N	120.47 E
Chichibu	64	35.59N	139.05 E
Chichijima-rettō II	28	27.06N	142.12 E
Chichiriviche	108	10.56N	68.16W
Chickasha	100	35.03N	97.56W
Chickerell	34	50.37N	2.30W
Chiclana de la Frontera	50	36.25N	6.08W
Chiclayo	110	6.46S	79.51W
Chico	104	39.43N	121.50W
Chico ≃, Arg.	112	49.56S	68.32W
Chico ≃, Arg.	112	43.48S	66.25W
Chicopee	102	42.08N	72.36W
Chicoutimi	98	48.26N	71.04W
Chidambaram	74	11.24N	79.42 E
Chiddingfold	34	51.06N	0.37W
Chiemsee ⊜	46	47.54N	12.29 E
Chieri	52	45.01N	7.49 E
Chieti	52	42.21N	14.10 E
Chieveley	34	51.27N	1.19W
Chifeng	62	42.18N	119.00 E
Chigasaki	64	35.19N	139.24 E
Chigwell	34	51.38N	0.05 E
Chihli, Gulf of →Bo Hai C	62	38.30N	120.00 E
Chihu	66	24.07N	117.51 E
Chihuahua	106	28.38N	106.05W
Chikmagalūr	74	13.19N	75.47 E
Chikugo ≃	64	33.09N	130.21 E
Chikuma ≃	64	36.59N	138.35 E
Chilās	76	35.26N	74.05 E
Chilcotin ≃	98	51.45N	122.24W
Chilcott Island I	94	16.58S	149.58 E
Childers	94	25.14S	152.17 E
Childress	100	34.25N	100.12W
Chile □[1]	112	30.00S	71.00W
Chile Basin +[1]	24	33.00S	80.00W
Chile Chico	112	46.33S	71.44W
Chilecito, Arg.	114	29.10S	67.30W
Chilecito, Arg.	114	33.53S	69.03W
Chile Rise +[3]	24	40.00S	90.00W
Chilete	110	7.14S	78.51W
Chilham	34	51.15N	0.57 E
Chilia, Braţul ≃[1]	54	45.18N	29.40 E
Chililabombwe (Bancroft)	84	12.18S	27.43 E
Chilin →Jilin	62	43.51N	126.33 E
Chilka Lake ⊜	76	19.45N	85.25 E
Chilko Lake ⊜	98	51.20N	124.05W
Chillagoe	94	17.09S	144.32 E
Chillán	114	36.36S	72.07W
Chillar	114	37.18S	59.59W
Chillicothe, Mo., U.S.	100	39.47N	93.33W
Chillicothe, Oh., U.S.	102	39.19N	82.58W
Chilliwack	98	49.10N	121.57W
Chiloé, Isla de I	112	42.30S	73.55W
Chilok	58	51.21N	110.28 E
Chilok ≃	58	51.19N	106.59 E
Chiloquin	104	42.34N	121.51W
Chilpancingo	106	17.33N	99.30W
Chiltern Hills ⋏[2]	34	51.42N	0.48W
Chilton	36	54.39N	1.33W
Chiluage	84	9.30S	21.47 E
Chilung	66	25.08N	121.44 E
Chilwa, Lake ⊜	84	15.12S	35.50 E
Chimbarongo	114	34.42S	71.03W
Chimbas	114	31.29S	68.32W
Chimborazo ∧[1]	110	1.28S	78.48W
Chimbote	110	9.05S	78.36W
Chimichagua	108	9.15N	73.49W
Chimkent →Čimkent	56	42.18N	69.36 E
Chimki	60	55.54N	37.26 E
Chimoio	86	19.08S	33.29 E
Chimpay	114	39.10S	66.09W
Chin □[8]	70	22.00N	93.30 E
China (Zhongguo) □[1]	62	35.00N	105.00 E
China Lake ⊜	104	35.46N	117.39W
Chinandega	108	12.37N	87.09W
Chincha Alta	110	13.27S	76.08W
Chinchaga ≃	98	58.50N	118.20W
Chinchiang →Quanzhou	66	24.54N	118.35 E
Chinchilla	94	26.45S	150.38 E
Chinchón	50	40.08N	3.25W
Chinchorro, Banco +[4]	106	18.35N	87.22W
Chincilla de Monte Aragón	50	38.55N	1.43W
Chincolco	114	32.13S	70.50W
Chincoteague	102	37.55N	75.22W
Chinde	86	18.37S	36.24 E
Chindwin ≃	70	21.26N	95.15 E
Ch'ingchiang →Qingjiang	66	33.35N	119.02 E
Chingola	84	12.32S	27.52 E
Ch'ingtao →Qingdao	62	36.06N	120.19 E
Chinguetti	80	20.27N	12.22W
Chinhae	62	35.09N	128.40 E
Chin Hills ⋏[2]	70	22.30N	93.30 E
Chinhoyi	84	17.22S	30.12 E
Chīni	76	31.32N	78.15 E
Chiniot	76	31.43N	72.59 E
Chinju	62	35.11N	128.05 E
Chinkiang →Zhenjiang	66	32.13N	119.26 E
Chinko ≃	82	4.50N	23.53 E
Chinkuashih	66	25.07N	121.51 E
Chinmen	66	24.27N	118.21 E
Chinmen Tao I	66	24.27N	118.23 E
Chinnor	34	51.43N	0.56W
Chino	104	34.00N	117.41W
Chinon	48	47.10N	0.15 E
Chinsali	84	10.34S	32.03 E
Chinú	108	9.06N	75.24W
Chioggia	52	45.13N	12.17 E
Chios →Khíos I	54	38.22N	26.00 E
Chipata	84	13.39S	32.40 E
Chippenham	34	51.28N	2.07W
Chippewa ≃, Mi., U.S.	102	43.35N	84.17W
Chippewa ≃, Wi., U.S.	100	44.25N	92.10W
Chippewa Falls	100	44.56N	91.23W
Chipping Campden	34	52.03N	1.46W
Chipping Norton	34	51.56N	1.32W
Chipping Ongar	34	51.43N	0.15 E
Chipping Sodbury	34	51.33N	2.24W
Chiquimula	106	14.48N	89.33W
Chiquinquirá	110	5.37N	73.50W
Chirāwa	76	28.15N	75.38 E
Chirfa	80	20.57N	12.21 E
Chīrgaon	76	25.35N	78.49 E
Chiricahua Peak ∧	100	31.52N	109.20W
Chiriguaná	108	9.22N	73.36W
Chiriquí, Golfo de C	106	8.00N	82.20W
Chiriquí, Laguna de C	108	9.03N	82.00W
Chiriquí Grande	108	8.57N	82.07W
Chirk	34	52.56N	3.03W
Chirnside	38	55.48N	2.13W
Chiromo	84	16.33S	35.08 E
Chirripó ≃	108	10.41N	83.41W
Chirripó, Cerro ∧	108	9.29N	83.30W
Chiseldon	34	51.31N	1.44W
Ch'ishan	66	22.53N	120.28 E
Chisholm	102	44.28N	70.12W
Chishtiān Mandi	76	29.48N	72.52 E
Chişineu-Criş	54	46.31N	21.31 E
Chislaviči	60	54.11N	32.10 E
Chisone ≃	52	44.49N	7.25 E
Chitado	84	17.20S	13.54 E
Chita-hantō ›[1]	64	34.50N	136.53 E
Chitembo	84	13.34S	16.40 E
Chitipa	84	9.43S	33.16 E
Chitorgarh	76	24.53N	74.38 E
Chitose	64a	42.49N	141.39 E
Chitradurga	74	14.14N	76.24 E
Chitrakūt Dham	76	25.11N	80.52 E
Chitrāl	76	35.51N	71.47 E
Chitré	106	7.58N	80.26W
Chittagong	76	22.20N	91.50 E
Chittering	90	31.29S	116.06 E
Chittoor	74	13.12N	79.07 E
Chíuchíu	114	22.21S	68.39W
Chiumbe ≃	84	7.00S	21.12 E
Chiusi	52	43.01N	11.57 E
Chiuta, Lake ⊜	84	14.55S	35.50 E
Chiva, Esp.	50	39.28N	0.43W
Chiva, S.S.S.R.	56	41.24N	60.22 E
Chivacoa	108	10.10N	68.54W
Chivasso	52	45.11N	7.53 E
Chivilcoy	114	34.53S	60.01W
Chivirira Falls L	86	21.14S	32.20 E
Chizu	64	35.16N	134.14 E
Chjargas nuur ⊜	62	49.12N	93.24 E
Chkalov →Orenburg	56	51.54N	55.06 E
Chloride	104	35.24N	114.11W
Chmel'nickij	56	49.25N	27.00 E
Chmielnik	46	50.37N	20.46 E
Chŏâm Khsant	70	14.13N	104.56 E
Choapa ≃	114	31.38S	71.34W
Chobe □[5]	86	18.30S	25.00 E
Chobe ≃	86	17.50S	25.05 E
Choceň	46	50.00N	16.13 E
Chochis, Cerro ∧	110	18.04S	60.03W
Chocianów	46	51.25N	15.55 E
Chociwel	46	53.28N	15.19 E
Chocolate Mountains ⋏	104	33.20N	115.15W
Chocope	110	7.47S	79.13W
Chodecz	46	52.24N	19.01 E
Chodžejli	56	42.48N	59.25 E
Chodziez	46	52.59N	16.56 E
Choele-Choel	114	39.16S	65.41W
Chohtan	76	25.29N	71.04 E
Choiseul I	88	7.05S	157.00 E
Chojna	46	52.58N	14.28 E
Chojnice	46	53.42N	17.34 E
Chojnów	46	51.17N	15.56 E
Chōkai-san ∧	64	39.06N	140.03 E
Cholame Creek ≃	104	35.39N	120.22W
Cholet	48	47.04N	0.53W
Cholm	60	57.09N	31.11 E
Cholmsk	58	47.03N	142.03 E
Cholsey	34	51.34N	1.10W
Choluj	60	56.34N	41.53 E
Choluteca	108	13.18N	87.12W
Choluteca ≃	108	13.07N	87.19W
Choma	84	16.48S	26.59 E
Chomo Lhāri ∧	76	27.50N	89.15 E
Chomu	76	27.10N	75.44 E
Chomutov	46	50.28N	13.26 E
Ch'ŏnan	62	36.48N	127.09 E
Chon Buri	70	13.22N	100.59 E
Chone	110	0.41S	80.06W
Chong'an	66	27.45N	118.02 E
Chongde	66	30.32N	120.26 E
Ch'ŏngjin	62	41.47N	129.50 E
Ch'ŏngju	62	36.39N	127.31 E
Chongming	66	31.37N	121.24 E
Chongqing	62	29.34N	106.35 E
Chongren, Zhg.	66	29.37N	120.43 E
Chongren, Zhg.	66	27.46N	116.01 E
Chongwu	66	24.53N	118.55 E
Chongyang	66	29.33N	114.00 E
Chongyi	66	25.44N	114.18 E
Chongzuo	62	22.21N	107.26 E
Chŏnju	62	35.49N	127.08 E
Chonkham	76	27.48N	96.02 E
Chonos, Archipiélago de los II	112	45.00S	74.00W
Chontaleña, Cordillera ⋏	108	11.50N	84.50W
Chonuu	58	66.27N	143.06 E
Chonzie, Ben ∧	38	56.27N	3.59W
Cho Oyu ∧	76	28.06N	86.39 E
Chopda	76	21.15N	75.18 E
Chopinzinho	114	25.51S	52.30W
Chop'or ≃	56	49.36N	42.19 E
Chopwell	36	54.55N	1.49W
Chor ≃	58	47.48N	134.43 E
Chorges	48	44.33N	6.17 E
Chorley	36	53.39N	2.39W
Chorlovo	60	55.20N	38.49 E
Chorog	76	37.31N	71.33 E
Choros, Isla I	114	29.16S	71.33W
Choroszcz	46	53.09N	22.59 E
Ch'ŏrwŏn	62	38.16N	127.12 E
Chorzele	46	53.16N	20.55 E
Chosedachard	56	67.02N	59.22 E
Chōshi	64	35.44N	140.50 E
Chos Malal	114	37.23S	70.16W
Choszczno	46	53.10N	15.26 E
Chotěboř	46	49.43N	15.40 E
Chotila	76	22.25N	71.11 E
Chotimsk	60	53.26N	32.35 E
Chot'kovo	60	56.15N	38.00 E
Chovd	62	48.01N	91.38 E
Chovd ≃	62	48.06N	92.11 E
Chövsgöl Nuur ⊜	62	51.00N	100.30 E
Chowchilla	104	37.07N	120.15W
Chowchilla ≃	104	37.07N	120.32W
Choya	114	28.30S	64.52W
Chrissiesmeer	86	26.16S	30.13 E
Christanshåb	98	68.50N	51.12W
Christchurch, N.Z.	96	43.32S	172.38 E
Christchurch, Eng., U.K.	34	50.44N	1.45W
Christian, Cape ›	98	70.31N	68.18W
Christiana	86	27.52S	25.08 E
Christian Island I	102	44.50N	80.13W
Christiansfeld	44	55.21N	9.29 E
Christiansø I	44	55.19N	15.12 E
Christiansted	108	17.45N	64.42W
Christie Bay C	98	62.32N	111.10W
Christina ≃	98	56.40N	111.03W
Christmas Creek	90	18.53S	125.55 E
Christmas Island □[2]	68	10.30S	105.40 E
Christmas Island →Kiritimati I[1]	28	1.52N	157.25W
Christmas Ridge +[3]	28	5.00N	160.00W
Christopher Lake ⊜	90	24.49S	127.42 E
Chroma ≃	58	71.36N	144.49 E
Chromtau	56	50.17N	58.27 E
Chrudim	46	49.57N	15.48 E
Chrzanów	46	50.09N	19.24 E
Chu ≃	68	19.53N	105.45 E
Chuansha	66	31.12N	121.42 E
Chubut ≃	112	43.20S	65.03W
Chudleigh	34	50.36N	3.38W
Chūgoku-sanchi ⋏	64	34.58N	132.57 E
Chuí	114	33.41S	53.27W
Chukai	72	4.15N	103.25 E
Chukchi Sea ⊤[2]	22	69.00N	171.00W
Chula Vista	104	32.38N	117.05W
Chulmleigh	34	50.55N	3.52W
Chulucanas	110	5.06S	80.10W
Chumbicha	114	28.52S	66.14W
Chumphon	70	10.30N	99.10 E
Chum Saeng	70	15.54N	100.19 E
Chunan, T'aiwan	66	24.41N	120.52 E
Chun'an, Zhg.	66	29.35N	118.58 E
Ch'unch'ŏn	62	37.52N	127.43 E
Ch'ungju	62	36.58N	127.58 E
Chungking →Chongqing	62	29.34N	106.35 E
Chungli	66	24.57N	121.13 E
Chungyang Shanmo ⋏	66	23.30N	121.00 E
Chuŏr Phnum Krâvanh ⋏	70	12.00N	103.15 E
Chuquicamata	114	22.19S	68.56W
Chur	48	46.51N	9.32 E
Churachandpur	76	24.20N	93.40 E
Churchdown	34	51.53N	2.10W
Churchill	98	58.46N	94.10W
Churchill ≃, Can.	98	58.47N	94.12W
Churchill ≃, Nf., Can.	98	53.30N	60.10W
Churchill, Cape ›	98	58.46N	93.12W
Churchill Falls L	98	53.35N	64.27W
Churchill Lake ⊜	98	55.55N	108.20W
Church Stretton	34	52.32N	2.49W
Churia Range ⋏	76	27.40N	83.40 E
Churn ≃	34	51.38N	1.53W
Churnet ≃	34	52.55N	1.50W
Churu	76	28.18N	74.57 E
Churubusco	102	41.13N	85.19W
Churuguara	108	10.49N	69.32W
Chushan	66	23.45N	120.40 E
Chushul	76	33.36N	78.39 E
Chust	56	48.10N	23.18 E
Chutag	62	49.23N	102.43 E
Chutung	66	24.44N	121.05 E
Chuxian	66	32.19N	118.17 E
Chuxiong	70	25.02N	101.30 E
Chuy	114	33.41S	53.27W
Chužir	58	53.11N	107.20 E
Chvalynsk	56	52.30N	48.07 E
Chvojnaja	60	58.54N	34.32 E
Chwefru ≃	34	52.09N	3.25W
Ciamis	72	7.20S	108.21 E
Cianjur	72	6.49S	107.08 E
Cianorte	114	23.37S	52.37W
Ciawi	72	6.40S	106.50 E
Cibatu	72	7.06S	107.59 E
Ćićarija ⋏	52	45.30N	13.54 E
Ciche, Sgurr na ∧	38	57.01N	5.27W
Cicheng	66	30.00N	121.22 E
Cicurug	72	6.47S	106.47 E
Cidacos ≃	50	42.19N	1.55W
Ciechanów	46	52.53N	20.38 E
Ciechanowiec	46	52.42N	22.31 E
Ciechocinek	46	52.52N	18.49 E
Ciego de Avila	108	21.51N	78.46W
Ciempozuelos	50	40.10N	3.37W
Ciénaga	110	11.01N	74.15W
Cienfuegos	108	22.09N	80.27W
Cieplice Śląskie-Zdrój	46	50.52N	15.41 E
Čierna [nad Tisou]	46	48.25N	22.05 E
Čierny Balog	46	48.45N	19.40 E
Cíes, Islas II	50	42.13N	8.54W
Cieszanów	46	50.16N	23.08 E
Cieszyn	46	49.45N	18.38 E
Cieza	50	38.14N	1.25W
Çifuentes	50	40.47N	2.37W
Čiganak	56	45.06N	73.58 E
Cigüela ≃	50	39.08N	3.44W
Čiili	56	44.10N	66.45 E
Cijara, Embalse de ⊜[1]	50	39.18N	4.52W
Cijulang	72	7.44S	108.27 E
Cikampek	72	6.24S	107.27 E
Čikoj ≃	58	51.02N	106.39 E
Cilacap	72	7.44S	109.00 E
Cilento +[1]	52	40.15N	15.10 E
Čilik	56	43.36N	78.15 E
Cill Airne →Killarney	40	52.03N	9.30W
Cill Chainnigh →Kilkenny	40	52.39N	7.15W
Cilleruelo de Bezana	50	42.58N	3.51W
Cimarron ≃	100	36.10N	96.17W
Čimbaj	56	42.57N	59.47 E
Čimkent	56	42.18N	69.36 E
Ciml'anskoje vodochranilišče ⊜[1]	56	48.00N	43.00 E
Cimone, Monte ∧	52	44.12N	10.42 E
Cîmpeni	54	46.22N	23.03 E
Cîmpia Turzii	54	46.33N	23.54 E
Cîmpina	54	45.08N	25.44 E
Cîmpulung	54	45.16N	25.03 E
Cîmpulung Moldovenesc	54	47.31N	25.34 E
Cina, Tanjung ›	72	5.56S	104.45 E
Cinca ≃	50	41.26N	0.21 E
Cincar ∧	52	43.54N	17.04 E
Cincinnati	102	39.09N	84.27W
Cinco Saltos	114	38.49S	68.04W
Cinderford	34	51.50N	2.29W
Çine	54	37.36N	28.04 E
Ciney	46	50.18N	5.06 E
Cingoli	52	43.22N	13.13 E
Cinto, Monte ∧	52	42.23N	8.56 E
Cinzas, Rio das ≃	114	22.56S	50.32W
Ciocăneşti	54	44.12N	27.04 E
Ciociaria +[1]	52	41.45N	13.15 E
Čiovo, Otok I	52	43.30N	16.20 E
Cipa ≃	58	55.23N	115.55 E
Cipolletti	114	38.56S	67.59W
Čirčik	56	41.29N	69.35 E
Circleville	102	39.36N	82.56W
Cirebon	72	6.44S	108.34 E
Ciremay, Gunung ∧	72	6.54S	108.24 E
Cirencester	34	51.44N	1.59W
Cirey-sur-Vezouze	48	48.35N	6.57 E
Ciriè	52	45.14N	7.36 E
Cîrlibaba	54	47.35N	25.07 E
Cirò Marina	52	39.22N	17.08 E
Čirpan	54	42.12N	25.20 E
Ciskei □[1]	86	32.50S	27.00 E
Cisnădie	54	45.43N	24.09 E
Cisterna di Latina	52	41.35N	12.49 E
Cistern Point ›	108	23.43N	77.35W
Cistierna	50	42.48N	5.07W
Čistoje	60	56.32N	43.02 E
Čistopol'	42	55.21N	50.37 E
Čita	58	52.03N	113.30 E
Citlaltépetl, Volcán ∧[1]	106	19.01N	97.16W
Citrusdal	86	32.36S	19.00 E
Citrus Heights	104	38.42N	121.16W
Cittadella	52	45.39N	11.47 E
Città di Castello	52	43.27N	12.14 E
Cittanova	52	38.21N	16.05 E
Ciucaş ∧	54	45.31N	25.55 E
Ciudad Acuña	106	29.18N	100.55W
Ciudad Bolívar	110	8.08N	63.33W
Ciudad Camargo	106	27.40N	105.10W
Ciudad Chetumal	106	18.30N	88.18W
Ciudad Darío	108	12.43N	86.08W
Ciudad del Carmen	106	18.38N	91.50W
Ciudad de México (Mexico City)	106	19.24N	99.09W
Ciudad de Valles	106	21.59N	99.01W
Ciudad de Villaldama	106	26.30N	100.26W
Ciudadela	50	40.02N	3.50 E
Ciudad Guayana	110	8.22N	62.40W
Ciudad Guerrero	106	28.33N	107.30W
Ciudad Guzmán	106	19.41N	103.29W
Ciudad Ixtepec	106	16.34N	95.06W
Ciudad Jiménez	106	27.08N	104.55W
Ciudad Juárez	106	31.44N	106.29W
Ciudad Mante	106	22.44N	98.57W
Ciudad Obregón	106	27.29N	109.56W
Ciudad Ojeda	110	10.12N	71.19W
Ciudad Real	50	38.59N	3.56W
Ciudad Rodrigo	50	40.36N	6.32W
Ciudad Trujillo →Santo Domingo	108	18.28N	69.54W
Ciudad Victoria, Méx.	104	32.20N	115.06W
Ciudad Victoria, Méx.	106	23.44N	99.08W
Ciurana ≃	50	41.08N	0.39 E
Cividale del Friuli	52	46.06N	13.25 E
Civil'sk	42	55.53N	47.29 E
Civita Castellana	52	42.17N	12.25 E
Civitanova Marche	52	43.18N	13.44 E
Civitavecchia	52	42.06N	11.48 E
Civray	48	46.09N	0.18 E
Cixi	66	30.11N	121.15 E
Cizre	78	37.20N	42.12 E
C.J. Strike Reservoir ⊜[1]	104	42.57N	115.53W
Čkalovsk, S.S.S.R.	56	40.09N	69.54 E
Čkalovsk, S.S.S.R.	60	56.46N	43.16 E
Clachan	38	55.45N	5.34W
Clackmannan	38	56.06N	3.46W
Clacton-on-Sea	34	51.48N	1.09 E
Cladich	38	56.21N	5.05W
Claerwen ≃	34	52.44N	3.37W
Claerwen Reservoir ⊜[1]	34	52.17N	3.43W
Clain ≃	48	46.47N	0.32 E
Claire, Lake ⊜	98	58.35N	112.05W
Clair Engle Lake ⊜[1]	104	40.52N	122.43W
Clairton	102	40.17N	79.52W
Clairvaux-les-Lacs	48	46.34N	5.45 E
Clam ≃	102	44.05N	85.00W
Clamecy	48	47.27N	3.31 E
Clampton	90	29.56S	119.06 E
Clan Alpine Mountains ⋏	104	39.40N	117.55W
Clane	40	53.18N	6.41W
Clanwilliam	86	32.11S	18.54 E
Claonaig	38	55.46N	5.22W
Clapham	34	52.09N	0.29W
Clapperton Island I	102	46.02N	82.13W
Clàr, Loch nan ⊜	38	58.17N	4.08W
Clara, Arg.	114	31.50S	58.49W
Clara, Ire.	40	53.20N	7.36W
Clara ≃	94	18.30S	141.18 E
Claraville	94	18.40S	141.43 E
Claraz	114	37.54S	59.17W
Clare, Austl.	90	33.50S	138.36 E
Clare, Austl.	94	33.25S	143.55 E
Clare, Eng., U.K.	34	52.25N	0.35 E
Clare, Mi., U.S.	102	43.49N	84.46W
Clare □[6]	40	52.50N	9.00W
Clare ≃	40	53.20N	9.03W
Clarecastle	40	52.49N	8.57W
Claregalway	40	53.21N	8.57W
Clare Island I	40	53.48N	10.00W
Claremont, Ca., U.S.	104	34.05N	117.43W
Claremont, N.H., U.S.	102	43.22N	72.20W
Claremont ∧	104	39.53N	120.57W
Claremorris	40	53.44N	9.00W
Clarence	96	42.10S	173.56 E
Clarence ≃, Austl.	94	29.25S	153.22 E
Clarence ≃, N.Z.	96	42.10S	173.57 E
Clarence Strait ʊ	92	12.00S	131.00 E
Clarence Town	108	23.06N	74.59W
Clarendon	102	41.46N	79.05W
Claresholm	98	50.02N	113.35W
Clarines	108	9.56N	65.10W
Clarion	102	41.12N	79.23W
Clarion ≃	102	41.07N	79.41W
Clarion Fracture Zone +	22	18.00N	122.00W
Clark, Point ›	102	44.04N	81.45W
Clarke ≃	94	19.12S	145.30 E
Clarke Island I	94	40.33S	148.10 E
Clarke Range ⋏	94	20.50S	148.33 E
Clarke River	94	19.13S	145.27 E
Clark Mountain ∧	104	35.32N	115.35W
Clarksburg	102	39.16N	80.20W
Clarksdale	100	34.12N	90.34W
Clarks Summit	102	41.29N	75.42W
Clarksville	100	36.31N	87.21W
Claro ≃	110	19.08S	50.40W
Clashmore	40	52.00N	7.48W
Clatteringshaws Lake ⊜	36	55.05N	4.17W
Claughton	36	54.06N	2.40W
Clausthal-Zellerfeld	46	51.48N	10.20 E
Clay	102	38.27N	81.05W
Clay City	102	37.51N	83.55W
Clay Cross	36	53.10N	1.24W
Claydon	34	52.06N	1.07 E
Claymont	102	39.48N	75.27W
Claysburg	102	40.17N	78.27W
Clayton, De., U.S.	102	39.17N	75.38W
Clayton, N.M., U.S.	100	36.27N	103.11W
Clayton, N.Y., U.S.	102	44.14N	76.05W
Clayton ≃	94	29.06S	138.05 E
Clayton-le-Moors	36	53.47N	2.23W
Clear, Cape ›	40	51.24N	9.30W
Clear, Lake ⊜	102	45.26N	77.12W
Clear Creek ≃	104	40.31N	122.22W
Clearfield	102	41.01N	78.26W
Clearfield Creek ≃	102	41.02N	78.24W
Clear Island I	40	51.26N	9.30W
Clear Lake ⊜[1]	104	39.02N	122.50W
Clear Lake Reservoir ⊜[1]	104	41.52N	121.08W
Clearwater	100	27.57N	82.48W
Clearwater ≃	98	56.44N	111.23W
Cleator Moor	36	54.31N	3.30W
Cleburne	100	32.20N	97.23W
Cleckheaton	36	53.43N	1.43W
Clee Hills ⋏[2]	34	52.25N	2.35W
Cleethorpes	36	53.34N	0.02W
Cleeve Cloud ∧[2]	34	51.34N	2.00W
Clefmont	48	48.06N	5.31 E
Cleggan	40	53.33N	10.09W
Clelles	48	44.50N	5.37 E
Clendenin	102	38.29N	81.20W
Cleobury Mortimer	34	52.23N	2.29W
Clerke Rocks II[1]	112	55.01S	34.41W
Clermont, Austl.	94	22.49S	147.39 E
Clermont, Fr.	48	49.23N	2.24 E
Clermont-en-Argonne	48	49.06N	5.04 E
Clermont-Ferrand	48	45.47N	3.05 E
Cles	52	46.22N	11.02 E
Cleve	94	33.42S	136.30 E
Clevedon	34	51.27N	2.51W
Cleveland, Ms., U.S.	100	33.44N	90.43W
Cleveland, Oh., U.S.	102	41.29N	81.41W
Cleveland, Tn., U.S.	100	35.09N	84.52W
Cleveland □[6]	36	54.35N	1.15W
Cleveland, Cape ›	94	19.11S	147.01 E
Cleveland, Mount ∧	94	41.25S	145.23 E
Cleveland Hills ⋏[2]	36	54.23N	1.05W
Clevelândia	114	26.24S	52.21W
Cleveleys	36	53.53N	3.03W
Cleves →Kleve	46	51.48N	6.09 E
Clew Bay C	40	53.50N	9.50W
Cley next the Sea	34	52.58N	1.03 E
Clifden	40	53.29N	10.01W
Clifden Bay C	40	53.28N	10.05W
Cliffdale Creek ≃	94	16.56S	138.48 E
Cliffe	34	51.28N	0.30 E
Clifton	94	27.56S	151.54 E
Clifton Forge	102	37.48N	79.49W
Clifton Gorge ∨	34	51.28N	2.37W
Clifton Hills	94	26.52S	138.50 E
Climax	102	42.14N	85.20W
Clingmans Dome ∧	100	35.35N	83.30W
Clinton, B.C., Can.	98	51.05N	121.35W
Clinton, On., Can.	102	43.37N	81.32W
Clinton, N.Z.	96	46.12S	169.22 E
Clinton, Ct., U.S.	102	41.16N	72.31W
Clinton, Ia., U.S.	100	41.50N	90.11W
Clinton, Me., U.S.	102	44.38N	69.30W
Clinton, Ma., U.S.	102	42.25N	71.41W
Clinton, Mi., U.S.	102	42.04N	83.58W
Clinton, Ok., U.S.	100	35.30N	98.58W
Clinton, Cape ›	94	22.32S	150.47 E
Clinton-Colden Lake ⊜	98	63.58N	107.27W
Clio	102	43.10N	83.44W
Clipperton, Île I[1]	22	10.17N	109.13W
Clipperton Fracture Zone +	22	10.00N	115.00W
Clisham ∧	38	57.57N	6.49W
Clisson	48	47.05N	1.17W
Clitheroe	36	53.53N	2.23W
Clive, Austl.	94	22.46S	149.18 E
Clive, N.Z.	96	39.35S	176.55 E
Cloates, Point ›	90	22.43S	113.40 E
Clocolan	86	29.00S	27.30 E
Clodomira	114	27.35S	64.08W
Cloghan, Ire.	40	54.51N	7.56W
Cloghan, Ire.	40	53.13N	7.53W
Cloghane	40	52.13N	10.12W
Clogheen	40	52.16N	8.00W
Clogher	40	54.25N	7.12W
Clogher Head ›	40	53.48N	6.12W
Cloghjordan	40	52.57N	8.02W
Clonakilty	40	51.37N	8.54W
Clonakilty Bay C	40	51.35N	8.50W
Cloncurry	94	20.42S	140.30 E
Cloncurry ≃	94	18.37S	140.40 E
Clondalkin	40	53.19N	6.24W
Clonee	40	53.25N	6.26W
Clones	40	54.11N	7.15W
Clonfert	40	53.14N	8.05W
Clonmany	40	55.14N	7.25W
Clonmel	40	52.21N	7.42W
Clonroche	40	52.27N	6.43W
Cloone	40	53.57N	7.46W
Cloppenburg	46	52.50N	8.02 E
Cloquet	100	46.43N	92.27W
Clorinda	114	25.17S	57.43W
Cloud Peak ∧	100	44.25N	107.10W
Cloudy Bay C	96	41.27S	174.10 E
Clough	40	54.18N	5.50W
Clova	38	56.50N	3.06W
Clova, Glen ∨	38	56.49N	3.04W
Clovelly	34	51.00N	4.24W
Clover Creek ≃	104	43.00N	115.11W
Cloverdale	104	38.48N	123.00W
Clovis, Ca., U.S.	104	36.49N	119.42W
Clovis, N.M., U.S.	100	34.24N	103.12W
Clowne	36	53.18N	1.16W
Cloyne	40	51.51N	8.08W
Cluain Meala →Clonmel	40	52.21N	7.42W
Cluanie, Loch ⊜	38	57.07N	5.05W
Cluj-Napoca	54	46.47N	23.36 E
Clun	34	52.26N	3.00W
Clun ≃	34	52.22N	2.53W
Clunes	94	37.18S	143.47 E
Clun Forest +[3]	34	52.28N	3.07W
Clunie Water ≃	38	57.00N	3.24W
Cluny, Austl.	94	24.31S	139.35 E
Cluny, Fr.	48	46.26N	4.39 E
Cluses	48	46.04N	6.36 E
Clusone	52	45.53N	9.57 E
Clutha ≃	96	46.21S	169.48 E
Clwyd □[6]	34	52.58N	3.20W
Clwyd ≃	36	53.20N	3.30W
Clwyd, Vale of ∨	36	53.12N	3.24W
Clwydian Range ⋏	36	53.10N	3.20W
Clydach	34	51.43N	3.50W
Clyde, N.Z.	96	45.11S	169.19 E
Clyde, N.Y., U.S.	102	43.05N	76.52W
Clyde, Oh., U.S.	102	41.18N	82.58W
Clyde ≃, On., Can.	102	44.58N	76.22W
Clyde ≃, Scot., U.K.	38	55.56N	4.29W
Clyde ≃, Vt., U.S.	102	44.56N	72.12W
Clyde, Firth of C[1]	38	55.42N	5.00W
Clydebank	38	55.54N	4.24W
Clydesdale ∨	38	55.42N	3.50W
Clymer	102	40.40N	79.00W
Clynnog-fawr	34	53.01N	4.23W
Clywedog ≃	34	52.27N	3.32W
Ćmielów	46	50.53N	21.31 E
Côa ≃	50	41.05N	7.06W
Coachella	104	33.40N	116.10W
Coachella Canal ≡	104	33.34N	116.00W
Coachford	40	51.53N	8.48W
Coahuila	104	32.12N	114.59W
Coalbrookdale	34	52.38N	2.30W
Coalburn	38	55.36N	3.54W
Coalcomán de Matamoros	106	18.47N	103.09W
Coal Creek Flat	96	45.29S	169.18 E
Coal Fork	102	38.19N	81.32W
Coalgate	96	43.29S	171.58 E
Coal Grove	102	38.30N	82.38W
Coalinga	104	36.08N	120.21W
Coalisland	40	54.33N	6.42W
Coal Island I	96	46.07S	166.38 E
Coalpit Heath	34	51.32N	2.28W
Coalport	102	40.44N	78.32W
Coal Valley ∨	104	38.00N	115.05W
Coalville	34	52.44S	1.20W
Coamo	108	18.05N	66.22W
Coari	110	4.05S	63.08W
Coari ≃	110	4.30S	63.33W
Coast Mountains ⋏	98	55.00N	129.00W
Coast Ranges ⋏	100	41.00N	123.30W
Coatbridge	38	55.52N	4.01W
Coatesville	102	39.58N	75.49W
Coaticook	102	45.08N	71.48W
Coats Island I	98	62.30N	83.00W
Coatzacoalcos	106	18.09N	94.25W
Cobadin	54	44.04N	28.13 E
Cobalt	98	47.24N	79.41W
Cobán	106	15.29N	90.19W
Cobar	94	31.30S	145.49 E
Cobargo	94	36.23S	149.53 E
Cobberas, Mount ∧	94	36.52S	148.10 E
Cobb Seamount +[3]	22	46.46N	130.49W
Cobden	102	45.38N	76.53W
Cobh	40	51.51N	8.17W
Cobham	34	51.20N	0.25W
Cobham ≃	98	53.15N	93.58W
Cobija, Bol.	110	11.02S	68.44W
Cobija, Chile	114	22.33S	70.16W
Coblenz →Koblenz	46	50.21N	7.35 E
Cobleskill	102	42.40N	74.29W
Cobourg	102	43.58N	78.10W
Cobourg Peninsula ›[1]	92	11.20S	132.15 E
Cobquecura	114	36.08S	72.47W
Cobram	94	35.55S	145.39 E
Cóbuè	84	12.04S	34.50 E
Coburg	46	50.15N	10.58 E
Coburg Island I	98	76.00N	79.25W
Coburn Mountain ∧	102	45.28N	70.06W
Cocentaina	50	38.45N	0.26W
Cochabamba	110	17.24S	66.09W
Cochagual	114	31.54S	68.23W
Coche, Isla I	108	10.45N	63.55W
Cochem	46	50.11N	7.09 E
Cochin	74	9.58N	76.14 E
Cochrane	98	49.04N	81.01W
Cochrane ≃	98	57.52N	101.38W
Cochrane, Lago (Lago Pueyrredón) ⊜	112	47.20S	72.00W
Cochranton	102	41.31N	80.02W
Cock Bridge	38	57.09N	3.14W
Cockburn	94	32.05S	141.00 E
Cockburn, Cape ›	92	11.20S	132.52 E
Cockburn, Mount ∧	90	22.46S	130.36 E
Cockburn Island I	102	45.55N	83.22W
Cockburnspath	38	55.56N	2.21W
Cockenzie	38	55.58N	2.58W
Cockerham	36	53.59N	2.50W
Cockermouth	36	54.40N	3.21W
Cockfield	36	54.37N	1.48W
Coco ≃	108	15.00N	83.10W
Coco, Cayo I	108	22.30N	78.28W
Coco, Isla del I	106	5.32N	87.04W
Cocoa	100	28.23N	80.44W
Coco Channel ʊ	70	13.45N	93.00 E
Coco Islands II	70	14.05N	93.18 E
Cocos (Keeling) Islands □[2]	26	12.10S	96.55 E
Cocos Ridge +[3]	22	5.30N	86.00W
Cocuiza ≃	108	10.59N	71.17W
Cod ≃	36	54.10N	1.22W
Cod, Cape ›[1]	102	41.42N	70.15W
Codăeşti	54	46.52N	27.46 E
Codajás	110	3.50S	62.05W
Coddenham	34	52.09N	1.07 E
Codera, Cabo ›	108	10.35N	66.05W
Codfish Island I	96	46.47S	167.38 E
Codigoro	52	44.49N	12.08 E
Cod Island I	98	57.45N	61.50W
Codlea	54	45.42N	25.27 E
Codnor	34	53.03N	1.23W
Codó	110	4.29S	43.53W
Codogno	52	45.09N	9.42 E
Codroipo	52	45.58N	12.59 E
Codru-Moma, Munţii ⋏	54	46.30N	22.20 E
Codsall	34	52.38N	2.12W
Coelemu	114	36.29S	72.42W
Coen	92	13.56S	143.12 E
Coen ≃	92	13.56S	142.02 E
Coetivy Island I	84	7.08S	56.16 E
Coeur d'Alene	100	47.40N	116.46W
Coffeyville	100	37.02N	95.36W
Coffin Bay C	90	34.27S	135.19 E
Coffin Bay Peninsula ›[1]	90	34.32S	135.15 E
Coffs Harbour	94	30.18S	153.08 E
Cofrentes	50	39.14N	1.04W
Coggeshall	34	51.52N	0.41 E
Cognac	48	45.42N	0.20W
Cogolin	48	43.15N	6.32 E
Cogolludo	50	40.57N	3.05W
Cohocton ≃	102	42.09N	77.05W
Cohoes	102	42.46N	73.42W
Cohuna	94	35.49S	144.13 E
Coiba, Isla de I	106	7.27N	81.45W
Coig ≃	112	50.58S	69.11W
Coigeach, Rubha ›	38	58.06N	5.26W
Coihaique	112	45.34S	72.04W
Coils Creek ≃	104	39.32N	116.16W
Coimbatore	74	11.00N	76.58 E
Coimbra	50	40.12N	8.25W
Coín	50	36.40N	4.45W
Coipasa, Salar de ⊻	110	19.26S	68.09W
Çoire, Loch ⊜	38	58.13N	4.21W
Čojbalsan	62	48.04N	114.30 E
Cojedes	108	9.37N	68.55W
Çojedes □[3]	108	9.20N	68.20W
Čokurdach	58	70.38N	147.55 E
Colac	94	38.20S	143.35 E
Colalao del Valle	114	26.22S	65.57W
Colares	50	38.48N	9.27W
Colatina	110	19.32S	40.37W
Colbinabbin	94	36.35S	144.49 E
Colborne	102	44.00N	77.53W
Colbún	114	35.42S	71.25W
Colburn	36	54.23N	1.41W
Colchester, Eng., U.K.	34	51.54N	0.54 E
Colchester, Ct., U.S.	102	41.34N	72.19W
Coldbackie	38	58.31N	4.23W
Cold Fell ∧	36	54.54N	2.36W
Coldingham	38	55.53N	2.10W
Coldsterworth	36	52.48N	0.37W
Coldstream	38	55.39N	2.15W
Coldwater, Mi., U.S.	102	41.56N	85.00W
Coldwater, Oh., U.S.	102	40.28N	84.37W
Cole ≃, Eng., U.K.	34	52.28N	1.44W
Cole ≃, Eng., U.K.	34	51.42N	1.42W
Colebrook	102	44.53N	71.29W
Coleford, Eng., U.K.	34	51.48N	2.36W
Coleford, Eng., U.K.	34	51.14N	2.27W
Coleman	102	43.45N	84.35W
Coleman ≃	92	15.06S	141.38 E
Colenso	86	28.50S	29.44 E
Coleraine, Austl.	94	37.36S	141.42 E
Coleraine, N. Ire., U.K.	40	55.08N	6.40W
Coleridge, Lake ⊜	96	43.17S	171.30 E
Colesberg	86	30.45S	25.05 E
Coleshill	34	52.30N	1.42W
Colfax, Ca., U.S.	104	39.06N	120.57W
Colfax, Wa., U.S.	100	46.52N	117.21W
Colgong	76	25.16N	87.13 E
Colgrave Sound ʊ	38	60.37N	0.58W
Colhué Huapi, Lago ⊜	112	45.30S	68.48W
Colico	52	46.08N	9.22 E
Coligny	86	26.17S	26.15 E
Colima, Méx.	104	32.25N	115.05W
Colima, Méx.	106	19.14N	103.43W
Colina	114	33.12S	70.41W
Colinas	110	6.02S	44.14W
Coll I	38	56.38N	6.34W
Collarenebri	94	29.33S	148.35 E
Collerina	94	29.41S	146.38 E
Collesalvetti	52	43.35N	10.28 E
Collie	90	33.21S	116.09 E
Collier Bay C	90	16.10S	124.15 E
Collier Law ∧[2]	36	54.46N	1.58W
Collier Range ⋏	90	24.43S	119.12 E
Collieston	38	57.21N	1.56W
Colliford Reservoir ⊜[1]	34	50.32N	4.33W
Colligan ≃	40	52.06N	7.38W
Collingbourne Kingston	34	51.18N	1.13W
Collingham	36	53.54N	1.24W
Collingwood, On., Can.	102	44.29N	80.13W
Collingwood, N.Z.	96	40.40S	172.41 E
Collins Bay	102	44.15N	76.36W
Collinsville	94	20.34S	147.51 E
Collipulli	114	37.57S	72.26W
Collon	40	53.47N	6.29W
Collooney	40	54.11N	8.29W
Colmar	48	48.05N	7.22 E
Colmars	48	44.11N	6.38 E
Colmenar	50	36.54N	4.20W
Colmenar de Oreja	50	40.06N	3.23W
Colmenar Viejo	50	40.40N	3.46W

Symbols in the Index entries are identified on page 122

Name	Page	Lat. °′	Long. °′
Cuilcagh ∧	40	54.10N	7.48W
Cuillin Hills ⋀[2]	38	57.15N	6.15W
Cuilo (Kwilu) ≃	84	3.22S	17.22 E
Cuiseaux	48	46.30N	5.24 E
Cuíto ≃	84	18.01S	20.48 E
Cuíto-Cuanavale	84	15.10S	19.10 E
Cuitzeo, Lago de ⊜	106	19.55N	101.05W
Čuja	58	59.12N	112.25 E
Čukotskij, mys ›	58	64.14N	173.10W
Čukotskij poluostrov ›[1]	58	66.00N	175.00W
Culcairn	94	35.40S	147.03 E
Culdaff	40	55.18N	7.11W
Culdaff Bay ⊂	40	55.17N	7.10W
Culebra, Isla de ❙	108	18.19N	65.17W
Culebra, Sierra de la ⋀	50	41.54N	6.20W
Culgoa ≃	94	29.56S	146.20 E
Culham Inlet ⊂	90	33.55S	120.04 E
Culiacán	106	24.48N	107.24W
Cúllar de Baza	50	37.35N	2.34W
Cullen	38	57.41N	2.49W
Cullen Point ›	92	11.57S	141.54 E
Cullera	50	39.10N	0.15W
Cullicudden	38	57.39N	4.13W
Cullin, Lough ⊜	40	53.57N	9.12W
Cullinan	86	25.40S	28.31 E
Cullman	100	34.10N	86.50W
Cullompton	34	50.52N	3.24W
Cullybackey	40	54.53N	6.21W
Culm ≃	34	50.46N	3.31W
Čul'man	58	56.52N	124.52 E
Culpeper	102	38.28N	77.59W
Culrain	38	57.55N	4.24W
Cults	38	57.07N	2.10W
Culuene ≃	110	12.56S	52.51W
Culvain ∧	38	56.56N	5.17W
Culver, Point ›	90	32.54S	124.43 E
Culverden	96	42.46S	172.51 E
Čulym	58	55.06N	80.58 E
Čulym ≃	58	57.43N	83.51 E
Cumaná	110	10.28N	64.10W
Cumanacoa	108	10.15N	63.55W
Cumbal, Nevado de ∧	110	0.57N	77.52W
Cumberland	102	39.39N	78.45W
Cumberland ≃	100	37.09N	88.25W
Cumberland Islands ❙❙	94	20.40S	149.09 E
Cumberland Peninsula ›[1]	98	66.50N	64.00W
Cumberland Sound ⊔	98	65.10N	65.30W
Cumbernauld	38	55.58N	3.59W
Cumborah	94	29.44S	147.46 E
Cumbria □[6]	36	54.30N	3.00W
Cumbrian Mountains ⋀	36	54.30N	3.05W
Čumikan	58	54.42N	135.19 E
Cuminestown	38	57.32N	2.20W
Cummins	94	34.16S	135.44 E
Cummins Range ⋀	90	19.05S	127.10 E
Cumnock	38	55.27N	4.16W
Cumnor	34	51.44N	1.20W
Cumwhinton	36	54.52N	2.51W
Čumyš ≃	58	53.31N	83.10 E
Čun'a ≃, S.S.S.R.	58	61.36N	96.30 E
Čuna ≃, S.S.S.R.	58	57.47N	95.26 E
Cunani	110	2.52N	51.06W
Cunco	114	38.55S	72.02W
Cuncumén	114	31.53S	70.38W
Cunderdin	90	31.39S	117.15 E
Cunene (Kunene) ≃	84	17.20S	11.50 E
Cuneo	52	44.23N	7.32 E
Cunha Porã	114	26.54S	53.09W
Cunlhat	48	45.38N	3.35 E
Cunnamulla	94	28.04S	145.41 E
Cunninghame □[9]	38	55.40N	4.30W
Cuokkaraš'ša ∧	42	69.57N	24.32 E
Cuorgnè	52	45.23N	7.39 E
Čupa	42	66.16N	33.00 E
Cupar	38	56.19N	3.01W
Ćuprija	54	43.56N	21.23 E
Curaçao ❙	108	12.11N	69.00W
Curacautín	114	38.26S	71.53W
Curacaví	114	33.24S	71.09W
Curacó ≃	114	38.49S	64.57W
Curanilahue	114	37.28S	73.21W
Curanipe	114	35.50S	72.38W
Čurapča	58	62.00N	132.24 E
Curaray ≃	110	2.20S	74.05W
Curcani	54	44.12N	26.35 E
Curcubăta ∧	54	46.27N	22.42 E
Curepipe	87c	20.19S	57.31 E
Curepto	114	35.05S	72.01W
Curiapo	108	8.33N	61.00W
Curicó	114	34.59S	71.14W
Curious, Mount ∧	90	27.28S	114.20 E
Curitiba	114	25.25S	49.15W
Curitibanos	114	27.18S	50.36W
Curiúva	114	24.02S	50.27W
Curlewis	94	31.07S	150.16 E
Curnamona	94	31.39S	139.32 E
Currais Novos	110	6.15S	36.31W
Curralinho	110	1.48S	49.47W
Currant Mountain ∧	104	38.55N	115.25W
Currie, Austl.	94	39.56S	143.52 E
Currie, Scot., U.K.	38	55.54N	3.20W
Currituck Seamount ✢[3]	28	30.00S	173.30W
Curry Rivel	34	51.02N	2.52W
Curtea-de-Argeș	54	45.08N	24.41 E
Curtina	114	32.09S	56.07W
Curtin Springs	90	25.20S	131.45 E
Curtis	50	43.07N	8.03W
Curtis, Port ⊤[3]	94	24.00S	151.30 E
Curtis Channel ⊔	94	23.30S	151.45 E
Curtis Island ❙	94	23.38S	151.09 E
Curtis Lake ⊜	98	66.38N	89.02W
Curuá ≃	110	5.23S	54.22W
Curuá, Ilha ❙	110	0.48N	50.10W
Čurug	54	45.29N	20.04 E
Curuguaty	114	24.31S	55.42W
Curup	72	3.28S	102.32 E
Cururupu	110	1.50S	44.52W
Curuzú Cuatiá	114	29.47S	58.03W
Curvelo	110	18.45S	44.25W
Curwensville	102	40.58N	78.31W
Cusco →Cuzco	110	13.31S	71.59W
Cushendall	40	55.06N	6.04W
Cushendun	40	55.07N	6.03W
Cushina ≃	40	53.11N	7.05W
Cusna, Monte ∧	52	44.17N	10.23 E
Čusovoj	56	58.17N	57.49 E
Cust	96	43.19S	172.22 E
Cutler, Ca., U.S.	104	36.31N	119.17W
Cutler, Me., U.S.	102	44.39N	67.12W
Cutral-Có	114	38.56S	69.14W
Cutro	52	39.02N	16.59 E
Cuttack	76	20.30N	85.50 E
Cuvier, Cape ›	90	24.05S	113.22 E
Cuvo ≃	84	10.50S	13.47 E
Cuxhaven	46	53.52N	8.42 E
Cuyahoga Falls	102	41.08N	81.29W
Cuyama ≃	104	34.54N	120.18W
Cuyamaca Peak ∧	104	32.57N	116.36W
Cuyo Islands ❙❙	68	11.04N	120.57 E
Cuyuni ≃	110	6.23N	58.41W
Cuzco	110	13.31S	71.59W
Cuzna ≃	50	38.04N	4.41W
Cwmbran	34	51.39N	3.00W
Cyangugu	84	2.29S	28.54 E
Cybinka	46	52.12N	14.48 E
Cyclades →Kikládhes ❙❙	54	37.30N	25.00 E
Cygnet Bay ⊂	90	16.35S	123.05 E
Cynin ≃	34	51.48N	4.29W
Cynthiana	102	38.23N	84.17W
Cynwyl Elfed	34	51.55N	4.22W
Cyprus (Kípros) □[1]	78	35.00N	33.00 E
Cyrenaica →Barqah □[9]	82	31.00N	22.30 E
Cyrus Field Bay ⊂	98	62.50N	64.55W
Cythera →Kíthira ❙	54	36.20N	22.58 E
Czaplinek	46	53.34N	16.14 E
Czarna Białostocka	46	53.19N	23.16 E
Czarna Woda	46	53.51N	18.06 E
Czarne	46	53.42N	16.57 E
Czarnków	46	52.55N	16.34 E
Czechoslovakia (Československo) □[1]	30	49.30N	17.00 E
Czechowice-Dziedzice	46	49.54N	19.00 E
Czempiń	46	52.10N	16.47 E
Czerniejewo	46	52.26N	17.30 E
Czersk	46	53.48N	18.00 E
Czerwieńsk	46	52.01N	15.25 E
Częstochowa	46	50.49N	19.06 E
Człopa	46	53.06N	16.08 E
Człuchów	46	53.41N	17.21 E
Czudec	46	49.57N	21.50 E
D			
Daan	70	23.19N	110.34 E
Dabajuro	108	11.02N	70.40W
Dabhoi	76	22.11N	73.26 E
Dąbie	46	52.06N	18.49 E
Dabie Shan ⋀	66	31.00N	115.40 E
Dabola	80	10.45N	11.07W
Dabra	76	25.54N	78.20 E
Dąbrowa Białostocka	46	53.39N	23.20 E
Dąbrowa Tarnowska	46	50.11N	21.00 E
Dacca →Dhaka	76	23.43N	90.25 E
Dachaidan	76	37.53N	95.07 E
Dachau	46	48.15N	11.27 E
Dačice	46	49.05N	15.26 E
Dadou ≃	48	43.44N	1.49 E
Dādu	76	26.44N	67.47 E
Dadu ≃	62	29.33N	103.45 E
Daet	68	14.05N	122.55 E
Dafeng	66	33.12N	120.30 E
Dagana	80	16.31N	15.30W
Dagang, Zhg.	66	33.12N	120.07 E
Dagang, Zhg.	66	32.12N	119.39 E
Dagang, Zhg.	66	22.49N	113.23 E
Dagg Sound ⊔	96	45.23S	166.46 E
Dagua	92	3.25S	143.20 E
Dagupan	68	16.03N	120.20 E
Da Hinggan Ling ⋀	62	49.00N	122.00 E
Dahlak Archipelago ❙❙	82	15.45N	40.30 E
Dahme	46	51.52N	13.25 E
Dahomey →Benin □[1]	80	9.30N	2.15 E
Dahra	82	29.34N	17.50 E
Dahūk □[4]	78	37.00N	43.00 E
Dahy, Nafūd ad- ✢[2]	74	22.20N	45.35 E
Daia	54	44.00N	25.59 E
Daibu	66	31.18N	119.30 E
Daijiayao	66	32.56N	120.19 E
Dailly	36	55.16N	4.43W
Daimanji-san ∧	64	36.15N	133.19 E
Daimiel	50	39.04N	3.37W
Dainan	66	32.43N	120.06 E
Daingean	40	53.18N	7.17W
Daintree	92	16.15S	145.19 E
Daiō-zaki ›	64	34.17N	136.54 E
Daireaux	114	36.36S	61.45W
Dairen →Lüda	62	38.53N	121.35 E
Dairsie	38	56.20N	2.56W
Dairy	38	55.43N	4.43W
Dai-sen ∧	64	35.22N	133.33 E
Daiyun Shan ⋀	66	25.46N	118.16 E
Dajabón	108	19.33N	71.42W
Dajarra	94	21.41S	139.31 E
Dajian Shan ∧	62	26.42N	103.34 E
Dajishan	66	24.38N	114.26 E
Dakar	80	14.40N	17.26W
Dak-gle	70	15.11N	107.48 E
Dākhilah, Al-Wāḥāt ad- ⊤[4]	82	25.30N	29.05 E
Dakhla	80	23.43N	15.57W
Đakovica	54	42.23N	20.25 E
Đakovo	54	45.19N	18.25 E
Dala-Järna	44	60.33N	14.21 E
Dalälven ≃	44	60.38N	17.27 E
Dalan Dzadgad	62	43.37N	104.29 E
Dalane ✢[1]	44	58.35N	6.20 E
Dalarna □[9]	44	61.01N	14.04 E
Dalarö	44	59.08N	18.24 E
Dalat, Malay.	72	2.44N	111.56 E
Da-lat, Viet.	70	11.56N	108.25 E
Dālbandin	78	28.53N	64.25 E
Dalbeattie	36	54.56N	3.49W
Dalbosjön ⊂	44	58.45N	12.48 E
Dalby, Austl.	94	27.11S	151.16 E
Dalby, Sve.	44	55.40N	13.20 E
Dalch ≃	34	50.52N	3.47W
Dale, Nor.	44	60.35N	5.49 E
Dale, Nor.	44	61.22N	5.25 E
Dale, Wales, U.K.	34	51.43N	5.11W
Dalecarlia →Dalarna □[9]	44	61.01N	14.04 E
Dale Lake ⊜	104	34.08N	115.42W
Dalen	44	59.27N	8.00 E
Daleszyce	46	50.48N	20.48 E
Dalgaranga	90	27.46S	117.02 E
Dalgaranger ∧	90	27.51S	117.06 E
Dalgety Bay	38	56.02N	3.20W
Dalgety Brook ≃	90	25.07S	115.47 E
Dalgety Downs	90	25.17S	116.15 E
Dalhalvaig	38	58.28N	3.54W
Dalhart	100	36.03N	102.30W
Dalhousie, N.B., Can.	98	48.04N	66.23W
Dalhousie, India	74	32.32N	75.59 E
Dalhousie, Cape ›	98	70.14N	129.42W
Dali	70	25.38N	100.09 E
Daliang Shan ⋀	62	28.00N	103.00 E
Dalías	50	36.49N	2.52W
Dalj	54	45.29N	18.59 E
Dalkeith	38	55.54N	3.04W
Dālkola	76	25.52N	87.51 E
Dallas, Scot., U.K.	38	57.33N	3.28W
Dallas, Or., U.S.	100	44.55N	123.18W
Dallas, Pa., U.S.	102	41.20N	75.57W
Dallas, Tx., U.S.	100	32.46N	96.47W
Dall Island ❙	98	54.50N	132.55W
Dalmā' ❙	78	24.30N	52.20 E
Dalmacija □[9]	52	43.00N	17.00 E
Dalmacio Vélez Sarsfield	114	32.36S	63.35W
Dalmally	38	56.24N	4.58W
Dalmatia →Dalmacija □[9]	52	43.00N	17.00 E
Dalmau	76	26.04N	81.02 E
Dalmellington	38	55.19N	4.24W
Dalnaspidal	38	56.50N	4.14W
Dal'negorsk	58	44.35N	135.35 E
Dal'nerečensk	58	45.55N	133.43 E
Daloa	80	6.53N	6.27W
Dalqū	82	20.07N	30.37 E
Dalry, Scot., U.K.	36	55.07N	4.10W
Dalry, Scot., U.K.	38	55.43N	4.44W
Dalrymple	36	55.23N	4.35W
Dalrymple, Mount ∧	94	21.02S	148.38 E
Dalsbruk (Taalintehdas)	44	60.02N	22.31 E
Dalsingh Sarai	76	25.40N	85.50 E
Dalsingpara	76	26.47N	89.22 E
Dalsjöfors	44	57.43N	13.05 E
Dalsland □[9]	44	58.30N	12.50 E
Dals-Långed	44	58.55N	12.18 E
Dalton, Ga., U.S.	100	34.47N	84.58W
Dalton, Ma., U.S.	102	42.28N	73.10W
Dalton, Pa., U.S.	102	41.32N	75.44W
Daltonganj	76	24.02N	84.04 E
Dalton-in-Furness	36	54.09N	3.11W
Dalupiri Island ❙	68	19.05N	121.14 E
Dalvík	42a	65.59N	18.32W
Dalwallinu	90	30.17S	116.40 E
Dalwhinnie	38	56.56N	4.14W
Daly ≃	92	13.20S	130.19 E
Daly Bay ⊂	98	64.00N	89.40W
Daly City	104	37.43N	122.31W
Daly Lake ⊜	98	56.33N	105.40W
Daly River	92	13.45S	130.50 E
Daly Waters	92	16.15S	133.22 E
Damān	74	20.25N	72.51 E
Damanhūr	82	31.02N	30.28 E
Damar, Pulau ❙	92	7.09S	128.40 E
Damaraland □[5]	86	21.00S	14.20 E
Damascus →Dimashq, Sūrīy.	78	33.30N	36.18 E
Damascus, Md., U.S.	102	39.17N	77.12W
Damāvand, Qolleh-ye ∧	78	35.56N	52.08 E
Damba	84	6.41S	15.08 E
Damerham	34	50.57N	1.52W
Dāmghān	78	39.09N	54.22 E
Damiaoshan	70	25.06N	109.15 E
Dămienești	54	46.44N	26.59 E
Damietta →Dumyāṭ	82	31.25N	31.48 E
Dammartin-en-Goële	48	49.03N	2.41 E
Dāmodar ≃	76	22.17N	88.05 E
Damoh	76	23.50N	79.27 E
Dampar, Tasek ⊜	72	3.02N	102.43 E
Dampier	90	20.39S	116.45 E
Dampier, Cape ›	92	6.02S	151.02 E
Dampier, Selat ⊔	92	0.40S	130.40 E
Dampier Archipelago ❙❙	90	20.35S	116.35 E
Dampier Land ›[1]	90	17.30S	122.55 E
Dampier Strait ⊔	92	5.36S	148.12 E
Da-nang	70	16.04N	108.13 E
Dānāpur	76	25.38N	85.03 E
Danbury, Eng., U.K.	34	51.44N	0.33 E
Danbury, Ct., U.S.	102	41.23N	73.27W
Danby Lake ⊜	104	34.14N	115.07W
Dancheng	66	33.39N	115.11 E
Dandaragan	90	30.40S	115.42 E
Dandenong	94	37.59S	145.12 E
Dandong	62	40.08N	124.20 E
Dane ≃	36	53.15N	2.31W
Danforth	102	45.39N	67.52W
Dang ≃	62	40.30N	94.42 E
Danger Point ›	86	34.40S	19.17 E
Dangila	82	11.16N	36.50 E
Dangshan	66	34.26N	116.21 E
Dangtu	66	31.34N	118.30 E
Danielskuil	86	28.11S	23.33 E
Danielson	102	41.48N	71.53W
Danilov	60	58.12N	40.12 E
Danjo-guntō ❙❙	64	32.02N	128.23 E
Dankov	60	53.15N	39.08 E
Danlí	108	14.00N	86.35W
Dannemora, Sve.	44	60.11N	17.49 E
Dannemora, N.Y., U.S.	102	44.43N	73.43W
Dannenberg	46	53.06N	11.05 E
Dannevirke	96	40.12S	176.07 E
Dannhauser	86	28.04S	30.04 E
Danshui	66	22.49N	114.27 E
Dansville	102	42.33N	77.41W
Danube ≃	30	45.20N	29.40 E
Danube, Mouths of the ≃[1]	54	45.10N	29.50 E
Danville, P.Q., Can.	102	45.47N	72.01W
Danville, Il., U.S.	100	40.07N	87.37W
Danville, Ky., U.S.	102	37.42N	84.46W
Danville, Pa., U.S.	102	40.57N	76.36W
Danville, Vt., U.S.	102	44.25N	72.07W
Danville, Va., U.S.	100	36.35N	79.23W
Danyang	66	32.00N	119.35 E
Danzig →Gdańsk	46	54.23N	18.40 E
Danzig, Gulf of ⊂	46	54.40N	19.15 E
Dâo ≃	50	40.20N	8.11W
Daocheng	62	29.06N	100.38 E
Daosa	76	26.53N	76.20 E
Daoulas	48	48.22N	4.15W
Daoxian	70	25.35N	111.27 E
Dapango	80	10.52N	0.12 E
Da Qaidam	62	37.53N	95.07 E
Daqiao	66	32.21N	119.41 E
Dar'ā	78	32.37N	36.06 E
Dārāb	78	28.45N	54.34 E
Darabani	54	48.11N	26.35 E
Darbhanga	76	26.10N	85.54 E
Darchan	62	49.29N	105.55 E
D'Archiac, Mount ∧	96	43.28S	170.35 E
Darda	54	45.37N	18.41 E
Dardanelle	104	38.20N	119.50W
Dardanelles →Çanakkale Boğazı ⊔	54	40.15N	26.25 E
Dar-el-Beida →Casablanca	80	33.39N	7.35W
Darent ≃	34	51.28N	0.13 E
Dar es Salaam	84	6.48S	39.17 E
Dargan-Ata	56	40.29N	62.10 E
Dargaville	96	35.56S	173.53 E
Dariense, Cordillera ⋀	108	12.55N	85.30W
Dariganga	62	45.18N	113.52 E
Darjeeling	76	27.02N	88.16 E
Darkan	90	33.20S	116.44 E
Darke Peak	94	33.28S	136.12 E
Darlag	62	33.48N	99.52 E
Darlaston	34	52.34N	2.02W
Darling	86	33.23S	18.23 E
Darling ≃	94	34.07S	141.55 E
Darling Downs ✢[1]	94	27.30S	150.30 E
Darling Range ⋀	90	31.25S	116.00 E
Darlington	36	54.31N	1.34W
Darlot, Lake ⊜	90	27.48S	121.35 E
Darłowo	46	54.26N	16.23 E
Darmstadt	46	49.53N	8.40 E
Darnah	82	32.46N	22.39 E
Darnall	86	29.23S	31.18 E
Darnétal	48	49.27N	1.09 E
Darney	48	48.05N	6.03 E
Darnick	94	32.51S	143.37 E
Darnley Bay ⊂	98	69.35N	123.30W
Daroca	50	41.07N	1.25W
Darr ≃	94	23.39S	143.50 E
Darregueira	114	37.42S	63.10W
Darreh Gaz	78	37.27N	59.07 E
Darsser Ort ›	46	54.29N	12.31 E
Dart ≃	34	50.20N	3.33W
Dartford	34	51.27N	0.14 E
Dartmoor	94	37.55S	141.17 E
Dartmoor ✢[3]	34	50.35N	4.00W
Dartmoor National Park ♦	34	50.37N	3.52W
Dartmouth, N.S., Can.	98	44.40N	63.34W
Dartmouth, Eng., U.K.	34	50.21N	3.35W
Dartmouth, Lake ⊜	94	26.04S	145.18 E
Darton	36	53.36N	1.32W
Dartuch, Cabo ›	50	39.56N	3.48 E
Daru	92	9.04S	143.21 E
Daruvar	52	45.36N	17.13 E
Darvaza	78	40.11N	58.24 E
Darvel	38	55.37N	4.18W
Darvel, Teluk ⊂	72	4.50N	118.30 E
Darwen	36	53.42N	2.28W
Darwen ≃	36	53.45N	2.41W
Darwin, Arg.	114	39.12S	65.46W
Darwin, Austl.	92	12.28S	130.50 E
Darwin River	92	12.49S	130.58 E
Daryāpur	76	20.56N	77.20 E
Dasāda	76	23.19N	71.50 E
Dasht ≃	78	25.10N	61.40 E
Dasht-e Āzādegān (Sūsangerd)	78	31.34N	48.11 E
Dašinčilen	62	47.51N	104.03 E
Daspalla	76	20.21N	84.51 E
Dasseneiland ❙	86	33.26S	18.04 E
Dassow	46	53.50N	10.59 E
Date	64a	42.27N	140.51 E
Datia	76	25.40N	78.28 E
Datian	66	25.42N	117.49 E
D'at'kovo	60	53.36N	34.20 E
D'atlovo	60	53.28N	25.24 E
Datong	62	40.05N	113.18 E
Datong ≃	62	36.20N	102.55 E
Datu, Tanjung ›	72	2.06N	109.39 E
Datuan	66	30.58N	121.44 E
Datu Piang	68	7.01N	124.30 E
Daudnagar	76	25.02N	84.24 E
Daugai	60	54.22N	24.20 E
Daugava (Zapadnaja Dvina) ≃	60	57.04N	24.03 E
Daugavpils	60	55.53N	26.32 E
Daulatābād (Shirin Tagāo)	76	36.26N	64.55 E
Daule ≃	110	2.10S	79.52W
Daun	46	50.11N	6.50 E
Dauphin	98	51.09N	100.03W
Dauphiné □[9]	48	44.50N	6.00 E
Dauphin Lake ⊜	98	51.17N	99.48W
Dāvangere	74	14.28N	75.55 E
Davao	68	7.04N	125.36 E
Davao Gulf ⊂	68	6.40N	125.55 E
Davel	86	26.24S	29.40 E
Davenport, Ia., U.S.	100	41.31N	90.34W
Davenport, Wa., U.S.	100	47.39N	118.08W
Davenport, Mount ∧	90	22.23S	130.51 E
Davenport Downs	94	24.08S	141.07 E
Davenport Range ⋀	90	20.47S	134.48 E
Daventry	34	52.16N	1.09W
Davey, Port ⊂	94	43.19S	145.55 E
David	106	8.26N	82.26W
Davies, Mount ∧	90	26.14S	129.16 E
Davington	38	55.18N	3.12W
Daviot	38	57.25N	4.08W
Davis, Ca., U.S.	104	38.32N	121.44W
Davis, W.V., U.S.	102	39.07N	79.27W
Davis ≃	90	21.42S	121.05 E
Davis, Mount ∧	102	39.47N	79.10W
Davis Dam	104	35.10N	114.33W
Davis Strait ⊔	98	67.00N	57.00W
Davlekanovo	56	54.13N	55.03 E
Davos	48	46.48N	9.50 E
Dawa (Daua) ≃	82	4.11N	42.06 E
Dawlish	34	50.35N	3.28W
Dawna Range ⋀	70	16.50N	98.15 E
Dawson	98	64.04N	139.25W
Dawson ≃	94	23.38S	149.46 E
Dawson, Isla ❙	112	53.55S	70.45W
Dawson Creek	98	55.46N	120.14W
Dawson Inlet ⊂	98	61.50N	93.25W
Dawson Range ⋀, Austl.	94	24.20S	149.45 E
Dawson Range ⋀, Yk., Can.	98	62.40N	139.00W
Dawu	66	31.34N	114.06 E
Dawusi	62	37.40N	91.50 E
Dax	48	43.43N	1.03W
Daxian	62	31.18N	107.30 E
Daxue Shan ⋀	62	30.10N	101.50 E
Dayao	70	25.43N	101.13 E
Dayboro	94	27.11S	152.50 E
Daye	66	30.06N	114.57 E
Dayingjiang (Taping) ≃	70	24.17N	97.14 E
Daylesford	94	37.21S	144.09 E
Daymán ≃	114	31.30S	58.02W
Dayr az-Zawr	78	35.20N	40.09 E
Dayrūṭ	82	27.33N	30.49 E
Dayton, Oh., U.S.	102	39.45N	84.11W
Dayton, Pa., U.S.	102	40.52N	79.14W
Dayton, Va., U.S.	102	38.24N	78.56W
Daytona Beach	100	29.12N	81.01W
Dayu	66	25.24N	114.22 E
Dayu Ling ⋀	66	25.20N	114.16 E
Da Yunhe (Grand Canal) ≊	62	32.12N	119.31 E
De Aar	86	30.39S	24.00 E
Deadman Hill ∧	90	23.48S	119.25 E
Deadmans Cay	108	23.14N	75.14W
Dead Sea ⊜	78	31.30N	35.30 E
Deadwood	100	44.22N	103.43W
Deakin	90	30.46S	128.58 E
Deal	34	51.14N	1.24 E
Deale	102	38.46N	76.33W
Dealesville	86	28.40S	25.37 E
Deal Island	102	38.09N	75.56W
De'an	66	29.20N	115.46 E
Dean ≃	36	53.20N	2.14W
Dean, Forest of ✢[3]	34	51.48N	2.30W
Deán Funes	114	30.26S	64.21W
Deans Dundas Bay ⊂	98	72.15N	118.25W
Dearborn	102	42.18N	83.10W
Dearg, Beinn ∧	38	57.47N	4.56W
Dearham	36	54.42N	3.26W
Dearne ≃	36	53.30N	1.16W
Dear Reservoir ⊜[1]	36	55.20N	3.37W
Dease ≃	98	59.54N	128.30W
Dease Arm ⊂	98	66.52N	119.37W
Dease Strait ⊔	98	68.40N	108.00W
Death Valley	104	36.18N	116.25W
Death Valley ∨	104	36.30N	117.00W
Deauville	48	49.22N	0.04 E
Debar	54	41.31N	20.30 E
Deben ≃	34	51.58N	1.24 E
Debenham	34	52.13N	1.11 E
Dębica	46	50.04N	21.24 E
De Bilt	46	52.06N	5.10 E
Dęblin	46	51.35N	21.50 E
Dębno	46	52.45N	14.40 E
Deborah West, Lake ⊜	90	30.45S	119.07 E
Deboyne Islands ❙❙	92	10.45S	152.25 E
Debrecen	46	47.32N	21.38 E
Debre Markos	82	10.20N	37.45 E
Debre Tabor	82	11.50N	38.05 E
Debrzno	46	53.33N	17.14 E
Decatur, Al., U.S.	100	34.36N	86.59W
Decatur, Il., U.S.	100	39.50N	88.57W
Decatur, In., U.S.	102	40.50N	84.56W
Decazeville	48	44.34N	2.15 E
Deccan ⋀[1]	74	17.00N	78.00 E
Dechu	76	26.47N	72.20 E
Decimomannu	52	39.19N	8.58 E
Děčín	46	50.48N	14.13 E
Decize	48	46.50N	3.27 E
Deckerville	102	43.31N	82.44W
Decorah	100	43.18N	91.47W
Decs	46	46.17N	18.46 E
Deda	54	46.57N	24.53 E
Deddington	34	51.59N	1.19W
Dediāpāda	76	21.38N	73.35 E
De Doorns	86	33.28S	19.41 E
Dédougou	80	12.28N	3.28W
Dedovsk	60	55.52N	37.07 E
Dee ≃, Ire.	40	53.52N	6.21W
Dee ≃, U.K.	34	53.04N	2.52W
Dee ≃, Eng., U.K.	36	54.18N	2.32W
Dee ≃, Scot., U.K.	38	57.09N	2.07W
Dee, Loch ⊜	36	55.05N	4.24W
Deep Creek ≃	104	42.15N	116.40W
Deeping Fen ⁘	34	52.44N	0.13W
Deep River, On., Can.	102	46.06N	77.30W
Deep River, Ct., U.S.	102	41.23N	72.26W
Deepwater	94	29.27S	151.51 E
Deep Well	90	24.25S	134.05 E
Deer ≃	102	44.55N	74.43W
Deer Creek ≃, U.S.	102	39.37N	76.09W
Deer Creek ≃, Ca., U.S.	104	39.56N	122.04W
Deer Creek ≃, Oh., U.S.	102	39.27N	83.00W
Deering, Mount ∧[2]	90	24.53S	129.04 E
Deer Isle	102	44.13N	68.40W
Deer Lake	98	49.10N	57.26W
Deer Lodge	100	46.23N	112.44W
Deer Mountain ∧	102	45.01N	70.56W
Deerpass Bay ⊂	98	65.56N	122.25W
Deer Sound ⊔	38	58.58N	2.48W
Deesa	76	24.15N	72.10 E
Defiance	102	41.17N	84.21W
Deganwy	36	53.18N	3.47W
Dêgê	62	31.50N	98.40 E
Degeberga	44	55.50N	14.05 E
Degeh Bur	82	8.13N	43.34 E
Degerby	44	60.02N	20.23 E
Degerfors	44	59.14N	14.26 E
Degerhamn	44	56.21N	16.24 E
Deggendorf	46	48.51N	12.59 E
De Graff	102	40.18N	83.54W
De Grey	90	20.10S	119.12 E
De Grey ≃	90	20.12S	119.11 E
Dehalak Deset ❙	82	15.40N	40.05 E
Dehej	76	21.42N	72.35 E
Dehiwala-Mount Lavinia	74	6.51N	79.52 E
Deh Kord	78	33.49N	48.53 E
Dehra Dūn	76	30.19N	78.02 E
Dehri	76	24.52N	84.11 E
Dehua	66	25.32N	118.15 E
Dehui	62	44.34N	125.43 E
Deinze	46	50.59N	3.32 E
Dej	54	47.09N	23.52 E
Deje	44	59.36N	13.28 E
Dejnau	78	39.15N	63.11 E
Dekese	84	3.27S	21.24 E
Delabole	34	50.37N	4.42W
Delamere	92	15.45S	131.33 E
Delamere Forest ✢[3]	36	53.14N	2.38W
Delanggu	72	7.37S	110.41 E
Delano	104	35.46N	119.14W
Delareyville	86	26.44S	25.29 E
Del'atin	54	48.32N	24.37 E
Delaware	102	40.17N	83.04W
Delaware □[3]	100	39.10N	75.30W
Delaware ≃	102	39.20N	75.25W
Delaware, East Branch ≃	102	41.55N	75.17W
Delaware, West Branch ≃	102	41.56N	75.17W
Delaware Bay ⊂	102	39.05N	75.15W
Delaware City	102	39.34N	75.35W
Del Campillo	114	34.22S	64.29W
Delegate	94	37.03S	148.58 E
Delémont	48	47.22N	7.21 E
Delft	46	52.00N	4.21 E
Delfzijl	46	53.19N	6.46 E
Delgado, Cabo ›	84	10.40S	40.35 E
Delgany	40	53.08N	6.05W
Delger ≃	62	49.17N	100.40 E
Delhi, On., Can.	102	42.51N	80.30W
Delhi, India	76	28.40N	77.13 E
Delhi, N.Y., U.S.	102	42.16N	74.54W
Delhi □[3]	76	28.37N	77.10 E
Deliblato	54	44.50N	21.03 E
Delicias	106	28.13N	105.28W
Delingde	58	70.08N	114.00 E
Delingha	62	37.14N	97.11 E
Delitua	70	3.30N	98.41 E
Delitzsch	46	51.31N	12.20 E
Dell	38	58.30N	6.20W
Delle	48	47.30N	7.00 E
Dellensjöarna ⊜	44	61.54N	16.41 E
Dellys	50	36.55N	3.55 E
Del Mar, Ca., U.S.	104	32.57N	117.15W
Delmar, De., U.S.	102	38.27N	75.34W
Delmenhorst	46	53.03N	8.38 E
Delnice	52	45.24N	14.48 E
De-Longa, ostrova ❙❙	58	76.30N	153.00 E
Deloraine	94	41.31S	146.39 E
Delorme, Lac ⊜	98	54.31N	69.52W
Delos →Dhílos ⊥	54	37.26N	25.16 E
Delph	36	53.34N	2.01W
Delphi →Dhelfoí ⊥	54	38.30N	22.29 E
Delphos	102	40.50N	84.20W
Delportshoop	86	28.22S	24.20 E
Delray Beach	108	26.27N	80.04W
Del Rio	100	29.21N	100.53W
Delsbo	44	61.48N	16.35 E
Delta, Méx.	104	32.22N	115.12W
Delta, Oh., U.S.	102	41.34N	84.00W
Delta Amacuro □[8]	108	9.00N	61.30W
Delta Downs	94	17.00S	141.18 E
Delta Peak ∧	98	56.39N	129.34W
Delungra	94	29.39S	150.50 E
Delvin	40	53.36N	7.05W
Delvinë	54	39.57N	20.06 E
Demak	72	6.53S	110.38 E
Dem'ansk	60	57.38N	32.28 E
Demarcation Point ›	98	69.40N	141.15W
Demavend, Mount →Damāvand, Qolleh-ye ∧	78	35.56N	52.08 E
Demba	84	5.30S	22.16 E
Dembi Dolo	82	8.32N	34.48 E
Demidov	60	55.16N	31.31 E
Deming	100	32.16N	107.45W
Demini ≃	110	0.46S	62.56W
Demirci	54	39.03N	28.40 E
Demir Kapija ∨	54	41.24N	22.15 E
Demjanka ≃	58	59.34N	69.17 E
Demjanskoje	56	59.36N	69.18 E
Demmin	46	53.54N	13.02 E
Demonte	52	44.19N	7.17 E
Dempo, Gunung ∧	72	4.02S	103.09 E
Dempster, Point ›	90	33.39S	123.52 E
Demta	92	2.20S	140.08 E
Denain	48	50.20N	3.23 E
Denakil ✢[1]	82	13.00N	41.00 E
Denau	56	38.16N	67.54 E
Denbigh	36	53.11N	3.25W
Den Burg	46	53.03N	4.48 E
Denby Dale	36	53.35N	1.38W
Dendermonde	46	51.02N	4.07 E
Dendron	86	23.25S	29.11 E
Denge Marsh ⁘	34	50.57N	0.55 E
Dengfeng	66	34.29N	113.04 E
Dêngqên	62	31.32N	95.27 E
Denham	90	25.55S	113.32 E
Denham, Mount ∧	108	18.13N	77.32W
Denham Island ❙	94	16.43S	139.09 E
Denham Range ⋀	94	21.55S	147.46 E
Denham Sound ⊔	90	25.40S	113.15 E
Den Helder	46	52.54N	4.45 E
Denia	50	38.51N	0.07 E
Denial Bay	90	32.06S	133.32 E
Deniliquin	94	35.32S	144.58 E
Denison	100	33.45N	96.32W
Denizli	30	37.46N	29.06 E
Denmark	90	34.57S	117.21 E
Denmark (Danmark) □[1]	30	56.00N	10.00 E
Denmark Bay ⊂	98	70.33N	103.20W
Denmark Strait ⊔	20	67.00N	25.00W
Denmead	34	50.54N	1.04W
Dennis Head ›	38	59.23N	2.23W
Dennison	102	40.23N	81.20W
Dennis Port	102	41.39N	70.07W
Denniston	96	41.44S	171.48 E
Denny	38	56.02N	3.55W
Denpasar	72	8.39S	115.13 E
Denton, Eng., U.K.	36	53.27N	2.07W
Denton, Md., U.S.	102	38.53N	75.49W
Denton, Tx., U.S.	100	33.12N	97.07W
D'Entrecasteaux, Point ›	90	34.50S	116.00 E
D'Entrecasteaux Islands ❙❙	92	9.30S	150.40 E
Denver, Co., U.S.	100	39.44N	104.59W
Denver, Pa., U.S.	102	40.13N	76.08W
Deoband	76	29.42N	77.41 E
Deogarh, India	76	21.32N	84.44 E
Deogarh, India	76	25.32N	73.54 E
Deogarh, India	76	24.33N	78.15 E
Deogarh Hills ⋀[2]	76	23.35N	82.30 E
Deoghar	76	24.29N	86.42 E
Deolāli	74	19.57N	73.50 E
Deoli	76	25.45N	75.23 E
Deoria	76	26.31N	83.47 E
Deori Khās	76	23.24N	79.01 E
Deosai Mountains ⋀	76	35.20N	75.12 E
Deosil	76	23.42N	82.15 E
Depew	102	42.54N	78.41W
Deposit	102	42.03N	75.25W
Depuch Island ❙	90	20.38S	117.43 E
Dêqên	62	28.38N	98.52 E
Deqing	66	30.33N	120.05 E
Dera, Lach ∨	84	0.35N	41.50 E
Derac	108	19.39N	71.49W
Dera Ghāzi Khān	76	30.03N	70.38 E
Dera Ismāīl Khān	76	31.50N	70.54 E
Derbent	56	42.03N	48.18 E
Derby, Austl.	90	17.18S	123.38 E
Derby, Austl.	94	41.09S	147.47 E
Derby, Eng., U.K.	34	52.55N	1.29W
Derby, Me., U.S.	102	45.14N	68.58W
Derby, N.Y., U.S.	102	42.40N	78.58W
Derby Line	102	45.00N	72.05W
Derbyshire □[6]	34	53.00N	1.33W
Derdepoort	86	24.42S	26.20 E
Derecske	46	47.21N	21.34 E
Derev'anka	42	61.34N	34.27 E
Derg ≃	40	54.44N	7.25W
Derg, Lough ⊜, Ire.	40	54.36N	7.53W
Derg, Lough ⊜, Ire.	40	53.00N	8.20W
Dergaon	76	26.42N	93.58 E
Déroute, Passage de la ⊔	35b	49.25N	2.00W
Derravaragh, Lough ⊜	40	53.40N	7.24W
Derry →Londonderry, N. Ire., U.K.	40	55.00N	7.19W
Derry, N.H., U.S.	102	42.52N	71.19W
Derrybrien	40	53.04N	8.36W
Derrykeevan	40	55.08N	6.29W
Derryveagh Mountains ⋀	40	55.00N	8.05W
Dersingham	34	52.51N	0.30 E
De Rust	86	33.30S	22.32 E
Derval	48	47.40N	1.40W
Derventa	54	44.58N	17.55 E
Derwent ≃, Austl.	94	43.03S	147.22 E
Derwent ≃, Eng., U.K.	36	53.45N	0.57W
Derwent ≃, Eng., U.K.	36	54.57N	1.41W
Derwent ≃, Eng., U.K.	36	54.38N	3.34W
Derwent Bridge	94	42.08S	146.13 E
Derwent Reservoir ⊜[1]	36	54.50N	2.00W
Derwent Water ⊜	36	54.34N	3.08W
Deržavinsk	56	51.03N	66.19 E
Desaguadero ≃, Arg.	114	34.13S	66.47W
Desaguadero ≃, Bol.	110	18.24S	67.05W
Désappointement, Îles du ❙❙	28	14.10S	141.20W
Desborough	34	52.27N	0.49W
Descabezado Grande, Volcán ∧[1]	114	35.36S	70.45W
Descanso, Bra.	114	26.50S	53.35W
Descanso, Ca., U.S.	104	32.51N	116.37W
Descanso, Punta ›	104	32.16N	117.03W
Descartes	48	46.58N	0.42 E
Deschambault Lake ⊜	98	54.40N	103.35W
Deschutes ≃	100	45.38N	120.54W
Dese	82	11.05N	39.41 E
Deseado ≃	112	47.45S	65.54W
Desengaño, Punta ›	112	49.15S	67.37W
Desenzano del Garda	52	45.28N	10.32 E
Deseronto	102	44.12N	77.03W
Desert Hot Springs	104	33.57N	116.30W
Desert Lake ⊜	104	36.58N	115.05W
Desert Peak ∧	104	41.11N	113.22W
Desert Valley ∨	104	41.15N	118.20W
Desford	34	52.39N	1.17W
Deshler	102	41.12N	83.53W
Deshnoke	76	27.48N	73.21 E
Desiderio Tello	114	31.13S	66.19W
Des Moines	100	41.36N	93.36W
Des Moines ≃	100	40.22N	91.26W
Desna ≃	56	50.33N	30.32 E
Desolación, Isla ❙	112	53.00S	74.10W
Despatch	86	33.46S	25.30 E
Despeñaperros, Desfiladero de)(	50	38.24N	3.30W
Despotovac	54	44.05N	21.33 E
Desroches, Île ❙	84	5.41S	53.41 E
Dessau	46	51.50N	12.14 E
Destruction, Mount ∧[2]	90	24.35S	127.59 E
Destruction Bay	98	61.15N	138.48W
Desvres	48	50.40N	1.50 E
Deta	54	45.24N	21.13 E
Detčino	60	54.49N	36.19 E
Detmold	46	51.56N	8.52 E
De Tour Village	102	46.00N	83.54W
Detrital Wash ∨	104	36.02N	114.28W
Detroit	102	42.20N	83.03W
Detroit Beach	102	41.55N	83.20W
Dettifoss ⌊	42a	65.50N	16.20W
Detva	46	48.31N	19.28 E
Deurne	46	51.28N	5.47 E
Deutsche Bucht ⊂	46	54.30N	7.30 E
Deutschlandsberg	46	46.49N	15.13 E
Deux-Sèvres □[5]	48	46.30N	0.20W
Deva	54	45.53N	22.55 E
Dévaványa	46	47.02N	20.58 E
Devecser	46	47.06N	17.26 E
Deventer	46	52.15N	6.10 E
Deveron ≃	38	57.40N	2.31W
Devès, Monts du ⋀	48	45.00N	3.45 E
Devgad Bāria	76	22.42N	73.54 E
Devīkot	76	26.42N	71.12 E

Symbols in the Index entries are identified on page 122.

Devi-Dunv

Name Page Lat.°′ Long.°′

Devil River Peak ∧ 96 40.58 S 172.39 E
Devil's Bridge 34 52.23 N 3.51 W
Devil's Island →Diable, Île du I 110 5.17 N 52.35 W
Devils Lake 100 48.06 N 98.51 W
Devil's Water ≃ 36 54.58 N 2.02 W
Devin 54 41.45 N 24.24 E
Devizes 34 51.22 N 1.59 W
Devoll ≃ 54 40.49 N 19.51 E
Devon □6 34 50.45 N 3.50 W
Devon ≃, Eng., U.K. 34 53.04 N 0.43 W
Devon ≃, Scot., U.K. 38 56.07 N 3.51 W
Devon Island I 22 75.00 N 87.00 W
Devonport, Austl. 94 41.11 S 146.21 E
Devonport, N.Z. 96 36.49 S 174.48 E
Devonport, Eng., U.K. 34 50.22 N 4.10 W
Devoto 114 31.24 S 62.19 W
Dewās 76 22.58 N 76.04 E
Dewa-sanchi ⩘2 64 39.05 N 140.10 E
Dewetsdorp 86 29.33 S 26.34 E
De Witt, Mi., U.S. 102 42.50 N 84.34 W
De Witt, N.Y., U.S. 102 43.02 N 76.03 W
Dewsbury 36 53.42 N 1.37 W
Dexing 66 28.54 N 117.36 E
Dexter, Me., U.S. 102 45.01 N 69.17 W
Dexter, Mi., U.S. 102 42.20 N 83.53 W
Dexter, N.Y., U.S. 102 44.00 N 76.02 W
Dexterity Fiord C2 98 71.11 N 73.03 W
Dey-Dey, Lake ⊜ 90 29.12 S 131.04 E
Dezfūl 78 32.23 N 48.24 E
Dezhou 62 37.27 N 116.18 E
Dežneva, mys › 58 66.06 N 169.45 W
Dháfni 54 37.48 N 22.01 E
Dhahab 78 28.29 N 34.32 E
Dhahran →Aẓ-Ẓahrān 78 26.18 N 50.08 E
Dhaka 76 23.43 N 90.25 E
Dhamār 74 14.46 N 44.23 E
Dhampur 76 29.19 N 78.31 E
Dhanaura 76 28.58 N 78.15 E
Dhānbād 76 23.48 N 86.27 E
Dhandhuka 76 22.22 N 71.59 E
Dhangarhi 74 28.41 N 80.36 E
Dhār 76 22.36 N 75.18 E
Dharangaon 76 21.01 N 75.16 E
Dhāri 76 21.20 N 71.01 E
Dharmjaygarh 76 22.28 N 83.13 E
Dharmsāla 76 32.13 N 76.19 E
Dhārwār 74 15.28 N 75.01 E
Dhaulāgiri ∧ 76 28.42 N 83.30 E
Dhelfoí ⊥ 54 38.30 N 22.29 E
Dhenkānāl 76 20.40 N 85.36 E
Dherue, Loch an ⊜ 38 58.25 N 4.27 W
Dheskáti 54 39.55 N 21.49 E
Dhiavolítsion 54 37.18 N 21.58 E
Dhidhimótikhon 54 41.21 N 26.30 E
Dhíkti ∧ 54 35.08 N 25.22 E
Dhílos ⊥ 54 37.26 N 25.16 E
Dhimitsána 54 37.37 N 22.03 E
Dhī Qār □4 78 31.00 N 46.15 E
Dhodhekánisos (Dodecanese) II 54 36.30 N 27.00 E
Dholka 76 22.43 N 72.28 E
Dholpur 76 26.42 N 77.54 E
Dhomhnull, Sgurr ∧ 38 56.45 N 5.27 W
Dhorāji 76 21.44 N 70.27 E
Dhoxáton 54 41.05 N 24.14 E
Dhrāngadhra 76 22.59 N 71.28 E
Dhrol 76 22.34 N 70.25 E
Dhubri 76 26.01 N 89.59 E
Dhule 76 20.54 N 74.47 E
Dhuliān 76 24.41 N 87.58 E
Dhupgāri 76 26.36 N 89.01 E
Día I 54 35.27 N 25.13 E
Diabaig 38 57.34 N 5.40 W
Diable, Île du I 110 5.17 N 52.35 W
Diablo, Mount ∧ 104 37.53 N 121.55 W
Diablo Range ⩘ 104 37.00 N 121.20 W
Diablotin, Morne ∧ 108 15.30 N 61.24 W
Diaka ≃1 80 15.13 N 4.14 W
Diamante 114 32.04 S 60.39 W
Diamante ≃ 114 34.31 S 66.56 W
Diamantina 110 18.15 S 43.36 W
Diamantina ≃ 94 26.45 S 139.10 E
Diamantina Fracture Zone ✦ 28 36.00 S 105.00 E
Diamantina Lakes 94 23.46 S 141.09 E
Diamantino 110 14.25 S 56.27 W
Diamond Harbour 76 22.12 N 88.12 E
Diamond Islets II 94 17.25 S 150.58 E
Diamond Lake ⊜ 104 43.10 N 122.09 W
Diamond Peak ∧ 104 43.33 N 122.09 W
Dianalund 44 55.32 N 11.30 E
Dianbai (Shuidong) 70 21.30 N 111.01 E
Dian Chi ⊜ 62 24.50 N 102.42 E
Dianópolis 110 11.38 S 46.50 W
Dibai 76 28.13 N 78.15 E
Dibaya 84 6.30 S 22.57 E
Dibeng 86 27.35 S 22.54 E
Dibrugarh 76 27.29 N 94.54 E
Dickinson 100 46.52 N 102.47 W
Dickins Seamount ✦3 22 54.30 N 137.00 W
Didbiran 58 51.58 N 139.20 E
Didcot 34 51.37 N 1.15 W
Dīdwāna 76 27.24 N 74.34 E
Die 48 44.45 N 5.22 E
Die Berg ∧ 86 25.12 S 30.09 E
Dieburg 46 49.54 N 8.50 E
Dieciocho de Julio 114 33.41 S 53.33 W
Diego de Almagro, Isla I 112 51.25 S 75.10 W
Diego de Ocampo, Pico ∧ 108 19.35 N 70.45 W
Diego Garcia I 26 7.20 S 72.25 E
Diego Ramírez, Islas II 112 56.30 S 68.44 W
Dien-bien-phu 70 21.23 N 103.01 E
Diepholz 46 52.35 N 8.21 E
Dieppe 48 49.56 N 1.05 E
Diest 46 50.59 N 5.03 E
Dietrich 104 42.54 N 114.15 W
Dieulefit 48 44.31 N 5.04 E
Dieuze 48 48.49 N 6.43 E
Dif 84 0.59 N 40.57 E
Differdange 46 49.32 N 5.52 E
Dīg 76 27.28 N 77.20 E
Digboi 76 27.23 N 95.38 E
Digby 98 44.37 N 65.46 W
Digges Islands II 98 62.35 N 77.50 W
Digne 48 44.06 N 6.14 E
Digoin 48 46.29 N 3.59 E
Digos 72 6.45 N 125.20 E
Digul ≃ 92 7.07 S 138.42 E
Dijon 48 47.19 N 5.01 E
Dikhil 82 11.06 N 42.22 E
Diksmuide 46 51.02 N 2.52 E
Dikson 56 73.30 N 80.35 E
Dikwa 80 12.02 N 13.56 E
Dili 72 8.33 S 125.35 E
Diligent Strait Ʉ 70 12.11 N 92.57 E
Dillenburg 46 50.44 N 8.17 E
Dillingen 46 49.21 N 6.44 E
Dillingen [an der Donau] 46 48.34 N 10.29 E
Dillon 100 45.12 N 112.38 W
Dillon Cone ∧ 96 42.16 S 173.13 E
Dillon Lake ⊜1 102 40.02 N 82.10 W
Dilolo 84 10.42 S 22.20 E
Dimāpur 76 25.54 N 93.44 E
Dimashq (Damascus) 78 33.30 N 36.18 E
Dimboola 94 36.27 S 142.02 E
Dîmbovița □6 54 45.00 N 25.30 E
Dîmbovița ≃ 54 44.14 N 26.27 E
Dimbulah 94 17.09 S 145.07 E
Dimitrovgrad, Blg. 54 42.03 N 25.36 E
Dimitrovgrad, Jugo. 54 43.01 N 22.47 E
Dimitrovgrad, S.S.S.R. 56 54.14 N 49.39 E
Dimitrovo →Pernik 54 42.36 N 23.02 E
Dimlang ∧ 80 8.24 N 11.47 E
Dimona 78 31.04 N 35.02 E
Dinagat Island I 68 10.12 N 125.35 E
Dinājpur 76 25.38 N 88.38 E
Dinan 48 48.27 N 2.02 W
Dinant 46 50.16 N 4.55 E
Dinara ⩘ 52 43.50 N 16.35 E
Dinard 48 48.38 N 2.04 W
Dinaric Alps →Dinara ⩘ 52 43.50 N 16.35 E
Dinas 34 52.00 N 4.54 W
Dinas Head › 34 52.02 N 4.55 W
Dinas Powys 34 51.26 N 3.14 W
Dindigul 74 10.21 N 77.57 E
Dindori 76 22.57 N 81.05 E
Dingalan Bay C 68 15.18 N 121.25 E
Dingan 70 19.44 N 110.21 E
Dinggyê 62 28.35 N 86.38 E
Dinghai 66 30.02 N 122.06 E
Dingle 40 52.08 N 10.15 W
Dingle Bay C 40 52.05 N 10.15 W
Dingnan 66 24.48 N 114.59 E
Dingo 94 23.39 S 149.20 E
Dingolfing 46 48.38 N 12.31 E
Dingqing 76 31.32 N 95.27 E
Dingri 76 28.35 N 86.38 E
Dingshuzhen 66 31.17 N 119.50 E
Dingwall 38 57.35 N 4.29 W
Dingxi 62 35.33 N 104.32 E
Dingxian 62 38.32 N 114.59 E
Dingyuan 66 32.32 N 117.40 E
Dīnhāta 76 26.08 N 89.28 E
Dinh-lap 70 21.33 N 107.06 E
Dinin ≃ 40 52.43 N 7.18 W
Dinkelsbühl 46 49.04 N 10.19 E
Dinnet 38 57.03 N 2.54 W
Dinnington 36 53.22 N 1.12 W
Dinuba 104 36.32 N 119.23 W
Diö 44 56.38 N 14.13 E
Diodār 76 24.06 N 71.47 E
Dionísio Cerqueira 114 26.15 S 53.38 W
Diourbel 80 14.40 N 16.15 W
Dipolog 68 8.35 N 123.20 E
Dippoldiswalde 46 50.54 N 13.40 E
Dipton 96 45.54 S 168.22 E
Dīr 76 35.12 N 71.53 E
Direction, Cape › 92 12.51 S 143.32 E
Dire Dawa 82 9.37 N 41.52 E
Diriamba 108 11.51 N 86.14 W
Dirico 84 17.58 S 20.47 E
Dirj 82 30.09 N 10.26 E
Dirk Hartog Island I 90 25.48 S 113.00 E
Dirranbandi 94 28.35 S 148.14 E
Disappointment, Cape ›, Falk. Is. 112 54.53 S 36.07 W
Disappointment, Cape ›, Wa., U.S. 100 46.18 N 124.03 W
Disappointment, Lake ⊜ 90 23.30 S 122.50 E
Disaster Bay C 94 37.17 S 150.00 E
Discovery Bay C 94 38.12 S 141.07 E
Disentis 48 46.43 N 8.51 E
Disko I 98 69.50 N 53.30 W
Disko Bugt C 98 69.15 N 52.00 W
Dismal Lakes ⊜ 98 67.26 N 117.07 W
Disna 60 55.33 N 28.10 E
Disraeli 102 45.54 N 71.21 W
Diss 34 52.23 N 1.07 E
Distington 36 54.36 N 3.32 W
Disūq 82 31.08 N 30.39 E
Dithmarschen ✦1 46 54.05 N 9.00 E
Ditton Priors 34 52.30 N 2.35 W
Diu 76 20.42 N 70.59 E
Dives ≃ 48 49.19 N 0.05 W
Divinópolis 110 20.09 S 44.54 W
Divisor, Serra do ⩘1 110 8.20 S 73.30 W
Divnoje 56 45.55 N 43.22 E
Dixfield 102 44.32 N 70.27 W
Dixie Valley ∨ 104 39.50 N 117.55 W
Dixon 104 38.19 N 121.49 W
Dixon Entrance Ʉ 98 54.25 N 132.30 W
Diyālā □4 78 34.00 N 45.00 E
Diyālā (Sīrvān) ≃ 78 33.14 N 44.31 E
Diyarbakır 78 37.55 N 40.14 E
Dizzard Point › 34 50.45 N 4.38 W
Dja ≃ 80 2.02 N 15.12 E
Djakarta →Jakarta 72 6.10 S 106.48 E
Djambala 84 2.33 S 14.45 E
Djanet 80 24.34 N 9.29 E
Djedi, Oued ∨ 80 34.28 N 6.05 E
Djénné 80 13.54 N 4.33 W
Djérem ≃ 80 5.20 N 13.24 E
Djibouti 82 11.36 N 43.09 E
Djibouti □1 82 11.30 N 43.00 E
Djokupunda 84 5.27 S 20.58 E
Djougou 80 9.42 N 1.40 E
Djúpivogur 42a 64.40 N 14.10 W
Djurås 44 60.33 N 15.08 E
Djurö I 44 58.52 N 13.28 E
Djursholm 44 59.24 N 18.05 E
Dmitrija Lapteva, proliv Ʉ 58 73.00 N 142.00 E
Dmitrijev-L'govskij 60 52.08 N 35.05 E
Dmitrov 60 56.21 N 37.31 E
Dmitrovsk-Orlovskij 60 52.30 N 35.09 E
Dnepr ≃ 56 46.30 N 32.18 E
Dneprodzeržinsk 56 48.30 N 34.37 E
Dnepropetrovsk 56 48.27 N 34.59 E
Dnestr ≃ 56 46.18 N 30.17 E
Dnieper →Dnepr ≃ 56 46.30 N 32.18 E
Dniester →Dnestr ≃ 56 46.18 N 30.17 E
Dno 60 57.50 N 29.59 E
Doany 87b 14.22 S 49.31 E
Doba 82 8.39 N 16.51 E
Dobbiaco 52 46.44 N 12.14 E
Dobbyn 94 19.48 S 140.00 E
Dobczyce 46 49.54 N 20.06 E
Döbeln 46 51.07 N 13.07 E
Doberai, Jazirah (Vogelkop) ›1 92 1.30 S 132.30 E
Dobiegniew 46 52.59 N 15.47 E
Dobo 92 5.46 S 134.13 E
Doboj 54 44.44 N 18.06 E
Dobra, Pol. 46 51.54 N 18.37 E
Dobra, Pol. 46 53.35 N 15.18 E
Dobra ≃ 52 45.33 N 15.31 E
Dobr'anka 56 58.27 N 56.25 E
Dobre Miasto 46 53.59 N 20.25 E
Dobříš 46 49.47 N 14.11 E
Dobrodzień 46 50.44 N 18.27 E
Dobroteasa 54 44.47 N 24.23 E
Dobrudžansko plato ⩘1 54 43.32 N 27.50 E
Dobruja ✦1 54 44.00 N 28.00 E
Dobruš 60 52.25 N 31.19 E
Dobruška 46 50.17 N 16.10 E
Dobrzany 46 53.22 N 15.25 E
Dobrzyń nad Wisłą 46 52.38 N 19.20 E
Dobšiná 46 48.49 N 20.23 E
Doce ≃ 110 19.37 S 39.49 W
Doce Leguas, Cayos de las II 108 20.55 N 79.05 W
Dochart ≃ 38 56.28 N 4.20 W
Docking 34 52.55 N 0.38 E
Doctor Cecilio Báez 114 25.03 S 56.19 W
Doctor Hicks Range ⩘ 90 28.40 S 124.20 E
Doctor Pedro P. Peña 114 22.26 S 62.22 W
Doddinghurst 34 51.40 N 0.18 E
Dodecanese →Dhodhekánisos II 54 36.30 N 27.00 E
Dodge City 100 37.45 N 100.01 W
Dodman Point › 34 50.13 N 4.48 W
Dodola 82 7.02 N 39.07 E
Dodoma 84 6.11 S 35.45 E
Doetinchem 46 51.58 N 6.17 E
Dogai Coring ⊜ 62 34.30 N 89.15 E
Dōgo I 64 36.15 N 133.16 E
Dogondoutchi 80 13.38 N 4.02 E
Doha →Ad-Dawḥah 78 25.17 N 51.32 E
Dohad 76 22.50 N 74.16 E
Dohhi 76 24.32 N 84.54 E
Dohrīghāt 76 26.16 N 83.31 E
Doiran, Lake ⊜ 54 41.13 N 22.44 E
Dokka 44 60.50 N 10.05 E
Dokkum 46 53.19 N 6.00 E
Dokšicy 60 54.54 N 27.46 E
Doksy 46 50.35 N 14.38 E
Dolbeau 98 48.53 N 72.14 W
Dol-de-Bretagne 48 48.33 N 1.45 W
Dole 48 47.06 N 5.30 E
Dolgarrog 36 53.11 N 3.51 W
Dolgellau 34 52.44 N 3.53 W
Dolgeville 102 43.06 N 74.46 W
Dolianova 52 39.22 N 9.10 E
Dolinsk 58 47.21 N 142.48 E
Dolisie 84 4.12 S 12.41 E
Dolj □6 54 44.15 N 23.45 E
Dollar 38 56.09 N 3.40 W
Dollar Law ∧ 38 55.33 N 3.17 W
Dolmatovskij 60 57.29 N 42.18 E
Dolni Dâbnik 54 43.24 N 24.26 E
Dolni Lom 54 43.31 N 22.47 E
Dolný Kubín 46 49.12 N 19.17 E
Dolomites →Dolomiti ⩘ 52 46.25 N 11.50 E
Dolomiti ⩘ 52 46.25 N 11.50 E
Dolores, Arg. 114 36.20 S 57.40 W
Dolores, Esp. 50 38.08 N 0.46 W
Dolores, Ur. 114 33.33 S 58.13 W
Dolphin and Union Strait Ʉ 98 69.05 N 114.45 W
Dolsk 46 52.00 N 17.03 E
Dolton 34 50.53 N 4.01 W
Dolwyddelan 34 53.03 N 3.53 W
Domažlice 46 49.27 N 12.56 E
Dombarovskij 56 50.46 N 59.32 E
Dombås 44 62.05 N 9.08 E
Dombes ✦1 48 46.00 N 5.03 E
Dombóvár 46 46.23 N 18.08 E
Dombrád 46 48.14 N 21.56 E
Dôme, Puy de ∧ 48 45.47 N 2.58 E
Domett 96 42.51 S 173.13 E
Domeyko 114 28.57 S 70.54 W
Domeyko, Cordillera ⩘ 114 24.30 S 69.00 W
Domfront 48 48.36 N 0.39 W
Domíngo M. Irala 114 25.54 S 54.43 W
Dominica □1 106 15.30 N 61.20 W
Dominica Channel Ʉ 108 15.10 N 61.15 W
Dominican Republic (República Dominicana) □1 106 19.00 N 70.40 W
Dominion, Cape › 98 66.13 N 74.28 W
Domnarvet 44 60.30 N 15.27 E
Domnești 54 44.25 N 25.56 E
Domo 82 7.54 N 46.52 E
Domodedovo 60 55.26 N 37.46 E
Domodossola 52 46.07 N 8.17 E
Dom Pedrito 114 30.59 S 54.40 W
Dompierre-sur-Besbre 48 46.31 N 3.41 E
Dompu 72 8.32 S 118.28 E
Domsjö 44 63.15 N 18.43 E
Domuyo, Volcán ∧1 114 36.38 S 70.26 W
Domžale 52 46.08 N 14.36 E
Don ≃, S.S.S.R. 56 47.04 N 39.18 E
Don ≃, Eng., U.K. 36 53.39 N 0.59 W
Don ≃, Scot., U.K. 38 57.08 N 2.05 W
Donadeu 114 26.43 S 62.44 W
Donaghadee 40 54.39 N 5.33 W
Donaghmore 40 54.32 N 6.49 W
Donald 94 36.22 S 143.00 E
Donard, Slieve ∧ 40 54.11 N 5.55 W
Donau →Danube ≃ 30 45.20 N 29.40 E
Donaueschingen 46 47.57 N 8.29 E
Donauwörth 46 48.43 N 10.46 E
Don Benito 50 38.57 N 5.52 W
Doncaster 36 53.32 N 1.07 W
Dondaicha 76 21.20 N 74.34 E
Dondo, Ang. 84 9.38 S 14.25 E
Dondo, Moç. 86 19.36 S 34.44 E
Dondra Head › 74 5.55 N 80.35 E
Doneck 56 48.00 N 37.48 E
Donegal 40 54.39 N 8.07 W
Donegal □6 40 54.50 N 8.00 W
Donegal Bay C 40 54.30 N 8.30 W
Doneraile 40 52.13 N 8.35 W
Donetsk →Doneck 56 48.00 N 37.48 E
Dong ≃ 66 23.06 N 114.00 E
Donga ≃ 80 8.19 N 9.58 E
Dongan 70 26.17 N 111.07 E
Dongara 90 29.15 S 114.56 E
Dongargarh 76 21.12 N 80.44 E
Dongba 66 31.18 N 119.03 E
Dongchuan 70 26.10 N 103.01 E
Dongen 46 51.37 N 4.56 E
Dongfang (Basuo) 70 19.05 N 108.39 E
Donggala 72 0.40 S 119.44 E
Donggou, Zhg. 66 33.38 N 119.40 E
Donggou, Zhg. 66 32.17 N 118.59 E
Dongguan 66 23.03 N 113.46 E
Donghaidao I 70 21.02 N 110.25 E
Dong-hoi 70 17.29 N 106.36 E
Donglong 66 23.36 N 116.50 E
Dong-nai ≃ 70 10.45 N 106.46 E
Dongola →Dunqulah 82 19.10 N 30.29 E
Dongpu 66 30.03 N 120.34 E
Dongshajiao 66 30.19 N 122.09 E
Dongshan 66 31.04 N 120.24 E
Dongshi 66 24.42 N 118.27 E
Dongtai 66 32.51 N 120.20 E
Dongting Hu ⊜ 66 29.20 N 112.54 E
Dongxiang 66 28.13 N 116.35 E
Dongyang 66 29.16 N 120.14 E
Dongzhi 66 30.07 N 116.59 E
Donington 34 52.55 N 0.12 W
Donja Stubica 52 45.59 N 15.58 E
Donjek ≃ 98 62.35 N 140.00 W
Donji Vakuf 52 44.09 N 17.25 E
Donnellys Crossing 96 35.43 S 173.37 E
Donner Pass)(104 39.19 N 120.20 W
Donner und Blitzen ≃ 104 43.17 N 118.49 W
Donnybrook, Austl. 90 33.35 S 115.49 E
Donnybrook, S. Afr. 86 30.00 S 29.48 E
Donora 102 40.10 N 79.51 W
Donors Hills 94 18.42 S 140.33 E
Donoughmore 40 51.57 N 8.45 W
Donskoj 60 53.58 N 38.20 E
Dooagh 40 53.59 N 10.09 W
Doogort 40 54.01 N 10.01 W
Doolow 82 4.10 N 42.05 E
Doomadgee Mission 94 17.56 S 138.49 E
Doon ≃ 38 55.26 N 4.38 W
Doon, Loch ⊜ 36 55.15 N 4.22 W
Doonbeg 40 52.44 N 9.32 W
Doonbeg ≃ 40 52.44 N 9.34 W
Doondi 94 28.15 S 148.28 E
Doornik →Tournai 46 50.36 N 3.23 E
Dora, Lake ⊜ 90 22.05 S 122.55 E
Dorain, Beinn ∧ 38 56.30 N 4.42 W
Dorback Burn ≃ 38 57.31 N 3.40 W
Dorchester, On., Can. 102 42.59 N 81.04 W
Dorchester, Eng., U.K. 34 51.39 N 1.10 W
Dorchester, Eng., U.K. 34 50.43 N 2.26 W
Dorchester, Cape › 98 65.29 N 77.30 W
Dordogne □5 48 45.10 N 0.45 E
Dordogne ≃ 48 45.02 N 0.35 W
Dordon 34 52.36 N 1.37 W
Dordrecht, Ned. 46 51.49 N 4.40 E
Dordrecht, S. Afr. 86 31.20 S 27.03 E
Dore ≃ 34 51.57 N 2.52 W
Dore, Monts ⩘ 48 45.30 N 2.45 E
Doré Lake ⊜ 98 54.46 N 107.17 W
Dores 38 57.22 N 4.15 W
Dores do Indaiá 110 19.27 S 45.36 W
Dorfen 46 48.17 N 12.08 E
Dorgali 52 40.17 N 9.35 E
Doring ≃ 86 31.54 S 18.39 E
Dorking 34 51.14 N 0.20 W
Dormans 48 49.04 N 3.38 E
Dornbirn 46 47.25 N 9.44 E
Dornie 38 57.17 N 5.31 W
Dornoch 38 57.52 N 4.02 W
Dornoch Firth C1 38 57.53 N 4.00 W
Dorochovo 60 55.33 N 36.23 E
Dorog 46 47.43 N 18.44 E
Dorogobuž 60 54.55 N 33.18 E
Dorohoi 54 47.57 N 26.24 E
Dorotea 44 64.16 N 16.24 E
Dorre Island I 90 25.09 S 113.07 E
Dorrigo 94 30.21 S 152.43 E
Dorris 104 41.58 N 121.55 W
Dorset □6 34 50.47 N 2.20 W
Dorset Peak ∧ 102 43.19 N 73.02 W
Dortmund 46 51.31 N 7.28 E
Doruma 82 4.44 N 27.42 E
Dosatuj 58 50.23 N 118.38 E
Dos Bahías, Cabo › 112 44.55 S 65.32 W
Dosčatoje 60 55.23 N 42.07 E
Dos Hermanas 50 37.17 N 5.55 W
Dos Palos 104 36.59 N 120.37 W
Dos Reyes, Punta › 114 24.33 S 70.35 W
Dossor 56 47.32 N 53.01 E
Dothan 100 31.13 N 85.23 W
Dotnuva 60 55.21 N 23.54 E
Douai 48 50.22 N 3.04 E
Douala 80 4.03 N 9.42 E
Douarnenez 48 48.06 N 4.20 W
Double Cone ∧ 96 45.04 S 168.48 E
Double Island Point › 94 25.56 S 153.11 E
Double Point › 94 17.39 S 146.09 E
Doubs □5 48 47.10 N 6.25 E
Doubs ≃ 46 46.54 N 5.02 E
Doubtful Sound Ʉ 96 45.17 S 166.51 E
Doubtless Bay C 96 34.55 S 173.25 E
Doudeville 48 49.43 N 0.48 E
Douentza 80 15.00 N 2.57 W
Doughboy Bay C 96 47.02 S 167.41 E
Douglas, I. of Man 36 54.09 N 4.28 W
Douglas, S. Afr. 86 29.04 S 23.46 E
Douglas, Scot., U.K. 38 55.33 N 3.51 W
Douglas ≃ 36 53.43 N 2.50 W
Douglas, Mount ∧2 90 28.39 S 123.53 E
Douglas Channel Ʉ 98 53.30 N 129.12 W
Douglas Water ≃ 38 55.38 N 3.46 W
Doulaincourt 48 48.19 N 5.12 E
Doulevant-le-Château 48 48.23 N 4.55 E
Doullens 48 50.09 N 2.21 E
Doune 38 56.12 N 4.05 W
Dour 48 50.24 N 3.47 E
Dourada, Serra ⩘1 110 13.10 S 48.45 W
Dourados 114 22.13 S 54.48 W
Dourdan 48 48.32 N 2.01 E
Dourdou ≃ 48 44.00 N 2.41 E
Douro (Duero) ≃ 50 41.08 N 8.40 W
Douvres 48 49.17 N 0.23 W
Douze ≃ 48 43.54 N 0.30 W
Dove ≃, Eng., U.K. 34 52.50 N 1.35 W
Dove ≃, Eng., U.K. 36 54.12 N 0.54 W
Dove Creek ≃ 104 41.42 N 113.22 W
Dover, Austl. 94 43.19 S 147.01 E
Dover, Eng., U.K. 34 51.08 N 1.19 E
Dover, De., U.S. 102 39.09 N 75.31 W
Dover, N.H., U.S. 102 43.11 N 70.52 W
Dover, N.J., U.S. 102 40.53 N 74.34 W
Dover, Oh., U.S. 102 40.31 N 81.28 W
Dover, Point › 90 32.32 S 125.32 E
Dover, Strait of (Pas de Calais) Ʉ 32 51.00 N 1.30 E
Dover-Foxcroft 102 45.11 N 69.13 W
Dovers Hills ⩘2 90 23.10 S 128.45 E
Dovey Valley ∨ 34 52.35 N 3.50 W
Dovre 44 61.59 N 9.15 E
Dovrefjell ⩘ 44 62.06 N 9.25 E
Dowally 38 56.36 N 3.37 W
Dowerin 90 31.12 S 117.02 E
Downderry 34 50.22 N 4.22 W
Downham 34 52.26 N 0.15 E
Downham Market 34 52.36 N 0.23 E
Downieville 104 39.33 N 120.49 W
Downingtown 102 40.00 N 75.42 W
Downpatrick 40 54.20 N 5.43 W
Downpatrick Head › 40 54.20 N 9.20 W
Downsville 102 42.04 N 74.59 W
Downton 34 51.00 N 1.44 W
Dow Rūd 78 33.28 N 49.04 E
Doyle 104 40.01 N 120.06 W
Doylestown, Oh., U.S. 102 40.58 N 81.41 W
Doylestown, Pa., U.S. 102 40.18 N 75.07 W
Dōzen II 64 36.05 N 133.05 E
Dra'a, Hamada du ✦2 80 29.00 N 6.45 W
Drâa, Oued ∨ 80 28.43 N 11.09 W
Drac ≃ 48 45.13 N 5.41 E
Dracena 114 21.32 S 51.29 W
Drachten 46 53.06 N 6.05 E
Dracut 102 42.40 N 71.18 W
Dragalina 54 44.26 N 27.20 E
Drăgănești-Olt 54 44.10 N 24.32 E
Drăgănești-Vlașca 54 44.06 N 25.36 E
Drăgășani 54 44.40 N 24.16 E
Drag Lake ⊜ 102 45.05 N 78.24 W
Dragonera, Isla I 50 39.35 N 2.19 E
Dragons Mouth Ʉ 108 10.45 N 61.46 W
Dragør 44 55.36 N 12.41 E
Draguignan 48 43.32 N 6.28 E
Drakensberg ⩘ 86 27.00 S 30.00 E
Drake Passage Ʉ 24 58.00 S 70.00 W
Drake Peak ∧ 104 42.19 N 120.07 W
Dráma 54 41.09 N 24.08 E
Drammen 44 59.44 N 10.15 E
Drangajökull ⊓ 42a 66.11 N 22.15 W
Dranov, Ostrovul I 54 44.52 N 29.15 E
Draperstown 40 54.48 N 6.47 W
Drās 76 34.27 N 75.46 E
Drau (Drava) (Dráva) ≃ 52 45.33 N 18.55 E
Drava (Drau) (Dráva) ≃ 52 45.33 N 18.55 E
Dravinja ≃ 52 46.22 N 15.57 E
Drawno 46 53.13 N 15.45 E
Drawsko Pomorskie 46 53.32 N 15.48 E
Drayton 34 51.38 N 1.18 W
Drayton Valley 98 53.13 N 114.59 W
Drenovec 54 43.42 N 22.59 E
Dresden, On., Can. 102 42.35 N 82.11 W
Dresden, D.D.R. 46 51.03 N 13.44 E
Dresden, Oh., U.S. 102 40.07 N 82.00 W
Dresden □5 46 51.10 N 14.00 E
Dreux 48 48.44 N 1.22 E
Drews Reservoir ⊜1 104 42.10 N 120.40 W
Drezdenko 46 52.51 N 15.50 E
Drienov 46 48.53 N 21.17 E
Drimnin 38 56.36 N 6.00 W
Drimoleague 40 51.38 N 9.14 W
Drin ≃ 54 41.45 N 19.34 E
Drina ≃ 54 44.53 N 19.21 E
Drinit, Pellg i C 54 41.45 N 19.28 E
Drjanovo 54 42.58 N 25.27 E
Drniš 52 43.51 N 16.09 E
Drøbak 44 59.39 N 10.39 E
Drobeta-Turnu-Severin 54 44.38 N 22.39 E
Drogheda (Droichead Átha) 40 53.43 N 6.21 W
Drogičin 60 52.11 N 25.09 E
Drohiczyn 46 52.24 N 22.41 E
Droichead Átha →Drogheda 40 53.43 N 6.21 W
Droichead Nua 40 53.11 N 6.48 W
Droitwich 34 52.16 N 2.09 W
Dromahair 40 54.14 N 8.19 W
Dromcolliher 40 52.20 N 8.54 W
Drôme □5 48 44.35 N 5.10 E
Drôme ≃ 48 44.46 N 4.46 E
Dromod 40 53.51 N 7.55 W
Dromore 40 54.25 N 6.09 W
Dromore West 40 54.15 N 8.53 W
Dronero 52 44.28 N 7.22 E
Dronfield 36 53.19 N 1.27 W
Drongan 36 55.26 N 4.27 W
Dronne ≃ 48 45.02 N 0.09 W
Dronninglund 44 57.09 N 10.18 E
Dr. Petru Groza 54 46.32 N 22.28 E
Druja 60 55.47 N 27.27 E
Drumbeg 38 58.14 N 5.12 W
Drumcliff 40 54.20 N 8.30 W
Drumheller 98 51.28 N 112.42 W
Drumlish 40 53.48 N 7.46 W
Drummond 96 46.09 S 168.09 E
Drummond Island I 102 46.00 N 83.40 W
Drummond Range ⩘ 94 23.30 S 147.15 E
Drummondville 102 45.53 N 72.29 W
Drummore 36 54.42 N 4.54 W
Drumquin 40 54.37 N 7.30 W
Drumshanbo 40 54.02 N 8.02 W
Druskininkai 60 54.01 N 23.58 E
Družba 56 45.15 N 82.26 E
Družina 58 68.14 N 145.18 E
Družnaja Gorka 60 59.17 N 30.08 E
Drvar 52 44.22 N 16.24 E
Drwęca ≃ 46 53.00 N 18.42 E
Dry ≃ 92 14.54 S 132.24 E
Dry Creek ≃, Ca., U.S. 104 38.35 N 122.51 W
Dry Creek ≃, Ca., U.S. 104 38.14 N 121.24 W
Dry Creek ≃, Or., U.S. 104 43.34 N 117.21 W
Dry Creek Mountain ∧ 104 41.22 N 116.22 W
Dryden 98 49.47 N 92.50 W
Dryfe Water ≃ 36 55.08 N 3.26 W
Drymen 38 56.04 N 4.27 W
Dry Ridge 102 38.40 N 84.35 W
Drysdale ≃ 92 13.59 S 126.51 E
Dry Tortugas II 108 24.38 N 82.55 W
Drzewica 46 51.27 N 20.28 E
Duan 70 24.06 N 108.10 E
Duaringa 94 23.43 S 149.40 E
Duarte, Pico ∧ 108 19.02 N 70.59 W
Duartina 114 22.24 S 49.25 W
Dubai →Dubayy 78 25.18 N 55.18 E
Dubawnt ≃ 98 64.33 N 100.06 W
Dubawnt Lake ⊜ 98 63.08 N 101.30 W
Dubayy 78 25.18 N 55.18 E
Dubbo 94 32.15 S 148.36 E
Dubh Artach II1 38 56.08 N 6.40 W
Dubica 52 45.11 N 16.48 E
Dublin (Baile Átha Cliath), Ire. 40 53.20 N 6.15 W
Dublin, Ga., U.S. 100 32.32 N 82.54 W
Dublin □6 40 53.20 N 6.15 W
Dublin Bay C 40 53.20 N 6.06 W
Dubna 60 56.44 N 37.10 E
Dubňany 46 48.55 N 17.06 E
Dubnica nad Váhom 46 48.58 N 18.09 E
Du Bois 102 41.07 N 78.45 W
Dubovka 56 49.03 N 44.50 E
Dubrājpur 76 23.48 N 87.23 E
Dubréka 80 9.48 N 13.31 W
Dubrovka, S.S.S.R. 60 53.42 N 33.30 E
Dubrovka, S.S.S.R. 60 59.51 N 30.56 E
Dubrovnik 54 42.38 N 18.07 E
Dubrovno 60 54.35 N 30.41 E
Dubuque 100 42.30 N 90.39 W
Duchang 66 29.15 N 116.13 E
Duchcov 46 50.37 N 13.45 E
Duchess 94 21.22 S 139.52 E
Duck Creek ≃ 104 40.06 N 114.43 W
Du Couedic, Cape › 94 36.04 S 136.42 E
Duddington 34 52.36 N 0.32 W
Duddon ≃ 36 54.15 N 3.13 W
Dudelange 46 49.28 N 6.05 E
Duderstadt 46 51.31 N 10.16 E
Dudinka 56 69.25 N 86.15 E
Dudley, Eng., U.K. 34 52.30 N 2.05 W
Dudley, Eng., U.K. 36 55.03 N 1.35 W
Dudorovskij 60 53.40 N 35.22 E
Dudweiler 46 49.17 N 7.02 E
Duerna ≃ 50 42.19 N 5.54 W
Duero (Douro) ≃ 50 41.08 N 8.40 W
Duffer Peak ∧ 104 41.40 N 118.44 W
Duffield, Austl. 90 25.50 S 134.40 E
Duffield, Eng., U.K. 34 52.58 N 1.29 W
Dufftown 38 57.26 N 3.08 W
Dufourspitze ∧ 48 45.55 N 7.52 E
Duga Resa 52 45.27 N 15.30 E
Dugi Otok I 52 44.00 N 15.04 E
Dugna 60 54.25 N 36.51 E
Du Gué ≃ 98 57.21 N 70.45 W
Duich, Loch C 38 57.14 N 5.30 W
Duifken Point › 92 12.33 S 141.38 E
Duirinish 38 57.19 N 5.41 W
Duisburg 46 51.25 N 6.46 E
Duitama 110 5.50 N 73.02 W
Duiwelskloof 86 23.42 S 30.06 E
Duke of York Bay C 98 65.25 N 84.50 W
Duke of York Island I 92 4.10 S 152.26 E
Duk Fadiat 82 7.45 N 31.25 E
Dukhān 78 25.25 N 50.48 E
Dukla 46 49.34 N 21.41 E
Dukla Pass)(46 49.25 N 21.43 E
Dūkštas 60 55.32 N 26.20 E
Dulais ≃ 34 51.41 N 3.47 W
Dulan 62 36.16 N 98.28 E
Dul'apino 60 57.15 N 40.49 E
Dulas ≃, Wales, U.K. 34 52.36 N 3.50 W
Dulas ≃, Wales, U.K. 34 52.16 N 3.22 W
Dulas Bay C 36 53.23 N 4.15 W
Dulce ≃ 114 30.31 S 62.32 W
Dul'durga 58 50.41 N 113.36 E
Duleek 40 53.39 N 6.25 W
Dulgalach ≃ 58 67.44 N 133.12 E
Dulkaninna 94 29.01 S 138.27 E
Dullstroom 86 25.27 S 30.07 E
Dülmen 46 51.51 N 7.16 E
Dulnain Bridge 38 57.16 N 3.41 W
Dulnan ≃ 38 57.18 N 3.40 W
Dulovo 54 43.49 N 27.09 E
Duluth 100 46.45 N 92.07 W
Dulverton 34 51.03 N 3.33 W
Dūmā 78 33.35 N 36.24 E
Dumaguete 68 9.18 N 123.18 E
Dumai 72 1.41 N 101.27 E
Dumaran Island I 68 10.33 N 119.51 E
Dumaresq ≃ 94 28.40 S 150.28 E
Dumaring 72 1.36 N 118.12 E
Dumbarton 38 55.57 N 4.35 W
Ďumbier ∧ 46 48.57 N 19.37 E
Dumbleyung 90 33.19 S 117.44 E
Dumbrăveni 54 46.14 N 24.35 E
Dume, Point › 104 34.00 N 118.48 W
Dumfries 36 55.04 N 3.37 W
Dumfries and Galloway □4 36 55.00 N 4.00 W
Duminiči 60 53.55 N 35.06 E
Dumka 76 24.16 N 87.15 E
Dummer Range ⩘ 90 20.11 S 125.59 E
Dumoine ≃ 102 46.13 N 77.51 W
Dumont, Lac ⊜ 102 46.04 N 76.27 W
Dumraon 76 25.33 N 84.09 E
Dumyāṭ 82 31.25 N 31.48 E
Duna →Danube ≃ 30 45.20 N 29.40 E
Dunaff Head › 40 55.17 N 7.33 W
Dunaföldvár 46 46.48 N 18.55 E
Dunaharaszti 46 47.21 N 19.05 E
Dunaj →Danube ≃ 30 45.20 N 29.40 E
Dunaj, ostrova II 58 73.52 N 124.29 E
Dunajec ≃ 46 50.14 N 20.44 E
Dunajská Streda 46 48.01 N 17.35 E
Dunakeszi 46 47.38 N 19.08 E
Dunărea →Danube ≃ 30 45.20 N 29.40 E
Dunărea Veche ≃ 54 45.17 N 28.02 E
Dunaújváros 46 46.58 N 18.57 E
Dunav →Danube ≃ 30 45.20 N 29.40 E
Dunavățu-de-Sus 54 44.59 N 29.13 E
Duna-Völgyi-főcsatorna ≍ 46 46.12 N 18.56 E
Dunback 96 45.23 S 170.38 E
Dunbar, Scot., U.K. 38 56.00 N 2.31 W
Dunbar, W.V., U.S. 102 38.21 N 81.44 W
Dunbeath 38 58.15 N 3.25 W
Dunblane 38 56.12 N 3.59 W
Dunboyne 40 53.24 N 6.28 W
Duncan, B.C., Can. 98 48.47 N 123.42 W
Duncan, Ok., U.S. 100 34.30 N 97.57 W
Duncan Lake ⊜1 98 50.20 N 117.00 W
Duncannon 102 40.23 N 77.01 W
Duncansby Head › 38 58.39 N 3.02 W
Dunchurch 34 52.20 N 1.16 W
Duncormick 40 52.14 N 6.39 W
Dundalk, On., Can. 102 44.10 N 80.24 W
Dundalk (Dún Dealgan), Ire. 40 54.01 N 6.25 W
Dundalk, Md., U.S. 102 39.15 N 76.31 W
Dundalk Bay C 40 53.57 N 6.17 W
Dundas 102 43.16 N 79.58 W
Dundas, Lake ⊜ 90 32.35 S 121.50 E
Dundas Peninsula ›1 98 74.50 N 111.30 W
Dundas Strait Ʉ 92 11.20 S 131.35 E
Dún Dealgan →Dundalk 40 54.01 N 6.25 W
Dundee, S. Afr. 86 28.12 S 30.16 E
Dundee, Scot., U.K. 38 56.28 N 3.00 W
Dundee, Mi., U.S. 102 41.57 N 83.39 W
Dundee, N.Y., U.S. 102 42.31 N 76.58 W
Dundonald 38 55.34 N 4.35 W
Dundoo 94 27.39 S 144.39 E
Dundrum, Ire. 40 53.17 N 6.15 W
Dundrum, N. Ire., U.K. 40 54.16 N 5.51 W
Dundrum Bay C 40 54.13 N 5.45 W
Duneaton Water ≃ 38 55.32 N 3.42 W
Dunedin 96 45.52 S 170.30 E
Dunedoo 94 32.01 S 149.24 E
Dunfanaghy 40 55.11 N 7.59 W
Dunfermline 38 56.04 N 3.29 W
Dungannon 40 54.31 N 6.46 W
Dūngarpur 76 23.50 N 73.43 E
Dungarvan 40 52.05 N 7.37 W
Dungarvan Harbour C 40 52.10 N 7.35 W
Dungeness › 34 50.55 N 0.58 E
Dungiven 40 54.55 N 6.55 W
Dunglow 40 54.57 N 8.22 W
Dungog 94 32.24 S 151.46 E
Dunholme 36 53.18 N 0.28 W
Dunhua 62 43.21 N 128.13 E
Dunhuang 62 40.12 N 94.41 E
Dunilovo 60 57.46 N 38.55 E
Dunkeld 38 56.34 N 3.35 W
Dunkellin ≃ 40 53.12 N 8.54 W
Dunkerque 48 51.03 N 2.22 E
Dunkerrin 40 52.55 N 7.55 W
Dunkery Hill ∧2 34 51.11 N 3.35 W
Dunkineely 40 54.38 N 8.23 W
Dunkirk →Dunkerque, Fr. 48 51.03 N 2.22 E
Dunkirk, Eng., U.K. 34 51.17 N 0.59 E
Dunkirk, In., U.S. 102 40.22 N 85.12 W
Dunkirk, N.Y., U.S. 102 42.28 N 79.20 W
Dunkirk, Oh., U.S. 102 40.47 N 83.38 W
Dunkwa 80 5.22 N 1.12 W
Dún Laoghaire 40 53.17 N 6.08 W
Dunlavin 40 53.02 N 6.41 W
Dunleary →Dún Laoghaire 40 53.17 N 6.08 W
Dunleer 40 53.50 N 6.24 W
Dun-le-Palestel 48 46.18 N 1.40 E
Dunlop 38 55.43 N 4.32 W
Dunloy 40 55.01 N 6.25 W
Dunmanus Bay C 40 51.35 N 9.45 W
Dunmanway 40 51.43 N 9.06 W
Dunmarra 92 16.42 S 133.25 E
Dunmore, Ire. 40 53.36 N 8.46 W
Dunmore, Pa., U.S. 102 41.25 N 75.37 W
Dunmore Cave ⌂5 40 52.44 N 7.15 W
Dunmore East 40 52.09 N 7.00 W
Dunmore Town 108 25.30 N 76.39 W
Dunmurry 40 54.33 N 6.01 W
Dunnamanagh 40 54.52 N 7.18 W
Dunnet 38 58.31 N 3.20 W
Dunnet Bay C 38 58.37 N 3.24 W
Dunnet Head › 38 58.40 N 3.24 W
Dunnington 36 53.57 N 0.59 W
Dunnville 102 42.54 N 79.36 W
Dunoon 38 55.57 N 4.56 W
Dunqulah 82 19.10 N 30.29 E
Dun Rig ∧ 38 55.34 N 3.10 W
Duns 38 55.47 N 2.20 W
Dunsandel 96 43.40 S 172.11 E
Dunsford 34 50.41 N 3.40 W
Dunsmuir 104 41.13 N 122.16 W
Dunstable 34 51.53 N 0.32 W
Dunstan Mountains ⩘ 96 44.57 S 169.32 E
Dunster 34 51.12 N 3.27 W
Dun-sur-Auron 48 46.53 N 2.34 E
Dun-sur-Meuse 48 49.23 N 5.11 E
Duntelchaig, Loch ⊜ 38 57.20 N 4.18 W
Dunton Green 34 51.18 N 0.11 E
Duntroon 96 44.52 S 170.41 E
Dunvegan 38 57.26 N 6.35 W
Dunvegan, Loch C 38 57.28 N 6.40 W

Symbols in the Index entries are identified on page 122.

Dunv-Ergu

Name Page Lat.°′ Long.°′

Dunvegan Head › 38 57.31N 6.43W
Duolun 62 42.15N 116.18E
Duomaer 62 34.15N 79.45E
Duomula 62 34.07N 82.30E
Duozhu 66 22.59N 114.43E
Duque de York, Isla I 112 50.40S 75.20W
Durack ≃ 92 15.33S 127.52E
Durack Range ⋀ 92 16.30S 128.00E
Durance ≃ 48 43.55N 4.44E
Durand 102 42.54N 83.59W
Durango, Esp. 50 43.10N 2.37W
Durango, Méx. 106 24.02N 104.40W
Durango, Co., U.S. 100 37.16N 107.52W
Durant 100 33.59N 96.22W
Duras 48 44.41N 0.11E
Duraton ≃ 50 41.37N 4.07W
Durazno 114 33.22S 56.31W
Durazzo →Durrës 54 41.19N 19.26E
Durban 86 29.55S 30.56E
Durbe 60 56.35N 21.21E
Durbin 102 38.32N 79.49W
Đurđevac 52 46.03N 17.04E
Düren 46 50.48N 6.28E
Durg 76 21.11N 81.17E
Durgāpur 76 23.29N 87.20E
Durham, On., Can. 102 44.10N 80.49W
Durham, Eng., U.K. 36 54.47N 1.34W
Durham, Ca., U.S. 104 39.38N 121.47W
Durham, N.H., U.S. 102 43.08N 70.55W
Durham, N.C., U.S. 100 35.59N 78.53W
Durham □6 36 54.45N 1.45W
Durham Downs 94 27.05S 141.54E
Durham Heights ∧ 98 71.08N 122.56W
Durmitor ∧ 54 43.08N 19.01E
Durness 38 58.33N 4.45W
Durness, Kyle of C 38 58.34N 4.49W
Dürnkrut 46 48.28N 16.51E
Durón 50 40.38N 2.43W
Durrës 54 41.19N 19.26E
Durrie 94 25.38S 140.16E
Durrington 34 51.13N 1.45W
Durrow 40 52.50N 7.22W
Durrus 40 51.36N 9.31W
Dursey Head › 40 51.35N 10.14W
Dursey Island I 40 51.36N 10.12W
Dursley 34 51.42N 2.21W
D'Urville Island I 96 40.50S 173.52E
Dury Voe C 38a 60.20N 1.08W
Dušanbe 56 38.35N 68.48E
Dušekan 58 60.39N 109.03E
Dusetos 60 55.45N 25.51E
Dushan 70 25.53N 107.30E
Dushanbe →Dušanbe 56 38.35N 68.48E
Dushanzi 62 44.20N 84.51E
Dushore 102 41.31N 76.24W
Dusky Sound ʮ 96 45.47S 166.28E
Düsseldorf 46 51.12N 6.47E
Dutton 102 42.39N 81.30W
Dutton ≃ 94 20.45S 143.12E
Duval, Lac ⊜ 102 46.19N 76.55W
Duved 44 63.24N 12.52E
Duvno 52 43.43N 17.14E
Duxun 66 23.55N 117.37E
Duyun 62 26.12N 107.31E
Dve Mogili 54 43.36N 25.52E
Dvinsk →Daugavpils 60 55.53N 26.32E
Dvinskaja guba C 42 65.00N 39.45E
Dvuch Cirkov, gora ∧ 58 67.35N 168.07E
Dvůr Králové [nad Labem] 46 50.26N 15.48E
Dwārka 76 22.14N 68.58E
Dwyfor ≃ 36 52.55N 4.17W
Dwyka 86 33.02S 21.30E
Dyce 38 57.12N 2.11W
Dyer, Cape › 98 66.37N 61.18W
Dyer Bay C 102 45.10N 81.18W
Dyersburg 100 36.02N 89.23W
Dyfed □6 34 52.00N 4.30W
Dyfi ≃ 34 52.32N 4.03W
Dyje (Thaya) ≃ 46 48.37N 16.56E
Dyke 38 57.36N 3.41W
Dymchurch 34 51.02N 1.00E
Dymock 34 51.59N 2.26W
Dynów 46 49.49N 22.14E
Dyrnesvågen 44 63.26N 7.51E
Dysart 38 56.08N 3.08W
Dysselsdorp 86 33.34S 22.28E
Dysynni ≃ 34 52.36N 4.05W
Džalal-Abad 56 40.56N 73.00E
Džalinda 58 53.29N 123.54E
Džambejty 56 50.16N 52.35E
Džambul 56 42.54N 71.22E
Džankoj 56 45.43N 34.24E
Džanybek 56 49.25N 46.51E
Dzaoudzi 87a 12.47S 45.17E
Džardžan 58 68.43N 124.02E
Dzavchan ≃ 62 48.54N 93.23E
Dzeržinsk 60 56.15N 43.24E
Dzeržinskoje 56 45.50N 81.07E
Džetygara 56 52.11N 61.12E
Džezkazgan 56 47.47N 67.46E
Dzhambul →Džambul 56 42.54N 71.22E
Działdowo 46 53.15N 20.10E
Działoszyce 46 50.22N 20.21E
Dzierzgoń 46 53.56N 19.21E
Dzierzoniów (Reichenbach) 46 50.44N 16.39E
Dziwnów 46 54.03N 14.45E
Džizak 56 40.06N 67.50E
Džugdžur, chrebet ⋀ 58 58.00N 136.00E
Džul'fa 78 38.58N 45.38E
Dzungarian Basin →Junggar Pendi ≚1 62 45.00N 88.00E
Džungarskij Alatau, chrebet ⋀ 56 45.00N 81.00E
Džusaly 56 45.28N 64.05E
Džüün Charaa 62 48.52N 106.28E
Dzuunmod 62 47.45N 106.55E

E

Eagle ≃ 98 53.35N 57.25W
Eagle Creek ≃ 102 38.36N 85.04W
Eaglehawk 94 36.43S 144.15E
Eagle Lake ⊜ 104 40.39N 120.44W
Eagle Mountain 104 33.49N 115.27W
Eagle Pass 100 28.42N 100.29W
Eagle Peak ∧ 104 41.17N 120.12W
Eaglesfield 36 55.03N 3.12W
Eaglesham 38 55.44N 4.18W
Ealing ✦8 34 51.31N 0.20W
Eamont ≃ 36 54.40N 2.39W
Earaheedy 90 25.34S 121.39E
Earby 36 53.56N 2.08W
Eardisley 34 52.08N 2.59W
Earlimart 104 35.53N 119.16W
Earlish 38 57.34N 6.23W
Earls Barton 34 52.15N 0.45W
Earls Colne 34 51.56N 0.42E
Earl Shilton 34 52.35N 1.20W
Earl Soham 34 52.14N 1.16E
Earlston 38 55.39N 2.40W
Earlville 102 42.44N 75.33W
Earn ≃ 38 56.21N 3.19W
Earn, Loch ⊜ 38 56.23N 4.14W
Earnslaw, Mount ∧ 96 44.37S 168.24E
Easington 36 54.47N 1.19W
Easingwold 36 54.07N 1.11W
Easky 40 54.18N 8.58W
East ≃ 102 45.20N 79.17W
East Allen ≃ 36 54.55N 2.19W
East Alligator ≃ 92 12.08S 132.42E
East-Angus 102 45.29N 71.40W
East Aurora 102 42.46N 78.36W
East Baines ≃ 92 15.38S 129.58E
East-Berlin →Berlin (Ost), D.D.R. 46 52.30N 13.25E
East Berlin, Pa., U.S. 102 39.56N 76.58W
Eastbourne, N.Z. 96 41.18S 174.54E
Eastbourne, Eng., U.K. 34 50.46N 0.17E
East Brady 102 40.59N 79.36W
East Caicos I 108 21.41N 71.30W
East Calder 38 55.54N 3.27W
East Canada Creek ≃ 102 43.00N 74.45W
East Cape › 96 37.41S 178.33E
East Caroline Basin ✦1 28 4.00N 146.45E
East China Sea ≂2 62 30.00N 126.00E
Eastchurch 34 51.25N 0.52E
East Cleddau ≃ 34 51.46N 4.52W
East Coast Bays 96 36.45S 174.46E
East Dean 34 50.45N 0.12E
East Dereham 34 52.41N 0.56E
East Ely 104 39.15N 114.53W
Easter Island →Pascua, Isla de I 24 27.07S 109.22W
Eastern Ghāts ⋀ 74 14.00N 78.50E
Eastern Highlands □5 92 6.30S 145.15E
Eastern Isles II 34a 49.57N 6.15W
Eastern Sayans →Vostočnyj Sajan ⋀ 58 53.00N 97.00E
East Falkland I 112 51.55S 59.00W
Eastfield 36 54.14N 0.24W
East Frisian Islands →Ostfriesische Inseln II 46 53.44N 7.25E
East Germany →German Democratic Republic □1 30 52.00N 12.30E
East Glacier Park 100 48.26N 113.13W
East Grand Rapids 102 42.56N 85.36W
East Greenwich 102 41.39N 71.27W
East Grinstead 34 51.08N 0.01W
Easthampton 102 42.16N 72.40W
East Harling 34 52.26N 0.55E
East Hoathly 34 50.55N 0.10E
East Horsley 34 51.15N 0.26W
East Ilsley 34 51.32N 1.17W
East Jordan 102 45.09N 85.07W
East Kilbride 38 55.46N 4.10W
Eastlake 102 41.39N 81.27W
East Lansing 102 42.44N 84.29W
East Leake 34 52.49N 1.10W
Eastleigh 34 50.58N 1.22W
East Linton 38 55.59N 2.39W
East Liverpool 102 40.37N 80.34W
East Loch Roag C 38 58.14N 6.48W
East Loch Tarbert C 38 57.52N 6.45W
East London (Oos-Londen) 86 33.00S 27.55E
East Looe 34 50.22N 4.27W
East Lynn Lake ⊜1 102 38.05N 82.20W
Eastmain 98 52.15N 78.30W
Eastmain ≃ 98 52.15N 78.35W
East Mariana Basin ✦1 28 12.00N 153.00E
East Markham 36 53.15N 0.54W
East Millinocket 102 45.37N 68.34W
East Novaya Zemlya Trough ✦1 20 73.30N 61.00E
Easton, Eng., U.K. 34 50.32N 2.26W
Easton, Md., U.S. 102 38.46N 76.04W
Easton, Pa., U.S. 102 40.41N 75.13W
East Palestine 102 40.50N 80.32W
East Peckham 34 51.15N 0.23E
Eastport 102 44.54N 66.59W
East Porterville 104 36.04N 118.56W
East Retford 36 53.19N 0.56W
Eastry 34 51.15N 1.18E
East Saint Louis 100 38.38N 90.09W
East Siberian Sea →Vostočno-Sibirskoje more ≂2 58 74.00N 166.00E
East Sister Island I 94 39.39S 148.00E
East Stour ≃ 34 51.08N 0.53E
East Stroudsburg 102 40.59N 75.10W
East Tawas 102 44.16N 83.29W
East Walker ≃ 104 38.53N 119.10W
East Wemyss 38 56.09N 3.04W
East Wittering 34 50.41N 0.53W
Eastwood 36 53.01N 1.18W
Eaton 102 39.44N 84.38W
Eaton Rapids 102 42.30N 84.39W
Eaton Socon 34 52.13N 0.18W
Eau ≃ 36 53.31N 0.44W
Eau Claire 100 44.48N 91.29W
Eau Claire, Lac à l' ⊜ 98 56.10N 74.25W
Eauripik I1 68 6.42N 143.03E
Eauripik Rise ✦3 28 3.00N 142.00E
Eauze 48 43.52N 0.06E
Ebbw ≃ 34 51.33N 2.59W
Ebbw Vale 34 51.47N 3.12W
Ebeltoft 44 56.12N 10.41E
Ebensburg 102 40.29N 78.43W
Ebensee 46 47.48N 13.46E
Eberbach 46 49.28N 8.59E
Ebermannstadt 46 49.43N 11.13E
Ebern 46 50.05N 10.47E
Eberndorf 46 46.35N 14.38E
Ebersbach 46 51.00N 14.35E
Ebersberg 46 48.05N 11.58E
Eberstein 46 46.48N 14.34E
Eberswalde 46 52.50N 13.49E
Ebetsu 64a 43.07N 141.34E
Ebingen 46 48.13N 9.01E
Ebino 64 32.03N 130.50E
Ebinur Hu ⊜ 62 44.55N 82.55E
Ebola ≃ 82 3.20N 20.57E
Eboli 52 40.37N 15.04E
Ebolowa 80 2.54N 11.09E
Ebon I1 28 4.35N 168.44E
Ebro ≃ 50 40.43N 0.54E
Ebro, Delta del ≚2 50 40.43N 0.54E
Ebro, Embalse del ⊜1 50 43.00N 3.58W
Ecclefechan 36 55.03N 3.17W
Eccles 36 53.29N 2.21W
Eccleshall 34 52.52N 2.15W
Eccleston 36 53.38N 2.43W
Echaporã 114 22.26S 50.12W
Ech Cheliff 80 36.10N 1.20E
Echeng 66 30.24N 114.51E
Echigo-sammyaku ⋀ 64 37.50N 139.50E
Echt, Ned. 46 51.06N 5.52E
Echt, Scot., U.K. 38 57.08N 2.26W
Echuca 94 36.08S 144.46E
Écija 50 37.32N 5.05W
Eck, Loch ⊜ 38 56.05N 5.00W
Eckernförde 46 54.28N 9.50E
Eckerö I 44 60.14N 19.35E
Eckington 36 53.19N 1.21W
Eclipse Sound ʮ 98 72.38N 79.00W
Ečmiadzin 56 40.10N 44.18E
Écommoy 48 47.50N 0.16E
Écouen 48 49.01N 2.23E
Écrins, Barre des ∧ 48 44.55N 6.22E
Ecuador □1 110 2.00S 79.00W
Écueillé 48 47.05N 1.21E
Ed 44 58.55N 11.55E
Edah 90 28.17S 117.10E
Edam 46 52.31N 5.03E
Eday I 38 59.11N 2.47W
Edderton 38 57.50N 4.10W
Eddleston 38 55.43N 3.13W
Eddrachillis Bay C 38 58.18N 5.15W
Eddystone Point › 94 41.00S 148.21E
Eddystone Rocks II1 34 50.12N 4.15W
Ede, Ned. 46 52.03N 5.40E
Ede, Nig. 80 7.44N 4.27E
Edéa 80 3.48N 10.08E
Edehon Lake ⊜ 98 60.25N 97.15W
Edelény 46 48.18N 20.44E
Eden, Austl. 94 37.04S 149.54E
Eden, N. Ire., U.K. 40 54.44N 5.47W
Eden ≃, Eng., U.K. 34 51.10N 0.11E
Eden ≃, Eng., U.K. 36 54.57N 3.01W
Eden ≃, Scot., U.K. 38 56.22N 2.50W
Eden ≃, Wales, U.K. 34 52.48N 3.53W
Edenbridge 34 51.12N 0.04E
Edenburg 86 29.45S 25.56E
Edendale, N.Z. 96 46.19S 168.47E
Edendale, S. Afr. 86 29.39S 30.18E
Edenderry 40 53.20N 7.03W
Edenside ∨ 36 54.40N 2.35W
Edenville 86 27.37S 27.34E
Edeowie 94 31.27S 138.27E
Eder ≃ 46 51.13N 9.27E
Ederny 40 54.32N 7.39W
Edessa →Édhessa 54 40.48N 22.03E
Edfu →Idfū 82 24.58N 32.52E
Edgar Ranges ⋀ 90 18.43S 123.25E
Edgartown 102 41.23N 70.30W
Edgecumbe 96 37.59S 176.50E
Edge Hill ∧2 34 52.08N 1.27W
Edgemont 100 43.18N 103.49W
Edgeøya I 20 77.45N 22.30E
Edgeroi 94 30.07S 149.48E
Edgerton 102 41.26N 84.44W
Edgewood 102 39.25N 76.17W
Édhessa 54 40.48N 22.03E
Edievale 96 45.48S 169.22E
Edinboro 102 41.52N 80.07W
Edinburg, Tx., U.S. 100 26.18N 98.09W
Edinburg, Va., U.S. 102 38.49N 78.33W
Edinburgh 38 55.57N 3.13W
Edirne 30 41.40N 26.34E
Edith River 92 14.11S 132.02E
Edith Weston 34 52.37N 0.37W
Edjeleh 80 27.38N 9.50E
Edjudina 90 29.48S 122.23E
Edmondbyers 36 54.51N 1.58W
Edmonton, Austl. 92 17.01S 145.45E
Edmonton, Ab., Can. 98 53.33N 113.28W
Edmore 102 43.24N 85.02W
Edmund 90 23.46S 116.02E
Edmundston 98 47.22N 68.20W
Edolo 52 46.11N 10.20E
Edremit 54 39.35N 27.01E
Edsbro 44 59.54N 18.29E
Edsbruk 44 58.02N 16.28E
Edsbyn 44 61.23N 15.49E
Edson 98 53.35N 116.26W
Edson Butte ∧ 104 42.52N 124.20W
Eduardo Castex 114 35.54S 64.18W
Edward ≃ 94 35.33S 144.58E
Edward, Lake ⊜ 84 0.25S 29.30E
Edward, Mount ∧ 90 23.22S 131.55E
Edwards 102 44.19N 75.15W
Edwards Creek 94 28.21S 135.51E
Edwards Plateau ⋀1 100 31.20N 101.00W
Edwinstowe 36 53.12N 1.04W
Edzell 38 56.48N 2.39W
Eeklo 46 51.11N 3.34E
Eel ≃ 104 40.40N 124.20W
Efate I 28 17.40S 168.25E
Eferding 46 48.18N 14.02E
Eforie Nord 54 44.06N 28.38E
Eforie Sud 54 44.03N 28.38E
Ega ≃ 50 42.19N 1.55W
Egadi, Isole II 52 37.58N 12.16E
Egaña 114 36.59S 59.06W
Egan Range ⋀ 104 39.10N 114.55W
Eganville 102 45.32N 77.06W
Egedesminde 98 68.42N 52.45W
Eger 46 47.54N 20.23E
Egersund 44 58.27N 6.00E
Eggenburg 46 48.39N 15.50E
Eggenfelden 46 48.25N 12.46E
Egg Harbor City 102 39.31N 74.38W
Egg Lagoon 94 39.39S 143.58E
Egham 34 51.26N 0.34W
Egijn ≃ 62 49.24N 103.36E
Egilsay I 38 59.09N 2.56W
Egilsstaðir 42a 65.16N 14.18W
Égletons 48 45.24N 2.03E
Eglinton 40 55.02N 7.11W
Egloskerry 34 50.39N 4.27W
Egmont, Cape › 96 39.17S 173.45E
Egmont, Mount ∧ 96 39.18S 174.04E
Egmont National Park ♦ 96 39.15S 174.05E
Egremont 36 54.29N 3.33W
Eğridir Gölü ⊜ 30 38.02N 30.53E
Egton 36 54.26N 0.45W
Egtved 44 55.37N 9.18E
Egvekinot 58 66.19N 179.10W
Egypt (Mişr) □1 82 27.00N 30.00E
Ehen ≃ 36 54.25N 3.30W
Ehime □5 64 33.40N 132.50E
Ehingen 46 48.17N 9.43E
Ehrenberg 104 33.36N 114.31W
Ehrenberg Range ⋀ 90 23.18S 130.20E
Ei 64 31.12N 130.30E
Eibar 50 43.11N 2.28W
Eibiswald 46 46.41N 15.15E
Eichstätt 46 48.54N 11.12E
Eide 44 62.55N 7.26E
Eidfjord 44 60.28N 7.05E
Eidsvåg, Nor. 44 60.27N 5.21E
Eidsvåg, Nor. 44 62.47N 8.03E
Eidsvold 94 25.22S 151.07E
Eidsvoll 44 60.19N 11.14E
Eifel ⋀ 46 50.15N 6.45E
Eigg I 38 56.54N 6.10W
Eigg, Sound of ʮ 38 56.51N 6.13W
Eigre, Carn ∧ 38 57.17N 5.07W
Eighty Mile Beach ⊥2 90 19.45S 121.00E
Eikeren ⊜ 44 59.38N 9.58E
Eikesdalsvatnet ⊜ 44 62.34N 8.11E
Eildon 94 37.14S 145.56E
Eildon, Lake ⊜1 94 37.11S 145.55E
Eilenburg 46 51.27N 12.37E
Eil Malk I 68 7.09N 134.22E
Eina 44 60.38N 10.36E
Einasleigh 94 18.31S 144.05E
Einasleigh ≃ 94 17.30S 142.17E
Einbeck 46 51.49N 9.52E
Eindhoven 46 51.26N 5.28E
Einsiedeln 48 47.08N 8.45E
Eire →Ireland □1 30 53.00N 8.00W
Eirunepé 110 6.40S 69.52W
Eisenach 46 50.59N 10.19E
Eisenberg 46 50.58N 11.53E
Eisenerz 46 47.33N 14.53E
Eisenerzer Alpen ⋀ 46 47.28N 14.45E
Eisenhüttenstadt 46 52.10N 14.39E
Eisenkappel 46 46.29N 14.35E
Eisenstadt 46 47.51N 16.32E
Eisfeld 46 50.26N 10.54E
Eishken 38 58.01N 6.32W
Eishort, Loch C 38 57.10N 5.59W
Eišiškes 60 54.10N 25.00E
Eisleben 46 51.31N 11.32E
Eislingen 46 48.42N 9.42E
Eithon ≃ 34 52.12N 3.27W
Eitorf 46 50.46N 7.26E
Ejby 44 55.26N 9.57E
Ejea de los Caballeros 50 42.08N 1.08W
Ejin Qi 62 41.50N 100.50E
Ekenäs (Taamisaari) 44 59.58N 23.26E
Ekenässjön 44 57.30N 15.00E
Ekeren 46 51.17N 4.25E
Eketahuna 96 40.39S 175.42E
Ekhínos 54 41.17N 24.59E
Ekiatapskij chrebet ⋀ 58 68.30N 179.00E
Ekibastuz 56 51.42N 75.22E
Ekimčan 58 53.04N 132.58E
Ekonda 58 65.47N 105.17E
Eksjö 44 57.40N 14.57E
Ekwan ≃ 98 53.14N 82.13W
El Aaiún 80 27.09N 13.12W
El Aguilar 114 23.12S 65.42W
Elaía 54 39.35N 20.20E
El Álamo 104 31.34N 116.02W
Elan ≃ 54 46.07N 28.04E
Elands ≃ 86 25.10S 29.10E
Elandsvlei 86 32.19S 19.33E
El Arahal 50 37.16N 5.33W
Elassón 54 39.54N 22.11E
Elat 78 29.33N 34.57E
Elat, Gulf of →Aqaba, Gulf of C 78 29.00N 34.40E
Elâzığ 78 38.41N 39.14E
Elba, Isola d' I 52 42.46N 10.17E
El Banco 110 9.00N 73.58W
El Barco de Avila 50 40.21N 5.31W
El Barco de Valdeorras 50 42.25N 6.59W
Elbasan 54 41.06N 20.05E
El Baúl 108 8.57N 68.17W
Elbe (Labe) ≃ 46 53.50N 9.00E
Elbe-Havel-Kanal ≍ 46 52.24N 12.23E
Elbert, Mount ∧ 100 39.07N 106.27W
Elbeuf 48 49.17N 1.00E
Elbing →Elbląg 46 54.10N 19.25E
Elbląg (Elbing) 46 54.10N 19.25E
El Bluff 108 11.59N 83.40W
El Bonillo 50 38.57N 2.32W
El Boulaïda 80 36.28N 2.50E
Elbow Cay I 108 23.57N 80.29W
El'brus, gora ∧ 56 43.21N 42.26E
Elbrus, Mount →El'brus, gora ∧ 56 43.21N 42.26E
El Burgo de Osma 50 41.35N 3.04W
Elburz Mountains →Alborz, Reshteh-ye Kūhhā-ye ⋀ 78 36.00N 53.00E
El Caburé 114 26.01S 62.22W
El Cajon 104 32.47N 116.57W
El Calverio 108 8.59N 67.00W
El Capitan ∧ 100 46.01N 114.23W
El Carmen 114 24.23S 65.16W
El Carmen de Bolívar 110 9.43N 75.08W
El Carril 114 25.05S 65.28W
El Castillo 108 11.01N 84.24W
El Cenajo, Embalse de ⊜1 50 38.25N 2.00W
El Centinela 104 32.38N 115.40W
El Centro 104 32.47N 115.33W
Elche 50 38.15N 0.42W
Elche de la Sierra 50 38.27N 2.03W
Elcho Island I 92 11.55S 135.45E
El Cholar 114 37.25S 70.39W
El Chorrillo 114 33.18S 66.16W
El Ciprés 104 31.50N 116.38W
El Colorado 114 26.18S 59.22W
El Cóndor, Cerro ∧ 114 26.38S 68.22W
El Corpus 108 13.16N 87.03W
Elda 50 38.29N 0.47W
El Descanso 104 32.12N 116.55W
El'dikan 58 60.48N 135.11E
El Djazaïr (Algiers) 80 36.47N 3.03E
Eldorado, Arg. 114 26.24S 54.38W
Eldorado, Bra. 114 24.32S 48.06W
El Dorado, Ar., U.S. 100 33.12N 92.39W
El Dorado, Ks., U.S. 100 37.49N 96.51W
Eldoret 84 0.31N 35.17E
Eldred 102 41.57N 78.23W
Eleanor 102 38.32N 81.55W
Elefantes, Rio dos (Olifants) ≃ 86 24.10S 32.40E
Elektrostal' 60 55.47N 38.28E
Elena 54 42.56N 25.53E
El Encanto 110 1.37S 73.14W
Elephant Butte Reservoir ⊜1 100 33.19N 107.10W
Elephant Mountain ∧ 102 44.46N 70.46W
El Eulma 50 36.08N 5.40E
Eleuthera I 108 25.10N 76.14W
Eleuthera Point › 108 24.40N 76.11W
Elevsís 54 38.02N 23.32E
Elevtheroúpolis 54 40.55N 24.16E
El Ferrol del Caudillo 50 43.29N 8.14W
El Galpón 114 25.23S 64.38W
Elgin, Scot., U.K. 38 57.39N 3.20W
Elgin, Il., U.S. 100 42.02N 88.16W
Elgol 38 57.09N 6.06W
El Golfo de Santa Clara 104 31.42N 114.30W
Elgon, Mount ∧ 84 1.08N 34.33E
El Grove 50 42.30N 8.52W
El Guamo 108 10.02N 74.59W
El Guapo 108 10.09N 65.58W
Elham 34 51.10N 1.07E
El Hank ⊥4 80 24.30N 7.00W
Elhovo 54 42.10N 26.34E
El Huecú 114 37.37S 70.36W
Elías Piña 108 18.53N 71.42W
Elila ≃ 84 2.45S 25.53E
Elim 86 34.35S 19.45E
Elin Pelin 54 42.40N 23.36E
Eliot 102 43.09N 70.48W
Élisabethville →Lubumbashi 84 11.40S 27.28E
Elista 56 46.16N 44.14E
Elizabeth, Austl. 94 34.43S 138.40E
Elizabeth, N.J., U.S. 102 40.39N 74.12W
Elizabeth, W.V., U.S. 102 39.03N 81.23W
Elizabeth City 100 36.18N 76.13W
Elizabeth Reef I1 88 29.56S 159.04E
Elizabethtown, N.Y., U.S. 102 44.12N 73.35W
Elizabethtown, Pa., U.S. 102 40.09N 76.36W
El-Jadida 80 33.16N 8.30W
Ełk 46 53.50N 22.22E
Ełk ≃, Pol. 46 53.31N 22.47E
Elk ≃, W.V., U.S. 102 38.21N 81.38W
Elk Creek 104 39.36N 122.32W
Elkedra ≃ 90 21.08S 136.22E
Elk Grove 104 38.24N 121.22W
Elkhart 100 41.40N 85.58W
Elkins 102 38.55N 79.50W
Elkland 102 41.59N 77.18W
Elko 104 40.49N 115.45W
Elk Rapids 102 44.53N 85.24W
Elkton, Md., U.S. 102 39.36N 75.50W
Elkton, Mi., U.S. 102 43.49N 83.10W
Elkton, Va., U.S. 102 38.24N 78.37W
Ell, Lake ⊜ 90 29.13S 127.46E
Elland 36 53.41N 1.50W
Ellavalla 90 25.05S 114.22E
Ellef Ringnes Island I 22 78.30N 104.00W
Elleker 90 35.00S 117.43E
Ellen ≃ 36 54.43N 3.30W
Ellendale, Austl. 90 17.56S 124.48E
Ellendale, N.D., U.S. 100 46.00N 98.31W
Ellensburg 100 46.59N 120.32W
Ellenville 102 41.43N 74.23W
Ellesmere 34 52.54N 2.54W
Ellesmere, Lake C 96 43.48S 172.25E
Ellesmere Island I 22 81.00N 80.00W
Ellesmere Port 36 53.17N 2.54W
Ellice ≃ 98 68.02N 103.26W
Ellice Islands →Tuvalu □1 28 8.00S 178.00E
Ellicott City 102 39.16N 76.47W
Ellicottville 102 42.16N 78.40W
Ellington 36 55.13N 1.34W
Elliot 86 31.18S 27.50E
Elliot, Mount ∧ 94 19.29S 146.58E
Elliotdale 86 31.55S 28.38E
Elliot Lake 98 46.23N 82.39W
Elliott 92 17.33S 133.32E
Elliott, Mount ∧ 90 20.29S 126.37E
Ellisras 86 23.40S 27.46E
Elliston 90 33.39S 134.55E
Ellon 38 57.22N 2.05W
Ellore →Elūru 74 16.42N 81.06E
Ellsworth, Me., U.S. 102 44.32N 68.25W
Ellsworth, Mi., U.S. 102 45.09N 85.14W
Ellwangen 46 48.57N 10.07E
Ellwood City 102 40.51N 80.17W
Elm, Schw. 48 46.55N 9.11E
Elm, Eng., U.K. 34 52.38N 0.10E
El Maneadero 104 31.45N 116.35W
El Menia 80 30.30N 2.50E
Elmer 102 39.35N 75.10W
El Milagro 114 31.01S 65.59W
Elmira, On., Can. 102 43.36N 80.33W
Elmira, N.Y., U.S. 102 42.05N 76.48W
El Mirage Lake ⊜ 104 34.38N 117.35W
Elmira Heights 102 42.07N 76.49W
El Molinillo 50 39.28N 4.13W
El Monte 114 33.41S 71.01W
Elmore, Austl. 94 36.30S 144.37E
Elmore, Oh., U.S. 102 41.28N 83.17W
El Mreyyé ✦1 80 19.30N 7.00W
Elmshorn 46 53.45N 9.39E
Elmsta 44 59.58N 18.48E
Elmswell 34 52.15N 0.53E
Elmvale 102 44.35N 79.52W
El Naranjo 114 25.44S 64.59W
Elne 48 42.36N 2.58E
El Nevado, Cerro ∧, Arg. 114 35.35S 68.30W
El Nevado, Cerro ∧, Col. 110 3.59N 74.04W
El-Obeid →Al-Ubayyiḍ 82 13.11N 30.13E
Elora 102 43.41N 80.26W
Elortondo 114 33.42S 61.37W
El Palmar 114 21.54S 63.39W
El Palqui 114 30.45S 70.59W
El Pao 108 9.38N 68.08W
El Paradero 108 10.38N 69.32W
El Paso 100 31.45N 106.29W
El Paso Peaks ⋀ 104 35.28N 117.43W
Elphin 40 53.51N 8.12W
El Pilar 108 10.32N 63.09W
El Piñón 108 10.24N 74.50W
El Pintado 114 24.38S 61.27W
El Piquete 114 24.13S 64.39W
El Portal 104 37.40N 119.46W
El Porvenir 104 32.05N 116.38W
El Puente del Arzobispo 50 39.48N 5.10W
El Puerto de Santa María 50 36.36N 6.13W
El Puesto 114 27.57S 67.38W
El Quebrachal 114 25.17S 64.04W
Elqui ≃ 114 29.54S 71.17W
El Rastro 108 9.03N 67.27W
El Reno 100 35.31N 97.57W
El Rio 104 34.13N 119.10W
Elsa 98 63.55N 135.28W
El Salado 114 26.25S 70.19W
El Salto 106 23.47N 105.22W
El Salvador □1 106 13.50N 88.55W
El Sauce 108 12.53N 86.32W
El Sauzal 104 31.54N 116.41W
Elsenham 34 51.55N 0.14E
Elsie 102 43.05N 84.23W
Elsinore →Helsingør 44 56.02N 12.37E
Elsinore, Lake ⊜1 104 33.39N 117.21W
Elsmere 102 39.44N 75.35W
El Socorro 108 8.59N 65.44W
El Sombrero 108 9.23N 67.03W
Elspe 46 51.09N 8.04E
Elstead 34 51.11N 0.43W
Elsterwerda 46 51.28N 13.31E
Elstree 34 51.39N 0.16W
El Tala 114 26.07S 65.17W
Eltham 96 39.26S 174.18E
El Tigre 110 8.55N 64.15W
Eltmann 46 49.58N 10.40E
El Tocuyo 108 9.47N 69.48W
El Tofo 114 29.27S 71.15W
El Tranco, Embalse de ⊜1 50 38.10N 2.45W
El Tránsito 114 28.52S 70.17W
El Trébol 114 32.12S 61.42W
El Triunfo 108 15.46N 87.26W
El Tunal 114 24.48S 65.45W
El Turbio 112 51.41S 72.05W
Elūru 74 16.42N 81.06E
Elva 60 58.13N 26.25E
Elvas 50 38.53N 7.10W
Elven 48 47.44N 2.35W
Elverum 44 60.53N 11.34E
El Viejo 108 12.40N 87.10W
Elvira 114 35.14S 59.29W
El Volcán, Arg. 114 33.15S 66.12W
El Volcán, Chile 114 33.49S 70.11W
El Wad 80 33.20N 6.58E
Elwy ≃ 36 53.16N 3.26W
Ely, Eng., U.K. 34 52.24N 0.16E
Ely, Nv., U.S. 104 39.14N 114.53W
Ely, Isle of ✦1 34 52.24N 0.10E
Elyria 102 41.22N 82.06W
Emāmshahr (Shāhrūd) 78 36.25N 55.01E
Emån ≃ 44 57.08N 16.30E
Emba 56 48.50N 58.08E
Emba ≃ 56 46.38N 53.14E
Embarcación 114 23.13S 64.06W
Embetsu 64a 44.44N 141.47E
Embid 50 40.58N 1.43W
Embira ≃ 110 7.19S 70.15W
Embleton 36 55.30N 1.37W
Embo 38 57.54N 3.59W
Embrun, On., Can. 102 45.16N 75.17W
Embrun, Fr. 48 44.34N 6.30E
Embsay 36 53.58N 1.59W
Emden 46 53.22N 7.12E
Emerald 94 23.32S 148.10E
Emilia-Romagna □4 52 44.35N 11.00E
Emine, nos › 54 42.42N 27.51E
Emita 94 40.00S 147.54E
Emlembe ∧ 86 25.57S 31.11E
Emlenton 102 41.11N 79.43W
Emmaboda 44 56.38N 15.32E
Emmaus 102 40.32N 75.29W
Emmaville 94 29.26S 151.36E
Emmen 46 52.47N 6.54E
Emmendingen 46 48.07N 7.50E
Emmerich 46 51.50N 6.15E
Emmet 94 24.40S 144.28E
Emmitsburg 102 39.42N 77.20W
Emneth 34 52.38N 0.11E
Emőd 46 47.56N 20.49E
Empalme 106 27.58N 110.51W
Empangeni 86 28.50S 31.48E
Empedrado, Arg. 114 27.57S 58.48W
Empedrado, Chile 114 35.36S 72.17W
Empire 104 40.34N 119.20W
Empoli 52 43.43N 10.57E
Emporia 100 38.24N 96.10W
Emporium 102 41.30N 78.14W
Emsdetten 46 52.10N 7.31E
Emsworth 34 50.51N 0.56W
Emukae 64 33.18N 129.38E
Emu Park 94 23.15S 150.50E
Emyvale 40 54.20N 6.59W
En (Inn) ≃ 48 48.35N 13.28E
Enånger 44 61.32N 17.00E
Enard Bay C 38 58.05N 5.20W
Enborne ≃ 34 51.24N 1.06W
Encantado 114 29.15S 51.53W
Encarnación 114 27.20S 55.54W
Encinitas 104 33.02N 117.17W
Encontrados 110 9.03N 72.14W
Encounter Bay C 94 35.35S 138.44E
Encruzilhada do Sul 114 30.32S 52.31W
Encs 46 48.20N 21.08E
Ende 72 8.50S 121.39E
Endeavour Strait ʮ 92 10.50S 142.15E
Enderbury I1 28 3.08S 171.05W
Enderby 34 52.36N 1.12W
Enderby Land ✦1 18 67.30S 53.00E
Endicott 102 42.05N 76.02W
Ene ≃ 110 11.09S 74.19W
Eneabba 90 29.50S 115.20E
Enewetak I1 28 11.30N 162.15E
Enfield, N.Z. 96 45.03S 170.52E
Enfield, N.H., U.S. 102 43.38N 72.08W
Enfield ✦8 34 51.40N 0.05W
Engaño, Cabo › 108 18.37N 68.20W
Engaru 64a 44.03N 143.31E
Engcobo 86 31.37S 28.00E
Engel's 56 51.30N 46.07E
Enggano, Pulau I 72 5.24S 102.16E
Engjan 44 63.09N 8.32E
England □8 32 52.30N 1.30W
Englefield, Cape › 98 69.51N 85.39W
Englehart 98 47.49N 79.52W
English ≃ 98 50.12N 95.00W
English Bāzār 76 25.00N 88.09E
English Channel (La Manche) ʮ 32 50.20N 1.00W
English Coast ⊥2 24 73.45S 73.00W
Enguera 50 38.59N 0.41W
Enid 100 36.23N 97.52W
Eniwa 64a 42.45N 141.33E
Eniwetok →Enewetak I1 28 11.30N 162.15E
eNjesuthi ∧ 86 29.09S 29.23E
Enkhuizen 46 52.42N 5.17E
Enköping 44 59.38N 17.04E
Enmelen 58 65.01N 175.54W
Enna 52 37.34N 14.16E
Ennadai Lake ⊜ 98 60.53N 101.15W
Ennedi ⋀1 82 17.15N 22.00E
Ennell, Lough ⊜ 40 53.28N 7.24W
Ennerdale Water ⊜ 36 54.31N 3.23W
Enngonia 94 29.19S 145.51E
Ennis 40 52.50N 8.59W
Enniscorthy 40 52.30N 6.34W
Enniskillen 40 54.21N 7.38W
Ennistimon 40 52.57N 9.15W
Enns 46 48.13N 14.29E
Enns ≃ 46 48.14N 14.32E
Eno 44 62.48N 30.09E
Enon 102 39.53N 83.56W
Enontekiö 42 68.23N 23.38E
Enosburg Falls 102 44.54N 72.48W
Enrekang 72 3.34S 119.47E
Enrique Urien 114 27.34S 60.32W
Enriquillo 108 17.54N 71.14W
Enriquillo, Lago ⊜ 108 18.27N 71.39W
Ensay 94 37.23S 147.50E
Ensay I 38 57.46N 7.05W
Enschede 46 52.12N 6.53E
Ensenada, Arg. 114 34.51S 57.55W
Ensenada, Méx. 106 31.52N 116.37W
Enshi 62 30.17N 109.19E
Enshū-nada ≂2 64 34.27N 137.38E
Entebbe 84 0.04N 32.28E
Enterprise, Ca., U.S. 104 39.32N 121.22W
Enterprise, Ut,. U.S. 104 37.34N 113.43W
Entinas, Punta › 50 36.41N 2.46W
Entraygues 48 44.39N 2.34E
Entrepeñas, Embalse de ⊜1 50 40.34N 2.42W
Entre Ríos □4 114 32.00S 59.00W
Entroncamento 50 39.28N 8.28W
Enugu 80 6.27N 7.27E
Enurmino 58 66.57N 171.49W
Envalira, Port d')(50 42.35N 1.45E
Envermeu 48 49.54N 1.16E
Enys, Mount ∧ 96 43.14S 171.38E
Enza ≃ 52 44.54N 10.31E
Eo ≃ 50 43.28N 7.03W
Eolie, Isole II 52 38.30N 14.50E
Epanomí 54 40.26N 22.56E
Epecuén, Lago ⊜ 114 37.10S 62.54W
Épernay 48 49.03N 3.57E
Ephraim 100 39.21N 111.35W
Ephrata 102 40.10N 76.10W
Epi I 28 16.43S 168.15E
Épila 50 41.36N 1.17W
Épinal 48 48.11N 6.27E
Epokiro 86 21.41S 19.08E
Eport, Loch C 38 57.33N 7.11W
Epping, Eng., U.K. 34 51.43N 0.07E
Epping, N.H., U.S. 102 43.02N 71.04W
Epping Forest ✦3 34 51.40N 0.03E
Epsom 34 51.20N 0.16W
Epte ≃ 48 49.04N 1.37E
Epukiro ≃ 86 20.45S 21.05E
Epworth 36 53.32N 0.49W
Equatorial Guinea □1 80 2.00N 9.00E
Eraclea 52 45.35N 12.40E
Eradu 90 28.41S 115.02E
Erba 52 45.48N 9.15E
Erbach 46 49.40N 8.59E
Erciyeş Dağı ∧ 78 38.32N 35.28E
Érd 46 47.23N 18.56E
Erdek 54 40.24N 27.48E
Erdene 62 44.15N 111.14E
Erdevik 54 45.07N 19.25E
Erding 46 48.18N 11.54E
Erechim 114 27.38S 52.17W
Ereğli 78 37.31N 34.04E
Erei, Monti ⋀ 52 37.27N 14.19E
Erenhot 62 43.46N 112.05E
Eresma ≃ 50 41.26N 4.45W
Eressós 54 39.18N 25.51E
Erétria 54 38.24N 23.48E
Erfoud 80 31.28N 4.10W
Erft ≃ 46 51.11N 6.44E
Erfurt 46 50.58N 11.01E
Erfurt □5 46 51.10N 10.45E
Erges (Erjas) ≃ 50 39.40N 7.01W
Ergun (Argun') ≃ 58 53.20N 121.28E

Symbols in the Index entries are identified on page 122.

Name	Page	Lat.°'	Long.°'

Name	Page	Lat.	Long.

Flinders Island I 94 40.00 S 148.00 E
Flinders Range ⋏ 88 31.25 S 138.45 E
Flinders Reefs ÷ 2 94 17.37 S 148.31 E
Flin Flon 98 54.46 N 101.53 W
Flint, Wales, U.K. 36 53.15 N 3.07 W
Flint, Mi., U.S. 102 43.00 N 83.41 W
Flint I 28 11.26 S 151.48 W
Flint ≃, Ga., U.S. 100 30.52 N 84.38 W
Flint ≃, Mi., U.S. 102 43.21 N 84.03 W
Flint Lake ⊜ 98 69.10 N 74.20 W
Flinton 94 27.54 S 149.34 E
Flisa 44 60.34 N 12.06 E
Flitwick 34 52.00 N 0.29 W
Flize 48 49.42 N 4.46 E
Floby 44 58.08 N 13.20 E
Floda 44 57.48 N 12.22 E
Flodden 38 55.38 N 2.10 W
Florac 48 44.19 N 3.36 E
Florence
→Firenze, It. 52 43.46 N 11.15 E
Florence, Al., U.S. 100 34.47 N 87.40 W
Florence, S.C., U.S. 100 34.11 N 79.45 W
Florencia 110 1.36 N 75.36 W
Florencio Sánchez 114 33.53 S 57.24 W
Florenville 46 49.42 N 5.18 E
Flores 110 7.51 S 37.59 W
Flores I, Indon. 72 8.30 S 121.00 E
Flores I, Port. 20 39.26 N 31.13 W
Flores, Laut (Flores Sea) ≃ 2 72 8.00 S 120.00 E
Flores da Cunha 114 29.02 S 51.11 W
Floriano 110 6.47 S 43.01 W
Florianópolis 114 27.35 S 48.34 W
Florida, Cuba 108 21.32 N 78.14 W
Florida, Ur. 114 34.06 S 56.13 W
Florida ◻ 3 108 28.00 N 82.00 W
Florida, Straits of ℧ 108 25.00 N 79.45 W
Florida Bay C 108 25.00 N 80.45 W
Florida Keys II 100 24.45 N 81.00 W
Floridia 52 37.05 N 15.09 E
Flórina 54 40.47 N 21.24 E
Florø 44 61.36 N 5.00 E
Florvåg 44 60.25 N 5.14 E
Flotta I 38 58.50 N 3.07 W
Flumen ≃ 50 41.43 N 0.09 W
Flumendosa ≃ 52 39.26 N 9.37 E
Fluminimaggiore 52 39.26 N 8.30 E
Flushing
→Vlissingen, Ned. 46 51.26 N 3.35 E
Flushing, Mi., U.S. 102 43.03 N 83.51 W
Fluvia ≃ 50 42.12 N 3.07 E
Fly ≃ 92 8.30 S 143.41 E
Flying Fish Cove 72 10.25 S 105.43 E
Foča 54 43.31 N 18.46 E
Fochabers 38 57.37 N 3.05 W
Fochville 86 26.30 S 27.30 E
Focșani 54 45.41 N 27.11 E
Foeni 54 45.30 N 20.53 E
Fogang (Shijiao) 66 23.52 N 113.32 E
Foggia 52 41.27 N 15.34 E
Fogo I 94 14.55 N 24.25 W
Fogo Island I 98 49.40 N 54.13 W
Fohnsdorf 46 47.13 N 14.41 E
Föhr I 46 54.43 N 8.30 E
Foia ⋏ 50 37.19 N 8.36 W
Foix 48 42.58 N 1.36 E
Foix ◻ 9 48 43.00 N 1.40 E
Fojnica 54 43.58 N 17.54 E
Fokino 60 53.27 N 34.24 E
Folarakardhuten ⋏ 44 60.37 N 7.45 E
Folda ≃ 2 44 67.36 N 14.50 E
Foley Island I 98 68.35 N 75.10 W
Folgefonni ☒ 44 60.00 N 6.20 E
Foligno 52 42.57 N 12.42 E
Folkestone 34 51.05 N 1.11 E
Folkingham 34 52.54 N 0.24 W
Follafoss 44 63.59 N 11.06 E
Folldal 44 62.08 N 10.03 E
Follebu 44 61.14 N 10.17 E
Föllinge 44 63.40 N 14.37 E
Follonica 52 42.55 N 10.45 E
Follonica, Golfo di C 52 42.54 N 10.43 E
Folsom 104 38.40 N 121.10 W
Folsom Lake ⊜1 104 38.43 N 121.08 W
Fomboni 87a 12.16 S 43.45 E
Fonda 102 42.57 N 74.22 W
Fond du Lac, Sk., Can. 98 59.19 N 107.10 W
Fond du Lac, Wi., U.S. 100 43.46 N 88.26 W
Fond du Lac ≃ 98 59.17 N 106.00 W
Fondi 52 41.21 N 13.25 E
Fonni 52 40.07 N 9.15 E
Fonsagrada 50 43.08 N 7.04 W
Fonseca 108 10.53 N 72.51 W
Fonseca, Golfo de C 106 13.10 N 87.40 W
Font ≃ 36 55.10 N 1.44 W
Fontainebleau 48 48.24 N 2.42 E
Fontana, Arg. 114 27.25 S 59.02 W
Fontana, Ca., U.S. 104 34.05 N 117.26 W
Fontas ≃ 98 58.20 N 121.50 W
Fonte Boa 110 2.32 S 66.01 W
Fontenay-le-Comte 48 46.28 N 0.48 W
Fontur ⊁ 42a 66.23 N 14.30 W
Fonyód 46 46.44 N 17.34 E
Foochow
→Fuzhou 66 26.06 N 119.17 E
Forbach, B.R.D. 46 48.41 N 8.21 E
Forbach, Fr. 46 49.11 N 6.54 E
Forbesganj 76 26.18 N 87.15 E
Forcalquier 48 43.58 N 5.47 E
Forchheim 46 49.43 N 11.04 E
Ford 38 56.10 N 5.26 W
Ford, Cape ⊁ 92 13.26 S 129.52 E
Ford City, Ca., U.S. 104 35.09 N 119.27 W
Ford City, Pa., U.S. 102 40.46 N 79.31 W
Ford Dry Lake ⊜ 104 33.38 N 115.00 W
Førde, Nor. 44 59.36 N 5.29 E
Førde, Nor. 44 61.27 N 5.52 E
Førdefjorden C 2 44 61.28 N 5.39 E
Forden 34 52.36 N 3.08 W
Fordingbridge 34 50.56 N 1.47 W
Fords Bridge 94 29.45 S 145.26 E
Forel, Mont ⋏ 96 67.00 N 37.00 W
Foreland Point ⊁ 34 51.16 N 3.47 W
Forest, On., Can. 102 43.06 N 82.00 W
Forest, Oh., U.S. 102 40.48 N 83.30 W
Forest City 102 41.39 N 75.28 W
Foresthill 104 39.01 N 120.49 W
Forestière Peninsula ⊁ 1 94 42.57 S 147.55 E
Forest Row 34 51.06 N 0.02 E
Forez, Monts du ⋏ 48 45.35 N 3.48 E
Forfar 38 56.38 N 2.54 W
Forli 52 44.13 N 12.03 E
Formby 36 53.34 N 3.05 W
Formby Point ⊁ 36 53.33 N 3.06 W
Formentera I 50 38.42 N 1.28 E
Formentor, Cabo de ⊁ 50 39.58 N 3.12 E
Formerie 48 49.39 N 1.44 E
Formia 52 41.15 N 13.37 E
Formiga 110 20.27 S 45.25 W
Formosa, Arg. 114 26.11 S 58.11 W
Formosa, Bra. 110 15.32 S 47.20 W
Formosa ◻ 4 114 25.00 S 60.00 W
Formosa, Serra ⋏ 1 110 12.00 S 55.00 W
Formosa Strait
→Taiwan Strait ℧ 66 24.00 N 119.00 E
Fornosovo 60 59.35 N 30.35 E
Fornovo di Taro 52 44.42 N 10.06 E
Forres, Arg. 114 27.53 S 63.58 W
Forres, Scot., U.K. 38 57.37 N 3.38 W

Forrest 90 30.51 S 128.06 E
Forrest ≃ 92 15.18 S 128.04 E
Forrest, Mount ⋏ 90 24.48 S 127.45 E
Forrest City 100 35.00 N 90.47 W
Forrest Lakes ⊜ 90 29.12 S 128.46 E
Forsayth 94 18.35 S 143.36 E
Forsbacka 44 60.37 N 16.53 E
Forsby 44 60.30 N 25.56 E
Forserum 44 57.42 N 14.28 E
Forshaga 44 59.32 N 13.28 E
Forssa 44 60.49 N 23.38 E
Forst 46 51.44 N 14.38 E
Forster 94 32.11 S 152.31 E
Forsyth Island I 94 16.50 S 139.06 E
Forsyth Range ⋏ 94 22.45 S 143.15 E
Fort Albany 98 52.15 N 81.37 W
Fort-Archambault
→Sarh 82 9.09 N 18.23 E
Fort Augustus 38 57.09 N 4.41 W
Fort Beaufort 86 32.46 S 26.40 E
Fort Bidwell 104 41.51 N 120.09 W
Fort Bragg 104 39.26 N 123.48 W
Fort Chipewyan 98 58.42 N 111.08 W
Fort Collins 100 40.35 N 105.05 W
Fort Constantine 94 20.28 S 140.37 E
Fort-Coulonge 102 45.51 N 76.44 W
Fort Covington 102 44.59 N 74.29 W
Fort Dodge 100 42.29 N 94.10 W
Forte dei Marmi 52 43.57 N 10.10 E
Fort Edward 102 43.16 N 73.35 W
Fort Erie 102 42.54 N 78.56 W
Fortescue ≃ 90 21.00 S 116.06 E
Fortevoit 38 56.20 N 3.32 W
Fortezza 52 46.47 N 11.37 E
Fort Fitzgerald 98 59.53 N 111.37 W
Fort Frances 98 48.36 N 93.24 W
Fort Franklin 98 65.11 N 123.46 W
Fort Gay 102 38.06 N 82.35 W
Fort Good Hope 98 66.15 N 128.38 W
Forth ≃ 38 55.47 N 3.41 W
Forth ≃ 38 56.03 N 3.44 W
Forth, Carse of ⩗ 38 56.08 N 4.05 W
Forth, Firth of C 38 56.10 N 2.45 W
Fortín Teniente Montaña 114 22.04 S 59.57 W
Fortín Uno 114 38.51 S 65.17 W
Fort Jones 104 41.36 N 122.50 W
Fort Klamath 104 42.42 N 121.59 W
Fort-Lamy
→N'Djamena 82 12.07 N 15.03 E
Fort Lauderdale 100 26.07 N 80.08 W
Fort Liard 98 60.15 N 123.28 W
Fort Loramie 102 40.21 N 84.22 W
Fort Macleod 98 49.43 N 113.25 W
Fort Madison 100 40.37 N 91.18 W
Fort McMurray 98 56.44 N 111.23 W
Fort McPherson 98 67.27 N 134.53 W
Fort Morgan 100 40.15 N 103.47 W
Fort Myers 100 26.38 N 81.52 W
Fort Nelson 98 58.49 N 122.43 W
Fort Nelson ≃ 98 59.30 N 124.00 W
Fort Norman 98 64.54 N 125.34 W
Fort Peck Lake ⊜1 100 47.45 N 106.50 W
Fort Pierce 100 27.26 N 80.19 W
Fort Plain 102 42.55 N 74.37 W
Fort Portal 84 0.40 N 30.17 E
Fort Providence 98 61.21 N 117.39 W
Fort Qu'Appelle 98 50.46 N 103.48 W
Fort Recovery 102 40.24 N 84.46 W
Fort Resolution 98 61.10 N 113.40 W
Fortrose, N.Z. 96 46.34 S 168.48 E
Fortrose, Scot., U.K. 38 57.34 N 4.09 W
Fort Saint James 98 54.26 N 124.15 W
Fort Saint John 98 56.15 N 120.51 W
Fort Sandeman 76 31.20 N 69.27 E
Fort Ševčenko 56 44.31 N 50.16 E
Fort Severn 98 56.00 N 87.38 W
Fort Simpson 98 61.52 N 121.23 W
Fort Smith, N.T., Can. 98 60.00 N 111.53 W
Fort Smith, Ar., U.S. 100 35.23 N 94.23 W
Fort Stockton 100 30.53 N 102.52 W
Fortuna, Arg. 114 35.07 S 65.23 W
Fortuna, Ca., U.S. 104 40.35 N 124.09 W
Fortune Bay C 98 47.25 N 55.25 W
Fortuneswell 34 50.34 N 2.27 W
Fort Vermilion 98 58.24 N 116.00 W
Fort Walton Beach 100 30.24 N 86.37 W
Fort Wayne 102 41.07 N 85.07 W
Fort William
→Thunder Bay, On., Can. 98 48.23 N 89.15 W
Fort William, Scot., U.K. 38 56.49 N 5.07 W
Fort Worth 100 32.43 N 97.19 W
Fort Yukon 98 66.34 N 145.17 W
Forty Foot Drain ⥿ 34 52.28 N 0.05 W
Foshan 66 23.03 N 113.09 E
Fosna ⊁1 44 64.00 N 10.30 E
Fosnavåg 44 62.21 N 5.39 E
Foss ≃ 36 53.57 N 1.06 W
Fossano 52 44.33 N 7.43 E
Fossil Downs 90 18.08 S 125.38 E
Fossil Lake ⊜ 104 43.18 N 120.15 W
Fossombrone 52 43.41 N 12.48 E
Foster 94 38.39 S 146.12 E
Foster ≃ 94 55.47 N 105.49 W
Fostoria 102 41.09 N 83.25 W
Fotan 66 22.24 N 117.53 E
Fotherhill 94 36.42 S 143.08 E
Fouesnant 48 47.54 N 4.01 W
Fougamou 84 1.13 S 10.36 E
Fougères 48 48.21 N 1.12 W
Foula I 38a 60.08 N 2.05 W
Foul Bay C 78 23.30 N 35.39 E
Foulness I 34 51.36 N 0.55 E
Foulness Point ⊁ 34 51.38 N 0.57 E
Foulsham 34 52.48 N 1.01 E
Foulwind, Cape ⊁ 96 41.45 S 171.28 E
Foumban 80 5.43 N 10.55 E
Fountain Peak ⋏ 104 34.57 N 115.32 W
Fouriesburg 86 28.38 S 28.14 E
Fourmies 48 50.00 N 4.03 E
Fournies ⊁ 80 11.30 N 12.30 W
Foveaux Strait ℧ 96 46.35 S 168.00 E
Foveran 38 57.18 N 2.02 W
Fowey 34 50.20 N 4.38 W
Fowler, Ca., U.S. 104 36.37 N 119.40 W
Fowler, Mi., U.S. 102 43.00 N 84.44 W
Fowler, Point ⊁ 90 32.02 S 132.29 E
Fowlers Bay 90 31.59 S 132.27 E
Fowlerville 102 42.39 N 84.04 W
Fowliang
→Jingdezhen 66 29.16 N 117.11 E
Foxe Basin C 98 68.25 N 77.00 W
Foxe Channel ℧ 98 64.30 N 80.00 W
Foxen ⊜ 44 59.23 N 11.52 E
Fox Glacier 96 43.28 S 170.00 E
Foxhole 34 53.58 N 9.08 W
Foxholes 36 54.10 N 0.29 W
Foxton 96 40.28 S 175.18 E
Foxton Beach 96 40.28 S 175.13 E
Foyers 38 57.14 N 4.29 W
Foyle ≃ 40 54.59 N 7.18 W
Foyle, Lough C 40 55.06 N 7.08 W
Foyle, Lough C 40 55.06 N 7.08 W
Foynes 40 52.37 N 9.06 W
Fóz do Cunene 86 17.16 S 11.50 E
Foz do Iguaçu 114 25.33 S 54.35 W

Foz Giraldo 50 40.00 N 7.43 W
Fraga, Arg. 114 33.30 S 65.48 W
Fraga, Esp. 50 41.31 N 0.21 E
Fraile Muerto 114 32.31 S 54.32 W
Framingham 102 42.16 N 71.25 W
Framlingham 34 52.13 N 1.21 E
Frampol 46 50.41 N 22.40 E
Frampton Cotterell 34 51.32 N 2.29 W
Frampton on Severn 34 51.46 N 2.22 W
Franca 110 20.32 S 47.24 W
Francavilla al Mare 52 42.25 N 14.17 E
Francavilla Fontana 52 40.31 N 17.35 E
France ◻ 1 30 46.00 N 2.00 E
Frances Creek 92 13.35 S 131.52 E
Frances Lake 98 61.25 N 129.30 W
Francés Viejo, Cabo ⊁ 108 19.39 N 69.55 W
Franceville 84 1.38 S 13.35 E
Franche-Comté ◻ 9 48 47.00 N 6.00 E
Francia 54 22.33 S 56.37 W
Francia, Peña de ⋏ 50 42.35 N 8.02 W
Francisca, Punta ⊁ 108 21.34 N 87.21 W
Francisco Beltrão 114 26.05 S 53.04 W
Francisco Zarco 104 32.06 N 116.30 W
Francistown 86 21.11 S 27.32 E
Francofonte 52 37.14 N 14.53 E
François Lake ⊜ 98 54.00 N 125.40 W
Francs Peak ⋏ 100 43.58 N 109.20 W
Frangy 48 46.01 S 5.56 E
Frankenberg 46 50.54 N 13.01 E
Frankenberg-Eder 46 51.03 N 8.48 E
Frankenmuth 102 43.19 N 83.44 W
Frankford 102 44.12 N 77.36 W
Frankfort, S. Afr. 86 32.44 S 27.28 E
Frankfort, Ky., U.S. 102 38.12 N 84.52 W
Frankfort, N.Y., U.S. 102 43.02 N 75.04 W
Frankfurt ◻ 5 46 39.24 N 83.10 W
Frankfurt ◻ 5 46 52.30 N 14.30 E
Frankfurt am Main 46 50.07 N 8.40 E
Frankfurt an der Oder 46 52.20 N 14.33 E
Frankland ≃ 90 34.58 S 116.49 E
Franklin, S. Afr. 86 30.18 S 29.30 E
Franklin, Me., U.S. 102 44.35 N 68.13 W
Franklin, N.H., U.S. 102 42.05 N 71.23 W
Franklin, N.H., U.S. 102 43.26 N 71.38 W
Franklin, N.J., U.S. 102 41.07 N 74.34 W
Franklin, Pa., U.S. 102 39.33 N 84.18 W
Franklin, Pa., U.S. 102 41.24 N 79.50 W
Franklin, W.V., U.S. 102 38.39 N 79.20 W
Franklin ◻ 5 98 81.00 N 100.00 W
Franklin Bay C 98 69.45 N 126.00 W
Franklin Harbor C 94 33.42 S 136.56 E
Franklin Lake ⊜, N.T., Can. 98 66.56 N 96.03 W
Franklin Lake ⊜, Nv., U.S. 104 40.24 N 115.12 W
Franklin Mountains ⋏, N.T., Can. 98 63.00 N 123.50 W
Franklin Mountains ⋏, N.Z. 96 44.55 S 167.45 E
Franklin Strait ℧ 98 72.00 N 96.00 W
Franklinville 102 42.20 N 78.27 W
Frånö 44 62.30 N 17.50 E
Fränsta 44 62.30 N 16.09 E
Franz Josef Glacier 96 43.24 S 170.11 E
Franz Josef Land
→Zeml'a Franca-Iosifa II 26 81.00 N 55.00 E
Frascati 52 41.48 N 12.41 E
Fraser ≃, B.C., Can. 98 49.09 N 123.12 W
Fraser ≃, Nf., Can. 98 56.35 N 61.55 W
Fraser, Mount ⋏ 90 25.35 S 118.23 E
Fraserburg 86 31.55 S 21.30 E
Fraserburgh 38 57.42 N 2.00 W
Fraser Island I 94 25.15 S 153.10 E
Fraser Plateau ⋏1 98 52.00 N 123.00 W
Fraser Range 90 32.03 S 122.48 E
Frasertown 96 38.58 S 177.24 E
Frauenfeld 48 47.34 N 8.54 E
Fray Bentos 114 33.08 S 58.18 W
Fray Luis Beltrán 114 32.29 S 65.46 W
Fray Marcos 114 34.11 S 55.44 W
Fr'azino 60 55.58 N 38.04 E
Frechilla 50 42.08 N 4.50 W
Fredensborg 44 55.58 N 12.24 E
Frederica 102 39.00 N 75.27 W
Fredericia 44 55.35 N 9.46 E
Frederick 102 39.24 N 77.24 W
Frederick Hills ⋏ 2 92 12.41 S 136.00 E
Frederick Island I 90 34.04 S 122.00 E
Frederick Reef ÷ 2 94 20.58 S 154.23 E
Fredericksburg 102 38.18 N 77.27 W
Fredericktown 102 40.29 N 82.33 W
Frederico Westphalen 114 27.22 S 53.24 W
Fredericton 98 45.58 S 66.39 W
Fredericton Junction 102 45.40 N 66.37 W
Frederikshåb 98 62.00 N 49.43 W
Frederikshavn 44 57.26 N 10.32 E
Frederikssund 44 55.50 N 12.04 E
Frederiksted 108 17.43 N 64.53 W
Frederiksværk 44 55.58 N 12.02 E
Fredonia 102 42.26 N 79.19 W
Fredrika 44 64.05 N 18.24 E
Fredriksberg 44 60.08 N 14.23 E
Fredrikstad 44 59.13 N 10.57 E
Freehold 102 40.15 N 74.16 W
Freeland, Mi., U.S. 102 43.31 N 84.07 W
Freeland, Pa., U.S. 102 41.01 N 75.53 W
Freeling, Mount ⋏ 90 22.35 S 133.06 E
Freel Peak ⋏ 104 38.52 N 119.54 W
Freels, Cape ⊁ 98 49.15 S 53.28 W
Freemount 40 52.16 N 8.53 W
Freeport, Ba. 108 26.30 N 78.45 W
Freeport, Me., U.S. 102 43.51 N 70.06 W
Freeport, N.Y., U.S. 102 40.39 N 73.35 W
Freeport, Tx., U.S. 100 28.57 N 95.21 W
Freetown 80 8.30 N 13.15 W
Fregenal de la Sierra 50 38.10 N 6.39 W
Freiberg 46 50.54 N 13.20 E
Freiburg
→Fribourg 48 46.48 N 7.09 E
Freiburg [im Breisgau] 46 47.59 N 7.51 E
Freirina 114 28.30 S 71.06 W
Freising 46 48.23 N 11.44 E
Freistadt 46 48.31 N 14.31 E
Freital 46 51.00 N 13.39 E
Fréjus 48 43.26 N 6.44 E
Fremantle 90 32.03 S 115.45 E
Fremington 34 51.04 N 4.07 W
Fremont, Ca., U.S. 104 37.33 N 121.59 W
Fremont, In., U.S. 102 41.44 N 84.56 W
Fremont, Ne., U.S. 100 41.26 N 96.29 W
Fremont, Oh., U.S. 102 41.21 N 83.07 W
Fremont ≃ 104 38.24 N 110.07 W
Fremont Island I 104 41.10 N 112.20 W
French ≃ 102 45.56 N 80.54 W
Frenchburg 102 37.57 N 83.37 W
French Frigate Shoals ÷ 28 23.45 N 166.10 W
French Guiana (Guyane français) ◻ 2 110 4.00 N 53.00 W
French Island I 94 38.21 S 145.21 E
Frenchman Bay C 102 44.30 N 68.10 W
Frenchman Lake ⊜ 104 39.54 N 120.12 W
Frenchmans Cap ⋏ 94 42.16 S 145.50 E
Frenchpark 40 53.52 N 8.26 W
French Pass 96 40.56 S 173.50 E
French Polynesia ◻ 2 28 15.00 S 140.00 W
Frenštát pod Radhoštěm 46 49.33 N 18.14 E
Fresco ≃ 110 6.39 S 51.59 W

Freshford 40 52.43 N 7.24 W
Freshwater 34 50.40 N 1.30 W
Fresne-Saint-Mamès 48 47.33 N 5.52 E
Fresnes-en-Woëvre 48 49.08 N 5.39 E
Fresnillo 106 23.10 N 102.53 W
Fresno 104 36.44 N 119.46 W
Fresno ≃ 104 37.05 N 120.33 W
Freu, Cabo del ⊁ 50 39.45 N 3.27 E
Freudenstadt 46 48.28 N 8.25 E
Frew ≃ 90 20.00 S 135.38 E
Frewash ≃ 34 52.53 N 1.14 W
Frewena 94 19.25 S 135.25 E
Frewsburg 102 42.03 N 79.09 W
Freycinet, Cape ⊁ 94 34.06 S 114.59 E
Freycinet Estuary C1 90 26.25 S 113.45 E
Freycinet Peninsula ⊁1 94 42.13 S 148.18 E
Freyre 114 31.10 S 62.06 W
Fria, Cape ⊁ 86 18.30 S 12.01 E
Friant 104 36.59 N 119.42 W
Frias 114 28.39 S 65.09 W
Fribourg (Freiburg) 48 46.48 N 7.09 E
Fridaythorpe 36 54.01 N 0.40 W
Friedberg, B.R.D. 46 50.20 N 8.45 E
Friedberg, B.R.D. 46 48.21 N 10.58 E
Friedberg, Öst. 46 47.27 N 16.03 E
Friedland 46 53.40 N 13.33 E
Friedrichshafen 46 47.39 N 9.28 E
Friedrichstadt 46 54.22 N 9.05 E
Friendship 102 42.12 N 78.08 W
Friesach 46 46.57 N 14.24 E
Friesland ◻ 9 46 53.00 N 5.40 E
Fritton-on-Sea 44 61.26 N 21.52 E
Frio, Cabo ⊁ 110 22.53 S 42.00 W
Friockheim 38 56.38 N 2.38 W
Frisa, Loch ⊜ 38 56.34 N 6.05 W
Frisian Islands II 30 53.35 N 6.40 E
Fristad 44 57.50 N 13.01 E
Fritsla 44 57.33 N 12.47 E
Fritzlar 46 51.08 N 9.16 E
Friuli-Venezia-Giulia ◻ 5 52 46.00 N 13.00 E
Friza, proliv ℧ 58 45.30 N 149.30 E
Frizington 36 54.32 N 3.30 W
Frobisher Bay 98 63.44 N 68.28 W
Frobisher Bay C 98 63.00 N 66.30 W
Frobisher Lake ⊜ 98 56.25 N 108.20 W
Frodsham 36 53.18 N 2.44 W
Frohavet ℧ 44 63.52 N 9.26 E
Frohnleiten 46 47.16 N 15.20 E
Frolovo 56 49.47 N 43.39 E
Frombork 46 54.22 N 19.41 E
Frome 34 51.14 N 2.20 W
Frome ≃, Austl. 94 29.06 S 137.52 E
Frome ≃, Eng., U.K. 34 52.03 N 2.38 W
Frome ≃, Eng., U.K. 34 50.41 N 2.04 W
Frome Downs 94 31.13 S 139.46 E
Front Royal 102 38.55 N 78.11 W
Frosinone 52 41.38 N 13.19 E
Frosna ⊁1 44 63.45 N 10.25 E
Fröson I 44 63.11 N 14.32 E
Frostburg 102 39.39 N 78.55 W
Frövi 44 59.28 N 15.22 E
Frøya I 44 63.43 N 8.42 E
Fruges 48 50.31 N 2.08 E
Fruitdale 104 42.24 N 123.20 W
Fruitland 104 41.59 N 75.37 W
Frumușița 54 45.40 N 28.04 E
Frunze 56 42.54 N 74.36 E
Frutigen 48 46.35 N 7.39 E
Frýdek-Mistek 46 49.41 N 18.22 E
Frýdlant 46 50.56 N 15.05 E
Fryeburg 102 44.00 N 70.58 W
Fu'an 66 27.08 N 119.40 E
Fuchow
→Fuzhou 66 26.06 N 119.17 E
Fuchū 64 34.34 N 133.14 E
Fuchun ≃ 66 30.10 N 120.09 E
Fuday I 38 57.00 N 7.23 W
Fuding 66 27.21 N 120.12 E
Fuencaliente 50 38.24 N 4.18 W
Fuensalida 50 40.03 N 4.12 W
Fuensanta, Embalse de ⊜1 50 38.23 N 2.13 W
Fuente de Cantos 50 38.15 N 6.18 W
Fuenteobejuna 50 38.16 N 5.25 W
Fuentesaúco 50 41.14 N 5.30 W
Fuentes de Ebro 50 41.31 N 0.38 W
Fuerte ≃ 106 25.54 N 109.22 W
Fuerteventura I 80 28.20 N 14.00 W
Fufeng 62 34.20 N 107.51 E
Fuga Island I 68 18.52 N 121.22 E
Fugløysund ℧ 44 70.12 N 20.20 E
Fugou 62 34.04 N 114.24 E
Fuji 64 35.09 N 138.38 E
Fuji ≃ 64 35.07 N 138.39 E
Fuji, Mount
→Fuji-san ⋀ 64 35.22 N 138.44 E
Fujian (Fukien) ◻ 4 66 26.00 N 118.00 E
Fujin 62 47.14 N 132.00 E
Fujinomiya 64 35.12 N 138.38 E
Fuji-san (Fujiyama) ⋀ 1 64 35.22 N 138.44 E
Fujisawa 64 35.21 N 139.29 E
Fuji-yoshida 64 35.29 N 138.48 E
Fukagawa 64a 43.43 N 142.03 E
Fukaya 64 36.12 N 139.17 E
Fukien
→Fujian ◻ 4 66 26.00 N 118.00 E
Fukuchiyama 64 35.18 N 135.07 E
Fukue 64 32.41 N 128.50 E
Fukue-jima I 64 32.40 N 128.45 E
Fukui 64 36.04 N 136.13 E
Fukui ◻ 5 64 36.00 N 136.15 E
Fukuoka 64 33.35 N 130.24 E
Fukuroi 64 34.45 N 137.55 E
Fukushima, Nihon 64 37.45 N 140.28 E
Fukushima, Nihon 64a 41.29 N 140.15 E
Fukuyama 64 34.29 N 133.22 E
Fülädï, Küh-e ⋀ 76 34.38 N 67.32 E
Fulda 46 50.33 N 9.41 E
Fulda ≃ 46 51.25 N 9.39 E
Fuling 62 29.42 N 107.21 E
Fullerton 104 33.52 N 117.55 W
Fulmes 46 47.10 N 11.21 E
Fulton 102 43.19 N 76.25 W
Fulufjället ⋀ 44 61.33 N 12.43 E
Fulwood 36 53.47 N 2.41 W
Fumel 48 44.30 N 0.58 E
Fumin 70 25.16 N 102.56 E
Funabashi 64 35.42 N 139.59 E
Funafuti 28 8.31 S 179.13 E
Funäsdalen 44 62.32 N 12.33 E
Funchal 80 32.38 N 16.54 W
Fundación 108 10.31 N 74.11 W
Fundão 50 40.08 N 7.30 W
Fundy, Bay of C 98 45.00 N 66.00 W
Funing 66 23.38 N 105.37 E
Funiu Shan ⋀ 62 33.47 N 112.21 E
Funing 62 33.47 N 119.48 E
Funtua 80 11.31 N 7.19 E
Fuqing 66 25.44 N 119.22 E
Furancungo 86 14.55 S 33.37 E
Furculești 54 43.52 N 25.09 E

Furmanov 60 57.15 N 41.07 E
Furnace 38 56.09 N 5.10 W
Furnas, Reprêsa de ⊜1 110 20.45 S 46.00 W
Furneaux Group II 94 40.10 S 148.05 E
Furnes
→Veurne 48 51.04 N 2.40 E
Furness Fells ⋏2 36 54.18 N 3.07 W
Fürstenberg/Havel 46 53.11 N 13.08 E
Fürstenfeld 46 47.03 N 16.05 E
Fürstenfeldbruck 46 48.10 N 11.15 E
Fürstenwalde 46 52.21 N 14.04 E
Furth im Wald 46 49.18 N 12.51 E
Furudal 44 61.10 N 15.08 E
Furukawa, Nihon 64 36.14 N 137.11 E
Furukawa, Nihon 64 38.34 N 140.58 E
Furusund 44 59.40 N 18.55 E
Fury and Hecla Strait ℧ 98 69.56 N 84.00 W
Fuse
→Higashiōsaka 64 34.39 N 135.35 E
Fushan 64 31.49 N 120.46 E
Fushun 62 41.52 N 123.53 E
Füssen 46 47.34 N 10.42 E
Fusui 66 22.32 N 107.56 E
Futuna, Île I 28 14.15 S 178.09 W
Fuxian, Zhg. 62 39.37 N 122.01 E
Fuxian, Zhg. 62 36.02 N 109.13 E
Fuxian Hu ⊜ 66 24.30 N 102.55 E
Fuxin 62 42.03 N 121.46 E
Fuyang, Zhg. 66 32.54 N 115.49 E
Fuyang, Zhg. 66 30.03 N 119.57 E
Fuyu 62 45.10 N 124.50 E
Fuyuan 70 25.39 N 104.12 E
Fuyu 70 24.28 N 111.22 E
Fuzhou, Zhg. 66 28.01 N 116.20 E
Fuzhou (Foochow), Zhg. 66 26.06 N 119.17 E
Fyfield 34 51.45 N 0.16 E
Fylde ⊁1 36 53.47 N 2.56 W
Fyn I 44 55.20 N 10.30 E
Fyne, Loch C 38 56.00 N 5.24 E
Fyresvatn ⊜ 44 59.06 N 8.12 E
Fyvie 38 57.25 N 2.23 W

G

Gaalkacyo 82 6.47 N 47.26 E
Gabare 54 43.19 N 23.55 E
Gabas ≃ 48 43.46 N 0.42 W
Gabbs 104 38.52 N 117.55 W
Gabela 84 10.48 S 14.20 E
Gaberones
→Gaborone 86 24.45 S 25.55 E
Gabès 80 33.53 N 10.07 E
Gabès, Golfe de C 80 34.00 N 10.25 E
Gabin 46 52.25 N 19.44 E
Gablonz
→Jablonec nad Nisou 46 50.44 N 15.10 E
Gabon ◻ 1 84 1.00 S 11.45 E
Gaborone 86 24.45 S 25.55 E
Gabriel Strait ℧ 98 61.45 N 65.30 W
Gabriel y Galan, Embalse de ⊜1 50 40.15 N 6.15 W
Gabrovo 54 42.52 N 25.19 E
Gacé 48 48.47 N 0.18 E
Gachsarān 78 30.12 N 50.47 E
Gacko 54 43.10 N 18.32 E
Gadag 74 15.25 N 75.37 E
Gadarwāra 76 22.55 N 78.47 E
Gäddede 44 64.30 N 14.09 E
Gádor ⋀ 50 36.57 N 2.29 W
Gádor, Sierra de ⋏ 50 36.56 N 15.05 E
Gadsden, Al., U.S. 100 34.00 N 86.00 W
Gadsden, Az., U.S. 104 32.33 N 114.47 W
Gaer (Geeryasha) 76 31.44 N 80.21 E
Gaerwen 36 53.13 N 4.16 W
Găești 54 44.43 N 25.19 E
Gaeta 52 41.13 N 13.35 E
Gaeta, Golfo di C 52 41.06 N 13.30 E
Gaferut I 68 9.14 N 145.23 E
Gafsa 80 34.25 N 8.48 E
Gagarin 60 55.33 N 35.00 E
Gagliano del Capo 52 39.50 N 18.22 E
Gagnoa 80 6.08 N 5.56 W
Gagnon, Lac ⊜ 102 46.07 N 75.07 W
Gagnon 98 51.53 N 68.10 W
Gaillac 48 43.54 N 1.55 E
Gaillimh
→Galway 40 53.16 N 9.03 W
Gailtaler Alpen ⋏ 46 46.42 N 13.10 E
Gainesville, Fl., U.S. 100 29.39 N 82.19 W
Gainesville, Ga., U.S. 100 34.17 N 83.49 W
Gainesville, Tx., U.S. 100 33.37 N 97.07 W
Gainford 36 54.32 N 1.44 W
Gainsborough 36 53.24 N 0.46 W
Gairdner, Lac ≃ 94 34.17 S 119.28 E
Gairdner, Lake C 90 31.35 S 135.55 E
Gairloch 38 57.42 N 5.42 W
Gairloch, Loch C 38 57.44 N 5.44 W
Gairn ≃ 38 57.03 N 3.06 W
Gaithersburg 102 39.08 N 77.12 W
Gaixian 62 40.24 N 122.22 E
Gaj 54 45.29 N 17.02 E
Gajny 60 60.15 N 54.15 E
Gakarosa ⋀ 86 27.54 S 23.33 E
Gal, Punta de ⊁ 50 39.10 N 1.05 E
Galán, Cerro ⋀ 114 25.55 S 66.52 W
Galanta 46 48.12 N 17.43 E
Galápagos Islands
→Colón, Archipiélago de II 24 0.30 S 90.30 W
Galaroza 50 37.55 N 6.42 W
Galashiels 38 55.37 N 2.49 W
Galatea 96 38.25 S 176.45 E
Galați 54 45.26 N 28.03 E
Galați ◻ 6 54 45.26 N 27.43 E
Galatina 52 40.10 N 18.10 E
Galax 102 36.39 N 80.55 W
Galaxidhion 54 38.22 N 22.23 E
Galbraith 94 16.25 S 141.30 E
Galdhøpiggen ⋀ 44 61.37 N 8.17 E
Galeana 106 24.50 N 100.04 W
Galena, Austl. 90 27.50 S 114.41 E
Galena, Il., U.S. 100 42.25 N 90.25 W
Galeota Point ⊁ 108 10.08 N 60.59 W
Galera, Punta ⊁, Chile 114 39.59 S 73.43 W
Galera, Punta ⊁, Ec. 110 0.49 N 80.03 W
Galesburg, Il., U.S. 100 40.56 N 90.22 W
Galesburg, Mi., U.S. 102 42.17 N 85.25 W
Galeton 102 41.43 N 77.38 W
Galgamácsa 46 47.42 N 19.21 E
Galič 60 58.23 N 42.21 E
Galilee, Lake ⊜ 94 22.21 S 145.48 E
Galion 102 40.44 N 82.47 W
Gallan Head ⊁ 38 58.14 N 7.00 W
Gallarate 52 45.40 N 8.47 E
Gallatin 100 36.24 N 86.26 W
Galle 74 6.02 N 80.13 E
Gállego ≃ 50 41.39 N 0.51 W
Gallegos ≃ 114 51.35 S 69.00 W
Galley Head ⊁ 40 51.32 N 8.57 W
Galliate 52 45.29 N 8.42 E
Gallinas, Punta ⊁ 110 12.28 N 71.40 W
Gallipoli, Austl. 94 19.10 S 137.55 E
Gallipoli, It. 52 40.03 N 17.58 E

Gallipoli
→Gelibolu, Tür. 54 40.24 N 26.40 E
Gallipoli Peninsula
→Gelibolu Yarimadası ⊁1 54 40.20 N 26.30 E
Gallipolis 102 38.48 N 82.12 W
Gällivare 42 67.07 N 20.45 E
Gallo, Capo ⊁ 52 38.13 N 13.19 E
Galloo Island I 102 43.54 N 76.25 W
Galloway ◻ 9 36 55.00 N 4.25 W
Galloway, Mull of ⊁ 36 54.38 N 4.50 W
Gallup 100 35.31 N 108.44 W
Gallur 50 41.52 N 1.19 W
Gallura ⋏1 52 41.00 N 9.13 E
Galston 38 55.36 N 4.24 W
Galt 104 38.15 N 121.17 W
Galtür 46 46.58 N 10.11 E
Galtymore Mountains ⋀ 40 52.22 N 8.10 W
Galty Mountains ⋏ 40 52.25 N 8.10 W
Galvarino 114 38.24 S 72.47 W
Galveston 100 29.17 N 94.47 W
Galway (Gaillimh) 40 53.16 N 9.03 W
Galway ◻ 6 40 53.20 N 9.00 W
Galway 40 53.16 N 9.15 W
Gamagōri 64 34.50 N 137.14 E
Gamarra 110 8.20 N 73.45 W
Gambela 82 8.18 N 34.37 E
Gambell 58 63.46 N 171.46 W
Gambia ◻ 1 80 13.30 N 15.30 W
Gambia (Gambie) ≃ 80 13.28 N 16.34 W
Gambier 102 40.22 N 82.23 W
Gamboa 108 9.07 N 79.42 W
Gamboma 84 1.53 S 15.51 E
Gamleby 44 57.54 N 16.24 E
Gamoep 86 29.55 S 18.25 E
Gamph, Slieve ⋏ 40 54.05 N 9.00 W
Gan ≃, Zhg. 62 49.12 N 125.14 E
Gan ≃, Zhg. 62 29.12 N 116.00 E
Gananoque 102 44.20 N 76.10 W
Gand
→Gent 46 51.03 N 3.43 E
Ganda 84 13.02 S 14.40 E
Gandak ≃ 76 25.39 N 85.13 E
Gandarbal 76 34.14 N 74.47 E
Gandesa 50 41.03 N 0.26 E
Gandevi 76 20.49 N 72.59 E
Gandía 50 38.58 N 0.11 W
Gangāpur, India 76 25.13 N 74.16 E
Gangāpur, India 76 26.29 N 76.43 E
Gängänrämpur 76 25.24 N 88.31 E
Gangaw 70 22.11 N 94.07 E
Gangdhār 76 23.57 N 75.37 E
Gangdisê Shan ⋏ 76 31.00 N 82.00 E
Gangdisi Shan ⋏ 76 32.29 N 80.45 E
Ganges 48 43.56 N 3.42 E
Ganges (Ganga) (Padma) ≃ 76 23.22 N 90.32 E
Ganges, Mouths of the ≃1 76 22.00 N 89.00 E
Gangi 52 37.49 N 14.13 E
Gangotri 76 30.56 N 79.02 E
Gangtok 76 27.20 N 88.37 E
Gangu 62 34.45 N 105.20 E
Gannat 48 46.06 N 3.12 E
Gannett Peak ⋏ 100 43.10 N 109.39 W
Gansbaai 86 34.35 S 19.22 E
Gänserndorf 46 48.20 N 16.43 E
Gansu (Kansu) ◻ 4 62 37.00 N 103.00 E
Gantang 66 26.56 N 119.40 E
Gantheaume, Cape ⊁ 94 36.05 S 137.27 E
Gantheaume Bay C 90 27.44 S 114.07 E
Gantheaume Point ⊁ 90 17.59 S 122.10 E
Ganu Mōr ⋀ 38 58.25 N 4.53 W
Ganyesa 86 26.35 S 24.10 E
Ganzhou 66 25.51 N 114.59 E
Ganzhenyi 66 33.33 N 113.21 E
Ganzhou 66 25.54 N 114.55 E
Gao 80 16.16 N 0.03 W
Gao'an 66 28.25 N 115.22 E
Gaochun 66 31.20 N 118.52 E
Gaogou 66 34.03 N 119.15 E
Gaohe 66 22.47 N 112.57 E
Gaokeng 66 55.55 N 5.28 W
Gaona 114 25.12 S 64.05 W
Gaoshan 66 25.29 N 119.34 E
Gaotang 62 36.52 N 116.13 E
Gaoyao 66 23.02 N 112.28 E
Gaoyou Hu ⊜ 66 32.50 N 119.20 E
Gaozhou 70 21.55 N 110.50 E
Gap 48 44.34 N 6.05 E
Gar 76 44.44 N 80.21 E
Gara, Lough ⊜ 40 53.55 N 8.25 W
Garah 94 29.04 S 149.38 E
Garanhuns 110 8.54 S 36.29 W
Garberville 104 40.06 N 123.47 W
Garboldisham 34 52.24 N 0.56 E
Garça 114 22.14 S 49.37 W
García de Sola, Embalse de ⊜1 50 39.15 N 5.05 W
Gard ◻ 5 48 43.51 N 4.37 E
Garda 52 45.34 N 10.42 E
Garda, Lago di ⊜ 52 45.40 N 10.41 E
Gardelegen 46 52.31 N 11.23 E
Garden City 100 37.58 N 100.52 W
Garden Grove 104 33.46 N 117.56 W
Garden Island I, Austl. 90 32.13 S 115.41 E
Garden Island I, Mi., U.S. 102 45.49 N 85.30 W
Garden Reach 76 22.33 N 88.17 E
Gardermoen 44 60.13 N 11.06 E
Gardey 114 37.17 S 59.21 W
Gardez 76 33.37 N 69.07 E
Gardiner Range ⋏ 90 23.50 S 131.46 E
Gardiners Bay C 102 41.08 N 72.10 W
Gardner 102 42.34 N 71.59 W
Gardnerville 104 38.56 N 119.44 W
Gardone Val Trompia 52 45.41 N 10.11 E
Gardunha, Serra da ⋏ 50 40.05 N 7.31 W
Gare Loch C 38 56.03 N 4.48 W
Garelochhead 38 56.05 N 4.50 W
Garešnica 52 45.35 N 16.56 E
Garessio 52 44.12 N 8.02 E
Garforth 36 53.48 N 1.22 W
Gargano, Testa del ⊁ 52 41.49 N 16.12 E
Gargia 44 59.59 N 80.03 W
Gargrave 36 53.59 N 2.06 W
Garhakota 76 23.47 N 79.09 E
Garibaldi 114 29.15 S 51.32 W
Garies 86 30.30 S 17.59 E
Gariglione, Monte ⋀ 52 39.09 N 16.41 E
Garin 114 34.25 N 71.05 W
Garissa 84 0.28 S 39.38 E
Garlasco 52 45.12 N 8.55 E
Garliestown 36 54.48 N 4.22 W
Garlin 48 43.33 N 0.16 W
Garmisch-Partenkirchen 46 47.29 N 11.05 E
Garmouth 38 57.40 N 3.07 W
Garnock 38 55.37 N 4.37 W
Garnpung, Lake ⊜ 94 33.30 S 143.12 E
Garonne ≃ 48 45.02 N 0.36 W

Name Page Lat.°′ Long.°′

Garoua 80 9.18N 13.24 E
Garpenberg 44 60.19N 16.12 E
Garrel 46 52.57N 8.01 E
Garrett 102 41.20N 85.08W
Garrison 40 54.25N 8.05W
Garron Point ❯ 40 55.03N 5.57W
Garros 38 57.37N 6.11W
Garrovillas 50 39.43N 6.33W
Garry ≃ 38 56.43N 3.47W
Garry Bay ⊂ 98 68.55N 85.05W
Garry Lake ⊜ 98 66.00N 100.00W
Garsdale Head 36 54.19N 2.20W
Garsen 84 2.16S 40.07 E
Garstang 36 53.55N 2.47W
Gartempe ≃ 48 46.48N 0.50 E
Garut 72 7.13S 107.54 E
Garve 38 57.37N 4.42W
Garvellachs ❙❙ 38 56.14N 5.47W
Garvie Mountains ⋀ 96 45.30S 168.50 E
Garwa 76 24.11N 83.49 E
Garwolin 46 51.54N 21.37 E
Gary 100 41.35N 87.20W
Garza 114 28.09S 63.32W
Garzón, Col. 110 2.12N 75.38W
Garzón, Ur. 114 34.36S 54.33W
Gasan-Kuli 78 37.27N 53.59 E
Gascogne ◻9 48 44.00N 0.05 E
Gascoyne ≃ 90 24.52S 113.37 E
Gascoyne, Mount ∧ 90 24.58S 116.38 E
Gascoyne Junction 90 25.03S 115.12 E
Gash (Nahr al-Qāsh) ≃ 82 16.48N 35.51 E
Gashaka 80 7.21N 11.27 E
Gaspar 114 26.56S 48.58W
Gaspé 98 48.50N 64.29W
Gas-san ∧ 64 38.32N 140.01 E
Gassaway 102 38.40N 80.46W
Gastonia 100 35.15N 81.11W
Gastoúni 54 37.51N 21.16 E
Gastre 112 42.17S 69.14W
Gästrikland ◻9 44 60.30N 16.27 E
Gata, Cabo de ❯ 50 36.43N 2.12W
Gata, Sierra de ⋀ 50 40.14N 6.45W
Gătaia 54 45.26N 21.26 E
Gatčina 60 59.34N 30.08 E
Gatehouse of Fleet 36 54.53N 4.11W
Gateshead 36 54.58N 1.37W
Gateshead Island ❙ 98 70.22N 100.27W
Gâtine, Hauteurs de ⋀2 48 46.40N 0.50W
Gatineau 102 45.29N 75.38W
Gatineau ≃ 98 45.27N 75.40W
Gattinara 52 45.37N 8.22 E
Gatton 94 27.33S 152.17 E
Gatún, Lago ⊜1 108 9.12N 79.55W
Gaucín 50 36.31N 5.19W
Gauer Lake ⊜ 98 57.00N 97.50W
Gauhāti 76 26.10N 91.45 E
Gaula ≃ 44 63.21N 10.14 E
Gauley ≃ 102 38.10N 81.12W
Gauley Bridge 102 38.10N 81.11W
Gaunless ≃ 36 54.40N 1.41W
Gaurama 114 27.34S 52.03W
Gaurela 76 22.45N 81.54 E
Gauri Sankar ∧ 76 27.57N 86.21 E
Gausta ∧ 44 59.50N 8.35 E
Gauting 46 48.04N 11.23 E
Gavá 50 41.18N 2.01 E
Gávdhos ❙ 54 34.50N 24.06 E
Gävle 44 60.40N 17.10 E
Gävleborgs Län ◻6 44 61.30N 16.15 E
Gavorrano 52 42.55N 10.54 E
Gavrilov-Jam 60 57.18N 39.51 E
Gavrilov Posad 60 56.33N 40.07 E
Gávrion 54 37.52N 24.46 E
Gawler 94 34.37S 138.44 E
Gawler Ranges ⋀ 90 32.30S 136.00 E
Gaxun Nur ⊜ 62 42.22N 100.34 E
Gaya 76 24.47N 85.00 E
Gaylord 102 45.01N 84.40W
Gayndah 94 25.37S 151.36 E
Gayton 34 52.45N 0.34 E
Gaza ◻5 86 23.30S 32.45 E
Gazelle Peninsula ❯1 92 4.40S 152.00 E
Gaziantep 78 37.05N 37.22 E
Gbarnga 80 7.00N 9.29W
Gdańsk (Danzig) 46 54.23N 18.40 E
Gdov 60 58.44N 27.48 E
Gdynia 46 54.32N 18.33 E
Gearhart Mountain ∧ 104 42.30N 120.53W
Geba ≃ 80 11.46N 15.36W
Gebe, Pulau ❙ 92 0.05S 129.20 E
Gebweiler →Guebwiller 48 47.55N 7.12 E
Gebze 54 40.48N 29.25 E
Geel 46 51.10N 5.00 E
Geelong 94 38.08S 144.21 E
Geelvink Channel ꓤ 90 28.30S 114.10 E
Geesthacht 46 53.26N 10.22 E
Geeveston 94 43.10S 146.55 E
Geikie ≃ 98 57.45N 103.52W
Geilo 44 60.31N 8.12 E
Geiranger 44 62.06N 7.12 E
Geisenfeld 46 48.41N 11.37 E
Geislingen 46 48.36N 9.50 E
Geistown 102 40.17N 78.52W
Geita 84 2.52S 32.10 E
Geithain 46 51.03N 12.41 E
Gejiu (Kokiu) 70 23.22N 103.06 E
Gela 52 37.04N 14.15 E
Gela, Golfo di ⊂ 52 37.03N 14.10 E
Gelang, Tanjong ❯ 72 3.58N 103.26 E
Gelasa, Selat ꓤ 72 2.40S 107.15 E
Geldrop 48 51.25N 5.33 E
Geleen 46 50.58N 5.52 E
Gelibolu 54 40.24N 26.40 E
Gelibolu Yarımadası (Gallipoli Peninsula) ❯1 54 40.20N 26.30 E
Gélise ≃ 48 44.11N 0.17 E
Gellibrand 94 38.32S 143.32 E
Gelsenkirchen 46 51.31N 7.07 E
Gelt ≃ 36 54.56N 2.47W
Gemas 72 2.35N 102.37 E
Gembloux 46 50.34N 4.41 E
Gembrook 94 37.57S 145.33 E
Gemena 82 3.15N 19.46 E
Gemert 46 51.34N 5.40 E
Gemla 44 56.52N 14.38 E
Gemlik 54 40.26N 29.09 E
Gemona del Friuli 52 46.16N 13.09 E
Gemünden 46 50.03N 9.41 E
Gen ≃ 62 50.16N 119.22 E
Genale (Jubba) ≃ 82 0.40N 42.45 E
Gençay 48 46.23N 0.24 E
Gending 72 7.48S 113.18 E
General Acha 114 37.23S 64.36W
General Alvear 114 34.58S 67.42W
General Aquino 114 24.26S 56.42W
General Arenales 114 34.18S 61.18W
General Belgrano 114 35.46S 58.30W
General Cabrera 114 32.48S 63.52W
General Câmara 114 29.54S 51.46W
General Campos 114 31.32S 58.24W
General Carrera, Lago (Lago Buenos Aires) ⊜ 112 46.35S 72.00W
General Conesa 114 36.30S 57.20W
General Daniel Cerri 114 38.42S 62.24W
General Elizardo Aquino 114 26.53S 56.17W
General Enrique Martínez 114 33.12S 53.48W
General Enrique Mosconi 114 22.36S 63.49W
General Eugenio A. Garay, Para. 110 20.31S 62.08W
General Eugenio A. Garay, Para. 114 25.55S 56.11W
General Galarza 114 32.43S 59.24W
General Guido 114 36.40S 57.46W
General Gutiérrez 114 32.57S 68.48W
General José de San Martín 114 26.33S 59.21W
General Juan Madariaga 114 37.00S 57.09W
General La Madrid 114 37.16S 61.17W
General Lavalle 114 36.24S 56.58W
General Levalle 114 34.01S 63.56W
General Manuel Belgrano, Cerro ∧ 114 29.01S 67.49W
General O'Brien 114 34.54S 60.45W
General Paz, Arg. 114 35.31S 58.19W
General Paz, Arg. 114 27.45S 57.37W
General Pico 114 35.40S 63.44W
General Pinedo 114 27.19S 61.17W
General Pinto 114 34.46S 61.53W
General Pizarro 114 24.13S 64.01W
General Roca 114 39.02S 67.35W
General Rojo 114 33.28S 60.17W
General San Martín 114 34.34S 58.32W
General Santos 72 6.07N 125.11 E
General Toševo 54 43.42N 28.02 E
General Vargas 114 29.42S 54.40W
General Viamonte (Los Toldos) 114 35.01S 61.01W
General Villegas 114 35.02S 63.01W
Genesee ≃ 102 43.16N 77.36W
Geneseo 102 42.47N 77.49W
Geneva →Genève, Schw. 48 46.12N 6.09 E
Geneva, In., U.S. 102 40.35N 84.57W
Geneva, N.Y., U.S. 102 42.52N 77.00W
Geneva, Oh., U.S. 102 41.48N 80.56W
Geneva, Lake ⊜ 48 46.25N 6.30 E
Genève 48 46.12N 6.09 E
Gengma 70 23.34N 99.06 E
Genil ≃ 50 37.42N 5.19W
Genk 46 50.58N 5.30 E
Genkai-nada ⥿2 64 34.00N 130.00 E
Genlis 48 47.14N 5.13 E
Gennargentu, Monti del ⋀ 52 40.01N 9.19 E
Gennes 48 47.20N 0.14W
Genoa, Austl. 94 37.29S 149.35 E
Genoa →Genova, It. 52 44.25N 8.57 E
Genoa, Oh., U.S. 102 41.31N 83.21W
Genova (Genoa) 52 44.25N 8.57 E
Genova, Golfo di ⊂ 52 44.10N 8.55 E
Genrijetty, ostrov ❙ 58 77.06N 156.30 E
Gent (Gand) 46 51.03N 3.43 E
Genthin 46 52.24N 12.09 E
Gentioux 48 45.47N 1.59 E
Genzano di Roma 52 41.42N 12.41 E
Geographe Bay ⊂ 90 33.35S 115.15 E
Geographe Channel ꓤ 90 24.40S 113.20 E
Geokčaj 78 40.39N 47.44 E
George 86 33.58S 22.24 E
George ≃, Austl. 90 20.50S 117.28 E
George ≃, P.Q., Can. 98 58.49N 66.10W
George, Lake ⊜, Austl. 90 22.37S 123.38 E
George, Lake ⊜, Austl. 94 35.05S 149.25 E
George, Lake ⊜, Ug. 84 0.02N 30.12 E
George, Lake ⊜, N.Y., U.S. 102 43.35N 73.35W
George Gill Range ⋀ 90 24.15S 131.36 E
Georges Bank ⥿4 22 41.15N 67.30W
George Sound ꓤ 96 44.50S 167.23 E
George Town, Austl. 94 41.06S 146.50 E
Georgetown, Austl. 94 18.18S 143.33 E
Georgetown, Cay. Is. 108 19.18N 81.23W
Georgetown, Gam. 80 13.30N 14.47W
Georgetown, Guy. 110 6.48N 58.10W
George Town (Pinang), Malay. 72 5.25N 100.20 E
Georgetown, St. Vin. 108 13.16N 61.08W
Georgetown, De., U.S. 102 38.41N 75.23W
Georgetown, Ky., U.S. 102 38.12N 84.33W
Georgetown, Oh., U.S. 102 38.51N 83.54W
Georgetown, S.C., U.S. 100 33.22N 79.17W
Georgia ◻3 100 32.50N 83.15W
Georgia, Strait of ꓤ 98 49.20N 124.00W
Georgian Bay ⊂ 102 45.15N 80.50W
Georgian Bay Islands National Park ♦ 102 44.54N 79.52W
Georgian Soviet Socialist Republic →Gruzinskaja Sovetskaja Socialističeskaja Respublika ◻3 56 42.00N 44.00 E
Georgijevsk 56 44.09N 43.28 E
Georgina ≃ 94 23.30S 139.47 E
Georgiu-Dež 56 50.59N 39.30 E
Gera 46 50.52N 12.04 E
Gera ◻5 46 50.45N 11.45 E
Geraardsbergen 46 50.46N 3.52 E
Geral, Serra ⋀4 114 26.30S 50.30W
Geral de Goiás, Serra ⋀4 110 13.00S 46.15W
Geraldine 96 44.05S 171.14 E
Geraldton, Austl. 90 28.46S 114.36 E
Geraldton, On., Can. 98 49.44N 86.57W
Gerard, Mount ∧ 90 27.13S 122.41 E
Gérardmer 48 48.04N 6.53 E
Gerber 104 40.03N 122.08W
Gerber Reservoir ⊜1 104 42.12N 121.06W
Gerdine, Mount ∧ 98 61.35N 152.26W
Gereshk 76 31.48N 64.34 E
Gérgal 50 37.07N 2.33W
Gerik 72 5.25N 101.08 E
Gerlachovský štít ∧ 46 49.12N 20.08 E
German Democratic Republic (Deutsche Demokratische Republik) ◻1 30 52.00N 12.30 E
Germany, Federal Republic of (Bundesrepublik Deutschland) ◻1 30 51.00N 9.00 E
Germiston 86 26.13S 28.11 E
Gero 64 35.48N 137.14 E
Gerolzhofen 46 49.54N 10.21 E
Gerona 50 41.59N 2.49 E
Gerrei ⥿1 52 39.28N 9.17 E
Gers ◻5 48 43.40N 0.30 E
Gers ≃ 48 44.09N 0.39 E
Geseke 46 51.38N 8.31 E
Geser 92 3.53S 130.54 E
Geta 44 60.23N 19.50 E
Getafe 50 40.18N 3.43W
Getinge 44 56.49N 12.44 E
Gettysburg 102 39.49N 77.13W
Getulina 114 21.49S 49.55W
Getúlio Vargas 114 27.50S 52.16W
Gevgelija 54 41.08N 22.30 E
Gévora ≃ 50 38.53N 6.57W
Gex 48 46.20N 6.04 E
Geyserville 104 38.42N 122.54W
Ghadāmis 82 30.08N 9.30 E
Ghāghra ≃ 76 25.47N 84.37 E
Ghana ◻1 80 8.00N 1.00W
Ghanzi 86 21.38S 21.45 E
Ghanzi ◻5 86 22.00S 23.00 E
Gharaunda 76 29.33N 76.58 E
Gharbīyah, As-Sahrā' al- (Western Desert) ⥿2 82 27.00N 27.00 E
Ghardaïa 80 32.31N 3.37 E
Gharghoda 76 22.10N 83.21 E
Gharyān 82 32.10N 13.01 E
Ghāt 82 24.58N 10.11 E
Ghātāl 76 22.40N 87.43 E
Ghātsīla 76 22.36N 86.29 E
Ghawdex ❙ 52 36.03N 14.15 E
Ghazāl, Bahr al- ≃ 82 9.31N 30.25 E
Ghazal, Bahr el ∨ 82 13.01N 15.28 E
Ghāziābād 76 28.40N 77.26 E
Ghāzīpur 76 25.35N 83.34 E
Ghaznī 76 33.33N 68.26 E
Ghaznī ◻4 76 33.00N 68.00 E
Ghazzah (Gaza) 78 31.30N 34.28 E
Ghedi 52 45.24N 10.16 E
Ghent →Gent 46 51.03N 3.43 E
Gheorghe Gheorghiu-Dej 54 46.14N 26.44 E
Gheorgheni 54 46.43N 25.36 E
Gherla 54 47.02N 23.55 E
Ghilizane 50 35.44N 0.30 E
Ghīn, Tall ∧ 78 32.39N 36.43 E
Ghlò, Beinn a ∧ 38 56.50N 3.43W
Ghowr ◻4 76 34.00N 65.00 E
Ghūrīān 76 34.21N 61.30 E
Gia-dinh 70 10.48N 106.42 E
Giannutri, Isola di ❙ 52 42.15N 11.06 E
Giant Mountain ∧ 102 44.10N 73.44W
Giant's Castle ∧ 86 29.21S 29.27 E
Giant's Causeway ♦ 36 55.14N 6.30W
Giarre 52 37.43N 15.11 E
Gibara 108 21.07N 76.08W
Gibb River 92 15.39S 126.38 E
Gibbs, Mount ∧ 90 32.55S 120.00 E
Gibeon 86 25.09S 17.43 E
Gibraleón 50 37.23N 6.58W
Gibraltar 50 36.08N 5.21W
Gibraltar ◻2 30 36.08N 5.21W
Gibraltar, Strait of (Estrecho de Gibraltar) ꓤ 50 35.57N 5.36W
Gibraltar Point ❯ 36 53.05N 0.19 E
Gibson 90 33.39S 121.48 E
Gibson Desert ⥿2 90 24.30S 126.00 E
Gideälven ≃ 44 63.20N 19.08 E
Gideåvallen 44 63.29N 18.58 E
Gidgee 90 27.16S 119.22 E
Gidgi, Lake ⊜ 90 29.16S 126.03 E
Gidrotorf 60 56.28N 43.33 E
Gien 48 47.42N 2.38 E
Giessen 46 50.35N 8.40 E
Gifford 38 55.54N 2.45W
Gifford ≃ 98 70.21N 83.05W
Gifford Creek 90 24.05S 116.11 E
Gifhorn 46 52.29N 10.33 E
Gifu 64 35.25N 136.45 E
Gigen 54 43.42N 24.29 E
Giggleswick 36 54.04N 2.17W
Gigha, Sound of ꓤ 38 55.41N 5.42W
Gigha Island ❙ 38 55.41N 5.46W
Giglio, Isola del ❙ 52 42.21N 10.54 E
Gijón 50 43.32N 5.40W
Gila ≃ 100 32.43N 114.33W
Gila Bend 100 32.56N 112.42W
Gilberdyke 36 53.45N 0.44W
Gilbert ≃ 94 16.35S 141.15 E
Gilbert Islands ❙❙ 28 0.30S 174.00 E
Gilbert River 94 18.09S 142.52 E
Gilbert Seamount ⥿3 22 52.50N 150.10W
Gilbués 110 9.50S 45.21W
Giles Creek ≃ 90 17.25S 130.50 E
Gilford 40 54.23N 6.22W
Gilgai 90 31.15S 119.56 E
Gilgandra 94 31.42S 148.39 E
Gil Gil Creek ≃ 94 29.10S 148.51 E
Gilgit 76 35.55N 74.18 E
Gilgit ≃ 76 35.44N 74.38 E
Gill, Lough ⊜ 40 54.16N 8.24W
Gillam 98 56.21N 94.43W
Gilleleje 44 56.07N 12.19 E
Gillen, Lake ⊜ 90 26.11S 124.38 E
Gilles, Lake ⊜ 94 32.50S 136.45 E
Gillette 100 44.17N 105.30W
Gillian, Lake ⊜ 98 69.32N 75.23W
Gillingham, Eng., U.K. 34 51.24N 0.33 E
Gillingham, Eng., U.K. 34 51.02N 2.17W
Gilo ≃ 82 8.10N 33.15 E
Gilroy 104 37.00N 121.34W
Gil'uj ≃ 58 53.58N 127.30 E
Giluwe, Mount ∧ 92 6.05S 143.50 E
Gilwern 34 51.51N 3.06W
Gimån ≃ 44 62.28N 16.20 E
Gimie, Mount ∧ 108 13.52N 61.01W
Gimli 98 50.38N 96.59W
Gimo 44 60.11N 18.11 E
Gimone ≃ 48 44.00N 1.06 E
Gimont 48 43.38N 0.53 E
Gingin, Austl. 90 31.21S 115.42 E
Gin Gin, Austl. 94 25.00S 151.58 E
Ginir 82 7.07N 40.46 E
Ginosa 52 40.35N 16.46 E
Ginowan 65b 26.17N 127.46 E
Ginzo de Limia 50 42.03N 7.43W
Gioia del Colle 52 40.48N 16.56 E
Gioia Tauro 52 38.26N 15.54 E
Gioiosa Ionica 52 38.20N 16.18 E
Gipping ≃ 34 52.04N 1.10 E
Giralia 90 22.41S 114.21 E
Giraltovce 46 49.07N 21.31 E
Girard, Oh., U.S. 102 41.09N 80.42W
Girard, Pa., U.S. 102 42.00N 80.19W
Girardot 110 4.18N 74.48W
Gîrbovu 54 44.44N 23.21 E
Girgarre 94 36.24S 144.59 E
Gir Hills ⋀2 76 21.18N 71.00 E
Giridih 76 24.11N 86.18 E
Girifalco 52 38.49N 16.25 E
Girilambone 94 31.15S 146.54 E
Giromagny 48 47.45N 6.50 E
Gironde ◻5 48 44.45N 0.35W
Gironde ⊂1 48 45.20N 0.45W
Girou ≃ 48 43.46N 1.23 E
Girton 34 52.14N 0.05 E
Giru 94 19.31S 147.06 E
Giruá 114 28.02S 54.21W
Girvan 38 55.15N 4.51W
Girvan, Water of ≃ 38 55.15N 4.51W
Girvas 42 62.30N 33.40 E
Girwa ≃ 76 28.15N 81.05 E
Gisborne 96 38.40S 178.01 E
Gisenyi 84 1.42S 29.15 E
Gislaved 44 57.18N 13.32 E
Gisors 48 49.17N 1.47 E
Gitega 84 3.26S 29.56 E
Giugliano [in Campania] 52 40.56N 14.12 E
Giulianova 52 42.45N 13.57 E
Giurgiu 54 43.53N 25.57 E
Give 44 55.51N 9.15 E
Givet 48 50.08N 4.50 E
Givors 48 45.35N 4.46 E
Givry 48 46.47N 4.45 E
Giyon 82 8.30N 38.00 E
Giza →Al-Jīzah 82 30.01N 31.13 E
Gižduvan 78 40.06N 64.41 E
Gižiga 58 62.03N 160.30 E
Gižiginskaja guba ⊂ 58 61.30N 158.00 E
Gizo 88 8.06S 156.51 E
Giżycko 46 54.03N 21.47 E
Gjirokastër 54 40.05N 20.10 E
Gjoa Haven 98 68.38N 95.57W
Gjøvik 44 60.48N 10.42 E
Gjuesevo 54 42.14N 22.28 E
Gjuhëzës, Kep i ❯ 54 40.25N 19.18 E
Glace Bay 98 46.12N 59.57W
Gladbach →Mönchengladbach 46 51.12N 6.28 E
Gladbeck 46 51.34N 6.59 E
Gladstone, Austl. 94 23.51S 151.16 E
Gladstone, Austl. 94 33.17S 138.22 E
Gladwin 102 43.58N 84.29W
Glafsfjorden ⊜ 44 59.34N 12.37 E
Gláma ∧ 42a 65.47N 23.00W
Glåma ≃ 44 59.12N 10.57 E
Glamis 38 56.36N 3.00W
Glamoč 52 44.03N 16.51 E
Glamsbjerg 44 55.16N 10.07 E
Glan ⊜ 44 58.37N 15.58 E
Glanamman 34 51.48N 3.54W
Glanmire 40 51.55N 8.24W
Glarner Alpen ⋀ 48 46.55N 9.00 E
Glarus 48 47.02N 9.04 E
Glascarnoch, Loch ⊜ 38 57.40N 4.50W
Glasgow, Scot., U.K. 38 55.53N 4.15W
Glasgow, Ky., U.S. 100 36.59N 85.54W
Glasgow, Mt., U.S. 100 48.11N 106.38W
Glaslyn ≃ 34 52.56N 4.06W
Glas Maol ∧ 38 56.52N 3.22W
Glass, Loch ⊜ 38 57.43N 4.30W
Glassan 40 53.28N 7.52W
Glassboro 102 39.42N 75.06W
Glastonbury 34 51.06N 2.43W
Glauchau 46 50.49N 12.32 E
Glaven ≃ 34 52.58N 1.03 E
Glazov 42 58.09N 52.40 E
Glazunovka 60 52.30N 36.19 E
Gleinalpe ⋀ 46 47.15N 15.03 E
Gleisdorf 46 47.06N 15.44 E
Gleiwitz →Gliwice 46 50.17N 18.40 E
Glemsford 34 52.06N 0.41 E
Glen ≃, Ire. 40 54.38N 8.40W
Glen ≃, Eng., U.K. 34 52.51N 0.06W
Glen Afton 96 37.37S 175.02 E
Glenamaddy 40 53.37N 8.35W
Glenamoy 40 54.14N 9.42W
Glenarm 40 54.58N 5.57W
Glenavy, N.Z. 96 44.55S 171.06 E
Glenavy, N. Ire., U.K. 40 54.36N 6.13W
Glenbeigh 40 52.02N 9.58W
Glen Burnie 102 39.09N 76.37W
Glencoe, Austl. 94 37.42S 140.37 E
Glencoe, On., Can. 102 42.45N 81.43W
Glencoe, S. Afr. 86 28.12S 30.07 E
Glencolumbkille 40 54.43N 8.45W
Glencoul, Loch ⊂ 38 58.14N 4.58W
Glen Cove 102 40.51N 73.38W
Glendale, Ca., U.S. 104 34.08N 118.15W
Glendale, Or., U.S. 104 42.44N 123.25W
Glendive 100 47.06N 104.42W
Glendoe Forest ⥿3 38 57.06N 4.37W
Glendowan 40 54.58N 7.56W
Glenelg 38 57.13N 5.38W
Glenelg ≃ 94 38.03S 141.00 E
Glenelly ≃ 40 54.44N 7.18W
Glenfarg 38 56.16N 3.24W
Glenfarne 40 54.17N 7.59W
Glenfield 34 52.39N 1.12W
Glenfinnan 38 56.52N 5.27W
Glen Florrie 90 22.55S 115.59 E
Glengarriff 40 51.45N 9.33W
Glengarry Range ⋀ 90 26.13S 118.59 E
Glengyle 94 24.48S 139.37 E
Glenhope 96 41.39S 172.39 E
Glen Innes 94 29.44S 151.44 E
Glenluce 36 54.53N 4.49W
Glen Lyon 102 41.10N 76.04W
Glenmorgan 94 27.15S 149.41 E
Glenns Ferry 104 42.57N 115.18W
Glenorchy 96 44.51S 168.23 E
Glenormiston 94 22.55S 138.48 E
Glenreagh 94 30.03S 152.59 E
Glen Robertson 102 45.21N 74.30W
Glen Rock 102 39.47N 76.43W
Glenrothes 38 56.12N 3.10W
Glenroy 90 21.46S 114.49 E
Glenroy ≃ 96 42.00S 172.20 E
Glens Falls 102 43.18N 73.38W
Glenshee ∨ 38 56.48N 3.30W
Glenties 40 54.47N 8.17W
Glenville, Ire. 40 52.03N 8.26W
Glenville, W.V., U.S. 102 38.56N 80.50W
Glide 104 43.18N 123.06W
Glífa 54 38.57N 22.58 E
Glimåkra 44 56.18N 14.08 E
Glimmingehus 44 55.30N 14.13 E
Glin 40 52.34N 9.17W
Glina 52 45.20N 16.06 E
Glina ≃ 52 45.26N 16.07 E
Glittertinden ∧ 44 61.39N 8.33 E
Gliwice (Gleiwitz) 46 50.17N 18.40 E
Globe 100 33.23N 110.47W
Glodeanu-Siliştea 54 44.50N 26.48 E
Gloggnitz 46 47.40N 15.57 E
Głogów, Pol. 46 51.40N 16.05 E
Głogów, Pol. 46 50.10N 21.58 E
Głogówek 46 50.22N 17.51 E
Glommersträsk 44 65.16N 19.38 E
Glória de Dourados 114 22.21S 54.13W
Glorieuses, Îles ❙❙ 84 11.30S 47.20 E
Glossop 36 53.27N 1.57W
Gloucester, Austl. 94 31.59S 151.58 E
Gloucester, Eng., U.K. 34 51.53N 2.14W
Gloucester, Ma., U.S. 102 42.36N 70.39W
Gloucester, Cape ❯ 92 5.27S 148.25 E
Gloucester, Vale of ∨ 34 51.55N 2.10W
Gloucester Island ❙ 94 20.01S 148.27 E
Gloucestershire ◻6 34 51.47N 2.15W
Glouster 102 39.30N 82.05W
Glovers Reef ⥿2 108 16.49N 87.48W
Gloversville 102 43.03N 74.20W
Głowno 46 51.58N 19.44 E
Głubczyce 46 50.13N 17.49 E
Glubokoje 60 55.08N 27.41 E
Głuchołazy 46 50.20N 17.22 E
Glücksburg 46 54.50N 9.33 E
Glückstadt 46 53.47N 9.25 E
Gluša 60 53.05N 28.52 E
Glusburn 36 53.54N 1.59W
Glusk 60 52.54N 28.41 E
Glyde ≃, Austl. 92 12.15S 135.03 E
Glyde ≃, Ire. 40 53.52N 6.21W
Glyder Fawr ∧ 34 53.06N 4.01W
Glyme ≃ 34 51.49N 1.22W
Glyngøre 44 56.46N 8.52 E
Glyn-Neath 34 51.45N 3.38W
Gmünd 46 48.47N 15.00 E
Gmunden 46 47.55N 13.48 E
Gnalta 94 31.03S 142.20 E
Gnaraloo 90 23.51S 113.31 E
Gnarp 44 62.03N 17.16 E
Gnesta 44 59.03N 17.18 E
Gnezdovo 60 54.47N 31.47 E
Gniew 46 53.51N 18.49 E
Gniewkowo 46 52.54N 18.25 E
Gniezno 46 52.31N 17.37 E
Gnjilane 54 42.28N 21.29 E
Gnoien 46 53.58N 12.42 E
Gnosall 34 52.47N 2.15W
Gnosjö 44 57.22N 13.44 E
Gnowangerup 90 33.56S 117.59 E
Gō ≃ 64 35.02N 132.13 E
Goalen Head ❯ 94 36.40S 150.05 E
Goālpāra 76 26.11N 90.37 E
Goat Fell ∧ 38 55.38N 5.12W
Goathland 36 54.23N 0.43W
Goba 82 7.02N 40.00 E
Gobabis 86 22.30S 18.58 E
Gobabis ◻5 86 22.30S 19.00 E
Gobernador Gregores 112 48.46S 70.15W
Gobernador Juan E. Martínez 114 28.55S 58.56W
Gobernador Racedo 114 31.34S 60.04W
Gobi ⥿2 62 43.00N 105.00 E
Gobowen 34 52.53N 3.02W
Goce Delčev 54 41.34N 23.44 E
Goch 46 51.41N 6.10 E
Godafoss ↳ 42a 65.40N 17.30W
Godalming 34 51.11N 0.37W
Godāvari ≃ 74 17.00N 81.45 E
Goderich 102 43.45N 81.43W
Goderville 48 49.39N 0.22 E
Godhavn 98 69.15N 53.33W
Godhra 76 22.45N 73.38 E
Godmanchester 34 52.19N 0.11W
Gödöllő 46 47.36N 19.22 E
Godoy Cruz 114 32.55S 68.50W
Gods ≃ 98 56.22N 92.51W
Godshill 34 50.38N 1.14W
Gods Lake ⊜ 98 54.45N 94.00W
Gods Mercy, Bay of ⊂ 98 63.30N 86.10W
Godstone 34 51.15N 0.04W
Godthåb 98 64.11N 51.44W
Godwin Austen →K2 ∧ 76 35.53N 76.30 E
Goéland, Lac au ⊜ 98 49.47N 76.48W
Goélands, Lac aux ⊜ 98 55.27N 64.17W
Goes 46 51.30N 3.54 E
Goffstown 102 43.01N 71.36W
Göggingen 46 48.20N 10.52 E
Gogha 76 21.41N 72.17 E
Gogolin 46 50.30N 18.02 E
Gohad 76 26.26N 78.27 E
Gohpur 76 26.53N 93.38 E
Goiana 110 7.33S 34.59W
Goiânia 110 16.40S 49.16W
Goiás 110 15.56S 50.08W
Goichran 76 31.04N 78.07 E
Goil, Loch ⊂ 38 56.08N 4.52W
Goio-Erê 114 24.12S 53.01W
Goio-Erê ≃ 114 24.14S 53.21W
Góis 50 40.09N 8.07W
Goito 52 45.15N 10.40 E
Gojō 64 34.21N 135.42 E
Gojōme 64 39.56N 140.07 E
Gojra 76 31.09N 72.41 E
Gokase ≃ 64 32.35N 131.42 E
Gökçeada ❙ 54 40.10N 25.50 E
Gol 44 60.42N 8.57 E
Golāghāt 76 26.31N 93.58 E
Gola Island ❙ 40 55.05N 8.22W
Gołańcz 46 52.57N 17.18 E
Gol'čicha 58 71.43N 83.36 E
Golconda 104 40.57N 117.29W
Gołdap 46 54.19N 22.19 E
Gold Beach 104 42.24N 124.25W
Gold Coast →Southport 94 27.58S 153.25 E
Golden, B.C., Can. 98 51.18N 116.58W
Golden, Ire. 40 52.29N 7.58W
Golden Bay ⊂ 96 40.40S 172.50 E
Golden Hinde ∧ 98 49.40N 125.45W
Golden Lake ⊜ 102 45.35N 77.20W
Golden Valley ∨ 34 52.02N 2.56W
Goldfield 104 37.42N 117.14W
Gold Mountain ∧ 104 37.15N 117.18W
Goldsworthy 90 20.20S 119.30 E
Goleen 40 51.28N 9.43W
Golela 86 27.20S 31.55 E
Goleniów 46 53.36N 14.50 E
Goleta 104 34.26N 119.49W
Golfito 106 8.38N 83.11W
Golicyno 60 55.37N 36.59 E
Golina 46 52.16N 18.05 E
Goljama Kamčija ≃ 54 43.03N 27.29 E
Goljam Perelik ∧ 54 41.36N 24.34 E
Golmud 62 36.22N 94.55 E
Golo ≃ 48 42.31N 9.32 E
Golpāyegān 78 33.27N 50.18 E
Golspie 38 57.58N 3.58W
Golub-Dobrzyń 46 53.08N 19.02 E
Golynki 60 54.52N 31.23 E
Golyšmanovo 56 56.23N 68.23 E
Goma 84 1.41S 29.14 E
Gomati ≃ 76 25.32N 83.10 E
Gomel' 60 52.25N 31.00 E
Gomera ❙ 80 28.06N 17.08W
Gometra ❙ 38 56.29N 6.17W
Gómez Palacio 106 25.34N 103.30W
Gomoh 76 23.52N 86.10 E
Gompa 76 35.02N 77.20 E
Gona 92 8.37S 148.17 E
Gonābād 78 34.20N 58.42 E
Gonaïves 108 19.27N 72.41W
Gonam 58 57.21N 131.12 E
Gonam ≃ 58 57.21N 131.14 E
Gonâve, Golfe de la ⊂ 108 19.00N 73.30W
Gonâve, Île de la ❙ 108 18.51N 73.03W
Gonbad-e Qābūs 78 37.17N 55.17 E
Gonda 76 27.08N 81.56 E
Gondal 76 21.58N 70.48 E
Gonder 82 12.40N 37.30 E
Gondia 76 21.27N 80.12 E
Gondomar 50 41.09N 8.32W
Gondrecourt-le-Château 48 48.31N 5.30 E
Gönen 54 40.06N 27.39 E
Gonesse 32 48.59N 2.27 E
Gong ≃ 66 28.00N 115.22 E
Gongbo'gyamda 62 29.56N 93.23 E
Gongcheng 70 24.49N 110.46 E
Gongchenqiao 66 30.20N 120.08 E
Gongga Shan ∧ 62 29.35N 101.51 E
Gonggeershan ∧ 76 38.37N 75.20 E
Gongola ≃ 80 9.30N 12.04 E
Gongping 66 23.05N 115.24 E
Gongxi 66 27.38N 115.52 E
Gongxian 62 34.48N 113.03 E
Goñi 114 33.31S 56.24W
Goniądz 46 53.30N 22.45 E
Gonnesa 52 39.16N 8.28 E
Gonoura 64 33.45N 129.41 E
Gonzaga 52 44.57N 10.49 E
Gonzales 104 36.30N 121.26W
González Chaves 114 38.02S 60.06W
González Moreno 114 35.33S 63.22W
González Ortega 104 32.40N 115.23W
Goodenough Island ❙ 92 9.20S 150.15 E
Gooderham 102 44.54N 78.23W
Good Hope 86 31.51S 21.55 E
Good Hope, Cape of ❯ 86 34.24S 18.30 E
Good Hope Mountain ∧ 98 51.09N 124.10W
Goodhouse 86 28.57S 18.13 E
Gooding 104 42.56N 114.42W
Goodland 100 39.21N 101.42W
Goodooga 94 29.07S 147.27 E
Goodwick 34 52.00N 5.00W
Goole 36 53.42N 0.52W
Goolgowi 94 33.59S 145.42 E
Goomalling 90 31.19S 116.49 E
Goombalie 94 29.59S 145.23 E
Goomburra 94 28.03S 152.07 E
Goondiwindi 94 28.32S 150.19 E
Goongarrie 90 30.03S 121.09 E
Goonyella 94 21.45S 147.55 E
Goose Bay 98 53.20N 60.25W
Goose Lake ⊜ 104 41.57N 120.25W
Gopālganj 76 26.28N 84.26 E
Göppingen 46 48.42N 9.40 E
Goqên 62 29.15N 96.59 E
Góra 46 51.40N 16.33 E
Góra Kalwaria 46 51.59N 21.12 E
Gorakhpur 76 26.45N 83.22 E
Goras 76 25.32N 76.56 E
Goražde 54 43.40N 18.56 E
Gorbatov 60 56.08N 43.04 E
Gorbatovka 60 56.15N 43.45 E
Gorčucha 60 57.43N 43.43 E
Gorda, Punta ❯, Cuba 108 22.24N 82.10W
Gorda, Punta ❯, Nic. 108 14.21N 83.12W
Gordon 38 55.41N 2.34W
Gordon, Lake ⊜1 94 42.42S 146.12 E
Gordon Downs 90 18.44S 128.35 E
Gordonsville 102 38.08N 78.11W
Gordonton 96 37.40S 175.18 E
Gordonvale 94 17.05S 145.47 E
Gore, Austl. 94 28.17S 151.29 E
Gore, Ityo. 82 8.08N 35.33 E
Gore, N.Z. 96 46.06S 168.58 E
Gore Bay 102 45.55N 82.28W
Gorebridge 38 55.51N 3.02W
Gore Mountain ∧ 102 44.55N 71.48W
Gore Point ❯ 92 17.38S 139.56 E
Gorey, Ire. 40 52.40N 6.18W
Gorey, Jersey 35b 49.12N 2.02W
Gorgān 78 36.50N 54.29 E
Gorgota 54 44.47N 26.05 E
Gorgova 54 45.11N 29.10 E
Gorham, Me., U.S. 102 43.40N 70.26W
Gorham, N.H., U.S. 102 44.23N 71.10W
Gori 56 41.58N 44.07 E
Gorinchem 46 51.50N 5.00 E
Goring 34 51.32N 1.09W
Goring-by-Sea 34 50.49N 0.25W
Goring Gap ∨ 34 51.32N 1.08W
Goris 78 39.31N 46.23 E
Gorizia 52 45.57N 13.38 E
Gorj ◻6 54 45.00N 23.20 E
Gorjani 54 45.24N 18.21 E
Gorki →Gor'kij, S.S.S.R. 60 56.20N 44.00 E
Gorki, S.S.S.R. 60 54.17N 30.59 E
Gor'kij (Gorky) 60 56.20N 44.00 E
Gor'kovskoje vodochranilišče ⊜1 60 57.00N 43.10 E
Gorleston on Sea 34 52.36N 1.43 E
Gorlice 46 49.40N 21.10 E
Görlitz 46 51.09N 14.59 E
Gorlovka 56 48.18N 38.03 E
Gorm, Loch ⊜ 38 55.48N 6.25W
Gorn'ackij 42 67.32N 64.03 E
Gorna Džhumaya →Blagoevgrad 54 42.01N 23.06 E
Gorn'ak 60 53.36N 39.29 E
Gorna Orjahovica 54 43.07N 25.41 E
Gornja Radgona 52 46.41N 16.00 E
Gornji Grad 52 46.18N 14.49 E
Gornji Milanovac 54 44.01N 20.27 E
Gornji Vakuf 52 43.56N 17.35 E
Gorno-Altajsk 56 51.58N 85.58 E
Gornozavodsk 58 46.34N 141.49 E
Gorochovec 60 56.12N 42.40 E
Gorodec 60 56.38N 43.30 E
Gorodeja 60 53.19N 26.32 E
Gorodišče 60 53.19N 26.00 E
Gorodok 60 55.28N 29.59 E
Goroka 92 6.05S 145.25 E
Gorontalo 72 0.33N 123.03 E
Górowo Iławeckie 46 54.17N 20.30 E
Gorseinon 34 51.40N 4.02W
Gort 40 53.04N 8.50W
Gortahork 40 55.08N 8.09W
Gorul ∧ 54 45.48N 26.25 E
Gorumna Island ❙ 40 53.15N 9.40W
Górzno 46 53.13N 19.38 E
Gorzów Śląski 46 51.02N 18.24 E
Gorzów Wielkopolski (Landsberg an der Warthe) 46 52.44N 15.15 E
Gosainthan ∧ 76 28.22N 85.50 E
Gosberton 34 52.51N 0.09W
Gosen 64 37.44N 139.11 E
Gosford 94 33.26S 151.21 E
Gosforth, Eng., U.K. 36 55.01N 1.37W
Gosforth, Eng., U.K. 36 54.26N 3.27W
Goshen, Ca., U.S. 104 36.21N 119.25W
Goshen, N.Y., U.S. 102 41.24N 74.19W
Goshogawara 64 40.48N 140.27 E
Goshute Lake ⊜ 104 40.08N 114.38W
Goshute Valley ∨ 104 40.40N 114.30W
Goslar 46 51.54N 10.25 E
Gosnells 90 32.04S 116.00 E
Gospić 52 44.33N 15.23 E
Gosport 34 50.48N 1.08W
Gostivar 54 41.47N 20.54 E
Gostyń 46 51.53N 17.00 E
Gostynin 46 52.26N 19.29 E
Göta älv ≃ 44 57.42N 11.52 E
Göta kanal ⩶ 44 58.50N 13.58 E
Göteborg (Gothenburg) 44 57.43N 11.58 E
Göteborgs Och Bohus Län ◻6 44 58.30N 11.30 E
Gotemba 64 35.18N 138.56 E
Götene 44 58.32N 13.29 E
Gotha 46 50.57N 10.41 E
Gothem 44 57.35N 18.43 E
Gothenburg →Göteborg 44 57.43N 11.58 E
Gotland ❙ 44 57.30N 18.33 E
Gotlands Län ◻6 44 57.30N 18.30 E
Gotō-rettō ❙❙ 64 32.50N 129.00 E
Gotska Sandön ❙ 44 58.23N 19.16 E
Gōtsu 64 35.00N 132.14 E
Göttingen 46 51.32N 9.55 E
Gottwaldov 46 49.13N 17.41 E
Götzis 46 47.20N 9.38 E
Gouarec 48 48.13N 3.11W
Gouda 46 52.01N 4.43 E
Goudge 114 34.40S 68.08W
Goudhurst 34 51.07N 0.28 E
Gough Island ❙ 20 40.20S 10.00W
Gouin, Réservoir ⊜1 98 48.38N 74.54W
Goulburn 94 34.45S 149.43 E
Goulburn Islands ❙❙ 92 11.33S 133.26 E
Gould City 102 46.05N 85.41W
Gouménissa 54 40.57N 22.27 E
Goundam 80 16.25N 3.40W
Gourdon 48 44.44N 1.23 E
Gouré 80 13.58N 10.18 E
Gourin 48 48.08N 3.36W
Gournay-en-Bray 48 49.29N 1.44 E
Gourock 38 55.58N 4.49W
Gouverneur 102 44.20N 75.27W
Govena, mys ❯ 58 59.48N 166.06 E
Gove Peninsula ❯1 92 12.20S 136.50 E

Symbols in the Index entries are identified on page 122.

Gove-Guss

Name Page Lat. Long.

Governador Valadares 110 18.51 S 41.56 W
Governors Harbour 108 25.10 N 76.14 W
Gowanda 102 42.27 N 78.56 W
Gowan Range ⋆ 94 25.00 S 145.00 E
Gower › [1] 34 51.36 N 4.10 W
Gowerton 34 51.39 N 4.01 W
Gowmal (Gumal) ≃ 76 31.56 N 70.22 E
Gowna, Lough ⊜ 40 53.51 N 7.34 W
Gowy ≃ 36 53.17 N 2.51 W
Goya 114 29.08 S 59.16 W
Goyder ≃ 92 12.38 S 135.11 E
Gozdnica 46 51.26 N 15.06 E
Gozo →Għawdex ■ 52 36.03 N 14.15 E
Graaff-Reinet 86 32.14 S 24.32 E
Grabow 46 53.16 N 11.34 E
Grabowiec 46 50.50 N 23.33 E
Grabów nad Prosną 46 51.31 N 18.06 E
Gračac 52 44.18 N 15.51 E
Gračanica 54 44.42 N 18.19 E
Graçay 48 47.08 N 1.51 E
Gracefield 102 46.06 N 76.03 W
Gracias a Dios, Cabo › 108 15.00 N 83.10 W
Gradačac 54 44.53 N 18.26 E
Gradaús 110 7.43 S 51.11 W
Gradaús, Serra dos ⋆[1] 110 8.00 S 50.45 W
Grado, Esp. 50 43.23 N 6.04 W
Grado, It. 52 45.40 N 13.23 E
Graemsay ■ 38 58.56 N 3.17 W
Grafenau 46 48.52 N 13.25 E
Gräfenhainichen 46 51.44 N 12.27 E
Grafham Water ⊜ 34 52.17 N 0.20 W
Grafing [bei München] 46 48.02 N 11.59 E
Gråfjell ▲ 44 60.16 N 9.29 E
Grafton, Austl. 94 29.41 S 152.56 E
Grafton, N.D., U.S. 100 48.24 N 97.24 W
Grafton, W.V., U.S. 102 39.20 N 80.01 W
Grafton, Cape › 94 16.52 S 145.55 E
Graham Island ■ 98 53.40 N 132.30 W
Graham Lake ⊜ 102 44.40 N 68.25 W
Graham Moore, Cape › 98 72.52 N 76.04 W
Graham Moore Bay c 98 75.26 N 101.25 W
Grahamstown 86 33.19 S 26.31 E
Graiguenamanagh 40 52.32 N 6.57 W
Grain 34 51.28 N 0.43 E
Grain, Isle of ■ 34 51.27 N 0.41 E
Grajaú 110 5.49 S 46.08 W
Grajaú ≃ 110 3.41 S 44.48 W
Grajewo 46 53.39 N 22.27 E
Gram 44 55.17 N 9.04 E
Gramada 54 43.50 N 22.39 E
Gramado 114 29.24 S 50.54 W
Gramat 48 44.47 N 1.43 E
Gramilla 114 27.18 S 64.37 W
Grammichele 52 37.13 N 14.38 E
Grampian ☐4 38 57.15 N 2.45 W
Grampian Mountains ⋆ 38 56.55 N 4.00 W
Gramsh 54 40.52 N 20.11 E
Granada, Esp. 50 37.13 N 3.41 W
Granada, Nic. 108 11.56 N 85.57 W
Granadella 50 41.21 N 0.40 E
Granard 40 53.47 N 7.30 W
Granby 102 45.24 N 72.44 W
Gran Canaria ■ 80 28.00 N 15.36 W
Gran Chaco ⚌ 112 23.00 S 60.00 W
Grand ≃, On., Can. 102 42.51 N 79.34 W
Grand ≃, Mi., U.S. 102 43.00 N 85.40 W
Grand ≃, Oh., U.S. 102 41.46 N 81.17 W
Grandas 50 43.13 N 6.52 W
Grandas de Salime, Embalse de ⊜[1] 50 43.10 N 6.45 W
Grand Bahama ■ 108 26.38 N 78.25 W
Grand Ballon ▲ 48 47.55 N 7.08 E
Grand Bank 98 47.06 N 55.46 W
Grand Banks of Newfoundland ✦[4] 22 45.00 N 53.00 W
Grand-Bassam 80 5.12 N 3.44 W
Grand Bend 102 43.15 N 81.45 W
Grand Blanc 102 42.55 N 83.37 W
Grand-Bourg 108 15.53 N 61.19 W
Grand Calumet, Île du ■ 102 45.44 N 76.41 W
Grand Canal ⚌ 40 53.21 N 6.14 W
Grand Canal →Da Yunhe ⚌ 62 32.12 N 119.31 E
Grand Canyon 100 36.03 N 112.08 W
Grand Cayman ■ 108 19.20 N 81.15 W
Grand Cess 80 4.36 N 8.10 W
Grand-Couronne 48 49.21 N 1.00 E
Grande ≃, Arg. 114 36.52 S 69.45 W
Grande ≃, Arg. 114 24.12 S 64.42 W
Grande ≃, Bol. 110 15.51 S 64.39 W
Grande ≃, Bra. 110 11.05 S 43.09 W
Grande ≃, Chile 114 30.35 S 71.11 W
Grande ≃, Esp. 50 39.07 N 0.44 W
Grande, Arroyo ≃ 114 33.08 S 57.09 W
Grande, Bahía c[3] 112 50.45 S 68.45 W
Grande, Boca ≃[1] 110 8.38 N 60.30 W
Grande, Corixa ≃ 110 17.31 S 57.52 W
Grande, Cuchilla ▲ 114 33.15 S 55.07 W
Grande, Ilha ■, Bra. 110 23.09 S 44.14 W
Grande, Ilha ■, Bra. 114 23.45 S 54.03 W
Grande, Punta › 114 25.06 S 70.30 W
Grande, Rio (Bravo del Norte) ≃ 100 25.55 N 97.09 W
Grande Cayemite ■ 108 18.37 N 73.45 W
Grande Comore ■ 87a 11.35 S 43.20 E
Grande de Matagalpa ≃ 108 12.54 N 83.32 W
Grande de Santa Marta, Ciénaga c 108 10.50 N 74.25 W
Grande de Tarija ≃ 114 22.53 S 64.21 W
Grande do Gurupá, Ilha ■ 110 1.00 S 51.30 W
Grande-Prairie 98 55.10 N 118.48 W
Grand Erg de Bilma ✦[2] 80 18.30 N 14.00 E
Grand Erg Occidental ✦[2] 80 30.30 N 0.30 E
Grand Erg Oriental ✦[2] 80 30.30 N 7.00 E
Grandes, Salinas ⚌ 114 30.05 S 65.05 W
Grande-Terre ■ 108 16.20 N 61.25 W
Grand Falls, N.B., Can. 98 47.03 N 67.44 W
Grand Falls, Nf., Can. 98 48.56 N 55.40 W
Grand Forks, B.C., Can. 98 49.02 N 118.27 W
Grand Forks, N.D., U.S. 100 47.55 N 97.01 W
Grand-Fougeray 48 47.44 N 1.44 W
Grand Hers ≃ 48 43.47 N 1.20 E
Grandin, Lac ⊜ 98 63.59 N 119.00 W
Grand Island 100 40.55 N 98.20 W
Grand Junction 100 39.03 N 108.33 W
Grand Lake ⊜, N.A. 102 45.43 N 67.50 W
Grand Lake ⊜, Mi., U.S. 102 45.18 N 83.30 W
Grand Lake ⊜, Oh., U.S. 102 40.30 N 84.32 W
Grand Ledge 102 42.45 N 84.44 W
Grand Lieu, Lac de ⊜ 48 47.06 N 1.40 W
Grand Manan Channel ɥ 102 44.45 N 66.52 W
Grand Manan Island ■ 102 44.40 N 66.50 W
Grândola 50 38.10 N 8.34 W
Grand Rapids, Mb., Can. 98 53.08 N 99.20 W
Grand Rapids, Mi., U.S. 102 42.58 N 85.40 W
Grand Rapids, Mn., U.S. 100 47.14 N 93.31 W
Grandrieu 48 44.47 N 3.38 E
Grand-Saint-Bernard, Tunnel du ✦[5] 48 45.51 N 7.11 E
Grand Teton ▲ 100 43.44 N 110.48 W
Grand Traverse Bay c 102 45.02 N 85.30 W
Grand Traverse Bay, East Arm c 102 44.52 N 85.28 W
Grand Traverse Bay, West Arm c 102 44.52 N 85.35 W
Grandtully 38 56.39 N 3.46 W
Grand Turk 108 21.28 N 71.08 W
Grandview 98 51.10 N 100.42 W
Grañén 50 41.56 N 0.22 W
Graneros 114 34.04 S 70.44 W
Graney, Lough ⊜ 40 52.59 N 8.40 W
Grangärde 44 60.16 N 14.59 E
Grangemouth 38 56.02 N 3.45 W
Grange-over-Sands 36 54.12 N 2.55 W
Grängesberg 44 60.05 N 14.59 E
Gran Guardia 114 25.52 S 58.53 W
Granite Downs 90 26.57 S 133.30 E
Granite Peak 90 25.38 S 121.21 E
Granite Peak ▲, Mt., U.S. 100 45.10 N 109.48 W
Granite Peak ▲, Nv., U.S. 104 41.40 N 117.35 W
Granite Peak ▲, Nv., U.S. 104 40.48 N 119.25 W
Granite Range ⋆ 104 41.00 N 119.35 W
Graniteville 102 44.09 N 72.29 W
Granity 96 41.38 S 171.51 E
Grankulla (Kauniainen) 44 60.13 N 24.45 E
Gränna 44 58.01 N 14.28 E
Grannoch, Loch ⊜ 36 55.00 N 4.17 W
Granollers 50 41.37 N 2.18 E
Granön 44 64.15 N 19.19 E
Gran Paradiso ▲ 52 45.32 N 7.16 E
Gran Sasso d'Italia ⋆ 52 42.27 N 13.42 E
Gransee 46 53.00 N 13.09 E
Grant, Mount ▲ 104 38.34 N 118.48 W
Granta ≃ 34 52.10 N 0.06 E
Grantham 34 52.55 N 0.39 W
Granton 38 55.59 N 3.14 W
Grantown on Spey 38 57.20 N 3.58 W
Grant Point › 98 68.19 N 98.53 W
Grant Range ⋆ 104 38.25 N 115.30 W
Grants 100 35.09 N 107.50 W
Grantshouse 38 55.53 N 2.19 W
Grants Pass 100 42.26 N 123.19 W
Grants Patch 90 30.27 S 121.07 E
Grant-Suttie Bay c 98 69.47 N 77.15 W
Grantsville 102 38.55 N 81.05 W
Granville, Fr. 48 48.50 N 1.36 W
Granville, N.Y., U.S. 102 43.24 N 73.15 W
Granville, Oh., U.S. 102 40.04 N 82.31 W
Granville, W.V., U.S. 102 39.38 N 79.59 W
Granville Lake ⊜ 98 56.18 N 100.30 W
Granvin 44 60.33 N 6.43 E
Grão Mogol 110 16.34 S 42.54 W
Grapevine Peak ▲ 104 36.57 N 117.09 W
Gras, Lac de ⊜ 98 64.30 N 110.30 W
Graskop 86 24.58 S 30.49 E
Grasmere, S. Afr. 86 26.26 S 27.52 E
Grasmere, Eng., U.K. 36 54.28 N 3.02 W
Gräsö ■ 44 60.24 N 18.25 E
Grasonville 102 38.57 N 76.12 W
Grass ≃, Mb., Can. 98 56.03 N 96.33 W
Grass ≃, N.Y., U.S. 102 44.59 N 74.46 W
Grassano 52 40.38 N 16.18 E
Grasse 48 43.40 N 6.55 E
Grassflat 102 41.00 N 78.07 W
Grassington 36 54.04 N 4.59 W
Grass Lake 102 42.15 N 84.13 W
Grass Patch 90 33.14 S 121.43 E
Grass Valley 104 39.13 N 121.03 W
Grassy 94 40.03 S 144.04 E
Gråsten 44 54.55 N 9.36 E
Grästorp 44 58.20 N 12.40 E
Gravatá 110 8.12 S 35.34 W
Gravelbourg 98 49.53 N 106.34 W
Gravelines 48 50.59 N 2.07 E
Gravell Point › 98 67.10 N 76.43 W
Gravelotte 86 23.56 S 30.34 E
Gravenhurst 102 44.55 N 79.22 W
Gravesend, Austl. 94 29.35 S 150.19 E
Gravesend, Eng., U.K. 34 51.27 N 0.24 E
Gravina in Puglia 52 40.49 N 16.25 E
Gray 48 47.27 N 5.35 E
Grayback Mountain ▲ 104 42.07 N 123.18 W
Grayling 102 44.39 N 84.42 W
Grays 34 51.29 N 0.20 E
Grayshott 34 51.11 N 0.45 W
Grayson 102 38.19 N 82.56 W
Grays Peak ▲ 100 39.37 N 105.45 W
Graz 46 47.05 N 15.27 E
Grazalema 50 36.46 N 5.22 W
Gr'azi 60 52.29 N 39.57 E
Gr'aznoje 60 54.02 N 39.07 E
Gr'azovec 60 58.53 N 40.14 E
Grdelica 54 42.54 N 22.04 E
Greåker 44 59.16 N 11.02 E
Great Abaco ■ 108 26.28 N 77.05 W
Great Artesian Basin ≃[1] 94 25.00 S 143.00 E
Great Australian Bight c[3] 90 35.00 S 130.00 E
Great Ayton 36 54.30 N 1.08 W
Great Baddow 34 51.43 N 0.29 E
Great Bahama Bank ✦[4] 22 23.15 N 78.00 W
Great Barford 34 52.09 N 0.21 W
Great Barrier Island ■ 96 36.10 S 175.25 E
Great Barrier Reef ✦[2] 88 18.00 S 145.50 E
Great Barrington 102 42.11 N 73.21 W
Great Basin ✦[1] 100 40.00 N 117.00 W
Great Bear Lake ⊜ 98 66.00 N 120.00 W
Great Bend 100 38.21 N 98.45 W
Great Bernera ■ 38 58.13 N 6.49 W
Great Blasket Island ■ 40 52.05 N 10.32 W
Great Channel ɥ 70 6.25 N 94.20 E
Great Chazy ≃ 102 44.56 N 73.23 W
Great Clifton 36 54.31 N 3.29 W
Great Cumbrae Island ■ 38 55.46 N 4.55 W
Great Dividing Range ⋆ 88 25.00 S 147.00 E
Great Driffield 36 54.00 N 0.27 W
Great Duck Island ■ 102 45.40 N 82.58 W
Great Dunmow 34 51.53 N 0.22 E
Great Eau ≃ 36 53.25 N 0.13 E
Greater Antilles ■■ 108 20.00 N 74.00 W
Greater Khingan Range →Da Hinggan Ling ⋆ 62 49.00 N 122.00 E
Greater London ☐6 34 51.30 N 0.10 W
Greater Manchester ☐6 36 53.30 N 2.20 W
Greater Sunda Islands ■■ 68 2.00 S 110.00 E
Great Exuma ■ 108 23.32 N 75.50 W
Great Falls 100 47.30 N 111.17 W
Great Gable ▲ 36 54.28 N 3.12 W
Great Guana Cay ■ 108 24.00 N 76.20 W
Great Harwood 36 53.48 N 2.24 W
Great Haywood 34 52.48 N 2.00 W
Great Himalaya Range ⋆ 76 29.00 N 83.00 E
Great Inagua ■ 108 21.05 N 73.18 W
Great Indian Desert (Thar Desert) ✦[2] 76 27.00 N 71.00 E
Great Island ■ 40 51.52 N 8.17 W
Great Karroo ⋆[1] 86 32.25 S 22.40 E
Great La Cloche Island ■ 102 46.01 N 81.52 W
Great Lake ⊜ 94 41.52 S 146.45 E
Great Malvern 34 52.07 N 2.19 W
Great Massingham 34 52.46 N 0.40 E
Great Mercury Island ■ 96 36.37 S 175.48 E
Great Meteor Tablemount ✦[3] 24 30.00 N 28.30 W
Great Miami ≃ 102 39.06 N 84.49 W
Great Missenden 34 51.43 N 0.43 W
Great Mis Tor ▲ 34 50.34 N 4.01 W
Great Namaqualand ☐9 86 25.00 S 17.00 E
Great Nicobar ■ 70 7.00 N 93.50 E
Great North East Channel ɥ 92 9.30 S 143.25 E
Great Ormes Head › 36 53.21 N 3.52 W
Great Ouse ≃ 34 52.47 N 0.22 E
Great Palm Island ■ 94 18.43 S 146.37 E
Great Plain of the Koukdjuak ⚌ 98 66.00 N 73.00 W
Great Plains ⚌ 22 42.00 N 100.00 W
Great Point › 102 41.23 N 70.03 W
Great Ruaha ≃ 84 7.56 S 37.52 E
Great Sacandaga Lake ⊜ 102 43.08 N 74.10 W
Great Salt Lake ⊜ 100 41.10 N 112.30 W
Great Salt Lake Desert ✦[2] 104 40.40 N 113.30 W
Great Sandy Desert ✦[2] 90 21.30 S 125.00 E
Great Sankey 36 53.23 N 2.37 W
Great Shelford 34 52.09 N 0.09 E
Great Slave Lake ⊜ 98 61.30 N 114.00 W
Great Stour ≃ 34 51.19 N 1.15 E
Great Torrington 34 50.57 N 4.08 W
Great Victoria Desert ✦[2] 90 28.30 S 127.45 E
Great Whernside ▲ 36 54.09 N 1.59 W
Great Wyrley 34 52.41 N 2.01 W
Great Yarmouth 34 52.37 N 1.44 E
Great Zab (Büyükzap) (Az-Zāb al-Kabīr) ≃ 78 36.00 N 43.21 E
Grebbestad 44 58.42 N 11.15 E
Gréboun ▲ 80 20.00 N 8.35 E
Greco 114 32.48 S 57.03 W
Gredos, Sierra de ⋆ 50 40.18 N 5.05 W
Greece 102 43.12 N 77.41 W
Greece (Elláς) ☐1 30 39.00 N 22.00 E
Greeley 100 40.25 N 104.42 W
Green ≃ 100 38.11 N 109.53 W
Green Bay 100 44.31 N 88.01 W
Green Bay c 100 45.00 N 87.30 W
Greenbrier ≃ 102 37.49 N 80.30 W
Greenbushes 90 33.51 S 116.03 E
Green Cape › 94 37.15 S 150.03 E
Greencastle, Ire. 40 55.12 N 6.59 W
Greencastle, Pa., U.S. 102 39.47 N 77.43 W
Greendale 102 39.06 N 84.51 W
Greene 102 42.19 N 75.46 W
Greenfield, Wales, U.K. 36 53.18 N 3.13 W
Greenfield, Ca., U.S. 104 36.19 N 121.14 W
Greenfield, Ma., U.S. 102 42.35 N 72.36 W
Greenfield, Oh., U.S. 102 39.21 N 83.22 W
Green Head › 90 30.05 S 114.58 E
Green Island, N.Z. 96 45.54 S 170.26 E
Greenisland, N. Ire., U.K. 40 54.42 N 5.52 W
Greenland (Kalaallit Nunaat) ☐2 22 70.00 N 40.00 W
Greenland Basin ✦[1] 22 73.30 N 5.00 W
Greenland-Iceland Rise ✦[3] 20 67.00 N 27.00 W
Greenland Sea ✦[2] 22 77.00 N 1.00 W
Greenlaw 38 55.43 N 2.28 W
Green Mountains ⋆ 102 43.45 N 72.45 W
Greenock 38 55.57 N 4.45 W
Greenodd 36 54.14 N 3.04 W
Greenore Point › 40 52.15 N 6.18 W
Greenough 90 28.57 S 114.44 E
Greenough ≃ 90 28.51 S 114.38 E
Greenport 102 41.06 N 72.21 W
Greensboro, Md., U.S. 102 38.58 N 75.48 W
Greensboro, N.C., U.S. 100 36.04 N 79.47 W
Greensburg 102 40.18 N 79.32 W
Green Springs 102 41.15 N 83.03 W
Greenstone Point › 38 57.55 N 5.38 W
Greenup 102 38.34 N 82.49 W
Greenvale 94 18.59 S 145.07 E
Greenville, Liber. 80 5.01 N 9.03 W
Greenville, Ca., U.S. 104 40.08 N 120.57 W
Greenville, Me., U.S. 102 45.28 N 69.35 W
Greenville, Mi., U.S. 102 43.10 N 85.15 W
Greenville, Ms., U.S. 100 33.24 N 91.03 W
Greenville, N.H., U.S. 102 42.46 N 71.48 W
Greenville, N.C., U.S. 100 35.36 N 77.22 W
Greenville, Oh., U.S. 102 40.06 N 84.37 W
Greenville, Pa., U.S. 102 41.24 N 80.23 W
Greenville, S.C., U.S. 100 34.51 N 82.23 W
Greenville, Tx., U.S. 100 33.08 N 96.06 W
Greenwich, Ct., U.S. 102 41.01 N 73.37 W
Greenwich, N.Y., U.S. 102 43.05 N 73.29 W
Greenwich, Oh., U.S. 102 41.01 N 82.30 W
Greenwich ✦[8] 34 51.28 N 0.02 E
Greenwood, Ms., U.S. 100 33.30 N 90.10 W
Greenwood, S.C., U.S. 100 34.11 N 82.09 W
Greerton 96 37.43 S 176.08 E
Gregory 102 42.27 N 84.05 W
Gregory ≃ 94 17.53 S 139.17 E
Gregory, Lake ⊜, Austl. 90 25.38 S 119.58 E
Gregory, Lake ⊜, Austl. 94 28.55 S 139.00 E
Gregory, Port c[3] 90 28.10 S 114.14 E
Gregory Lake ⊜ 90 20.10 S 127.20 E
Gregory Range ⋆ 94 19.00 S 143.05 E
Greifswald 46 54.05 N 13.23 E
Greifswalder Bodden c 46 54.15 N 13.35 E
Grein 46 48.14 N 14.51 E
Greiz 46 50.39 N 12.12 E
Grem'ačinsk 56 58.34 N 57.51 E
Gremicha 42 68.03 N 39.27 E
Grenå 44 56.25 N 10.53 E
Grenada ☐1 106 12.07 N 61.40 W
Grenadine Islands ■■ 108 12.40 N 61.15 W
Grenagh 40 52.00 N 8.37 W
Grenchen 48 47.11 N 7.24 E
Grenen ›[2] 44 57.44 N 10.40 E
Grenfell 94 33.54 S 148.10 E
Grenoble 48 45.10 N 5.43 E
Grenville, Cape › 92 11.58 S 143.14 E
Gréoux-les-Bains 48 43.45 N 5.53 E
Gresik 72 7.09 S 112.38 E
Gresten 46 48.00 N 15.02 E
Greta ≃, Eng., U.K. 36 54.32 N 1.53 W
Greta ≃, Eng., U.K. 36 54.36 N 3.10 W
Greta ≃, Eng., U.K. 36 54.09 N 2.36 W
Gretna 36 54.59 N 3.04 W
Greven 46 52.05 N 7.36 E
Grevená 54 40.05 N 21.25 E
Grevenbroich 46 51.05 N 6.35 E
Grevesmühlen 46 53.51 N 11.10 E
Grey ≃ 96 42.27 S 171.12 E
Grey, Cape › 92 13.00 S 136.40 E
Greyabbey 40 54.32 N 5.33 W
Grey Islands ■■ 98 50.50 N 55.37 W
Greylock, Mount ▲ 102 42.38 N 73.10 W
Greymouth 96 42.28 S 171.12 E
Grey Range ⋆ 94 27.00 S 143.35 E
Greystoke 36 54.40 N 2.52 W
Greystones 40 53.09 N 6.04 W
Greytown, N.Z. 96 41.05 S 175.27 E
Greytown, S. Afr. 86 29.07 S 30.30 E
Gribanovskij 56 51.27 N 41.58 E
Gribbin Head › 34 50.19 N 4.40 W
Gridley 104 39.21 N 121.41 W
Griekwastad 86 28.49 S 23.15 E
Griesbach 46 48.28 N 13.11 E
Griesheim 46 49.50 N 8.34 E
Griffin 100 33.14 N 84.15 W
Griffith 94 34.17 S 146.03 E
Griffith Island ■ 98 74.35 N 95.30 W
Grignan 48 44.25 N 4.54 E
Grignols 48 44.23 N 0.03 W
Grijalva ≃ 106 18.36 N 92.39 W
Grim, Cape › 94 40.41 S 144.41 E
Grimma 46 51.14 N 12.43 E
Grimmen 46 54.07 N 13.02 E
Grimsby, On., Can. 102 43.12 N 79.34 W
Grimsby, Eng., U.K. 36 53.35 N 0.05 W
Grimselpass)(48 46.34 N 8.21 E
Grímsey ■ 42a 66.34 N 18.00 W
Grímsstaðir 42a 65.40 N 16.01 W
Grimstad 44 58.20 N 8.36 E
Grindavík 42a 63.52 N 22.27 W
Grindelwald 48 46.37 N 8.02 E
Grindsted 44 55.45 N 8.56 E
Grinnell Peninsula ›[1] 98 76.40 N 95.00 W
Grintavec ▲ 52 46.21 N 14.32 E
Grip 44 63.14 N 7.37 E
Griqualand East ☐9 86 30.30 S 29.00 E
Griqualand West ☐9 86 28.20 S 23.30 E
Gris-Nez, Cap › 48 50.52 N 1.35 E
Grisslehamn 44 60.06 N 18.50 E
Grizzly Bear Mountain ▲ 98 65.22 N 121.00 W
Grmeč ⋆ 52 44.40 N 16.30 E
Grobiņa 60 56.33 N 21.10 E
Groblersdal 86 25.15 S 29.25 E
Groblershoop 86 28.55 S 20.59 E
Grodków 46 50.43 N 17.22 E
Grodno 60 53.41 N 23.50 E
Grodzisk Mazowiecki 46 52.07 N 20.37 E
Grodzisk [Wielkopolski] 46 52.14 N 16.22 E
Groen ≃, S. Afr. 86 29.00 S 22.10 E
Groen ≃, S. Afr. 86 30.40 S 23.17 E
Groix 48 47.38 N 3.28 W
Groix, Île de ■ 48 47.38 N 3.27 W
Grójec 46 51.52 N 20.52 E
Gronau 46 52.13 N 7.00 E
Grong 42 64.28 N 12.18 E
Grongemouth 36 56.01 N 3.44 W
Groningen 46 53.13 N 6.33 E
Groom Lake ⊜ 104 37.15 N 115.48 W
Groot ≃, S. Afr. 86 33.45 S 24.36 E
Groot ≃, S. Afr. 86 33.54 S 21.39 E
Groot-Berg ≃ 86 32.47 S 18.08 E
Groot-Brakrivier 86 34.01 S 21.46 E
Grootdraaidam ⊜[1] 86 26.56 S 29.20 E
Groote Eylandt ■ 92 14.00 S 136.40 E
Grootfontein 86 19.32 S 18.05 E
Groot Karasberge ⋆ 86 27.20 S 18.40 E
Groot-Kei ≃ 86 32.41 S 28.22 E
Groot Laagte ≃ 86 20.37 S 21.37 E
Groot-Letaba ≃ 86 23.58 S 31.50 E
Groot-Marico 86 25.37 S 26.26 E
Groot-Swartberge ⋆ 86 33.22 S 22.20 E
Groot-Vis ≃ 86 33.30 S 27.08 E
Grootvloer ⚌ 86 30.00 S 20.40 E
Gropeni 54 45.04 N 27.53 E
Gros Morne ▲ 98 49.36 N 57.48 W
Grosnez Point › 35b 49.16 N 2.15 W
Grossenhain 46 51.17 N 13.31 E
Grosse Pointe 102 42.23 N 82.54 W
Grosser Arber ▲ 46 49.07 N 13.07 E
Grosser Beerberg ▲ 46 50.37 N 10.44 E
Grosser Feldberg ▲ 46 50.14 N 8.26 E
Grosser Priel ▲ 46 47.43 N 14.04 E
Grosseto 52 42.46 N 11.08 E
Gross-Gerau 46 49.55 N 8.29 E
Grossglockner ▲ 46 47.04 N 12.42 E
Grossräschen 46 51.35 N 14.00 E
Grossvenediger ▲ 46 47.06 N 12.21 E
Groswater Bay c 98 54.20 N 57.30 W
Groton, Ct., U.S. 102 41.21 N 72.04 W
Groton, N.Y., U.S. 102 42.35 N 76.22 W
Grottaglie 52 40.32 N 17.26 E
Grottaminarda 52 41.04 N 15.02 E
Grottammare 52 42.59 N 13.52 E
Grottoes 102 38.16 N 78.49 W
Grouard Mission 98 55.31 N 116.09 W
Groundhog ≃ 98 49.43 N 81.58 W
Grouse Creek ≃ 104 41.22 N 113.55 W
Grove 34 51.36 N 1.25 W
Grove City, Oh., U.S. 102 39.52 N 83.05 W
Grove City, Pa., U.S. 102 41.09 N 80.05 W
Grovely Ridge ▲ 34 51.08 N 2.04 W
Grover City 104 35.07 N 120.37 W
Groveton 102 44.35 N 71.30 W
Growa Point › 80 4.21 N 7.37 W
Groznyj 56 43.20 N 45.42 E
Grubišno Polje 52 45.42 N 17.10 E
Grudovo 54 42.21 N 27.10 E
Grudziądz 46 53.29 N 18.45 E
Gruia 54 44.16 N 22.42 E
Gruinard Bay c 38 57.53 N 5.31 W
Gruinart, Loch c 38 55.52 N 6.20 W
Grumo Appula 52 41.01 N 16.42 E
Grums 44 59.21 N 13.06 E
Grünau [im Almtal] 46 47.51 N 13.57 E
Grunavat, Loch ⊜ 38 58.10 N 6.55 W
Gruting 38 60.14 N 1.30 W
Gruzinskaja Sovetskaja Socialističeskaja Respublika ☐3 56 42.00 N 44.00 E
Grybów 46 49.38 N 20.56 E
Gryfice 46 53.56 N 15.12 E
Gryfino 46 53.12 N 14.30 E
Grythyttan 44 59.42 N 14.32 E
Gstaad 48 46.28 N 7.17 E
Gua 76 22.12 N 85.23 E
Guabu 66 32.16 N 118.53 E
Guacanayabo, Golfo de c 108 20.28 N 77.30 W
Guacara 108 10.14 N 67.53 W
Guadajira ≃ 50 38.52 N 6.41 W
Guadajoz ≃ 50 37.50 N 4.51 W
Guadalajara, Esp. 50 40.38 N 3.10 W
Guadalajara, Méx. 106 20.40 N 103.20 W
Guadalamar ≃ 50 38.05 N 3.06 W
Guadalaviar ≃ 50 40.21 N 1.08 W
Guadalcanal 50 38.06 N 5.49 W
Guadalcanal ■ 88 9.32 S 160.12 E
Guadalén ≃ 50 38.05 N 3.32 W
Guadalén, Embalse de ⊜[1] 50 38.25 N 3.15 W
Guadalentín ≃ 50 37.59 N 1.04 W
Guadalete ≃ 50 36.35 N 6.13 W
Guadalhorce ≃ 50 36.41 N 4.27 W
Guadalmena ≃ 50 38.19 N 2.56 W
Guadalmez ≃ 50 38.46 N 5.04 W
Guadalope ≃ 50 41.15 N 0.03 W
Guadalquivir ≃ 50 36.47 N 6.22 W
Guadalupe 104 34.58 N 120.34 W
Guadalupe ≃ 104 32.05 N 116.53 W
Guadalupe, Isla ■ 100 29.00 N 118.16 W
Guadalupe, Sierra de ⋆ 50 39.26 N 5.25 W
Guadalupe Peak ▲ 100 31.50 N 104.52 W
Guadalupe Seamount ✦[3] 28 27.50 N 168.45 E
Guadarrama, Puerto de)(50 40.43 N 4.10 W
Guadarrama, Sierra de ⋆ 50 40.55 N 4.00 W
Guadazaón ≃ 50 39.42 N 1.36 W
Guadeloupe ☐2 106 16.15 N 61.35 W
Guadeloupe Passage ɥ 108 16.45 N 61.30 W
Guadiana ≃ 50 37.14 N 7.22 W
Guadiana Menor ≃ 50 37.56 N 3.15 W
Guadiaro ≃ 50 36.17 N 5.17 W
Guadiela ≃ 50 40.22 N 2.49 W
Guadix 50 37.18 N 3.08 W
Guafo, Isla ■ 112 43.36 S 74.43 W
Guaíba 114 30.06 S 51.19 W
Guaimaca 108 14.32 N 86.51 W
Guainía ≃ 110 2.01 N 67.07 W
Guaíra 114 24.04 S 54.15 W
Guairá ☐5 114 25.45 S 56.30 W
Guajaba, Cayo ■ 108 21.50 N 77.30 W
Guajará Mirim 110 10.48 S 65.22 W
Gualala 104 38.45 N 123.31 W
Gualdo Tadino 52 43.14 N 12.47 E
Gualeguay 114 33.09 S 59.20 W
Gualeguay ≃ 114 33.19 S 59.39 W
Gualeguaychú 114 33.01 S 58.31 W
Gualicho, Salina del ⚌ 112 40.24 S 65.15 W
Guam ☐2 28 13.28 N 144.47 E
Guamal 108 9.09 N 74.14 W
Guamini 114 37.02 S 62.25 W
Gua Musang 72 4.53 N 101.58 E
Guanabacoa 108 23.07 N 82.18 W
Guanacaste, Cordillera de ⋆ 108 10.45 N 85.05 W
Guanahacabibes, Golfo de c 108 22.08 N 84.35 W
Guanaja 108 16.27 N 85.54 W
Guanaja, Isla de ■ 108 16.30 N 85.55 W
Guanajay 108 22.55 N 82.42 W
Guanajuato 106 21.01 N 101.15 W
Guanambi 110 14.13 S 42.47 W
Guanare 110 9.03 N 69.45 W
Guancheng 66 30.11 N 121.25 E
Guandacol 114 29.31 S 68.32 W
Guandian 66 32.40 N 118.04 E
Guane 108 22.12 N 84.05 W
Guang'an 62 30.28 N 106.39 E
Guangchang 66 26.50 N 116.14 E
Guangde 66 30.54 N 119.26 E
Guangdong (Kwangtung) ☐4 62 23.00 N 113.00 E
Guangfeng 66 28.25 N 118.11 E
Guanghua 62 32.25 N 111.36 E
Guangji 66 29.52 N 115.34 E
Guangnan 62 24.10 N 105.06 E
Guangshan 66 32.02 N 114.52 E
Guangshui 66 31.40 N 114.00 E
Guangxi Zhuangzu Zizhiqu (Kwangsi Chuang) ☐4 62 24.00 N 109.00 E
Guangyuan 62 32.26 N 105.52 E
Guangze 66 27.32 N 117.20 E
Guangzhou (Canton) 66 23.06 N 113.16 E
Guanhu 66 34.26 N 117.59 E
Guanipa ≃ 108 9.56 N 62.26 W
Guanlin 66 31.32 N 119.42 E
Guanling 70 25.57 N 105.29 E
Guannan (Xin'anzhen) 66 34.07 N 119.23 E
Guano Creek ≃ 104 42.12 N 119.31 W
Guanpata 108 15.01 N 85.02 W
Guanta 108 10.14 N 64.36 W
Guantánamo 108 20.08 N 75.12 W
Guantou 66 26.08 N 119.33 E
Guanxian 62 31.00 N 103.40 E
Guanyun (Dayishan) 66 34.20 N 119.17 E
Guapí 110 2.36 N 77.54 W
Guapiara 114 24.10 S 48.32 W
Guápiles 108 10.13 N 83.46 W
Guaporé 114 28.51 S 51.54 W
Guaporé ≃, Bra. 114 29.10 S 51.54 W
Guaporé (Iténez) ≃, S.A. 110 11.54 S 65.01 W
Guaqui 110 16.35 S 68.51 W
Guara, Sierra de ⋆ 50 42.17 N 0.10 W
Guarabira 110 6.51 S 35.29 W
Guaraci 114 22.57 S 51.40 W
Guaramirim 114 26.27 S 49.00 W
Guaranda 110 1.36 S 79.00 W
Guaraniaçu 114 25.06 S 52.52 W
Guarani das Missões 114 28.08 S 54.34 W
Guarapuava 114 25.23 S 51.27 W
Guaraqueçaba 114 25.17 S 48.21 W
Guaratuba 114 25.54 S 48.34 W
Guarda 50 40.32 N 7.16 W
Guardafui, Cape →Caseyr › 82 11.49 N 51.15 E
Guardavalle 52 38.30 N 16.30 E
Guardia Escolta 114 28.59 S 62.08 W
Guardiagrele 52 42.11 N 14.13 E
Guardiato ≃ 50 38.20 N 5.22 W
Guardo 50 42.47 N 4.50 W
Guareim (Quaraí) ≃ 114 30.12 S 57.36 W
Guareña 50 38.51 N 6.06 W
Guareña ≃ 50 41.29 N 5.23 W
Guarenas 108 10.28 N 66.37 W
Guarico 108 9.32 N 69.48 W
Guárico ☐3 108 9.00 N 66.35 W
Guárico, Embalse del ⊜[1] 108 9.05 N 67.25 W
Guarulhos 114 23.28 S 46.32 W
Guasare ≃ 108 11.03 N 72.02 W
Guasave 106 25.34 N 108.27 W
Guasdualito 110 7.15 N 70.44 W
Guasipati 110 7.28 N 61.54 W
Guastalla 52 44.55 N 10.39 E
Guatemala 106 14.38 N 90.31 W
Guatemala ☐1 106 15.30 N 90.15 W
Guatemala Basin ✦[1] 22 11.00 N 95.00 W
Guatimozín 114 33.27 S 62.27 W
Guatire 108 10.28 N 66.32 W
Guatraché 114 37.40 S 63.32 W
Guaviare ≃ 110 4.03 N 67.44 W
Guaxupé 114 21.18 S 46.42 W
Guayabal 108 20.42 N 77.36 W
Guayacán 114 29.58 S 71.22 W
Guayama 108 17.59 N 66.07 W
Guayana →Ciudad Guayana 110 8.22 N 62.40 W
Guayape ≃ 108 14.26 N 85.58 W
Guayaquil 110 2.10 S 79.50 W
Guayaquil, Golfo de c 110 3.00 S 80.30 W
Guayatayoc, Laguna de ⊜ 114 23.25 S 65.51 W
Guaymas 106 27.56 N 110.54 W
Guayquiraró ≃ 114 30.10 S 58.34 W
Guazhou 66 32.15 N 119.23 E
Gubacha 56 58.52 N 57.36 E
Gubbio 52 43.21 N 12.35 E
Gubin 46 51.56 N 14.45 E
Gubkin 56 51.18 N 37.32 E
Gúdar, Sierra de ⋆ 50 40.27 N 0.42 W
Gudbrandsdalen ∨ 44 61.30 N 10.00 E
Gudenå ≃ 44 56.29 N 10.13 E
Gudermes 56 43.20 N 46.08 E
Gudhjem 44 55.13 N 14.59 E
Gudiyāttam 74 12.57 N 78.52 E
Gudvangen 44 60.52 N 6.50 E
Guebwiller 48 47.55 N 7.12 E
Guelma 80 36.28 N 7.26 E
Guelph 102 43.33 N 80.15 W
Guémené-sur-Scorff 48 48.04 N 3.12 W
Guer 32 47.54 N 2.07 W
Guérande 48 47.20 N 2.26 W
Güere ≃ 108 9.50 N 65.08 W
Guéret 48 46.10 N 1.52 E
Guerla Mandatashan ▲ 76 30.26 N 81.20 E
Guerneville 104 38.30 N 123.00 W
Guernica y Luno 50 43.19 N 2.41 W
Guernsey ☐2 30 49.28 N 2.35 W
Guga 58 52.43 N 137.35 E
Guge ▲ 82 6.10 N 37.26 E
Guguan ■ 68 17.19 N 145.51 E
Guiana Basin ✦[1] 24 11.00 N 52.00 W
Guibes 86 26.41 S 16.42 E
Guichen 48 47.58 N 1.48 W
Guichi 66 30.40 N 117.28 E
Guichón 114 32.21 S 57.12 W
Guide 62 36.03 N 101.28 E
Guide Post 36 55.10 N 1.35 W
Guiding 70 26.34 N 107.14 E
Guidong 66 26.05 N 113.57 E
Guijuelo 50 40.33 N 5.40 W
Guildford 34 51.14 N 0.35 W
Guildhall 102 44.33 N 71.33 W
Guildtown 38 56.28 N 3.24 W
Guilford 102 45.10 N 69.23 W
Guilin (Kweilin) 70 25.17 N 110.17 E
Guillaume-Delisle, Lac ⊜ 98 56.15 N 76.17 W
Guillaumes 48 44.05 N 6.51 E
Guillestre 48 44.40 N 6.39 E
Guilsfield 34 52.42 N 3.09 W
Guilvinec 48 47.47 N 4.17 W
Guimarães 50 41.27 N 8.18 W
Guimaras Island ■ 68 10.35 N 122.37 E
Guimeishan 66 24.44 N 114.52 E
Guinea (Guinée) ☐1 80 11.00 N 10.00 W
Guinea, Gulf of c 80 2.00 N 2.30 E
Guinea Basin ✦[1] 20 0.00 5.00 W
Guinea-Bissau (Guiné-Bissau) ☐1 80 12.00 N 15.00 W
Guinea Rise ✦[3] 20 8.00 S 0.00
Güines, Cuba 108 22.50 N 82.02 W
Guînes, Fr. 48 50.52 N 1.52 E
Guingamp 48 48.33 N 3.11 W
Güinope 108 13.51 N 86.55 W
Guiping 70 23.20 N 110.09 E
Guipúzcoa ☐4 50 43.10 N 2.10 W
Güira de Melena 108 22.48 N 82.30 W
Guiratinga 110 16.21 S 53.45 W
Güiria 110 10.34 N 62.18 W
Guisachan Forest ✦[3] 38 57.17 N 4.55 W
Guisborough 36 54.32 N 1.04 W
Guise 48 49.54 N 3.38 E
Guiseley 36 53.53 N 1.42 W
Guitiriz 50 43.11 N 7.54 W
Guîtres 48 45.03 N 0.11 W
Guiuan 68 11.02 N 125.43 E
Guixi 66 28.16 N 117.10 E
Guixian 70 23.06 N 109.39 E
Guiyang, Zhg. 66 25.46 N 112.43 E
Guiyang (Kweiyang), Zhg. 70 26.35 N 106.43 E
Guizhou (Kweichow) ☐4 62 27.00 N 107.00 E
Gujarat ☐3 76 22.00 N 72.00 E
Gujrānwāla 76 32.26 N 74.33 E
Gujrāt 76 32.34 N 74.05 E
Gulargambone 94 31.20 S 148.28 E
Gulbarga 74 17.20 N 76.50 E
Gulbene 60 57.11 N 26.45 E
Gulf of Alaska Seamount Province ✦[3] 22 56.00 N 147.00 W
Gulfport 100 30.22 N 89.05 W
Gulgong 94 32.22 S 149.32 E
Gulian 62 52.55 N 122.19 E
Gulistan, Pāk. 76 30.36 N 66.35 E
Gulistan, S.S.S.R. 56 40.30 N 68.46 E
Guljanci 54 43.38 N 24.42 E
Gulland Rock ■■[1] 34 50.34 N 4.59 W
Gullane 38 56.02 N 2.50 W
Gullfoss ⌊ 42a 64.24 N 20.08 W
Gullholmen 44 58.11 N 11.24 E
Gullion, Slieve ▲[2] 40 54.08 N 6.27 W
Gull Lake 98 50.08 N 108.27 W
Gullspång 44 58.59 N 14.06 E
Gulsvik 44 60.23 N 9.35 E
Gulu 82 2.47 N 32.18 E
Gumal (Gowmal) ≃ 76 31.56 N 70.22 E
Gumla 76 23.03 N 84.33 E
Gumma ☐5 64 36.30 N 139.00 E
Gummersbach 46 51.02 N 7.34 E
Gümüşhane 78 40.27 N 39.29 E
Guna 76 24.39 N 77.19 E
Gunbar 94 34.01 S 145.25 E
Gundagai 94 35.04 S 148.07 E
Gungu 84 5.44 S 19.19 E
Gunisao ≃ 98 53.54 N 97.58 W
Gunnar 98 59.23 N 108.53 W
Gunnarn 44 65.00 N 17.40 E
Gunnbjørn Fjeld ▲ 22 68.55 N 29.53 W
Gunnebo 44 57.43 N 16.32 E
Gunnedah 94 30.59 S 150.15 E
Gunnislake 34 50.31 N 4.12 W
Guntramsdorf 46 48.03 N 16.19 E
Guntūr 74 16.18 N 80.27 E
Gunungsitoli 70 1.17 N 97.37 E
Gunyidi 90 30.08 S 116.04 E
Günzburg 46 48.27 N 10.16 E
Gunzenhausen 46 49.07 N 10.45 E
Guoyang 66 33.32 N 116.12 E
Gupei 66 34.09 N 117.54 E
Gurahonț 54 46.16 N 22.21 E
Gura Humorului 54 47.33 N 25.54 E
Gurais 76 34.38 N 74.50 E
Gurara ≃ 80 8.12 N 6.41 E
Gurdāspur 76 32.02 N 75.31 E
Gurgaon 76 28.28 N 77.02 E
Gurghiului, Munții ⋆ 54 46.41 N 25.12 E
Gurguéia ≃ 110 6.50 S 43.24 W
Guri, Embalse ⊜[1] 110 7.30 N 62.50 W
Gurjev 56 47.07 N 51.56 E
Gurjevsk, S.S.S.R. 56 54.17 N 85.56 E
Gurjevsk, S.S.S.R. 60 54.47 N 20.38 E
Gurk ≃ 46 46.36 N 14.31 E
Gurkha 76 28.00 N 84.37 E
Gurla Mandhata →Guerla Mandatashan ▲ 76 30.26 N 81.20 E
Gurskøy ■ 44 62.15 N 5.41 E
Gurupá 110 1.25 S 51.39 W
Gurupi 110 11.43 S 49.04 W
Gurupi ≃ 110 1.13 S 46.06 W
Gusau 80 12.12 N 6.40 E
Gus'-Chrustal'nyj 60 55.37 N 40.40 E
Gusev 60 54.36 N 22.12 E
Gusevskij 60 55.40 N 40.34 E
Gushi 66 32.12 N 115.41 E
Gushikawa 65b 26.21 N 127.52 E
Gusi 72 6.07 N 117.08 E
Gusinoozersk 58 51.17 N 106.30 E
Guspini 52 39.32 N 8.37 E
Güssing 46 47.04 N 16.20 E

Symbols in the Index entries are identified on page 122

Name	Page	Lat.°′	Long.°′
Hertzogville	86	28.08 S	25.33 E
Hervás	50	40.16 N	5.51 W
Hervel d'Oeste	114	27.13 S	51.34 W
Hervey Bay c	94	25.00 S	153.00 E
Herzberg	46	51.41 N	13.14 E
Herzberg [am Harz]	46	51.39 N	10.20 E
Herzogenburg	46	48.17 N	15.42 E
Hesdin	48	50.22 N	2.02 E
Hess ≃	98	63.34 N	133.57 W
Hesselø I	44	56.12 N	11.43 E
Hessen □3	46	50.30 N	9.15 E
Hessisch Lichtenau	46	51.12 N	9.43 E
Hessle	36	53.44 N	0.26 W
Hesso	94	32.08 S	137.27 E
Hess Tablemount ✦3	28	17.50 N	174.15 W
Heswall	36	53.20 N	3.06 W
Hetch Hetchy Aqueduct ☲1	104	37.29 N	122.19 W
Hethersett	34	52.36 N	1.11 E
Hetian	76	37.08 N	79.54 E
Hetton-le-Hole	36	54.50 N	1.27 W
Hettstedt	46	51.38 N	11.30 E
Heuvelton	102	44.37 N	75.24 W
Heves	46	47.36 N	20.17 E
Heves □6	46	47.50 N	20.15 E
Hexham	36	54.58 N	2.06 W
Hexian, Zhg.	62	24.15 N	111.43 E
Hexian, Zhg.	66	31.43 N	118.22 E
Hexton	96	38.37 S	177.58 E
Heyburn	104	42.33 N	113.45 W
Heyrieux	48	45.38 N	5.03 E
Heysham	36	54.02 N	2.54 W
Heyuan	66	23.44 N	114.41 E
Heywood, Austl.	94	38.08 S	141.38 E
Heywood, Eng., U.K.	36	53.36 N	2.13 W
Hialeah	108	25.51 N	80.16 W
Hibaldstow	36	53.31 N	0.32 W
Hibbing	100	47.25 N	92.56 W
Hibbs, Point ≻	94	42.38 S	145.15 E
Hibernia Reef ✦2	88	12.00 S	123.23 E
Hicks, Point ≻	94	37.48 S	149.17 E
Hicks Bay	96	37.36 S	178.18 E
Hicksville	102	41.17 N	84.45 W
Hidaka-sammyaku ⋏	64a	42.35 N	142.45 E
Hidalgo	106	24.15 N	99.26 W
Hidalgo del Parral	106	26.56 N	105.40 W
Hida-sammyaku ⋏	64	36.25 N	137.40 E
Hieflau	46	47.36 N	14.44 E
Hierro I	80	27.45 N	18.00 W
Higashihiroshima	64	34.26 N	132.42 E
Higashiichiki	64	31.40 N	130.20 E
Higashine	64	38.26 N	140.24 E
Higashiōsaka	64	34.39 N	135.35 E
Higgins Lake ◎	102	44.30 N	84.45 W
Higginsville	90	31.45 S	121.43 E
Higham Ferrers	34	52.18 N	0.36 W
Higham Upshire	34	51.26 N	0.28 E
High Bentham	36	54.08 N	2.30 W
Highbridge	34	51.13 N	2.49 W
Highbury	92	16.25 S	143.09 E
Higher Walton	36	53.44 N	2.39 W
High Force ⱡ	36	54.38 N	2.13 W
High Hesket	36	54.48 N	2.48 W
High Island I	102	45.42 N	85.40 W
Highland	104	34.07 N	117.12 W
Highland □4	38	57.40 N	5.00 W
Highland Peak ▲	104	38.33 N	119.45 W
Highlands	102	40.24 N	73.59 W
Highley	34	52.27 N	2.23 W
High Peak ✦1	36	53.22 N	1.50 W
High Point	100	35.57 N	80.00 W
High Point ▲	102	41.19 N	74.40 W
High River	98	50.35 N	113.52 W
High Rock ▲	102	39.33 N	79.06 W
High Seat ▲	36	54.24 N	2.18 W
High Street ▲	36	54.29 N	2.52 W
Hightown	36	53.31 N	3.03 W
Hightstown	102	40.16 N	74.31 W
High Willhays ▲	34	50.41 N	3.59 W
Highworth	34	51.38 N	1.43 W
High Wycombe	34	51.38 N	0.46 W
Higüero, Punta ≻	108	18.22 N	67.16 W
Higuerote	108	10.29 N	66.06 W
Hiiumaa I	60	58.52 N	22.40 E
Híjar	50	41.10 N	0.27 W
Hikari	64	33.58 N	131.56 E
Hikone	64	35.15 N	136.15 E
Hikueru I1	28	17.36 S	142.37 W
Hikurangi	96	35.36 S	174.18 E
Hikurangi ▲	96	37.55 S	178.04 E
Hikutaia	96	37.17 S	175.39 E
Hildburghausen	46	50.25 N	10.44 E
Hilden	46	51.10 N	6.56 E
Hildesheim	46	52.09 N	9.57 E
Hillaby, Mount ▲	108	13.12 N	59.35 W
Hillcrest Center	104	35.23 N	118.57 W
Hillerød	44	55.56 N	12.19 E
Hillingdon ✦8	34	51.32 N	0.27 W
Hill Island Lake ◎	98	60.29 N	109.50 W
Hillman	102	45.03 N	83.54 W
Hill of Fearn	38	57.45 N	3.56 W
Hillsboro, N.H., U.S.	102	43.06 N	71.53 W
Hillsboro, Oh., U.S.	102	39.12 N	83.36 W
Hillsborough	40	54.28 N	6.05 W
Hillsborough, Cape ≻	94	20.54 S	149.03 E
Hillsdale	102	41.55 N	84.37 W
Hillside, Austl.	90	21.44 S	119.23 E
Hillside, Scot., U.K.	38	56.44 N	2.29 W
Hillston	94	33.29 S	145.32 E
Hillswick	38a	60.28 N	1.30 W
Hilltown	40	54.12 N	6.09 W
Hilo	105a	19.43 N	155.05 W
Hilo Bay c	105a	19.44 N	155.05 W
Hilpsford Point ≻	36	54.03 N	3.12 W
Hiltaba, Mount ▲	90	32.09 S	135.03 E
Hilton	102	43.17 N	77.47 W
Hilversum	46	52.14 N	5.10 E
Himachal Pradesh □8	76	32.00 N	77.00 E
Himalayas ⋏	76	28.00 N	84.00 E
Himanka	44	64.04 N	23.39 E
Himarë	54	40.07 N	19.44 E
Himatnagar	76	23.36 N	72.57 E
Himeji	64	34.49 N	134.42 E
Himi	64	36.51 N	136.59 E
Himmerland ✦1	44	56.50 N	9.45 E
Hims (Homs)	78	34.44 N	36.43 E
Hinche	108	19.09 N	72.01 W
Hinchinbrook Island I	94	18.23 S	146.17 E
Hinckley	34	52.33 N	1.21 W
Hindaun	76	26.43 N	77.01 E
Hindenburg →Zabrze	46	50.18 N	18.46 E
Hindhead	34	51.07 N	0.44 W
Hindley	36	53.32 N	2.35 W
Hindmarsh, Lake ◎	94	36.03 S	141.55 E
Hindon	34	51.06 N	2.08 W
Hinds	96	44.00 S	171.34 E
Hindu Kush ⋏	76	36.00 N	71.30 E
Hines	104	43.33 N	119.04 W
Hingham, Eng., U.K.	34	52.35 N	0.59 E
Hingham, Ma., U.S.	102	42.14 N	70.53 W
Hingol ≃	78	25.23 N	65.28 E
Hinish Bay c	38	56.28 N	6.50 W
Hinkston Creek ≃	102	38.18 N	84.14 W
Hinnerjoki	44	61.00 N	22.00 E
Hinnøya I	42	68.30 N	16.00 E
Hino ≃	64	35.27 N	133.23 E
Hinojosa del Duque	50	38.30 N	5.09 W
Hinokage	64	32.39 N	131.24 E
Hinsdale	102	42.47 N	72.29 W
Hinterrhein ≃	48	46.49 N	9.25 E
Hinton	98	53.25 N	117.34 W
Hipólito Yrigoyen	114	32.55 S	66.20 W
Hirado	64	33.22 N	129.33 E
Hirado-shima I	64	33.20 N	129.30 E
Hiraizumi	64	38.59 N	141.07 E
Hīrākud	76	21.31 N	83.57 E
Hiram	102	43.52 N	70.48 W
Hīrāpur	76	24.22 N	79.13 E
Hirara	62	24.48 N	125.17 E
Hirata	64	35.26 N	132.49 E
Hiratsuka	64	35.19 N	139.21 E
Hîrlău	54	47.25 N	26.54 E
Hiroo	64a	42.17 N	143.19 E
Hirosaki	64	40.35 N	140.28 E
Hiroshima	64	34.24 N	132.27 E
Hirson	48	49.55 N	4.05 E
Hîrşova	54	44.41 N	27.57 E
Hirtshals	44	57.35 N	9.58 E
Hirwaun	34	51.45 N	3.30 W
Hisār	76	29.10 N	75.43 E
Hispaniola I	108	19.00 N	71.00 W
Histon	34	52.15 N	0.06 E
Hisua	76	24.50 N	85.25 E
Hita	64	33.19 N	130.56 E
Hitachi	64	36.36 N	140.39 E
Hitachi-ōta	64	36.32 N	140.31 E
Hitchin	34	51.57 N	0.17 W
Hitchins	102	38.16 N	82.55 W
Hitoyoshi	64	32.13 N	130.45 E
Hitra I	44	63.33 N	8.45 E
Hittarp	44	56.06 N	12.38 E
Hiuchiga-dake ▲	64	36.57 N	139.17 E
Hiwasa	64	33.44 N	134.32 E
Hjälmaren ◎	44	59.15 N	15.45 E
Hjelmelandsvågen	44	59.14 N	6.11 E
Hjeltefjorden c2	44	60.40 N	4.55 E
Hjo	44	58.18 N	14.17 E
Hjørring	44	57.28 N	9.59 E
Hjørundfjorden c2	44	62.21 N	6.23 E
Hkakabo Razi ▲	62	28.20 N	97.32 E
Hkok (Kok) ≃	70	20.14 N	100.09 E
Hlatikulu	86	27.00 S	31.25 E
Hlinsko	46	49.45 N	15.55 E
Hlobane	86	27.42 S	31.00 E
Hlohovec	46	48.25 N	17.47 E
Hlučín	46	49.54 N	18.12 E
Hluhluwe	86	28.01 S	32.15 E
Ho	80	6.35 N	0.30 E
Hoa-binh	70	20.50 N	105.20 E
Hoare Bay c	98	65.18 N	62.30 W
Hobart	94	42.53 S	147.19 E
Hobbs	100	32.42 N	103.08 W
Hobhole Drain ☲	36	52.59 N	0.02 E
Hoboken	46	51.10 N	4.21 E
Hobro	44	56.38 N	9.48 E
Hobyo	82	5.21 N	48.32 E
Hochalmspitze ▲	46	47.01 N	13.19 E
Hochgolling ▲	46	47.16 N	13.45 E
Hochkönig ▲	46	47.25 N	13.04 E
Hochschwab ▲	46	47.37 N	15.09 E
Höchstadt an der Aisch	46	49.42 N	10.44 E
Hockenheim	46	49.19 N	8.33 E
Hocking ≃	102	39.12 N	81.45 W
Hockley	34	51.37 N	0.40 E
Hodal	76	27.54 N	77.22 E
Hodder ≃	36	53.50 N	2.25 W
Hoddesdon	34	51.46 N	0.01 W
Hodeida →Al-Hudaydah	74	14.48 N	42.57 E
Hodgson ≃	92	14.48 S	134.35 E
Hódmezővásárhely	46	46.25 N	20.20 E
Hodna, Chott el ◎	80	35.25 N	4.45 E
Hodnet	34	52.51 N	2.35 W
Hodonín	46	48.51 N	17.08 E
Hoek van Holland	46	51.59 N	4.09 E
Hof, B.R.D.	46	50.18 N	11.55 E
Hof, Ísland	42a	64.34 N	14.39 W
Höfðakaupstaður	42a	65.50 N	20.19 W
Hofei →Hefei	66	31.51 N	117.17 E
Hofgeismar	46	51.30 N	9.22 E
Hofheim in Unterfranken	46	50.08 N	10.31 E
Hofmeyr	86	31.39 S	25.50 E
Höfn	42a	64.17 N	15.10 W
Hofors	44	60.33 N	16.17 E
Hofsjökull ⊠	42a	64.48 N	18.50 W
Hōfu	64	34.03 N	131.34 E
Hofuf →Al-Hufūf	78	25.22 N	49.34 E
Hog, Tanjong ≻	72	5.18 N	119.16 E
Höganäs	44	56.12 N	12.33 E
Hogan Lake ◎	102	45.52 N	78.30 W
Hogarth, Mount ▲2	94	21.48 S	136.58 E
Hoggar →Ahaggar ⋏	80	23.00 N	6.30 E
Hog Island I	102	45.48 N	85.22 W
Hogs Back ▲4	34	51.13 N	0.40 W
Högsby	44	57.10 N	16.02 E
Hohe Acht ▲	46	50.23 N	7.00 E
Hohenau	114	27.05 S	55.45 W
Hohenau an der March	46	48.36 N	16.55 E
Hohenlimburg	46	51.21 N	7.35 E
Hohen Neuendorf	46	52.40 N	13.16 E
Hohenthurn	46	46.33 N	13.40 E
Hoher Dachstein ▲	46	47.28 N	13.35 E
Hohe Tauern ⋏	46	47.10 N	12.30 E
Hohhot	62	40.51 N	111.40 E
Hohoe	80	7.09 N	0.28 W
Hōhoku	64	34.17 N	130.57 E
Hohultslätt	44	56.58 N	15.39 E
Hoh Xil Shan ⋏	76	35.20 N	90.00 E
Hoi-an	70	15.52 N	108.19 E
Hojai	76	26.00 N	92.51 E
Højer	44	54.58 N	8.43 E
Hōjō	64	33.58 N	132.46 E
Hokitika	96	42.43 S	170.58 E
Hokkaidō □5	64a	44.00 N	143.00 E
Hokkaidō I	64a	44.00 N	143.00 E
Hokksund	44	59.47 N	9.59 E
Holbæk	44	55.43 N	11.43 E
Holbeach	34	52.49 N	0.01 E
Holbeach Marsh ⊞	34	52.52 N	0.05 E
Holbrook, Austl.	94	35.44 S	147.19 E
Holbrook, Az., U.S.	104	34.54 N	110.09 W
Holden	102	37.49 N	82.03 W
Holderness ≻1	36	53.47 N	0.10 W
Hole in the Mountain Peak ▲	104	40.55 N	115.05 W
Holešov	46	49.20 N	17.35 E
Holgate	102	41.14 N	84.07 W
Holguín	108	20.53 N	76.15 W
Holič	46	48.49 N	17.10 E
Holice	46	50.04 N	15.59 E
Höljes	44	60.54 N	12.36 E
Hollabrunn	46	48.34 N	16.05 E
Holland	102	42.47 N	86.06 W
Holland →Netherlands □1	30	52.15 N	5.30 E
Holland, Mount ▲	90	32.12 S	119.44 E
Holland Fen ⊞	34	53.00 N	0.10 W
Hollandia →Jayapura	92	2.32 S	140.42 E
Hollandsbird Island I	86	24.45 S	14.34 E
Hollandstoun	38	59.21 N	2.16 W
Holleton	90	31.57 S	119.02 E
Holley	102	43.13 N	78.01 W
Hollidaysburg	102	40.25 N	78.23 W
Hollister	104	36.51 N	121.24 W
Hollister, Mount ▲2	90	22.08 S	114.01 E
Hollywood, Ire.	40	53.06 N	6.35 W
Hollywood, Fl., U.S.	100	26.00 N	80.08 W
Hólmavík	42a	65.43 N	21.43 W
Holme ≃	36	53.41 N	1.43 W
Holmen	44	60.40 N	10.22 E
Holmenkollen	44	59.58 N	10.40 E
Holme-on-Spaulding-Moor	36	53.50 N	0.46 W
Holmes Chapel	36	53.12 N	2.22 W
Holmes Reefs ✦2	92	16.27 S	148.00 E
Holmestrand	44	59.29 N	10.18 E
Holmfirth	36	53.35 N	1.46 W
Holmön I	44	63.47 N	20.53 E
Holmsbu	44	59.33 N	10.27 E
Holmsjön ◎, Sve.	44	62.41 N	16.33 E
Holmsjön ◎, Sve.	44	62.25 N	15.20 E
Holmsund	44	63.42 N	20.21 E
Holod	54	46.47 N	22.08 E
Holroyd ≃	92	14.10 S	141.36 E
Holstebro	44	56.21 N	8.38 E
Holsteinsborg	98	66.55 N	53.40 W
Holsworthy	34	50.49 N	4.21 W
Holt, Eng., U.K.	34	52.55 N	1.05 E
Holt, Wales, U.K.	34	53.05 N	2.53 W
Holt, Mi., U.S.	102	42.38 N	84.30 W
Holtville	104	32.48 N	115.22 W
Holycross	40	52.38 N	7.52 W
Holyhead	36	53.19 N	4.38 W
Holyhead Bay c	36	53.23 N	4.37 W
Holy Island I, Eng., U.K.	36	55.41 N	1.48 W
Holy Island I, Scot., U.K.	38	55.32 N	5.04 W
Holy Island I, Wales, U.K.	36	53.18 N	4.37 W
Holyoke	102	42.12 N	72.37 W
Holýšov	46	49.36 N	13.05 E
Holywell	36	53.17 N	3.13 W
Holywood	40	54.38 N	5.50 W
Holzkirchen	46	47.52 N	11.42 E
Holzminden	46	51.50 N	9.27 E
Homalin	70	24.52 N	94.55 E
Homberg	46	51.02 N	9.24 E
Hombori Tondo ▲	80	15.16 N	1.40 W
Hombre Muerto, Salar del ⩶	114	25.23 S	67.06 W
Homburg	46	49.19 N	7.20 E
Home Bay c	98	68.45 N	67.10 W
Home Hill	94	19.40 S	147.25 E
Homer, Ak., U.S.	98	59.39 N	151.33 W
Homer, Mi., U.S.	102	42.08 N	84.48 W
Homer, N.Y., U.S.	102	42.38 N	76.10 W
Homer City	102	40.32 N	79.09 W
Homer Wash ∨	104	34.20 N	115.02 W
Home Seamount ✦3	28	12.55 S	175.37 W
Homestead, Austl.	94	20.22 S	145.39 E
Homestead, Fl., U.S.	108	25.28 N	80.28 W
Hommersåk	44	58.58 N	5.42 E
Hommura	64	34.22 N	139.15 E
Homs →Al-Khums	82	32.39 N	14.16 E
Homs →Hims	78	34.44 N	36.43 E
Honan →Henan □4	62	34.00 N	114.00 E
Honbetsu	64a	43.07 N	143.37 E
Honda	110	5.12 N	74.45 W
Honda, Bahía c	108	12.21 N	71.47 W
Honddu ≃, Wales, U.K.	34	51.57 N	3.23 W
Honddu ≃, Wales, U.K.	34	51.54 N	2.58 W
Hondeklipbaai	86	30.20 S	17.18 E
Hondo	64	32.27 N	130.12 E
Hondsrug ⋏2	46	52.55 N	6.50 E
Honduras □1	106	15.00 N	86.30 W
Honduras, Cabo de ≻	108	16.01 N	86.02 W
Honduras, Gulf of c	106	16.10 N	87.50 W
Hønefoss	44	60.10 N	10.18 E
Honesdale	102	41.34 N	75.15 W
Honey Lake ◎	104	40.16 N	120.19 W
Honfleur	48	49.25 N	0.14 E
Høng	44	55.31 N	11.18 E
Hong'an	66	31.18 N	114.37 E
Hon-gay	70	20.57 N	107.05 E
Honghe	70	23.23 N	102.25 E
Honghu	66	29.48 N	113.27 E
Hongjiang	62	27.07 N	109.56 E
Hong Kong □2	62	22.15 N	114.10 E
Hong Kong I	66	22.15 N	114.11 E
Honglai	66	25.08 N	118.32 E
Hongliuyuan	62	41.04 N	95.26 E
Hongqiao	66	28.14 N	121.01 E
Hongshui ≃	62	23.45 N	109.30 E
Hongtong	62	36.19 N	111.39 E
Honguedo, Détroit d' ꓴ	98	49.15 N	64.00 W
Hongxingqiao	66	30.55 N	119.52 E
Hongze	66	33.19 N	118.53 E
Hongze Hu ◎	66	33.16 N	118.34 E
Honiara	88	9.26 S	159.57 E
Honiton	34	50.48 N	3.13 W
Honjō	64	39.23 N	140.03 E
Honkamäki ▲2	44	62.58 N	27.05 E
Honningsvåg	42	70.59 N	25.59 E
Hönö	44	57.42 N	11.39 E
Honokaa	105a	20.04 N	155.28 W
Honolulu	105a	21.18 N	157.51 W
Honomu	105a	19.52 N	155.07 W
Honshū I	64	36.00 N	138.00 E
Honuapo Bay c	105a	19.05 N	155.33 W
Hood ≃	98	67.26 N	108.53 W
Hood, Mount ▲	100	45.23 N	121.41 W
Hood Point ≻	90	34.23 S	119.34 E
Hoods Range ⋏	94	28.35 S	144.30 E
Hoogeveen	46	52.43 N	6.29 E
Hoogezand	46	53.09 N	6.45 E
Hook	34	51.17 N	0.58 W
Hooker Creek	90	18.20 S	130.40 E
Hook Head ≻	40	52.07 N	6.55 W
Hookina	94	31.45 S	138.20 E
Hook Island I	94	20.08 S	148.55 E
Hook Norton	34	51.59 N	1.29 W
Hook Point ≻	94	25.48 S	153.05 E
Hoolehua	105a	21.10 N	157.04 W
Hoonah	98	58.07 N	135.26 W
Hoopa	104	41.03 N	123.40 W
Hoopstad	86	27.54 S	25.58 E
Höör	44	55.56 N	13.32 E
Hoorn	46	52.38 N	5.04 E
Hoosick Falls	102	42.54 N	73.21 W
Hoover Dam ✦6	104	36.00 N	114.27 W
Hooversville	102	40.08 N	78.54 W
Hopatcong	102	40.55 N	74.39 W
Hope, B.C., Can.	98	49.23 N	121.26 W
Hope, Ar., U.S.	100	33.40 N	93.35 W
Hope, Ben ▲	38	58.24 N	4.37 W
Hope, Loch ◎	38	58.27 N	4.39 W
Hopedale	98	55.28 N	60.13 W
Hopefield	86	33.04 S	18.22 E
Hopeh →Hebei □4	62	38.00 N	116.00 E
Hopelchén	106	19.46 N	89.51 W
Hopeman	38	57.42 N	3.25 W
Hopes Advance, Cap ≻	98	61.04 N	69.34 W
Hopetoun	94	35.44 S	142.22 E
Hopetown	86	29.34 S	24.03 E
Hope Valley	102	41.30 N	71.43 W
Hopewell Islands II	98	58.25 N	78.00 W
Hopkins ≃	94	38.24 S	142.31 E
Hopkins, Lake ◎	90	24.15 S	128.50 E
Hopkinsville	100	36.51 N	87.29 W
Hopland	104	38.58 N	123.06 W
Hopwood, Mount ▲	94	21.49 S	144.26 E
Hoquiam	100	46.58 N	123.53 W
Horažďovice	46	49.20 N	13.43 E
Horb	46	48.26 N	8.41 E
Hörby	44	55.51 N	13.39 E
Hordaland □6	44	60.15 N	6.30 E
Horden	36	54.46 N	1.18 W
Horezu	54	45.08 N	23.59 E
Horgen	48	47.15 N	8.36 E
Hořice	46	50.22 N	15.38 E
Horizon Tablemount ✦3	28	19.40 N	168.30 W
Horizontina	114	27.37 S	54.19 W
Horley	34	51.11 N	0.11 W
Hormoz, Jazīreh-ye I	78	27.04 N	56.28 E
Hormuz, Strait of ꓴ	78	26.34 N	56.15 E
Horn	46	48.40 N	15.40 E
Horn ≻	42a	66.28 N	22.28 W
Horn ≃	98	61.30 N	118.01 W
Horn, Ben ▲2	38	58.01 N	4.02 W
Horn, Cape →Hornos, Cabo de ≻	112	55.59 S	67.16 W
Hornaday ≃	98	69.22 N	123.50 W
Hornafjörður c	42a	64.17 N	15.16 W
Hornavan ◎	42	66.10 N	17.30 E
Hornbrook	104	41.55 N	122.33 W
Hornby	96	43.33 S	172.32 E
Hornby Bay c	98	66.35 N	117.50 W
Horncastle	36	53.13 N	0.07 W
Horndal	44	60.18 N	16.25 E
Horndean	34	50.55 N	1.00 W
Horne, Îles de II	28	14.16 S	178.05 W
Hörnefors	44	63.38 N	19.54 E
Hornell	102	42.19 N	77.39 W
Hornepayne	98	49.13 N	84.47 W
Horn Head ≻	40	55.14 N	7.59 W
Hornindal	44	61.58 N	6.31 E
Hornindalsvatnet ◎	44	61.56 N	6.22 E
Horní Počernice	46	50.06 N	14.38 E
Horn Island I	92	10.37 S	142.17 E
Horní Slavkov	46	50.07 N	12.46 E
Hornos, Cabo de (Cape Horn) ≻	112	55.59 S	67.16 W
Horn Plateau ⋏1	98	62.15 N	119.15 W
Hornsea	36	53.55 N	0.10 W
Hornslet	44	56.19 N	10.20 E
Horoshiri-dake ▲	64a	42.43 N	142.41 E
Horotiu	96	37.43 S	175.12 E
Hořovice	46	49.50 N	13.54 E
Horqin Youyi Qianqi	62	46.05 N	122.05 E
Horqueta	114	23.24 S	56.53 W
Horrabridge	34	50.31 N	4.05 W
Horrelville	96	43.20 S	172.20 E
Horseback Knob ▲2	102	39.14 N	83.06 W
Horseheads	102	42.10 N	76.49 W
Horse Islands II	98	50.13 N	55.45 W
Horsens	44	55.52 N	9.52 E
Horse Shoe Reef ✦2	108	18.40 N	64.12 W
Horsford	34	52.41 N	1.15 E
Horsforth	36	53.51 N	1.39 W
Horsham	94	36.43 S	142.13 E
Hørsholm	44	55.53 N	12.30 E
Horšovský Týn	46	49.32 N	12.56 E
Horsted Keynes	34	51.02 N	0.01 W
Horten	44	59.25 N	10.30 E
Hortobágy □9	46	47.35 N	21.00 E
Horton ≃	98	70.00 N	126.53 W
Horton in Ribblesdale	36	54.09 N	2.17 W
Horton Lake ◎	98	67.29 N	122.31 W
Horwich	36	53.37 N	2.33 W
Hosaina	82	7.38 N	37.52 E
Hösbach	46	50.00 N	9.12 E
Hoséré Vokré ▲	80	8.20 N	13.15 E
Hoshangābād	76	22.45 N	77.43 E
Hoshiārpur	76	31.32 N	75.54 E
Hospet	74	15.16 N	76.24 E
Hospital	40	52.29 N	8.25 W
Hospital de Orbigo	50	42.28 N	5.53 W
Hospitalet	50	41.22 N	2.08 E
Hossegor	48	43.40 N	1.27 W
Hoste, Isla I	112	55.15 S	69.00 W
Hotagen	44	63.59 N	14.15 E
Hotagen ◎	44	63.53 N	14.29 E
Hotagsfjällen ⋏	44	64.20 N	14.30 E
Hotaka-dake ▲	64	36.17 N	137.39 E
Hotan	62	37.08 N	79.54 E
Hotan ≃	62	40.30 N	80.45 E
Hotarele	54	44.10 N	26.22 E
Hotazel	86	27.15 S	23.00 E
Hot Creek Range ⋏	104	38.30 N	116.25 W
Hoting	44	64.07 N	16.10 E
Hot Springs, S.D., U.S.	100	43.25 N	103.28 W
Hot Springs, Va., U.S.	102	37.59 N	79.49 W
Hot Springs National Park	100	34.30 N	93.04 W
Hot Springs Peak ▲, Ca., U.S.	104	40.22 N	120.07 W
Hot Springs Peak ▲, Nv., U.S.	104	41.22 N	117.26 W
Hottah Lake ◎	98	65.04 N	118.29 W
Hotte, Massif de la ⋏	108	18.25 N	73.55 W
Houdan	48	48.47 N	1.36 E
Houeillès	48	44.12 N	0.02 E
Houghton	102	47.06 N	88.34 W
Houghton Lake	102	44.18 N	84.45 W
Houghton Lake ◎	102	44.20 N	84.45 W
Houghton-le-Spring	36	54.51 N	1.28 W
Houghton Regis	34	51.55 N	0.31 W
Houjie	66	22.58 N	113.39 E
Houlton	102	46.07 N	67.50 W
Houma, La., U.S.	100	29.35 N	90.43 W
Houma, Zhg.	62	35.36 N	111.21 E
Hounslow ✦8	34	51.29 N	0.22 W
Hourn, Loch c	38	57.07 N	5.35 W
Housatonic	102	42.15 N	73.22 W
Houston	100	29.45 N	95.21 W
Hout ≃	86	23.04 S	29.36 E
Houtkraal	86	30.23 S	24.05 E
Houtman Abrolhos II	90	28.43 S	113.48 E
Houtskär I	44	60.12 N	21.22 E
Houtzdale	102	40.49 N	78.21 W
Hova	44	58.52 N	14.13 E
Hove	34	50.49 N	0.10 W
Hovmantorp	44	56.47 N	15.08 E
Howard, Austl.	94	25.19 S	152.34 E
Howard, Pa., U.S.	102	40.57 N	77.39 W
Howard City	102	43.23 N	85.28 W
Howardian Hills ⋏2	36	54.07 N	1.00 W
Howard Island I	92	12.10 S	135.24 E
Howard Prairie Lake ◎1	104	42.15 N	122.20 W
Howden	36	53.45 N	0.52 W
Howe, Cape ≻	94	37.31 S	149.59 E
Howe Island I	102	44.17 N	76.15 W
Howell	102	42.36 N	83.55 W
Howick	86	29.28 S	30.14 E
Howitt, Mount ▲	94	37.10 S	146.40 E
Howland	102	45.14 N	68.39 W
Howland Island I	28	0.48 N	176.38 W
Howmore	38	57.18 N	7.23 W
Howrah	76	22.35 N	88.20 E
Howth	40	53.23 N	6.04 W
Howth Head ≻	40	53.22 N	6.03 W
Höxter	46	51.46 N	9.23 E
Hoy I	38	58.51 N	3.18 W
Høyanger	44	61.13 N	6.05 E
Hoyerswerda	46	51.26 N	14.14 E
Hoylake	36	53.23 N	3.11 W
Hoyos	50	40.10 N	6.43 W
Höytiäinen ◎	44	62.48 N	29.39 E
Hradec Králové	46	50.12 N	15.50 E
Hrádek nad Nisou	46	50.51 N	14.51 E
Hranice	46	49.33 N	17.44 E
Hriňová	46	48.36 N	19.31 E
Hron ≃	46	47.49 N	18.45 E
Hronov	46	50.29 N	16.12 E
Hrubieszów	46	50.49 N	23.55 E
Hrubý Jeseník ⋏	46	50.00 N	17.20 E
Hrvatska (Croatia) □3	52	45.10 N	15.30 E
Hsiamen →Xiamen	66	24.28 N	118.07 E
Hsihu	66	23.58 N	120.28 E
Hsilo	66	23.48 N	120.27 E
Hsinchu	66	24.48 N	120.58 E
Hsinchuang	66	25.02 N	121.27 E
Hsinghua →Xinghua	66	32.57 N	119.50 E
Hsinhua	66	23.02 N	120.18 E
Hsintien	66	24.57 N	121.32 E
Hsipaw	70	22.37 N	97.18 E
Hsüehchia	66	23.14 N	120.10 E
Hua'an	66	25.02 N	117.34 E
Huabu	66	29.00 N	118.20 E
Huacho	110	11.07 S	77.37 W
Huaco	114	30.09 S	68.31 W
Huadian	62	42.58 N	126.43 E
Hua Hin	70	12.34 N	99.58 E
Huai ≃	66	32.58 N	118.17 E
Huai'an	66	33.32 N	119.10 E
Huaibin	66	32.28 N	115.24 E
Huaide	62	43.32 N	124.50 E
Huailai	62	40.23 N	115.33 E
Huainan	66	32.40 N	117.00 E
Huaining	66	30.25 N	116.38 E
Huaiyang	66	33.44 N	114.53 E
Huaiyuan	66	32.57 N	117.12 E
Huajuapan de León	106	17.48 N	97.46 W
Hualalai ▲1	105a	19.42 N	155.52 W
Hualañé	114	34.59 S	71.49 W
Hualapai Mountains ⋏	104	34.50 N	113.55 W
Hualapai Peak ▲	104	35.04 N	113.54 W
Hualfín	114	27.14 S	66.50 W
Hualien	66	23.59 N	121.36 E
Huallaga ≃	110	5.10 S	75.32 W
Huallanca	110	8.49 S	77.52 W
Huamachuco	110	7.48 S	78.04 W
Huambo (Nova Lisboa)	84	12.44 S	15.47 E
Huancavelica	110	12.46 S	75.02 W
Huancayo	110	12.04 S	75.14 W
Huanchaca	110	20.20 S	66.39 W
Huang ≃, Asia	70	17.49 N	101.33 E
Huang (Yellow) ≃, Zhg.	62	37.32 N	118.19 E
Huangchuan	66	32.09 N	115.03 E
Huangdu	66	31.16 N	121.13 E
Huanggang	66	30.27 N	114.52 E
Huanggang Shan ▲	66	27.50 N	117.45 E
Huangho →Huang ≃	62	37.32 N	118.19 E
Huangjinbu	66	28.27 N	116.47 E
Huangli	66	31.39 N	119.42 E
Huangling	62	35.41 N	109.09 E
Huangmei	66	30.04 N	115.56 E
Huangpi	66	30.53 N	114.22 E
Huangqi	66	26.21 N	119.54 E
Huangqiao	66	32.15 N	120.13 E
Huangshi	66	30.13 N	115.05 E
Huanguelén	114	37.02 S	61.57 W
Huangyan	66	28.39 N	121.15 E
Huangyuan	66	36.40 N	101.12 E
Huangze	66	29.35 N	120.55 E
Huaning	70	24.14 N	102.56 E
Huanjiang	70	24.54 N	108.21 E
Huánuco	110	9.55 S	76.14 W
Huanuni	110	18.16 S	66.51 W
Huaral	110	11.30 S	77.12 W
Huarong	66	29.30 N	112.34 E
Huascarán, Nevado ▲	110	9.07 S	77.37 W
Huasco	114	28.28 S	71.14 W
Huasco ≃	114	28.27 S	71.13 W
Huashi	66	31.50 N	120.28 E
Huatabampo	106	26.50 N	109.38 W
Huaxian	66	23.22 N	113.12 E
Huazhou	70	21.40 N	110.33 E
Hubbard Lake ◎	102	44.49 N	83.34 W
Hubei (Hupeh) □4	62	31.00 N	112.00 E
Huberdeau	102	45.58 N	74.38 W
Hubli	74	15.21 N	75.10 E
Hucclecote	34	51.51 N	2.11 W
Huckitta Creek ≃	90	22.38 S	135.30 E
Hucknall	34	53.02 N	1.11 W
Huddersfield	36	53.39 N	1.47 W
Huddinge	44	59.14 N	17.59 E
Hudiksvall	44	61.44 N	17.07 E
Hudong	66	22.51 N	115.56 E
Hudson, Ma., U.S.	102	42.23 N	71.34 W
Hudson, Mi., U.S.	102	41.51 N	84.21 W
Hudson, N.H., U.S.	102	42.45 N	71.26 W
Hudson, N.Y., U.S.	102	42.15 N	73.47 W
Hudson, Oh., U.S.	102	41.14 N	81.26 W
Hudson ≃	102	40.42 N	74.02 W
Hudson Bay	98	52.52 N	102.25 W
Hudson Bay c	98	60.00 N	86.00 W
Hudson Falls	102	43.18 N	73.35 W
Hudson Strait ꓴ	98	62.30 N	72.00 W
Hue	70	16.28 N	107.36 E
Huebra ≃	50	41.02 N	6.48 W
Huedin	54	46.52 N	23.02 E
Huehuetenango	106	15.20 N	91.28 W
Huelgoat	48	48.22 N	3.45 W
Huelma	50	37.39 N	3.27 W
Huelva	50	37.16 N	6.57 W
Huelva, Río de ≃	50	37.27 N	6.00 W
Huentelauquén	114	31.35 S	71.32 W
Huércal-Overa	50	37.23 N	1.57 W
Huesca	50	42.08 N	0.25 W
Huéscar	50	37.49 N	2.32 W
Huetamo de Núñez	106	18.35 N	100.53 W
Huete	50	40.08 N	2.41 W
Hugh ≃	90	25.01 S	134.01 E
Hughenden	94	20.51 S	144.12 E
Hughes	90	30.42 S	129.31 E
Hughes, South Fork ≃	102	39.08 N	81.20 W
Hughesville	102	41.14 N	76.43 W
Hughson	104	37.36 N	120.52 W
Hugh Town	34a	49.55 N	6.17 W
Hugo	100	34.00 N	95.30 W
Hugou	66	33.23 N	117.08 E
Hui'an	66	25.04 N	118.47 E
Huiarau Range ⋏	96	38.45 S	177.00 E
Huichang	66	25.34 N	115.49 E
Hŭich'ŏn	62	40.10 N	126.17 E
Huidong	70	26.41 N	102.36 E
Huila, Nevado del ▲	110	3.00 N	76.00 W
Huilai	66	23.04 N	116.18 E
Huili	70	26.43 N	102.10 E
Huillapima	114	28.44 S	65.59 W
Huimin	62	37.29 N	117.29 E
Huinan	62	42.40 N	126.00 E
Huinca Renancó	114	34.50 S	64.23 W
Huishui	70	26.07 N	106.24 E
Huittinen (Lauttakylä)	44	61.11 N	22.42 E
Huixtla	106	15.09 N	92.28 W
Huize	70	26.27 N	103.09 E
Huizhou	66	23.05 N	114.24 E
Hukeng	66	27.29 N	114.18 E
Hukou	66	29.45 N	116.13 E
Hukusima →Fukushima	64	37.45 N	140.28 E
Hulan	62	46.00 N	126.38 E
Hulan Ergi	62	47.13 N	123.39 E
Huldrefossen ⱡ	44	61.28 N	5.58 E
Hulín, Česko.	46	49.19 N	17.28 E
Hulin, Zhg.	62	45.46 N	132.59 E
Hull	102	45.26 N	75.43 W
Hull ≃	36	53.44 N	0.19 W
Hullavington	34	51.33 N	2.09 W
Hullbridge	34	51.37 N	0.37 E
Hultsfred	44	57.29 N	15.50 E
Hulun Nur ◎	62	49.01 N	117.32 E
Huma	62	51.43 N	126.38 E
Huma ≃	62	51.40 N	126.44 E
Humacao	108	18.09 N	65.50 W
Humahuaca	114	23.12 S	65.21 W
Humaitá, Bra.	110	7.31 S	63.02 W
Humaitá, Para.	114	27.03 S	58.33 W
Humansdorp	86	34.02 S	24.46 E
Humbe	84	16.40 S	14.55 E
Humber ≃	36	53.40 N	0.10 W
Humber, Mouth of the ≃1	36	53.32 N	0.08 E
Humberside □6	36	53.55 N	0.40 W
Humberston	36	53.32 N	0.02 W
Humberto Primo	114	30.52 S	61.22 W
Humboldt	98	52.12 N	105.07 W
Humboldt ≃	104	40.02 N	118.31 W
Humboldt Bay c	104	40.47 N	124.11 W
Humboldt Lake ◎	104	39.58 N	118.38 W
Humboldt Salt Marsh ⊞	104	39.50 N	117.55 W
Hume	104	36.47 N	118.55 W
Hume, Lake ◎1	94	36.06 S	147.05 E
Humeburn	94	27.24 S	145.14 E
Humenné	46	48.56 N	21.55 E
Hummelfjell ▲	44	62.27 N	11.17 E
Humphreys, Mount ▲	104	37.17 N	118.40 W
Humphreys Peak ▲	100	35.20 N	111.40 W
Humpolec	46	49.32 N	15.22 E
Humppila	44	60.56 N	23.22 E
Húnaflói c	42a	65.50 N	20.50 W
Hunan □4	62	28.00 N	111.00 E
Hunchun	62	42.54 N	130.22 E
Hundested	44	55.58 N	11.52 E
Hundorp	44	61.33 N	9.54 E
Hundred	102	39.41 N	80.27 W
Hunedoara	54	45.45 N	22.54 E
Hunedoara □6	54	45.45 N	23.00 E
Hünfeld	46	50.40 N	9.46 E
Hungary (Magyarország) □1	30	47.00 N	20.00 E
Hungerford, Austl.	94	29.00 S	144.25 E
Hungerford, Eng., U.K.	34	51.26 N	1.30 W
Hŭngnam	62	39.50 N	127.38 E
Hungry Law ▲2	38	55.21 N	2.24 W
Hung-yen	70	20.39 N	106.04 E
Huningue	48	47.36 N	7.35 E
Hunish, Rubha ≻	38	57.41 N	6.21 W
Hunjiang	62	41.56 N	126.29 E
Hunkurāb, Ra's ≻	78	24.34 N	35.10 E
Hunmanby	36	54.10 N	0.19 W
Hunnebostrand	44	58.27 N	11.18 E
Hunsberge ⋏	86	27.45 S	17.12 E
Hunsrück ⋏	46	49.50 N	6.40 E
Hunstanton	34	52.57 N	0.30 E
Hunstein Range ⋏	92	4.30 S	142.40 E
Hunte ≃	46	52.30 N	8.19 E
Hunter ≃, Austl.	94	32.50 S	151.42 E
Hunter ≃, N.Z.	96	44.22 S	169.25 E
Hunter, Île I	28	22.24 S	172.03 E
Hunter Island I	94	40.32 S	144.45 E
Hunter Mountain ▲	102	42.10 N	74.14 W
Hunter Mountains ⋏	96	45.42 S	167.25 E
Hunter Ridge ✦3	28	21.30 S	174.30 E
Hunter's Quay	38	55.58 N	4.55 W
Hunterville	96	39.56 S	175.34 E
Huntingdon, P.Q., Can.	102	45.05 N	74.10 W
Huntingdon, Eng., U.K.	34	52.20 N	0.12 W
Huntingdon, Pa., U.S.	102	40.29 N	78.00 W
Huntington, Eng., U.K.	36	54.01 N	1.04 W
Huntington, N.Y., U.S.	102	40.51 N	73.25 W
Huntington, W.V., U.S.	102	38.25 N	82.26 W
Huntington Beach	104	33.39 N	117.59 W
Huntington Creek ≃	104	40.37 N	115.43 W
Huntly, N.Z.	96	37.33 S	175.10 E
Huntly, Scot., U.K.	38	57.27 N	2.47 W
Huntsville, On., Can.	102	45.20 N	79.13 W
Huntsville, Al., U.S.	100	34.43 N	86.35 W
Huntsville, Tx., U.S.	100	30.43 N	95.33 W
Hunucmá	106	21.01 N	89.52 W
Hunyani ≃	84	15.37 S	30.39 E
Hunyuan	62	39.48 N	113.41 E
Huon Gulf c	92	7.10 S	147.25 E
Huon Peninsula ≻1	92	6.25 S	147.25 E
Huonville	94	43.01 S	147.02 E
Huoqiu	66	32.20 N	116.16 E
Huoshan	66	31.25 N	116.20 E
Huotong	66	26.53 N	119.25 E
Hupeh →Hubei □4	62	31.00 N	112.00 E
Hurd, Cape ≻	102	45.13 N	81.44 W
Hurdalssjøen ◎	44	60.20 N	11.05 E
Huriel	48	46.23 N	2.29 E
Hurlford	38	55.36 N	4.28 W
Hurliness	38	58.47 N	3.15 W
Hurlock	102	38.37 N	75.51 W
Huron, Ca., U.S.	104	36.12 N	120.06 W
Huron, Oh., U.S.	102	41.22 N	82.33 W
Huron, S.D., U.S.	100	44.21 N	98.12 W
Huron ≃	102	42.03 N	83.14 W
Huron, Lake ◎	102	44.30 N	82.15 W
Hurricane	102	38.25 N	82.01 W
Hursley	34	51.02 N	1.24 W
Hurstbourne Tarrant	34	51.17 N	1.23 W
Hurstbridge	94	37.38 S	145.12 E
Hurstpierpoint	34	50.56 N	0.11 W
Hurtado ≃	114	30.35 S	71.11 W
Hurunui ≃	96	42.55 S	173.17 E
Hurup	44	56.45 N	8.25 E
Hurworth-on-Tees	36	54.29 N	1.31 W
Husainīwāla	76	30.59 N	74.34 E
Húsavík	42a	66.04 N	17.18 W
Hushu	66	31.52 N	118.59 E
Huşi	54	46.40 N	28.04 E
Huskvarna	44	57.48 N	14.16 E
Husum, B.R.D.	46	54.28 N	9.03 E
Husum, Sve.	44	63.20 N	19.10 E
Hutanopan	70	0.41 N	99.42 E
Hutchinson, S. Afr.	86	31.30 S	23.09 E
Hutchinson, Ks., U.S.	100	38.03 N	97.55 W
Huthwaite	36	53.09 N	1.17 W
Hüttental	46	50.54 N	8.02 E
Hutte Sauvage, Lac de la ◎	98	56.15 N	64.45 W
Hutton, Mount ▲	94	25.51 S	148.20 E
Hutton Rudby	36	54.27 N	1.17 W
Huwei	66	23.43 N	120.26 E
Huy	46	50.31 N	5.14 E
Huyton-with-Roby	36	53.25 N	2.52 W
Huzhen	66	28.50 N	120.15 E
Huzhou	66	30.52 N	120.06 E
Hvannadalshnúkur ▲	42a	64.01 N	16.41 W
Hvar	52	43.10 N	16.27 E
Hvar, Otok I	52	43.09 N	16.45 E
Hvarski Kanal ꓴ	52	43.15 N	16.37 E
Hveragerði	42a	64.03 N	21.10 W
Hvide Sande	44	55.59 N	8.08 E
Hvittingfoss	44	59.29 N	10.01 E
Hvolsvöllur	42a	63.45 N	20.10 W
Hwainan →Huainan	66	32.40 N	117.00 E
Hwange	86	18.22 S	26.29 E
Hwang Ho →Huang ≃	62	37.32 N	118.19 E
Hyannis	102	41.39 N	70.17 W
Hyde, N.Z.	96	45.18 S	170.15 E
Hyde, Eng., U.K.	36	53.27 N	2.05 W

Symbols in the Index entries are identified on page 122

Hyde-Jaff

Name	Page	Lat. °′	Long. °′
Hyden	90	32.27 S	118.53 E
Hyde Park, Guy.	110	6.30 N	58.16 W
Hyde Park, N.Y., U.S.	102	41.47 N	73.56 W
Hyde Park, Vt., U.S.	102	44.35 N	72.37 W
Hyderābād, India	74	17.23 N	78.29 E
Hyderābād, Pāk.	76	25.22 N	68.22 E
Hydra →Ídhra I	54	37.20 N	23.32 E
Hydrographers Passage ɥ	94	20.00 S	150.00 E
Hyères	48	43.07 N	6.07 E
Hyères, Îles d' II	50	43.00 N	6.20 E
Hyesan	62	41.23 N	128.12 E
Hyland ≃	98	59.50 N	128.10 W
Hylestad	44	59.05 N	7.32 E
Hyltebruk	44	57.00 N	13.14 E
Hyndman	102	39.49 N	78.43 W
Hyndman Peak ∧	100	43.45 N	114.08 W
Hyōgo □ 5	64	35.00 N	135.00 E
Hyrynsalmi	44	64.40 N	28.32 E
Hythe, Austl.	94	43.25 S	146.59 E
Hythe, Eng., U.K.	34	51.05 N	1.05 E
Hythe, Eng., U.K.	34	50.51 N	1.24 W
Hyūga	64	32.25 N	131.38 E
Hyūga-nada ⊤ 2	64	32.00 N	131.35 E
Hyvinkää	44	60.38 N	24.52 E
I			
Iacanga	114	21.54 S	49.01 W
Iaco (Yaco) ≃	110	9.03 S	68.34 W
Ialomiţa □ 6	54	44.30 N	27.20 E
Ialomiţa ≃	54	44.42 N	27.51 E
Iaşi	54	47.10 N	27.35 E
Iaşi □ 6	54	47.15 N	27.15 E
Iazu	54	44.44 N	27.25 E
Ibadan	80	7.17 N	3.30 E
Ibagué	110	4.27 N	75.14 W
Ibaiti	114	23.50 S	50.10 W
Ibăneşti	54	48.04 N	26.22 E
Ibapah Peak ∧	104	39.50 N	113.55 W
Ibar ≃	54	43.44 N	20.45 E
Ibaraki □ 5	64	36.30 N	140.30 E
Ibarra	110	0.21 N	78.07 W
Ibarreta	114	25.13 S	59.51 W
Ibb	74	14.01 N	44.10 E
Ibbenbüren	46	52.16 N	7.43 E
Ibérico, Sistema ⋏	50	41.00 N	2.30 W
Iberville, Mont d' (Mount Caubvick) ∧	98	58.53 N	63.43 W
Ibiá	110	19.29 S	46.32 W
Ibicaraí	110	14.51 S	39.36 W
Ibicuí ≃	114	29.25 S	56.47 W
Ibicuy	114	33.44 S	59.10 W
Ibirama	114	27.04 S	49.31 W
Ibirubá	114	28.38 S	53.06 W
Ibitinga	114	21.45 S	48.49 W
Ibiza	50	38.54 N	1.26 E
Ibiza I	50	39.00 N	1.25 E
Iblei, Monti ⋏	52	37.10 N	14.50 E
Ibo	84	12.20 S	40.35 E
Ibor ≃	50	39.49 N	5.33 W
'Ibrī	78	23.14 N	56.30 E
Ibstock	34	52.42 N	1.23 W
Ibusuki	64	31.16 N	130.39 E
Ica	110	14.04 S	75.42 W
Ica ≃, Perú	110	14.54 S	75.34 W
Içá (Putumayo) ≃, S.A.	110	3.07 S	67.58 W
Içana ≃	110	0.26 N	67.19 W
Icaño, Arg.	114	28.54 S	65.19 W
Icaño, Arg.	114	28.41 S	62.54 W
Iceland (Ísland) □ 1	30	65.00 N	18.00 W
Iceland Basin + 1	20	69.00 N	10.00 W
Ichalkaranji	74	16.42 N	74.28 E
Ichikawa	64	35.44 N	139.55 E
Ichilo ≃	110	15.57 S	64.42 W
Ichinohe	64	40.13 N	141.17 E
Ichinomiya, Nihon	64	35.18 N	136.48 E
Ichinomiya, Nihon	64	32.57 N	131.07 E
Ichinoseki	64	38.55 N	141.08 E
Ich Ovoo uul ∧	62	44.40 N	95.08 E
Ičinskaja Sopka, vulkan ∧ 1	58	55.42 N	157.35 E
Icó	110	6.24 S	38.51 W
Icoraci	110	1.18 S	48.28 W
Ida	102	41.54 N	83.34 W
Ida, Mount ∧	90	29.14 S	120.25 E
Idaho □ 3	100	45.00 N	115.00 W
Idaho Falls	100	43.28 N	112.02 W
Idanha-a-Nova	50	39.55 N	7.14 W
Idar	76	23.50 N	73.00 E
Idar-Oberstein	46	49.42 N	7.19 E
Idel'	42	64.08 N	34.14 E
Iderijn ≃	62	49.16 N	100.41 E
Idfū	82	24.58 N	32.52 E
Ídhi Óros ∧	54	35.18 N	24.43 E
Ídhra	54	37.20 N	23.29 E
Ídhra I	54	37.20 N	23.32 E
Idi	70	4.57 N	97.46 E
Idiofa	84	5.02 S	19.36 E
Idkerberget	44	60.23 N	15.14 E
Idlib	78	35.55 N	36.38 E
Idre	44	61.52 N	12.43 E
Idrica	60	56.21 N	28.53 E
Idrigill Point ›	38	57.20 N	6.35 W
Idrija	52	46.00 N	14.01 E
Idutywa	86	32.02 S	28.16 E
Idyllwild	104	33.45 N	116.43 W
Iepê	114	22.40 S	51.05 W
Ieper	46	50.51 N	2.53 E
Ierápetra	54	35.00 N	25.45 E
Ierisós	54	40.24 N	23.52 E
Iesi	52	43.31 N	13.14 E
Iesolo	52	45.32 N	12.38 E
Ifalik I 1	68	7.15 N	144.27 E
Ife	80	7.30 N	4.30 E
Iferouâne	80	19.04 N	8.24 E
Ifni □ 9	80	29.15 N	10.08 W
Ifôghas, Adrar des ⋏	80	20.00 N	2.00 E
Ifould Lake ⊜	90	30.53 S	132.09 E
Igal	46	46.31 N	17.55 E
Igan	72	2.49 N	111.43 E
Igarka	56	67.28 N	86.35 E
Iggesund	44	61.38 N	17.04 E
Iglesia	114	30.24 S	69.13 W
Iglesias	52	39.19 N	8.32 E
Iglesiente + 1	52	39.18 N	8.40 E
Igloolik	98	69.24 N	81.49 W
Ignalina	60	55.21 N	26.10 E
Igombe ≃	84	4.38 S	31.40 E
Igoumenítsa	54	39.30 N	20.16 E
Iguaçu ≃	114	25.36 S	54.36 W
Iguaçu, Saltos do ⌊	114	25.41 S	54.26 W
Iguala	106	18.21 N	99.32 W
Igualada	50	41.35 N	1.38 E
Iguape	114	24.43 S	47.33 W
Iguaraçu	114	23.11 S	51.50 W
Iguassu Falls →Iguaçu, Saltos do ⌊	114	25.41 S	54.26 W
Iguatemi	114	23.40 S	54.34 W
Iguatu	110	6.22 S	39.18 W
Iguéla	84	1.55 S	9.19 E
Iguîdi, 'Erg ⊥ 8	80	26.35 N	5.40 W
Igžej	58	53.59 N	103.10 E
Iheya-shima I	65b	27.04 N	127.58 E
Ihosy	87b	22.24 S	46.08 E
Ihtiman	54	42.26 N	23.49 E
Ii	44	65.19 N	25.22 E
Iida	64	35.31 N	137.50 E
Iijoki ≃	44	65.20 N	25.17 E
Iisalmi	44	63.34 N	27.11 E
Iittala	44	61.04 N	24.10 E
Iivaara ∧ 2	44	65.47 N	29.40 E
Iiyama	64	36.51 N	138.22 E
Iizuka	64	33.38 N	130.41 E
Ijâfene + 2	80	20.30 N	8.00 W
IJmuiden	46	52.27 N	4.36 E
IJsselmeer (Zuiderzee) ⊤ 2	46	52.45 N	5.25 E
Ijuí	114	28.23 S	53.55 W
Ika	58	59.18 N	106.12 E
Ikaalinen	44	61.46 N	23.03 E
Ikamatua	96	42.16 S	171.41 E
Ikaría I	54	37.41 N	26.20 E
Ikast	44	56.08 N	9.10 E
Ikawhenua Range ⋏	96	38.20 S	176.56 E
Ikeda, Nihon	64	34.01 N	133.48 E
Ikeda, Nihon	64a	42.55 N	143.27 E
Ikela	84	1.11 S	23.16 E
Iki I	64	33.47 N	129.43 E
Ikša	60	56.10 N	37.31 E
Ikuno	64	35.10 N	134.48 E
Ilagan	68	17.10 N	121.54 E
Ilan	66	24.46 N	121.45 E
Ilanskij	58	56.14 N	96.03 E
Ilanz	48	46.46 N	9.12 E
Iława	46	53.37 N	19.33 E
Ilbenge	58	62.49 N	124.24 E
Ilbunga	90	26.25 S	135.03 E
Ilchester	34	51.01 N	2.41 W
Île-à-la-Crosse	98	55.27 N	107.53 W
Île-à-la-Crosse, Lac ⊜	98	55.40 N	107.45 W
Ilebo	84	4.19 S	20.35 E
Île-de-France □ 9	48	49.00 N	2.20 E
Ilek ≃	56	51.30 N	53.20 E
Ilen ≃	40	51.33 N	9.19 W
Ilesha	80	7.38 N	4.45 E
Ileza	42	60.43 N	43.54 E
Ilfov □ 6	54	44.30 N	26.00 E
Ilfracombe, Austl.	94	23.30 S	144.30 E
Ilfracombe, Eng., U.K.	34	51.13 N	4.08 W
Ilhabela	114	23.47 S	45.21 W
Ilhavo	50	40.36 N	8.40 W
Ilhéus	110	14.49 S	39.02 W
Ili ≃	62	45.24 N	74.02 E
Ilia	54	45.56 N	22.39 E
Iliamna Lake ⊜	98	59.30 N	155.00 W
Iligan	68	8.14 N	124.14 E
Ilimsk	58	56.46 N	103.52 E
Ilion	102	43.00 N	75.02 W
Ilio Point ›	105a	21.13 N	157.15 W
Ilirska Bistrica	52	45.34 N	14.15 E
Ilizi	80	26.29 N	8.28 E
Iljinskij, S.S.S.R.	42	61.02 N	32.41 E
Iljinskij, S.S.S.R.	58	47.58 N	142.12 E
Ilkeston	34	52.59 N	1.18 W
Ilkley	36	53.55 N	1.50 W
Illampu, Nevado ∧	110	15.50 S	68.34 W
Illapel	114	31.38 S	71.10 W
Illbillee, Mount ∧	90	27.02 S	132.30 E
Ille-et-Vilaine □ 5	48	48.10 N	1.30 W
Illéla	80	14.28 N	5.15 E
Iller ≃	46	48.23 N	9.58 E
Illertissen	46	48.13 N	10.06 E
Illescas	50	40.07 N	3.50 W
Illiers	48	48.18 N	1.15 E
Illimani, Nevado ∧	110	16.39 S	67.48 W
Illinois □ 3	100	40.00 N	89.00 W
Illinois ≃, Il., U.S.	100	38.58 N	90.27 W
Illinois ≃, Or., U.S.	104	42.33 N	124.03 W
Illminster	34	50.56 N	2.55 W
Illovo	86	30.05 S	30.50 E
Ilmajoki	44	62.44 N	22.34 E
Il'men', ozero ⊜	60	58.17 N	31.20 E
Ilmenau	46	50.41 N	10.55 E
Ilo	110	17.38 S	71.20 W
Iloilo	68	10.42 N	122.34 E
Ilomantsi	44	62.40 N	30.55 E
Ilorin	80	8.30 N	4.32 E
Iłowa	46	51.30 N	15.12 E
Il'pyrskij	58	59.56 N	164.10 E
Ilūkste	60	55.58 N	26.18 E
Ilwaki	72	7.56 S	126.26 E
Iłża	46	51.11 N	21.14 E
Imabari	64	34.03 N	133.00 E
Imaichi	64	36.43 N	139.41 E
Imandra, ozero ⊜	42	67.30 N	33.00 E
Imanombo	87b	24.26 S	45.49 E
Imari	64	33.16 N	129.53 E
Imaruí	114	28.21 S	48.49 W
Imaruí, Lagoa C	114	28.21 S	48.52 W
Imatra	44	61.10 N	28.46 E
Imbituba	114	28.14 S	48.40 W
Imbituva	114	25.12 S	50.35 W
Ime, Beinn ∧	38	56.14 N	4.49 W
Imeni C'urupy	60	55.30 N	38.39 E
Imeni Kirova	58	59.42 N	128.12 E
Imeni Vorovskogo	60	55.43 N	41.06 E
Imeni Žel'abova	60	58.57 N	36.36 E
Imi	82	6.28 N	42.18 E
Imías	108	20.04 N	74.38 W
Imilac	114	24.14 S	68.53 W
Imlay	104	40.39 N	118.08 W
Imlay City	102	43.01 N	83.04 W
Immarna	90	30.30 S	132.09 E
Immenstadt	46	47.33 N	10.13 E
Immingham	36	53.36 N	0.13 W
Imola	52	44.21 N	11.42 E
Imotski	52	43.27 N	17.13 E
Imperatriz	110	5.32 S	47.29 W
Imperia	52	43.53 N	8.03 E
Imperial	104	32.50 N	115.34 W
Imperial ≃	114	38.48 S	73.24 W
Imperial Beach	104	32.35 N	117.06 W
Imperial de Aragón, Canal ≊	50	42.02 N	1.33 W
Imperial Valley ∨	104	32.50 N	115.30 W
Impfondo	84	1.37 N	18.04 E
Imphāl	76	24.49 N	93.57 E
Imst	46	47.14 N	10.44 E
Ina, Nihon	64	35.50 N	137.57 E
In'a, S.S.S.R.	58	59.24 N	144.48 E
In'a ≃	58	59.23 N	144.54 E
Inaccessible Island I	20	37.17 S	12.45 W
In Amnas	80	28.05 N	9.30 E
Inangahua Junction	96	41.51 S	171.57 E
Inanwatan	92	2.08 S	132.10 E
In'aptuk, gora ∧	56	56.22 N	110.11 E
Inari	42	68.54 N	27.01 E
Inari ⊜	42	69.00 N	28.00 E
Inarigda	58	63.14 N	107.27 E
Inawashiro-ko ⊜	64	37.29 N	140.06 E
Inca	50	39.43 N	2.54 E
Inca de Oro	114	26.45 S	69.54 W
Incaguasi	114	29.13 S	71.03 W
Inch	40	52.08 N	9.59 W
Inchard, Loch C	38	58.27 N	5.04 W
Inchbare	38	56.47 N	2.38 W
Inchcape I 2	38	56.26 N	2.23 W
Inchmarnock I	38	55.47 N	5.09 W
Inchnadamph	38	58.09 N	4.59 W
Inch'ŏn	62	37.28 N	126.38 E
Inchture	38	56.26 N	3.10 W
Incline Village	104	39.16 N	119.56 W
Incomáti (Komati) ≃	86	25.46 S	32.43 E
Indaal, Loch C	38	55.45 N	6.21 W
Indalsälven ≃	44	62.31 N	17.27 E
Indaw	70	23.40 N	94.46 E
Independence, Ca., U.S.	104	36.48 N	118.11 W
Independence, Ks., U.S.	100	37.13 N	95.42 W
Independence, Ky., U.S.	102	38.56 N	84.32 W
Independence ≃	102	43.45 N	75.20 W
Independence Mountains ⋏	104	41.15 N	115.55 W
Independenţa	54	43.58 N	28.05 E
Inderborskij	56	48.33 N	51.44 E
India (Bhārat) □ 1	74	20.00 N	77.00 E
Indian ≃	102	44.24 N	75.39 W
Indiana	102	40.37 N	79.09 W
Indiana □ 3	100	40.00 N	86.15 W
Indianapolis	100	39.46 N	86.09 W
Indian Head	98	50.32 N	103.40 W
Indian Lake	102	43.46 N	74.16 W
Indian Ocean ⊤ 1	18	10.00 S	70.00 E
Indian Peak ∧	104	38.16 N	113.53 W
Indian River	102	45.24 N	84.36 W
Indian Springs	104	36.34 N	115.40 W
Indigirka ≃	58	70.48 N	148.54 E
Inđija	54	45.03 N	20.05 E
Indio	104	33.43 N	116.12 W
Indispensable Reefs + 2	88	12.40 S	160.25 E
Indochina + 1	26	16.00 N	107.00 E
Indonesia □ 1	68	5.00 S	120.00 E
Indore	76	22.43 N	75.50 E
Indragiri ≃	72	0.22 S	103.26 E
Indramayu	72	6.20 S	108.19 E
Indrāvati ≃	74	18.44 N	80.16 E
Indre □ 5	48	46.45 N	1.30 E
Indre ≃	48	47.16 N	0.19 E
Indre-et-Loire □ 5	48	47.15 N	0.45 E
Indus ≃	76	24.20 N	67.47 E
Indwe	86	31.27 S	27.23 E
İnegöl	54	40.05 N	29.31 E
Ineu	54	46.26 N	21.49 E
Inez	102	37.51 N	82.32 W
Infante, Kaap ›	86	34.29 S	20.51 E
Infiernillo, Presa del ⊜ 1	106	18.35 N	101.45 W
Infiesto	50	43.21 N	5.22 W
Ingal	80	16.47 N	6.56 E
Ingatestone	34	51.41 N	0.22 E
Ingelheim	46	49.59 N	8.05 E
Ingelstad	44	56.45 N	14.55 E
Ingende	84	0.15 S	18.57 E
Ingeniero Luiggi	114	35.25 S	64.29 W
Ingeniero Luis A. Huergo	114	39.05 S	67.14 W
Ingeniero White	114	38.47 S	62.16 W
Ingenio La Esperanza	114	24.13 S	64.51 W
Ingenio Santa Ana	114	27.28 S	65.41 W
Ingersoll	102	43.02 N	80.53 W
Ingham	94	18.39 S	146.10 E
Ingleborough ∧	36	54.11 N	2.23 W
Ingleton	36	54.10 N	2.27 W
Inglewood, Austl.	94	28.25 S	151.05 E
Inglewood, Austl.	94	36.34 S	143.52 E
Inglewood, N.Z.	96	39.09 S	174.12 E
Inglewood, Ca., U.S.	104	33.57 N	118.21 W
Inglewood Forest + 3	36	54.45 N	2.50 W
Ingoda ≃	58	51.42 N	115.48 E
Ingolstadt	46	48.46 N	11.27 E
In Guezzam	80	19.32 N	5.42 E
Ingwavuma	86	27.09 S	32.00 E
Ingwiller	48	48.52 N	7.29 E
Inhaca, Ilha da I	86	26.03 S	32.57 E
Inhambane	86	23.51 S	35.29 E
Inhambane □ 5	86	23.00 S	34.30 E
Inhambupe	110	11.47 S	38.21 W
Inhaminga	86	18.24 S	35.00 E
Inharrime	86	24.29 S	35.01 E
Iniesta	50	39.26 N	1.45 W
Inírida ≃	110	3.55 N	67.52 W
Inishbofin I, Ire.	40	55.09 N	8.11 W
Inishbofin I, Ire.	40	53.37 N	10.15 W
Inishcrone	40	54.12 N	9.06 W
Inisheer I	40	53.02 N	9.26 W
Inishmaan I	40	53.05 N	9.32 W
Inishmore I	40	53.07 N	9.45 W
Inishowen › 1	40	55.12 N	7.20 W
Inishowen Point ›	40	55.14 N	6.56 W
Inishshark I	40	53.37 N	10.18 W
Inishtrahull I	40	55.26 N	7.14 W
Inishturk I	40	53.43 N	10.08 W
Inistioge	40	52.29 N	7.04 W
Injune	94	25.51 S	148.34 E
Inkeroinen	44	60.42 N	26.51 E
Inland Kaikoura Range ⋏	96	42.00 S	173.40 E
Inland Sea →Seto-naikai ⊤ 2	64	34.20 N	133.30 E
Inle Lake ⊜	70	20.32 N	96.55 E
Inn (En) ≃	48	48.35 N	13.28 E
Innamincka	94	27.45 S	140.44 E
Innellan	38	55.54 N	4.57 W
Inner Hebrides II	38	56.30 N	6.00 W
Innerleithen	38	55.38 N	3.05 W
Inner Mongolia →Nei Monggol Zizhiqu □ 4	62	43.00 N	115.00 E
Inner Sound ɥ	38	57.25 N	5.56 W
Innisfail	94	17.32 S	146.02 E
Innoshima	64	34.17 N	133.11 E
Innsbruck	46	47.16 N	11.24 E
Innviertel + 1	48	48.10 N	13.15 E
Inny ≃, Ire.	40	53.33 N	7.48 W
Inny ≃, Eng., U.K.	34	50.35 N	4.17 W
Ino	64	33.33 N	133.26 E
Inongo	84	1.57 S	18.16 E
Inowrocław	46	52.48 N	18.15 E
In Salah	80	27.12 N	2.28 E
Insar	42	53.52 N	44.21 E
Insch	38	57.21 N	2.37 W
Inscription, Cape ›	90	25.29 S	112.59 E
Insein	70	16.53 N	96.07 E
Insjön	44	60.41 N	15.05 E
Ińsko	46	53.27 N	15.33 E
Inta	42	66.02 N	60.08 E
Intendente Alvear	114	35.14 S	63.35 W
Interlaken	48	46.41 N	7.51 E
International Falls	100	48.36 N	93.24 W
Inthanon, Doi ∧	70	18.35 N	98.29 E
Intiyaco	114	28.39 S	60.05 W
Intracoastal Waterway ≊	102	38.10 N	76.20 W
Inubō-saki ›	64	35.42 N	140.53 E
Inuvik	98	68.25 N	133.30 W
Inver	38	57.49 N	3.55 W
Inverallochy	38	57.40 N	1.55 W
Inveraray	38	56.13 N	5.05 W
Inverarity	38	56.35 N	2.53 W
Inverbervie	38	56.51 N	2.17 W
Invercargill	96	46.24 S	168.21 E
Inverdruie	38	57.10 N	3.48 W
Inverell	94	29.47 S	151.07 E
Invergarry	38	57.02 N	4.47 W
Invergordon	38	57.42 N	4.10 W
Inverkeilor	38	56.38 N	2.32 W
Inverkeithing	38	56.02 N	3.25 W
Inverkeithny	38	57.30 N	2.37 W
Invermoriston	38	57.13 N	4.38 W
Inverness, Scot., U.K.	38	57.27 N	4.15 W
Inverness, Ca., U.S.	104	38.06 N	122.51 W
Inveruglas	38	56.15 N	4.43 W
Inverurie	38	57.17 N	2.23 W
Inverway	90	17.50 S	129.38 E
Investigator Group II	90	33.45 S	134.30 E
Investigator Shoal + 2	68	8.09 N	114.44 E
Investigator Strait ɥ	94	35.25 S	137.10 E
Inyangani ∧	86	18.20 S	32.50 E
Inyo, Mount ∧	104	36.44 N	117.59 W
Inyokern	104	35.38 N	117.48 W
Inyo Mountains ⋏	104	36.40 N	118.10 W
Inza	42	53.51 N	46.21 E
Inžavino	60	52.19 N	42.30 E
Ioánnina	54	39.40 N	20.50 E
Iō-jima (Iwo Jima) I	28	24.47 N	141.20 E
Iona I	38	56.19 N	6.25 W
Iona, Sound of ɥ	38	56.19 N	6.24 W
Ione	104	38.21 N	120.55 W
Ionia	102	42.59 N	85.04 W
Ionian Islands →Iónioi Nísoi II	54	38.30 N	20.30 E
Ionian Sea ⊤ 2	30	39.00 N	19.00 E
Iónioi Nísoi II	54	38.30 N	20.30 E
Iony, ostrov I	58	56.26 N	143.25 E
Íos	54	36.44 N	25.17 E
Íos I	54	36.42 N	25.24 E
Iō-shima I	65b	30.48 N	130.18 E
Iowa □ 3	100	42.15 N	93.15 W
Iowa City	100	41.39 N	91.31 W
Ipameri	110	17.43 S	48.09 W
Ípeiros □ 9	54	39.40 N	20.50 E
Ipel'(Ipoly) ≃	46	47.49 N	18.52 E
Ipiales	110	0.50 N	77.37 W
Ipiaú	110	14.08 S	39.44 W
Ipin →Yibin	62	28.47 N	104.38 E
Ipiranga	114	25.01 S	50.35 W
Ipoh	72	4.35 N	101.05 E
Ipoly (Ipel') ≃	46	47.49 N	18.52 E
Iporá, Bra.	110	16.28 S	51.07 W
Iporã, Bra.	114	23.59 S	53.37 W
Ipplepen	34	50.29 N	3.38 W
Ipswich, Austl.	94	27.36 S	152.46 E
Ipswich, Eng., U.K.	34	52.04 N	1.10 E
Ipswich, Ma., U.S.	102	42.40 N	70.50 W
Ipu	110	4.20 S	40.42 W
Iquique	110	20.13 S	70.10 W
Iquitos	110	3.46 S	73.15 W
Iraí	114	27.11 S	53.15 W
Iráklion	54	35.20 N	25.09 E
Iran (Īrān) □ 1	74	32.00 N	53.00 E
Iran, Pegunungan ⋏	72	2.05 N	114.55 E
Īrānshahr	78	27.13 N	60.41 E
Irapa	108	10.34 N	62.35 W
Irapuato	106	20.41 N	101.21 W
Iraq (Al-'Irāq) □ 1	74	33.00 N	44.00 E
Irati	114	25.27 S	50.39 W
Irati ≃	50	42.35 N	1.16 W
Irazú, Volcán ∧ 1	108	9.58 N	83.53 W
Irbid	78	32.33 N	35.51 E
Irbīl	78	36.11 N	44.01 E
Irbīl □ 4	78	36.10 N	44.00 E
Irbit	56	57.41 N	63.03 E
Irchester	34	52.16 N	0.38 W
Irdning	46	47.33 N	14.01 E
Iregua ≃	50	42.27 N	2.24 W
Ireland (Eire) □ 1	30	53.00 N	8.00 W
Irene	86	25.53 S	28.13 E
Irene, Mount ∧	96	45.10 S	167.22 E
Irfon ≃	34	52.09 N	3.24 W
Irgiz	56	48.37 N	61.16 E
Iri	62	35.56 N	126.57 E
Irian Jaya □ 4	92	5.00 S	138.00 E
Iringa	84	7.46 S	35.42 E
Iriomote-jima I	62	24.20 N	123.50 E
Iriri ≃	110	3.52 S	52.37 W
Irish, Mount ∧	104	37.38 N	115.24 W
Irish Sea ⊤ 2	32	53.30 N	5.20 W
Irishtown	94	40.55 S	145.08 E
Irkutsk	58	52.16 N	104.20 E
Irlam	36	53.28 N	2.25 W
Iroise C	48	48.15 N	4.55 W
Iron Baron	94	32.59 S	137.09 E
Iron Bridge, On., Can.	102	46.17 N	83.14 W
Iron Bridge, Eng., U.K.	34	52.38 N	2.29 W
Irondequoit	102	43.12 N	77.36 W
Iron Gate ∨	54	44.41 N	22.31 E
Iron Gate Reservoir ⊜ 1	54	44.30 N	22.00 E
Iron Knob	94	32.44 S	137.08 E
Iron Mountain	100	45.49 N	88.03 W
Iron Range	92	12.42 S	143.18 E
Ironton	102	38.32 N	82.40 W
Ironwood	100	46.27 N	90.10 W
Iroquois	102	44.51 N	75.19 W
Irō-zaki ›	64	34.36 N	138.51 E
Irrawaddy □ 8	70	17.00 N	95.00 E
Irrawaddy ≃	70	15.50 N	95.06 E
Irregully Creek ≃	90	23.06 S	116.21 E
Irsina	52	40.45 N	16.15 E
Irt ≃	36	54.22 N	3.26 W
Irthing ≃	36	54.55 N	2.50 W
Irthlingborough	34	52.20 N	0.37 W
Irtyš (Ertix) ≃	56	61.04 N	68.52 E
Irtyšsk	58	53.21 N	75.27 E
Irumu	84	1.27 N	29.52 E
Irún	50	43.21 N	1.47 W
Irurzun	50	42.55 N	1.50 W
Irvine, Scot., U.K.	38	55.37 N	4.40 W
Irvine, Ky., U.S.	102	37.42 N	83.58 W
Irvine ≃	38	55.37 N	4.41 W
Irvinestown	40	54.28 N	7.38 W
Irwell ≃	36	53.27 N	2.17 W
Irwin	90	29.12 S	115.04 E
Irwin ≃	90	29.15 S	114.56 E
Irwin, Point ›	90	35.04 S	116.56 E
Isaac ≃	94	22.52 S	149.20 E
Isaba	50	42.52 N	0.55 W
Isabela, Cabo ›	108	19.56 N	71.01 W
Isabela, Isla I	24	0.30 S	91.06 W
Isabelia, Cordillera ⋏	108	13.45 N	85.15 W
Isabella Lake ⊜ 1	104	35.40 N	118.26 W
Isábena ≃	50	42.11 N	0.21 E
Isaccea	54	45.16 N	28.28 E
Ísafjarđardjúp C 2	42a	66.10 N	23.00 W
Ísafjörđur	42a	66.08 N	23.13 W
Isahaya	64	32.50 N	130.03 E
Isak	70	4.28 N	96.55 E
Işalniţa	54	44.24 N	23.44 E
Isar ≃	46	48.49 N	12.58 E
Isbister	38	60.36 N	1.19 W
Ischia	52	40.44 N	13.57 E
Ischia, Isola d' I	52	40.43 N	13.54 E
Isdell ≃	90	16.27 S	124.51 E
Ise (Uji-yamada)	64	34.29 N	136.42 E
Isefjord C	44	55.52 N	11.49 E
Iseo, Lago d' ⊜	52	45.43 N	10.04 E
Isère □ 5	48	45.10 N	5.50 E
Isère ≃	48	44.59 N	4.51 E
Iserlohn	46	51.22 N	7.41 E
Isernia	52	41.36 N	14.14 E
Isesaki	64	36.19 N	139.12 E
Iset' ≃	56	56.36 N	66.24 E
Ise-wan C	64	34.43 N	136.43 E
Iseyin	80	7.58 N	3.36 E
Isfahan →Eşfahān	78	32.40 N	51.38 E
Ishigaki-shima I	62	24.24 N	124.12 E
Ishikari ≃	64a	43.15 N	141.23 E
Ishikari-dake ∧	64a	43.33 N	143.02 E
Ishikari-heiya ≚	64a	43.15 N	141.23 E
Ishikari-wan C	64a	43.25 N	141.01 E
Ishikawa	65b	26.25 N	127.50 E
Ishikawa □ 5	64	36.45 N	136.45 E
Ishinomaki	64	38.25 N	141.18 E
Ishinomaki-wan C	64	38.18 N	141.18 E
Ishioka	64	36.11 N	140.16 E
Ishizuchi-san ∧	64	33.46 N	133.07 E
Isigny	48	49.19 N	1.06 W
Isil'kul'	56	54.55 N	71.16 E
Išim	56	56.09 N	69.27 E
Išim ≃	56	57.45 N	71.12 E
Išimbaj	56	53.28 N	56.02 E
Išimskaja step' ≚	56	55.00 N	70.00 E
Isimu	72	0.40 N	122.51 E
Isiolo	84	0.21 N	37.35 E
Isipingo	86	29.59 S	30.56 E
Isiro	82	2.47 N	27.37 E
Isis	94	25.12 S	152.13 E
Isisford	94	24.16 S	144.26 E
Iskâr ≃	54	43.44 N	24.27 E
İskenderun	78	36.37 N	36.07 E
İskenderun Körfezi C	30	36.30 N	35.40 E
Iskitim	58	54.38 N	83.18 E
Iskut ≃	98	56.42 N	131.45 W
Isla ≃	38	57.30 N	2.47 W
Isla, Salar de la ≚	114	25.49 S	68.53 W
Isla Cristina	50	37.12 N	7.19 W
Isla de Maipo	114	33.45 S	70.54 W
Islāmābād	76	33.42 N	73.10 E
Islāmpur, India	76	25.09 N	85.12 E
Islāmpur, India	76	26.16 N	88.12 E
Isla Mujeres	108	21.12 N	86.43 W
Island Falls	102	46.00 N	68.16 W
Island Lagoon ⊜	94	31.30 S	136.40 E
Island Lake ⊜	98	53.47 N	94.25 W
Island Point ›	90	30.20 S	115.02 E
Island Pond	102	44.48 N	71.52 W
Islands, Bay of C, Nf., Can.	98	49.10 N	58.15 W
Islands, Bay of C, N.Z.	96	35.12 S	174.10 E
Isla Patrulla	114	32.59 S	54.35 W
Isla Verde	114	33.14 S	62.24 W
Isla Vista	104	34.25 N	119.50 W
Islay I	38	55.46 N	6.10 W
Islay, Sound of ɥ	38	55.50 N	6.01 W
Isle ≃, Fr.	48	44.55 N	0.15 W
Isle ≃, Eng., U.K.	34	50.59 N	2.53 W
Isle of Man □ 2	30	54.15 N	4.30 W
Isle of Wight □ 6	34	50.40 N	1.20 W
Islesboro Island I	102	44.20 N	68.53 W
Isleton	104	38.09 N	121.36 W
Islington + 8	34	51.34 N	0.06 W
Islip	34	51.50 N	1.14 W
Islivig	38	58.05 N	7.11 W
Islón	114	29.54 S	71.12 W
Ismael Cortinas	114	33.58 S	57.06 W
Ismailia →Al-Ismā'īlīyah	82	30.35 N	32.16 E
Isny	46	47.41 N	10.02 E
Isojoki	44	62.07 N	21.58 E
Isokyrö	44	63.00 N	22.19 E
Isola della Scala	52	45.16 N	11.00 E
Isola del Liri	52	41.41 N	13.34 E
Isola di Capo Rizzuto	52	38.58 N	17.06 E
Isosyöte ∧ 2	44	65.37 N	27.35 E
Isparta	30	37.46 N	30.33 E
Isperih	54	43.43 N	26.50 E
Ispica	52	36.47 N	14.55 E
Israel (Yisra'el) □ 1	74	31.30 N	35.00 E
Israel ≃	102	44.29 N	71.35 W
Issigeac	48	44.44 N	0.36 E
Issoire	48	45.33 N	3.15 E
Issoudun	48	46.57 N	2.00 E
Is-sur-Tille	48	47.31 N	5.06 E
Issyk-Kul', ozero ⊜	56	42.25 N	77.15 E
İstanbul	30	41.01 N	28.58 E
İstanbul Boğazı ɥ	54	41.06 N	29.04 E
Isteren ⊜	44	61.58 N	11.48 E
Istiaía	54	38.57 N	23.09 E
Isto, Mount ∧	98	69.12 N	143.48 W
Istok	54	42.47 N	20.29 E
Istra	60	55.55 N	36.52 E
Istra › 1	52	45.15 N	14.00 E
Istranca Dağları ⋏	54	41.50 N	27.30 E
Istria →Istra › 1	52	45.15 N	14.00 E
Iswepe	86	26.50 S	30.31 E
Itá	114	25.29 S	57.21 W
Itabaiana, Bra.	110	7.20 S	35.20 W
Itabaiana, Bra.	110	10.41 S	37.26 W
Itaberá	114	23.51 S	49.09 W
Itaberaí	110	16.02 S	49.48 W
Itabira	110	19.37 S	43.13 W
Itabuna	110	14.48 S	39.16 W
Itacoatiara	110	3.08 S	58.25 W
Itacurubí del Rosario	114	24.29 S	56.41 W
Itaguajé	114	22.37 S	51.59 W
Itagüi	110	6.10 N	75.36 W
Itaí	114	23.24 S	49.06 W
Itá-Ibaté	114	27.26 S	57.20 W
Itaiópolis	114	26.20 S	49.56 W
Itaituba	110	4.17 S	55.59 W
Itajaí	114	26.53 S	48.39 W
Itajubá	114	22.26 S	45.27 W
Italy (Italia) □ 1	30	42.50 N	12.50 E
Itami	64	34.46 N	135.25 E
Itanhaém	114	24.11 S	46.47 W
Itapecuru ≃	110	2.52 S	44.12 W
Itapecuru-Mirim	110	3.24 S	44.20 W
Itapemirim	110	21.01 S	40.50 W
Itaperuna	110	21.12 S	41.54 W
Itapetinga	110	15.15 S	40.15 W
Itapetininga	114	23.36 S	48.03 W
Itapeva	114	23.58 S	48.52 W
Itapicuru ≃	110	11.47 S	37.32 W
Itapira	114	22.26 S	46.50 W
Itapiranga	114	27.08 S	53.43 W
Itápolis	114	21.35 S	48.46 W
Itaporã	114	22.01 S	54.54 W
Itaporanga	114	23.42 S	49.29 W
Itapúa □ 5	114	26.50 S	55.50 W
Itaquari	110	20.20 S	40.22 W
Itaqui	114	29.08 S	56.33 W
Itaquyry	114	24.56 S	55.13 W
Itararé	114	24.07 S	49.20 W
Itararé ≃	114	23.10 S	49.42 W
Itārsi	76	22.37 N	77.45 E
Itata ≃	114	36.23 S	72.52 W
Itatí	114	27.16 S	58.15 W
Itatiba	114	23.00 S	46.51 W
Itatinga	114	23.07 S	48.36 W
Itaúna	110	20.04 S	44.34 W
Itbayat Island I	68	20.46 N	121.50 E
Itéa	54	38.26 N	22.24 E
Iténez (Guaporé) ≃	110	11.54 S	65.01 W
Ithaca, Mi., U.S.	102	43.17 N	84.36 W
Ithaca, N.Y., U.S.	102	42.26 N	76.29 W
Itháki	54	38.23 N	20.42 E
Itháki I	54	38.24 N	20.42 E
Itirapina	114	22.15 S	47.49 W
Itō	64	34.58 N	139.05 E
Itoigawa	64	37.02 N	137.51 E
Itoman	65b	26.08 N	127.40 E
Itsuki	64	32.24 N	130.50 E
Itsuwa	64	32.30 N	130.10 E
Ittiri	52	40.36 N	8.34 E
Itu	114	23.16 S	47.19 W
Itu ≃	114	29.25 S	55.51 W
Ituango	110	7.04 N	75.45 W
Ituí ≃	110	4.38 S	70.19 W
Ituiutaba	110	18.58 S	49.28 W
Itumbiara	110	18.25 S	49.13 W
Ituporanga	114	27.25 S	49.36 W
Iturbe	114	26.01 S	56.30 W
Ituri ≃	84	1.40 N	27.01 E
Iturup, ostrov (Etorofu-tō) I	58	44.54 N	147.30 E
Ituxi ≃	110	7.18 S	64.51 W
Ituzaingó	114	27.36 S	56.41 W
Itzehoe	46	53.55 N	9.31 E
Iul'tin	58	67.50 N	178.48 W
Ivacevići	60	52.43 N	25.21 E
Ivaí ≃	114	23.18 S	53.42 W
Ivaiporã	114	24.15 S	51.45 W
Ivajlovgrad	54	41.32 N	26.08 E
Ivalo	42	68.42 N	27.30 E
Ivalojoki ≃	42	68.43 N	27.36 E
Ivančice	46	49.06 N	16.23 E
Ivanec	52	46.13 N	16.08 E
Ivangorod	60	59.24 N	28.10 E
Ivangrad	54	42.50 N	19.52 E
Ivanhoe, Austl.	94	32.54 S	144.18 E
Ivanhoe, Ca., U.S.	104	36.23 N	119.13 W
Ivanić Grad	52	45.42 N	16.24 E
Ivanišči	60	55.46 N	40.26 E
Ivanjica	54	43.35 N	20.14 E
Ivan'kovo	60	54.44 N	37.57 E
Ivan'kovskij	60	56.39 N	40.05 E
Ivano-Frankovsk	56	48.55 N	24.43 E
Ivanovo	60	57.00 N	40.59 E
Ivanpah Lake ⊜	104	35.35 N	115.25 W
Ivatuva	114	23.37 S	52.13 W
Ivdel'	56	60.42 N	60.24 E
Ivenec	60	53.53 N	26.45 E
Ivigtut	98	61.12 N	48.10 W
Ivinghoe	34	51.50 N	0.37 W
Ivory Coast (Côte d'Ivoire) □ 1	80	8.00 N	5.00 W
Ivösjön ⊜	44	56.06 N	14.27 E
Ivot	60	53.42 N	34.12 E
Ivrea	52	45.28 N	7.52 E
Ivujivik	98	62.24 N	77.55 W
Ivybridge	34	50.23 N	3.56 W
Iwaizumi	64	39.50 N	141.48 E
Iwaki (Taira)	64	37.03 N	140.55 E
Iwaki-san ∧	64	40.39 N	140.18 E
Iwakuni	64	34.09 N	132.11 E
Iwami	64	35.35 N	134.20 E
Iwamizawa	64a	43.12 N	141.46 E
Iwanai	64a	42.58 N	140.30 E
Iwanuma	64	38.06 N	140.52 E
Iwata	64	34.42 N	137.48 E
Iwate □ 5	64	39.37 N	141.22 E
Iwate-san ∧	64	39.51 N	141.00 E
Iwo	80	7.38 N	4.11 E
Iwo Jima →Iō-jima I	28	24.47 N	141.20 E
Ixmiquilpan	106	20.29 N	99.14 W
Ixopo	86	30.08 S	30.00 E
Ixworth	34	52.18 N	0.50 E
Iyo	64	33.46 N	132.42 E
Iyo-mishima	64	33.58 N	133.33 E
Iyo-nada ⊤ 2	64	33.40 N	132.20 E
Izberbaš	56	42.33 N	47.52 E
Izbica, Pol.	46	50.54 N	23.09 E
Izbica, Pol.	46	54.42 N	17.26 E
Izegem	46	50.55 N	3.12 E
Izena-shima I	65b	26.56 N	127.56 E
Ižma ≃	42	65.19 N	52.54 E
Izmail	56	45.21 N	28.50 E
İzmir	30	38.25 N	27.09 E
İzmit	30	40.46 N	29.55 E
Iznajar, Embalse de ⊜ 1	50	37.15 N	4.30 W
Iznalloz	50	37.23 N	3.31 W
Izoplit	60	56.38 N	36.12 E
Izozog, Bañados de ⋮	110	18.48 S	62.10 W
Izsák	46	46.48 N	19.22 E
Izu-hantō › 1	64	34.45 N	139.00 E
Izuhara	64	34.12 N	129.17 E
Iz'um	56	49.12 N	37.19 E
Izumi, Nihon	64	32.05 N	130.22 E
Izumi, Nihon	64	34.29 N	135.26 E
Izumi, Nihon	64	38.20 N	140.53 E
Izumo	64	35.22 N	132.46 E
Izu-shotō II	64	34.30 N	139.30 E
Izvestij CIK, ostrova II	58	75.55 N	82.30 E
J			
Jääsjärvi ⊜	44	61.36 N	26.07 E
Jabal, Baḩr al- →Mountain Nile ≃	82	9.30 N	30.30 E
Jabal al-Awliyā'	82	15.14 N	32.30 E
Jabalón ≃	50	38.53 N	4.05 W
Jabalpur	76	23.10 N	79.57 E
Jablah	78	35.21 N	35.55 E
Jablanac	52	44.42 N	14.54 E
Jablanica	52	43.39 N	17.45 E
Jablanica ≃	54	43.07 N	21.57 E
Jablaničko Jezero ⊜ 1	52	43.40 N	17.50 E
Jablonec nad Nisou	46	50.44 N	15.10 E
Jablonica	46	48.37 N	17.25 E
Jabłonka	46	49.29 N	19.41 E
Jablonovyj chrebet ⋏	58	53.30 N	115.00 E
Jabłonowo	46	53.24 N	19.09 E
Jablunkov	46	49.35 N	18.47 E
Jaboatão	110	8.07 S	35.01 W
Jabrīn ⊤ 4	74	23.17 N	48.58 E
Jaca	50	42.34 N	0.33 W
Jacareí	114	23.19 S	45.58 W
Jacarezinho	114	23.09 S	49.59 W
Jaceel ∨	82	10.25 N	51.01 E
Jáchal ≃	114	30.44 S	68.08 W
Jacinto Aráuz	114	38.04 S	63.26 W
Jacinto Machado	114	29.00 S	49.46 W
Jack Creek ≃	104	42.59 N	121.32 W
Jackman	102	45.38 N	70.15 W
Jackpot	104	41.59 N	114.40 W
Jackson, Ca., U.S.	104	38.20 N	120.46 W
Jackson, Mi., U.S.	102	42.14 N	84.24 W
Jackson, Ms., U.S.	100	32.17 N	90.11 W
Jackson, Oh., U.S.	102	39.03 N	82.38 W
Jackson, Tn., U.S.	100	35.36 N	88.48 W
Jackson ≃	102	37.47 N	79.46 W
Jackson, Mount ∧, Ant.	24	71.23 S	63.22 W
Jackson, Mount ∧, Austl.	90	30.15 S	119.16 E
Jackson, Port C	94	33.50 S	151.16 E
Jackson Bay C	96	43.58 S	168.42 E
Jackson Center	102	40.27 N	84.02 W
Jackson Mountain ∧	102	44.46 N	70.32 W
Jacksons Head ›	96	43.58 S	168.37 E
Jacksonville, Al., U.S.	100	33.48 N	85.45 W
Jacksonville, Fl., U.S.	100	30.19 N	81.39 W
Jacksonville, N.C., U.S.	100	34.45 N	77.25 W
Jacksonville, Or., U.S.	104	42.18 N	122.57 W
Jacmel	108	18.14 N	72.32 W
Jacobābād	76	28.17 N	68.26 E
Jacobina	110	11.11 S	40.31 W
Jacobsdal	86	29.13 S	24.41 E
Jacques-Cartier, Détroit de ɥ	98	50.00 N	63.30 W
Jacques-Cartier, Mont ∧	98	48.59 N	65.57 W
Jacuí ≃	114	30.02 S	51.15 W
Jacumba	104	32.37 N	116.11 W
Jacupiranga	114	24.42 S	48.00 W
Jadebusen C	46	53.30 N	8.10 E
J.A.D. Jensens Nunatakker ∧	98	62.45 N	48.00 W
Jadotville →Likasi	84	10.59 S	26.44 E
Jadraque	50	40.55 N	2.55 W
Jaén, Esp.	50	37.46 N	3.47 W
Jaén, Perú	110	5.42 S	78.47 W
Jæren + 1	44	58.45 N	5.45 E
Jāfarābād	76	20.52 N	71.22 E
Jaffa, Cape ›	94	36.58 S	139.40 E
Jaffa, Tel Aviv- →Tel Aviv-Yafo	78	32.04 N	34.46 E
Jaffna	74	9.40 N	80.00 E

Symbols in the Index entries are identified on page 122.

Name	Page	Lat. °′	Long. °′
Jaffrey	102	42.48N	72.01W
Jagādhri	76	30.10N	77.18 E
Jagatsingpur	76	20.16N	86.10 E
Jagdalpur	74	19.04N	82.02 E
Jagersfontein	86	29.44S	25.29 E
Jagodnoje	58	62.33N	149.40 E
Jagraon	76	30.47N	75.29 E
Jagst ≃	46	49.14N	9.11 E
Jaguarão	114	32.34S	53.23W
Jaguarão (Yaguarón) ≃	114	32.39S	53.12W
Jaguari	114	29.30S	54.41W
Jaguariaíva	114	24.15S	49.42W
Jaguaribe ≃	110	4.25S	37.45W
Jaguaruna	114	28.36S	49.02W
Jagüé	114	28.38S	68.24W
Jagüey Grande	108	22.32N	81.08W
Jahānābād	76	25.13N	84.59 E
Jahrom	78	28.31N	53.33 E
Jailolo	68	1.05N	127.30 E
Jainti	76	26.42N	89.36 E
Jaipur	76	26.55N	75.49 E
Jāis	76	26.15N	81.32 E
Jaisalmer	76	26.55N	70.54 E
Jaito	76	30.28N	74.53 E
Jaja	58	56.12N	86.26 E
Jajce	52	44.21N	17.16 E
Jājpur	76	20.51N	86.20 E
Jakarta	72	6.10S	106.48 E
Jake Creek Mountain ∧	104	41.13N	116.54W
Jākhal	76	29.48N	75.50 E
Jakhāu	76	23.13N	68.43 E
Jakobshavn	98	69.13N	51.06W
Jakobstad (Pietarsaari)	44	63.40N	22.42 E
Jakupica ⋏	54	41.43N	21.26 E
Jakutsk	58	62.00N	129.40 E
Jalālābād, Afg.	76	34.26N	70.28 E
Jalālābād, India	76	30.37N	74.15 E
Jalālpur	76	26.19N	82.44 E
Jalapa Enríquez	106	19.32N	96.55W
Jalasjärvi	44	62.30N	22.45 E
Jālaun	76	26.09N	79.21 E
Jalesar	76	27.29N	78.19 E
Jaleswar	76	21.49N	87.13 E
Jālgaon	76	21.01N	75.34 E
Jallas ≃	50	42.54N	9.08W
Jālna	74	19.50N	75.53 E
Jalón ≃	50	41.47N	1.04W
Jālor	76	25.21N	72.37 E
Jalpaiguri	76	26.31N	88.44 E
Jalta	56	44.30N	34.10 E
Jaluit I[1]	28	6.00N	169.35 E
Jalutorovsk	56	56.40N	66.18 E
Jamaame	84	0.04N	42.45 E
Jamaica □[1]	106	18.15N	77.30W
Jamaica Channel ⩌	108	18.00N	75.30W
Jamal, poluostrov ›[1]	58	70.00N	70.00 E
Jamālpur, Bngl.	76	24.55N	89.56 E
Jamālpur, India	76	25.18N	86.30 E
Jamantau, gora ∧	56	54.15N	58.06 E
Jamanxim ≃	110	4.43S	56.18W
Jamarovka	58	50.38N	110.16 E
Jambes	46	50.28N	4.52 E
Jambi	72	1.36S	103.37 E
Jambi □[4]	72	1.30S	103.00 E
Jambin	94	24.12S	150.22 E
Jambol	54	42.29N	26.30 E
Jambongan, Pulau I	72	6.40N	117.27 E
Jambusar	76	22.03N	72.48 E
James ≃, Austl.	94	20.36S	137.41 E
James ≃, U.S.	100	42.52N	97.18W
James Bay C	98	53.30N	80.30W
James Craik	114	32.09S	63.28W
James Price Point ›	90	17.30S	122.08 E
James Ranges ⋏	90	24.06S	132.30 E
James Ross, Cape ›	98	74.40N	114.25W
James Ross Strait ⩌	98	69.40N	95.30W
Jamestown, Austl.	94	33.12S	138.36 E
Jamestown, Ire.	40	53.55N	8.02W
Jamestown, S. Afr.	86	31.06S	26.45 E
Jamestown, Ca., U.S.	104	37.57N	120.25W
Jamestown, N.Y., U.S.	102	42.05N	79.14W
Jamestown, N.D., U.S.	100	46.54N	98.42W
Jamestown, Oh., U.S.	102	39.39N	83.44W
Jamiltepec	106	16.17N	97.49W
Jamjodhpur	76	21.54N	70.01 E
Jammerbugten C	44	57.20N	9.30 E
Jammu	76	32.42N	74.52 E
Jammu and Kashmir □[2]	76	34.00N	76.00 E
Jāmnagar	76	22.28N	70.04 E
Jamnotri	76	31.01N	78.27 E
Jampang-kulon	72	7.16S	106.37 E
Jämsä	44	61.52N	25.12 E
Jämsänkoski	44	61.55N	25.11 E
Jamshedpur	76	22.48N	86.11 E
Jamsk	58	59.35N	154.10 E
Jämtland □[9]	44	63.30N	14.00 E
Jämtlands Län □[6]	44	63.00N	14.40 E
Jamūi	76	24.55N	86.13 E
Jamuna ≃	76	23.51N	89.45 E
Jāmuria	76	23.44N	87.02 E
Jana ≃	58	71.31N	136.32 E
Janaucu, Ilha I	110	0.30N	50.10W
Janda, Laguna de la ⊜	50	36.15N	5.51W
Jandaia do Sul	114	23.36S	51.39W
Jandiāla	76	31.36N	75.03 E
Jandowae	94	26.47S	151.06 E
Jándula ≃	50	38.03N	4.06W
Jándula, Embalse de ⊜[1]	50	38.30N	4.00W
Jane Peak ∧	96	45.20S	168.19 E
Janesville, Ca., U.S.	104	40.17N	120.31W
Janesville, Wi., U.S.	100	42.40N	89.01W
Jangany	87b	23.14S	45.27 E
Jangijul'	56	41.07N	69.03 E
Jangipur	76	24.28N	88.04 E
Janikowo	46	52.45N	18.07 E
Janīn	78	32.28N	35.18 E
Janja	54	44.40N	19.15 E
Janjina	52	42.56N	17.26 E
Jan Kempdorp (Andalusia)	86	27.55S	24.51 E
Jan Mayen I	20	71.00N	8.20W
Jan Mayen Ridge ✦[3]	20	69.00N	8.00W
Jánoshalma	46	46.18N	19.20 E
Jánosháza	46	47.08N	17.10 E
Janoviči	60	55.17N	30.42 E
Janowiec Wielkopolski	46	52.46N	17.31 E
Janów Lubelski	46	50.43N	22.24 E
Jansenville	86	32.56S	24.40 E
Janskij	58	68.28N	134.48 E
Janskij zaliv C	58	71.50N	136.00 E
Jantarnyj	60	54.52N	19.57 E
Jantra ≃	54	43.38N	25.34 E
Januária	110	15.29S	44.22W
Janzé	48	47.58N	1.30W
Jaora	76	23.38N	75.08 E
Japan (Nihon) □[1]	62	36.00N	138.00 E
Japan, Sea of ⊤[2]	62	40.00N	135.00 E
Japan Basin ✦[1]	26	40.00N	135.00 E
Japtiksal'a	58	69.21N	72.32 E
Japurá (Caquetá) ≃	110	3.08S	64.46W
Jaraguá do Sul	114	26.29S	49.04W
Jaraicejo	50	39.40N	5.49W
Jaraiz de la Vera	50	40.04N	5.45W
Jarama ≃	50	40.02N	3.39W
Jarandilla	50	40.08N	5.39W
Jaransk	42	57.19N	47.54 E
Jarānwāla	76	31.20N	73.26 E
Jarash	78	32.17N	35.54 E
Jarbidge ≃	104	42.19N	115.39W
Järbo	44	60.43N	16.36 E
Jarcevo	60	55.04N	32.41 E
Jardín América	114	27.03S	55.14W
Jardine ≃	92	10.55S	142.13 E
Jardines de la Reina, Archipiélago de los II	108	20.50N	78.55W
Jarega	56	63.27N	53.26 E
Jarensk	42	62.11N	49.02 E
Jargeau	48	47.52N	2.07 E
Jari ≃	110	1.09S	51.54W
Jaridih	76	23.38N	86.04 E
Jarmen	46	53.55N	13.20 E
Järna	44	59.06N	17.34 E
Jarnac	48	45.41N	0.10W
Jarocin	46	51.59N	17.31 E
Jaroměř	46	50.21N	15.55 E
Jaroslavl'	60	57.37N	39.52 E
Jarosław	46	50.02N	22.42 E
Järpen	44	63.21N	13.29 E
Jarrahdale	90	32.21S	116.04 E
Jarrow	36	54.59N	1.29W
Jar-Sale	56	66.50N	70.50 E
Järvelä	44	60.52N	25.17 E
Järvenpää	44	60.28N	25.06 E
Jarvis	102	42.53N	80.06W
Jarvis Island I	28	0.23S	160.02W
Järvsö	44	61.43N	16.10 E
Jaša Tomić	54	45.27N	20.51 E
Jasdan	76	22.02N	71.12 E
Jasień	46	51.46N	15.01 E
Jāsk	78	25.38N	57.46 E
Jasło	46	49.45N	21.29 E
Jasnogorsk	60	54.29N	37.42 E
Jasnyj	58	53.17N	127.59 E
Jason Islands II	112	51.05S	61.00W
Jasper, Ab., Can.	98	52.53N	118.05W
Jasper, Al., U.S.	100	33.49N	87.16W
Jasra	76	25.17N	81.48 E
Jastarnia	46	54.43N	18.40 E
Jastrebarsko	52	45.40N	15.39 E
Jastrowie	46	53.26N	16.49 E
Jászapáti	46	47.31N	20.09 E
Jászberény	46	47.30N	19.55 E
Jataí	110	17.53S	51.43W
Játiva	50	38.59N	0.31W
Jatni	76	20.10N	85.42 E
Jaú	114	22.18S	48.33W
Jaú ≃	110	1.54S	61.26W
Jauja	110	11.48S	75.30W
Jaunjelgava	60	56.37N	25.05 E
Jaunpur	76	25.44N	82.41 E
Java → Jawa I	72	7.30S	110.00 E
Javalambre ∧	50	40.06N	1.03W
Javari (Yavarí) ≃	110	4.21S	70.02W
Javas	60	54.26N	42.51 E
Java Sea → Jawa, Laut ⊤[2]	72	5.00S	110.00 E
Java Trench ✦[1]	26	10.30S	110.00 E
Jávea	50	38.47N	0.10 E
Javor ⋏	54	44.05N	18.55 E
Javorie ∧	46	48.27N	19.18 E
Javorník	46	50.23N	17.00 E
Javorová skála ∧	46	49.31N	14.30 E
Jävre	44	65.09N	21.59 E
Jawa (Java) I	72	7.30S	110.00 E
Jawa, Laut (Java Sea) ⊤[2]	72	5.00S	110.00 E
Jawa Barat □[4]	72	7.00S	107.00 E
Jawa Tengah □[4]	72	7.30S	110.00 E
Jawa Timur □[4]	72	8.00S	113.00 E
Jawor	46	51.03N	16.11 E
Jaworzno	46	50.13N	19.15 E
Jaya, Puncak ∧	92	4.05S	137.11 E
Jayapura (Sukarnapura)	92	2.32S	140.42 E
Jay Peak ∧	102	44.55N	72.32W
Jaywick	34	51.47N	1.08 E
Jaz Mūrīān, Hāmūn-e ⊜	78	27.20N	58.55 E
Jebāl Bārez, Kūh-e ⋏	78	28.30N	58.20 E
Jebba	80	9.08N	4.50 E
Jebel	54	45.33N	21.14 E
Jedburgh	38	55.29N	2.34W
Jędrzejów	46	50.39N	20.18 E
Jed Water ≃	38	55.32N	2.33W
Jefferson	102	41.44N	80.46W
Jefferson, Mount ∧	104	38.46N	116.55W
Jefferson City	100	38.34N	92.10W
Jeffersonton	102	38.38N	77.55W
Jeffersonville	102	39.39N	83.33W
Jefremov	60	53.09N	38.07 E
Jegorjevsk	60	55.23N	39.02 E
Jejsk	56	46.42N	38.16 E
Jeju → Cheju	62	33.31N	126.32 E
Jēkabpils	60	56.29N	25.51 E
Jekateriny, proliv ⩌	58	44.30N	146.45 E
Jelabuga	42	55.47N	52.04 E
Jelancy	58	52.49N	106.25 E
Jelat'ma	60	54.58N	41.45 E
Jelec	60	52.37N	38.30 E
Jelenia Góra (Hirschberg)	46	50.55N	15.46 E
Jelenskij	60	53.29N	35.23 E
Jelgava	60	56.39N	23.42 E
Jelizavety, mys ›	58	54.26N	142.42 E
Jelizovo	60	53.24N	29.01 E
Jelling	44	55.45N	9.26 E
Jel'n'a	60	54.35N	33.11 E
Jeloguj ≃	56	63.13N	87.45 E
Jelšava	46	48.39N	20.14 E
Jemanželinsk	56	54.45N	61.20 E
Jember	72	8.10S	113.42 E
Jemca	42	63.04N	40.20 E
Jemnice	46	49.01N	15.35 E
Jena	46	50.56N	11.35 E
Jenašimskij Polkan, gora ∧	58	59.50N	92.52 E
Jenbach	46	47.24N	11.47 E
Jeneponto	72	5.41S	119.42 E
Jenisej ≃	56	71.50N	82.40 E
Jenisejsk	56	58.27N	92.10 E
Jenisejskij kr'až ⋏	58	59.00N	93.00 E
Jenisejskij zaliv C	58	72.30N	80.00 E
Jenkins, Mount ∧	90	25.36S	129.41 E
Jenkintown	102	40.05N	75.07W
Jennersdorf	46	46.57N	16.08 E
Jens Munk Island I	98	69.42N	79.30W
Jepara	72	6.35S	110.39 E
Jeparit	94	36.09S	141.59 E
Jepifan'	60	53.49N	38.33 E
Jepua (Jeppo)	44	63.24N	22.37 E
Jequié	110	13.51S	40.05W
Jequitinhonha ≃	110	15.51S	38.53W
Jerada	80	34.17N	2.13W
Jerba, Île de I	80	33.48N	10.54 E
Jerbogačon	58	61.16N	108.00 E
Jérémie	108	18.39N	74.07W
Jeremoabo	110	10.04S	38.21W
Jerevan	56	40.11N	44.30 E
Jerez de la Frontera	50	36.41N	6.08W
Jerez de los Caballeros	50	38.19N	6.46W
Jergeni ⋏[2]	56	47.00N	44.00 E
Jericho, Austl.	94	23.36S	146.08 E
Jericho → Arīḥā, Urd.	78	31.52N	35.27 E
Jerid, Chott ⋮	80	33.42N	8.26 E
Jerilderie	94	35.22S	145.44 E
Jerimoth Hill ∧[2]	102	41.52N	71.47W
Jermiš'	60	54.46N	42.16 E
Jermolino	60	55.12N	36.36 E
Jerofej Pavlovič	58	53.58N	122.01 E
Jerome	104	42.43N	114.31W
Jeropol	58	65.15N	168.40 E
Jersey □[2]	30	49.15N	2.10W
Jersey City	102	40.43N	74.04W
Jersey Shore	102	41.12N	77.16W
Jeršov	56	51.20N	48.17 E
Jerte ≃	50	39.58N	6.17W
Jerusalem → Yerushalayim	78	31.46N	35.14 E
Jervis, Cape ›	94	35.38S	138.06 E
Jervis Bay C	94	35.05S	150.44 E
Jervois Range ⋏	90	22.38S	136.05 E
Jesenice, Česko.	46	50.04N	13.29 E
Jesenice, Jugo.	52	46.27N	14.04 E
Jeseník	46	50.14N	17.13 E
Jesil'	56	51.58N	66.24 E
Jessej	58	68.29N	102.10 E
Jesselton → Kota Kinabalu	72	5.59N	116.04 E
Jessen	46	51.47N	12.58 E
Jessentuki	56	44.03N	42.51 E
Jessheim	44	60.09N	11.11 E
Jessore	76	23.10N	89.13 E
Jessup	102	41.28N	75.33W
Jesús	114	27.03S	55.47W
Jesús Carranza	106	17.26N	95.02W
Jesús María	114	30.59S	64.06W
Jetpur	76	21.44N	70.37 E
Jeumont	48	50.18N	4.06 E
Jever	46	53.34N	7.54 E
Jevlach	78	40.36N	47.09 E
Jevnaker	44	60.15N	10.28 E
Jevpatorija	56	45.12N	33.22 E
Jewett City	102	41.36N	71.58W
Jezerce ∧	54	42.26N	19.49 E
Jeziorany	46	53.58N	20.46 E
Jhābua	76	22.46N	74.36 E
Jhajha	76	24.46N	86.22 E
Jhajjar	76	28.37N	76.39 E
Jhālawār	76	24.36N	76.09 E
Jhang Maghiāna	76	31.16N	72.19 E
Jhānsi	76	25.26N	78.35 E
Jhārgrām	76	22.27N	86.59 E
Jharia	76	23.45N	86.24 E
Jhārsuguda	76	21.51N	84.02 E
Jhelum	76	32.56N	73.44 E
Jhelum ≃	76	31.12N	72.08 E
Jhinkpāni	76	22.25N	85.47 E
Jhūnjhunu	76	28.08N	75.24 E
Jiading	66	31.23N	121.15 E
Jiaganj	76	24.14N	88.16 E
Jiali	62	30.47N	93.24 E
Jialing ≃	62	29.34N	106.35 E
Jiamusi	62	46.50N	130.21 E
Ji'an	66	27.07N	114.58 E
Jianchuan	70	26.34N	99.53 E
Jiande	66	29.29N	119.16 E
Jiangba	66	33.08N	118.45 E
Jiangcheng	70	22.40N	101.48 E
Jiangdu	66	32.26N	119.34 E
Jiangjin	62	29.17N	106.15 E
Jiangkou	62	23.31N	110.17 E
Jiangle	66	26.42N	117.25 E
Jiangmen	66	22.35N	113.05 E
Jiangning	66	31.58N	118.50 E
Jiangpu	66	32.04N	118.37 E
Jiangshan	66	28.45N	118.37 E
Jiangsu (Kiangsu) □[4]	62	33.00N	120.00 E
Jiangtian	66	25.52N	119.34 E
Jiangxi (Kiangsi) □[4]	62	28.00N	116.00 E
Jiangyin	66	31.55N	120.16 E
Jiangzi	76	28.57N	89.35 E
Jianhu	66	33.28N	119.50 E
Jianli	66	29.49N	112.53 E
Jianning	66	26.50N	116.49 E
Jian'ou	66	27.03N	118.19 E
Jianshui	70	23.38N	102.49 E
Jianyang	66	27.22N	118.04 E
Jiaohe	62	43.42N	127.19 E
Jiaoling	66	24.41N	116.10 E
Jiaoxian	62	36.18N	119.58 E
Jiaozuo	62	35.15N	113.13 E
Jiapu	66	31.06N	119.56 E
Jiashan, Zhg.	66	32.47N	118.00 E
Jiashan, Zhg.	66	30.51N	120.54 E
Jiashun Hu ⊜	62	34.35N	86.05 E
Jiawang	66	34.27N	117.27 E
Jiaxian	66	33.58N	113.13 E
Jiaxing	66	30.46N	120.45 E
Jiayu	66	29.58N	113.55 E
Jiazi	66	22.55N	116.04 E
Jičín	46	50.26N	15.21 E
Jiddah	74	21.30N	39.12 E
Jiesheng	66	22.45N	115.25 E
Jieshi	66	22.51N	115.49 E
Jieshou	66	33.18N	115.20 E
Jiexi	66	23.28N	115.56 E
Jieyang	66	23.35N	116.21 E
Jiezhongdian	66	32.41N	112.29 E
Jieznas	60	54.36N	24.10 E
Jigel	50	36.48N	5.46 E
Jiggalong Mission	90	23.25S	120.47 E
Jiguaní	108	20.22N	76.26W
Jigüey, Bahía de C	108	22.08N	78.05W
Jihlava	46	49.24N	15.36 E
Jihlava ≃	46	48.55N	16.37 E
Jihočeský Kraj □[4]	46	49.05N	14.30 E
Jihomoravský Kraj □[4]	46	49.10N	16.40 E
Jijia ≃	54	46.54N	28.05 E
Jijiashi	66	32.08N	120.18 E
Jijiga	82	9.22N	42.47 E
Jijona	50	38.32N	0.30W
Jilib	84	0.29N	42.46 E
Jili Hu ⊜	62	46.57N	87.27 E
Jilin	62	43.51N	126.33 E
Jilin (Kirin) □[4]	62	44.00N	126.00 E
Jill, Kediet ej ∧	80	22.38N	12.33W
Jiloca ≃	50	41.21N	1.39W
Jima	82	7.36N	36.50 E
Jimbolia	54	45.47N	20.43 E
Jimena de la Frontera	50	36.26N	5.27W
Jim Thorpe	102	40.52N	75.43W
Jinan (Tsinan)	62	36.40N	116.57 E
Jincheng	62	35.30N	112.50 E
Jīnd	76	29.19N	76.19 E
Jindabyne	94	36.25S	148.38 E
Jindřichův Hradec	46	49.09N	15.00 E
Jinfeng	66	26.01N	119.36 E
Jing'an	66	28.52N	115.20 E
Jingde	66	30.19N	118.31 E
Jingdezhen (Kingtechen)	66	29.16N	117.11 E
Jingdong	70	24.28N	100.52 E
Jinggang	66	28.28N	112.46 E
Jinggangshan	62	26.36N	114.05 E
Jinghai	66	23.03N	116.31 E
Jinghong	70	22.01N	100.49 E
Jingshan	66	31.02N	113.05 E
Jingxi	70	23.08N	106.29 E
Jingxian, Zhg.	62	37.42N	116.16 E
Jingxian, Zhg.	66	30.42N	118.24 E
Jinhua	66	29.07N	119.39 E
Jining, Zhg.	62	40.57N	113.02 E
Jining, Zhg.	62	35.25N	116.36 E
Jinja	84	0.26N	33.12 E
Jinjiang	66	24.50N	118.35 E
Jinjing	66	24.37N	118.36 E
Jinkou	66	30.22N	114.10 E
Jinning	70	24.41N	102.35 E
Jinotega	108	13.06N	86.00W
Jinotepe	108	11.51N	86.12W
Jinping	70	26.38N	109.03 E
Jinsha	66	32.06N	121.05 E
Jinsha ≃	62	28.50N	104.36 E
Jinshan	66	30.54N	121.09 E
Jinshanwei	66	30.44N	121.19 E
Jinshi	62	29.39N	111.52 E
Jintan	66	31.45N	119.34 E
Jinxi, Zhg.	62	40.45N	120.50 E
Jinxi, Zhg.	66	27.54N	116.43 E
Jinxian, Zhg.	62	39.04N	121.40 E
Jinxian, Zhg.	66	28.22N	116.14 E
Jinxiang	66	27.26N	120.35 E
Jinyun	66	28.40N	120.03 E
Jinzhai	66	31.44N	115.54 E
Jinzhou	62	41.07N	121.08 E
Jinzū ≃	64	36.46N	137.13 E
Jiparaná ≃	110	8.03S	62.52W
Jipijapa	110	1.20S	80.35W
Jirjā	82	26.20N	31.53 E
Jirkov	46	50.30N	13.27 E
Jishui	66	27.14N	115.06 E
Jisr ash-Shughūr	78	35.48N	36.19 E
Jitarning	90	32.48S	117.59 E
Jiu ≃	54	43.47N	23.48 E
Jiufeng	66	24.20N	117.02 E
Jiujiang, Zhg.	66	29.44N	115.59 E
Jiujiang, Zhg.	66	22.51N	113.02 E
Jiujiang, Zhg.	66	29.36N	115.52 E
Jiulian Shan ⋏	66	24.40N	114.46 E
Jiuling Shan ⋏	66	28.46N	114.45 E
Jiuquan	62	39.45N	98.34 E
Jiutai	62	44.08N	125.50 E
Jiuyuhang	66	30.17N	119.56 E
Jiuzhen	66	24.05N	117.42 E
Jixi, Zhg.	62	45.17N	130.59 E
Jixi, Zhg.	66	30.06N	118.35 E
Jixian	62	40.03N	117.24 E
Jiyang	66	27.10N	118.07 E
Jizera ≃	46	50.10N	14.43 E
Joaçaba	114	27.10S	51.30W
João Pessoa	110	7.07S	34.52W
Joaquim Távora	114	23.30S	49.58W
Joaquín V. González	114	25.05S	64.11W
Jobat	76	22.25N	74.34 E
Job Peak ∧	104	39.35N	118.14W
Jocolí	114	32.35S	68.41W
Jódar	50	37.50N	3.21W
Jodhpur	76	26.17N	73.02 E
Jodiya	76	22.42N	70.18 E
Joensuu	44	62.36N	29.46 E
Joetsu	64	37.06N	138.15 E
Jõgeva	60	58.45N	26.24 E
Jōhana	64	36.31N	136.54 E
Johannesburg, S. Afr.	86	26.12S	28.05 E
Johannesburg, Ca., U.S.	104	35.22N	117.38W
Jōhen	64	32.57N	132.35 E
John O'Groats	38	58.38N	3.05W
Johnshaven	38	56.47N	2.20W
Johnson	102	44.38N	72.40W
Johnsonburg	102	41.29N	78.40W
Johnson City, N.Y., U.S.	102	42.06N	75.57W
Johnson City, Tn., U.S.	100	36.18N	82.21W
Johnsondale	104	35.58N	118.32W
Johnsonville	96	41.14S	174.47 E
Johnston	34	51.46N	5.00W
Johnston, Lake ⊜	90	32.25S	120.30 E
Johnston Atoll I[1]	28	16.45N	169.32W
Johnstone	38	55.50N	4.31W
Johnstown, N.Y., U.S.	102	43.00N	74.22W
Johnstown, Oh., U.S.	102	40.09N	82.41W
Johnstown, Pa., U.S.	102	40.19N	78.55W
Johor □[3]	72	2.00N	103.30 E
Johor Baharu	72	1.28N	103.45 E
Joigny	48	47.59N	3.24 E
Joinvile	114	26.18S	48.50W
Joinville	48	48.27N	5.08 E
Jokioinen	44	60.49N	23.28 E
Jokkmokk	42	66.37N	19.50 E
Jökulsá á Brú ≃	42a	65.41N	14.13W
Joliet	100	41.31N	88.04W
Joliette	102	46.01N	73.27W
Jolo	68	6.03N	121.00 E
Jolo Island I	68	5.58N	121.06 E
Jølstravatnet ⊜	44	61.32N	6.13 E
Jombang	72	7.33S	112.14 E
Jomda	62	31.27N	98.15 E
Jonesboro	100	35.50N	90.42W
Jonesport	102	44.31N	67.35W
Jones Sound ⩌	98	76.00N	85.00W
Jonesville	102	41.59N	84.40W
Jongkha	76	28.57N	85.15 E
Jongunjärvi ⊜	44	65.17N	27.15 E
Joniškis	60	56.14N	23.37 E
Jönköping	44	57.47N	14.11 E
Jönköpings Län □[6]	44	57.30N	14.30 E
Jonquière	98	48.24N	71.15W
Jonuta	106	18.05N	92.08W
Jonzac	48	45.27N	0.26W
Joplin	100	37.05N	94.30W
Jora	76	26.20N	77.49 E
Jordan, Mt., U.S.	100	47.19N	106.54W
Jordan, N.Y., U.S.	102	43.03N	76.28W
Jordan (Al-Urdunn) □[1]	74	31.00N	36.00 E
Jordan ≃	78	31.46N	35.33 E
Jordan Creek ≃	104	42.52N	117.38W
Jordanów	46	49.40N	19.50 E
Jordan Valley	104	42.58N	117.03W
Jordão ≃	114	25.46S	52.07W
Jordet	44	61.25N	12.09 E
Jorhāt	76	26.46N	94.13 E
Jörn	44	65.04N	20.02 E
Joroinen	44	62.11N	27.50 E
Jørpeland	44	59.01N	6.03 E
Jos	80	9.55N	8.53 E
José Batlle y Ordóñez	114	33.28S	55.07W
José de San Martín	112	44.02S	70.29W
José Francisco Vergara	114	22.28S	69.38W
José Pedro Varela	114	33.27S	54.32W
Joseph, Lac ⊜	98	52.45N	65.15W
Joseph, Lake ⊜	102	45.10N	79.44W
Joseph Bonaparte Gulf C	92	14.15S	128.30 E
Joshīmath	76	30.34N	79.34 E
Joshua Tree	104	34.08N	116.18W
Joškar-Ola	42	56.38N	47.52 E
Josselin	48	47.57N	2.33W
Jostedalsbreen ⊏	44	61.40N	7.00 E
Jotunheimen ⋏	44	61.38N	8.18 E
Joubertina	86	33.50S	23.51 E
Joutsa	44	61.44N	26.07 E
Joutseno	44	61.06N	28.30 E
Joutsijärvi	42	66.40N	28.00 E
Jovellanos	108	22.48N	81.12W
Jowai	76	25.27N	92.12 E
Jowhar	82	2.46N	45.31 E
Jowlaenga, Mount ∧	90	17.21S	122.56 E
Jowzjān □[4]	76	36.30N	66.00 E
Józefów	46	52.09N	21.12 E
Juan B. Arruabarrena	114	30.20S	58.19W
Juan de Fuca, Strait of ⩌	100	48.18N	124.00W
Juan de Garay	114	38.52S	64.34W
Juan de Mena	114	24.55S	56.44W
Juan de Nova, Île I	84	17.03S	42.45 E
Juan E. Barra	114	37.48S	60.29W
Juan Fernández, Archipiélago II	112	33.00S	80.00W
Juangriego	108	11.05N	63.57W
Juan Jorba	114	33.37S	65.16W
Juan José Castelli	114	25.57S	60.37W
Juanjuí	110	7.11S	76.45W
Juankoski	44	63.04N	28.21 E
Juan L. Lacaze	114	34.26S	57.27W
Juan N. Fernández	114	38.00S	59.16W
Juan Viñas	108	9.54N	83.45W
Juárez, Arg.	114	37.40S	59.48W
Juárez → Ciudad Juárez, Méx.	106	31.44N	106.29W
Juárez, Sierra de ⋏	104	32.00N	115.50W
Juàzeiro	110	9.25S	40.30W
Juàzeiro do Norte	110	7.12S	39.20W
Jūbā	82	4.51N	31.37 E
Jubba ≃	84	0.15S	42.38 E
Jubbulpore → Jabalpur	76	23.10N	79.57 E
Jubilee Downs	90	18.22S	125.17 E
Jubilee Lake ⊜	90	29.12S	126.38 E
Juby, Cap ›	80	27.58N	12.55W
Júcar ≃	50	39.09N	0.14W
Júcaro	108	21.37N	78.51W
Juchitán	106	16.26N	95.01W
Juchnov	60	54.45N	35.14 E
Judenburg	46	47.10N	14.40 E
Judoma ≃	58	59.08N	135.06 E
Juelsminde	44	55.43N	10.01 E
Juexi	66	29.27N	121.57 E
Jugon	48	48.25N	2.20W
Juidongshan	66	23.46N	117.31 E
Juigalpa	108	12.05N	85.24W
Juillac	48	45.19N	1.19 E
Juist I	46	53.40N	7.00 E
Juiz de Fora	110	21.45S	43.20W
Jujuy → San Salvador de Jujuy	114	24.11S	65.18W
Jujuy □[4]	114	23.00S	66.00W
Jukagirskoje ploskogorje ⋏[1]	58	66.00N	155.00 E
Jukta	58	63.23N	105.41 E
Juliaca	110	15.30S	70.08W
Julia Creek	94	20.39S	141.45 E
Julia Creek ≃	94	20.00S	141.11 E
Julian Alps ⋏	52	46.00N	14.00 E
Juliana Top ∧	110	3.41N	56.32W
Julianehåb	98	60.43N	46.01W
Jülich	46	50.55N	6.21 E
Júlio de Castilhos	114	29.14S	53.41W
Jullundur	76	31.19N	75.34 E
Jumboo	84	0.15S	42.38 E
Jumbo Peak ∧	104	36.12N	114.11W
Jumentos Cays II	108	22.42N	75.55W
Jumet	46	50.26N	4.25 E
Jumilla	50	38.29N	1.17W
Jumt uul ∧	62	44.30N	97.06 E
Junāgadh	76	21.31N	70.28 E
Junction City	100	39.01N	96.49W
Jundiaí	114	23.11S	46.52W
Jundiaí do Sul	114	23.27S	50.17W
Juneau	98	58.20N	134.27W
Junee	94	34.52S	147.35 E
June Lake	104	37.46N	119.04W
Jungar Qi	62	39.49N	111.10 E
Jungfrau ∧	48	46.32N	7.58 E
Junggar Pendi ≚[1]	62	45.00N	88.00 E
Juniata ≃	102	40.24N	77.01W
Junín	114	34.35S	60.57W
Junín, Lago ⊜	110	11.02S	76.06W
Junín de los Andes	112	39.56S	71.05W
Junior	102	38.59N	79.57W
Junipero Serra Peak ∧	104	36.08N	121.25W
Juniville	48	49.24N	4.23 E
Junqueirópolis	114	21.32S	51.26W
Junsele	44	63.41N	16.54 E
Junxian	62	32.31N	111.30 E
Juojärvi ⊜	44	62.43N	28.33 E
Juquiá	114	24.19S	47.38W
Jur, Česko.	46	48.15N	17.13 E
Jur, S.S.S.R.	58	59.52N	137.39 E
Jur ≃	82	8.39N	29.18 E
Jura □[5]	48	46.50N	5.50 E
Jura ⋏	48	46.45N	6.30 E
Jura I	38	56.00N	5.50W
Jura, Sound of ⩌	38	55.57N	5.48W
Jurbarkas	60	55.05N	22.48 E
Jurga	58	55.42N	84.51 E
Jurjevec	60	57.18N	43.06 E
Jūrmala	60	56.58N	23.42 E
Jurong	66	31.57N	119.10 E
Jurty	58	56.03N	97.37 E
Juruá ≃	110	2.37S	65.44W
Juruena ≃	110	7.20S	58.03W
Jur'uzan'	56	54.52N	58.26 E
Jurva	44	62.41N	21.59 E
Jusepín	108	9.45N	63.31W
Jussey	48	47.49N	5.54 E
Justiniano Posse	114	32.53S	62.40W
Justo Daract	114	33.52S	65.11W
Jutaí ≃	110	2.43S	66.57W
Jüterbog	46	51.59N	13.04 E
Juti	114	22.52S	54.37W
Jutiapa	106	14.17N	89.54W
Juticalpa	108	14.42N	86.15W
Jutland → Jylland ›[1]	44	56.00N	9.15 E
Jutrosin	46	51.40N	17.10 E
Juupajoki	44	61.47N	24.27 E
Juva	44	61.54N	27.51 E
Juventud, Isla de la (Isla de Pinos) I	108	21.40N	82.50W
Juvuln ⊜	44	63.43N	13.09 E
Juža	60	56.35N	42.01 E
Južno-Aličurskij chrebet ⋏	76	37.30N	73.20 E
Južno-Jenisejskij	58	58.48N	94.39 E
Južno-Sachalinsk	58	46.58N	142.42 E
Južno-Ural'sk	56	54.26N	61.15 E
Južnyj, mys ›	58	57.45N	156.45 E
Južnyj Bug ≃	56	46.59N	31.58 E
Jwayyā	78	33.14N	35.19 E
Jyderup	44	55.40N	11.26 E
Jylland ›[1]	44	56.00N	9.15 E
Jyväskylä	44	62.14N	25.44 E
K			
K2 (Godwin Austen) ∧	76	35.53N	76.30 E
Kaachka	78	37.21N	59.36 E
Kaala ∧	105a	21.31N	158.09W
Kaapmuiden	86	25.33S	31.20 E
Kaap Plato ⋏[1]	86	28.20S	23.57 E
Kaapstad → Cape Town	86	33.55S	18.22 E
Kaavi	44	62.59N	28.30 E
Kabaena, Pulau I	72	5.15S	121.55 E
Kabale	84	1.15S	29.59 E
Kabalega Falls ∟	82	2.17N	31.41 E
Kabalo	84	6.03S	26.55 E
Kabambare	84	4.42S	27.43 E
Kåbdalis	42	66.10N	20.00 E
Kab-hegy ∧	46	47.03N	17.39 E
Kabinda	84	6.08S	24.29 E
Kabīr Kūh ⋏	78	33.25N	46.45 E
Kabompo ≃	84	14.10S	23.11 E
Kabongo	84	7.19S	25.35 E
Kābul	76	34.30N	69.11 E
Kābul □[4]	76	34.30N	69.00 E
Kābul ≃	76	33.55N	72.14 E
Kaburuang, Pulau I	68	3.48N	126.48 E
Kačanik	54	42.13N	21.14 E
Kachin □[3]	70	26.00N	97.30 E
Kachovskoje vodochranilišče ⊜[1]	56	47.25N	34.10 E
K'achta	58	50.26N	106.25 E
Kačug	58	53.58N	105.52 E
Kadaň	46	50.20N	13.15 E
Kadanai (Kadaney) ≃	76	31.02N	66.09 E
Kadaney (Kadanai) ≃	76	31.02N	66.09 E
Kadan Kyun I	70	12.30N	98.22 E
Kade	80	6.05N	0.50W
Kadéï ≃	82	3.31N	16.05 E
Kadgo, Lake ⊜	90	26.42S	127.18 E
Kadhimain	78	33.22N	44.20 E
Kadi	76	23.18N	72.20 E
Kadina	94	33.58S	137.43 E
Kādīpur	76	26.10N	82.23 E
Kadirli	78	37.23N	36.05 E
Kadnikov	60	59.30N	40.20 E
Kadogawa	64	32.28N	131.39 E
Kadom	60	54.34N	42.30 E
Kadoma	86	18.21S	29.55 E
Kaduj	60	59.12N	37.09 E
Kaduna	80	10.33N	7.27 E
Kaduna ≃	80	8.45N	5.45 E
Kāduqlī	82	11.01N	29.43 E
Kadykčan	58	63.02N	146.50 E
Kadžerom	42	64.41N	55.54 E
Kaédi	80	16.09N	13.30W
Kaena Point ›	105a	21.35N	158.17W
Kaeo	96	35.06S	173.47 E
Kaesŏng	62	37.59N	126.33 E
Kafan	78	39.13N	46.24 E
Kafia Kingi	82	9.16N	24.25 E
Kafirévs, Ákra ›	54	38.09N	24.36 E
Kafo ≃	84	1.08N	31.05 E
Kafue ≃	84	15.56S	28.55 E
Kaga	64	36.18N	136.18 E
Kagan	78	39.43N	64.33 E
Kagawa □[5]	64	34.15N	134.00 E
Kagawong, Lake ⊜	102	45.49N	82.18W
Kåge	44	64.50N	20.59 E
Kagera ≃	84	0.57S	31.47 E
Kagoshima	64	31.36N	130.33 E
Kagoshima □[5]	65b	29.00N	129.30 E
Kagoshima-wan C	64	31.25N	130.38 E
Kagul	56	45.54N	28.11 E
Kahama	84	3.50S	32.36 E
Kahayan ≃	72	3.20S	114.04 E
Kahemba	84	7.17S	19.00 E
Kahiu Point ›	105a	21.13N	156.58W
Kahler Asten ∧	46	51.11N	8.29 E
Kahoolawe I	105a	20.33N	156.37W
Kahuku	105a	21.40N	157.57W
Kahuku Point ›	105a	21.43N	157.59W
Kahului	105a	20.54N	156.28W
Kahului Bay C	105a	20.54N	156.28W
Kahurangi Point ›	96	40.47S	172.13 E
Kai, Kepulauan II	92	5.35S	132.45 E
Kaiapoi	96	43.23S	172.40 E
Kai Besar I	92	5.35S	133.00 E
Kaidu ≃	62	41.55N	86.38 E
Kaieteur Fall ∟	110	5.10N	59.28W
Kaifeng	62	34.51N	114.21 E
Kaihu	96	35.46S	173.42 E
Kaihua	66	29.09N	118.23 E
Kai-Iwi	96	39.51S	174.56 E
Kai Kecil I	92	5.45S	132.40 E
Kaikohe	96	35.25S	173.48 E
Kaikoura	96	42.25S	173.41 E
Kaikoura Peninsula ›[1]	96	42.26S	173.42 E
Kailāshahar	76	24.20N	92.01 E
Kailu	62	43.36N	121.14 E
Kailua	105a	21.24N	157.44W
Kailua Kona	105a	19.22N	155.59W
Kaimai Range ⋏	96	37.45S	175.55 E
Kaïmakchalán ∧	54	40.58N	21.48 E
Kaimana	92	3.39S	133.45 E
Kaimanawa Mountains ⋏	96	39.15S	175.54 E
Kaimon-dake ∧	64	31.11N	130.32 E
Kainan	64	34.09N	135.12 E
Kainantu	92	6.15S	145.55 E
Kaintragarh	76	20.43N	84.32 E
Kaiping	62	22.23N	112.35 E
Kairāna	76	29.24N	77.12 E
Kairouan	80	35.41N	10.07 E
Kairuku	92	8.50S	146.35 E
Kaiserslautern	46	49.26N	7.46 E
Kaitaia	96	35.07S	173.16 E
Kaitangata	96	46.18S	169.51 E
Kaithal	76	29.48N	76.23 E
Kaiwaka	96	36.10S	174.27 E
Kaiwi Channel ⩌	105a	21.15N	157.30W
Kaiyuan, Zhg.	62	42.32N	124.01 E
Kaiyuan, Zhg.	70	23.44N	103.11 E
Kajaani	44	64.14N	27.41 E
Kajabbi	94	20.02S	140.02 E
Kajang	72	2.59N	101.47 E
Kajiki	64	31.44N	130.40 E
Kajnar	56	49.12N	77.25 E
Kakamas	86	28.45S	20.33 E
Kakamigahara	64	35.24N	136.54 E
Kakanui Mountains ⋏	96	45.09S	170.26 E
Kaka Point	96	46.23S	169.47 E
Kakaramea	96	39.43S	174.27 E
Kakatahi	96	39.41S	175.20 E
Kākdwīp	76	21.53N	88.11 E
Kake	64	34.36N	132.19 E
Kakegawa	64	34.46N	138.01 E
Kākināda	74	16.56N	82.13 E
Kakisa Lake ⊜	98	60.55N	117.40W
Kakizaki	64	37.15N	138.25 E
Kakogawa	64	34.46N	134.51 E
Kakuda	64	37.58N	140.47 E
Kakunodate	64	39.35N	140.34 E
Kalabahi	72	8.13S	124.31 E
Kalabáka	54	39.42N	21.43 E
Kalabakan	72	4.25N	117.29 E
Kalabo	84	14.57S	22.40 E
Kalač	56	50.25N	41.01 E
Kalačinsk	56	55.03N	74.34 E
Kalač-na-Donu	56	48.43N	43.31 E
Kaladan ≃	70	20.09N	92.57 E
Ka Lae ›	105a	18.55N	155.41W
Kalahari Desert ✦[2]	86	24.00S	21.30 E
Kalahari Gemsbok National Park ♠	86	25.30S	20.30 E
Kalajoki	44	64.15N	23.57 E
Kalajoki ≃	44	64.17N	23.55 E
Kalakan	58	55.08N	116.45 E
Kalakashihe ≃	76	37.00N	79.45 E
Kalām	76	35.32N	72.35 E
Kalámai	54	37.04N	22.07 E
Kalamariá	54	40.35N	22.58 E
Kalamazoo	100	42.17N	85.35W
Kalampáka	54	39.42N	21.39 E
Kalannie	90	30.21S	117.04 E
Kalao, Pulau I	72	7.18S	120.58 E
Kalaotoa, Pulau I	72	7.22S	121.47 E
Kalapana	105a	19.21N	154.58W
Kälarne	44	62.59N	16.05 E
Kalasin	70	16.29N	103.30 E
Kalašnikovo	60	57.17N	35.13 E
Kalāt	76	29.02N	66.35 E
Kalavárdha	54	36.20N	27.57 E
Kalávrita	54	38.01N	22.06 E
Kalaw	70	20.38N	96.34 E

Symbols in the Index entries are identified on page 122.

Kala-Kew

Name Page Lat. °′ Long. °′

Kal'azin 60 57.15N 37.52 E
Kalb, Ra's al- › 74 14.02N 48.40 E
Kalbā' 78 25.03N 56.21 E
Kalemie (Albertville) 84 5.56 S 29.12 E
Kalemyo 70 23.12N 94.10 E
Kalety 46 50.34N 18.54 E
Kalevala 42 65.13N 31.08 E
Kalewa 70 23.12N 94.17 E
Kale Water ≃ 38 55.32N 2.28W
Kälfafell 42a 63.58N 17.40W
Kalgan 90 34.53 S 118.01 E
Kalgoorlie 90 30.45 S 121.28 E
Kāli (Sārda) ≃ 76 27.21N 81.23 E
Kaliakra, nos › 54 43.21N 28.27 E
Kalibo 68 11.43N 122.22 E
Kalima 84 2.34 S 26.37 E
Kalimantan
→Borneo I 72 0.30N 114.00 E
Kalimantan Barat □4 72 0.30N 110.00 E
Kalimantan Selatan □4 72 2.30 S 115.30 E
Kalimantan Tengah □4 72 2.00 S 113.30 E
Kalimantan Timur □4 72 1.30N 116.30 E
Kálimnos 54 36.57N 26.59 E
Kálimnos I 54 37.00N 27.00 E
Kalimpong 76 27.04N 88.29 E
Kalinin 60 56.52N 35.55 E
Kaliningrad (Königsberg) 60 54.43N 20.30 E
Kalinkoviči 60 52.08N 29.21 E
Kalinovik 54 43.31N 18.26 E
Kalisat 72 8.08 S 113.48 E
Kalispell 100 48.11N 114.18W
Kalisz 46 51.46N 18.06 E
Kalisz Pomorski 46 53.19N 15.54 E
Kalix 44 65.51N 23.08 E
Kalixälven ≃ 42 65.50N 23.11 E
Kålka 76 30.50N 76.56 E
Kalkaska 102 44.44N 85.10W
Kalkfonteindam ⊜1 86 29.30 S 25.15 E
Kallakoopah Creek ≃ 94 27.29 S 138.15 E
Källandsö I 44 58.40N 13.09 E
Kallaste 60 58.39N 27.09 E
Kallavesi ⊜ 44 62.50N 27.45 E
Kallinge 44 56.14N 15.17 E
Kallsjön ⊜ 44 63.37N 13.00 E
Kalmar 44 56.40N 16.22 E
Kalmar Län □6 44 57.20N 16.00 E
Kalmarsund 𝔘 44 56.40N 16.25 E
Kālna 76 23.13N 88.22 E
Kalničko Gorje ✱ 52 46.10N 16.30 E
Kalocsa 46 46.32N 18.59 E
Kalofer 54 42.37N 24.59 E
Kalohi Channel 𝔘 105a 21.00N 156.56W
Kālol, India 76 23.15N 72.29 E
Kālol, India 76 22.36N 73.27 E
Kaloli Point › 105a 19.38N 154.57W
Kalomo 84 17.02 S 26.30 E
Kalpāki 54 39.55N 20.28 E
Kalpeni Island I 74 10.05N 73.38 E
Kālpi 76 26.07N 79.44 E
Kalsūbai ▲ 74 19.36N 73.43 E
Kaltan 56 53.30N 87.17 E
Kaluga 60 54.31N 36.16 E
Kalumba, Mount ▲ 94 31.49 S 146.22 E
Kalumburu 92 14.18 S 126.39 E
Kalundborg 44 55.41N 11.06 E
Kałuszyn 46 52.13N 21.49 E
Kalvåg 44 61.46N 4.53 E
Kalvarija 60 54.21N 23.14 E
Kälviä 44 63.52N 23.26 E
Kalwang 46 47.26N 14.46 E
Kalwaria Zebrzydowska 46 49.52N 19.41 E
Kalyān 74 19.15N 73.09 E
Kama ≃ 56 55.45N 52.00 E
Kamae 64 32.48N 131.56 E
Kamaishi 64 39.16N 141.53 E
Kamakou ▲ 105a 21.07N 156.52W
Kamakura 64 35.19N 139.33 E
Kamālia 76 30.44N 72.39 E
Kāman 76 27.39N 77.16 E
Kamaniskeg Lake ⊜ 102 45.25N 77.42W
Kamarān I 74 15.21N 42.34 E
Kamba 76 28.17N 88.32 E
Kamballie 90 30.48 S 121.30 E
Kambar 76 27.36N 68.00 E
Kambarka 56 56.17N 54.12 E
Kambing, Pulau I 72 8.13 S 125.35 E
Kamčatka ≃ 58 56.15N 162.30 E
Kamčatka, poluostrov ›1 58 56.00N 160.00 E
Kamčatskij zaliv c 58 55.35N 162.21 E
Kamčija ≃ 54 43.02N 27.53 E
Kameda 64 37.52N 139.07 E
Kamen', gora ▲ 58 69.06N 94.48 E
Kamenec-Podol'skij 56 48.41N 26.36 E
Kamenjak, Rt › 52 44.46N 13.55 E
Kamenka 56 53.13N 44.03 E
Kamen'-na-Obi 56 53.47N 81.20 E
Kamennogorsk 42 60.58N 29.07 E
Kamenskoje 58 62.30N 166.12 E
Kamensk-Ural'skij 56 56.28N 61.54 E
Kamenz 46 51.16N 14.06 E
Kames 38 55.54N 5.15W
Kameškovo 60 56.21N 41.00 E
Kāmet ▲ 76 30.54N 79.37 E
Kamień Krajeński 46 53.33N 17.32 E
Kamienna ≃ 46 51.06N 21.47 E
Kamienna Góra 46 50.47N 16.01 E
Kamień Pomorski 46 53.58N 14.46 E
Kamieńsk 46 51.12N 19.30 E
Kamieskroon 86 30.09 S 17.56 E
Kamiiso 64a 41.49N 140.39 E
Kamikawa 64a 43.51N 142.46 E
Kamilukuak Lake ⊜ 98 62.22N 101.40W
Kamina 84 8.44 S 25.00 E
Kaminak Lake ⊜ 98 62.10N 95.00W
Kaminokuni 64a 41.48N 140.06 E
Kaminoyama 64 38.09N 140.17 E
Kaminskij 60 57.10N 41.28 E
Kaminuriak Lake ⊜ 98 63.00N 95.40W
Kamioka 64 36.16N 137.18 E
Kamisunagawa 64a 43.30N 142.00 E
Kamitsushima 64 34.50N 129.28 E
Kamku 76 27.30N 96.30 E
Kamloops 98 50.40N 120.20W
Kamnik 52 46.13N 14.37 E
Kamo, N.Z. 96 35.41 S 174.19 E
Kamo, Nihon 64 37.39N 139.03 E
Kamo, S.S.S.R. 78 40.22N 45.08 E
Kamojima 64 34.04N 134.21 E
Kāmoke 76 31.58N 74.13 E
Kamp ≃ 46 48.23N 15.48 E
Kampala 84 0.19N 32.25 E
Kampar 72 4.18N 101.09 E
Kampar ≃ 72 0.32N 103.08 E
Kampen 46 52.33N 5.54 E
Kamphaeng Phet 70 16.28N 99.30 E
Kâmpóng Cham 70 12.00N 105.27 E
Kâmpóng Chhnăng 70 12.15N 104.40 E
Kâmpóng Saôm 70 10.38N 103.30 E
Kâmpóng Saôm, Chhāk c 70 10.50N 103.32 E
Kampong Sebuyau 72 1.31N 110.56 E
Kâmpóng Thum 70 12.42N 104.54 E
Kâmpôt 70 10.37N 104.11 E
Kampuchea □1 68 13.00N 105.00 E
Kamrau, Teluk c 72 3.32 S 133.37 E
Kamsack 98 51.34N 101.54W
Kamskoje vodochranilišče ⊜1 42 58.52N 56.15 E
Kāmthi 76 21.14N 79.12 E

Kamuela (Waimea) 105a 20.01N 155.48W
Kamui-misaki › 64a 43.20N 140.21 E
Kámuk, Cerro ▲ 108 9.17N 83.04W
Kamyšin 56 50.06N 45.24 E
Kamyšlov 56 56.52N 62.43 E
Kanaaupscow ≃ 98 53.39N 77.09W
Kanagawa □5 64 35.30N 139.30 E
Kanairiktok ≃ 98 55.05N 60.20W
Kananga (Luluabourg) 84 5.54 S 22.25 E
Kanaš 42 55.31N 47.30 E
Kanaudi 76 23.36N 81.23 E
Kanawha ≃ 102 38.50N 82.08W
Kanazawa 64 36.34N 136.39 E
Kanbe 70 16.42N 96.01 E
Kanchanaburi 70 14.01N 99.32 E
Kānchenjunga ▲ 76 27.42N 88.08 E
Kānchipuram 74 12.50N 79.43 E
Kańczuga 46 49.59N 22.24 E
Kanda 64 33.47N 130.59 E
Kandalakša 42 67.09N 32.21 E
Kandangan 72 2.47 S 115.16 E
Kandanghaur 72 6.21 S 108.06 E
Kandava 60 57.05N 22.49 E
Kandavu Island I 28 19.03 S 178.13 E
Kandel 46 49.05N 8.11 E
Kandhkot 76 28.14N 69.11 E
Kāndi 76 23.57N 88.02 E
Kandos 94 32.52 S 149.58 E
Kandy 74 7.18N 80.38 E
Kane 102 41.39N 78.48W
Kaneohe 105a 21.25N 157.48W
Kaneohe Bay c 105a 21.28N 157.49W
Kangalassy 58 62.23N 129.59 E
Kangar 72 6.26N 100.12 E
Kangaroo Island I 94 35.50 S 137.06 E
Kangasala 44 61.28N 24.05 E
Kangasniemi 44 61.59N 26.38 E
Kangding 62 30.03N 102.02 E
Kangean, Kepulauan II 72 6.55 S 115.30 E
Kanggye 62 40.58N 126.34 E
Kangnŭng 62 37.45N 128.54 E
Kango 84 0.09N 10.08 E
Kāngpokpi 76 25.08N 93.58 E
Kangrinboqê Feng ▲ 62 31.04N 81.18 E
Kangshan 66 22.48N 120.17 E
Kangto ▲ 76 27.52N 92.30 E
Kaniama 84 7.31 S 24.11 E
Kaniere 96 42.45 S 171.00 E
Kaniere, Lake ⊜ 96 42.50 S 171.09 E
Kaniet Islands II 92 0.53 S 145.30 E
Kanin, poluostrov ›1 42 68.00N 45.00 E
Kanin Nos 42 68.39N 43.14 E
Kanin Nos, mys › 42 68.39N 43.16 E
Kaniva 94 36.23 S 141.15 E
Kanjiža 54 46.04N 20.04 E
Kankaanpää 44 61.48N 22.25 E
Kankakee 100 41.07N 87.51W
Kankan 80 10.23N 9.18W
Kankunskij 58 57.37N 126.08 E
Kanmaw Kyun I 70 11.40N 98.28 E
Kanmen 66 28.06N 121.16 E
Kanmuri-yama ▲ 64 34.28N 132.05 E
Kannapolis 100 35.29N 80.37W
Kannauj 76 27.04N 79.55 E
Kannod 76 22.40N 76.44 E
Kannonkoski 44 62.58N 25.15 E
Kannus 44 63.54N 23.54 E
Kano 80 12.00N 8.30 E
Kanonji 64 34.07N 133.39 E
Kanowit 72 2.06N 112.09 E
Kanowna 90 30.36 S 121.36 E
Kanoya 64 31.23N 130.51 E
Kānpur 76 26.28N 80.21 E
Kansas □3 100 38.45N 98.15W
Kansas City, Ks., U.S. 100 39.06N 94.37W
Kansas City, Mo., U.S. 100 39.05N 94.34W
Kanshan 66 30.12N 120.25 E
Kansk 58 56.13N 95.41 E
Kansu
→Gansu □4 62 37.00N 103.00 E
Kant 56 42.55N 74.55 E
Kantang 70 7.25N 99.31 E
Kānth 76 29.04N 78.38 E
Kantishna ≃ 98 64.45N 149.58W
Kantō-heiya ≚ 64 36.00N 139.30 E
Kanton I 28 2.50 S 171.41W
Kantō-sanchi ✱ 64 35.50N 138.50 E
Kantunilkín 108 21.06N 87.29W
Kanturk 40 52.10N 8.55W
Kanuma 64 36.33N 139.44 E
Kanye 86 24.59 S 25.19 E
Kaohiung
→Kaohsiung 66 22.38N 120.17 E
Kaohsiung 66 22.38N 120.17 E
Kaohsiunghsien 66 22.38N 120.21 E
Kaokoland □5 86 18.15 S 13.00 E
Kaoko Veld ✱1 86 20.00 S 14.00 E
Kaolack 80 14.09N 16.04W
Kaoma 84 14.47 S 24.48 E
Kapaa 105a 22.04N 159.19W
Kapadvanj 76 23.01N 73.04 E
Kapanga 84 8.21 S 22.35 E
Kapaonik ✱ 54 43.20N 20.50 E
Kapčagaj 56 43.53N 77.12 E
Kapčagajskoje vodochranilišče ⊜1 56 43.50N 78.00 E
Kapfenberg 46 47.26N 15.18 E
Kapingamarangi I1 28 1.04N 154.46 E
Kāpīsā □4 76 34.50N 69.35 E
Kapiskau ≃ 98 52.47N 81.55W
Kapit 72 2.01N 112.56 E
Kapiti Island I 96 40.52 S 174.54 E
Kaplice 46 48.45N 14.30 E
Kaponga 96 39.26 S 174.09 E
Kapos ≃ 46 46.44N 18.30 E
Kaposvár 46 46.22N 17.47 E
Kapp 44 60.42N 10.52 E
Kappeln 46 54.40N 9.56 E
Kappelshamn 44 57.51N 18.47 E
Kaprun 46 47.16N 12.46 E
Kapsukas 60 54.33N 23.21 E
Kaptol 54 45.26N 17.44 E
Kapuas ≃ 72 0.25 S 109.40 E
Kapuas Hulu, Pegunungan ✱ 72 1.25N 113.30 E
Kapunda 94 34.21 S 138.54 E
Kapūrthala 76 31.23N 75.23 E
Kapuskasing 98 49.25N 82.26W
Kapuskasing ≃ 98 49.49N 82.00W
Kapuvár 46 47.36N 17.02 E
Kara 56 69.14N 65.00 E
Kara ≃ 56 68.57N 65.24 E
Karaaul 56 48.57N 79.15 E
Kara-Balta 56 42.50N 73.52 E
Karabanovo 60 56.19N 38.42 E
Karabaš 56 55.29N 60.14 E
Kara-Bogaz-Gol, zaliv c 56 41.00N 53.15 E
Karabük 30 41.12N 32.36 E
Karabula 58 58.08N 97.23 E
Karacabey 54 40.13N 28.21 E
Karačev 60 53.07N 35.00 E
Karāchi 76 24.52N 67.03 E
Karadeniz
→Black Sea ⊤2 30 43.00N 35.00 E
Karaganda 56 49.50N 73.10 E
Karaginskij, ostrov I 58 58.50N 164.00 E
Karaginskij zaliv c 58 58.50N 164.00 E
Karagoš, gora ▲ 58 51.44N 89.24 E
Karaj 78 35.48N 50.59 E
Karakelong, Pulau I 68 4.15N 126.48 E
Karakoram Range ✱ 76 35.30N 77.00 E

Karakul' 78 39.32N 63.50 E
Karakumskij kanal ≊ 56 37.35N 61.50 E
Karakumy ⊹2 56 39.00N 60.00 E
Karaman 78 37.11N 33.14 E
Karamay 62 45.30N 84.55 E
Karamea 96 41.15 S 172.07 E
Karamea ≃ 96 41.16 S 172.06 E
Karamea Bight c3 96 41.30 S 171.40 E
Karamürsel 54 40.42N 29.36 E
Karangasem 72 8.27 S 115.37 E
Karangnunggal 72 7.38 S 108.06 E
Karanjia 76 21.47N 85.58 E
Karasburg 86 28.00 S 18.43 E
Karasburg □5 86 28.00 S 18.45 E
Kara Sea
→Karskoje more ⊤2 56 76.00N 80.00 E
Karašjåkka ≃ 42 69.26N 25.49 E
Karasjok 42 69.27N 25.30 E
Karasuk 56 53.44N 78.02 E
Karatau 56 43.10N 70.28 E
Karatau, chrebet ✱ 56 43.50N 68.30 E
Karaton 56 46.25N 53.30 E
Karatsu 64 33.26N 129.58 E
Karaul 56 70.06N 83.08 E
Karauli 76 26.30N 77.01 E
Karavas 54 36.21N 22.57 E
Karawanken ✱ 52 46.30N 14.25 E
Karažal 56 48.02N 70.49 E
Karbalā' 78 32.36N 44.02 E
Karbalā' □4 78 32.00N 42.15 E
Kårböle 44 61.59N 15.19 E
Karcag 46 47.19N 20.56 E
Karczew 46 52.06N 21.15 E
Kardhámaina 54 36.47N 27.09 E
Kardhámila 54 38.32N 26.05 E
Kardhítsa 54 39.21N 21.55 E
Kärdžali 54 41.39N 25.22 E
Kareli 76 22.55N 79.04 E
Karelia □9 42 63.00N 32.00 E
Karen 70 12.51N 92.53 E
Karen □3 70 17.30N 97.45 E
Karesuando 42 68.25N 22.30 E
Kargasok 56 59.07N 80.53 E
Kargil 76 34.34N 76.06 E
Kargopol' 42 61.30N 38.58 E
Karhijärvi ⊜ 44 61.35N 22.30 E
Karhula 44 60.31N 26.57 E
Kariai 54 40.16N 24.15 E
Kariba 84 16.32 S 28.45 E
Kariba, Lake ⊜1 84 17.00 S 28.00 E
Karibib 86 21.58 S 15.51 E
Karibib □5 86 22.00 S 16.00 E
Kariega ≃ 86 33.03 S 23.28 E
Karigasniemi 42 69.24N 25.50 E
Karikari, Cape › 96 34.47 S 173.24 E
Karimata, Kepulauan II 72 1.25 S 109.05 E
Karimata, Selat (Karimata Strait) 𝔘 72 2.05 S 108.40 E
Karīmnagar 74 18.26N 79.09 E
Karimunjawa, Kepulauan II 72 5.50 S 110.25 E
Karin 82 10.51N 45.47 E
Karin Seamount ⊹3 28 17.55N 168.58W
Karis (Karjaa) 44 60.05N 23.40 E
Karisimbi, Volcan ▲1 84 1.30 S 29.27 E
Káristos 54 38.00N 24.24 E
Kariya 64 34.59N 136.59 E
Karjala ⊹1 44 60.00N 32.00 E
Karkaralinsk 56 49.23N 75.21 E
Karkkila 44 60.32N 24.11 E
Karkku 44 61.25N 23.01 E
Karlholmsbruk 44 60.31N 17.35 E
Karlino 46 54.03N 15.51 E
Karl-Marx-Stadt (Chemnitz) 46 50.50N 12.55 E
Karl-Marx-Stadt □5 46 50.45N 12.45 E
Karlobag 52 44.32N 15.05 E
Karlovac 52 45.29N 15.34 E
Karlovo 54 42.38N 24.48 E
Karlovy Vary 46 50.11N 12.52 E
Karlsbad
→Karlovy Vary 46 50.11N 12.52 E
Karlsborg, Sve. 44 58.32N 14.31 E
Karlsborg, Sve. 44 65.48N 23.17 E
Karlshamn 44 56.10N 14.51 E
Karlskoga 44 59.20N 14.31 E
Karlskrona 44 56.10N 15.35 E
Karlsöarna II 44 57.17N 17.58 E
Karlsruhe 46 49.03N 8.24 E
Karlstad 44 59.22N 13.30 E
Karlstadt 46 49.57N 9.46 E
Karmøy I 44 59.15N 5.15 E
Karnāl 76 29.41N 76.59 E
Karnāli ≃ 76 28.45N 81.16 E
Karnaphuli Reservoir ⊜1 76 22.42N 92.12 E
Karnobat 54 42.39N 26.59 E
Kärnten □3 46 46.50N 13.50 E
Karonga 84 9.56 S 33.56 E
Karonie 90 30.58 S 122.32 E
Karoonda 94 35.06 S 139.54 E
Kárpathos 54 35.30N 27.14 E
Kárpathos I 54 35.40N 27.10 E
Karpenísion 54 38.55N 21.40 E
Karpinsk 56 59.45N 60.01 E
Karridale 90 34.13 S 115.05 E
Kars 78 40.36N 43.05 E
Karsakpaj 56 47.49N 66.41 E
Kärsämäki 44 63.58N 25.46 E
Karši 78 38.53N 65.48 E
Karsin 46 53.54N 17.56 E
Karskije Vorota, proliv 𝔘 56 70.30N 58.00 E
Karskoje more (Kara Sea) ⊤2 58 76.00N 80.00 E
Karstula 44 62.52N 24.47 E
Kartala ▲ 87a 11.45 S 43.22 E
Kartaly 56 53.03N 60.40 E
Kartārpur 76 31.27N 75.30 E
Karthaus 102 41.07N 78.07W
Karttula 44 62.53N 26.58 E
Kartuzy 46 54.20N 18.12 E
Karufa 72 3.50 S 133.27 E
Karumba 92 17.29 S 140.50 E
Karungi 44 66.03N 23.57 E
Karunjie 92 16.18 S 127.12 E
Karunki 44 66.02N 24.01 E
Karup 44 56.18N 9.10 E
Karūr 74 10.57N 78.05 E
Karviná 46 49.50N 18.30 E
Kārwār 74 14.48N 74.08 E
Karymskoje 58 51.37N 114.21 E
Kasai (Cassai) ≃ 84 3.02 S 16.57 E
Kasaji 84 10.22 S 23.27 E
Kasama, Nihon 64 36.23N 140.16 E
Kasama, Zam. 84 10.13 S 31.12 E
Kasanga 84 8.28 S 31.09 E
Kasaoka 64 34.30N 133.30 E
Kasba 76 25.51N 87.33 E
Kasba Lake ⊜ 98 60.18N 102.07W
Kåseberga 44 55.23N 14.04 E
Kasempa 84 13.27 S 25.50 E
Kasenga 84 10.22 S 28.38 E
Kasese, Ug. 84 0.10N 30.05 E
Kasese, Zaïre 84 1.38 S 27.07 E
Kāsganj 76 27.49N 78.39 E
Kāshān 78 33.59N 51.29 E
Kashi 62 39.29N 75.59 E
Kashihara 64 34.30N 135.46 E
Kashima 64 33.06N 130.06 E
Kashima-nada ⊤2 64 36.15N 140.45 E
Kashīpur 76 29.13N 78.57 E

Kashiwazaki 64 37.22N 138.33 E
Kāshmar 78 35.12N 58.27 E
Kashmir
→Jammu and Kashmir □2 76 34.00N 76.00 E
Kasia 74 26.45N 83.55 E
Kasimov 60 54.56N 41.24 E
Kašin 60 57.21N 37.37 E
Kašira 60 54.51N 38.10 E
Kasiruta, Pulau I 68 0.25 S 127.12 E
Kaskattama ≃ 98 57.03N 90.07W
Kaskö (Kaskinen) 44 62.23N 21.13 E
Kasli 56 55.53N 60.46 E
Kasongo 84 4.27 S 26.40 E
Kasongo-Lunda 84 6.28 S 16.49 E
Kásos I 54 35.22N 26.56 E
Kaspijsk 56 42.52N 47.38 E
Kaspijskij 56 45.22N 47.24 E
Kaspijskoje more
→Caspian Sea ⊤2 56 42.00N 50.30 E
Kasr, Ra's › 82 18.02N 38.35 E
Kassalā 82 15.28N 36.24 E
Kassándra ›1 54 40.06N 23.22 E
Kassándras, Kólpos c 54 40.06N 23.30 E
Kassel 46 51.19N 9.29 E
Kasserine 80 35.11N 8.48 E
Kastamonu 30 41.22N 33.47 E
Kastanéai 54 41.38N 26.28 E
Kastelholm 44 60.14N 20.04 E
Kastl 46 49.22N 11.42 E
Kastoría 54 40.31N 21.15 E
Kastorías, Límni ⊜ 54 40.30N 21.17 E
Kastrávion, Tekhnití Límni ⊜1 54 38.50N 21.20 E
Kasugai 64 35.14N 136.58 E
Kasumi 64 35.38N 134.38 E
Kasumi-ura ⊜ 64 36.00N 140.25 E
Kasūr 76 31.07N 74.27 E
Kaszuby ⊹1 46 54.10N 18.15 E
Katahdin, Mount ▲ 102 45.55N 68.55W
Katanga □9 84 10.00 S 26.00 E
Katanga ≃ 58 60.08N 102.13 E
Katangi 76 23.27N 79.47 E
Katangli 58 51.42N 143.14 E
Katanning 90 33.42 S 117.33 E
Katchall Island I 70 7.57N 93.22 E
Katerini 54 40.16N 22.30 E
Katesbridge 40 54.18N 6.08W
Kates Needle ▲ 98 57.03N 132.03W
Katha 70 24.11N 96.21 E
Katherine 92 14.28 S 132.16 E
Katherine ≃ 92 14.39 S 131.42 E
Katherine Creek ≃ 94 23.48 S 143.42 E
Kāthgodām 76 29.16N 79.32 E
Kathiār 76 25.32N 87.35 E
Kāthiāwār ›1 76 22.00N 71.00 E
Kathla 76 31.59N 76.47 E
Kathleen Valley 90 27.23 S 120.38 E
Kathmandu 76 27.43N 85.19 E
Kathor 76 21.18N 72.56 E
Kathua 76 32.22N 75.31 E
Katihār 76 25.32N 87.35 E
Katikati 96 37.33 S 175.55 E
Katiola 80 8.08N 5.06W
Kāto Akhaïa 54 38.09N 21.32 E
Kātol 76 21.16N 78.35 E
Katoomba 94 33.42 S 150.18 E
Katoúna 54 38.47N 21.07 E
Katowice 46 50.16N 19.00 E
Katrīnā, Jabal ▲ 82 28.31N 33.57 E
Katrine, Loch ⊜ 38 56.15N 4.31W
Katrineholm 44 59.00N 16.12 E
Katsina 80 13.00N 7.32 E
Katsina Ala ≃ 80 7.48N 8.52 E
Katsuta 64 36.24N 140.30 E
Katsuura 64 35.08N 140.18 E
Katsuyama, Nihon 64 36.03N 136.30 E
Katsuyama, Nihon 64 35.05N 133.41 E
Kattakurgan 56 39.55N 66.15 E
Kattavià 54 35.57N 27.46 E
Kattegat 𝔘 44 57.00N 11.00 E
Katthammarsvik 44 57.26N 18.50 E
Kattonghu ⊜ 76 35.30N 92.00 E
Kattowitz
→Katowice 46 50.16N 19.00 E
Katun' ≃ 58 52.25N 85.05 E
Katunki 60 56.50N 43.14 E
Kātwa 76 23.39N 88.08 E
Katwijk aan Zee 46 52.13N 4.24 E
Katy Wrocławskie 46 51.02N 16.46 E
Katzenbuckel ▲ 46 49.28N 9.02 E
Kauai I 105a 22.00N 159.30W
Kauai Channel 𝔘 105a 21.45N 158.50W
Kau Desert ⊹2 105a 19.21N 155.19W
Kaufbeuren 46 47.53N 10.37 E
Kauhajoki 44 62.26N 22.11 E
Kauhava 44 63.06N 23.05 E
Kauiki Head › 105a 20.45N 155.59W
Kaukapakapa 96 36.37 S 174.30 E
Kaukau Veld ✱1 86 19.30 S 20.30 E
Kaukura I1 28 15.45 S 146.42W
Kaula I 105a 21.45N 160.30W
Kauliranta 42 66.27N 23.41 E
Kaumalapau 105a 20.47N 156.59W
Kaunakakai 105a 21.05N 157.01W
Kaunas 60 54.54N 23.54 E
Kaupanger 44 61.11N 7.14 E
Kaura Namoda 80 12.35N 6.35 E
Kausala 44 60.54N 26.22 E
Kaustinen 44 63.32N 23.42 E
Kautokeino 42 69.00N 23.02 E
Kauttua 44 61.06N 22.10 E
Kavača 58 60.16N 169.51 E
Kavadarci 54 41.26N 22.00 E
Kavajë 54 41.11N 19.33 E
Kavála 54 40.56N 24.25 E
Kavalerovo 58 44.15N 135.04 E
Kavango □5 86 18.30 S 20.15 E
Kavaratti Island I 74 10.33N 72.38 E
Kavarna 54 43.25N 28.20 E
Kavieng 92 2.35 S 150.50 E
Kavīr, Dasht-e ⊹2 78 34.40N 54.30 E
Kävlinge 44 55.48N 13.06 E
Kawagama Lake ⊜ 102 45.18N 78.45W
Kawagoe 64 35.55N 139.29 E
Kawaguchi 64 35.48N 139.43 E
Kawaihae Bay c 105a 20.02N 155.50W
Kawaikini ▲ 105a 22.05N 159.29W
Kawakawa 96 35.23 S 174.04 E
Kawambwa 84 9.47 S 29.05 E
Kawanoe 64 34.01N 133.34 E
Kawardha 76 22.01N 81.15 E
Kawasaki 64 35.32N 139.43 E
Kawatana 64 33.04N 129.52 E
Kawau Island I 96 36.25 S 174.51 E
Kaweka ▲ 96 39.17 S 176.23 E
Kaweka Range ✱ 96 39.15 S 176.20 E
Kawerau 96 38.03 S 176.43 E
Kawhia 96 38.04 S 174.49 E
Kawich Peak ▲ 104 37.58N 116.27W
Kawich Range ✱ 104 37.40N 116.30W
Kawm Umbū 82 24.28N 32.57 E
Kawthaung 70 9.59N 98.33 E
Kaxgar ≃ 62 39.46N 78.15 E
Kayah □3 70 19.15N 97.30 E
Kayak Island I 98 59.52N 144.30W
Kayan 70 16.54N 96.34 E
Kayan ≃ 72 2.55N 117.35 E
Kayangel Islands II 68 8.04N 134.43 E
Kayes, Congo 84 4.25 S 11.41 E
Kayes, Mali 80 14.27N 11.26W
Kayseri 78 38.43N 35.30 E
Kayuagung 72 3.24 S 104.50 E

Kazachskaja Sovetskaja Socialističeskaja Respublika □3 56 48.00N 68.00 E
Kazachskij melkosopočnik ✱2 56 49.00N 72.00 E
Kazačinskoje 58 57.49N 93.17 E
Kazačje 58 70.44N 136.13 E
Kazakh Soviet Socialist Republic
→Kazachskaja Sovetskaja Socialističeskaja Respublika □3 56 48.00N 68.00 E
Kazalinsk 56 45.46N 62.07 E
Kazan' 42 55.49N 49.08 E
Kazan ≃ 98 64.02N 95.30W
Kazandžik 78 39.16N 55.32 E
Kazanlăk 54 42.38N 25.21 E
Kazanovka 60 53.46N 38.34 E
Kazan-rettō II 28 25.00N 141.00 E
Kazbek, gora ▲ 56 42.42N 44.31 E
Kāzerūn 78 29.37N 51.38 E
Kažim 42 60.20N 51.30 E
Kazi-Magomed 78 40.03N 48.56 E
Kazimierza Wielka 46 50.16N 20.30 E
Kazimierz Dolny 46 51.20N 21.58 E
Kazincbarcika 46 48.16N 20.37 E
Kazinka 60 52.32N 39.42 E
Kazungula 84 17.45 S 25.20 E
Kazuno 64 40.11N 140.47 E
Kazym 56 63.40N 67.14 E
Kazym ≃ 56 63.54N 65.50 E
Kazyr ≃ 58 53.47N 92.53 E
Kcynia 46 53.00N 17.30 E
Kdyně 46 49.23N 13.02 E
Kéa 54 37.38N 24.21 E
Kéa I 54 37.34N 24.22 E
Keaau 105a 19.37N 155.02W
Keady 40 54.15N 6.42W
Keahole Point › 105a 19.44N 156.03W
Keal, Loch na c 38 56.28N 6.04W
Kealaikahiki Channel 𝔘 105a 20.37N 156.50W
Kealakekua Bay c 105a 19.28N 155.56W
Keanapapa Point › 105a 20.54N 157.04W
Kearney 100 40.41N 99.04W
Keban Gölü ⊜1 78 38.50N 39.15 E
Kebnekaise ▲ 42 67.53N 18.33 E
Kebock Head › 38 58.01N 6.20W
Kebri Dehar 82 6.47N 44.17 E
Kecel 46 46.32N 19.16 E
Kech ≃ 78 26.00N 62.44 E
Kechika ≃ 98 59.36N 127.05W
Kecskemét 46 46.54N 19.42 E
Kedah □3 72 6.00N 100.40 E
Kedainiai 60 55.17N 24.00 E
Kédhron 54 39.13N 22.03 E
Kediri 72 7.49 S 112.01 E
Kedon 58 64.08N 159.14 E
Kédougou 80 12.33N 12.11W
Kędzierzyn 46 50.20N 18.12 E
Keelby 36 53.34N 0.15W
Keele 34 53.00N 2.17W
Keele ≃ 98 64.24N 124.50W
Keele Peak ▲ 98 63.26N 130.19W
Keeling Islands
→Cocos Islands □2 26 12.10 S 96.55 E
Keelung
→Chilung 66 25.08N 121.44 E
Keen, Mount ▲ 38 56.58N 2.54W
Keene, Ky., U.S. 102 37.56N 84.38W
Keene, N.H., U.S. 102 42.56N 72.16W
Keer-Weer, Cape › 92 13.58 S 141.30 E
Keerzong 76 32.11N 79.59 E
Keeseville 102 44.30N 73.28W
Keetmanshoop 86 26.36 S 18.08 E
Keetmanshoop □5 86 26.30 S 19.00 E
Keewatin □5 98 65.00N 95.00W
Kefallinia I 54 38.15N 20.35 E
Kéfalos 54 36.45N 27.00 E
Kefamenanu 72 9.27 S 124.29 E
Keffi 80 8.51N 7.52 E
Keflavík 42a 64.02N 22.36W
Keg River 98 57.48N 117.52W
Kegworth 34 52.50N 1.16W
Ke-hsi Mānsām 70 21.56N 97.50 E
Keig 38 57.15N 2.39W
Keighley 36 53.52N 1.54W
Keila 60 59.18N 24.25 E
Keimoes 86 28.41 S 21.00 E
Keiskammahoek 86 32.41 S 27.09 E
Keitele 44 63.11N 26.22 E
Keitele ⊜ 44 62.55N 26.00 E
Keith, Austl. 94 36.06 S 140.21 E
Keith, Scot., U.K. 38 57.32N 2.57W
Keith Arm c 98 65.20N 122.15W
Kejaman 72 2.39N 113.45 E
Kekaha 105a 21.58N 159.42W
Kekerengu 96 42.00 S 174.01 E
Kékes ▲ 46 47.55N 20.02 E
Kekexili 62 35.31N 93.35 E
Kekri 76 25.58N 75.09 E
Kelafo 82 5.40N 44.20 E
Kelai ≃ 72 2.10N 117.29 E
Kelang 72 3.02N 101.27 E
Kelantan □3 72 5.20N 102.00 E
Kelantan ≃ 72 6.11N 102.15 E
Keleti-főcsatorna ≊ 46 48.01N 21.20 E
Kelheim 46 48.55N 11.52 E
Keliyahe ≃ 62 38.05N 82.40 E
Kellerberrin 90 31.38 S 117.43 E
Keller Lake ⊜ 98 63.58N 121.36W
Kellett, Cape › 98 71.59N 125.34W
Kelleys Island I 102 41.36N 82.42W
Kelloe 36 54.43N 1.28W
Kellojärvi ⊜ 44 64.16N 29.03 E
Kelloselkä 42 66.56N 28.50 E
Kells
→Ceanannus Mór 40 53.44N 6.53W
Kelme 60 55.38N 22.56 E
Kelo 82 9.19N 15.48 E
Kelolokan 72 1.10N 117.54 E
Keloottijärvi 42 68.31N 22.04 E
Kelowna 98 49.53N 119.29W
Kelsall 36 53.13N 2.43W
Kelsey Head › 34 50.24N 5.08W
Kelseyville 104 38.58N 122.50W
Kelso 38 55.36N 2.25W
Kelty 38 56.08N 3.23W
Keluang 72 2.02N 103.19 E
Kelvedon 34 51.51N 0.42 E
Kelvin Seamount ⊹3 22 38.50N 64.00W
Kem' 42 64.57N 34.36 E
Kem' ≃ 42 64.57N 34.41 E
Kemerovo 56 55.20N 86.05 E
Kemi 44 65.49N 24.32 E
Kemie 72 0.39N 115.39 E
Kemijärvi 42 66.40N 27.25 E
Kemijärvi ⊜ 42 66.36N 27.24 E
Kemijoki ≃ 44 65.47N 24.30 E
Kemmuna I 52 36.00N 14.20 E
Kemnath 46 49.52N 11.54 E
Kemnay 38 57.14N 2.27W
Kempele 44 64.55N 25.30 E
Kempen 46 51.22N 6.25 E
Kemps Bay 108 24.02N 77.33W
Kempsey, Austl. 94 31.05 S 152.50 E
Kempsey, Eng., U.K. 34 52.08N 2.12W
Kempston 34 52.07N 0.30W
Kempt, Lac ⊜ 102 47.25N 74.22W
Kempten [Allgäu] 46 47.43N 10.19 E
Kemptville 102 45.01N 75.38W
Kemul, Kong ▲ 72 1.52N 116.11 E
Ken, Loch ⊜ 36 55.02N 4.02W

Ken, Water of ≃ 36 55.04N 4.08W
Kendai 76 22.45N 82.37 E
Kendal, Indon. 72 6.55 S 110.12 E
Kendal, S. Afr. 86 26.04 S 28.58 E
Kendal, Eng., U.K. 36 54.20N 2.45W
Kendall 94 31.38 S 152.43 E
Kendall, Cape › 98 63.36N 87.09W
Kendall, Mount ▲ 96 41.22 S 172.24 E
Kendallville 102 41.26N 85.15W
Kendari 72 3.57 S 122.35 E
Kendawangan 72 2.32 S 110.12 E
Kendenup 90 34.29 S 117.39 E
Kendrāpāra 76 20.30N 86.25 E
Kendrew 86 32.31 S 24.30 E
Kenema 80 7.52N 11.12W
Kenge 84 4.52 S 16.59 E
Kēng Tung 70 21.17N 99.36 E
Kenhardt 86 29.19 S 21.12 E
Kenilworth 34 52.21N 1.34W
Keningau 72 5.20N 116.10 E
Kenitra 80 34.16N 6.40W
Kenmare, Ire. 40 51.53N 9.35W
Kenmare, N.D., U.S. 100 48.40N 102.04W
Kenmare River ≃ 40 51.45N 10.00W
Kenmore 38 56.34N 3.59W
Kennebec ≃ 102 44.00N 69.50W
Kennebunk 102 43.23N 70.32W
Kennedy, Cape
→Canaveral, Cape › 100 28.27N 80.32W
Kennedy, Mount ▲ 98 60.30N 139.00W
Kennedy Range ✱ 90 24.30 S 115.00 E
Kennet ≃, Eng., U.K. 34 51.28N 0.57W
Kennet ≃, Eng., U.K. 34 52.26N 0.28 E
Kennett Square 102 39.50N 75.42W
Kennington, Eng., U.K. 34 51.43N 1.15W
Kennington, Eng., U.K. 34 51.10N 0.54 E
Kenn Reef ⊹2 88 21.12 S 155.46 E
Kenogami ≃ 98 51.06N 84.28W
Keno Hill 98 63.55N 135.18W
Kenora 98 49.47N 94.29W
Kenosha 100 42.35N 87.49W
Kenova 102 38.23N 82.34W
Kent 102 41.09N 81.21W
Kent □6 34 51.15N 0.40 E
Kent ≃ 36 54.15N 2.48W
Kent, Vale of ∨ 34 51.10N 0.30 E
Kentallen 38 56.39N 5.15W
Kentau 56 43.36N 68.36 E
Kent Group II 94 39.27 S 147.20 E
Kenton, Eng., U.K. 34 50.38N 3.28W
Kenton, Oh., U.S. 102 40.38N 83.36W
Kent Peninsula ›1 98 68.30N 107.00W
Kentucky □3 100 37.30N 85.15W
Kentucky ≃ 102 38.40N 85.09W
Kentucky Lake ⊜1 100 36.25N 88.05W
Kentville 98 45.05N 64.30W
Kenya □1 84 1.00N 38.00 E
Kenya, Mount
→Kirinyaga ▲ 84 0.10 S 37.20 E
Keokea 105a 20.42N 156.21W
Keokuk 100 40.23N 91.23W
Keo Neua, Col de)(70 18.23N 105.09 E
Keonjhargarh 76 21.38N 85.35 E
Kepi 92 6.32 S 139.19 E
Kępice 46 54.15N 16.52 E
Kępno 46 51.17N 17.59 E
Keppel Bay c 94 23.21 S 150.55 E
Kerang 94 35.44 S 143.55 E
Keratéa 54 37.48N 23.59 E
Keraudren, Cape › 90 19.57 S 119.45 E
Kerava 44 60.24N 25.07 E
Keravat 92 4.19 S 152.01 E
Kerbela
→Karbalā' 78 32.36N 44.02 E
Kerby 104 42.11N 123.39W
Kerč' 56 45.22N 36.27 E
Kerčevskij 42 59.55N 56.17 E
Kerch
→Kerč' 56 45.22N 36.27 E
Kerema 92 8.00 S 145.45 E
Keren 82 15.46N 38.28 E
Keret' 42 66.16N 33.34 E
Kerguélen, Îles II 18 49.15 S 69.10 E
Kericho 84 0.22 S 35.17 E
Kerikeri 96 35.13 S 173.58 E
Kerimäki 44 61.55N 29.17 E
Kerinci, Gunung ▲ 72 1.42 S 101.16 E
Kerion 54 37.40N 20.48 E
Keriya ≃ 62 38.30N 82.10 E
Kerkebet 82 16.18N 37.24 E
Kerkenna, Îles II 80 34.44N 11.12 E
Kerki 78 37.50N 65.12 E
Kérkira (Corfu) 54 39.36N 19.56 E
Kérkira I 54 39.40N 19.42 E
Kerkrade [-Holz] 46 50.52N 6.04 E
Kermadec Islands II 28 29.16 S 177.55W
Kermadec Ridge ⊹3 28 30.30 S 178.30W
Kermadec Trench ⊹1 28 30.00 S 177.00W
Kermajärvi ⊜ 44 62.28N 28.40 E
Kermān, Īrān 78 30.17N 57.05 E
Kerman, Ca., U.S. 104 36.43N 120.04W
Kermit Roosevelt Seamount ⊹3 22 39.35N 146.00W
Kern ≃ 104 35.13N 119.17W
Kernville 104 35.45N 118.25W
Keroh 72 5.43N 101.00 E
Kerrera I 38 56.23N 5.34W
Kerrobert 98 51.55N 109.08W
Kerrville 100 30.02N 99.08W
Kerry 34 52.30N 3.16W
Kerry □6 40 52.10N 9.30W
Kerry Head › 40 52.25N 9.57W
Kerteh 72 4.31N 103.27 E
Kerteminde 44 55.27N 10.40 E
Kerulen (Cherlen) (Herlen) ≃ 62 48.48N 117.00 E
Kesagami Lake ⊜ 98 50.23N 80.15W
Kesälahti 44 61.54N 29.50 E
Keşan 30 40.51N 26.37 E
Kesennuma 64 38.54N 141.35 E
Kesh 40 54.32N 7.43W
Keshod 76 21.18N 70.15 E
Keski-Suomen lääni □4 44 62.30N 25.30 E
Kessingland 34 52.25N 1.42 E
Kestell 86 28.19 S 28.38 E
Kestilä 44 64.21N 26.17 E
Keswick 36 54.37N 3.08W
Keszthely 46 46.46N 17.15 E
Ket' ≃ 58 58.55N 81.32 E
Keta 80 5.55N 1.00 E
Keta, ozero ⊜ 58 68.44N 90.00 E
Ketapang 72 1.52 S 109.59 E
Ketchikan 98 55.21N 131.35W
Ketchum 100 43.40N 114.21W
Kete Krachi 80 7.46N 0.03W
Ketoj, ostrov I 58 47.20N 152.28 E
Kętrzyn (Rastenburg) 46 54.06N 21.23 E
Kettering, Eng., U.K. 34 52.24N 0.44W
Kettering, Oh., U.S. 102 39.41N 84.10W
Kettle Creek ≃ 102 41.18N 77.51W
Kettlewell 36 54.09N 2.02W
Kęty 46 49.53N 19.13 E
Keudepasi 70 4.18N 95.56 E
Keudeteunom 70 4.27N 95.48 E
Keuka Lake ⊜ 102 42.27N 77.10W
Keurusselkä ⊜ 44 62.10N 24.40 E
Keuruu 44 62.16N 24.42 E
Kevelaer 46 51.35N 6.15 E
Kew 108 21.54N 72.02W

Symbols in the Index entries are identified on page 122.

Name	Page	Lat. °′	Long. °′
Konžakovskij Kamen', gora ∧	56	59.38 N	59.08 E
Kookynie	90	29.20 S	121.29 E
Koolamarra	94	20.12 S	140.14 E
Koolatah	92	15.53 S	142.27 E
Koolau Range ⋀	105a	21.35 N	158.00 W
Kooloonong	94	34.53 S	143.09 E
Koolyanobbing	90	30.50 S	119.35 E
Koondrook	94	35.39 S	144.08 E
Koonibba	90	31.58 S	133.27 E
Koorawatha	94	34.02 S	148.33 E
Koorda	90	30.50 S	117.29 E
Kootjieskolk	86	31.15 S	20.21 E
Kopāganj	76	26.01 N	83.34 E
Kópasker	42a	66.20 N	16.24 W
Kópavogur	42a	64.06 N	21.50 W
Kopejsk	56	55.07 N	61.37 E
Koper	52	45.33 N	13.44 E
Kopervik	44	59.17 N	5.18 E
Köping	44	59.31 N	16.00 E
Koplik	54	42.13 N	19.26 E
Köpmanholmen	44	63.10 N	18.34 E
Koppang	44	61.34 N	11.04 E
Koppány ≃	46	46.35 N	18.26 E
Kopparberg	44	59.52 N	14.59 E
Kopparbergs Län □6	44	61.00 N	14.30 E
Koppeh Dāgh ⋀	78	37.50 N	58.00 E
Kopperå	44	63.24 N	11.51 E
Koppies	86	27.20 S	27.30 E
Koppom	44	59.43 N	12.09 E
Koprivnica	52	46.10 N	16.50 E
Kopyl'	60	53.09 N	27.05 E
Korab ⋀	54	41.47 N	20.34 E
Korablino	60	53.55 N	40.01 E
Kor'akskaja Sopka, vulkan ∧1	58	53.20 N	158.43 E
Kor'akskoje nagorje ⋀	58	62.30 N	172.00 E
Koralpe ⋀	46	46.50 N	14.58 E
Koraput	74	18.49 N	82.43 E
Korba	76	22.21 N	82.41 E
Korbach	46	51.16 N	8.52 E
Korçë	54	40.37 N	20.46 E
Korčula	52	42.58 N	17.08 E
Korčula, Otok I	52	42.57 N	16.50 E
Korčulanski Kanal ʊ	52	43.03 N	16.40 E
Kordestān □4	78	35.30 N	47.00 E
Kord Kūy	78	36.48 N	54.07 E
Korea, North □1	62	40.00 N	127.00 E
Korea, South □1	62	36.30 N	128.00 E
Korea Bay C	62	39.00 N	124.00 E
Korea Strait ʊ	62	34.00 N	129.00 E
Korf	58	60.19 N	165.50 E
Korfovskij	58	48.13 N	135.03 E
Korhogo	80	9.27 N	5.38 W
Korinthiakós Kólpos C	54	38.19 N	22.04 E
Kórinthos (Corinth)	54	37.56 N	22.56 E
Korínthou, Dhiórix ⌅	54	37.57 N	22.56 E
Kőris-hegy ∧	46	47.18 N	17.45 E
Koritsa →Korçë	54	40.37 N	20.46 E
Kōriyama	64	37.24 N	140.23 E
Korkino	56	54.54 N	61.23 E
Korla	62	41.44 N	86.09 E
Korliki	58	61.31 N	82.22 E
Korma	60	53.08 N	30.48 E
Körmend	46	47.01 N	16.37 E
Kornat, Otok I	52	43.50 N	15.16 E
Korneuburg	46	48.21 N	16.20 E
Kórnik	46	52.17 N	17.04 E
Kornsjø	44	58.57 N	11.39 E
Korogwe	84	5.09 S	38.29 E
Koroit	94	38.17 S	142.22 E
Koronadal	72	6.30 N	124.51 E
Koróni	54	36.48 N	21.56 E
Korónia, Límni ⊜	54	40.41 N	23.05 E
Koronowo	46	53.19 N	17.57 E
Koropíon	54	37.54 N	23.53 E
Koror	68	7.20 N	134.29 E
Körös ≃	46	46.43 N	20.12 E
Koro Sea ⊤2	28	18.00 S	179.50 E
Korosten'	56	50.57 N	28.39 E
Korpilahti	44	62.01 N	25.33 E
Korpo (Korppoo)	44	60.10 N	21.34 E
Korsakov	58	46.38 N	142.46 E
Korselbränna	44	64.27 N	15.35 E
Korsnäs, Suomi	44	62.47 N	21.12 E
Korsnäs, Sve.	44	60.35 N	15.43 E
Korso	44	60.21 N	25.06 E
Korsør	44	55.20 N	11.09 E
Korsze	46	54.10 N	21.09 E
Kortrijk (Courtrai)	46	50.50 N	3.16 E
Korumburra	94	38.26 S	145.49 E
Kos	54	36.53 N	27.18 E
Kos I	54	36.50 N	27.10 E
Kosa	42	59.56 N	54.55 E
Koš-Agač	56	50.00 N	88.40 E
Kosai	64	34.43 N	137.33 E
Kosaja Gora	60	54.07 N	37.33 E
Kosaka	64	40.19 N	140.44 E
Koščagyl	56	46.51 N	53.48 E
Kościan	46	52.06 N	16.38 E
Kościerzyna	46	54.08 N	18.00 E
Kosciusko, Mount ∧	94	36.27 S	148.16 E
Koshikijima-rettō II	64	31.45 N	129.49 E
Kōshoku	64	36.32 N	138.06 E
Kosi	76	27.48 N	77.26 E
Košice	46	48.43 N	21.15 E
Kosimeer ⊜	86	26.55 S	32.52 E
Koski	44	60.39 N	23.09 E
Koskullskulle	42	67.12 N	20.50 E
Koslan	56	63.28 N	48.52 E
Kosovska Mitrovica	54	42.53 N	20.52 E
Kosrae I	28	5.19 N	162.59 E
Kossovo	60	52.45 N	25.09 E
Kosta	44	56.51 N	15.23 E
Kostajnica	52	45.14 N	16.33 E
Kostenec	54	42.16 N	23.49 E
Koster	86	25.57 S	26.42 E
Kosterevo	60	55.56 N	39.37 E
Kosteröarna I	44	58.54 N	11.02 E
Kostonjärvi ⊜	44	65.47 N	28.27 E
Kostroma	60	57.46 N	40.55 E
Kostrzyn	46	52.37 N	14.39 E
Koszalin (Köslin)	46	54.12 N	16.09 E
Kőszeg	46	47.23 N	16.33 E
Koszyce	46	50.11 N	20.35 E
Kota, India	76	22.18 N	82.02 E
Kota, India	76	25.11 N	75.50 E
Kotaagung	72	5.30 S	104.38 E
Kota Baharu	72	6.08 N	102.15 E
Kotabaru	72	3.14 S	116.13 E
Kota Belud	72	6.25 N	116.31 E
Kotabumi	72	4.50 S	104.54 E
Kotadabok	72	0.30 S	104.33 E
Kota Kinabalu (Jesselton)	72	5.59 N	116.04 E
Kotamobagu	72	0.46 N	124.19 E
Kotari ⋀	52	44.05 N	15.30 E
Kota Tinggi	72	1.44 N	103.54 E
Kotcho Lake ⊜	98	59.05 N	121.10 W
Kotel	54	42.53 N	26.27 E
Kotel'nič	42	58.18 N	48.20 E
Kotel'nikovo	56	47.38 N	43.09 E
Kotel'nyj, ostrov I	58	75.45 N	138.44 E
Köthen	46	51.45 N	11.58 E
Kotka	44	60.28 N	26.55 E
Kot Kapūra	76	30.35 N	74.54 E
Kotlas	42	61.16 N	46.35 E
Kotlenski prohod)(	54	42.53 N	26.27 E
Kotor	54	42.25 N	18.46 E
Kotoriba	52	46.21 N	16.49 E
Kotor Varoš	52	44.37 N	17.23 E
Kotovsk, S.S.S.R.	56	47.45 N	29.32 E
Kotovsk, S.S.S.R.	60	52.36 N	41.32 E
Kot Pūtli	76	27.43 N	76.12 E
Kotra	76	24.22 N	73.10 E
Kotri	76	25.22 N	68.18 E
Kötschach [-Mauthen]	46	46.40 N	13.00 E
Kottagūdem	74	17.33 N	80.38 E
Kottayam	74	9.35 N	76.31 E
Kotto ≃	82	4.14 N	22.02 E
Kotuj ≃	58	71.55 N	102.05 E
Kötzting	46	49.11 N	12.52 E
Kou'an	66	32.19 N	119.52 E
Koudougou	80	12.15 N	2.22 W
Kougaberge ⋀	86	33.40 S	23.50 E
Koukdjuak ≃	98	66.45 N	73.09 W
Koulamoutou	84	1.08 S	12.29 E
Koulikoro	80	12.53 N	7.33 W
Koumala	94	21.37 S	149.15 E
Koumi	64	36.05 N	138.29 E
Koumra	82	8.55 N	17.33 E
Kounradskij	56	46.59 N	75.00 E
Kouroussa	80	10.39 N	9.53 W
Koussi, Emi ∧	82	19.50 N	18.30 E
Koutiala	80	12.23 N	5.28 W
Kouvola	44	60.52 N	26.42 E
Kovarskas	60	55.26 N	24.55 E
Kovdor	42	67.34 N	30.22 E
Kovel'	56	51.14 N	24.41 E
Kovin	54	44.45 N	20.59 E
Kovno →Kaunas	60	54.54 N	23.54 E
Kovrov	60	56.22 N	41.18 E
Kovylkino	42	54.02 N	43.56 E
Kowal	46	52.32 N	19.09 E
Kowalewo Pomorskie	46	53.10 N	18.53 E
Kowhitirangi	96	42.52 S	171.01 E
Kowkcheh ≃	76	37.10 N	69.23 E
Kowloon (Jiulong)	66	22.18 N	114.10 E
Kowt-e 'Ashrow	76	34.27 N	68.48 E
Kō-zaki ›	64	34.05 N	129.13 E
Kozan	78	37.27 N	35.49 E
Kozáni	54	40.18 N	21.47 E
Kozara ⋀	52	45.00 N	16.50 E
Kozarac	52	44.58 N	16.51 E
Kozhikode →Calicut	74	11.15 N	75.46 E
Koziegłowy	46	50.36 N	19.09 E
Kozienice	46	51.35 N	21.33 E
Koźle	46	50.20 N	18.08 E
Kozlovo	60	56.31 N	36.16 E
Koźmin	46	51.50 N	17.28 E
Koz'modemjansk	42	56.20 N	46.36 E
Kozuchów	46	51.45 N	15.35 E
Kōzu-shima I	64	34.13 N	139.10 E
Kpandu	80	7.00 N	0.18 E
Kra, Isthmus of ⊥3	70	10.20 N	99.00 E
Kraai ≃	86	30.40 S	26.45 E
Krâchéh	70	12.29 N	106.01 E
Kragan	72	6.42 S	111.37 E
Kragerø	44	58.52 N	9.25 E
Kragujevac	54	44.01 N	20.55 E
Krajenka	46	53.19 N	17.00 E
Kraków	46	50.03 N	19.58 E
Kralendijk	108	12.10 N	68.17 W
Kraljevica	52	45.16 N	14.34 E
Kraljevo	54	43.43 N	20.41 E
Kralovice	46	49.59 N	13.29 E
Kralupy nad Vltavou	46	50.11 N	14.18 E
Kramatorsk	56	48.43 N	37.32 E
Kramfors	44	62.56 N	17.47 E
Krångede	44	63.09 N	16.05 E
Kranídhion	54	37.22 N	23.10 E
Kranj	52	46.15 N	14.21 E
Kranskop	86	29.00 S	30.47 E
Krapina	52	46.10 N	15.52 E
Krapkowice	46	50.29 N	17.56 E
Krasavino	42	60.58 N	46.26 E
Krasino	56	70.45 N	54.27 E
Krasnaja Gorka	60	56.12 N	43.04 E
Krasneno	58	64.38 N	174.48 E
Kraśnik	46	50.56 N	22.13 E
Kraśnik Fabryczny	46	50.58 N	22.12 E
Krasnoarmejsk	60	56.08 N	38.08 E
Krasnoarmejskij	58	69.35 N	172.00 E
Krasnobród	46	50.33 N	23.13 E
Krasnodar	56	45.02 N	39.00 E
Krasnogorsk, S.S.S.R.	58	48.24 N	142.06 E
Krasnogorsk, S.S.S.R.	60	55.50 N	37.20 E
Krasnoj Armii, proliv ʊ	58	80.00 N	94.35 E
Krasnojarsk	58	56.01 N	92.50 E
Krasnojarskoje vodochranilišče ⊜1	58	55.00 N	92.00 E
Krasnoje, ozero ⊜	58	64.30 N	174.24 E
Krasnoje-na-Volge	60	57.31 N	41.14 E
Krasnoje Selo	60	59.44 N	30.05 E
Krasnokamsk	56	58.04 N	55.48 E
Krasnoostrovskij	60	60.18 N	28.40 E
Krasnopolje	60	53.20 N	31.24 E
Krasnosel'kup	56	65.41 N	82.28 E
Krasnosielc	46	53.03 N	21.10 E
Krasnoslobodsk	56	48.42 N	44.34 E
Krasnoturjinsk	56	59.46 N	60.12 E
Krasnoural'sk	56	58.21 N	60.03 E
Krasnovišersk	42	60.23 N	56.59 E
Krasnovodsk	78	40.00 N	53.00 E
Krasnoyarsk →Krasnojarsk	58	56.01 N	92.50 E
Krasnozatonskij	42	61.41 N	50.58 E
Krasnozavodsk	60	56.27 N	38.13 E
Krasnoznamenskij	56	51.03 N	69.30 E
Krasnoz'orskoje	58	53.59 N	79.14 E
Krasnyj Cholm	60	58.03 N	37.07 E
Krasnyj Kut	56	50.57 N	46.58 E
Krasnyj Luč	56	48.08 N	38.56 E
Krasnyj Majak	60	56.03 N	41.23 E
Krasnystaw	46	50.59 N	23.10 E
Kraszna (Crasna) ≃	54	48.09 N	22.20 E
Kratke Range ⋀	92	6.25 S	145.35 E
Kratovo	54	42.05 N	22.11 E
Kravaře	46	49.56 N	18.01 E
Krawang	72	6.19 S	107.17 E
Krbava ◆1	52	44.40 N	15.35 E
Krečevicy	60	58.37 N	31.21 E
Krefeld	46	51.20 N	6.34 E
Kremastón, Tekhnití Límni ⊜1	54	38.55 N	21.30 E
Kremenčug	56	49.04 N	33.25 E
Kremenčugskoje vodochranilišče ⊜1	56	49.20 N	32.30 E
Kremnica	46	48.43 N	18.54 E
Krems an der Donau	46	48.25 N	15.36 E
Krepoljin	54	44.16 N	21.37 E
Kresta, zaliv C	58	66.00 N	179.15 W
Krest-Major	58	67.37 N	144.45 E
Krestovaja Guba	56	74.07 N	55.33 E
Kretinga	60	55.53 N	21.13 E
Kría Vrísi	54	40.41 N	22.18 E
Kribi	80	2.57 N	9.55 E
Kričov	60	53.42 N	31.43 E
Kriens	48	47.02 N	8.17 E
Křimice	46	49.46 N	13.15 E
Krimml	46	47.13 N	12.11 E
Krishna ≃	74	15.57 N	80.59 E
Krishnanagar	76	23.24 N	88.30 E
Kristdala	44	57.24 N	16.11 E
Kristiania →Oslo	44	59.55 N	10.45 E
Kristianopel	44	56.15 N	16.02 E
Kristiansand	44	58.10 N	8.00 E
Kristianstad	44	56.02 N	14.08 E
Kristianstads Län □6	44	56.15 N	14.00 E
Kristiansund	44	63.07 N	7.45 E
Kristineberg	44	65.04 N	18.35 E
Kristinehamn	44	59.20 N	14.07 E
Kristinestad (Kristiinankau-Punki)	44	62.17 N	21.23 E
Kriti (Crete) I	54	35.29 N	24.42 E
Kritikón Pélagos (Sea of Crete) ⊤2	54	35.46 N	23.54 E
Krivaja ≃	54	44.27 N	18.09 E
Kriva Palanka	54	42.12 N	22.20 E
Krivodol	54	43.23 N	23.29 E
Krivoj Rog	56	47.55 N	33.21 E
Križevci	52	46.02 N	16.33 E
Krk, Otok I	52	45.05 N	14.35 E
Krnov	46	50.05 N	17.41 E
Krobia	46	51.47 N	16.58 E
Krøderen ⊜	44	60.15 N	9.38 E
Krokek	44	58.40 N	16.24 E
Kroken	42	65.22 N	14.20 E
Krokodil ≃, S. Afr.	86	24.12 S	26.52 E
Krokodil ≃, S. Afr.	86	25.26 S	31.58 E
Krokom	44	63.19 N	14.30 E
Krokowa	46	54.48 N	18.11 E
Kroměříž	46	49.18 N	17.24 E
Krompachy	46	48.56 N	20.52 E
Kronach	46	50.14 N	11.20 E
Krong Ana ⊜1	70	12.30 N	108.00 E
Krŏng Kaôh Kŏng	70	11.37 N	102.59 E
Krŏng Kêb	70	10.29 N	104.19 E
Kronobergs Län □6	44	56.40 N	14.40 E
Kronoby (Kruunupyy)	44	63.43 N	23.02 E
Kronockij zaliv C	58	54.12 N	160.36 E
Kronoki	58	54.36 N	161.10 E
Kronštadt	60	59.59 N	29.45 E
Kroonstad	86	27.46 S	27.12 E
Kropotkin, S.S.S.R.	56	45.26 N	40.34 E
Kropotkin, S.S.S.R.	58	58.30 N	115.17 E
Krościenko	46	49.27 N	20.26 E
Krośniewice	46	52.16 N	19.10 E
Krosno	46	49.42 N	21.46 E
Krosno Odrzańskie	46	52.04 N	15.05 E
Krotoszyn	46	51.42 N	17.26 E
Kroya	72	7.38 S	109.14 E
Krško	52	45.58 N	15.29 E
Kruger National Park ♦	86	24.00 S	31.40 E
Krugersdorp	86	26.05 S	27.35 E
Krui	72	5.11 S	103.56 E
Kruidfontein	86	32.51 S	21.57 E
Kruisfontein	86	34.00 S	24.43 E
Krujë	54	41.30 N	19.48 E
Kr'ukovo	58	66.30 N	159.31 E
Krumbach [Schwaben]	46	48.14 N	10.22 E
Krumovgrad	54	41.28 N	25.39 E
Krung Thep (Bangkok)	70	13.45 N	100.31 E
Krupka	46	50.43 N	13.46 E
Kruså	44	54.50 N	9.25 E
Kruševac	54	43.35 N	21.20 E
Kruševo	54	41.22 N	21.14 E
Krušné hory (Erzgebirge) ⋀	48	50.30 N	13.15 E
Kruszwica	46	52.41 N	18.19 E
Kruzenšterna, proliv ʊ	58	48.30 N	153.50 E
Kruzof Island I	98	57.10 N	135.40 W
Krylbo	44	60.08 N	16.13 E
Krymskij poluostrov ›1	56	45.00 N	34.00 E
Krynica	46	49.25 N	20.56 E
Krzepice	46	50.58 N	18.44 E
Krzeszowice	46	50.09 N	19.39 E
Krzna ≃	46	52.08 N	23.31 E
Krzywiń	46	51.58 N	16.49 E
Krzyz	46	52.54 N	16.01 E
Ksar-El-Kebir	80	35.01 N	5.54 W
Ksenjevka	58	53.34 N	118.44 E
Książ Wielkopolski	46	52.05 N	17.14 E
Kstovo	42	56.11 N	44.11 E
Kuah	72	6.19 N	99.51 E
Kuala Dungun	72	4.47 N	103.26 E
Kuala Kangsar	72	4.46 N	100.56 E
Kualakapuas	72	3.01 S	114.21 E
Kuala Kerai	72	5.32 N	102.12 E
Kuala Kubu Baharu	72	3.34 N	101.39 E
Kualakurun	72	1.07 S	113.53 E
Kuala Lipis	72	4.11 N	102.03 E
Kuala Lumpur	72	3.10 N	101.42 E
Kuala Lumpur □3	72	3.10 N	101.42 E
Kuala Nerang	72	6.15 N	100.36 E
Kuala Pilah	72	2.44 N	102.15 E
Kuala Terengganu	72	5.20 N	103.08 E
Kuamut	72	5.13 N	117.30 E
Kuandang	72	0.52 N	122.55 E
Kuantan	72	3.48 N	103.20 E
Kuba	56	41.22 N	48.31 E
Kuban' ≃	56	45.20 N	37.30 E
Kubokawa	64	33.12 N	133.08 E
Kubor, Mount ∧	92	6.05 S	144.45 E
Kubrat	54	43.48 N	26.30 E
Kučevo	54	44.27 N	21.44 E
Kuchaiburi	76	22.16 N	86.10 E
Kuchāman	76	27.09 N	74.52 E
Kuching	72	1.33 N	110.20 E
Kuchinoerabu-jima I	65b	30.28 N	130.12 E
Kuchino-shima I	65b	29.57 N	129.57 E
Kūd	76	33.05 N	75.17 E
Kudamatsu	64	34.00 N	131.52 E
Kudat	72	6.53 N	116.50 E
Kudus	72	6.48 S	110.50 E
Kudymkar	42	59.01 N	54.37 E
Kufstein	46	47.35 N	12.10 E
Kuga	62	41.43 N	82.54 E
Kuhmo	44	64.08 N	29.31 E
Kuhmoinen	44	61.34 N	25.11 E
Kuiseb ≃	86	22.59 S	14.31 E
Kuitan	66	23.05 N	115.58 E
Kuito	84	12.22 S	16.56 E
Kuiu Island I	98	57.45 N	134.10 W
Kuivaniemi	44	65.35 N	25.11 E
Kujawy ◆1	46	52.45 N	18.30 E
Kujbyšev, S.S.S.R.	42	53.12 N	50.09 E
Kujbyšev, S.S.S.R.	56	55.27 N	78.19 E
Kujbyševskij	56	37.52 N	68.44 E
Kujbyševskoje vodochranilišče ⊜1	42	54.30 N	48.30 E
Kuji	64	40.11 N	141.46 E
Kuji ≃	64	36.29 N	140.37 E
Kujūkuri-heiya ⊥2	64	35.35 N	140.30 E
Kujū-san ∧	64	33.05 N	131.15 E
Kukalaya ≃	108	13.39 N	83.37 W
Kukawa	80	12.56 N	13.35 E
Kukerin	90	33.11 S	118.05 E
Kukës	54	42.05 N	20.24 E
Kukkola	44	65.59 N	24.04 E
Kukshi	76	22.12 N	74.45 E
Kukup	72	1.19 N	103.27 E
Kula, Blg.	54	43.53 N	22.31 E
Kula, Jugo.	54	45.36 N	19.32 E
Kula, Tür.	54	38.32 N	28.40 E
Kul'ab	76	37.55 N	69.46 E
Kula Kangri ∧	76	28.03 N	90.27 E
Kuldīga	60	56.58 N	21.59 E
Kulebaki	60	55.24 N	42.32 E
Kulen Vakuf	52	44.34 N	16.06 E
Kulgera	90	25.50 S	133.18 E
Kulim	72	5.22 N	100.34 E
Kulin	90	32.40 S	118.10 E
Kulju	44	61.23 N	23.46 E
Kulmbach	46	50.06 N	11.27 E
Kuloj	42	61.02 N	42.29 E
Kul'sary	56	46.59 N	54.01 E
Kulti	76	23.44 N	86.51 E
Kulu	76	31.58 N	77.06 E
Kulumadau	92	9.03 S	152.43 E
Kulundinskaja step' ≚	56	53.00 N	79.00 E
Kulundinskoje, ozero ⊜	58	53.00 N	79.36 E
Kulwin	94	35.02 S	142.33 E
Kuma ≃, Nihon	64	32.30 N	130.34 E
Kuma ≃, S.S.S.R.	56	44.56 N	47.00 E
Kumagaya	64	36.08 N	139.23 E
Kumaishi	64a	42.08 N	139.59 E
Kumamoto	64	32.48 N	130.43 E
Kumano	64	33.54 N	136.05 E
Kumano ≃	64	33.44 N	136.01 E
Kumano-nada ⊤2	64	33.47 N	136.20 E
Kumanovo	54	42.08 N	21.43 E
Kumara	96	42.38 S	171.11 E
Kumarl	90	32.47 S	121.33 E
Kumasi	80	6.41 N	1.35 W
Kumba	80	4.38 N	9.25 E
Kumbakonam	74	10.58 N	79.23 E
Kumbarilla	94	27.19 S	150.53 E
Kum-Dag	78	39.16 N	54.35 E
Kume-jima I	65b	26.20 N	126.47 E
Kumertau	56	52.46 N	55.47 E
Kumla	44	59.08 N	15.08 E
Kumlinge I	44	60.16 N	20.47 E
Kummerower See ⊜	46	53.49 N	12.52 E
Kumo	80	10.03 N	11.13 E
Kumora	58	55.53 N	111.13 E
Kumukahi, Cape ›	105a	19.31 N	154.49 W
Kuna	104	43.29 N	116.25 W
Kunašir, ostrov (Kunashiri-tō) I	58	44.10 N	146.00 E
Kundam	76	23.13 N	80.21 E
Kundar ≃	76	31.56 N	69.19 E
Kundiān	76	32.27 N	71.28 E
Kundiawa	92	6.00 S	145.00 E
Kundip	90	33.42 S	120.10 E
Kundla	76	21.20 N	71.18 E
Kunene (Cunene) ≃	84	17.20 S	11.50 E
Kunes	42	70.21 N	26.31 E
Kungälv	44	57.52 N	11.58 E
Kungrad	56	43.06 N	58.54 E
Kungsbacka	44	57.29 N	12.04 E
Kungshamn	44	58.22 N	11.15 E
Kungsör	44	59.25 N	16.05 E
Kungur	56	57.25 N	56.57 E
Kungurri	94	21.05 S	148.44 E
Kunhegyes	46	47.22 N	20.38 E
Kuningan	72	6.59 S	108.29 E
Kunisaki	64	33.33 N	131.45 E
Kunisaki-hantō ›1	64	33.30 N	131.40 E
Kunkuri	76	22.45 N	83.57 E
Kunlun Shan ⋀	76	36.30 N	88.00 E
Kunming	70	25.05 N	102.40 E
Kunovice	46	49.03 N	17.29 E
Kunsan	62	35.58 N	126.41 E
Kunshan	66	31.23 N	120.57 E
Kunszentmárton	46	46.51 N	20.18 E
Kununurra	92	15.47 S	128.44 E
Künzelsau	46	49.16 N	9.41 E
Kuopio	44	62.54 N	27.41 E
Kuopion lääni □4	44	63.00 N	27.30 E
Kuortane	44	62.48 N	23.30 E
Kupa ≃	52	45.28 N	16.24 E
Kupang	72	10.10 S	123.35 E
Kup'ansk	56	49.42 N	37.38 E
Kupanskoje	60	56.51 N	38.43 E
Kupino	56	54.22 N	77.18 E
Kupreanof Island I	98	56.50 N	133.30 W
Kupres	52	44.00 N	17.17 E
Kura ≃	56	39.24 N	49.24 E
Kurashiki	64	34.35 N	133.46 E
Kurauli	76	27.24 N	78.59 E
Kurayoshi	64	35.26 N	133.49 E
Kurchatov	56	51.38 N	35.29 E
K'urdamir	78	40.21 N	48.08 E
Kurdistan □9	74	37.00 N	45.00 E
Kure, Austl.	92	15.27 S	124.33 E
Kure, Nihon	64	34.14 N	132.34 E
Kure Island I1	28	28.25 N	178.25 W
Kurejka ≃	58	66.30 N	87.12 E
Kurenalus	44	65.21 N	26.59 E
Kuressaare	60	58.15 N	22.28 E
Kurgan	56	55.26 N	65.18 E
Kurgan-T'ube	76	37.50 N	68.48 E
Kuria I	28	0.14 N	173.25 E
Kuria Muria Islands →Khūryān Mūryān II	74	17.30 N	56.00 E
Kuridala	94	21.17 S	140.30 E
Kurikka	44	62.37 N	22.25 E
Kuril Islands →Kuril'skije ostrova II	58	46.10 N	152.00 E
Kuril'sk	58	45.14 N	147.53 E
Kuril'skije ostrova (Kuril Islands) II	58	46.10 N	152.00 E
Kuřim	46	49.18 N	16.32 E
Kurinskaja kosa ›2	78	39.03 N	49.13 E
Kurinwás ≃	108	12.49 N	83.41 W
Kuripapango	96	39.23 S	176.21 E
Kuriyama	64a	43.03 N	141.47 E
Kurmuk	82	10.33 N	34.17 E
Kurnool	74	15.50 N	78.03 E
Kurobe	64	36.51 N	137.26 E
Kuroishi	64	40.38 N	140.36 E
Kuro-shima I	65b	30.50 N	129.57 E
Kurovskoje	60	55.34 N	38.55 E
Kurow	96	44.44 S	170.28 E
Kurseong	76	26.53 N	88.17 E
Kursk	56	51.42 N	36.12 E
Kuršumlija	54	43.08 N	21.17 E
Kūrtī	82	18.07 N	31.33 E
Kurtistown	105a	19.36 N	155.03 W
Kuru	44	61.52 N	23.44 E
Kuruman	86	27.28 S	23.28 E
Kuruman ≃	86	26.56 S	20.39 E
Kurumanheuwels ⋀2	86	27.40 S	23.25 E
Kurume	64	33.19 N	130.31 E
Kurumkan	58	54.18 N	110.18 E
Kurunegala	74	7.29 N	80.22 E
Kusa	56	55.20 N	59.29 E
Kusawa Lake ⊜	98	60.20 N	136.15 W
Kusel	46	49.32 N	7.24 E
Kushālgarh	76	23.10 N	74.27 E
Kushikino	64	31.44 N	130.16 E
Kushima	64	31.29 N	131.14 E
Kushimoto	64	33.28 N	135.47 E
Kushiro	64a	42.58 N	144.23 E
Kushtia	76	23.55 N	89.07 E
Kushui	62	42.11 N	94.25 E
Kuška	78	35.16 N	62.20 E
Kuška ≃	78	36.00 N	62.40 E
Kuskokwim ≃	22	60.17 N	162.27 W
Kušmurun	56	52.27 N	64.36 E
Küsnacht	48	47.19 N	8.35 E
Kussharo-ko ⊜	64a	43.38 N	144.21 E
Küssnacht	48	47.05 N	8.27 E
Kustanaj	56	53.10 N	63.35 E
Kūstī	82	13.10 N	32.40 E
Kusu	64	33.16 N	131.09 E
K'us'ur	58	70.39 N	127.15 E
Kušva	56	58.18 N	59.45 E
Kut, Ko I	70	11.40 N	102.35 E
Kütahya	30	39.25 N	29.59 E
Kutaisi	56	42.15 N	42.40 E
Kūt al-Imāra	74	32.25 N	45.49 E
Kutarere	96	38.03 S	177.09 E
Kutch, Gulf of C	76	22.36 N	69.30 E
Kutch, Rann of ≚	76	24.05 N	70.10 E
Kutchan	64a	42.54 N	140.45 E
Kutcharo-ko ⊜	64a	45.09 N	142.19 E
Kutina	52	45.29 N	16.46 E
Kutiyāna	76	21.38 N	69.59 E
Kutná Hora	46	49.57 N	15.16 E
Kutno	46	52.15 N	19.23 E
Kuttura	42	68.24 N	26.28 E
Kuttusoja	42	67.46 N	28.50 E
Kutu	84	2.44 S	18.09 E
Kutubu, Lake ⊜	92	6.23 S	143.18 E
Kúty	46	48.40 N	17.03 E
Kutztown	102	40.31 N	75.46 W
Kuusamo	44	65.58 N	29.11 E
Kuusankoski	44	60.54 N	26.38 E
Kuvandyk	56	51.28 N	57.21 E
Kuvšinovo	60	57.02 N	34.10 E
Kuwait (Al-Kuwayt) □1	74	29.30 N	47.45 E
Kuwana	64	35.04 N	136.42 E
Kuwayt, Khalīj al- C	78	29.30 N	48.00 E
Kuženkino	60	57.44 N	33.59 E
Kuz'movka	58	62.19 N	92.02 E
Kuzneck	42	53.07 N	46.36 E
Kuzneckij Alatau ⋀	58	54.45 N	88.00 E
Kuzuryū ≃	64	36.13 N	136.08 E
Kvænangen C2	42	70.05 N	21.13 E
Kvaløya I, Nor.	42	69.40 N	18.30 E
Kvaløya I, Nor.	42	70.37 N	23.52 E
Kvam	44	61.40 N	9.42 E
Kvanndal	44	60.29 N	6.36 E
Kvarner C	52	44.45 N	14.15 E
Kvarnerić ʊ	52	44.45 N	14.35 E
Kvenna ≃	44	60.01 N	7.56 E
Kverkfjöll ∧	42a	64.43 N	16.38 W
Kvikkjokk	42	66.55 N	17.50 E
Kvina ≃	44	58.17 N	6.56 E
Kvissleby	44	62.17 N	17.21 E
Kwai →Khwae Noi ≃	70	14.00 N	99.33 E
Kwajalein I1	28	9.05 N	167.20 E
Kwakoegron	110	5.15 N	55.20 W
Kwando (Cuando) ≃	84	18.27 S	23.32 E
Kwangchow →Guangzhou	66	23.06 N	113.16 E
Kwangju	62	35.09 N	126.54 E
Kwango (Cuango) ≃	84	3.14 S	17.23 E
Kwangsi Chuang Autonomous Region →Guangxi Zhuangzu Zizhiqu □4	62	24.00 N	109.00 E
Kwangtung →Guangdong □4	62	23.00 N	113.00 E
Kweisui →Hohhot	62	40.51 N	111.40 E
Kwekwe	86	18.55 S	29.49 E
Kweneng □5	86	24.00 S	24.00 E
Kwenge ≃	84	4.50 S	18.42 E
Kwidzyn	46	53.45 N	18.56 E
Kwilu (Cuilo) ≃	84	3.22 S	17.22 E
Kwinana	90	32.15 S	115.48 E
Kwobrup	90	33.37 S	117.46 E
Kyabra	94	26.18 S	143.10 E
Kyabram	94	36.19 S	145.03 E
Kyaiklat	70	16.26 N	95.44 E
Kyaikto	70	17.18 N	97.01 E
Kyancutta	94	33.08 S	135.34 E
Kyaukpyu	70	19.05 N	93.52 E
Kyauktaw	70	20.51 N	92.59 E
Kyjov	46	49.01 N	17.08 E
Kyle □9	36	55.29 N	4.24 W
Kyle, Lake ⊜1	86	20.14 S	31.00 E
Kyleakin	38	57.16 N	5.44 W
Kyle of Lochalsh	38	57.17 N	5.43 W
Kylerhea	38	57.14 N	5.41 W
Kylestrome	38	58.16 N	5.02 W
Kym ≃	34	52.14 N	0.17 W
Kymen lääni □4	44	61.00 N	28.00 E
Kymijoki ≃	44	60.30 N	26.52 E
Kyneton	94	37.15 S	144.27 E
Kynšperk nad Ohří	46	50.04 N	12.32 E
Kynuna	94	21.35 S	141.55 E
Kyoga, Lake ⊜	84	1.30 N	33.00 E
Kyōga-misaki ›	64	35.46 N	135.13 E
Kyogle	94	28.37 S	153.00 E
Kyŏngju	62	35.51 N	129.14 E
Kyōto	64	35.00 N	135.45 E
Kyren	58	51.41 N	102.08 E
Kyritz	46	52.56 N	12.23 E
Kyrkheden	44	60.10 N	13.29 E
Kyrksæterøra	44	63.17 N	9.06 E
Kyrkslätt (Kirkkonummi)	44	60.07 N	24.26 E
Kyrö	44	60.42 N	22.45 E
Kyrönjoki ≃	44	63.14 N	21.45 E
Kyrösjärvi ⊜	44	61.45 N	23.10 E
Kyröskoski	44	61.40 N	23.11 E
Kyštovka	58	56.33 N	76.38 E
Kyštym	56	55.42 N	60.34 E
Kyūroku-jima I	64	40.32 N	139.29 E
Kyūshū I	64	33.00 N	131.00 E
Kyushu-Palau Ridge ◆3	28	20.00 N	136.00 E
Kyūshū-sanchi ⋀	64	32.35 N	131.17 E
Kywong	94	34.59 S	146.44 E
Kyyjärvi	44	63.02 N	24.34 E
Kyzyl	58	51.42 N	94.27 E
Kyzyl-Kija	56	40.16 N	72.08 E
Kyzylkum ◆2	56	42.00 N	64.00 E
Kzyl-Orda	56	44.48 N	65.28 E
Kzyltu	56	53.38 N	72.20 E
L			
Laa an der Thaya	46	48.43 N	16.23 E
La Aguja, Cabo de ›	108	11.18 N	74.12 W
Laakajärvi ⊜	44	63.50 N	27.55 E
La Albuera	50	38.43 N	6.49 W
La Albufera ⊜	50	39.20 N	0.22 W
La Alcarria ◆1	50	40.30 N	2.45 W
La Algaba	50	37.28 N	6.01 W
La Almarcha	50	39.41 N	2.22 W
La Almunia de Doña Godina	50	41.29 N	1.22 W
La Araucanía □4	114	38.45 S	72.30 W
Laas Caanood	82	8.28 N	47.21 E
La Asunción	110	11.02 N	63.53 W
Laau Point ›	105a	21.06 N	157.19 W
L'Abacou, Pointe ›	108	18.03 N	73.47 W
La Baie	98	48.19 N	70.53 W
La Banda	114	27.44 S	64.15 W
La Bañeza	50	42.18 N	5.54 W
La Barca	106	20.17 N	102.34 W
La Bassée	48	50.32 N	2.48 E
Labastide-Murat	48	44.39 N	1.34 E
La Baule	48	47.17 N	2.24 W
Labé	80	11.19 N	12.17 W
Labe (Elbe) ≃	46	53.50 N	9.00 E
Labelle	102	46.16 N	74.44 W
Laberge, Lake ⊜	98	61.11 N	135.12 W
Laberinto de las Doce Leguas II	108	20.35 N	78.30 W
Labin	52	45.05 N	14.07 E
Labinsk	56	44.38 N	40.44 E
Labis	72	2.23 N	103.02 E
La Bisbal	50	41.57 N	3.03 E
Łabiszyn	46	52.57 N	17.55 E
Laboe	46	54.24 N	10.15 E
Laborde	114	33.09 S	62.51 W
Laborec ≃	46	48.36 N	22.00 E
Labouchere, Mount ∧	90	25.12 S	118.18 E
Labouheyre	48	44.13 N	0.55 W
Laboulaye	114	34.07 S	63.24 W
Labrador ◆1	98	54.00 N	62.00 W
Labrador Basin ◆1	22	53.00 N	48.00 W
Labrador City	98	52.57 N	66.55 W
Labrador Sea ⊤2	98	57.00 N	53.00 W
Lábrea	110	7.16 S	64.47 W
Labrède	48	44.41 N	0.31 W
Labrit	48	44.07 N	0.33 W
Labuan, Pulau I	72	5.21 N	115.13 E
Labuha	92	0.37 S	127.29 E
Labuhan	72	6.22 S	105.50 E
Labuhanbajo	72	8.29 S	119.54 E
Labuk ≃	72	5.54 N	117.30 E
Labutta	70	16.09 N	94.46 E
Labytnangi	56	66.39 N	66.21 E
Laç	54	41.38 N	19.43 E
L'Acadie ≃	102	45.29 N	73.16 W
La Calera	114	32.47 S	71.12 W
La Campana	50	37.34 N	5.26 W
La Canada	104	34.12 N	118.12 W
Lacanau	48	44.59 N	1.05 W
Lacanau, Étang de C	48	44.58 N	1.07 W
La Candelaria	114	26.06 S	65.06 W
La Cañiza	50	42.13 N	8.16 W
La Canourgue	48	44.26 N	3.13 E
La Capelle95-En-Thierache]	48	49.58 N	3.55 E
Lacapelle-Marival	48	44.44 N	1.54 E
La Carlota	114	33.26 S	63.18 W
La Carolina	50	38.15 N	3.37 W
Lacaune	48	43.43 N	2.42 E
Laccadive Sea ⊤2	26	7.00 N	76.00 E
Laceby	36	53.32 N	0.10 W
Lacedonia	52	41.03 N	15.25 E
La Ceiba, Hond.	108	15.47 N	86.50 W
La Ceiba, Ven.	108	9.28 N	71.04 W
Lacepede Bay C	94	36.47 S	139.45 E
Lac-giao	70	12.40 N	108.03 E
La Chaise-Dieu	48	45.19 N	3.42 E
La Chambre	48	45.22 N	6.18 E
La Chapelle-d'Angillon	48	47.22 N	2.26 E
La Chartre-sur-le-Loir	48	47.44 N	0.35 E
La Châtaigneraie	48	46.39 N	0.44 W
La Châtre	48	46.35 N	1.59 E
La Chaux-de-Fonds	48	47.06 N	6.50 E
Lachdenpochja	42	61.31 N	30.08 E
Lachhmangarh	76	27.49 N	75.02 E
Lachine	102	45.26 N	73.40 W
Lachlan ≃	94	34.21 S	143.57 E
La Chorrera, Col.	110	0.44 S	73.01 W
La Chorrera, Pan.	106	8.53 N	79.47 W
L'achovskije ostrova II	58	73.30 N	141.00 E
Lachute	102	45.38 N	74.20 W
La Ciénaga	114	27.30 S	66.57 W
La Ciotat	48	43.10 N	5.36 E
Lack	40	54.33 N	7.35 W
Lackawanna	102	42.49 N	78.49 W
Läckö	44	58.41 N	13.13 E
Lac la Biche	98	54.46 N	111.58 W
La Clayette	48	46.18 N	4.19 E
La Clotilde	114	27.08 S	60.40 W
Lac-Mégantic	102	45.36 N	70.53 W
La Cocha	114	27.47 S	65.34 W
Lacombe	98	52.28 N	113.44 W
La Concepción	108	10.38 N	71.50 W
Laconia	102	43.31 N	71.28 W
La Consulta	114	33.44 S	69.07 W
La Coruña	50	43.22 N	8.23 W
La Courtine	48	45.42 N	2.16 E
La Crosse	100	43.48 N	91.14 W
La Cruz, Arg.	114	29.10 S	56.38 W
La Cruz, Col.	110	1.35 N	76.58 W
La Cruz, Ur.	114	33.56 S	56.15 W
La Cruz de Río Grande	108	13.06 N	84.10 W
La Cumbre	114	30.58 S	64.30 W
Ladākh ◆1	74	34.45 N	76.30 E
Ladākh Range ⋀	76	34.00 N	78.00 E
La Désirade I	108	16.19 N	61.03 W
Ládhi	54	41.27 N	26.17 E
La Digue I	84	4.21 S	55.50 E
Ladismith	86	33.30 S	21.16 E
Ladispoli	52	41.56 N	12.05 E
Lādīz	78	28.56 N	61.19 E
Lādnun	76	27.39 N	74.23 E
Ladoga, Lake →Ladožskoje ozero ⊜	42	61.00 N	31.30 E
La Dorada	110	5.27 N	74.40 W
La Dormida	114	33.21 S	67.55 W
Ladožskoje ozero (Lake Ladoga) ⊜	42	61.00 N	31.30 E
Laduškin	60	54.36 N	20.11 E
Ladva	42	61.21 N	34.34 E
Lady Ann Strait ʊ	98	75.40 N	79.50 W
Ladybank	38	56.16 N	3.08 W
Lady Barron	94	40.12 S	148.14 E
Ladybower Reservoir ⊜1	36	53.20 N	1.45 W
Ladybrand	86	29.19 S	27.25 E
Lady Elliot Island I	94	24.07 S	152.42 E
Lady Grey	86	30.45 S	27.13 E
Ladysmith, B.C., Can.	98	48.58 N	123.49 W
Ladysmith, S. Afr.	86	28.34 S	29.45 E
Lae	92	6.45 S	147.00 E
Lae I1	28	8.56 N	166.14 E
La Encantada, Cerro de ∧	106	31.00 N	115.24 W
Lærdalsøyri	44	61.06 N	7.29 E
La Esmeralda	114	22.13 S	62.38 W
Læsø I	44	57.16 N	11.01 E
La Esperanza, Cuba	108	22.46 N	83.44 W
La Esperanza, Méx.	104	32.06 N	114.47 W
La Estrada	50	42.41 N	8.29 W
La Falda	114	31.05 S	64.30 W
Lafayette, Ca., U.S.	104	37.53 N	122.07 W
Lafayette, In., U.S.	100	40.25 N	86.52 W
Lafayette, La., U.S.	100	30.13 N	92.01 W
Lafayette, Mount ∧	102	44.10 N	71.38 W
La Fère	48	49.40 N	3.22 E
La Ferté-Bernard	48	48.11 N	0.40 E
La Ferté-Gaucher	48	48.47 N	3.18 E
La Ferté-Macé	48	48.36 N	0.22 W
La Ferté-Saint-Aubin	48	47.43 N	1.56 E
Lafia	80	8.30 N	8.30 E
La Flèche	48	47.42 N	0.05 W
Lafnitz ≃	46	46.57 N	16.16 E
La Fortuna	108	10.30 N	84.35 W
La Fragua	114	26.05 S	64.20 W
La Francia	114	31.24 S	62.38 W
La Fregeneda	50	40.59 N	6.52 W
La Fuente de San Esteban	50	40.48 N	6.15 W
La Galite I	80	37.32 N	8.56 E
La Gallareta	114	29.34 S	60.23 W
La Gallega	50	41.54 N	3.16 W
Lagan	44	56.55 N	13.59 E
Lagan ≃, Sve.	44	56.33 N	12.56 E
Lagan ≃, N. Ire., U.K.	36	54.37 N	5.53 W
Lagawe	68	16.49 N	121.06 E
Lage	50	43.13 N	9.00 W
Lågen ≃, Nor.	44	59.03 N	10.05 E
Lågen ≃, Nor.	44	61.08 N	10.25 E
Laggan	38	57.02 N	4.16 W
Laggan, Loch ⊜1	38	56.57 N	4.28 W
Laggan Bay C	38	55.41 N	6.19 W
Laghmān □4	76	35.00 N	70.15 E
Laghouat	80	33.50 N	2.59 E
Laghy	40	54.37 N	8.05 W
Lagoa Vermelha	114	28.13 S	51.32 W
Lagonegro	52	40.07 N	15.46 E
Lagos, Nig.	80	6.27 N	3.24 E
Lagos, Port.	50	37.06 N	8.40 W
Lagos de Moreno	106	21.21 N	101.55 W
La Gouèra	80	20.48 N	17.08 W

Symbols in the Index entries are identified on page 122.

Symbols in the Index entries are identified on page 122.

Name	Page	Lat. °'	Long. °'
León, Esp.	50	42.36N	5.34W
Léon, Fr.	48	43.53N	1.18W
León, Méx.	106	21.07N	101.40W
León, Nic.	108	12.26N	86.53W
León □9	50	42.40N	6.00W
Leonardtown	102	38.17N	76.38W
Leona Vicario	104	32.10N	115.10W
Leomberg	48	48.48N	9.01 E
Leones	114	32.39S	62.18W
Leongatha	94	38.53S	145.57 E
Leonidhion	54	37.10N	22.52 E
Leonora	90	28.53S	121.20 E
León Rougés	114	27.13S	65.32W
Leopold Downs	90	17.52S	125.25 E
Leopoldina	110	21.32S	42.38W
Léopoldville →Kinshasa	84	4.18S	15.18 E
Le Palais	48	47.21N	3.09W
Lepanto →Návpaktos	54	38.23N	21.50 E
Lepe	50	37.15N	7.12W
Le Pellerin	48	47.12N	1.45W
Leping	66	28.57N	117.05 E
L'Epiphanie	102	45.51N	73.30W
Le Pont-de-Beauvoisin	48	45.32N	5.40 E
Lepontine, Alpi ⋌	48	46.25N	8.40 E
Le Port	87c	20.55S	55.18 E
Leppävirta	44	62.29N	27.47 E
Lepperton	96	39.04S	174.13 E
Lepsy	56	46.15N	78.55 E
Le Puy	48	45.02N	3.53 E
Lequeitio	50	43.22N	2.30W
Lercara Friddi	52	37.45N	13.36 E
Leri	34	52.32N	4.02W
Leribe	86	28.53S	28.00 E
Lerici	52	44.04N	9.55 E
Lérida	50	41.37N	0.37 E
Lerma	50	42.02N	3.45W
Léros I	54	37.08N	26.52 E
Lerum	44	57.46N	12.16 E
Lerwick	38a	60.09N	1.09W
Les Aix-d'Angillon	48	47.12N	2.34 E
Les Andelys	48	49.15N	1.25 E
Lesbos →Lésvos I	54	39.10N	26.20 E
Lesbury	36	55.24N	1.36W
Les Cayes	108	18.12N	73.45W
Leschenault, Cape ⋋	90	31.18S	115.27 E
Les Échelles	48	45.26N	5.45 E
Les Essarts	48	46.46N	1.14W
Lesever, Mount ⋀	90	30.10S	115.11 E
Leshan	66	29.34N	103.45 E
Les Herbiers	48	46.52N	1.01W
Lesina, Lago di ⊂	52	41.53N	15.26 E
Lesjaskog	44	62.15N	8.22 E
Lesjöfors	44	59.59N	14.11 E
Lesko	46	49.29N	22.21 E
Leskovac	54	42.59N	21.57 E
Leskov Island I	24	56.40S	28.10W
Leslie, S. Afr.	86	26.27S	28.55 E
Leslie, Scot., U.K.	38	56.12N	3.13W
Leslie, Mi., U.S.	102	42.27N	84.25W
Leslie, W.V., U.S.	102	38.02N	80.43W
Lesmahagow	38	55.39N	3.53W
Leśna	46	51.02N	15.16 E
Lesneven	32	48.34N	4.19W
Lešnica	54	44.39N	19.19 E
Lesný ⋀	46	50.02N	12.37 E
Lesotho □¹	84	29.30S	28.30 E
Lesozavodsk	58	45.28N	133.27 E
Lesozavodskij	42	66.44N	32.49 E
Lesparre-Médoc	48	45.18N	0.56W
Les Pieux	48	49.31N	1.48W
Les Riceys	48	47.59N	4.22 E
Les Sables-d'Olonne	48	46.30N	1.47W
Lessay	48	49.13N	1.32W
Lessebo	44	56.45N	15.16 E
Lesser Antilles II	108	15.00N	61.00W
Lesser Khingan Range →Xiao Hinggan Ling ⋀	62	48.45N	127.00 E
Lesser Slave Lake ⊚	98	55.25N	115.30W
Lesser Sunda Islands →Nusa Tenggara II	68	9.00S	120.00 E
Lestijärvi ⊚	44	63.32N	24.39 E
Lestijoki ⋍	44	64.04N	23.38 E
Les Vans	48	44.24N	4.08 E
Lésvos I	54	39.10N	26.20 E
Leszno	46	51.51N	16.35 E
Letchworth	34	51.58N	0.14W
Letea, Ostrovul I	54	45.20N	29.20 E
Letenye	46	46.26N	16.43 E
Lethbridge	98	49.42N	112.50W
Lethem	110	3.23N	59.48W
Le Thillot	48	47.53N	6.46 E
Leti, Kepulauan II	92	8.13S	127.50 E
Leticia	110	4.09S	69.57W
Letjiesbos	86	32.34S	22.16 E
Letpadan	70	17.47N	95.45 E
Le Trayas	48	43.28N	6.55 E
Le Tréport	48	50.04N	1.22 E
Letsök-aw Kyun I	70	11.37N	98.15 E
Lettermullan	40	53.13N	9.43W
Letterkenny	40	54.57N	7.44W
Letterston	34	51.56N	5.00W
Leu	54	44.11N	24.00 E
Leucadia	104	33.04N	117.18W
Leucate, Étang de ⊂	48	42.51N	3.00 E
Leuchars	38	56.23N	2.53W
Leuk	48	46.19N	7.38 E
Leuna	46	51.19N	12.01 E
Leuser, Gunung ⋀	70	3.45N	97.11 E
Leutkirch	46	47.49N	10.01 E
Leuven	46	50.53N	4.42 E
Levádhia	54	38.26N	22.53 E
Levanger	44	63.45N	11.18 E
Levante, Riviera di ⋋²	52	44.10N	9.30 E
Levanto	52	44.10N	9.38 E
Levanzo, Isola di I	52	38.00N	12.20 E
Leven, Eng., U.K.	36	53.53N	0.19W
Leven, Scot., U.K.	38	56.12N	3.00W
Leven ⋍, Eng., U.K.	36	54.14N	3.01W
Leven, Loch ⊚, Scot., U.K.	38	56.41N	5.07W
Leven, Loch ⊚, Scot., U.K.	38	56.12N	3.22W
Leverano	52	40.17N	18.00 E
Leverburgh	38a	57.46N	7.00W
Leverkusen	46	51.03N	6.59 E
Levice	46	48.13N	18.37 E
Levier	48	46.57N	6.08 E
Le Vigan	48	43.59N	3.36 E
Levin	96	40.37S	175.17 E
Lévis	102	46.48N	71.11W
Levisa Fork ⋍	102	38.06N	82.36W
Levittown, N.Y., U.S.	102	40.44N	73.30W
Levittown, Pa., U.S.	102	40.09N	74.49W
Lévka Óri ⋀	54	35.18N	24.01 E
Levkás	54	38.50N	20.41 E
Levkás I	54	38.39N	20.27 E
Levkímmi	54	39.25N	20.04 E
Levkôsia (Nicosia)	78	35.10N	33.22 E
Levoča	46	49.02N	20.36 E
Levroux	48	46.59N	1.37 E
Levski	54	43.22N	25.08 E
Lewes, Eng., U.K.	34	50.52N	0.01 E
Lewes, De., U.S.	102	38.46N	75.08W
Lewin Brzeski	46	50.46N	17.37 E
Lewis, Butt of ⋋	38	58.31N	6.16W
Lewis, Isle of I	38	58.10N	6.40W
Lewis, Mount ⋀	104	40.24N	116.51W
Lewisburg, Pa., U.S.	102	40.57N	76.53W
Lewisburg, W.V., U.S.	102	37.48N	80.26W
Lewisham ✦⁸	34	51.27N	0.01 E
Lewis Pass ⨯	96	42.23S	172.24 E
Lewis Range ⋀	90	20.20S	128.40 E
Lewis Run	102	41.52N	78.39W
Lewiston, Ca., U.S.	104	40.43N	122.48W
Lewiston, Id., U.S.	100	46.25N	117.01W
Lewiston, Me., U.S.	102	44.06N	70.12W
Lewiston, N.Y., U.S.	102	43.10N	79.02W
Lewistown, Mt., U.S.	100	47.03N	109.25W
Lewistown, Pa., U.S.	102	40.35N	77.34W
Lexington, Ky., U.S.	102	38.02N	84.30W
Lexington, Ma., U.S.	102	42.26N	71.13W
Lexington, Mi., U.S.	102	43.16N	82.31W
Lexington Park	102	38.16N	76.27W
Leyburn	36	54.19N	1.49W
Leyden →Leiden	46	52.09N	4.30 E
Leyland	36	53.42N	2.42W
Leyre ⋍	48	44.39N	1.01W
Leysdown-on-Sea	34	51.24N	0.55 E
Leyte I	68	10.50N	124.50 E
Leyte Gulf ⊂	68	10.50N	125.25 E
Lezajsk	46	50.16N	22.24 E
Lezama	108	9.43N	66.24W
Lezhë	54	41.47N	19.39 E
L'gov	56	51.43N	35.17 E
Lhanbryde	38	57.37N	3.13W
Lhasa	76	29.40N	91.09 E
Lhoknga	70	5.29N	95.15 E
Lhokseumawe	70	5.10N	97.08 E
Lhoksukon	70	5.03N	97.19 E
Lhorong	62	30.45N	96.09 E
Li	62	29.24N	112.01 E
Liancheng	66	25.44N	116.46 E
Liangyuan	66	32.00N	117.34 E
Lianhua	66	27.07N	113.57 E
Lianjiang, Zhg.	66	26.12N	119.31 E
Lianjiang, Zhg.	70	21.38N	110.15 E
Lianping	66	24.22N	114.31 E
Lianshui	66	33.47N	119.16 E
Lianxian	62	24.48N	112.25 E
Lianyungang	62	34.39N	119.16 E
Liao ⋍	62	40.50N	121.48 E
Liaocheng	62	36.30N	115.59 E
Liaodong Bandao ⋋¹	62	40.00N	122.20 E
Liaodong Wan ⊂	62	40.00N	121.30 E
Liaoning □⁴	62	41.00N	123.00 E
Liaotong, Gulf of →Liaodong Wan ⊂	62	40.30N	121.30 E
Liaotung Peninsula →Liaodong Bandao ⋋¹	62	40.00N	122.20 E
Liaoyang	62	41.17N	123.11 E
Liaoyuan	62	42.54N	125.07 E
Liapádhes	54	39.40N	19.44 E
Liard ⋍	98	61.52N	121.18W
Liathach ⋀	38	57.35N	5.29W
Libagon	68	8.19N	125.00 E
Libenge	84	3.39N	18.38 E
Liberal	100	37.02N	100.55W
Liberec	46	50.46N	15.03 E
Liberia	108	10.38N	85.27W
Liberia □¹	80	6.30N	9.30W
Libertad, Ur.	114	34.38S	56.39W
Libertad, Ven.	108	9.23N	68.44W
Libertador General Bernardo O'Higgins □⁴	114	34.30S	71.00W
Libertador General San Martín	114	23.48S	64.48W
Liberty, In., U.S.	102	39.38N	84.55W
Liberty, N.Y., U.S.	102	41.48N	74.44W
Liberty Center	102	41.26N	84.00W
Lībiyah, Aş-Sahrā' al- (Libyan Desert) ⋍²	82	24.00N	25.00 E
Libo	86	25.26N	107.53 E
Libode	86	31.33S	29.02 E
Libourne	48	44.55N	0.14W
Libramont	46	49.55N	5.23 E
Librazhd	54	41.11N	20.19 E
Libreville	84	0.23N	9.27 E
Libya (Lībiyā) □¹	82	27.00N	17.00 E
Libyan Desert →Lībiyah, Aş-Sahrā' al- ⋍²	82	24.00N	25.00 E
Licantén	114	34.59S	72.00W
Licata	52	37.06N	13.56 E
Lich	46	50.31N	8.50 E
Lichfield	34	52.42N	1.48W
Lichinga	84	13.18S	35.14 E
Lichtenburg	86	26.23S	27.17 E
Lichtenvoorde	46	51.59N	6.34 E
Lichuan	66	30.18N	108.51 E
Lickershamn	44	57.50N	18.31 E
Licking ⋍	102	39.06N	84.30W
Licosa, Punta ⋋	52	40.15N	14.54 E
Lida	60	53.53N	25.18 E
Lidar ⋍	76	33.58N	75.10 E
Liddel Water ⋍	36	55.04N	2.57W
Liddon Gulf ⊂	98	75.03N	113.00W
Liden	44	62.42N	16.48 E
Lidingö	44	59.22N	18.08 E
Lidköping	44	58.30N	13.10 E
Lido di Ostia	52	41.44N	12.14 E
Lidzbark	46	53.16N	19.49 E
Lidzbark Warmiński	46	54.09N	20.35 E
Liechtenstein □¹	30	47.09N	9.35 E
Liège	46	50.38N	5.34 E
Liegnitz →Legnica	46	51.13N	16.09 E
Lieksa	44	63.19N	30.01 E
Lienz	46	46.50N	12.47 E
Liepāja	60	56.31N	21.01 E
Lier	46	51.08N	4.34 E
Liestal	48	47.29N	7.44 E
Lieşti	54	45.38N	27.32 E
Lièvre, Rivière du ⋍	98	45.31N	75.26W
Liffey ⋍	40	53.21N	6.14W
Lifford	40	54.50N	7.29W
Liffré	48	48.13N	1.30W
Lifjell ⋀	44	59.30N	8.52 E
Lifou I	28	20.53S	167.13 E
Lifton	34	50.39N	4.17W
Lighthouse Point ⋋	104	25.31N	80.05W
Lighthouse Reef ⋫²	108	17.25N	87.32W
Ligny-en-Barrois	48	48.41N	5.20 E
Ligonha ⋍	84	16.54S	39.09 E
Ligonier	102	40.15N	79.14W
Liguel	114	21.40S	49.45W
Liguria □⁴	52	44.30N	8.50 E
Ligurian Sea ⊤²	52	43.30N	9.00 E
Lihir Group I	92	3.05S	152.40 E
Lihou Reef and Cays ⋫²	92	17.25S	151.40 E
Lihue	105a	21.58N	159.22W
Liji	66	33.48N	117.36 E
Lijiang	66	26.57N	100.15 E
Likasi (Jadotville)	84	10.59S	26.44 E
Likino-Dulevo	60	55.43N	38.58 E
Liknes	44	58.19N	6.59 E
Likoma Island I	84	12.05S	34.45 E
Likouala ⋍	84	1.13S	16.48 E
L'Île-Bouchard	48	47.07N	0.25 E
L'Île-Rousse	48	42.38N	8.56 E
Lili	66	31.00N	120.42 E
Lilienfeld	46	48.03N	15.36 E
Liling	66	27.40N	113.30 E
Lilla Edet	44	58.08N	12.08 E
Lilby	44	63.28N	23.00 E
Lille	48	50.38N	3.04 E
Lillebonne	48	49.31N	0.33 E
Lillehammer	44	61.08N	10.30 E
Lillers	48	50.34N	2.29 E
Lillesand	44	58.15N	8.24 E
Lilleshall	34	52.44N	2.21W
Lillestrøm	44	59.57N	11.05 E
Lillhärdal	44	61.51N	14.04 E
Lillo	50	39.43N	3.18W
Lillooet	98	50.42N	121.56W
Liloy	68	13.59S	33.44 E
Lilydale	94	41.15S	147.13 E
Lim ⋍	54	43.45N	19.13 E
Lima, Pará.	114	23.45S	50.05W
Lima, Perú	110	12.03S	77.03W
Lima, Sve.	44	60.56N	13.26 E
Lima, N.Y., U.S.	102	42.54N	77.36W
Lima, Oh., U.S.	102	40.44N	84.06W
Lima (Limia) ⋍	50	41.41N	8.50W
Limache	114	33.01S	71.16W
Limanowa	46	49.43N	20.26 E
Limarí ⋍	114	30.44S	71.43W
Limassol →Lemesós	78	34.40N	33.02 E
Limavady	40	55.03N	6.57W
Limay ⋍	114	38.59S	68.00W
Limay Mahuida	114	37.12S	66.42W
Limbang ⋍	72	4.45N	115.00 E
Limbara, Monte ⋀	52	40.51N	9.10 E
Limbdi	76	22.34N	71.48 E
Limbunya	92	17.14S	129.50 E
Limburg an der Lahn	46	50.23N	8.04 E
Limeira	114	22.34S	47.24W
Limerick (Luimneach)	40	52.40N	9.00W
Limerick (Luimneach) □⁶	40	52.30N	8.38W
Limestone	90	21.11S	119.50 E
Limfjorden ⋃	44	56.55N	9.10 E
Limia (Lima) ⋍	50	41.41N	8.50W
Liminka	44	64.49N	25.24 E
Liminzhen	66	34.31N	115.56 E
Limmared	44	57.32N	13.21 E
Limmen Bight ⊂³	92	14.45S	135.40 E
Limmen Bight ⋍	92	15.07S	135.44 E
Límnos I	54	39.54N	25.21 E
Limoeiro	110	7.52S	35.27W
Limoges	48	45.50N	1.16 E
Limogne	48	44.24N	1.46 E
Limón, C.R.	108	10.00N	83.02W
Limón, Hond.	108	15.52N	85.33W
Limone Piemonte	52	44.12N	7.34 E
Limours	32	48.39N	2.05 E
Limousins, Plateau du ⋋¹	48	45.30N	1.15 E
Limoux	48	43.04N	2.14 E
Limpopo ⋍	86	25.15S	33.30 E
Limpsfield	34	51.16N	0.01 E
Lin'an	66	30.14N	119.43 E
Linapacan Island I	68	11.27N	119.49 E
Linares, Chile	114	35.51S	71.36W
Linares, Esp.	50	38.05N	3.38W
Linares, Méx.	106	24.52N	99.34W
Linariá	54	37.24N	24.57 E
Lincang	70	23.45N	100.20 E
Lincoln, Arg.	114	34.52S	61.32W
Lincoln, N.Z.	96	43.39S	172.29 E
Lincoln, Eng., U.K.	36	53.14N	0.33W
Lincoln, Il., U.S.	100	40.08N	89.21W
Lincoln, Me., U.S.	102	45.22N	68.30W
Lincoln, Mi., U.S.	102	44.41N	83.24W
Lincoln, Ne., U.S.	100	40.48N	96.40W
Lincoln, N.H., U.S.	102	44.02N	71.40W
Lincoln Gap	94	32.37S	137.35 E
Lincoln Park	102	42.15N	83.10W
Lincoln Sea ⊤²	22	83.00N	56.00W
Lincolnshire □⁶	36	53.00N	0.10W
Lincoln Village	104	38.00N	121.19W
L'Incudine ⋀	52	41.51N	9.12 E
Linda	104	39.07N	121.32W
Lindau	46	47.33N	9.41 E
Linde ⋍	58	64.57N	124.36 E
Linden	102	42.49N	83.46W
Lindesay, Mount ⋀	90	34.49S	117.18 E
Lindesberg	44	59.35N	15.15 E
Lindesnes ⋋	44	58.00N	7.02 E
Lindfield	94	33.59S	148.00 E
Lindi	84	10.00S	39.43 E
Lindi ⋍	84	0.33N	25.05 E
Lindis Pass ⨯	96	44.35S	169.40 E
Lindley	86	27.51S	27.58 E
Lindome	44	57.34N	12.05 E
Lindsay, On., Can.	102	44.21N	78.44W
Lindsay, Ca., U.S.	104	36.12N	119.05W
Line Islands II	28	0.05N	157.00W
Lineville	102	36.09N	80.26W
Linfen	62	36.05N	111.32 E
Linganamakki Reservoir ⊚	74	14.11N	74.50 E
Lingao	70	19.54N	109.40 E
Lingayen	68	16.01N	120.14 E
Lingayen Gulf ⊂	68	16.15N	120.14 E
Lingbi	66	33.33N	117.33 E
Lingbo	44	61.03N	16.41 E
Lingdale	36	54.32N	0.55W
Lingen	46	52.31N	7.19 E
Lingfield	34	51.11N	0.01W
Lingga, Kepulauan II	72	0.05S	104.35 E
Lingga, Pulau I	72	0.10S	104.35 E
Lingling	66	26.13N	111.37 E
Lingshan	70	22.25N	109.17 E
Lingshi	62	36.50N	111.46 E
Lingshui	66	18.31N	110.01 E
Linguère	80	15.24N	15.07W
Lingwood	34	52.37N	1.29 E
Lingxian	62	37.20N	116.34 E
Linh, Ngoc ⋀	70	15.04N	107.59 E
Linhai	66	28.51N	121.08 E
Linhe	62	40.51N	107.30 E
Linhuaiguan	66	32.56N	117.37 E
Linjiang	62	41.51N	126.55 E
Linköping	44	58.25N	15.37 E
Linkou	62	45.18N	130.17 E
Linkuva	60	56.05N	23.57 E
Linlithgow	38	55.59N	3.37W
Linney Head ⋋	34	51.38N	5.04W
Linnhe, Loch ⊂	38	56.39N	5.21W
Linnich	46	50.59N	6.16 E
Linosa, Isola di I	52	35.51N	12.52 E
Linpu	66	30.03N	120.15 E
Linquan	66	33.06N	115.13 E
Lins	114	21.40S	49.45W
Linslade	34	51.55N	0.41W
Lintao	62	35.27N	103.46 E
Linthal	48	46.55N	9.00 E
Linton, Eng., U.K.	34	52.06N	0.17 E
Linton, N.D., U.S.	100	46.16N	100.13W
Linxi	62	43.30N	118.00 E
Linxia	62	35.31N	103.00 E
Linxiang	66	29.28N	113.30 E
Linyanti ⋍	86	17.58S	24.16 E
Linyi	62	35.04N	118.22 E
Linying	66	33.50N	113.57 E
Linz	46	48.18N	14.18 E
Lio Matoh	72	3.10N	115.14 E
Lion, Golfe du ⊂	48	43.00N	4.00 E
Liozno	60	55.02N	30.48 E
Lipa	68	13.57N	121.10 E
Lipany	46	49.09N	20.58 E
Lipari	52	38.28N	14.57 E
Lipari, Isola I	52	38.29N	14.56 E
Lipcani	60	52.37N	39.35 E
Lipeck	44	62.32N	29.22 E
Lipeck →Lipeck	60	52.37N	39.35 E
Lipez, Cerro ⋀	110	21.53S	66.52W
Liphook	34	51.05N	0.49W
Liping	70	26.17N	109.08 E
Lipki	60	53.58N	37.42 E
Lipnik nad Bečvou	46	49.31N	17.35 E
Lipno	46	52.51N	19.10 E
Lipova	54	46.05N	21.40 E
Lipová, údolní nádrž ⊚¹	46	48.43N	14.04 E
Lippe ⋍	46	51.39N	6.38 E
Lippstadt	46	51.40N	8.19 E
Lipsko	46	51.09N	21.39 E
Lipsoí I	54	37.20N	26.45 E
Liptovská Teplička	46	48.59N	20.06 E
Liptovský Mikuláš	46	49.06N	19.37 E
Liptrap, Cape ⋋	94	38.54S	145.55 E
Lipu	70	24.25N	110.29 E
Lira	84	2.15N	32.54 E
Liri ⋍	52	39.38N	0.36W
Lisakovsk	84	2.09N	21.31 E
Lisala	84	2.09N	21.31 E
Lisboa (Lisbon)	50	38.43N	9.08W
Lisbon →Lisboa, Port.	50	38.43N	9.08W
Lisbon, N.H., U.S.	102	44.12N	71.54W
Lisbon, Oh., U.S.	102	40.46N	80.46W
Lisbon Falls	102	43.59N	70.03W
Lisburn	40	54.31N	6.03W
Liscannor Bay ⊂	40	52.55N	9.25W
Liscarney	40	53.43N	9.35W
Liscia ⋍	52	41.11N	9.19 E
Lisdoonvarna	40	53.01N	9.15W
Lishi	66	37.31N	111.06 E
Lishui, Zhg.	66	28.27N	119.54 E
Lishui, Zhg.	66	31.39N	119.01 E
Lisianski Island I	28	26.02N	174.00 E
Lisieux	48	49.09N	0.14 E
Liskeard	34	50.28N	4.28W
L'Isle-Jourdain, Fr.	48	46.14N	0.41 E
L'Isle-Jourdain, Fr.	48	43.37N	1.05 E
L'Isle-sur-le-Doubs	48	47.27N	6.35 E
Lismore, Austl.	94	28.48S	153.17 E
Lismore, Ire.	40	52.08N	7.55W
Lismore Island I	38	56.30N	5.33W
Lisnaskea	40	54.15N	7.27W
Lišov	46	49.01N	14.37 E
Liss	34	51.03N	0.55W
Lista ⋋¹	44	58.07N	6.40 E
Lištica	52	43.23N	17.36 E
Listowel, On., Can.	102	43.44N	80.57W
Listowel, Ire.	40	52.27N	9.29W
Lit	44	63.19N	14.49 E
Litang, Malay.	72	5.20N	118.31 E
Litang, Zhg.	100	30.00N	100.16 E
Litang, Zhg.	62	23.11N	109.05 E
Litang ⋍	62	28.04N	101.30 E
Litcham	34	52.44N	0.47 E
Litchfield	102	42.02N	84.45W
Litherland	36	53.28N	2.59W
Lithgow	94	33.29S	150.09 E
Líthinon, Ákra ⋋	54	34.55N	24.44 E
Lithuania →Litovskaja Sovetskaja Socialističeskaja Respublika □³	60	56.00N	24.00 E
Litija	52	46.03N	14.50 E
Lititz	102	40.09N	76.18W
Litókhoron	54	40.06N	22.30 E
Litoměřice	46	50.33N	14.09 E
Litovel	46	49.42N	17.05 E
Litovko	58	49.15N	135.11 E
Litovskaja Sovetskaja Socialističeskaja Respublika □³	60	56.00N	24.00 E
Little Abaco Island I	108	26.53N	77.43W
Little Andaman I	70	10.45N	92.30 E
Little Avon ⋍	34	51.42N	2.28W
Little Barrier Island I	96	36.12S	175.05 E
Littleborough	36	53.39N	2.05W
Little Brosna ⋍	40	53.09N	8.03W
Little Buffalo ⋍	98	61.00N	113.46W
Little Cayman I	108	19.41N	80.03W
Little Cumbrae Island I	38	55.43N	4.57W
Little Current	102	45.58N	81.56W
Little Current ⋍	102	50.57N	84.36W
Little Dart ⋍	34	50.54N	3.51W
Little Deschutes ⋍	104	43.51N	121.27W
Little Desert ⋍²	94	36.35S	141.20 E
Little Falls	102	43.02N	74.51W
Little Gold ⋍	98	64.00N	140.20W
Little Humboldt ⋍	104	41.00N	117.43W
Little Inagua I	108	21.30N	73.00W
Little Juniata ⋍	102	40.34N	78.03W
Little Kanawha ⋍	102	39.16N	81.34W
Little Karroo ⋋¹	86	33.45S	21.30 E
Little Mecatina ⋍	98	50.28N	59.35W
Little Minch ⋃	38	57.35N	6.55W
Little Missouri ⋍	100	47.30N	102.25W
Little Namaqualand □⁹	86	29.00S	17.00 E
Little Nicobar I	70	7.20N	93.40 E
Little Ouse ⋍	34	52.30N	0.22 E
Little Paxton	34	52.14N	0.15W
Little Rann of Kutch ⋍	76	23.25N	71.15 E
Little River	96	43.46S	172.47 E
Little Rock	100	34.44N	92.17W
Little Sandy ⋍	102	38.35N	82.51W
Little Scarcies ⋍	80	8.51N	13.09W
Little Smoky ⋍	98	55.42N	117.38W
Little Stukeley	34	52.20N	0.10W
Little Traverse Bay ⊂	102	45.24N	85.03W
Little Walsingham	34	52.53N	0.51 E
Little Wood ⋍	104	42.57N	114.21W
Livada	54	47.52N	23.07 E
Livanátai	54	38.42N	23.03 E
Livarot	48	49.01N	0.09 E
Live Oak	104	39.16N	121.39W
Liveringa	90	18.03S	124.10 E
Livermore	104	37.40N	121.46W
Livermore Falls	102	44.28N	70.11W
Liverpool, N.S., Can.	98	44.02N	64.43W
Liverpool, Eng., U.K.	36	53.25N	2.55W
Liverpool, Pa., U.S.	102	40.34N	76.59W
Liverpool ⋍	92	12.02S	134.13 E
Liverpool, Cape ⋋	98	73.38N	78.06W
Liverpool Bay ⊂	36	53.30N	3.16W
Liverpool Range ⋀	94	31.40S	150.30 E
Livigno	52	46.32N	10.04 E
Livingston, Guat.	106	15.50N	88.45W
Livingston, Scot., U.K.	38	55.53N	3.32W
Livingston, Ca., U.S.	104	37.23N	120.43W
Livingston, Mt., U.S.	100	45.39N	110.33W
Livingstone	84	17.50S	25.53 E
Livingstone, Chutes de ⊾	84	4.50S	14.30 E
Livingstone Falls →Livingstone, Chutes de ⊾	84	4.50S	14.30 E
Livingstone Manor	102	41.54N	74.49W
Livingstonia	84	10.36S	34.07 E
Livny	60	52.25N	37.37 E
Livojoki ⋍	44	65.24N	26.48 E
Livonia, Mi., U.S.	102	42.22N	83.21W
Livonia, N.Y., U.S.	102	42.49N	77.40W
Livorno (Leghorn)	52	43.33N	10.19 E
Liwale	84	9.46S	37.56 E
Lixi	66	29.15N	114.46 E
Lixin	66	33.08N	116.08 E
Lixoúrion	54	38.12N	20.26 E
Liyang	66	31.26N	119.29 E
Liyujiang	66	25.57N	113.15 E
Lizard	34	49.58N	5.12W
Lizard Point ⋋	34	49.56N	5.13W
Lizhu	66	29.56N	120.30 E
Ljan	44	59.16N	10.48 E
Ljubija	52	44.56N	16.37 E
Ljubinje	54	42.57N	18.05 E
Ljubljana	52	46.03N	14.31 E
Ljubovija	54	44.11N	19.22 E
Ljugarn	44	57.19N	18.42 E
Ljungan ⋍	44	62.19N	17.23 E
Ljungaverk	44	62.29N	16.03 E
Ljungby	44	56.50N	13.56 E
Ljungbyhed	44	56.04N	13.12 E
Ljungbyholm	44	56.38N	16.10 E
Ljungdalen	44	62.51N	12.47 E
Ljungsbro	44	58.31N	15.30 E
Ljungskile	44	58.14N	11.55 E
Ljusnan ⋍	44	61.12N	17.08 E
Ljusne	44	61.13N	17.08 E
Ljusterö I	44	59.31N	18.37 E
Ljutomer	44	46.31N	16.12 E
Llaima, Volcán ⋀¹	114	38.43S	71.43W
Llanaber	34	52.45N	4.05W
Llanaelhaearn	34	52.59N	4.24W
Llanarth	34	52.12N	4.18W
Llanarthney	34	51.52N	4.09W
Llanbedrog	34	52.51N	4.29W
Llanberis	34	53.06N	4.07W
Llanberis, Pass of ⨯	34	53.06N	4.04W
Llanbister	34	52.21N	3.27W
Llanboidy	34	51.54N	4.36W
Llanbrynmair	34	52.37N	3.57W
Llancanelo, Laguna ⊚	114	35.35S	69.09W
Llandaff	34	51.30N	3.14W
Llanddewi Brefi	34	52.10N	3.57W
Llandinam	34	52.27N	3.26W
Llandissilio	34	51.52N	3.59W
Llandovery	34	51.59N	3.48W
Llandrindod Wells	34	52.15N	3.23W
Llandudno	34	53.19N	3.49W
Llandybie	34	51.49N	3.58W
Llandysul	34	52.02N	4.19W
Llanelli	34	51.42N	4.10W
Llanenddwyn	34	52.45N	4.06W
Llanerchymedd	34	53.20N	4.22W
Llanes	50	43.25N	4.45W
Llanfaethlu	34	53.21N	4.32W
Llanfair-Caereinion	34	52.39N	3.20W
Llanfair-pwllgwyngyll	34	53.13N	4.12W
Llanfrynach	34	51.56N	3.18W
Llanfyllin	34	52.46N	3.16W
Llanfynydd	34	51.57N	4.09W
Llangadog	34	51.56N	3.53W
Llangefni	34	53.16N	4.19W
Llangelynin	34	52.37N	4.06W
Llangollen	34	52.58N	3.10W
Llangranog	34	52.10N	4.28W
Llangurig	34	52.25N	3.36W
Llangwyryfon	34	52.19N	4.02W
Llangynog	34	52.50N	3.24W
Llanharan	34	51.33N	3.26W
Llanidloes	34	52.27N	3.32W
Llanilar	34	52.21N	4.01W
Llanllyfni	34	53.03N	4.17W
Llano Colorado	104	32.38N	115.55W
Llanon	34	52.17N	4.10W
Llanos ⋍	110	5.00N	70.00W
Llanquihue, Lago ⊚	114	41.08S	72.47W
Llanrhaeadr-ym-Mochnant	34	52.51N	3.11W
Llanrhidian	34	51.37N	4.11W
Llanrhystud	34	52.19N	4.09W
Llanrwst	34	53.08N	3.48W
Llansantffraid-ym-Mechain	34	52.47N	3.09W
Llansawel	34	52.01N	4.00W
Llantrisant	114	26.20S	69.49W
Llantwit Major	34	51.25N	3.30W
Llanuwchllyn	34	52.52N	3.40W
Llanwenog	34	52.06N	4.12W
Llanwnen	34	52.08N	4.09W
Llanwrda	34	51.58N	3.50W
Llanwrtyd Wells	34	52.07N	3.38W
Llay	34	53.06N	2.59W
Lleyn Peninsula ⋋¹	34	52.54N	4.30W
Llobregat ⋍	50	41.19N	2.09 E
Lloydminster	98	53.17N	110.00W
Lluchmayor	50	39.29N	2.54 E
Llullaillaco, Volcán ⋀¹	114	24.43S	68.33W
Lobitos	110	4.26S	81.17W
Lobn'a	60	56.01N	37.30 E
Lobos	114	35.11S	59.06W
Lobos, Cay I	108	22.24N	77.32W
Lobos de Afuera, Islas II	110	6.57S	80.42W
Lobos de Tierra, Isla I	110	6.27S	80.52W
Lobzenica	46	53.16N	17.15 E
Locarno	48	46.10N	8.48 E
Lochaber ✦¹	38	56.57N	5.00W
Lochailort	38	56.53N	5.40W
Lochaline	38	56.32N	5.47W
Locharbriggs	36	55.06N	3.34W
Lochboisdale	38	57.09N	7.19W
Lochcarron	38	57.24N	5.30W
Lochdonhead	38	56.26N	5.41W
Lochearnhead	38	56.23N	4.17W
Loches	48	47.08N	1.00 E
Lochgair	38	56.03N	5.20W
Loch Garman →Wexford	40	52.20N	6.27W
Lochgelly	38	56.08N	3.19W
Lochgilphead	38	56.03N	5.26W
Lochindorb ⊚	38	57.24N	3.43W
Lochinver	38	58.09N	5.15W
Lochmaben	38	55.08N	3.27W
Lochmaddy	38	57.36N	7.11W
Lochnagar ⋀	38	56.57N	3.16W
Lochranza	38	55.42N	5.18W
Loch Sport	94	38.03S	147.36 E
Lochwinnoch	38	55.48N	4.39W
Lochy, Loch ⊚	38	56.57N	4.53W
Lock	94	33.34S	135.46 E
Lockerbie	36	55.07N	3.22W
Lockhart	94	35.14S	146.43 E
Lock Haven	102	41.08N	77.26W
Löcknitz	46	53.27N	14.12 E
Lockport	102	43.10N	78.41W
Locks Heath	34	50.52N	1.15W
Loc-ninh	70	11.51N	106.36 E
Locri	52	38.14N	16.16 E
Lod	78	31.58N	34.54 E
Loddon	34	52.32N	1.29 E
Loddon ⋍, Austl.	94	35.32S	143.52 E
Loddon ⋍, Eng., U.K.	34	51.30N	0.53W
Lodejnoje Pole	60	60.44N	33.30 E
Lodève	48	43.43N	3.19 E
Lodi, It.	52	45.19N	9.30 E
Lodi, Ca., U.S.	104	38.08N	121.16W
Lodi, Oh., U.S.	102	41.02N	82.00W
Lodja	84	3.29S	23.26 E
Lodosa	50	42.25N	2.05W
Lodwar	82	3.07N	35.36 E
Łódź	46	51.46N	19.30 E
Loei	70	17.29N	101.35 E
Loen	44	61.52N	6.52 E
Loeriesfontein	86	30.56S	19.26 E
Lofa ⋍	80	6.36N	11.08W
Lofer	46	47.35N	12.41 E
Lofoten II	42	68.30N	15.00 E
Lofoten Basin ⇥¹	20	70.00N	4.00 E
Lofthouse	36	54.11N	1.29W
Loftus	36	54.33N	0.53W
Logan, Oh., U.S.	102	39.32N	82.24W
Logan, Ut., U.S.	102	41.44N	111.50W
Logan, W.V., U.S.	102	37.50N	81.59W
Logan, Mount ⋀	98	60.34N	140.24W
Logandale	104	36.35N	114.29W
Logansport	100	40.45N	86.21W
Lögdeälven ⋍	44	63.39N	19.25 E
Logone ⋍	82	12.06N	15.02 E
Logroño	50	42.28N	2.27W
Logrosán	50	39.20N	5.29W
Løgstør	44	56.58N	9.15 E
Logudoro ⋋¹	52	40.38N	8.40 E
Løgumkloster	44	55.03N	8.57 E
Lohärdaga	76	23.26N	84.41 E
Lohilahti	44	61.53N	28.27 E
Lohja	44	60.15N	24.05 E
Lohjanjärvi ⊚	44	60.15N	24.05 E
Lohne	46	52.42N	8.12 E
Lohr	46	50.00N	9.34 E
Loi-kaw	70	21.19N	100.44 E
Loimaa	44	60.51N	23.03 E
Loir ⋍	48	47.33N	0.32W
Loire □⁵	48	45.30N	4.00 E
Loire ⋍	48	47.16N	2.11W
Loire-Atlantique □⁵	48	47.20N	1.35W
Loiret □⁵	48	47.55N	2.20 E
Loir-et-Cher □⁵	48	47.30N	1.30 E
Loitz	46	53.58N	13.07 E
Loja, Ec.	110	4.00S	79.13W
Loja, Esp.	50	37.10N	4.09W
Lokandu	84	2.31S	25.47 E
Løken	44	59.48N	11.29 E
Løken tekojärvi ⊚¹	42	68.40N	27.40 E
Lokeren	46	51.06N	3.59 E
Loket	46	50.11N	12.45 E
Lokka	42	67.49N	27.44 E
Løkken verk	44	63.08N	9.43 E
Lol ⋍	82	9.13N	28.59 E
Lola, Mount ⋀	104	39.26N	120.22W
Loleta	104	40.38N	124.13W
Lolland I	44	54.46N	11.30 E
Lolworth Range ⋀	94	20.20S	145.15 E
Lom, Blg.	54	43.49N	23.14 E
Lom, Nor.	44	61.50N	8.33 E
Lomami ⋍	84	0.46N	24.16 E
Lomas de Zamora	114	34.46S	58.24W
Lombardia □⁴	52	45.40N	9.30 E
Lomblen, Pulau I	72	8.30S	123.30 E
Lombok I	72	8.45S	116.30 E
Lomé	80	6.08N	1.13 E
Lomela	84	2.19S	23.17 E
Lomela ⋍	84	0.14S	20.42 E
Lomié	80	3.10N	13.37 E
Lo Miranda	114	34.11S	70.59W
Lomond, Loch ⊚	38	56.08N	4.38W
Lomonosov	60	59.55N	29.46 E
Lompoc	104	34.38N	120.27W
Lom Sak	70	16.47N	101.15 E
Łomazy	46	51.55N	23.11 E
Łomża	46	53.11N	22.05 E
Lonāvale	74	18.45N	73.25 E
Loncoche	114	39.22S	72.38W
Loncopué	114	38.04S	70.37W
Londinières	32	49.50N	1.24 E
London, On., Can.	102	42.59N	81.14W
London, Eng., U.K.	34	51.30N	0.10W
London, Oh., U.S.	102	39.53N	83.26W
Londonderry (Derry)	40	55.00N	7.19W
Londonderry, Cape ⋋	92	13.45S	126.55 E

Name Page Lat. °′ Long. °′

Londonderry, Isla I 112 55.03S 70.35W
Londres 114 27.43S 67.07W
Londrina 114 23.18S 51.09W
Lone Mountain ▲ 104 38.02N 117.29W
Lone Pine 104 36.36N 118.03W
Long, Loch C 36 56.04N 4.50W
Longa ≃ 84 10.15S 13.30E
Longa, proliv ⊻ 58 70.20N 178.00E
Long Akah 72 3.19N 114.47E
Longarone 52 46.16N 12.18E
Longavi 114 35.58S 71.41W
Long Beach, Ca., U.S. 104 33.46N 118.11W
Long Beach, N.Y., U.S. 102 40.35N 73.39W
Long Belepai 72 2.45N 114.04E
Longbenton 36 55.02N 1.35W
Long Branch 102 40.18N 73.59W
Long Buckby 34 52.19N 1.04W
Longchang 62 29.21N 105.17E
Longchuan 66 24.07N 115.17E
Longchuanjiang (Shweli) ≃ 70 23.56N 96.17E
Long Crendon 34 51.47N 1.01W
Long Eaton 34 52.54N 1.15W
Longeau 48 47.46N 5.18E
Longford, Austl. 94 38.10S 147.05E
Longford, Ire. 40 53.44N 7.47W
Longford □6 40 53.40N 7.40W
Longframlington 36 55.18N 1.47W
Longhorsley 36 55.15N 1.46W
Longhoughton 36 55.26N 1.36W
Longiram 72 0.02S 115.38E
Long Island I, Austl. 94 22.09S 149.54E
Long Island I, Ba. 108 23.15N 75.07W
Long Island I, N.T., Can. 98 54.50N 79.20W
Long Island I, N.Y., U.S. 102 40.50N 73.00W
Long Island Sound ⊻ 102 41.05N 72.58W
Longitudinal, Valle ∨ 114 36.00S 72.00W
Longjiang 62 47.19N 123.12E
Longkou 62 37.38N 120.18E
Long Lake 102 43.58N 74.25W
Long Lake ⊜, Mi., U.S. 102 45.12N 83.30W
Long Lake ⊜, N.Y., U.S. 102 44.04N 74.20W
Long Lama 72 3.46N 114.24E
Longli 70 26.26N 106.58E
Longling 70 24.39N 98.40E
Longmeadow 102 42.03N 72.35W
Long Melford 34 52.05N 0.43E
Longmen 66 23.44N 114.15E
Longmont 100 40.10N 105.06W
Longmorn 38 57.36N 3.17W
Long Mountain ▲2 34 52.39N 3.09W
Longnan 66 24.54N 114.48E
Longnawan 72 1.54N 114.53E
Longniddry 38 55.58N 2.53W
Longny 48 48.32N 0.45E
Longping 66 29.53N 115.41E
Long Point ❯1 102 42.34N 80.15W
Long Point Bay C 102 42.40N 80.14W
Long Preston 36 54.02N 2.15W
Longquan 66 28.04N 119.07E
Long Range Mountains ⁂ 98 49.20N 57.30W
Longreach 94 23.26S 144.15E
Long Reef ✢2 92 11.11S 151.40E
Longridge 36 53.51N 2.36W
Long-Sault 102 45.02N 74.53W
Longsheng 70 25.48N 110.00E
Longs Peak ▲ 100 40.15N 105.37W
Long Stratton 34 52.29N 1.14E
Long Sutton 34 52.47N 0.08E
Longtan 66 32.11N 119.04E
Long Teru 72 3.52N 114.15E
Longtian 66 25.38N 119.28E
Longton 36 53.43N 2.47W
Longtown 36 55.01N 2.58W
Longué 48 47.23N 0.06W
Longueuil 102 45.32N 73.30W
Longuyon 48 49.26N 5.36E
Longview, Tx., U.S. 100 32.30N 94.44W
Longview, Wa., U.S. 100 46.08N 122.56W
Longwy 48 49.31N 5.46E
Longxi 62 34.56N 104.47E
Long-xuyen 70 10.23N 105.25E
Longyan 66 25.08N 117.02E
Longyou 66 29.02N 119.10E
Longzhou 70 22.22N 106.52E
Lonigo 52 45.23N 11.23E
Löningen 46 52.44N 7.46E
Lönsboda 44 56.24N 14.19E
Lønsdal 42 66.44N 15.28E
Lons-le-Saunier 48 46.40N 5.33E
Looking Glass ≃ 102 42.52N 84.54W
Lookout, Cape ❯ 100 34.35N 76.32W
Loongana 90 30.57S 127.02E
Loon op Zand 46 51.38N 5.04E
Loop Head ❯ 40 52.34N 9.56W
Lopatina, gora ▲ 58 50.52N 143.10E
Lopatka, mys ❯ 58 50.52N 156.40E
Lop Buri 70 14.48N 100.37E
Lopez, Cap ❯ 84 0.37S 8.43E
Lop Nor →Lop Nur ⊜ 62 40.20N 90.15E
Lop Nur (Lop Nor) ⊜ 62 40.20N 90.15E
Lopori ≃ 84 1.14N 19.49E
Loppi 44 60.43N 24.27E
Łopuszno 46 50.57N 20.15E
Lora ≃ 90 9.25N 72.25W
Lora, Hāmūn-i- ⊜ 78 29.20N 64.50E
Lora del Rio 50 37.39N 5.32W
Lorain 102 41.27N 82.10W
Lorca 50 37.40N 1.42W
Lord Howe Island I 88 31.33S 159.05E
Lord Howe Rise ✢3 28 32.00S 162.00E
Lord Howe Seamounts ✢3 28 28.00S 159.00E
Lord Mayor Bay C 98 69.44N 92.00W
Lordsburg 100 32.21N 108.42W
Lorengau 92 2.00S 147.15E
Lorenzo Geyres (Queguay) 114 32.05S 57.55W
Lorestān □8 78 33.30N 48.30E
Loreto, Arg. 114 27.46S 57.17W
Loreto, Bra. 110 7.05S 45.09W
Loreto, Méx. 106 26.01N 111.21W
Loreto, Para. 114 23.16S 57.11W
Lorica 110 9.14N 75.49W
Lorient 48 47.45N 3.22W
L'Orignal 102 45.37N 74.42W
Loriol 48 44.45N 4.49E
Lormes 48 47.17N 3.49E
Lorn, Firth of C1 38 56.20N 5.45W
Lorna Glen 90 26.14S 121.33E
Lorne 94 38.33S 143.59E
Lörrach 46 47.37N 7.40E
Lorraine □9 48 49.00N 6.00E
Lorris 48 47.53N 2.31E
Los 44 61.44N 15.10E
Los Alamos, Ca., U.S. 104 34.44N 120.16W
Los Alamos, N.M., U.S. 100 35.53N 106.19W
Los Andes 114 32.50S 70.37W
Los Ángeles, Chile 114 37.28S 72.21W
Los Angeles, Ca., U.S. 104 34.03N 118.14W
Los Angeles Aqueduct ⌶1 104 35.22N 118.05W
Losap I1 28 6.54N 152.44E
Los Banos 104 37.03N 120.50W
Los Berros 114 31.57S 68.39W
Los Blancos 114 23.36S 62.36W
Los Cerrillos 114 31.57S 65.28W
Los Conquistadores 114 30.36S 58.28W
Los Coronados, Islas II 104 32.25N 117.15W
Los Frentones 114 26.25S 61.25W
Los Gatos 104 37.13N 121.58W
Los Hermanos, Islas II 108 11.45N 64.25W
Łosice 46 52.14N 22.43E
Lošinj, Otok I 52 44.36N 14.24E
Losinoborskaja 58 58.27N 89.28E
Los Juríes 114 28.28S 62.06W
Loskopdam ⊜1 86 25.23S 29.20E
Los Lagos 112 39.51S 72.50W
Los Mochis 106 25.45N 108.57W
Los Molinos 104 40.01N 122.05W
Los Navalmorales 50 39.43N 4.38W
Los Palacios, Arg. 114 29.22S 68.11W
Los Palacios, Cuba 108 22.35N 83.15W
Los Palacios y Villafranca 50 37.10N 5.56W
Los Quirquinchos 114 33.22S 61.43W
Los Roques, Islas II 110 11.50N 66.45W
Los Santos de Maimona 50 38.27N 6.23W
Los Sauces 114 37.58S 72.50W
Losser 46 52.15N 7.00E
Lossie ≃ 38 57.43N 3.16W
Lossiemouth 38 57.43N 3.18W
Lost ≃, U.S. 104 41.56N 121.30W
Lost ≃, W.V., U.S. 102 39.05N 78.36W
Los Taques 108 11.50N 70.16W
Los Telares 114 28.59S 63.26W
Los Teques 108 10.21N 67.02W
Los Testigos, Islas II 108 11.22N 63.06W
Lost Hills 104 35.36N 119.41W
Lostwithiel 34 50.25N 4.40W
Losuia 92 8.32S 151.04E
Los Vilos 114 31.55S 71.31W
Los Yébenes 50 39.34N 3.53W
Lot □5 48 44.35N 1.40E
Lot ≃ 48 44.18N 0.20E
Lota 114 37.05S 73.10W
Løten 44 60.49N 11.19E
Lot-et-Garonne □5 48 44.20N 0.20E
Lothair 86 26.26S 30.27E
Lothian □4 38 55.55N 3.05W
Lotrului, Munţii ⁂ 54 45.30N 23.52E
Lotsane ≃ 86 22.41S 28.11E
Lotta ≃ 42 68.36N 31.06E
Lotung 66 24.41N 121.46E
Louang Namtha 70 20.57N 101.25E
Louangphrabang 70 19.52N 102.08E
Loudéac 48 48.10N 2.45W
Loudonville 102 40.38N 82.14W
Loudun 48 47.01N 0.05E
Loué 48 48.00N 0.09W
Louga 80 15.37N 16.13W
Louge 114 36.57S 61.40W
Louge ≃ 48 43.27N 1.20E
Loughborough 34 52.47N 1.11W
Loughor 34 51.40N 4.04W
Loughor ≃ 34 51.40N 4.04W
Loughrea 40 53.12N 8.34W
Loughros More Bay C 40 54.47N 8.35W
Louhans 48 46.38N 5.13E
Louisa, Ky., U.S. 102 38.06N 82.36W
Louisa, Va., U.S. 102 38.01N 78.00W
Louisburgh 40 53.46N 9.51W
Louiseville 102 46.15N 72.57W
Louisiade Archipelago II 88 11.00S 153.00E
Louisiana □3 100 31.15N 92.15W
Louis Trichardt 86 23.01S 29.43E
Louisville, Ky., U.S. 100 38.15N 85.45W
Louisville, Oh., U.S. 102 40.50N 81.15W
Louisville Ridge ✢3 28 31.00S 172.30W
Louisville Seamount ✢3 28 31.15S 172.15W
Louis-XIV, Pointe ❯ 98 54.37N 79.45W
Loulé 50 37.08N 8.02W
Louny 46 50.19N 13.46E
Lourdes 48 43.06N 0.03W
Lourenço Marques →Maputo 86 25.58S 32.35E
Loures 50 38.50N 9.10W
Lourinhã 50 39.14N 9.19W
Lourosa 50 40.19N 7.56W
Lousã 50 40.07N 8.15W
Louth, Austl. 94 30.32S 145.07E
Louth, Ire. 40 53.37N 6.53W
Louth, Eng., U.K. 36 53.22N 0.01W
Louth □6 40 53.55N 6.30W
Louth Bay C 94 34.34S 136.02E
Loutrá Aidhipsoú 54 38.51N 23.02E
Louvain →Leuven 46 50.53N 4.42E
Louviers 48 49.13N 1.10E
Louvigné-du-Désert 48 48.29N 1.08W
Louwsburg 86 27.37S 31.07E
Lövånger 44 64.22N 21.18E
Lovat' ≃ 60 58.14N 31.28E
Loveč 54 43.08N 24.43E
Loveland 100 40.23N 105.04W
Lovelock 104 40.10N 118.28W
Lovere 52 45.49N 10.04E
Lovisa (Loviisa) 44 60.27N 26.14E
Lovosice 46 50.31N 14.03E
Lövstabruk 44 60.24N 17.53E
Low 102 45.48N 75.57W
Low, Cape ❯ 98 63.07N 85.18W
Lowa ≃ 84 1.24S 25.51E
Lowell, Ma., U.S. 102 42.38N 71.19W
Lowell, Mi., U.S. 102 42.56N 85.20W
Lowell, Lake ⊜1 104 43.33N 116.40W
Löwenberg 46 52.54N 13.09E
Lower Hutt 96 41.13S 174.55E
Lower Klamath Lake ⊜ 104 41.55N 121.42W
Lower Lake ⊜ 104 41.15N 120.02W
Lower Post 98 59.55N 128.30W
Lower Red Lake ⊜ 100 48.00N 94.50W
Lowestoft 34 52.29N 1.45E
Lowgar □4 76 33.50N 69.00E
Lowick 36 55.38N 2.00W
Łowicz 46 52.07N 19.56E
Lowrah (Pishīn Lora) ≃ 76 29.09N 64.55E
Low Rocky Point ❯ 94 43.00S 145.30E
Lowther ≃ 36 54.39N 2.44W
Lowther Hills ⁂2 36 55.19N 3.39W
Lowville 102 43.47N 75.29W
Loxton, Austl. 94 34.27S 140.35E
Loxton, S. Afr. 86 31.30S 22.22E
Loyal, Loch ⊜ 38 58.23N 4.22W
Loyalsock Creek ≃ 102 41.14N 76.56W
Loyalton 104 39.40N 120.14W
Loyauté, Îles II 28 21.00S 167.00E
Loyne, Loch ⊜ 38 57.06N 5.00W
Lozère □5 48 44.30N 3.30E
Loznica 54 44.32N 19.13E
Lozoyuela 50 40.55N 3.37W
Lua ≃ 82 2.46N 18.26E
Lualaba ≃ 84 0.26N 25.20E
Luama ≃ 84 4.46S 26.53E
Lu'an 66 31.44N 116.31E
Luan ≃ 62 39.20N 119.10E
Luanda 84 8.48S 13.14E
Luando ≃ 84 10.19S 16.40E
Luang Prabang Range ⁂ 70 18.30N 101.15E
Luangue (Loange) ≃ 84 4.17S 20.02E
Luanguinga ≃ 84 15.11S 22.56E
Luangwa ≃ 84 15.36S 30.25E
Luanshya 84 13.08S 28.24E
Luán Toro 114 36.12S 65.06W
Luapula ≃ 84 9.26S 28.33E
Luarca 50 43.32N 6.32W
Luba 80 3.27N 8.33E
Lubaczów 46 50.10N 23.07E
Lubań, Pol. 46 51.08N 15.18E
L'uban', S.S.S.R. 60 59.21N 31.13E
Lubang Islands II 68 13.46N 120.15E
Lubango 84 14.55S 13.30E
Lubartów 46 51.28N 22.38E
Lubawa 46 53.30N 19.45E
Lübben 46 51.56N 13.53E
Lübbenau 46 51.52N 13.57E
Lubbock 100 33.34N 101.51W
Lubec 102 44.51N 66.59W
Lübeck 46 53.52N 10.40E
Lübecker Bucht C 46 54.00N 10.55E
Lubefu 84 4.43S 24.25E
Lubelska, Wyżyna ⁂2 46 51.00N 23.00E
L'ubercy 60 55.41N 37.53E
Lubersac 48 45.27N 1.24E
Lubiana →Ljubljana 52 46.03N 14.31E
Lubień Kujawski 46 52.25N 19.10E
Lubilash ≃ 84 6.02S 23.45E
L'ubim 60 58.22N 40.41E
Lubin 46 51.24N 16.13E
Lublin 46 51.15N 22.35E
Lubliniec 46 50.40N 18.41E
Lubny 56 50.01N 33.00E
Lubomierz 46 51.01N 15.30E
Luboń 46 52.23N 16.54E
L'ubotin 56 49.57N 35.57E
Lubraniec 46 52.33N 18.50E
Lubsko 46 51.46N 14.59E
Lübtheen 46 53.18N 11.04E
Lubudi 84 9.57S 25.58E
Lubudi ≃ 84 9.13S 25.38E
Lubukbkinggau 72 3.18S 102.52E
Lubuksikaping 72 0.08N 100.10E
Lubumbashi (Élisabethville) 84 11.40S 27.28E
Lubutu 84 0.44S 26.35E
Lübz 46 53.27N 12.01E
Lucan, On., Can. 102 43.11N 81.24W
Lucan, Ire. 40 53.22N 6.27W
Lucania □9 52 40.30N 16.00E
Lucania, Mount ▲ 98 61.01N 140.28W
Lucas González 114 32.24S 59.33W
Lucasville 102 38.52N 82.59W
Lucca 52 43.50N 10.29E
Luce, Water of ≃ 36 54.52N 4.48W
Luce Bay C 36 54.47N 4.50W
Lucena, Esp. 50 37.24N 4.29W
Lucena, Pil. 68 13.56N 121.37E
Lucena del Cid 50 40.08N 0.17W
Lucenay-L'Évêque 48 47.05N 4.15E
Luc-en-Diois 48 44.37N 5.27E
Lučenec 46 48.20N 19.40E
Lucera 52 41.30N 15.20E
Lucerne →Luzern, Schw. 48 47.03N 8.18E
Lucerne, Ca., U.S. 104 39.05N 122.47W
Lucerne, Lake →Vierwaldstätter See ⊜ 48 47.00N 8.28E
Lucerne Lake ⊜ 104 34.31N 116.57W
Luch 60 57.01N 42.15E
Luchena ≃ 50 37.44N 1.50W
Lücheng 66 31.55N 119.44E
Luchovicy 60 54.59N 39.03E
Lüchow, B.R.D. 46 52.58N 11.10E
Luchow →Luzhou, Zhg. 62 28.54N 105.27E
Lucindale 94 36.59S 140.22E
Lucipara, Kepulauan II 92 5.30S 127.33E
Lucira 84 13.51S 12.31E
Luck 56 50.44N 25.20E
Luck, Mount ▲2 90 28.47S 123.33E
Luckau 46 51.51N 13.43E
Luckenwalde 46 52.05N 13.10E
Luckhoff 86 29.44S 24.43E
Lucknow, On., Can. 102 43.57N 81.31W
Lucknow, India 76 26.51N 80.55E
Lucky Peak Lake ⊜1 104 43.33N 116.00W
Luçon 48 46.27N 1.10W
Lucy Creek 94 22.25S 136.20E
Lüda (Dairen) 62 38.53N 121.35E
Lúda Kamčija ≃ 54 43.03N 27.29E
Ludbreg 52 46.15N 16.37E
Lüdenscheid 46 51.13N 7.38E
Lüderitz 86 26.38S 15.10E
Lüderitz □5 86 26.30S 15.45E
Ludgershall 34 51.16N 1.37W
Ludhiāna 76 30.54N 75.51E
Lüdinghausen 46 51.46N 7.26E
L'udinovo 60 53.52N 34.27E
Ludlow, Eng., U.K. 34 52.22N 2.43W
Ludlow, Ma., U.S. 102 42.09N 72.28W
Ludlow, Vt., U.S. 102 43.23N 72.42W
Ludogorie ✢1 54 43.46N 26.56E
Luduş 54 46.29N 24.05E
Ludvika 44 60.09N 15.11E
Ludwigsburg 46 48.53N 9.11E
Ludwigsfelde 46 52.17N 13.16E
Ludwigshafen 46 49.29N 8.26E
Ludwigslust 46 53.19N 11.30E
Luebo 84 5.21S 21.25E
Luena, Ang. 84 11.47S 19.52E
Luena, Zaïre 84 9.27S 25.47E
Luena ≃ 84 12.31S 22.34E
Lufeng, Zhg. 66 22.57N 115.38E
Lufeng, Zhg. 70 25.07N 102.07E
Lufira ≃ 84 8.16S 26.27E
Lufkin 100 31.20N 94.43W
Luga 60 58.44N 29.52E
Luga ≃ 60 59.40N 28.18E
Lugano 48 46.01N 8.58E
Lugano, Lago di ⊜ 48 46.00N 9.00E
Lugansk →Vorošilovgrad 56 48.34N 39.20E
Lugenda ≃ 84 11.25S 38.33E
Lugg ≃ 34 52.02N 2.38W
Lugnaquillia Mountain ▲ 40 52.58N 6.27W
Lugo, Esp. 50 43.00N 7.34W
Lugo, It. 52 44.25N 11.54E
Lugoj 54 45.41N 21.54E
Luhanka 44 61.47N 25.42E
Luhit ≃ 76 27.48N 95.28E
Lui, Beinn ▲ 38 56.24N 4.49W
Luichart, Loch ⊜ 38 57.37N 4.46W
Luik →Liège 46 50.38N 5.34E
Luilaka ≃ 84 0.52S 20.12E
Luimneach →Limerick 40 52.40N 8.38W
Luing I 38 56.13N 5.40W
Luino 52 46.00N 8.44E
Luís Alves 114 26.44S 48.57W
Luishia 84 11.10S 27.02E
Luisiânia 114 21.41S 50.17W
Luiza 84 7.12S 22.25E
Luján, Arg. 114 33.03S 68.52W
Luján, Arg. 114 32.22S 65.57W
Lujiang 66 31.14N 117.17E
Lukang 66 24.03N 120.25E
Lukanga Swamp ⁝⁝ 84 14.25S 27.45E
Luke, Mount ▲ 90 27.13S 116.48E
Lukenie ≃ 84 2.44S 18.09E
Lukojanov 60 55.02N 44.30E
Lukolela 84 1.03S 17.12E
Lukou 66 31.48N 118.52E
Lukovit 54 43.12N 24.10E
Łuków 46 51.56N 22.23E
Lukulu 84 14.25S 23.12E
Luleå 44 65.34N 22.10E
Luleälven ≃ 42 65.35N 22.03E
Lüleburgaz 54 41.24N 27.21E
Lules 114 26.56S 65.21W
Luliang 70 25.05N 103.36E
Lüliang Shan ⁂ 62 37.25N 111.20E
Lulonga ≃ 84 0.43N 18.23E
Lulua ≃ 84 5.02S 21.07E
Lulworth, Mount ▲ 90 26.53S 117.42E
Lumajang 72 8.08S 113.13E
Lumberport 102 39.22N 80.20W
Lumberton 100 34.37N 79.00W
Lumbrales 50 40.56N 6.43W
Lumbres 48 50.42N 2.08E
Lumding 76 25.45N 93.10E
Lumphanan 38 57.07N 2.41W
Lumsden, N.Z. 96 45.44S 168.27E
Lumsden, Scot., U.K. 38 57.15N 2.54W
Lumut 72 4.14N 100.38E
Lumut, Tanjung ❯ 72 3.50S 105.57E
Lunan Bay C 38 56.39N 2.28W
Luna Pier 102 41.48N 83.26W
Lūnāvāda 76 23.08N 73.37E
Luncarty 38 56.27N 3.28W
Lund, Sve. 44 55.42N 13.11E
Lund, Nv., U.S. 104 38.51N 115.00W
Lundale 102 37.48N 81.44W
Lundazi 84 12.19S 33.13E
Lundevatn ⊜ 44 58.22N 6.36E
Lundi ≃ 86 21.43S 32.34E
Lundy I 34 51.10N 4.40W
Lune ≃ 36 54.02N 2.50W
Lüneburg 46 53.15N 10.23E
Lüneburger Heide ✢1 46 53.10N 10.20E
Lunel 48 43.41N 4.08E
Lünen 46 51.36N 7.32E
Lunéville 48 48.36N 6.30E
Lunga I 38 56.13N 5.42W
Lunga ≃ 84 14.34S 26.25E
Lungi 80 8.38N 13.13W
Lungleh 76 22.53N 92.44E
Lungué-Bungo ≃ 84 14.19S 23.14E
Lūni 76 26.00N 73.00E
Lūni ≃ 76 24.41N 71.15E
Lunjiao 66 22.53N 113.13E
Lünkaransar 76 28.29N 73.44E
Lunndörrsfjällen ▲ 44 63.00N 13.00E
Luo ≃ 62 34.42N 110.15E
Luoding 70 22.47N 111.31E
Luogosanto 52 41.03N 9.13E
Luohe 66 33.35N 114.01E
Luolong 70 30.45N 96.09E
Luoping 70 24.59N 104.21E
Luopu 76 37.02N 80.15E
Luoshan 66 32.13N 114.32E
Luotian 66 30.48N 115.22E
Luoyang 66 34.41N 112.28E
Luoyuan 66 26.31N 119.32E
Łupawa 46 54.26N 17.24E
Lupeni 54 45.22N 23.13E
Luqiao, Zhg. 66 32.34N 117.14E
Luqiao, Zhg. 66 28.35N 121.22E
Luqu 62 34.41N 102.22E
Luque 114 25.16S 57.34W
Luray 102 38.39N 78.27W
Lure 48 47.41N 6.30E
Luremo 84 8.31S 17.50E
Lurgan 40 54.28N 6.20W
Lurín 110 12.17S 76.52W
Lúrio 84 13.35S 40.30E
Lúrio ≃, Moç. 84 13.35S 40.32E
Lurio ≃, Suomi 42 67.08N 27.29E
Lurö I 44 58.48N 13.14E
Lusaka 84 15.25S 28.17E
Lusambo 84 4.58S 23.27E
Lusanga 84 4.50S 18.44E
Lush, Mount ▲ 92 17.02S 127.30E
Lushan, Zhg. 62 30.15N 102.58E
Lushan, Zhg. 66 33.45N 112.53E
Lu Shan ▲ 66 29.31N 115.58E
Lushnje 54 40.56N 19.42E
Lushoto 84 4.47S 38.17E
Lüshun (Port Arthur) 62 38.48N 121.16E
Lüsi 66 32.03N 121.36E
Lusignan 48 46.26N 0.07E
Lusikisiki 86 31.25S 29.30E
Lusk 100 42.45N 104.27W
Luspebryggan 42 67.01N 19.51E
Lussac-les-Châteaux 48 46.24N 0.44E
Lustenau 46 47.26N 9.39E
Luster 44 61.26N 7.24E
Lustrafjorden C2 44 61.20N 7.22E
Lūt, Dasht-e ✢2 78 33.00N 57.00E
Luther 102 44.02N 85.40W
Luther Lake ⊜ 102 43.55N 80.26W
Luthrie 38 56.21N 3.05W
Luton 34 51.53N 0.25W
Lutong 72 4.28N 114.00E
Lutterworth 34 52.28N 1.10W
Lützow 46 53.40N 11.11E
Lutzputs 86 28.03S 20.40E
Lutzville 86 31.33S 18.22E
Luuq 82 3.48N 42.33E
Luvua ≃ 84 6.46S 26.58E
Luvuvhu ≃ 86 22.40S 30.55E
Luwegu ≃ 84 8.31S 37.23E
Luwuk 72 0.56S 122.47E
Luxembourg 46 49.36N 6.09E
Luxembourg □1 30 49.45N 6.05E
Luxeuil-les-Bains 48 47.49N 6.23E
Luxi (Mangshi) 70 24.20N 98.25E
Luxor →Al-Uqṣur 82 25.41N 32.39E
Luy ≃ 48 43.39N 1.08W
Luyi 66 33.53N 115.28E
Luza 60 60.39N 47.10E
Luzarches 48 49.07N 2.25E
Luzern 48 47.03N 8.18E
Luzhai 70 24.31N 109.50E
Luzhou 62 28.54N 105.27E
Luziânia 110 16.15S 47.56W
Lužnice ≃ 46 49.14N 14.23E
Luzon I 68 16.00N 121.00E
Luzon Strait ⊻ 68 20.30N 121.00E
Luzy 48 46.48N 3.58E
L'vov 56 49.50N 24.00E
Lwówek 46 52.28N 16.10E
Lwówek Śląski 46 51.07N 15.35E
Lyall, Mount ▲ 96 45.17S 167.34E
Lybster 38 58.18N 3.18W
Lyck →Ełk 46 53.50N 22.22E
Lyckeby 44 56.12N 15.39E
Lycksele 44 64.36N 18.40E
Lycoming Creek ≃ 102 41.13N 77.02W
Lydd 34 50.57N 0.55E
Lydda →Lod 78 31.58N 34.54E
Lydden ∨ 34 50.56N 2.22W
Lydenburg 86 25.10S 30.29E
Lydford 34 50.39N 4.06W
Lydham 34 52.31N 2.58W
Lydney 34 51.44N 2.32W
Lyell Brown, Mount ▲ 90 23.21S 130.24E
Lygnern ⊜ 44 57.29N 12.20E
Lykens 102 40.34N 76.42W
Lyme Bay C 34 50.38N 3.00W
Lyme Regis 34 50.44N 2.57W
Lyminge 34 51.08N 1.05E
Lymington 34 50.46N 1.33W
Lympne 34 51.05N 1.02E
Lympstone 34 50.39N 3.25W
Łyna (Lava) ≃ 60 54.37N 21.14E
Lynch, Lac ⊜ 102 46.25N 77.05W
Lynchburg, Oh., U.S. 102 39.14N 83.47W
Lynchburg, Va., U.S. 100 37.24N 79.08W
Lynd ≃ 94 16.28S 143.18E
Lyndhurst, Austl. 94 19.12S 144.23E
Lyndhurst, Austl. 94 30.17S 138.21E
Lyndhurst, Eng., U.K. 34 50.52N 1.34W
Lyndon 90 23.37S 115.15E
Lyndon ≃ 90 23.29S 114.06E
Lyndonville 102 44.32N 72.00W
Lyndora 102 40.51N 79.55W
Lyne ≃ 36 54.58N 3.01W
Lyneham 34 51.31N 1.58W
Lynemouth 36 55.12N 1.31W
Lyne Water ≃ 38 54.39N 3.16W
Lyngdal 44 58.08N 7.05E
Lyngen 42 69.34N 20.10E
Lyngen C2 42 69.58N 20.30E
Lyngør 44 58.38N 9.10E
Lynher ≃ 34 50.28N 4.12W
Lynmouth 34 51.15N 3.50W
Lynn, In., U.S. 102 40.02N 84.56W
Lynn, Ma., U.S. 102 42.28N 70.57W
Lynn Lake 98 56.51N 101.03W
Lynton 34 51.15N 3.50W
Lynx Lake ⊜ 98 62.25N 106.15W
Lyon 48 45.45N 4.51E
Lyon ≃ 38 56.37N 4.01W
Lyon, Glen ∨ 38 56.35N 4.20W
Lyon, Loch ⊜ 38 56.32N 4.36W
Lyon Inlet C 98 66.32N 83.53W
Lyon Mountain 102 44.43N 73.54W
Lyon Mountain ▲ 102 44.41N 73.53W
Lyonnais, Monts du ⁂ 48 45.40N 4.30E
Lyons, Mi., U.S. 102 42.58N 84.56W
Lyons, N.Y., U.S. 102 43.03N 76.59W
Lyons ≃ 90 25.02S 115.09E
Lyracrumpane 40 52.20N 9.30W
Lys (Leie) ≃ 46 51.03N 3.43E
Lysaker 44 59.54N 10.36E
Lysá pod Makytou 46 49.12N 18.13E
Lysefjorden C2 44 59.00N 6.14E
Lysekil 44 58.16N 11.26E
Łysica ▲ 46 50.54N 20.55E
Lyskovo 60 56.04N 45.02E
Lys'va 56 58.07N 57.47E
Lytham Saint Anne's 36 53.45N 2.57W
Lyttelton 96 43.35S 172.42E

M

Ma ≃ 70 19.47N 105.56E
Maalaea Bay C 105a 20.47N 156.29W
Maam Cross 40 53.27N 9.31W
Ma'ān 78 30.12N 35.44E
Maaninka 44 63.09N 27.18E
Maanshan 66 31.42N 118.30E
Ma'arrat an-Nu'mān 78 35.38N 36.40E
Maas 40 54.50N 8.22W
Maas (Meuse) ≃ 46 51.49N 5.01E
Maaseik 46 51.06N 5.48E
Maastricht 46 50.52N 5.43E
Mababe Depression ⊥7 86 18.50S 24.15E
Mabel Creek 90 29.01S 134.17E
Maberry, Loch ⊜ 36 55.02N 4.41W
Mabi 66 26.21N 119.36E
Mablethorpe 36 53.21N 0.15E
Mača 58 59.54N 117.35E
Macachín 114 37.09S 63.39W
McAdam 102 45.36N 67.20W
McAdoo 102 40.54N 75.59W
Macaé 110 22.23S 41.47W
McAlester 100 34.56N 95.46W
Macalister ≃ 94 38.02S 146.59E
McAlister, Mount ▲ 94 34.27S 149.45E
McAllen 100 26.12N 98.13W
McAlpine Lake ⊜ 98 66.40N 103.15W
Macão 50 39.33N 8.00W
Macao →Macau □2 66 22.10N 113.33E
Macapá 110 0.02N 51.03W
Macará 110 4.23S 79.57W
Macareo, Caño ≃1 108 9.47N 61.37W
McArthur 102 39.14N 82.28W
McArthur ≃ 92 15.54S 136.40E
McArthur River 92 16.27S 136.07E
Macaterick, Loch ⊜ 36 55.12N 4.26W
Macau, Bra. 110 5.07S 36.38W
Macau (Aomen), Macau 66 22.14N 113.35E
Macau □2 66 22.10N 113.33E
Macaya, Pic de ▲ 108 18.25N 74.00W
McBain 102 44.11N 85.12W
McBeth Fjord C2 98 69.38N 68.30W
Macclesfield 36 53.16N 2.07W
McCloud 104 41.15N 122.08W
McCloud ≃ 104 40.46N 122.18W
McClure 102 40.42N 77.18W
McClure, Lake ⊜1 104 37.37N 120.16W
McComb, Ms., U.S. 100 31.14N 90.27W
McComb, Oh., U.S. 102 41.06N 83.47W
McConnellsburg 102 39.55N 77.59W
McConnelsville 102 39.38N 81.51W
McCook 100 40.12N 100.37W
McCoy Creek ≃ 104 43.02N 118.50W
McCulloch, Mount ▲ 90 25.10S 129.52E
McCullough Mountain ▲ 104 35.36N 115.11W
McDermitt 104 41.59N 117.43W
McDermott 102 38.50N 83.03W
Macdhui, Ben ▲ 86 30.39S 27.58E
Macdonald, Lake ⊜ 90 23.30S 129.00E
MacDonald Downs 90 22.27S 135.13E
Macdonnell Ranges ⁂ 90 23.45S 133.20E
McDouall Peak 90 29.51S 134.55E
Macduff 38 57.40N 2.29W
Macdui, Ben ▲ 38 57.05N 3.38W
Macedo de Cavaleiros 50 41.32N 6.58W
Macedonia →Makedonija □3 54 41.50N 22.00E
Macedonia □9 54 41.00N 23.00E
Maceió 110 9.40S 35.43W
Macenta 80 8.33N 9.28W
Macerata 52 43.18N 13.27E
McFarland 104 35.40N 119.13W
MacFarlane ≃ 98 59.12N 107.58W
Macfarlane, Lake ⊜ 94 31.55S 136.42E
Macfarlane, Mount ▲ 96 43.56S 169.23E
McGill 104 39.24N 114.46W
McGillivray, Lac ⊜ 102 46.04N 77.06W
Macgillycuddy's Reeks ⁂ 40 51.55N 9.45W
McGraw 102 42.35N 76.05W
McGregor 98 54.11N 122.00W
McGregor ≃ 94 26.40S 142.45E
McGregor Range ⁂ 94 27.00S 142.45E
Machačkala 56 42.58N 47.30E
Machado 114 21.41S 45.56W
Machadodorp 86 25.40S 30.14E
Machagai 114 26.56S 60.03W
Machakos 84 1.31S 37.16E
Machala 110 3.16S 79.58W
Machali 114 34.11S 70.40W
Machattie, Lake ⊜ 94 24.50S 139.48E
Machecoul 48 47.00N 1.50W
Macheng 66 31.13N 115.00E
Machias 102 44.42N 67.27W
Machias ≃ 102 44.43N 67.22W
Machias Bay C 102 44.40N 67.20W
Machichaco, Cabo ❯ 50 43.27N 2.45W
Machilīpatnam 74 16.10N 81.08E
Mchinji 84 13.41S 32.55E
Machiques 110 10.04N 72.34W
Machupicchu 110 13.07S 72.34W
Machynlleth 34 52.35N 3.51W
Maciá 114 32.10S 59.23W
Măcin 54 45.15N 28.08E
Macintyre ≃, Austl. 94 29.25S 148.45E
Macintyre ≃, Austl. 94 28.38S 150.47E
Mackay 94 21.09S 149.11E
Mackay, Lake ⊜ 90 22.30S 129.00E
McKay, Mount ▲ 90 22.26S 120.01E
MacKay Lake ⊜ 98 63.55N 110.25W
McKeand ≃ 98 65.26N 68.10W
McKeesport 102 40.20N 79.51W
Mackenzie 110 6.00N 58.17W
Mackenzie □5 98 65.00N 115.00W
Mackenzie ≃, Austl. 94 23.38S 149.46E
Mackenzie ≃, N.T., Can. 98 69.15N 134.08W
Mackenzie Bay C 98 69.00N 136.30W
Mackenzie Mountains ⁂ 98 64.00N 130.00W
McKerrow, Lake ⊜ 96 44.26S 168.03E
Mackinac, Straits of ⊻ 102 45.49N 84.42W
Mackinac Island 102 45.50N 84.37W
Mackinac Island I 102 45.51N 84.38W
Mackinaw City 102 45.47N 84.43W
McKinlay 94 21.16S 141.17E
McKinlay ≃ 94 20.50S 141.28E
McKinley, Mount ▲ 98 63.30N 151.00W
McKinleyville 104 40.56N 124.05W
Mackinnon Road 84 3.44S 39.03E
McKittrick Summit ▲ 104 35.18N 119.46W
Macksville 94 30.43S 152.55E
McLarty Hills ⁂2 90 19.29S 123.33E
Maclean 94 29.28S 153.13E
Maclear 86 31.02S 28.23E
Macleay ≃ 94 30.52S 153.01E
McLennan 98 55.42N 116.54W
McLeod ≃ 98 54.08N 115.42W
Macleod, Lake ⊜ 90 24.00S 113.35E
McLeod Bay C 98 62.53N 110.00W
McLoughlin, Mount ▲ 104 42.27N 122.19W
McLoughlin Bay C 98 67.50N 99.00W
Macmillan ≃ 98 62.52N 135.55W
Macomer 52 40.16N 8.47E
Mâcon, Fr. 48 46.18N 4.50E
Macon, Ga., U.S. 100 32.50N 83.37W
Mâconnais, Monts du ⁂ 48 46.18N 4.45E
Macoris, Cabo ❯ 108 19.47N 70.28W
McPherson 100 38.22N 97.39W
McPherson Range ⁂ 94 28.20S 153.00E
Macquarie ≃ 94 30.07S 147.24E
Macquarie, Lake ⊜ 94 33.05S 151.35E
Macquarie Harbour C 94 42.19S 145.23E
McRae, Mount ▲ 90 22.17S 117.35E
Macroom 40 51.54N 8.57W
MacTier 102 45.08N 79.47W
Macumba ≃ 94 27.52S 137.12E
Macuro 108 10.39N 61.56W
Mad ≃, On., Can. 102 44.25N 79.54W
Mad ≃, Ca., U.S. 104 40.57N 124.07W
Mad ≃, Oh., U.S. 102 39.46N 84.11W
Mad ≃, Vt., U.S. 102 44.18N 72.41W
Mada ≃ 80 7.59N 7.55E
Ma'dabā 78 31.43N 35.48E
Madagascar (Madagasikara) □1 84 19.00S 46.00E
Madagascar Basin ✢1 20 27.00S 53.00E
Madagascar Plateau ✢3 20 30.00S 45.00E
Madan 54 41.30N 24.57E
Madang 92 5.15S 145.50E
Mādārīpur 76 23.10N 90.12E
Madawaska ≃ 98 45.27N 76.21W
Madawaska Highlands ⁂1 102 45.15N 77.35W
Maddalena, Isola I 52 41.14N 9.25E
Maddaloni 52 41.02N 14.23E
Madden, Mount ▲ 90 33.12S 119.51E
Maddy, Loch C 38 57.36N 7.08W
Madeira ≃ 110 3.22S 58.45W
Madeira, Arquipélago da (Madeira Islands) II 80 32.40N 16.45W
Mädelegabel ▲ 48 47.18N 10.18E
Madeleine, Îles de la II 98 47.30N 61.45W
Madeley, Eng., U.K. 34 52.59N 2.20W
Madeley, Eng., U.K. 34 52.39N 2.28W
Madera 104 36.57N 120.03W
Madhipura 76 25.55N 86.47E
Mādhopur 76 32.22N 75.36E
Madhubani 76 26.22N 86.05E
Madhupur 76 24.16N 86.39E
Madhya Pradesh □3 76 23.00N 79.00E
Madibogo 86 26.25S 25.10E
Madidi ≃ 110 12.32S 66.52W
Madimba 84 4.58S 15.08E
Madīnat ash-Sha'b 74 12.50N 44.56E
Madingou 84 4.09S 13.34E
Madison, Me., U.S. 102 44.47N 69.52W
Madison, Oh., U.S. 102 41.46N 81.03W
Madison, S.D., U.S. 100 44.00N 97.06W
Madison, Va., U.S. 102 38.22N 78.15W
Madison, W.V., U.S. 102 38.04N 81.49W
Madison, Wi., U.S. 100 43.04N 89.24W
Madisonville 100 37.19N 87.29W
Madiun 72 7.37S 111.31E
Madley, Mount ▲ 90 24.31S 123.58E
Madoc 102 44.30N 77.28W
Mado Gashi 84 0.44S 39.10E
Madoi 62 34.53N 98.24E
Madonna di Campiglio 52 46.14N 10.49E
Madrakah, Ra's al- ❯ 74 19.00N 57.50E
Madras 74 13.05N 80.17E
Madre, Laguna C, Méx. 106 25.00N 97.40W
Madre, Laguna C, Tx., U.S. 100 27.00N 97.35W
Madre, Sierra ⁂ 68 16.20N 122.00E
Madre de Dios ≃ 110 10.59S 66.08W
Madre de Dios, Isla I 112 50.15S 75.05W
Madre del Sur, Sierra ⁂ 106 17.00N 100.00W
Madre Occidental, Sierra ⁂ 106 25.00N 105.00W
Madre Oriental, Sierra ⁂ 106 22.00N 99.30W
Madrid 50 40.24N 3.41W
Madridejos 50 39.28N 3.32W
Madrigalejo 50 39.08N 5.37W
Madroñera 50 39.26N 5.46W
Madura 90 31.55S 127.00E
Madura I 72 7.00S 113.20E
Madurai 74 9.56N 78.07E
Madyan ✢1 78 27.40N 35.35E
Maebaru 64 33.33N 130.12E
Maebashi 64 36.23N 139.04E
Mae Hong Son 70 19.16N 97.56E
Mae Klong ≃ 70 13.21N 100.00E
Maenclochog 34 51.54N 4.48W
Mae Sariang 70 18.10N 97.56E
Mae Sot 70 16.43N 98.34E

Symbols in the Index entries are identified on page 122.

Name	Page	Lat. °′	Long. °′
Maesteg	34	51.37N	3.40W
Maestra, Sierra ✱	108	20.00N	76.45W
Maestu	50	42.44N	2.27W
Maevatanana	87b	16.56S	46.49E
Maewo I	28	15.10S	168.10E
Mafeteng	86	29.51S	27.15E
Maffra	94	37.58S	146.59E
Mafia Island I	84	7.50S	39.50E
Mafikeng	86	25.53S	25.39E
Mafra, Bra.	114	26.07S	49.49W
Mafra, Port.	50	38.56N	9.20W
Magadan	58	59.34N	150.48E
Magadi	84	1.54S	36.17E
Magaguadavic Lake ⊜	102	45.43N	67.12W
Magallanes, Estrecho de (Strait of Magellan) Ʊ	112	54.00S	71.00W
Magangué	110	9.14N	74.45W
Magdagači	58	53.27N	125.48E
Magdalena, Arg.	114	35.04S	57.32W
Magdalena, Bol.	110	13.20S	64.08W
Magdalena □[5]	108	10.00N	74.00W
Magdalena ≃	110	11.06N	74.51W
Magdalena, Isla I	112	44.40S	73.10W
Magdalena de Kino	106	30.38N	110.57W
Magdeburg	46	52.07N	11.38E
Magdeburg □[5]	46	52.15N	11.30E
Magee, Island ›[1]	40	54.49N	5.42W
Magelang	72	7.28S	110.13E
Magellan, Strait of →Magallanes, Estrecho de Ʊ	112	54.00S	71.00W
Magenta	52	45.28N	8.53E
Magenta, Lake ⊜	90	33.26S	119.10E
Magerøya I	42	71.03N	25.45E
Magetan	72	7.39S	111.20E
Maggie Creek ≃	104	40.43N	116.05W
Maggieville	94	17.27S	141.10E
Maggiorasca, Monte ∧	52	44.33N	9.29E
Maggiore, Lago ⊜	52	46.00N	8.40E
Maghera	40	54.51N	6.40W
Magherafelt	40	54.45N	6.36W
Maghull	36	53.32N	2.57W
Magic Reservoir ⊜[1]	104	43.17N	114.23W
Magina ∧	50	37.43N	3.28W
Magione	52	43.08N	12.12E
Maglaj	54	44.33N	18.06E
Maglie	52	40.07N	18.19E
Magnetawan ≃	102	45.46N	80.37W
Magnetic Island I	94	19.08S	146.50E
Magnitogorsk	56	53.27N	59.04E
Magnolia	100	33.16N	93.14W
Magnor	44	59.57N	12.12E
Magny-en-Vexin	48	49.09N	1.47E
Magog	102	45.16N	72.09W
Magpie, Lac ⊜	98	51.00N	64.41W
Magro ≃	50	39.11N	0.25W
Magruder Mountain ∧	104	37.25N	117.33W
Maguari, Cabo ›	110	0.18S	48.22W
Maguse Lake ⊜	98	61.40N	95.10W
Magwe	70	20.09N	94.55E
Magwe □[8]	70	23.00N	95.00E
Mahābād	78	36.45N	45.43E
Mahābaleshwar	74	17.55N	73.40E
Mahābalipuram	74	12.37N	80.12E
Mahābhārat Range ✱	76	27.40N	84.30E
Mahabo	87b	20.23S	44.40E
Mahajamba, Helodranon' i C	87b	15.24S	47.05E
Mahājan	76	28.47N	73.50E
Mahajanga	87b	15.43S	46.19E
Mahajanga □[4]	87b	17.00S	46.00E
Mahakam ≃	72	0.35S	117.17E
Mahalatswe	86	23.05S	26.51E
Maham	76	28.59N	76.18E
Mahānadi ≃	74	20.19N	86.45E
Mahanoro	87b	19.54S	48.48E
Mahanoy City	102	40.48N	76.08W
Mahārājganj	76	26.07N	84.29E
Mahārājpur	76	25.01N	79.44E
Mahārāshtra □[3]	76	21.00N	79.00E
Mahāsamund	76	21.06N	82.06E
Maha Sarakham	70	16.11N	103.18E
Mahates	108	10.14N	75.12W
Maḥaṭṭat al-Qaṭrānah	78	31.15N	36.03E
Mahbūbnagar	74	16.44N	77.59E
Mahd adh-Dhahab	78	23.30N	40.52E
Mahe	74	11.42N	75.32E
Mahébourg	87c	20.24S	57.42E
Mahé Island I	84	4.40S	55.28E
Mahendraganj	76	25.20N	89.45E
Mahendragarh	76	28.17N	76.09E
Mahenge	84	8.41S	36.43E
Maheno	96	45.10S	170.50E
Maheshwar	76	22.11N	75.35E
Mahia Peninsula ›[1]	96	39.10S	177.53E
Mahinerangi, Lake ⊜	96	45.51S	169.57E
Mahlabatini	86	28.14S	31.30E
Mahmūdābād	76	27.18N	81.07E
Mahoba	76	25.17N	79.52E
Mahogany Mountain ∧	104	43.14N	117.16W
Mahón	50	39.53N	4.15E
Mahora	50	39.13N	1.44W
Mahroni	76	24.35N	78.43E
Mahuva	76	21.05N	71.48E
Mahwah	76	27.03N	76.56E
Maia	50	41.14N	8.37W
Maicao	108	11.23N	72.13W
Maîche	48	47.15N	6.48E
Maicurú ≃	110	2.14S	54.17W
Maidenhead	34	51.32N	0.44W
Maiden Newton	34	50.46N	2.35W
Maidstone	34	51.17N	0.32E
Maiduguri	80	11.51N	13.10E
Maignelay	48	49.33N	2.31E
Maihar	76	24.16N	80.45E
Maikala Range ✱	76	22.30N	81.30E
Maiko ≃	84	0.14N	25.33E
Maikoor, Pulau I	92	6.15S	134.15E
Mailāni	76	28.17N	80.21E
Maillezais	48	46.22N	0.44W
Main ≃, B.R.D.	46	50.00N	8.18E
Main ≃, N. Ire., U.K.	36	54.43N	6.18W
Maināguri	76	26.34N	88.49E
Mainburg	46	48.38N	11.47E
Main Channel Ʊ	102	45.22N	81.50W
Mai-Ndombe, Lac ⊜	84	2.00S	18.20E
Maine □[9]	48	48.15N	0.05W
Maine □[3]	100	45.15N	69.15W
Maine ≃	40	52.09N	9.45W
Maine-et-Loire □[5]	48	47.25N	0.30W
Mainhardt	46	49.04N	9.33E
Mainland I, Scot., U.K.	38	59.00N	3.15W
Mainland I, Scot., U.K.	38a	60.16N	1.16W
Mainoru	92	14.02S	134.05E
Mainpuri	76	27.14N	79.01E
Maintenon	48	48.35N	1.35E
Maintirano	87b	18.03S	44.01E
Mainz	46	50.01N	8.16E
Maio I	80	15.15N	23.10W
Maipo ≃	114	33.37S	71.39W
Maipo, Volcán ∧[1]	114	34.10S	69.50W
Maipú, Arg.	114	36.52S	57.52W
Maipú, Arg.	114	32.58S	68.47W
Maipú, Chile	114	33.31S	70.46W
Maiquetía	110	10.36N	66.57W
Mairabāri	76	26.28N	92.26E
Maitengwe ≃	86	19.59S	26.26E
Maitland, Austl.	94	34.22S	137.40E
Maitland, Austl.	94	32.44S	151.33E
Maitland ≃	102	43.45N	81.43W
Maitland, Lake ⊜	90	27.11S	121.03E
Maíz, Islas del II	108	12.15N	83.00W
Maizuru	64	35.28N	135.24E
Maja ≃	58	60.24N	134.30E
Majene	72	3.33S	118.57E
Majevica ✱	54	44.30N	18.55E
Maji	82	6.11N	35.38E
Majja	58	61.44N	130.18E
Majkain	58	51.27N	75.52E
Majkop	56	44.35N	40.07E
Major, Puig ∧	50	39.48N	2.48E
Majorca →Mallorca I	50	39.30N	3.00E
Majskij	58	52.18N	129.38E
Majskoje	58	50.55N	78.15E
Majuro I[1]	28	7.09N	171.12E
Makabana	84	2.48S	12.29E
Makahuena Point ›	105a	21.52N	159.27W
Makale	72	3.06S	119.51E
Makallé	114	27.13S	59.17W
Makālu ∧	76	27.54N	87.06E
Makanza	84	1.36N	19.07E
Makapuu Head ›	105a	21.19N	157.39W
Makarewa	96	46.20S	168.21E
Makarjev	60	57.52N	43.48E
Makarov	58	48.38N	142.48E
Makarska	52	43.18N	17.02E
Makasar →Ujung Pandang	72	5.07S	119.24E
Makasar, Selat (Makassar Strait) Ʊ	72	2.00S	117.30E
Makassar Strait →Makasar, Selat Ʊ	72	2.00S	117.30E
Makat	56	47.39N	53.19E
Makatea I	28	15.50S	148.15W
Makawao	105a	20.51N	156.18W
Makedonija □[3]	54	41.50N	22.00E
Makejevka	56	48.02N	37.58E
Makemo I[1]	28	16.35S	143.40W
Makeni	80	8.53N	12.03W
Maketu	96	37.46S	176.27E
Makgadikgadi ≚	86	20.45S	25.30E
Maki	64	37.45N	138.53E
Makika, Lua •[6]	105a	20.34N	156.34W
Makikihi	96	44.38S	171.09E
Makindu	84	2.17S	37.49E
Makinsk	56	52.37N	70.26E
M'akit	58	61.24N	152.09E
Makkah (Mecca)	74	21.27N	39.49E
Makó	46	46.13N	20.29E
Makokou	84	0.34N	12.52E
Makorako ∧	96	39.09S	176.02E
Makotuku	96	40.07S	176.14E
Makoua	84	0.01N	15.39E
Makov	46	49.23N	18.30E
Maków Mazowiecki	46	52.52N	21.06E
Maków Podhalański	46	49.44N	19.41E
Makrai	76	22.04N	77.06E
Makrāna	76	27.03N	74.43E
Makumbi	84	5.51S	20.41E
Makung (P'enghu)	66	23.34N	119.34E
Makurazaki	64	31.16N	130.19E
Makurdi	80	7.45N	8.32E
Makwassie	86	27.26S	26.00E
Māl	76	26.52N	88.44E
Malå	44	65.11N	18.44E
Malabang	68	7.38N	124.03E
Malabar Coast •[2]	74	11.00N	75.00E
Malabo	80	3.45N	8.47E
Malacca, Strait of Ʊ	70	2.30N	101.20E
Malacky	46	48.27N	17.00E
Málaga, Col.	110	6.42N	72.44W
Málaga, Esp.	50	36.43N	4.25W
Malagasy Republic →Madagascar □[1]	84	19.00S	46.00E
Malagón	50	39.10N	3.51W
Malagón ≃	50	37.35N	7.29W
Malahide	40	53.27N	6.09W
Malaimbandy	87b	20.20S	45.36E
Malaita I	28	9.00S	161.00E
Malaja Kuril'skaja Gr'ada (Habomai-shotō) II	58	43.30N	146.10E
Malaja Višera	42	58.51N	32.14E
Malakāl	82	9.31N	31.39E
Mala Kapela ✱	52	44.50N	15.30E
Malang	72	7.59S	112.37E
Malanville	80	11.52N	3.23E
Malanzán	114	30.48S	66.37W
Mała Panew ≃	46	50.44N	17.52E
Mälaren ⊜	44	59.30N	17.12E
Malargüe	114	35.28S	69.35W
Malartic	98	48.08N	78.08W
Malaspina Glacier ⊓	98	59.50N	140.30W
Malåträsk	42	65.11N	18.44E
Malatya	78	38.21N	38.19E
Malaucène	48	44.10N	5.08E
Malaut	76	30.13N	74.29E
Malawali, Pulau I	72	7.03N	117.18E
Malawi □[1]	84	13.30S	34.00E
Malawi, Lake →Nyasa, Lake ⊜	84	12.00S	34.30E
Malaya □[9]	72	4.00N	102.00E
Malaybalay	68	8.09N	125.05E
Malāyer	78	34.17N	48.50E
Malay Peninsula ›[1]	70	6.00N	101.00E
Malay Reef +[2]	94	17.59S	149.18E
Malaysia □[1]	68	2.30N	112.30E
Malazgirt	78	39.09N	42.31E
Malbon	94	21.04S	140.18E
Malbooma	90	30.41S	134.11E
Malbork	46	54.02N	19.01E
Malbrán	114	29.21S	62.27W
Malchin	46	53.44N	12.46E
Malchow	46	53.28N	12.25E
Malcolm	90	28.56S	121.30E
Malcolm, Point ›	90	33.48S	123.45E
Malczyce	46	51.14N	16.29E
Malden I	28	4.03S	154.59W
Maldive Islands →Maldives □[1]	26	3.15N	73.00E
Maldives □[1]	26	3.15N	73.00E
Maldon	34	51.45N	0.40E
Maldonado	114	34.54S	54.57W
Malé, It.	52	46.21N	10.55E
Male, Mald.	26	4.10N	73.30E
Maléa, Ákra ›	54	36.26N	23.12E
Mālegaon	74	20.33N	74.32E
Malé Karpaty ✱	46	48.30N	17.20E
Malek Sīāh, Kūh-e ∧	78	29.51N	60.52E
Malekula I	28	16.15S	167.30E
Malen'ga	42	63.50N	36.25E
Malente	46	54.10N	10.33E
Māler Kotla	76	30.31N	75.53E
Malesherbes	48	48.18N	2.25E
Malestroit	48	47.49N	2.23W
Malgomaj ⊜	44	64.47N	16.12E
Malha Wells	82	15.08N	26.12E
Malheur, South Fork ≃	104	43.33N	118.10W
Malheur Lake ⊜	104	43.20N	118.45W
Mali □[1]	80	17.00N	4.00W
Mali ≃	70	25.43N	97.29E
Malik, Wādī al- ∨	82	18.02N	30.58E
Mali Kyun I	70	13.06N	98.16E
Malili	72	2.38S	121.06E
Målilla	44	57.23N	15.48E
Malin, Ire.	40	55.18N	7.15W
Malin, Or., U.S.	104	42.00N	121.24W
Malinau	72	3.35N	116.38E
Malin Beg	40	54.40N	8.48E
Malindi	84	3.13S	40.07E
Malines →Mechelen	46	51.02N	4.28E
Malingping	72	6.46S	106.01E
Malin Head ›	40	55.23N	7.24W
Malino, Bukit ∧	72	0.45N	120.47E
Mali Rajinac ∧	52	44.48N	15.02E
Māliya	76	23.05N	70.46E
Malka	58	53.20N	157.30E
Malkāpur	76	20.53N	76.12E
Malkara	54	40.53N	26.54E
Malko Târnovo	54	41.59N	27.32E
Mallaig	38	57.00N	5.50W
Mallala	94	34.26S	138.30E
Mallapunyah	92	16.59S	135.49E
Mallaranny	40	53.54N	9.49W
Mallawī	82	27.44N	30.50E
Mallersdorf	46	48.47N	12.16E
Mallery Lake ⊜	98	63.55N	98.25W
Mallet	114	25.55S	50.50W
Malligasta	114	29.11S	67.26W
Mallina	90	20.53S	118.02E
Mallnitz	46	46.59N	13.10E
Mallorca I	50	39.30N	3.00E
Mallow	40	52.08N	8.39W
Malm	44	64.04N	11.13E
Malmbäck	44	57.35N	14.28E
Malmberget	42	67.10N	20.40E
Malmédy	46	50.25N	6.02E
Malmesbury, S. Afr.	86	33.28S	18.44E
Malmesbury, Eng., U.K.	34	51.36N	2.06W
Malmesbury, Vale of ∨	34	51.22N	2.10W
Malmköping	44	59.08N	16.44E
Malmö	44	55.36N	13.00E
Malmöhus Län □[6]	44	55.45N	13.30E
Malmslätt	44	58.25N	15.30E
Malmyž	42	56.31N	50.41E
Maloelap I[1]	28	8.45N	171.03E
Maloja	48	46.24N	9.41E
Malojaroslavec	60	55.01N	36.28E
Malone	102	44.50N	74.17W
Malonga	84	10.24S	23.10E
Małopolska ◆[1]	46	50.10N	21.30E
Małowice	46	51.34N	15.27E
Måløy	44	61.56N	5.07E
Malpartida de Plasencia	50	39.59N	6.02W
Malpas, Austl.	94	34.43S	140.37E
Malpas, Eng., U.K.	34	53.01N	2.46W
Malpelo, Isla de I	110	3.59N	81.35W
Mālpura	76	26.17N	75.23E
Målselva ≃	42	69.14N	18.30E
Malta	102	39.38N	81.51W
Malta □[1]	30	35.50N	14.35E
Malta I	52	35.53N	14.27E
Malta Channel Ʊ	52	36.20N	15.00E
Maltahöhe	86	24.50S	17.00E
Maltahöhe □[5]	86	25.00S	16.30E
Maltby	36	53.26N	1.11W
Malte Brun, Mount ∧	96	43.34S	170.18E
Malton	36	54.08N	0.48W
Maluku □[4]	72	3.00S	126.00E
Maluku (Moluccas) II	68	2.00S	128.00E
Maluku, Laut (Molucca Sea) ⊤[2]	68	0.00	125.00E
Malu Mare	54	44.15N	23.51E
Malung	44	60.40N	13.44E
Malvern	102	40.41N	81.10W
Malvern Hills	94	24.29S	145.10E
Malvern Hills ✱[2]	34	52.05N	2.21W
Malvern Link	34	52.08N	2.18W
Malvinas	114	29.37S	58.59W
Malý Dunaj ≃	46	47.45N	18.09E
Malyj An'uj ≃	58	68.30N	160.49E
Malyje Karmakuly	56	72.23N	52.44E
Malyj Jenisej ≃	58	51.43N	94.26E
Malyj Kavkaz ✱	56	41.00N	44.35E
Malyj Tajmyr, ostrov I	58	78.08N	107.12E
Malyj Uzen' ≃	56	48.50N	49.39E
Mama	58	58.18N	112.54E
Mamadyš	42	55.44N	51.25E
Mamaia	54	44.15N	28.37E
Mamaku	96	38.06S	176.05E
Mamasa	72	2.56S	119.22E
Mamberamo ≃	92	1.26S	137.53E
Mambéré ≃	82	3.31N	16.03E
Mamburao	68	13.14N	120.35E
Mamers	48	48.21N	0.23E
Mamfe	80	5.46N	9.17E
Mammola	52	38.22N	16.15E
Mammoth	102	38.15N	81.22W
Mammoth Lakes	104	37.38N	118.58W
Mamonovo	60	54.28N	19.57E
Mamoré ≃	110	10.23S	65.23W
Mamou	80	10.23N	12.05W
Mampikony	87b	16.06S	47.38E
Mamry, Jezioro ⊜	46	54.08N	21.42E
Mamuju	72	2.41S	118.54E
Man, C. Iv.	80	7.24N	7.33W
Man, India	76	33.51N	78.32E
Man, Isle of →Isle of Man □[2]	30	54.15N	4.30W
Mana	105a	22.02N	159.46W
Mana ≃	110	5.44N	53.54W
Manacapuru	110	3.18S	60.37W
Manacle Point ›	34	50.03N	5.03W
Manacor	50	39.34N	3.12E
Manado	72	1.29N	124.51E
Managua	108	12.09N	86.17W
Managua, Lago de ⊜	108	12.20N	86.20W
Manaia	96	39.33S	174.08E
Manakara	87b	22.08S	48.01E
Manakau	96	40.43S	175.13E
Manakau ∧	96	42.14S	173.37E
Manāli	76	32.15N	77.10E
Manama →Al-Manāmah	78	26.13N	50.35E
Manam Island I	92	4.05S	145.05E
Mánamo, Caño ≃[1]	108	9.55N	62.16W
Mananara	87b	16.10S	49.46E
Mananjary	87b	21.13S	48.20E
Manapire ≃	108	8.40N	66.15W
Manapouri	96	45.34S	167.36E
Manapouri, Lake ⊜	96	45.30S	167.30E
Manas	62	44.18N	86.13E
Manās ≃	76	26.13N	90.38E
Manas Hu ⊜	62	45.45N	85.55E
Manāslu ∧	76	28.33N	84.33E
Manasquan	102	40.07N	74.02W
Manassas	102	38.45N	77.28W
Manatí, Col.	108	10.27N	74.58W
Manatí, P.R.	108	18.26N	66.29W
Manatuto	72	8.30S	126.01E
Manaus	110	3.08S	60.01W
Manāwar	76	22.14N	75.05E
Manawatu ≃	96	40.28S	175.13E
Mancelona	102	44.54N	85.03W
Mancha Real	50	37.47N	3.37W
Manche □[5]	48	49.00N	1.10W
Manchester, Eng., U.K.	36	53.30N	2.15W
Manchester, Ct., U.S.	102	41.46N	72.31W
Manchester, Ma., U.S.	102	42.34N	70.46W
Manchester, Mi., U.S.	102	42.09N	84.02W
Manchester, N.H., U.S.	102	42.59N	71.27W
Manchester, Oh., U.S.	102	38.41N	83.36W
Manchester, Vt., U.S.	102	43.09N	73.04W
Manchuria □[9]	62	47.00N	125.00E
Manciano	52	42.35N	11.31E
Mand ≃	78	28.11N	51.17E
Manda	84	10.28S	34.35E
Mandabe	87b	21.03S	44.55E
Mandaguaçu	114	23.20S	52.05W
Mandaguari	114	23.32S	51.42W
Mandal	44	58.02N	7.27E
Mandala, Puncak ∧	92	4.44S	140.20E
Mandalay	70	22.00N	96.05E
Mandalay □[5]	70	22.00N	96.00E
Mandalgov'	62	45.45N	106.12E
Mandalī	78	33.45N	45.32E
Mandalselva ≃	44	58.02N	7.28E
Mandan	100	46.49N	100.53W
Mandara Mountains ✱	80	10.45N	13.40E
Mandas	52	39.38N	9.07E
Mandasor	76	24.04N	75.04E
Mandeb, Bab el Ʊ	82	12.40N	43.20E
Mandeville, Jam.	108	18.02N	77.30W
Mandeville, N.Z.	96	46.00S	168.49E
Mandi	76	31.43N	76.55E
Mandi Bahāuddīn	76	32.35N	73.30E
Mandi Būrewāla	76	30.09N	72.41E
Mandi Dabwāli	76	29.58N	74.42E
Mandimba	84	14.21S	35.39E
Mandinga	108	9.27N	79.04W
Mandioli, Pulau I	68	0.44S	127.14E
Mandla	76	22.36N	80.23E
Mandora	90	19.44S	120.51E
Mandritsara	87b	15.50S	48.49E
Mandurah	90	32.32S	115.43E
Manduri	114	23.01S	49.19W
Manduria	52	40.24N	17.38E
Māndvi, India	76	21.15N	73.18E
Māndvi, India	76	22.50N	69.22E
Måne ≃	44	59.00N	9.40E
Manea	34	52.30N	0.11E
Manendragarh	76	23.13N	82.13E
Manerbio	52	45.21N	10.08E
Manfalūṭ	82	27.19N	30.58E
Manfredonia	52	41.38N	15.55E
Manfredonia, Golfo di C	52	41.35N	16.05E
Mangabeiras, Chapada das ✱[2]	110	10.00S	46.30W
Mangahao ≃	96	40.23S	175.50E
Mangaia I	28	21.55S	157.55W
Mangakino	96	38.22S	175.47E
Mangaldai	76	26.26N	92.02E
Mangalia	54	43.50N	28.35E
Mangalkot	76	23.33N	87.54E
Mangalore	74	12.52N	74.53E
Mangamahu	96	39.49S	175.22E
Mangapehi	96	38.31S	175.18E
Mangawān	76	24.41N	81.33E
Mangaweka	96	39.48S	175.47E
Mangaweka ∧	96	39.49S	176.05E
Mangchang	62	25.08N	107.31E
Mangerton Mountain ∧	40	51.57N	9.29W
Manggar	72	2.53S	108.16E
Mangkalihat, Tanjung ›	72	1.02N	118.59E
Mangochi	84	14.28S	35.16E
Mangoky ≃	87b	23.27S	45.13E
Mangole, Pulau I	72	1.53S	125.50E
Mangonui	96	34.59S	173.32E
Mangotsfield	34	51.28N	2.28W
Māngrol	76	21.07N	70.07E
Mangrove Cay I	108	24.10N	77.45W
Mangualde	50	40.36N	7.46W
Mangueira, Lagoa C	114	33.06S	52.48W
Mangueirinha	114	25.57S	52.09W
Mangya	62	37.40N	90.50E
Manhattan	100	39.11N	96.34W
Manhauçu	110	20.15S	42.02W
Maniago	52	46.10N	12.43E
Maniamba	84	12.43S	35.00E
Manica □[5]	86	19.00S	33.15E
Manicaland □[4]	86	19.30S	32.15E
Manicoré	110	5.49S	61.17W
Manicouagan ≃	98	49.11N	68.13W
Manicouagan, Réservoir ⊜[1]	98	51.30N	68.19W
Manihiki I[1]	28	10.24S	161.01W
Mānikpur	76	25.04N	81.07E
Manila	68	14.35N	121.00E
Manila Bay C	68	14.30N	120.45E
Manilla	94	30.45S	150.43E
Manily	58	62.29N	165.36E
Maningrida	92	12.03S	134.13E
Manipa, Selat Ʊ	92	3.20S	127.23E
Manipur □[8]	76	25.00N	94.00E
Manipur ≃	70	22.52N	94.05E
Manisa	30	38.36N	27.26E
Manistee ≃	102	44.22N	85.51W
Manitoba □[4]	98	54.00N	97.00W
Manitoba, Lake ⊜	98	51.00N	98.45W
Manitou, Lake ⊜	102	45.48N	82.00W
Manitoulin Island I	102	45.50N	82.20W
Manitowaning	102	45.45N	81.49W
Manitowoc	100	44.05N	87.39W
Maniwaki	102	46.23N	75.58W
Manizales	110	5.05N	75.32W
Manja	87b	21.26S	44.20E
Manjacaze	86	24.44S	33.53E
Manjimup	90	34.14S	116.09E
Mankato	100	44.09N	93.59W
Mankayane	86	26.42S	31.00E
Manlléu	50	42.00N	2.17E
Mann ≃	92	12.20S	134.07E
Mann, Mount ∧	90	25.59S	129.42E
Manna	72	4.27S	102.55E
Mannahill	94	32.26S	139.59E
Mannar, Gulf of C	74	8.30N	79.00E
Mannheim	46	49.29N	8.29E
Mannington	102	39.31N	80.20W
Manningtree	34	51.57N	1.04E
Mann Ranges ✱	90	26.00S	129.30E
Mannu ≃	52	40.50N	8.23E
Manoharpur	76	22.23N	85.12E
Manokwari	92	0.52S	134.05E
Manono	84	7.18S	27.25E
Manorbier	34	51.39N	4.48W
Manorhamilton	40	54.18N	8.10W
Manosque	48	43.50N	5.47E
Manouane, Lac ⊜	98	50.41N	70.45W
Manra I[1]	28	4.27S	171.15W
Manresa	50	41.44N	1.50E
Mānsa, India	76	29.59N	75.23E
Mānsa, India	76	23.26N	72.40E
Mansa, Zam.	84	11.12S	28.53E
Mānsehra	76	34.20N	73.12E
Mansel Island I	98	62.00N	79.50W
Mansfield, Austl.	94	37.03S	146.05E
Mansfield, Eng., U.K.	36	53.09N	1.11W
Mansfield, Ma., U.S.	102	42.02N	71.13W
Mansfield, Oh., U.S.	102	40.45N	82.30W
Mansfield, Pa., U.S.	102	41.48N	77.04W
Mansfield, Mount ∧	102	44.33N	72.49W
Mansfield Woodhouse	36	53.11N	1.12W
Mansle	48	45.53N	0.11E
Manta	110	0.57S	80.44W
Manteca	104	37.47N	121.12W
Mantekamuhu ⊜	76	34.30N	89.15E
Mantes-la-Jolie	48	48.59N	1.43E
Mantiqueira, Serra da ✱	110	22.00S	44.45W
Manton	102	44.24N	85.23W
Mantos Blancos	114	23.25S	70.05W
Mantova	52	45.09N	10.48E
Mänttä	44	62.02N	24.38E
Mantua, Cuba	108	22.17N	84.17W
Mantua →Mantova, It.	52	45.09N	10.48E
Mantua, Oh., U.S.	102	41.17N	81.13W
Manturovo	60	58.20N	44.46E
Mäntyharju	44	61.25N	26.53E
Mäntyluoto	44	61.35N	21.29E
Manú ≃	110	12.16S	70.51W
Manuae I[1], Cook Is.	28	19.21S	158.56W
Manuae I[1], Poly. fr.	28	16.30S	154.40W
Manua Islands II	28	14.13S	169.35W
Manuel Derqui	114	27.50S	58.48W
Manuel Ribas	114	24.31S	51.39W
Manuhangi I[1]	28	19.12S	141.16W
Manuherikia ≃	96	45.16S	169.24E
Manui, Pulau I	72	3.35S	123.08E
Manukau	96	37.02S	174.54E
Manulla ≃	40	53.57N	9.12W
Manunui	96	38.53S	175.20E
Manuoha ∧	96	38.39S	177.07E
Manus Island I	92	2.05S	147.00E
Manutahi	96	39.40S	174.24E
Manutuke	96	38.41S	177.55E
Manyara, Lake ⊜	84	3.35S	35.50E
Manyč ≃	56	47.15N	40.00E
Manyoni	84	5.45S	34.50E
Many Peaks	94	24.33S	151.23E
Manzanares	50	39.00N	3.22W
Manzanares ≃	50	40.19N	3.32W
Manzanillo, Cuba	108	20.21N	77.07W
Manzanillo, Méx.	106	19.03N	104.20W
Manzanillo, Punta ›	108	9.38N	79.32W
Manzanillo Bay C	108	19.45N	71.46W
Manzhouli	62	49.35N	117.22E
Manzini	86	26.30S	31.25E
Mao, Rep. Dom.	108	19.34N	71.05W
Mao, Tchad	82	14.07N	15.19E
Maoke, Pegunungan ✱	92	4.00S	138.00E
Maoming	70	21.39N	110.54E
Maouri, Dallol ∨	80	12.05N	3.32E
Mapi	92	7.07S	139.23E
Mapia, Kepulauan II	68	0.50N	134.20E
Maple ≃	102	42.59N	84.57W
Maple Creek	98	49.55N	109.27W
Maprik	92	3.40S	143.05E
Mapuera ≃	110	1.05S	57.02W
Maputo (Lourenço Marques)	86	25.58S	32.35E
Maputo □[5]	86	26.00S	32.25E
Maputo ≃	86	26.11S	32.42E
Maqueda	50	40.04N	4.22W
Maquela do Zombo	84	6.03S	15.07E
Maquinchao	112	41.15S	68.44W
Mar, Serra do •[4]	114	26.00S	48.00W
Mara	76	28.11N	94.06E
Mara ≃	84	1.31S	33.56E
Marabá	110	5.21S	49.07W
Maracá, Ilha de I	110	2.05N	50.25W
Maracaí	114	22.36S	50.39W
Maracaibo	110	10.40N	71.37W
Maracaibo, Lago de ⊜	110	9.50N	71.30W
Maracay	110	10.15N	67.36W
Marādah	82	29.14N	19.13E
Maradi	80	13.29N	7.06E
Marāgheh	78	37.23N	46.13E
Maragogipe	110	12.46S	38.55W
Marahuaca, Cerro ∧	110	3.34N	65.27W
Marajó, Baía de C	110	1.00S	48.30W
Marajó, Ilha de I	110	1.00S	49.30W
Marakabei	86	29.32S	28.09E
Maralal	84	1.06N	36.42E
Maram	76	25.25N	94.06E
Marampa	80	8.41N	12.28W
Maramureş □[6]	54	47.40N	24.00E
Maramureşului, Munţii ✱	54	47.50N	24.45E
Maran	72	3.35N	102.46E
Maranalgo	90	29.23S	117.48E
Maranboy	92	14.30S	132.45E
Maranchón	50	41.03N	2.12W
Marand	78	38.26N	45.46E
Marang	72	5.12N	103.13E
Maranguape	110	3.53S	38.40W
Maranoa ≃	94	27.50S	148.37E
Marano [di Napoli]	52	40.54N	14.11E
Marañón ≃	110	4.30S	73.27W
Marans	48	46.19N	1.00W
Marapanim	110	0.42S	47.42W
Mararoa ≃	96	45.34S	167.36E
Maraş	78	37.36N	36.55E
Mărăşeşti	54	45.52N	27.14E
Maratea	52	39.59N	15.45E
Marathon, Austl.	94	20.49S	143.34E
Marathon, On., Can.	98	48.43N	86.23W
Marathón, Ellás	54	38.10N	23.58E
Marathon, N.Y., U.S.	102	42.26N	76.01W
Marau	114	28.27S	52.12W
Maravilha	114	26.47S	53.09W
Marawī	82	18.29N	31.49E
Marayes	114	31.29S	67.20W
Marazion	34	50.08N	5.28W
Marbella	50	36.31N	4.53W
Marble Bar	90	21.11S	119.44E
Marble Hall	86	24.57S	29.13E
Marblehead	102	41.32N	82.44W
Marburg	86	30.44S	30.26E
Marburg an der Lahn	46	50.49N	8.46E
Marca, Ponta da ›	84	16.31S	11.42E
Marcal ≃	46	47.41N	17.32E
Marcali	46	46.35N	17.25E
Marcaria	52	45.07N	10.32E
Marcelino Ramos	114	27.28S	51.54W
March	34	52.33N	0.06E
March (Morava) ≃	46	48.10N	16.59E
Marcha	58	60.37N	123.18E
Marcha ≃	58	63.28N	118.50E
Marche □[4]	52	43.30N	13.15E
Marche □[9]	48	46.05N	2.10E
Marche-en-Famenne	46	50.12N	5.20E
Marchegg	46	48.17N	16.55E
Marchena	50	37.20N	5.24W
Marchinbar Island I	92	11.15S	136.45E
Mar Chiquita, Laguna C	114	37.37S	57.24W
Mar Chiquita, Laguna ⊜	114	30.42S	62.36W
Marcigny	48	46.17N	4.02E
Marcillac-Vallon	48	44.29N	2.28E
Marcos Juárez	114	32.42S	62.06W
Marcos Paz	114	34.46S	58.50W
Marcus Baker, Mount ∧	98	61.26N	147.45W
Marcy, Mount ∧	102	44.07N	73.56W
Marda	90	30.13S	119.17E
Mardalsfossen ∟	44	62.30N	8.07E
Mardān	76	34.12N	72.02E
Mar del Plata	114	38.00S	57.33W
Marden	34	51.10N	0.29E
Mardie	90	21.11S	115.57E
Mardin	78	37.18N	40.44E
Maré I	28	21.30S	168.00E
Mare, Muntele ∧	54	46.29N	23.14E
Marechal Cândido Rondon	114	24.34S	54.04W
Maree, Loch ⊜	38	57.42N	5.30W
Mareeba	94	17.00S	145.26E
Mareetsane	86	26.09S	25.25E
Maremma ◆[1]	52	42.30N	11.30E
Marennes	48	45.50N	1.06W
Marettimo, Isola I	52	37.58N	12.03E
Mareuil-sur-Belle	48	45.28N	0.28E
Mar Forest ◆[3]	38	57.00N	3.35W
Margam	34	51.34N	3.44W
Marganec	56	47.38N	34.40E
Margaret ≃	90	18.10S	125.37E
Margaret Creek ≃	94	29.26S	137.07E
Margaret River, Austl.	90	33.57S	115.04E
Margaret River, Austl.	90	18.38S	126.52E
Margaretville	102	42.08N	74.38W
Margarita, Isla de I	110	11.00N	64.00W
Margarita Belén	114	27.16S	58.58W
Margate, S. Afr.	86	30.55S	30.15E
Margate, Eng., U.K.	34	51.24N	1.24E
Margate City	102	39.19N	74.30W
Margecany	46	48.54N	21.01E
Margeride, Monts de la ✱	48	44.50N	3.30E
Mārgherita	76	27.17N	95.41E
Margherita di Savoia	52	41.23N	16.09E
Margherita Peak ∧	84	0.22N	29.51E
Marghita	54	47.21N	22.21E
Margilan	56	40.28N	71.44E
Margonin	46	52.59N	17.05E
Mārgow, Dasht-e ◆[2]	78	30.45N	63.10E
Maria, Îles II	28	21.48S	154.41W
María Elena	114	22.21S	69.40W
Maria Gail	46	46.36N	13.52E
Mariager	44	56.39N	10.00E
Maria Island I	94	42.39S	148.04E
María la Baja	108	9.59N	75.17W
Mariana Basin +[1]	28	17.30N	145.00E
Mariana Islands II	68	16.00N	145.30E
Marianao	108	23.05N	82.26W
Mariana Ridge +[3]	28	17.00N	146.00E
Mariana Trench +[1]	28	15.00N	147.30E
Mariāni	76	26.40N	94.20E
Marian Lake ⊜	98	63.00N	116.10W
Mariannelund	44	57.37N	15.34E
Mariano I. Loza	114	29.22S	58.12W
Mariano Moreno	114	38.44S	70.01W
Mariánské Lázně	46	49.59N	12.43E
Marías, Islas II	106	21.25N	106.28W
María Teresa	114	34.01S	61.54W
Mariato, Punta ›	106	7.13N	80.53W
Maria van Diemen, Cape ›	96	34.28S	172.39E
Mariazell	46	47.47N	15.19E
Maribo	44	54.46N	11.31E
Maribor	52	46.33N	15.39E
Marica	54	42.02N	25.50E
Marica (Évros) (Meriç) ≃	54	40.52N	26.12E
Marico ≃	86	24.12S	26.52E
Maricopa	104	35.03N	119.24W
Maricunga, Salar de ≚	114	26.55S	69.05W
Marie Byrd Land ◆[1]	18	80.00S	120.00W
Mariefred	44	59.16N	17.13E
Marie-Galante I	108	15.56N	61.16W
Mariehamn	44	60.06N	19.57E
Marienbad →Mariánské Lázně	46	49.59N	12.43E
Marienburg →Malbork	46	54.02N	19.01E
Mariental	86	24.36S	17.59E
Mariental □[5]	86	25.00S	19.00E
Marienville	102	41.28N	79.07W
Mariestad	44	58.43N	13.51E
Marietta, Ga., U.S.	100	33.57N	84.33W
Marietta, Oh., U.S.	102	39.24N	81.27W
Marieville	102	45.26N	73.10W
Mariga ≃	80	9.40N	5.55E
Marignane	48	43.25N	5.13E
Marigot, Dom.	108	15.32N	61.18W
Marigot, Guad.	108	18.04N	63.06W
Mariinsk	58	56.13N	87.45E
Marikana	86	25.42S	27.30E
Marília	114	22.13S	49.56W
Marimba	84	8.28S	17.08E
Marín	50	42.23N	8.42W
Marina di Gioiosa Ionica	52	38.18N	16.20E
Marina di Ravenna	52	44.29N	12.17E
Marinduque Island I	68	13.24N	121.58E
Marine City	102	42.43N	82.29W
Marinette	100	45.06N	87.37W
Maringá	114	23.25S	51.55W
Maringa ≃	84	1.14N	19.48E
Marinha Grande	50	39.45N	8.56W
Marino	52	41.46N	12.39E
Marinskij Posad	42	56.07N	47.43E
Marion, In., U.S.	100	40.33N	85.39W
Marion, Mi., U.S.	102	44.06N	85.08W
Marion, Oh., U.S.	102	40.35N	83.07W
Marion, Lake ⊜[1]	100	33.30N	80.25W
Marion Bay C	94	42.48S	147.55E
Marion Downs	94	23.22S	139.39E
Marion Reef +[2]	94	19.10S	152.17E
Marióplis	114	26.20S	52.33W
Mariposa	104	37.29N	119.57W
Mariscal Estigarribia	114	22.02S	60.38W
Maritime Alps ✱	48	44.15N	7.10E
Mariusa, Caño ≃[1]	108	9.43N	61.26W
Marka	82	1.43N	44.53E
Markaryd	44	56.26N	13.36E
Markdale	102	44.19N	80.39W
Markerwaard ◆[1]	46	52.33N	5.15E
Market Bosworth	34	52.37N	1.24W
Market Deeping	34	52.41N	0.19W
Market Drayton	34	52.54N	2.29W
Market Harborough	34	52.29N	0.55W
Market Lavington	34	51.18N	1.59W
Market Rasen	36	53.24N	0.21W
Market Weighton	36	53.52N	0.40W
Markfield	34	52.40N	1.17W
Markham	102	43.52N	79.16W
Markham Bay C	98	63.30N	71.48W
Markinch	38	56.12N	3.08W
Markle	102	40.50N	85.20W
Markleeville	104	38.41N	119.46W
Markovo	58	64.40N	170.25E
Marks	56	51.42N	46.46E
Marks Tey	34	51.52N	0.47E
Marktheidenfeld	46	49.50N	9.36E
Marktoberdorf	46	47.47N	10.37E
Marktredwitz	46	50.00N	12.06E
Marlboro	102	41.36N	73.58W
Marlborough, Austl.	94	22.49S	149.53E
Marlborough, Eng., U.K.	34	51.26N	1.43W
Marlborough, Ma., U.S.	102	42.20N	71.33W
Marlborough Downs ✱[1]	34	51.30N	1.45W
Marldon	34	50.28N	3.36W
Marle	48	49.44N	3.46E
Marlette	102	43.19N	83.04W
Marlinton	102	38.13N	80.05W
Marlow	34	51.35N	0.48W
Marma	44	61.16N	16.52E
Marmande	48	44.30N	0.10E
Marmara, Sea of →Marmara Denizi ⊤[2]	54	40.40N	28.15E
Marmara Denizi (Sea of Marmara) ⊤[2]	54	40.40N	28.15E
Marmelos, Rio dos ≃	110	6.06S	61.46W
Marmet	102	38.14N	81.34W
Marmora	102	44.29N	77.41W
Marnay	48	47.17N	5.46E
Marne	46	53.57N	9.00E
Marne □[5]	48	48.55N	4.10E
Marne ≃	48	48.49N	2.24E
Marne au Rhin, Canal de la ⌶	48	48.35N	7.47E
Marnhull	34	50.58N	2.18W
Maroa	110	2.43N	67.33W

Symbols in the Index entries are identified on page 122.

Maro-Mick

Name	Page	Lat. °′	Long. °′
Maroantsetra	87b	15.26 S	49.44 E
Maromme	48	49.28 N	1.02 E
Maromokotro ∧	87b	14.01 S	48.59 E
Marondera	86	18.10 S	31.36 E
Maroni ≃	110	5.45 N	53.58 W
Maros (Mureş) ≃	54	46.15 N	20.13 E
Marotiri, Îles II	28	27.55 S	143.26 W
Maroua	80	10.36 N	14.20 E
Marovoay	87b	16.06 S	46.39 E
Marple	36	53.24 N	2.03 W
Marquard	86	28.54 S	27.28 E
Marquesas Keys II	108	24.34 N	82.08 W
Marquette	100	46.32 N	87.23 W
Marquina-Jemein	50	43.16 N	2.30 W
Marquise	48	50.49 N	1.42 E
Marquises, Îles II	18	9.00 S	139.30 W
Marra Creek ≃	94	30.05 S	147.05 E
Marradi	52	44.04 N	11.37 E
Marrah, Jabal ∧	82	13.04 N	24.21 E
Marrakech	80	31.38 N	8.00 W
Marrawah	94	40.56 S	144.41 E
Marree	94	29.39 S	138.04 E
Marromeu	86	18.20 S	35.56 E
Mars	102	40.41 N	80.00 W
Marsā al-Burayqah	82	30.25 N	19.34 E
Marsabit	82	2.20 N	37.59 E
Marsala	52	37.48 N	12.26 E
Marsā Maṭrūḥ	82	31.21 N	27.14 E
Marsciano	52	42.54 N	12.20 E
Marsden	94	33.45 S	147.32 E
Marseille	48	43.18 N	5.24 E
Marseille-en-Beauvaisis	48	49.35 N	1.57 E
Marsfjället ∧	42	65.05 N	15.28 E
Marshall, Liber.	80	6.10 N	10.23 W
Marshall, Mi., U.S.	102	42.16 N	84.57 W
Marshall, Mo., U.S.	100	39.07 N	93.11 W
Marshall, Tx., U.S.	100	32.32 N	94.22 W
Marshall, Va., U.S.	102	38.51 N	77.51 W
Marshall ≃	94	22.59 S	136.59 E
Marshall Bennett Islands II	92	8.50 S	151.50 E
Marshall Islands □[2]	28	11.00 N	168.00 E
Marshall Islands II	28	9.00 N	168.00 E
Marshalltown	100	42.02 N	92.54 W
Marshfield	34	51.28 N	2.19 W
Marsh Harbour	108	26.33 N	77.03 W
Marshyhope Creek ≃	102	38.32 N	75.45 W
Marsing	104	43.32 N	116.48 W
Marske-by-the-Sea	36	54.36 N	1.01 W
Märsta	44	59.37 N	17.51 E
Marstal	44	54.51 N	10.31 E
Marston Moor ≚	36	53.57 N	1.17 W
Marstrand	44	57.53 N	11.35 E
Martaban	70	16.32 N	97.37 E
Martaban, Gulf of C	70	16.30 N	97.00 E
Martapura, Indon.	72	3.25 S	114.51 E
Martapura, Indon.	72	4.19 S	104.22 E
Marteg ≃	34	52.20 N	3.33 W
Martel	48	44.56 N	1.37 E
Marthaguy Creek ≃	94	30.16 S	147.35 E
Martham	34	52.42 N	1.38 E
Martha's Vineyard I	102	41.25 N	70.40 W
Martí	108	21.09 N	77.27 W
Martigny	48	46.06 N	7.04 E
Martigues	48	43.24 N	5.03 E
Martin	46	49.05 N	18.55 E
Martín ≃	50	41.18 N	0.19 W
Martin, Isle I	38	57.55 N	5.14 W
Martina Franca	52	40.42 N	17.21 E
Martinborough	96	41.13 S	175.28 E
Mărtineşti	54	45.30 N	27.18 E
Martinez	104	38.01 N	122.07 W
Martinique □[2]	106	14.40 N	61.00 W
Martinniemi	44	65.13 N	25.18 E
Martinsberg	46	48.22 N	15.09 E
Martinsburg, Pa., U.S.	102	40.18 N	78.19 W
Martinsburg, W.V., U.S.	102	39.27 N	77.57 W
Martins Ferry	102	40.05 N	80.43 W
Martinsville	100	36.41 N	79.52 W
Martin Vaz, Ilhas II	112	20.30 S	28.51 W
Martock	34	50.59 N	2.46 W
Marton	96	40.05 S	175.23 E
Martos	50	37.43 N	3.58 W
Martre, Lac la ⊜	98	63.15 N	117.55 W
Martti	42	67.28 N	28.28 E
Marudi	72	4.11 N	114.19 E
Marugame	64	34.17 N	133.47 E
Maruia	96	42.11 S	172.13 E
Maruia ≃	96	41.47 S	172.12 E
Marungu ⋏	84	7.42 S	30.00 E
Maruoka	64	36.09 N	136.16 E
Marutea I[1]	28	17.00 S	143.10 W
Marv Dasht	78	29.50 N	52.40 E
Marvejols	48	44.33 N	3.18 E
Marvel Loch	90	31.28 S	119.28 E
Marviken	44	58.34 N	16.51 E
Mārwār	76	25.44 N	73.36 E
Mary	78	37.36 N	61.50 E
Mary ≃	94	25.26 S	152.55 E
Mary Anne Group II	90	21.13 S	115.32 E
Maryborough, Austl.	94	25.32 S	152.42 E
Maryborough, Austl.	94	37.03 S	143.45 E
Maryborough →Port Laoise	40	53.02 N	7.17 W
Marydale	86	29.23 S	22.05 E
Mary Kathleen	94	20.49 S	139.58 E
Maryland □[3]	100	39.00 N	76.45 W
Marypark	38	57.26 N	3.21 W
Maryport	36	54.43 N	3.30 W
Marys ≃	104	41.04 N	115.16 W
Marys Creek ≃	104	42.18 N	115.48 W
Marysville, Ca., U.S.	104	39.08 N	121.35 W
Marysville, Mi., U.S.	102	42.54 N	82.29 W
Marysville, Oh., U.S.	102	40.14 N	83.22 W
Marysville, Pa., U.S.	102	40.20 N	76.55 W
Maryville	100	40.20 N	94.52 W
Marywell	38	57.02 N	2.42 W
Marzūq	82	25.55 N	13.55 E
Marzūq, Ṣaḥrā' ◆[2]	82	24.30 N	13.00 E
Masai Steppe ⋏[1]	84	4.45 S	37.00 E
Masaka	84	0.20 S	31.44 E
Masalembo-besar I	72	5.34 S	114.26 E
Masamba	72	2.32 S	120.20 E
Masan	62	35.11 N	128.32 E
Masasi	84	10.43 S	38.48 E
Masatepe	108	11.55 N	86.09 W
Masaya	108	11.58 N	86.06 W
Masbate	68	12.22 N	123.36 E
Masbate Island I	68	12.15 N	123.30 E
Mascarene Basin ⊹[1]	26	15.00 S	56.00 E
Mascarene Islands II	87c	21.00 S	57.00 E
Mascarene Plateau ⊹[3]	26	10.00 S	60.00 E
Mascasín	114	31.22 S	66.59 W
Maseru	86	29.28 S	27.30 E
Mashaba Mountains ⋏	86	18.45 S	30.32 E
Mashābih I	78	25.37 N	36.29 E
Masham	36	54.13 N	1.40 W
Mashan	70	23.50 N	108.16 E
Masherbrum ∧	76	35.43 N	76.18 E
Mashhad	78	36.18 N	59.36 E
Mashike	64a	43.51 N	141.31 E
Mashiko	64	36.28 N	140.06 E
Māshkel (Māshkīd) ≃	78	28.02 N	63.25 E
Māshkel, Hāmūn-i- ⊜	78	28.15 N	63.00 E
Māshkīd (Māshkel) ≃	78	28.02 N	63.25 E
Mashonaland South □[4]	86	18.15 S	30.45 E
Mashra'ur-Raqq	82	8.25 N	29.16 E
Mashū-ko ⊜	64a	43.35 N	144.32 E
Masi Manimba	84	4.46 S	17.55 E
Masindi	84	1.41 N	31.43 E
Maṣīrah, Khalīj al- C	74	20.10 N	58.15 E
Masjed Soleymān	78	31.58 N	49.18 E
Mask, Lough ⊜	40	53.35 N	9.20 W
Masku	44	60.34 N	22.06 E
Masoala, Presqu'île de ≻[1]	87b	15.40 S	50.12 E
Mason, Mi., U.S.	102	42.34 N	84.26 W
Mason, Oh., U.S.	102	39.21 N	84.18 W
Mason, W.V., U.S.	102	39.01 N	82.01 W
Mason, Lake ⊜	90	27.39 S	119.34 E
Mason Bay C	96	46.56 S	167.44 E
Mason City	100	43.09 N	93.12 W
Masqaṭ (Muscat)	78	23.37 N	58.35 E
Massa	52	44.01 N	10.09 E
Massachusetts □[3]	100	42.15 N	71.50 W
Massachusetts Bay C	102	42.20 N	70.50 W
Massacre Lake ⊜	104	41.39 N	119.35 W
Massafra	52	40.35 N	17.07 E
Massa Marittima	52	43.03 N	10.53 E
Massangena	86	21.32 S	32.57 E
Massarosa	52	43.52 N	10.20 E
Massawa →Mitsiwa	82	15.38 N	39.28 E
Massena	102	44.55 N	74.53 W
Massenya	82	11.24 N	16.10 E
Masseube	48	43.26 N	0.35 E
Massey	102	46.12 N	82.05 W
Massiac	48	45.15 N	3.12 E
Massif Central →Central, Massif ⋏	48	45.00 N	3.10 E
Massillon	102	40.48 N	81.32 W
Massina ◆[1]	80	14.30 N	5.00 W
Massinga	86	23.20 S	35.25 E
Massive, Mount ∧	100	39.12 N	106.28 W
Maštaga	78	40.32 N	50.00 E
Masterton	96	40.57 S	175.40 E
Mastung	76	29.48 N	66.51 E
Masuda	64	34.40 N	131.51 E
Maszewo	46	53.29 N	15.02 E
Mat ≃	54	41.39 N	19.34 E
Matabeleland North □[4]	86	19.00 S	27.15 E
Matabeleland South □[4]	86	21.00 S	29.15 E
Matabuena	50	41.10 N	3.40 W
Matachel ≃	50	38.50 N	6.17 W
Matadi	84	5.49 S	13.27 E
Matagalpa	108	12.55 N	85.55 W
Mataiva I[1]	28	14.53 S	148.40 W
Matakana, Austl.	94	33.00 S	145.54 E
Matakana, N.Z.	96	36.21 S	174.43 E
Matakana Island I	96	37.35 S	176.05 E
Matakitaki ≃	96	41.48 S	172.19 E
Matam	80	15.40 N	13.15 W
Matamata	96	37.49 S	175.47 E
Matamoras	102	41.22 N	74.42 W
Matamoros	106	25.53 N	97.30 W
Matamoros de la Laguna	106	25.32 N	103.15 W
Matandu ≃	84	8.45 S	39.19 E
Matane	98	48.51 N	67.32 W
Matangi	96	37.49 S	175.25 E
Matanzas	108	23.03 N	81.35 W
Matapu	96	39.29 S	174.14 E
Mataquito ≃	114	34.59 S	72.12 W
Matara	74	5.56 N	80.33 E
Mataram	72	8.35 S	116.07 E
Mataranka	92	14.56 S	133.07 E
Mataró	50	41.32 N	2.27 E
Matarraña ≃	50	41.14 N	0.22 E
Mätäsvaara	44	63.26 N	29.36 E
Matata	96	37.53 S	176.45 E
Matatiele	86	30.24 S	28.43 E
Mataura	96	46.11 S	168.52 E
Mataura ≃	96	46.34 S	168.43 E
Matawai	96	38.21 S	177.32 E
Matehuala	106	23.39 N	100.39 W
Matelica	52	43.15 N	13.00 E
Matera	52	40.40 N	16.37 E
Mátészalka	46	47.57 N	22.19 E
Matfors	44	62.21 N	17.02 E
Matha	48	45.52 N	0.19 W
Mathematicians Seamounts ⊹[3]	22	15.00 N	111.00 W
Mather	102	39.56 N	80.04 W
Mathry	34	51.57 N	5.05 W
Mathura	76	27.30 N	77.41 E
Matícora ≃	108	11.03 N	71.09 W
Matiere	96	38.45 S	175.06 E
Matignon	48	48.36 N	2.18 W
Matinicus Island I	102	43.54 N	68.55 W
Matlock	36	53.08 N	1.32 W
Mato, Cerro ∧	110	7.15 N	65.14 W
Matočkin Šar	56	73.16 N	56.27 E
Matočkin Šar, proliv ⊔	56	73.20 N	55.21 E
Mato Grosso	110	15.00 S	59.57 W
Mato Grosso, Planalto do ⋏[1]	110	15.30 S	56.00 W
Matosinhos	50	41.11 N	8.42 W
Matou, T'aiwan	66	23.11 N	120.14 E
Matou, Zhg.	66	25.14 N	118.22 E
Matoury	110	4.51 N	52.20 W
Mátra ⋏	46	47.55 N	20.00 E
Maṭraḥ	78	23.38 N	58.34 E
Matrei in Osttirol	46	47.00 N	12.32 E
Matsudo	64	35.47 N	139.54 E
Matsue	64	35.28 N	133.04 E
Matsumae	64	41.26 N	140.07 E
Matsumoto	64	36.14 N	137.58 E
Matsusaka	64	34.34 N	136.32 E
Matsushima	64	38.22 N	141.04 E
Matsu Tao I	66	26.09 N	119.56 E
Matsutō	64	36.31 N	136.34 E
Matsuura	64	33.22 N	129.42 E
Matsuyama	64	33.50 N	132.45 E
Mattagami ≃	98	50.43 N	81.29 W
Mattāncheri	74	9.59 N	76.16 E
Mattaponi ≃	102	37.51 N	77.10 W
Mattawa	102	46.19 N	78.42 W
Mattawa ≃	102	46.19 N	78.43 W
Mattawamkeag	102	45.30 N	68.21 W
Mattawamkeag ≃	102	45.30 N	68.24 W
Matterhorn ∧, Europe	48	45.59 N	7.43 E
Matterhorn ∧, Nv., U.S.	104	41.49 N	115.23 W
Mattersburg	46	47.44 N	16.25 E
Matthew Town	108	20.57 N	73.40 W
Mattighofen	46	48.06 N	13.09 E
Mattishall	34	52.39 N	1.02 E
Mattole ≃	104	40.18 N	124.21 W
Mattoon	100	39.28 N	88.22 W
Mattydale	102	43.05 N	76.08 W
Matu	72	2.41 N	111.32 E
Maturín	110	9.45 N	63.11 W
Maú ≃	110	3.33 N	59.51 W
Maúa	84	13.51 S	37.10 E
Mau Aimma	76	25.42 N	81.55 E
Maubeuge	48	50.17 N	3.58 E
Ma-ubin	70	16.44 N	95.39 E
Mauchline	38	55.31 N	4.24 W
Maud	38	57.31 N	2.06 W
Maud, Point ≻	90	23.06 S	113.45 E
Maudaha	76	25.41 N	80.07 E
Maude	94	34.28 S	144.18 E
Maués	110	3.24 S	57.42 W
Mauganj	76	24.41 N	81.53 E
Maughold	36	54.18 N	4.17 W
Maug Islands II	68	20.01 N	145.13 E
Maui I	105a	20.45 N	156.15 W
Mauke I	28	20.09 S	157.23 W
Maule □[4]	114	35.30 S	71.30 W
Maule ≃	114	35.19 S	72.25 W
Maule, Laguna del ⊜	114	36.04 S	70.30 W
Mauléon	48	46.56 N	0.45 W
Mauléon-Licharre	48	43.14 N	0.53 W
Maumee	102	41.33 N	83.39 W
Maumee ≃	102	41.42 N	83.28 W
Maumere	72	8.37 S	122.14 E
Maun	86	20.00 S	23.25 E
Mauna Kea ∧[1]	105a	19.50 N	155.28 W
Maunaloa	105a	21.08 N	157.13 W
Mauna Loa ∧[1]	105a	19.29 N	155.36 W
Maunath Bhanjan	76	25.57 N	83.33 E
Maungatapere	96	35.45 S	174.12 E
Maungaturoto	96	36.06 S	174.22 E
Maunoir, Lac ⊜	98	67.30 N	125.00 W
Maupihaa I[1]	28	16.50 S	153.55 W
Mau Rānīpur	76	25.15 N	79.08 E
Maure-de-Bretagne	48	47.54 N	1.59 W
Maures ⋏	48	43.16 N	6.23 E
Mauriac	48	45.13 N	2.20 E
Maurice, Lake ⊜	90	29.28 S	130.58 E
Mauriceville	96	40.47 S	175.42 E
Mauritania (Mauritanie) □[1]	80	20.00 N	12.00 W
Mauritius □[1]	84	20.17 S	57.33 E
Mauritius I	87c	20.17 S	57.33 E
Mauron	48	48.05 N	2.18 W
Maurs	48	44.43 N	2.11 E
Maury ≃	102	37.50 N	79.25 W
Maury Channel ⊔	98	75.44 N	94.40 W
Mauterndorf	46	47.08 N	13.40 E
Mauthausen	46	48.14 N	14.32 E
Mauvezin	48	43.44 N	0.55 E
Mavinga	84	15.50 S	20.21 E
Maw-Daung Pass)(	70	11.47 N	99.39 E
Mawgan	34	50.06 N	5.06 W
Maw Taung ∧	70	11.39 N	99.35 E
Maxiang	66	24.41 N	118.15 E
Maxixe	86	23.51 S	35.21 E
Maxville	102	45.17 N	74.51 W
Maxwell	104	39.16 N	122.11 W
Maxwell Bay C	98	74.35 N	89.00 W
May ≃	90	17.07 S	123.50 E
May, Cape ≻[1]	102	38.58 N	74.55 W
May, Isle of I	38	56.11 N	2.34 W
Mayaguana I	108	22.23 N	72.57 W
Mayaguana Passage ⊔	108	22.32 N	73.15 W
Mayagüez	108	18.12 N	67.09 W
Mayari	108	20.40 N	75.41 W
Maybole	36	55.21 N	4.41 W
Maydena	94	42.55 S	146.30 E
Mayen	46	50.19 N	7.13 E
Mayenne	48	48.18 N	0.37 W
Mayenne □[5]	48	48.05 N	0.40 W
Mayenne ≃	48	47.30 N	0.33 W
Mayfield, N.Z.	96	43.49 S	171.25 E
Mayfield, Eng., U.K.	34	53.01 N	1.45 W
Mayfield, Eng., U.K.	34	51.01 N	0.15 E
Mayfield, Scot., U.K.	38	55.52 N	3.02 W
Mayfield, Ky., U.S.	100	36.44 N	88.38 W
May Inlet C	98	76.15 N	100.45 W
Maykop →Majkop	56	44.35 N	40.07 E
Mayland	34	51.39 N	0.47 E
Maymyo	70	22.02 N	96.28 E
Mayne ≃	94	23.34 S	141.18 E
Maynooth	40	53.23 N	6.35 W
Mayo	98	63.35 N	135.54 W
Mayo □[6]	40	53.50 N	9.30 W
Mayola ≃	36	54.45 N	6.31 W
Mayon Volcano ∧[1]	68	13.15 N	123.41 E
Mayor Buratovich	114	39.15 S	62.37 W
Mayor Island I	96	37.18 S	176.16 E
Mayotte □[2]	84	12.50 S	45.10 E
May Pen	108	17.58 N	77.14 W
Mayrhofen	46	47.10 N	11.52 E
Maysān □[4]	78	32.00 N	47.00 E
Mays Landing	102	39.27 N	74.43 W
Maysville	102	38.38 N	83.44 W
Mayumba	84	3.25 S	10.39 E
Māyūram	74	11.06 N	79.40 E
Mayville, Mi., U.S.	102	43.20 N	83.21 W
Mayville, N.Y., U.S.	102	42.15 N	79.30 W
Mayville, N.D., U.S.	100	47.29 N	97.19 W
Maza	114	36.50 S	63.19 W
Mazabuka	84	15.51 S	27.46 E
Mazagão	110	0.07 S	51.17 W
Mazamet	48	43.30 N	2.24 E
Mazara, Val di ◆[1]	52	37.50 N	13.00 E
Mazara del Vallo	52	37.39 N	12.35 E
Mazār-e Sharīf	76	36.42 N	67.06 E
Mazarrón	50	37.36 N	1.19 W
Mazarrón, Golfo de C	50	37.30 N	1.18 W
Mazaruni ≃	110	6.25 N	58.38 W
Mazatenango	106	14.32 N	91.30 W
Mazatlán	106	23.13 N	106.25 W
Mazoe ≃	84	16.32 S	33.25 E
Mazsalaca	60	57.52 N	25.03 E
Mazury ◆[1]	46	53.45 N	21.00 E
Mbabane	86	26.18 S	31.06 E
Mbaïki	82	3.53 N	18.00 E
Mbala	84	8.50 S	31.22 E
Mbale	84	1.05 N	34.10 E
Mbalmayo	80	3.31 N	11.30 E
Mbamba Bay	84	11.17 S	34.46 E
Mbandaka (Coquilhatville)	84	0.04 N	18.16 E
M'banza Congo	84	6.16 S	14.15 E
Mbanza-Ngungu	84	5.15 S	14.52 E
Mbarara	84	0.37 S	30.39 E
Mbari ≃	82	4.34 N	22.43 E
Mbashe ≃	86	32.15 S	28.53 E
Mbeya	84	8.54 S	33.27 E
Mbinda	84	2.00 S	12.55 E
Mbini	84	1.35 N	9.37 E
Mbomou (Bomu) ≃	82	4.08 N	22.26 E
Mbout	80	16.02 N	12.35 W
Mbuji-Mayi (Bakwanga)	84	6.09 S	23.38 E
Mburucuyá	114	28.03 S	58.14 W
M'Clintock Channel ⊔	98	72.00 N	102.00 W
M'Clure Strait ⊔	98	74.30 N	116.00 W
Mead, Lake ⊜[1]	104	36.05 N	114.25 W
Meadie, Loch ⊜	38	58.20 N	4.33 W
Meadow Valley Wash ∨	104	36.39 N	114.35 W
Meadville	102	41.38 N	80.09 W
Meaford	102	44.36 N	80.35 W
Me-akan-dake ∧	64a	43.23 N	144.01 E
Mealasta Isle I	38	58.05 N	7.08 W
Mealhada	50	40.22 N	8.27 W
Méan	46	50.22 N	5.20 E
Meandarra	94	27.20 S	149.53 E
Meander River	98	59.02 N	117.42 W
Measham	34	52.43 N	1.29 W
Meath □[6]	40	53.35 N	6.40 W
Meath □[9]	40	53.40 N	7.00 W
Meaux	48	48.57 N	2.52 E
Mecca →Makkah	74	21.27 N	39.49 E
Mechanic Falls	102	44.06 N	70.23 W
Mechanicsburg	102	40.04 N	83.33 W
Mechanicville	102	42.54 N	73.41 W
Mechelen	46	51.02 N	4.28 E
Mechita	114	35.04 S	60.24 W
Mechlin →Mechelen	46	51.02 N	4.28 E
Meckering	90	31.38 S	117.01 E
Mecklenburg □[9]	46	53.30 N	13.00 E
Mecklenburger Bucht C	46	54.20 N	11.40 E
Mecsek ⋏	46	46.15 N	18.05 E
Meda	50	40.58 N	7.16 W
Medan	70	3.35 N	98.40 E
Médanos	114	38.50 S	62.41 W
Medanosa, Punta ≻	112	48.06 S	65.55 W
Mede	52	45.06 N	8.44 E
Medellín	110	6.15 N	75.35 W
Medelpad □[9]	44	62.40 N	16.15 E
Médenine	80	33.21 N	10.30 E
Medevi	44	58.40 N	14.57 E
Medford	100	42.19 N	122.52 W
Medgidia	54	44.15 N	28.16 E
Mediaş	54	46.10 N	24.21 E
Medicina	52	44.28 N	11.38 E
Medicine Hat	98	50.03 N	110.40 W
Medina →Al-Madīnah, Ar. Su.	78	24.28 N	39.36 E
Medina, N.Y., U.S.	102	43.13 N	78.23 W
Medina, Oh., U.S.	102	41.08 N	81.51 W
Medinaceli	50	41.10 N	2.26 W
Medina del Campo	50	41.18 N	4.55 W
Medina de Ríoseco	50	41.53 N	5.02 W
Medina-Sidonia	50	36.27 N	5.55 W
Mediterranean Sea ⊤[2]	20	35.00 N	20.00 E
Medkovec	54	43.37 N	23.10 E
Mednogorsk	56	51.24 N	57.37 E
Mednyj, ostrov I	58	54.45 N	167.35 E
Médoc ◆[1]	48	45.20 N	1.00 W
Médouneu	84	0.57 N	10.47 E
Medstead	34	51.08 N	1.04 W
Meductic	102	46.00 N	67.29 W
Medveđa	54	42.50 N	21.35 E
Medvedica ≃	56	49.35 N	42.41 E
Medvežjegorsk	42	62.55 N	34.23 E
Medvežji ostrova II	58	70.52 N	161.26 E
Medway ≃	34	51.27 N	0.44 E
Medyn'	60	54.58 N	35.52 E
Medzilaborce	46	49.16 N	21.55 E
Meeberrie	90	26.58 S	115.58 E
Meekatharra	90	26.36 S	118.29 E
Meeks Bay	104	39.02 N	120.08 W
Meentheena	90	21.17 S	120.28 E
Meerane	46	50.51 N	12.28 E
Meersburg	46	47.41 N	9.16 E
Meerut	76	28.59 N	77.42 E
Meese ≃	34	52.40 N	2.39 W
Mega	82	4.07 N	38.16 E
Mega, Pulau I	72	4.00 S	101.02 E
Megálon Khoríon	54	36.27 N	27.21 E
Megalópolis	54	37.24 N	22.08 E
Mégantic, Lac ⊜	102	45.32 N	70.53 W
Mégara	54	38.01 N	23.21 E
Megget Reservoir ⊜[1]	38	55.29 N	3.17 W
Meghna ≃	76	22.50 N	90.50 E
Mehadia	54	44.55 N	22.22 E
Meharry, Mount ∧	90	22.59 S	118.35 E
Mehedinţi □[6]	54	44.30 N	22.50 E
Mehetia I	28	17.52 S	148.03 W
Mehidpur	76	23.49 N	75.40 E
Mehndāwal	76	26.59 N	83.07 E
Mehsāna	76	23.36 N	72.24 E
Mehtar Lām	76	34.39 N	70.10 E
Mehun-sur-Yèvre	48	47.09 N	2.13 E
Meichuan	66	30.10 N	115.36 E
Meig ≃	38	57.34 N	4.41 W
Meigle	38	56.35 N	3.09 W
Meihua	66	26.02 N	119.40 E
Meikle Millyea ∧	36	55.07 N	4.19 W
Meikle Says Law ∧	38	55.55 N	2.40 W
Meiktila	70	20.52 N	95.52 E
Meiners Oaks	104	34.26 N	119.17 W
Meiningen	46	50.34 N	10.25 E
Meiringen	48	46.43 N	8.12 E
Meissen	46	51.10 N	13.28 E
Meiss Lake ⊜	104	41.52 N	122.04 W
Meixian	66	24.21 N	116.08 E
Meizhou	66	23.50 N	117.20 E
Meizhu	66	31.16 N	119.13 E
Mejillones	114	23.06 S	70.27 W
Mejillones, Península ≻[1]	114	23.17 S	70.34 W
Mejillones del Sur, Bahía de C	114	23.03 S	70.27 W
Mejnypil'gyno	58	62.32 N	177.02 E
Meka	90	27.26 S	116.48 E
Mékambo	84	1.01 N	13.56 E
Mekele	82	13.33 N	39.30 E
Meknès	80	33.53 N	5.37 W
Mekong ≃	70	10.33 N	105.24 E
Mékrou ≃	80	12.24 N	2.49 E
Melado ≃	114	35.43 S	71.05 W
Melaka	72	2.12 N	102.15 E
Melaka □[3]	72	2.15 N	102.15 E
Melalap	72	5.14 N	116.00 E
Melanesia II	28	13.00 S	164.00 E
Melanesian Basin ⊹[1]	28	0.05 N	160.35 E
Melawi ≃	72	0.05 N	111.29 E
Melbost	38	58.15 N	6.22 W
Melbourn	34	52.05 N	0.01 E
Melbourne, Austl.	94	37.49 S	144.58 E
Melbourne, Eng., U.K.	34	52.49 N	1.25 W
Melbourne, Fl., U.S.	100	28.04 N	80.36 W
Melbourne Island I	98	68.30 N	104.45 W
Melby House	38	60.18 N	1.39 W
Melderskin ∧	44	60.01 N	6.05 E
Meldorf	46	54.05 N	9.05 E
Meldrum Bay	102	45.56 N	83.07 W
Melegnano	52	45.21 N	9.19 E
Melenki	60	55.20 N	41.38 E
Meleuz	56	52.58 N	55.55 E
Mélèzes, Rivière aux ≃	98	57.40 N	69.29 W
Melfi, It.	52	41.00 N	15.39 E
Melfi, Tchad	82	11.04 N	17.56 E
Melfort	98	52.52 N	104.36 W
Melfort, Loch C	38	56.15 N	5.31 W
Melgaço	50	42.07 N	8.16 W
Melghir, Chott ⊜	80	34.20 N	6.20 E
Melhus	44	63.17 N	10.16 E
Meligalás	54	37.13 N	21.59 E
Melilla	80	35.19 N	2.58 W
Melincué	114	33.39 S	61.27 W
Melipilla	114	33.42 S	71.13 W
Melita	98	49.16 N	101.00 W
Melito di Porto Salvo	52	37.55 N	15.47 E
Melitopol'	56	46.50 N	35.22 E
Melívoia	54	39.45 N	22.48 E
Melk	46	48.14 N	15.20 E
Melksham	34	51.23 N	2.09 W
Mellansel	44	63.26 N	18.19 E
Melle	48	46.13 N	0.09 W
Mellerud	44	58.42 N	12.28 E
Mellid	50	42.55 N	8.00 W
Mellish Reef I[1]	88	17.25 S	155.50 E
Mellish Rise ⊹[3]	28	17.00 S	156.00 E
Mellon Udrigle	38	57.55 N	5.39 W
Melmerby	36	54.44 N	2.35 W
Melmoth	86	28.38 S	31.24 E
Mělník	46	50.20 N	14.29 E
Melo	114	32.22 S	54.11 W
Melrose, Austl.	90	27.56 S	121.19 E
Melrose, Austl.	94	32.42 S	146.58 E
Melrose, Scot., U.K.	38	55.36 N	2.44 W
Melsungen	46	51.08 N	9.32 E
Meltaus	42	66.54 N	25.22 E
Meltham	36	53.35 N	1.51 W
Melton Constable	34	52.53 N	1.01 E
Melton Mowbray	34	52.46 N	0.53 W
Meluan	72	1.52 N	111.56 E
Melun	48	48.32 N	2.40 E
Melvaig	38	57.48 N	5.49 W
Melvich	38	58.33 N	3.55 W
Melville	98	50.55 N	102.48 W
Melville, Cape ≻	92	14.11 S	144.30 E
Melville, Lake ⊜	98	53.45 N	59.30 W
Melville Bugt C	22	75.30 N	63.00 W
Melville Island I, Austl.	92	11.40 S	131.00 E
Melville Island I, N.T., Can.	22	75.15 N	110.00 W
Melville Peninsula ≻[1]	98	68.00 N	84.00 W
Melville Sound ⊔	98	68.05 N	107.30 W
Melvin, Lough ⊜	40	54.26 N	8.10 W
Mélykút	46	46.13 N	19.24 E
Melzo	52	45.30 N	9.25 E
Memboro	72	9.22 S	119.32 E
Memel →Klaipeda, S.S.S.R.	60	55.43 N	21.07 E
Memel, S. Afr.	86	27.43 S	29.30 E
Memmingen	46	47.59 N	10.11 E
Memo ≃	108	9.16 N	66.40 W
Mempawah	72	0.22 N	108.58 E
Memphis, Mi., U.S.	102	42.54 N	82.46 W
Memphis, Tn., U.S.	100	35.08 N	90.02 W
Memphremagog, Lake ⊜	102	45.05 N	72.15 W
Memsie	38	57.39 N	2.02 W
Menai Bridge	36	53.14 N	4.10 W
Menai Strait ⊔	36	53.12 N	4.12 W
Ménaka	80	15.55 N	2.24 E
Menangina	90	29.50 S	121.54 E
Mendawai ≃	72	3.17 S	113.21 E
Mende	48	44.30 N	3.30 E
Menden	46	51.26 N	7.47 E
Mendi, Ityo.	82	9.50 N	35.06 E
Mendi, Pap. N. Gui.	92	6.10 S	143.40 E
Mendip Hills ⋏[2]	34	51.15 N	2.40 W
Mendlesham	34	52.16 N	1.05 E
Mendocino	104	39.18 N	123.47 W
Mendocino, Cape ≻	104	40.25 N	124.25 W
Mendocino Fracture Zone ⊹	22	40.00 N	145.00 W
Mendon	102	42.00 N	85.27 W
Mendota	104	36.45 N	120.22 W
Mendoza	114	32.53 S	68.49 W
Mendoza □[4]	114	34.30 S	68.30 W
Mendoza ≃	114	32.21 S	68.18 W
Ménéac	48	48.09 N	2.28 W
Mene de Mauroa	108	10.43 N	71.01 W
Mene Grande	108	9.49 N	70.56 W
Menemen	54	38.36 N	27.04 E
Menén	46	50.48 N	3.07 E
Menfi	52	37.36 N	12.58 E
Mengalum, Pulau I	72	6.16 N	115.12 E
Mengcheng	66	33.17 N	116.33 E
Menggala	72	4.28 S	105.17 E
Menghai	70	22.00 N	100.26 E
Menghe	66	32.03 N	119.47 E
Menglian	70	22.20 N	99.38 E
Mengzhi	70	24.10 N	99.46 E
Mengzi	70	23.22 N	103.20 E
Menihek Lakes ⊜	98	54.00 N	66.35 W
Menindee	94	32.24 S	142.26 E
Menindee Lake ⊜	94	32.21 S	142.20 E
Meningie	94	35.42 S	139.20 E
Menlo Park	104	37.27 N	122.10 W
Menongue	84	14.36 S	17.48 E
Menor, Mar C	50	37.43 N	0.48 W
Menorca I	50	40.00 N	4.00 E
Mens	48	44.49 N	5.45 E
Menston	36	53.53 N	1.44 W
Mentawai, Kepulauan II	72	3.00 S	100.10 E
Mentawai, Selat ⊔	72	1.56 S	100.12 E
Menton	48	43.47 N	7.30 E
Mentor	102	41.39 N	81.20 W
Mentzdam ⊜[1]	86	33.10 S	25.09 E
Menzel Bourguiba	80	37.10 N	9.48 E
Menzelinsk	42	55.43 N	53.08 E
Menzies	90	29.41 S	121.02 E
Meon ≃	34	50.48 N	1.15 W
Meoqui	106	28.17 N	105.29 W
Mepal	34	52.24 N	0.07 E
Meppel	46	52.42 N	6.11 E
Meppen	46	52.41 N	7.17 E
Meqerghane, Sebkha ≚	80	26.19 N	1.20 E
Mer	48	47.42 N	1.30 E
Meråker	44	63.26 N	11.45 E
Meramangye, Lake ⊜	90	28.25 S	132.13 E
Merambéllou, Kólpos C	54	35.14 N	25.47 E
Merano (Meran)	52	46.40 N	11.09 E
Merate	52	45.42 N	9.25 E
Merauke	92	8.28 S	140.20 E
Merbein	94	34.11 S	142.04 E
Mercāra	74	12.25 N	75.44 E
Mercato Saraceno	52	43.57 N	12.12 E
Merced	104	37.18 N	120.28 W
Merced ≃	104	37.21 N	120.58 W
Mercedario, Cerro ∧	114	31.59 S	70.07 W
Mercedes, Arg.	114	33.40 S	65.28 W
Mercedes, Arg.	114	34.39 S	59.27 W
Mercedes, Arg.	114	29.12 S	58.05 W
Mercedes, Ur.	114	33.16 S	58.01 W
Mercer, N.Z.	96	37.16 S	175.03 E
Mercer, Pa., U.S.	102	41.13 N	80.14 W
Mercersburg	102	39.49 N	77.54 W
Merchants Bay C	98	67.10 N	62.50 W
Mercury	104	36.40 N	115.59 W
Mercury Islands II	96	36.35 S	175.55 E
Mercy Bay C	98	74.05 N	119.00 W
Mere	34	51.06 N	2.16 W
Meredith	102	43.39 N	71.30 W
Mereeg	82	3.46 N	47.18 E
Merenkurkku (Norra Kvarken) ⊔	44	63.36 N	20.43 E
Mergui (Myeik)	70	12.26 N	98.36 E
Mergui Archipelago II	70	12.00 N	98.00 E
Meribah	94	34.42 S	140.51 E
Meriç (Marica) (Évros) ≃	54	40.52 N	26.12 E
Mérida, Esp.	50	38.55 N	6.20 W
Mérida, Méx.	106	20.58 N	89.37 W
Mérida, Ven.	110	8.36 N	71.08 W
Mérida, Cordillera de ⋏	110	8.40 N	71.00 W
Meriden, Eng., U.K.	34	52.26 N	1.37 W
Meriden, Ct., U.S.	102	41.32 N	72.48 W
Meridian	100	32.21 N	88.42 W
Mérignac	48	44.50 N	0.42 W
Merikarvia	44	61.51 N	21.30 E
Merimbula	94	36.53 S	149.54 E
Merín, Laguna (Lagoa Mirim) C	114	32.45 S	52.50 W
Merinda	94	20.01 S	148.10 E
Meringur	94	34.24 S	141.16 E
Merinos	114	32.24 S	56.54 W
Merir I	68	4.19 N	132.19 E
Merkendorf	46	49.12 N	10.42 E
Merlin, On., Can.	102	42.14 N	82.14 W
Merlin, Or., U.S.	104	42.31 N	123.25 W
Merlo	114	32.21 S	65.02 W
Mernye	46	46.30 N	17.50 E
Meron, Hare ∧	78	32.58 N	35.25 E
Merotai Besar	72	4.26 N	117.46 E
Merredin	90	31.29 S	118.16 E
Merrick ∧	36	55.08 N	4.29 W
Merrickville	102	44.55 N	75.50 W
Merrill, Mi., U.S.	102	43.24 N	84.19 W
Merrill, Or., U.S.	104	42.01 N	121.35 W
Merrimack ≃	102	42.49 N	70.49 W
Merriott	34	50.54 N	2.48 W
Merritt	98	50.07 N	120.47 W
Merriwa	94	32.08 S	150.21 E
Merrygoen	94	31.50 S	149.14 E
Mersa Matruh →Marsā Maṭrūḥ	82	31.21 N	27.14 E
Merse ∨	38	55.39 N	2.15 W
Mersea Island I	34	51.47 N	0.55 E
Merseburg	46	51.21 N	11.59 E
Mersey ≃, Austl.	94	41.10 S	146.22 E
Mersey ≃, Eng., U.K.	36	53.25 N	3.00 W
Merseyside □[6]	36	53.25 N	2.50 W
Mersin	78	36.48 N	34.38 E
Mersing	72	2.26 N	103.50 E
Merta	76	26.39 N	74.02 E
Merta Road	76	26.43 N	73.55 E
Merthyr Tydfil	34	51.46 N	3.23 W
Mértola	50	37.38 N	7.40 W
Merton ◆[8]	34	51.25 N	0.12 W
Méru, Fr.	48	49.14 N	2.08 E
Meru, Kenya	84	0.03 N	37.39 E
Meru, Mount ∧	84	3.14 S	36.45 E
Merweville	86	32.40 S	21.31 E
Méry	48	48.30 N	3.53 E
Merzig	46	49.27 N	6.36 E
Mesa	100	33.25 N	111.49 W
Mesa ≃	50	41.15 N	1.48 W
Mesagne	52	40.33 N	17.49 E
Mesarás, Kólpos C	54	34.58 N	24.36 E
Meschede	46	51.20 N	8.17 E
Mesgouez, Lac ⊜	98	51.24 N	75.05 W
Meshed →Mashhad	78	36.18 N	59.36 E
Mesick	102	44.24 N	85.42 W
Meslay-du-Maine	48	47.57 N	0.33 W
Mesocco	48	46.23 N	9.14 E
Mesolóngion	54	38.21 N	21.17 E
Mesopotamia □[9]	78	34.00 N	44.00 E
Mesquite	104	36.48 N	114.03 W
Messalo ≃	84	11.40 S	40.26 E
Messina, It.	52	38.11 N	15.33 E
Messina, S. Afr.	86	22.23 S	30.00 E
Messina, Stretto di ⊔	52	38.15 N	15.35 E
Messingham	36	53.32 N	0.39 W
Messíni	54	37.04 N	22.00 E
Messiniakós Kólpos C	54	36.58 N	22.00 E
Messkirch	46	47.59 N	9.07 E
Messojacha ≃	58	67.52 N	77.27 E
Mestá	54	38.15 N	25.55 E
Mesta (Néstos) ≃	54	40.41 N	24.44 E
Mestghanem	80	35.51 N	0.07 E
Mestre	52	45.29 N	12.15 E
Meta ≃	110	6.12 N	67.28 W
Metallifere, Colline ⋏	52	43.15 N	11.00 E
Metán	114	25.29 S	64.57 W
Metheringham	36	53.08 N	0.24 W
Methil	38	56.10 N	3.01 W
Methlick	38	57.25 N	2.14 W
Methóni	54	36.50 N	21.43 E
Methven	96	43.38 S	171.39 E
Methwold	34	52.31 N	0.33 E
Methyen	38	56.25 N	3.34 W
Metković	52	43.03 N	17.39 E
Metlika	52	45.39 N	15.19 E
Métsovon	54	39.46 N	21.11 E
Mettmann	46	51.15 N	6.58 E
Metz	48	49.08 N	6.10 E
Metzingen	46	48.32 N	9.17 E
Meu ≃	48	48.02 N	1.47 W
Meulaboh	70	4.09 N	96.08 E
Meulan	48	49.01 N	1.54 E
Meurthe ≃	48	48.47 N	6.09 E
Meurthe-et-Moselle □[5]	48	48.35 N	6.10 E
Meuse □[5]	48	49.00 N	5.30 E
Meuse (Maas) ≃	46	51.49 N	5.01 E
Meuselwitz	46	51.02 N	12.17 E
Mevagissey	34	50.16 N	4.48 W
Mexborough	36	53.30 N	1.17 W
Mexiana, Ilha I	110	0.02 S	49.35 W
Mexicali	106	32.40 N	115.29 W
Mexico, Me., U.S.	102	44.33 N	70.32 W
Mexico, Mo., U.S.	100	39.10 N	91.52 W
Mexico, N.Y., U.S.	102	43.27 N	76.13 W
Mexico (México) □[1]	106	23.00 N	102.00 W
Mexico, Gulf of C	106	25.00 N	90.00 W
Mexico Basin ⊹[1]	22	25.00 N	92.00 W
Mexico Bay C	102	43.31 N	76.17 W
Mexico City →Ciudad de México	106	19.24 N	99.09 W
Meximieux	48	45.54 N	5.12 E
Meyersdale	102	39.48 N	79.01 W
Meymac	48	45.32 N	2.09 E
Meymaneh	76	35.55 N	64.47 E
Meyrargues	48	43.38 N	5.32 E
Meyrueis	48	44.10 N	3.26 E
Mezdra	54	43.09 N	23.42 E
Meždurečensk	58	53.42 N	88.03 E
Mèze	48	43.25 N	3.36 E
Mézel	48	43.59 N	6.12 E
Mezen' ≃	42	66.11 N	43.59 E
Mézenc, Mont ∧	48	44.55 N	4.11 E
Mézières-en-Brenne	48	46.49 N	1.13 E
Mézin	48	44.03 N	0.16 E
Mezőberény	46	46.50 N	21.02 E
Mezőcsát	46	47.49 N	20.55 E
Mezőkovácsháza	46	46.25 N	20.55 E
Mezőkövesd	46	47.50 N	20.34 E
Mezőtúr	46	47.00 N	20.38 E
Mezzolombardo	52	46.13 N	11.05 E
Mfolozi ≃	86	28.25 S	32.26 E
M'goun, Irhil ∧	80	31.31 N	6.25 W
Mholach, Beinn ∧[2]	38	56.45 N	4.18 W
Mhòr, Beinn ∧	38	57.17 N	7.19 W
Mhòr, Loch ⊜	38	57.14 N	4.26 W
Mhow	76	22.33 N	75.46 E
Miahuatlán de Porfirio Díaz	106	16.20 N	96.36 W
Miajadas	50	39.09 N	5.54 W
Miājlar	76	26.15 N	70.23 E
Miami	100	25.46 N	80.11 W
Miami Beach	100	25.47 N	80.07 W
Miamisburg	102	39.38 N	84.17 W
Miān Channūn	76	30.27 N	72.22 E
Mīāndowāb	78	36.58 N	46.06 E
Miandrivazo	87b	19.31 S	45.28 E
Mīāneh	78	37.26 N	47.42 E
Miang, Phu ∧	70	17.42 N	101.01 E
Miangas, Pulau I	68	5.35 N	126.35 E
Mianhu	66	23.28 N	116.09 E
Miāni	76	21.51 N	69.23 E
Mianyang, Zhg.	62	31.30 N	104.49 E
Mianyang, Zhg.	66	30.23 N	113.25 E
Miaoli	66	24.34 N	120.49 E
Miass	56	54.59 N	60.06 E
Miasteczko Krajeńskie	46	53.06 N	17.01 E
Miastko	46	54.01 N	17.00 E
Mica	86	24.10 S	30.48 E
Michajlov	60	54.14 N	39.02 E
Michajlovka	56	50.05 N	43.15 E
Michalovce	46	48.45 N	21.55 E
Micheldever	34	51.09 N	1.15 W
Miches	108	18.59 N	69.03 W
Michigan □[3]	100	44.00 N	85.00 W
Michigan, Lake ⊜	100	44.00 N	87.00 W
Michigan Center	102	42.13 N	84.19 W
Michigan City	100	41.42 N	86.53 W
Michipicoten Island I	98	47.45 N	85.45 W
Michoacán	104	32.28 N	115.20 W
Michów	46	51.32 N	22.19 E
Mickle Fell ∧	36	54.37 N	2.18 W

Symbols in the Index entries are identified on page 122

Name	Page	Lat. °′	Long. °′
Mickleover	34	52.24N	1.34W
Micronesia II	28	11.00N	159.00 E
Micronesia, Federated States of □[2]	28	5.00N	152.00 E
Mičurin	54	42.10N	27.51 E
Mičurinsk	60	52.54N	40.30 E
Mid-Atlantic Ridge +[3]	20	20.00S	12.00W
Middalya	90	23.55S	114.45 E
Middelburg, Ned.	46	51.30N	3.37 E
Middelburg, S. Afr.	86	31.30S	25.00 E
Middelburg, S. Afr.	86	25.47S	29.28 E
Middelfart	44	55.30N	9.45 E
Middelharnis	46	51.45N	4.11 E
Middelpos	86	31.55S	20.13 E
Middelwater	86	23.17S	30.16 E
Middelwit	86	24.58S	27.00 E
Middle Alkali Lake ⊜	104	41.28N	120.04W
Middle America Trench +[1]	22	15.00N	95.00W
Middle Andaman I	70	12.30N	92.50 E
Middle Barton	34	51.56N	1.22W
Middleboro	102	41.53N	70.54W
Middlebourne	102	39.29N	80.54W
Middleburg, N.Y., U.S.	102	42.36N	74.20W
Middleburg, Pa., U.S.	102	40.47N	77.02W
Middlebury	102	44.00N	73.10W
Middle Caicos I	108	21.47N	71.43W
Middlefield	102	41.27N	81.04W
Middleham	36	54.17N	1.49W
Middle Island I	90	34.07S	123.12 E
Middle Level Main Drain ☲	34	52.43N	0.22 E
Middlemarch	96	45.31S	170.07 E
Middle Point	102	40.51N	84.27W
Middleport	102	39.00N	82.02W
Middlesboro	100	36.36N	83.43W
Middlesbrough	36	54.35N	1.14W
Middleton, Austl.	94	22.22S	141.32 E
Middleton, Eng., U.K.	34	52.43N	0.28 E
Middleton, Eng., U.K.	36	53.33N	2.13W
Middleton, Mi., U.S.	102	43.11N	84.42W
Middleton ≃	94	22.35S	141.51 E
Middleton in Teesdale	36	54.38N	2.04W
Middleton Island I	98	59.25N	146.25W
Middleton-on-the-Wolds	36	53.56N	0.33W
Middleton Reef I[1]	88	29.28S	159.06 E
Middleton Saint George	36	54.30N	1.28W
Middletown, N. Ire., U.K.	40	54.18N	6.50W
Middletown, Ca., U.S.	104	38.45N	122.36W
Middletown, Ct., U.S.	102	41.33N	72.39W
Middletown, De., U.S.	102	39.26N	75.43W
Middletown, Md., U.S.	102	39.26N	77.32W
Middletown, N.Y., U.S.	102	41.26N	74.25W
Middletown, Oh., U.S.	102	39.30N	84.23W
Middletown, Pa., U.S.	102	40.11N	76.43W
Middletown, R.I., U.S.	102	41.32N	71.17W
Middletown, Va., U.S.	102	39.01N	78.16W
Middleville	102	42.42N	85.27W
Middlewich	34	53.11N	2.27W
Middle Yuba ≃	104	39.22N	121.12W
Mid Glamorgan □[6]	34	51.40N	3.30W
Midhurst	34	50.59N	0.45W
Midi, Canal du ☲	48	43.26N	1.58 E
Midi de Bigorre, Pic du ∧	48	42.56N	0.08 E
Mid-Indian Basin +[1]	26	10.00S	80.00 E
Mid-Indian Ridge +[3]	26	14.00S	66.00 E
Midland, On., Can.	102	44.45N	79.53W
Midland, Ca., U.S.	104	33.52N	114.48W
Midland, Mi., U.S.	102	43.36N	84.14W
Midland, Tx., U.S.	100	31.59N	102.04W
Midlands □[4]	86	19.00S	29.45 E
Midleton	40	51.55N	8.10W
Midnapore	76	22.26N	87.20 E
Midongy Sud	87b	23.35S	47.01 E
Midori ≃	64	32.42N	130.37 E
Midou ≃	48	43.54N	0.30W
Mid-Pacific Mountains +[3]	28	20.00N	170.00 E
Midsomer Norton	34	51.18N	2.28W
Midway	102	38.09N	84.41W
Midway Islands □[2]	28	28.13S	177.22W
Midžor (Midžur) ∧	54	43.23N	22.42 E
Mie	64	32.58N	131.35 E
Mie □[5]	64	34.30N	136.30 E
Miechów	46	50.23N	20.01 E
Międzybórz	46	51.24N	17.40 E
Międzychód	46	52.36N	15.55 E
Międzylesie	46	50.10N	16.40 E
Międzyrzec Podlaski	46	52.00N	22.47 E
Międzyrzecz	46	52.28N	15.35 E
Międzyzdroje	46	53.55N	14.28 E
Miejska Górka	46	51.40N	16.58 E
Miélan	48	43.26N	0.19 E
Mielec	46	50.18N	21.25 E
Mielno	46	54.16N	16.01 E
Mien ⊜	44	56.25N	14.51 E
Miercurea-Ciuc	54	46.22N	25.48 E
Mieres	50	43.15N	5.46W
Mieroszów	46	50.41N	16.10 E
Miersig	54	46.53N	21.51 E
Miesbach	46	47.47N	11.50 E
Mieszkowice	46	52.46N	14.30 E
Mifflinburg	102	40.55N	77.02W
Migennes	48	47.58N	3.31 E
Miguel Alemán, Presa ⊜[1]	106	18.13N	96.32W
Miguel Riglos	114	36.51S	63.42W
Migvie	38	57.08N	2.56W
Mihăeşti	54	45.07N	25.00 E
Mihai Viteazu	54	44.39N	28.41 E
Mihajlovgrad	54	43.25N	23.13 E
Mihara	64	34.24N	133.05 E
Mihara-yama ∧	64	34.43N	139.23 E
Mijares ≃	50	39.55N	0.01W
Mikame	64	33.25N	132.27 E
Mikasa	64a	43.14N	141.53 E
Mikindani	84	10.17S	40.07 E
Mikkeli	44	61.41N	27.15 E
Mikkelin lääni □[4]	44	62.00N	27.30 E
Mikkwa ≃	98	58.25N	114.45W
Mikołajki	46	53.49N	21.36 E
Mikolów	46	50.11N	18.55 E
Míkonos	54	37.26N	25.20 E
Míkonos I	54	37.29N	25.25 E
Mikre	54	43.02N	24.31 E
Mikrí Préspa, Límni ⊜	54	40.46N	21.04 E
Mikstat	46	51.32N	17.59 E
Mikulov	46	48.49N	16.39 E
Mikumi	84	7.24S	36.59 E
Mikun'	42	62.21N	50.06 E
Mikuni	64	36.13N	136.09 E
Mikura-jima I	64	33.52N	139.36 E
Milagro	110	2.07S	79.36W
Milan →Milano, It.	52	45.28N	9.12 E
Milan, Mi., U.S.	102	42.05N	83.40W
Milang	94	35.25S	138.58 E
Milano (Milan)	52	45.28N	9.12 E
Milâs	54	37.19N	27.47 E
Milazzo	52	38.13N	15.14 E
Milbank	100	45.13N	96.38W
Milborne Port	34	50.58N	2.27W
Mildenhall	34	52.21N	0.30 E
Mildmay	102	44.03N	81.07W
Mildred	102	41.28N	76.22W
Mildura	94	34.12S	142.09 E
Mile	70	24.26N	103.26 E
Miléai	54	39.20N	23.09 E
Miles	94	26.40S	150.11 E
Miles City	100	46.24N	105.50W
Miletto, Monte ∧	52	41.27N	14.22 E
Mileura	90	26.23S	117.20 E
Milevsko	46	49.27N	14.22 E
Milford, Eng., U.K.	34	51.11N	1.38W
Milford, Ct., U.S.	102	41.13N	73.04W
Milford, De., U.S.	102	38.54N	75.25W
Milford, Me., U.S.	102	44.56N	68.38W
Milford, Ma., U.S.	102	42.08N	71.31W
Milford, Mi., U.S.	102	42.35N	83.35W
Milford, N.H., U.S.	102	42.50N	71.38W
Milford, N.J., U.S.	102	40.34N	75.05W
Milford, Pa., U.S.	102	41.19N	74.48W
Milford Center	102	40.10N	83.26W
Milford Haven	34	51.40N	5.02W
Milford Haven C	34	51.42N	5.03W
Milford on Sea	34	50.44N	1.36W
Milford Sound	96	44.40S	167.54 E
Milford Sound U	96	44.35S	167.47 E
Milgoo ∧	90	28.51S	118.07 E
Mili I[1]	28	6.08N	171.55 E
Milicz	46	51.32N	17.17 E
Miling	90	30.30S	116.21 E
Milk ≃	100	48.05N	106.15W
Milk Hill ∧[2]	34	51.23N	1.51W
Mil'kovo	58	54.43N	158.37 E
Millau	48	44.06N	3.05 E
Millboro	102	37.59N	79.36W
Millbrook, On., Can.	102	44.09N	78.27W
Millbrook, Eng., U.K.	34	50.20N	4.13W
Millbrook, N.Y., U.S.	102	41.47N	73.41W
Millcreek, Pa., U.S.	102	42.05N	80.10W
Mill Creek, W.V., U.S.	102	38.43N	79.58W
Milledgeville	100	33.04N	83.13W
Mille Lacs, Lac des ⊜	98	48.50N	90.30W
Mille Lacs Lake ⊜	100	46.15N	93.40W
Miller	100	44.31N	98.59W
Miller Mountain ∧	104	38.03N	118.12W
Millerovo	56	48.55N	40.25 E
Millersburg, Ky., U.S.	102	38.18N	84.08W
Millersburg, Mi., U.S.	102	45.20N	84.03W
Millersburg, Oh., U.S.	102	40.33N	81.55W
Millersburg, Pa., U.S.	102	40.32N	76.57W
Miller Seamount +[3]	22	53.30N	144.20W
Millers Flat	96	45.40S	169.25 E
Millersport	102	39.54N	82.32W
Millersville	102	39.59N	76.21W
Millerton	102	41.57N	73.30W
Millerton Lake ⊜[1]	104	37.01N	119.41W
Milleur Point ›	36	55.01N	5.06W
Millevaches, Plateau de ⋀[1]	48	45.30N	2.10 E
Millford	40	55.07N	7.43W
Mill Hall	102	41.06N	77.29W
Millicent	94	37.36S	140.22 E
Millington	102	43.16N	83.31W
Millinocket	102	45.39N	68.42W
Mill Island I	98	64.00N	78.00W
Millisle	40	54.36N	5.32W
Millmerran	94	27.52S	151.16 E
Millom	36	54.13N	3.18W
Millport	38	55.46N	4.55W
Mills Creek ≃	94	22.23S	143.05 E
Mills Lake ⊜	98	61.30N	118.10W
Millstatt	46	46.48N	13.35 E
Millstream	90	21.35S	117.04 E
Millstreet	40	52.03N	9.04W
Milltown Malbay	40	52.50N	9.23W
Mill Valley	104	37.54N	122.32W
Millville	102	39.24N	75.02W
Millwood	102	39.04N	78.02W
Milne Bay C	92	10.22S	150.30 E
Milngavie	38	55.57N	4.20W
Milnrow	36	53.37N	2.06W
Milnthorpe	36	54.14N	2.46W
Milo	102	45.15N	68.59W
Mílos	54	36.45N	24.27 E
Mílos I	54	36.41N	24.15 E
Miłosław	46	52.13N	17.29 E
Milparinka	94	29.44S	141.53 E
Milpitas	104	37.25N	121.54W
Milpitas Wash V	104	33.18N	114.44W
Milroy	102	40.42N	77.35W
Miltenberg	46	49.42N	9.15 E
Milton, On., Can.	102	43.31N	79.53W
Milton, N.Z.	96	46.07S	169.58 E
Milton, Eng., U.K.	34	52.14N	0.09W
Milton, De., U.S.	102	38.46N	75.18W
Milton, Pa., U.S.	102	41.00N	76.50W
Milton, Vt., U.S.	102	44.38N	73.06W
Milton, W.V., U.S.	102	38.26N	82.07W
Milton Abbot	34	50.35N	4.15W
Milton Keynes	34	52.02N	0.42W
Milverton, On., Can.	102	43.34N	80.55W
Milverton, Eng., U.K.	34	51.02N	3.16W
Milwaukee	100	43.02N	87.54W
Mimi ≃	64	32.20N	131.37 E
Mimizan	48	44.12N	1.14W
Mimmaya	64	41.12N	140.26 E
Mimoň	46	50.40N	14.44 E
Min ≃, Zhg.	62	28.46N	104.38 E
Min ≃, Zhg.	66	26.05N	119.32 E
Mina	104	38.23N	118.06W
Mīnā' al-Aḥmadī	78	29.04N	48.08 E
Minahasa ›[1]	72	1.00N	124.35 E
Minakuchi	64	34.58N	136.10 E
Minamata	64	32.13N	130.24 E
Minami-Daitō-jima I	62	25.50N	131.15 E
Minami-Iō-jima I	28	24.14N	141.28 E
Minami-Tori-shima (Marcus Island) I	28	24.18N	153.58 E
Mina Pirquitas	114	22.41S	66.31W
Minard	38	56.07N	5.15W
Minas, Cuba	108	21.29N	77.37W
Minas, Ur.	114	34.23S	55.14W
Minas de Corrales	114	31.35S	55.28W
Minas de Matahambre	108	22.35N	83.57W
Minas de Oro	108	14.46N	87.20W
Minas de Ríotinto	50	37.42N	6.35W
Minas Novas	110	17.15S	42.36W
Mînăstirea	54	44.13N	26.54 E
Minatitlán	106	17.59N	94.31W
Minchinhampton	34	51.42N	2.10W
Minčol ∧	46	49.15N	20.59 E
Mindanao I	68	8.00N	125.00 E
Mindanao Sea ⊤[2]	68	9.10N	124.25 E
Mindelheim	46	48.03N	10.29 E
Mindelo	80	16.53N	25.00W
Mindemoya	102	45.44N	82.10W
Minden, B.R.D.	46	52.17N	8.55 E
Minden, On., Can.	102	44.55N	78.43W
Minden, Nv., U.S.	104	38.57N	119.45W
Minden, W.V., U.S.	102	37.58N	81.07W
Minden City	102	43.40N	82.46W
Minderoo	90	22.00S	115.02 E
Mindoro I	68	12.50N	121.05 E
Mindoro Strait U	68	12.20N	120.40 E
Mine	64	34.10N	131.13 E
Minehead	34	51.13N	3.29W
Mineiros	110	17.34S	52.34W
Mineral'nyje Vody	56	44.12N	43.08 E
Mineral Wells	100	32.48N	98.06W
Minersville	102	40.41N	76.16W
Minerva	102	40.43N	81.06W
Minervino Murge	52	41.05N	16.05 E
Mineville	102	44.05N	73.31W
Minfeng	62	37.05N	82.40 E
Mingary	94	32.08S	140.44 E
Mingečaur	56	40.45N	47.03 E
Mingela	94	19.53S	146.38 E
Mingenew	90	29.11S	115.26 E
Mingera Creek ≃	94	20.38S	138.10 E
Minggang	66	32.29N	114.03 E
Minggao	66	34.20N	112.15 E
Minglanilla	50	39.32N	1.36W
Mingo Junction	102	40.19N	80.36W
Mingorría	50	40.45N	4.40W
Mingulay I	38	56.49N	7.38W
Minhang	66	31.01N	121.24 E
Minho □[9]	50	41.40N	8.30W
Minho (Miño) ≃	50	41.52N	8.51W
Minhou	66	26.12N	119.06 E
Minićevo	54	43.41N	22.18 E
Minicoy Island I	74	8.17N	73.02 E
Minigwal, Lake ⊜	90	29.35S	123.12 E
Minilya	90	23.51S	113.58 E
Minilya ≃	90	23.56S	113.51 E
Minlaton	94	34.46S	137.36 E
Minle	62	38.27N	100.56 E
Minna	80	9.37N	6.33 E
Minneapolis	100	44.58N	93.15W
Minnedosa	98	50.14N	99.51W
Minnesota □[3]	100	46.00N	94.15W
Minnesota ≃	100	44.54N	93.10W
Minnie Creek	90	24.02S	115.42 E
Minnigaff	36	54.58N	4.30W
Minnipa	90	32.51S	135.09 E
Minnoch, Water of ≃	36	55.02N	4.33W
Mino	64	35.32N	136.55 E
Miño (Minho) ≃	50	41.52N	8.51W
Mino-Mikawa-kōgen ⋀[1]	64	35.11N	137.23 E
Minorca →Menorca I	50	40.00N	4.00 E
Minot	100	48.13N	101.17W
Minqing	66	26.12N	118.51 E
Minsk	60	53.54N	27.34 E
Mińsk Mazowiecki	46	52.11N	21.34 E
Minster, Eng., U.K.	34	51.20N	1.19 E
Minster, Eng., U.K.	34	51.26N	0.49 E
Minster, Oh., U.S.	102	40.24N	84.23W
Minsterley	34	52.39N	2.55W
Mintaka Pass)(	76	37.00N	74.50 E
Mintlaw	38	57.31N	2.00W
Minto, Lac ⊜	98	57.13N	75.00W
Minto Inlet C	98	71.20N	117.00W
Minturno	52	41.15N	13.45 E
Minusinsk	58	53.43N	91.42 E
Minutang	76	28.13N	96.32 E
Minxian	62	34.26N	104.02 E
Minya Konka →Gongga Shan ∧	62	29.35N	101.51 E
Mio	102	44.39N	84.07W
Mionica	54	44.15N	20.05 E
Mipi	76	28.57N	95.48 E
Mir	60	53.27N	26.28 E
Mira, It.	52	45.26N	12.08 E
Mira, Port.	50	40.26N	8.44W
Mira ≃	50	37.43N	8.47W
Miracema do Norte	110	9.33S	48.24W
Mirador	110	6.22S	44.22W
Miraflores, Arg.	114	28.36S	65.55W
Miraflores, Col.	110	5.12N	73.12W
Miraj	74	16.50N	74.38 E
Miramar, Arg.	114	38.16S	57.51W
Miramar, Arg.	114	30.54S	62.40W
Miramas	48	43.35N	5.00 E
Mirambeau	48	45.23N	0.34W
Miramichi Bay C	98	47.08N	65.08W
Miranda	104	40.14N	123.49W
Miranda □[3]	108	10.15N	66.25W
Miranda ≃	110	19.25S	57.20W
Miranda de Ebro	50	42.41N	2.57W
Miranda do Douro	50	41.30N	6.16W
Mirande	48	43.31N	0.25 E
Mirandela	50	41.29N	7.11W
Mirandola	52	44.53N	11.04 E
Mirante do Paranapanema	114	22.17S	51.54W
Miravalles, Volcán ∧[1]	108	10.45N	85.10W
Miravete, Puerto de)(	50	39.43N	5.43W
Mirbāṭ	74	17.00N	54.45 E
Mirebeau-sur-Bèze	48	47.24N	5.19 E
Mirecourt	48	48.18N	6.08 E
Mirfield	36	53.40N	1.41W
Miri	72	4.23N	113.59 E
Miriam Vale	94	24.20S	151.34 E
Mirim, Lagoa (Laguna Merín) C	114	32.45S	52.50W
Mírina	54	39.52N	25.04 E
Miriñay ≃	114	30.10S	57.39W
Mirnyj	58	62.33N	113.53 E
Mironeasa	54	46.58N	27.25 E
Miroslav	46	48.57N	16.18 E
Mirosławiec	46	53.21N	16.05 E
Mirow	46	53.16N	12.49 E
Mīrpur	76	33.11N	73.47 E
Mīrpur Khās	76	25.32N	69.00 E
Mirtóön Pélagos ⊤[2]	54	36.51N	23.18 E
Mirzāpur	76	25.09N	82.35 E
Misāḥah, Bi'r ⊤[4]	82	22.12N	27.57 E
Misasa	64	35.24N	133.54 E
Misawa	64	40.41N	141.24 E
Mishan	62	45.33N	131.52 E
Mi-shima I	64	34.46N	131.09 E
Mishmi Hills ⋀[2]	76	29.00N	96.00 E
Misilmeri	52	38.02N	13.27 E
Misima Island I	92	10.40S	152.45 E
Misiones □[4]	114	27.00S	55.00W
Misiones □[5]	114	27.00S	57.00W
Misión San Francisco de Laishí	114	26.14S	58.38W
Miskitos, Cayos II	108	14.23N	82.46W
Miskolc	46	48.06N	20.47 E
Mislivna ∧	46	48.40N	14.44 E
Misool, Pulau I	92	1.52S	130.10 E
Misrātah	82	32.23N	15.06 E
Misrikh	76	27.27N	80.31 E
Missinaibi ≃	98	50.44N	81.29W
Missinaibi Lake ⊜	98	48.23N	83.40W
Mississauga	102	43.35N	79.39W
Mississippi □[3]	100	32.50N	89.30W
Mississippi ≃, On., Can.	102	45.26N	76.16W
Mississippi ≃, U.S.	100	29.00N	89.15W
Mississippi Bay C	90	34.00S	122.17 E
Mississippi Delta ⊻[2]	100	29.10N	89.15W
Mississippi Lake ⊜	102	45.05N	76.12W
Missoula	100	46.52N	113.59W
Missouri □[3]	100	38.30N	93.30W
Missouri ≃	100	38.50N	90.08W
Mistake Creek	92	17.06S	129.04 E
Mistake Creek ≃	94	21.38S	146.50 E
Mistassibi ≃	98	48.53N	72.13W
Mistassini, Lac ⊜	98	51.00N	73.37W
Mistelbach an der Zaya	46	48.34N	16.35 E
Misterbianco	52	37.31N	15.00 E
Misterton, Eng., U.K.	34	50.52N	2.47W
Misterton, Eng., U.K.	36	53.27N	0.51W
Misti, Volcán ∧[1]	110	16.18S	71.24W
Mistley	34	51.56N	1.05 E
Mistretta	52	37.56N	14.22 E
Misumi, Nihon	64	32.37N	130.27 E
Misumi, Nihon	64	34.46N	131.58 E
Mita, Punta ›	106	20.47N	105.33W
Mitcheldean	34	51.53N	2.30W
Mitchell, Austl.	94	26.29S	147.58 E
Mitchell, On., Can.	102	43.28N	81.12W
Mitchell, S.D., U.S.	100	43.42N	98.01W
Mitchell ≃, Austl.	92	15.12S	141.35 E
Mitchell ≃, Austl.	94	37.53S	147.41 E
Mitchell, Mount ∧	100	35.46N	82.16W
Mitchell River Mission	92	15.28S	141.44 E
Mitchelstown	40	52.16N	8.16W
Mithapur	76	22.25N	69.00 E
Míthimna	54	39.22N	26.10 E
Mitiaro I	28	19.49S	157.43W
Mitilíni	54	39.06N	26.32 E
Mito	64	36.22N	140.28 E
Mitre ∧	96	40.48S	175.27 E
Mitre Peak ∧	96	44.38S	167.50 E
Mitsio, Nosy I	87b	12.54S	48.36 E
Mitsiwa	82	15.38N	39.28 E
Mitsukaidō	64	36.01N	139.59 E
Mitsuke	64	37.32N	138.56 E
Mitsushima	64	34.16N	129.19 E
Mittellandkanal ☲	46	52.16N	11.41 E
Mittenwald	46	47.27N	11.15 E
Mittersill	46	47.16N	12.29 E
Mittweida	46	50.59N	12.59 E
Mitú	110	1.08N	70.03W
Mitumba, Monts ⋀	84	6.00S	29.00 E
Mitwaba	84	8.38S	27.20 E
Mitzic	84	0.47N	11.34 E
Miura	64	35.08N	139.37 E
Miura-hantō ›[1]	64	35.15N	139.39 E
Mixian	66	34.31N	113.22 E
Miya ≃	64	34.32N	136.44 E
Miyagi □[5]	64	38.22N	140.52 E
Miyajima	64	34.18N	132.19 E
Miyake-jima I	64	34.05N	139.32 E
Miyako	64	39.38N	141.57 E
Miyako-jima I	62	24.47N	125.20 E
Miyakonojō	64	31.44N	131.04 E
Miyama	64	34.06N	136.14 E
Miyanojō	64	31.54N	130.27 E
Miyanoura-dake ∧	65b	30.20N	130.31 E
Miyazaki	64	31.54N	131.26 E
Miyazu	64	35.32N	135.11 E
Miyoshi	64	34.48N	132.51 E
Miyun	62	40.22N	116.50 E
Mizdah	82	31.26N	12.59 E
Mizen Head ›, Ire.	40	51.27N	9.49W
Mizen Head ›, Ire.	40	52.51N	6.01W
Mizil	54	45.00N	26.26 E
Mizo Hills ⋀[2]	76	22.50N	93.00 E
Mizoram □[8]	76	23.30N	93.00 E
Mizpe Ramon	78	30.36N	34.48 E
Mizque	110	17.56S	65.19W
Mizusawa	64	39.08N	141.08 E
Mjällom	44	62.59N	18.26 E
Mjölby	44	58.19N	15.08 E
Mjøndalen	44	59.45N	10.01 E
Mjörn ⊜	44	57.54N	12.25 E
Mjøsa ⊜	44	60.40N	11.00 E
Mkalama	84	4.07S	34.38 E
Mkomazi ≃	86	30.12S	30.50 E
Mkuze	86	27.37S	32.02 E
Mkuze ≃	86	27.53S	32.29 E
Mladá Boleslav	46	50.23N	14.59 E
Mladenovac	54	44.26N	20.42 E
Mlava ≃	54	44.45N	21.13 E
Mława	46	53.06N	20.23 E
Mljet, Otok I	52	42.45N	17.30 E
Mljetski Kanal U	52	42.48N	17.35 E
Mmabatho	86	25.51S	25.38 E
Mníšek pod Brdy	46	49.52N	14.16 E
Mo	42	66.15N	14.08 E
Moa ≃	80	6.59N	11.36W
Moa, Pulau I	92	8.10S	127.56 E
Moab	100	38.34N	109.32W
Moa Island I	92	10.12S	142.16 E
Moama	94	36.07S	144.47 E
Moanda	84	1.34S	13.11 E
Moate	40	53.24N	7.58W
Moawhango	96	39.35S	175.52 E
Mobara	64	35.25N	140.18 E
Mobaye	82	4.19N	21.11 E
Moberly	100	39.25N	92.26W
Mobile	100	30.41N	88.02W
Mobridge	100	45.32N	100.25W
Moca	108	19.24N	70.31W
Moçambique	84	15.03S	40.45 E
Moçâmedes	84	15.10S	12.09 E
Mocha →Al-Mukhā	74	13.19N	43.15 E
Mocha, Isla I	114	38.22S	73.56W
Mochudi	86	24.28S	26.05 E
Mocímboa da Praia	84	11.20S	40.21 E
Möckeln ⊜	44	56.40N	14.10 E
Mockfjärd	44	60.30N	14.58 E
Môco, Serra ∧	84	12.28S	15.10 E
Mococa	114	21.28S	47.01W
Mocoretá	114	30.38S	57.58W
Mocorito	106	25.29N	107.55W
Moctezuma	106	29.48N	109.42W
Mocuba	84	16.50S	36.59 E
Močurica ≃	54	42.31N	26.32 E
Modane	48	45.12N	6.40 E
Modāsa	76	23.28N	73.18 E
Modbury	34	50.21N	3.53W
Modder ≃	86	29.02S	24.37 E
Modderrivier	86	29.02S	24.38 E
Modena	52	44.40N	10.55 E
Modesto	104	37.38N	120.59W
Modica	52	36.52N	14.46 E
Mödling	46	48.05N	16.17 E
Modowi	92	4.05S	134.39 E
Modra	46	48.21N	17.17 E
Modriča	54	44.57N	18.18 E
Moe	94	38.10S	146.15 E
Moehau ∧	96	36.35S	175.24 E
Moel Fferna ∧	34	52.57N	3.18W
Moelv	44	60.56N	10.42 E
Moengo	110	5.37N	54.24W
Moeranyah Lake ⊜	94	33.02S	143.58 E
Moerewa	96	35.23S	174.02 E
Moers	46	51.27N	6.37 E
Moffat	36	55.20N	3.27W
Moffat Peak ∧	96	45.02S	168.07 E
Moffat Water ≃	38	55.18N	3.25W
Moga	76	30.48N	75.10 E
Mogadiscio →Muqdisho	82	2.04N	45.22 E
Mogador →Essaouira	80	31.30N	9.47W
Mogadouro	50	41.20N	6.39W
Mogalakwena ≃	86	23.00S	28.40 E
Mogami ≃	64	38.55N	139.48 E
Mogaung	70	25.18N	96.56 E
Mogi das Cruzes	114	23.31S	46.11W
Mogielnica	46	51.42N	20.43 E
Mogilno	46	52.40N	17.58 E
Mogil'ov	60	53.54N	30.21 E
Mogil'ov-Podol'skij	56	48.27N	27.48 E
Mogi-Mirim	114	22.26S	46.57W
Mogincual	84	15.35S	40.25 E
Mogliano Veneto	52	45.33N	12.14 E
Mogoča	58	53.44N	119.44 E
Mogočin	56	57.43N	83.34 E
Mogotón, Pico ∧	108	13.45N	86.23W
Moguer	50	37.16N	6.50W
Mogzon	58	51.45N	111.58 E
Mohács	46	45.59N	18.42 E
Mohaka	96	39.07S	177.11 E
Mohaka ≃	96	39.07S	177.12 E
Mohammedia	80	33.44N	7.24W
Mohana	76	25.54N	77.45 E
Mohania	76	25.11N	83.37 E
Mohave, Lake ⊜[1]	104	35.25N	114.38W
Mohawk ≃	102	42.47N	73.42W
Mohawk Mountain ∧	102	41.49N	73.17W
Mohe	62	53.29N	122.19 E
Moheda	44	57.00N	14.34 E
Mohéli I	87a	12.15S	43.45 E
Mohelnice	46	49.46N	16.55 E
Moher, Cliffs of ⊥[4]	40	52.57N	9.26W
Mohican ≃	102	40.22N	82.09W
Mohill	40	53.54N	7.52W
Mohns Ridge +[3]	20	72.30N	5.00 E
Moi	44	58.28N	6.32 E
Moineşti	54	46.28N	26.29 E
Mointy	56	47.13N	73.21 E
Moira	40	54.30N	6.17W
Moira ≃	102	44.09N	77.23W
Moisdon	48	47.37N	1.22W
Moisés Ville	114	30.43S	61.29W
Moisie ≃	98	50.11N	66.05W
Moissac	48	44.06N	1.05 E
Moita	50	38.39N	8.59W
Möja I	44	59.26N	18.55 E
Mojácar	50	37.08N	1.51W
Mojave	104	35.03N	118.10W
Mojave ≃	104	35.06N	116.04W
Mojave Desert +[2]	104	35.00N	117.00W
Moji-Guaçu ≃	110	20.53S	48.10W
Mojjero ≃	58	68.44N	103.42 E
Mōka	64	36.26N	140.01 E
Mokai	96	38.32S	175.54 E
Mokameh	76	25.24N	85.55 E
Mokapu Peninsula ›[1]	105a	21.27N	157.45W
Mokau	96	38.41S	174.37 E
Mokau ≃	96	38.42S	174.37 E
Mokelumne ≃	104	38.13N	121.28W
Mokhotlong	86	29.22S	29.02 E
Mokil I[1]	28	6.40N	159.47 E
Moknine	80	35.38N	10.54 E
Mokohinau Islands II	96	35.55S	175.07 E
Mokokchūng	76	26.20N	94.32 E
Mokolo ≃	86	23.14S	27.43 E
Mokoreta ≃	96	46.21S	168.51 E
Mokp'o	62	34.48N	126.22 E
Mokša ≃	56	54.44N	41.53 E
Mol	46	51.11N	5.06 E
Mola di Bari	52	41.04N	17.05 E
Moláoi	54	36.48N	22.52 E
Molat, Otok I	52	44.15N	14.49 E
Mold	36	53.10N	3.08W
Moldau →Vltava ≃	46	50.21N	14.30 E
Moldavia →Moldavskaja Sovetskaja Socialističeskaja Respublika □[3]	56	47.00N	29.00 E
Moldavia □[9]	54	47.00N	27.15 E
Moldavskaja Sovetskaja Socialističeskaja Respublika □[3]	56	47.00N	29.00 E
Molde	44	62.44N	7.11 E
Moldova ≃	54	46.54N	26.58 E
Moldova-Nouă	54	44.44N	21.40 E
Moldoveanu ∧	54	45.36N	24.44 E
Mole ≃, Eng., U.K.	34	50.57N	3.54W
Mole ≃, Eng., U.K.	34	51.24N	0.21W
Môle, Cap du ›	108	19.50N	73.25W
Mole Creek	94	41.33S	146.24 E
Molepolole	86	24.25S	25.30 E
Molfetta	52	41.12N	16.36 E
Molina	114	35.07S	71.17W
Molina de Aragón	50	40.51N	1.53W
Molina de Segura	50	38.03N	1.12W
Moline	100	41.30N	90.30W
Molinella	52	44.37N	11.40 E
Molinos	114	25.25S	66.19W
Molins de Rey	50	41.25N	2.01 E
Molise □[4]	52	41.35N	14.30 E
Molkom	44	59.36N	13.43 E
Mölle	44	56.17N	12.29 E
Mollendo	110	17.02S	72.01W
Mölln	46	53.37N	10.41 E
Mollösund	44	58.04N	11.28 E
Mölndal	44	57.39N	12.01 E
Mölnlycke	44	57.39N	12.09 E
Molodečno	60	54.19N	26.49 E
Molokai I	105a	21.07N	157.00W
Molong	94	33.06S	148.52 E
Molopo ≃	86	28.30S	20.13 E
Molotov →Perm'	56	58.00N	56.15 E
Molsheim	48	48.32N	7.29 E
Molson Lake ⊜	98	54.12N	96.45W
Molteno	86	31.22S	26.22 E
Molu, Pulau I	92	6.45S	131.33 E
Moluccas →Maluku II	68	2.00S	128.00 E
Molucca Sea →Maluku, Laut ⊤[2]	68	0.00	125.00 E
Moma	84	16.44S	39.14 E
Moma ≃	58	66.26N	143.06 E
Mombasa	84	4.03S	39.40 E
Mombetsu	64a	44.21N	143.22 E
Mombuey	50	42.02N	6.20W
Momčilgrad	54	41.32N	25.25 E
Momotombo, Volcán ∧[1]	108	12.26N	86.33W
Mompós	110	9.14N	74.26W
Momskij chrebet ⋀	58	66.00N	146.00 E
Mon □[8]	70	17.30N	97.00 E
Møn I	44	55.00N	12.20 E
Mona, Canal de la U	108	18.30N	67.45W
Mona, Isla de I	108	18.05N	67.54W
Mona, Punta ›	108	9.38N	82.37W
Monaca	102	40.41N	80.16W
Monach, Sound of U	38	57.34N	7.35W
Monaco	48	43.42N	7.23 E
Monaco □[1]	30	43.45N	7.25 E
Monadhliath Mountains ⋀	38	57.10N	4.00W
Monadnock Mountain ∧	102	42.52N	72.07W
Monagas □[3]	108	9.20N	63.00W
Monaghan	40	54.15N	6.58W
Monaghan □[6]	40	54.10N	7.00W
Monamolin	40	52.33N	6.20W
Monar, Loch ⊜	38	57.25N	5.06W
Monasterevin	40	53.07N	7.02W
Moncalieri	52	45.00N	7.41 E
Monção, Bra.	110	3.30S	45.15W
Moncão, Port.	50	42.05N	8.29W
Mončegorsk	42	67.54N	32.58 E
Mönchengladbach	46	51.12N	6.28 E
Monchique	50	37.19N	8.33W
Monclova	106	26.54N	101.25W
Moncontour	48	48.21N	2.39W
Moncoutant	48	46.43N	0.35W
Moncton	98	46.06N	64.47W
Mondaí	114	27.05S	53.25W
Monday ≃	114	25.33S	54.41W
Mondego ≃	50	40.09N	8.52W
Mondego, Cabo ›	50	40.11N	8.55W
Mondoñedo	50	43.26N	7.22W
Mondoubleau	48	47.59N	0.54 E
Mondovì	52	44.23N	7.49 E
Mondragone	52	41.07N	13.53 E
Mondrain Island I	90	34.08S	122.15 E
Monemvasía	54	36.41N	23.03 E
Monessen	102	40.08N	79.53W
Monesterio	50	38.05N	6.16W
Moneygall	40	52.53N	7.57W
Moneymore	40	54.42N	6.40W
Monfalcone	52	45.49N	13.32 E
Monferrato □[9]	52	44.55N	8.05 E
Monflanquin	48	44.32N	0.46 E
Monforte	50	39.03N	7.26W
Monforte de Lemos	50	42.31N	7.30W
Mongaguá	114	24.06S	46.37W
Mongala ≃	82	1.53N	19.46 E
Mongalla	82	5.12N	31.46 E
Mongaup ≃	102	41.25N	74.45W
Mong-cai	70	21.32N	107.58 E
Mongers Lake ⊜	90	29.15S	117.05 E
Möng Hsat	70	20.32N	99.15 E
Monghyr	76	25.23N	86.28 E
Mongo	82	12.11N	18.42 E
Mongol Altajn nuruu ⋀	62	46.30N	93.00 E
Mongolia (Mongol Ard Uls) □[1]	62	46.00N	105.00 E
Mongu	84	15.15S	23.09 E
Monheim	46	48.50N	10.51 E
Moniaive	36	55.12N	3.55W
Monifieth	38	56.29N	2.49W
Monimail	38	56.18N	3.08W
Monino	60	55.50N	38.11 E
Monistrol-sur-Loire	48	45.17N	4.10 E
Monitor Range ⋀	104	38.45N	116.30W
Monitor Valley V	104	39.00N	116.40W
Monívea	40	53.23N	8.43W
Mońki	46	53.24N	22.49 E
Monkira	94	24.49S	140.34 E
Monmouth	34	51.50N	2.43W
Monnow ≃	34	51.48N	2.42W
Mono ≃	80	6.17N	1.51 E
Mono Lake ⊜	104	38.00N	119.00W
Monongahela ≃	102	40.27N	80.00W
Monopoli	52	40.57N	17.19 E
Monor	46	47.21N	19.27 E
Monóvar	50	38.26N	0.50W
Monowai, Lake ⊜	96	45.52S	167.27 E
Monreal	50	42.42N	1.30W
Monreal del Campo	50	40.47N	1.21W
Monreale	52	38.05N	13.17 E
Monroe, La., U.S.	100	32.30N	92.07W
Monroe, Mi., U.S.	102	41.54N	83.23W
Monroe, N.Y., U.S.	102	41.19N	74.11W
Monroeville, In., U.S.	102	40.58N	84.52W
Monroeville, Oh., U.S.	102	41.14N	82.41W
Monroeville, Pa., U.S.	102	40.26N	79.47W
Monrovia	80	6.18N	10.47W
Mons	46	50.27N	3.56 E
Monschau	46	50.33N	6.14 E
Monselice	52	45.14N	11.45 E
Monserrato	52	39.15N	9.08 E
Monson	102	45.17N	69.30W
Mönsterås	44	57.02N	16.26 E
Montabaur	46	50.26N	7.50 E
Montagnana	52	45.14N	11.28 E
Montagrier	48	45.16N	0.29 E
Montagu	86	33.45S	20.08 E
Montague	104	41.43N	122.31W
Montague, Isla I	104	31.45N	114.48W
Montague Island I	98	60.00N	147.30W
Montagu Island I	24	58.25S	26.20W
Montaigu	48	46.59N	1.19W
Montaigut-en-Combraille	48	46.11N	2.48 E
Montalbán	50	40.50N	0.48W
Montalbano Elicona	52	38.02N	15.01 E
Montalbano Ionico	52	40.17N	16.34 E
Montalcino	52	43.03N	11.29 E
Montalegre	50	41.49N	7.48W
Montalto ∧	52	38.10N	15.55 E
Montalto di Castro	52	42.21N	11.37 E
Montalto Uffugo	52	39.25N	16.10 E
Montana	48	46.18N	7.29 E
Montana □[3]	100	47.00N	110.00W
Montánchez	50	39.13N	6.09W
Montargil	50	39.05N	8.10W
Montargis	48	48.00N	2.45 E
Montauban	48	44.01N	1.21 E
Montauk	102	41.02N	71.57W
Montauk Point ›	102	41.04N	71.52W
Montbard	48	47.37N	4.20 E
Montbarrey	48	47.01N	5.39 E
Montbéliard	48	47.31N	6.48 E
Montblanch	50	41.22N	1.10 E
Montbrison	48	45.36N	4.03 E
Montbron	48	45.40N	0.30 E
Montceau [-les-Mines]	48	46.40N	4.22 E
Montchanin	48	46.45N	4.27 E
Montclair, Ca., U.S.	104	34.06N	117.41W
Montclair, N.J., U.S.	102	40.49N	74.12W
Mont-de-Marsan	48	43.53N	0.30W
Montdidier	48	49.39N	2.34 E
Monte, Laguna del ⊜	114	37.00S	62.28W
Monteagudo	110	19.49S	63.59W
Monte Alegre	110	2.01S	54.04W
Monte Azul	110	15.09S	42.53W
Montebello	102	45.39N	74.56W
Montebello Iónico	52	37.59N	15.45 E
Montebello Islands II	90	20.25S	115.32 E
Monte Buey	114	32.55S	62.27W
Montecarlo	114	26.34S	54.47W
Monte Caseros	114	30.15S	57.39W
Montecassino, Abbazia di ♁[1]	52	41.29N	13.48 E
Montecatini Terme	52	43.53N	10.46 E
Montecito	104	34.26N	119.37W
Monte Comán	114	34.36S	67.54W
Monte Cristo, Cerro ∧	106	14.25N	89.21W
Montecristo, Isola di I	52	42.20N	10.19 E
Montefalco	52	42.54N	12.39 E
Montefiascone	52	42.32N	12.02 E
Montefrío	50	37.19N	4.01W
Montego Bay	108	18.28N	77.55W
Monte Grande	114	30.06S	70.31W
Montejicar	50	37.34N	3.30W
Montejinni	92	16.40S	131.45 E
Montélimar	48	44.34N	4.45 E
Montelindo ≃	114	23.56S	57.12W
Montella	52	40.51N	15.01 E
Montellano	50	37.00N	5.34W
Montello	104	41.15N	114.11W
Monte Maíz	114	33.12S	62.36W
Montemorelos	106	25.12N	99.49W
Montemor-o-Novo	50	38.39N	8.13W
Montemor-o-Vehlo	50	40.10N	8.41W
Montendre	48	45.17N	0.24W
Montenegro	114	29.42S	51.28W
Montenegro →Crna Gora □[3]	54	42.30N	19.18 E
Montenero di Bisaccia	52	41.57N	14.47 E
Monte Patria	114	30.42S	70.58W
Montepuez	84	13.07S	39.00 E
Montepulciano	52	43.05N	11.47 E
Monte Quemado	114	25.48S	62.52W
Montereau-Faut-Yonne	48	48.23N	2.57 E
Monterey, Ca., U.S.	104	36.36N	121.53W
Monterey, Va., U.S.	102	38.24N	79.34W
Monterey Bay C	104	36.45N	121.55W
Montería	110	8.46N	75.53W
Monteros	114	27.10S	65.30W
Monterotondo	52	42.03N	12.37 E
Monterrey	106	25.40N	100.19W
Montesano	52	40.16N	15.43 E
Monte Sant'Angelo	52	41.42N	15.57 E
Monte Santu, Capo di ›	52	40.05N	9.44 E
Montesarchio	52	41.04N	14.38 E

Symbols in the Index entries are identified on page 122.

Mont-Mzim

Name	Page	Lat. °′	Long. °′
Montes Claros	110	16.43 S	43.52 W
Montevarchi	52	43.31 N	11.34 E
Montevideo	114	34.53 S	56.11 W
Montfaucon	48	45.10 N	4.18 E
Montfort	48	48.08 N	1.58 W
Montgenèvre, Col de)(	48	44.56 N	6.44 E
Montgomery →Sāhiwāl, Pāk.	76	30.40 N	73.06 E
Montgomery, Wales, U.K.	34	52.33 N	3.03 W
Montgomery, Al., U.S.	100	32.23 N	86.18 W
Montgomery, Pa., U.S.	102	41.10 N	76.52 W
Montgomery, W.V., U.S.	102	38.11 N	81.19 W
Montguyon	48	45.13 N	0.11 W
Monthermé	48	49.53 N	4.44 E
Monthey	48	46.15 N	6.57 E
Monthois	48	49.19 N	4.43 E
Monticello	102	41.39 N	74.41 W
Montichiari	52	45.25 N	10.23 E
Montiel, Campo de ⩧	50	38.46 N	2.44 W
Montignac	48	45.04 N	1.10 E
Montigny-le-Roi	48	48.00 N	5.30 E
Montigny-sur-Aube	48	47.57 N	4.46 E
Montijo, Esp.	50	38.55 N	6.37 W
Montijo, Port.	50	38.42 N	8.58 W
Montilla	50	37.35 N	4.38 W
Montivilliers	48	49.33 N	0.12 E
Mont-Joli	98	48.35 N	68.11 W
Mont-Laurier	98	46.33 N	75.30 W
Mont-Louis	48	42.31 N	2.07 E
Montluçon	48	46.21 N	2.36 E
Montluel	48	45.51 N	5.03 E
Montmagny	98	46.59 N	70.33 W
Montmédy	48	49.31 N	5.22 E
Montmirail	48	48.52 N	3.32 E
Montmoreau-Saint-Cybard	48	45.24 N	0.08 E
Montmorillon	48	46.26 N	0.52 E
Montmort	48	48.55 N	3.49 E
Monto	94	24.52 S	151.07 E
Montorio al Vomano	52	42.35 N	13.38 E
Montoro	50	38.01 N	4.23 W
Montour Falls	102	42.20 N	76.50 W
Montoursville	102	41.15 N	76.55 W
Montpelier, In., U.S.	102	40.33 N	85.16 W
Montpelier, Oh., U.S.	102	41.35 N	84.36 W
Montpelier, Vt., U.S.	102	44.15 N	72.34 W
Montpellier	48	43.36 N	3.53 E
Montpon-Ménesterol	48	45.00 N	0.10 E
Montréal	102	45.31 N	73.34 W
Montreal Lake ⊜	98	54.20 N	105.40 W
Montrésor	48	47.09 N	1.12 E
Montreuil	48	50.28 N	1.46 E
Montreuil-Bellay	48	47.08 N	0.09 W
Montreux	48	46.26 N	6.55 E
Montrevel [-en-Bresse]	48	46.20 N	5.08 E
Montrichard	48	47.21 N	1.11 E
Montrose, Scot., U.K.	38	56.43 N	2.29 W
Montrose, Co., U.S.	100	38.28 N	107.52 W
Montrose, Mi., U.S.	102	43.10 N	83.53 W
Montrose, Pa., U.S.	102	41.50 N	75.52 W
Montross	102	38.05 N	76.49 W
Mont-Saint-Michel →Le Mont Saint-Michel ♜ 1	48	48.38 N	1.32 W
Montserrat □ 2	106	16.45 N	62.12 W
Montuenga	50	41.03 N	4.37 W
Monument Peak ∧	104	42.07 N	114.14 W
Monymusk	38	57.13 N	2.31 W
Monywa	70	22.05 N	95.08 E
Monza	52	45.35 N	9.16 E
Monzen	64	37.17 N	136.46 E
Monzie	38	56.24 N	3.48 W
Monzón	50	41.55 N	0.12 E
Moodie Island I	98	64.37 N	65.30 W
Mooi ≃	86	28.45 S	30.34 E
Mooirivier	86	29.13 S	29.50 E
Mooketsi	86	23.35 S	30.05 E
Moolawatana	94	29.55 S	139.43 E
Mooloogool	90	26.06 S	119.05 E
Moonah Creek ≃	94	22.03 S	138.33 E
Moonie ≃	94	29.19 S	148.43 E
Moonta	94	34.04 S	137.35 E
Moonyoonooka	90	28.47 S	114.43 E
Moora	90	30.39 S	116.00 E
Mooraberree	94	25.14 S	140.59 E
Moorarie	90	25.56 S	117.35 E
Moore ≃	90	31.22 S	115.29 E
Moore, Lake ⊜	90	29.50 S	117.35 E
Moorea I	28	17.32 S	149.50 W
Moorefield	102	39.03 N	78.58 W
Moore Reservoir ⊜ 1	102	44.25 N	71.50 W
Moorfoot Hills ⋀ 2	38	55.45 N	3.02 W
Moorhead	100	46.52 N	96.46 W
Moorreesburg	86	33.08 S	18.40 E
Moosburg	46	48.29 N	11.57 E
Moosehead Lake ⊜	102	45.40 N	69.40 W
Moose Jaw	98	50.23 N	105.32 W
Mooselookmeguntic Lake ⊜	102	44.53 N	70.48 W
Moosomin	98	50.07 N	101.40 W
Moosonee	98	51.17 N	80.39 W
Mopane	86	22.37 S	29.52 E
Mopti	80	14.30 N	4.12 W
Moquegua	110	17.12 S	70.56 W
Mór	46	47.23 N	18.12 E
Mòr, Glen v	38	57.10 N	4.40 W
Mor, Sgurr ∧	38	57.42 N	5.03 W
Mora, Esp.	50	39.41 N	3.46 W
Mora, Port.	50	38.56 N	8.10 W
Mora, Sve.	44	61.00 N	14.33 E
Morādābād	76	28.50 N	78.47 E
Mora de Rubielos	50	40.15 N	0.45 W
Morado Primero, Cerro ∧	114	22.49 S	65.26 W
Morafenobe	87b	17.49 S	44.55 E
Morąg	46	53.56 N	19.56 E
Mórahalom	46	46.13 N	19.54 E
Mor'akovskij Zaton	56	56.45 N	84.41 E
Moral de Calatrava	50	38.50 N	3.35 W
Moraleda, Canal de ⋓	112	44.30 S	73.30 W
Moran	102	45.59 N	84.49 W
Moran ≃	92	15.16 S	125.33 E
Morant Bay	108	17.53 N	76.25 W
Morant Cays II	108	17.24 N	75.59 W
Morant Point >	108	17.55 N	76.10 W
Morar, Loch ⊜	38	56.57 N	5.43 W
Morasverdes	50	40.36 N	6.16 W
Moratalla	50	38.12 N	1.53 W
Moratuwa	74	6.46 N	79.53 E
Morava □ 9	46	49.20 N	17.00 E
Morava (March) ≃	46	48.10 N	16.59 E
Moravia	102	42.42 N	76.25 W
Moravia →Morava □ 9	46	49.20 N	17.00 E
Moravská Třebová	46	49.45 N	16.40 E
Moravské Budějovice	46	49.03 N	15.49 E
Moravský Krumlov	46	49.03 N	16.19 E
Morawa	90	29.13 S	116.00 E
Morawhanna	110	8.16 N	59.45 W
Moray Firth C 1	38	57.50 N	3.30 W
Morbegno	52	46.08 N	9.34 E
Morbihan □ 5	48	47.55 N	2.50 W
Mörbylånga	44	56.31 N	16.23 E
Morcenx	48	44.02 N	0.55 W
Morden	98	49.11 N	98.05 W
Mordy	46	52.13 N	22.31 E
More, Ben ∧, Scot., U.K.	38	56.25 N	6.01 W
More, Ben ∧, Scot., U.K.	38	56.21 N	4.35 W
More, Loch ⊜	38	58.17 N	4.52 W
More Assynt, Ben ∧	38	58.08 N	4.53 W
Moreau ≃	100	45.18 N	100.43 W
Morecambe	36	54.04 N	2.53 W
Morecambe Bay C	36	54.07 N	3.00 W
Moree, Austl.	94	29.28 S	149.51 E
Morée, Fr.	48	47.54 N	1.14 E
Morehead	102	38.11 N	83.25 W
Morelia	106	19.42 N	101.07 W
Morella, Austl.	94	22.59 S	143.52 E
Morella, Esp.	50	40.37 N	0.06 W
Morena	76	26.30 N	78.09 E
Morena, Sierra ⋀	50	38.00 N	5.00 W
Morenci	102	41.43 N	84.13 W
Moreni	54	45.00 N	25.39 E
Moreno, Bahía C	114	23.35 S	70.30 W
Møre og Romsdal □ 6	44	62.40 N	7.50 E
Moresby Island I	98	52.50 N	131.55 W
Mores Island I	108	26.18 N	77.33 W
Morestel	48	45.40 N	5.28 E
Moreton, Austl.	92	12.28 S	142.38 E
Moreton, Eng., U.K.	36	53.24 N	3.07 W
Moretonhampstead	34	50.40 N	3.45 W
Moreton-in-Marsh	34	51.59 N	1.42 W
Moreton Island I	94	27.10 S	153.25 E
Moreuil	48	49.46 N	2.29 E
Morey Peak ∧	104	38.37 N	116.17 W
Morez	48	46.31 N	6.02 E
Morfa Nefyn	34	52.56 N	4.33 W
Morgan	94	34.02 S	139.40 E
Morgan City	100	29.41 N	91.12 W
Morgan Hill	104	37.07 N	121.39 W
Morgantown	102	39.37 N	79.57 W
Morgenzon	86	26.45 S	29.36 E
Morghāb (Murgab) ≃	78	38.18 N	61.12 E
Morgongåva	44	59.56 N	16.57 E
Morguilla, Punta >	114	37.46 S	73.40 W
Mori	64a	42.06 N	140.35 E
Mori ≃	92	10.00 S	148.30 E
Moriah, Mount ∧	104	39.17 N	114.12 W
Morichal Largo ≃	108	9.27 N	62.25 W
Morie, Loch ⊜	38	57.44 N	4.28 W
Moringen	46	51.42 N	9.52 E
Morioka	64	39.42 N	141.09 E
Morisset	94	33.06 S	151.29 E
Moriston ≃	38	57.12 N	4.36 W
Moriyoshi-zan ∧	64	39.58 N	140.33 E
Morkoka ≃	58	65.10 N	115.52 E
Morlaix	48	48.35 N	3.50 W
Morley, Eng., U.K.	36	53.46 N	1.36 W
Morley, Mi., U.S.	102	43.29 N	85.26 W
Mörlunda	44	57.19 N	15.51 E
Mormanno	52	39.53 N	16.00 E
Mormon Peak ∧	104	36.57 N	114.30 W
Mormon Reservoir ⊜ 1	104	43.16 N	114.49 W
Morney	94	25.22 S	141.28 E
Morningstar ≃	40	52.27 N	8.41 W
Mornington	94	38.13 S	145.03 E
Mornington, Isla I	112	49.45 S	75.23 W
Mornington Island I	94	16.33 S	139.24 E
Morobe	92	7.45 S	147.35 E
Morocco (Al-Magreb) □ 1	80	32.00 N	5.00 W
Morogoro	84	6.49 S	37.40 E
Moro Gulf C	68	6.51 N	123.00 E
Morokweng	86	26.12 S	23.45 E
Morombe	87b	21.45 S	43.22 E
Morón, Arg.	114	34.39 S	58.37 W
Morón, Cuba	108	22.06 N	78.38 W
Mörön, Mong.	62	49.38 N	100.10 E
Morón, Ven.	108	10.29 N	68.11 W
Morona ≃	110	4.45 S	77.04 W
Morondava	87b	20.17 S	44.17 E
Morón de Almazán	50	41.25 N	2.25 W
Morón de la Frontera	50	37.08 N	5.27 W
Moroni	87a	11.41 S	43.16 E
Moron Us ≃	62	34.42 N	94.50 E
Moros ≃	50	41.03 N	4.15 W
Morošečnoje	58	56.24 N	156.12 E
Morotai I	68	2.20 N	128.25 E
Morozovsk	56	48.22 N	41.50 E
Morpeth	36	55.10 N	1.41 W
Morretes	114	25.28 S	48.49 W
Morrinhos	110	17.44 S	49.07 W
Morrinsville	96	37.39 S	175.32 E
Morris	98	49.21 N	97.22 W
Morris, Mount ∧	90	26.09 S	131.04 E
Morrisburg	102	44.54 N	75.11 W
Morris Jesup, Kap >	22	83.38 N	33.52 W
Morrison	114	32.36 S	62.50 W
Morrisville, N.Y., U.S.	102	42.53 N	75.38 W
Morrisville, Pa., U.S.	102	40.12 N	74.47 W
Morrisville, Vt., U.S.	102	44.33 N	72.35 W
Morro, Punta >	114	27.07 S	70.57 W
Morro Bay	104	35.21 N	120.50 W
Morro do Chapéu	110	11.33 S	41.09 W
Morrosquillo, Golfo de C	108	9.35 N	75.40 W
Mörrum	44	56.11 N	14.45 E
Morrumbene	86	23.39 S	35.20 E
Mörrumsån ≃	44	56.09 N	14.44 E
Mors I	44	56.50 N	8.45 E
Moršansk	60	53.26 N	41.49 E
Morsi	76	21.21 N	78.00 E
Mortagne	48	48.31 N	0.33 E
Mortagne-sur-Sèvre	48	47.00 N	0.57 W
Mortain	48	48.39 N	0.56 W
Mortana	90	33.02 S	134.07 E
Mortara	52	45.15 N	8.44 E
Morteau	48	47.04 N	6.37 E
Morte Point >	34	51.11 N	4.13 W
Morteros	114	30.42 S	62.00 W
Mortes, Rio das ≃	110	11.45 S	50.44 W
Mortimer	34	51.22 N	1.04 W
Mortlake	94	38.05 S	142.48 E
Morton Craig Range ⋀	90	28.12 S	124.41 E
Moruya	94	35.55 S	150.05 E
Morvan ⋀	48	47.05 N	4.00 E
Morven, Austl.	94	26.25 S	147.07 E
Morven, N.Z.	96	44.50 S	171.07 E
Morven ∧, Scot., U.K.	38	57.07 N	3.02 W
Morven ∧, Scot., U.K.	38	58.14 N	3.42 W
Morvi	76	22.49 N	70.50 E
Morwell	94	38.14 S	146.24 E
Morwenstow	34	50.54 N	4.33 W
Moryń	46	52.49 N	14.13 E
Mosbach	46	49.21 N	9.08 E
Mosborough	36	53.19 N	1.22 W
Mosby	44	58.14 N	7.54 E
Moscos Islands II	70	14.00 N	97.45 E
Moscow →Moskva, S.S.S.R.	60	55.45 N	37.35 E
Moscow, Id., U.S.	100	46.43 N	116.59 W
Mosel (Moselle) ≃	48	50.22 N	7.36 E
Moselle □ 5	48	49.00 N	6.30 E
Moselle (Mosel) ≃	48	50.22 N	7.36 E
Mosgiel	96	45.53 S	170.21 E
Moshaweng ≃	86	26.35 S	22.50 E
Moshi	84	3.21 S	37.20 E
Mosina	46	52.16 N	16.51 E
Mosjøen	42	65.50 N	13.10 E
Moskenesøya I	42	67.59 N	13.00 E
Moskva (Moscow)	60	55.45 N	37.35 E
Moskva ≃	60	55.05 N	38.50 E
Mosonmagyaróvár	46	47.51 N	17.17 E
Mosopa	86	24.50 S	25.31 E
Mosquera	110	2.30 N	78.29 W
Mosquito, Punta >	108	9.07 N	77.53 W
Mosquito Creek Lake ⊜ 1	102	41.22 N	80.45 W
Mosquitos, Costa de □ 9	108	13.00 N	83.45 W
Mosquitos, Golfo de los C	108	9.00 N	81.15 W
Moss	44	59.26 N	10.42 E
Mossaka	84	1.13 S	16.48 E
Mossbank	38	60.27 N	1.12 W
Mossburn	96	45.40 S	168.15 E
Mosselbaai	86	34.11 S	22.08 E
Mossendjo	84	2.57 S	12.44 E
Mossman	92	16.28 S	145.22 E
Mossoró	110	5.11 S	37.20 W
Moss Vale	94	34.33 S	150.22 E
Most	46	50.32 N	13.39 E
Mosta	60	56.32 N	42.10 E
Mostar	52	43.20 N	17.49 E
Mostardas	114	31.06 S	50.57 W
Møsting, Kap >	98	64.00 N	41.00 W
Mostiştea ≃	54	44.15 N	27.10 E
Mostrim (Edgeworthstown)	40	53.42 N	7.36 W
Mostyn, Malay.	72	4.40 N	118.11 E
Mostyn, Wales, U.K.	36	53.19 N	3.16 W
Mosul →Al-Mawṣil	78	36.20 N	43.08 E
Møsvatnet ⊜	44	59.52 N	8.05 E
Mota	82	11.02 N	37.52 E
Mota del Cuervo	50	39.30 N	2.52 W
Mota del Marqués	50	41.38 N	5.10 W
Motagua ≃	106	15.44 N	88.14 W
Motala	44	58.33 N	15.03 E
Motatán	108	9.24 N	70.36 W
Motherwell	38	55.48 N	4.00 W
Motīhāri	76	26.39 N	84.55 E
Motilla del Palancar	50	39.34 N	1.53 W
Motiti Island I	96	37.38 S	176.26 E
Motril	50	36.45 N	3.31 W
Motru	54	44.50 N	23.00 E
Mottisfont	34	51.02 N	1.32 W
Mottola	52	40.38 N	17.03 E
Motu ≃	96	37.51 S	177.35 E
Motueka	96	41.07 S	173.00 E
Motueka ≃	96	41.05 S	173.01 E
Motu One I 1	28	15.48 S	154.33 W
Motygino	58	58.11 N	94.40 E
Motyklejka	58	59.26 N	148.38 E
Mouaskar	80	35.45 N	0.01 E
Mouchoir Passage ⋓	108	21.10 N	71.00 W
Moúdhros	54	39.52 N	25.16 E
Mouding	70	25.24 N	101.35 E
Moudjéria	80	17.53 N	12.20 W
Moudon	48	46.40 N	6.48 E
Mouila	84	1.52 S	11.01 E
Moulamein	94	35.05 S	144.02 E
Moulay-Idriss	80	34.02 N	5.27 W
Moulins	48	46.34 N	3.20 E
Moulins-la-Marche	48	48.39 N	0.29 E
Moulmein	70	16.30 N	97.38 E
Moulmeingyun	70	16.23 N	95.16 E
Moulouya, Oued ≃	80	35.05 N	2.25 W
Moulton	36	53.14 N	2.31 W
Moultrie	100	31.10 N	83.47 W
Moundou	82	8.34 N	16.05 E
Moundsville	102	39.55 N	80.44 W
Moungahaumi ∧	96	38.18 S	177.40 E
Mountain ≃	98	65.41 N	128.50 W
Mountain Ash	34	51.42 N	3.24 W
Mountain City	104	41.50 N	115.57 W
Mountain Home	104	43.07 N	115.41 W
Mountain Nile (Baḥr al-Jabal) ≃	82	9.30 N	30.30 E
Mountain View	104	37.23 N	122.04 W
Mount Airy	102	39.22 N	77.09 W
Mount Alida	86	29.09 S	30.18 E
Mount Augustus	90	24.19 S	116.54 E
Mount Ayliff	86	30.54 S	29.20 E
Mount Barker, Austl.	90	34.38 S	117.40 E
Mount Barker, Austl.	94	35.04 S	138.52 E
Mount Bellew Bridge	40	53.28 N	8.29 W
Mount Brydges	102	42.54 N	81.29 W
Mount Carmel	102	40.47 N	76.24 W
Mount Cavenagh	90	25.58 S	133.15 E
Mount Clare	102	39.13 N	80.21 W
Mount Clemens	102	42.35 N	82.52 W
Mount Cook National Park ♠	96	43.35 S	170.15 E
Mount Desert Island I	102	44.20 N	68.20 W
Mount Doreen	90	22.03 S	131.18 E
Mount Dutton	90	27.50 S	135.43 E
Mount Eba	94	30.12 S	135.40 E
Mount Elizabeth	92	16.15 S	126.12 E
Mount Forest	102	43.59 N	80.44 W
Mount Frere	86	31.00 S	28.58 E
Mount Gambier	94	37.50 S	140.46 E
Mount Garnet	94	17.41 S	145.07 E
Mount Gay	102	37.51 N	82.00 W
Mount Gilead	102	40.32 N	82.49 W
Mount Hagen	92	5.50 S	144.15 E
Mount Hawke	34	50.17 N	5.12 W
Mount Holly Springs	102	40.07 N	77.11 W
Mount Hope, Austl.	94	34.07 S	135.23 E
Mount Hope, W.V., U.S.	102	37.53 N	81.09 W
Mount Howitt	94	26.31 S	142.16 E
Mount Isa	94	20.44 S	139.30 E
Mount Jackson	102	38.44 N	78.38 W
Mount Jewett	102	41.43 N	78.38 W
Mount Kisco	102	41.12 N	73.43 W
Mount Lebanon	102	40.21 N	80.02 W
Mount Magnet	90	28.04 S	117.49 E
Mount Manara	94	32.29 S	143.56 E
Mount Margaret	94	26.54 S	143.21 E
Mount Maunganui	96	37.37 S	176.11 E
Mountmellick	40	53.07 N	7.20 W
Mount Molloy	92	16.41 S	145.20 E
Mount Monger	90	30.59 S	121.53 E
Mount Morgan	94	23.39 S	150.23 E
Mount Morris, Mi., U.S.	102	43.07 N	83.41 W
Mount Morris, N.Y., U.S.	102	42.43 N	77.52 W
Mount Mulligan	94	16.51 S	144.52 E
Mount Olivet	102	38.31 N	84.02 W
Mount Orab	102	39.01 N	83.55 W
Mount Perry	94	25.11 S	151.39 E
Mount Pleasant, On., Can.	102	43.05 N	80.19 W
Mount Pleasant, Mi., U.S.	102	43.35 N	84.46 W
Mount Pleasant, Pa., U.S.	102	40.08 N	79.32 W
Mount Pleasant, Tx., U.S.	100	33.09 N	94.58 W
Mountrath	40	53.00 N	7.27 W
Mount Rebecca	90	26.48 S	135.10 E
Mount Riddock	90	23.03 S	134.40 E
Mount Roskill	96	36.55 S	174.45 E
Mount Sandiman	90	24.24 S	115.23 E
Mount Savage	102	39.41 N	78.52 W
Mount's Bay C	34	50.03 N	5.25 W
Mount Shasta	104	41.18 N	122.18 W
Mount Somers	96	43.43 S	171.24 E
Mountsorrel	34	52.44 N	1.07 W
Mount Sterling, Ky., U.S.	102	38.03 N	83.56 W
Mount Sterling, Oh., U.S.	102	39.43 N	83.15 W
Mount Stewart	86	33.10 S	24.26 E
Mount Surprise	94	18.09 S	144.19 E
Mount Union	102	40.23 N	77.52 W
Mount Vernon, Austl.	90	24.13 S	118.14 E
Mount Vernon, Il., U.S.	100	38.19 N	88.54 W
Mount Vernon, Oh., U.S.	102	40.23 N	82.29 W
Mount Vernon, Wa., U.S.	100	48.25 N	122.19 W
Mount Victory	102	40.32 N	83.31 W
Mount Wedge	90	33.29 S	135.10 E
Mount Wellington	96	36.54 S	174.51 E
Mount Willoughby	90	27.58 S	134.08 E
Mount Wolf	102	40.03 N	76.42 W
Moura, Austl.	94	24.35 S	149.58 E
Moura, Bra.	110	1.27 S	61.38 W
Moura, Port.	50	38.08 N	7.27 W
Mourdi, Dépression du ⊥ 7	82	18.10 N	23.00 E
Mourne ≃	40	54.49 N	7.28 W
Mourne Beg ≃	40	54.41 N	7.39 W
Mourne Mountains ⋀	40	54.10 N	6.04 W
Mousa I	38	60.00 N	1.11 W
Mouscron	46	50.44 N	3.13 E
Moussoro	82	13.39 N	16.29 E
Moutier	48	47.17 N	7.23 E
Moûtiers	48	45.29 N	6.32 E
Moutohora	96	38.17 S	177.32 E
Moutong	72	0.28 N	121.13 E
Mouzákion	54	39.26 N	21.40 E
Mouzon	48	49.36 N	5.05 E
Moville	40	55.11 N	7.03 W
Mowang	66	30.31 N	113.34 E
Moy	40	54.27 N	6.42 W
Moy ≃	40	54.12 N	9.08 W
Moy, Cnoc ∧ 2	38	55.22 N	5.46 W
Moyagee	90	27.45 S	117.54 E
Moyale	82	3.32 N	39.03 E
Moyamba	80	8.10 N	12.26 W
Moycullen	40	53.21 N	9.09 W
Moyen Atlas ⋀	80	33.30 N	5.00 W
Moyeuvre-Grande	48	49.15 N	6.02 E
Moyle ≃	40	52.24 N	7.39 W
Moyo, Pulau I	72	8.15 S	117.34 E
Moyobamba	110	6.03 S	76.58 W
Moyu	76	37.17 N	79.44 E
Možajsk	60	55.30 N	36.01 E
Mozambique (Moçambique) □ 1	84	18.15 S	35.00 E
Mozambique Channel ⋓	84	19.00 S	41.00 E
Mozambique Plateau + 3	20	32.00 S	35.00 E
Mozdok	56	43.44 N	44.38 E
Možga	42	56.23 N	52.17 E
Mozyr'	56	52.03 N	29.14 E
Mpanda	84	6.22 S	31.02 E
Mpika	84	11.54 S	31.26 E
Mpraeso	80	6.35 N	0.44 W
Mpwapwa	84	6.21 S	36.29 E
Mrągowo	46	53.52 N	21.19 E
Mrkonjić Grad	52	44.25 N	17.05 E
Mrkopalj	52	45.19 N	14.51 E
Mrocza	46	53.14 N	17.36 E
Mstislavl'	60	54.02 N	31.42 E
Mszana Dolna	46	49.42 N	20.05 E
Mszczonów	46	51.58 N	20.31 E
Mtamvuna ≃	86	31.06 S	30.12 E
Mtubatuba	86	28.30 S	32.08 E
Mtwara	84	10.16 S	40.11 E
Mu ≃	64a	42.33 N	141.56 E
Mu, Cerro ∧	108	9.29 N	73.07 W
Muanda	84	5.56 S	12.21 E
Muang Khammouan	70	17.24 N	104.48 E
Muang Không	70	14.07 N	105.51 E
Muang Khôngxédôn	70	15.34 N	105.49 E
Muang Ngoy	70	20.43 N	102.41 E
Muang Pak-Lay	70	18.12 N	101.25 E
Muang Pakxan	70	18.22 N	103.39 E
Muang Sing	70	21.11 N	101.09 E
Muang Vangviang	70	18.56 N	102.27 E
Muang Xaignabouri	70	19.15 N	101.45 E
Muang Xépôn	70	16.41 N	106.14 E
Muar (Bandar Maharani)	72	2.02 N	102.34 E
Muar ≃	72	2.03 N	102.35 E
Muara	72	5.02 N	115.02 E
Muaradua	72	4.32 S	104.05 E
Muaraenim	72	3.39 S	103.48 E
Muaralabuh	72	1.29 S	101.03 E
Muarasiberut	68	1.36 S	99.11 E
Muaratebo	72	1.30 S	102.26 E
Muaratembesi	72	1.42 S	103.07 E
Muaratewe	72	0.57 S	114.53 E
Muasdale	38	55.36 N	5.41 W
Mubārakpur	76	26.05 N	83.18 E
Mubende	84	0.35 N	31.23 E
Mucajaí ≃	110	2.25 N	60.52 W
Muccan	90	20.38 S	120.04 E
Much Dewchurch	34	51.59 N	2.46 W
Muchea	90	31.35 S	115.59 E
Mücheln	46	51.18 N	11.48 E
Muchinga Mountains ⋀	84	12.20 S	31.00 E
Much Wenlock	34	52.36 N	2.34 W
Muck I	38	56.50 N	6.15 W
Muckadilla	94	26.35 S	148.23 E
Muckle Roe I	38a	60.22 N	1.27 W
Muckno Lake ⊜	40	54.07 N	6.42 W
Mucucuaú ≃	110	0.37 S	61.24 W
Mucugê	110	13.00 S	41.23 W
Muçum	114	29.10 S	51.53 W
Mucuri ≃	110	18.05 S	39.34 W
Mud ≃	102	38.25 N	82.17 W
Muda ≃	72	5.33 N	100.22 E
Mudan ≃	62	46.22 N	129.33 E
Mudanjiang	62	44.35 N	129.36 E
Muddy ≃	104	36.27 N	114.22 W
Muddy Peak ∧	104	36.18 N	114.42 W
Mudgee	94	32.36 S	149.35 E
Mud Lake ⊜	104	37.52 N	117.04 W
Mudon	70	16.15 N	97.44 E
Mudu	66	31.15 N	120.30 E
Muelle de los Bueyes	108	12.04 N	84.32 W
Mueller, Mount ∧	90	19.54 S	127.51 E
Muerto ≃	114	23.02 S	62.29 W
Mufulira	84	12.33 S	28.14 E
Mughalsarai	76	25.18 N	83.07 E
Mugi	64	33.40 N	134.25 E
Mu Gia, Deo)(	70	17.40 N	105.47 E
Muğla	30	37.12 N	28.22 E
Mugron	48	43.45 N	0.45 W
Muhamdi	76	27.57 N	80.13 E
Muḥammad, Ra's >	82	27.44 N	34.15 E
Mühlacker	46	48.57 N	8.50 E
Mühldorf	46	48.15 N	12.32 E
Mühlhausen	46	51.12 N	10.27 E
Mühlviertel ◆ 1	46	48.25 N	14.10 E
Muhola	44	63.20 N	25.05 E
Muhos	44	64.48 N	25.59 E
Mui Ca-mau >	70	8.38 N	104.44 E
Muick, Loch ⊜	38	56.55 N	3.10 W
Mui Ke-ga >	70	12.53 N	109.28 E
Muine Bheag	40	52.41 N	6.58 W
Muirdrum	38	56.31 N	2.42 W
Muirkirk	38	55.31 N	4.04 W
Muir of Ord	38	57.31 N	4.27 W
Muiron Islands II	90	21.35 S	114.20 E
Mui Ron-ma >	70	18.07 N	106.22 E
Muir Seamount + 3	22	33.41 N	62.30 W
Muirtown	38	56.16 N	3.45 W
Muja	58	56.24 N	115.39 E
Mujnak	56	43.48 N	59.02 E
Mukačevo	56	48.27 N	22.45 E
Mukah	72	2.54 N	112.06 E
Mukalla →Al-Mukallā	74	14.32 N	49.08 E
Mukandwara	76	24.49 N	75.59 E
Mukden →Shenyang	62	41.48 N	123.27 E
Mukeriān	76	31.57 N	75.37 E
Mukinbudin	90	30.54 S	118.13 E
Mukomuko	72	2.35 S	101.07 E
Mukoshima-rettō II	28	27.37 N	142.10 E
Mukry	78	37.36 N	65.44 E
Muktsar	76	30.29 N	74.31 E
Mula	50	38.03 N	1.30 W
Mulanje	84	16.03 S	35.31 E
Mulas, Punta de >	108	21.01 N	75.35 W
Mulatupo	108	8.57 N	77.45 W
Mulben	38	57.31 N	3.06 W
Mulchén	114	37.43 S	72.14 W
Mulde ≃	46	51.52 N	12.15 E
Mulga Downs	90	22.08 S	118.26 E
Mulgathing	90	30.15 S	134.00 E
Mulgathing Rocks ∧	90	30.14 S	133.58 E
Mulgowie	94	27.43 S	152.22 E
Mulgul	90	24.49 S	118.26 E
Mulhacén ∧	50	37.03 N	3.19 W
Mulhouse	48	47.45 N	7.20 E
Mulkear ≃	40	52.40 N	8.33 W
Mull, Island of I	38	56.27 N	6.00 W
Mull, Sound of ⋓	38	56.32 N	5.50 W
Mullagh	40	53.49 N	6.57 W
Mullaghareirk Mountains ⋀	40	52.20 N	9.10 W
Mullaghcleevaun ∧	40	53.06 N	6.24 W
Mullaghmore ∧	40	54.52 N	6.51 W
Mullengudgery	94	31.41 S	147.26 E
Muller, Pegunungan ⋀	72	0.40 N	113.50 E
Muller Range ⋀	92	5.35 S	142.15 E
Mullet Peninsula > 1	40	54.12 N	10.00 W
Mullett Lake ⊜	102	45.30 N	84.30 W
Mullewa	90	28.33 S	115.31 E
Mull Head >, Scot., U.K.	38	58.58 N	2.43 W
Mull Head >, Scot., U.K.	38	59.23 N	2.54 W
Müllheim	46	47.48 N	7.38 E
Mullica ≃	102	39.33 N	74.25 W
Mulligan ≃	94	25.00 S	138.30 E
Mullinahone	40	52.30 N	7.30 W
Mullinavat	40	52.21 N	7.10 W
Mullingar	40	53.32 N	7.20 W
Mullion	34	50.01 N	5.15 W
Mullsjö	44	57.55 N	13.53 E
Mullumbimby	94	28.33 S	153.30 E
Multai	76	21.46 N	78.15 E
Multān	76	30.11 N	71.29 E
Multia	44	62.25 N	24.47 E
Mulu, Gunong ∧	72	4.04 N	114.56 E
Mulyah Mountain ∧	94	30.37 S	144.31 E
Mumbles Head >	34	51.35 N	3.59 W
Mumbwa	84	14.59 S	27.04 E
Mun ≃	70	15.19 N	105.30 E
Muna ≃	58	67.52 N	123.06 E
Muna, Pulau I	72	5.00 S	122.30 E
Munābāo	76	25.45 N	70.17 E
Münchberg	46	50.11 N	11.47 E
München (Munich)	46	48.08 N	11.34 E
Muncie	100	40.11 N	85.23 W
Muncy	102	41.12 N	76.47 W
Mundaring	90	31.54 S	116.10 E
Münden	46	51.25 N	9.39 E
Mundesley	34	52.53 N	1.26 E
Mundiwindi	90	23.52 S	120.09 E
Mundo ≃	50	38.19 N	1.40 W
Mundra	76	22.51 N	69.44 E
Mundrabilla	90	31.52 S	127.51 E
Mundubbera	94	25.36 S	151.18 E
Munera	50	39.02 N	2.28 W
Mungallala	94	26.27 S	147.33 E
Mungallala Creek ≃	94	28.05 S	147.15 E
Mungana	94	17.07 S	144.24 E
Mungar Junction	94	25.36 S	152.36 E
Mungbere	82	2.38 N	28.30 E
Mungeli	76	22.04 N	81.41 E
Mungeranie	94	28.00 S	138.36 E
Mungindi	94	28.58 S	148.59 E
Munhango	84	12.12 S	18.42 E
Munich →München	46	48.08 N	11.34 E
Muniesa	50	41.02 N	0.48 W
Munkedal	44	58.29 N	11.41 E
Munkfors	44	59.50 N	13.32 E
Munksund	44	65.17 N	21.29 E
Munku-Sardyk, gora ∧	58	51.45 N	100.32 E
Munlochy	38	57.32 N	4.15 W
Münsingen, B.R.D.	46	48.25 N	9.29 E
Münsingen, Schw.	48	46.53 N	7.34 E
Munsons Corners	102	42.35 N	76.13 W
Munster, B.R.D.	46	52.59 N	10.05 E
Münster, B.R.D.	46	51.57 N	7.37 E
Munster, Fr.	48	48.03 N	7.08 E
Munster □ 9	40	52.25 N	8.20 W
Munster ≃	40	52.33 N	7.12 W
Muntadgin	90	31.45 S	118.34 E
Muntok	72	2.04 S	105.11 E
Munuscong Lake ⊜	102	46.10 N	84.08 W
Muojärvi ⊜	44	65.56 N	29.36 E
Muonio	42	67.57 N	23.42 E
Muoro	52	40.20 N	9.20 E
Muqayshit I	78	24.12 N	53.42 E
Muqdisho (Mogadishu)	82	2.04 N	45.22 E
Mur (Mura) ≃	46	46.18 N	16.53 E
Mura (Mur) ≃	46	46.18 N	16.53 E
Muradiye	54	38.39 N	27.21 E
Murakami	64	38.14 N	139.29 E
Muráň	46	48.46 N	20.02 E
Murana	92	3.33 S	133.49 E
Muraši	42	59.24 N	48.55 E
Murat	48	45.07 N	2.52 E
Murat ≃	30	38.39 N	39.50 E
Murau	46	47.07 N	14.10 E
Muravera	52	39.25 N	9.34 E
Murayama	64	38.28 N	140.22 E
Murča	50	41.24 N	7.27 W
Murchison, Austl.	94	36.37 S	145.14 E
Murchison, N.Z.	96	41.48 S	172.20 E
Murchison ≃	90	27.42 S	114.09 E
Murchison, Mount ∧, Austl.	90	26.46 S	116.25 E
Murchison, Mount ∧, N.Z.	96	43.01 S	171.22 E
Murchison Falls →Kabalega Falls ʟ	82	2.17 N	31.41 E
Murchison Range ⋀	90	20.11 S	134.26 E
Murcia	50	37.59 N	1.07 W
Mur-de-Barrez	48	44.51 N	2.39 E
Mureck	46	46.42 N	15.46 E
Mureş □ 6	54	46.35 N	24.40 E
Mureş (Maros) ≃	54	46.15 N	20.13 E
Muret	48	43.28 N	1.21 E
Murfreesboro	100	35.50 N	86.23 W
Murgab	56	38.10 N	73.59 E
Murgab (Morghāb) ≃	78	38.18 N	61.12 E
Murgeni	54	46.12 N	28.01 E
Murgon	94	26.15 S	151.57 E
Murguia	50	42.57 N	2.49 W
Murias de Paredes	50	42.51 N	6.11 W
Murilo I 1	28	8.40 N	152.11 E
Müritz ⊜	46	53.25 N	12.43 E
Muriwai	96	38.46 S	177.55 E
Murkong Selek	76	27.49 N	95.16 E
Murliganj	76	25.54 N	86.59 E
Murmansk	42	68.58 N	33.05 E
Murmansk Rise + 3	20	75.00 N	37.00 E
Murnau	46	47.40 N	11.12 E
Muro, Capo di >	52	41.44 N	8.40 E
Muro Lucano	52	40.45 N	15.29 E
Murom	60	55.34 N	42.02 E
Muroran	64a	42.18 N	140.59 E
Muros	50	42.47 N	9.02 W
Muros y Noya, Ría de C 1	50	42.45 N	9.00 W
Muroto	64	33.18 N	134.09 E
Muroto-zaki >	64	33.15 N	134.11 E
Murowana Goślina	46	52.35 N	17.01 E
Murphy	104	43.13 N	116.33 W
Murphys	104	38.08 N	120.27 W
Murra Murra	94	28.16 S	146.48 E
Murray	100	36.36 N	88.18 W
Murray ≃, Austl.	94	35.22 S	139.22 E
Murray ≃, B.C., Can.	98	55.40 N	121.10 W
Murray, Lake ⊜	92	7.00 S	141.30 E
Murray Bay →La Malbaie	98	47.39 N	70.10 W
Murray Bridge	94	35.07 S	139.17 E
Murray City	102	39.30 N	82.09 W
Murray Downs	90	21.04 S	134.40 E
Murray Fracture Zone +	22	34.00 N	135.00 W
Murray Maxwell Bay C	98	70.00 N	80.00 W
Murraysburg	86	31.58 S	23.47 E
Murree	76	33.54 N	73.24 E
Murrhardt	46	48.59 N	9.34 E
Murrin Murrin	90	28.55 S	121.49 E
Murrumbidgee ≃	94	34.43 S	143.12 E
Murrumburrah	94	34.33 S	148.21 E
Murrurundi	94	31.46 S	150.50 E
Murshidābād	76	24.11 N	88.16 E
Murska Sobota	52	46.40 N	16.10 E
Murtee	94	31.35 S	143.30 E
Murten	48	46.56 N	7.07 E
Murter, Otok I	52	43.48 N	15.37 E
Murtoa	94	36.37 S	142.28 E
Murton	36	54.49 N	1.24 W
Murtosa	50	40.44 N	8.38 W
Murud, Gunong ∧	72	3.52 N	115.30 E
Murukta	58	67.46 N	102.01 E
Murupara	96	38.28 S	176.42 E
Murwāra	76	23.51 N	80.24 E
Murwillumbah	94	28.19 S	153.24 E
Mürzzuschlag	46	47.36 N	15.41 E
Muş	78	38.44 N	41.30 E
Mūsā, Jabal (Mount Sinai) ∧	78	28.32 N	33.59 E
Musaid	82	31.35 N	25.03 E
Musala ∧	54	42.11 N	23.34 E
Musay'īd	78	24.59 N	51.32 E
Muscat →Masqaṭ	78	23.37 N	58.35 E
Muscat and Oman →Oman □ 1	74	22.00 N	58.00 E
Muscatine	100	41.25 N	91.03 W
Mus-Chaja, gora ∧	58	62.35 N	140.50 E
Muscongus Bay C	102	43.55 N	69.20 W
Musgrave	92	14.47 S	143.30 E
Musgrave, Mount ∧	96	43.48 S	170.43 E
Musgrave Ranges ⋀	90	26.10 S	131.50 E
Mushie	84	3.01 S	16.54 E
Mushin	80	6.32 N	3.22 E
Musi ≃	72	2.20 S	104.56 E
Musishan ∧	76	36.03 N	80.07 E
Muskegon	100	43.14 N	86.14 W
Muskegon ≃	102	43.25 N	85.42 W
Muskingum ≃	102	39.27 N	81.30 W
Muskö I	44	59.00 N	18.06 E
Muskogee	100	35.44 N	95.22 W
Muskoka, Lake ⊜	102	45.00 N	79.25 W
Muskrat Lake ⊜	102	45.40 N	76.55 W
Muskwa ≃	98	58.45 N	122.35 W
Musoma	84	1.30 S	33.48 E
Mussau Island I	92	1.30 S	149.40 E
Musselburgh	38	55.57 N	3.04 W
Mussidan	48	45.02 N	0.22 E
Mussomeli	52	37.35 N	13.45 E
Mussuma	84	14.14 S	21.59 E
Mustafakemalpaşa	54	40.02 N	28.24 E
Mustla	60	58.14 N	25.52 E
Muswellbrook	94	32.16 S	150.53 E
Muszyna	46	49.21 N	20.54 E
Mutare	86	18.58 S	32.40 E
Muthill	38	56.19 N	3.50 W
Mutoraj	58	61.20 N	100.30 E
Mutsamudu	87a	12.09 S	44.25 E
Mutsu	64	41.17 N	141.10 E
Mutsu-wan C	64	41.05 N	140.55 E
Muttaburra	94	22.36 S	144.33 E
Mutton Bird Islands II	96	47.15 S	167.24 E
Muxima	84	9.31 S	13.56 E
Muyang	66	27.06 N	119.34 E
Muyumba	84	7.15 S	26.59 E
Muzaffarābād	76	34.22 N	73.28 E
Muzaffarnagar	76	29.28 N	77.41 E
Muzaffarpur	76	26.07 N	85.24 E
Muzat ≃	62	41.15 N	83.27 E
Muži	56	65.22 N	64.40 E
Muzillac	48	47.33 N	2.29 W
Muztag ∧	62	36.25 N	87.25 E
Mvuma	86	19.19 S	30.35 E
Mwadui	84	3.33 S	33.36 E
Mwanza	84	2.31 S	32.54 E
Mweelrea ∧	40	53.38 N	9.50 W
Mweka	84	4.51 S	21.34 E
Mwenezi	86	21.22 S	30.45 E
Mweru, Lake ⊜	84	9.00 S	28.45 E
Mwinilunga	84	11.44 S	24.26 E
Myanaung	70	18.17 N	95.19 E
Myaungmya	70	16.36 N	94.56 E
Mybster	38	58.27 N	3.25 W
Myckelgensjö	44	63.34 N	17.37 E
Myerstown	102	40.22 N	76.19 W
Myingyan	70	21.28 N	95.23 E
Myitkyinā	70	25.23 N	97.24 E
Myjava	46	48.45 N	17.34 E
Myllymäki	44	62.32 N	24.17 E
Mynämäki	44	60.40 N	22.00 E
Mynfontein	86	30.55 S	23.57 E
Mynydd Bach ∧ 2	34	52.15 N	4.05 W
Mynydd Eppynt ∧	34	52.05 N	3.30 W
Mynydd Hiraethog ∧	34	53.05 N	3.33 W
Mynydd Pencarreg ∧ 2	34	52.04 N	4.04 W
Mynydd Preseli ∧	34	51.58 N	4.42 W
Myōkō-san ∧	64	36.52 N	138.07 E
Mýrdalsjökull ⊓	42a	63.40 N	19.05 W
Myroodah	90	18.08 S	124.16 E
Myrskylä (Mörskom)	44	60.40 N	25.51 E
Myrtle Creek	104	43.01 N	123.17 W
Myrtle Point	104	43.03 N	124.08 W
Myrtletowne	104	40.47 N	124.04 W
Mysen	44	59.33 N	11.20 E
Myski	58	53.42 N	87.48 E
Myślenice	46	49.51 N	19.56 E
Myślibórz	46	52.55 N	14.52 E
Mysłowice	46	50.15 N	19.07 E
Mysore	74	12.18 N	76.39 E
Mys Šmidta	58	68.56 N	179.26 W
Mystic	102	41.21 N	71.58 W
Mys Vchodnoj	56	73.53 N	86.43 E
Mys Želanija	56	76.56 N	68.35 E
Myszków	46	50.36 N	19.20 E
My-tho	70	10.21 N	106.21 E
Mytilene →Mitilíni	54	39.06 N	26.32 E
Mytišči	60	55.55 N	37.46 E
Mývatn ⊜	42a	65.37 N	16.58 W
Mzimba	84	11.52 S	33.34 E

Symbols in the Index entries are identified on page 122

Name	Page	Lat. °′	Long. °′
Mzimvubu ≃	86	31.38 S	29.32 E
Mzuzu	84	11.27 S	33.55 E
N			
Na (Tengtiaohe) ≃	70	22.05 N	103.09 E
Naab ≃	46	49.01 N	12.02 E
Naalehu	105a	19.03 N	155.35 W
Naantali	44	60.27 N	22.02 E
Naas	40	53.13 N	6.39 W
Nababiep	86	29.36 S	17.46 E
Nabadwīp	76	23.25 N	88.22 E
Nabari	64	34.37 N	136.05 E
Nabberu, Lake ⊜	90	25.36 S	120.30 E
Nabburg	46	49.28 N	12.11 E
Nabeul	80	36.27 N	10.44 E
Nābha	76	30.22 N	76.09 E
Nabire	92	3.22 S	135.29 E
Nabī Shu'ayb, Jabal an- ∧	74	15.18 N	43.59 E
Naboomspruit	86	24.32 S	28.36 E
Nabq	78	28.04 N	34.25 E
Nābulus	78	32.13 N	35.16 E
Nachičevan'	78	39.13 N	45.24 E
Nachi-katsuura	64	33.30 N	135.55 E
Nachingwea	84	10.23 S	38.46 E
Nāchna	76	27.30 N	71.43 E
Náchod	46	50.25 N	16.10 E
Nachodka	58	42.48 N	132.52 E
Nachvak Fiord c [2]	98	59.03 N	63.45 W
Nacimiento	114	37.30 S	72.40 W
Nacimiento ≃	104	35.49 N	120.45 W
Nacimiento, Lake ⊜ [1]	104	35.45 N	121.00 W
Nacka	44	59.18 N	18.10 E
Nacogdoches	100	31.36 N	94.39 W
Nacozari	106	30.24 N	109.39 W
Ñacunday	114	26.01 S	54.46 W
Nadder ≃	34	51.03 N	1.48 W
Nadela	50	42.58 N	7.30 W
Nadiād	76	22.42 N	72.52 E
Nădlac	54	46.10 N	20.45 E
Nador	80	35.12 N	2.55 W
Nadym	56	65.35 N	72.42 E
Nadym ≃	56	66.12 N	72.00 E
Naenwa	76	25.46 N	75.51 E
Nærbø	44	58.40 N	5.39 E
Næstved	44	55.14 N	11.46 E
Näfels	48	47.06 N	9.04 E
Naga	68	13.37 N	123.11 E
Nagahama, Nihon	64	33.36 N	132.29 E
Nagahama, Nihon	64	35.23 N	136.16 E
Naga Hills ✱	70	26.00 N	95.00 E
Nagai	64	38.06 N	140.02 E
Nāgāland □ [3]	76	26.00 N	95.00 E
Nagano	64	36.39 N	138.11 E
Nagaoka	64	37.27 N	138.51 E
Nāgappattinam	74	10.46 N	79.50 E
Nagara ≃	64	35.01 N	136.43 E
Nagarote	108	12.16 N	86.34 W
Nagasaki	64	32.48 N	129.55 E
Nagato	64	34.21 N	131.10 E
Nāgaur	76	27.12 N	73.44 E
Nāgda	76	23.27 N	75.25 E
Nāgercoil	74	8.10 N	77.26 E
Nagīna	76	29.27 N	78.27 E
Nagles Mountains ✱	40	52.05 N	8.30 W
Nagłowice	46	50.41 N	20.06 E
Nago	65b	26.35 N	127.59 E
Nagold	46	48.33 N	8.43 E
Nagornyj	58	55.58 N	124.57 E
Nagorsk	42	59.18 N	50.48 E
Nagoya	64	35.10 N	136.55 E
Nāgpur	76	21.09 N	79.06 E
Nagqu	62	31.34 N	92.00 E
Nagu I	44	60.10 N	21.48 E
Nagua	108	19.23 N	69.50 W
Nagyatád	46	46.14 N	17.22 E
Nagybajom	46	46.23 N	17.31 E
Nagyecsed	46	47.52 N	22.24 E
Nagykálló	46	47.53 N	21.51 E
Nagykanizsa	46	46.27 N	17.00 E
Nagykáta	46	47.25 N	19.45 E
Nagykőrös	46	47.02 N	19.43 E
Nagy-Milic ∧	46	48.35 N	21.28 E
Naha	65b	26.13 N	127.40 E
Nāhan	76	30.33 N	77.18 E
Nahang (Nihing) ≃	78	26.00 N	62.44 E
Nahariyya	78	33.00 N	35.05 E
Nahe	62	48.28 N	124.52 E
Nahe ≃	46	49.58 N	7.57 E
Nahuel Huapí, Lago ⊜	112	40.58 S	71.30 W
Naila	46	50.19 N	11.42 E
Nailsea	34	51.26 N	2.43 W
Nailsworth	34	51.42 N	2.14 W
Nain, Nf., Can.	98	56.32 N	61.41 W
Nā'īn, Īrān	78	32.52 N	53.05 E
Naini Tāl	76	29.23 N	79.27 E
Nainpur	76	22.26 N	80.07 E
Nairn	38	57.35 N	3.53 W
Nairn ≃	38	57.35 N	3.52 W
Nairobi	84	1.17 S	36.49 E
Naivasha	84	0.43 S	36.26 E
Najac	48	44.13 N	1.59 E
Najafābād	78	32.37 N	51.21 E
Najasa ≃	108	20.42 N	77.55 W
Nájera	50	42.25 N	2.44 W
Najībābād	76	29.38 N	78.20 E
Najin	62	42.15 N	130.18 E
Naka ≃	64	36.20 N	140.36 E
Nakadōri-shima I	64	32.57 N	129.04 E
Nakajō	64	38.03 N	139.24 E
Nakama	64	33.50 N	130.43 E
Nakaminato	64	36.21 N	140.36 E
Nakamura	64	32.59 N	132.56 E
Nakanai Mountains ✱	92	5.35 S	151.10 E
Nakano	64	36.45 N	138.22 E
Nakano-shima I	65b	29.49 N	129.52 E
Nakanoshima-suidō I	65b	29.44 N	129.49 E
Nakashibetsu	64a	43.33 N	144.59 E
Nakatsu	64	33.34 N	131.13 E
Nakatsugawa	64	35.29 N	137.30 E
Nakhola	76	26.07 N	92.11 E
Nakhon Nayok	70	14.12 N	101.13 E
Nakhon Pathom	70	13.49 N	100.03 E
Nakhon Phanom	70	17.24 N	104.47 E
Nakhon Ratchasima	70	14.58 N	102.07 E
Nakhon Sawan	70	15.41 N	100.07 E
Nakhon Si Thammarat	70	8.26 N	99.58 E
Nakhtarana	76	23.20 N	69.15 E
Nakina	98	50.10 N	86.42 W
Nakło nad Notecią	46	53.08 N	17.35 E
Nakodar	76	31.07 N	75.29 E
Nakskov	44	54.50 N	11.09 E
Näkten ⊜	44	62.52 N	14.38 E
Nakuru	84	0.17 S	36.04 E
Nalajch	62	47.45 N	107.16 E
Nālanda	76	25.07 N	85.25 E
Nalbāri	76	26.25 N	91.26 E
Nal'čik	56	43.29 N	43.37 E
Näldsjön ⊜	44	63.23 N	14.17 E
Nałęczów	46	51.18 N	22.11 E
Nalgonda	74	17.03 N	79.16 E
Nalón ≃	50	43.32 N	6.04 W
Nālūt	82	31.52 N	10.59 E
Nam ≃	70	21.33 N	98.38 E
Namak, Daryācheh-ye ⊜	78	34.45 N	51.36 E
Namakzār, Daryācheh-ye ⊜	78	34.00 N	60.30 E
Namaland □ [5]	86	25.50 S	18.00 E
Namangan	56	41.00 N	71.40 E
Namapa	84	13.43 S	39.50 E
Nambi	90	28.54 S	121.41 E
Nambour	94	26.38 S	152.58 E
Nambucca Heads	94	30.39 S	153.00 E
Namcha Barwa →Namjagbarwa Feng ∧	62	29.38 N	95.04 E
Nam Co ⊜	62	30.42 N	90.30 E
Nam-dinh	70	20.25 N	106.10 E
Nam-du, Quan-dao II	70	9.42 N	104.22 E
Namerikawa	64	36.46 N	137.20 E
Námestovo	46	49.25 N	19.30 E
Namib Desert ◆ [2]	86	23.00 S	15.00 E
Namibia (South West Africa) □ [2]	84	22.00 S	17.00 E
Namie	64	37.29 N	141.00 E
Namies	86	29.18 S	19.13 E
Namjagbarwa Feng ∧	62	29.38 N	95.04 E
Namlea	92	3.18 S	127.06 E
Namoi ≃	94	30.00 S	148.07 E
Namoluk I [1]	28	5.55 N	153.08 E
Namonuito I [1]	28	8.46 N	150.02 E
Namorik I [1]	28	5.36 N	168.07 E
Nampa	100	43.32 N	116.33 W
Namp'o	62	38.45 N	125.23 E
Nampula	84	15.07 S	39.15 E
Namsang	70	20.53 N	97.43 E
Namsen ≃	42	64.27 N	11.28 E
Namsos	42	64.29 N	11.30 E
Namtu	70	23.05 N	97.24 E
Namu	98	51.49 N	127.52 W
Namu I [1]	28	8.00 N	168.10 E
Namur	46	50.28 N	4.52 E
Namutoni	86	18.49 S	16.55 E
Namysłów	46	51.05 N	17.42 E
Nan	70	18.47 N	100.47 E
Nan ≃	70	15.42 N	100.09 E
Nanaimo	98	49.10 N	123.56 W
Nanam	62	41.43 N	129.41 E
Nan'an	66	24.58 N	118.23 E
Nanango	94	26.40 S	152.00 E
Nanao	64	37.03 N	136.58 E
Nanao-wan c	64	37.06 N	137.00 E
Nanatsu-jima II	64	37.36 N	136.53 E
Nanchang, Zhg.	66	28.41 N	115.53 E
Nanchang (Liantang), Zhg.	66	28.34 N	115.56 E
Nancheng	66	27.35 N	116.40 E
Nanchong	62	30.48 N	106.04 E
Nancowry Island I	70	7.59 N	93.32 E
Nancy	48	48.41 N	6.12 E
Nanda Devi ∧	76	30.23 N	79.59 E
Nandaime	108	11.46 N	86.03 W
Nandan	64	34.15 N	134.43 E
Nānded	74	19.09 N	77.20 E
N'andoma	42	61.40 N	40.12 E
Nandu	66	31.27 N	119.19 E
Nandurbār	76	21.22 N	74.15 E
Nanfeng	66	27.15 N	116.32 E
Nanga Parbat ∧	76	35.15 N	74.36 E
Nangapinoh	72	0.20 S	111.44 E
Nangarhār □ [4]	76	34.15 N	70.30 E
Nangatayap	72	1.32 S	110.34 E
Nangis	48	48.33 N	3.00 E
Nangō	64	31.32 N	131.23 E
Nangqian (Xiangda)	76	32.22 N	96.21 E
Nanhui	66	31.03 N	121.45 E
Nanjing, Zhg.	66	24.32 N	117.22 E
Nanjing (Nanking), Zhg.	66	32.03 N	118.47 E
Nankang	66	25.42 N	114.44 E
Nanking →Nanjing	62	32.03 N	118.47 E
Nankoku	64	33.39 N	133.44 E
Nanling	66	30.56 N	118.20 E
Nan Ling ✱	62	25.00 N	112.00 E
Nannine	90	26.53 S	118.20 E
Nanning	70	22.48 N	108.20 E
Nannup	90	33.59 S	115.45 E
Nānpāra	76	27.52 N	81.30 E
Nanping	66	26.38 N	118.10 E
Nansa ≃	50	43.22 N	4.29 W
Nansei	64	34.22 N	136.41 E
Nansei-shotō (Ryukyu Islands) II	62	26.30 N	128.00 E
Nanshan →Qilian Shan ✱	62	39.06 N	98.40 E
Nanshan Island I	68	10.45 N	115.49 E
Nanson	90	28.34 S	114.46 E
Nant	48	44.01 N	3.18 E
Nantais, Lac ⊜	98	60.59 N	74.00 W
Nantai-zan ∧	64	36.46 N	139.29 E
Nant Bran ≃	34	51.57 N	3.28 W
Nantes	48	47.13 N	1.33 W
Nanteuil-le-Haudouin	48	49.08 N	2.48 E
Nanticoke	102	41.12 N	76.00 W
Nanticoke ≃	102	38.16 N	75.56 W
Nanto	64	34.20 N	136.31 E
Nantong	66	32.02 N	120.53 E
Nant'ou, T'aiwan	66	23.55 N	120.41 E
Nantou, Zhg.	66	22.33 N	113.55 E
Nantua	48	46.09 N	5.37 E
Nantucket	102	41.17 N	70.06 W
Nantucket Island I	102	41.16 N	70.03 W
Nantucket Sound ʊ	102	41.30 N	70.15 W
Nantwich	34	53.04 N	2.32 W
Nanty Glo	102	40.28 N	78.50 W
Nant-y-Moch Reservoir ⊜ [1]	34	52.27 N	3.50 W
Nanumanga I	28	6.18 S	176.20 E
Nanumea I [1]	28	5.39 S	176.08 E
Nanuque	110	17.50 S	40.21 W
Nanusa, Pulau-pulau II	68	4.42 N	127.06 E
Nanxiang	66	31.17 N	121.18 E
Nanxiong	66	25.10 N	114.20 E
Nanyang	66	33.00 N	112.32 E
Nan-yō	64	38.03 N	140.10 E
Nanyuki	84	0.01 N	37.04 E
Nanzhao	66	33.30 N	112.27 E
Nanzhaoji	66	32.38 N	115.58 E
Nao, Cabo de la ›	50	38.44 N	0.14 E
Naococane, Lac ⊜	98	52.52 N	70.40 W
Naogaon	76	24.47 N	88.56 E
Não-me-Toque	114	28.28 S	52.49 W
Náousa	54	40.37 N	22.05 E
Napa	104	38.17 N	122.17 W
Napa ≃	104	38.07 N	122.18 W
Napajedla	46	49.10 N	17.31 E
Napalkovo	56	70.03 N	73.47 E
Napanee	102	44.15 N	76.57 W
Napenay	114	26.44 S	60.37 W
Napier, N.Z.	96	39.29 S	176.55 E
Napier, S. Afr.	86	34.29 S	19.53 E
Napier, Mount ∧	90	17.32 S	129.10 E
Naples →Napoli, It.	52	40.51 N	14.17 E
Naples, Fl., U.S.	108	26.08 N	81.47 W
Naples, N.Y., U.S.	102	42.36 N	77.24 W
Napo ≃	110	3.20 S	72.40 W
Napoleon	102	41.23 N	84.07 W
Napoli (Naples)	52	40.51 N	14.17 E
Nappamerry	94	27.36 S	141.07 E
Napton on the Hill	34	52.15 N	1.24 W
Nar ≃	34	52.45 N	0.24 E
Nara, Mali	80	15.10 N	7.17 W
Nara, Nihon	64	34.41 N	135.50 E
Naracoorte	94	36.58 S	140.44 E
Naradhan	94	33.37 S	146.19 E
Naraini	76	25.11 N	80.29 E
Narao	64	32.50 N	129.04 E
Narathiwat	70	6.26 N	101.50 E
Nārāyanganj	76	23.37 N	90.30 E
Narberth	34	51.48 N	4.45 W
Narbonne	48	43.11 N	3.00 E
Narcea ≃	50	43.28 N	6.06 W
Nardò	52	40.11 N	18.02 E
Narembeen	90	32.04 S	118.24 E
Naretha	90	31.00 S	124.50 E
Narew ≃	46	52.26 N	20.42 E
Narinda, Baie de c	87b	14.55 S	47.30 E
Narita	64	35.47 N	140.19 E
Nar'jan-Mar	42	67.39 N	53.00 E
Narkatiāganj	76	27.06 N	84.28 E
Närke □ [9]	44	59.06 N	15.03 E
Narmada ≃	74	21.38 N	72.36 E
Nārnaul	76	28.03 N	76.07 E
Narni	52	42.31 N	12.31 E
Naro	52	37.18 N	13.47 E
Narodnaja, gora ∧	42	65.04 N	60.09 E
Naro-Fominsk	60	55.23 N	36.43 E
Narol	46	50.22 N	23.21 E
Narón	50	43.32 N	8.10 W
Narooma	94	36.14 S	150.03 E
Närpes (Närpiö)	44	62.28 N	21.20 E
Narrabri	94	30.19 S	149.47 E
Narran ≃	94	29.45 S	147.20 E
Narrandera	94	34.45 S	146.33 E
Narrogin	90	32.56 S	117.10 E
Narromine	94	32.14 S	148.15 E
Narsimhapur	76	22.57 N	79.12 E
Narsinghgarh	76	23.42 N	77.06 E
Narssaq	98	60.54 N	46.00 W
Naru	64	32.49 N	128.56 E
Naruko	64	38.44 N	140.43 E
Naruto	64	34.11 N	134.37 E
Narva	60	59.23 N	28.12 E
Narvik	42	68.26 N	17.25 E
Narwāna	76	29.37 N	76.07 E
Narwietooma	90	23.15 S	132.35 E
Naryn	56	41.26 N	75.59 E
Naryn ≃	56	40.54 N	71.45 E
Narynkol	56	42.43 N	80.12 E
Naryškino	60	52.58 N	35.44 E
Nås	44	60.27 N	14.29 E
Näsåker	44	63.26 N	16.54 E
Năsăud	54	47.17 N	24.24 E
Nasbinals	48	44.40 N	3.03 E
Naschel	114	32.55 S	65.23 W
Nase →Naze	65b	28.23 N	129.30 E
Naseby, N.Z.	96	45.02 S	170.09 E
Naseby, Eng., U.K.	34	52.25 N	0.58 W
Nashua	102	42.45 N	71.28 W
Nashville, Mi., U.S.	102	42.36 N	85.05 W
Nashville, Tn., U.S.	100	36.09 N	86.47 W
Našice	54	45.29 N	18.06 E
Nasielsk	46	52.36 N	20.48 E
Näsijärvi ⊜	44	61.37 N	23.42 E
Nāsik	74	19.59 N	73.48 E
Nāṣir	82	8.36 N	33.04 E
Nāṣir, Buḥayrat ⊜ [1]	82	22.40 N	32.00 E
Nasirābād, Bngl.	76	24.45 N	90.24 E
Nasīrābād, India	76	26.18 N	74.44 E
Naskaupi ≃	98	53.45 N	60.50 W
Nass ≃	98	55.00 N	129.50 W
Nassau, Ba.	108	25.05 N	77.21 W
Nassau, N.Y., U.S.	102	42.30 N	73.36 W
Nassau Island I	28	11.33 S	165.25 W
Nassereith	46	47.19 N	10.50 E
Nässjö	44	57.39 N	14.41 E
Nastapoca ≃	98	56.55 N	76.33 W
Nastapoka Islands II	98	57.00 N	76.50 W
Nasu	64	37.01 N	140.07 E
Nasu-dake ∧	64	37.07 N	139.58 E
Nata	86	20.12 S	26.12 E
Nata ≃	86	20.14 S	26.10 E
Natal, Bra.	110	5.47 S	35.13 W
Natal, Indon.	70	0.33 N	99.07 E
Natal □ [4]	86	28.40 S	30.40 E
Natal Basin ✢ [1]	20	30.00 S	40.00 E
Natashquan ≃	98	50.06 N	61.49 W
Natchez	100	31.33 N	91.24 W
Natchitoches	100	31.45 N	93.05 W
Nāthdwāra	76	24.56 N	73.49 E
Natimuk	94	36.45 S	141.57 E
National City	104	32.40 N	117.05 W
Native Bay c	98	63.52 N	82.30 W
Natividade	110	11.43 S	47.47 W
Natori	64	38.08 N	140.55 E
Natron, Lake ⊜	84	2.25 S	36.00 E
Nattastunturit ∧	42	68.12 N	27.20 E
Natuna Besar I	72	4.00 N	108.15 E
Naturaliste, Cape ›	90	33.32 S	115.01 E
Naturaliste Channel ʊ	90	25.25 S	113.00 E
Naucelle	48	44.12 N	2.20 E
Nauders	46	46.53 N	10.30 E
Nauen	46	52.36 N	12.52 E
Naugatuck	102	41.30 N	73.05 W
Naulavaara ∧ [2]	44	63.53 N	28.13 E
Naumburg	46	51.09 N	11.48 E
Nauru □ [1]	28	0.32 S	166.55 E
Naust	38	57.47 N	5.39 W
Naustdal	44	61.31 N	5.43 E
Nautanwa	76	27.26 N	83.25 E
Nautla	106	20.13 N	96.47 W
Nava del Rey	50	41.20 N	5.05 W
Navahermosa	50	39.38 N	4.28 W
Navalcarnero	50	40.18 N	4.00 W
Navalmoral de la Mata	50	39.54 N	5.32 W
Navalvillar de Pela	50	39.06 N	5.28 W
Navan →An Uaimh	40	52.07 N	7.16 W
Navāpur	76	21.09 N	73.48 E
Navarin, mys ›	58	62.16 N	179.10 E
Navarino →Pílos	54	36.55 N	21.43 E
Navarino, Isla I	112	55.05 S	67.40 W
Navarra □ [4]	50	42.40 N	1.30 W
Navarre	102	40.43 N	81.31 W
Navarro	114	35.01 S	59.16 W
Navarro ≃	104	39.11 N	123.45 W
Navašino	60	55.32 N	42.12 E
Navassa Island I	108	18.24 N	75.01 W
Naver ≃	38	58.32 N	4.15 W
Naver, Loch ⊜	38	58.17 N	4.23 W
Navia, Arg.	114	34.47 S	66.35 W
Navia, Esp.	50	43.32 N	6.43 W
Navia ≃	50	43.33 N	6.44 W
Navibandar	76	21.26 N	69.48 E
Navidad	114	33.57 S	71.50 W
Naviraí	114	23.08 S	54.13 W
Navl'a	60	52.51 N	34.30 E
Navoi	56	40.15 N	65.15 E
Navojoa	106	27.06 N	109.26 W
Návpaktos	54	38.23 N	21.50 E
Návplion	54	37.34 N	22.48 E
Navsāri	76	20.51 N	72.55 E
Nawābganj, Bngl.	76	24.36 N	88.17 E
Nawābganj, India	76	26.56 N	81.13 E
Nawābshāh	76	26.15 N	68.25 E
Nawāda	76	24.53 N	85.32 E
Nawalgarh	76	27.51 N	75.16 E
Náxos	54	37.06 N	25.23 E
Náxos I	54	37.02 N	25.35 E
Nayāgarh	76	20.08 N	85.06 E
Nayarit	104	32.20 N	115.19 W
Nayland	34	51.59 N	0.52 E
Nayoro	64a	44.21 N	142.28 E
Nazaré, Bra.	110	13.02 S	39.00 W
Nazaré, Port.	50	39.36 N	9.04 W
Nazaré da Mata	110	7.44 S	35.14 W
Nazareth	102	40.44 N	75.18 W
Nazareth Bank ✢ [4]	26	14.30 S	60.45 E
Nazarovo	58	56.01 N	90.26 E
Nazas	106	25.14 N	104.08 W
Nazca	110	14.50 S	74.57 W
Naze	65b	28.23 N	129.30 E
Nazilli	54	37.55 N	28.21 E
Nāzira	76	26.55 N	94.44 E
Nazret	82	8.33 N	39.16 E
Nazwā	78	22.56 N	57.32 E
Nazyvajevsk	56	55.34 N	71.21 E
N'dalatando	84	9.18 S	14.54 E
Ndélé	82	8.24 N	20.39 E
Ndendé	84	2.23 S	11.23 E
N'Djamena	82	12.07 N	15.03 E
Ndjolé	84	0.11 S	10.45 E
Nea ≃	44	63.13 N	11.02 E
Neabul Creek ≃	94	27.45 S	147.32 E
Neagh, Lough ⊜	40	54.38 N	6.24 W
Neajlov ≃	54	44.11 N	26.12 E
Neale, Lake ⊜	90	24.22 S	130.00 E
Neales ≃	94	28.08 S	136.47 E
Neamţ □ [6]	54	47.00 N	26.30 E
Néa Páfos (Paphos)	78	34.45 N	32.25 E
Neápolis, Ellás	54	35.15 N	25.37 E
Neápolis, Ellás	54	36.30 N	23.04 E
Néa Psará	54	38.23 N	23.48 E
Neath	34	51.40 N	3.48 W
Neath ≃	34	51.37 N	3.50 W
Nebine Creek ≃	94	29.07 S	146.56 E
Nebit-Dag	78	39.30 N	54.22 E
Neblina, Pico da ∧	110	0.48 N	66.02 W
Nebolči	60	59.08 N	33.18 E
Nebraska □ [3]	100	41.30 N	100.00 W
Nebraska City	100	40.40 N	95.51 W
Nebrodi ✱	52	37.54 N	14.35 E
Nechako ≃	98	53.56 N	122.42 W
Neckar ≃	46	49.31 N	8.26 E
Neckarsulm	46	49.12 N	9.13 E
Necker Island I	28	23.35 N	164.42 W
Necker Ridge ✢ [3]	28	22.00 N	167.15 W
Necochea	114	38.33 S	58.45 W
Nêdong	62	29.14 N	91.46 E
Nedre Soppero	42	68.01 N	21.44 E
Nedstrand	44	59.21 N	5.51 E
Needham Market	34	52.09 N	1.03 E
Needles	104	34.50 N	114.36 W
Ñeembucú □ [5]	114	27.00 S	58.00 W
Neepawa	98	50.13 N	99.29 W
Nefern ≃	34	52.02 N	4.50 W
Nefyn	34	52.57 N	4.31 W
Negage	84	7.45 S	15.16 E
Negara	72	8.22 S	114.37 E
Negele	82	5.20 N	39.36 E
Negeri Sembilan □ [3]	72	2.45 N	102.10 E
Negev Desert →HaNegev ◆ [2]	78	30.30 N	34.55 E
Negombo	74	7.13 N	79.50 E
Negonego I [1]	28	18.47 S	141.48 W
Negotin	54	44.14 N	22.32 E
Negra, Laguna ⊜	114	34.03 S	53.40 W
Negra, Punta ›	110	6.06 S	81.09 W
Negreira	50	42.54 N	8.44 W
Negreşti	54	46.50 N	27.27 E
Negreşti-Oaş	54	47.52 N	23.25 E
Negritos	110	4.38 S	81.19 W
Negro ≃, Arg.	112	41.02 S	62.47 W
Negro ≃, Bra.	114	26.01 S	50.30 W
Negro ≃, Para.	114	24.23 S	57.11 W
Negro ≃, S.A.	110	3.08 S	59.55 W
Negro ≃, S.A.	114	33.24 S	58.22 W
Negro ≃, Ven.	108	9.36 N	72.15 W
Negros I	68	10.00 N	123.00 E
Negru-Vodă	54	43.50 N	28.12 E
Nehbandān	78	31.32 N	60.02 E
Neheim-Hüsten	46	51.27 N	7.57 E
Neiba	108	18.28 N	71.25 W
Neiba, Bahía de c	108	18.15 N	71.02 W
Neiges, Piton des ∧	87c	21.05 S	55.29 E
Neijiang	62	29.35 N	105.03 E
Neilston	38	55.47 N	4.27 W
Nei Monggol Zizhiqu (Inner Mongolia) □ [4]	62	43.00 N	115.00 E
Neisse (Nysa Łuzycka) (Nisa) ≃	46	52.04 N	14.46 E
Neiva	110	2.56 N	75.18 W
Neja	60	58.18 N	43.54 E
Nejdek	46	50.17 N	12.42 E
Nekemte	82	9.02 N	36.31 E
Nekrasovskoje	60	57.41 N	40.22 E
Neksø	44	55.04 N	15.09 E
Nelidovo	60	56.13 N	32.46 E
Nel'kan	58	57.40 N	136.13 E
Nellore	74	14.26 N	79.58 E
Nel'ma	58	47.39 N	139.09 E
Nelson, B.C., Can.	98	49.29 N	117.17 W
Nelson, N.Z.	96	41.17 S	173.17 E
Nelson, Eng., U.K.	36	53.51 N	2.13 W
Nelson ≃	98	57.04 N	92.30 W
Nelson, Cape ›	94	38.26 S	141.33 E
Nelsonville	102	39.27 N	82.14 W
Nelspoort	86	32.07 S	23.00 E
Nelspruit	86	25.30 S	30.58 E
Néma	80	16.37 N	7.15 W
Neman	60	55.02 N	22.02 E
Neman (Nemunas) ≃	60	55.18 N	21.23 E
Nemira ∧	54	46.15 N	26.19 E
Nemours	48	48.16 N	2.42 E
Nemuna, Bjeshkët e ✱	54	42.27 N	19.47 E
Nemunas (Neman) ≃	60	55.18 N	21.23 E
Nemuro	64a	43.20 N	145.35 E
Nemuro-hantō › [1]	64a	43.21 N	145.42 E
Nemuro Strait ʊ	64a	44.00 N	145.20 E
Nen ≃	62	45.25 N	124.40 E
Nenagh	40	52.52 N	8.12 W
Nenagh ≃	40	52.56 N	8.17 W
Nenana ≃	98	64.30 N	149.00 W
Nendo I	28	10.45 S	165.54 E
Nene ≃	34	52.48 N	0.13 E
Nenggiri ≃	72	4.53 N	101.48 E
Néon Karlovásion	54	37.48 N	26.44 E
Nepa ≃	58	59.16 N	108.16 E
Nepal (Nepāl) □ [1]	74	28.00 N	84.00 E
Nepālganj	76	28.03 N	81.37 E
Nepa Nagar	76	21.28 N	76.23 E
Nepewassi Lake ⊜	102	46.20 N	80.40 W
Nephin ∧	40	54.01 N	9.22 W
Nephin Beg Range ✱	40	54.00 N	9.35 W
Nepomuk	46	49.29 N	13.36 E
Neptune	102	40.12 N	74.02 W
Nera ≃, Europe	54	44.49 N	21.22 E
Nera ≃, It.	52	42.26 N	12.24 E
Nérac	48	44.08 N	0.20 E
Nerča ≃	58	51.56 N	116.40 E
Nerčinsk	58	51.58 N	116.35 E
Nerčinskij Zavod	58	51.19 N	119.36 E
Nerechta	60	57.28 N	40.34 E
Neretva ≃	52	43.01 N	17.27 E
Neriquinha	84	15.58 S	21.42 E
Nerja	50	36.44 N	3.52 W
Nérondes	48	47.00 N	2.49 E
Nerrima	90	18.24 S	124.29 E
Nerva	50	37.42 N	6.32 W
Nes, Ned.	46	53.26 N	5.45 E
Nes, Nor.	44	60.34 N	9.59 E
Nesbyen	44	60.34 N	9.09 E
Nesebâr	54	42.39 N	27.44 E
Neskaupstaður	42a	65.10 N	13.43 W
Nesle	48	49.46 N	2.55 E
Nesna	42	66.12 N	13.02 E
Ness, Loch ⊜	38	57.15 N	4.30 W
Nesselrode, Mount ∧	98	58.58 N	134.18 W
Nesselwang	46	47.37 N	10.30 E
Neston	36	53.18 N	3.04 W
Néstos (Mesta) ≃	54	40.41 N	24.44 E
Nesttun	44	60.19 N	5.20 E
Nesviž	60	53.13 N	26.40 E
Netanya	78	32.20 N	34.51 E
Nethan ≃	38	55.42 N	3.52 W
Netherdale	94	21.08 S	148.32 E
Netherlands (Nederland) □ [1]	30	52.15 N	5.30 E
Netherlands Antilles (Nederlandse Antillen) □ [2]	106	12.15 N	68.45 W
Nethy Bridge	38	57.16 N	3.38 W
Netley Marsh	34	50.53 N	1.21 W
Neto ≃	52	39.13 N	17.08 E
Netolice	46	49.03 N	14.12 E
Netrakona	76	24.53 N	90.43 E
Nettilling Fiord c [2]	98	66.02 N	68.12 W
Nettilling Lake ⊜	98	66.30 N	70.40 W
Nettlebed	34	51.35 N	1.00 W
Nettleham	36	53.16 N	0.29 W
Nettuno	52	41.27 N	12.39 E
Neubrandenburg	46	53.33 N	13.15 E
Neubrandenburg □ [5]	46	53.30 N	13.15 E
Neuburg an der Donau	46	48.44 N	11.11 E
Neuchâtel	48	46.59 N	6.56 E
Neuchâtel, Lac de ⊜	48	46.52 N	6.50 E
Neuenhagen	46	52.32 N	13.41 E
Neuerburg	46	50.00 N	6.17 E
Neuf-Brisach	48	48.01 N	7.32 E
Neufchâteau, Bel.	46	49.50 N	5.26 E
Neufchâteau, Fr.	48	48.21 N	5.42 E
Neufchâtel-en-Bray	48	49.44 N	1.27 E
Neugersdorf	46	50.59 N	14.36 E
Neuillé-Pont-Pierre	48	47.33 N	0.33 E
Neu-Isenburg	46	50.03 N	8.41 E
Neumarkt [im Hausruckkreis]	46	48.16 N	13.45 E
Neumarkt in der Oberpfalz	46	49.16 N	11.28 E
Neumarkt in Steiermark	46	47.04 N	14.25 E
Neumarkt-Sankt Veit	46	48.22 N	12.30 E
Neumünster	46	54.04 N	9.59 E
Neunburg vorm Wald	46	49.21 N	12.24 E
Neunkirchen	46	47.43 N	16.05 E
Neunkirchen/Saar	46	49.20 N	7.10 E
Neuquén	114	38.57 S	68.04 W
Neuquén ≃	114	38.59 S	68.00 W
Neurara	114	24.10 S	68.29 W
Neuruppin	46	52.55 N	12.48 E
Neusiedl am See	46	47.57 N	16.51 E
Neusiedler See ⊜	46	47.50 N	16.45 E
Neuss	46	51.12 N	6.41 E
Neustadt, B.R.D.	46	47.54 N	8.13 E
Neustadt, D.D.R.	46	50.44 N	11.44 E
Neustadt [an der Aisch]	46	49.34 N	10.37 E
Neustadt an der Waldnaab	46	49.44 N	12.11 E
Neustadt an der Weinstrasse	46	49.21 N	8.08 E
Neustadt bei Coburg	46	50.19 N	11.07 E
Neustadt in Holstein	46	54.06 N	10.48 E
Neustrelitz	46	53.21 N	13.04 E
Neutral Zone □ [2]	74	29.10 N	45.30 E
Neu-Ulm	46	48.23 N	10.01 E
Neuvic	48	45.23 N	2.16 E
Neuville-de-Poitou	48	46.41 N	0.15 E
Neuville-sur-Saône	48	45.52 N	4.51 E
Neuwied	46	50.25 N	7.27 E
Neva ≃	60	59.57 N	30.20 E
Nevada, Mo., U.S.	100	37.50 N	94.21 W
Nevada, Oh., U.S.	102	40.49 N	83.07 W
Nevada □ [3]	100	39.00 N	117.00 W
Nevada, Sierra ✱, Esp.	50	37.05 N	3.10 W
Nevada, Sierra ✱, Ca., U.S.	104	38.00 N	119.15 W
Nevada City	104	39.15 N	121.00 W
Nevel'	60	56.02 N	29.55 E
Nevel'sk	58	46.40 N	141.53 E
Never	58	53.58 N	124.05 E
Nevers	48	47.00 N	3.09 E
Nevertire	94	31.52 S	147.39 E
Nevesinje	54	43.15 N	18.07 E
Nevinnomyssk	56	44.38 N	41.56 E
Nevis I	108	17.10 N	62.34 W
Nevis ≃	38	56.50 N	5.00 W
Nevis, Ben ∧	38	56.48 N	5.01 W
Nevis, Loch c	38	57.01 N	5.43 W
Nevjansk	56	57.32 N	60.13 E
Nevlunghamn	44	58.58 N	9.52 E
Nevşehir	78	38.38 N	34.43 E
New ≃, N.A.	104	33.08 N	115.44 W
New ≃, U.S.	102	38.10 N	81.12 W
New Abbey	36	54.59 N	3.38 W
New Albany	100	38.17 N	85.49 W
New Alresford	34	51.06 N	1.10 W
New Amsterdam	110	6.15 N	57.31 W
New Angledool	94	29.07 S	147.57 E
Newark, De., U.S.	102	39.41 N	75.45 W
Newark, N.J., U.S.	102	40.44 N	74.10 W
Newark, N.Y., U.S.	102	43.02 N	77.05 W
Newark, Oh., U.S.	102	40.04 N	82.24 W
Newark Lake ⊜	104	39.41 N	115.44 W
Newark-on-Trent	34	53.05 N	0.49 W
Newark Valley	102	42.13 N	76.11 W
New Baltimore	102	42.40 N	82.44 W
New Bedford	102	41.38 N	70.56 W
New Bedford ≃	34	52.35 N	0.20 E
New Berlin	102	42.37 N	75.19 W
New Bern	100	35.06 N	77.02 W
Newberry	100	34.16 N	81.37 W
New Bethlehem	102	41.00 N	79.19 W
Newbiggin-by-the-Sea	36	55.11 N	1.30 W
New Bloomfield	102	40.25 N	77.11 W
Newborough	36	53.09 N	4.22 W
New Boston	102	38.45 N	82.56 W
New Bremen	102	40.26 N	84.22 W
Newbridge →Droichead Nua	40	53.11 N	6.48 W
Newbridge on Wye	34	52.13 N	3.27 W
New Brighton	96	43.31 S	172.44 E
New Britain	102	41.39 N	72.46 W
New Britain I	92	6.00 S	150.00 E
New Britain Trench ✢ [1]	28	6.00 S	153.00 E
New Brunswick	102	40.29 N	74.27 W
New Brunswick □ [4]	98	46.30 N	66.15 W
Newbuildings	40	54.57 N	7.21 W
Newburgh, On., Can.	102	44.19 N	76.52 W
Newburgh, Scot., U.K.	38	56.20 N	3.15 W
Newburgh, Scot., U.K.	38	57.18 N	2.00 W
Newburgh, N.Y., U.S.	102	41.30 N	74.00 W
Newburn	36	54.59 N	1.43 W
Newbury	34	51.25 N	1.20 W
Newburyport	102	42.48 N	70.52 W
Newby	36	54.20 N	0.28 W
Newby Bridge	36	54.16 N	2.58 W
New Caledonia (Nouvelle-Calédonie) □ [2]	28	21.30 S	165.30 E
New-Carlisle, P.Q., Can.	98	48.01 N	65.20 W
New Carlisle, Oh., U.S.	102	39.56 N	84.01 W
Newcastle, Austl.	94	32.56 S	151.46 E
Newcastle, N.B., Can.	98	47.00 N	65.34 W
Newcastle, On., Can.	102	43.55 N	78.35 W
Newcastle, Ire.	40	52.16 N	7.48 W
Newcastle, S. Afr.	86	27.49 S	29.55 E
Newcastle, Eng., U.K.	34	52.26 N	3.06 W
Newcastle, N. Ire., U.K.	40	54.12 N	5.54 W
Newcastle, Ca., U.S.	104	38.53 N	121.08 W
New Castle, De., U.S.	102	39.39 N	75.34 W
New Castle, Pa., U.S.	102	41.00 N	80.20 W
Newcastle Bay c	92	10.50 S	142.37 E
Newcastle Creek ≃	92	17.20 S	133.23 E
Newcastle Emlyn	34	52.02 N	4.28 W
Newcastleton	36	55.11 N	2.49 W
Newcastle-under-Lyme	34	53.00 N	2.14 W
Newcastle upon Tyne	36	54.59 N	1.35 W
Newcastle Waters	92	17.24 S	133.24 E
Newcastle West	40	52.27 N	9.03 W
Newcestown	40	51.47 N	8.51 W
Newchurch	34	52.09 N	3.08 W
New City	102	41.08 N	73.59 W
Newcomerstown	102	40.16 N	81.36 W
New Concord	102	39.59 N	81.44 W
New Cumberland	102	40.29 N	80.36 W
New Cumnock	36	55.24 N	4.12 W
New Deer	38	57.30 N	2.12 W
Newdegate	90	33.06 S	119.01 E
New Delhi	76	28.36 N	77.12 E
New Egypt	102	40.04 N	74.31 W
Newell	102	40.37 N	80.36 W
Newell, Lake ⊜	90	24.50 S	126.10 E
New England Range ✱	94	30.00 S	151.50 E
Newent	34	51.56 N	2.24 W
Newfane, N.Y., U.S.	102	43.17 N	78.42 W
Newfane, Vt., U.S.	102	42.59 N	72.39 W
New Florence	102	40.22 N	79.04 W
New Forest ◆ [3]	34	50.53 N	1.35 W
Newfoundland □ [4]	98	52.00 N	56.00 W
Newfoundland I	98	48.30 N	56.00 W
Newfoundland Basin ✢ [1]	22	45.00 N	45.00 W
Newfoundland Ridge ✢ [3]	22	40.30 N	48.00 W
New Freedom	102	39.44 N	76.42 W
New Galloway	36	55.05 N	4.10 W
New Georgia I	88	8.15 S	157.30 E
New Glasgow	98	45.35 N	62.39 W
New Guinea I	92	5.00 S	140.00 E
New Guinea, Territory of →Papua New Guinea □ [1]	92	6.00 S	150.00 E
Newhall, Eng., U.K.	34	52.48 N	1.34 W
Newhall, Ca., U.S.	104	34.23 N	118.31 W
Newham ◆ [8]	34	51.32 N	0.03 E
New Hamburg	102	43.23 N	80.42 W
New Hampshire □ [3]	100	43.35 N	71.40 W
New Hanover	86	29.28 S	30.28 E
New Hanover I	92	2.30 S	150.15 E
New Hartford	102	41.52 N	72.58 W
Newhaven, Eng., U.K.	34	50.47 N	0.03 E
New Haven, Ct., U.S.	102	41.18 N	72.56 W
New Haven, In., U.S.	102	41.04 N	85.00 W
New Haven, W.V., U.S.	102	38.59 N	81.58 W
New Hebrides →Vanuatu □ [1]	28	16.00 S	167.00 E
New Hebrides II	28	16.00 S	167.00 E
New Hebrides Trench ✢ [1]	28	22.30 S	170.00 E
New Hogan Lake ⊜ [1]	104	38.09 N	120.48 W
New Holland, Eng., U.K.	36	53.42 N	0.22 W
New Holland, Oh., U.S.	102	39.33 N	83.15 W
New Holland, Pa., U.S.	102	40.06 N	76.05 W
New Iberia	100	30.00 N	91.49 W
Newick	34	50.58 N	0.01 E
Newington	34	51.05 N	1.08 E
New Inn	40	52.26 N	7.53 W
New Ireland I	92	3.20 S	152.00 E
New Jersey □ [3]	100	40.15 N	74.30 W
New Kensington	102	40.34 N	79.45 W
New Kowloon (Xinjiulong)	68	22.20 N	114.10 E
Newland Range ✱	90	27.53 S	123.58 E
New Lexington	102	39.42 N	82.12 W
New Liskeard	98	47.30 N	79.40 W
New London, Ct., U.S.	102	41.21 N	72.07 W
New London, N.H., U.S.	102	43.24 N	71.59 W
New London, Oh., U.S.	102	41.05 N	82.24 W
Newlyn East	34	50.22 N	5.03 W
Newmachar	38	57.16 N	2.11 W
Newmains	36	55.47 N	3.53 W
Newman, Austl.	90	23.20 S	119.46 E
Newman, Ca., U.S.	104	37.18 N	121.01 W
Newman, Mount ∧	90	23.16 S	119.33 E
Newmarket, On., Can.	102	44.03 N	79.28 W
Newmarket, Ire.	40	52.13 N	9.00 W
Newmarket, Eng., U.K.	34	52.15 N	0.25 E
Newmarket, N.H., U.S.	102	43.04 N	70.56 W
New Market, Va., U.S.	102	38.39 N	78.40 W
Newmarket on Fergus	40	52.45 N	8.53 W
New Marske	36	54.34 N	1.02 W
New Martinsville	102	39.38 N	80.51 W
New Mexico □ [3]	100	34.30 N	106.00 W
New Milford, Ct., U.S.	102	41.34 N	73.24 W
New Milford, Pa., U.S.	102	41.52 N	75.43 W
New Mills	36	53.23 N	2.00 W
Newmilns	38	55.37 N	4.20 W
New Milton	34	50.44 N	1.40 W
Newnham	34	51.49 N	2.27 W
New Norcia	90	30.58 S	116.13 E
New Norfolk	94	42.47 S	147.03 E
New Orleans	100	29.57 N	90.04 W
New Oxford	102	39.51 N	77.03 W
New Paltz	102	41.44 N	74.05 W
New Paris	102	39.51 N	84.47 W
New Philadelphia	102	40.30 N	81.27 W
New Pine Creek	104	41.59 N	120.17 W
New Pitsligo	38	57.35 N	2.11 W
New Plymouth	96	39.04 S	174.05 E
Newport, Ire.	40	53.53 N	9.34 W
Newport, Ire.	40	52.42 N	8.24 W
Newport, Eng., U.K.	34	50.42 N	1.18 W
Newport, Eng., U.K.	34	52.47 N	2.22 W
Newport, Eng., U.K.	34	51.59 N	0.15 E
Newport, Wales, U.K.	34	52.01 N	4.51 W
Newport, Wales, U.K.	34	51.35 N	3.00 W
Newport, Ky., U.S.	102	39.05 N	84.29 W
Newport, Me., U.S.	102	44.50 N	69.16 W
Newport, N.H., U.S.	102	43.21 N	72.10 W
Newport, Pa., U.S.	102	40.28 N	77.07 W
Newport, R.I., U.S.	102	41.29 N	71.18 W
Newport, Vt., U.S.	102	44.56 N	72.12 W
Newport Beach	104	33.37 N	117.55 W
Newport News	100	36.58 N	76.25 W
Newport-on-Tay	38	56.26 N	2.55 W
Newport Pagnell	34	52.05 N	0.44 W
New Providence I	108	25.02 N	77.24 W
Newquay, Eng., U.K.	34	50.25 N	5.05 W

Symbols in the Index entries are identified on page 122.

Name	Page	Lat.	Long.
New Quay, Wales, U.K.	34	52.13N	4.22W
New Richmond	102	38.56N	84.16W
New Rochelle	102	40.54N	73.46W
New Romney	34	50.59N	0.57 E
New Ross	40	52.24N	6.56W
New Rossington	36	53.29N	1.04W
Newry	40	54.11N	6.20W
New Scone	38	56.25N	3.24W
New South Wales □3	88	33.00 S	146.00 E
Newton, Eng., U.K.	36	53.57N	2.27W
Newton, Ia., U.S.	100	41.41N	93.02W
Newton, Ks., U.S.	100	38.02N	97.20W
Newton, Ma., U.S.	102	42.20N	71.12W
Newton, N.J., U.S.	102	41.03N	74.45W
Newton Abbot	34	50.32N	3.36W
Newton Arlosh	36	54.53N	3.15W
Newton Aycliffe	36	54.36N	1.32W
Newton Falls	102	44.12N	74.59W
Newton Ferrers	34	50.18N	4.02W
Newton Flotman	36	52.32N	1.16 E
Newton-le-Willows	36	53.28N	2.37W
Newton Longville	34	51.58N	0.46W
Newtonmore	38	57.04N	4.08W
Newton Stewart	34	54.57N	4.29W
Newtown	34	52.32N	3.19W
Newtownabbey	40	54.42N	5.54W
Newtownards	40	54.36N	5.41W
Newtownbutler	40	54.12N	7.23W
Newtown Crommelin	40	54.59N	6.13W
Newtown Forbes	40	53.46N	7.50W
Newtownhamilton	40	54.12N	6.35W
Newtown Mount Kennedy	40	53.05N	6.07W
Newtown Saint Boswells	38	55.34N	2.40W
Newtownstewart	40	54.43N	7.24W
New Tredegar	34	51.43N	3.14W
New Ulm	100	44.19N	94.27W
New Vienna	102	39.19N	83.41W
Newville	102	40.10N	77.23W
New Vineyard	102	44.48N	70.07W
New Waltham	36	53.32N	0.04W
New Washington	102	40.57N	82.51W
New Waterford	98	46.15N	60.05W
New Westminster	98	49.12N	122.55W
New Wilmington	102	41.07N	80.19W
New York	102	40.43N	74.01W
New York □3	102	43.00N	75.00W
New York State Barge Canal ≡	102	43.05N	78.43W
New Zealand □1	96	41.00 S	174.00 E
Nexon	34	45.41N	1.11 E
Neyland	34	51.43N	4.57W
Neyríz	78	29.12N	54.19 E
Neyshābūr	78	36.12N	58.50 E
Nezahualcóyotl, Presa @1	106	17.10N	93.40W
Nežin	56	51.03N	31.54 E
Ngabang	72	0.23N	109.57 E
Ngahere	96	42.24 S	171.27 E
Ngami, Lake ⊚	86	20.37 S	22.40 E
Ngamiland □5	86	19.09 S	22.47 E
Nganglong Kangri ⋟	76	32.00N	83.00 E
Nganjuk	72	7.36 S	111.55 E
Ngaoundéré	80	7.19N	13.35 E
Ngapara	96	44.57 S	170.45 E
Ngaruawahia	96	37.40 S	175.09 E
Ngatea	96	39.34 S	176.56 E
Ngatea	96	37.17 S	175.30 E
Ngatik I1	28	5.51N	157.16 E
Ngauruhoe, Mount ⋀	96	39.09 S	175.38 E
Ngawi	96	7.24 S	111.26 E
Ng'iro, Ewaso ≃	84	0.28N	39.55 E
Ngoko ≃	84	1.40N	16.03 E
Ngongotaha	96	38.05 S	176.12 E
Ngoring Hu ⊚	62	34.50N	97.35 E
Nguigmi	80	14.15N	13.07 E
Ngulu I1	28	8.27N	137.29 E
Nguru	80	12.52N	10.27 E
Nhamundá ≃	110	2.12 S	56.41W
Nha-trang	70	12.15N	109.11 E
Nhill	94	36.20 S	141.39 E
Nhlangano	86	27.06 S	31.12 E
Nhulunbuy	92	12.11 S	136.47 E
Niafounké	80	15.56N	4.00W
Niagara Falls, On., Can.	102	43.06N	79.04W
Niagara Falls, N.Y., U.S.	102	43.05N	79.03W
Niagara-on-the-Lake	102	43.15N	79.04W
Niah	72	3.52N	113.44 E
Niamey	82	13.31N	2.07 E
Niangara	82	3.42N	27.52 E
Nias, Pulau I	70	1.05N	97.35 E
Nibe	44	56.59N	9.38 E
Nica	56	57.29N	64.33 E
Nicaragua □1	106	13.00N	85.00W
Nicaragua, Lago de ⊚	106	11.30 S	85.30W
Nicastro (Lamezia Terme)	52	38.59N	16.20 E
Nice	48	43.42N	7.15 E
Nichinan	64	31.36N	131.23 E
Nicholas Channel ⋃	108	23.25N	80.05W
Nicholasville	102	37.52N	84.34W
Nicholson, Austl.	90	18.02 S	128.54 E
Nicholson, Pa., U.S.	102	41.37N	75.46W
Nicholson ≃, Austl.	90	17.34 S	128.38 E
Nicholson ≃, Austl.	94	17.31 S	139.36 E
Nicholson Range ⋟	90	27.15 S	116.45 E
Nickol Bay C	90	20.39 S	116.52 E
Nicobar Islands II	70	8.00N	93.30 E
Nicolae Bălcescu	54	47.34N	26.52 E
Nicolet	102	46.13N	72.37W
Nicolet Sud-Ouest ≃	102	46.13N	72.36W
Nicolls Town	108	25.08N	78.00W
Nicosia, It.	52	37.45N	14.24 E
Nicosia →Levkosía, Kípros	78	35.10N	33.22 E
Nicotera	52	38.34N	15.57 E
Nicoya	108	10.09N	85.27W
Nicoya, Golfo de C	108	9.47N	84.48W
Nicoya, Peninsula de ⋟1	108	10.00N	85.25W
Nida ≃	46	50.18N	20.52 E
Nidd ≃	36	54.01N	1.12W
Nidelva ≃	44	58.24N	8.48 E
Nidzica	46	53.22N	20.26 E
Niebüll	46	54.48N	8.50 E
Niederbronn-les-Bains	48	48.57N	7.38 E
Nedere Tauern ⋟	46	47.18N	14.00 E
Niedermarsberg	46	51.28N	8.50 E
Niederösterreich □3	46	48.20N	15.50 E
Niedersachsen □3	46	52.47N	9.00 E
Niekerkshoop	86	29.15 S	22.51 E
Niemodlin	46	50.39N	17.37 E
Nienburg	46	52.38N	9.13 E
Niepołomice	46	50.03N	20.13 E
Nier ≃	40	52.17N	7.48W
Niesky	46	51.17N	14.49 E
Nieszawa	46	52.52N	18.55 E
Nieu Bethesda	86	31.51 S	24.34 E
Nieuw Amsterdam	110	5.53N	55.05W
Nieuw Nickerie	110	5.57N	56.59W
Nieuwoudtville	86	31.23 S	19.07 E
Nieuwpoort	46	51.08N	2.45 E
Nièvre □5	48	47.05N	3.30 E
Niğde	78	37.59N	34.42 E
Nigel	86	26.26 S	28.28 E
Niger □1	80	16.00N	8.00 E
Niger ≃	80	5.33N	6.33 E
Nigeria □1	80	10.00N	8.00 E
Nigg	38	57.43N	4.00W
Nightcaps	96	45.58 S	168.02 E
Nightingale Island I	20	37.24 S	12.28W
Nigríta	54	40.55N	23.30 E
Nihing (Nahang) ≃	78	26.00N	62.44 E
Nihommatsu	64	37.35N	140.26 E
Nihuil, Embalse del @1	114	35.05 S	68.45W
Niigata	64	37.55N	139.03 E
Niihama	64	33.58N	133.16 E
Niihau I	105a	21.55N	160.10W
Nii-jima I	64	34.22N	139.16 E
Niimi	64	34.59N	133.28 E
Niinisalo	44	61.50N	22.29 E
Niitsu	64	37.48N	139.07 E
Nijar	50	36.58N	2.12W
Nijkerk	46	52.13N	5.30 E
Nijmegen	46	51.50N	5.50 E
Nijvel →Nivelles	46	50.36N	4.20 E
Nikel'	42	69.24N	30.12 E
Nikkō	64	36.45N	139.37 E
Nikolajev	54	46.58N	32.00 E
Nikolajevsk-na-Amure	58	53.08N	140.44 E
Nikol'sk	56	53.45N	46.05 E
Nikol'skoje	58	55.12N	166.00 E
Nikopol, Blg.	54	43.42N	24.54 E
Nikopol', S.S.S.R.	54	47.35N	34.25 E
Nikšić	54	42.46N	18.56 E
Nikumaroro I1	28	4.40 S	174.32W
Nikunau I1	28	1.23 S	176.26 E
Nila, Pulau I	92	6.44 S	129.31 E
Nilakka ⊚	44	63.07N	26.33 E
Niland	104	33.14N	115.31W
Nile (Nahr an-Nīl) ≃	82	30.10N	31.06 E
Nîleh, Kūh-e ⋀	78	32.59N	50.32 E
Niles	102	41.10N	80.45W
Nīlgiri	64	21.28N	86.46 E
Nilsiä	44	63.12N	28.05 E
Nîmach	76	24.28N	74.52 E
Nimba, Mont ⋀	80	7.37N	8.25W
Nimbahera	76	24.37N	74.41 E
Nimba Range ⋟	80	7.30N	8.30W
Nîmes	48	43.50N	4.21 E
Nimmitabel	94	36.31 S	149.16 E
Nimrūz □4	78	30.30N	62.00 E
Nimule	82	3.36N	32.03 E
Ninawá □6	78	36.10N	42.35 E
Nindigully	94	28.21 S	148.49 E
Ninetyeast Ridge ⋗3	26	4.00 S	90.00 E
Ninety Mile Beach ≃, Austl.	94	38.13 S	147.23 E
Ninety Mile Beach ≃, N.Z.	96	34.48 S	173.00 E
Nineveh ⋏	78	36.25N	43.10 E
Ninfield	34	50.53N	0.25 E
Ningbo	66	29.52N	121.31 E
Ningcheng	62	41.33N	119.20 E
Ningde	66	26.43N	119.33 E
Ningdu	66	26.31N	115.58 E
Ningguo	66	30.38N	118.58 E
Ninghai	66	29.17N	121.25 E
Ninghua	66	26.15N	116.38 E
Ningling	66	34.27N	115.21 E
Ningming	66	22.07N	107.05 E
Ningnan	62	27.04N	102.45 E
Ningwu	66	39.01N	112.21 E
Ningxia Huizu Zizhiqu (Ningsia Hui) □4	62	37.00N	106.00 E
Ningxiang	66	28.15N	112.33 E
Ningyuan	66	25.37N	111.46 E
Ninh-binh	70	20.15N	105.59 E
Ninhue	114	36.24 S	72.24W
Ninigo Group II	92	1.15 S	144.15 E
Ninohe	64	40.16N	141.18 E
Ninove	46	50.50N	4.02 E
Nioaque	110	22.45 S	55.48W
Niobrara ≃	100	42.45N	98.00W
Nioki	84	2.43 S	17.41 E
Niono	80	14.15N	6.00W
Nioro du Sahel	80	15.15N	9.35W
Niort	48	46.19N	0.27W
Nipawin	98	53.22N	104.00W
Nipe, Bahía de C	108	20.47N	75.42W
Nipigon	102	49.01N	88.16W
Nipigon, Lake ⊚	102	49.50N	88.30W
Nipissing, Lake ⊚	102	46.17N	80.00W
Nipomo	104	35.02N	120.28W
Niquero	108	20.03N	77.35W
Niquivil	114	30.25 S	68.42W
Nirasaki	64	35.42N	138.27 E
Nirgua	108	10.09N	68.34W
Niš	54	43.19N	21.54 E
Nisa	50	39.31N	7.39W
Nisa (Neisse) (Nysa Łużycka) ≃	46	52.04N	14.46 E
Nišava ≃	54	43.22N	21.46 E
Niscemi	52	37.09N	14.23 E
Nishinoomote	64	30.44N	131.00 E
Nishio	64	34.52N	137.03 E
Nishiwaki	64	34.59N	134.58 E
Nisiros I	54	36.35N	27.10 E
Niskibi ≃	98	56.40N	88.00W
Nissan ≃	44	56.40N	12.51 E
Nissan Bredning C	44	56.38N	8.22 E
Nissum Fjord C2	44	56.21N	8.14 E
Niterói	110	22.53 S	43.07W
Nith ≃, On., Can.	102	43.12N	80.22W
Nith ≃, Scot., U.K.	36	55.00N	3.35W
Nithsdale ⋁	36	55.14N	3.46W
Niton	34	50.35N	1.16W
Nitra	46	48.20N	18.05 E
Nitra ≃	46	47.46N	18.10 E
Nitro	102	38.24N	81.50W
Nitsie Óros (Nidže) ⋀	54	40.58N	21.48 E
Nittedal	44	60.04N	10.53 E
Niue □2	28	19.02 S	169.52W
Niulakita I1	28	10.45 S	179.30 E
Niut, Gunung ⋀	72	1.00N	109.55 E
Niutao I1	28	6.06 S	177.17 E
Nivala	44	63.55N	24.58 E
Nive ≃, Austl.	94	26.02 S	146.25 E
Nive ≃, Fr.	48	43.30N	1.29W
Nive Downs	94	25.30 S	146.32 E
Nivelles	46	50.36N	4.20 E
Nivernais □9	48	47.00N	3.30 E
Nixon	104	39.49N	119.21W
Niyodo ≃	64	33.27N	133.29 E
Nizamghāt	76	28.16N	95.42 E
Nizhny Novgorod →Gor'kij	60	56.20N	44.00 E
Nizke Tatry ⋟	46	48.54N	19.40 E
Nizza Monferrato	52	44.46N	8.21 E
Njombe ≃	84	9.20 S	34.46 E
Njurunda	44	62.16N	17.22 E
Nkhata Bay	84	11.33 S	34.18 E
Nkhotakota	84	12.57 S	34.17 E
Nkongsamba	80	4.57N	9.56 E
Nkwalini	86	28.45 S	31.33 E
Nmai ≃	70	25.42N	97.30 E
Noākhāli	76	22.49N	91.06 E
Nobeoka	64	32.35N	131.40 E
Noboribetsu	64a	42.27N	141.11 E
Noccundra	94	27.50 S	142.36 E
Noce ≃	52	46.09N	11.04 E
Nocera [Inferiore]	52	40.45N	14.38 E
Noci	52	40.48N	17.08 E
Nockatunga	94	27.43 S	142.43 E
Noetinger	114	32.22 S	62.19W
Nogales, Chile	114	32.45 S	71.15W
Nogales, Az., U.S.	100	31.20N	110.56W
Nogara	52	45.11N	11.04 E
Nogaro	48	43.46N	0.02W
Nōgata	64	33.44N	130.44 E
Nogent-le-Rotrou	48	48.19N	0.50 E
Nogent-sur-Seine	48	48.29N	3.30 E
Noginsk	60	55.51N	38.27 E
Nogoa ≃	94	23.33 S	148.32 E
Nogoyá	114	32.24 S	59.48W
Nógrád □6	46	48.00N	19.35 E
Noguera Pallaresa ≃	50	42.15N	0.54 E
Noguera Ribagorzana ≃	50	41.40N	0.43 E
Nohar	76	29.11N	74.46 E
Noheji	64	40.52N	141.08 E
Nohta	76	23.40N	79.34 E
Noir, Causse ⋏1	48	44.10N	3.15 E
Noir, Montagne ⋀	48	43.28N	2.18 E
Noire ≃	102	45.54N	76.57W
Noirétable	48	45.49N	3.46 E
Noirmoutier	48	47.00N	2.14W
Noirmoutier, Île de I	48	47.00N	2.15W
Nojima-zaki ⋗	64	34.54N	139.53 E
Nokha	76	27.35N	73.29 E
Nokia	64	61.28N	23.30 E
Nola	52	40.55N	14.33 E
Nolinsk	42	57.33N	49.57 E
Nombre de Dios	108	9.35N	79.28W
Nome	22	64.30N	165.24W
Nomgon	62	42.50N	105.07 E
Nominingue	102	46.24N	75.02W
Nomoi Islands II	28	5.27N	153.40 E
Nomozaki	64	32.35N	129.45 E
Nonacho Lake ⊚	98	61.42N	109.40W
Nonancourt	48	48.46N	1.12 E
Nondalton	22	60.00N	154.49W
Nondweni	86	28.11 S	30.49 E
Nong'an	62	44.25N	125.10 E
Nong Khai	70	17.52N	102.44 E
Nongoma	86	27.58 S	31.35 E
Nongpoh	76	25.54N	91.53 E
Nongstoin	76	25.31N	91.16 E
Nonning	94	32.30 S	136.30 E
Nonoai	114	27.21 S	52.47W
Nonogasta	114	29.18 S	67.30W
Nonouti I1	28	0.40 S	174.21 E
Nonthaburi	70	13.50N	100.29 E
Nontron	48	45.32N	0.40 E
Nookawarra	90	26.19 S	116.52 E
Noonamah	92	12.38 S	131.04 E
Noonkanbah	92	18.30 S	124.50 E
Noordoost Polder ⋗1	46	52.42N	5.45 E
Noordwijk aan Zee	46	52.14N	4.26 E
Noosaville	94	26.24 S	153.04 E
Nootka Island I	98	49.32N	126.42W
Nóqui	84	5.51 S	13.25 E
Nora	44	59.31N	15.02 E
Nora Islands II	82	16.02N	40.03 E
Noranda	98	48.15N	79.02W
Norberg	44	60.04N	15.56 E
Norberto de la Riestra	114	35.16 S	59.46W
Norcia	52	42.48N	13.05 E
Norcott, Mount ⋀	90	32.07 S	121.59 E
Nord □5	48	50.20N	3.40 E
Nordaustlandet I	26	79.48N	22.24 E
Nordborg	44	55.03N	9.45 E
Norden	46	53.36N	7.12 E
Nordenham	46	53.29N	8.28 E
Norderney I	46	53.42N	7.10 E
Norderstedt	46	53.43N	10.00 E
Nordfjord C2	44	61.54N	5.12 E
Nordfjordeid	44	61.54N	6.00 E
Nordfold	44	67.46N	15.12 E
Nordhausen	46	51.30N	10.47 E
Nordhorn	46	52.27N	7.05 E
Nordingrå	44	62.56N	18.16 E
Nordkapp ⋗	42	71.11N	25.48 E
Nordkinnhalvøya ⋗1	42	70.55N	27.45 E
Nordland □6	44	66.30N	13.30 E
Nördlingen	46	48.51N	10.30 E
Nordmaling	44	63.34N	19.30 E
Nordmark ⋁	44	59.54N	14.08 E
Nordostrundingen ⋗	22	81.36N	12.09W
Nord-Ostsee-Kanal ≡	46	53.53N	9.08 E
Nordreisa	44	69.46N	21.03 E
Nordre Strømfjord C2	98	67.50N	52.00W
Nordrhein-Westfalen □3	46	51.30N	7.30 E
Nordstrand I	46	54.30N	8.53 E
Nord-Trøndelag □6	44	64.25N	12.00 E
Nordvik	58	74.02N	111.32 E
Nore	44	60.10N	9.01 E
Nore ≃	40	52.25N	6.58W
Norfolk, Ne., U.S.	100	42.02N	97.25W
Norfolk, Va., U.S.	100	36.50N	76.17W
Norfolk □6	34	52.40N	1.00 E
Norfolk Broads ⋗1	34	52.43N	1.32 E
Norfolk Island □2	28	29.02 S	167.57 E
Norfolk Ridge ⋗3	28	29.00 S	168.00 E
Norham	36	55.43N	2.10W
Norheimsund	44	60.22N	6.08 E
Norikura-dake ⋀	64	36.06N	137.33 E
Noril'sk	58	69.20N	88.06 E
Norman	100	35.13N	97.26W
Norman ≃	94	17.28 S	140.49 E
Normanby I	92	10.05 S	151.05 E
Normanby Island I	92	14.25 S	144.08 E
Normandie □9	48	49.00N	0.10 E
Normandie, Collines de ⋟2	48	48.40N	0.30W
Normandy →Normandie □9	48	49.00N	0.05 E
Normanhurst, Mount ⋀	90	25.04 S	122.30 E
Normanton, Austl.	94	17.40 S	141.05 E
Normanton, Eng., U.K.	36	53.41N	1.27W
Norman Wells	98	65.17N	126.51W
Nornalup	90	35.00 S	116.49 E
Norquay	98	51.48N	102.05W
Norrahammar	44	57.42N	14.06 E
Norra Kvarken (Merenkurkku) ⋃	44	63.36N	20.43 E
Norra Storfjället ⋀	44	65.52N	15.18 E
Norrbotten ≃	42	66.45N	23.00 E
Norrbottens Län □6	42	66.50N	20.00 E
Nørresundby	44	57.04N	9.55 E
Norridgewock	102	44.43N	69.47W
Norristown	102	40.07N	75.20W
Norrköping	44	58.36N	16.11 E
Norrsundet	44	60.56N	17.08 E
Norrtälje	44	59.46N	18.42 E
Norseman	92	32.12 S	121.46 E
Norsewood	96	40.04 S	176.13 E
Norsjö	44	59.18N	9.20 E
Norsjö	44	64.55N	19.29 E
Norsk	58	52.20N	129.55 E
Norte, Canal do ⋃	110	0.30N	50.30W
Norte, Punta ⋗	114	36.17 S	56.47W
Norte, Serra do ⋏1	110	11.20 S	59.00W
Norte ≃	98	57.30N	62.05W
North, Cape ⋗	98	47.02N	60.25W
North Adams, Ma., U.S.	102	42.42N	73.06W
North Adams, Mi., U.S.	102	41.58N	84.32W
Northallerton	36	54.20N	1.26W
Northam, Austl.	90	31.39 S	116.40 E
Northam, S. Afr.	86	25.03 S	27.11 E
Northam, Eng., U.K.	34	51.02N	4.12W
North America ⋀1	22	45.00N	100.00W
North American Basin ⋗1	22	30.00N	60.00W
Northampton, Austl.	90	28.21 S	114.37 E
Northampton, Eng., U.K.	34	52.14N	0.54W
Northampton, Ma., U.S.	102	42.19N	72.38W
Northamptonshire □6	34	52.20N	0.50W
North Andaman I	70	13.15N	92.55 E
North Anna ≃	102	37.50N	77.29W
North Anson	102	44.51N	69.54W
North Aulatsivik Island I	98	59.50N	64.00W
North Australian Basin ⋗1	26	14.30 S	116.30 E
North Baltimore	102	41.10N	83.40W
North Battleford	98	52.47N	108.17W
North Bay	102	46.19N	79.28W
North Bend	104	43.24N	124.13W
North Bennington	102	42.55N	73.14W
North Berwick, Scot., U.K.	38	56.04N	2.44W
North Berwick, Me., U.S.	102	43.18N	70.44W
North Bourke	94	30.03 S	145.57 E
North Branch	102	43.13N	83.11W
North Caicos I	108	21.56N	71.59W
North Canton	102	40.52N	81.24W
North Cape ⋗, N.Z.	96	34.25 S	173.02 E
North Cape →Nordkapp ⋗, Nor.	42	71.11N	25.48 E
North Caribou Lake ⊚	98	52.50N	90.40W
North Carolina □3	100	35.30N	80.00W
North Channel ⋃, On., Can.	102	46.02N	82.50W
North Channel ⋃, U.K.	36	55.10N	5.40W
Northcliffe	90	34.36 S	116.07 E
North College Hill	102	39.13N	84.33W
North Collins	102	42.35N	78.56W
North Conway	102	44.03N	71.07W
North Creek	102	43.41N	73.59W
North Dakota □3	100	47.30N	100.15W
North Downs ⋏1	34	51.20N	0.10 E
North East, Md., U.S.	102	39.36N	75.56W
North East, Pa., U.S.	102	42.12N	79.50W
North-East □3	86	21.00 S	27.30 E
Northeast Point ⋗, Ba.	108	21.20N	73.01W
Northeast Point ⋗, Ba.	108	22.43N	73.50W
Northeast Providence Channel ⋃	108	25.40N	77.09W
Northeim	46	51.42N	10.00 E
Northern Cook Islands II	28	10.00 S	161.00W
Northern Dvina →Severnaja Dvina ≃	42	64.32N	40.30 E
Northern Indian Lake ⊚	98	57.20N	97.20W
Northern Ireland □8	32	54.40N	6.45W
Northern Mariana Islands □2	28	16.00N	149.00 E
Northern Territory □8	92	20.00 S	134.00 E
North Esk ≃, Scot., U.K.	38	56.44N	2.25W
North Esk ≃, Scot., U.K.	38	56.46N	2.25W
North Ferriby	36	53.43N	0.27W
Northfield, Ma., U.S.	102	42.42N	72.27W
Northfield, Mn., U.S.	100	44.27N	93.09W
Northfield, Vt., U.S.	102	44.09N	72.39W
Northfleet	34	51.27N	0.21 E
North Flinders Range ⋏	94	31.00 S	139.00 E
North Foreland ⋗	34	51.23N	1.27 E
North Fork	104	37.13N	119.30W
North Frisian Islands II	46	54.50N	8.12 E
North Hero	102	44.49N	73.17W
North Highlands	104	38.41N	121.23W
North Hill	34	50.34N	4.25W
North Hinksey	34	51.45N	1.16W
Northiam	34	50.59N	0.36 E
North Island I	96	39.00 S	176.00 E
North Kingsville	102	41.54N	80.42W
North Knife Lake ⊚	98	58.05N	97.05W
North Lakhimpur	76	27.14N	94.07 E
North Las Vegas	104	36.11N	115.07W
Northleach	34	51.50N	1.50W
North Luconia Shoals ⋈	72	5.40N	112.35 E
North Palisade ⋀	104	37.06N	118.31W
North Petherton	34	51.06N	3.01W
North Platte	100	41.07N	100.46W
North Platte ≃	100	41.07N	100.42W
North Point ⋗	102	45.02N	83.16W
North Pole	122	90.00N	0.00
Northport	102	45.08N	85.37W
North Queensferry	38	56.00N	3.24W
North Ronaldsay I	38	59.23N	2.26W
North Ronaldsay Firth ⋃	38	59.22N	2.25W
North Saskatchewan ≃	98	53.15N	105.05W
North Saugeen ≃	102	44.25N	81.17W
North Sea ⋕2	32	56.00N	3.00 E
North Seaton Colliery	36	55.11N	1.32W
North Shields	36	55.01N	1.27W
North Shoshone Peak ⋀	104	39.09N	117.29W
North Siberian Lowland →Severo-Sibirskaja nizmennost' ≃	58	73.00N	100.00 E
North Somercotes	36	53.28N	0.09 E
North Sound ⋃, Ire.	40	53.10N	9.43W
North Sound ⋃, Scot., U.K.	38	59.18N	2.46W
North Spicer Island I	98	68.30N	78.55W
North Stradbroke Island I	94	27.35 S	153.28 E
North Sunderland	36	55.34N	1.39W
North Taranaki Bight C3	96	38.42 S	174.15 E
North Tawton	34	50.48N	3.53W
North Tea Lake ⊚	102	45.56N	79.03W
North Thompson ≃	98	50.41N	120.21W
North Tidworth	34	51.16N	1.40W
North Tolsta	38	58.20N	6.13W
North Troy	102	44.59N	72.24W
North Tyne ≃	36	54.59N	2.08W
North Uist I	38	57.36N	7.18W
Northumberland □6	36	55.15N	2.05W
Northumberland Isles II	94	21.40 S	150.00 E
Northumberland National Park ⋔	36	55.15N	2.20W
Northumberland Strait ⋃	98	46.00N	63.30W
North Umpqua ≃	104	43.16N	123.20W
North Vancouver	98	49.19N	123.04W
Northville	102	43.13N	74.10W
North Walsham	34	52.50N	1.24 E
North Weald Bassett	34	51.43N	0.10 E
North West Cape ⋗	90	21.45 S	114.10 E
Northwest Frontier □4	76	34.00N	72.00 E
Northwest Providence Channel ⋃	108	26.10N	78.20W
North West River	98	53.32N	60.08W
Northwest Territories □4	98	70.00N	100.00W
Northwich	36	53.16N	2.32W
North Windham	102	43.50N	70.26W
Northwold	34	52.33N	0.35 E
Northwood	34	50.44N	1.19W
North York	102	43.46N	79.25W
North York Moors ⋏2	36	54.24N	0.53W
North York Moors National Park ⋔	36	54.23N	0.48W
North Yorkshire □6	36	54.15N	1.30W
North Yuba ≃	104	39.22N	121.08W
Norton	36	54.09N	0.47W
Norton Fitzwarren	34	51.02N	3.09W
Norton Sound ⋃	22	63.50N	164.00W
Nortorf	46	54.10N	9.50 E
Nort-sur-Erdre	48	47.26N	1.30W
Norwalk, Ct., U.S.	102	41.07N	73.24W
Norwalk, Oh., U.S.	102	41.14N	82.36W
Norway	102	44.12N	70.32W
Norway (Norge) □1	42	62.00N	10.00 E
Norway Bay C	102	71.08N	104.35W
Norway House	98	53.59N	97.50W
Norwegian Basin ⋗1	20	68.00N	2.00 E
Norwegian Sea ⋕2	20	70.00N	2.00 E
Norwegian Trench ⋗1	20	59.00N	4.30 E
Norwich, Eng., U.K.	34	52.38N	1.18 E
Norwich, Ct., U.S.	102	41.32N	72.05W
Norwich, N.Y., U.S.	102	42.31N	75.31W
Norwood, On., Can.	102	44.23N	77.59W
Norwood, Ma., U.S.	102	42.11N	71.12W
Norwood, N.Y., U.S.	102	44.45N	74.59W
Norwood, Oh., U.S.	102	39.10N	84.27W
Nosbonsing, Lake ⊚	102	46.12N	79.14W
Noshiro	64	40.12N	140.02 E
Nosop (Nossob) ≃	86	26.55 S	20.37 E
Noss, Isle of I	38a	60.09N	1.01W
Nossebro	44	58.11N	12.43 E
Noss Head ⋗	38	58.28N	3.04W
Nossob (Nosop) ≃	86	26.55 S	20.37 E
Nosy Varika	87b	20.35 S	48.32 E
Noteć ≃	46	52.44N	15.26 E
Notikewin ≃	98	57.15N	117.05W
Noto, It.	52	36.53N	15.04 E
Noto, Nihon	64	37.18N	137.09 E
Noto, Golfo di C	52	36.50N	15.12 E
Notodden	44	59.34N	9.17 E
Noto-hantō ⋗1	64	37.20N	137.00 E
Notoro-ko ⊚	64a	44.05N	144.10 E
Notozero ⊚	42	68.30N	31.05 E
Notre-Dame, Monts ⋀	98	48.10N	68.40W
Notre Dame Bay C	98	49.45N	55.15W
Notre-Dame-du-Laus	102	46.05N	75.37W
Nottawasaga	102	44.19N	80.04W
Nottawasaga Bay C	102	44.35N	80.15W
Nottaway ≃	98	51.22N	78.55W
Nottingham	34	52.58N	1.10W
Nottingham Island I	98	63.20N	77.55W
Nottingham Road	86	29.22 S	30.00 E
Nottinghamshire □6	34	53.00N	1.00W
Nouâdhibou	80	20.54N	17.04W
Nouâdhibou, Râs ⋗	80	20.46N	17.03W
Nouakchott	80	18.06N	15.57W
Nouamrhâr	80	19.22N	16.31W
Nouméa	28	22.16 S	166.27 E
Noupoort	86	31.10 S	24.57 E
Nouveau-Québec, Cratère du @6	98	61.17N	73.40W
Nouvelle-Calédonie I	28	21.30 S	165.30 E
Nouvelle-France, Cap de ⋗	98	62.27N	73.42W
Nova Andradina	114	22.14 S	53.15W
Nová Baňa	46	48.26N	18.39 E
Nová Bystřice	46	49.01N	15.06 E
Nova Caipemba	84	7.26 S	14.38 E
Nova Esperança	114	23.09 S	52.13W
Nova Feltria	52	43.53N	12.17 E
Nova Friburgo	110	22.16 S	42.32W
Nova Gradiška	52	45.16N	17.23 E
Nova Iguaçu	110	22.45 S	43.27W
Novaja Kachovka	56	46.45N	33.23 E
Novaja Kazanka	56	48.57N	49.36 E
Novaja Ladoga	60	60.05N	32.16 E
Novaja Sibir', ostrov I	58	75.00N	149.00 E
Novaja Zeml'a II	58	74.00N	57.00 E
Nováky	46	48.43N	18.32 E
Nova Lima	110	19.59 S	43.51W
Nova Lisboa →Huambo	84	12.44 S	15.47 E
Nova Mambone	86	21.04 S	35.01 E
Nova Paka	46	50.29N	15.31 E
Nova Prata	114	28.47 S	51.36W
Nova Scotia □4	98	45.00N	63.00W
Nova Sofala	86	20.09 S	34.42 E
Novato	104	38.06N	122.34W
Nova Varoš	54	43.23N	19.48 E
Nova Veneza	114	28.39 S	49.30W
Nova Zagora	54	42.29N	26.01 E
Nové Hrady	46	48.47N	14.47 E
Nové Město nad Váhom	46	48.45N	17.49 E
Nové Město na Moravě	46	49.34N	16.04 E
Nové Zámky	46	47.59N	18.11 E
Novgorod	60	58.31N	31.17 E
Novi Bečej	54	45.36N	20.08 E
Novi di Modena	52	44.54N	10.54 E
Novi Ligure	52	44.46N	8.47 E
Novinger	100	40.14N	92.43W
Novi Pazar, Blg.	54	43.21N	27.12 E
Novi Pazar, Jugo.	54	43.08N	20.31 E
Novi Sad	54	45.15N	19.50 E
Novi Vinodolski	52	45.08N	14.48 E
Novoaltajsk	58	53.24N	83.58 E
Novoanninskij	56	50.32N	42.41 E
Novo Aripuanã	110	5.08 S	60.22W
Novočerkassk	56	47.25N	40.06 E
Novodvinsk	42	64.26N	40.47 E
Novograd-Volynskij	56	50.36N	27.36 E
Novogrudok	60	53.36N	25.50 E
Novo Hamburgo	114	29.41 S	51.08W
Novo Horizonte	114	21.28 S	49.13W
Novoil'insk	58	50.51N	38.15 E
Novokazalinsk	58	45.50N	62.10 E
Novokujbyševsk	42	53.07N	49.58 E
Novokuzneck	58	53.45N	87.06 E
Novol'vovsk	60	53.45N	38.47 E
Novo Mesto	52	45.48N	15.10 E
Novomoskovsk	60	54.05N	38.13 E
Novopetrovskoje	60	55.59N	36.28 E
Novopolock	60	55.32N	28.38 E
Novorossijsk	56	44.45N	37.45 E
Novorybnoje	58	72.50N	105.50 E
Novošachtinsk	56	47.47N	39.56 E
Novosibirsk	58	55.02N	82.55 E
Novosibirskie ostrova II	58	75.00N	142.00 E
Novosibirskoje vodochranilišče @1	58	54.35N	82.35 E
Novosil'	60	52.58N	37.03 E
Novosokol'niki	60	56.21N	30.10 E
Novotroick	56	51.12N	58.20 E
Novouzensk	56	50.28N	48.08 E
Novov'atsk	42	58.29N	49.44 E
Novovolynsk	56	50.50N	24.05 E
Novozybkov	60	52.32N	31.56 E
Novska	52	45.21N	16.59 E
Nový Bohumín	46	49.56N	18.20 E
Nový Bor	46	50.45N	14.33 E
Novyje Gorki	60	56.42N	41.06 E
Nový Jičín	46	49.36N	18.00 E
Novyj Port	42	67.40N	72.52 E
Novyj Uzen	58	43.18N	52.48 E
Nowa Dęba	46	50.26N	21.46 E
Nowa Ruda	46	50.35N	16.31 E
Nowa Sól (Neusalz)	46	51.48N	15.44 E
Nowe	46	53.40N	18.43 E
Nowe Miasteczko	46	51.42N	15.45 E
Nowe Miasto Lubawskie	46	53.27N	19.35 E
Nowe Miasto nad Pilicą	46	51.38N	20.35 E
Nowendoc	94	31.32 S	151.43 E
Nowe Warpno	46	53.44N	14.16 E
Nowgong	76	26.20N	92.41 E
Nowingi	94	34.36 S	142.14 E
Nowitna ≃	22	65.55N	154.17W
Nowogard	46	53.40N	15.08 E
Nowogród	46	53.15N	21.53 E
Nowogrodziec	46	51.12N	15.25 E
Nowra	94	34.53 S	150.36 E
Nowy Dwór Gdański	46	54.13N	19.07 E
Nowy Dwór Mazowiecki	46	52.26N	20.43 E
Nowy Sącz	46	49.38N	20.42 E
Nowy Staw	46	54.09N	19.00 E
Nowy Targ	46	49.29N	20.02 E
Nowy Tomyśl	46	52.20N	16.07 E
Noxen	102	41.25N	76.03W
Noya	50	42.47N	8.53W
Noya ≃	50	41.28N	1.56 E
Noyon	48	49.35N	3.00 E
Nozay	48	47.34N	1.38W
Nsanje	84	16.55 S	35.12 E
Nsawam	80	5.50N	0.20W
Nsukka	80	6.52N	7.24 E
Ntem ≃	80	2.15N	9.45 E
Nuanetsi	86	22.40 S	31.50 E
Nuasjärvi ⊚	44	64.10N	28.05 E
Nūbah, Jibāl an- ⋏	82	11.00N	30.45 E
Nubian Desert ⋟2	82	21.30N	33.30 E
Nûble □4	114	36.39 S	72.27W
Nueces ≃	100	27.50N	97.30W
Nueltin Lake ⊚	98	60.20N	99.50W
Nuestra Señora de Talavera	114	25.26 S	63.48W
Nueva, Isla I	112	55.13 S	66.30W
Nueva California	114	32.45 S	68.20W
Nueva Casas Grandes	106	30.25N	107.55W
Nueva Esparta □3	108	11.00N	64.00W
Nueva Francia	114	28.35 S	64.10W
Nueva Galia	114	35.07 S	65.15W
Nueva Germania	114	23.53 S	56.45W
Nueva Gerona	108	21.53N	82.48W
Nueva Helvecia	114	34.19 S	57.13W
Nueva Imperial	114	38.44 S	72.57W
Nueva Palmira	114	33.53 S	58.25W
Nueva Rosita	106	27.57N	101.13W
Nueve de Julio	114	35.27 S	60.52W
Nuevitas	108	21.33N	77.16W
Nuevo, Golfo C	112	42.42 S	64.36W
Nuevo Berlín	114	32.59 S	58.03W
Nuevo Laredo	106	27.30N	99.31W
Nuevo León □3	106	25.00N	100.00W
Nugget Point ⋗	96	46.27 S	169.49 E
Nûgssuaq ⋗1	98	70.25N	52.30W
Nuguria Islands II	28	3.20 S	154.45 E
Nui I1	28	7.15 S	177.10 E
Nuits-Saint-Georges	48	47.08N	4.57 E
N'uja ≃	58	60.32N	116.20 E
Nukey Bluff ⋀4	94	32.33 S	135.40 E
Nuku'alofa	28	21.08 S	175.12W
Nukufetau I1	28	8.00 S	178.22 E
Nukulaelae I1	28	9.23 S	179.52 E
Nukumanu Islands II	28	4.35 S	159.25 E
Nukunonu I1	28	9.12 S	171.54W
Nukus	58	42.50N	59.29 E
Nules	50	39.51N	0.09W
Nullagine	90	21.53 S	120.06 E
Nullarbor	90	31.26 S	130.55 E
Nullarbor Plain ⋍	90	31.00 S	129.00 E
Numan	80	9.28N	12.02 E
Numata, Nihon	64	36.38N	139.03 E
Numata, Nihon	64a	43.48N	141.57 E
Numazu	64	35.06N	138.52 E
Numbargulme, Mount ⋀	92	14.56 S	145.03 E
Numedal v	44	60.06N	9.06 E
Numfoor, Pulau I	92	1.03 S	134.54 E
Numto	58	63.40N	71.20 E
Nuneaton	34	52.32N	1.28W
Nunivak Island I	22	60.00N	166.30W
Nunjikompita	90	32.16 S	134.19 E
Nunkun ≃	76	33.59N	76.01 E
Nuomin ≃	62	48.06N	124.26 E
Nura ≃	58	50.30N	69.59 E
Nurallao	52	39.47N	9.04 E
Nurata	58	40.33N	65.41 E
Nürburg	46	50.20N	6.57 E
Nuremberg →Nürnberg	46	49.27N	11.04 E
Nurlat	42	54.26N	50.46 E
Nurmes	44	63.33N	29.07 E
Nurmijärvi	44	60.28N	24.48 E
Nürnberg (Nuremberg)	46	49.27N	11.04 E
Nurmo	44	62.50N	22.54 E
Nurri	52	39.43N	9.14 E
Nurri, Punta ⋗1	52	39.01N	9.05 E

Symbols in the Index entries are identified on page 122

Name Page Lat. °′ Long. °′

Nurri 52 39.43N 9.14 E
Nurri, Mount ∧ 94 31.42S 146.02 E
Nürtingen 46 48.38N 9.20 E
Nuruhak Dağı ∧ 78 38.04N 37.29 E
Nusa Tenggara (Lesser Sunda Islands) II 68 9.00S 120.00 E
Nusa Tenggara Barat □[4] 72 8.50S 117.30 E
Nusa Tenggara Timur □[4] 72 9.30S 122.00 E
Nusaybin 78 37.03N 41.13 E
Nu Shan ✶ 62 27.00N 99.00 E
Nushki 76 29.33N 66.01 E
Nutter Fort 102 39.15N 80.19W
Nutwood Downs 92 15.49S 134.10 E
Nuwara-Eliya 74 6.58N 80.46 E
Nuwaybi'al-Muzayyinah 78 28.58N 34.39 E
Nuwerus 86 31.08S 18.24 E
Nuweveldberge ✶ 86 32.13S 22.10 E
Nuyts, Point › 90 35.04S 116.37 E
Nuyts Archipelago II 90 32.35S 133.17 E
Nyabing 90 33.32S 118.09 E
Nyack 102 41.05N 73.55W
Nyah West 94 35.11S 143.22 E
Nyainqêntanglha Shan ✶ 62 30.00N 90.00 E
Nyala 82 12.03N 24.53 E
Nyanga, Lake ⊜ 90 29.57S 126.10 E
Nyanza 84 2.21S 29.45 E
Nyasa, Lake ⊜ 84 12.00S 34.30 E
Nyaunglebin 70 17.57N 96.44 E
Nybergsund 44 61.15N 12.19 E
Nyborg 44 55.19N 10.48 E
Nybro 44 56.45N 15.54 E
Nyda 58 66.36N 72.54 E
Nyenyam 76 28.11N 85.58 E
Nyfer ≃ 34 52.02N 4.50W
Nyíradony 46 47.41N 21.55 E
Nyírbátor 46 47.50N 22.08 E
Nyíregyháza 46 47.59N 21.43 E
Nykøbing, Dan. 44 54.46N 11.53 E
Nykøbing, Dan. 44 55.55N 11.41 E
Nykøbing, Dan. 44 56.48N 8.52 E
Nyköping 44 58.45N 17.00 E
Nykroppa 44 59.38N 14.18 E
Nyland 44 63.00N 17.46 E
Nylstroom 86 24.42S 28.20 E
Nymagee 94 32.04S 146.20 E
Nymboida ≃ 94 29.39S 152.30 E
Nymburk 46 50.11N 15.03 E
Nynäshamn 44 58.54N 17.57 E
Nyngan 94 31.34S 147.11 E
Nyoma 76 33.11N 78.38 E
Nyon 48 46.23N 6.14 E
Nyong ≃ 80 3.17N 9.54 E
Nyons 48 44.22N 5.08 E
Nýrsko 46 49.18N 13.09 E
Nysa 46 50.29N 17.20 E
Nysa Kłodzka ≃ 46 50.49N 17.50 E
Nysa Łuzycka (Neisse) (Nisa) ≃ 46 52.04N 14.46 E
Nysted 44 54.40N 11.45 E
Nytva 42 57.56N 55.20 E
Nyūdō-zaki › 64 40.00N 139.42 E
Nyuri 76 27.42N 92.13 E
Nyūzen 64 36.56N 137.30 E
Nzérékoré 80 7.45N 8.49W
N'zeto 84 7.14S 12.52 E
Nzheleledam ⊜[1] 86 22.44S 30.06 E
Nzi ≃ 80 5.57N 4.50W

O

Oa, Mull of › 38 55.35N 6.20W
Oadby 34 52.36N 1.04W
Oahe, Lake ⊜[1] 100 45.30N 100.25W
Oahu I 105a 21.30N 158.00W
O-Akan-dake ∧ 64a 43.27N 144.10 E
Oakbank 94 33.03S 140.35 E
Oak Bluffs 102 41.27N 70.33W
Oakdale, Austl. 90 34.26S 119.00 E
Oakdale, Ca., U.S. 104 37.46N 120.50W
Oakengates 34 52.42N 2.28W
Oakey 94 27.26S 151.43 E
Oakfield, Me., U.S. 102 46.05N 68.09W
Oakfield, N.Y., U.S. 102 43.03N 78.16W
Oakham 34 52.40N 0.43W
Oak Hill, Oh., U.S. 102 38.54N 82.34W
Oak Hill, W.V., U.S. 102 37.58N 81.08W
Oakhurst 104 37.19N 119.40W
Oak Knolls 104 34.51N 120.27W
Oakland, Ca., U.S. 104 37.48N 122.16W
Oakland, Me., U.S. 102 44.32N 69.43W
Oakland, Md., U.S. 102 39.24N 79.24W
Oakland, Or., U.S. 104 43.25N 123.17W
Oakley, Eng., U.K. 34 51.15N 1.11W
Oakley, Scot., U.K. 38 56.04N 3.33W
Oakley, Id., U.S. 104 42.14N 113.52W
Oakover ≃ 90 20.43S 120.33 E
Oak Ridge 100 36.00N 84.16W
Oakura 96 39.07S 173.57 E
Oak View 104 34.24N 119.18W
Oakville 102 43.27N 79.41W
Oakwood 102 41.05N 84.22W
Oamaru 96 45.06S 170.58 E
Oancea 54 45.55N 28.06 E
Ōarai 64 36.18N 140.34 E
Oaro 96 42.31S 173.30 E
Oatka Creek ≃ 102 43.01N 77.44W
Oatlands 94 42.18S 147.21 E
Oatman 104 35.01N 114.22W
Oaxaca 106 17.03N 96.43W
Ob' ≃ 56 66.45N 69.30 E
Obama, Nihon 64 35.30N 135.45 E
Obama, Nihon 64 32.43N 130.13 E
Oban, Austl. 94 21.14S 139.03 E
Oban, Scot., U.K. 38 56.25N 5.29W
Obanazawa 64 38.36N 140.24 E
Obbola 44 63.42N 20.19 E
Obelisk ∧ 96 45.20S 169.12 E
Oberá 114 27.29S 55.08W
Oberdrauburg 46 46.45N 12.58 E
Obergurgl 46 46.52N 11.01 E
Oberhausen 46 51.28N 6.50 E
Oberlin 102 41.17N 82.13W
Obernai 48 48.28N 7.29 E
Obernburg am Main 46 49.50N 9.08 E
Oberon 94 33.43S 149.52 E
Oberösterreich □[3] 46 48.15N 14.00 E
Oberpullendorf 46 47.31N 16.31 E
Oberursel 46 50.11N 8.35 E
Obervellach 46 46.56N 13.12 E
Oberviechtach 46 49.28N 12.25 E
Oberwart 46 47.17N 16.13 E
Oberwölz Stadt 46 47.13N 14.17 E
Obi, Kepulauan II 92 1.30S 127.45 E
Obi, Pulau I 92 1.30S 127.45 E
Óbidos 110 1.55S 55.31W
Obihiro 64a 42.55N 143.12 E
Obilatu, Pulau I 68 1.25S 127.20 E
Obing 46 48.00N 12.24 E
Obira 64a 44.00N 141.35 E
Oblučje 58 49.03N 131.04 E
Obninsk 60 55.05N 36.37 E
Obnova 54 43.26N 24.59 E
Obock 82 11.59N 43.16 E
Oborniki 46 52.39N 16.51 E
Obra ≃ 46 52.36N 15.28 E
Obrenovac 54 44.39N 20.12 E
O'Brien 104 42.04N 123.42W
Obrovac 52 44.12N 15.41 E
Obščij Syrt ∧ 56 52.00N 51.30 E
Observation Peak ∧ 104 40.46N 120.10W
Observatoire, Caye de l' I 88 21.25S 158.50 E
Obskaja guba ⊂ 56 69.00N 73.00 E
Ob' Trench +[1] 28 33.00S 98.00 E
Obuasi 80 6.14N 1.39W
Ocala 100 29.11N 82.08W
Ocaña, Col. 110 8.15N 73.20W
Ocaña, Esp. 50 39.56N 3.31W
Occidental, Cordillera ✶, Col. 110 5.00N 76.00W
Occidental, Cordillera ✶, Perú 110 10.00S 77.00W
Ocean Cape › 98 59.30N 139.45W
Ocean City, Md., U.S. 102 38.20N 75.05W
Ocean City, N.J., U.S. 102 39.16N 74.34W
Ocean Falls 98 52.21N 127.40W
Ocean Island → Banaba I 28 0.52S 169.35 E
Oceano 104 35.06N 120.37W
Oceanside 104 33.11N 117.22W
Očer 42 57.53N 54.42 E
Ocha 58 53.34N 142.56 E
Ōchi 64 34.16N 134.18 E
Ochil Hills ✶[2] 38 56.14N 3.40W
Ochiltree 38 55.28N 4.23W
Ocho Rios 108 18.25N 77.07W
Ochota ≃ 58 59.20N 143.04 E
Ochotsk 58 59.23N 143.18 E
Ochsenfurt 46 49.40N 10.03 E
Ochtrup 46 52.13N 7.11 E
Ock ≃ 34 51.39N 1.17W
Ockelbo 44 60.53N 16.43 E
Öckerö 44 57.43N 11.39 E
Ocna Mureş 54 46.23N 23.51 E
Ocoa, Bahía de ⊂ 108 18.22N 70.39W
Ocoña ≃ 110 16.28S 73.07W
Ocotal 108 13.38N 86.29W
Ocotlán 106 20.21N 102.46W
Ocozingo 106 16.54N 92.07W
Ocreza, Ribeira da ≃ 50 39.32N 7.50W
Ocumare del Tuy 110 10.07N 66.46W
Ocussi 72 9.12S 124.21 E
Oda, Ghana 80 5.55N 0.59W
Ōda, Nihon 64 35.11N 132.30 E
Oda, Jabal ∧ 82 20.21N 36.39 E
Ōdaigahara-zan ∧ 64 34.11N 136.05 E
Odaka 64 37.34N 141.00 E
Ōdate 64 40.16N 140.34 E
Odawara 64 35.15N 139.10 E
Odda 44 60.04N 6.33 E
Odder 44 55.58N 10.10 E
Odeleite, Ribeira de ≃ 50 37.21N 7.27W
Odell Lake ⊜ 104 43.34N 122.00W
Odemira 50 37.36N 8.38W
Ödemiş 54 38.13N 27.59 E
Odendaalsrus 86 27.48S 26.45 E
Odense 44 55.24N 10.23 E
Odenwald ✶ 46 49.40N 9.00 E
Oder (Odra) ≃ 46 53.32N 14.38 E
Oderberg 46 52.52N 14.02 E
Oderhaff (Zalew Szczeciński) ⊂ 46 53.46N 14.14 E
Oderzo 52 45.47N 12.29 E
Ödeshög 44 58.14N 14.39 E
Odessa, On., Can. 102 44.17N 76.43W
Odessa, S.S.S.R. 56 46.28N 30.44 E
Odessa, Tx., U.S. 100 31.50N 102.22W
Odesskoje 56 54.13N 72.58 E
Odiel ≃ 50 37.10N 6.54W
Odienné 80 9.30N 7.34W
Odiham 34 51.15N 0.57W
Odin, Mount ∧ 98 50.33N 118.08W
Odincovo 60 55.41N 37.17 E
Odobeşti 54 45.45N 27.04 E
Odolanów 46 51.35N 17.39 E
O'Donnell ≃ 90 18.22S 126.36 E
Odorheiu Secuiesc 54 46.18N 25.18 E
Odry 46 49.39N 17.50 E
Odrzywół 46 51.32N 20.33 E
Odžaci 54 45.30N 19.16 E
Oebisfelde 46 52.25N 10.59 E
Oeiras 110 7.01S 42.08W
Oelde 46 51.49N 8.08 E
Oelsnitz 46 50.24N 12.10 E
Oenpelli Mission 92 12.20S 133.04 E
Oettingen in Bayern 46 48.57N 10.36 E
Oetz 46 47.12N 10.54 E
Ofanto ≃ 52 41.22N 16.13 E
Offaly □[6] 40 53.20N 7.30W
Offenbach 46 50.08N 8.47 E
Offenburg 46 48.28N 7.57 E
Offerdal 44 63.28N 14.00 E
Offida 52 42.56N 13.41 E
Oficina Chile 114 25.09S 69.54W
Oficina Pedro de Valdivia 114 22.36S 69.40W
Ofotfjorden ⊂[2] 42 68.23N 16.10 E
Ōfunato 64 39.04N 141.43 E
Oga 64 39.53N 139.51 E
Ogaden +[1] 82 8.00N 44.00 E
Oga-hantō ›[1] 64 39.55N 139.50 E
Ōgaki 64 35.21N 136.37 E
Ogallala 100 41.07N 101.43W
Ogasawara-guntō (Bonin Islands) II 28 27.00N 142.10 E
Ogatsu 64 38.31N 141.28 E
Ogawa 64 32.35N 130.43 E
Ogawara-ko ⊜ 64 40.47N 141.20 E
Ogbomosho 80 8.08N 4.15 E
Ogden 100 41.13N 111.58W
Ogdensburg 102 44.41N 75.29W
Ogilvie 90 28.09S 114.38 E
Ogilvie Mountains ✶ 98 65.00N 139.30W
Ogliastra +[1] 52 39.56N 9.37 E
Oglio ≃ 52 45.02N 10.39 E
Ogmore 94 22.37S 149.40 E
Ogmore ≃ 34 51.28N 3.38W
Ogmore Vale 34 51.38N 3.31W
Ognon ≃ 48 47.20N 5.29 E
Ogoja 80 6.40N 8.48 E
Ogoki ≃ 98 51.38N 85.57W
Ogooué ≃ 84 0.49S 9.00 E
Ogōri 64 34.06N 131.24 E
Ogosta ≃ 54 43.45N 23.51 E
Ogre 60 56.51N 24.36 E
Ogrodzieniec 46 50.27N 19.31 E
Ogulin 52 45.16N 15.14 E
Oguni 64 38.04N 139.45 E
Ogunquit 102 43.14N 70.35W
Ohai 96 45.55S 167.57 E
Ohakune 96 39.25S 175.24 E
Ohanet 80 28.45N 8.55 E
Ōhara 64 35.15N 140.23 E
Ōhata 64 41.24N 141.10 E
Ohau, Lake ⊜ 96 44.15S 169.51 E
Ohaupo 96 37.55S 175.19 E
O'Higgins, Lago (Lago San Martín) ⊜ 112 49.00S 72.40W
Ohingaiti 96 39.52S 175.43 E
Ohio □[3] 100 40.15N 82.45W
Ohio ≃ 100 36.59N 89.08W
Ohio City 102 40.46N 84.36W
Ohře ≃ 46 50.32N 14.08 E
Ohrid 54 41.07N 20.47 E
Ohrid, Lake ⊜ 54 41.02N 20.43 E
Ohrigstad 86 24.49S 30.33 E
Öhringen 46 49.12N 9.29 E
Ohura 96 38.50S 174.59 E
Ōi ≃ 64 34.46N 138.18 E
Oiapoque 110 3.50N 51.50W
Oiapoque (Oyapock) ≃ 110 4.08N 51.40W
Oil City 102 41.26N 79.42W
Oil Creek ≃ 102 41.26N 79.42W
Oildale 104 35.25N 119.01W
Oir, Beinn an ∧ 38 55.54N 6.00W
Oise □[5] 48 49.30N 2.30 E
Oise ≃ 48 49.00N 2.04 E
Oisemont 48 49.57N 1.46 E
Oissel 48 49.20N 1.06 E
Ōita 64 33.14N 131.36 E
Oituz, Pasul)(54 46.03N 26.23 E
Ojai 104 34.26N 119.14W
Öje 44 60.49N 13.51 E
Ojinaga 106 29.34N 104.25W
Ojiya 64 37.18N 138.48 E
Ojm'akon 58 63.28N 142.49 E
Ojos del Salado, Nevado ∧ 114 27.06S 68.32W
Oka ≃, S.S.S.R. 56 56.20N 43.59 E
Oka ≃, S.S.S.R. 58 55.15N 102.10 E
Okaba 92 8.06S 139.42 E
Okahandja 86 21.59S 16.58 E
Okahandja □[5] 86 21.30S 17.00 E
Okahukura 96 38.47S 175.13 E
Okaihau 96 35.19S 173.47 E
Okanagan Lake ⊜ 98 50.00N 119.28W
Okanogan ≃ 100 48.06N 119.43W
Okāra 76 30.49N 73.27 E
Okarito 96 43.14S 170.11 E
Okato 96 39.12S 173.53 E
Okaukuejo 86 19.10S 15.54 E
Okavango (Cubango) ≃ 84 18.50S 22.25 E
Okavango Delta ≚[2] 86 18.45S 22.45 E
Ōkawa 64 33.12N 130.23 E
Okaya 64 36.03N 138.03 E
Okayama 64 34.39N 133.55 E
Okazaki 64 34.57N 137.10 E
Okeechobee, Lake ⊜ 100 26.55N 80.45W
Okehampton 34 50.44N 4.00W
Okement ≃ 34 50.50N 4.01W
Okemos 102 42.43N 84.25W
Okene 80 7.33N 6.15 E
Okhotsk, Sea of (Ochotskoje more) ⊤[2] 58 53.00N 150.00 E
Okhotsk Basin +[1] 26 53.00N 148.00 E
Oki-Daitō-jima I 28 24.28N 131.11 E
Okiep 86 29.39S 17.53 E
Okinawa 65b 26.20N 127.50 E
Okinawa □[5] 65b 26.31N 127.59 E
Okinawa-jima I 65b 26.30N 128.00 E
Okinawa-shotō II 65b 26.40N 128.00 E
Okino-Daitō-jima I 62 24.28N 131.11 E
Okino-Erabu-shima I 65b 27.22N 128.35 E
Okino-Tori-shima (Parece Vela) I 62 20.25N 136.00 E
Oki-shotō II 64 36.15N 133.15 E
Oklahoma □[3] 100 35.30N 98.00W
Oklahoma City 100 35.28N 97.30W
Okmulgee 100 35.37N 95.57W
Okonek 46 53.33N 16.50 E
Oksbøl 44 55.38N 8.17 E
Oksskolten ∧ 42 65.59N 14.15 E
Okt'abr'sk 56 49.28N 57.25 E
Okt'abr'skij 56 54.28N 53.28 E
Okt'abr'skoje 56 62.28N 66.03 E
Okt'abr'skoj Revol'ucii, ostrov I 58 79.30N 97.00 E
Okučani 52 45.16N 17.12 E
Ōkuchi 64 32.04N 130.37 E
Okuku ≃ 96 43.16S 172.28 E
Okulovka 60 58.26N 33.18 E
Okushiri 64a 42.10N 139.31 E
Okushiri-tō I 64a 42.10N 139.27 E
Okwa (Chapman's) ≃ 86 22.30S 23.00 E
Ola 58 59.35N 151.17 E
Ólafsfjörður 42a 66.06N 18.38W
Olancha 104 36.16N 118.00W
Olancha Peak ∧ 104 36.16N 118.07W
Olanchito 108 15.30N 86.35W
Öland I 44 56.45N 16.38 E
Olary 94 32.17S 140.19 E
Olascoaga 114 35.12S 60.36W
Olavarría 114 36.54S 60.17W
Oława 46 50.57N 17.17 E
Olbia 52 40.55N 9.31 E
Ol'chon, ostrov I 58 53.09N 107.24 E
Olcott 102 43.20N 78.42W
Old Bahama Channel ⋓ 108 22.30N 78.50W
Old Bedford ≃ 34 52.35N 0.20 E
Old Bight 108 24.15N 75.21W
Oldbury 34 52.30N 2.00W
Oldcastle 40 53.46N 7.10W
Old Colwyn 36 53.18N 3.43W
Old Cork 94 22.56S 141.52 E
Old Crow 98 67.35N 139.50W
Old Crow ≃ 98 67.35N 139.50W
Oldebroek 46 52.26N 5.54 E
Olden 44 61.50N 6.49 E
Oldenburg 46 53.08N 8.13 E
Oldenburg □[9] 46 53.00N 8.00 E
Oldenburg [in Holstein] 46 54.17N 10.52 E
Oldenzaal 46 52.19N 6.56 E
Old Forge, N.Y., U.S. 102 43.42N 74.58W
Old Forge, Pa., U.S. 102 41.22N 75.44W
Oldham 36 53.33N 2.07W
Old Howe ≃ 36 53.57N 0.21W
Oldmeldrum 38 57.20N 2.20W
Old Nene ≃ 34 52.40N 0.10 E
Old Noranside 94 22.13S 140.04 E
Old Orchard Beach 102 43.31N 70.22W
Olds 98 51.47N 114.06W
Old Saybrook 102 41.17N 72.22W
Old Speck Mountain ∧ 102 44.34N 70.57W
Old Tate 86 21.22S 27.46 E
Old Town 102 44.56N 68.38W
Old Wives Lake ⊜ 98 50.06N 106.00W
Olean 102 42.04N 78.25W
Olecko 46 54.03N 22.30 E
Ølen 44 59.36N 5.48 E
Olenegorsk 42 68.09N 33.15 E
Olenij, ostrov I 56 72.25N 77.45 E
Olen'ok 58 68.33N 112.18 E
Olen'ok ≃ 58 73.00N 119.55 E
Olen'okskij zaliv ⊂ 58 73.20N 121.00 E
Oléron, Île d' I 48 45.56N 1.15W
Oleśnica 46 51.13N 17.23 E
Olesno 46 50.53N 18.25 E
Ol'ga 58 43.45N 135.18 E
Olga, Mount ∧ 90 25.19S 130.46 E
Ölgij 62 48.56N 89.57 E
Ølgod 44 55.49N 8.37 E
Olhão 50 37.02N 7.50W
Olib, Otok I 52 44.22N 14.48 E
Oliena 52 40.16N 9.24 E
Olifants (Rio dos Elefantes) ≃, Afr. 86 24.10S 32.40 E
Olifants ≃, S. Afr. 86 31.42S 18.12 E
Olifantshoek 86 27.57S 22.42 E
Olimarao I[1] 68 7.41N 145.52 E
Ólimbos 54 35.44N 27.11 E
Ólimbos ∧, Ellás 54 40.05N 22.21 E
Ólimbos ∧, Kípros 78 34.56N 32.52 E
Olímpia 110 20.44S 48.54W
Olinda 110 8.01S 34.51W
Olio 94 21.54S 143.13 E
Olite 50 42.29N 1.39W
Oliva, Arg. 114 32.03S 63.34W
Oliva, Esp. 50 38.55N 0.07W
Oliva de la Frontera 50 38.16N 6.55W
Olivare, Cerro de ∧ 114 30.18S 69.55W
Olive Hill 102 38.18N 83.10W
Olivehurst 104 39.05N 121.33W
Oliveira 110 20.41S 44.49W
Olivenza 50 38.41N 7.06W
Olivet 102 42.26N 84.55W
Olivine Range ✶ 96 44.18S 168.30 E
Ollagüe 112 21.14S 68.16W
Ollatrim ≃ 40 52.52N 8.13W
Olmedillo de Roa 50 41.47N 3.56W
Olmedo 50 41.23N 4.41W
Olmos 110 5.59S 79.46W
Olney 34 52.09N 0.42W
Olofström 44 56.16N 14.30 E
Oloj ≃ 58 66.29N 159.29 E
Ol'okma ≃ 58 60.22N 120.42 E
Ol'okminsk 58 60.24N 120.24 E
Olomouc 46 49.36N 17.16 E
Olonec 42 61.00N 32.57 E
Olongapo 68 14.50N 120.16 E
Oloron, Gave d' ≃ 48 43.33N 1.05W
Oloron-Sainte-Marie 48 43.12N 0.36W
Olot 50 42.11N 2.29 E
Olov'annaja 58 50.56N 115.35 E
Olpe 46 51.02N 7.52 E
Olshammar 44 58.45N 14.48 E
Olsztyn (Allenstein) 46 53.48N 20.29 E
Olsztynek 46 53.36N 20.17 E
Olt □[6] 54 44.20N 24.30 E
Olt ≃ 54 43.43N 24.51 E
Olta 114 30.37S 66.16W
Olten 48 47.21N 7.54 E
Olteni 54 44.10N 25.18 E
Olteniţa 54 44.05N 26.39 E
Olteţ ≃ 54 44.14N 24.27 E
Oltul ≃ 54 45.38N 24.16 E
Oluan Pi › 66 21.54N 120.51 E
Ol'utorskij, mys › 58 59.55N 170.27 E
Ol'utorskij zaliv ⊂ 58 60.15N 168.30 E
Olvera 50 36.56N 5.16W
Olympia 100 47.02N 122.53W
Olympus, Mount → Ólimbos ∧ 54 40.05N 22.21 E
Olympus, Mount ∧ 100 47.48N 123.43W
Olympus, Mount ∧[2] 102 38.03N 83.39W
Om' ≃ 56 54.59N 73.22 E
Ōma 64 41.32N 140.55 E
Ōmachi 64 36.30N 137.52 E
Omae-zaki › 64 34.36N 138.14 E
Ōmagari 64 39.27N 140.29 E
Omagh 40 54.36N 7.18W
Omaha 100 41.15N 95.56W
Omak 100 48.24N 119.31W
Omakau 96 45.05S 169.36 E
Oman ('Umān) □[1] 74 22.00N 58.00 E
Oman, Gulf of ⊂ 74 24.30N 58.30 E
Omarama 96 44.29S 169.58 E
Omaruru 86 21.28S 15.56 E
Omaruru □[5] 86 21.00S 16.00 E
Omatako ≃ 86 17.59S 20.30 E
Ōma-zaki › 64a 41.32N 140.55 E
Ombersley 34 52.17N 2.13W
Omboué 84 1.34S 9.15 E
Ombrone ≃ 52 42.39N 11.00 E
Omčak 58 61.38N 147.55 E
Omdraaisvlei 86 30.08S 23.08 E
Omdurman → Umm Durmān 82 15.38N 32.30 E
Ōme 64 35.47N 139.15 E
Omegna 52 45.53N 8.24 E
Omemee 102 44.18N 78.33W
Omeo 94 37.06S 147.36 E
Ometepe, Isla de I 108 11.30N 85.35W
Ometepec 106 16.41N 98.25W
Ōmi-hachiman 64 35.08N 136.06 E
Ōminato → Mutsu 64 41.17N 141.10 E
Omineca ≃ 98 56.05N 124.30W
Omineca Mountains ✶ 98 56.00N 125.00W
Omišalj 52 45.13N 14.34 E
Ōmiya 64 35.54N 139.38 E
Ommanney Bay ⊂ 98 73.07N 100.11W
Ommen 46 52.32N 6.25 E
Omo ≃ 82 4.31N 35.59 E
Omodeo, Lago ⊜ 52 40.08N 8.55 E
Omoloj ≃ 58 71.10N 132.08 E
Omolon ≃ 58 68.42N 158.36 E
Omono ≃ 64 39.46N 140.03 E
Omsk 56 55.00N 73.24 E
Omsukčan 58 62.32N 155.48 E
Ōmu 64a 44.34N 142.58 E
Omu, Vîrful ∧ 54 45.26N 25.26 E
Omulew ≃ 46 53.05N 21.32 E
Ōmura 64 32.54N 129.57 E
Omurtag 54 43.06N 26.25 E
Ōmuta 64 33.02N 130.27 E
Omutninsk 42 58.40N 52.12 E
Ona 44 62.52N 6.34 E
Onagawa 64 38.26N 141.27 E
Onaway 102 45.21N 84.13W
Oncativo 114 31.55S 63.40W
Onchan 36 54.11N 4.27W
Onda 50 39.58N 0.15W
Ondangwa 86 17.55S 16.00 E
Ondava ≃ 46 48.27N 21.48 E
Ondo, Nig. 80 7.04N 4.47 E
Ondo, Nihon 64 34.11N 132.32 E
Öndörchaan 62 47.19N 110.39 E
Onega 42 63.55N 38.05 E
Onega ≃ 42 63.58N 37.55 E
Onega, Lake → Onežskoje ozero ⊜ 42 61.30N 35.45 E
Oneida 102 43.05N 75.39W
Oneida Lake ⊜ 102 43.13N 76.00W
O'Neill 100 42.27N 98.38W
Onekotan, ostrov I 58 49.25N 154.45 E
Oneonta 102 42.27N 75.03W
Onežskoje ozero (Lake Onega) ⊜ 42 61.30N 35.45 E
Ongaonga 96 39.55S 176.25 E
Ongarue 96 38.43S 175.17 E
Ongerup 90 33.58S 118.29 E
Onich 38 56.42N 5.13W
Onitsha 80 6.09N 6.47 E
Onkivesi ⊜ 44 63.18N 27.18 E
Onny ≃ 34 52.23N 2.45W
Ōno 64 35.59N 136.29 E
Onoda 64 33.59N 131.11 E
Ono-I-Lau I 28 20.39S 178.42W
Onomichi 64 34.25N 133.12 E
Onon ≃ 62 51.42N 115.50 E
Onoto 108 9.36N 65.12W
Onotoa I[1] 28 1.52S 175.34 E
Ons, Isla de I 50 42.23N 8.56W
Onseepkans 86 28.46S 19.14 E
Onset 102 41.44N 70.39W
Onslow 90 21.39S 115.06 E
Ontake-san ∧ 64 35.53N 137.29 E
Ontario, Ca., U.S. 104 34.03N 117.39W
Ontario, Oh., U.S. 102 40.45N 82.35W
Ontario, Or., U.S. 100 44.01N 116.57W
Ontario □[4] 98 51.00N 85.00W
Ontario, Lake ⊜ 102 43.45N 78.00W
Onteniente 50 38.49N 0.37W
Ontojärvi ⊜ 44 64.08N 29.09 E
Ontong Java I[1] 28 5.20S 159.30 E
Onverwacht 110 5.36N 55.12W
Oobagooma 90 16.46S 123.59 E
Oodnadatta 90 27.33S 135.28 E
Ooldea 90 30.27S 131.50 E
Ooratippra 90 22.00S 136.00 E
Ooratippra Creek ≃ 90 21.55S 136.05 E
Oostelijk Flevoland +[1] 46 52.30N 5.45 E
Oostende (Ostende) 46 51.13N 2.55 E
Oosterhout 46 51.38N 4.51 E
Oost-Vlieland 46 53.17N 5.04 E
Ootacamund 74 11.24N 76.42 E
Opaka 54 43.27N 26.10 E
Opala 84 0.37S 24.21 E
Opalenica 46 52.19N 16.23 E
Oparino 42 59.52N 48.17 E
Opatija 52 45.21N 14.19 E
Opatów 46 50.49N 21.26 E
Opava 46 49.56N 17.54 E
Opava ≃ 46 49.50N 18.13 E
Opelika 100 32.38N 85.22W
Opelousas 100 30.32N 92.04W
Opeongo ≃ 102 45.30N 77.57W
Opeongo Lake ⊜ 102 45.42N 78.23W
Opequon Creek ≃ 102 39.35N 77.52W
Ophir 104 42.33N 124.22W
Ophthalmia Range ✶ 90 23.17S 119.30 E
Opihikao 105a 19.25N 154.53W
Opinaca ≃ 98 52.15N 78.02W
Opinan 38 57.43N 5.47W
Opiscotéo, Lac ⊜ 98 53.10N 68.10W
Opladen 46 51.04N 7.00 E
Opočka 60 56.43N 28.38 E
Opoczno 46 51.23N 20.17 E
Opole (Oppeln) 46 50.41N 17.55 E
Opole Lubelskie 46 51.09N 21.58 E
Oporto → Porto 50 41.11N 8.36W
Opotiki 96 38.00S 177.17 E
Oppdal 44 62.36N 9.40 E
Oppeln → Opole 46 50.41N 17.55 E
Oppido Mamertina 52 38.16N 16.00 E
Oppland □[6] 44 61.10N 9.40 E
Opua 96 35.19S 174.07 E
Opunake 96 39.27S 173.51 E
Or, Côte d' ∧ 48 47.10N 4.50 E
Ora 52 46.21N 11.18 E
Ora Banda 90 30.22S 121.04 E
Oradea 54 47.03N 21.57 E
Öræfajökull ⊓ 42a 64.03N 16.38W
Orahovica 54 45.31N 17.53 E
Orai 76 25.59N 79.28 E
Oran → Wahran 80 35.43N 0.43W
Orange, Austl. 94 33.17S 149.06 E
Orange, Fr. 48 44.08N 4.48 E
Orange, Ma., U.S. 102 42.35N 72.18W
Orange, Tx., U.S. 100 30.05N 93.44W
Orange, Va., U.S. 102 38.14N 78.06W
Orange (Oranje) ≃ 86 28.41S 16.28 E
Orange, Cabo › 110 4.24N 51.33W
Orangeburg 100 33.29N 80.51W
Orange Cove 104 36.37N 119.19W
Orange Free State (Oranje-Vrystaat) □[4] 86 28.30S 27.00 E
Orangemouth → Oranjemund 86 28.38S 16.24 E
Orangeville 102 43.55N 80.06W
Oranienburg 46 52.45N 13.14 E
Oranje → Orange ≃ 86 28.41S 16.28 E
Oranjefontein 86 23.25S 27.41 E
Oranjemund 86 28.38S 16.24 E
Oranjerivier 86 29.40S 24.12 E
Oranjestad 108 12.33N 70.06W
Oranmore 40 53.16N 8.54W
Orari ≃ 96 44.15S 171.25 E
Orăştie 54 45.50N 23.12 E
Oravais (Oravainen) 44 63.18N 22.23 E
Oraviţa 54 45.02N 21.41 E
Orawia 96 46.03S 167.49 E
Orb ≃ 48 43.15N 3.18 E
Orbe 48 46.43N 6.32 E
Orbetello 52 42.27N 11.13 E
Orbieu ≃ 48 43.14N 2.54 E
Orbigo ≃ 50 41.58N 5.40W
Orbisonia 102 40.15N 77.54W
Orbost 94 37.42S 148.27 E
Örbyhus 44 60.14N 17.42 E
Orce ≃ 50 37.44N 2.28W
Orcera 50 38.19N 2.39W
Orchard Park 102 42.46N 78.44W
Orchies 48 50.28N 3.14 E
Orchila, Isla I 110 11.48N 66.09W
Orchon ≃ 62 50.21N 106.05 E
Orco ≃ 52 45.10N 7.52 E
Ord ≃ 92 15.30S 128.21 E
Ord, Mount ∧ 90 17.20S 125.34 E
Ordenes 50 43.04N 8.24W
Ord Mountain ∧ 104 34.40N 116.49W
Ordoqui 114 35.54S 61.10W
Ord River 90 17.23S 128.51 E
Ordu 30 41.00N 37.53 E
Ordžonikidze 56 43.03N 44.40 E
Ore ≃ 38 56.10N 3.15W
Öreälven ≃ 44 63.32N 19.44 E
Örebro 44 59.17N 15.13 E
Örebro Län □[6] 44 59.30N 15.00 E
Orechovo-Zujevo 60 55.49N 38.59 E
Orechovsk 60 54.41N 30.30 E
Oregon 102 41.38N 83.29W
Oregon □[3] 100 44.00N 121.00W
Oregon City 100 45.21N 122.36W
Öregrund 44 60.20N 18.26 E
Orel → Or'ol 60 52.59N 36.05 E
Orellana, Embalse de ⊜[1] 50 39.00N 5.25W
Orenburg 56 51.54N 55.06 E
Orense, Arg. 114 38.40S 59.47W
Orense, Esp. 50 42.20N 7.51W
Orepuki 96 46.17S 167.44 E
Orestiás 54 41.30N 26.31 E
Oreti ≃ 96 46.28S 168.17 E
Orewa 96 36.34S 174.42 E
Orfanoú, Kólpos ⊂ 54 40.40N 23.50 E
Orford 34 52.06N 1.31 E
Orford Ness › 34 52.05N 1.34 E
Orgaz 50 39.39N 3.54W
Orgelet 48 46.31N 5.37 E
Orgūn 76 32.51N 69.07 E
Orick 104 41.17N 124.03W
Oriental, Cordillera ✶, Col. 110 6.00N 73.00W
Oriental, Cordillera ✶, Perú 110 11.00S 74.00W
Orientaliă, Poarta)(54 45.06N 22.18 E
Oriente 114 38.44S 60.37W
Orientos 94 28.05S 141.14 E
Orihuela 50 38.05N 0.57W
Orillia 102 44.37N 79.25W
Orimattila 44 60.48N 25.45 E
Orini 96 37.34S 175.18 E
Orinoco ≃ 110 8.37N 62.15W
Orinoco, Delta del ≚[2] 108 9.15N 61.30W
Oripää 44 60.51N 22.41 E
Oriskany 102 43.09N 75.19W
Orissa □[3] 76 20.00N 84.00 E
Oristano 52 39.54N 8.36 E
Orituco ≃ 108 8.45N 67.27W
Orivesi 44 61.41N 24.21 E
Orivesi ⊜ 44 62.16N 29.24 E
Oriximiná 110 1.45S 55.52W
Orizaba 106 18.51N 97.06W
Orizaba, Pico de → Citlaltépetl, Volcán ∧[1] 106 19.01N 97.16W
Orjahovo 54 43.45N 23.57 E
Ørje 44 59.29N 11.39 E
Orjen ∧ 54 42.30N 18.38 E
Orjiva 50 36.54N 3.25W
Ork, Ness of › 38 59.05N 2.48W
Orkanger 44 63.19N 9.52 E
Örkelljunga 44 56.17N 13.17 E
Orkla ≃ 44 63.18N 9.50 E
Orkney 86 27.00S 26.39 E
Orkney Islands □[4] 38 59.00N 3.00W
Orkney Islands II 38 59.00N 3.00W
Orland 104 39.44N 122.11W
Orlando 100 28.32N 81.22W
Orleães 114 28.21S 49.18W
Orléanais □[9] 48 47.50N 2.00 E
Orléans, On., Can. 102 45.28N 75.31W
Orléans, Fr. 48 47.55N 1.54 E
Orleans, Ca., U.S. 104 41.18N 123.32W
Orleans, Ma., U.S. 102 41.47N 69.59W
Orleans, Vt., U.S. 102 44.48N 72.12W
Orléans, Canal d' ≍ 48 47.54N 1.55 E
Orléansville → Ech Cheliff 80 36.10N 1.20 E
Orlik 58 52.30N 99.55 E
Orlová 46 49.50N 18.24 E
Ormāra 78 25.12N 64.38 E
Ormesby 36 54.33N 1.11W
Ormesby Saint Margaret 34 52.40N 1.42 E
Ormoc 68 11.00N 124.37 E
Ormož 52 46.25N 16.09 E
Ormsjön ⊜ 44 64.23N 16.03 E
Ormskirk 36 53.35N 2.54W
Ornans 48 47.06N 6.09 E
Orne □[5] 48 48.40N 0.05 E
Orne ≃ 48 49.19N 0.14W
Ornes 44 61.18N 7.22 E
Orneta 46 54.08N 20.08 E
Ornö I 44 59.04N 18.24 E
Örnsköldsvik 44 63.18N 18.43 E
Oročen 58 58.28N 125.26 E
Orocué 110 4.48N 71.20W
Oro Grande 104 34.35N 117.20W
Or'ol 60 52.59N 36.05 E
Oroluk I[1] 28 7.32N 155.18 E
Oromocto 98 45.51N 66.29W
Oromocto Lake ⊜ 102 45.36N 67.00W
Orona I[1] 28 4.29S 172.10W
Orono, On., Can. 102 43.59N 78.37W
Orono, Me., U.S. 102 44.52N 68.40W
Oronsay I 38 56.01N 6.16W
Orosei, Golfo di ⊂ 52 40.15N 9.44 E
Orosháza 46 46.34N 20.40 E
Oroszlány 46 47.30N 18.19 E
Oroville 104 39.30N 121.33W
Oroville, Lake ⊜[1] 104 39.32N 121.25W
Orrefors 44 56.50N 15.45 E
Orrell 36 53.32N 2.42W
Orrin, Glen v 38 57.30N 4.46W
Orrin, Loch ⊜ 38 57.30N 4.45W
Orroroo 94 32.44S 138.37 E
Orrs Island 102 43.45N 69.58W
Orrville 102 40.50N 81.45W
Orša, S.S.S.R. 60 54.30N 30.24 E
Orsa, Sve. 44 61.07N 14.37 E
Orsasjön ⊜ 44 61.07N 14.34 E
Orsières 48 46.02N 7.09 E
Orsjön ⊜ 44 61.35N 16.20 E
Orsk 56 51.12N 58.34 E
Orşova 54 44.42N 22.24 E
Ørsta 44 62.12N 6.09 E
Orta Nova 52 41.19N 15.42 E
Ortegal, Cabo › 50 43.45N 7.53W
Orthez 48 43.29N 0.46W
Orthon ≃ 110 10.50S 66.04W
Ortigueira, Bra. 114 24.12S 50.55W
Ortigueira, Esp. 50 43.41N 7.51W
Ortigueira, Ría de ⊂[1] 50 43.42N 7.51W
Ortisei 52 46.34N 11.40 E
Ortiz 108 9.37N 67.17W
Ortona 52 42.21N 14.24 E
Ortonville 100 45.18N 96.26W
Orto-Tokoj 56 42.21N 76.01 E
Örträsk 44 64.08N 18.59 E
Oruanui 96 38.35S 176.02 E
Orūmīyeh (Rezā'īyeh) 78 37.33N 45.04 E
Orūmīyeh, Daryācheh-ye (Lake Urmia) ⊜ 78 37.40N 45.30 E
Oruro 110 17.59S 67.09W
Orust I 44 58.10N 11.38 E
Orūzgān (Qala-i-Hazār Qadam) 76 32.56N 66.38 E
Orūzgān □[4] 76 33.15N 66.00 E
Orvieto 52 42.43N 12.07 E
Orwell 102 41.32N 80.52W
Orwell ≃ 34 51.57N 1.17 E
Orxon ≃ 62 49.00N 117.41 E
Orzinuovi 52 45.24N 9.55 E
Orzyc ≃ 46 52.47N 21.13 E
Orzysz 46 53.49N 21.56 E
Os, Nor. 44 62.30N 11.12 E
Oš, S.S.S.R. 56 40.33N 72.48 E
Osa, Peninsula de ›[1] 106 8.34N 83.31W
Ōsaka 64 34.40N 135.30 E
Ōsaka-wan ⊂ 64 34.30N 135.18 E
Osâm ≃ 54 43.42N 24.51 E
Osby 44 56.22N 13.59 E
Osceola Mills 102 40.51N 78.16W
Oschatz 46 51.17N 13.07 E
Oschersleben 46 52.01N 11.13 E
Oscoda 102 44.26N 83.20W
Osečina 54 44.23N 19.36 E
Osen 42 64.17N 10.30 E
Oshamambe 64a 42.30N 140.22 E
O'Shanassy ≃ 94 18.59S 138.46 E
Oshawa 102 43.54N 78.51W
Oshika 64 38.16N 141.32 E
Oshika-hantō ›[1] 64 38.20N 141.30 E
Ōshima, Nihon 64 34.45N 139.21 E
Ōshima, Nihon 64 33.03N 129.33 E
Ō-shima I 64a 41.30N 139.22 E
Oshima-hantō ›[1] 64a 42.00N 140.30 E
Oshkosh 100 44.01N 88.32W
Oshogbo 80 7.47N 4.34 E
Oshwe 84 3.24S 19.30 E
Osica de Jos 54 44.15N 24.17 E
Osiek 46 50.31N 21.28 E
Osijek 54 45.33N 18.41 E
Osilo 52 40.45N 8.40 E
Osimo 52 43.29N 13.29 E
Osinniki 58 53.37N 87.21 E
Osintorf 60 54.42N 30.39 E
Osipaonica 54 44.33N 21.04 E
Osipoviči 60 53.18N 28.38 E
Oskaloosa 100 41.17N 92.38W
Oskarshamn 44 57.16N 16.26 E
Oskarström 44 56.48N 12.58 E
Oskū 78 37.55N 46.06 E
Oslava ≃ 46 49.05N 16.22 E
Oslo 44 59.55N 10.45 E
Oslofjorden ⊂[2] 44 59.20N 10.35 E
Osmānābād 74 18.10N 76.02 E
Osmaniye 78 37.05N 36.14 E
Osmington 34 50.38N 2.22W
Ösmo 44 58.59N 17.54 E
Osnabrück 46 52.16N 8.02 E
Ośno 46 52.28N 14.50 E
Osore-yama ∧ 64 41.18N 141.05 E
Osório 112 29.54S 50.16W
Osorno, Chile 112 40.34S 73.09W
Osorno, Esp. 50 42.24N 4.22W
Osøyra 44 60.11N 5.28 E
Ospino 108 9.18N 69.27W
Osprey Reef +[2] 92 13.55S 146.38 E
Oss 46 51.46N 5.31 E
Ossa, Mount ∧ 94 41.54S 146.01 E

Symbols in the Index entries are identified on page 122.

Symbols in the Index entries are identified on page 122

Symbols in the Index entries are identified on page 122.

Symbols in the Index entries are identified on page 122

Name	Page	Lat.°'	Long.°'

Symbols in the Index entries are identified on page 122.

Symbols in the Index entries are identified on page 122.

Name Page Lat.°′ Long.°′
Sant-Sela

Santa Bárbara, Chile 114 37.40S 72.01W
Santa Bárbara, Méx. 106 26.48N 105.49W
Santa Barbara, Ca., U.S. 104 34.25N 119.42W
Santa Barbara Channel ↯ 104 34.15N 119.55W
Santa Bárbara de Samaná 108 19.13N 69.19W
Santa Bárbara do Sul 114 28.22S 53.15W
Santa Barbara Island I 104 33.28N 119.02W
Santa Branca 114 23.24S 45.53W
Santa Catalina 114 21.57S 66.04W
Santa Catalina, Gulf of C 104 33.20N 117.45W
Santa Catalina de Armara 50 43.02N 8.49W
Santa Catalina Island I 104 33.23N 118.24W
Santa Catarina 114 31.37N 115.48W
Santa Catarina □3 114 27.00S 50.00W
Santa Catarina, Ilha de I 114 27.36S 48.30W
Santa Cecília 114 26.56S 50.27W
Santa Cesarea Terme 52 40.02N 18.29 E
Santa Clara, Arg. 114 29.33S 68.31W
Santa Clara, Cuba 108 22.24N 79.58W
Santa Clara, Ca., U.S. 104 37.20N 121.56W
Santa Clara ≃ 104 34.14N 119.16W
Santa Clara de Olimar 114 32.55S 54.58W
Santa Coloma de Farnés 50 41.52N 2.40 E
Santa Comba Dão 50 40.24N 8.08W
Santa Cruz, Arg. 112 50.01S 68.31W
Santa Cruz, Bol. 110 17.48S 63.10W
Santa Cruz, Chile 114 34.38S 71.22W
Santa Cruz, C.R. 108 10.16N 85.36W
Santa Cruz, Ca., U.S. 104 36.58N 122.01W
Santa Cruz ≃ 112 50.08S 68.20W
Santa Cruz, Isla I 24 0.38S 90.23W
Santa Cruz Basin ✦1 28 12.00S 163.00 E
Santa Cruz de el Seibo 108 18.46N 69.02W
Santa Cruz de la Palma 80 28.41N 17.45W
Santa Cruz de la Zarza 50 39.58N 3.10W
Santa Cruz del Sur 108 20.43N 78.00W
Santa Cruz de Mudela 50 38.38N 3.28W
Santa Cruz de Tenerife 80 28.27N 16.14W
Santa Cruz do Rio Pardo 114 22.55S 49.37W
Santa Cruz do Sul 114 29.43S 52.26W
Santa Cruz Island I 104 34.01N 119.45W
Santa Cruz Islands II 28 11.00S 166.15 E
Santa Elena 114 30.57S 59.48W
Santa Elena, Cabo › 108 10.54N 85.57W
Santa Eufemia 50 38.36N 4.54W
Santa Eugenia 50 42.33N 9.00W
Santa Eulalia 50 40.34N 1.19W
Santa Eulalia del Río 50 38.59N 1.31 E
Santa Fe, Arg. 114 31.38S 60.42W
Santa Fé, Bra. 114 23.01S 51.48W
Santa Fé, Cuba 108 21.45N 82.45W
Santa Fe, Esp. 50 37.11N 3.43W
Santa Fe, N.M., U.S. 100 35.41N 105.56W
Santa Fe □4 114 31.00S 61.00W
Santa Fe Baldy ∧ 100 35.50N 105.46W
Santa Filomena 110 9.07S 45.56W
Sant'Agata di Militello 52 38.04N 14.38 E
Santai 62 31.10N 105.02 E
Santa Inés, Isla I 112 53.45S 72.45W
Santa Isabel, Arg. 114 36.15S 66.56W
Santa Isabel, Arg. 114 33.54S 61.42W
Santa Isabel →Malabo, Gui. Ecu. 80 3.45N 8.47 E
Santa Isabel I 88 8.00S 159.00 E
Santa Isabel de las Lajas 108 22.25N 80.18W
Sāntalpur 76 23.45N 71.10 E
Santa Lucía, Arg. 114 28.59S 59.06W
Santa Lucía, Arg. 114 31.32S 68.29W
Santa Lucía, Cuba 108 21.02N 76.00W
Santa Lucía, Ur. 114 34.27S 56.24W
Santa Lucia Range ✱ 104 36.00N 121.20W
Santa Luzia 50 37.44N 8.24W
Santa Luzia I 80 16.46N 24.45W
Santa Magdalena 114 34.30S 63.56W
Santa Magdalena, Isla I 106 24.55N 112.15W
Santa Margarita 104 35.23N 120.36W
Santa Margarita, Isla de I 106 24.27N 111.50W
Santa Margherita Ligure 52 44.20N 9.12 E
Santa Maria, Arg. 114 26.41S 66.02W
Santa Maria, Bra. 114 29.41S 53.48W
Santa Maria, Ca., U.S. 104 34.57N 120.26W
Santa Maria I 20 36.58N 25.06W
Santa Maria ≃ 114 29.48S 54.56W
Santa Maria, Cabo › 114 34.40S 54.10W
Santa Maria, Cabo de ›, Ang. 84 13.25S 12.32 E
Santa Maria, Cabo de ›, Port. 50 36.58N 7.54W
Santa Maria, Cape › 108 23.41N 75.19W
Santa María, Isla I 114 37.02S 73.33W
Santa Maria Capua Vetere 52 41.05N 14.15 E
Santa María de Ipire 108 8.49N 65.19W
Santa Maria Island I 28 14.15S 167.30 E
Santa Maria la Real de Nieva 50 41.04N 4.24W
Santa-Maria-Siché 52 41.52N 8.59 E
Santa Marinella 52 42.02N 11.51 E
Santa Marta 110 11.15N 74.13W
Santa Marta Grande, Cabo de › 114 28.38S 48.45W
Santa Monica 104 34.01N 118.29W
Santa Monica Bay C 104 33.54N 118.25W
Santana, Coxilha de ✱2 114 31.15S 55.15W
Santana da Boa Vista 114 30.52S 53.07W
Santana do Livramento 114 30.53S 55.31W
Santander, Esp. 50 43.28N 3.48W
Santander, Pil. 68 9.25N 123.20 E
Santander, Norte de □3 108 9.15N 73.00W
Sant'Angelo dei Lombardi 52 40.56N 15.11 E
Santanilla, Islas II 108 17.25N 83.55W
Sant'Antioco 52 39.04N 8.27 E
Sant'Antioco, Isola di I 52 39.02N 8.25 E
Santañy 50 39.22N 3.07 E
Santa Paula 104 34.21N 119.03W
Santa Pola, Cabo de › 50 38.12N 0.31W
Sant'Arcangelo 52 40.15N 16.17 E
Santarém, Bra. 110 2.26S 54.42W
Santarém, Port. 50 39.14N 8.41W
Santaren Channel ↯ 108 24.00N 79.30W
Santa Rita, Hond. 106 15.09N 87.53W
Santa Rita, Ven. 108 10.32N 71.32W
Santa Rita de Catuna 114 30.57S 66.13W
Santa Rosa, Arg. 114 28.02S 67.37W
Santa Rosa, Arg. 114 36.37S 64.17W
Santa Rosa, Arg. 114 23.22S 64.30W
Santa Rosa, Arg. 114 32.20S 65.12W
Santa Rosa, Bra. 114 27.52S 54.29W
Santa Rosa, Ec. 110 3.27S 79.58W
Santa Rosa, Méx. 104 31.59N 116.45W
Santa Rosa, Para. 114 26.52S 56.49W
Santa Rosa, Ca., U.S. 104 38.26N 122.42W
Santa Rosa de Copán 106 14.47N 88.46W
Santa Rosa de Leales 114 27.09S 65.15W
Santa Rosa de Río Primero 114 31.09S 63.23W
Santa Rosa Island I 104 33.58N 120.06W
Santa Rosalía, Méx. 106 27.19N 112.17W
Santa Rosalía, Ven. 108 9.02N 69.01W
Santa Rosa Range ✱ 104 41.35N 117.40W
Šantarskije ostrova II 58 55.00N 137.36 E
Santa Sylvina 114 27.49S 61.09W
Santa Teresa 114 33.26S 60.47W
Santa Teresa, Embalse de ⊜1 50 40.40N 5.30W
Santa Teresa del Tuy 108 10.14N 66.40W
Santa Teresa Gallura 52 41.14N 9.11 E
Santa Vitória do Palmar 114 33.31S 53.21W
Santa Ynez ≃ 104 34.41N 120.36W
Santee 104 32.50N 116.58W
Sant'Eufemia, Golfo di C 52 38.50N 16.00 E
Santhià 52 45.22N 8.10 E
Santiago, Bra. 114 29.11S 54.53W
Santiago, Chile 114 33.27S 70.40W
Santiago, Pan. 106 8.06N 80.59W
Santiago, Para. 114 27.09S 56.47W
Santiago I 80 15.05N 23.40W
Santiago ≃ 110 4.27S 77.38W
Santiago de Compostela 50 42.53N 8.33W
Santiago de Cuba 108 20.01N 75.49W
Santiago del Estero 114 27.47S 64.16W
Santiago del Estero □4 114 28.00S 63.30W
Santiago [de los Caballeros] 108 19.27N 70.42W
Santiago do Cacém 50 38.01N 8.42W
Santiago Larre 114 35.34S 59.10W
Santiago Papasquiaro 106 25.03N 105.25W
Santiago Peak ∧ 104 33.42N 117.32W
San Timoteo 108 9.48N 71.04W
Sāntipur 76 23.15N 88.26 E
Säntis ∧ 48 47.15N 9.21 E
Santisteban del Puerto 50 38.15N 3.12W
Santo Amaro 110 12.32S 38.43W
Santo Anastácio 114 21.58S 51.39W
Santo André 114 23.40S 46.31W
Santo Ângelo 114 28.18S 54.16W
Santo Antão I 80 17.05N 25.10W
Santo Antônio, Bra. 114 29.50S 50.32W
Santo António, S. Tom./P. 84 1.39N 7.26 E
Santo Antônio, Ilha de I 86 21.58S 35.28 E
Santo Antônio de Jesus 110 12.58S 39.16W
Santo Antônio do Içá 110 3.05S 67.57W
Santo Antônio do Sudoeste 114 26.02S 53.44W
Santo Augusto 114 27.51S 53.47W
Santo Cristo 114 27.50S 54.40W
Santo Domingo, Arg. 114 29.16S 63.56W
Santo Domingo, Nic. 108 12.16N 85.05W
Santo Domingo, Rep. Dom. 108 18.28N 69.54W
Santo Domingo, Arroyo ≃ 104 30.43N 116.03W
Santo Domingo de la Calzada 50 42.26N 2.57W
Santolea, Embalse de ⊜1 50 40.47N 0.19W
San Tomé 108 8.58N 64.08W
Santoña 50 43.27N 3.27W
Santorini →Thíra I 54 36.24N 25.29 E
Santos 114 23.57S 46.20W
Santos Dumont 110 21.28S 43.34W
Santo Tirso 50 41.21N 8.28W
Santo Tomás, Col. 108 10.46N 74.45W
Santo Tomás, Méx. 104 31.33N 116.24W
Santo Tomás, Nic. 108 12.04N 85.05W
Santo Tomás, Ven. 108 8.53N 64.33W
Santo Tomás ≃ 104 31.32N 116.40W
Santo Tomás, Punta › 104 31.34N 116.42W
Santo Tomé, Arg. 114 31.40S 60.46W
Santo Tomé, Arg. 114 28.33S 56.03W
Sanuki-sammyaku ✱ 64 34.09N 134.11 E
San Valentín, Cerro ∧ 112 46.36S 73.20W
San Vicente, Arg. 114 28.30S 64.09W
San Vicente, El Sal. 106 13.38N 88.48W
San Vicente, Méx. 104 31.20N 116.15W
San Vicente de Baracaldo 50 43.18N 2.59W
San Vicente de Cañete 110 13.05S 76.24W
San Vicente de la Barquera 50 43.26N 4.24W
San Vicente del Caguán 110 2.07N 74.46W
San Vicente de Tagua-Tagua 114 34.26S 71.05W
San Vincenzo 52 43.06N 10.32 E
San Vito 52 39.26N 9.32 E
San Vito, Capo › 52 38.11N 12.44 E
San Vito al Tagliamento 52 45.54N 12.52 E
San Vito dei Normanni 52 40.39N 17.42 E
Sanyō 64 34.02N 131.10 E
Sanyuan 62 34.35N 108.54 E
Sanza Pombo 84 7.19S 15.59 E
São Bento 110 2.42S 44.50W
São Bento do Sul 114 26.15S 49.23W
São Borja 114 28.39S 56.00W
São Brás de Alportel 50 37.09N 7.53W
São Caetano do Sul 114 23.36S 46.34W
São Carlos, Bra. 114 27.04S 52.59W
São Carlos, Bra. 114 22.01S 47.54W
São Cristóvão 110 11.01S 37.12W
São Domingos, Bra. 110 13.24S 46.19W
São Domingos, Bra. 114 26.34S 52.32W
São Francisco 110 15.57S 44.52W
São Francisco ≃ 110 10.30S 36.24W
São Francisco, Baía de C 114 26.10S 48.34W
São Francisco de Assis 114 29.33S 55.08W
São Francisco de Paula 114 29.27S 50.35W
São Francisco do Sul 114 26.14S 48.39W
São Gabriel 114 30.20S 54.19W
São Gonçalo do Sapucaí 114 21.54S 45.36W
São Hill 84 8.20S 35.12 E
São Jerônimo 114 29.58S 51.43W
São Jerônimo da Serra 114 23.43S 50.44W
São João da Barra 110 21.38S 41.03W
São João da Boa Vista 114 21.58S 46.47W
São João da Madeira 50 40.54N 8.30W
São João del Rei 110 21.09S 44.16W
São João do Araguaia 110 5.23S 48.46W
São João do Caiuá 114 22.48S 52.22W
São João do Triunfo 114 25.40S 50.20W
São Joaquim 114 28.18S 49.56W
São Joaquim da Barra 110 20.35S 47.53W
São Jorge 114 23.24S 52.17W
São Jorge I 20 38.38N 28.03W
São José 114 27.38S 48.39W
São José do Cedro 114 26.30S 53.30W
São José do Norte 114 32.01S 52.03W
São José do Rio Prêto 110 20.48S 49.23W
São José dos Campos 114 23.11S 45.53W
São José dos Pinhais 114 25.31S 49.13W
São Leopoldo 114 29.46S 51.09W
São Lourenço ≃ 110 17.53S 57.27W
São Lourenço d'Oeste 114 26.24S 52.46W
São Lourenço do Sul 114 31.22S 51.58W
São Luís 110 2.31S 44.16W
São Luís Gonzaga 114 28.24S 54.58W
São Manuel 114 22.44S 48.34W
São Manuel ≃ 110 7.21S 58.03W
São Mateus 110 18.44S 39.51W
São Mateus do Sul 114 25.52S 50.23W
São Miguel I 20 37.47N 25.30W
São Miguel d'Oeste 114 26.45S 53.34W
Saona, Isla I 108 18.09N 68.40W
Saône ≃ 48 45.44N 4.50 E
Saône-et-Loire □5 48 46.42N 4.45 E
São Nicolau I 80 16.35N 24.15W
São Paulo 114 23.32S 46.37W
São Paulo de Olivença 110 3.27S 68.48W
São Pedro do Ivaí 114 23.51S 51.51W
São Pedro do Sul, Bra. 114 29.37S 54.10W
São Pedro do Sul, Port. 50 40.45N 8.04W
São Raimundo Nonato 110 9.01S 42.42W
São Roque 114 23.32S 47.08W
São Roque, Cabo de › 110 5.29S 35.16W
São Sebastião 114 23.48S 45.25W
São Sebastião, Ilha de I 114 23.50S 45.18W
São Sebastião, Ponta › 86 22.07S 35.30 E
São Sebastião do Paraíso 110 20.55S 47.00W
São Sepé 114 30.10S 53.34W
São Simão 110 21.30S 47.33W
São Tomé 84 0.20N 6.44 E
São Tomé I 84 0.12N 6.39 E
São Tomé, Cabo de › 110 21.59S 40.59W
Sao Tome and Principe □1 84 1.00N 7.00 E
Saoura, Oued ∨ 80 29.00N 0.55W
São Vicente 114 23.58S 46.23W
São Vicente I 80 16.50N 25.00W
São Vicente, Cabo de › 50 37.01N 9.00W
Sápai 54 41.02N 25.41 E
Sapé 110 7.06S 35.13W
Sapele 80 5.54N 5.41 E
Sapitwa ∧ 84 15.57S 35.36 E
Sapporo 64a 43.03N 141.21 E
Sapri 52 40.04N 15.38 E
Sapt Kosi ≃ 76 26.31N 86.58 E
Sapulpa 100 35.59N 96.06W
Saqqez 78 36.14N 46.16 E
Sarāb 78 37.56N 47.32 E
Sara Buri 70 14.32N 100.55 E
Saragossa →Zaragoza 50 41.38N 0.53W
Sarai 60 53.44N 41.00 E
Saraipali 76 21.20N 83.00 E
Säräisniemi 44 64.27N 26.47 E
Sarajevo 54 43.52N 18.25 E
Saraji 94 22.21S 148.18 E
Sarakhs 78 36.32N 61.11 E
Saran' 56 49.46N 72.52 E
Saranac 102 42.55N 85.12W
Saranac ≃ 102 44.42N 73.27W
Saranac Lake 102 44.19N 74.07W
Sarandë 54 39.52N 20.00 E
Sarandi 114 27.56S 52.55W
Sarandí del Yi 114 33.21S 55.38W
Sarandí Grande 114 33.44S 56.20W
Sarangani Islands II 72 5.25N 125.26 E
Sārangpur 76 23.34N 76.28 E
Saranpaul' 42 64.15N 60.55 E
Saransk 42 54.11N 45.11 E
Sarapul 42 56.28N 53.48 E
Sarare 108 9.47N 69.10W
Sarasota 100 27.20N 82.31W
Saratoga 104 37.15N 122.01W
Saratoga Springs 102 43.04N 73.47W
Saratok 72 1.44N 111.20 E
Saratov 56 51.34N 46.02 E
Saratovskoje vodochranilišče ⊜1 42 53.15N 48.30 E
Saravan 70 15.43N 106.25 E
Sarawak □3 72 2.30N 113.30 E
Sarayköy 54 37.55N 28.58 E
Sárbogárd 46 46.53N 18.38 E
Sarcidano ✦1 52 39.55N 9.05 E
Sarclet 38 58.22N 3.07W
Sarda (Kāli) ≃ 76 27.22N 81.23 E
Sardārshahr 76 28.26N 74.29 E
Sardegna □4 52 40.00N 9.00 E
Sardegna (Sardinia) I 52 40.00N 9.00 E
Sardinia →Sardegna I 52 40.00N 9.00 E
Sarektjåkkå ∧ 42 67.25N 17.46 E
Sar-e Pol 78 36.14N 65.55 E
Sargans 48 47.03N 9.26 E
Sargodha 76 32.05N 72.40 E
Sarh 80 9.09N 18.23 E
Sārī 78 36.34N 53.04 E
Saria I 54 35.50N 27.15 E
Sarigan I 68 16.42N 145.47 E
Sarikei 72 2.07N 111.31 E
Sarina 94 21.26S 149.13 E
Sariñena 50 41.48N 0.10W
Sariwŏn 62 38.31N 125.44 E
Şarıyer 54 41.10N 29.03 E
Sarja 42 58.24N 45.30 E
Sark I 35b 49.26N 2.21W
Sark ≃ 36 54.58N 3.04W
Sarkad 46 46.45N 21.23 E
Sarlat-la-Canéda 48 44.53N 1.13 E
Sărmaşu 54 46.46N 24.11 E
Sármellék 46 46.44N 17.10 E
Sarmi 92 1.51S 138.44 E
Sarmiento 112 45.36S 69.05W
Sarmiento, Cerro ∧ 112 54.27S 70.50W
Särna 44 61.41N 13.08 E
Sarnen 48 46.54N 8.15 E
Sărnena ✱ 54 42.35N 25.10 E
Sarnia 102 42.58N 82.23W
Sarno 52 40.49N 14.37 E
Sarnowa 46 51.38N 16.54 E
Sarolangun 72 2.18S 102.42 E
Saroma-ko ⊜ 64a 44.08N 143.50 E
Saron 86 33.11S 19.01 E
Saronikós Kólpos C 54 37.54N 23.12 E
Saronno 52 45.38N 9.02 E
Saros Körfezi C 54 40.30N 26.20 E
Sárospatak 46 48.19N 21.34 E
Šar Planina ✱ 54 42.05N 20.50 E
Sarpsborg 44 59.17N 11.07 E
Sarralbe 48 49.00N 7.01 E
Sarrebourg 48 48.44N 7.03 E
Sarreguemines 48 49.06N 7.03 E
Sarre-Union 48 48.56N 7.05 E
Sarria 50 42.47N 7.24W
Sartang ≃ 58 67.44N 133.12 E
Sartène 52 41.36N 8.59 E
Sarthe □5 48 48.00N 0.05 E
Sarthe ≃ 48 47.30N 0.32W
Sartilly 48 48.45N 1.27W
Sarufutsu 64a 45.16N 142.12 E
Sárvár 46 47.15N 16.57 E
Sárvíz ≃ 46 46.24N 18.41 E
Saryg-Sep 58 51.30N 95.36 E
Saryozek 56 44.22N 77.59 E
Sarysu ≃ 56 45.12N 66.36 E
Sary-Taš 56 39.44N 73.15 E
Saryžaz 56 42.55N 79.38 E
Sarzana 52 44.07N 9.58 E
Sarzeau 48 47.32N 2.46W
Sasarām 76 24.57N 84.02 E
Sasayama 64 35.04N 135.13 E
Sásd 46 46.15N 18.06 E
Sasebo 64 33.10N 129.43 E
Saskatchewan □4 98 54.00N 105.00W
Saskatchewan ≃ 98 53.12N 99.16W
Saskatoon 98 52.07N 106.38W
Saskylach 58 71.55N 114.01 E
Saslaya, Cerro ∧ 108 13.45N 85.03W
Sasolburg 86 26.48S 27.45 E
Sasovo 60 54.21N 41.54 E
Sassandra 80 4.58N 6.05W
Sassandra ≃ 80 4.58N 6.05W
Sassari 52 40.44N 8.33 E
Sassnitz 46 54.31N 13.38 E
Sassoferrato 52 43.26N 12.51 E
Sasso Marconi 52 44.24N 11.15 E
Sassuolo 52 44.33N 10.47 E
Sastown 80 4.40N 8.26W
Sastre 114 31.45S 61.50W
Satakunta ✦1 44 61.30N 23.00 E
Sata-misaki › 64 30.59N 130.40 E
Sátão 50 40.44N 7.44W
Sātāra 74 17.41N 73.59 E
Satarar Uskamp 86 24.29S 31.47 E
Säter 44 60.21N 15.45 E
Satka 56 55.03N 59.01 E
Satna 76 24.35N 80.50 E
Sátoraljaújhely 46 48.24N 21.39 E
Sātpura Range ✱ 76 22.00N 78.00 E
Satsuma-hantō ›1 64 31.25N 130.25 E
Satsunan-shotō II 65b 29.00N 130.00 E
Sattahip 70 12.40N 100.54 E
Satu Mare 54 47.48N 22.53 E
Satu Mare □6 54 47.40N 23.00 E
Satun 70 6.37N 100.04 E
Šatura 60 55.34N 39.32 E
Saturnino M. Laspiur 114 31.42S 62.29W
Sauce, Arg. 114 30.05S 58.46W
Sauce, Ur. 114 34.39S 56.04W
Sauce Chico ≃ 114 38.47S 62.18W
Sauce Grande ≃ 114 38.59S 61.07W
Saucillo 106 28.01N 105.17W
Sauda 44 59.39N 6.20 E
Sauđárkrókur 42a 65.46N 19.41W
Saudi Arabia (Al-'Arabīyah as-Sa'ūdīyah) □1 74 25.00N 45.00 E
Sauerland ✦1 46 51.10N 8.00 E
Saugeen ≃ 102 44.30N 81.22W
Saugerties 102 42.04N 73.57W
Saujil 114 28.11S 66.14W
Saujon 48 45.40N 0.56W
Saül 110 3.37N 53.12W
Saulgau 46 48.01N 9.30 E
Saulieu 48 47.16N 4.14 E
Sault-de-Vaucluse 48 44.05N 5.25 E
Sault Sainte Marie, On., Can. 98 46.31N 84.20W
Sault Sainte Marie, Mi., U.S. 100 46.29N 84.20W
Saumarez Reef ✦2 94 21.50S 153.40 E
Saumlaki 92 7.57S 131.19 E
Saumon, Rivière au ≃ 102 45.41N 71.27W
Saumur 48 47.16N 0.05W
Saundersfoot 34 51.43N 4.43W
Saunders Island I 24 57.47S 26.27W
Saunders Point ∧2 90 27.52S 125.38 E
Sauquoit 102 43.00N 75.16W
Saurimo 84 9.39S 20.24 E
Sausalito 104 37.51N 122.29W
Sauveterre-de-Béarn 48 43.24N 0.56W
Sauveterre-de-Guyenne 48 44.42N 0.05W
Sauvo 44 60.21N 22.42 E
Sauwald ✦3 46 48.28N 13.40 E
Sava, It. 52 40.24N 17.34 E
S'ava, S.S.S.R. 42 58.01N 46.22 E
Sava ≃ 54 44.50N 20.26 E
Savage 102 39.08N 76.49W
Savai'i I 28 13.35S 172.25W
Savalen ⊜ 44 62.15N 10.29 E
Savannah 100 32.05N 81.06W
Savannah ≃ 100 32.02N 80.53W
Savannakhét 70 16.33N 104.45 E
Savanna-la-Mar 108 18.13N 78.08W
Sävar 44 63.54N 20.34 E
Savé 80 8.02N 2.29 E
Save (Sabi) ≃, Afr. 86 21.00S 35.02 E
Save ≃, Fr. 48 43.47N 1.17 E
Sāveh 78 35.01N 50.20 E
Savelli 52 39.19N 16.47 E
Savenay 48 47.22N 1.57W
Săveni 54 47.57N 26.52 E
Saverdun 48 43.14N 1.35 E
Savernake Forest ✦3 34 51.24N 1.38W
Saverne 48 48.44N 7.22 E
Savigliano 52 44.38N 7.40 E
Savigny-sur-Braye 48 47.53N 0.49 E
Savino 60 56.35N 41.13 E
Săvîrşin 54 46.01N 22.14 E
Savitaipale 44 61.12N 27.42 E
Šavnik 54 42.57N 19.05 E
Savoie □5 48 45.30N 6.25 E
Savolaks ✦1 44 62.00N 28.00 E
Savona 52 44.17N 8.30 E
Savonlinna 44 61.52N 28.53 E
Savonranta 44 62.11N 29.12 E
Savory Creek ≃ 90 23.22S 122.37 E
Sävsjö 44 57.25N 14.40 E
Savu Basin ✦1 28 9.15S 123.15 E
Savu Sea →Sawu, Laut ≂2 72 9.40S 122.00 E
Sawahlunto 72 0.40S 100.47 E
Sawai Mādhopur 76 25.59N 76.22 E
Sawākin 82 19.07N 37.20 E
Sawang 72 0.45N 103.21 E
Sawankhalok 70 17.19N 99.50 E
Sawara 64 35.53N 140.30 E
Sawata 64 38.00N 138.16 E
Sawbridgeworth 34 51.50N 0.09 E
Sawdā', Jabal as- ✱2 82 28.40N 15.30 E
Sawdā', Qurnat as- ∧ 78 34.18N 36.07 E
Sawel Mountain ∧ 40 54.49N 7.02W
Sawhāj 82 26.33N 31.42 E
Sawknah 82 29.04N 15.47 E
Sawqarah, Dawhat C 74 18.35N 57.15 E
Sawston 34 52.07N 0.10 E
Sawtry 34 52.27N 0.17W
Sawu, Laut (Savu Sea) ≂2 72 9.40S 122.00 E
Sawu, Pulau I 72 10.30S 121.54 E
Saxby ≃ 94 18.25S 140.53 E
Saxilby 36 53.17N 0.40W
Saxis 102 37.55N 75.43W
Saxmundham 34 52.13N 1.29 E
Saxon 46 46.09N 7.11 E
Saxton 102 40.12N 78.14W
Saya de Malha Bank ✦4 26 10.30S 61.30 E
Sayan Mountains (Sajany) ✱ 56 52.45N 96.00 E
Şaydā (Sidon) 78 33.33N 35.22 E
Şayhūt 74 15.12N 51.14 E
Säynätsalo 44 62.08N 25.46 E
Sayre 102 41.58N 76.30W
Sayreville 102 40.27N 74.21W
Sayula 106 19.52N 103.37W
Say'ūn 74 15.56N 48.47 E
Saza 64 33.14N 129.39 E
Sazanit I 54 40.30N 19.16 E
Sazlijka ≃ 54 42.02N 25.52 E
Sazonovo 60 59.04N 35.14 E
Scaddan 90 33.27S 121.43 E
Scaër 48 48.02N 3.42W
Scafell Pikes ∧ 36 54.27N 3.12W
Scalasaig 38 56.04N 6.11W
Scalby 36 54.18N 0.27W
Scalea 52 39.49N 15.48 E
Scalloway 38a 60.08N 1.18W
Scalpay I, Scot., U.K. 38 57.17N 5.59W
Scalpay I, Scot., U.K. 38 57.52N 6.40W
Scampton 36 53.18N 0.34W
Scansano 52 42.41N 11.20 E
Scapa Flow C 38 58.55N 3.06W
Scapegoat Mountain ∧ 100 47.19N 112.50W
Ščapino 58 55.19N 159.25 E
Scarba I 38 56.11N 5.43W
Scarborough, On., Can. 102 43.47N 79.15W
Scarborough, Trin. 108 11.11N 60.44W
Scarborough, Eng., U.K. 36 54.17N 0.24W
Scardroy 38 57.31N 4.59W
Scargill 96 42.56S 172.57 E
Scarinish 38 56.29N 6.48W
Scărişoara 54 44.00N 24.35 E
Scarp I 38 58.02N 7.08W
Scarriff 40 52.55N 8.31W
Scartaglin 40 52.10N 9.26W
Scavaig, Loch C 38 57.09N 6.10W
Scawfell Island I 94 20.52S 149.36 E
Sceale Bay 90 33.01S 134.12 E
Ščeljajur 42 65.21N 53.21 E
Ščelkovo 60 55.55N 38.00 E
Ščerbakovo 58 65.15N 160.30 E
Ščerbinka 60 55.31N 37.35 E
Schaffhausen 48 47.42N 8.38 E
Schärding 46 48.27N 13.26 E
Schefferville 98 54.48N 66.50W
Scheibbs 46 48.00N 15.10 E
Scheinfeld 46 49.40N 10.27 E
Schelde (Escaut) ≃ 46 51.22N 4.15 E
Schell Creek Range ✱ 104 39.10N 114.40W
Schenectady 102 42.48N 73.56W
Schenevus Creek ≃ 102 42.29N 74.59W
Schesslitz 46 49.59N 11.01 E
Schichallion ∧ 38 56.40N 4.06W
Schiedam 46 51.55N 4.24 E
Schiermonnikoog I 46 53.28N 6.15 E
Schiltigheim 48 48.36N 7.45 E
Schio 52 45.43N 11.21 E
Schjetman Reef ✦2 28 15.10N 178.40W
Schkeuditz 46 51.24N 12.13 E
Schladming 46 47.23N 13.41 E
Schleiden 46 50.31N 6.28 E
Schleinitz Range ✱ 92 3.10S 151.40 E
Schleiz 46 50.34N 11.49 E
Schleswig 46 54.31N 9.33 E
Schleswig-Holstein □3 46 54.20N 9.40 E
Schleusingen 46 50.31N 10.45 E
Schlitz 46 50.40N 9.33 E
Schloss Neuhaus 46 51.44N 8.43 E
Schlüchtern 46 50.20N 9.31 E
Schmalkalden 46 50.43N 10.26 E
Schmidmühlen 46 49.16N 11.56 E
Schmölln 46 50.53N 12.20 E
Schneeberg 46 50.36N 12.38 E
Schneverdingen 46 53.07N 9.47 E
Schodn'a 60 55.57N 37.18 E
Schoharie 102 42.39N 74.18W
Schoharie Creek ≃ 102 42.57N 74.18W
Scholes 36 53.49N 1.25W
Schönebeck 46 52.01N 11.44 E
Schongau 46 47.49N 10.54 E
Schopfheim 46 47.39N 7.49 E
Schorndorf 46 48.48N 9.31 E
Schouten Island I 94 42.19S 148.17 E
Schouten Islands II 92 3.30S 144.40 E
Schouwen I 46 51.43N 3.50 E
Schrader Range ✱ 92 5.05S 144.15 E
Schramberg 46 48.13N 8.23 E
Schreiber 98 48.48N 87.15W
Schrobenhausen 46 48.33N 11.17 E
Schroon ≃ 102 43.29N 73.49W
Schroon Lake ⊜ 102 43.47N 73.46W
Schruns 46 47.04N 9.55 E
Schultz Lake ⊜ 98 64.45N 97.30W
Schuylkill ≃ 102 39.53N 75.12W
Schuylkill Haven 102 40.37N 76.10W
Schwabach 46 49.20N 11.01 E
Schwaben □9 46 48.20N 10.30 E
Schwäbische Alb ✱ 46 48.25N 9.30 E
Schwäbisch Gmünd 46 48.48N 9.47 E
Schwäbisch Hall 46 49.07N 9.44 E
Schwabmünchen 46 48.11N 10.45 E
Schwandorf in Bayern 46 49.20N 12.08 E
Schwaner, Pegunungan ✱ 72 0.40S 112.40 E
Schwarza 46 50.41N 11.19 E
Schwarza ≃ 46 47.43N 16.13 E
Schwarzach im Pongau 46 47.19N 13.09 E
Schwarzenburg 48 46.49N 7.21 E
Schwarzwald ✱ 46 48.00N 8.15 E
Schwaz 46 47.20N 11.42 E
Schwechat 46 48.08N 16.29 E
Schwedt 46 53.03N 14.17 E
Schweidnitz →Świdnica 46 50.51N 16.29 E
Schweinfurt 46 50.03N 10.14 E
Schweizer-Reneke 86 27.11S 25.18 E
Schwerin 46 53.38N 11.25 E
Schwerin □5 46 53.30N 11.30 E
Schweriner See ⊜ 46 53.45N 11.28 E
Schwetzingen 46 49.23N 8.34 E
Schwyz 48 47.02N 8.40 E
Sciacca 52 37.31N 13.03 E
Scicli 52 36.47N 14.42 E
Scilla 52 38.15N 15.44 E
Scilly, Isles of II 34a 49.55N 6.20W
Ścinawa 46 51.25N 16.27 E
Scio 102 40.23N 81.05W
Scioto ≃ 102 38.44N 83.01W
Ščit ∧ 52 44.02N 17.47 E
Ščokino 60 54.01N 37.31 E
Scole 34 52.22N 1.10 E
Scolt Head › 34 52.58N 0.42 E
Scone 94 32.03S 150.52 E
Scordia 52 37.18N 14.51 E
Scorno, Punta di › 52 41.07N 8.19 E
Scotia 102 42.49N 73.57W
Scotia Ridge ✦3 24 54.00S 50.00W
Scotland 102 43.01N 80.22W
Scotland □8 32 57.00N 4.00W
Scott ≃ 104 41.48N 123.02W
Scott, Mount ∧ 104 42.56N 122.01W
Scottburgh 86 30.19S 30.40 E
Scottdale 102 40.06N 79.35W
Scotter 36 53.29N 0.40W
Scott Islands II 98 50.48N 128.40W
Scott Reef ✦2 88 14.00S 121.50 E
Scottsbluff 100 41.52N 103.40W
Scottsdale, Austl. 94 41.10S 147.31 E
Scottsdale, Az., U.S. 100 33.30N 111.53W
Scour ≃ 38 55.13N 3.46W
Scourie 38 58.20N 5.08W
Scranton 102 41.24N 75.39W
Scremerston 36 55.44N 1.59W
Screw ≃ 92 3.55S 142.50 E
Scridain, Loch C 38 56.21N 6.07W
Scrooby 36 53.25N 1.01W
Ščučinsk 56 52.56N 70.12 E
Scugog, Lake ⊜ 102 44.10N 78.51W
Scunthorpe 36 53.36N 0.38W
Scuol 48 46.48N 10.18 E
Scurrival Point › 38 57.04N 7.31W
Scutari →Shkodër 54 42.05N 19.30 E
Scutari, Lake ⊜ 54 42.12N 19.18 E
Seabrook, Lake ⊜ 90 30.56S 119.40 E
Seaford, Eng., U.K. 34 50.46N 0.06 E
Seaford, De., U.S. 102 38.38N 75.36W
Seaforth 102 43.33N 81.24W
Seaforth, Loch C 38 57.54N 6.40W
Seafox Seamount ✦3 28 30.30S 172.45W
Seaham 36 54.52N 1.21W
Seahorse Point › 98 63.47N 80.09W
Seahorse Shoal ✦2 72 5.30N 112.37 E
Seahouses 36 55.35N 1.38W
Sea Islands II 100 31.20N 81.20W
Sea Isle City 102 39.09N 74.41W
Seal ≃ 98 59.04N 94.48W
Sea Lake 94 35.30S 142.51 E
Seal Cove 102 44.39N 66.51W
Seal Lake ⊜ 98 54.18N 61.40W
Seamer 36 54.14N 0.26W
Seara 114 27.07S 52.17W
Searchlight 104 35.27N 114.55W
Searcy 100 35.15N 91.44W
Searles Lake ⊜ 104 35.43N 117.20W
Searsport 102 44.27N 68.55W
Seascale 36 54.24N 3.29W
Seaside 104 36.36N 121.51W
Seaside Park 102 39.55N 74.04W
Seaton, Eng., U.K. 34 50.43N 3.05W
Seaton, Eng., U.K. 36 54.41N 3.33W
Seaton, Eng., U.K. 36 53.54N 0.14W
Seaton ≃ 34 50.22N 4.22W
Seaton Delaval 36 55.04N 1.31W
Seaton Sluice 36 55.05N 1.28W
Seattle 100 47.36N 122.19W
Seaview 34 50.43N 1.06W
Seaward Kaikoura Range ✱ 96 42.14S 173.39 E
Sébaco 108 12.51N 86.06W
Sebago Lake ⊜ 102 43.50N 70.35W
Šebalino 58 51.17N 85.40 E
Sebastian, Cape › 104 42.19N 124.26W
Sebastián Vizcaíno, Bahía C 106 28.00N 114.30W
Sebastopol 104 38.24N 122.49W
Sebec Lake ⊜ 102 45.18N 69.18W
Seberi 114 27.29S 53.24W
Sebeş 54 45.58N 23.34 E
Sebes Körös (Crişu Repede) ≃ 54 46.55N 20.59 E
Sebeşului, Munţii ✱ 54 45.38N 23.27 E
Sebewaing 102 43.43N 83.27W
Sebiş 54 46.23N 22.08 E
Sebnitz 46 50.58N 14.16 E
Sechura, Bahía de C 110 5.42S 81.00W
Seclantas 114 25.18S 66.15W
Seco, Arroyo ≃ 104 36.25N 121.20W
Sečovce 46 48.43N 21.40 E
Sečovská Polianka 46 48.47N 21.42 E
Secretary Island I 96 45.15S 166.55 E
Séd ≃ 46 47.00N 18.31 E
Seda 62 32.20N 100.41 E
Sedalia 100 38.42N 93.13W
Sedan, Austl. 94 34.35S 139.18 E
Sedan, Fr. 48 49.42N 4.57 E
Sedano 50 42.43N 3.45W
Sedayu 72 6.59S 112.33 E
Sedbergh 36 54.20N 2.31W
Seddon 96 41.40S 174.05 E
Seddonville 96 41.33S 171.59 E
Sedel'nikovo 58 56.57N 75.18 E
Séderon 48 44.12N 5.32 E
Sedgefield 36 54.39N 1.26W
Sedini 52 40.51N 8.49 E
Sedlčany 46 49.40N 14.26 E
Sedova, pik ∧ 56 73.29N 54.58 E
Sędziszów 46 50.04N 21.41 E
Seefeld in Tirol 46 47.20N 11.11 E
Seefin ∧2 40 52.18N 8.32W
Seehausen 46 52.53N 11.45 E
Seeheim 86 26.50S 17.45 E
Seekoei ≃ 86 30.18S 25.01 E
Seelow 46 52.32N 14.23 E
Seemore Downs 90 30.42S 125.15 E
Sées 48 48.36N 0.10 E
Seesen 46 51.53N 10.10 E
Sefton 96 43.15S 172.40 E
Sefton, Mount ∧ 96 43.41S 170.03 E
Segama ≃ 72 5.27N 118.48 E
Segamat 72 2.30N 102.49 E
Şegarcea 54 44.06N 23.45 E
Segeža 42 63.44N 34.19 E
Segni 52 41.41N 13.01 E
Segorbe 50 39.51N 0.29W
Ségou 80 13.27N 6.16W
Segovia 50 40.57N 4.07W
Segré 48 47.41N 0.53W
Segre ≃ 50 41.40N 0.43 E
Séguédine 80 20.12N 12.59 E
Seguí 114 31.57S 60.08W
Segundo ≃ 114 31.21S 62.59W
Segura 50 39.50N 6.59W
Segura ≃ 50 38.06N 0.38W
Segura, Sierra de ✱ 50 38.00N 2.43W
Sehore 76 23.12N 77.05 E
Seia 50 40.25N 7.42W
Seiches-sur-le-Loir 48 47.35N 0.22W
Seil I 38 56.18N 5.39W
Seiland I 42 70.25N 23.15 E
Seilhac 48 45.22N 1.42 E
Sein, Île de I 48 48.02N 4.51W
Seinäjoki 44 62.47N 22.50 E
Seine ≃, On., Can. 98 48.40N 92.49W
Seine ≃, Fr. 48 49.26N 0.26 E
Seine, Baie de la C 48 49.30N 0.30W
Seine-et-Marne □5 48 48.30N 3.00 E
Seine-Maritime □5 48 49.45N 1.00 E
Seixal 50 38.38N 9.06W
Sejerø I 44 55.53N 11.09 E
Sejm ≃ 56 51.27N 32.34 E
Sejmčan 58 62.53N 152.26 E
Sejny 46 54.07N 23.20 E
Sekayu 72 2.51S 103.51 E
Seki, Nihon 64 35.29N 136.55 E
Šeki (Nucha), S.S.S.R. 56 41.12N 47.12 E
Sekondi-Takoradi 80 4.59N 1.43W
Šelagskij, mys › 58 70.06N 170.26 E
Selama 72 5.13N 100.42 E
Selangor □3 72 3.20N 101.30 E
Selaön I 44 59.24N 17.12 E
Selaru, Pulau I 92 8.09S 131.00 E

Symbols in the Index entries are identified on page 122.
165

Name Page Lat.°′ Long.°′

Selatan, Tanjung ❯ 72 4.10 S 114.38 E
Selatpanjang 72 1.00 N 102.43 E
Selayar, Pulau I 72 6.05 S 120.30 E
Selb 46 50.10 N 12.08 E
Selborne 34 51.06 N 0.56 W
Selbu 44 63.13 N 11.02 E
Selbusjøen ⊜ 44 63.14 N 10.54 E
Selby 36 53.48 N 1.04 W
Selbyville 102 38.27 N 75.13 W
Selçuk 54 37.56 N 27.22 E
Selemdža ≈ 58 51.42 N 128.53 E
Selenga (Selenge) ≈ 58 52.16 N 106.16 E
Selenge (Selenga) ≈ 58 52.16 N 106.16 E
Selenicë 54 40.32 N 19.38 E
Selenn'ach ≈ 58 67.48 N 144.54 E
Sélestat 48 48.16 N 7.27 E
Seletyteniz, ozero ⊜ 56 53.15 N 73.15 E
Selfoss 42a 63.56 N 20.57 W
Sélibaby 80 15.10 N 12.11 W
Šelichova, zaliv C 58 60.00 N 158.00 E
Seliger, ozero ⊜ 60 57.13 N 33.05 E
Selinsgrove 102 40.47 N 76.51 W
Selišče 60 56.53 N 33.16 E
Selje 44 62.03 N 5.22 E
Seljord 44 59.29 N 8.37 E
Selkämeri (Bottenhavet) C 44 62.00 N 20.00 E
Selkirk, Mb., Can. 98 50.09 N 96.52 W
Selkirk, Scot., U.K. 38 55.33 N 2.50 W
Selle, Chaîne de la ▲ 108 18.22 N 71.59 W
Selles-sur-Cher 48 47.16 N 1.33 E
Selly Oak ✦8 34 52.25 N 1.52 W
Selm 46 51.42 N 7.28 E
Selma, Al., U.S. 100 32.24 N 87.01 W
Selma, Ca., U.S. 104 36.34 N 119.36 W
Selong 72 8.39 S 116.32 E
Selsey 34 50.44 N 0.48 W
Selsey Bill ❯ 34 50.43 N 0.48 W
Selston 34 53.04 N 1.20 W
Seltz 48 48.53 N 8.06 E
Selu, Pulau I 92 7.32 S 130.54 E
Selva 114 29.46 S 62.03 W
Selvagens, Ilhas II 80 30.05 N 15.55 W
Selvas ✦3 110 5.00 S 68.00 W
Selwyn 94 21.32 S 140.30 E
Selwyn Lake ⊜ 98 59.55 N 104.35 W
Selwyn Mountains ✱ 98 63.10 N 130.20 W
Selwyn Range ✱ 94 21.35 S 140.35 E
Šemacha 78 40.38 N 48.39 E
Seman ≈ 54 40.56 N 19.24 E
Semarang 72 6.58 S 110.25 E
Sematan 72 1.48 N 109.46 E
Semau, Pulau I 72 10.13 S 123.22 E
Semberong ≈ 72 2.27 N 103.37 E
Šemdinli 78 37.18 N 44.35 E
Semenic, Munţii ✱ 54 45.05 N 22.05 E
Semeru, Gunung ▲ 72 8.06 S 112.55 E
Semibratovo 60 57.18 N 39.32 E
Semily 46 50.36 N 15.20 E
Seminole, Lake ⊜1 100 30.46 N 84.50 W
Semipalatinsk 56 50.28 N 80.13 E
Semitau 72 0.33 N 111.58 E
Semnān 78 35.33 N 53.24 E
Šemonaicha 58 50.39 N 81.54 E
Sem'onov 42 56.48 N 44.30 E
Sem'onovka 60 52.10 N 32.35 E
Semporna 72 4.28 N 118.36 E
Semuliki ≈ 84 1.14 N 30.28 E
Semur-en-Auxois 48 47.29 N 4.20 E
Seňa, Česko. 46 48.34 N 21.15 E
Sena, Moç. 84 17.27 S 35.00 E
Senador Pompeu 110 5.35 S 39.22 W
Senaja 72 6.45 N 117.03 E
Sena Madureira 110 9.04 S 68.40 W
Senanga 84 16.06 S 23.16 E
Sendai, Nihon 64 31.49 N 130.18 E
Sendai, Nihon 64 38.15 N 140.53 E
Sendai ≈ 64 31.51 N 130.12 E
Sendai-heiya ≚ 64 38.15 N 141.00 E
Sendurjana 76 21.32 N 78.17 E
Senec 46 48.14 N 17.24 E
Seneca, Mount ▲ 102 42.01 N 78.49 W
Seneca Falls 102 42.54 N 76.47 W
Seneca Lake ⊜ 102 42.40 N 76.57 W
Senecaville Lake ⊜1 102 39.55 N 81.25 W
Senegal (Sénégal) ◻1 80 14.00 N 14.00 W
Sénégal ≈ 80 15.48 N 16.32 W
Senekal 86 28.19 S 27.36 E
Senetosa, Punta di ❯ 52 41.33 N 8.47 E
Senftenberg 46 51.31 N 14.00 E
Sengés 114 24.06 S 49.29 W
Senghenydd 34 51.36 N 3.16 W
Sengilej 42 53.58 N 48.46 E
Senhor do Bonfim 110 10.27 S 40.11 W
Senica 46 48.41 N 17.22 E
Senigallia 52 43.43 N 13.13 E
Senise 52 40.09 N 16.18 E
Senj 52 44.59 N 14.54 E
Senja I 42 69.20 N 17.30 E
Šenkursk 42 62.08 N 42.53 E
Senlis 48 49.12 N 2.35 E
Senmonorom 70 12.27 N 107.12 E
Sennen 34 50.04 N 5.42 W
Sennestadt 46 51.59 N 8.37 E
Senneterre 98 48.23 N 77.15 W
Senno 60 54.49 N 29.43 E
Sennokura-yama ▲ 64 36.49 N 138.50 E
Sennori 52 40.48 N 8.35 E
Sennybridge 34 51.57 N 3.34 W
Sens 48 48.12 N 3.17 E
Senta 54 45.56 N 20.04 E
Šentjur 52 46.13 N 15.24 E
Senyavin Islands II 28 6.55 N 158.00 E
Seo de Urgel 50 42.21 N 1.28 E
Seoni 76 22.05 N 79.32 E
Seoni Mālwa 76 22.27 N 77.28 E
Seoul → Sŏul 62 37.33 N 126.58 E
Separation Point ❯ 96 40.47 S 173.00 E
Šepetovka 56 50.11 N 27.04 E
Sepik ≈ 92 3.51 S 144.34 E
Sępólno Krajeńskie 46 53.28 N 17.32 E
Sępopol 46 54.15 N 21.00 E
Sept-Îles (Seven Islands) 98 50.12 N 66.23 W
Sepúlveda 50 41.18 N 3.45 W
Sequeros 50 40.31 N 6.01 W
Sequillo ≈ 50 41.45 N 5.30 W
Sequoia National Park ✦ 104 36.30 N 118.30 W
Serafimovič 56 49.36 N 42.43 E
Seraing 46 50.36 N 5.29 E
Seram (Ceram) I 92 3.00 S 129.00 E
Seram, Laut (Ceram Sea) ▾2 68 2.30 S 128.00 E
Serang 72 6.07 S 106.09 E
Serbia → Srbija ◻3 54 44.00 N 21.00 E
Serdobsk 56 52.28 N 44.13 E
Sered' 46 48.17 N 17.44 E
Seredejskij 60 54.03 N 35.14 E
Seremban 72 2.43 N 101.56 E
Serengeti Plain ≚ 84 2.50 S 35.00 E
Serenje 84 13.15 S 30.14 E
Sergač 42 55.32 N 45.28 E
Sergeja Kirova, ostrova II 58 77.12 N 89.30 E
Sergejevka 58 43.21 N 133.22 E
Sergino 56 62.30 N 65.38 E
Seria 72 4.39 N 114.23 E
Serian 72 1.10 N 110.34 E
Sérifos 54 37.09 N 24.31 E
Sérifos I 54 37.11 N 24.31 E
Sérigny ≈ 98 56.47 N 66.00 W
Seringapatam 74 12.25 N 76.42 E
Šerlovaja Gora 58 50.34 N 116.15 E
Sermata, Pulau I 68 8.10 S 128.40 E
Serock 46 52.31 N 21.03 E
Serodino 114 32.37 S 60.57 W
Serov 56 59.29 N 60.31 E
Serowe 86 22.25 S 26.44 E
Serpa 50 37.56 N 7.36 W
Serpeddi, Punta ▲ 52 39.22 N 9.18 E
Serpentine Lakes ⊜ 90 28.32 S 129.09 E
Serpents Mouth ꞩ 108 10.00 N 62.00 W
Serpis ≈ 50 38.59 N 0.09 W
Serpuchov 60 54.55 N 37.25 E
Serracapriola 52 41.48 N 15.09 E
Serra do Navio 110 0.59 N 52.03 W
Sérrai 54 41.05 N 23.32 E
Serramanna 52 39.25 N 8.55 E
Serrania 114 21.33 S 46.03 W
Serra San Bruno 52 38.35 N 16.20 E
Serra Talhada 110 7.59 S 38.18 W
Serravalle Scrivia 52 44.43 N 8.51 E
Serres 48 44.26 N 5.43 E
Serrezuela 114 30.38 S 65.23 W
Serri 52 39.42 N 9.08 E
Serrières 48 45.19 N 4.45 E
Serrinha 110 11.39 S 39.00 W
Sersale 52 39.01 N 16.44 E
Sertã 50 39.48 N 8.06 W
Sertaneja 114 23.03 S 50.50 W
Sertânia 110 8.05 S 37.16 W
Serua, Pulau I 92 6.18 S 130.01 E
Serui 92 1.53 S 136.14 E
Sérvia 54 40.11 N 22.00 E
Sêrxu 62 33.04 N 97.45 E
Şes, Munţii ✱ 54 47.05 N 22.30 E
Sesajap ≈ 72 3.36 N 117.15 E
Sesfontein 86 19.07 S 13.39 E
Sesheke 84 17.28 S 24.18 E
Sesia ≈ 52 45.05 N 8.37 E
Seskarö 44 65.44 N 23.44 E
Sespe Creek ≈ 104 34.23 N 118.57 W
Sessa Aurunca 52 41.14 N 13.56 E
Sestao 50 43.18 N 3.00 W
Sestri Levante 52 44.16 N 9.24 E
Sestroreck 60 60.06 N 29.58 E
Šešupe ≈ 60 55.03 N 22.12 E
Setana 64a 42.26 N 139.51 E
Sète 48 43.24 N 3.41 E
Sete Barras 114 24.23 S 47.55 W
Sete Lagoas 110 19.27 S 44.14 W
Sete Quedas, Salto das ㇄ 114 24.02 S 54.16 W
Setesdal ∨ 44 59.25 N 7.25 E
Seto 64 35.14 N 137.06 E
Seto-naikai ▾2 64 34.20 N 133.30 E
Setouchi 65b 28.10 N 129.15 E
Settat 80 33.04 N 7.37 W
Setté Cama 84 2.32 S 9.45 E
Sette-Daban, chrebet ✱ 58 62.00 N 138.00 E
Settle 36 54.04 N 2.16 W
Settlers 86 25.02 S 28.30 E
Setúbal 50 38.32 N 8.54 W
Setúbal, Baía de C 50 38.27 N 8.53 W
Seui 52 39.50 N 9.19 E
Seul, Lac ⊜ 98 50.20 N 92.30 W
Seul Choix Point ❯ 102 45.56 N 85.52 W
Seurre 48 47.00 N 5.09 E
Sevagram 74 20.45 N 78.30 E
Sevan, ozero ⊜ 56 40.20 N 45.20 E
Sevastopol' 56 44.36 N 33.32 E
Ševčenko 56 43.35 N 51.05 E
Seven ≈ 36 54.11 N 0.52 W
Seven Islands → Sept-Îles 98 50.12 N 66.23 W
Sevenmile Creek ≈ 102 39.28 N 84.33 W
Sevenoaks 34 51.16 N 0.12 E
Seven Sisters 34 51.46 N 3.43 W
Sévérac-le-Château 48 44.19 N 3.04 E
Severn ≈, On., Can. 98 56.02 N 87.36 W
Severn ≈, On., Can. 102 44.52 N 79.41 W
Severn ≈, U.K. 34 51.35 N 2.40 W
Severn, Mouth of the ≈ 34 51.25 N 3.00 W
Severnaja Dvina ≈ 42 64.32 N 40.30 E
Severnaja Sos'va ≈ 56 64.10 N 65.28 E
Severnaja Zeml'a II 58 79.30 N 98.00 E
Severna Park 102 39.04 N 76.32 W
Severnyj 42 67.38 N 64.06 E
Severnyje uvaly ✱2 42 59.30 N 49.00 E
Severočeský Kraj ◻4 46 50.30 N 14.00 E
Severodvinsk 42 64.34 N 39.50 E
Severo-Jenisejskij 58 60.22 N 93.01 E
Severo-Kuril'sk 58 50.40 N 156.08 E
Severomoravský Kraj ◻4 46 49.45 N 17.50 E
Severomorsk 42 69.05 N 33.24 E
Severo-Sibirskaja nizmennost' ≚ 58 73.00 N 100.00 E
Severoural'sk 56 60.09 N 59.57 E
Severo-Zadonsk 60 54.02 N 38.24 E
Severskij Donec ≈ 56 47.35 N 40.54 E
Sevettijärvi 42 69.26 N 28.38 E
Sevier ≈ 100 39.04 N 113.06 W
Sevier Lake ⊜ 100 38.55 N 113.09 W
Sevilla, Col. 110 4.16 N 75.57 W
Sevilla, Esp. 50 37.23 N 5.59 W
Seville → Sevilla, Esp. 50 37.23 N 5.59 W
Seville, Oh., U.S. 102 41.00 N 81.51 W
Sevlievo 54 43.01 N 25.06 E
Sevsk 60 52.09 N 34.30 E
Seward, Ak., U.S. 98 60.06 N 149.26 W
Seward, Ne., U.S. 100 40.54 N 97.05 W
Seward, Pa., U.S. 102 40.25 N 79.01 W
Sewell 114 34.05 S 70.23 W
Seychelles ◻1 84 4.35 S 55.40 E
Seychelles Bank ✦4 26 4.45 S 55.30 E
Seyches 48 44.33 N 0.18 E
Seyðisfjörður 42a 65.16 N 14.00 W
Seylac 82 11.21 N 43.29 E
Seymour, Austl. 94 37.02 S 145.08 E
Seymour, Ciskei 86 32.33 S 26.46 E
Seymour, Ct., U.S. 102 41.23 N 73.04 W
Seyne 48 44.21 N 6.21 E
Seyssel 48 45.57 N 5.49 E
Sežana 52 45.42 N 13.52 E
Sézanne 48 48.43 N 3.43 E
Sezela 86 30.24 S 30.38 E
Sezimbra 50 38.26 N 9.06 W
Sezimovo Ústí 46 49.23 N 14.42 E
Sezze 52 41.30 N 13.03 E
Sfax 80 34.44 N 10.46 E
Sfîntu Gheorghe 54 45.52 N 25.47 E
Sfîntu Gheorghe, Braţul ≈1 54 44.53 N 29.36 E
Sfîntu Gheorghe, Ostrov I 54 45.07 N 29.22 E
's-Gravenhage (The Hague) 46 52.06 N 4.18 E
Sgritheall, Beinn ▲ 38 57.08 N 5.35 W
Shaanxi (Shensi) ◻4 62 35.00 N 109.00 E
Shabeelle (Shebele) ≈ 82 0.50 N 43.10 E
Shache (Yarkand) 62 38.25 N 77.16 E
Shady Cove 104 42.04 N 122.36 W
Shadyside 102 39.58 N 80.45 W
Shafter 104 35.30 N 119.16 W
Shaftesbury 34 51.01 N 2.12 W
Shag ≈ 96 45.29 S 170.49 E
Shag Rocks II1 112 53.33 S 42.02 W
Shāhābād 76 30.10 N 76.53 E
Shah Alam 72 3.04 N 101.33 E
Shahdād, Namakzār-e ≚ 78 30.30 N 58.30 E
Shāhdādkot 76 27.51 N 67.54 E
Shāhdādpur 76 25.56 N 68.37 E
Shahdol 76 23.20 N 81.21 E
Shāhganj 76 26.03 N 82.41 E
Shāhjahānpur 76 27.53 N 79.55 E
Shāhpura 76 25.38 N 74.56 E
Shahrezā 78 32.01 N 51.52 E
Shakawe 86 18.23 S 21.50 E
Shaker Heights 102 41.28 N 81.32 W
Shaki 80 8.39 N 3.25 E
Shakotan-hantō ❯1 64a 43.20 N 140.30 E
Shala, Lake ⊜ 82 7.25 N 38.30 E
Shaler Mountains ✱ 98 72.35 N 110.45 W
Shām, Bādiyat ash- ✦2 78 32.00 N 40.00 E
Shām, Jabal ash- ▲ 78 23.13 N 57.16 E
Shamattawa 98 55.52 N 92.05 W
Shāmli 76 29.27 N 77.19 E
Shamokin 102 40.47 N 76.33 W
Shamva 84 17.18 S 31.34 E
Shan ◻3 70 22.00 N 98.00 E
Shandī 82 16.42 N 33.26 E
Shandong (Shantung) ◻4 62 36.00 N 118.00 E
Shandong Bandao ❯1 62 37.00 N 121.00 E
Shangani ≈ 86 18.41 S 27.10 E
Shangcai 66 33.16 N 114.15 E
Shangcheng 66 31.48 N 115.24 E
Shangdian 66 34.07 N 112.23 E
Shanggan 66 25.56 N 119.22 E
Shanggang 66 33.30 N 120.04 E
Shanggao 66 28.18 N 114.54 E
Shanghai 66 31.14 N 121.28 E
Shanghai Shi ◻7 66 31.10 N 121.30 E
Shanghang 66 25.06 N 116.25 E
Shangqiu, Zhg. 66 34.23 N 115.37 E
Shangqiu (Zhuji), Zhg. 66 34.27 N 115.42 E
Shangrao 66 28.26 N 117.58 E
Shangshui 66 33.33 N 114.34 E
Shangsi 70 22.09 N 107.57 E
Shangxian 62 33.51 N 109.54 E
Shangyou 66 25.51 N 114.30 E
Shangyu 66 30.02 N 120.54 E
Shangzhi 62 45.13 N 127.59 E
Shanhaiguan 62 40.01 N 119.44 E
Shanklin 34 50.38 N 1.10 W
Shannon, Ire. 40 52.43 N 8.53 W
Shannon, N.Z. 96 40.33 S 175.25 E
Shannon, S. Afr. 86 29.08 S 26.18 E
Shannon ≈ 40 52.36 N 9.41 W
Shannon, Mouth of the ≈1 40 52.30 N 9.50 W
Shannon Airport ⊠ 40 52.41 N 8.55 W
Shansi → Shanxi ◻4 62 37.00 N 112.00 E
Shantou (Swatow) 66 23.23 N 116.41 E
Shantung Peninsula → Shandong Bandao ❯1 62 37.00 N 121.00 E
Shanwei 66 22.47 N 115.21 E
Shanxi (Shansi) ◻4 62 37.00 N 112.00 E
Shanxian 62 34.48 N 116.03 E
Shanyin 62 39.33 N 112.50 E
Shaobo 66 32.30 N 119.32 E
Shaoguan 66 24.50 N 113.37 E
Shaowu 66 27.20 N 117.28 E
Shaoxing 66 30.00 N 120.35 E
Shaoyang 66 27.15 N 111.28 E
Shap 36 54.32 N 2.41 W
Shapinsay I 38 59.03 N 2.53 W
Sharbatāt, Ra's ash- ❯ 74 17.52 N 56.22 E
Sharbot Lake 102 44.46 N 76.41 W
Shari 64a 43.55 N 144.50 E
Shari-dake ▲ 64a 43.46 N 144.43 E
Shark Bay C 90 25.30 S 113.30 E
Sharktooth Mountain ▲ 98 58.35 N 127.57 W
Sharm ash-Shaykh 78 27.51 N 34.17 E
Sharnbrook 34 52.13 N 0.32 W
Sharon 102 41.13 N 80.29 W
Sharqīyah, Aṣ-Ṣaḥrā' ash- (Arabian Desert) ✦2 82 28.00 N 32.00 E
Shashe ≈ 86 22.14 S 29.20 E
Shashi 62 30.19 N 112.14 E
Shasta 104 40.36 N 122.29 W
Shasta ≈ 104 41.50 N 122.35 W
Shasta, Mount ▲1 104 41.20 N 122.20 W
Shasta Lake ⊜1 104 40.50 N 122.25 W
Shaunavon 98 49.40 N 108.25 W
Shavington 36 53.04 N 2.27 W
Shaw 36 53.34 N 2.05 W
Shaw ≈ 90 20.20 S 119.17 E
Shawanaga Inlet C 102 45.32 N 80.24 W
Shawbury 34 52.47 N 2.39 W
Shawinigan 98 46.33 N 72.45 W
Shawnee, Oh., U.S. 102 39.36 N 82.12 W
Shawnee, Ok., U.S. 100 35.19 N 96.55 W
Shaw River 90 20.43 S 119.20 E
Shawville 102 45.36 N 76.30 W
Shaxi 66 31.34 N 121.04 E
Shaxian 66 26.24 N 117.47 E
Shayang 66 30.42 N 112.33 E
Shaybārā I 78 25.26 N 36.47 E
Shay Gap 90 20.25 S 120.03 E
Shaykh, Jabal ash- ▲ 78 33.26 N 35.51 E
Shaykh 'Uthmān 74 12.52 N 44.59 E
Sheaf ≈ 36 53.23 N 1.26 W
Shebele (Shabeelle) ≈ 82 0.50 N 43.10 E
Sheberghān 76 36.41 N 65.45 E
Sheboygan 100 43.45 N 87.42 W
Shediac 98 46.13 N 64.32 W
Sheelin, Lough ⊜ 40 53.48 N 7.22 W
Sheenjek ≈ 98 66.45 N 144.33 W
Sheep Creek ≈ 104 42.27 N 115.36 W
Sheep Haven C 40 55.10 N 7.52 W
Sheep Mountain ▲ 104 32.32 N 114.14 W
Sheep Range ✱ 104 36.45 N 115.05 W
Sheerness 34 51.27 N 0.45 E
Sheffield, N.Z. 96 43.23 S 172.01 E
Sheffield, Eng., U.K. 36 53.23 N 1.30 W
Sheffield, Al., U.S. 100 34.45 N 87.41 W
Sheffield, Pa., U.S. 102 41.42 N 79.02 W
Shefford 34 52.02 N 0.20 W
Shehy Mountains ✱ 40 51.48 N 9.15 W
Shekhūpura 76 31.42 N 73.59 E
Shelagyote Peak ▲ 98 55.58 N 127.12 W
Shelburne, N.S., Can. 98 43.46 N 65.19 W
Shelburne, On., Can. 102 44.04 N 80.12 W
Shelburne Bay C 92 11.49 S 143.00 E
Shelburne Falls 102 42.36 N 72.44 W
Shelby, Mt., U.S. 100 48.30 N 111.51 W
Shelby, Oh., U.S. 102 40.52 N 82.39 W
Shell, Loch C 38 58.00 N 6.30 W
Shellbrook 98 53.13 N 106.24 W
Shellharbour 94 34.35 S 150.52 E
Shell Lakes ⊜ 90 29.21 S 127.25 E
Shelton 102 41.18 N 73.05 W
Shenandoah, Ia., U.S. 100 40.45 N 95.22 W
Shenandoah, Pa., U.S. 102 40.49 N 76.12 W
Shenandoah, Va., U.S. 102 38.29 N 78.37 W
Shenandoah ≈ 102 39.19 N 77.44 W
Shenandoah, North Fork ≈ 102 38.57 N 78.12 W
Shenandoah, South Fork ≈ 102 38.57 N 78.12 W
Shenandoah National Park ✦ 102 38.48 N 78.12 W
Shengou 66 34.08 N 113.13 E
Shengxian 66 29.36 N 120.48 E
Shengze 66 30.55 N 120.39 E
Shenhu 66 24.38 N 118.39 E
Shenqiu 66 33.24 N 115.02 E
Shenquan 66 22.59 N 116.20 E
Shensi → Shaanxi ◻4 62 35.00 N 109.00 E
Shenton, Mount ▲ 90 28.00 S 123.22 E
Shenyang (Mukden) 62 41.48 N 123.27 E
Sheo 76 26.11 N 71.15 E
Sheopur 76 25.40 N 76.42 E
Shepherd 102 43.31 N 84.41 W
Shepherdstown 102 39.25 N 77.48 W
Shepparton 94 36.23 S 145.25 E
Shepperd, Lake ⊜ 90 29.55 S 123.09 E
Sheppey, Isle of I 34 51.24 N 0.50 E
Shepshed 34 52.47 N 1.18 W
Shepton Mallet 34 51.12 N 2.33 W
Sheqi 66 33.03 N 112.57 E
Sherard, Cape ❯ 98 74.36 N 80.25 W
Sherborne 34 50.57 N 2.31 W
Sherborne Saint John 34 51.18 N 1.07 W
Sherbro Island I 80 7.45 N 12.55 W
Sherbrooke 102 45.25 N 71.54 W
Sherburne 102 42.40 N 75.29 W
Sherburn in Elmet 36 53.48 N 1.15 W
Shercock 40 54.00 N 6.54 W
Sheridan 100 44.47 N 106.57 W
Sheringa 90 33.51 S 135.15 E
Sheringham 34 52.57 N 1.12 E
Sherlock ≈ 90 20.44 S 117.35 E
Sherman, N.Y., U.S. 102 42.09 N 79.35 W
Sherman, Tx., U.S. 100 33.38 N 96.36 W
Sherman Creek ≈ 102 40.23 N 77.02 W
Sherman Mills 102 45.52 N 68.23 W
Sherman Station 102 45.53 N 68.25 W
Sherpur 76 25.01 N 90.01 E
Sherridon 98 55.07 N 101.05 W
Sherrill 102 43.04 N 75.35 W
's-Hertogenbosch 46 51.41 N 5.19 E
Sherwood 102 41.17 N 84.33 W
Sherwood Forest ✦3 36 53.08 N 1.08 W
Shetland Islands ◻4 38a 60.30 N 1.15 W
Shetland Islands II 38a 60.30 N 1.15 W
Shexian 66 29.53 N 118.26 E
Sheyang, Zhg. 66 33.20 N 119.38 E
Sheyang, Zhg. 66 33.46 N 120.18 E
Sheyenne ≈ 100 47.05 N 96.50 W
Shiant, Sound of ꞩ 38 57.55 N 6.25 W
Shiant Islands II 38 57.53 N 6.21 W
Shibām 74 15.56 N 48.38 E
Shibata 64 37.57 N 139.20 E
Shibecha 64a 43.17 N 144.36 E
Shibetsu, Nihon 64a 43.40 N 145.08 E
Shibetsu, Nihon 64a 44.10 N 142.23 E
Shibukawa 64 36.29 N 139.00 E
Shibushi 64 31.28 N 131.07 E
Shicheng 66 26.22 N 116.22 E
Shickshinny 102 41.09 N 76.09 W
Shidao 62 36.53 N 122.23 E
Shiel, Loch ⊜ 38 56.47 N 5.35 W
Shiel Bridge 38 57.12 N 5.25 W
Shieldaig 38 57.31 N 5.39 W
Shieldhill 38 55.58 N 3.46 W
Shifnal 34 52.40 N 2.21 W
Shiga ◻5 64 35.15 N 136.00 E
Shijiazhuang 62 38.03 N 114.28 E
Shikārpur 76 27.57 N 68.38 E
Shikohābād 76 27.06 N 78.36 E
Shikoku I 64 33.45 N 133.30 E
Shikoku-sanchi ✱ 64 33.47 N 133.30 E
Shikotsu-ko ⊜ 64a 42.45 N 141.20 E
Shilbottle 36 55.23 N 1.42 W
Shildon 36 54.38 N 1.39 W
Shillelagh 40 52.45 N 6.32 W
Shillingstone 34 50.54 N 2.14 W
Shillington 102 40.18 N 75.57 W
Shillong 76 25.34 N 91.53 E
Shiloh 102 39.49 N 84.13 W
Shilong 66 23.07 N 113.48 E
Shima 64 34.13 N 136.51 E
Shimabara 64 32.47 N 130.22 E
Shimada 64 34.49 N 138.11 E
Shimane ◻5 64 35.00 N 132.30 E
Shimanto ≈ 64 32.56 N 133.00 E
Shimber Berris ▲ 82 10.44 N 47.15 E
Shimian 62 29.18 N 102.22 E
Shimizu, Nihon 64 35.01 N 138.29 E
Shimizu, Nihon 64a 43.01 N 142.53 E
Shimminato 64 36.47 N 137.04 E
Shimoda 64 34.40 N 138.57 E
Shimodate 64 36.18 N 139.59 E
Shimoga 74 13.55 N 75.34 E
Shimokawa 64a 44.18 N 142.39 E
Shimokita-hantō ❯1 64 41.15 N 141.00 E
Shimonoseki 64 33.57 N 130.57 E
Shin, Loch ⊜ 38 58.06 N 4.34 W
Shinano ≈ 64 37.56 N 139.03 E
Shīndand 78 33.18 N 62.08 E
Shinglehouse 102 41.57 N 78.11 W
Shingū, Nihon 64 34.55 N 134.33 E
Shingū, Nihon 64 33.44 N 135.59 E
Shingwidzi 86 23.05 S 31.25 E
Shingwidzi (Singuédeze) ≈ 86 23.53 S 32.17 E
Shinji-ko ⊜ 64 35.27 N 132.58 E
Shinjō 64 38.46 N 140.18 E
Shinkolobwe 84 11.02 S 26.35 E
Shinnel Water ≈ 36 55.13 N 3.49 W
Shinness 38 58.05 N 4.28 W
Shinnston 102 39.23 N 80.18 W
Shinyanga 84 3.40 S 33.26 E
Shiogama 64 38.19 N 141.01 E
Shiojiri 64 36.06 N 137.58 E
Shiono-misaki ❯ 64 33.26 N 135.45 E
Shioya-zaki ❯, Nihon 64 33.26 N 135.45 E
Shioya-zaki ❯, Nihon 64 36.59 N 140.59 E
Shipdham 34 52.37 N 0.53 E
Shiping 70 23.47 N 102.30 E
Shipley 36 53.50 N 1.47 W
Shippensburg 102 40.03 N 77.31 W
Shipston-on-Stour 34 52.04 N 1.37 W
Shipton-under-Wychwood 34 51.51 N 1.35 W
Shipu 66 29.13 N 121.55 E
Shiqiao 66 33.12 N 112.36 E
Shirahama 64 33.40 N 135.20 E
Shirakami-misaki ❯ 64a 41.24 N 140.12 E
Shirakawa 64 37.07 N 140.13 E
Shiranuka 64a 42.57 N 144.05 E
Shiraoi 64a 42.33 N 141.21 E
Shīrāz 78 29.36 N 52.32 E
Shire ≈ 84 17.42 S 35.19 E
Shirebrook 36 53.12 N 1.13 W
Shiretoko-hantō ❯1 64a 44.00 N 145.00 E
Shiretoko-misaki ❯ 64a 44.14 N 145.17 E
Shīr Kūh ▲ 78 31.37 N 54.04 E
Shiroishi 64 38.00 N 140.37 E
Shirone 64 37.46 N 139.01 E
Shirpur 76 21.21 N 74.53 E
Shirrell Heath 34 50.55 N 1.12 W
Shīrvān 78 37.24 N 57.55 E
Shishi 66 24.48 N 118.38 E
Shitan 66 27.44 N 112.42 E
Shitang 66 28.16 N 121.36 E
Shitara 64 35.05 N 137.35 E
Shivpuri 76 25.26 N 77.39 E
Shiwan 66 23.01 N 113.04 E
Shixing 66 24.58 N 114.03 E
Shizhenjie 66 28.51 N 116.56 E
Shizugawa 64 38.40 N 141.27 E
Shizunai 64a 42.20 N 142.22 E
Shizuoka 64 34.58 N 138.23 E
Shizuoka ◻5 64 35.00 N 138.00 E
Shkodër 54 42.05 N 19.30 E
Shkumbin ≈ 54 41.01 N 19.26 E
Shō ≈ 64 36.47 N 137.04 E
Shoal Cape ❯ 90 33.53 S 121.07 E
Shoalhaven ≈ 94 34.52 S 150.44 E
Shoalwater Bay C 94 22.02 S 150.25 E
Shōbara 64 34.51 N 133.01 E
Shōdo-shima I 64 34.30 N 134.17 E
Shoeburyness 34 51.32 N 0.48 E
Sholāpur 74 17.41 N 75.55 E
Shona, Eilean I 38 56.47 N 5.52 W
Shoreham-by-Sea 34 50.49 N 0.16 W
Shortsville 102 42.57 N 77.13 W
Shoshone 104 42.56 N 114.24 W
Shoshone Mountains ✱ 104 39.00 N 117.30 W
Shoshone Peak ▲ 104 36.56 N 116.16 W
Shoshone Range ✱ 104 40.20 N 116.50 W
Shoshong 86 22.59 S 26.30 E
Shotley Gate 34 51.58 N 1.15 E
Shotton Colliery 36 54.44 N 1.20 W
Shotts 38 55.49 N 3.48 W
Shouchang 66 29.22 N 119.13 E
Shouning 66 27.27 N 119.30 E
Shournagh ≈ 40 51.53 N 8.35 W
Shouxian 66 32.35 N 116.47 E
Shreve 102 40.40 N 82.01 W
Shreveport 100 32.30 N 93.44 W
Shrewsbury, Eng., U.K. 34 52.43 N 2.45 W
Shrewsbury, Ma., U.S. 102 42.17 N 71.42 W
Shrewton 34 51.12 N 1.55 W
Shrivenham 34 51.36 N 1.39 W
Shropshire ◻6 34 52.40 N 2.40 W
Shrule 40 53.30 N 9.08 W
Shuajingsi 62 32.00 N 103.05 E
Shuangcheng 62 45.21 N 126.17 E
Shuanggou, Zhg. 66 32.12 N 112.21 E
Shuanggou, Zhg. 66 33.16 N 118.10 E
Shuanggou, Zhg. 66 34.03 N 117.37 E
Shuangjiang 70 23.37 N 99.41 E
Shuangliao 62 43.31 N 123.30 E
Shuanglin 66 30.47 N 120.19 E
Shuangpai 70 25.57 N 111.32 E
Shuangqiao 66 32.29 N 116.41 E
Shuangyashan 62 46.37 N 131.22 E
Shubrā al-Khaymah 82 30.06 N 31.15 E
Shucheng 66 31.27 N 116.57 E
Shuicheng 70 26.41 N 104.50 E
Shuidong 66 30.47 N 118.57 E
Shuiji 66 27.26 N 118.20 E
Shuitou 66 24.43 N 118.25 E
Shuiyang 66 31.14 N 118.47 E
Shule ≈ 62 40.50 N 94.10 E
Shunchang 66 26.50 N 117.48 E
Shunde 66 22.50 N 113.14 E
Shundian 66 34.15 N 113.20 E
Shupīyan 76 33.43 N 74.50 E
Shuqrah 74 13.21 N 45.42 E
Shurugwi 86 19.40 S 30.00 E
Shūshtar 78 32.03 N 48.51 E
Shuswap Lake ⊜ 98 50.57 N 119.15 W
Shuyang 66 34.08 N 118.47 E
Shwebo 70 22.34 N 95.42 E
Shweli (Longchuanjiang) ≈ 70 23.56 N 96.17 E
Shyok ≈ 76 35.13 N 75.53 E
Siāhān Range ✱ 76 27.25 N 64.30 E
Siaksriinderapura 72 0.46 N 102.04 E
Siālkot 76 32.30 N 74.31 E
Siam → Thailand ◻1 68 15.00 N 100.00 E
Siam, Gulf of → Thailand, Gulf of C 70 10.00 N 101.00 E
Sian → Xi'an, Zhg. 62 34.15 N 108.52 E
Si'an, Zhg. 66 30.54 N 119.39 E
Sianów 46 54.15 N 16.16 E
Siargao Island I 68 9.53 N 126.02 E
Siasconset 102 41.15 N 69.58 W
Šiaškotan, ostrov I 58 48.49 N 154.06 E
Siátista 54 40.16 N 21.33 E
Siau, Pulau I 72 2.42 N 125.24 E
Šiauliai 60 55.56 N 23.19 E
Sibaj 56 52.42 N 58.39 E
Sibasa 86 22.53 S 30.33 E
Sibayi ⊜ 86 27.20 S 32.40 E
Sibbo 44 60.22 N 25.16 E
Šibenik 52 43.44 N 15.54 E
Siberia → Sibir' ✦1 58 65.00 N 110.00 E
Siberut, Pulau I 68 1.20 S 98.55 E
Sibi 76 29.33 N 67.53 E
Sibir' (Siberia) ✦1 58 65.00 N 110.00 E
Sibir'akova, ostrov I 58 72.50 N 79.00 E
Sibiti 84 3.41 S 13.21 E
Sibiu 54 45.48 N 24.09 E
Sibiu ◻6 54 46.00 N 24.15 E
Sible Hedingham 34 51.58 N 0.35 E
Sibolga 70 1.45 N 98.48 E
Sibsāgar 76 26.59 N 94.39 E
Sibu 72 2.18 N 111.49 E
Sibu, Pulau I 72 2.13 N 104.04 E
Sibuti 72 4.03 N 113.48 E
Sibutu Island I 68 4.46 N 119.29 E
Sibuyan Island I 68 12.25 N 122.34 E
Sibuyan Sea ▾2 68 12.50 N 122.40 E
Siccus ≈ 90 31.26 S 139.30 E
Sichote-Alin' ✱ 58 48.00 N 138.00 E
Sichuan (Szechwan) ◻4 62 31.00 N 105.00 E
Sicié, Cap ❯ 48 43.03 N 5.51 E
Sicilia ◻4 52 37.30 N 14.00 E
Sicilia (Sicily) I 52 37.30 N 14.00 E
Sicily → Sicilia I 52 37.30 N 14.00 E
Sicily, Strait of ꞩ 52 37.20 N 11.20 E
Sico ≈ 108 15.58 N 84.58 W
Sicuani 110 14.16 S 71.13 W
Šid 54 45.08 N 19.13 E
Sidareja 72 7.29 S 108.47 E
Siderno 52 38.16 N 16.18 E
Siderópolis 114 28.35 S 49.26 W
Sidhauli 76 27.17 N 80.50 E
Sidheros, Ákra ❯ 54 35.19 N 26.19 E
Sidhi 76 24.25 N 81.53 E
Sidhirókastron 54 41.14 N 23.22 E
Sidhpur 76 23.55 N 72.23 E
Sīdī Barrānī 82 31.36 N 25.55 E
Sidi bel Abbès 80 35.13 N 0.10 W
Sidi Bennour 80 32.30 N 8.30 W
Sidi Ifni 80 29.24 N 10.12 W
Sidlaw Hills ✱2 38 56.30 N 3.10 W
Sidmouth 34 50.41 N 3.15 W
Sidney, Mt., U.S. 100 47.43 N 104.09 W
Sidney, Ne., U.S. 100 41.08 N 102.58 W
Sidney, N.Y., U.S. 102 42.18 N 75.23 W
Sidney, Oh., U.S. 102 40.17 N 84.09 W
Sidney Lanier, Lake ⊜1 100 34.15 N 83.57 W
Sidon → Ṣaydā 78 33.33 N 35.22 E
Sidra, Gulf of → Surt, Khalīj C 82 31.30 N 18.00 E
Sidu 66 23.48 N 117.18 E
Siedlce 46 52.11 N 22.16 E
Siegburg 46 50.47 N 7.12 E
Siegen 46 50.52 N 8.02 E
Siemianowice Śląskie 46 50.19 N 19.01 E
Siemiatycze 46 52.26 N 22.53 E
Siěmréab 70 13.22 N 103.51 E
Siena 52 43.19 N 11.21 E
Sieniawa 46 50.11 N 22.36 E
Sieradz 46 51.36 N 18.45 E
Sieraków 46 52.39 N 16.04 E
Sierck-les-Bains 48 49.26 N 6.21 E
Sierpc 46 52.52 N 19.41 E
Sierra Chica 114 36.50 S 60.13 W
Sierra Colorada 112 40.35 S 67.48 W
Sierra de Outes 50 42.51 N 8.54 W
Sierra Gorda 114 22.54 S 69.19 W
Sierra Leone ◻1 80 8.30 N 11.30 W
Sierra Leone Basin ✦1 20 5.00 N 17.00 W
Sierra Leone Rise ✦3 20 5.30 N 21.00 W
Sierras Bayas 114 36.57 S 60.09 W
Sierre 48 46.18 N 7.32 E
Siete Puntas ≈ 114 23.34 S 57.20 W
Sífnos I 54 36.59 N 24.40 E
Sigean 48 43.02 N 2.59 E
Sighetu Marmaţiei 54 47.56 N 23.54 E
Sighişoara 54 46.13 N 24.48 E
Sighty Crag ▲ 36 55.07 N 2.37 W
Siglan 58 59.02 N 152.25 E
Sigli 70 5.23 N 95.57 E
Siglufjörður 42a 66.10 N 18.56 W
Sigmaringen 46 48.05 N 9.13 E
Signal Mountain ▲ 102 44.12 N 72.20 W
Signy-l'Abbaye 48 49.42 N 4.25 E
Sigsig 110 3.01 S 78.45 W
Sigtuna 44 59.37 N 17.43 E
Siguanea, Ensenada de la C 108 21.38 N 83.05 W
Sigüenza 50 41.04 N 2.38 W
Sigües 50 42.38 N 1.00 W
Siguiri 80 11.25 N 9.10 W
Sigulda 60 57.09 N 24.51 E
Sihanoukville → Kâmpóng Saôm 70 10.38 N 103.30 E
Sihong 66 33.28 N 118.11 E
Sihor 76 21.42 N 71.58 E
Siikajoki ≈ 44 64.50 N 24.44 E
Siilinjärvi 44 63.05 N 27.40 E
Siirt 78 37.56 N 41.57 E
Sijunjung 72 0.42 S 100.58 E
Sikandarābād 76 28.27 N 77.42 E
Sikanni Chief ≈ 98 58.20 N 121.50 W
Sīkar 76 27.37 N 75.09 E
Sikasso 80 11.19 N 5.40 W
Sikéai 54 36.46 N 22.56 E
Sikeston 100 36.52 N 89.35 W
Sikiá 54 40.02 N 23.56 E
Síkinos 54 36.39 N 25.06 E
Síkinos I 54 36.39 N 25.06 E
Sikkim ◻3 76 27.35 N 88.35 E
Šikotan, ostrov (Shikotan-tō) I 58 43.47 N 146.45 E
Sikt'ach 58 69.55 N 125.02 E
Sikuati 72 6.53 N 116.40 E
Sil ≈ 50 42.27 N 7.43 W
Silandro 52 46.38 N 10.46 E
Silay 68 10.48 N 122.58 E
Silba 52 44.23 N 14.42 E
Silchar 76 24.49 N 92.48 E
Sileby 34 52.43 N 1.06 W
Silesia ◻9 46 51.00 N 16.45 E
Silhouette I 84 4.29 S 55.14 E
Silifke 78 36.22 N 33.56 E
Silīguri 76 26.42 N 88.26 E
Siling Co ⊜ 62 31.50 N 89.00 E
Silistra 54 44.07 N 27.16 E
Šiljak ▲ 54 43.45 N 21.50 E
Siljan ⊜ 44 60.50 N 14.45 E
Siljansnäs 44 60.45 N 14.42 E
Šilka 58 51.51 N 116.02 E
Šilka ≈ 58 53.22 N 121.32 E
Silkeborg 44 56.10 N 9.34 E
Sillamäe 60 59.24 N 27.45 E
Sillé-le-Guillaume 48 48.12 N 0.08 W
Sillem Island I 98 70.55 N 71.30 W
Sillian 46 46.45 N 12.25 E
Sillon de Talbert ❯1 48 48.53 N 3.05 W
Silloth 36 54.52 N 3.23 W
Šilovo 60 54.19 N 40.53 E
Silsden 36 53.55 N 1.55 W
Šilute 60 55.21 N 21.29 E
Silvânia 110 16.42 S 48.38 W
Silver Bank Passage ꞩ 108 20.45 N 70.15 W
Silver City 100 32.46 N 108.16 W
Silver Creek 102 42.32 N 79.10 W
Silver Creek ≈ 104 43.16 N 119.13 W
Silverdale, N.Z. 96 36.37 S 174.40 E
Silverdale, Eng., U.K. 36 54.10 N 2.49 W
Silverdalen 44 57.32 N 15.44 E
Silver End 34 51.51 N 0.37 E
Silver Lake 104 43.07 N 121.02 W
Silver Lake ⊜, Or., U.S. 104 43.06 N 120.53 W
Silver Lake ⊜, Or., U.S. 104 43.22 N 119.24 W
Silvermine Mountains ✱ 40 52.45 N 8.15 W
Silvermines 40 52.47 N 8.13 W
Silver Peak Range ✱ 104 37.35 N 117.45 W
Silver Spring 102 38.59 N 77.01 W
Silverstone 34 52.05 N 1.02 W
Silver Streams 86 28.20 S 23.33 E
Silverton, Austl. 94 31.53 S 141.13 E
Silverton, Eng., U.K. 34 50.48 N 3.28 W
Silves 50 37.11 N 8.26 W
Silvi 52 42.34 N 14.05 E
Silvretta ✱ 48 46.50 N 10.10 E
Simanggang 72 1.15 N 111.26 E
Šimanosk 58 52.00 N 127.42 E
Simao 62 22.50 N 101.00 E
Simbach 46 48.34 N 12.45 E
Simcoe 102 42.50 N 80.18 W
Simcoe, Lake ⊜ 102 44.20 N 79.20 W
Simeria 54 45.51 N 23.01 E
Simeto ≈ 52 37.24 N 15.06 E
Simeulue, Pulau I 70 2.35 N 96.00 E
Simferopol' 56 44.57 N 34.06 E
Sími 54 36.36 N 27.50 E
Sími I 54 36.35 N 27.52 E
Simití 110 7.58 N 73.57 W
Simi Valley 104 34.16 N 118.47 W
Simla, India 74 22.47 N 88.16 E
Simla, India 76 31.06 N 77.10 E
Şimleu Silvaniei 54 47.14 N 22.48 E
Simmern 46 49.59 N 7.31 E
Simnas 60 54.24 N 23.39 E
Simoca 114 27.16 S 65.21 W
Simojärvi ⊜ 44 66.06 N 27.03 E
Simojoki ≈ 44 65.37 N 25.03 E
Simon, Lac ⊜ 102 45.58 N 75.05 W
Simonsbath 34 51.09 N 3.45 W
Simonstad 86 34.14 S 18.26 E
Simoom Sound 98 50.45 N 126.29 W
Simpele 44 61.26 N 29.22 E
Simplon Pass)(48 46.15 N 8.02 E
Simpson Desert ✦2 90 25.00 S 137.00 E
Simpson Peninsula ❯1 98 68.34 N 88.45 W
Simpson Strait ꞩ 98 68.27 N 97.45 W
Simrishamn 44 55.33 N 14.20 E
Simsbury 102 41.52 N 72.48 W
Simunjan 72 1.23 N 110.45 E
Simušir, ostrov I 58 46.58 N 152.02 E
Sīnā', Shibh Jazīrat (Sinai Peninsula) ❯1 82 29.30 N 34.00 E
Sinabang 70 2.29 N 96.23 E
Sinaia 54 45.21 N 25.33 E
Sinai, Mount → Mūsā, Jabal ▲ 78 28.32 N 33.59 E
Sinai Peninsula → Sīnā', Shibh Jazīrat ❯1 82 29.30 N 34.00 E
Sin'aja ≈ 58 61.06 N 126.50 E
Sinalunga 52 43.12 N 11.44 E
Sinamaica 108 11.05 N 71.51 W
Sinan 62 27.54 N 108.18 E
Sīnāwin 82 31.02 N 10.36 E
Sincé 108 9.15 N 75.09 W
Sincelejo 110 9.18 N 75.24 W
Sinclair, Point ❯ 90 32.06 S 133.00 E
Sinclair's Bay C 38 58.30 N 3.07 W
Sind ◻4 76 25.30 N 69.00 E
Sindal 44 57.28 N 10.13 E

Symbols in the Index entries are identified on page 122

Symbols in the Index entries are identified on page 122.

Symbols in the Index entries are identified on page 122.

Name	Page	Lat. °′	Long. °′
Suspiro del Moro, Puerto)(	50	37.04N	3.39W
Susquehanna	102	41.56N	75.36W
Susquehanna ≃	102	39.33N	76.05W
Susquehanna, West Branch ≃	102	40.53N	76.47W
Susques	114	23.25S	66.29W
Sussex, N.B., Can.	98	45.43N	65.31W
Sussex, N.J., U.S.	102	41.12N	74.36W
Sussex, East □ [6]	34	50.55N	0.15 E
Sussex, Vale of ∨	34	50.57N	0.17W
Susui	72	4.56N	116.41 E
Susuman	58	62.47N	148.10 E
Susurluk	54	39.54N	28.10 E
Susz	46	53.44N	19.20 E
Sutherland	86	32.24S	20.40 E
Sutherlin	104	43.23N	123.18W
Sutlej (Satluj) (Langchuhe) ≃	76	29.23N	71.02 E
Sutter	104	39.10N	121.45W
Sutter Buttes ∧	104	39.12N	121.50W
Sutter Creek	104	38.23N	120.48W
Sutton, Eng., U.K.	34	52.23N	0.07 E
Sutton, W.V., U.S.	102	38.39N	80.42W
Sutton ✦ [8]	34	51.22N	0.12W
Sutton Bridge	34	52.46N	0.12 E
Sutton Coldfield	34	52.34N	1.48W
Sutton Courtenay	34	51.39N	1.17W
Sutton in Ashfield	36	53.08N	1.15W
Sutton Lake ⊜ [1]	102	38.40N	80.40W
Sutton on Sea	36	53.19N	0.17 E
Sutton on Trent	36	53.10N	0.49W
Suttons Bay	102	44.58N	85.39W
Sutton Scotney	34	51.10N	1.21W
Sutton Valence	34	51.12N	0.36 E
Sutton Veny	34	51.11N	2.08W
Sutton West	102	44.18N	79.22W
Suttor ≃	94	21.25S	147.45 E
Suttsu	64a	42.48N	140.14 E
Suurbraak	86	34.00S	20.39 E
Suure-Jaani	60	58.33N	25.28 E
Suva	28	18.08S	178.25 E
Suva Planina ✱	54	43.10N	22.10 E
Suvasvesi ⊜	44	62.39N	28.12 E
Suvorov	60	54.07N	36.30 E
Suwa	64	36.02N	138.08 E
Suwałki	46	54.07N	22.56 E
Suwanose-jima I	65b	29.38N	129.43 E
Suwanose-suidō ⋓	65b	29.32N	129.40 E
Suwarrow I [1]	28	13.15S	163.05W
Suways, Khalīj as- c	82	29.00N	32.50 E
Suways, Qanāt as- ☲	82	29.55N	32.33 E
Suwŏn	62	37.17N	127.01 E
Suxian	66	33.38N	116.58 E
Suzak	56	44.07N	68.28 E
Suzaka	64	36.39N	138.19 E
Suzdal'	60	56.25N	40.26 E
Suzhou (Soochow)	66	31.18N	120.37 E
Suzu	64	37.25N	137.17 E
Suzuka	64	34.51N	136.35 E
Suzuka-sammyaku ✱	64	35.00N	136.25 E
Suzu-misaki ›	64	37.31N	137.21 E
Suzzara	52	45.00N	10.45 E
Svalbard □ [2]	26	78.00N	20.00 E
Svalöv	44	55.55N	13.06 E
Svaneke	44	55.08N	15.09 E
Svängsta	44	56.16N	14.46 E
Svanskog	44	59.11N	12.33 E
Svappavaara	42	67.39N	21.04 E
Svärdsjö	44	60.45N	15.55 E
Svartå	44	59.08N	14.31 E
Svartån ≃	44	59.37N	16.33 E
Svartenhuk › [1]	98	71.55N	55.00W
Svartisen ⌓	42	66.38N	14.00 E
Svataj	58	67.57N	151.54 E
Sv'atoj Nos, mys ›, S.S.S.R.	42	68.10N	39.45 E
Sv'atoj Nos, mys ›, S.S.S.R.	58	72.52N	140.42 E
Svay Riěng	70	11.05N	105.48 E
Svedala	44	55.30N	13.14 E
Sveg	44	62.02N	14.21 E
Svelgen	44	61.47N	5.15 E
Svelvik	44	59.37N	10.24 E
Sven'	60	53.09N	34.21 E
Švenčioneliai	60	55.10N	26.00 E
Svendborg	44	55.03N	10.37 E
Svenljunga	44	57.30N	13.07 E
Svenstrup	44	56.59N	9.52 E
Sverdlovsk, S.S.S.R.	56	56.51N	60.36 E
Sverdlovsk, S.S.S.R.	56	48.05N	39.40 E
Sverdrup, ostrov I	58	74.35N	79.30 E
Sveti Nikole	54	41.52N	21.58 E
Svetlaja	58	46.33N	138.18 E
Světlá nad Sázavou	46	49.40N	15.25 E
Svetlyj	58	58.26N	115.55 E
Svetogorsk	42	61.07N	28.51 E
Svetozarevo	54	43.58N	21.16 E
Svidník	46	49.18N	21.35 E
Svilajnac	54	44.14N	21.13 E
Svilengrad	54	41.46N	26.12 E
Svindal	44	58.30N	7.28 E
Svinecea ∧	54	44.48N	22.09 E
Svinesund	44	59.06N	11.16 E
Svinninge	44	55.43N	11.28 E
Svir' ≃	60	60.30N	32.48 E
Svirica	60	60.29N	32.51 E
Svirsk	58	53.04N	103.21 E
Svir'stroj	60	60.48N	33.43 E
Svisloč'	60	53.02N	24.06 E
Svištov	54	43.37N	25.20 E
Svit	46	49.03N	20.12 E
Svitávka	46	49.30N	16.37 E
Svitavy	46	49.45N	16.27 E
Svobodnyj	58	51.24N	128.08 E
Svoge	54	42.58N	23.21 E
Svolvær	42	68.14N	14.34 E
Svorkmo	44	63.10N	9.45 E
Svratka ≃	46	49.11N	16.38 E
Svullrya	44	60.25N	12.24 E
Swadlincote	34	52.47N	1.33W
Swaffham	34	52.39N	0.41 E
Swain Reefs ✦ [2]	94	21.40S	152.15 E
Swains Island I [1]	28	11.03S	171.05W
Swakop ≃	86	22.38S	14.36 E
Swakopmund	86	22.41S	14.34 E
Swakopmund □ [5]	86	23.00S	15.00 E
Swale ≃	36	54.06N	1.20W
Swaledale ∨	36	54.25N	1.47W
Swan ≃	90	32.03S	115.45 E
Swanage	34	50.37N	1.58W
Swan Hill	94	35.21S	143.34 E
Swan Islands → Santanilla, Islas II	108	17.25N	83.55W
Swan Lake ⊜	98	52.30N	100.45W
Swanland	36	53.44N	0.29W
Swanley	34	51.24N	0.12 E
Swanlinbar	40	54.10N	7.42W
Swan River	98	52.06N	101.16W
Swansea, Austl.	94	42.08S	148.04 E
Swansea, Wales, U.K.	34	51.38N	3.57W
Swansea Bay c	34	51.35N	3.52W
Swans Island I	102	44.10N	68.25W
Swanton, Oh., U.S.	102	41.35N	83.53W
Swanton, Vt., U.S.	102	44.55N	73.07W
Swartruggens	86	25.40S	26.42 E
Swartz Creek	102	42.57N	83.49W
Swarzędz	46	52.26N	17.05 E
Swatara Creek ≃	102	40.11N	76.44W
Swatow → Shantou	62	23.23N	116.41 E
Sway	34	50.47N	1.37W
Swaziland □ [1]	84	26.30S	31.30 E
Sweden (Sverige) □ [1]	30	62.00N	15.00 E
Swedru	80	5.32N	0.43W
Sween, Loch c	38	55.59N	5.39W
Sweetwater	100	32.28N	100.24W
Swellendam	86	34.02S	20.26 E
Świdnica (Schweidnitz)	46	50.51N	16.29 E
Świdnik	46	51.14N	22.41 E
Świdwin	46	53.47N	15.47 E
Świebodzice	46	50.52N	16.19 E
Świebodzin	46	52.15N	15.32 E
Świecie	46	53.25N	18.28 E
Świerzawa	46	51.01N	15.54 E
Świętokrzyskie, Góry ✱	46	50.55N	21.00 E
Swift ≃	34	52.23N	1.16W
Swift Current	98	50.17N	107.50W
Swilly ≃	40	54.57N	7.42W
Swilly, Lough c	40	55.10N	7.38W
Swinburne, Cape ›	98	71.14N	98.34W
Swindon	34	51.34N	1.47W
Swineshead	34	52.56N	0.09W
Swinford	40	53.57N	8.57W
Świnoujście (Swinemünde)	46	53.53N	14.14 E
Swinton, Eng., U.K.	36	53.28N	1.20W
Swinton, Scot., U.K.	38	55.43N	2.15W
Switzerland □ [1]	30	47.00N	8.00 E
Swona I	38	58.45N	3.03W
Swordfish Seamount ✦ [3]	28	18.25N	158.25W
Swords	40	53.28N	6.13W
Swords Range ✱	94	21.57S	141.32 E
Syalach	58	66.12N	124.00 E
Sycamore	102	40.56N	83.10W
Sycan ≃	104	42.27N	121.15W
Syčovka	60	55.50N	34.17 E
Syców	46	51.19N	17.43 E
Sydenham	102	44.25N	76.36W
Sydney, Austl.	94	33.52S	151.13 E
Sydney, N.S., Can.	98	46.09N	60.11W
Sydney Mines	98	46.14N	60.14W
Syke	46	52.54N	8.49 E
Sykesville, Md., U.S.	102	39.22N	76.58W
Sykesville, Pa., U.S.	102	41.03N	78.49W
Sykkylven	44	62.24N	6.35 E
Syktyvkar	42	61.40N	50.46 E
Sylarna ∧	44	63.02N	12.13 E
Sylhet	76	24.54N	91.52 E
Sylsjön ⊜	44	62.56N	12.11 E
Sylt I	46	54.54N	8.20 E
Sylvania	102	41.43N	83.42W
Sym	56	60.20N	88.23 E
Symmes Creek ≃	102	38.26N	82.27W
Syracuse → Siracusa, It.	52	37.04N	15.18 E
Syracuse, N.Y., U.S.	102	43.02N	76.08W
Syrdarja	56	40.52N	68.38 E
Syrdarja (Syr Darya) ≃	56	46.03N	61.00 E
Syre	38	58.22N	4.14W
Syria (As-Sūrīyah) □ [1]	74	35.00N	38.00 E
Syriam	70	16.46N	96.15 E
Syrian Desert → Shām, Bādiyat ash- ✦ [2]	78	32.00N	40.00 E
Sysmä	44	61.30N	25.41 E
Sysslebäck	44	60.44N	12.52 E
Systert'	56	56.29N	60.49 E
Syston	34	52.42N	1.04W
Syväri ⊜	44	63.16N	28.06 E
Syzran'	42	53.09N	48.27 E
Szabadka → Subotica	54	46.06N	19.39 E
Szabolcs-Szatmár □ [6]	46	48.00N	22.10 E
Szamocin	46	53.02N	17.08 E
Szamos (Someş) ≃	54	48.07N	22.20 E
Szamotuły	46	52.37N	16.35 E
Szarvas	46	46.52N	20.34 E
Szczawnica	46	49.26N	20.30 E
Szczecin (Stettin)	46	53.24N	14.32 E
Szczecinek (Neustettin)	46	53.43N	16.42 E
Szczeciński, Zalew (Oderhaff) c	46	53.46N	14.14 E
Szczekociny	46	50.38N	19.50 E
Szczuczyn	46	53.34N	22.18 E
Szczytno	46	53.34N	21.00 E
Szechwan → Sichuan □ [4]	62	31.00N	105.00 E
Szécsény	46	48.06N	19.31 E
Szeged	46	46.15N	20.09 E
Szeghalom	46	47.01N	21.11 E
Székesfehérvár	46	47.12N	18.25 E
Szekszárd	46	46.21N	18.42 E
Szentendre	46	47.40N	19.05 E
Szentes	46	46.39N	20.16 E
Szentgotthárd	46	46.57N	16.17 E
Szerencs	46	48.09N	21.13 E
Szlichtyngowa	46	51.43N	16.15 E
Szob	46	47.50N	18.52 E
Szolnok	46	47.10N	20.12 E
Szolnok □ [6]	46	47.12N	20.11 E
Szombathely	46	47.14N	16.38 E
Szprotawa	46	51.34N	15.33 E
Sztum	46	53.56N	19.01 E
Szubin	46	53.00N	17.44 E
Szydłowiec	46	51.14N	20.51 E
Szypliszki	46	54.15N	23.05 E
T			
Taavetti	44	60.55N	27.34 E
Tabacal	114	23.16S	64.15W
Tábara	50	41.49N	5.57W
Tabar Islands II	92	2.50S	152.00 E
Tabas	78	33.36N	56.54 E
Tabasco	104	32.35N	114.55W
Tabelbala	80	29.23N	3.15W
Taber	98	49.47N	112.08W
Taberg	44	57.41N	14.05 E
Tabernes de Valldigna	50	39.04N	0.16W
Tabiteuea I [1]	28	1.20S	174.50 E
Tablas, Cabo ›	114	31.51S	71.34W
Tablas Island I	68	12.24N	122.02 E
Table Bay c	86	33.53S	18.27 E
Table Cape ›	96	39.06S	178.00 E
Tableland	90	17.17S	127.00 E
Tabletop ∧	90	22.32S	123.55 E
Tábor, Česko.	46	49.25N	14.41 E
Tabor, S.S.S.R.	58	71.16N	150.12 E
Tabora	84	5.01S	32.48 E
Tabou	80	4.25N	7.21W
Tabrīz	78	38.05N	46.18 E
Tabuaço	50	41.07N	7.34W
Tabuaeran I [1]	28	3.52N	159.20W
Tabūk	78	28.23N	36.35 E
Täby	44	59.30N	18.03 E
Tacañitas	114	28.38S	62.36W
Taché, Lac ⊜	98	64.00N	120.00W
Tacheng	62	46.45N	82.57 E
Tachiataš	56	42.22N	59.35 E
Tachikawa	64	35.42N	139.25 E
Tachov	46	49.48N	12.38 E
Tachta-Bazar	78	35.57N	62.50 E
Tachtamygda	58	54.06N	123.34 E
Tacloban	68	11.15N	125.00 E
Tacna	110	18.01S	70.15W
Tacoma	100	47.15N	122.26W
Taconic Range ✱	102	42.30N	73.20W
Taco Pozo	114	25.37S	63.17W
Tacuarembó	114	31.44S	55.59W
Tacuarembó ≃	114	32.25S	55.29W
Tacuarí ≃	114	32.46S	53.18W
Tacuatí	114	23.27S	56.35W
Tacutu (Takutu) ≃	110	3.01N	60.29W
Tadami	64	37.21N	139.19 E
Tadcaster	36	53.53N	1.16W
Tademaït, Plateau du ✱ [1]	80	28.30N	2.00 E
Tadjoura	82	11.47N	42.54 E
Tadley	34	51.21N	1.08W
Tadotsu	64	34.16N	133.45 E
Tadoule Lake ⊜	98	58.36N	98.20W
Tadoussac	98	48.09N	69.43W
Tādpatri	74	14.55N	78.01 E
Tadworth	34	51.17N	0.14W
Tadžikskaja Sovetskaja Socialističeskaja Respublika □ [3]	56	39.00N	71.00 E
T'aebaek-sanmaek ✱	62	37.40N	128.50 E
Taegu	62	35.52N	128.35 E
Taejŏn	62	36.20N	127.26 E
Tafahi I	28	15.51S	173.43W
Tafalla	50	42.31N	1.40W
Tafassâsset, Oued ∨	80	20.56N	10.12 E
Taff ≃	34	51.27N	3.09W
Tafí Viejo	114	26.44S	65.16W
Taft	104	35.08N	119.27W
Tagajō	64	38.20N	141.00 E
Taganrog	56	47.12N	38.56 E
Tagawa	64	33.38N	130.49 E
Tagaytay	68	14.06N	120.56 E
Tagbilaran	68	9.39N	123.51 E
Taghmon	40	52.18N	6.39W
Tagish Lake ⊜	98	59.45N	134.15W
Tagliacozzo	52	42.04N	13.14 E
Taglio di Po	52	45.00N	12.12 E
Tagon Harbour c	90	33.53S	123.00 E
Taguatinga	110	12.25S	46.26W
Taguke	62	32.07N	84.35 E
Tagula Island I	92	11.30S	153.30 E
Tagus (Tejo) (Tajo) ≃	50	38.40N	9.24W
Tahaa I	28	16.38S	151.30W
Tahakopa	96	46.31S	169.23 E
Tahan, Gunong ∧	72	4.38N	102.14 E
Tahat ∧	80	23.18N	5.47 E
Taheke	96	35.27S	173.39 E
Tahiryuak Lake ⊜	98	70.56N	112.20W
Tahiti I	28	17.37S	149.27W
Tahlequah	100	35.54N	94.58W
Tahoe, Lake ⊜	104	39.07N	120.03W
Tahoe City	104	39.10N	120.08W
Tahoe Lake ⊜	98	70.15N	108.45W
Tahoe Valley	104	38.55N	120.00W
Tahoua	80	14.54N	5.16 E
Ṭahṭā	82	26.46N	31.30 E
Tahulandang, Pulau I	72	2.20N	125.25 E
Tahuna	72	3.37N	125.29 E
Tai'an	62	36.12N	117.07 E
Taibai Shan ∧	62	33.54N	107.46 E
Taibilla, Sierra de ✱	50	38.10N	2.10W
Taicang	66	31.26N	121.07 E
T'aichung	66	24.09N	120.41 E
Taieri ≃	96	46.03S	170.11 E
Taihang Shan ✱	62	38.00N	114.00 E
Taihape	96	39.40S	175.48 E
Taihe, Zhg.	66	33.11N	115.36 E
Taihe, Zhg.	66	26.49N	114.55 E
Taihu	66	30.26N	116.16 E
Tai Hu ⊜	62	31.15N	120.10 E
Taikang	66	34.04N	114.50 E
Tailai	62	46.23N	123.27 E
Tailem Bend	94	35.16S	139.27 E
Taimba	58	60.18N	98.58 E
Tain	38	57.48N	4.04W
T'ainan	66	23.00N	120.12 E
T'ainanhsien	66	23.18N	120.19 E
Taínaron, Ákra ›	54	36.22N	22.30 E
Taining	66	26.54N	117.09 E
Tai O	66	22.15N	113.51 E
Tai Pang Wan c	66	22.30N	114.24 E
T'aipei	66	25.03N	121.30 E
T'aipeihsien	66	25.00N	121.27 E
Taiping, Malay.	72	4.51N	100.44 E
Taiping, Zhg.	66	30.18N	118.12 E
Taiping, Zhg.	66	22.49N	113.41 E
Taira → Iwaki	64	37.03N	140.55 E
Tais	72	4.06S	102.34 E
Taisha	64	35.24N	132.40 E
Taishun	66	27.33N	119.43 E
Taitao, Península de › [1]	112	46.30S	74.25W
Taitapu	96	43.40S	172.33 E
T'aitung	66	22.45N	121.09 E
Taivalkoski	44	65.34N	28.15 E
Taiwan (T'aiwan) □ [1]	62	23.30N	121.00 E
Taiwan Strait ⋓	66	24.00N	119.00 E
Taixian	66	32.31N	120.09 E
Taixing	66	32.11N	120.01 E
Taíyetos Óros ✱	54	37.16N	22.12 E
Taiyuan	62	37.55N	112.30 E
Taizhou	66	32.30N	119.58 E
Ta'izz	74	13.38N	44.04 E
Tajga	58	56.04N	85.37 E
Tajgonos, poluostrov › [1]	58	61.20N	161.00 E
Tajik Soviet Socialist Republic → Tadžikskaja Sovetskaja Socialističeskaja Respublika □ [3]	56	39.00N	71.00 E
Tajima	64	37.12N	139.46 E
Tajimi	64	35.19N	137.08 E
Tajmura ≃	58	63.46N	98.01 E
Tajmyr, ozero ⊜	58	74.30N	102.30 E
Tajmyr, poluostrov › [1]	58	76.00N	104.00 E
Tajo → Tagus ≃	50	38.40N	9.24W
Tajrīsh	78	35.48N	51.25 E
Tajšet	58	55.57N	98.00 E
Tajumulco, Volcán ∧ [1]	106	15.02N	91.55W
Tajuña ≃	50	40.07N	3.35W
Tak	70	16.52N	99.08 E
Takachiho	64	32.42N	131.18 E
Takahagi	64	36.43N	140.43 E
Takahashi	64	34.47N	133.37 E
Takaka	96	40.51S	172.48 E
Takalar	72	5.28S	119.24 E
Takamatsu	64	34.20N	134.03 E
Takanabe	64	32.08N	131.30 E
Takanosu	64	40.13N	140.22 E
Takaoka	64	36.45N	137.01 E
Takapau	96	40.02S	176.21 E
Takapuna	96	36.47S	174.47 E
Takara-jima I	65b	29.09N	129.13 E
Takasago	64	34.45N	134.48 E
Takasaki	64	36.20N	139.01 E
Takashima	64	32.39N	129.45 E
Takatsuki	64	34.51N	135.37 E
Takayama	64	36.08N	137.15 E
Takefu	64	35.54N	136.10 E
Takeo	64	33.12N	130.01 E
Tåkern ⊜	44	58.21N	14.48 E
Take-shima I	65b	30.49N	130.26 E
Taketa	64	32.58N	131.24 E
Takêv	70	10.59N	104.47 E
Takhār □ [4]	76	36.30N	69.30 E
Ta Khli	70	15.15N	100.21 E
Takikawa	64a	43.33N	141.54 E
Takingeun	70	4.38N	96.50 E
Takitimu Mountains ✱	96	45.41S	167.53 E
Takla Lake ⊜	98	55.25N	125.53W
Takla Makan → Taklimakan Shamo ✦ [2]	62	39.00N	83.00 E
Taklimakan Shamo ✦ [2]	62	39.00N	83.00 E
Taku	64	33.17N	130.08 E
Takutea I	28	19.49S	158.18W
Takutu (Tacutu) ≃	110	3.01N	60.29W
Tala	114	34.21S	55.46W
Talagante	114	33.40S	70.56W
Tālāla	76	21.02N	70.32 E
Talamanca, Cordillera de ✱	108	9.30N	83.40W
Talana	86	28.10S	30.15 E
Talangbetutu	72	2.53S	104.41 E
Talangpadang	72	5.21S	104.11 E
Talara	110	4.34S	81.17W
Talarrubias	50	39.02N	5.14W
Talas	56	42.32N	72.14 E
Talasea	92	5.20S	150.05 E
Talata Mafara	80	12.35N	6.04 E
Talaud, Kepulauan II	68	4.20N	126.50 E
Talavera de la Reina	50	39.57N	4.50W
Talawanta	94	18.38S	140.16 E
Talawdī	82	10.38N	30.23 E
Talbot, Cape ›	92	13.48S	126.43 E
Talbot Islands II	92	9.15S	142.08 E
Talbragar ≃	94	32.12S	148.37 E
Talca	114	35.26S	71.40W
Talcahuano	114	36.43S	73.07W
Taldom	60	56.44N	37.32 E
Taldy-Kurgan	56	45.00N	78.23 E
Talent	104	42.14N	122.47W
Talgar	56	43.18N	77.18 E
Talgarreg	34	52.08N	4.18W
Talgarth	34	52.00N	3.15W
Talia	90	33.19S	134.54 E
Taliabu, Pulau I	72	1.48S	124.48 E
Talica	56	57.00N	63.43 E
Talisay	68	10.44N	122.58 E
Talisker	38	57.17N	6.27W
Taliwang	72	8.44S	116.52 E
Talladale	38	57.42N	5.29W
Talladega	100	33.26N	86.06W
Tall 'Afar	78	36.22N	42.27 E
Tallaght	40	53.26N	6.21W
Tallahassee	100	30.26N	84.16W
Tallangatta	94	36.13S	147.15 E
Tallard	48	44.28N	6.03 E
Talla Reservoir ⊜ [1]	38	55.29N	3.24W
Tällberg	44	60.49N	15.00 E
Tallinn	60	59.25N	24.45 E
Tallmadge	102	41.06N	81.27W
Tallow	40	52.05N	8.00W
Tallulah	100	32.24N	91.11W
Talmage	104	39.08N	123.10W
Tal'menka	58	53.51N	83.35 E
Talmine	38	58.31N	4.26W
Talmont	48	46.28N	1.37W
Talo ∧	82	10.44N	37.55 E
Taloda	76	21.34N	74.13 E
Talok	72	1.03N	118.48 E
Talon, Lake ⊜	102	46.18N	79.05W
Tāloqān	76	36.44N	69.33 E
Talsarnau	34	52.54N	4.03W
Talsi	60	57.15N	22.36 E
Taltal	114	25.24S	70.29W
Taltson ≃	98	61.23N	112.45W
Talu	72	0.14N	99.59 E
Taluk	72	0.32S	101.35 E
Talwood	94	28.30S	149.30 E
Talybont	34	52.29N	3.59W
Tama	114	30.31S	66.32W
Tamala	90	26.42S	113.45 E
Tamale	80	9.25N	0.50W
Tamalpais, Mount ∧	104	37.56N	122.35W
Tamana	64	32.55N	130.33 E
Tamana I	28	2.29S	175.59 E
Tamanaco ≃	108	9.25N	65.23W
Taman Negara ♠	72	4.43N	102.23 E
Tamano	64	34.30N	133.56 E
Tamaqua	102	40.47N	75.58W
Tamar ≃, Austl.	94	41.04S	146.47 E
Tamar ≃, Eng., U.K.	34	50.22N	4.10W
Tamarite de Litera	50	41.52N	0.26 E
Tamási	46	46.38N	18.18 E
Tamazunchale	106	21.16N	98.47W
Tambacounda	80	13.47N	13.40W
Tamba-kōchi ✱ [1]	64	35.20N	135.30 E
Tambej	58	71.30N	71.50 E
Tambelan, Kepulauan II	72	1.00N	107.30 E
Tambellup	90	34.02S	117.39 E
Tamberías	114	31.28S	69.25W
Tambo	94	24.53S	146.15 E
Tambo ≃, Austl.	94	37.51S	147.48 E
Tambo ≃, Perú	110	17.10S	71.51W
Tamboara	114	23.09S	52.33W
Tambohorano	87b	17.30S	43.58 E
Tamboritha, Mount ∧	94	37.28S	146.41 E
Tambov	60	52.43N	41.25 E
Tambre ≃	50	42.49N	8.53W
Tambunan	72	5.40N	116.22 E
Tambura	82	5.36N	27.28 E
Tamchaket	80	17.15N	10.40W
Tame	110	6.28N	71.44W
Tame ≃	34	52.44N	1.43W
Tâmega ≃	50	41.05N	8.21W
Tamel Aike	112	48.19S	70.58W
Tamenghest	80	22.56N	5.30 E
Tamerton Foliot	34	50.26N	4.08W
Tamiahua	106	21.16N	97.27W
Tamiahua, Laguna de c	106	21.35N	97.35W
Tamiš (Timiş) ≃	54	44.51N	20.39 E
Tamkuhi	76	26.41N	84.11 E
Tam-ky	70	15.34N	108.29 E
Tāmma	76	25.11N	93.42 E
Tämnaren ⊜	44	60.10N	17.20 E
Tampa	100	27.56N	82.27W
Tampa Bay c	100	27.45N	82.35W
Tampere	44	61.30N	23.45 E
Tampico	106	22.13N	97.51W
Tampin	72	2.28N	102.14 E
Tamsagbulag	62	47.14N	117.21 E
Tamsweg	46	47.08N	13.48 E
Tamworth	94	31.05S	150.55 E
Tana	42	70.28N	28.18 E
Tana I	28	19.30S	169.20 E
Tana ≃, Europe	42	70.30N	28.23 E
Tana ≃, Kenya	84	2.32S	40.31 E
Tana, Lake ⊜	82	12.00N	37.20 E
Tanabe	64	33.44N	135.22 E
Tanafjorden c [2]	42	70.54N	28.40 E
Tanahbala, Pulau I	70	0.25S	98.25 E
Tanahgrogot	72	1.55S	116.12 E
Tanahjampea, Pulau I	72	7.05S	120.42 E
Tanahmasa, Pulau I	70	0.12S	98.27 E
Tanahmerah, Indon.	92	6.05S	140.17 E
Tanah Merah, Malay.	72	5.48N	102.09 E
Tanami	90	19.59S	129.43 E
Tanami Desert ✦ [2]	90	20.00S	129.30 E
Tan-an	70	10.32N	106.25 E
Tanana	98	65.10N	152.05W
Tanana ≃	98	65.09N	151.55W
Tananarive → Antananarivo	87b	18.55S	47.31 E
Tanaro ≃	52	45.01N	8.47 E
Tanat ≃	34	52.46N	3.07W
Tanbar	94	25.50S	141.55 E
Tanchoj	58	51.33N	105.07 E
Tanch'ŏn	62	40.27N	128.54 E
Tānda	76	26.33N	82.39 E
Tandag	68	9.04N	126.12 E
Ţăndărei	54	44.38N	27.40 E
Tandil	114	37.19S	59.09W
Tando Ādam	76	25.46N	68.40 E
Tando Allāhyār	76	25.28N	68.43 E
Tando Muhammad Khān	76	25.08N	68.32 E
Tandou Lake ⊜	94	32.38S	142.05 E
Tandragee	40	54.20N	6.25W
Taneatua	96	38.04S	177.01 E
Tanega-shima I	64	30.40N	131.00 E
Taneichi	64	40.26N	141.43 E
Tanew ≃	46	50.31N	22.16 E
Taneytown	102	39.39N	77.10W
Tanezrouft ✦ [2]	80	24.00N	0.45W
Tanga	84	5.04S	39.06 E
Tangail	76	24.15N	89.55 E
Tanga Islands II	28	3.30S	153.15 E
Tanganyika → Tanzania □ [1]	84	6.00S	35.00 E
Tanganyika, Lake ⊜	84	6.00S	29.30 E
Tangará	114	27.08S	51.13W
Tanger (Tangier)	80	35.48N	5.45W
Tangerang	72	6.11S	106.37 E
Tangerhütte	46	52.26N	11.48 E
Tangermünde	46	52.32N	11.58 E
Tanggou	66	33.59N	118.57 E
Tanggu	62	39.01N	117.40 E
Tanggulahu ⊜	76	31.00N	86.20 E
Tanggula Shan ✱	76	33.00N	90.00 E
Tanghe	66	32.43N	112.48 E
Tangi	76	34.18N	71.40 E
Tangier → Tanger	80	35.48N	5.45W
Tangjiagou	66	30.48N	117.28 E
Tangjiang	66	25.51N	114.44 E
Tangmarg	76	34.02N	74.26 E
Tango-hantō › [1]	64	35.40N	135.10 E
Tangowahine	96	35.52S	173.56 E
Tangqi	66	30.29N	120.11 E
Tangra Yumco ⊜	62	31.00N	86.20 E
Tangshan	62	39.38N	118.11 E
Tangxi	66	29.04N	119.23 E
Tangzha	66	32.05N	120.49 E
Tanigawa-dake ∧	64	36.50N	138.56 E
Tanimbar, Kepulauan II	92	7.30S	131.30 E
Taninges	48	46.07N	6.36 E
Tanjore → Thanjāvūr	74	10.48N	79.09 E
Tanjung	72	8.21S	116.09 E
Tanjungbalai	70	2.58N	99.48 E
Tanjungbatu	72	0.38N	103.26 E
Tanjungkarang	72	5.25S	105.16 E
Tanjungmengedar	72	2.39N	100.01 E
Tanjungpandan	72	2.45S	107.39 E
Tanjungpinang	72	0.55N	104.27 E
Tanjungraja	72	3.21S	104.40 E
Tanjungredep	72	2.09N	117.29 E
Tanjungselor	72	2.51N	117.22 E
Tännäs	44	62.27N	12.40 E
Tannila	44	65.29N	25.59 E
Tannis Bugt c	44	57.40N	10.15 E
Tannu-Ola, chrebet ✱	58	51.00N	94.00 E
Tannūrah, Ra's at- ›	78	26.40N	50.30 E
Tânout	80	14.58N	8.53 E
Tanshui	66	25.10N	121.26 E
Ṭanṭā	82	30.47N	31.00 E
Tantou	66	26.03N	119.35 E
Tanumshede	44	58.44N	11.19 E
Tanvald	46	50.45N	15.19 E
Tanworth	34	52.20N	1.50W
Tanworth-in-Arden	34	52.39N	1.40W
Tanzania □ [1]	84	6.00S	35.00 E
Tao ≃	62	35.52N	103.16 E
Tao'er ≃	62	45.42N	124.05 E
Taongi I [1]	28	14.37N	168.58 E
Taormina	52	37.51N	15.17 E
Taoudenni	80	22.40N	4.00W
Taoxi	66	31.33N	117.00 E
Tapa	60	59.16N	25.58 E
Tapachula	106	14.54N	92.17W
Tapah	72	4.11N	101.16 E
Tapajós ≃	110	2.24S	54.41W
Tapalquén	114	36.21S	60.01W
Tapanahony ≃	110	4.22N	54.27W
Tapanui	96	45.57S	169.16 E
Tapauá ≃	110	5.40S	64.21W
Tapawera	96	41.24S	172.49 E
Tapejara	114	28.04S	52.00W
Tapera	114	28.38S	52.52W
Tapes	114	30.40S	51.23W
Taphan Hin	70	16.13N	100.26 E
Tāpi ≃	76	21.06N	72.41 E
Tapiche ≃	110	4.59S	73.51W
Taping (Dayingjiang) ≃	70	24.17N	97.14 E
Tapis, Gunong ∧	72	4.03N	102.54 E
Tapolca	46	46.53N	17.27 E
Tappahannock	102	37.55N	76.51W
Tappi-zaki ›	64	41.15N	140.21 E
Tapuaenuku ∧	96	42.00S	173.40 E
Tapurucuara	110	0.24S	65.02W
Taqāṭu'Hayyā	82	18.20N	36.22 E
Taquara	114	29.39S	50.47W
Taquaras, Ponta das ›	114	27.01S	48.34W
Taquari	114	29.48S	51.51W
Taquari ≃, Bra.	110	19.15S	57.17W
Taquari ≃, Bra.	114	29.56S	51.44W
Taquaritinga	114	21.24S	48.30W
Tara, Austl.	94	27.17S	150.28 E
Tara, S.S.S.R.	58	56.54N	74.22 E
Tara ✱	54	43.55N	19.25 E
Tara ≃	54	43.21N	18.51 E
Taraba ≃	80	8.30N	10.15 E
Ṭarābulus (Tripoli), Lībiyā	82	32.54N	13.11 E
Ṭarābulus (Tripoli), Lubnān	78	34.26N	35.51 E
Ṭarābulus (Tripolitania) □ [9]	82	31.00N	15.00 E
Taradale	96	39.32S	176.51 E
Tarakan	72	3.18N	117.38 E
Taralga	94	34.24S	149.49 E
Taramakau ≃	96	42.34S	171.08 E
Tarancón	50	40.01N	3.00W
Taranga Island I	96	35.58S	174.43 E
Taransay I	38	57.54N	7.01W
Taranto	52	40.28N	17.15 E
Taranto, Golfo di c	52	40.10N	17.20 E
Tarapoto	110	6.30S	76.25W
Taraquá	110	0.06N	68.28W
Tarare	48	45.54N	4.26 E
Tarariras	114	34.17S	57.37W
Tararua Range ✱	96	40.46S	175.23 E
Tarāsa Dwīp I	70	8.15N	93.10 E
Tarascon	48	42.51N	1.36 E
Tarata	110	17.37S	66.01W
Tarauacá	110	8.10S	70.46W
Tarauacá ≃	110	6.42S	69.48W
Taravo ≃	52	41.42N	8.49 E
Tarawa I [1]	28	1.25N	173.00 E
Tarawera	96	39.02S	176.35 E
Tarawera, Lake ⊜	96	38.12S	176.27 E
Tarazona	50	41.54N	1.44W
Tarazona de la Mancha	50	39.15N	1.55W
Tarbagataj, chrebet ✱	56	47.12N	83.00 E
Tarbat Ness ›	38	57.51N	3.47W
Tarbert, Ire.	40	52.32N	9.23W
Tarbert, Scot., U.K.	38	55.52N	5.26W
Tarbert, Scot., U.K.	38	57.54N	6.49W
Tarbert, Loch c	38	55.57N	6.00W
Tarbes	48	43.14N	0.05 E
Tarbet	38	56.12N	4.43W
Tarbolton	38	55.31N	4.29W
Tarbū	82	26.02N	15.10 E
Tarcăului, Munţii ✱	54	46.45N	26.20 E
Tarcento	52	46.13N	13.13 E
Tarcoola	90	30.41S	134.33 E
Tarcoon	94	30.16S	146.43 E
Tardajos	50	42.21N	3.49W
Tardoki-Jani, gora ∧	58	48.55N	138.04 E
Tardun	90	28.48S	115.45 E
Taree	94	31.54S	152.28 E
Tareja	58	73.20N	90.37 E
Tärendö	42	67.10N	22.38 E
Tarentum	102	40.36N	79.45W
Tarfaya	80	27.58N	12.55W
Tarfside	38	56.54N	2.50W
Tarf Water ≃	36	54.55N	4.35W
Targon	48	44.44N	0.16W
Târgovişte	54	43.15N	26.34 E
Tarhūnah	82	32.26N	13.38 E
Tari	92	5.50S	143.00 E
Tarifa	50	36.01N	5.36W
Tarifa, Punta de ›	50	36.00N	5.37W
Tarija	110	21.31S	64.45W
Tariki	96	39.14S	174.15 E
Tariku ≃	92	3.04S	138.09 E
Tarim ≃	62	41.05N	86.40 E
Tarim Pendi ⌣ [1]	62	39.00N	83.00 E
Taritatu ≃	92	2.54S	138.27 E
Tarkastad	86	32.00S	26.16 E
Tarko-Sale	56	64.55N	77.49 E
Tarkwa	80	5.19N	1.59W
Tarlac	68	15.29N	120.35 E
Tarland	38	57.08N	2.52W
Tarleton	36	53.41N	2.50W
Tarm	44	55.55N	8.32 E
Tarma	110	11.25S	75.42W
Tarn □ [5]	48	43.50N	2.00 E
Tarn ≃	48	44.05N	1.06 E
Tarna ≃	46	47.31N	19.59 E
Tärnaby	42	65.43N	15.16 E
Tarna Mare, Rom.	54	48.04N	23.12 E
Tarna Mare, Rom.	54	47.29N	26.20 E
Tarn-et-Garonne □ [5]	48	44.05N	1.20 E
Tarnobrzeg	46	50.35N	21.41 E
Tarnogród	46	50.23N	22.45 E
Tarnów	46	50.01N	21.00 E
Tarnowskie Góry	46	50.27N	18.52 E
Tärnsjö	44	60.09N	16.56 E
Taro ≃	52	45.00N	10.15 E
Tarong	94	26.46S	151.51 E
Taroom	94	25.39S	149.49 E
Tarouca	50	41.00N	7.40W
Tarporley	36	53.09N	2.40W
Tarquinia	52	42.15N	11.45 E
Tarrabool, Lake ⊜	90	18.15S	135.04 E
Tarragona	50	41.07N	1.15 E
Tarraleah	94	42.18S	146.27 E
Tarran Hills ✱ [2]	94	32.27S	146.27 E
Tarrant Hinton	34	50.53N	2.05W
Tarras	96	44.50S	169.25 E
Tarrasa	50	41.34N	2.01 E
Tárrega	50	41.39N	1.09 E
Tarsus	78	36.55N	34.53 E
Tartagal, Arg.	114	22.32S	63.49W
Tartagal, Arg.	114	28.40S	59.52W
Tartas	48	43.50N	0.48W
Tartu	60	58.23N	26.43 E
Ṭarṭūs	78	34.53N	35.53 E
Tarumizu	64	31.29N	130.42 E
Tarusa	60	54.43N	37.11 E
Tarutung	70	2.01N	98.58 E
Tarves	38	57.22N	2.13W
Tarvisio	52	46.30N	13.35 E
Tas ≃	34	52.36N	1.18 E
Tašauz	56	41.50N	59.58 E
Tasejeva ≃	58	58.06N	94.01 E
Tasejevo	58	57.12N	94.54 E
Ṭashk, Daryācheh-ye ⊜	78	29.45N	53.35 E
Tashkent → Taškent	56	41.20N	69.18 E
Tasikmalaya	72	7.20S	108.12 E
Tåsinge I	44	55.00N	10.36 E
Tåsjö	44	64.13N	15.54 E
Tåsjön ⊜	44	64.15N	15.47 E
Taškent	56	41.20N	69.18 E
Taškepri	78	36.18N	62.38 E
Tasman, Mount ∧	96	43.34S	170.09 E
Tasman Basin ✦ [1]	28	43.00S	158.00 E
Tasman Bay c	96	41.00S	173.20 E
Tasmania □ [3]	88	43.00S	147.00 E
Tasmania I	94	42.00S	147.00 E
Tasman Mountains ✱	96	41.07S	172.33 E
Tasman Peninsula › [1]	94	43.05S	147.50 E
Tasman Sea ⊤ [2]	28	40.00S	163.00 E
Tăşnad	54	47.29N	22.35 E
Tassialouc, Lac ⊜	98	59.03N	74.00W
Taštagol	58	52.47N	87.53 E
Tata	46	47.39N	18.18 E
Tatabánya	46	47.34N	18.26 E
Tatarsk	56	55.13N	75.58 E
Tatarskij proliv ⋓	58	50.00N	141.15 E
Tatar Strait → Tatarskij proliv ⋓	58	50.00N	141.15 E
Tate ≃	94	17.22S	143.44 E
Tateyama	64	34.59N	139.52 E
Tate-yama ∧	64	36.35N	137.37 E
Tathlina Lake ⊜	98	60.32N	117.32W
Tathra	94	36.44S	149.59 E
Tatnam, Cape ›	98	57.16N	91.00W
Tatsuno, Nihon	64	34.52N	134.33 E
Tatsuno, Nihon	64	35.59N	137.59 E
Tatta	76	24.45N	67.55 E
Tattenhall	36	53.06N	2.46W
Tatvan	78	38.30N	42.16 E
Tau	44	59.04N	5.54 E
Taubaté	114	23.02S	45.33W
Tauber ≃	46	49.46N	9.31 E
Tauberbischofsheim	46	49.37N	9.40 E
Taučik	56	44.21N	51.19 E
Taujskaja guba c	58	59.20N	150.20 E
Taumarunui	96	38.52S	175.17 E
Taung	86	27.33S	24.47 E
Taungdwingyi	70	20.01N	95.33 E
Taunggyi	70	20.47N	97.02 E
Taungup Pass)(	70	18.40N	94.45 E
Taunton, Eng., U.K.	34	51.01N	3.06W
Taunton, Ma., U.S.	102	41.54N	71.05W
Taunton, Vale of ∨	34	51.02N	3.08W
Taupiri	96	37.37S	175.11 E
Taupo	96	38.41S	176.05 E
Taupo, Lake ⊜	96	38.49S	175.55 E
Taurage	42	55.15N	22.17 E
Tauranga	96	37.42S	176.10 E
Taurianova	52	38.21N	16.01 E
Tauroa Point ›	96	35.10S	173.04 E
Taurus Mountains → Toros Dağları ✱	30	37.00N	33.00 E
Tauste	50	41.55N	1.15W
Tauu Islands II	28	4.45S	157.00 E
Tavaí	114	26.07S	55.32W
Tavda	56	58.03N	65.15 E
Tavda ≃	56	57.47N	67.16 E
Taverham	34	52.41N	1.12 E
Taveuni I	28	16.51S	179.58 E
Tavira	50	37.07N	7.39W
Tavistock, On., Can.	102	43.19N	80.50W
Tavistock, Eng., U.K.	34	50.33N	4.08W
Tavolžan	56	52.44N	77.27 E
Távora ≃	50	41.09N	7.35W
Tavoy	70	14.05N	98.12 E
Tavşanlı	54	39.33N	29.30 E
Tavy ≃	34	50.16N	4.10W
Taw ≃	34	51.04N	4.11W
Tawa	96	41.10S	174.51 E
Tawas City	102	44.16N	83.30W
Tawau	72	4.15N	117.54 E
Tawe ≃	34	51.37N	3.55W
Tawitawi Island I	68	5.10N	120.00 E
Ṭawkar	82	18.26N	37.44 E
Taxco de Alarcón	106	18.33N	99.36W
Taxkorgan	62	37.47N	75.14 E
Tay ≃	38	56.22N	3.21W
Tay, Firth of c [1]	38	56.26N	3.00W

Symbols in the Index entries are identified on page 122.

Tay -Tol

Name Page Lat.°′ Long.°′

Tay, Lake ◎ 90 32.55S 120.48E
Tay, Loch ◎ 38 56.31N 4.10W
Taymā' 78 27.38N 38.29E
Taymyr Peninsula →Tajmyr, poluostrov ≻1 58 76.00N 104.00E
Tay-ninh 70 11.18N 106.06E
Taynuilt 38 56.25N 5.14W
Tayport 38 57.27N 2.53W
Tayside □4 38 56.30N 3.30W
Taytay 68 10.49N 119.31E
Tayu 72 6.32S 111.02E
Taz ≃ 58 67.32N 78.40E
Taza 80 34.16N 4.01W
Tazawa-ko ◎ 64 39.43N 140.40E
Tazin ≃ 98 60.26N 110.45W
Tazin Lake ◎ 98 59.47N 109.03W
Tazovskaja guba c 58 69.05N 76.00E
Tazovskij 56 67.28N 78.42E
Tazovskij poluostrov ≻1 56 68.35N 76.00E
Tbessa 80 35.28N 8.09E
Tbilisi 56 41.43N 44.49E
Tchibanga 84 2.51S 11.02E
Tchien 80 6.04N 8.08W
Tczew 46 54.06N 18.47E
Teaca 54 46.55N 24.31E
Te Anau 96 45.25S 167.43E
Te Anau, Lake ◎ 96 45.12S 167.48E
Teangue 38 57.07N 5.50W
Teano 52 41.15N 14.04E
Teapa 106 17.33N 92.57W
Te Araroa 96 37.38S 178.22E
Te Aroha 96 37.33S 175.43E
Tea Tree 90 22.11S 133.17E
Te Awamutu 96 38.01S 175.19E
Teba 50 36.58N 4.56W
Tebakang 72 1.06N 110.30E
Tebay 36 54.26N 2.35W
Tebicuary ≃ 114 26.36S 58.16W
Tebingtinggi 70 3.20N 99.09E
Tebingtinggi, Pulau I 72 0.54N 102.45E
Tecate 104 32.34N 116.38W
Tech ≃ 48 42.36N 3.03E
Techirghiol 54 44.03N 28.36E
Tecka 112 43.29S 70.48W
Tecklenburg 46 52.13N 7.48E
Tecopa 104 35.50N 116.13W
Tecpan de Galeana 106 17.15N 100.41W
Tecuci 54 45.50N 27.26E
Tecumseh 102 42.00N 83.56W
Tedžen 78 37.23N 60.31E
Tedžen (Harīrūd) ≃ 78 37.24N 60.38E
Teeli 58 51.07N 90.14E
Teels Marsh ⩩ 104 38.12N 118.21W
Tees ≃ 36 54.34N 1.16W
Tees Bay c 36 54.39N 1.07W
Teesdale v 36 54.38N 2.07W
Teeswater 102 44.00N 81.17W
Tefé 110 3.22S 64.42W
Tefé ≃ 110 3.35S 64.47W
Tegal 72 6.52S 109.08E
Tegernsee 46 47.43N 11.45E
Tegid, Llyn ◎ 36 52.53N 3.36W
Tegucigalpa 108 14.06N 87.13W
Tehachapi 104 35.07N 118.26W
Tehachapi Mountains ⊀ 104 35.00N 118.40W
Tehachapi Pass)(104 35.06N 118.18W
Te Hapua 96 34.31S 172.54E
Te Haroto 96 39.08S 176.36E
Tehek Lake ◎ 98 64.55N 95.38W
Teheran →Tehrān 78 35.40N 51.26E
Tehrān 78 35.40N 51.26E
Tehri 76 30.23N 78.29E
Tehuacán 106 18.27N 97.23W
Tehuantepec 106 16.20N 95.14W
Tehuantepec, Golfo de c 106 16.00N 94.50W
Tehuantepec, Istmo de ⊥3 106 17.00N 95.00W
Tehuantepec Ridge ⊹3 22 13.30N 98.00W
Teide, Pico de ▲ 80 28.16N 16.38W
Teifi ≃ 34 52.07N 4.42W
Teifiside ⊹1 34 52.02N 4.22W
Teign ≃ 34 50.33N 3.29W
Teignmouth 34 50.33N 3.30W
Teith ≃ 38 56.08N 3.59W
Teixeira Soares 114 25.22S 50.27W
Tejakula 72 8.08S 115.20E
Tejkovo 60 56.52N 40.34E
Tejo →Tagus ≃ 50 38.40N 9.24W
Tejon Pass)(104 34.48N 118.52W
Te Kaha 96 37.44S 177.41E
Te Kao 96 34.39S 172.57E
Tekapo, Lake ◎ 96 43.53S 170.31E
Te Karaka 96 38.28S 177.52E
Te Kauwhata 96 37.24S 175.09E
Tekeli 56 44.48N 78.57E
Tekeze ≃ 82 14.20N 35.50E
Tekirdağ 30 40.59N 27.31E
Tekonsha 102 42.05N 84.59W
Te Kopuru 96 36.02S 173.56E
Te Kuiti 96 38.20S 175.10E
Tela 108 15.44N 87.27W
Telavåg 44 60.16N 4.49E
Tel Aviv-Yafo 78 32.03N 34.46E
Telč 46 49.11N 15.27E
Telechany 60 52.31N 25.51E
Teleckoje, ozero ◎ 58 51.35N 87.40E
Telefomin 92 5.10S 141.35E
Telegraph Creek 98 57.55N 131.10W
Telemark □6 44 59.30N 8.40E
Telén 114 36.16S 65.30W
Telen ≃ 72 0.26S 116.42E
Teleño ▲ 50 42.21N 6.23W
Teleorman □6 54 44.00N 25.15E
Teleorman ≃ 54 43.52N 25.26E
Telerig 54 43.51N 27.40E
Telertheba, Djebel ▲ 80 24.10N 6.51E
Telescope Peak ▲ 104 36.10N 117.05W
Telford 34 52.40N 2.28W
Telfs 46 47.18N 11.04E
Telok Anson 70 4.02N 101.01E
Telsen 112 42.24S 66.57W
Telšiai 60 55.59N 22.15E
Telti 52 40.52N 9.21E
Teltow 46 52.23N 13.16E
Telukbayur 72 1.00S 100.22E
Telukbetung 72 5.27S 105.16E
Telukdalem 70 0.34N 97.49E
Temagami, Lake ◎ 98 47.00N 80.05W
Tematagi I1 28 21.41S 140.40W
Temax 106 21.09N 88.56W
Tembeling ≃ 72 4.04N 102.20E
Tembenči ≃ 58 64.36N 99.58E
Tembesi ≃ 72 1.43S 103.06E
Tembilahan 72 0.19S 103.09E
Temblador 108 8.59N 62.44W
Tembleque 50 39.42N 3.30W
Temblor Range ⊀ 104 35.20N 119.55W
Tembuland □9 86 31.30S 27.40E
Teme ≃ 34 52.09N 2.18W
Temecula 104 33.29N 117.08W
Temerin 54 45.24N 19.53E
Temerloh 72 3.27N 102.25E
Teminabuan 92 1.26S 132.01E
Temir 56 49.08N 57.06E
Temirtau, S.S.S.R. 56 50.05N 72.56E
Temirtau, S.S.S.R. 58 53.08N 87.28E
Temora 94 34.26S 147.32E
Tempe 100 33.24N 111.54W
Temperance 102 41.46N 83.34W
Tempio Pausania 52 40.54N 9.06E
Temple 100 31.05N 97.20W
Templecombe 34 51.00N 2.25W
Temple Ewell 34 51.09N 1.16E
Templemore 40 52.48N 7.50W
Temple Sowerby 36 54.39N 2.35W
Templeton 94 18.26S 142.28E
Templeton ≃ 94 21.14S 138.13E
Templin 46 53.07N 13.30E
Tempy 60 56.38N 37.18E
Temr'uk 56 45.17N 37.23E
Temuco 114 38.44S 72.36W
Temuka 96 44.15S 171.17E
Tena 110 0.59S 77.49W
Tenāli 74 16.15N 80.35E
Tenasserim 70 12.05N 99.01E
Tenasserim □8 70 12.00N 99.00E
Tenbury Wells 34 52.19N 2.35W
Tenby 34 51.41N 4.43W
Tendaho 82 11.48N 40.52E
Tende 48 44.05N 7.36E
Tende, Col de)(48 44.09N 7.34E
Ten Degree Channel ꭒ 70 10.00N 93.00E
Tendō 64 38.21N 140.22E
Tenente Portela 114 27.22S 53.45W
Ténéré ⊹2 80 19.00N 10.30E
Tenerife I 80 28.19N 16.34W
Tengchong 70 25.04N 98.29E
Tenggarong 72 0.24S 116.58E
Tenggol, Pulau I 72 4.48N 103.38E
Tenghilan 72 6.14N 116.19E
Tengiz, ozero ◎ 56 50.24N 68.57E
Tengtiaohe (Na) ≃ 70 22.05N 103.09E
Tengxian, Zhg. 62 35.08N 117.10E
Tengxian, Zhg. 70 23.21N 110.53E
Tenke 84 10.35S 26.07E
Tenkeli 58 70.01N 140.58E
Tenkodogo 80 11.47N 0.22W
Tenmile Creek ≃ 102 40.08N 80.22W
Tennant Creek 90 19.40S 134.10E
Tennessee □3 100 35.50N 85.30W
Tennessee ≃ 100 37.04N 88.33W
Teno 114 34.52S 71.11W
Tenom 72 5.08N 115.57E
Tenosique de Pino Suárez 106 17.29N 91.26W
Tenryū 64 34.52N 137.49E
Tenryū ≃ 64 34.39N 137.47E
Tenterden 34 51.05N 0.42E
Tenterfield 94 29.03S 152.01E
Ten Thousand Islands II 108 25.50N 81.33W
Teodelina 114 34.11S 61.32W
Tepa 92 7.52S 129.31E
Tepatitlán 106 20.49N 102.44W
Tepelenë 54 40.18N 20.01E
Tepic 106 21.30N 104.54W
Teplice 46 50.39N 13.48E
Te Pohue 96 39.15S 176.41E
Te Puia 96 38.04S 178.18E
Te Puke 96 37.47S 176.20E
Ter ≃, Esp. 50 42.01N 3.12E
Ter ≃, Eng., U.K. 34 51.50N 0.36E
Téra 80 14.01N 0.45E
Tera ≃ 50 41.54N 5.44W
Teradomari 64 37.38N 138.46E
Teraina I 28 4.43N 160.24W
Teramo 52 42.39N 13.42E
Terang 94 38.14S 142.55E
Terceira I 20 38.43N 27.13W
Tercero ≃ 114 32.55S 62.19W
Terechovka 60 52.13N 31.27E
Te Rehunga 96 40.13S 176.01E
Terek ≃ 56 43.44N 46.33E
Terengganu □3 72 5.00N 103.00E
Terengganu ≃ 72 5.17N 103.05E
Teresina 110 5.05S 42.49W
Teresópolis 110 22.26S 42.59W
Terespol 46 52.05N 23.36E
Teriang ≃ 72 3.19N 102.31E
Terib'orka 42 69.08N 35.08E
Terjärv (Teerijärvi) 44 63.32N 23.30E
Termez 56 37.14N 67.16E
Termini Imerese 52 37.59N 13.42E
Termini Imerese, Golfo di c 52 38.01N 13.45E
Terminillo, Monte ▲ 52 42.28N 13.00E
Términos, Laguna de c 106 18.37N 91.33W
Termoli 52 42.00N 15.00E
Termonde →Dendermonde 46 51.02N 4.07E
Tern ≃ 34 52.47N 2.32W
Ternate 68 0.48N 127.24E
Ternberg 46 47.58N 14.22E
Ternej 58 45.03N 136.37E
Terneuzen 46 51.20N 3.50E
Terni 52 42.34N 12.37E
Ternitz 46 47.44N 16.03E
Ternopol' 56 49.34N 25.36E
Terpenija, mys ≻ 58 48.39N 144.44E
Terpenija, zaliv c 58 49.00N 143.30E
Terra Alta 102 39.26N 79.32W
Terra Bella 104 35.58N 119.03W
Terra Boa 114 23.45S 52.27W
Terrace 98 54.31N 128.35W
Terracina 52 41.17N 13.15E
Terralba 52 39.43N 8.39E
Terra Rica 114 22.43S 52.38W
Terra Roxa d'Oeste 114 24.08S 53.59W
Terrasson-la-Villedieu 48 45.08N 1.18E
Terre Haute 100 39.28N 87.24W
Terrington Saint Clement 34 52.45N 0.18E
Terschelling I 46 53.24N 5.20E
Teruel 50 40.21N 1.06W
Tervakoski 44 60.48N 24.37E
Tervel 54 43.45N 27.24E
Tervola 44 66.05N 24.48E
Tešanj 54 44.37N 18.00E
Tes-Chem (Tesijn) ≃ 58 50.28N 93.04E
Teseney 82 15.07N 36.41E
Teshikaga 64a 43.29N 144.28E
Teshio 64a 44.53N 141.44E
Teshio ≃ 64a 44.53N 141.44E
Teshio-sanchi ⊀ 64a 44.15N 142.05E
Tesijn (Tes-Chem) ≃ 58 50.28N 93.04E
Teslić 54 44.37N 17.51E
Teslin 98 60.09N 132.45W
Teslin ≃ 98 61.34N 134.54W
Teslin Lake ◎ 98 60.15N 132.57W
Tessalit 80 20.12N 1.00E
Tessaoua 80 13.45N 7.59E
Tessy-sur-Vire 48 48.58N 1.04W
Test ≃ 34 50.55N 1.29W
Testa, Capo ≻ 52 41.14N 9.08E
Têt ≃ 48 42.44N 3.02E
Tetas, Punta ≻ 114 23.31S 70.38W
Tetbury 34 51.39N 2.10W
Tete 84 16.13S 33.35E
Te Teko 96 38.02S 176.48E
Teterow 46 53.46N 12.34E
Teteven 54 42.55N 24.16E
Tetiaroa I1 28 17.05S 149.32W
Tetica de Bacares ▲ 50 37.15N 2.25W
Tétouan 80 35.34N 5.23W
Tetovo 54 42.01N 20.58E
Tetschen →Děčín 46 50.48N 14.13E
Tettenhall 34 52.36N 2.09W
Tet'uši 42 54.57N 48.50E
Teuco ≃ 114 25.38S 60.12W
Teulada 52 38.58N 8.46E
Teun, Pulau I 92 6.59S 129.08E
Teuri-tō I 64a 44.25N 141.19E
Teutoburger Wald ⊹3 46 52.10N 8.15E
Teuva 44 62.29N 21.44E
Tevere (Tiber) ≃ 52 41.44N 12.14E
Teverya 78 32.47N 35.32E
Teviot ≃ 38 55.36N 2.26W
Teviotdale v 36 55.25N 2.50W
Teviothead 38 55.21N 2.56W
Te Waewae Bay c 96 46.15S 167.30E
Te Whaiti 96 38.35S 176.47E
Tewkesbury 34 51.59N 2.09W
Texarkana 100 33.25N 94.02W
Texas 94 28.51S 151.11E
Texas □3 100 31.30N 99.00W
Texas City 100 29.23N 94.54W
Texel I 46 53.05N 4.45E
Texoma, Lake ◎1 100 33.55N 96.37W
Teynham 34 51.20N 0.50E
Teyvareh 76 33.21N 64.25E
Teziutlán 106 19.49N 97.21W
Tezpur 76 26.37N 92.48E
Tha-anne ≃ 98 60.31N 94.37W
Thabana-Ntlenyana ▲ 86 29.28S 29.16E
Thaba Nchu 86 29.17S 26.52E
Thabazimbi 86 24.41S 27.21E
Thai-binh 70 20.27N 106.20E
Thailand (Prathet Thai) □1 68 15.00N 100.00E
Thailand, Gulf of c 70 10.00N 101.00E
Thai-nguyen 70 21.36N 105.50E
Thal 76 33.22N 70.33E
Thal Desert ⊹2 76 31.30N 71.40E
Thale 46 51.45N 11.02E
Thalfang 46 49.45N 6.59E
Thālith, Ash-Shallāl ath- ⱶ 82 19.49N 30.19E
Thallon 94 28.38S 148.52E
Thalwil 48 47.17N 8.34E
Thame 34 51.45N 0.59W
Thames 96 37.08S 175.33E
Thames ≃, On., Can. 102 42.19N 82.27W
Thames ≃, Eng., U.K. 34 51.28N 0.43E
Thamesford 102 43.04N 81.00W
Thamesville 102 42.33N 81.59W
Thāna 74 19.12N 72.58E
Thanet, Isle of I 34 51.22N 1.20E
Thangoo 90 18.10S 122.22E
Thangool 94 24.29S 150.35E
Thanh-hoa 70 19.48N 105.46E
Thanh-pho Ho Chi Minh (Sai-gon) 70 10.45N 106.40E
Thanjāvūr 74 10.48N 79.09E
Thann 48 47.49N 7.05E
Thar Desert (Great Indian Desert) ⊹2 76 27.00N 71.00E
Thargomindah 94 28.00S 143.49E
Tharrawaddy 70 17.39N 95.48E
Tharsuinn, Beinn ▲ 38 57.47N 4.21W
Thásos 54 40.47N 24.42E
Thásos I 54 40.41N 24.47E
Thatcham 34 51.25N 1.15W
Thaton 70 16.55N 97.22E
Thau, Bassin de c 48 43.23N 3.36E
Thaungyin ≃ 70 17.50N 97.42E
Thaxted 34 51.57N 0.20E
Thaya (Dyje) ≃ 46 48.37N 16.56E
Thayetmyo 70 19.19N 95.11E
Thazi 70 20.51N 96.05E
The Aldermen Islands II 96 36.58S 176.05E
Theale 34 51.27N 1.04W
Thealka 102 37.49N 82.47W
Thebes →Thívai 54 38.21N 23.19E
The Bight 108 24.19N 75.24W
The Cheviot ▲ 36 55.28N 2.09W
The Dalles 100 45.35N 121.10W
The Deeps c 38a 60.09N 1.23W
The Downs ⊹3 34 51.13N 1.27E
Theebine 94 25.57S 152.33E
The English Companys Islands II 92 11.50S 136.32E
The Everglades ⩩ 100 26.00N 80.40W
The Father ▲ 92 5.03S 151.20E
The Fens ⩩ 34 52.38N 0.02E
The Glenkens ⊹1 36 55.10N 4.15W
The Granites 90 20.35S 130.21E
The Granites ▲ 90 20.35S 130.20E
The Hague →'s-Gravenhage 46 52.06N 4.18E
The Heads ≻ 104 42.44N 124.31W
The Hunters Hills ⊀2 96 44.30S 170.50E
Thelon ≃ 98 64.16N 96.05W
The Long Mynd ▲ 34 52.35N 2.48W
The Lynd 94 18.56S 144.30E
The Machars □8 36 54.50N 4.30W
The Machars ⊹1 36 55.20N 4.33W
The Minch ꭒ 38 58.10N 5.50W
The Moors ⊹1 36 54.56N 4.40W
The Mumbles 34 51.34N 4.00W
The Naze ≻ 34 51.53N 1.16E
The Needles ≻ 34 50.39N 1.34W
Thénezay 48 46.43N 0.02W
The Oa ⊹1 38 55.37N 6.16W
Theodore 94 24.57S 150.05E
Theólogos 54 40.39N 24.41E
The Paps ▲ 40 52.00N 9.17W
The Pas 98 53.50N 101.15W
The Pilot ▲ 94 36.45S 148.13E
The Rand →Witwatersrand ⊹1 86 26.00S 27.00E
Theresa 102 44.12N 75.47W
The Rhins ≻1 36 54.50N 5.00W
Thermaïkós Kólpos c 54 40.23N 22.47E
Thermopílai ⊥ 54 38.48N 22.33E
Thermopolis 100 43.38N 108.12W
Thermopylae →Thermopílai ⊥ 54 38.48N 22.33E
The Road c 34a 49.56N 6.20W
The Rock 94 35.16S 147.07E
Thesiger Bay c 98 71.30N 124.05W
The Solent ꭒ 34 50.46N 1.20W
The Sound ꭒ 44 55.50N 12.40E
Thesprotikón 54 39.15N 20.47E
Thessalia □9 54 39.30N 22.00E
Thessalon 102 46.15N 83.34W
Thessaloníki (Salonika) 54 40.38N 22.56E
The Storr ▲ 38 57.31N 6.12W
The Swale ꭒ 34 51.22N 0.56E
Thet ≃ 34 52.27N 0.33E
Thetford 34 52.25N 0.45E
Thetford-Mines 102 46.05N 71.18W
The Thumbs ▲ 96 43.35S 170.44E
The Twelve Pins ▲ 40 53.31N 9.50W
The Twins ▲ 96 41.14S 172.39E
Theunissen 86 28.30S 26.41E
The Valley 108 18.13N 63.04W
Thevenard 90 32.09S 133.38E
Thevenard Island I 90 21.27S 115.00E
The Wash c 34 52.55N 0.15E
The Weald ⊹1 34 51.05N 0.20E
The Wrekin ▲2 34 52.41N 2.34W
Thief River Falls 100 48.07N 96.10W
Thielsen, Mount ▲ 104 43.09N 122.04W
Thiene 52 45.42N 11.29E
Thiers 48 45.51N 3.34E
Thiès 80 14.48N 16.56W
Thiesi 52 40.31N 8.43E
Thika 84 1.03S 37.05E
Thimbu 76 27.28N 89.39E
Thingvallavatn ◎ 42a 64.12N 21.10W
Thingvellir 42a 64.17N 21.07W
Thionville 48 49.22N 6.10E
Thira 54 36.25N 25.26E
Thíra I 54 36.24N 25.29E
Thirlmere ◎ 36 54.33N 3.04W
Thirsk 36 54.14N 1.20W
Thisted 44 56.57N 8.42E
Thistilfjördur c 42a 66.20N 15.25W
Thistle Island I 94 35.00S 136.09E
Thívai (Thebes) 54 38.21N 23.19E
Thiviers 48 45.25N 0.56E
Thizy 48 46.02N 4.19E
Thjórsá ≃ 42a 63.47N 20.48W
Thlewiaza ≃ 98 60.28N 94.45W
Thoa ≃ 98 60.30N 109.47W
Tho-chu, Dao II 70 9.20N 103.28E
Thohoyandou 86 23.00S 30.29E
Thomas 102 39.08N 79.29W
Thomaston, Ct., U.S. 102 41.40N 73.04W
Thomaston, Me., U.S. 102 44.04N 69.10W
Thomastown 40 52.31N 7.08W
Thomasville 100 30.50N 83.58W
Thomes Creek ≃ 104 39.59N 122.06W
Thompson 98 55.45N 97.45W
Thompson Peak ▲ 104 41.00N 123.03W
Thompson Sound ꭒ 96 45.09S 166.57E
Thomsen ≃ 98 74.08N 119.35W
Thomson ≃ 94 25.11S 142.53E
Thongwa 70 16.46N 96.32E
Thonon-les-Bains 48 46.22N 6.29E
Thonze 70 17.38N 95.47E
Thórisvatn ◎ 42a 64.50N 19.26W
Thorlákshöfn 42a 63.53N 21.18W
Thormanby 36 54.10N 1.14W
Thornaby-on-Tees 36 54.34N 1.18W
Thornbury, On., Can. 102 44.34N 80.26W
Thornbury, N.Z. 96 46.17S 168.06E
Thornbury, Eng., U.K. 34 51.37N 2.32W
Thorndon 34 52.17N 1.08E
Thorne 36 53.37N 0.58W
Thorney 34 52.37N 0.07W
Thorngumbald 36 53.43N 0.10W
Thornhill 36 55.15N 3.46W
Thornton, Eng., U.K. 36 53.53N 3.02W
Thornton, Scot., U.K. 38 56.10N 3.09W
Thornton Dale 36 54.14N 0.43W
Thorpe-le-Soken 34 51.52N 1.10E
Thorshavn →Tórshavn 30 62.01N 6.46W
Thórshöfn 42a 66.13N 15.17W
Thouars 48 46.59N 0.13W
Thouin, Cape ≻ 90 20.20S 118.12E
Thousand Oaks 104 34.10N 118.50W
Thousand Springs Creek ≃ 104 41.17N 113.51W
Thrace □9 54 41.20N 26.45E
Thrakikón Pélagos ⊹2 54 40.15N 24.28E
Thrapston 34 52.24N 0.32W
Three Hummock Island I 94 40.26S 144.55E
Three Kings Islands II 96 34.10S 172.05E
Three Pagodas Pass)(70 15.18N 98.23E
Three Points, Cape ≻ 80 4.45N 2.06W
Three Rivers 90 25.07S 119.09E
Three Sisters 86 31.54S 23.06E
Three Springs 90 29.32S 115.45E
Threlkeld 36 54.38N 3.03W
Throckley 36 54.59N 1.45W
Throssel, Lake ◎ 90 27.24S 124.16E
Throssel Range ⊀ 90 22.03S 121.43E
Thrushel ≃ 34 50.39N 4.15W
Thueyts 48 44.41N 4.13E
Thuin 46 50.20N 4.17E
Thule 22 76.34N 68.47W
Thun 48 46.45N 7.37E
Thunder Bay 98 48.23N 89.15W
Thunder Bay c 102 45.00N 83.22W
Thunder Bay ≃ 102 45.04N 83.25W
Thunersee ◎ 48 46.40N 7.45E
Thurcroft 36 53.24N 1.16W
Thüringen □9 46 51.00N 11.00E
Thüringer Wald ⊀ 46 50.40N 10.50E
Thurles 40 52.41N 7.49W
Thurmont 102 39.37N 77.24W
Thurnscoe 36 53.31N 1.19W
Thurnwald Range ⊀ 92 4.45S 141.15E
Thursby 36 54.51N 3.03W
Thursday Island 92 10.35S 142.13E
Thurso 38 58.35N 3.32W
Thurso ≃ 38 58.36N 3.30W
Thurston 34 52.15N 0.49E
Thurston Island I 24 72.20S 99.00W
Thury-Harcourt 48 48.59N 0.29W
Thusis 48 46.42N 9.26E
Thy ⊹1 44 57.00N 8.30E
Thyborøn 44 56.42N 8.13E
Thylungra 94 26.04S 143.28E
Thyolo 84 16.10S 35.10E
Tía Juana 108 10.16N 71.22W
Tianchang 66 32.41N 119.01E
Tiandong 70 23.36N 107.08E
Tianjin (Tientsin) 62 39.08N 117.12E
Tianjun 62 37.25N 98.58E
Tianlin 70 24.14N 106.03E
Tianmen 66 30.39N 113.06E
Tianmu Shan ⊀ 66 30.25N 119.30E
Tianshui 62 34.30N 105.58E
Tiantai 66 29.09N 121.02E
Tianwangsi 66 31.45N 119.12E
Tianyang 70 23.51N 106.34E
Tianzhu 62 37.14N 102.59E
Tiaro 94 25.44S 152.35E
Tibagi 114 24.30S 50.24W
Tibasti, Sarīr ⊹2 82 24.00N 17.00E
Tibbermore 38 56.22N 3.32W
Tiber →Tevere ≃ 52 41.44N 12.14E
Tiberias →Teverya 78 32.47N 35.32E
Tibesti ⊀ 82 21.30N 17.30E
Tibet →Xizang Zizhiqu □4 62 32.00N 88.00E
Tibleş, Munţii ⊀ 54 47.38N 24.05E
Tibro 44 58.26N 14.10E
Tiburón, Isla I 106 29.00N 112.23W
Ticehurst 34 51.03N 0.25E
Tichít 80 18.28N 9.30W
Tichmenevo 60 58.00N 38.36E
Tichoreck 56 45.51N 40.09E
Tichvin 60 59.39N 33.31E
Ticino ≃ 52 45.09N 9.14E
Tickhill 36 53.26N 1.06W
Ticonderoga 102 43.50N 73.25W
Tidaholm 44 58.11N 13.57E
Tideswell 36 53.16N 1.46W
Tidioute 102 41.41N 79.24W
Tidjikja 80 18.33N 11.25W
Tidore 68 0.40N 127.26E
Tiel 46 51.54N 5.25E
Tieli 62 46.59N 128.02E
Tieling 62 42.18N 123.49E
Tielt 46 51.00N 3.19E
T'ienchung 66 23.52N 120.35E
Tienen 46 50.48N 4.57E
Tien Shan ⊀ 62 42.00N 80.00E
Tientsin →Tianjin 62 39.08N 117.12E
Tierga 50 41.37N 1.36W
Tierp 44 60.20N 17.30E
Tierra Amarilla 114 27.29S 70.17W
Tierra de Campos ⊹1 50 42.10N 4.50W
Tierra del Fuego, Isla Grande de I 112 54.00S 69.00W
Tietar ≃ 50 39.50N 6.01W
Tietê 114 23.07S 47.43W
Tietê ≃ 114 21.30S 49.45W
Tiffin 102 41.07N 83.11W
Tifton 100 31.27N 83.30W
Tiga, Pulau I 72 5.43N 115.39E
Tighvein ▲2 38 55.30N 5.10W
Tigil' 58 57.48N 158.40E
Tigre ≃, Perú 110 4.26S 74.05W
Tigre ≃, Ven. 108 9.20N 62.30W
Tigris (Dicle) (Dijlah) ≃ 78 31.00N 47.25E
Tiguabos 108 20.14N 75.21W
Tiguentourine 80 27.50N 9.18E
Tihert 80 35.28N 1.21E
Tijesno 52 43.48N 15.39E
Tijuana 106 32.32N 117.01W
Tijuana ≃ 104 32.33N 117.07W
Tijucas 114 27.14S 48.38W
Tijucas do Sul 114 25.55S 49.12W
Tikei, Île I 28 14.58S 144.32W
Tikitiki 96 37.48S 178.24E
Tiko 80 4.05N 9.22E
Tikokino 96 39.49S 176.27E
Tikrīt 78 34.36N 43.42E
Tiksi 58 71.36N 128.48E
Tilamuta 72 0.30N 122.20E
Tilburg 46 51.34N 5.05E
Tilbury, On., Can. 102 42.16N 82.26W
Tilbury, Eng., U.K. 34 51.28N 0.23E
Tilcara 114 23.34S 65.22W
Tilcha 94 29.36S 140.54E
Tilemsi, Vallée du v 80 16.15N 0.02E
Tilhar 76 27.59N 79.44E
Tilimsen 80 34.52N 1.15W
Tilisarao 114 32.44S 65.18W
Till ≃, Eng., U.K. 36 53.16N 0.37W
Till ≃, Eng., U.K. 38 55.41N 2.12W
Tillaberi 80 14.13N 1.27E
Tillanchāng Dwīp I 70 8.30N 93.37E
Tillberga 44 59.41N 16.37E
Tillicoultry 38 56.09N 3.45W
Tillson 102 41.49N 74.04W
Tillsonburg 102 42.51N 80.44W
Tillyfourie 38 57.11N 2.35W
Tilos I 54 36.25N 27.25E
Tilpa 94 30.57S 144.24E
Tilsit →Sovetsk 60 55.05N 21.53E
Tilt ≃ 38 56.46N 3.50W
Tilton 102 43.26N 71.35W
Tiltonsville 102 40.10N 80.41W
Timanskij kr'až ▲ 56 65.00N 51.00E
Timaru 96 44.24S 171.15E
Timbákion 54 35.04N 24.46E
Timbedgha 80 16.15N 8.10W
Timbó 114 26.50S 49.18W
Timboon 94 38.29S 142.59E
Timbuktu →Tombouctou 80 16.46N 3.01W
Timimoun 80 29.14N 0.16E
Timir'azevskij 58 56.29N 84.54E
Timirist, Râs ≻ 80 19.23N 16.32W
Timiş □6 54 45.40N 21.20E
Timiş (Tamiš) ≃ 54 44.51N 20.39E
Timişoara 54 45.45N 21.13E
Timmendorfer Strand 46 54.00N 10.46E
Timmernabben 44 56.58N 16.26E
Timmins 98 48.28N 81.20W
Timok ≃ 54 44.13N 22.40E
Timor I 72 9.00S 125.00E
Timor Sea ⊹2 68 11.00S 128.00E
Timor Timur □4 72 8.35S 126.00E
Timor Trough ⊹1 28 9.50S 126.00E
Timotes 108 8.59N 70.44W
Timpton ≃ 58 58.43N 127.12E
Timšer 56 62.06N 54.45E
Tina ≃ 86 31.18S 29.14E
Tinaca Point ≻ 68 5.33N 125.20E
Tinaco 108 9.42N 68.26W
Tinahely 40 52.48N 6.28W
Tinapagee 94 29.28S 144.23E
Tinaquillo 108 9.55N 68.18W
Tindouf 80 27.50N 8.04W
Tineo 50 43.20N 6.25W
Tinggi, Pulau I 72 2.18N 104.07E
Tingha 94 29.57S 151.13E
Tinghert, Plateau du (Hamādat Tinghert) ⊹1 80 29.00N 9.00E
Tinglev 44 54.56N 9.15E
Tingo María 110 9.09S 75.56W
Tingsryd 44 56.32N 14.59E
Tingstäde 44 57.44N 18.36E
Tingvoll 44 62.54N 8.12E
Tingvollfjorden c2 44 62.50N 8.11E
Tingwon Group II 92 2.35S 149.45E
Tinharé, Ilha de I 110 13.30S 38.58W
Tinian I 68 15.00N 145.38E
Tinkisso ≃ 80 11.21N 9.10W
Tinnoset 44 59.43N 9.02E
Tinnsjø ◎ 44 59.54N 8.55E
Tinogasta 114 28.04S 67.34W
Tinos 54 37.32N 25.10E
Tinos I 54 37.38N 25.10E
Tinsukia 76 27.30N 95.22E
Tintagel 34 50.40N 4.45W
Tintagel Head ≻ 34 50.41N 4.46W
Tinte, Cerro ▲ 114 22.40S 67.02W
Tintern Parva 34 51.42N 2.40W
Tintina 114 27.02S 62.43W
Tintinara 94 35.54S 140.03E
Tinto ▲ 38 55.36N 3.39W
Tinto ≃ 50 37.12N 6.55W
Tinui 96 40.53S 176.04E
Tinwald 96 43.55S 171.43E
Tioga 102 41.55N 77.08W
Tioga ≃ 102 42.09N 77.05W
Tiojala 44 61.10N 23.52E
Tioman, Pulau I 72 2.48N 104.10E
Tione di Trento 52 46.02N 10.43E
Tionesta 102 41.30N 79.27W
Tionesta Creek ≃ 102 41.28N 79.22W
Tioro, Selat ꭒ 72 4.40S 122.20E
Tioughnioga ≃ 102 42.14N 75.51W
Tipitapa 108 12.12N 86.06W
Tipperary, Austl. 92 13.44S 131.02E
Tipperary, Ire. 40 52.29N 8.10W
Tipperary □6 40 52.40N 8.20W
Tipton, Eng., U.K. 34 52.32N 2.05W
Tipton, Ca., U.S. 104 36.03N 119.18W
Tipton, Mount ▲ 104 35.32N 114.12W
Tip Top Mountain ▲ 98 48.16N 85.59W
Tiptree 34 51.49N 0.45E
Tiracambu, Serra do ⊀1 110 3.15S 46.30W
Tirān, Jazīrat I 78 27.56N 34.34E
Tirān, Madīq ꭒ 78 27.58N 34.28E
Tirana →Tiranë 54 41.20N 19.50E
Tiranë 54 41.20N 19.50E
Tirano 52 46.13N 10.10E
Tiraspol' 56 46.51N 29.38E
Tirat Karmel 78 32.46N 34.58E
Tirau 96 37.59S 175.45E
Tire 54 38.04N 27.45E
Tiree I 38 56.31N 6.49W
Tîrgovişte 54 44.56N 25.27E
Tîrgu Bujor 54 45.52N 27.54E
Tîrgu-Cărbuneşti 54 44.58N 23.31E
Tîrgu-Frumos 54 47.13N 27.00E
Tîrgu-Jiu 54 45.02N 23.17E
Tîrgu-Lăpuş 54 47.27N 23.52E
Tîrgu Mureş 54 46.33N 24.33E
Tîrgu-Neamţ 54 47.12N 26.22E
Tîrgu-Ocna 54 46.15N 26.37E
Tîrgu-Secuiesc 54 46.00N 26.08E
Tirgusor 54 44.28N 28.25E
Tirich Mīr ▲ 76 36.15N 71.50E
Tîrnava Mare ≃ 54 46.09N 23.42E
Tîrnava Mică ≃ 54 46.11N 23.55E
Tîrnăveni 54 46.20N 24.17E
Tirnavos 54 39.45N 22.17E
Tirnovo →Veliko Tărnovo 54 43.04N 25.39E
Tirol □3 46 47.15N 11.20E
Tirry ≃ 38 58.02N 4.26W
Tirschenreuth 46 49.53N 12.21E
Tirso ≃ 52 39.53N 8.32E
Tiruchchirāppalli 74 10.49N 78.41E
Tirunelveli 74 8.44N 77.42E
Tiruppur 74 11.06N 77.21E
Tisa (Tisza) ≃ 54 45.15N 20.17E
Tisbury 34 51.04N 2.03W
Tisdale 98 52.51N 104.04W
Tisisat Falls ⱶ 82 11.29N 37.35E
Tisjön ◎ 44 60.55N 12.58E
Tisnaren ◎ 44 58.57N 15.57E
Tišnov 46 49.21N 16.25E
Tisovec 46 48.43N 19.57E
Tista ≃ 76 25.23N 89.43E
Tisza (Tisa) ≃ 54 45.15N 20.17E
Tiszaföldvár 46 46.59N 20.15E
Tiszafüred 46 47.37N 20.46E
Tiszavasvári 46 47.58N 21.22E
Tit-Ary 58 71.58N 127.01E
Titel 54 45.12N 20.18E
Titicaca, Lago ◎ 110 15.50S 69.20W
Titograd 54 42.26N 19.14E
Titova Korenica 52 44.45N 15.43E
Titovo Užice 54 43.51N 19.51E
Titov Veles 54 41.41N 21.48E
Titov vrh ▲ 54 42.00N 20.51E
Titran 44 63.40N 8.18E
Tittabawassee ≃ 102 43.23N 83.59W
Titterstone Clee Hill ▲2 34 52.23N 2.35W
Tittling 46 48.44N 13.23E
Tittmoning 46 48.04N 12.46E
Titu 54 44.41N 25.32E
Titule 82 3.17N 25.32E
Titusville, Fl., U.S. 100 28.36N 80.48W
Titusville, Pa., U.S. 102 41.37N 79.40W
Tiumpan Head ≻ 38 58.16N 6.09W
Tiverton 34 50.55N 3.29W
Tivoli 52 41.58N 12.48E
Tizimín 106 21.10N 88.10W
Tizi-Ouzou 80 36.48N 4.02E
Tiznados ≃ 108 8.50N 67.47W
Tjøme I 44 59.07N 10.24E
Tjörn I 44 58.00N 11.38E
Tlahualilo de Zaragoza 106 26.07N 103.27W
Tlaxcala 106 19.19N 98.14W
Tlaxiaco 106 17.16N 97.41W
Tłuszcz 46 52.26N 21.26E
Toaca ▲ 54 46.59N 25.57E
Toamasina 87b 18.10S 49.23E
Toamasina □4 87b 18.00S 48.40E
Toano 52 44.23N 10.34E
Toano Draw v 104 41.17N 114.35W
Toano Range ⊀ 104 40.50N 114.20W
Toay 114 36.40S 64.21W
Toba 64 34.29N 136.51E
Toba, Danau ◎ 70 2.35N 98.50E
Tobacco ≃ 102 43.49N 84.24W
Tobago I 108 11.15N 60.40W
Toba Kākar Range ⊀ 76 31.15N 68.00E
Tobarra 50 38.35N 1.41W
Tobas 114 28.08S 62.42W
Tobe Jube, Bahía c 108 9.15N 60.45W
Tobelo 68 1.44N 128.01E
Tobercurry 40 54.03N 8.43W
Tobermorey 94 22.15S 138.00E
Tobermory, Austl. 94 27.17S 143.41E
Tobermory, Scot., U.K. 38 56.37N 6.05W
Toberonochy 38 56.13N 5.38W
Tōbetsu 64a 43.13N 141.31E
Tobi I 68 3.00N 131.10E
Tobin, Mount ▲ 104 40.22N 117.32W
Tobin Lake ◎ 90 21.45S 125.49E
Tobi-shima I 64 39.12N 139.34E
Toboali 72 3.00S 106.30E
Tobol 56 52.40N 62.39E
Tobol ≃ 56 58.10N 68.12E
Toboli 72 0.43S 120.05E
Tobol'sk 56 58.12N 68.16E
Tobruk →Tubruq 82 32.05N 23.59E
Tobyhanna 102 41.10N 75.25W
Tocantínia 110 9.33S 48.22W
Tocantinópolis 110 6.20S 47.25W
Tocantins ≃ 110 1.45S 49.10W
Tochigi 64 36.23N 139.44E
Tochigi □5 64 36.45N 139.45E
Tochio 64 37.28N 139.00E
Töcksfors 44 59.30N 11.50E
Toco 114 22.05S 69.35W
Tocoa 108 15.41N 86.03W
Toconao 114 23.11S 68.01W
Tocopilla 114 22.05S 70.12W
Tocumwal 94 35.49S 145.34E
Tocuyo ≃ 108 11.03N 68.23W
Tocuyo de la Costa 108 11.02N 68.23W
Toda Rai Singh 76 26.01N 75.29E
Todd ≃ 90 24.52S 135.48E
Toddington 34 51.57N 0.32W
Todi 52 42.47N 12.24E
Todmorden, Austl. 90 27.08S 134.48E
Todmorden, Eng., U.K. 36 53.43N 2.05W
Todoga-saki ≻ 64 39.33N 142.05E
Todos Santos 110 16.48S 65.08W
Todos Santos, Bahía c 104 31.48N 116.42W
Todtnau 46 47.50N 7.56E
Toe Head ≻ 38 57.50N 7.08W
Toetoes Bay c 96 46.38S 168.43E
Tofte 44 59.33N 10.34E
Togi 64 37.08N 136.44E
Togian, Kepulauan II 72 0.20S 122.00E
Togo □1 80 8.00N 1.10E
Togučin 58 55.16N 84.23E
Tōhaku 64 35.30N 133.40E
Tohakum Peak ▲ 104 40.11N 119.27W
Toholampi 44 63.46N 24.15E
Toi-misaki ≻ 64 31.20N 131.22E
Toiyabe Range ⊀ 104 39.10N 117.10W
Tōjō 64 34.53N 133.16E
Tokaanu 96 38.58S 175.46E
Tokachi ≃ 64a 42.44N 143.42E
Tokachi-dake ▲ 64a 43.25N 142.41E
Tokachi-heiya ⩩ 64a 43.00N 143.30E
Tōkamachi 64 37.08N 138.46E
Tokanui 96 46.34S 168.56E
Tokara-kaikyō ꭒ 65b 30.10N 130.10E
Tokara-rettō II 65b 29.36N 129.43E
Tokashiki-jima I 65b 26.11N 127.21E
Tokat 78 40.19N 36.34E
Tokelau □2 28 9.00S 171.45W
Tokko 58 59.59N 119.52E
Tokmak 56 42.55N 75.18E
Toko 96 39.20S 174.24E
Tokomaru 96 40.28S 175.30E
Tokomaru Bay 96 38.08S 178.18E
Toko Range ⊀ 94 23.05S 138.20E
Tokoro ≃ 64a 44.07N 144.05E
Tokoroa 96 38.14S 175.52E
Toksovo 60 60.09N 30.31E
Toku Island I 28 18.10S 174.11W
Tokuno-shima I 65b 27.45N 128.58E
Tokushima 64 34.04N 134.34E
Tokuyama 64 34.03N 131.49E
Tōkyō 64 35.42N 139.46E
Tokyo Bay →Tōkyō-wan c 64 35.25N 139.47E
Tōkyō-wan c 64 35.25N 139.47E
Tol I 28 7.22N 151.37E

Symbols in the Index entries are identified on page 122

Name	Page	Lat. °′	Long. °′
Tolaga Bay	96	38.22 S	178.18 E
Tolbuhin	54	43.34 N	27.50 E
Toledo, Bra.	114	24.44 S	53.45 W
Toledo, Esp.	50	39.52 N	4.01 W
Toledo, Oh., U.S.	102	41.39 N	83.33 W
Toledo, Montes de ⩘	50	39.33 N	4.20 W
Toledo Bend Reservoir ⊜[1]	100	31.30 N	93.45 W
Tolentino	52	43.12 N	13.17 E
Tolga	44	62.25 N	11.00 E
Toliara	87b	23.21 S	43.40 E
Toliara □[4]	87b	24.00 S	45.00 E
Tolima, Nevado del ∧	110	4.40 N	75.19 W
Tolitoli	72	1.02 N	120.49 E
Toljatti	42	53.31 N	49.26 E
Tol'ka	56	64.02 N	81.55 E
Tolkmicko	46	54.20 N	19.31 E
Tollarp	44	55.56 N	13.59 E
Tollense ≃	46	53.54 N	13.02 E
Tollesbury	34	51.46 N	0.50 E
Tolloche	114	25.30 S	63.32 W
Tølløse	44	55.37 N	11.45 E
Tolmačovo	60	58.52 N	29.55 E
Tolmezzo	52	46.24 N	13.01 E
Tolmin	52	46.11 N	13.44 E
Tolna	46	46.26 N	18.46 E
Tolna □[6]	46	46.30 N	18.35 E
Tolo, Teluk c	72	2.00 S	122.30 E
Tolob	38a	59.53 N	1.19 W
Tolosa	50	43.08 N	2.04 W
Tolpuddle	34	50.45 N	2.18 W
Tolsta Head ›	38	58.20 N	6.10 W
Tolstoj, mys ›	58	59.10 N	155.12 E
Toltén	112	39.13 S	73.14 W
Tolú	110	9.31 N	75.35 W
Toluca	106	19.17 N	99.40 W
Tolvdalselva ≃	44	58.10 N	8.00 E
Tom' ≃	58	56.50 N	84.27 E
Tomakomai	64a	42.38 N	141.36 E
Tomani	72	4.50 N	115.55 E
Tomar	50	39.36 N	8.25 W
Tomás Gomensoro	114	30.26 S	57.26 W
Tomaszów Lubelski	46	50.28 N	23.25 E
Tomaszów Mazowiecki	46	51.32 N	20.01 E
Tomatin	38	57.20 N	3.59 W
Tomazina	114	23.46 S	49.58 W
Tombigbee ≃	100	31.04 N	87.58 W
Tombouctou (Timbuktu)	80	16.46 N	3.01 W
Tombstone Mountain ∧	98	64.25 N	138.30 W
Tom Burke	86	23.05 S	28.00 E
Tomdoun	38	57.04 N	5.03 W
Tomé	114	36.37 S	72.57 W
Tomelilla	44	55.33 N	13.57 E
Tomelloso	50	39.10 N	3.01 W
Tomich	38	57.18 N	4.48 W
Tomini	72	0.30 N	120.32 E
Tomini, Teluk c	72	0.20 S	121.00 E
Tomintoul	38	57.14 N	3.22 W
Tomioka	64	36.15 N	138.54 E
Tomkinson Ranges ⩘	90	26.11 S	129.05 E
Tommot	58	58.58 N	126.19 E
Tomnavoulin	38	57.18 N	3.19 W
Tomo ≃	110	5.20 N	67.48 W
Tom Price	90	22.41 S	117.43 E
Tom Price, Mount ∧	90	22.39 S	117.40 E
Tomptokan	58	57.06 N	133.59 E
Tomra	44	62.35 N	6.56 E
Toms ≃	102	39.57 N	74.07 W
Tomsk	58	56.30 N	84.58 E
Toms River	102	39.58 N	74.12 W
Tonalá	106	16.04 N	93.45 W
Tonami	64	36.38 N	136.54 E
Tonawanda	102	43.01 N	78.52 W
Tonbridge	34	51.12 N	0.16 E
Tondano	72	1.19 N	124.54 E
Tønder	44	54.56 N	8.54 E
Tone ≃	64	35.44 N	140.51 E
Tonekābon	78	36.49 N	50.53 E
Tonga □[1]	28	20.00 S	175.00 W
Tongaat	86	29.37 S	31.03 E
Tong'an	66	24.46 N	118.08 E
Tonga Ridge ✢[3]	28	21.00 S	175.00 W
Tongariro, Mount ∧	96	39.08 S	175.38 E
Tongatapu I	28	21.10 S	175.10 W
Tongatapu Group II	28	21.10 S	175.10 W
Tonga Trench ✢[1]	28	20.00 S	173.00 W
Tongbai	66	32.22 N	113.24 E
Tongcheng, Zhg.	66	31.03 N	116.58 E
Tongcheng, Zhg.	66	32.53 N	118.58 E
Tongcheng, Zhg.	66	29.11 N	113.49 E
Tongchuan	62	35.01 N	109.01 E
Tongeren	46	50.47 N	5.28 E
Tonggu	66	28.33 N	114.21 E
Tongguan, Zhg.	62	34.38 N	110.20 E
Tongguan, Zhg.	66	28.29 N	112.48 E
Tonghai	70	24.07 N	102.49 E
Tonghua	62	41.41 N	125.55 E
Tongjing	66	31.47 N	118.33 E
Tongjosŏn-man c	62	39.30 N	128.00 E
Tongli	66	31.10 N	120.43 E
Tongliao	62	43.39 N	122.14 E
Tongling	66	30.53 N	117.46 E
Tonglu	66	29.48 N	119.40 E
Tongo	94	30.30 S	143.45 E
Tongololo Creek ≃	90	22.06 S	121.08 E
Tongoy	114	30.15 S	71.30 W
Tongren	62	27.38 N	109.03 E
Tongsa Dzong	76	27.31 N	90.30 E
Tongtian ≃	62	33.25 N	96.32 E
Tongtianheyan	62	33.50 N	92.28 E
Tongue	38	58.28 N	4.25 W
Tongue, Kyle of c	38	58.30 N	4.26 W
Tongxian	62	39.55 N	116.39 E
Tongxiang	66	30.38 N	120.32 E
Tongxu	66	34.29 N	114.28 E
Tongyu	62	44.48 N	123.05 E
Tongzi	62	28.08 N	106.49 E
Tonk	76	26.10 N	75.47 E
Tonkin, Gulf of c	70	20.00 N	108.00 E
Tonle Sap →Sab, Tônlé ⊜	70	13.00 N	104.00 E
Tonnay-Boutonne	48	45.58 N	0.42 W
Tonneins	48	44.23 N	0.19 E
Tonnerre	48	47.51 N	3.58 E
Tönning	46	54.19 N	8.56 E
Tōno	64	39.19 N	141.32 E
Tonopah	104	38.04 N	117.13 W
Tonoshō	64	34.29 N	134.11 E
Tonota	86	21.29 S	27.29 E
Tønsberg	44	59.17 N	10.25 E
Tonstad	44	58.40 N	6.43 E
Tonyrefail	34	51.36 N	3.25 W
Toobeah	94	28.25 S	149.52 E
Toodyay	90	31.33 S	116.28 E
Tooele	100	40.31 N	112.17 W
Toogoolawah	94	27.06 S	152.23 E
Toomebridge	40	54.45 N	6.27 W
Toompine	94	27.13 S	144.22 E
Toomyvara	40	52.50 N	8.02 W
Toora-Chem	58	52.28 N	96.17 E
Toormakeady	40	53.39 N	9.24 W
Toowoomba	94	27.33 S	151.57 E
Topeka	100	39.02 N	95.40 W
Topki	58	55.16 N	85.36 E
Topko, gora ∧	58	57.08 N	137.24 E
Topl'a ≃	46	48.45 N	21.45 E
Toplica ≃	54	43.13 N	21.49 E
Toplița	54	46.55 N	25.21 E
Topocalma, Punta ›	114	34.08 S	72.01 W
Topol'čany	46	48.34 N	18.10 E
Topolobampo	106	25.36 N	109.03 W
Topolog	54	44.53 N	28.22 E
Topolovățu Mare	54	45.46 N	21.37 E
Topolovgrad	54	42.05 N	26.20 E
Topozero, ozero ⊜	56	65.40 N	32.00 E
Tops, Mount ∧	90	21.50 S	134.00 E
Topsham, Eng., U.K.	34	50.41 N	3.27 W
Topsham, Me., U.S.	102	43.55 N	69.58 W
Top Springs	92	16.38 S	131.50 E
Toquima Range ⩘	104	38.45 N	116.55 W
Toquop Wash v	104	36.45 N	114.11 W
Torawitan, Tanjung ›	72	1.46 N	124.58 E
Torbalı	54	38.10 N	27.21 E
Torbat-e Heydarīyeh	78	35.16 N	59.13 E
Torbat-e Jām	78	35.14 N	60.36 E
Tor Bay c	34	50.25 N	3.30 W
Torch ≃	98	53.50 N	103.05 W
Torch Lake ⊜	102	45.00 N	85.19 W
Tordera ≃	50	41.39 N	2.47 E
Tordesillas	50	41.30 N	5.00 W
Tordino ≃	52	42.44 N	13.59 E
Töre	44	65.54 N	22.39 E
Töreboda	44	58.43 N	14.08 E
Torekov	44	56.26 N	12.37 E
Toreno	50	42.42 N	6.30 W
Torez	56	48.01 N	38.37 E
Torgau	46	51.34 N	13.00 E
Torgelow	46	53.37 N	14.00 E
Torhamn	44	56.05 N	15.50 E
Torhout	46	51.04 N	3.06 E
Torino (Turin)	52	45.03 N	7.40 E
Torio ≃	50	42.35 N	5.34 W
Torit	82	4.24 N	32.34 E
Torkoviči	60	58.52 N	30.20 E
Torment, Point ›	90	17.02 S	123.36 E
Tormes ≃	50	41.18 N	6.29 W
Torne ≃	36	53.36 N	0.44 W
Torneälven ≃	42	65.48 N	24.08 E
Torneträsk ⊜	42	68.20 N	19.10 E
Torngat Mountains ⩘	98	59.00 N	64.00 W
Tornio	44	65.51 N	24.08 E
Tornquist	114	38.06 S	62.14 W
Toro	50	41.31 N	5.24 W
Toro, Punta ›	114	33.47 S	71.49 W
Törökszentmiklós	46	47.11 N	20.25 E
Toronto, On., Can.	102	43.39 N	79.23 W
Toronto, Oh., U.S.	102	40.27 N	80.36 W
Toro Peak ∧	104	33.32 N	116.25 W
Toropec	60	56.30 N	31.39 E
Tororo	84	0.42 N	34.11 E
Toros Dağları ⩘	30	37.00 N	33.00 E
Torphins	38	57.06 N	2.37 W
Torpo	44	60.40 N	8.43 E
Torpoint	34	50.22 N	4.11 W
Torquay (Torbay)	34	50.28 N	3.30 W
Torquemada	50	42.02 N	4.19 W
Torrance	104	33.50 N	118.20 W
Torrão	50	38.18 N	8.13 W
Torre Annunziata	52	40.45 N	14.27 E
Torre Baja	50	40.07 N	1.15 W
Torreblanca	50	40.13 N	0.12 E
Torrecilla ∧	50	37.36 N	2.31 W
Torrecilla en Cameros	50	42.16 N	2.37 W
Torre del Campo	50	37.46 N	3.53 W
Torre de Moncorvo	50	41.10 N	7.03 W
Torredonjimeno	50	37.46 N	3.57 W
Torrejón, Embalse de ⊜[1]	50	39.50 N	5.50 W
Torrejoncillo	50	39.54 N	6.28 W
Torrejón de Ardoz	50	40.27 N	3.29 W
Torrelaguna	50	40.50 N	3.32 W
Torrelavega	50	43.21 N	4.03 W
Torremaggiore	52	41.41 N	15.17 E
Torremolinos	50	36.37 N	4.30 W
Torrens, Lake ⊜	94	31.00 S	137.50 E
Torrens Creek	94	20.46 S	145.02 E
Torrent	114	28.50 S	56.28 W
Torrente	50	39.26 N	0.28 W
Torreón	106	25.33 N	103.26 W
Torre Pellice	52	44.49 N	7.13 E
Torreperogil	50	38.02 N	3.17 W
Tôrres	114	29.21 S	49.44 W
Torres Islands II	28	13.15 S	166.37 E
Torres Novas	50	39.29 N	8.32 W
Torres Strait ʊ	92	10.25 S	142.10 E
Torres Vedras	50	39.06 N	9.16 W
Torrevieja	50	37.59 N	0.41 W
Torricelli Mountains ⩘	92	3.25 S	142.20 E
Torridge ≃	34	51.03 N	4.11 W
Torridon	38	57.33 N	5.31 W
Torridon, Loch c	38	57.35 N	5.46 W
Torriglia	52	44.31 N	9.10 E
Torrijos	50	39.59 N	4.17 W
Torrin	38	57.12 N	6.02 W
Torrington, Ct., U.S.	102	41.48 N	73.07 W
Torrington, Wy., U.S.	100	42.03 N	104.10 W
Torrinha	114	22.26 S	48.09 W
Torröjen ⊜	44	63.55 N	12.56 E
Torrox	50	36.46 N	3.58 W
Torsås	44	56.24 N	16.00 E
Torsby	44	60.08 N	13.00 E
Torshälla	44	59.25 N	16.28 E
Tórshavn	30	62.01 N	6.46 W
Torsö I	44	58.48 N	13.50 E
Torteval	35b	49.27 N	2.38 W
Tortola I	108	18.27 N	64.36 W
Tortoli	52	39.55 N	9.39 E
Tortona	52	44.54 N	8.52 E
Tortorici	52	38.02 N	14.49 E
Tortosa	50	40.48 N	0.31 E
Tortosa, Cabo de ›	50	40.43 N	0.55 E
Tortue, Île de la I	108	20.04 N	72.49 W
Toruń	46	53.02 N	18.35 E
Torup	44	56.58 N	13.05 E
Tõrva	60	58.00 N	25.56 E
Tory Island I	40	55.16 N	8.14 W
Torysa ≃	46	48.39 N	21.21 E
Tory Sound ʊ	40	55.14 N	8.14 W
Toržok	60	57.03 N	34.58 E
Torzym	46	52.20 N	15.04 E
Tosa	64	33.29 N	133.25 E
Tosas, Puerto de)(	50	42.19 N	2.01 E
Tosa-shimizu	64	32.46 N	132.57 E
Tosa-wan c	64	33.20 N	133.40 E
Tosca	86	25.53 S	23.58 E
Toscaig	38	57.24 N	5.50 W
Toscana □[4]	52	43.25 N	11.00 E
To-shima I	64	34.31 N	139.17 E
Tosno	60	59.33 N	30.53 E
T'osovo-Netyl'skij	60	58.57 N	31.04 E
T'osovskij	60	58.48 N	30.52 E
Tostado	114	29.14 S	61.46 W
Tosu	64	33.22 N	130.31 E
Toszek	46	50.28 N	18.32 E
Totana	50	37.46 N	1.30 W
Toteng	86	20.22 S	22.58 E
Tôtes	48	49.41 N	1.03 E
Totes Gebirge ⩘	46	47.42 N	13.55 E
Tot'ma	60	59.57 N	42.45 E
Totnes	34	50.25 N	3.41 W
Totness	110	5.53 N	56.19 W
Totoras	114	32.35 S	61.11 W
Tottenham, Austl.	94	32.14 S	147.21 E
Tottenham, On., Can.	102	44.01 N	79.49 W
Tottington	36	53.37 N	2.20 W
Totton	34	50.56 N	1.29 W
Tottori	64	35.30 N	134.14 E
Touba	80	8.17 N	7.41 W
Toubkal, Jebel ∧	80	31.05 N	7.55 W
Toucy	48	47.44 N	3.18 E
Touggourt	80	33.10 N	6.00 E
Toul	48	48.41 N	5.54 E
Touliu	66	23.43 N	120.32 E
Toulnustouc ≃	98	49.35 N	68.24 W
Toulon	48	43.07 N	5.56 E
Toulon Lake ⊜	104	40.01 N	118.40 W
Toulon-sur-Arroux	48	46.42 N	4.08 E
Toulouse	48	43.36 N	1.26 E
Tounan	66	23.41 N	120.28 E
Toungoo	70	18.56 N	96.26 E
Touques ≃	48	49.22 N	0.06 E
Touraine	102	45.34 N	75.47 W
Touraine □[9]	48	47.12 N	1.30 E
Tourcoing	48	50.43 N	3.09 E
Tourinan, Cabo ›	50	43.03 N	9.18 W
Tournai	46	50.36 N	3.23 E
Tournon	48	45.04 N	4.50 E
Tournus	48	46.34 N	4.54 E
Tours	48	47.23 N	0.41 E
Toury	48	48.12 N	1.56 E
Toussidé, Pic ∧	82	21.02 N	16.25 E
Touws ≃	86	33.45 S	21.11 E
Touwsrivier	86	33.20 S	20.00 E
Toužim	46	50.04 N	13.00 E
Tove ≃	34	52.05 N	0.38 W
Towada	64	40.37 N	141.13 E
Towada-ko ⊜	64	40.28 N	140.55 E
Towai	96	35.29 S	174.08 E
Towanda	102	41.46 N	76.26 W
Towanda Creek ≃	102	41.45 N	76.26 W
Towan Head ›	34	50.25 N	5.07 W
Towcester	34	52.08 N	1.00 W
Tower City	102	40.35 N	76.33 W
Tower Hamlets ✦[8]	34	51.32 N	0.03 W
Tower Hill	94	22.03 S	144.36 E
Towerhill Creek ≃	94	22.29 S	144.39 E
Tow Law	36	54.44 N	1.49 W
Townsend, Mount ∧	94	36.25 S	148.15 E
Townshend Island I	94	22.15 S	150.30 E
Townsville	94	19.16 S	146.48 E
Towson	102	39.24 N	76.36 W
Towuti, Danau ⊜	72	2.45 S	121.32 E
Toyama	64	36.41 N	137.13 E
Toyama-heiya ≚	64	36.40 N	137.15 E
Toyama-wan c	64	36.50 N	137.10 E
Tōyō, Nihon	64	33.30 N	134.16 E
Tōyo, Nihon	64	33.55 N	133.05 E
Toyohashi	64	34.46 N	137.23 E
Toyokawa	64	34.49 N	137.24 E
Toyonaka	64	34.47 N	135.28 E
Toyooka	64	35.32 N	134.50 E
Toyosaka	64	37.56 N	139.13 E
Toyota	64	35.05 N	137.09 E
Toyoura	64	34.08 N	130.58 E
Tozer, Mount ∧	92	12.45 S	143.13 E
Tozeur	80	33.55 N	8.08 E
Trabiju	114	22.03 S	48.18 W
Trabzon	30	41.00 N	39.43 E
Tracy, P.Q., Can.	102	46.01 N	73.09 W
Tracy, Ca., U.S.	104	37.44 N	121.25 W
Trafalgar, Cabo ›	50	36.11 N	6.02 W
Tragacete	50	40.21 N	1.51 W
Traid	50	40.40 N	1.49 W
Traiguén	114	38.15 S	72.41 W
Trail	98	49.06 N	117.42 W
Trakai	60	54.38 N	24.56 E
Trakt	42	62.44 N	51.11 E
Tralee	40	52.16 N	9.42 W
Tralee Bay c	40	52.15 N	9.59 W
Trá Lí →Tralee	40	52.16 N	9.42 W
Tramore	40	52.10 N	7.10 W
Trân	54	42.50 N	22.39 E
Tranås	44	58.03 N	14.59 E
Trancas	114	26.13 S	65.17 W
Trancoso	50	40.47 N	7.21 W
Tranebjerg	44	55.50 N	10.36 E
Tranemo	44	57.29 N	13.21 E
Tranent	38	55.57 N	2.58 W
Trang	70	7.33 N	99.36 E
Trangan, Pulau I	92	6.35 S	134.20 E
Trangie	94	32.02 S	147.59 E
Trängslet	44	61.25 N	13.40 E
Trani	52	41.17 N	16.26 E
Trannon ≃	34	52.31 N	3.25 W
Tranqueras	114	31.12 S	55.45 W
Transkei □[1]	86	31.20 S	29.00 E
Transtrand	44	61.05 N	13.19 E
Transvaal □[4]	86	25.00 S	29.00 E
Transylvania □[9]	54	46.30 N	24.00 E
Transylvanian Alps →Carpații Meridionali ⩘	54	45.30 N	24.15 E
Trapani	52	38.01 N	12.31 E
Traralgon	94	38.12 S	146.32 E
Trasacco	52	41.57 N	13.32 E
Trăscau, Munții ⩘	54	46.23 N	23.33 E
Trasimeno, Lago ⊜	52	43.08 N	12.06 E
Träslövsläge	44	57.04 N	12.16 E
Trás-os-Montes □[9]	50	41.30 N	7.15 W
Trâstenik	54	43.31 N	24.28 E
Traun	46	48.13 N	14.14 E
Traun ≃	46	48.16 N	14.22 E
Traunstein	46	47.52 N	12.38 E
Travellers Lake ⊜	94	33.18 S	142.00 E
Travers, Mount ∧	96	42.01 S	172.44 E
Traverse City	102	44.45 N	85.37 W
Travnik	52	44.14 N	17.40 E
Trawbreaga Bay c	40	55.17 N	7.18 W
Trawsfynydd	34	52.54 N	3.55 W
Trayning	90	31.07 S	117.48 E
Trbovlje	52	46.10 N	15.03 E
Trebbia ≃	52	45.04 N	9.41 E
Třebechovice pod Orebem	46	50.12 N	16.00 E
Třebíč	46	49.13 N	15.53 E
Trebinje	54	42.43 N	18.20 E
Trebisacce	52	39.52 N	16.32 E
Trebišov	46	48.40 N	21.47 E
Trebizond →Trabzon	74	41.00 N	39.43 E
Treblinka	46	52.39 N	22.03 E
Třeboň	46	49.00 N	14.47 E
Trecate	52	45.26 N	8.44 E
Tredegar	34	51.47 N	3.16 W
Treene ≃	46	54.22 N	9.05 E
Tregaron	34	52.13 N	3.55 W
Tregosse Islets II	94	17.41 S	150.43 E
Tréguier	48	48.47 N	3.14 W
Treharris	34	51.41 N	3.16 W
Trehörningsjö	44	63.42 N	18.48 E
Treig, Loch ⊜[1]	38	56.50 N	4.44 W
Treinta y Tres	114	33.14 S	54.23 W
Trélazé	48	47.27 N	0.28 W
Trelew	112	43.15 S	65.18 W
Trelleborg	44	55.22 N	13.10 E
Tremadog	36	52.56 N	4.09 W
Tremadog Bay c	36	52.52 N	4.15 W
Tremblant, Mont ∧	102	46.16 N	74.35 W
Tremont	102	40.37 N	76.23 W
Tremp	50	42.10 N	0.54 E
Trenčín	46	48.54 N	18.04 E
Trenel	114	35.42 S	64.08 W
Trenggalek	72	8.03 S	111.43 E
Trenque Lauquen	114	35.58 S	62.42 W
Trent ≃, On., Can.	102	44.06 N	77.34 W
Trent ≃, Eng., U.K.	36	53.42 N	0.41 W
Trent, Vale of v	34	52.44 N	1.50 W
Trente et un Milles, Lac des ⊜	102	46.12 N	75.49 W
Trentino-Alto Adige □[4]	52	46.30 N	11.20 E
Trento	52	46.04 N	11.08 E
Trenton, On., Can.	102	44.06 N	77.35 W
Trenton, N.J., U.S.	102	40.13 N	74.44 W
Trepuzzi	52	40.24 N	18.05 E
Tres Algarrobos	114	35.12 S	62.46 W
Tres Árboles	114	32.24 S	56.43 W
Tres Arroyos	114	38.23 S	60.17 W
Tresco I	34a	49.57 N	6.19 W
Três Coroas	114	29.32 S	50.48 W
Três de Maio	114	27.47 S	54.14 W
Tres Esquinas	110	0.43 N	75.16 W
Treshnish Isles II	38	56.30 N	6.24 W
Treshnish Point ›	38	56.33 N	6.21 W
Tres Isletas	114	26.21 S	60.26 W
Três Lagoas	110	20.48 S	51.43 W
Três Marias, Reprêsa ⊜[1]	110	18.12 S	45.15 W
Três Passos	114	27.27 S	53.56 W
Tres Picos, Cerro ∧	114	38.09 S	61.57 W
Tres Puntas, Cabo ›	112	47.06 S	65.53 W
Třešť	46	49.18 N	15.30 E
Tresta	38	60.14 N	1.21 W
Tretten	44	61.19 N	10.19 E
Treuchtlingen	46	48.57 N	10.54 E
Treuen	46	50.32 N	12.18 E
Treuenbrietzen	46	52.06 N	12.52 E
Treviglio	52	45.31 N	9.35 E
Treviño	50	42.44 N	2.45 W
Treviso	52	45.40 N	12.15 E
Trevorton	102	40.46 N	76.40 W
Trevose Head ›	34	50.33 N	5.01 W
Trévoux	48	45.56 N	4.46 E
Trgovište	54	42.21 N	22.05 E
Trhové Sviny	46	48.51 N	14.39 E
Triabunna	94	42.30 S	147.55 E
Triánda	54	36.24 N	28.10 E
Triangle	102	38.32 N	77.20 W
Triberg	46	48.08 N	8.13 E
Tricao Malal	114	37.03 S	70.19 W
Tricarico	52	40.37 N	16.09 E
Tricase	52	39.56 N	18.22 E
Trichardt	86	26.28 S	29.13 E
Trichūr	74	10.31 N	76.13 E
Trida	94	33.01 S	145.01 E
Trident Peak ∧	104	41.54 N	118.25 W
Trieben	46	47.29 N	14.30 E
Trier	46	49.45 N	6.38 E
Trieste	52	45.40 N	13.46 E
Triglav ∧	52	46.23 N	13.50 E
Trigno ≃	52	42.04 N	14.48 E
Trigueros	50	37.23 N	6.50 W
Trikala	54	39.34 N	21.46 E
Trikhonis, Límni ⊜	54	38.34 N	21.28 E
Trikora, Puncak (Wilhelmina Peak) ∧	92	4.15 S	138.45 E
Trillick	40	54.27 N	7.30 W
Trim	40	53.34 N	6.47 W
Trimdon	36	54.42 N	1.25 W
Trincomalee	74	8.34 N	81.14 E
Trindade I	112	20.31 S	29.19 W
Třinec	46	49.41 N	18.40 E
Tring	34	51.48 N	0.40 W
Trinidad, Bol.	110	14.47 S	64.47 W
Trinidad, Col.	110	5.25 N	71.40 W
Trinidad, Cuba	108	21.48 N	79.59 W
Trinidad, Co., U.S.	100	37.10 N	104.30 W
Trinidad, Ur.	114	33.32 S	56.54 W
Trinidad I	108	10.30 N	61.15 W
Trinidad, Isla I	114	39.08 S	61.58 W
Trinidad and Tobago □[1]	106	11.00 N	61.00 W
Trinity ≃, Ca., U.S.	104	41.11 N	123.42 W
Trinity ≃, Tx., U.S.	100	29.47 N	94.42 W
Trinity Bay c	98	48.00 N	53.40 W
Trinity Mountains ⩘	104	41.00 N	122.30 W
Trinity Peak ∧	104	40.14 N	118.45 W
Trinkat Island I	70	8.05 N	93.30 E
Trino	52	45.12 N	8.18 E
Triolet	87c	20.03 S	57.32 E
Tripoli →Țarābulus, Lībiyā	82	32.54 N	13.11 E
Tripoli →Țarābulus, Lubnān	78	34.26 N	35.51 E
Trípolis	54	37.31 N	22.21 E
Tripolitania →Țarābulus □[9]	82	31.00 N	15.00 E
Tripura □[4]	76	24.00 N	92.00 E
Tristan da Cunha Group II	20	37.15 S	12.30 W
Triste	50	42.23 N	0.43 W
Triste, Golfo c	108	10.40 N	68.10 W
Trivandrum	74	8.29 N	76.55 E
Trivento	52	41.47 N	14.33 E
Trnava	46	48.23 N	17.35 E
Troarn	48	49.11 N	0.11 W
Trobriand Islands II	92	8.35 S	151.05 E
Trogir	52	43.31 N	16.15 E
Troglav ∧	52	43.57 N	16.36 E
Troia	52	41.22 N	15.18 E
Troick	56	54.06 N	61.35 E
Troicko-Pečorsk	42	62.44 N	56.06 E
Troina	52	37.47 N	14.36 E
Troisdorf	46	50.49 N	7.08 E
Trois-Rivières	102	46.21 N	72.33 W
Trojan	54	42.51 N	24.43 E
Trojanski prohod)(	54	42.47 N	24.37 E
Trollhättan	44	58.16 N	12.18 E
Trollheimen ∧	44	62.51 N	9.05 E
Trombetas ≃	110	1.55 S	55.35 W
Trombudo Central	114	27.18 S	49.47 W
Tromelin, Île I	84	15.52 S	54.25 E
Trompsburg	86	30.01 S	25.46 E
Troms □[6]	42	69.15 N	19.40 E
Tromsø	42	69.40 N	18.58 E
Trona	104	35.45 N	117.22 W
Tronador, Monte ∧	112	41.10 S	71.54 W
Trondheim	44	63.25 N	10.25 E
Trondheimsfjorden c[2]	44	63.39 N	10.49 E
Trondheimsleia ʊ	44	63.30 N	9.00 E
Trooilapspan	86	28.40 S	21.25 E
Troon, Eng., U.K.	34	50.12 N	5.16 W
Troon, Scot., U.K.	38	55.32 N	4.40 W
Tropea	52	38.41 N	15.54 E
Tropojë	54	42.24 N	20.10 E
Trosa	44	58.54 N	17.33 E
Trostan ∧	40	55.03 N	6.09 W
Trotuș ≃	54	46.03 N	27.14 E
Trotwood	102	39.47 N	84.18 W
Trou-du-Nord	108	19.38 N	72.01 W
Troup Head ›	38	57.41 N	2.18 W
Trout ≃	98	61.19 N	119.51 W
Trout Creek ≃	104	42.23 N	118.36 W
Trout Lake ⊜, N.T., Can.	98	60.35 N	121.10 W
Trout Lake ⊜, On., Can.	98	51.13 N	93.20 W
Trout Lake ⊜, On., Can.	102	46.13 N	80.35 W
Trout Lake ⊜, On., Can.	102	46.18 N	79.20 W
Trouville [-sur-Mer]	48	49.22 N	0.05 E
Trowbridge	34	51.20 N	2.13 W
Troy, Al., U.S.	100	31.48 N	85.58 W
Troy, N.H., U.S.	102	42.49 N	72.10 W
Troy, N.Y., U.S.	102	42.43 N	73.41 W
Troy, Oh., U.S.	102	40.02 N	84.12 W
Troy, Pa., U.S.	102	41.47 N	76.47 W
Troy ⊥	54	39.57 N	26.15 E
Troyes	48	48.18 N	4.05 E
Troy Lake ⊜	104	34.49 N	116.33 W
Troy Peak ∧	104	38.19 N	115.30 W
Trpanj	52	43.00 N	17.17 E
Trst →Trieste	52	45.40 N	13.46 E
Trstená	46	49.22 N	19.37 E
Trstenik	54	43.37 N	21.00 E
Trubč'ovsk	60	52.37 N	33.44 E
Truc-giang	70	10.14 N	106.23 E
Trucial States →United Arab Emirates □[1]	74	24.00 N	54.00 E
Truckee	104	39.19 N	120.10 W
Truckee ≃	104	39.51 N	119.24 W
Trud	60	57.37 N	33.58 E
Truim ≃	38	57.02 N	4.10 W
Trujillo, Esp.	50	39.28 N	5.53 W
Trujillo, Hond.	108	15.55 N	86.00 W
Trujillo, Perú	110	8.07 S	79.02 W
Trujillo, Ven.	110	9.22 N	70.26 W
Trujillo □[3]	108	9.25 N	70.30 W
Truk Islands II	28	7.25 N	151.47 E
Trumansburg	102	42.32 N	76.39 W
Trumbull	102	41.14 N	73.12 W
Trumon	70	2.49 N	97.38 E
Trundle	94	32.55 S	147.43 E
Truro, Austl.	94	34.25 S	139.07 E
Truro, N.S., Can.	98	45.22 N	63.16 W
Truro, Eng., U.K.	34	50.16 N	5.03 W
Trușești	54	47.46 N	27.01 E
Trust Territory of the Pacific Islands □[2]	28	10.00 N	155.00 E
Trutnov	46	50.34 N	15.55 E
Truyère ≃	48	44.39 N	2.34 E
Trwyn Cilan ›	34	52.46 N	4.30 W
Trysil	44	61.19 N	12.16 E
Trysilelva (Klarälven) ≃	44	59.23 N	13.32 E
Tryweryn ≃	34	52.24 N	3.35 W
Trzcianka	46	53.03 N	16.28 E
Trzciel	46	52.23 N	15.52 E
Trzcińsko-Zdrój	46	52.58 N	14.35 E
Trzebiatów	46	54.04 N	15.14 E
Trzebież	46	53.42 N	14.31 E
Trzebinia	46	50.10 N	19.18 E
Trzebnica	46	51.19 N	17.03 E
Trzemeszno	46	52.35 N	17.50 E
Tržič	52	46.22 N	14.19 E
Tsaratanana	87b	16.47 S	47.39 E
Tsaratanana, Massif du ⩘	87b	14.00 S	49.00 E
Tsau	86	20.12 S	22.22 E
Tsavo	84	2.59 S	38.28 E
Tsévié	80	6.25 N	1.13 E
Tshabong	86	26.03 S	22.29 E
Tshane	86	24.05 S	21.54 E
Tshangalele, Lac ⊜	84	10.55 S	27.03 E
Tshela	84	4.59 S	12.56 E
Tshidilamolomo	86	25.50 S	24.41 E
Tshikapa	84	6.25 S	20.48 E
Tshofa	84	5.14 S	25.15 E
Tshuapa ≃	84	0.14 S	20.42 E
Tshwaane	86	22.29 S	22.03 E
Tsiafajavona ∧	87b	19.21 S	47.15 E
Tsihombe	87b	25.18 S	45.29 E
Tsineng	86	27.06 S	23.04 E
Tsinghai →Qinghai □[4]	62	36.00 N	96.00 E
Tsingtao →Qingdao	62	36.06 N	120.19 E
Tsinling Shan →Qin Ling ⩘	62	34.00 N	108.00 E
Tsiribihina ≃	87b	19.42 S	44.31 E
Tsiroanomandidy	87b	18.46 S	46.02 E
Tsitsihar →Qiqihar	62	47.19 N	123.55 E
Tsolo	86	31.18 S	28.37 E
Tsomo ≃	86	32.25 S	27.50 E
Tsoying	66	22.41 N	120.17 E
Tsu	64	34.43 N	136.31 E
Tsubame	64	37.39 N	138.56 E
Tsuchiura	64	36.05 N	140.12 E
Tsugaru-hantō ›[1]	64	41.00 N	140.30 E
Tsugaru-heiya ≚	64	40.49 N	140.27 E
Tsugaru-kaikyō ʊ	64a	41.35 N	141.00 E
Tsukumi	64	33.04 N	131.52 E
Tsukushi-sanchi ⩘	64	33.30 N	130.30 E
Tsumeb	86	19.13 S	17.42 E
Tsumeb □[5]	86	19.00 S	17.30 E
Tsumis Park	86	23.43 S	17.28 E
Tsuruga	64	35.39 N	136.04 E
Tsurugi-san ∧	64	33.51 N	134.06 E
Tsuruoka	64	38.44 N	139.50 E
Tsushima II	64	34.30 N	129.22 E
Tsushima-kaikyō (Eastern Channel) ʊ	64	34.00 N	129.00 E
Tsuwano	64	34.28 N	131.46 E
Tsuyama	64	35.03 N	134.00 E
Tua ≃	50	41.13 N	7.26 W
Tuakau	96	37.16 S	174.57 E
Tual	92	5.40 S	132.45 E
Tuam	40	53.31 N	8.50 W
Tuamarina	96	41.26 S	173.57 E
Tuamotu, Îles (Tuamotu Archipelago) II	28	19.00 S	142.00 W
Tuanfeng	66	30.38 N	114.51 E
Tuapeka Mouth	96	46.01 S	169.31 E
Tuapse	56	44.07 N	39.05 E
Tuaran	72	6.11 N	116.14 E
Tuatapere	96	46.08 S	167.41 E
Tuath, Loch ʊ	38	56.30 N	6.12 W
Tuban	72	6.54 S	112.03 E
Tubarão	114	28.30 S	49.01 W
Tubau	72	3.08 N	113.42 E
Tübingen	46	48.31 N	9.02 E
Ṭubruq	82	32.05 N	23.59 E
Tucacas	110	10.48 N	68.19 W
Tucacas, Punta ›	108	10.50 N	68.14 W
Tucano	110	10.58 S	38.48 W
Tuchola	46	53.35 N	17.50 E
Tuchów	46	49.54 N	21.03 E
Tuckanarra	90	27.07 S	118.05 E
Tuckerton	102	39.36 N	74.20 W
Tuckfield, Mount ∧	90	18.44 S	124.54 E
Tučkovo	60	55.36 N	36.28 E
Tucson	100	32.13 N	110.55 W
Tucumán →San Miguel de Tucumán	114	26.49 S	65.13 W
Tucumán □[4]	114	27.00 S	65.30 W
Tucumcari	100	35.10 N	103.43 W
Tucunduva	114	27.39 S	54.27 W
Tucunuco	114	30.36 S	68.38 W
Tucupido	108	9.17 N	65.47 W
Tucupita	110	9.04 N	62.03 W
Tucuruí	110	3.42 S	49.27 W
Tuczna	46	51.54 N	23.26 E
Tud ≃	34	52.38 N	1.15 E
Tudcum	114	30.14 S	69.15 W
Tudela	50	42.05 N	1.36 W
Tudela de Duero	50	41.35 N	4.35 W
Tudmur (Palmyra)	78	34.33 N	38.17 E
Tudweiliog	34	52.54 N	4.35 W
Tuela ≃	50	41.30 N	7.12 W
Tufi	92	9.05 S	149.20 E
Tugela ≃	86	29.14 S	31.30 E
Tug Fork ≃	102	38.06 N	82.36 W
Tuggerah Lake c	94	33.18 S	151.30 E
Tuguegarao	68	17.37 N	121.44 E
Tugur	58	53.48 N	136.48 E
Tuirc, Beinn an ∧[2]	38	55.34 N	5.34 W
Tujmazy	56	54.36 N	53.42 E
T'ukalinsk	58	55.52 N	72.12 E
Tukangbesi, Kepulauan II	72	5.40 S	123.50 E
Tukituki ≃	96	39.36 S	176.57 E
Tuktoyaktuk	98	69.27 N	133.02 W
Tula, Méx.	106	23.00 N	99.43 W
Tula, S.S.S.R.	60	54.12 N	37.37 E
Tulaghi	88	9.06 S	160.09 E
Tulancingo	106	20.05 N	98.22 W
Tulangbawang ≃	72	4.24 S	105.52 E
Tulare	104	36.12 N	119.20 W
Tulare Lake Bed ⊜	104	36.03 N	119.49 W
Tulbagh	86	33.17 S	19.09 E
Tulcán	110	0.48 N	77.43 W
Tulcea	54	45.11 N	28.48 E
Tulcea □[6]	54	45.00 N	29.00 E
Tule ≃	104	36.03 N	119.50 W
Tulelake	104	41.57 N	121.29 W
Tule Lake Sump ⊜[1]	104	41.54 N	121.32 W
Tuli	86	21.59 S	29.15 E
Tuli ≃	86	21.48 S	29.04 E
Tuliszków	46	52.05 N	18.17 E
Ṭūlkarm	78	32.19 N	35.02 E
Tulla	40	52.52 N	8.45 W
Tullahoma	100	35.21 N	86.12 W
Tullamore, Austl.	94	32.38 S	147.34 E
Tullamore, Ire.	40	53.16 N	7.30 W
Tulle	48	45.16 N	1.46 E
Tullibigeal	94	33.25 S	146.44 E
Tullins	48	45.18 N	5.29 E
Tulln	46	48.20 N	16.03 E
Tullow	40	52.48 N	6.44 W
Tully	94	17.56 S	145.56 E
Tulsa	100	36.09 N	95.59 W
Tulsequah	98	58.35 N	133.35 W
Tulsk	40	53.47 N	8.16 W
Tuluá	110	4.06 N	76.11 W
Tulum	108	20.13 N	87.28 W
Tulumaya (Lavalle)	114	32.43 S	68.35 W
Tulun	58	54.35 N	100.33 E
Tulungagung	72	8.04 S	111.54 E
Tuma ≃	108	13.03 N	84.44 W
Tumaco	110	1.49 N	78.46 W
Tuman-gang (Tumen) ≃	62	42.18 N	130.41 E
Tumany	58	60.56 N	155.56 E
Tumba	44	59.12 N	17.49 E
Tumba, Lac ⊜	84	0.48 S	18.03 E
Tumbarumba	94	35.47 S	148.01 E
Tumbaya	114	23.51 S	65.28 W
Tumbes	110	3.34 S	80.28 W
Tumbes, Punta ›	114	36.37 S	73.07 W
Tumby Bay	94	34.22 S	136.06 E
Tumča ≃	42	66.36 N	30.48 E
T'umen', S.S.S.R.	56	57.09 N	65.32 E
Tumen, Zhg.	62	42.58 N	129.49 E
Tumeremo	110	7.18 N	61.30 W
Tumkūr	74	13.21 N	77.05 E
Tummel ≃	38	56.38 N	3.40 W
Tummo	82	22.40 N	14.10 E
Tumos ≃	86	22.55 S	14.37 E
Tumpat	72	6.12 N	102.10 E
Tumsar	76	21.23 N	79.44 E
Tumuc-Humac Mountains ⩘	110	2.20 N	55.00 W
Tumut	94	35.18 S	148.13 E
Tunas de Zaza	108	21.38 N	79.33 W
Tunchang	70	19.28 N	110.08 E
Tūndla	76	27.12 N	78.17 E
Tunduru	84	11.07 S	37.21 E
Tundža ≃	54	41.40 N	26.34 E
T'ung ≃	58	63.46 N	121.35 E
Tungkang	66	22.28 N	120.26 E
Tungku	72	5.01 N	118.53 E
Tungla	108	13.18 N	84.26 W
Tungsha Tao (Pratas Island) I	62	20.42 N	116.43 E
Tungshih	66	24.15 N	120.49 E
Tunguska Crater •[6]	56	60.05 N	100.55 E
Tunis	80	36.48 N	10.11 E
Tunis, Golfe de c	80	37.00 N	10.30 E
Tunisia (Tunisie) □[1]	80	34.00 N	9.00 E
Tunja	110	5.31 N	73.22 W
Tunkhannock	102	41.32 N	75.56 W
Tunnelton	102	39.23 N	79.44 W
Tunnsjøen ⊜	42	64.43 N	13.24 E
Tunungayualok Island I	98	56.05 N	61.05 W
Tunuyán	114	33.34 S	69.01 W
Tunuyán ≃	114	34.03 S	66.45 W
Tunxi	66	29.44 N	118.18 E
Tuo ≃	62	28.57 N	105.27 E
Tuobuja	58	62.00 N	122.02 E
Tuoj-Chaja	58	62.32 N	111.18 E
Tuokusidawanling ∧	76	37.14 N	85.47 E
Tuolumne	104	37.57 N	120.14 W
Tuolumne ≃	104	37.36 N	121.10 W
Tupã	114	21.56 S	50.30 W
Tupaciguara	110	18.35 S	48.42 W
Tupanciretã	114	29.05 S	53.51 W
Tupelo	100	34.15 N	88.42 W
Tupiza	110	21.27 S	65.43 W
Tuplice	46	51.41 N	14.50 E
Tupper Lake	102	44.13 N	74.29 W
Tupuai, Île I	28	23.18 S	149.30 W
Tupungato	114	33.22 S	69.08 W
Tupungato, Cerro ∧	114	33.22 S	69.47 W
Túquerres	110	1.05 N	77.37 W
Tura, India	76	25.31 N	90.13 E
Tura, S.S.S.R.	58	64.17 N	100.15 E
Tura ≃	56	57.12 N	66.56 E
Turakina	96	40.02 S	175.13 E
Turakina ≃	96	40.04 S	175.08 E
Turan	58	52.08 N	93.55 E
Turangi	96	39.00 S	175.49 E
Turano ≃	52	42.26 N	12.47 E
Turbaco	108	10.20 N	75.25 W
Turbacz ∧	46	49.33 N	20.08 E
Turbat	78	25.59 N	63.04 E
Turbo	110	8.06 N	76.43 W
Turda	54	46.34 N	23.47 E
Turee Creek	90	23.37 S	118.39 E
Turek	46	52.02 N	18.30 E
Turenki	44	60.55 N	24.38 E
Turfan Depression →Turpan Pendi •[7]	62	42.40 N	89.10 E
Turgaj	56	49.38 N	63.28 E
Turgaj ≃	56	48.01 N	62.45 E
Turgajskoje plato ⩘[1]	56	51.00 N	64.00 E
Turginovo	60	56.30 N	36.00 E
Turgutlu	54	38.30 N	27.43 E
Türi	60	58.48 N	25.26 E
Turia ≃	50	39.27 N	0.19 W
Turimiquire, Cerro ∧	108	10.07 N	63.53 W
Turin →Torino	52	45.03 N	7.40 E
Turinsk	56	58.03 N	63.42 E
Turkestan	56	43.18 N	68.15 E
Túrkeve	46	47.06 N	20.45 E
Turkey □[1]	30	39.00 N	35.00 E
Turkey Creek	92	17.02 S	128.12 E
Turkmenskaja Sovetskaja Socialističeskaja Respublika □[3]	56	40.00 N	60.00 E
Turkmen Soviet Socialist Republic →Turkmenskaja Sovetskaja Socialističeskaja Respublika □[3]	56	40.00 N	60.00 E
Turks and Caicos Islands □[2]	106	21.45 N	71.35 W
Turks Island Passage ʊ	108	21.25 N	71.19 W
Turks Islands II	108	21.24 N	71.07 W
Turku (Åbo)	44	60.27 N	22.17 E
Turkwel ≃	82	3.06 N	36.06 E
Turlock	104	37.29 N	120.50 W
Turnagain ≃	98	59.06 N	127.35 W
Turnagain, Cape ›	96	40.29 S	176.37 E
Turnagain Island I	92	9.34 S	142.18 E
Turňa nad Bodvou	46	48.37 N	20.53 E
Turnbull, Mount ∧[2]	90	21.03 S	131.57 E
Turneffe Islands II	106	17.22 N	87.51 W
Turner	90	17.50 S	128.17 E
Turner ≃	90	20.21 S	118.25 E
Turners Falls	102	42.36 N	72.33 W
Turnhout	46	51.19 N	4.57 E
Türnitz	46	47.57 N	15.30 E
Turnor Lake ⊜	98	56.32 N	108.38 W
Turnov	46	50.35 N	15.10 E
Tǔrnovo →Veliko Târnovo	54	43.04 N	25.39 E
Turnu-Măgurele	54	43.45 N	24.53 E
Turnu Roșu, Pasul)(	54	45.33 N	24.16 E
Turobin	46	50.50 N	22.45 E
Turpan	62	42.56 N	89.10 E
Turpan Pendi •[7]	62	42.40 N	89.10 E
Turquino, Pico ∧	108	19.59 N	76.50 W
Turriff	38	57.32 N	2.28 W
Turritano ✦[1]	52	40.45 N	8.35 E
Turskaja ložbina v	56	51.00 N	64.30 E
Turu ≃	58	64.38 N	100.00 E

Symbols in the Index entries are identified on page 122.

Name	Page	Lat. °′	Long. °′
Turua	96	37.14 S	175.34 E
Turuchan ≃	58	65.56 N	87.42 E
Turuchansk	56	65.49 N	87.59 E
Turvo	114	28.56 S	49.41 W
Turzovka	46	49.25 N	18.39 E
Tuscaloosa	100	33.12 N	87.34 W
Tuscarora Mountain ∧	102	40.10 N	77.45 W
Tuscarora Mountains ⋏	104	41.00 N	116.20 W
Tushan	66	34.14 N	117.51 E
Tusker Rock II [1]	34	51.27 N	3.40 W
Tustumena Lake ⊜	98	60.12 N	150.50 W
Tuszyn	46	51.37 N	19.34 E
Tutaekuri ≃	96	39.30 S	176.54 E
Tutajev	60	57.53 N	39.32 E
Tutbury	34	52.51 N	1.41 W
Tuticorin	74	8.47 N	78.08 E
Tutin	54	42.59 N	20.20 E
Tutóia	110	2.45 S	42.16 W
Tutoko, Mount ∧	96	44.36 S	168.00 E
Tutova ≃	54	46.06 N	27.32 E
Tutrakan	54	44.03 N	26.37 E
Tutuila I	28	14.18 S	170.42 W
Tutupaca, Volcán ∧ [1]	110	17.01 S	70.22 W
Tutzing	46	47.54 N	11.17 E
Tuul ≃	62	48.57 N	104.48 E
Tuupovaara	44	62.29 N	30.36 E
Tuusniemi	44	62.49 N	28.30 E
T'uva-Guba	42	69.08 N	33.32 E
Tuvalu □ [1]	28	8.00 S	178.00 E
Ţuwayq, Jabal ⋏	74	23.00 N	46.00 E
Tuxford	36	53.13 N	0.53 W
Tuxiaqiao	66	28.47 N	121.29 E
Tuxpan	106	21.57 N	105.18 W
Tuxpan de Rodríguez Cano	106	20.57 N	97.24 W
Tuxtla Gutiérrez	106	16.45 N	93.07 W
Túy	50	42.03 N	8.38 W
Tuyen-hoa	70	17.50 N	106.10 E
Tuyen-quang	70	21.49 N	105.13 E
Tuy-hoa	70	13.05 N	109.18 E
Tuz Gölü ⊜	78	38.45 N	33.25 E
Tuzla	54	44.32 N	18.41 E
Tvârdica	54	43.42 N	25.52 E
Tvedestrand	44	58.37 N	8.55 E
Tveitsund	44	59.01 N	8.32 E
Twardogóra	46	51.22 N	17.28 E
Tweed	102	44.29 N	77.19 W
Tweed ≃	38	55.46 N	2.00 W
Tweeddale ∨	38	55.37 N	2.55 W
Tweed Heads	94	28.10 S	153.31 E
Tweedmouth	36	55.45 N	2.01 W
Tweeling	86	27.38 S	28.31 E
Twee Rivieren	86	26.27 S	20.37 E
Tweespruit	86	29.11 S	27.01 E
Twentynine Palms	104	34.08 N	116.03 W
Twilight Cove C	90	32.16 S	126.03 E
Twin Creek ≃	102	39.33 N	84.21 W
Twin Falls	104	42.33 N	114.27 W
Twin Heads ⋏	90	20.13 S	126.30 E
Twin Peak Islands II	90	34.00 S	122.50 E
Twinsburg	102	41.18 N	81.26 W
Twitchell Reservoir ⊜ [1]	104	35.00 N	120.19 W
Twitya ≃	98	64.10 N	128.12 W
Twofold Bay C	94	37.06 S	149.55 E
Two Thumb Range ⋏	96	43.45 S	170.43 E
Twrch ≃, Wales, U.K.	34	52.42 N	3.29 W
Twrch ≃, Wales, U.K.	34	51.46 N	3.46 W
Twyford, Eng., U.K.	34	51.29 N	0.53 W
Twyford, Eng., U.K.	34	51.01 N	1.19 W
Twymyn ≃	34	52.38 N	3.44 W
Tychy	46	50.09 N	18.59 E
Tyczyn	46	49.58 N	22.02 E
Tydal	44	63.04 N	11.34 E
Tyin ⊜	44	61.17 N	8.13 E
Tyldesley	36	53.31 N	2.28 W
Tyler	100	32.21 N	95.18 W
Tylösand	44	56.39 N	12.44 E
Tym ≃	58	59.25 N	80.04 E
Tymovskoje	58	50.51 N	142.39 E
Tynagh	40	53.09 N	8.22 W
Tyndinskij	58	55.10 N	124.43 E
Tyndrum	38	56.27 N	4.44 W
Tyne ≃, Eng., U.K.	36	55.01 N	1.26 W
Tyne ≃, Scot., U.K.	38	56.01 N	2.37 W
Tyne and Wear □ [6]	36	54.55 N	1.35 W
Tynemouth	36	55.01 N	1.24 W
Týn nad Vltavou	46	49.14 N	14.26 E
Tynset	44	62.17 N	10.47 E
Tyre →Şūr	78	33.16 N	35.11 E
Tyrifjorden ⊜	44	60.02 N	10.08 E
Tyringe	44	56.10 N	13.35 E
Tyrma	58	50.03 N	132.12 E
Tyrone	102	40.40 N	78.14 W
Tyrrell, Lake ⊜	94	35.21 S	142.50 E
Tyrrellspass	40	53.23 N	7.22 W
Tyrrhenian Sea (Mare Tirreno) ⊤ [2]	52	40.00 N	12.00 E
Tysnesøy I	44	60.00 N	5.35 E
Tysse	44	60.22 N	5.45 E
Tyssedal	44	60.07 N	6.34 E
Tywardreath	34	50.22 N	4.41 W
Tywi ≃	34	51.46 N	4.22 W
Tywyn	34	52.35 N	4.05 W
Tzaneen	86	23.50 S	30.09 E

U

Name	Page	Lat. °′	Long. °′
Uatumã ≃	110	2.26 S	57.37 W
Uaupés (Vaupés) ≃	110	0.02 N	67.16 W
Ubá	110	21.07 S	42.56 W
Ubangi (Oubangui) ≃	80	1.30 N	18.07 E
Ube	64	33.56 N	131.15 E
Úbeda	50	38.01 N	3.22 W
Uberaba	110	19.45 S	47.55 W
Uberlândia	110	18.56 S	48.18 W
Überlingen	46	47.46 N	9.10 E
Ubl'a	46	48.55 N	22.23 E
Ubly	102	43.42 N	82.55 W
Ubombo	86	27.33 S	32.00 E
Ubon Ratchathani	70	15.14 N	104.54 E
Ubrique	50	36.41 N	5.27 W
Ubundu	84	0.21 S	25.29 E
Ucacha	114	33.02 S	63.31 W
Učaly	56	54.19 N	59.27 E
Učami	58	63.50 N	96.29 E
Ucayali ≃	110	4.30 S	73.27 W
Uchinoura	64	31.16 N	131.05 E
Uchiura-wan C	64a	42.20 N	140.40 E
Uchiza	110	8.29 S	76.23 W
Uchta	42	63.33 N	53.38 E
Uckermark □ [9]	46	53.10 N	13.35 E
Uckfield	34	50.58 N	0.06 E
Učur ≃	58	58.48 N	130.35 E
Uda ≃, S.S.S.R.	58	56.05 N	99.34 E
Uda ≃, S.S.S.R.	58	51.47 N	107.33 E
Uda ≃, S.S.S.R.	58	54.42 N	135.14 E
Udaipur	76	24.35 N	73.41 E
Udaquiola	114	36.34 S	58.31 W
Udbina	52	44.32 N	15.46 E
Uddeholm	44	60.01 N	13.37 E
Uddevalla	44	58.21 N	11.55 E
Uddingston	38	55.50 N	4.06 W
Uddjaur ⊜	42	65.55 N	17.49 E
Udhampur	76	32.56 N	75.08 E
Udine	52	46.03 N	13.14 E
Udoml'a	60	57.52 N	35.01 E
Udono	64	33.44 N	136.01 E
Udon Thani	70	17.26 N	102.46 E
Udor, Mount ∧	90	23.30 S	131.01 E
Udskaja guba C	58	54.50 N	135.45 E
Udža	58	71.14 N	117.10 E
Ueckermünde	46	53.44 N	14.03 E
Ueda	64	36.24 N	138.16 E
Uele ≃	82	4.09 N	22.26 E
Uelen	58	66.10 N	169.48 W
Uel'kal'	58	65.32 N	179.17 W
Uelzen	46	52.58 N	10.33 E
Ueno	64	34.45 N	136.08 E
Uere ≃	82	3.42 N	25.24 E
Uetersen	46	53.41 N	9.39 E
Ufa	56	54.44 N	55.56 E
Uffculme	34	50.54 N	3.20 W
Uffenheim	46	49.32 N	10.14 E
Ugab ≃	86	21.08 S	13.40 E
Uganda □ [1]	84	1.00 N	32.00 E
Ugârčin	54	43.06 N	24.25 E
Ugie	86	31.10 S	28.13 E
Ugie ≃	38	57.30 N	1.47 W
Ugíjar	50	36.57 N	3.03 W
Ugine	48	45.45 N	6.25 E
Uglegorsk	58	49.02 N	142.03 E
Uglič	60	57.32 N	38.19 E
Ugljan, Otok I	52	44.05 N	15.10 E
Ugoma ∧	84	4.00 S	28.45 E
Uh (Už) ≃	46	48.34 N	22.00 E
Uherské Hradiště	46	49.05 N	17.28 E
Uherský Brod	46	49.02 N	17.39 E
Uhrichsville	102	40.23 N	81.20 W
Uig	38	57.35 N	6.22 W
Uíge	84	7.37 S	15.03 E
Uil ≃	56	48.36 N	52.30 E
Uimaharju	44	62.55 N	30.15 E
Uitenhage	86	33.40 S	25.28 E
Uithuizermeeden	46	53.24 N	6.42 E
Uj ≃	56	54.17 N	64.58 E
Ujae I [1]	28	9.05 N	165.40 E
Ujandina ≃	58	68.23 N	145.50 E
Ujar	58	55.48 N	94.20 E
Ujazd	46	50.24 N	18.22 E
Ujedinenija, ostrov I	56	77.28 N	82.28 E
Ujelang I [1]	28	9.49 N	160.55 E
Újfehértó	46	47.48 N	21.40 E
Uji	64	34.53 N	135.48 E
Uji-guntō II	64	31.11 N	129.27 E
Ujiji	84	4.55 S	29.41 E
Ujjain	76	23.11 N	75.46 E
'Ujmān	78	25.25 N	55.27 E
Ujście	46	53.04 N	16.43 E
Ujung Pandang (Makasar)	72	5.07 S	119.24 E
Uka	58	57.50 N	162.06 E
Ukerewe Island I	84	2.03 S	33.00 E
Ukhrul	76	25.07 N	94.22 E
Ukiah	104	39.09 N	123.12 W
Ukmergė	60	55.15 N	24.45 E
Ukraine →Ukrainskaja Sovetskaja Socialističeskaja Respublika □ [3]	56	49.00 N	32.00 E
Ukrainskaja Sovetskaja Socialističeskaja Respublika □ [3]	56	49.00 N	32.00 E
Ukrina ≃	52	45.05 N	17.56 E
Ukyr	58	49.28 N	108.52 E
Ulaanbaatar	62	47.55 N	106.53 E
Ulaangom	62	49.58 N	92.02 E
Ulan Bator →Ulaanbaatar	62	47.55 N	106.53 E
Ulanów	46	50.30 N	22.16 E
Ulan-Ude	58	51.50 N	107.37 E
Ułazów	46	50.17 N	23.00 E
Ulcinj	54	41.55 N	19.11 E
Ulco	86	28.21 S	24.15 E
Ulefoss	44	59.17 N	9.16 E
Ulfborg	44	56.16 N	8.20 E
Ulhāsnagar	74	19.13 N	73.07 E
Uliastaj	62	47.45 N	96.49 E
Ulindi ≃	84	1.40 S	25.52 E
Ulithi I [1]	68	9.58 N	139.40 E
Ulja	58	58.51 N	141.50 E
Uljanovka	60	59.38 N	30.46 E
Uljanovsk	42	54.20 N	48.24 E
Ulla	60	55.14 N	29.15 E
Ulla ≃	50	42.39 N	8.44 W
Ulladulla	94	35.21 S	150.29 E
Ullapool	38	57.54 N	5.10 W
Ullswater ⊜	36	54.34 N	2.54 W
Ullún	114	31.28 S	68.42 W
Ullŭng-do I	64	37.29 N	130.52 E
Ulm	46	48.24 N	10.00 E
Ulma	54	47.53 N	25.18 E
Ulmarra	94	29.37 S	153.02 E
Ulmeni	54	45.04 N	26.39 E
Ulricehamn	44	57.47 N	13.25 E
Ulrum	46	53.22 N	6.20 E
Ulsan	62	35.34 N	129.19 E
Ulsta	38	60.30 N	1.09 W
Ulsteinvik	44	62.20 N	5.53 E
Ulster □ [9]	40	54.35 N	7.00 W
Ulster Canal ≍	40	54.08 N	7.22 W
Ulu	58	60.19 N	127.24 E
Ulul I	28	8.35 N	149.40 E
Ulu Laho, Bukit ∧	72	5.43 N	101.27 E
Ulungur ≃	62	46.59 N	87.27 E
Ulungur Hu ⊜	62	47.15 N	87.20 E
Ulva I	38	56.29 N	6.14 W
Ulverston	36	54.12 N	3.06 W
Ulverstone	94	41.09 S	146.10 E
Ulvöarna II	44	63.01 N	18.40 E
Ulzë	54	41.41 N	19.54 E
Umag	52	45.25 N	13.32 E
Uman'	56	48.44 N	30.14 E
Umanak	98	70.40 N	52.07 W
Umanak Fjord C [2]	98	70.55 N	53.00 W
Umarkot	76	25.22 N	69.44 E
Umba	42	66.41 N	34.15 E
Umbertide	52	43.18 N	12.20 E
Umbria □ [4]	52	43.00 N	12.30 E
Umeå	44	63.50 N	20.15 E
Umeälven ≃	44	63.47 N	20.16 E
Umfors	42	65.56 N	15.00 E
Umhlanga Rocks	86	29.43 S	31.06 E
Umkomaas	86	30.15 S	30.42 E
Umm al-Qaywayn	78	25.35 N	55.34 E
Umm Durmān (Omdurman)	82	15.38 N	32.30 E
Umnäs	42	65.24 N	16.10 E
Um'ot	60	54.08 N	42.42 E
Umpqua ≃	104	43.32 N	123.30 W
'Umrān	74	15.50 N	43.56 E
Umreth	76	22.42 N	73.07 E
Umtata	86	31.35 S	28.47 E
Umtentweni	86	30.42 S	30.28 E
Umuarama	114	23.45 S	53.20 W
Umzimkulu	86	30.16 S	29.56 E
Umzinto	86	30.22 S	30.33 E
Una	76	20.49 N	71.02 E
Una ≃	52	45.16 N	16.55 E
Una, Mount ∧	96	42.13 S	172.35 E
Unac ≃	52	44.30 N	16.09 E
Unadilla	102	42.19 N	75.18 W
Unadilla ≃	102	42.20 N	75.25 W
Unalaska	22	53.52 N	166.32 W
Unare ≃	108	10.03 N	65.14 W
'Unayzah	78	26.06 N	43.56 E
Uncia	110	18.27 S	66.37 W
Uncompahgre Peak ∧	100	38.04 N	107.28 W
Unden ⊜	44	58.47 N	14.26 E
Underberg	86	29.50 S	29.22 E
Undersåker	44	63.20 N	13.23 E
Uneča	60	52.50 N	32.40 E
Ungarie	94	33.38 S	146.58 E
Ungava, Péninsule d' › [1]	98	60.00 N	74.00 W
Ungava Bay C	98	59.30 N	67.30 W
Uni	42	57.46 N	51.30 E
União	110	4.35 S	42.52 W
União da Vitória	114	26.13 S	51.05 W
União dos Palmares	110	9.10 S	36.02 W
Uniejów	46	51.58 N	18.49 E
Unije, Otok I	52	44.38 N	14.15 E
Unini ≃	110	1.41 S	61.31 W
Unión, Arg.	114	35.09 S	65.57 W
Unión, Para.	114	24.48 S	56.33 W
Union, N.J., U.S.	102	40.41 N	74.15 W
Union, S.C., U.S.	100	34.42 N	81.37 W
Union City, Mi., U.S.	102	42.04 N	85.09 W
Union City, Oh., U.S.	102	40.11 N	84.48 W
Union City, Pa., U.S.	102	41.53 N	79.50 W
Union City, Tn., U.S.	100	36.25 N	89.03 W
Uniondale	86	33.40 S	23.08 E
Unión de Reyes	108	22.48 N	81.32 W
Union of Soviet Socialist Republics □ [1]	26	60.00 N	80.00 E
Union Seamount ◂ [3]	22	49.35 N	132.45 W
Union Springs	102	42.50 N	76.41 W
Uniontown	102	39.54 N	79.44 W
Unionville	102	43.39 N	83.27 W
United	102	40.13 N	79.29 W
United Arab Emirates □ [1]	74	24.00 N	54.00 E
United Kingdom □ [1]	30	54.00 N	2.00 W
United States □ [1]	100	38.00 N	97.00 W
United States Military Academy ▪	102	41.23 N	73.58 W
United States Naval Academy ▪	102	38.59 N	76.30 W
Unity	98	52.27 N	109.10 W
Unjha	76	23.48 N	72.24 E
Unna	46	51.32 N	7.41 E
Unnão	76	26.32 N	80.30 E
Unquillo	114	31.14 S	64.19 W
Unst I	38a	60.45 N	0.53 W
Unstrut ≃	46	51.10 N	11.48 E
Unža ≃	60	57.20 N	43.08 E
Unzen-dake ∧	64	32.45 N	130.17 E
Uozu	64	36.48 N	137.24 E
Upata	110	8.01 N	62.24 W
Upavon	34	51.18 N	1.49 W
Upemba, Lac ⊜	84	8.36 S	26.26 E
Upernavik	98	72.47 N	56.10 W
Upington	86	28.25 S	21.15 E
Upire ≃	108	11.27 N	68.58 W
Upleta	76	21.44 N	70.17 E
Upolu I	28	13.55 S	171.45 W
Upolu Point ›	105a	20.16 N	155.51 W
Upper Arlington	102	40.00 N	83.03 W
Upper Arrow Lake ⊜	98	50.30 N	117.55 W
Upper Darby	102	39.55 N	75.16 W
Upper Hutt	96	41.08 S	175.04 E
Upper Klamath Lake ⊜	104	42.23 N	121.55 W
Upper Lake	104	39.10 N	122.54 W
Upper Lake ⊜	104	41.44 N	120.08 W
Upper Moutere	96	41.16 S	173.00 E
Upper Red Lake ⊜	100	48.10 N	94.40 W
Upper Sandusky	102	40.49 N	83.16 W
Upper Takaka	96	41.02 S	172.50 E
Upper Tean	34	52.57 N	1.58 W
Uppingham	34	52.35 N	0.43 W
Uppland □ [9]	44	59.59 N	17.48 E
Upplands Väsby	44	59.31 N	17.54 E
Uppsala	44	59.52 N	17.38 E
Uppsala Län □ [6]	44	60.00 N	17.45 E
Upstart, Cape ›	94	19.42 S	147.45 E
Upton	36	53.37 N	1.17 W
Upton upon Severn	34	52.04 N	2.13 W
Upwell	34	52.36 N	0.12 E
Ur ⊥	78	30.57 N	46.09 E
Uracoa	108	9.00 N	62.21 W
Urahoro	64a	42.48 N	143.39 E
Uraj	56	60.08 N	64.48 E
Urakawa	64a	42.09 N	142.47 E
Ural ≃	56	47.00 N	51.48 E
Uralla	94	30.39 S	151.30 E
Ural Mountains →Ural'skije gory ⋏	56	60.00 N	60.00 E
Ural'sk	56	51.14 N	51.22 E
Ural'skije gory (Ural Mountains) ⋏	56	60.00 N	60.00 E
Urana	94	35.20 S	146.16 E
Urandangi	94	21.36 S	138.18 E
Urangan	94	25.18 S	152.54 E
Uranium City	98	59.34 N	108.36 W
Urarey	90	27.26 S	122.18 E
Uraricoera ≃	110	3.02 N	60.30 W
Urasoe	65b	26.15 N	127.43 E
Ura-T'ube	56	39.55 N	68.59 E
Urawa	64	35.51 N	139.39 E
Urbana	102	40.06 N	83.45 W
Urbania	52	43.40 N	12.31 E
Urbiña, Peña ∧	50	43.01 N	5.57 W
Urbino	52	43.43 N	12.38 E
Urdinarrain	114	32.41 S	58.53 W
Urdoma	42	61.47 N	48.32 E
Ure ≃	36	54.01 N	1.12 W
Urenui	96	39.00 S	174.23 E
Ures	106	29.26 N	110.24 W
Ureshino	64	33.06 N	129.59 E
Urewera National Park ♠	96	38.40 S	177.00 E
Urfa	78	37.08 N	38.46 E
Urgenč	56	41.33 N	60.38 E
Ürgüp	78	38.38 N	34.56 E
Uribia	110	11.43 N	72.16 W
Urie ≃	38	57.19 N	2.30 W
Urjala	44	61.05 N	23.32 E
Urlaţi	54	44.59 N	26.14 E
Urlingford	40	52.42 N	7.35 W
Urmar Tanda	76	31.42 N	75.38 E
Urmia →Orūmīyeh	78	37.33 N	45.04 E
Urmia, Lake →Orūmīyeh, Daryācheh-ye ⊜	78	37.40 N	45.30 E
Urmston	36	53.27 N	2.21 W
Uroševac	54	42.22 N	21.09 E
Urquhart, Glen ∨	38	57.20 N	4.35 W
Urrao	110	6.20 N	76.11 W
Urr Water ≃	36	54.53 N	3.49 W
Ursus	46	52.12 N	20.53 E
Uruapan	106	19.25 N	102.04 W
Urubamba ≃	110	10.44 S	73.45 W
Urubu ≃	110	2.55 S	58.25 W
Uruguaiana	114	29.45 S	57.05 W
Uruguay □ [1]	112	33.00 S	56.00 W
Uruguay (Uruguai) ≃	114	34.12 S	58.18 W
Urukthapel I	68	7.15 N	134.24 E
Urumchi →Ürümqi	62	43.48 N	87.35 E
Ürümqi	62	43.48 N	87.35 E
Urundel	114	23.33 S	64.25 W
Ur'ung-Chaja	58	72.48 N	113.23 E
Urup, ostrov I	58	46.00 N	150.00 E
Ur'upinsk	56	50.47 N	41.59 E
Urussanga	114	28.31 S	49.19 W
Urutaú	114	25.42 S	63.04 W
Uruti	96	38.57 S	174.32 E
Urziceni	54	44.43 N	26.38 E
Uržum	42	57.08 N	50.00 E
Usa	64	33.31 N	131.22 E
Usa ≃	42	65.57 N	56.55 E
Ušači	60	55.11 N	28.37 E
Uşak	54	38.41 N	29.25 E
Usakos	86	22.01 S	15.32 E
Ušće	54	43.28 N	20.37 E
Usedom I	46	54.00 N	14.00 E
Ushibuka	64	32.11 N	130.01 E
Ushuaia	112	54.48 S	68.18 W
Usingen	46	50.20 N	8.32 E
Usk	34	51.43 N	2.54 W
Usk ≃	34	51.36 N	2.58 W
Uskedal	44	59.56 N	5.52 E
Üsküb →Skopje	54	41.59 N	21.26 E
Üsküdar	30	41.01 N	29.01 E
Uslar	46	51.39 N	9.38 E
Usman'	60	52.02 N	39.44 E
Usolje	42	59.25 N	56.41 E
Usolje-Sibirskoje	58	52.47 N	103.38 E
Uspallata	114	32.35 S	69.20 W
Ussel	48	45.33 N	2.18 E
Ussuri (Wusuli) ≃	58	48.27 N	135.04 E
Ussurijsk	58	43.48 N	131.59 E
Ustaoset	44	60.30 N	8.04 E
Ustaritz	48	43.24 N	1.27 W
Ust'-Barguzin	58	53.27 N	108.59 E
Ust'-Belaja	58	65.30 N	173.20 E
Ust'-Bol'šereck	58	52.48 N	156.14 E
Ust'-Čaun	58	68.47 N	170.30 E
Ust'-Cil'ma	42	65.27 N	52.06 E
Uster	48	47.21 N	8.43 E
Ustica, Isola di I	52	38.42 N	13.11 E
Ust'-Ilimsk	56	58.00 N	102.39 E
Ust'-Ilimskoje vodochranilišče ⊜ [1]	58	57.00 N	102.15 E
Ústí nad Labem	46	50.40 N	14.02 E
Ústí nad Orlicí	46	49.58 N	16.24 E
Ustinov	42	56.51 N	53.14 E
Ust'-Išim	56	57.42 N	71.10 E
Ustka	46	54.35 N	16.50 E
Ust'-Kamčatsk	58	56.15 N	162.30 E
Ust'-Kamenogorsk	56	49.58 N	82.38 E
Ust'-Katav	56	54.56 N	58.10 E
Ust'-Koksa	58	50.18 N	85.36 E
Ust'-Kujda	58	70.01 N	135.36 E
Ust'-Kut	58	56.46 N	105.40 E
Ust'-Maja	58	60.25 N	134.32 E
Ust'-Manja	56	62.11 N	60.20 E
Ust'-Nera	58	64.34 N	143.12 E
Ust'-N'ukža	58	56.34 N	121.37 E
Uštobe	56	45.16 N	78.00 E
Ust'-Omčug	58	61.09 N	149.38 E
Ust'-Ordynskij	58	52.48 N	104.45 E
Ust'-Oz'ornoje	58	58.54 N	87.48 E
Ustroń	46	49.43 N	18.49 E
Ustrzyki Dolne	46	49.26 N	22.37 E
Ust'-Šonoša	42	61.10 N	41.18 E
Ust'-Tym	56	59.26 N	80.08 E
Ustupo Yantupo	108	9.27 N	78.34 W
Ust'urt, plato ⋏ [1]	56	43.00 N	56.00 E
Ust'-Usa	42	65.59 N	56.54 E
Ust'užna	60	58.51 N	36.26 E
Usu	62	44.27 N	84.37 E
Usuki	64	33.08 N	131.49 E
Usumacinta ≃	106	18.24 N	92.38 W
Usumbura →Bujumbura	84	3.23 S	29.22 E
Ušumun	58	52.49 N	126.27 E
Usu-zan ∧	64a	42.32 N	140.51 E
Utah □ [3]	100	39.30 N	111.30 W
Utah Lake ⊜	100	40.13 N	111.49 W
Utajärvi	44	64.45 N	26.23 E
Utashinai	64a	43.31 N	142.03 E
Utembo ≃	84	17.06 S	22.01 E
Utena	60	55.30 N	25.36 E
Utersum	46	54.43 N	8.24 E
Utete	84	7.59 S	38.47 E
Uthai Thani	70	15.22 N	100.03 E
Utiariti	110	13.02 S	58.17 W
Utica, Mi., U.S.	102	42.37 N	83.02 W
Utica, N.Y., U.S.	102	43.06 N	75.13 W
Utica, Oh., U.S.	102	40.14 N	82.27 W
Utiel	50	39.34 N	1.12 W
Utila	108	16.06 N	86.54 W
Utila, Isla de I	108	16.06 N	86.56 W
Utirik I [1]	28	11.15 N	169.48 E
Utlängan I	44	56.01 N	15.47 E
Uto	64	32.41 N	130.40 E
Utö I	44	58.56 N	18.16 E
Utopia	90	22.14 S	134.33 E
Utrecht, Ned.	46	52.05 N	5.08 E
Utrecht, S. Afr.	86	27.38 S	30.20 E
Utrera	50	37.11 N	5.47 W
Utsira	44	59.18 N	4.54 E
Utsjoki	42	69.53 N	27.00 E
Utsunomiya	64	36.33 N	139.52 E
Uttaradit	70	17.38 N	100.06 E
Uttarkāshi	76	30.44 N	78.27 E
Uttar Pradesh □ [3]	76	27.00 N	80.00 E
Uttoxeter	34	52.54 N	1.51 W
Utuado	108	18.16 N	66.42 W
Utupua I	28	11.16 S	166.29 E
Uudenmaan lääni □ [4]	44	60.30 N	25.00 E
Uusikaarlepyy (Nykarleby)	44	63.32 N	22.32 E
Uusikaupunki (Nystad)	44	60.48 N	21.25 E
Uusimaa ◂ [1]	44	60.30 N	25.00 E
Uvá ≃	110	3.57 N	68.24 W
Uvalde	100	29.12 N	99.47 W
Uvarovka	60	55.32 N	35.37 E
Uvarovo	60	51.59 N	42.15 E
Uvat	56	59.09 N	68.54 E
Uvdal	44	60.16 N	8.44 E
Uvinza	84	5.06 S	30.22 E
Uvira	84	3.24 S	29.08 E
Uvongo Beach	86	30.51 S	30.23 E
Uvs nuur ⊜	58	50.20 N	92.45 E
Uwa	64	33.20 N	132.30 E
Uwajima	64	33.13 N	132.34 E
'Uwaynāt, Jabal al- ∧	82	21.54 N	24.58 E
Uxbridge	102	44.06 N	79.07 W
Uyuni	110	20.28 S	66.50 W
Uyuni, Salar de ≚	110	20.20 S	67.42 W
Už (Uh) ≃	46	48.34 N	22.00 E
Uzbekskaja Sovetskaja Socialističeskaja Respublika □ [3]	56	41.00 N	64.00 E
Uzbek Soviet Socialist Republic →Uzbekskaja Sovetskaja Socialističeskaja Respublika □ [3]	56	41.00 N	64.00 E
Uzdin	54	45.12 N	20.38 E
Uzerche	48	45.26 N	1.34 E
Uzès	48	44.01 N	4.25 E
Užgorod	56	48.37 N	22.18 E
Užice →Titovo Užice	54	43.51 N	19.51 E
Uzlovaja	60	53.59 N	38.10 E
Uzunköprü	54	41.16 N	26.41 E
Užur	58	55.20 N	89.50 E
Užventis	60	55.47 N	22.39 E

V

Name	Page	Lat. °′	Long. °′
Vä	44	55.59 N	14.05 E
Vaajakoski	44	62.16 N	25.54 E
Vääksy	44	61.11 N	25.33 E
Vaal ≃	86	29.04 S	23.38 E
Vaala	44	64.26 N	26.48 E
Vaaldam ⊜ [1]	86	26.55 S	28.12 E
Vaalkop ∧	86	31.21 S	26.31 E
Vaalserberg ∧	46	50.46 N	6.01 E
Vaalwater	86	24.20 S	28.03 E
Vaanta (Vanda)	44	60.16 N	25.03 E
Vaasa (Vasa)	44	63.06 N	21.36 E
Vaasan lääni □ [4]	44	63.00 N	23.00 E
Vác	46	47.47 N	19.08 E
Vača	60	55.48 N	42.46 E
Vacacai ≃	114	29.55 S	53.06 W
Vacaria	114	28.30 S	50.56 W
Vacaville	104	38.21 N	121.59 W
Vaccarès, Étang de C	48	43.32 N	4.34 E
Vach ≃	56	60.45 N	76.45 E
Vache, Île à I	108	18.05 N	73.38 W
Vachš ≃	56	37.06 N	68.18 E
Vacoas	87c	20.18 S	57.29 E
Väddö I	44	60.00 N	18.50 E
Vădeni	54	45.22 N	27.56 E
Vadheim	44	61.13 N	5.49 E
Vado Ligure	52	44.17 N	8.27 E
Vadsø	42	70.05 N	29.46 E
Vadstena	44	58.27 N	14.54 E
Vaduz	48	47.09 N	9.31 E
Værøy I	42	67.40 N	12.39 E
Vaga ≃	42	62.48 N	42.56 E
Vagaj	58	57.56 N	69.01 E
Vågåmo	44	61.53 N	9.06 E
Vaganski Vrh ∧	52	44.22 N	15.31 E
Vaggeryd	44	57.30 N	14.07 E
Váh ≃	46	47.55 N	18.00 E
Vaich, Loch ⊜	38	57.43 N	4.46 W
Vaihingen	46	48.56 N	8.58 E
Vaila I	38a	60.12 N	1.37 W
Vailly-sur-Aisne	48	49.25 N	3.31 E
Vaison-la-Romaine	48	44.14 N	5.04 E
Vaitupu I	28	7.28 S	178.41 E
Vajgač	56	70.25 N	58.46 E
Vajgač, ostrov I	56	70.00 N	59.30 E
Vākhān ◂ [1]	76	37.00 N	73.00 E
Vaksdal	44	60.29 N	5.44 E
Vålådalen	44	63.10 N	12.57 E
Valandovo	54	41.19 N	22.34 E
Valašské Klobouky	46	49.08 N	18.01 E
Valašské Meziříčí	46	49.28 N	17.58 E
Valatie	102	42.24 N	73.40 W
Vålberg	44	59.24 N	13.12 E
Valbo	44	60.40 N	17.04 E
Vâlcĕdrâm	54	43.42 N	23.27 E
Valcheta	112	40.42 S	66.09 W
Valdagno	52	45.39 N	11.18 E
Valdai Hills →Valdajskaja vozvyšennost' ⋏ [2]	42	57.00 N	33.30 E
Valdaj, S.S.S.R.	42	63.26 N	35.30 E
Valdaj, S.S.S.R.	60	57.59 N	33.14 E
Valdajskaja vozvyšennost' ⋏ [2]	42	57.00 N	33.30 E
Valdarno ∨	52	43.45 N	11.15 E
Valdavia ≃	50	42.24 N	4.16 W
Valdecañas, Embalse de ⊜ [1]	50	39.45 N	5.30 W
Valdemarsvik	44	58.12 N	16.36 E
Valdepeñas	50	38.46 N	3.23 W
Valderaduey ≃	50	41.31 N	5.42 W
Valderas	50	42.05 N	5.27 W
Valderrobres	50	40.53 N	0.09 E
Valdés, Península › [1]	112	42.30 S	64.00 W
Val-des-Bois	102	45.54 N	75.35 W
Valdez	98	61.08 N	146.22 W
Val-d'Isère	48	45.27 N	6.59 E
Valdivia	112	39.48 S	73.14 W
Valdobbiadene	52	45.54 N	12.00 E
Val-d'Oise □ [5]	48	49.10 N	2.10 E
Val-d'Or	98	48.07 N	77.47 W
Valdosta	100	30.49 N	83.16 W
Valdoviño	50	43.36 N	8.08 W
Valdres ∨	44	60.55 N	9.10 E
Vale	35b	49.29 N	2.31 W
Valea lui Mihai	54	47.31 N	22.09 E
Valença, Bra.	110	13.22 S	39.05 W
Valença, Port.	50	42.02 N	8.38 W
Valençay	48	47.09 N	1.34 E
Valence	48	44.56 N	4.54 E
Valencia, Esp.	50	39.28 N	0.22 W
Valencia, Ven.	110	10.11 N	68.00 W
Valencia □ [4]	50	39.30 N	0.45 W
Valencia, Golfo de C	50	39.50 N	0.30 E
Valencia de Alcántata	50	39.25 N	7.14 W
Valencia de Don Juan	50	42.18 N	5.31 W
Valencia Island I	40	51.52 N	10.20 W
Valenciennes	48	50.21 N	3.32 E
Vălenii-de-Munte	54	45.12 N	26.03 E
Valentine	100	42.52 N	100.33 W
Valenza	52	45.01 N	8.38 E
Våler	44	60.40 N	11.50 E
Valera	110	9.19 N	70.37 W
Valga	60	57.47 N	26.02 E
Valguarnera Caropepe	52	37.30 N	14.23 E
Valiente, Península › [1]	108	9.05 N	81.51 W
Valjevo	54	44.16 N	19.53 E
Valka	60	57.46 N	26.00 E
Valkeakoski	44	61.16 N	24.02 E
Valkenburg	46	50.52 N	5.50 E
Valkenswaard	46	51.21 N	5.28 E
Valladolid, Esp.	50	41.39 N	4.43 W
Valladolid, Méx.	106	20.41 N	88.12 W
Vallauris	48	43.35 N	7.03 E
Valldal	44	62.20 N	7.21 E
Vall de Uxó	50	39.49 N	0.14 W
Valle	50	43.14 N	4.18 W
Valle d'Aosta □ [4]	52	45.45 N	7.25 E
Valle de Guanape	108	9.54 N	65.41 W
Valle de la Pascua	110	9.13 N	66.00 W
Valledolmo	52	37.45 N	13.49 E
Valledupar	110	10.29 N	73.15 W
Valle Edén	114	31.50 S	56.09 W
Vallegrande	110	18.29 S	64.06 W
Valle Hermoso	114	31.07 S	64.29 W
Vallejo	104	38.06 N	122.15 W
Vallelunga Pratameno	52	37.41 N	13.50 E
Vallenar	114	28.35 S	70.46 W
Vallentuna	44	59.32 N	18.05 E
Valle Redondo	104	32.31 N	116.46 W
Vallet	48	47.10 N	1.16 W
Valletta	52	35.54 N	14.31 E
Valley Bend	102	38.46 N	79.56 W
Valley City	100	46.55 N	97.59 W
Valleyfield	102	45.15 N	74.08 W
Valley Head	102	38.32 N	80.02 W
Valleyview	98	55.04 N	117.17 W
Vallgrund I	44	63.12 N	21.14 E
Vallo della Lucania	52	40.14 N	15.17 E
Vallon-Pont-d'Arc	48	44.24 N	4.24 E
Vallorbe	48	46.43 N	6.22 E
Valls	50	41.17 N	1.15 E
Valmaseda	50	43.12 N	3.12 W
Valmiera	60	57.33 N	25.24 E
Valognes	48	49.31 N	1.28 W
Valona →Vlorë	54	40.27 N	19.30 E
Valongo	50	41.11 N	8.30 W
Valoria la Buena	50	41.48 N	4.32 W
Valparai	74	10.22 N	76.58 E
Valparaíso, Chile	114	33.02 S	71.38 W
Valparaíso, Méx.	106	22.46 N	103.34 W
Valpovo	54	45.39 N	18.26 E
Valréas	48	44.23 N	4.59 E
Vals ≃	86	27.23 S	26.30 E
Vals, Tanjung ›	92	8.26 S	137.38 E
Valsbaai C	86	34.12 S	18.40 E
Valsjöbyn	44	64.04 N	14.08 E
Valtimo	44	63.40 N	28.48 E
Valujki	56	50.13 N	38.08 E
Valverde del Camino	50	37.34 N	6.45 W
Våmhus	44	61.08 N	14.28 E
Vammala	44	61.20 N	22.54 E
Van	78	38.28 N	43.20 E
Vanajanselkä ⊜	44	61.09 N	24.15 E
Vanavana I [1]	28	20.47 S	139.09 W
Vanavara	58	60.22 N	102.16 E
Van Buren	100	35.26 N	94.20 W
Vanč	56	38.23 N	71.26 E
Vanceboro	102	45.33 N	67.25 W
Vanceburg	102	38.35 N	83.19 W
Vancouver, B.C., Can.	98	49.16 N	123.07 W
Vancouver, Wa., U.S.	100	45.38 N	122.39 W
Vancouver, Cape ›	90	35.01 S	118.12 E
Vancouver Island I	98	49.45 N	126.00 W
Vandalia	102	39.53 N	84.11 W
Vanderbijlpark	86	26.42 S	27.54 E
Vanderbilt	102	45.08 N	84.39 W
Vandergrift	102	40.36 N	79.33 W
Vanderhoof	98	54.01 N	124.01 W
Vanderlin Island I	92	15.44 S	137.02 E
Van Diemen, Cape ›, Austl.	92	11.10 S	130.23 E
Van Diemen, Cape ›, Austl.	92	16.31 S	139.41 E
Van Diemen Gulf C	92	11.50 S	132.00 E
Van Duzen ≃	104	40.33 N	124.08 W
Vänern ⊜	44	58.55 N	13.30 E
Vänersborg	44	58.22 N	12.19 E
Vangaindrano	87b	23.21 S	47.36 E
Vängelälven ≃	44	63.41 N	16.25 E
Van Gölü ⊜	78	38.33 N	42.46 E
Vangsnes	44	61.11 N	6.38 E
Vangunu I	88	8.38 S	158.00 E
Vanier	102	45.26 N	75.40 W
Vanikolo I	28	11.39 S	166.54 E
Vanimo	92	2.40 S	141.20 E
Vanino	58	49.05 N	140.15 E
Vankarem	58	67.51 N	175.50 W
Vankleek Hill	102	45.31 N	74.39 W
Van Lear	102	37.46 N	82.45 W
Vanna I	42	70.09 N	19.51 E
Vännäs	44	63.55 N	19.45 E
Vannes	48	47.39 N	2.46 W
Vanoise, Massif de la ⋏	48	45.20 N	6.40 E
Van Reenen	86	28.22 S	29.24 E
Van Rees, Pegunungan ⋏	92	2.35 S	138.15 E
Vanrhynsdorp	86	31.36 S	18.44 E
Vanrook	94	16.57 S	141.57 E
Vansbro	44	60.31 N	14.13 E
Vansittart Island I	98	65.50 N	84.00 W
Vanstadensrus	86	29.59 S	27.02 E
Vantaa ≃	44	60.13 N	24.59 E
Vanua Lava I	28	13.48 S	167.28 E
Vanua Levu I	28	16.33 S	179.15 E
Vanuatu □ [1]	28	16.00 S	167.00 E
Van Wert	102	40.52 N	84.35 W
Vanwyksdorp	86	33.46 S	21.28 E
Vanwyksvlei	86	30.18 S	21.49 E
Vanzylsrus	86	26.52 S	22.04 E
Var □ [5]	48	43.30 N	6.20 E
Var ≃	48	43.39 N	7.12 E
Vara	44	58.16 N	12.57 E
Varades	48	47.23 N	1.02 W
Varakļāni	60	56.37 N	26.44 E
Varallo	52	45.49 N	8.15 E
Varāmīn	78	35.20 N	51.39 E
Vārānasi (Benares)	74	25.20 N	83.00 E
Varangerfjorden C [2]	42	70.00 N	30.00 E
Varangerhalvøya › [1]	42	70.25 N	29.30 E
Varano, Lago di C	52	41.53 N	15.45 E
Varaždin	52	46.19 N	16.20 E
Varazze	52	44.22 N	8.34 E
Varberg	44	57.06 N	12.15 E
Vardak □ [4]	76	34.15 N	68.00 E
Vardar (Axiós) ≃	54	40.35 N	22.50 E
Varde	44	55.38 N	8.29 E
Vardhoúsia Óri ⋏	54	38.44 N	22.07 E
Vardø	42	70.21 N	31.02 E
Varegovo	60	57.47 N	39.17 E
Varel	46	53.22 N	8.10 E
Vareļa	114	34.07 S	66.27 W
Varena	60	54.13 N	24.34 E
Varennes-sur-Allier	48	46.19 N	3.24 E
Vareš	54	44.09 N	18.19 E
Varese	52	45.48 N	8.48 E
Varese Ligure	52	44.22 N	9.37 E
Vårgårda	44	58.02 N	12.48 E
Varginha	110	21.33 S	45.26 W
Vargön	44	58.22 N	12.22 E
Varkaus	44	62.19 N	27.55 E
Värmeln ⊜	44	59.32 N	12.54 E
Värmland □ [9]	44	59.48 N	13.03 E
Värmlands Län □ [6]	44	59.45 N	13.15 E
Värmlandsnäs › [1]	44	59.00 N	13.10 E
Varna	54	43.13 N	27.55 E
Värnamo	44	57.11 N	14.02 E
Varnenski zaliv C	54	43.11 N	27.56 E
Varnhem	44	58.23 N	13.39 E
Varnsdorf	46	50.52 N	14.40 E
Värö	44	57.16 N	12.11 E
Varpaisjärvi	44	63.22 N	27.45 E
Várpalota	46	47.12 N	18.09 E
Vâršec	54	43.12 N	23.17 E
Varsinais-Suomi ◂ [1]	44	60.40 N	22.30 E
V'artsil'a, S.S.S.R.	42	62.11 N	30.41 E
Värtsilä, Suomi	44	62.15 N	30.40 E
Varvarin	54	43.43 N	21.19 E
Várzea, Rio da ≃	114	27.13 S	53.19 W
Varzeão	114	24.34 S	49.26 W
Varzo	52	46.12 N	8.15 E
Varzy	48	47.22 N	3.23 E
Vas □ [6]	46	47.05 N	16.45 E
Vascão ≃	50	37.31 N	7.31 W
Vaşcău	54	46.28 N	22.28 E
Vasiliká	54	40.28 N	23.08 E
Vaslui	54	46.38 N	27.44 E
Vaslui □ [6]	54	46.30 N	27.45 E
Väsman ⊜	44	60.11 N	15.04 E
Vassar	102	43.22 N	83.35 W
Vassdalsegga ∧	44	59.46 N	7.10 E
Västerås	44	59.37 N	16.33 E
Västerbotten □ [9]	44	64.36 N	20.04 E
Västerbottens Län □ [6]	44	64.00 N	17.30 E
Västerdalälven ≃	44	60.33 N	15.08 E
Västergötland □ [9]	44	58.01 N	13.03 E
Västerhaninge	44	59.07 N	18.06 E
Västernorrlands Län □ [6]	44	63.00 N	17.30 E
Västervik	44	57.45 N	16.38 E
Västmanland □ [9]	44	59.38 N	15.15 E
Västmanlands Län □ [6]	44	59.45 N	16.20 E
Vasto	52	42.07 N	14.42 E
Vas'ugan ≃	58	59.07 N	80.46 E
Vas'uganje ⁝⁝	58	58.00 N	77.00 E
Vasvár	46	47.03 N	16.49 E
Vaţa de Jos	54	46.10 N	22.35 E
Vatan	48	47.05 N	1.48 E
Vaternish Point ›	38	57.36 N	6.38 W
Vatersay I	38	56.55 N	7.32 W
Vathí	54	37.45 N	26.59 E
Vatican City □ [1]	50	41.54 N	12.27 E
Vaticano, Capo ›	52	38.38 N	15.50 E
V'atka ≃	42	55.36 N	51.30 E
Vatnajökull ⊏	42a	64.25 N	16.50 W
Vatneyri	42a	65.38 N	23.57 W
Vatomandry	87b	19.20 S	48.59 E
Vatra Dornei	54	47.21 N	25.21 E
V'atskije Pol'any	42	56.14 N	51.04 E
Vättern ⊜	44	58.24 N	14.36 E
Vaucluse □ [5]	48	44.00 N	5.10 E
Vaucouleurs	48	48.36 N	5.40 E
Vaughan	102	43.47 N	79.36 W
Vaughn	100	34.36 N	105.12 W
Vaupés (Uaupés) ≃	110	0.02 N	67.16 W
Vauvert	48	43.42 N	4.17 E
Vava'u Group II	28	18.40 S	174.00 W
Växjö	44	56.52 N	14.49 E
V'azemskij	58	47.32 N	134.48 E
V'az'ma	60	55.13 N	34.18 E
V'azniki	60	56.15 N	42.10 E
Veazie	102	44.50 N	68.42 W
Vechta	46	52.43 N	8.16 E
Vecsés	46	47.25 N	19.16 E

Symbols in the Index entries are identified on page 122

Name	Page	Lat. °′	Long. °′
Veddige	44	57.16 N	12.19 E
Vedea	54	44.47 N	24.37 E
Vedea ≃	54	43.43 N	25.32 E
Vedia	114	34.30 S	61.32 W
Veendam	46	53.06 N	6.58 E
Veenendaal	46	52.02 N	5.34 E
Vefsna ≃	42	65.50 N	13.12 E
Vega I	42	65.39 N	11.50 E
Vegreville	98	53.30 N	112.03 W
Veil, Loch ⊜	38	56.20 N	4.25 W
Veinticinco de Mayo, Arg.	114	35.26 S	60.10 W
Veinticinco de Mayo, Ur.	114	34.12 S	56.22 W
Vejen	44	55.29 N	9.09 E
Vejer de la Frontera	50	36.15 N	5.58 W
Vejle	44	55.42 N	9.32 E
Vela Luka	52	42.58 N	16.43 E
Velas, Cabo ›	108	10.22 N	85.53 W
Velázquez	114	34.02 S	54.17 W
Velbert	46	51.20 N	7.02 E
Velddrif	86	32.47 S	18.11 E
Velden	46	48.19 N	12.16 E
Veldhoven	46	51.24 N	5.24 E
Velebit ⋀	52	44.38 N	15.03 E
Velebitski Kanal ⊔	52	45.00 N	14.50 E
Veleka ≃	54	42.04 N	27.58 E
Velencei-tó ⊜	46	47.12 N	18.35 E
Velenje	52	46.21 N	15.06 E
Velestínon	54	39.23 N	22.45 E
Velet'ma	60	55.20 N	42.25 E
Vélez-Málaga	50	36.47 N	4.06 W
Vélez Rubio	50	37.39 N	2.04 W
Vel'gija	60	58.23 N	33.59 E
Velhas, Rio das ≃	110	17.13 S	44.49 W
Velika Gorica	52	45.43 N	16.05 E
Velika Gubavica ∟	52	43.26 N	16.54 E
Velikaja ≃, S.S.S.R.	58	64.40 N	176.20 E
Velikaja ≃, S.S.S.R.	60	57.48 N	28.20 E
Velika Kapela ⋀	52	45.15 N	15.00 E
Velika Morava ≃	54	44.43 N	21.03 E
Velika Plana	54	44.20 N	21.04 E
Velike Lašče	52	45.50 N	14.38 E
Velikije Luki	60	56.20 N	30.32 E
Velikij Ust'ug	42	60.48 N	46.18 E
Veliki kanal Ξ	54	45.45 N	18.50 E
Veliki Vitorog ∧	52	44.07 N	17.03 E
Veliko Gradište	54	44.45 N	21.32 E
Velikoje	60	57.21 N	39.47 E
Velikookt'abr'skij	60	57.26 N	33.49 E
Veliko Târnovo	54	43.04 N	25.39 E
Veli Lošinj	52	44.31 N	14.30 E
Vélingara	80	13.09 N	14.07 W
Velingrad	54	42.04 N	24.00 E
Velino, Monte ∧	52	42.09 N	13.23 E
Veliž	60	55.38 N	31.12 E
Velká Bíteš	46	49.17 N	16.13 E
Vel'ké Kapušany	46	48.33 N	22.04 E
Velké Meziříčí	46	49.21 N	16.00 E
Vella Lavella I	88	7.45 S	156.40 E
Velletri	52	41.41 N	12.47 E
Vellinge	44	55.28 N	13.01 E
Vellore	74	12.56 N	79.08 E
Vel'sk	42	61.05 N	42.05 E
Velten	46	52.41 N	13.10 E
Vemdalen	44	62.27 N	13.52 E
Ven I	44	55.54 N	12.41 E
Venachar, Loch ⊜	38	56.13 N	4.19 W
Venaco	52	42.14 N	9.10 E
Venado Tuerto	114	33.45 S	61.58 W
Venafro	52	41.29 N	14.02 E
Venâncio Aires	114	29.36 S	52.11 W
Vence	48	43.43 N	7.07 E
Venceslau Brás	114	23.51 S	49.48 W
Venda □1	86	23.00 S	30.30 E
Venda Nova	50	41.40 N	7.58 W
Vendas Novas	50	38.41 N	8.28 W
Vendée □5	48	46.40 N	1.20 W
Vendée ◆1	48	46.40 N	1.10 W
Vendeuvre-sur-Barse	48	48.14 N	4.28 E
Vendôme	48	47.48 N	1.04 E
Vendrell	50	41.13 N	1.32 E
Vendsyssel ◆1	44	57.20 N	10.00 E
Venecia	108	10.22 N	84.17 W
Veneto □4	48	45.30 N	11.45 E
Venev	60	54.21 N	38.16 E
Venezia (Venice)	52	45.27 N	12.21 E
Venezuela □1	110	8.00 N	66.00 W
Venezuela, Golfo de ⊂	110	11.30 N	71.00 W
Venezuelan Basin ◆1	22	15.00 N	68.00 W
Vengerovo	58	55.41 N	76.45 E
Venice →Venezia	52	45.27 N	12.21 E
Venice, Gulf of ⊂	52	45.15 N	13.00 E
Vénissieux	48	45.41 N	4.53 E
Venjan	44	60.57 N	13.55 E
Venjansjön ⊜	44	60.54 N	14.00 E
Venlo	46	51.24 N	6.10 E
Vennesla	44	58.17 N	7.59 E
Venosa	52	40.57 N	15.49 E
Venraij	46	51.32 N	5.59 E
Vent	46	46.52 N	10.56 E
Ventersburg	86	28.09 S	27.08 E
Ventersdorp	86	26.17 S	26.48 E
Venterstad	86	30.47 S	25.48 E
Ventimiglia	52	43.47 N	7.36 E
Ventnor	34	50.36 N	1.11 W
Ventotene, Isola I	52	40.47 N	13.25 E
Ventry	40	52.08 N	10.22 W
Ventspils	60	57.24 N	21.36 E
Ventuari ≃	110	3.58 N	67.02 W
Ventura	104	34.16 N	119.17 W
Ver ≃	34	51.42 N	0.20 W
Vera, Arg.	114	29.28 S	60.13 W
Vera, Esp.	50	37.15 N	1.52 W
Veracruz	106	19.12 N	96.08 W
Veranópolis	114	28.57 S	51.33 W
Verāval	76	20.54 N	70.22 E
Verbania	52	45.56 N	8.33 E
Verbilki	60	56.32 N	37.36 E
Vercelli	52	45.19 N	8.25 E
Vercel-Villedieu- le-Camp	48	47.11 N	6.24 E
Verchn'aja Amga	58	59.30 N	126.08 E
Verchn'aja Inta	42	66.00 N	60.20 E
Verchn'aja Salda	56	58.02 N	60.33 E
Verchn'aja Tajmyra ≃	58	74.15 N	99.48 E
Verchn'aja Tura	56	58.22 N	59.49 E
Verchneimbatskoje	58	63.11 N	87.58 E
Verchnetulomskij	42	68.38 N	31.45 E
Verchnevil'ujsk	58	63.27 N	120.18 E
Verchnij Baskunčak	56	48.14 N	46.44 E
Verchnij Ufalej	56	56.04 N	60.14 E
Verchojansk	58	67.35 N	133.27 E
Verchojanskij chrebet ⋀	58	67.00 N	129.00 E
Verchoturje	56	58.52 N	60.48 E
Vercors ◆1	48	44.57 N	5.25 E
Verdalsøra	44	63.48 N	11.29 E
Verde ≃, Bra.	110	21.12 S	51.53 W
Verde ≃, Para.	114	23.09 S	57.37 W
Verden	46	52.55 N	9.13 E
Verdi	104	39.31 N	119.59 W
Verdon ≃	48	43.43 N	5.46 E
Verdun, P.Q., Can.	102	45.27 N	73.34 W
Verdun, Fr.	48	43.52 N	1.14 E
Verdun, Fr.	48	49.10 N	5.23 E
Verdun-sur-le-Doubs	48	46.54 N	5.01 E
Verdun-sur-Meuse	46	49.10 N	5.23 E
Vereeniging	86	26.38 S	27.57 E
Vereja	60	55.21 N	36.11 E
Vereščagino, S.S.S.R.	42	58.05 N	54.40 E
Vereščagino, S.S.S.R.	58	64.14 N	87.37 E
Vergara, Esp.	50	43.07 N	2.25 W
Vergara, Ur.	114	32.56 S	53.57 W
Vergemont Creek ≃	94	24.12 S	143.17 E
Vergennes	102	44.10 N	73.15 W
Vergt	48	45.02 N	0.43 E
Verin	50	41.56 N	7.26 W
Verkhoyansk →Verchojansk	58	67.35 N	133.27 E
Vermenton	48	47.40 N	3.44 E
Vermilion	102	41.25 N	82.21 W
Vermillion	100	42.46 N	96.55 W
Vermont □3	100	43.50 N	72.45 W
Verneuil	48	48.44 N	0.56 E
Verneukpan ≚	86	30.00 S	21.10 E
Vernon, B.C., Can.	98	50.16 N	119.16 W
Vernon, Fr.	48	49.05 N	1.29 E
Vernon, Ct., U.S.	102	41.49 N	72.28 W
Verny	48	49.01 N	6.12 E
Vero ≃	50	42.00 N	0.10 E
Vero Beach	100	27.38 N	80.23 W
Véroia	54	40.31 N	22.12 E
Verona, On., Can.	102	44.29 N	76.42 W
Verona, It.	52	45.27 N	11.00 E
Verónica	114	35.22 S	57.20 W
Verran	94	33.51 S	136.18 E
Verrès	52	45.40 N	7.42 E
Verrettes	108	19.03 N	72.28 W
Versailles, Fr.	48	48.48 N	2.08 E
Versailles, Ky., U.S.	102	38.03 N	84.43 W
Versailles, Oh., U.S.	102	40.13 N	84.29 W
Veršino-Darasunskij	58	52.20 N	115.32 E
Veršino-Šachtaminskij	58	51.21 N	117.50 E
Vert, Cap ›	80	14.43 N	17.30 W
Verteillac	48	45.21 N	0.22 E
Vertientes	108	21.16 N	78.09 W
Vertou	48	47.10 N	1.29 W
Vertus	48	48.54 N	4.00 E
Verulam	86	29.45 S	31.02 E
Verviers	46	50.35 N	5.52 E
Vervins	48	49.50 N	3.54 E
Verwood	34	50.53 N	1.52 W
Veryan	34	50.13 N	4.54 W
Verzy	48	49.09 N	4.10 E
Vesanto	44	62.56 N	26.25 E
Vescovato	48	42.30 N	9.26 E
Veselí nad Lužnicí	46	49.11 N	14.43 E
Veselí nad Moravou	46	48.58 N	17.22 E
Vesijärvi ⊜	44	61.06 N	25.32 E
Vesjegonsk	60	58.40 N	37.16 E
Vesoul	48	47.38 N	6.10 E
Vesta	108	9.43 N	83.03 W
Vest-Agder □6	44	58.30 N	7.10 E
Vestbygd	44	58.06 N	6.35 E
Vesterålen II	42	68.45 N	15.00 E
Vesterø Havn	44	57.18 N	10.56 E
Vestfjorden ⊂2	42	68.08 N	15.00 E
Vestfold □6	44	59.15 N	10.10 E
Vestmannaeyjar	42a	63.26 N	20.12 W
Vestvågøya I	42	68.15 N	13.50 E
Vesuvio ∧1	52	40.49 N	14.26 E
Vesuvius →Vesuvio ∧1	52	40.49 N	14.26 E
Veszprém	46	47.06 N	17.55 E
Veszprém □6	46	46.50 N	17.30 E
Vésztő	46	46.55 N	21.16 E
Vetka	60	52.33 N	31.10 E
Vetlanda	44	57.26 N	15.04 E
Vetluga	42	57.51 N	45.47 E
Vetovo	54	43.42 N	26.16 E
Vetralla	52	42.19 N	12.03 E
Vetren	54	42.16 N	24.03 E
Vetrino	60	55.25 N	28.28 E
Vetrişoaia	54	46.26 N	28.13 E
Vetschau	46	51.47 N	14.04 E
Vettisfossen ∟	44	61.22 N	7.55 E
Vettore, Monte ∧	52	42.49 N	13.16 E
Veurne	46	51.04 N	2.40 E
Vevelstad	42	65.43 N	12.30 E
Vevey	48	46.28 N	6.51 E
Veynes	48	44.32 N	5.49 E
Vézelise	48	48.29 N	6.05 E
Vézère ≃	48	44.53 N	0.53 E
Viacha	110	16.39 S	68.18 W
Viadana	52	44.56 N	10.31 E
Viadutos	114	27.34 S	52.01 W
Viale	114	31.53 S	60.01 W
Viamão	114	30.05 S	51.02 W
Viamonte	114	33.44 S	63.06 W
Viana	110	3.13 S	45.00 W
Viana del Bollo	50	42.11 N	7.06 W
Viana do Alentejo	50	38.20 N	8.00 W
Viana do Castelo	50	41.42 N	8.50 W
Viangchan (Vientiane)	70	17.58 N	102.36 E
Viar ≃	50	37.36 N	5.50 W
Viareggio	52	43.52 N	10.14 E
Viaur ≃	48	44.08 N	2.23 E
Viborg, Dan.	44	56.26 N	9.24 E
Viborg →Vyborg, S.S.S.R.	60	60.42 N	28.45 E
Vibo Valentia	52	38.40 N	16.06 E
Vibraye	48	48.03 N	0.44 E
Vic-en-Bigorre	48	43.23 N	0.03 E
Vicente López	114	34.32 S	58.28 W
Vicente Noble	108	18.23 N	71.11 W
Vicenza	52	45.33 N	11.33 E
Vich	50	41.56 N	2.15 E
Vichada ≃	110	4.55 N	67.50 W
Vichadero	114	31.48 S	54.43 W
Vichigasta	114	29.29 S	67.31 W
Vichuquén	114	34.53 S	72.00 W
Vichy	48	46.08 N	3.26 E
Vicksburg, Mi., U.S.	102	42.07 N	85.31 W
Vicksburg, Ms., U.S.	100	32.21 N	90.52 W
Vico	52	42.10 N	8.48 E
Vic-sur-Cère	48	44.59 N	2.37 E
Victor Harbor	94	35.34 S	138.37 E
Victoria, Arg.	114	32.37 S	60.10 W
Victoria, Cam.	80	4.01 N	9.12 E
Victoria, B.C., Can.	98	48.25 N	123.22 W
Victoria, Chile	114	38.13 S	72.20 W
Victoria, Gren.	108	12.12 N	61.42 W
Victoria (Xianggang), H.K.	66	22.17 N	114.09 E
Victoria, Malay.	72	5.17 N	115.15 E
Victoria, Rom.	54	45.45 N	24.41 E
Victoria, Sey.	84	4.38 S	55.27 E
Victoria, Tx., U.S.	100	28.48 N	97.00 W
Victoria □3	88	38.00 S	145.00 E
Victoria □4	86	20.54 S	31.21 E
Victoria ≃	92	15.12 S	129.43 E
Victoria, Lake ⊜, Afr.	84	1.00 S	33.00 E
Victoria, Lake ⊜, Austl.	94	34.00 S	141.16 E
Victoria, Mount ∧, Mya.	70	21.14 N	93.55 E
Victoria, Mount ∧, Pap. N. Gui.	92	8.55 S	147.35 E
Victoria de las Tunas	108	20.58 N	76.57 W
Victoria Falls ∟	86	17.55 S	25.51 E
Victoria Falls National Park ♠	86	17.55 S	25.40 E
Victoria Harbour	102	44.45 N	79.46 W
Victoria Island I	98	71.00 N	110.00 W
Victoria Nile ≃	82	2.14 N	31.26 E
Victoria Peak ∧	106	16.48 N	88.37 W
Victoria Range ⋀	96	42.09 S	172.08 E
Victoria River Downs	92	16.24 S	131.00 E
Victoria Strait ⊔	98	69.15 N	100.30 W
Victoriaville	102	46.03 N	71.57 W
Victoria West	86	31.25 S	23.04 E
Victorica	114	36.13 S	65.27 W
Victorino de la Plaza	114	36.36 S	62.40 W
Victorville	104	34.32 N	117.17 W
Vičuga	60	57.13 N	41.56 E
Vicuña	114	30.02 S	70.44 W
Vicuña Mackenna	114	33.54 S	64.23 W
Vidal Ramos	114	27.23 S	49.22 W
Vidauban	48	43.26 N	6.26 E
Videbæk	44	56.05 N	8.38 E
Videira	114	27.00 S	51.08 W
Videle	54	44.16 N	25.31 E
Vidigueira	50	38.13 N	7.48 W
Vidin	54	43.59 N	22.52 E
Vidisha	76	23.32 N	77.49 E
Vidöstern ⊜	44	57.04 N	14.01 E
Vidra, Rom.	54	44.16 N	26.11 E
Vidra, Rom.	54	45.55 N	26.54 E
Vidsel	42	65.51 N	20.24 E
Viechtach	46	49.05 N	12.53 E
Viedma	112	40.48 S	63.00 W
Viedma, Lago ⊜	112	49.35 S	72.35 W
Vieira do Minho	50	41.39 N	8.09 W
Viella	50	42.42 N	0.48 E
Vienna →Wien, Öst.	46	48.13 N	16.20 E
Vienna, Md., U.S.	102	38.29 N	75.49 W
Vienna, W.V., U.S.	102	39.19 N	81.32 W
Vienne	48	45.31 N	4.52 E
Vienne □5	48	46.35 N	0.30 E
Vienne ≃	48	47.13 N	0.05 E
Vientiane →Viangchan	70	17.58 N	102.36 E
Vieques	108	18.09 N	65.27 W
Vieques, Isla de I	108	18.08 N	65.25 W
Vieremä	44	63.45 N	27.01 E
Vierfontein	86	27.03 S	26.46 E
Viersen	46	51.15 N	6.23 E
Vierumäki	44	61.06 N	25.57 E
Vierwaldstätter See ⊜	48	47.00 N	8.28 E
Vierzon	48	47.13 N	2.05 E
Vieste	52	41.53 N	16.10 E
Vietnam □1	68	16.00 N	108.00 E
Viet-tri	70	21.18 N	105.26 E
Vieux Fort	108	13.44 N	60.57 W
Vieytes	114	35.16 S	57.35 W
Vif	48	45.03 N	5.40 E
Vigan	68	17.34 N	120.23 E
Vigeland	44	58.05 N	7.18 E
Vigevano	52	45.19 N	8.51 E
Vigneulles-lès-Hattonchâtel	48	48.59 N	5.43 E
Vignola	52	44.29 N	11.00 E
Vigo	50	42.14 N	8.43 W
Vigo, Ría de ⊂1	50	42.15 N	8.45 W
Vigrestad	44	58.34 N	5.42 E
Vihanti	44	64.29 N	25.00 E
Vihiers	48	47.09 N	0.32 W
Vihti	44	60.25 N	24.20 E
Viiala	44	61.13 N	23.47 E
Viinijärvi	44	62.39 N	29.14 E
Viinijärvi ⊜	44	62.44 N	29.17 E
Viitasaari	44	63.04 N	25.52 E
Vijāpur	76	23.34 N	72.45 E
Vijayapuri	74	16.52 N	79.35 E
Vijayawāda	74	16.31 N	80.37 E
Vijosë (Aóös) ≃	54	40.37 N	19.20 E
Vikajärvi	42	66.37 N	26.12 E
Vikbolandet ›1	44	58.32 N	16.40 E
Viken	44	56.09 N	12.34 E
Viken ⊜	44	58.39 N	14.20 E
Vikersund	44	59.59 N	10.02 E
Vikmanshyttan	44	60.17 N	15.49 E
Vikna	42	64.57 N	10.58 E
Vikramasingapuram	74	8.43 N	77.24 E
Viksøyri	44	61.05 N	6.35 E
Vila de Manica	86	18.56 S	32.53 E
Vila de Rei	50	39.40 N	8.09 W
Vila do Bispo	50	37.05 N	8.55 W
Vila do Conde	50	41.21 N	8.45 W
Vila Flor	50	41.18 N	7.09 W
Vila Fontes	86	17.50 S	35.21 E
Vilafranca del Penedés	50	41.21 N	1.42 E
Vila Franca de Xira	50	38.57 N	8.59 W
Vilaine ≃	48	47.30 N	2.27 W
Viļaka	60	57.11 N	27.41 E
Vilama, Laguna de ⊜	114	22.36 S	66.55 W
Vilanculos	86	22.01 S	35.19 E
Viļāni	60	56.33 N	26.57 E
Vila Nova de Famalicão	50	41.25 N	8.32 W
Vila Nova de Foz Côa	50	41.05 N	7.12 W
Vila Nova de Gaia	50	41.08 N	8.37 W
Vila Novo de Ourém	50	39.39 N	8.35 W
Vila Real	50	41.18 N	7.45 W
Vila Real de Santo António	50	37.12 N	7.25 W
Vilar Formoso	50	40.37 N	6.50 W
Vila Velha	110	20.20 S	40.17 W
Vila Velha de Ródão	50	39.38 N	7.40 W
Vila Verde	50	41.39 N	8.26 W
Vila Viçosa	50	38.47 N	8.13 W
Vîlcea □6	54	45.19 N	24.00 E
Vildbjerg	44	56.12 N	8.46 E
Vilelas	114	27.57 S	62.38 W
Vilhelmina	44	64.37 N	16.39 E
Vilhena	110	12.43 S	60.07 W
Viljandi	60	58.22 N	25.36 E
Viljoenskroon	86	27.12 S	27.00 E
Vil'kickogo, ostrov I	56	73.29 N	75.50 E
Vil'kickogo, proliv ⊔	58	77.55 N	103.00 E
Vilkija	60	55.03 N	23.35 E
Villa Aberastain	114	31.39 S	68.35 W
Villa Ahumada	106	30.37 N	106.31 W
Villa Alberdi	114	27.35 S	65.37 W
Villa Alemana	114	33.03 S	71.23 W
Villa Allende	114	31.18 S	64.18 W
Villa Ana	114	28.29 S	59.37 W
Villa Ángela	114	27.35 S	60.43 W
Villa Atamisqui	114	28.29 S	63.48 W
Villa Atuel	114	34.50 S	67.54 W
Villa Bella	110	10.23 S	65.24 W
Villa Berthet	114	27.17 S	60.25 W
Villablino	50	42.56 N	6.19 W
Villa Bruzual	108	9.20 N	69.06 W
Villa Bustos	114	29.17 S	67.02 W
Villa Cañás, Arg.	114	34.00 S	61.36 W
Villacañas, Esp.	50	39.38 N	3.20 W
Villa Carlos Paz	114	31.24 S	64.31 W
Villacarriedo	50	43.14 N	3.48 W
Villacarrillo	50	38.07 N	3.05 W
Villa Castelli	114	29.00 S	68.11 W
Villacastín	50	40.47 N	4.25 W
Villach	46	46.36 N	13.50 E
Villacidro	52	39.27 N	8.44 E
Villa Colón (Caucete)	112	31.39 S	68.17 W
Villa Concepción del Tío	114	31.19 S	62.50 W
Villa Constitución	114	33.14 S	60.20 W
Villada	50	42.15 N	4.58 W
Villa de Cura	108	10.02 N	67.29 W
Villa del Carmen	114	32.57 S	65.03 W
Villa del Río	50	37.59 N	4.17 W
Villa del Rosario, Arg.	114	31.35 S	63.32 W
Villa del Rosario, Arg.	114	30.47 S	57.55 W
Villa de María	114	29.54 S	63.43 W
Villa de Soto	114	30.51 S	64.59 W
Villa Diego, Arg.	114	33.01 S	60.37 W
Villadiego, Esp.	50	42.31 N	4.00 W
Villa Dolores	114	31.56 S	65.12 W
Villa El Alto	114	28.18 S	65.22 W
Villa Elisa	114	32.10 S	58.24 W
Villa Florida	114	26.23 S	57.09 W
Villafranca del Bierzo	50	42.36 N	6.48 W
Villafranca de los Barros	50	38.34 N	6.20 W
Villafranca di Verona	52	45.21 N	10.50 E
Villagarcía	50	42.36 N	8.45 W
Villa General Roca	114	32.39 S	66.28 W
Villaguay	114	31.51 S	59.01 W
Villa Guillermina	114	28.14 S	59.28 W
Villa Hayes	114	25.06 S	57.34 W
Villahermosa	106	17.59 N	92.55 W
Villa Hernandarias	114	31.13 S	59.59 W
Villa Hidalgo	104	30.59 N	116.10 W
Villa Huidobro	114	34.50 S	64.35 W
Villaines-la-Juhel	48	48.21 N	0.17 W
Villa Iris	114	38.10 S	63.15 W
Villajoyosa	50	38.30 N	0.14 W
Villa Krause	114	31.34 S	68.32 W
Villa La Paz	114	33.27 S	67.38 W
Villa Larca	114	32.37 S	64.59 W
Villa Larroque	114	33.02 S	59.01 W
Villalba	50	43.18 N	7.41 W
Villalón de Campos	50	42.06 N	5.02 W
Villalonga	112	39.53 S	62.35 W
Villalpando	50	41.52 N	5.24 W
Villa María	114	32.25 S	63.15 W
Villa María Grande	114	31.39 S	59.54 W
Villamartín	50	36.52 N	5.38 W
Villa Matoque	114	25.49 S	63.49 W
Villa Mazán	114	28.40 S	66.34 W
Villa Mercedes	114	30.07 S	68.42 W
Villa Montes	110	21.15 S	63.30 W
Villandraut	48	44.28 N	0.23 W
Villanova Monteleone	52	40.30 N	8.28 E
Villa Nueva, Arg.	114	32.54 S	68.47 W
Villa Nueva, Arg.	114	32.26 S	63.15 W
Villanueva, Col.	108	10.37 N	72.59 W
Villanueva de Córdoba	50	38.20 N	4.37 W
Villanueva de la Serana	50	38.58 N	5.48 W
Villanueva de la Sierra	50	40.12 N	6.24 W
Villanueva de los Infantes	50	38.44 N	2.59 W
Villanueva del Río y Minas	50	37.39 N	5.42 W
Villanueva y Geltrú	50	41.14 N	1.44 E
Villa Ocampo	114	28.28 S	59.22 W
Villa Ojo de Agua	114	29.31 S	63.42 W
Villa Oliva	114	26.01 S	57.53 W
Villa Quinteros	114	27.14 S	65.33 W
Villa Ramírez	114	32.11 S	60.12 W
Villarcayo	50	42.56 N	3.34 W
Villard-de-Lans	48	45.04 N	5.33 E
Villardefrades	50	41.43 N	5.15 W
Villar del Arzobispo	50	39.44 N	0.49 W
Villa Regina	114	39.06 S	67.04 W
Villa Reynolds	114	33.43 S	65.23 W
Villarreal	50	39.56 N	0.06 W
Villarrica, Chile	112	39.16 S	72.13 W
Villarrica, Para.	114	25.45 S	56.26 W
Villarrobledo	50	39.16 N	2.36 W
Villarrubia de los Ojos	50	39.13 N	3.36 W
Villas	102	39.01 N	74.56 W
Villa Sandino	108	12.03 N	84.59 W
Villa San Giovanni	52	38.13 N	15.38 E
Villa San José	114	32.12 S	58.13 W
Villa San Martín	114	28.18 S	64.12 W
Villasayas	50	41.21 N	2.37 W
Villasimius	52	39.08 N	9.31 E
Villasor	52	39.23 N	8.56 E
Villa Unión, Arg.	114	29.18 S	68.12 W
Villa Unión, Arg.	114	29.24 S	62.47 W
Villa Unión, Méx.	106	23.12 N	106.14 W
Villa Valeria	114	34.20 S	64.55 W
Villa Vázquez	108	19.45 N	71.27 W
Villavicencio	110	4.09 N	73.37 W
Villaviciosa	50	43.29 N	5.26 W
Villaviciosa de Córdoba	50	38.05 N	5.01 W
Villazón	110	22.06 S	65.36 W
Villa Zorraquín	114	31.19 S	58.02 W
Villé	48	48.20 N	7.18 E
Villedieu	48	48.50 N	1.13 W
Villefort	48	44.26 N	3.56 E
Villefranche	48	45.59 N	4.43 E
Villefranche-de-Rouergue	48	44.21 N	2.02 E
Villena	50	38.38 N	0.51 W
Villenauxe-la-Grande	48	48.35 N	3.33 E
Villeneuve-d'Aveyron	48	44.26 N	2.02 E
Villeneuve-de-Berg	48	44.33 N	4.30 E
Villeneuve-Saint-Georges	48	48.44 N	2.27 E
Villeneuve-sur-Lot	48	44.25 N	0.42 E
Villeneuve-sur-Yonne	48	48.05 N	3.18 E
Villers-Bocage	48	49.05 N	0.39 W
Villers-Cotterêts	48	49.15 N	3.05 E
Villersexel	48	47.33 N	6.26 E
Villerupt	48	49.28 N	5.56 E
Villeurbanne	48	45.46 N	4.53 E
Villiers	86	27.03 S	28.35 E
Villingen-Schwenningen	46	48.04 N	8.28 E
Vilna →Vilnius	60	54.41 N	25.19 E
Vilnius	60	54.41 N	25.19 E
Vilppula	44	62.01 N	24.31 E
Vilsbiburg	46	48.27 N	12.12 E
Vilshofen	46	48.39 N	13.12 E
Vil'uj ≃	58	64.24 N	126.26 E
Vil'ujsk	58	63.45 N	121.35 E
Vil'ujskoje vodochranilišče ⊜1	58	62.30 N	111.00 E
Vilvoorde	46	50.56 N	4.26 E
Vimianzo	50	43.07 N	9.02 W
Vimmerby	44	57.40 N	15.51 E
Vimoutiers	48	48.55 N	0.12 E
Vimpeli	44	63.09 N	23.48 E
Vimperk	46	49.03 N	13.47 E
Vina	104	39.55 N	122.03 W
Vina ≃	80	7.45 N	15.36 E
Viña del Mar	114	33.02 S	71.34 W
Vinalhaven	102	44.02 N	68.49 W
Vinalhaven Island I	102	44.05 N	68.52 W
Vinaroz	50	40.28 N	0.29 E
Vincennes	100	38.40 N	87.31 W
Vinchina	114	28.46 S	68.10 W
Vindelälven ≃	44	63.54 N	19.52 E
Vindeln	44	64.12 N	19.44 E
Vinden, Mount ∧	90	27.01 S	115.38 E
Vinderup	44	56.29 N	8.47 E
Vindhya Range ⋀	76	23.00 N	77.00 E
Vineland	102	39.29 N	75.01 W
Vineyard Haven	102	41.27 N	70.36 W
Vineyard Sound ⊔	102	41.25 N	70.46 W
Vingåker	44	59.02 N	15.52 E
Vinh	70	18.40 N	105.40 E
Vinhais	50	41.50 N	7.00 W
Vinh Cam-ranh ⊂	70	11.53 N	109.10 E
Vinh-long	70	10.15 N	105.58 E
Vinica	52	45.28 N	15.15 E
Vînju Mare	54	44.26 N	22.52 E
Vinkovci	54	45.17 N	18.49 E
Vinnica	56	49.14 N	28.29 E
Vinnitsa →Vinnica	56	49.14 N	28.29 E
Vinslöv	44	56.06 N	13.55 E
Vinson Massif ∧	18	78.35 S	85.25 W
Vinstra	44	61.36 N	9.45 E
Vintilă Vodă	54	45.28 N	26.44 E
Vipava	52	45.51 N	13.58 E
Vipiteno	52	46.54 N	11.26 E
Vipos	114	26.29 S	65.22 W
Vir, Otok I	52	44.18 N	15.04 E
Virac	68	13.35 N	124.15 E
Viramgām	76	23.07 N	72.02 E
Virbalis	60	54.38 N	22.49 E
Virden	98	49.51 N	100.55 W
Vire	48	48.50 N	0.53 W
Vire ≃	48	49.20 N	1.07 W
Vîrfurile	54	46.19 N	22.31 E
Virgin ≃	104	36.31 N	114.20 W
Virgin Gorda I	108	18.30 N	64.24 W
Virginia, Ire.	40	53.49 N	7.04 W
Virginia, S. Afr.	86	28.12 S	26.49 E
Virginia, Mn., U.S.	100	47.31 N	92.32 W
Virginia □3	100	37.30 N	78.45 W
Virginia Beach	100	36.51 N	75.58 W
Virginia City	104	39.18 N	119.38 W
Virginia Falls ∟	98	61.38 N	125.42 W
Virginia Peak ∧	104	39.45 N	119.28 W
Virgin Islands □2	108	18.20 N	64.50 W
Virieu-le-Grand	48	45.51 N	5.39 E
Virihaure ⊜	42	67.20 N	16.35 E
Virje	52	46.04 N	16.59 E
Virkie	38	59.53 N	1.18 W
Virkkala	44	60.12 N	24.01 E
Virojoki	44	60.35 N	27.42 E
Virovitica	52	45.50 N	17.23 E
Virpazar	54	42.15 N	19.05 E
Virrat	44	62.14 N	23.47 E
Virsbo	44	59.52 N	16.02 E
Virserum	44	57.19 N	15.35 E
Virtaniemi	42	68.53 N	28.27 E
Virton	46	49.34 N	5.32 E
Vîrtopu	54	44.12 N	23.21 E
Virudunagar	74	9.36 N	77.58 E
Virungu	84	7.04 S	29.46 E
Vis	52	43.03 N	16.12 E
Vis (Fish) ≃, Namibia	86	28.07 S	17.45 E
Vis ≃, S. Afr.	86	30.53 S	20.23 E
Vis, Otok I	52	43.02 N	16.11 E
Visalia	104	36.19 N	119.17 W
Visayan Sea ⊤2	68	11.35 N	123.51 E
Visby	44	57.38 N	18.18 E
Viscount Melville Sound ⊔	98	74.10 N	108.00 W
Višegrad	54	43.47 N	19.17 E
Viseu	50	40.39 N	7.55 W
Vişeu ≃	54	47.55 N	24.09 E
Vişeu de Sus	54	47.44 N	24.22 E
Vishākhapatnam	74	17.42 N	83.18 E
Vishoek	86	34.08 S	18.26 E
Visingsö I	44	58.03 N	14.20 E
Viskafors	44	57.38 N	12.50 E
Viskan ≃	44	57.14 N	12.12 E
Vislanda	44	56.47 N	14.27 E
Vislinskij Zaliv ⊂	46	54.27 N	19.40 E
Visnagar	76	23.42 N	72.33 E
Viso, Monte ∧	52	44.40 N	7.07 E
Visoko	54	43.59 N	18.11 E
Visokoi Island I	24	56.42 S	27.12 W
Visp	48	46.18 N	7.53 E
Vissefjärda	44	56.32 N	15.35 E
Visselhövede	46	52.59 N	9.35 E
Vista	104	33.12 N	117.14 W
Vista Alegre	114	38.45 S	68.11 W
Vista Flores	114	33.38 S	69.09 W
Vistula →Wisła ≃	46	54.22 N	18.55 E
Vit ≃	54	43.41 N	24.45 E
Vitanje	52	46.23 N	15.18 E
Vitarte	110	12.02 S	76.56 W
Vitebsk	60	55.12 N	30.11 E
Viterbo	52	42.25 N	12.06 E
Vitiaz Strait ⊔	92	5.50 S	147.20 E
Vitigudino	50	41.01 N	6.26 W
Viti Levu I	28	18.00 S	178.00 E
Vitim	58	59.28 N	112.34 E
Vitim ≃	58	59.26 N	112.34 E
Vítkov	46	49.46 N	17.45 E
Vitória, Bra.	110	20.19 S	40.21 W
Vitoria, Esp.	50	42.51 N	2.40 W
Vitória da Conquista	110	14.51 S	40.51 W
Vitré	48	48.08 N	1.12 W
Vitry-le-François	48	48.44 N	4.35 E
Vittangi	42	67.41 N	21.36 E
Vitteaux	48	47.24 N	4.32 E
Vittel	48	48.12 N	5.57 E
Vittoria	52	36.57 N	14.32 E
Vittorio Veneto	52	45.59 N	12.18 E
Vittsjö	44	56.20 N	13.40 E
Vivarais, Monts du ⋀	48	44.55 N	4.15 E
Viver	50	39.55 N	0.36 W
Vivero	50	43.40 N	7.35 W
Vivi ≃	58	63.52 N	97.50 E
Viviers	48	44.29 N	4.41 E
Vivonne	48	46.26 N	0.16 E
Vivoratá	114	37.40 S	57.39 W
Vivsta	44	62.29 N	17.19 E
Vizcaya □4	50	43.20 N	2.45 W
Vize, ostrov I	56	79.30 N	77.00 E
Vizianagaram	74	18.07 N	83.25 E
Vizille	48	45.05 N	5.46 E
Vižinada	52	45.20 N	13.46 E
Vizzini	52	37.10 N	14.53 E
Vlaardingen	46	51.54 N	4.21 E
Vlădeasa ∧	54	46.45 N	22.48 E
Vlădeni	54	47.25 N	27.20 E
Vladičin Han	54	42.42 N	22.04 E
Vladimir	60	56.10 N	40.25 E
Vladivostok	58	43.10 N	131.56 E
Vlasenica	54	44.11 N	18.56 E
Vlašim	46	49.42 N	14.54 E
Vlasotince	54	42.58 N	22.08 E
Vlasovo	58	70.48 N	135.00 E
Vlieland I	46	53.15 N	5.00 E
Vlissingen (Flushing)	46	51.26 N	3.35 E
Vlorë	54	40.27 N	19.30 E
Vlorës, Gji i ⊂	54	40.25 N	19.25 E
Vltava ≃	46	50.21 N	14.30 E
Vočin	52	45.37 N	17.32 E
Vöcklabruck	46	48.01 N	13.39 E
Vodňany	46	49.09 N	14.11 E
Vodnjan	52	44.57 N	13.51 E
Vogel Peak →Dimlang ∧	80	8.24 N	11.47 E
Vogelsberg ⋀	46	50.30 N	9.15 E
Voghera	52	44.59 N	9.01 E
Vohenstrauss	46	49.37 N	12.21 E
Vohibinany	87b	18.49 S	49.04 E
Vohimarina	87b	13.21 S	50.02 E
Voi	84	3.23 S	38.34 E
Void	48	48.41 N	5.37 E
Voikkaa	44	60.56 N	26.37 E
Voineşti	54	47.05 N	27.26 E
Voinjama	80	8.25 N	9.45 W
Voiron	48	45.22 N	5.35 E
Voitsberg	46	47.03 N	15.10 E
Vojens	44	55.15 N	9.19 E
Vojmsjön ⊜	44	64.55 N	16.40 E
Vojnić	52	45.19 N	15.42 E
Voj-Vož	42	62.56 N	54.56 E
Volary	46	48.55 N	13.54 E
Volcán	114	23.54 S	65.27 W
Volcano	105a	19.25 N	155.14 W
Volcano Islands →Kazan-rettō II	28	25.00 N	141.00 E
Volchov	60	59.55 N	32.20 E
Volchov ≃	60	60.08 N	32.20 E
Volda	44	62.09 N	6.06 E
Volga	60	57.57 N	38.24 E
Volga ≃	56	45.55 N	47.52 E
Volga-Baltic Canal →Volgo-Baltijskij kanal Ξ	42	59.00 N	38.00 E
Volgo-Baltijskij kanal Ξ	60	59.00 N	38.00 E
Volgodonsk	56	47.33 N	42.08 E
Volgograd (Stalingrad)	56	48.44 N	44.25 E
Volgogradskoje vodochranilišče ⊜1	56	49.20 N	45.00 E
Volissós	54	38.29 N	25.58 E
Volkach	46	49.52 N	10.13 E
Völkermarkt	46	46.39 N	14.38 E
Völklingen	46	49.15 N	6.50 E
Volkovysk	60	53.10 N	24.28 E
Volksrust	86	27.24 S	29.53 E
Voločanka	58	71.00 N	94.28 E
Volodarskoje	56	53.18 N	68.08 E
Vologda	60	59.12 N	39.55 E
Volokolamsk	60	56.02 N	35.57 E
Volonne	48	44.07 N	6.01 E
Vólos	54	39.21 N	22.56 E
Vol'sk	56	52.02 N	47.23 E
Volta, Lake ⊜1	80	7.30 N	0.15 E
Volta Blanche (White Volta) ≃	80	9.10 N	1.15 W
Voltaire, Cape ›	92	14.16 S	125.35 E
Volta Noire (Black Volta) ≃	80	8.41 N	1.33 E
Volta Redonda	110	22.32 S	44.07 W
Volterra	52	43.24 N	10.51 E
Voltri	52	44.26 N	8.45 E
Volturino, Monte ∧	52	40.25 N	15.49 E
Volturno ≃	52	41.01 N	13.55 E
Vólvi, Límni ⊜	54	40.41 N	23.23 E
Volyně	46	49.10 N	13.53 E
Volžsk	42	55.53 N	48.21 E
Volžskij	56	48.50 N	44.44 E
Von Treuer Tableland ⋀1	90	26.38 S	122.53 E
Vopnafjörður	42a	65.47 N	14.44 W
Vopnafjörður ⊂	42a	65.52 N	14.40 W
Vörå (Vöyri)	44	63.09 N	22.15 E
Vorarlberg □3	46	47.15 N	9.55 E
Vorau	46	47.25 N	15.54 E
Vorderrhein ≃	48	46.49 N	9.25 E
Vordingborg	44	55.01 N	11.55 E
Vorga	60	53.45 N	32.45 E
Voríai Sporádhes II	54	39.17 N	23.23 E
Vøringsfossen ∟	44	60.26 N	7.15 E
Vórios Evvoïkós Kólpos ⊂	54	38.40 N	23.15 E
Vorkuta	42	67.27 N	63.58 E
Vorlich, Ben ∧	38	56.20 N	4.14 W
Vorma ≃	44	60.09 N	11.27 E
Voronež	56	51.40 N	39.10 E
Voronovo	60	54.09 N	25.19 E
Vorošilovgrad	56	48.34 N	39.20 E
Vorpommern □9	46	53.40 N	13.45 E
Vorsma	60	55.59 N	43.16 E
Võru	60	57.50 N	27.01 E
Vosburg	86	30.33 S	22.52 E
Vosges □5	48	48.10 N	6.20 E
Vosges ⋀	48	48.30 N	7.10 E
Voskresensk	60	55.19 N	38.42 E
Voss	44	60.39 N	6.26 E
Vostočno-Sibirskoje more (East Siberian Sea) ⊤2	58	74.00 N	166.00 E
Vostočnyj Sajan ⋀	58	53.00 N	97.00 E
Vostok I	28	10.06 S	152.23 W
Votice	46	49.38 N	14.39 E
Votkinsk	42	57.03 N	53.59 E
Votuporanga	110	20.24 S	49.59 W
Vouga ≃	50	40.41 N	8.40 W
Vouillé	48	46.39 N	0.10 E
Vouziers	48	49.24 N	4.42 E
Voves	48	48.16 N	1.38 E
Voxnan ≃	44	61.17 N	16.26 E
Vožega	60	60.29 N	40.12 E
Voznesensk	56	47.34 N	31.20 E
Vrå	44	57.21 N	9.57 E
Vráble	46	48.15 N	18.19 E
Vraca	54	43.12 N	23.33 E
Vrådal	44	59.20 N	8.25 E
Vrancea □6	54	45.45 N	27.00 E
Vrancei, Munţii ⋀	54	46.00 N	26.30 E
Vrangel'a, ostrov I	58	71.00 N	179.30 W
Vranje	54	42.33 N	21.54 E
Vranov [nad Topl'ou]	46	48.54 N	21.41 E
Vrbas	54	45.35 N	19.39 E
Vrbas ≃	52	45.06 N	17.31 E
Vrbovec	52	45.53 N	16.25 E
Vrbovsko	52	45.23 N	15.05 E
Vrchlabí	46	50.38 N	15.37 E
Vrede	86	27.30 S	29.06 E
Vredefort	86	27.05 S	27.16 E
Vredenburg	86	32.54 S	17.59 E
Vredendal	86	31.41 S	18.35 E
Vrena	44	58.52 N	16.41 E
Vrginmost	52	45.21 N	15.52 E
Vrhnika	52	45.58 N	14.18 E
Vrigstad	44	57.21 N	14.28 E
Vrindāvan	76	27.35 N	77.42 E
Vrlika	52	43.55 N	16.24 E
Vrnograč	52	45.10 N	15.57 E
Vrondádhes	54	38.24 N	26.08 E
Vršac	54	45.07 N	21.18 E
Vrútky	46	49.07 N	18.55 E
Vryburg	86	26.55 S	24.45 E
Vryheid	86	27.46 S	30.48 E
Vsetín	46	49.21 N	17.59 E
Vsevoložsk	60	60.01 N	30.40 E
Vučitrn	54	42.49 N	20.58 E
Vught	46	51.40 N	5.17 E
Vukovar	54	45.21 N	19.00 E
Vulcan	54	45.23 N	23.17 E
Vulcano, Isola I	52	38.27 N	14.58 E
Vung-tau (Cap-saint-jacques)	70	10.21 N	107.04 E
Vuoggatjålme	42	66.36 N	16.22 E
Vuohijärvi ⊜	44	61.12 N	26.42 E
Vuoksenniska	44	61.13 N	28.49 E
Vuoksi ≃	44	61.03 N	30.11 E
Vuotso	42	68.08 N	27.08 E
Vyborg	60	60.42 N	28.45 E
Vyčegda ≃	56	61.18 N	46.36 E
Východočeský Kraj □4	46	50.10 N	16.00 E
Východoslovenský Kraj □4	46	49.00 N	21.15 E
Vygozero, ozero ⊜	42	63.35 N	34.42 E
Vyksa	60	55.18 N	42.11 E
Vypolzovo	60	57.53 N	33.42 E
Vyrica	60	59.25 N	30.21 E
Vyrnwy, Lake ⊜	34	52.47 N	3.30 W
Vyša	60	53.52 N	42.24 E
Vyškov, Česko.	46	49.16 N	17.00 E
Vyškov, S.S.S.R.	60	52.29 N	31.41 E
Vyšná Radvaň	46	49.07 N	21.56 E
Vyšnij Voločok	60	57.35 N	34.34 E
Vysock	60	60.36 N	28.34 E
Vysoké Mýto	46	49.57 N	16.10 E
Vysoké Tatry ⋀	46	49.12 N	20.05 E
Vysokiniči	60	54.54 N	36.55 E
Vysokogornyj	58	50.09 N	139.09 E
Vysokovsk	60	56.19 N	36.33 E
Vyšši Brod	46	48.37 N	14.19 E
Vytegra	42	61.00 N	36.24 E

W

Name	Page	Lat. °′	Long. °′
Wa	80	10.04 N	2.29 W
Waal ≃	46	51.49 N	4.58 E
Waalwijk	46	51.42 N	5.04 E
Wabag	92	5.30 S	143.40 E
Wabana	98	47.38 N	52.57 W
Wabasca	98	56.00 N	113.53 W
Wabasca ≃	98	58.22 N	115.20 W
Wabash ≃	100	37.46 N	88.02 W
Wabe Gestro ≃	82	4.17 N	42.02 E
Wabowden	98	54.55 N	98.38 W
Wąbrzeźno	46	53.17 N	18.57 E
Wachau ◆1	46	48.18 N	15.24 E
Wachusett Mountain ∧	102	42.29 N	71.53 W
Waco	100	31.32 N	97.08 W
Wadayama	64	35.19 N	134.52 E
Waddeneilanden II	46	53.26 N	5.30 E
Waddenzee ⊤2	46	53.15 N	5.15 E
Wadderin Hill	90	32.00 S	118.27 E
Waddesdon	34	51.51 N	0.56 W
Waddingham	36	53.27 N	0.31 W
Waddington, Eng., U.K.	36	53.10 N	0.32 W

Symbols in the Index entries are identified on page 122.

Name	Page	Lat. °′	Long. °′
Waddington, N.Y., U.S.	102	44.51N	75.12W
Waddington, Mount ∧	98	51.23N	125.15W
Wadebridge	34	50.32N	4.50W
Wadena	98	51.57N	103.47W
Wädenswil	48	47.14N	8.40 E
Wadhurst	34	51.04N	0.21 E
Wādī Ḥalfā'	82	21.56N	31.20 E
Wad Madanī	82	14.25N	33.28 E
Wadowice	46	49.53N	19.30 E
Wadsworth, Nv., U.S.	104	39.38N	119.17W
Wadsworth, Oh., U.S.	102	41.01N	81.43W
Wafrah	78	28.33N	48.02 E
Wageningen	46	51.58N	5.40 E
Wager Bay C	98	65.26N	88.40W
Wagga Wagga	94	35.07S	147.22 E
Wagin	90	33.18S	117.21 E
Waging am See	46	47.56N	12.43 E
Wagontire Mountain ∧	104	43.21N	119.53W
Wagrien ✦[1]	46	54.15N	10.45 E
Wągrowiec	46	52.49N	17.11 E
Wah	76	33.48N	72.42 E
Waha	82	28.16N	19.54 E
Wahai	92	2.48S	129.30 E
Waharoa	96	37.46S	175.46 E
Wahiawa	105a	21.30N	158.01W
Wahpeton	100	46.15N	96.36W
Wahran (Oran)	80	35.43N	0.43W
Waialeale ∧	105a	22.04N	159.30W
Waialua	105a	21.34N	158.07W
Waianae	105a	21.26N	158.11W
Waiapu ≃	96	37.47S	178.29 E
Waiatoto ≃	96	43.59S	168.47 E
Waiau	96	42.39S	173.03 E
Waiau ≃, N.Z.	96	42.47S	173.22 E
Waiau ≃, N.Z.	96	46.12S	167.38 E
Waiau ≃, N.Z.	96	38.58S	177.24 E
Waiblingen	46	48.50N	9.19 E
Waidhofen an der Thaya	46	48.49N	15.18 E
Waidhofen an der Ybbs	46	47.58N	14.47 E
Waigeo, Pulau I	92	0.14S	130.45 E
Waihao Downs	96	44.48S	170.55 E
Waiheke Island I	96	36.48S	175.06 E
Waihi	96	37.24S	175.51 E
Waihola	96	46.02S	170.06 E
Waihopai ≃	96	41.31S	173.44 E
Waihou ≃	96	37.10S	175.32 E
Waikabubak	72	9.38S	119.25 E
Waikaia	96	45.44S	168.51 E
Waikaia ≃	96	45.53S	168.48 E
Waikanae	96	40.53S	175.04 E
Waikare, Lake ⊜	96	37.26S	175.13 E
Waikaremoana, Lake ⊜	96	38.46S	177.07 E
Waikari	96	42.58S	172.41 E
Waikato ≃	96	37.23S	174.43 E
Waikelo	72	9.24S	119.14 E
Waikerie	94	34.11S	139.59 E
Waikino	96	37.25S	175.46 E
Waikouaiti	96	45.36S	170.41 E
Wailuku	105a	20.53N	156.30W
Waimahaka	96	46.31S	168.49 E
Waimakariri ≃	96	43.24S	172.42 E
Waimamaku	96	35.33S	173.29 E
Waimana	96	38.09S	177.05 E
Waimana ≃	96	38.04S	177.00 E
Waimangaroa	96	41.43S	171.46 E
Waimarama	96	39.48S	176.59 E
Waimate	96	44.44S	171.02 E
Waimea	105a	21.38N	158.03W
Wainfleet All Saints	36	53.07N	0.14 E
Wainganga ≃	74	18.50N	79.55 E
Waingapu	72	9.39S	120.16 E
Wainuiomata	96	41.16S	174.57 E
Wainwright	98	52.49N	110.52W
Waiohau	96	38.14S	176.51 E
Waiotira	96	35.56S	174.12 E
Waiouru	96	39.29S	175.40 E
Waipa ≃	96	37.41S	175.09 E
Waipahi	96	46.07S	169.15 E
Waipaoa	96	38.32S	177.54 E
Waipara	96	43.04S	172.45 E
Waipara ≃	96	43.09S	172.48 E
Waipawa	96	39.56S	176.36 E
Waipiro	96	38.01S	178.20 E
Waipu	96	35.59S	174.27 E
Waipukurau	96	40.00S	176.34 E
Wairakei	96	38.38S	176.06 E
Wairarapa, Lake ⊜	96	41.13S	175.15 E
Wairau ≃	96	41.30S	174.04 E
Wairau Valley	96	41.34S	173.32 E
Wairio	96	46.00S	168.02 E
Wairoa	96	39.02S	177.25 E
Wairoa ≃	96	39.04S	177.26 E
Waitahanui	96	38.47S	176.05 E
Waitahuna	96	45.59S	169.46 E
Waitakaruru	96	37.15S	175.23 E
Waitaki ≃	96	44.57S	171.09 E
Waitara	96	39.00S	174.13 E
Waitara ≃	96	38.59S	174.14 E
Waitarere	96	40.33S	175.12 E
Waitati	96	45.45S	170.34 E
Waitemata	96	36.56S	174.42 E
Waitoa	96	37.37S	175.38 E
Waitotara	96	39.48S	174.44 E
Waitotara ≃	96	39.51S	174.41 E
Waiuku	96	37.15S	174.45 E
Waiuta	96	42.18S	171.49 E
Waiwera South	96	46.13S	169.30 E
Wajima	64	37.24N	136.54 E
Wajir	82	1.45N	40.04 E
Waka	82	7.07N	37.26 E
Wakasa-wan C	64	35.45N	135.40 E
Wakatipu, Lake ⊜	96	45.05S	168.34 E
Wakayama	64	34.13N	135.11 E
Wakayanagi	64	38.46N	141.08 E
Wakefield, N.Z.	96	41.24S	173.03 E
Wakefield, Eng., U.K.	36	53.42N	1.29W
Wakefield, R.I., U.S.	102	41.26N	71.30W
Wake Island □[2]	28	19.17N	166.36 E
Wakema	70	16.36N	95.11 E
Waki	64	34.04N	134.09 E
Wakkanai	64a	45.25N	141.40 E
Wakkerstroom	86	27.24S	30.10 E
Walberswick	34	52.19N	1.39 E
Wałbrzych (Waldenburg)	46	50.46N	16.17 E
Walbury Hill ∧[2]	34	51.21N	1.30W
Walcha	94	30.59S	151.36 E
Walcheren I	46	51.33N	3.35 E
Walcott, Lake ⊜[1]	104	42.40N	113.23W
Wałcz	46	53.17N	16.28 E
Waldbröl	46	50.53N	7.37 E
Waldeck	46	51.12N	9.04 E
Walden	102	41.33N	74.11W
Waldkirchen	46	48.44N	13.37 E
Waldmünchen	46	49.23N	12.43 E
Waldoboro	102	44.05N	69.22W
Waldon ≃	34	50.22N	4.14W
Waldorf	102	38.37N	76.56W
Waldron	102	41.43N	84.25W
Waldshut	46	47.37N	8.13 E
Walenstadt	48	47.07N	9.19 E
Wales □[8]	32	52.30N	3.30W
Wales Island I	98	68.00N	86.43W
Walgett	94	30.01S	148.07 E
Walhalla	100	48.55N	97.55W
Walkaway	90	28.57S	114.48 E
Walkden	36	53.32N	2.24W
Walker ≃	104	38.54N	118.47W
Walker Lake ⊜	104	38.44N	118.43W
Walkersville	102	39.29N	77.21W
Walkerton	102	44.07N	81.09W
Wallace	100	47.28N	115.55W
Wallaceburg	102	42.36N	82.23W
Wallachia □[9]	54	44.00N	25.00 E
Wallal Downs	90	19.47S	120.40 E
Wallam Creek ≃	94	28.40S	147.20 E
Wallangarra	94	28.56S	151.56 E
Wallaroo	94	33.56S	137.38 E
Wallasey	36	53.26N	3.03W
Walla Walla	100	46.03N	118.20W
Wallingford, Eng., U.K.	34	51.37N	1.08W
Wallingford, Ct., U.S.	102	41.27N	72.49W
Wallingford, Vt., U.S.	102	43.28N	72.58W
Wallis, Îles II	28	13.18S	176.10W
Wallis and Futuna □[2]	28	14.00S	177.00W
Walls	38a	60.14N	1.35W
Wallsend	36	55.00N	1.31W
Walmer	34	51.13N	1.24 E
Walney, Isle of I	36	54.07N	3.15W
Walnut Creek ≃	102	39.41N	82.59W
Walpeup	94	35.08S	142.02 E
Walpole, Austl.	90	34.57S	116.44 E
Walpole, N.H., U.S.	102	43.04N	72.25W
Walpole Saint Peter	34	52.42N	0.15 E
Walsall	34	52.35N	1.58W
Walsenburg	100	37.37N	104.46W
Walsh	92	16.39S	143.54 E
Walsh ≃	92	16.31S	143.42 E
Walsrode	46	52.52N	9.35 E
Waltershausen	46	50.53N	10.33 E
Waltham, Eng., U.K.	36	53.31N	0.06W
Waltham, Ma., U.S.	102	42.22N	71.14W
Waltham Abbey	34	51.42N	0.01 E
Waltham Forest ✦[8]	34	51.35N	0.01W
Waltham on the Wolds	34	52.49N	0.49W
Walton, Eng., U.K.	34	51.24N	0.25W
Walton, Eng., U.K.	34	51.58N	1.21 E
Walton, Ky., U.S.	102	38.52N	84.36W
Walton, N.Y., U.S.	102	42.10N	75.07W
Walton-le-Dale	36	53.45N	2.39W
Walton on the Naze	34	51.51N	1.16 E
Walvisbaai (Walvis Bay)	86	22.59S	14.31 E
Walvisbaai C	86	22.57S	14.30 E
Walvis Bay →Walvisbaai	86	22.59S	14.31 E
Walvis Bay □[8]	86	22.59S	14.31 E
Walvis Ridge ✦[3]	20	28.00S	3.00 E
Wamba ≃	84	3.56S	17.12 E
Wami ≃	84	6.08S	38.49 E
Wampool ≃	36	54.54N	3.14W
Wampsville	102	43.04N	75.42W
Wampum	102	40.53N	80.20W
Wanaaring	94	29.42S	144.09 E
Wanaka	96	44.42S	169.09 E
Wanaka, Lake ⊜	96	44.30S	169.08 E
Wan'an	66	26.30N	114.49 E
Wanapitei ≃	102	46.02N	80.51W
Wanbi	94	34.46S	140.19 E
Wanborough	34	51.33N	1.42W
Wandana	90	32.04S	133.49 E
Wandoan	94	26.08S	149.57 E
Wandsworth ✦[8]	34	51.27N	0.11W
Wanfoxia	62	40.04N	95.55 E
Wanganui	96	39.56S	175.03 E
Wanganui ≃	96	39.56S	175.00 E
Wangaratta	94	36.22S	146.20 E
Wangary	94	34.33S	135.29 E
Wangdian	66	30.37N	120.44 E
Wangen [im Allgäu]	46	47.41N	9.50 E
Wangerooge I	46	53.46N	7.55 E
Wangingsha	66	22.44N	113.33 E
Wangiwangi, Pulau I	72	5.20S	123.35 E
Wangjiang	66	30.09N	116.41 E
Wangpan Yang C	66	30.30N	121.46 E
Wanigela	92	9.22S	149.10 E
Wānkāner	76	22.37N	70.56 E
Wanli	66	31.06N	120.16 E
Wanna Lakes ⊜	90	28.30S	128.27 E
Wanne-Eickel	46	51.32N	7.09 E
Wannian	66	28.42N	117.03 E
Wanstead	96	40.08S	176.32 E
Wantage	34	51.36N	1.25W
Wanxian	62	30.52N	108.22 E
Wanzai	66	28.06N	114.27 E
Wanzleben	46	52.03N	11.26 E
Wapakoneta	102	40.34N	84.11W
Wapiti ≃	98	55.08N	118.18W
Wappingers Falls	102	41.35N	73.54W
Warangal	74	18.00N	79.35 E
Waratah	94	41.27S	145.32 E
Waratah Bay C	94	38.51S	146.04 E
Warboys	34	52.24N	0.04W
Warbreccan	94	24.18S	142.51 E
Warburg	46	51.29N	9.08 E
Warburton	94	37.46S	145.41 E
Warburton Bay C	98	63.50N	111.30W
Warburton Creek ≃	94	27.55S	137.28 E
Warburton Range ∧∧	90	26.09S	126.38 E
Ward	96	41.50S	174.08 E
Ward ≃	94	26.32S	146.06 E
Ward, Mount ∧	96	43.52S	169.50 E
Warden	86	27.56S	29.00 E
Wardha	74	20.45N	78.37 E
Wardha ≃	74	19.38N	79.48 E
Ward Hill ∧[2], Scot., U.K.	38	58.57N	3.09W
Ward Hill ∧[2], Scot., U.K.	38	58.54N	3.20W
Wardle	36	53.39N	2.08W
Wardour, Vale of ∨	34	51.05N	2.00W
Ward's Stone ∧	36	54.02N	2.38W
Ware, Eng., U.K.	34	51.49N	0.02W
Ware, Ma., U.S.	102	42.15N	72.14W
Ware ≃	102	42.11N	72.22W
Wareham, Eng., U.K.	34	50.41N	2.07W
Wareham, Ma., U.S.	102	41.45N	70.43W
Waremme	46	50.41N	5.15 E
Waren, D.D.R.	46	53.31N	12.40 E
Waren, Indon.	92	2.16S	136.20 E
Warenda	94	22.37S	140.32 E
Warendorf	46	51.57N	7.59 E
Wargla	80	31.59N	5.25 E
Warialda	94	29.32S	150.34 E
Warin Chamrap	70	15.12N	104.53 E
Warka	46	51.47N	21.10 E
Warks Burn ≃	36	55.03N	2.08W
Warkworth, On., Can.	102	44.12N	77.53W
Warkworth, N.Z.	96	36.24S	174.40 E
Warkworth, Eng., U.K.	36	55.21N	1.36W
Warlingham	34	51.19N	0.04W
Warlington	34	51.39N	1.01W
Warmbad, Namibia	86	28.29S	18.41 E
Warmbad, S. Afr.	86	24.55S	28.15 E
Warmington	34	52.08N	1.24W
Warminster, Eng., U.K.	34	51.13N	2.12W
Warminster, Pa., U.S.	102	40.12N	75.06W
Warm Springs	102	38.02N	79.47W
Warm Springs Reservoir ⊜[1]	104	43.37N	118.14W
Warnemünde ✦[8]	46	54.10N	12.04 E
Warner	102	43.16N	71.49W
Warner Lakes ⊜	104	42.25N	119.50W
Warner Mountains ∧∧	104	41.40N	120.20W
Warner Peak ∧	104	42.27N	119.44W
Warnes	114	34.55S	60.31W
Warnow ≃	46	54.06N	12.09 E
Waroona	90	32.50S	115.55 E
Warra	94	26.56S	150.55 E
Warracknabeal	94	36.15S	142.24 E
Warragul	94	38.10S	145.56 E
Warrawagine	90	20.51S	120.42 E
Warrego ≃	94	30.24S	145.21 E
Warrego Range ∧∧	94	25.00S	146.30 E
Warren, Austl.	94	31.42S	147.50 E
Warren, Mi., U.S.	102	42.28N	83.01W
Warren, Oh., U.S.	102	41.14N	80.49W
Warren, Pa., U.S.	102	41.50N	79.08W
Warren ≃	90	34.35S	115.50 E
Warrenpoint	40	54.06N	6.15W
Warrensburg, Mo., U.S.	100	38.45N	93.44W
Warrensburg, N.Y., U.S.	102	43.29N	73.46W
Warrenton, S. Afr.	86	28.09S	24.47 E
Warrenton, Va., U.S.	102	38.42N	77.47W
Warri	80	5.31N	5.45 E
Warriedar Hill ∧[2]	90	29.06S	117.06 E
Warrina	94	28.12S	135.50 E
Warrington, N.Z.	96	45.43S	170.35 E
Warrington, Eng., U.K.	36	53.24N	2.37W
Warrior Reefs ✦[2]	92	9.35S	143.10 E
Warrnambool	94	38.23S	142.29 E
Warsaw →Warszawa, Pol.	46	52.15N	21.00 E
Warsaw, Ky., U.S.	102	38.47N	84.54W
Warsaw, N.Y., U.S.	102	42.44N	78.07W
Warsaw, Oh., U.S.	102	40.20N	82.00W
Warsaw, Va., U.S.	102	37.57N	76.45W
Warsop	36	53.13N	1.09W
Warszawa (Warsaw)	46	52.15N	21.00 E
Warta	46	51.42N	18.38 E
Warta ≃	46	52.35N	14.39 E
Wartburg ⊥	46	50.58N	10.18 E
Warthe →Warta ≃	46	52.35N	14.39 E
Warton	36	54.09N	2.47W
Warud	76	21.28N	78.16 E
Warwick, Austl.	94	28.13S	152.02 E
Warwick, P.Q., Can.	102	45.56N	71.59W
Warwick, Eng., U.K.	34	52.17N	1.34W
Warwick, R.I., U.S.	102	41.41N	71.22W
Warwick Channel ʉ	92	13.51S	136.16 E
Warwickshire □[6]	34	52.13N	1.37W
Wasaga Beach	102	44.31N	80.01W
Wasbank	86	28.24S	30.05 E
Wasbister	38	59.10N	3.07W
Wasco	104	35.35N	119.20W
Washburn Lake ⊜	98	70.03N	106.50W
Washdyke	96	44.21S	171.14 E
Washington, Eng., U.K.	36	54.55N	1.30W
Washington, D.C., U.S.	102	38.53N	77.02W
Washington, Ky., U.S.	102	38.36N	83.48W
Washington, Pa., U.S.	102	40.10N	80.14W
Washington, Va., U.S.	102	38.42N	78.09W
Washington □[3]	100	47.30N	120.30W
Washington, Mount ∧	102	44.15N	71.15W
Washington Court House	102	39.32N	83.26W
Washoe Lake ⊜	104	39.16N	119.48W
Washurn ≃	36	53.54N	1.39W
Wasian	92	1.54S	133.17 E
Wasilków	46	53.12N	23.12 E
Wasior	92	2.43S	134.30 E
Wāsiṭ □[4]	78	32.45N	45.25 E
Wąsosz	46	51.34N	16.42 E
Waspam	108	14.44N	83.58W
Wassen	48	46.42N	8.36 E
Wasseralfingen	46	48.52N	10.06 E
Wasserburg am Inn	46	48.04N	12.13 E
Wasserkuppe ∧	46	50.30N	9.56 E
Wassy	48	48.30N	4.57 E
Wast Water ⊜	36	54.26N	3.18W
Watampone (Bone)	72	4.32S	120.20 E
Watansoppeng	72	4.21S	119.53 E
Watatic, Mount ∧	102	42.42N	71.53W
Watchet	34	51.12N	3.20W
Waterbeach	34	52.16N	0.11 E
Waterberge ∧∧	86	24.30S	28.00 E
Waterbury, Ct., U.S.	102	41.33N	73.02W
Waterbury, Vt., U.S.	102	44.20N	72.45W
Waterdown	102	43.20N	79.53W
Waterford, On., Can.	102	42.56N	80.17W
Waterford (Port Láirge), Ire.	40	52.15N	7.06W
Waterford, Ca., U.S.	104	37.38N	120.46W
Waterford, Pa., U.S.	102	41.56N	79.59W
Waterford □[6]	40	52.10N	7.40W
Waterford Harbour C	40	52.10N	6.55W
Watergate Bay C	34	50.27N	5.05W
Watergrasshill	40	52.01N	8.21W
Waterhen Lake ⊜	98	52.06N	99.34W
Waterhouse Range ∧∧	90	24.01S	133.25 E
Waterloo, Austl.	92	16.38S	129.18 E
Waterloo, Bel.	46	50.43N	4.23 E
Waterloo, On., Can.	102	43.28N	80.31W
Waterloo, P.Q., Can.	102	45.21N	72.31W
Waterloo, Eng., U.K.	36	53.28N	3.02W
Waterloo, Ia., U.S.	100	42.29N	92.20W
Waterloo, N.Y., U.S.	102	42.54N	76.51W
Waterlooville	34	50.53N	1.02W
Watertown, N.Y., U.S.	102	43.58N	75.54W
Watertown, S.D., U.S.	100	44.53N	97.06W
Waterval-Boven	86	25.40S	30.20 E
Waterville, Ire.	40	51.49N	10.13W
Waterville, Me., U.S.	102	44.33N	69.37W
Waterville, Oh., U.S.	102	41.30N	83.43W
Watervliet	102	42.43N	73.42W
Watford, On., Can.	102	42.57N	81.53W
Watford, Eng., U.K.	34	51.40N	0.25W
Watford City	100	47.48N	103.16W
Wathaman ≃	98	57.16N	102.52W
Watheroo	90	30.17S	116.04 E
Wath upon Dearne	36	53.29N	1.20W
Watkins Glen	102	42.22N	76.52W
Watling Island →San Salvador I	108	24.02N	74.28W
Watlington	34	51.37N	1.00W
Watrous	98	51.40N	105.28W
Watson	90	30.29S	131.31 E
Watson Lake	98	60.07N	128.48W
Watsontown	102	41.05N	76.51W
Watsonville	104	36.54N	121.45W
Watten, Loch ⊜	38	58.29N	3.19W
Wattens	46	47.17N	11.36 E
Wattenscheid	46	51.29N	7.08 E
Wattiwarriganna ≃	90	28.57S	136.10 E
Watton	34	52.35N	0.48 E
Wattwil	48	47.18N	9.06 E
Watubela, Kepulauan II	92	4.35S	131.40 E
Wat Wat	92	4.29S	152.21 E
Watzmann ∧	46	47.33N	12.55 E
Wauchope	94	31.27S	152.44 E
Waukaringa	94	32.18S	139.26 E
Waukarlycarly, Lake ⊜	90	21.25S	121.50 E
Waukegan	100	42.21N	87.50W
Wausau	100	44.57N	89.37W
Wauseon	102	41.32N	84.08W
Wave Hill	90	17.29S	130.57 E
Waveney ≃	34	52.28N	1.45 E
Waver ≃	36	54.52N	3.17W
Waverley	96	39.46S	174.38 E
Waverly, N.Y., U.S.	102	42.00N	76.31W
Waverly, Oh., U.S.	102	39.07N	82.59W
Wavre	48	50.43N	4.37 E
Wāw	82	7.42N	28.00 E
Wawa	98	47.59N	84.47W
Wawa ≃	108	13.53N	83.28W
Wāw al-Kabīr	82	25.20N	16.43 E
Way, Lake ⊜	90	26.48S	120.18 E
Wayabula	68	2.17N	128.12 E
Waycross	100	31.12N	82.21W
Wayland	102	42.34N	77.35W
Wayne, Mi., U.S.	102	42.16N	83.23W
Wayne, Ne., U.S.	100	42.13N	97.01W
Wayne, N.J., U.S.	102	40.55N	74.16W
Wayne, W.V., U.S.	102	38.13N	82.26W
Waynesboro, Pa., U.S.	102	39.45N	77.34W
Waynesboro, Va., U.S.	102	38.04N	78.53W
Waynesburg, Oh., U.S.	102	40.40N	81.15W
Waynesburg, Pa., U.S.	102	39.53N	80.10W
Wazīrābād	76	32.27N	74.07 E
Wda ≃	46	53.25N	18.29 E
We, Pulau I	70	5.51N	95.18 E
Wear ≃	36	54.55N	1.22W
Wearhead	36	54.45N	2.13W
Wearyan ≃	92	15.57S	136.51 E
Weatherford	100	35.31N	98.42W
Weatherly	102	40.56N	75.50W
Weaver ≃	34	53.04N	2.32W
Weaverham	36	53.16N	2.35W
Weaverville	104	40.43N	122.56W
Webbwood	102	46.16N	81.53W
Webster	102	42.03N	71.52W
Webster Springs	102	38.28N	80.24W
Weda	68	0.21N	127.52 E
Weddell Sea ∓[2]	24	72.00S	45.00W
Wedderburn	94	36.25S	143.37 E
Wedel	46	53.35N	9.41 E
Wedmore	34	51.14N	2.49W
Weebo	90	28.01S	121.03 E
Weed	104	41.25N	122.23W
Weedon Beck	34	52.14N	1.05W
Weedsport	102	43.02N	76.33W
Weedville	102	41.17N	78.30W
Weeley	34	51.51N	1.07 E
Weenen	86	28.57S	30.03 E
Weert	46	51.15N	5.43 E
Weethalle	94	33.53S	146.38 E
Weeting	34	52.27N	0.37 E
Wee Waa	94	30.14S	149.26 E
Węgliniec	46	51.17N	15.13 E
Węgorzewo	46	54.14N	21.44 E
Węgorzyno	46	53.32N	15.33 E
Węgrów	46	52.25N	22.01 E
Wegscheid	46	48.36N	13.48 E
Wei ≃	62	34.30N	110.20 E
Weichuan	66	34.17N	113.58 E
Weida	46	50.45N	12.04 E
Weiden in der Oberpfalz	46	49.41N	12.10 E
Weifang	62	36.42N	119.04 E
Weihai	62	37.28N	122.07 E
Weilburg	46	50.29N	8.15 E
Weilheim	46	47.50N	11.08 E
Weilmoringle	94	29.15S	146.51 E
Weimar	46	50.59N	11.19 E
Weinan	62	34.29N	109.29 E
Weinheim	46	49.33N	8.39 E
Weipa	92	12.41S	141.52 E
Weir ≃	94	28.50S	149.06 E
Weirton	102	40.25N	80.35W
Weisburd	114	27.18S	62.36W
Weiser	100	44.15N	116.58W
Weishan, Zhg.	66	29.20N	120.25 E
Weishan, Zhg.	70	25.15N	100.20 E
Weishi	66	34.25N	114.11 E
Weissenburg in Bayern	46	49.01N	10.58 E
Weissenfels	46	51.12N	11.58 E
Weisswasser	46	51.30N	14.38 E
Weitra	46	48.42N	14.54 E
Weiz	46	47.13N	15.37 E
Wejherowo	46	54.37N	18.15 E
Welbourn Hill	90	27.21S	134.06 E
Welker Seamount ✦[3]	22	55.07N	140.20W
Welkom	86	27.59S	26.45 E
Welland	102	42.59N	79.15W
Welland ≃, On., Can.	102	43.04N	79.03W
Welland ≃, Eng., U.K.	34	52.53N	0.02 E
Wellesbourne	34	52.12N	1.35W
Wellesley Islands II	94	16.42S	139.30 E
Wellfleet	102	41.56N	70.02W
Wellingborough	34	52.19N	0.42W
Wellington, Austl.	94	32.33S	148.57 E
Wellington, On., Can.	102	43.57N	77.21W
Wellington, N.Z.	96	41.18S	174.47 E
Wellington, S. Afr.	86	33.38S	18.57 E
Wellington, Eng., U.K.	34	50.59N	3.14W
Wellington, Eng., U.K.	34	52.43N	2.31W
Wellington, Oh., U.S.	102	41.10N	82.13W
Wellington, Isla I	112	49.20S	74.40W
Wellington Bay C	98	69.30N	106.30W
Wellington Channel ʉ	98	75.00N	93.00W
Wells, Eng., U.K.	34	51.13N	2.39W
Wells, Nv., U.S.	104	41.06N	114.57W
Wells, N.Y., U.S.	102	43.24N	74.17W
Wells, Lake ⊜	90	26.43S	123.10 E
Wellsboro	102	41.44N	77.18W
Wellsburg	102	40.16N	80.36W
Wellsford	96	36.17S	174.31 E
Wells-next-the-Sea	34	52.58N	0.51 E
Wellston	102	39.07N	82.31W
Wellsville, N.Y., U.S.	102	42.07N	77.56W
Wellsville, Oh., U.S.	102	40.36N	80.38W
Wellton	104	32.40N	114.08W
Welney	34	52.31N	0.15 E
Wels	46	48.10N	14.02 E
Welshpool	34	52.40N	3.09W
Welwyn Garden City	34	51.50N	0.13W
Wem	34	52.51N	2.44W
Wembere ≃	84	4.10S	34.11 E
Wembury	34	50.19N	4.05W
Wenatchee	100	47.25N	120.18W
Wenchang	70	19.41N	110.48 E
Wencheng	66	27.50N	120.05 E
Wenchow →Wenzhou	62	28.01N	120.39 E
Wendell	104	42.46N	114.42W
Wendover, Eng., U.K.	34	51.46N	0.46W
Wendover, Ut,. U.S.	100	40.44N	114.02W
Wengyuan	66	24.21N	114.08 E
Wenjiazhen	66	28.20N	116.05 E
Wenling	66	28.22N	121.20 E
Wenlock	92	13.06S	142.58 E
Wenlock ≃	92	12.02S	141.55 E
Wenlock Edge ⩤[4]	34	52.30N	2.40W
Wenning ≃	36	54.07N	2.39W
Wenshan	70	23.30N	104.20 E
Wensleydale ∨	36	54.19N	2.00W
Wensum ≃	34	52.37N	1.19 E
Went ≃	36	53.39N	0.59W
Wentworth	94	34.07S	141.55 E
Wenzhou	66	28.01N	120.39 E
Weobley	34	52.09N	2.51W
Wepener	86	29.46S	27.00 E
Werdau	46	50.44N	12.22 E
Werder	46	52.23N	12.56 E
Werdohl	46	51.15N	7.45 E
Werl	46	51.33N	7.54 E
Wernadinga	94	18.07S	139.58 E
Werne [an der Lippe 96	46	51.40N	7.38 E
Wernigerode	46	51.50N	10.47 E
Werra ≃	46	51.26N	9.39 E
Werribee	94	37.54S	144.40 E
Werrimull	94	34.24S	141.26 E
Werris Creek	94	31.21S	150.39 E
Wertheim	46	49.46N	9.31 E
Wertingen	46	48.34N	10.41 E
Wervik	46	50.47N	3.02 E
Wesel	46	51.40N	6.38 E
Weser ≃	46	53.32N	8.34 E
Weslemkoon Lake ⊜	102	45.02N	77.25W
Wesleyville	102	42.08N	80.00W
Wessel, Cape ›	92	10.59S	136.46 E
Wessel Islands II	92	11.30S	136.25 E
Wesselsbron	86	27.50S	25.23 E
West ≃	102	42.52N	72.33W
West Alexandria	102	39.44N	84.31W
Westall, Point ›	90	32.55S	134.04 E
West Allen ≃	36	54.55N	2.19W
West Baines ≃	92	15.36S	129.58 E
West Bengal □[3]	76	24.00N	88.00 E
West Bergholt	34	51.55N	0.51 E
West-Berlin →Berlin (West)	46	52.30N	13.20 E
West Branch	102	44.16N	84.14W
West Bridgford	34	52.56N	1.08W
West Bromwich	34	52.31N	1.56W
Westbrook	102	43.40N	70.22W
West Burra I	38a	60.05N	1.21W
Westbury, Eng., U.K.	34	52.41N	2.57W
Westbury, Eng., U.K.	34	51.16N	2.11W
Westbury-on-Severn	34	51.50N	2.24W
Westby	94	35.30S	147.25 E
West Caicos I	108	21.39N	72.28W
West Calder	38	55.52N	3.35W
West Cape ›	96	45.54S	166.26 E
West Cape Howe ›	90	35.08S	117.36 E
West Caroline Basin ✦[1]	28	4.00N	138.00 E
West Chester	102	39.57N	75.36W
West Cleddau ≃	34	51.46N	4.54W
West End	108	26.41N	78.58W
Westerdale	38	58.27N	3.30W
Westerham	34	51.16N	0.05 E
Westerland	46	54.54N	8.18 E
Westerly	102	41.22N	71.49W
Western ≃	94	22.22S	142.25 E
Western Australia □[3]	88	25.00S	122.00 E
Western Desert →Gharbīyah, Aṣ-Ṣaḥrā' al- ✦[2]	82	27.00N	27.00 E
Western Ghāts ∧∧	74	14.00N	75.00 E
Western Isles □[4]	38	57.40N	7.00W
Westernport	102	39.29N	79.02W
Western Port C	94	38.22S	145.20 E
Western Sahara □[2]	80	24.30N	13.00W
Western Samoa □[1]	28	13.55S	172.00W
Western Sayans →Zapadnyj Sajan ∧∧	58	53.00N	94.00 E
Westerstede	46	53.15N	7.55 E
Westerville	102	40.07N	82.55W
Westerwald ∧∧	46	50.40N	7.55 E
West European Basin ✦[1]	20	47.00N	15.00W
West Falkland I	112	51.50S	60.00W
Westfield, Eng., U.K.	34	50.55N	0.35 E
Westfield, Ma., U.S.	102	42.07N	72.45W
Westfield, N.J., U.S.	102	40.39N	74.20W
Westfield, N.Y., U.S.	102	42.19N	79.34W
Westfield, Pa., U.S.	102	41.55N	77.32W
West Fiord C[2]	98	76.02N	90.00W
West Frisian Islands →Waddeneilanden II	46	53.26N	5.30 E
Westgate	94	26.35S	146.12 E
Westgate on Sea	34	51.23N	1.21 E
West Germany →Germany, Federal Republic of □[1]	46	51.00N	9.00 E
West Glamorgan □[6]	34	51.35N	3.35W
West Hamlin	102	38.17N	82.11W
West Harbour	96	45.51S	170.35 E
West Hartford	102	41.45N	72.44W
Westhaven, Ca., U.S.	104	41.03N	124.06W
West Haven, Ct., U.S.	102	41.16N	72.57W
Westhill	38	57.09N	2.17W
West Indies II	108	19.00N	70.00W
West Irian →Irian Jaya □[4]	92	5.00S	138.00 E
West Island I	92	15.36S	136.34 E
West Jan Mayen Ridge ✦[3]	20	71.00N	13.00W
West Jefferson	102	39.56N	83.16W
West Kilbride	38	55.42N	4.51W
West Kingsdown	34	51.21N	0.17 E
West Kingston	102	41.28N	71.33W
West Kirby	36	53.22N	3.10W
West Lafayette	102	40.16N	81.45W
West Liberty, Ky., U.S.	102	37.55N	83.15W
West Liberty, Oh., U.S.	102	40.15N	83.45W
West Linton	38	55.46N	3.22W
West Little Owyhee ≃	104	42.28N	117.15W
West Loch Roag C	38	58.13N	6.53W
West Loch Tarbert C, Scot., U.K.	38	57.55N	6.54W
West Loch Tarbert C, Scot., U.K.	38	55.48N	5.32W
West Looe	34	50.21N	4.28W
West Lorne	102	42.36N	81.36W
West Lulworth	34	50.38N	2.15W
West Malling	34	51.18N	0.25 E
Westmeath □[6]	40	53.30N	7.30W
West Meon	34	51.01N	1.05W
West Mersea	34	51.47N	0.55 E
West Midlands □[6]	34	52.30N	2.00W
West Mifflin	102	40.22N	79.52W
Westminster	102	39.34N	76.59W
Westmont	102	40.18N	78.57W
West Moors	34	50.49N	1.55W
Westmorland	104	33.02N	115.37W
West Mountain ∧	102	43.51N	74.43W
West Nicholson	86	21.06S	29.25 E
West Novaya Zemlya Trough ✦[1]	20	73.30N	50.00 E
Weston, Malay.	72	5.13N	115.36 E
Weston, Oh., U.S.	102	41.20N	83.47W
Weston, W.V., U.S.	102	39.02N	80.28W
Weston-super-Mare	34	51.21N	2.59W
Weston upon Trent	34	52.45N	2.02W
Westover	102	39.38N	79.58W
West Palm Beach	100	26.42N	80.03W
West Paris	102	44.19N	70.34W
West Point, Ca., U.S.	104	38.23N	120.31W
West Point, Ms., U.S.	100	33.36N	88.39W
West Point, N.Y., U.S.	102	41.23N	73.57W
Westport, On., Can.	102	44.41N	76.26W
Westport, Ire.	40	53.48N	9.32W
Westport, N.Z.	96	41.45S	171.36 E
Westport, Ct., U.S.	102	41.08N	73.21W
West Portsmouth	102	38.45N	83.01W
West Quoddy Head ›	102	44.49N	66.57W
Westray I	38	59.18N	3.00W
Westray Firth ʉ	38	59.12N	2.55W
West Rutland	102	43.35N	73.02W
West Sacramento	104	38.34N	121.31W
West Salem	102	40.58N	82.06W
West Scotia Basin ✦[1]	24	57.00S	53.00W
West Siberian Plain →Zapadno-Sibirskaja ravnina ⩧	56	60.00N	75.00 E
West Sussex □[6]	34	50.55N	0.35W
West Union, Oh., U.S.	102	38.47N	83.32W
West Union, W.V., U.S.	102	39.17N	80.46W
West Unity	102	41.35N	84.26W
West Virginia □[3]	100	38.45N	80.30W
West Walker ≃	104	38.53N	119.10W
Westward Ho90	34	51.02N	4.15W
West Warwick	102	41.42N	71.31W
West Water ≃	38	56.47N	2.38W
West Webster	102	43.12N	77.29W
West Wellow	34	50.58N	1.35W
Westwood	104	40.18N	121.00W
West Wyalong	94	33.55S	147.13 E
West Wycombe	34	51.39N	0.49W
West Yorkshire □[6]	36	53.45N	1.40W
Wetar, Pulau I	72	7.48S	126.18 E
Wetaskiwin	98	52.58N	113.22W
Wete	84	5.04S	39.43 E
Wetherby	36	53.56N	1.23W
Wethersfield	102	41.43N	72.40W
Wetwang	36	54.01N	0.34W
Wetzlar	46	50.33N	8.29 E
Wewak	92	3.35S	143.40 E
Wexford	40	52.20N	6.27W
Wexford □[6]	40	52.20N	6.40W
Wexford Harbour C	40	52.20N	6.55W
Wey ≃	34	51.23N	0.28W
Weybridge	34	51.23N	0.28W
Weyburn	98	49.41N	103.52W
Weyer Markt	46	47.52N	14.41 E
Weymouth, Eng., U.K.	34	50.36N	2.28W
Weymouth, Ma., U.S.	102	42.13N	70.56W
Weymouth, Cape ›	92	12.37S	143.27 E
Whakatane	96	37.58S	177.00 E
Whakatane ≃	96	37.57S	177.00 E
Whaley Bridge	36	53.20N	1.59W
Whalley	36	53.50N	2.24W
Whalsay I	38a	60.20N	0.59W
Whangaehu ≃	96	40.03S	175.06 E
Whangamata	96	37.12S	175.52 E
Whangamomona	96	39.09S	174.44 E
Whangara	96	38.34S	178.13 E
Whangarei	96	35.43S	174.19 E
Whaplode	34	52.48N	0.02W
Wharfe ≃	36	53.51N	1.07W
Wharfedale ∨	36	54.01N	1.56W
Wharton	102	37.54N	81.40W
Wharton Basin ✦[1]	26	21.00S	100.00 E
Wharton Lake ⊜	98	64.00N	99.55W
Whataroa	96	43.17S	170.25 E
Whatatutu	96	38.23S	177.50 E
Whauphill	36	54.49N	4.29W
Wheao ≃	96	38.34S	176.39 E
Wheathampstead	34	51.49N	0.17W
Wheatland	104	39.00N	121.25W
Wheatley, On., Can.	102	42.06N	82.27W
Wheatley, Eng., U.K.	36	51.44N	1.08W
Wheatley Hill	36	54.45N	1.23W
Wheaton	102	39.02N	77.03W
Wheelbarrow Peak ∧	104	37.27N	116.05W
Wheeler ≃	98	57.02N	67.13W
Wheeler Peak ∧, Ca., U.S.	104	38.25N	119.17W
Wheeler Peak ∧, Nv., U.S.	104	38.59N	114.19W
Wheeler Peak ∧, N.M., U.S.	100	36.34N	105.25W
Wheeling	102	40.03N	80.43W
Wheelock ≃	36	53.12N	2.26W
Wheelwright	114	33.47S	61.13W
Whela Creek ≃	90	26.17S	116.50 E
Whelan, Mount ∧[2]	94	23.25S	138.54 E
Whernside ∧	36	54.14N	2.23W
Whickham	36	54.56N	1.41W
Whidbey Islands II	90	34.45S	135.04 E
Whiddon Down	34	50.43N	3.51W
Whim Creek	90	20.50S	117.50 E
Whinham, Mount ∧	90	26.04S	130.15 E
Whitburn, Eng., U.K.	36	54.57N	1.22W
Whitburn, Scot., U.K.	38	55.52N	3.42W
Whitby, On., Can.	102	43.52N	78.56W
Whitby, Eng., U.K.	36	54.29N	0.37W
Whitchurch, Eng., U.K.	34	51.53N	0.51W
Whitchurch, Eng., U.K.	34	51.14N	1.20W
Whitchurch, Eng., U.K.	34	51.52N	2.39W
Whitchurch, Eng., U.K.	34	52.58N	2.41W
Whitchurch-Stouffville	102	43.58N	79.15W
Whitcombe, Mount ∧	96	43.13S	170.55 E
White ≃, N.A.	98	63.11N	139.36W
White ≃, U.S.	100	43.45N	99.30W
White ≃, U.S.	100	33.53N	91.03W
White ≃, In., U.S.	102	40.09N	85.20W
White ≃, Nv., U.S.	104	37.42N	115.10W
White ≃, Vt., U.S.	102	43.37N	72.20W
White, Lake ⊜	90	21.05S	129.00 E
White Bay C	98	50.00N	56.30W
White Cap Mountain ∧	102	45.35N	69.13W
White Cliffs	94	30.51S	143.05 E
White Cloud	102	43.33N	85.46W
White Coomb ∧	36	55.26N	3.20W
Whitecourt	98	54.09N	115.41W
White Esk ≃	36	55.12N	3.10W
Whiteface Mountain ∧	102	44.22N	73.54W
Whitefield, Eng., U.K.	36	53.33N	2.18W
Whitefield, N.H., U.S.	102	44.22N	71.36W
Whitefish	100	48.24N	114.20W
Whitefish Lake ⊜	98	62.41N	106.48W
Whiteford Point ›	34	51.38N	4.14W
Whitegate	40	51.50N	8.14W
Whitehall (Paulstown), Ire.	40	52.41N	7.01W
Whitehall, Scot., U.K.	38	59.07N	2.37W
Whitehall, N.Y., U.S.	102	43.33N	73.24W
Whitehaven, Eng., U.K.	36	54.33N	3.35W
White Haven, Pa., U.S.	102	41.03N	75.46W
Whitehead	40	54.46N	5.43W
Whitehorse	98	60.43N	135.03W
White Horse, Vale of ∨	34	51.37N	1.37W
Whitehorse Hill ∧[2]	34	51.34N	1.34W
Whitehouse	38	57.13N	2.37W
White Island I, N.T., Can.	98	65.50N	84.50W
White Island I, N.Z.	96	37.31S	177.11 E
White Lake ⊜	102	45.18N	76.31W
Whiteman Range ∧∧	92	5.50S	149.55 E
Whitemark	94	40.07S	148.01 E
White Mountain Peak ∧	104	37.38N	118.15W
White Mountains ∧∧, U.S.	104	37.30N	118.15W
White Mountains ∧∧, N.H., U.S.	102	44.10N	71.35W
Whiten Head ›	38	58.34N	4.36W
White Nile (Al-Bahr al-Abyad) ≃	82	15.38N	32.31 E
White Plains	102	41.02N	73.45W
White River Junction	102	43.38N	72.19W
White Sea →Beloje more ∓[2]	42	65.30N	38.00 E
Whitesville	102	37.58N	81.31W
White Volta (Volta Blanche) ≃	80	9.10N	1.15W
Whitewater ≃, U.S.	102	39.10N	84.47W
Whitewater ≃, Ca., U.S.	104	33.30N	116.03W

Symbols in the Index entries are identified on page 122.

Name | Page | Lat.°′ | Long.°′

Whitewood 94 21.28 S 143.36 E
Whitfield 34 51.09 N 1.18 E
Whithorn 36 54.44 N 4.25 W
Whitianga 96 36.50 S 175.42 E
Whiting Bay 36 55.29 N 5.06 W
Whitland 34 51.50 N 4.37 W
Whitley Bay 36 55.03 N 1.25 W
Whitman 102 42.04 N 70.56 W
Whitney 102 45.30 N 78.14 W
Whitney, Mount ▲ 104 36.35 N 118.18 W
Whitney Point 102 42.19 N 75.58 W
Whitstable 34 51.22 N 1.02 E
Whitsunday Island I 94 20.17 S 148.59 E
Whittemore 102 44.14 N 83.48 W
Whittingham 36 55.24 N 1.54 W
Whittington 34 52.52 N 3.00 W
Whittle, Cap > 98 50.11 N 60.08 W
Whittlesea, Austl. 94 37.31 S 145.07 E
Whittlesea, Ciskei 86 32.10 S 26.50 E
Whittlesey 34 52.34 N 0.08 W
Whitwick 34 52.44 N 1.21 W
Whitworth 36 53.40 N 2.10 W
Wholdaia Lake ⊜ 98 60.43 N 104.10 W
Whyalla 94 33.02 S 137.35 E
Wiarton 102 44.45 N 81.09 W
Wiay I 38 57.23 N 7.13 W
Wiązów 46 50.49 N 17.11 E
Wichita 100 37.41 N 97.20 W
Wichita Falls 100 33.54 N 98.29 W
Wick 38 58.26 N 3.06 W
Wick ≈ 38 58.27 N 3.05 W
Wickepin 90 32.46 S 117.30 E
Wickford 34 51.38 N 0.31 E
Wickham 34 50.54 N 1.10 W
Wickham ≈ 92 16.22 S 131.06 E
Wickham, Cape > 94 39.36 S 143.57 E
Wickham Market 34 52.09 N 1.22 E
Wicklow 40 52.59 N 6.03 W
Wicklow □6 40 53.00 N 6.30 W
Wicklow Head > 40 52.58 N 6.00 W
Wicklow Mountains ✱ 40 53.02 N 6.24 W
Widdrington Station 36 55.15 N 1.36 W
Widecombe in the Moor 34 50.35 N 3.48 W
Widemouth Bay 34 50.47 N 4.32 W
Widen 102 38.27 N 80.51 W
Wide Open 36 55.03 N 1.38 W
Widgiemooltha 90 31.30 S 121.34 E
Widnes 36 53.22 N 2.44 W
Więcbork 46 53.22 N 17.30 E
Wiehl 46 50.57 N 7.31 E
Wiek 46 54.37 N 13.17 E
Wieleń 46 52.54 N 16.10 E
Wielichowo 46 52.08 N 16.21 E
Wieliczka 46 49.59 N 20.04 E
Wielkopolska ✦1 46 51.50 N 17.20 E
Wieluń 46 51.14 N 18.34 E
Wien (Vienna) 46 48.13 N 16.20 E
Wiener Neustadt 46 47.49 N 16.15 E
Wienerwald ✱ 46 48.10 N 16.00 E
Wieprz ≈ 46 51.34 N 21.49 E
Wieprza ≈ 46 54.26 N 16.22 E
Wierden 46 52.22 N 6.35 E
Wieruszów 46 51.18 N 18.08 E
Wierzyca ≈ 46 53.51 N 18.50 E
Wiesbaden 46 50.05 N 8.14 E
Wieselburg 46 48.08 N 15.09 E
Wiesloch 46 49.17 N 8.42 E
Wietze 46 52.39 N 9.50 E
Wigan 36 53.33 N 2.38 W
Wigglesworth 36 54.01 N 2.17 W
Wight, Isle of I 34 50.40 N 1.20 W
Wigmore 34 52.19 N 2.51 W
Wigston 34 52.36 N 1.05 W
Wigton 36 54.49 N 3.09 W
Wigtown 36 54.52 N 4.26 W
Wigtown Bay C 36 54.46 N 4.15 W
Wil 46 47.27 N 9.03 E
Wilberforce Falls ⌊ 98 67.07 N 108.47 W
Wilcannia 94 31.34 S 143.23 E
Wilcox 102 41.34 N 78.41 W
Wildon 46 46.53 N 15.31 E
Wildspitze ▲ 46 46.53 N 10.52 E
Wildwood 102 38.59 N 74.48 W
Wilge ≈ 86 27.03 S 28.20 E
Wilgena 90 30.46 S 134.44 E
Wilhelm, Mount ▲ 92 5.45 S 145.05 E
Wilhelmina Peak →Trikora, Puncak ▲ 92 4.15 S 138.45 E
Wilhelm-Pieck-Stadt Guben 46 51.57 N 14.43 E
Wilhelmshaven 46 53.31 N 8.08 E
Wilkes-Barre 102 41.14 N 75.52 W
Wilkes Land ✦1 18 69.00 S 120.00 E
Wilkhaven 38 57.52 N 3.45 W
Wilkie 98 52.25 N 108.43 W
Wilkinson Lakes ⊜ 90 29.40 S 132.39 E
Willard 102 41.03 N 82.44 W
Willaumez Peninsula >1 92 5.05 S 150.05 E
Willemstad 108 12.06 N 68.56 W
Willenhall 34 52.36 N 2.02 W
Willeroo 92 15.17 S 131.35 E
William, Mount ▲ 94 37.17 S 142.36 E
William Creek 94 28.55 S 136.21 E
Williams, Austl. 90 33.01 S 116.52 E
Williams, Ca., U.S. 104 39.09 N 122.08 W
Williams ≈ 94 20.04 S 141.08 E
Williamsburg 102 40.27 N 78.12 W
Williams Lake 98 52.08 N 122.09 W
Williamson, N.Y., U.S. 102 43.13 N 77.11 W
Williamson, W.V., U.S. 100 37.40 N 82.16 W
Williamson ≈ 104 42.28 N 121.57 W
Williamsport 102 41.14 N 77.00 W
Williamston 102 42.41 N 84.16 W
Williamstown, Ky., U.S. 102 38.38 N 84.33 W
Williamstown, Ma., U.S. 102 42.42 N 73.12 W
Williamstown, N.J., U.S. 102 39.41 N 74.59 W
Williamstown, Vt., U.S. 102 44.07 N 72.32 W
Williamstown, W.V., U.S. 102 39.24 N 81.27 W
Willich 48 51.16 N 6.33 E
Willimantic 102 41.42 N 72.12 W
Willingboro 102 40.01 N 74.52 W
Willingdon 34 50.47 N 0.15 E
Willingham 34 52.19 N 0.04 E
Willington, Eng., U.K. 34 52.50 N 1.33 W
Willington, Eng., U.K. 36 54.43 N 1.41 W
Willis Group II 92 16.18 S 150.00 E
Williston, S. Afr. 86 31.20 S 20.53 E
Williston, N.D., U.S. 100 48.08 N 103.37 W
Williston Lake ⊜1 98 55.40 N 123.40 W
Williton 34 51.10 N 3.20 W
Willits 104 39.24 N 123.21 W
Willoughby 102 41.38 N 81.25 W
Willoughby, Cape > 94 35.51 S 138.07 E
Willow Brook ≈ 34 52.32 N 0.24 W
Willow Creek 104 40.56 N 123.38 W
Willow Creek ≈ 104 38.10 N 116.35 W
Willowick 102 41.37 N 81.28 W
Willow Lake ⊜ 98 62.11 N 119.10 W
Willowlake ≈ 98 62.52 N 123.08 W
Willowmore 86 33.17 S 23.29 E
Willowra 90 21.15 S 132.35 E
Willows 104 39.31 N 122.11 W
Willowvale 86 32.16 S 28.30 E
Wills, Lake ⊜ 88 21.25 S 128.51 E
Wills Creek ≈, Austl. 94 22.43 S 140.02 E
Wills Creek ≈, Oh., U.S. 102 40.09 N 81.55 W
Willshire 102 40.45 N 84.48 W
Willunga 94 35.17 S 138.33 E
Wilmington, Austl. 94 32.39 S 138.07 E
Wilmington, De., U.S. 102 39.44 N 75.32 W
Wilmington, N.C., U.S. 100 34.13 N 77.56 W
Wilmington, Oh., U.S. 102 39.26 N 83.49 W
Wilmington, Vt., U.S. 102 42.52 N 72.52 W
Wilmore 102 37.51 N 84.39 W
Wilmslow 36 53.20 N 2.15 W
Wilna →Vilnius 60 54.41 N 25.19 E
Wilnecote 34 52.36 N 1.40 W
Wilshamstead 34 52.05 N 0.27 W
Wilson, Austl. 94 32.00 S 138.22 E
Wilson, N.Y., U.S. 102 43.18 N 78.49 W
Wilson, N.C., U.S. 100 35.43 N 77.54 W
Wilson ≈ 94 27.38 S 141.24 E
Wilson, Cape > 98 66.59 N 81.28 W
Wilson, Mount ▲, Ca., U.S. 104 34.13 N 118.04 W
Wilson, Mount ▲, Nv., U.S. 104 38.15 N 114.23 W
Wilson Cliffs ✦4 90 22.03 S 127.09 E
Wilson Range ✱ 90 28.50 S 124.25 E
Wilsons Beach 102 44.56 N 66.56 W
Wilsons Promontory > 94 38.55 S 146.20 E
Wilton, Eng., U.K. 34 51.05 N 1.52 W
Wilton, Me., U.S. 102 44.35 N 70.13 W
Wilton, N.H., U.S. 102 42.50 N 71.44 W
Wilton ≈ 92 14.45 S 134.33 E
Wiltshire □6 34 51.15 N 1.50 W
Wiluna 90 26.36 S 120.13 E
Wimborne Minster 34 50.48 N 1.59 W
Winburg 86 28.37 S 27.00 E
Wincanton 34 51.04 N 2.25 W
Winchcombe 34 51.57 N 1.58 W
Winchelsea 34 50.55 N 0.42 E
Winchendon 102 42.41 N 72.02 W
Winchester, On., Can. 102 45.06 N 75.21 W
Winchester, N.Z. 96 44.12 S 171.17 E
Winchester, Eng., U.K. 34 51.04 N 1.19 W
Winchester, In., U.S. 102 40.10 N 84.58 W
Winchester, Ky., U.S. 102 37.59 N 84.10 W
Winchester, N.H., U.S. 102 42.46 N 72.23 W
Winchester, Va., U.S. 102 39.11 N 78.10 W
Wind ≈ 98 65.49 N 135.18 W
Windber 102 40.14 N 78.50 W
Windera 94 26.03 S 151.50 E
Windermere 36 54.23 N 2.54 W
Windermere ⊜ 36 54.22 N 2.56 W
Windhoek 86 22.34 S 17.06 E
Windhoek □5 86 22.30 S 17.00 E
Windischgarsten 46 47.44 N 14.20 E
Windorah 94 25.26 S 142.39 E
Windrush ≈ 34 51.42 N 1.25 W
Windsor, Austl. 94 33.37 S 150.49 E
Windsor, N.S., Can. 98 44.59 N 64.08 W
Windsor, On., Can. 102 42.18 N 83.01 W
Windsor, P.Q., Can. 102 45.34 N 72.00 W
Windsor, Eng., U.K. 34 51.29 N 0.38 W
Windsor, Ca., U.S. 104 38.33 N 122.49 W
Windsor, Ct., U.S. 102 41.51 N 72.38 W
Windsor, Vt., U.S. 102 43.29 N 72.23 W
Windsor Forest ✦3 34 51.27 N 0.43 W
Windsor Locks 102 41.55 N 72.37 W
Windsorton 86 28.16 S 24.44 E
Windward Islands II 108 13.00 N 61.00 W
Windward Passage ⅄ 108 20.00 N 73.50 W
Winfield, Ks., U.S. 100 37.14 N 96.59 W
Winfield, W.V., U.S. 102 38.31 N 81.53 W
Wingate 36 55.44 N 1.23 W
Wingate Mountains ✱ 92 14.29 S 130.42 E
Wingerworth 36 53.12 N 1.26 W
Wingham, Austl. 94 31.52 S 152.22 E
Wingham, On., Can. 102 43.53 N 81.19 W
Wingham, Eng., U.K. 34 51.17 N 1.13 E
Winifreda 114 36.15 S 64.14 W
Winisk 98 55.15 N 85.12 W
Winisk ≈ 98 55.17 N 85.05 W
Winisk Lake ⊜ 98 52.55 N 87.22 W
Winklern 46 46.52 N 12.52 E
Winneba 80 5.25 N 0.36 W
Winnebago, Lake ⊜ 100 44.00 N 88.25 W
Winnecke, Mount ▲2 90 18.47 S 130.20 E
Winnemucca 104 40.58 N 117.44 W
Winnemucca Lake ⊜ 104 40.09 N 119.20 W
Winning 90 23.09 S 114.32 E
Winnipeg 98 49.53 N 97.09 W
Winnipeg ≈ 98 50.38 N 96.19 W
Winnipeg, Lake ⊜ 98 52.00 N 97.00 W
Winnipegosis, Lake ⊜ 98 52.30 N 100.00 W
Winnipesaukee, Lake ⊜ 102 43.35 N 71.20 W
Winona 100 44.03 N 91.38 W
Winooski 102 44.29 N 73.11 W
Winooski ≈ 102 44.30 N 73.15 W
Winooski, North Branch ≈ 102 44.15 N 72.35 W
Winschoten 46 53.08 N 7.02 E
Winscombe 34 51.18 N 2.50 W
Winsen 46 53.22 N 10.12 E
Winsford, Eng., U.K. 34 51.06 N 3.33 W
Winsford, Eng., U.K. 36 53.12 N 2.32 W
Winshill 34 52.48 N 1.36 W
Winslow, Eng., U.K. 34 51.57 N 0.54 W
Winslow, Az., U.S. 100 35.01 N 110.41 W
Winslow, Me., U.S. 102 44.32 N 69.37 W
Winslow Reef ✦2 28 1.36 S 174.57 W
Winsted 102 41.55 N 73.03 W
Winston 104 43.07 N 123.24 W
Winston-Salem 100 36.05 N 80.14 W
Winterberge ✱ 86 32.28 S 26.15 E
Winterbourne Abbas 34 50.43 N 2.34 W
Winter Harbor 102 44.23 N 68.05 W
Winterhaven, Ca., U.S. 104 32.44 N 114.38 W
Winter Haven, Fl., U.S. 100 28.01 N 81.43 W
Winter Island I 98 66.14 N 83.04 W
Winterport 102 44.38 N 68.51 W
Winters 104 38.31 N 121.58 W
Winterswijk 46 51.58 N 6.44 E
Winterthur 46 47.30 N 8.43 E
Winterton 36 53.39 N 0.36 W
Winterton-on-Sea 34 52.43 N 1.42 E
Winthrop 102 44.18 N 69.58 W
Wintinna 90 27.41 S 134.07 E
Winton, Austl. 94 22.23 S 143.02 E
Winton, N.Z. 96 46.09 S 168.20 E
Wipperfürth 46 51.07 N 7.23 E
Wirksworth 36 53.05 N 1.34 W
Wirral >1 36 53.20 N 3.03 W
Wirraminna 94 31.12 S 136.15 E
Wirrulla 90 32.24 S 134.31 E
Wisbech 34 52.40 N 0.10 E
Wiscasset 102 44.00 N 69.39 W
Wisconsin □3 100 44.45 N 89.30 W
Wisconsin ≈ 100 43.00 N 91.10 W
Wisconsin Rapids 100 44.23 N 89.49 W
Wisdom, Lake ⊜ 92 5.20 S 147.05 E
Wishaw 38 55.47 N 3.56 W
Wisła 46 49.40 N 18.52 E
Wisła ≈ 46 54.22 N 18.55 E
Wisłok ≈ 46 50.13 N 22.32 E
Wisłoka ≈ 46 50.27 N 21.23 E
Wismar, D.D.R. 46 53.53 N 11.28 E
Wismar, Guy. 110 6.00 N 58.18 W
Wissembourg 48 49.02 N 7.57 E
Wissey ≈ 34 52.33 N 0.21 E
Wisznice 46 51.48 N 23.12 E
Witbank 86 25.56 S 29.07 E
Witdraai 86 26.58 S 20.45 E
Witham 34 51.48 N 0.38 E
Witham ≈ 36 53.06 N 0.13 W
Witheridge 34 50.55 N 3.42 W
Withernsea 36 53.44 N 0.02 E
Witkowo 46 52.27 N 17.47 E
Witley 34 51.09 N 0.38 W
Witney 34 51.48 N 1.29 W
Witnica 46 52.40 N 14.55 E
Witrivier 86 24.40 S 31.00 E
Witsand 86 34.24 S 20.50 E
Wittabrenna Creek ≈ 94 29.20 S 142.43 E
Witten 46 51.26 N 7.20 E
Wittenberg 46 51.52 N 12.39 E
Wittenberge 46 53.00 N 11.44 E
Wittenburg 46 53.31 N 11.04 E
Wittenoom 90 22.17 S 118.19 E
Wittering 34 52.37 N 0.27 W
Wittingen 46 52.43 N 10.44 E
Wittlich 46 49.59 N 6.53 E
Wittmund 46 53.34 N 7.47 E
Wittstock 46 53.10 N 12.29 E
Witu Islands II 92 4.40 S 149.25 E
Witwatersrand ✦1 86 26.00 S 27.00 E
Witzenhausen 46 51.20 N 9.51 E
Wiveliscombe 34 51.03 N 3.19 W
Wivenhoe 34 51.52 N 0.58 E
Wiżajny 46 54.23 N 22.51 E
W. J. van Blommestein Meer ⊜1 110 4.45 N 55.00 W
Wkra ≈ 46 52.27 N 20.44 E
Władysławowo 46 54.49 N 18.25 E
Wleń 46 51.01 N 15.40 E
Włocławek 46 52.39 N 19.02 E
Włodawa 46 51.34 N 23.32 E
Włoszczowa 46 50.52 N 19.59 E
Wnion ≈ 34 52.45 N 3.54 W
Woburn 102 42.28 N 71.09 W
Woburn Sands 34 52.01 N 0.39 W
Wodgina 90 21.11 S 118.40 E
Wodonga 94 36.07 S 146.54 E
Wodzisław Śląski 46 50.00 N 18.28 E
Wojcieszów 46 50.58 N 15.56 E
Wokam, Pulau I 92 5.37 S 134.30 E
Wokha 76 26.06 N 94.16 E
Woking 34 51.20 N 0.34 W
Wokingham 34 51.25 N 0.51 W
Wokingham Creek ≈ 94 22.19 S 142.30 E
Wolbrom 46 50.24 N 19.46 E
Wolcott 102 43.13 N 76.48 W
Wolcottville 102 41.32 N 85.22 W
Wołczyn 46 51.01 N 18.03 E
Wolds, The ✦2 36 53.20 N 0.10 W
Woleai I1 68 7.21 N 143.52 E
Wolfach 46 48.17 N 8.13 E
Wolf Creek 104 42.41 N 123.23 W
Wolfeboro 102 43.35 N 71.12 W
Wolfe Island I 102 44.12 N 76.20 W
Wolfen 46 51.40 N 12.16 E
Wolfenbüttel 46 52.10 N 10.32 E
Wolfhagen 46 51.19 N 9.10 E
Wolfratshausen 46 47.54 N 11.25 E
Wolf Rock I2 32 49.57 N 5.49 W
Wolfsberg 46 46.51 N 14.51 E
Wolfsburg 46 52.28 N 10.47 E
Wolf's Castle 34 51.54 N 4.58 W
Wolgast 46 54.03 N 13.46 E
Wolin 46 53.50 N 14.35 E
Wollaston 34 52.15 N 0.40 W
Wollaston, Islas II 112 55.40 S 67.30 W
Wollaston Lake ⊜ 98 58.15 N 103.20 W
Wollaston Peninsula >1 98 70.00 N 115.00 W
Wollogorang 94 17.13 S 137.57 E
Wollongong 94 34.25 S 150.54 E
Wolmaransstad 86 27.12 S 26.13 E
Wołomin 46 52.21 N 21.14 E
Wołów 46 51.21 N 16.39 E
Wolseley, Sk., Can. 98 50.25 N 103.19 W
Wolseley, S. Afr. 86 33.26 S 19.12 E
Wolsingham 36 54.44 N 1.52 W
Wolsztyn 46 52.08 N 16.06 E
Wolverhampton 34 52.36 N 2.08 W
Wolverine 102 45.16 N 84.36 W
Wolverton 34 52.04 N 0.50 W
Wombourne 34 52.32 N 2.13 W
Wombwell 36 53.31 N 1.24 W
Wonarah 90 19.55 S 136.20 E
Wondai 94 26.19 S 151.52 E
Wonderland 104 40.24 N 121.19 W
Wondinong 90 27.52 S 118.25 E
Wongan Hills 90 30.53 S 116.42 E
Wonju 72 37.22 N 127.58 E
Wonogiri 72 7.49 S 110.55 E
Wonosari 72 7.58 S 110.35 E
Wonosobo 72 7.22 S 109.54 E
Wŏnsan 62 39.09 N 127.25 E
Wonthaggi 94 38.36 S 145.35 E
Woocalla 94 31.42 S 137.13 E
Woodbine 102 39.14 N 74.48 W
Woodbridge, Eng., U.K. 34 52.06 N 1.19 E
Woodbridge, Va., U.S. 102 38.39 N 77.15 W
Woodbury, Eng., U.K. 34 50.41 N 3.24 W
Woodbury, Ct., U.S. 102 41.32 N 73.12 W
Woodbury, N.J., U.S. 102 39.50 N 75.09 W
Woodchurch 34 51.05 N 0.46 E
Woodcock, Mount ▲ 90 19.16 S 134.02 E
Wooded Bluff ✦4 94 29.22 S 153.22 E
Woodenbong 94 28.23 S 152.37 E
Woodford 40 53.03 N 8.23 W
Woodford Halse 34 52.10 N 1.12 W
Woodhall Spa 36 53.09 N 0.13 W
Woodlake 104 36.25 N 119.06 W
Woodland, Ca., U.S. 104 38.40 N 121.46 W
Woodland, Me., U.S. 102 45.09 N 67.24 W
Woodlands 96 46.22 S 168.33 E
Woodlark Island I 92 9.05 S 152.50 E
Woodley 34 51.28 N 0.53 W
Woodmansey 36 53.50 N 0.29 W
Woodrarung Range ✱ 90 27.10 S 115.30 E
Woodroffe ≈ 94 21.28 S 137.58 E
Woodroffe, Mount ▲ 90 26.20 S 131.45 E
Woods, Lake ⊜ 90 17.50 S 133.30 E
Woods, Lake of the ⊜ 98 49.15 N 94.45 W
Woodsfield 102 39.45 N 81.06 W
Woods Hole 102 41.31 N 70.40 W
Woodside 94 38.31 S 146.52 E
Woodstock, Austl. 94 22.15 S 141.57 E
Woodstock, N.B., Can. 98 46.09 N 67.34 W
Woodstock, On., Can. 102 43.08 N 80.45 W
Woodstock, Eng., U.K. 34 51.52 N 1.21 W
Woodstock, N.Y., U.S. 102 42.02 N 74.07 W
Woodstock, Vt., U.S. 102 43.37 N 72.31 W
Woodstock, Va., U.S. 102 38.52 N 78.30 W
Woodsville 102 44.09 N 72.02 W
Woodville, N.Z. 96 40.20 S 175.52 E
Woodville, Oh., U.S. 102 41.27 N 83.21 W
Woodward 100 36.26 N 99.23 W
Woodward Reservoir ⊜1 104 37.51 N 120.52 W
Wool 34 50.41 N 2.14 W
Woolacombe 34 51.10 N 4.13 W
Wooler 36 55.33 N 2.01 W
Woolgangie 90 31.10 S 120.32 E
Woolgoolga 94 30.07 S 153.12 E
Woolpit 34 52.13 N 0.54 E
Woomera 94 31.31 S 137.10 E
Woonsocket 102 42.00 N 71.30 W
Woorabinda 94 24.08 S 149.28 E
Wooramel 90 25.44 S 114.17 E
Wooramel ≈ 90 25.47 S 114.10 E
Wooster 102 40.48 N 81.56 W
Wootton 34 52.11 N 0.53 W
Wootton Bassett 34 51.33 N 1.54 W
Wootton Wawen 34 52.16 N 1.47 W
Worb 46 46.56 N 7.34 E
Worcester, S. Afr. 86 33.39 S 19.27 E
Worcester, Eng., U.K. 34 52.11 N 2.13 W
Worcester, Ma., U.S. 102 42.15 N 71.48 W
Wörgl 46 47.29 N 12.04 E
Workington 36 54.39 N 3.35 W
Worksop 36 53.18 N 1.07 W
Worland 100 44.01 N 107.57 W
Wormit 38 56.25 N 2.59 W
Worms 46 49.38 N 8.22 E
Worms Head > 34 51.34 N 4.20 W
Worsbrough 36 53.31 N 1.29 W
Worthen 34 52.38 N 3.00 W
Wörther See ⊜ 46 46.37 N 14.10 E
Worthing 34 50.48 N 0.23 W
Worthington, Mn., U.S. 100 43.37 N 95.35 W
Worthington, Oh., U.S. 102 40.05 N 83.01 W
Worthington Peak ▲ 104 37.55 N 115.37 W
Wotho I1 28 10.06 N 165.59 E
Wotje I1 28 9.27 N 170.02 E
Wotton-under-Edge 34 51.39 N 2.21 W
Wounta 108 13.33 N 83.32 W
Wowan 94 23.55 S 150.12 E
Wowoni, Pulau I 72 4.08 S 123.06 E
Woy Woy 94 33.30 S 151.20 E
Woźniki 46 50.36 N 19.03 E
Wragby 36 53.18 N 0.19 W
Wrangel Island →Vrangel'a, ostrov I 58 71.00 N 179.30 W
Wrangell 98 56.28 N 132.23 W
Wrangell Mountains ✱ 98 62.00 N 143.00 W
Wrath, Cape > 38 58.37 N 5.01 W
Wreck Reef ✦2 94 22.13 S 155.17 E
Wrentham 34 52.23 N 1.40 E
Wrexham 36 53.03 N 3.00 W
Wright, Mount ▲ 94 31.12 S 142.26 E
Wright Peak ▲ 104 38.59 N 122.46 W
Wrightwood 104 34.21 N 117.37 W
Wrigley 98 63.16 N 123.37 W
Writtle 34 51.44 N 0.26 E
Wrocław (Breslau) 46 51.06 N 17.00 E
Wronki 46 52.43 N 16.23 E
Wrotham 34 51.19 N 0.19 E
Wroughton 34 51.31 N 1.46 W
Wroxham 34 52.42 N 1.24 E
Września 46 52.20 N 17.34 E
Wschowa 46 51.48 N 16.19 E
Wu ≈ 62 29.43 N 107.24 E
Wubin 90 30.06 S 116.38 E
Wuchang →Wuhan 66 30.36 N 114.17 E
Wuchuan 70 21.25 N 110.40 E
Wudian 66 32.42 N 117.18 E
Wuding 70 25.32 N 102.23 E
Wudinna 94 33.03 S 135.28 E
Wudu 62 33.24 N 104.50 E
Wugang 62 26.44 N 110.38 E
Wugong Shan ✱ 66 27.21 N 113.50 E
Wuhai 62 39.39 N 106.41 E
Wuhan 66 30.36 N 114.17 E
Wuhe 66 33.10 N 117.54 E
Wuhu, Zhg. 66 31.21 N 118.22 E
Wuhu, Zhg. 66 31.11 N 118.35 E
Wuhua 66 23.57 N 115.48 E
Wujiang 66 31.10 N 120.38 E
Wukang 66 30.33 N 119.58 E
Wuliang Shan ✱ 62 24.30 N 100.45 E
Wuliaru, Pulau I 92 7.27 S 131.04 E
Wuluhan 72 8.21 S 113.33 E
Wuming 70 23.10 N 108.18 E
Wundowie 90 31.46 S 116.22 E
Wuning 66 29.17 N 115.06 E
Wunnummin Lake ⊜ 98 52.55 N 89.10 W
Wunstorf 46 52.25 N 9.26 E
Wuping 66 25.08 N 116.06 E
Wuppertal, B.R.D. 46 51.16 N 7.11 E
Wuppertal, S. Afr. 86 32.15 S 19.15 E
Wurarga 90 28.25 S 116.17 E
Würzburg 46 49.48 N 9.56 E
Wurzen 46 51.22 N 12.44 E
Wushan 62 31.05 N 109.48 E
Wusheng 66 29.56 N 119.25 E
Wushenqi 62 38.58 N 109.01 E
Wusong 66 31.23 N 121.29 E
Wusuli (Ussuri) ≈ 58 48.27 N 135.04 E
Wutai 62 38.44 N 113.17 E
Wutai Shan ▲ 62 39.04 N 113.35 E
Wutongqiao 62 29.26 N 103.51 E
Wuvulu Island I 92 1.45 S 142.50 E
Wuwei, Zhg. 62 37.58 N 102.49 E
Wuwei, Zhg. 66 31.18 N 117.54 E
Wuxi (Wuhsi) 66 31.35 N 120.18 E
Wuyang 66 33.26 N 113.34 E
Wuyi, Zhg. 66 32.13 N 118.26 E
Wuyi, Zhg. 66 28.54 N 119.48 E
Wuyi Shan ✱ 66 27.52 N 117.40 E
Wuyuan, Zhg. 62 41.06 N 108.29 E
Wuyuan, Zhg. 66 29.15 N 117.49 E
Wuzhi Shan ▲ 62 18.57 N 109.43 E
Wuzhong 62 37.57 N 106.18 E
Wuzhou (Wuchow) 70 23.30 N 111.27 E
Wyaaba ≈ 94 16.27 S 141.35 E
Wyaaba Creek ≈ 94 16.27 S 141.35 E
Wyalkatchem 90 31.10 S 117.22 E
Wyalusing 102 41.40 N 76.15 W
Wyandotte 102 42.12 N 83.09 W
Wyandra 94 27.15 S 145.59 E
Wyangala Reservoir ⊜1 94 33.58 S 148.55 E
Wycheproof 94 36.05 S 143.14 E
Wydgee 90 28.51 S 117.49 E
Wye 34 51.11 N 0.56 E
Wye ≈, U.K. 34 51.37 N 2.39 W
Wye ≈, Eng., U.K. 36 53.12 N 1.37 W
Wyemandoo ▲ 90 28.31 S 118.32 E
Wyk 46 54.42 N 8.34 E
Wyke Regis 34 50.36 N 2.29 W
Wylye ≈ 34 51.04 N 1.52 W
Wymeswold 34 52.47 N 1.06 W
Wymondham 34 52.34 N 1.07 E
Wynberg 86 34.02 S 18.28 E
Wynbring 90 30.33 S 133.32 E
Wyndham, Austl. 92 15.28 S 128.06 E
Wyndham, N.Z. 96 46.20 S 168.51 E
Wynniatt Bay C 98 72.55 N 110.30 W
Wynyard, Austl. 94 40.59 S 145.41 E
Wynyard, Sk., Can. 98 51.47 N 104.10 W
Wyola Lake ⊜ 90 29.08 S 130.17 E
Wyoming 102 42.57 N 82.07 W
Wyoming □3 100 43.00 N 107.30 W
Wyong 94 33.17 S 151.25 E
Wyre ≈ 36 53.55 N 3.00 W
Wyre Forest ✦3 34 52.23 N 2.23 W
Wyrzysk 46 53.10 N 17.15 E
Wyśmierzyce 46 51.38 N 20.49 E
Wysoka 46 53.11 N 17.05 E
Wysokie Mazowieckie 46 52.56 N 22.32 E
Wyszków 46 52.36 N 21.28 E
Wyszogród 46 52.23 N 20.11 E
Wyvis, Ben ▲ 38 57.42 N 4.35 W

X

Xainza 62 30.57 N 88.38 E
Xam Nua 70 20.25 N 104.02 E
Xangongo 84 16.43 S 15.01 E
Xánthi 54 41.08 N 24.53 E
Xanxerê 114 26.53 S 52.23 W
Xapuri 110 10.39 S 68.31 W
Xar Moron ≈ 62 43.25 N 121.41 E
Xarrama ≈ 50 38.14 N 8.20 W
Xau, Lake ⊔ 86 21.15 S 24.38 E
Xaxim 114 26.56 S 52.31 W
X-Can 108 20.50 N 87.43 W
Xenia 102 39.41 N 83.55 W
Xertigny 48 48.03 N 6.24 E
Xi ≈ 62 22.25 N 113.23 E
Xiaguanpi 66 24.04 N 117.06 E
Xiahe 62 35.18 N 102.30 E
Xiajiang 66 27.32 N 115.08 E
Xiamen (Amoy) 66 24.28 N 118.07 E
Xi'an (Sian) 62 34.15 N 108.52 E
Xiang ≈ 62 29.00 N 112.56 E
Xiang'an 66 31.12 N 117.46 E
Xiangcheng, Zhg. 66 33.28 N 114.53 E
Xiangcheng, Zhg. 66 33.53 N 113.29 E
Xiangfan 62 32.03 N 112.01 E
Xiangkhoang 70 19.20 N 103.22 E
Xiangride 62 36.02 N 98.08 E
Xiangshan 66 29.28 N 121.51 E
Xiangtan 66 27.51 N 112.54 E
Xiangtang 66 28.26 N 115.58 E
Xiangyin 66 28.40 N 112.53 E
Xiangyun 70 25.30 N 100.30 E
Xianju 66 28.51 N 120.44 E
Xianning 66 29.53 N 114.17 E
Xianyou 66 25.23 N 118.40 E
Xiaodanyang 66 31.38 N 118.43 E
Xiaofeng 66 30.36 N 119.32 E
Xiaogan 66 30.55 N 113.54 E
Xiao Hinggan Ling ✱ 62 48.45 N 127.00 E
Xiaoji 66 32.38 N 119.48 E
Xiaolan 66 22.41 N 113.14 E
Xiaoshan 66 30.10 N 120.15 E
Xiaoxian 66 34.11 N 116.56 E
Xiapu 66 26.52 N 120.01 E
Xiayang 66 26.46 N 117.59 E
Xiayi 66 34.14 N 116.06 E
Xichang 62 27.58 N 102.13 E
Xiegeer 76 28.38 N 87.04 E
Xigazê 76 29.17 N 88.53 E
Xihua 66 33.47 N 114.31 E
Xihuashan 66 25.28 N 114.20 E
Xiliao ≈ 62 43.24 N 123.42 E
Xilókastron 54 38.05 N 22.38 E
Ximakou 66 30.33 N 113.47 E
Ximiao 62 41.09 N 100.17 E
Xin'an 66 23.02 N 114.56 E
Xinavane 86 25.02 S 32.47 E
Xincai 66 32.44 N 114.59 E
Xinchang, Zhg. 66 29.30 N 120.53 E
Xinchang, Zhg. 66 31.02 N 121.38 E
Xindian 66 33.07 N 112.38 E
Xinfeng, Zhg. 66 25.24 N 114.56 E
Xinfeng, Zhg. 66 24.04 N 114.12 E
Xing'an 62 25.37 N 110.31 E
Xingguo 66 26.21 N 115.19 E
Xinghua 66 32.57 N 119.50 E
Xingkai Hu (ozero Chanka) ⊜ 62 45.00 N 132.24 E
Xingning 66 24.09 N 115.45 E
Xingren 70 25.27 N 105.13 E
Xingtai 62 37.04 N 114.29 E
Xingtan 66 22.46 N 113.07 E
Xingu ≈ 110 1.30 S 51.53 W
Xingyi 70 25.06 N 104.58 E
Xinhe 66 28.30 N 121.27 E
Xinhua 62 27.37 N 111.02 E
Xinhui 62 22.32 N 113.02 E
Xining 62 36.38 N 101.55 E
Xinjian, Zhg. 66 28.46 N 120.02 E
Xinjian, Zhg. 66 28.34 N 115.47 E
Xinjiang 62 35.40 N 111.11 E
Xinjiang Uygur Zizhiqu (Sinkiang) □4 62 40.00 N 85.00 E
Xinning 66 26.19 N 110.45 E
Xinping 70 24.06 N 101.58 E
Xinshi 66 30.37 N 120.19 E
Xintang 66 23.08 N 113.36 E
Xinxian 66 31.38 N 114.51 E
Xinxiang 62 35.20 N 113.51 E
Xinyang 66 32.08 N 114.04 E
Xinyi (Xin'anzhen) 66 34.22 N 118.21 E
Xinyu 66 27.49 N 114.57 E
Xinzhan 66 33.33 N 114.50 E
Xinzheng 66 34.25 N 113.43 E
Xinzhou 66 30.50 N 114.47 E
Xiping, Zhg. 66 28.27 N 119.29 E
Xiping, Zhg. 66 33.23 N 114.02 E
Xique-Xique 110 10.50 S 42.44 W
Xisha Qundao (Paracel Islands) II 68 16.30 N 112.15 E
Xishui 66 30.27 N 115.13 E
Xiuning 66 29.47 N 118.10 E
Xiushui 66 29.04 N 114.33 E
Xiwu 66 29.40 N 121.30 E
Xixian 66 32.21 N 114.44 E
Xizang Zizhiqu (Tibet) □4 62 32.00 N 88.00 E
Xuancheng 66 30.58 N 118.45 E
Xuanfeng 66 27.42 N 114.08 E
Xuanhua 62 40.37 N 115.03 E
Xuchang 66 34.03 N 113.49 E
Xuefeng 66 33.21 N 118.22 E
Xueyanqiao 66 31.30 N 120.06 E
Xuguanzhen 66 31.23 N 120.30 E
Xun ≈ 62 23.28 N 111.18 E
Xunwu 66 24.58 N 115.38 E
Xupu 66 31.45 N 120.54 E
Xuwan 66 27.55 N 116.31 E
Xuwen 70 20.21 N 110.11 E
Xuyi 66 33.01 N 118.29 E
Xuyong 62 28.10 N 105.24 E
Xuzhou (Süchow) 66 34.16 N 117.11 E

Y

Yaan 62 30.03 N 103.02 E
Yaapeet 94 35.46 S 142.03 E
Yablis 108 14.10 N 83.49 W
Yablonovy Range →Jablonovyj chrebet ✱ 58 53.30 N 115.00 E
Yaco (Iaco) ≈ 110 9.03 S 68.34 W
Yacuiba 110 22.02 S 63.45 W
Yadong 62 27.29 N 88.55 E
Yafran 82 32.04 N 12.31 E
Yagishiri-tō I 64a 44.26 N 141.25 E
Yagoua 80 10.20 N 15.14 E
Yagradagzê Shan ▲ 62 35.12 N 95.20 E
Yaguajay 108 22.19 N 79.14 W
Yaguaraparo 108 10.34 N 62.49 W
Yaguari 114 31.31 S 54.58 W
Yaguarón (Jaguarão) ≈ 114 32.39 S 53.12 W
Yai, Khao ▲ 70 12.27 N 99.26 E
Yainax Butte ▲ 104 42.20 N 121.16 W
Yaita 64 36.48 N 139.56 E
Yaizu 64 34.52 N 138.20 E
Yakima 100 46.36 N 120.30 W
Yakoma 82 4.05 N 22.27 E
Yakumo 64a 42.15 N 140.16 E
Yaku-shima I 65b 30.20 N 130.30 E
Yakutat Bay C 98 59.40 N 140.00 W
Yakutat Seamount ✦3 22 35.15 N 48.00 W
Yakutsk →Jakutsk 58 62.00 N 129.40 E
Yala 70 6.33 N 101.18 E
Yalahán, Laguna de C 108 21.30 N 87.15 W
Yalata 90 31.29 S 131.52 E
Yale 102 43.07 N 82.47 W
Yalgar ≈ 90 26.09 S 117.57 E
Yalgoo 90 28.20 S 116.41 E
Yalinga 82 6.31 N 23.15 E
Yalleroi 94 24.04 S 145.45 E
Yalong ≈ 62 26.37 N 101.48 E
Yalta →Jalta 56 44.30 N 34.10 E
Yalu (Amnok-kang) ≈ 62 39.55 N 124.22 E
Yamada 64 39.28 N 141.57 E
Yamaga 64 33.01 N 130.41 E
Yamagata 64 38.15 N 140.20 E
Yamagawa 64 31.12 N 130.39 E
Yamaguchi 64 34.10 N 131.29 E
Yamanaka 64 36.15 N 136.22 E
Yamanashi □5 64 35.30 N 138.30 E
Yamasaki 64 35.00 N 134.33 E
Yamaska ≈ 102 46.06 N 72.56 W
Yamba 94 29.26 S 153.22 E
Yambio 82 4.34 N 28.23 E
Yamdena, Pulau I 92 7.36 S 131.25 E
Yame 64 33.28 N 130.34 E
Yamethin 70 20.26 N 96.09 E
Y'Ami Island I 68 21.07 N 121.57 E
Yamma Yamma, Lake ⊜ 94 26.20 S 141.25 E
Yamoussoukro 80 6.49 N 5.17 W
Yamsay Mountain ▲ 104 42.56 N 121.22 W
Yamuna ≈ 76 25.25 N 81.50 E
Yanac 94 36.08 S 141.26 E
Yanagawa 64 33.10 N 130.24 E
Yanai 64 33.58 N 132.07 E
Yanam 74 16.44 N 82.13 E
Yan'an 62 36.36 N 109.28 E
Yanbu', Ar. Su. 78 24.05 N 38.03 E
Yanbu, Zhg. 66 23.05 N 113.10 E
Yanchang 62 36.31 N 110.08 E
Yancheng, Zhg. 66 33.36 N 113.57 E
Yancheng, Zhg. 66 33.24 N 120.09 E
Yanchi 62 37.52 N 107.22 E
Yanco 94 34.36 S 146.25 E
Yandal 90 27.33 S 121.07 E
Yandoon 70 17.02 N 95.39 E
Yangce 66 32.58 N 113.14 E
Yangchow →Yangzhou 66 32.24 N 119.26 E
Yanghe 66 33.47 N 118.23 E
Yangjiang 62 21.51 N 111.56 E
Yangjiaqiao 66 27.44 N 112.46 E
Yangluo 66 30.41 N 114.34 E
Yangquan 62 37.52 N 113.36 E
Yangshuo 70 24.45 N 110.24 E
Yangtze →Chang ≈ 62 31.48 N 121.10 E
Yangxin 66 29.51 N 115.12 E
Yangzhong (Sanmaozhen) 66 32.16 N 119.49 E
Yangzhou 66 32.24 N 119.26 E
Yangzhuoyonghu ⊜ 76 28.58 N 90.44 E
Yanji 62 42.57 N 129.32 E
Yankton 100 42.52 N 97.23 W
Yanling 66 34.07 N 114.11 E
Yanna 94 26.56 S 146.03 E
Yannarie ≈ 90 22.28 S 114.48 E
Yanqi 62 42.00 N 86.15 E
Yanrey 90 22.31 S 114.48 E
Yanshan 66 28.18 N 117.41 E
Yantabulla 94 29.21 S 145.00 E
Yantai (Chefoo) 62 37.33 N 121.20 E
Yanzhou 62 35.33 N 116.50 E
Yao 64 34.37 N 135.36 E
Yaoan 70 25.32 N 101.12 E
Yaoundé 80 3.52 N 11.31 E
Yaowan 66 34.12 N 118.03 E
Yap I 68 9.31 N 138.06 E
Yapacani 110 16.45 S 64.18 W
Yapen, Pulau I 92 1.45 S 136.15 E
Yapeyú 114 29.28 S 56.49 W
Yappar ≈ 94 18.22 S 141.16 E
Yap Trench ✦1 28 8.30 N 138.00 E
Yaque del Norte ≈ 108 19.51 N 71.41 W
Yaqui ≈ 106 27.37 N 110.39 W
Yaracuy □3 108 10.20 N 69.10 W
Yaraka 94 24.53 S 144.04 E
Yarcombe 34 50.52 N 3.05 W
Yardea 94 32.23 S 135.32 E
Yare ≈ 34 52.35 N 1.44 E
Yari ≈ 110 0.23 S 72.16 W
Yariga-take ▲ 64 36.20 N 137.39 E
Yarim 78 14.29 N 44.21 E
Yaring 70 6.52 N 101.22 E
Yaritagua 108 10.05 N 69.08 W
Yarkant (Yarkand) ≈ 62 40.28 N 80.52 E
Yarkhūn ≈ 76 36.17 N 72.30 E
Yarlarweelor 90 25.35 S 117.59 E
Yarle Lakes ⊜ 90 30.15 S 131.27 E
Yarloop 90 32.57 S 115.54 E
Yarmouth, N.S., Can. 98 43.50 N 66.07 W
Yarmouth, Eng., U.K. 34 50.42 N 1.29 W
Yarmouth, Me., U.S. 102 43.48 N 70.11 W
Yarraloola 90 21.34 S 115.52 E
Yarram 94 38.33 S 146.41 E
Yarraman 94 26.50 S 151.59 E
Yarrawonga 94 36.01 S 146.00 E
Yarra Yarra Lakes ⊜ 90 29.40 S 115.47 E
Yarrow 38 55.32 N 3.01 W
Yarrow Water ≈ 36 55.34 N 2.51 W
Yarty ≈ 34 50.47 N 3.01 W
Yarumal 110 6.58 N 75.24 W
Yashiro-jima I 64 33.55 N 132.15 E
Yasothon 70 15.45 N 104.08 E
Yass 94 34.50 S 148.55 E
Yasugi 64 35.26 N 133.15 E
Yāsūj 78 30.42 N 51.06 E
Yata ≈ 110 10.29 S 65.26 W
Yatate-yama ▲ 64 34.10 N 129.10 E
Yatesboro 102 40.48 N 79.20 W
Yathkyed Lake ⊜ 98 62.41 N 98.00 W
Yatsuga-take ▲ 64 35.59 N 138.23 E
Yatsuo 64 36.34 N 137.08 E
Yatsushiro 64 32.30 N 130.36 E
Yatsushiro-kai C 64 32.20 N 130.25 E
Yatta Plateau ✱1 84 2.00 S 38.00 E
Yatton 34 51.24 N 2.49 W
Yauco 108 18.02 N 66.51 W
Yavari (Javari) ≈ 110 4.21 S 70.02 W
Yavi, Cerro ▲ 110 5.32 N 65.59 W
Yawata →Kitakyūshū 64 33.53 N 130.50 E
Yawatahama 64 33.27 N 132.24 E
Yaxian 70 18.20 N 109.30 E
Yaxley 34 52.31 N 0.16 W
Yazd 78 31.53 N 54.25 E
Yazoo ≈ 100 32.22 N 91.00 W
Ybbs ≈ 46 48.10 N 15.06 E
Ybbs an der Donau 46 48.11 N 15.05 E
Ybycuí 114 26.01 S 57.03 W
Yding Skovhøj ▲2 44 56.00 N 9.48 E
Ydstebøhavn 44 59.08 N 5.15 E
Ye 70 15.15 N 97.51 E
Yeadon 36 53.52 N 1.41 W
Yealm ≈ 34 50.18 N 4.03 W
Yealmpton 34 50.21 N 3.59 W
Yecheng 76 37.54 N 77.25 E
Yecla 50 38.37 N 1.07 W
Yeeda 90 17.36 S 123.39 E
Yeelanna 94 34.09 S 135.43 E
Yeelirrie 90 27.17 S 120.06 E
Yegros 114 26.24 S 56.25 W
Yeguas, Rio de las ≈ 50 37.22 N 4.45 W
Yei ≈ 82 6.15 N 30.13 E

Symbols in the Index entries are identified on page 122.

Name	Page	Lat.	Long.